THE
HOTEL
GUIDE
2017

Published by AA Publishing, a trading name of AA Media Limited,
whose registered office is Fanum House, Basing View, Basingstoke,
Hampshire RG21 4EA. Registered number 06112600

First published by the Automobile Association as the Hotel and
Restaurant Guide, 1967
© AA Media Limited 2016.
50th edition September 2016.

Please contact:
Advertising Sales Department: advertisingsales@theAA.com
Hotel Services: hotelservices@theAA.com
Editorial Department: lifestyleguides@theAA.com
AA Hotel Scheme Enquiries: 01256 844455

Website addresses are included in some entries and specified by the
respective establishment. Such websites are not under the control of
AA Media Limited and as such AA Media Limited will not accept any
responsibility or liability in respect of any and all matters whatsoever
relating to such web sites including access, content, material and
functionality. By including the addresses of third party websites the AA
does not intend to solicit business or offer any security to any person in
any country, directly or indirectly.

Typesetting and Repro by Servis Filmsetting Ltd, Stockport
Printed in Italy by Printer Trento SRL, Trento

This directory is compiled by AA Lifestyle Guides; managed in the Librios
Information Management System and generated by the AA establishment
database system.

Maps prepared by the Mapping Services Department of AA Publishing.

Maps © AA Media Limited 2016.

Contains Ordnance Survey data © Crown copyright and database
right 2016.

This is based upon Crown Copyright and is reproduced
with the permission of Land & Property Services under
delegated authority from the Controller of Her Majesty's
Stationery Office.
© Crown copyright and database rights 2016 PMLPA No. 100497

Republic of Ireland mapping based on © Ordnance
Survey Ireland/Government of Ireland Copyright
Permit No. MP0000616

Information on National Parks in England provided by the Countryside
Agency (Natural England).

Information on National Parks in Scotland provided by Scottish
Natural Heritage.

Information on National Parks in Wales provided by The Countryside
Council for Wales.

A CIP catalogue record for this book is available from the British Library.

ISBN: 978-0-7495-7828-2

A05407

AA Lifestyle Guides

Contents

Welcome to the AA Hotel Guide 2017

For 50 years our readers have been using the AA Hotel Guide to find different types of accommodation, for a variety of reasons. As the AA inspects such a wide range of establishments, we hope that this guide will prove an invaluable asset in helping you to find the right place to stay.

Who's in the guide?

From the most opulent and sophisticated of London's elite hotels to personally run small hotels in the British countryside; from the practical and convenient budget hotel aimed at business or air travellers, to the luxurious country house hotel catering for leisure and sporting guests, *The AA Hotel Guide 2017* has it all. All year round our specially trained team of expert inspectors are visiting, grading and advising the hotels that appear in this guide. Each one is judged on presentation, quality of accommodation leisure and sporting facilities, food operation, service, hospitality, conference facilities and cleanliness. It is then rated according to our classification system (see pages 18–19).

Any hotel applying for AA recognition receives an annual unannounced visit to check standards. If the hotel changes hands, the new owners must reapply for classification, as AA recognition is not transferable.

Our inspectors have also chosen their Hotels of the Year, for England, London, Scotland, Wales, and Northern Ireland, as well as Hotel Group of the Year (see pages 13–17).

Red Stars and Inspectors' Choice

All of the hotels in this guide should be of a high standard, but some are a cut above, and these are specially selected by our inspectors. At these establishments you can expect a little more of everything: more comfort, more facilities, more extras and more attention. From 2 Red Stars to 5 Red Stars, these are the best of British hotels. Every Red Star hotel is highlighted as an INSPECTORS' CHOICE, but these are not the only places that are singled out in this way.

Silver Stars and Highly Recommended

Hotels with silver stars ★ have been selected for their superior level of quality, high standards of hotel keeping and for the quality of food within its star rating. These are highlighted as HIGHLY RECOMMENDED.

Rosettes

Most of the hotels in this guide have their own restaurants, and a large proportion of them serve food that has attained an AA Rosette award; including some that have reached the four and five Rosette level, making them among the finest restaurants in the world. These are regularly visited by the AA inspectorate and awarded Rosettes strictly on the basis of the inspector's experience alone.

Some of the establishments in the guide are known as Restaurants with Rooms. Most will have been awarded AA Rosettes for their food, and the accommodation they offer meets the required AA standard, making them worthy of inclusion in this guide.

Anonymous inspection

All hotel and restaurant inspections are made anonymously. After taking a meal or staying overnight at the hotel, the inspector will announce to a member of staff and ask to speak to the manager, or the chef, in the case of a Rosette visit.

Tell us what you think

We welcome your feedback about the hotels included in this guide, and about the guide itself. A Readers' Report form appears at the back of the guide, so please write in, or email us at: **lifestyleguides@theaa.com**.

The hotels, along with guest accommodation, pubs, golf courses, days out and restaurants feature on the AA website: **theAA.com**.

How to use the guide

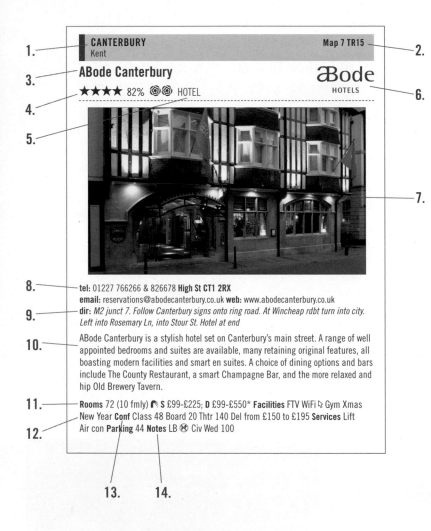

1. Location

Town listed alphabetically within country (the county name appears under the town name)

2. Map reference

Map page number followed by a National Grid reference (see also page 9)

3. Hotel name

Where the name appears in italic type the information that follows has not been confirmed by the establishment for 2017

4. Grading

Hotels are listed in star rating and merit score order within each location (for full explanation of ratings and awards see page 18-19)

★ Star rating

% Merit score

◉ Rosette award

≗ Breakfast award

5. Type of hotel

See page 10

6. Hotel logo

If a symbol appears here it represents a hotel group or consortium (see pages 31–39)

7. Picture

Optional photograph supplied by the establishment

8. Address and contact details

9. Directions
Brief details of how to find the hotel

10. Description
Written by the AA inspector at the time of the last visit

11. Rooms
Number of rooms and prices (see page 8)

12. Facilities
Additional facilities including those for children and for leisure activities

13. Conference
Conference facilities as available (see page 8)

14. Notes
Additional information (see pages 8–9)

Key to symbols and abbreviations

★	Black stars
★	Red stars – indicate AA Inspectors' Choice
★	Silver stars – indicate superior level of quality – Highly Recommended
◉	AA Rosettes – indicate an AA award for food
♨	Breakfast Award
%	Inspectors' Merit score (see page 8)
A	Associate Hotels (see page 10)
O	Hotel due to open during the currency of the guide
U	Star rating not confirmed (see page 10)
Fmly	Number of family rooms available
GF	Ground floors rooms available
🚿	Bedrooms with walk-in showers available
Smoking	Number of bedrooms allocated for smokers
prt facs	Bedroom with separate private facilities (Restaurant with Rooms only)
S	Single room
D	Double room
✳	2016 prices
fr	From
incl. bkfst	Breakfast included in the price
FTV	Freeview television
STV	Satellite television
WiFi	Wireless network connection

⚲	High speed internet connection (bedrooms)
HL	Hearing loop installed
Air con	Air conditioning
🏊	Heated indoor swimming pool
🏊	Outdoor swimming pool
🏊	Heated outdoor swimming pool
🎵	Entertainment
Child facilities	Children's facilities (see page 8)
Xmas/New Year	Special programme for Christmas/New Year
🎾	Tennis court
🏑	Croquet lawn
⛳	Golf course
CONF	Conference facilities
Thtr	Number of theatre style seats
Class	Number of classroom style seats
Board	Number of boardroom style seats
🐕	No dogs allowed (guide dogs for the blind and assist dogs should be allowed)
No children	Children cannot be accommodated
RS	Restricted opening time
Civ Wed	Establishment licensed for civil weddings (+ maximum number of guests at ceremony)
LB	Special leisure breaks available
Spa	Hotel has its own spa

How to use the guide *continued*

Merit score (%)

AA inspectors supplement their reports with an additional quality assessment of everything the hotel provides, including hospitality, based on their findings as a 'mystery guest'. This wider ranging quality assessment results in an overall Merit Score which is shown as a percentage beside the hotel name. When making your selection of hotel accommodation this enables you to see at a glance that a three star hotel with a Merit Score of 79% offers a higher standard overall than one in the same star classification but with a Merit Score of 69%. To gain AA recognition, a hotel must achieve a minimum score of 50%.

AA Awards

Every year the AA presents a range of awards to the finest AA-inspected and rated hotels from England, London, Scotland, Wales, and Northern Ireland. The Hotel of the Year is our ultimate accolade and is awarded to those hotels that are recognised as outstanding examples in their field. Often innovative, the winning hotels always set high standards in hotel keeping. The winners for all the 2016–2017 awards are listed on pages 13–17.

Rooms

Each entry shows the total number of en suite rooms available (this total will include any annexe rooms). The total number may be followed by a breakdown of the type of rooms available, i.e. the number of annexe rooms; number of family rooms (fmly); number of ground-floor rooms (GF); and number of rooms available for smokers.

Bedrooms in an annexe or extension are only noted if they are at least equivalent in quality to those in the main building, but facilities and prices may differ. In some hotels all bedrooms are in an annexe or extension.

If the hotel has highspeed or broadband internet access in the bedrooms, this may be chargeable.

Prices

Prices are per room per night and are provided by the hoteliers in good faith. These prices are indications and not firm quotations. An asterisk (*) indicates 2016 prices. Many hotels have special rates so it is worth looking at their websites for the latest information.

Payment

Credit cards may be subject to a surcharge – check when booking if this is how you intend to pay.

Children

Child facilities may include baby intercom, baby-sitting service, playroom, playground, laundry, drying/ironing facilities, cots, high chairs or special meals. In some hotels children can sleep in parents' rooms at no extra cost – check when booking.

If 'No children' is indicated, a minimum age may be also given e.g. No children 4yrs indicates that no children under 4 years of age would be accepted.

Some hotels, although accepting children, may not have any special facilities for them.

Leisure breaks (LB)

Some hotels offer special leisure breaks. The cost of these may differ from those quoted in this guide and availability may vary through the year.

Parking

We indicate the number of parking spaces available for guests. This may include covered parking. Please note that some hotels make a charge for the use of their car park.

Civil weddings (Civ Wed)

Indicates that the establishment holds a civil wedding licence, and we indicate the number of guests that can be accommodated at the ceremony.

Conference facilities

We include three types of meeting layouts – Theatre, Classroom and Boardroom style – and state the maximum number of delegates for each. The price shown is the maximum 24-hour rate per delegate. Please note that as arrangements vary between a hotel and a business client, VAT may or may not be included in the price quoted in the guide. We also show if WiFi connectivity is available, but please check with the hotel that this is suitable for your requirements.

Dogs

Although many hotels allow dogs, they may be excluded from some areas of the hotel and some breeds, particularly those requiring an exceptional licence, may not be acceptable at all. Under the Equality Act 2010 access should be allowed for guide dogs and assistance dogs. Please check the hotel's policy when making your booking.

Entertainment (♫)
This indicates that live entertainment will be available at least once a week all year. Some hotels provide live entertainment only in summer or on special occasions.

Hotel logos
If an establishment belongs to a hotel group or consortium their logo is included in their entry (see pages 31–39).

Map references
Each town is given a map reference – the map page number and a map reference based on the National Grid. For example: **Map 05 SU48**:
05 refers to the page number of the map section at back of the guide
SU is the National Grid lettered square (representing 100,000sq metres) in which the location will be found
4 is the figure reading across the top or bottom of the map page
8 is the figure reading down at each side of the map page

Restricted service
Some hotels have restricted service (RS) during quieter months, usually during the winter, and at this time some of the listed facilities will not be available. If your booking is out-of-season, check with the hotel and enquire specifically.

Smoking regulations
If a bedroom has been allocated for smokers, the hotel is obliged to clearly indicate that this is the case. If either the freedom to smoke, or to be in a non-smoking environment is important to you, please check with the hotel when you book.

Spa
For the purposes of this guide the word Spa in an entry indicates that the hotel has its own spa which is either managed by themselves or outsourced to an external management company. Facilities will vary but will include a minimum of two treatment rooms. Any specific details are also given, and these are as provided to us by the establishment (i.e. steam room, beauty therapy etc).

Types of hotel

The majority of establishments in this guide come under the category of Hotel; other categories are listed below.

Town House Hotel A small, individual city or town centre property, which provides a high degree of personal service and privacy.

Country House Hotel These are quietly located in a rural area.

Small Hotel Has fewer than 20 bedrooms and is owner-managed.

Metro Hotel A hotel in an urban location that does not offer an evening meal.

Budget Hotel These are usually purpose-built modern properties offering inexpensive accommodation. Often located near motorways and in town or city centres.

Restaurant with Rooms This category of accommodation is now assessed under the AA's Guest Accommodation scheme, therefore, although they continue to have an entry in this guide, we do not include their star rating.

   Most Restaurants with Rooms have been awarded AA Rosettes for their food and the rooms will meet the required AA standard. For more detailed information about any Restaurant with Rooms please consult *The AA Bed and Breakfast Guide* or visit: www.theAA.com/bed-and-breakfast-and-hotel.

A These are establishments that have not been inspected by the AA, but by one of the national tourist boards in Britain and Northern Ireland. An establishment marked as 'Associate' has paid to belong to the AA Associate Hotel Scheme and therefore receives a limited entry in the guide. Descriptions of these hotels can be found on theAA.com.

U A small number of hotels in the guide have this symbol because their star classification was not confirmed at the time of going to press. This may be due to a change of ownership or because the hotel has only recently joined the AA rating scheme.

AA Advertised
   These establishments are not rated or inspected by the AA, but are displayed for advertising purposes only.

O These hotels were not open at the time of going to press, but will open in late 2016, or in 2017.

Breakfast Award

This year sees the launch of the AA Hotel Breakfast Award, given by inspectors to those hotels who serve the most impressive morning meals.

The Breakfast Award is given to those establishments which serve a breakfast that "showcases the very best sourced ingredients, cooked with skill and passion, served with great hospitality and service." Simple enough, but what exactly does an AA Inspector look for in an award-winning breakfast? Here are a few details.

Hot Drinks

There should be a good range of quality teas, both in bags and in pots; as well as a good range of coffees, presented in a variety of ways, e.g. cappacino, latte, Americano etc.

Cold Drinks

At least two freshly squeezed juices should be on offer, as well as the option to order other juices or smoothies. Water should also be readily available.

Starters

Plenty of fruit, whether whole, in salads, fruit compotes, preserves, with yogurt etc; seasonal produce where appropriate.

Good choice of cereals, with various options like a choice of milk, cream, yogurt etc. Cereals can be home-made or bought in, as often people like their brand of cereal to be the same as they'd get at home.

Bread/Toast

Bread should be freshly baked on the premises, or very high quality bought-in produce. A choice of breads should be offered, alongside the offer for toast to be brought to the table. A good quality toaster or toasting machine is also acceptable.

Jams and marmalades should be good quality, locally sourced or home-made where possible, or best quality if not. Butter should be high quality and never foil wrapped.

Pastries

These should be made in house, or top quality if bought in. There should be a good range, fresh, served warm if suitable or required. Cakes and cereal/granola bars should also be offered.

Cooked Breakfast

As well as variations on the 'Full English/Welsh/Scottish', the menu should include at least four special breakfasts, along the lines of pancakes, kedgeree, eggs Benedict, omelettes, or kippers, as well as local or artisan specialities. There should also be a reasonable assortment of dishes that are suitable for various dietary needs – a standard requirement expected across all aspects of an AA-rated Hotels cuisine.

Breakfasts should be cooked to order or if a hot buffet is offered; all should be hot and kept replenished. A chef on hand to prepare simple dishes is a good option.

A choice of eggs as well as ways of cooking them should be on offer, and there should also be a choice of sausages and possibly different types of bacon. Vegetarian options should always be available.

Continental Breakfast

An appropriate range of cooked meats and cheeses should be on offer, as well as smoked salmon or other smoked or cured fish. Hard-boiled eggs are also a welcome option.

Service

Napkins should be cloth or of very high quality and of a generous size. Tables should be cleared quickly, and top-ups offered as appropriate. Staff should also be ready to help and explain what's on offer, and how to operate any relevant technology (eg toast machines or juice makers).

YOU KNOW WHEN YOU'VE ARRIVED

Stunning scenery encompassing rolling parkland, manicured formal gardens, fountains, lakes, woodland, quintessential English villages, the country's newest National Park and the UK's sunniest seaside resort are just some of the southerly splendours awaiting our guests.

Welcome to the world of Elite Hotels - Gourmet restaurants with a sense of old world charm, our beautifully appointed bedrooms and suites, and the wealth of health, leisure and beauty amenities available are all complemented by unparalleled levels of service.

Ashdown Park Hotel & Country Club
East Sussex, 01342 824988
★★★★

Luton Hoo Hotel, Golf & Spa
Bedfordshire
01582 734437
★★★★★

Tylney Hall Hotel & Gardens
Hampshire
01256 764881
★★★★

The Grand Hotel, Eastbourne
East Sussex
01323 412345
★★★★★

4 Distinctive Hotels, 4 Distinctive Experiences

www.elitehotels.co.uk

AA Hotels of the Year

ENGLAND

NORTHCOTE ★★★★ ◉◉◉◉

LANGHO page 220

Having secured long-term investment at the end of 2012, joint managing directors Craig Bancroft and Nigel Haworth looked to complete the vision for Northcote that they set out back in 1984. The hotel has gone from strength to strength and now boasts 4 AA Red Stars and 4 AA Rosettes. Investment has brought a completely new state-of-the-art kitchen, chef's table, and small cookery school. There are now 26 luxurious rooms spread between the original Manor House and the newly-created Garden Lodge set in beautiful gardens. The rest of the hotel has also been upgraded, and the kitchen garden and terraces have been extended. For over 15 years Northcote has been home to Obsession - an annual homage to gastronomy with world class chefs and dinner events over a two week period. Obsession also benefits charities like Hospitality Action. Executive chef, Lisa Allen, is now renowned as one of the country's best, and Craig and Nigel have recently set up an innovative scholarship scheme and apprenticeship programme in conjunction with Blackburn College. It is a bespoke training programme where Nigel offers students advice, as well as allowing them to gain experience at the hotel.

LONDON

THE BEAUMONT ★★★★★ 87% ◉ ⬯

LONDON page 276

Located in the heart of Mayfair on a site that dates back to the 1920s, this stylish Art Deco hotel is privately owned by renowned restaurateurs Corbin & King, who are responsible for iconic restaurants such as The Wolseley and The Delaunay. This is their first hotel venture and as you would expect from their restaurant operations, it is very grand in style. It's a short walk from Selfridges in one direction and Mayfair's shops in the other. Quality is exceedingly high throughout with great attention to detail and lots of extra touches. The 73 stylish bedrooms include 23 suites and all are appointed to a very high standard with lots of thoughtful extras. *Room*, commissioned by Anthony Gormley is a stunning feature. Inside it is a one bedroom suite, but from outside it is sculpted to represent a crouching figure based on the artist's body. In terms of dining, there is The Colony Grill Room as well as The American Bar and a further residents' bar/lounge. There is also a small, very high quality spa and gym with an Art Deco Hamam (Turkish bath). Staffing levels are very impressive with a very high staff-to-guest ratio. Service is slick and very attentive. This is a great example of something unique in hotels.

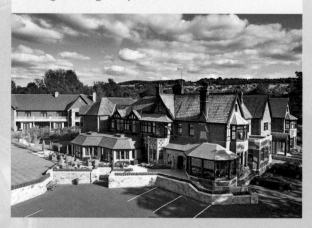

AA Hotels of the Year *continued*

SCOTLAND

CROMLIX AND CHEZ ROUX ★★★★★ 86% ◉◉◉ ◒
DUNBLANE page 486

This elegant Victorian mansion set in Perthshire countryside
was acquired by tennis champion Andy Murray in 2013,
and has been lovingly refurbished and transformed into a
beautiful 15 bedroom country house hotel. It re-opened
two years ago and has certainly put itself on the map. The
hotel is run by Inverlochy Castle Management International
who have considerable experience in running quality hotels
in Scotland. Service and hospitality are outstanding, while
bedrooms and suites are stylish and individually beautifully
appointed with rich fabrics, quality furnishings and state-of-
the-art technology. All have stunning views over the beautiful
grounds and gardens. The Chez Roux restaurant, is headed
up by chef Darin Campbell whose pedigree includes a stint
as head chef for Andrew Fairlie and executive chef at One
Devonshire Gardens. Cuisine is classic French and the
menus often draw from the kitchen gardens. As you would
expect with a sporting owner, the hotel boasts a range of
activities on its estate that include tennis, archery, clay
pigeon shooting and fishing.

WALES

ANGEL HOTEL ★★★ 82% ◉
ABERGAVENNY page 532

Set in a historic market town, this old posting inn started
life in 1829. While retaining plenty of character, it has
been modernised and upgraded by a series of extensive
refurbishments. Working with a local business called The
Art Shop, the company that own the hotel have introduced
artwork, paints and decorating techniques that enhance
the décor and ensure that this a very individual property.
Over the years, many well-known people have stayed here,
including film royalty such as Gregory Peck, Elizabeth Taylor
and Richard Burton. Lounges and bars are always bustling
with locals having a coffee, guests relaxing after exploring
the local area or people enjoying the very special afternoon
tea. It is one of only nine hotels outside of London that are
members of the prestigious Tea Guild and they hold an
award of excellence, so you can be assured of a very special
experience. The restaurant serves brasserie style food which
has achieved an AA Rosette. The bedrooms are beautifully
furnished, with Villeroy & Boch or Fired Earth bathroom
fittings, pocket-sprung beds, and Lewis and Wood fabrics.
They are very stylish and sumptuous.

NORTHERN IRELAND

MANOR HOUSE COUNTRY HOTEL ★★★★ 83% ◉
ENNISKILLEN page 566

Originally dating back to the 17th century, the interior of this charming manor house was reworked in 1860 by Italian workmen, and the results can still be seen today. During WW2, the property was a USAF officers' mess. Over the last four years the whole of this delightful hotel has been refurbished. It is set in a fantastic location with views down onto Lough Erne, and guests are able to take a cruise to enjoy the beauty of the lough. The property retains much of its original character but even so bedrooms have been given a stylish, more modern theme. There is an up-to-date leisure club and spa, a smart restaurant and bar, as well as a less formal bar/bistro. Service is attentive, with wonderful Irish hospitality, and the team are always happy to engage socially with the guests; the gift of real Irish charm always comes to the forefront and the atmosphere is very relaxed and friendly. This impressive hotel has gone from strength to strength over the last few years and investment continues from great owners.

AA HOTEL GROUP OF THE YEAR 2016 - 17

BREWERS SINCE 1807
THWAITES

It is over two centuries since Daniel Thwaites set out from the Lake District to make a new life away from his family farm. He built up his brewery with an eye for quality and a generous blend of innovation, craftsmanship and warm northern hospitality.

Six generations later, his family continues the adventure, still striving for brewing perfection, and now with a growing collection of pubs, inns and hotels & spas.

Our Hotels began life in 1980, under the name Shire Inns, evolving into Shire Hotels & Spas. Their development over nearly 40 years has been always founded on the quality of the experience and attention to detail. The latest achievement - being awarded AA Hotel Group of the Year 2016-17 - would have brought a twinkle to Daniel's eye.

Today, our Company remains steadfastly faithful to his principles. Independent and full of character, we proudly continue the journey he started, constantly looking for improvement, always seeking to give you an experience that's second to none.

Cottons Hotel & Spa Cheshire	Thorpe Park Hotel & Spa Yorkshire	Aztec Hotel & Spa Bristol
North Lakes Hotel & Spa Cumbria	Solent Hotel & Spa Hampshire	Kettering Park Hotel & Spa Northamptonshire

www.thwaites.co.uk

AA Hotel Group of the Year

Thwaites Hotels

Thwaites Hotels is an independently-owned group of six hotels based around the UK. All properties have extensive spa and conference facilities with a strong food and beverage ethos. Much of its success has been achieved by sound investment not only in the hotels but the staff who are seen as the key to Thwaites' success. Investment has also been made in technology at the hotels to help improve efficiency and the guest experience. Over a million pounds has been invested in reservation systems to automate reservation input and improve check-in, which allows the reception team more time to engage with guests.

Investment continues with all 480 bedrooms across the estate being refurbished. Spa development is taking place at Kettering Park Hotel, with restaurant and bar redevelopment taking place at Solent, North Lakes and Aztec Hotel. Work to other spa facilities will see the creation of additional space; also in development are garden rooms with heat experiences.

Charity and community work is a key part of each hotels focus with all six adopting a local charity, chosen by the staff. National charities are also supported, especially Macmillan and Clean for the Queen.

Thwaites also work with local colleges and schools to promote the hospitality industry and encourage young people to learn more. A number of the team also attend local colleges, while the senior members of the kitchen brigade spend time helping to develop the chefs of the future.

The group worked with Blackburn Youth Zone to make a film about recycling; many of the youth group appeared in the film too. This is used as part of the company induction. Support has also been given to young athletes.

This group has certainly come a long way in the last two years and is fully deserving of AA Hotel Group of the Year.

Thorpe Park Hotel & Spa – Leeds ★★★★ 84% ◉
Solent Hotel & Spa – Fareham ★★★★ 82% ◉
Kettering Park Hotel & Spa – Kettering ★★★★ 81% ◉
Aztec Hotel & Spa – Bristol ★★★★ 81% ◉
North Lakes Hotel & Spa – Penrith ★★★★ 79%
Cottons Hotel & Spa – Knutsford ★★★★ 79% ◉

AA classifications and awards

AA assessment

In 2006, in collaboration with VisitBritain, VisitScotland and VisitWales, the AA developed Common Quality Standards for inspecting and rating accommodation. These standards and rating categories are applied throughout the British Isles.

Any hotel applying for AA recognition receives an unannounced visit from an AA inspector to check standards. Although AA inspectors do not stay overnight at Budget Hotels, they do carry out regular visits to verify standards and procedures.

A guide to some of the general expectations for each star classification is as follows:

★ One Star

Polite, courteous staff providing a relatively informal yet competent style of service, available during the day and evening to receive guests
- At least one designated eating area open to residents for breakfast
- If dinner is offered it should be on at least five days a week, with last orders no earlier than 6.30pm
- Television in bedroom
- All rooms en suite, or private facilities with bath or shower room available at all times

★★ Two Star

As for one star, plus
- At least one restaurant or dining room open to residents for breakfast (and for dinner at least five days a week)
- Last orders for dinner no earlier than 7pm
- Easy access to both sides of beds for double occupancy.

★★★ Three Star

- Management and staff smartly and professionally presented and usually uniformed
- A dedicated receptionist on duty at peak times
- At least one restaurant or dining room open to residents and non-residents for breakfast and dinner whenever the hotel is open
- Last orders for dinner no earlier than 8pm
- Remote-control television, direct-dial telephone
- En suite bath or shower and WC

★★★★ Four Star

- A formal, professional staffing structure with smartly presented, uniformed staff anticipating and responding to your needs or requests. Usually spacious, well-appointed public areas
- Reception staffed 24 hours by well-trained staff
- Express checkout facilities where appropriate
- Porterage available on request
- Night porter available
- At least one restaurant open to residents and non-residents for breakfast and dinner seven days per week, and lunch to be available in a designated eating area
- Last orders for dinner no earlier than 9pm
- En suite bath with fixed overhead shower and WC

★★★★★ Five Star

- Luxurious accommodation and public areas with a range of extra facilities.
- First time guests shown to their bedroom
- Multilingual service
- Guest accounts well explained and presented
- Porterage offered
- Guests greeted at hotel entrance, full concierge service provided
- At least one restaurant open to residents and non-residents for all meals seven days per week
- Last orders for dinner no earlier than 10pm
- High-quality menu and wine list
- Evening service to turn down the beds. Remote-control television, direct-dial telephone at bedside and desk, a range of luxury toiletries, bath sheets and robes. En suite bathroom incorporating fixed overhead shower and WC

★ Inspectors' Choice

Each year we select the best hotels in each rating. These hotels stand out as the very best in the British Isles, regardless of style. Red Star hotels appear in highlighted panels throughout the guide. Inspectors' Choice Restaurants with Rooms are establishments that have been awarded the highest accommodation rating under the AA Guest Accommodation scheme.

★ Highly Recommended

Hotels with silver stars ★ have been selected for their superior level of quality, high standards of hotel keeping and for the quality of food within their star rating.

AA Rosette awards

Out of the many thousands of restaurants in the UK, the AA identifies over 2,000 as the best. The following is an outline of what to expect from restaurants with AA Rosette awards.

◉ Excellent local restaurants serving food prepared with care, understanding and skill, using good quality ingredients.

◉◉ The best local restaurants, which aim for and achieve higher standards, and better consistency; where a greater precision is apparent in the cooking. There will be obvious attention to the selection of quality ingredients.

◉◉◉ Outstanding restaurants that demand recognition well beyond their local area.

◉◉◉◉ Among the very best restaurants in the British Isles, where the cooking demands national recognition.

◉◉◉◉◉ The finest restaurants in the British Isles, where the cooking stands comparison with the best in the world.

Additional information

Hints on booking your stay

It's always worth booking as early as possible, particularly for the peak holiday period from the beginning of June to the end of September. Bear in mind that Easter and other public holidays may be busy too and in some parts of Scotland, the ski season is a peak holiday period.

Some hotels will ask for a deposit or full payment in advance, especially for one-night bookings. Some hotels charge half-board (bed, breakfast and dinner) whether you require the meals or not, while others may only accept full-board bookings. Not all hotels will accept advance bookings for bed and breakfast, overnight or short stays. Some will not take reservations from mid week.

Once a booking is confirmed, let the hotel know at once if you are unable to keep your reservation. If the hotel cannot re-let your room you may be liable to pay about two-thirds of the room price (a deposit will count towards this payment). In Britain a legally binding contract is made when you accept an offer of accommodation, either in writing or by telephone, and illness is not accepted as a release from this contract. You are advised to take out insurance against possible cancellation, for example AA Single Trip Insurance (telephone 0800 912 5002).

AA Hotels online

Locating and booking somewhere to stay can be a time-consuming process, but all the hotels inspected and rated by the AA are searchable online at www.theaa.com/bed-and-breakfast-and-hotel.

Facilities for disabled guests

The Equality Act 2010 provides legal rights for disabled people including access to goods, services and facilities, and means that service providers may have to consider making adjustments to their premises. For more information about the Act see: www.gov.uk/rights-disabled-person/the-equality-act-2010-and-un-convention or www.gov.uk/definition-of-disability-under-equality-act-2010

The establishments in this guide should be aware of their obligations under the Act. We recommend that you always telephone in advance to ensure that the establishment you have chosen has appropriate facilities.

Please note: AA inspectors are not accredited to make inspections under the National Accessible Scheme. We indicate in entries if an establishment has ground floor rooms, walk-in showers and whether the hotel has a hearing loop system; and if a hotel tells us that they have disabled facilities this is included in the description.

Food allergies

From December 2014 a new EU regulation came into force making it easier for those with food allergies to make safer food choices when eating out. There are 14 allergens listed in the regulation, and pubs and restaurants are required to list any of these that are used in the dishes they offer. These may be highlighted on the menus or customers can ask staff for full information. Remember, if you are allergic to a food and are in any doubt speak to a member of the hotel's staff. For further information see: www.food.gov.uk/science/allergy-intolerance/label/labelling-changes

Licensing laws

Licensing laws differ in England, Wales, Scotland, the Republic of Ireland, the Isle of Man, the Isles of Scilly and the Channel Islands. Public houses are generally open from mid morning to early afternoon, and from about 6 or 7pm until 11pm, although closing times may be earlier or later and some pubs are open all afternoon. Unless otherwise stated, establishments listed are licensed to serve alcohol. Hotel residents can obtain alcoholic drinks at all times, if the licensee is prepared to serve them. Non-residents eating at the hotel restaurant can have drinks with meals. Children under 14 may be excluded from bars where no food is served. Those under 18 may not purchase or consume alcoholic drinks.

Club licence means that drinks are served to club members only, 48 hours must lapse between joining and ordering.

The Fire Safety Order 2005 does not apply to the Channel Islands, Republic of Ireland, or the Isle of Man, which have their own rules. As far as we are aware, all hotels listed in Great Britain have applied for and not been refused a fire certificate.

For information on Ireland see page 562.

Bank and Public Holidays 2017

New Year's Day	2nd January	Spring Bank Holiday	29th May
2nd January (Scotland) (Substitute Day)	3rd January	Orangemen's Day (NI)	12th July
St Patrick's Day (NI & ROI)	17th March	Summer Bank Holiday (Scotland)	7th August
Good Friday	14th April	Summer Bank Holiday	28th August
Easter Monday	17th April	St Andrew's Day (Scotland)	30th November
Early May Bank Holiday	1st May	Christmas Day (Substitute Day)	25th December
		Boxing Day	26th December

Fifty Years On

By Mark Taylor

In 1966, The AA launched the first edition of a combined guide to Great Britain's hotels and restaurants. 50 years later, it is still going strong. Mark Taylor looks at the past and present of one of our longest-running publications.

Singer Rick Astley, DJ Chris Evans, chefs Gordon Ramsay and Heston Blumenthal, and the Ford Cortina MK II — The AA Hotel Guide certainly shares its 50th birthday with some notable Britons.

Originally including Great Britain's best restaurants as well as hotels, the guide was launched in the same year that The Beatles played their final concert, boxer Henry Cooper was floored by Muhammad Ali and England's football team lifted the World Cup.

In 1966, Britain was in the midst of the Swinging Sixties. Mini-skirts were the fashion item of choice for women, as hemlines got shorter and men's hair got longer. With the likes of The Rolling Stones, Small Faces and Dusty Springfield topping the charts and cinema audiences queueing around the block for *Alfie*, *Born Free* and *Carry on Screaming*, Britain was booming.

The weekly wage was £23 for men and £12 for women (apart from doctors and footballers who were earning more like £100 a week) and the average UK house price was £3,500. The first credit card had just been launched for those who needed to treat themselves, perhaps on a ticket for the new Inter-City train, or a colour TV ready for the start of BBC colour broadcasts in 1967.

In 1966 a pint of beer would cost you 9p in today's money, with a loaf of bread around 6p and a pint of milk 4p. If you were lucky enough to secure a ticket to see England in the World Cup, it would have set you back the equivalent of £11 (the cheapest ticket for the 2014 World Cup Brazil was £288).

The changing face of the AA Hotel Guide, 1966-1985 ▷

△ Some hotels that were in the 1st edition are still featured in the guide. This is how they appeared in 1966.

With all the changes that half a century have brought in technology and guest expectations, it's hard to imagine quite how basic facilities in hotels were 50 years ago. Today's guest expects 'rain' showers, sumptuous king-size beds and free high-speed WiFi as a matter of course. All those years ago, a typical stay in many hotels might include a night spent in a dimly-lit room with no central heating and single bed with a sagging mattress.

Nowadays, rooms have tea and coffee making facilities – often via a state-of-the-art coffee pod machine – but there weren't even kettles in most of the bedrooms 50 years ago. If you wanted to warm up with a cup of tea or instant coffee, you would have to head back down to the lounge and order one, usually walking past the queue of guests waiting to use the shared bathroom and toilet. At the time, en suite or private

AA Guide

Hotels and Restaurants in Great Britain

An AA Service Publication

AA Guide

Hotels and restaurants in Great Britain 1968

AA Guide

HOTELS AND RESTAURANTS in Great Britain

1970

AA GUIDE

Hotels and Restaurants in Great Britain and Ireland 1971

£1.50

AA GUIDE TO HOTELS AND RESTAURANTS IN GREAT BRITAIN AND IRELAND 1972

£1.50 to members

AA Guide to Hotels and Restaurants in Great Britain and Ireland 1973

£1.35 to members

AA Guide to Hotels & Restaurants In Great Britain and Ireland

Nearly 3000 AA-approved Hotels & Restaurants and 200 maps

AA Guide to Hotels & Restaurants in Great Britain & Ireland

STONE'S CHOP HOUSE

Nearly 5,000 AA-approved hotels and restaurants 200 maps

AA 1977 EDITION

GUIDE TO HOTELS AND RESTAURANTS

NEARLY 5,000 AA APPROVED HOTELS & RESTAURANTS IN GREAT BRITAIN & IRELAND

AA

HOTELS AND RESTAURANTS IN BRITAIN

Nearly 5000 AA approved hotels and restaurants Plus Red Star line-up · 32 pages in full colour

AA 1982

HOTELS and RESTAURANTS IN BRITAIN

INSIDE: New merit awards

AA 75th anniversary edition

HOTELS AND RESTAURANTS IN BRITAIN 1985

Seven £1 Money-off Vouchers inside

BTA

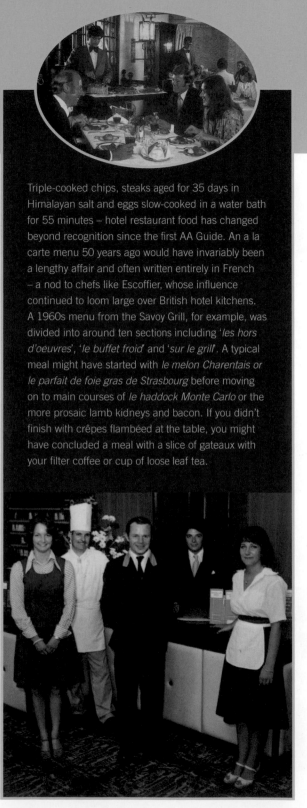

Triple-cooked chips, steaks aged for 35 days in Himalayan salt and eggs slow-cooked in a water bath for 55 minutes – hotel restaurant food has changed beyond recognition since the first AA Guide. An a la carte menu 50 years ago would have invariably been a lengthy affair and often written entirely in French – a nod to chefs like Escoffier, whose influence continued to loom large over British hotel kitchens. A 1960s menu from the Savoy Grill, for example, was divided into around ten sections including 'les hors d'oeuvres', 'le buffet froid' and 'sur le grill'. A typical meal might have started with le melon Charentais or le parfait de foie gras de Strasbourg before moving on to main courses of le haddock Monte Carlo or the more prosaic lamb kidneys and bacon. If you didn't finish with crêpes flambéed at the table, you might have concluded a meal with a slice of gateaux with your filter coffee or cup of loose leaf tea.

bathrooms were a luxury, being found in around 10% of three-star bedrooms and 20% of four-star establishments.

In 1966, there were no televisions in bedrooms, but one communal television in a room that was often separate from the residents' lounge. Not that there was much choice when it came to watching TV back then, with just three channels (BBC1, BBC2 and ITV) transmitting in black and white, although colour was just around the corner, with BBC2 broadcasting its first colour pictures from Wimbledon in 1967. Five decades later and hotel guests are usually able to watch a gazillion satellite channels on gigantic flat-screen TVs without leaving the luxury of their room, or plug their iPod into a 21st-century music/entertainment system.

The Early Days

Prior to the first edition of the Guide, information on hotels and restaurants formed part of the AA Members' Handbook or was printed as a supplement to the handbook. The amount of information became so great though, that it was decided to create a proper book. So it came to pass that in 1966, the first edition of the combined hotel and restaurant guide was printed. It had 888 pages, and contained over 4,000 hotels and restaurants. Intended entirely for members, it had no price information appearing anywhere on the cover. It was a drab affair apart from the colourful cover, as it had no photographs or images of any kind, apart from a basic atlas section.

The book, which didn't feature Ireland at the time, contained no advertising - that came in the 1970s - and the hotel information included was detailed, if limited in scope. Descriptive text was almost non-existent, with descriptions concise and tersely written - often a partial sentence of less than ten words - and a far cry from today when entries provide a detailed overview of the hotels featured, including information about the location, standards of service and other items of interest.

In 1967, facilities such as 'night porter' - now a standard feature for the majority of establishments - were still a

Shopping List		
	1966	2016
White loaf	1/4 (6.5p)	£1
Pint of milk	9d (4p)	45p
Lard	1/7 (8p)	60p
Dozen eggs	3/6 (18p)	£2
Cabbage	1/3 (6p)	50p
Filter coffee (227g)	5/ (26p)	£4

feature to be prominently listed, as were prices for 'bed and breakfast'. These days, hotels and B&Bs (aka Guest Accommodation) are clearly separated and contained in their own AA guide books.

Now printed in full colour with photographs of many hotels and plenty of informative advertising, the guide that you hold in your hands is much easier to navigate, with striking page design and handy colour-coding for each country.

The 1966 guide was arranged alphabetically by location, as it is now, and has been through the majority of the book's history. (There was a brief period in the 2000s when the contents were ordered by county, and then town, but those who had come to depend on the guide weren't keen, so the format was restored to its original style.) Each location also featured mileage distances that told guests how far it was from London and other notable places.

Enticing colour images of hotels are now commonplace in the book, which became full colour throughout in 1996, but early editions of the monochrome book relied on town plans and something that is rarely seen in books these days: line drawings, usually of of significant local buildings or natural features of interest.

Going through Changes

As time has moved on, the guide has also reflected major social changes. Editions published prior to 1971 and decimalisation list prices in shillings and pence or guineas, and as STD codes were only just being introduced in 1967, phone numbers – often only three or four digits – had no dialling codes. Similarly, and hard to believe when so many of us rely on sat-nav technology, establishment addresses were often so brief that they were sometimes simply a road name or village. Other than London, post codes were still being introduced and were rarely used in 1966.

As this was before the separation of hotels and restaurants into separate books – that came in 1991, the first AA Hotel Guide listed prices for lunch, tea, dinner and wine, as well as a description of the style of cuisine served, although in the

"Technology has to be the big thing. I can remember when opening the post was quite a lengthy job, normally accompanied by a morning cup of tea..."

late 1960s, hotel restaurants would have rarely strayed too far from English or French cooking. Fusion was still a futuristic concept.

Some hotels still appear in the guide, 50 years later, so I contacted a few to see if they could cast a light on how things have changed in the last half century. Kate Firth has worked at Ye Olde Bell Hotel in Barnby Moor, Nottinghamshire, for the past 34 years and she says the changes to the Guide have mirrored the changes to hotel life.

"Technology has to be the big thing. I can remember when opening the post was quite a lengthy job, normally accompanied by a morning cup of tea. We used to get piles of post with the confirmations, invoices and enquiries. Since email, the letter knife has long been discarded into the bottom drawer."

"We used typewriters back then and I can remember having to type menus for events - you had to do each one individually.

Looking at our original entry in the first Guide, "the biggest change must be the ratio of bedrooms with private bathrooms, just over half in 1966, almost unthinkable these days."

THE LOUIS XVI RESTAURANT

The top restaurant in Blackpool, combining superb decor with a high standard of French cuisine and excellent service.

L'APERITIF BAR

△ L'Aperitif – the cocktail bar at The Imperial Hotel, Blackpool. 1960s cocktails would have included the Bloody Mary, the Manhattan, the Moscow Mule, and the Mint Julep; all drinks that are still popular today.

◁ The Louis XVI Restaurant at The Imperial Hotel, Blackpool. As the name indicates, French cuisine was the standard approach to luxury dining; and the faux-Versailles decor certainly reflects this.

◁ The Imperial Hotel, Blackpool as it appeared in the mid-1960s. A grand 19th-century building, it doesn't look so different in 2016.

"It's also interesting to see garage accommodation available, too.

I remember the garages from my early days at the hotel but they were derelict at that time. They must have housed a fancy motor or two back in the '60s though."

Another hotel to have featured in the first edition as well as the 2017 Guide is The Imperial in Blackpool, which still celebrates notable past employees and their stories on the walls of the hotel. In the 1960s, the head cocktail barman at the hotel's L'Aperitif bar was the formidable Freddie Robinson, who invented many cocktails including *The Mayflower Spirit*, which can still be sampled in the bar to this day.

"Freddie, you can't buy publicity like this - great job, my friend!"

Freddie was a stickler for a strict suit and tie dress code in the bar and on one occasion he had to turn away a guest who turned up wearing a pullover. The next morning, the front page of the local Gazette newspaper carried the headline '*Coronation Street* Producer Refused Service at the Imperial'. Quaking in his boots, Freddie headed to the office of Jack White, the General Manager, to check if he was still in employment. Mr White's straight-faced response was: "Freddie, you can't buy publicity like this - great job, my friend!"

Peter Sweeney in 2016

It's not just the AA Hotel Guide that has clocked up a half century in the world of hospitality.

Doorman Peter Sweeney joined the iconic London hotel The Goring in 1965; the year *The Sound of Music* was first released in cinemas, and the nation said goodbye to Sir Winston Churchill.

Inspired by his brother, who was a doorman before him, he welcomed his first guest, Lord Moray of Scotland, through the front doors and over the last 50 years has continued this ritual, greeting the great and the good as they arrive at the hotel.

Despite admitting that so many of The Goring's guests have been memorable, his favourite remains the legendary actress Jean Simmons who, he says, arrived at the hotel with poise and grace. This is certainly in contrast to the time that Peter had to carry a rather worse for wear guest to their room – one of the more unusual items of luggage he has transported over the past half-century.

As The Goring's longest-serving member of staff, Peter has been given a number of gifts over the years for his service, including a gold watch, a holiday in the USA and two tickets to anywhere in the world.

Although he has met several members of the Royal family, it's an encounter with screen star Elizabeth Taylor that still ranks as one of the high points of his career.

"She drove up and as she got out of the car she looked at me and said: 'you must be Peter because of those beautiful blue eyes'. That was something I won't forget!"

Peter Sweeney in 1966

So Many Stories

There are endless celebrity stories from the early days of the Hotel Guide still being regaled by owners and past members of staff.

In the 1960s, The Maids Head Hotel in Norwich used to attract some of the biggest celebrities around, including actor Wilfred Hyde-White, who always used to ask for room 402 and who was known as a generous tipper.

Staff also had plenty of fun with comedy duo Eric Morecambe and Ernie Wise. One night Eric asked for Ernie's breakfast to be brought to him first. When the two boiled eggs appeared the next morning, Eric emptied the eggs through a hole in the bottom and they were presented to Ernie, who proceeded to knock the tops off two empty eggs, with a grinning Eric hovering nearby.

Back at Ye Olde Bell Hotel in Barnby Moor, long-serving General Manager Kate Firth still hears stories about past famous guests including Charlie Chaplin, Bing Crosby, Margaret Thatcher, Shirley Bassey and Cilla Black.

One of her favourite non-celebrity stories came from a guest of the 1960s and relates to the private owner at that time, Mr Hans Nielsen.

It was Christmas Day, 150 guests were expected for lunch, and the chefs were refusing to work unless they were paid extra. Mr Nielsen was not fazed by this and promptly saw them all off the premises. "As the guests arrived he explained that the format had changed this year and they were providing a whole turkey for each table that the guests were invited to carve themselves. It went down a treat and remained a Christmas Day tradition for many years!"

50 years has seen a mass of changes in our guide, and in Britain's hotels. We hope that both have retained a sense of integrity, and stayed true to their collective mission; to provide an important and worthwhile service, to the readers and guests who use both.

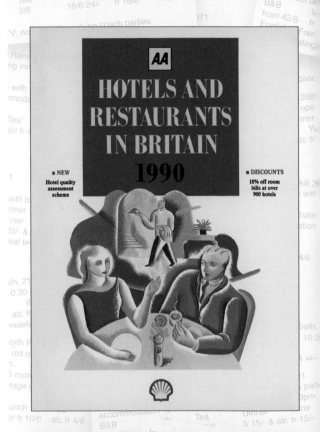

More Hotel Guides, 1990-2016 ▷

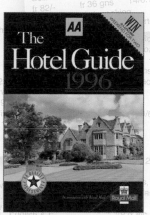

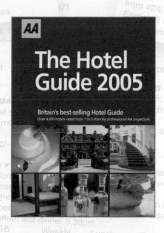

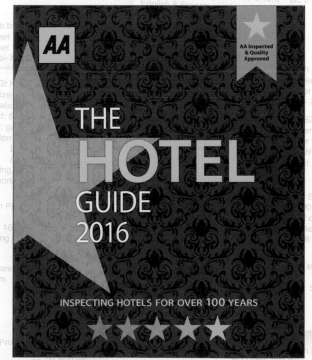

AA GUIDES

YOUR TRUSTED GUIDE

▸ THE BEST PLACES TO VISIT

▸ CLEAR TOWN PLANS AND MAPPING

▸ WRITTEN BY LOCAL EXPERTS

▸ RECOMMENDED PLACES TO EAT

▸ TRUSTED LISTINGS

Follow @TheAA_Lifestyle

Hotel groups information

Æbode HOTELS	**Abode Hotels** A contemporary collection of four city centre hotels in Canterbury, Chester, Exeter and Manchester that have a wide variety of dining outlets and are well geared to both corporate and leisure markets.	www.abodehotels.co.uk
BW Best Western.	**Best Western** Britain's largest consortia group has over 280 independently owned and managed hotels, modern and traditional, in the two, three and four star range. Many have leisure facilities and rosette awards.	0845 767676 *(Calls cost 7p per minute plus your phone company's access charge)* www.bestwestern.co.uk
BW Best Western PLUS	**Best Western Plus** 30 independently owned and managed hotels that offer that little something extra in the three and four star range. Some of these hotels have AA Rosette awards.	0845 767676 *(Calls cost 7p per minute plus your phone company's access charge)* www.bestwestern.co.uk
PREMIER | BEST WESTERN	**Best Western Premier** These hotels are selected for their beautiful settings, range of facilities and enhanced levels of service. There are currently 4 Best Western Great Britain hotels that have achieved Premier status. These join over 45 Best Western Premier accredited hotels across Europe and Asia.	0845 767676 *(Calls cost 7p per minute plus your phone company's access charge)* www.bestwestern.co.uk
Brend Hotels	**Brend** A privately owned group of 11 three and four star hotels in Devon and Cornwall.	01271 344496 www.brend-hotels.co.uk
Andrew BROWNSWORD HOTELS	**Brownsword Hotels** A small group of country hotels each with unique qualities, personalised service, memorable locations and a strong focus on food and wine.	www.brownswordhotels.co.uk
CHOICE HOTELS EUROPE	**Choice Hotels** Choice has four different brands in the UK: Clarion and Quality Hotels are three and four star hotels, Comfort Inns are two and three star hotels, and Sleep Inns are budget hotels.	0800 444444 www.choicehotelseurope.com
CLASSIC BRITISH HOTELS	**Classic British Hotels** An exclusive upmarket collection of four star and quality three star independent hotels throughout the UK, noted for its comfort, fine dining, spas, golf and event facilities.	0845 070 7090 *(Calls cost 7p per minute plus your phone company's access charge)* www.classicbritishhotels.com
COTSWOLD INNS & HOTELS	**Cotswold Inns & Hotels** Charming three and four star small hotels located in the Cotswolds.	www.cotswold-inns-hotels.co.uk
CROWNE PLAZA HOTELS & RESORTS	**Crowne Plaza** Four star hotels predominantly found in key city centre locations.	0871 423 4876 *(Calls cost 13p per minute plus your phone company's access charge)* www.crowneplaza.co.uk
DAYS INN	**Days Inn** Good quality modern budget hotels with good coverage across the UK.	0800 028 0400 www.daysinn.com
EDEN HOTEL COLLECTION	**Eden Hotel Collection** A privately owned collection of individual hotels, featuring award winning dining in quality surroundings.	0845 351 0980 *(Calls cost 7p per minute plus your phone company's access charge)* www.edenhotelcollection.com

Hotel groups information *continued*

English Lakes Hotels Resorts & Venues	**English Lakes Hotels** A collection of individually styled four star hotels located in and around the Lake District.	*015394 33773 www.englishlakes.co.uk*
EXCLUSIVE HOTELS and VENUES	**Exclusive Hotels** A small privately owned group of luxury five star hotels, all located in the south of England.	*01276 471774 www.exclusivehotels.co.uk*
FBD Hotels & Resorts	**FBD Hotels & Resorts** An Irish owned and operated group offering quality hotels in convenient locations.	*00 353 1 428 2400 www.fdbhotels.com*
fOCUShotels	**Focus Hotels** A group of 3 and 4 star hotels in both city and country locations across England. All offer WiFi and a number have spa facilities.	**0844 225 1625** *(Calls cost 7p per minute plus your phone company's access charge)* *www.focushotels.co.uk*
FOUR PILLARS HOTELS	**Four Pillars Hotels** A group of mainly 4 star hotels located in Oxfordshire and Gloucestershire. Most have leisure facilities and all offer free WiFi.	*0800 374692 www.four-pillars.co.uk*
hallmark	**Hallmark Hotels** A collection of 20 hotels that provide comfortable accommodation; some have leisure facilities.	*0113 307 6760 www.hallmarkhotels.co.uk*
Hand PICKED HOTELS BUILT FOR PLEASURE	**Hand Picked Hotels** A collection of predominantly four star, high quality country house hotels, with a real emphasis on quality food and service. Some have stylish spa facilities.	*01642 706606 www.handpickedhotels.co.uk*
Hillbrooke QUIRKY LUXURY	**Hillbrooke Hotels** A growing portfolio of hotels and inns under the banner 'Quirky Luxury'. Excellent locations, comfortable surroundings, relaxed informal service.	*www.hillbrookehotels.co.uk*
Holiday Inn	**Holiday Inn** A major international group with many hotels across the UK.	*0871 423 4896* *(Calls cost 10p per minute plus your phone company's access charge)* *www.holidayinn.co.uk*
Holiday Inn **Express**	**Holiday Inn Express** A major international hotel brand with over 100 hotels in the UK.	*www.hiexpress.co.uk*
Hotel du Vin & Bistro	**Hotel du Vin** A small expanding group of high quality 4 star hotels, with a strong emphasis on its destination restaurant concept and appealing menus.	*0871 943 0345* *(Calls cost 10p per minute plus your phone company's access charge)* *www.hotelduvin.com*
THE **HOTEL** COLLECTION	**The Hotel Collection** operates 11 four star hotels across the UK.	*0800 808 9596 www.thehotelcollection.co.uk*
ibis	**Ibis** A growing chain of modern budget hotels with properties across the UK. Now includes the Ibis Budget and Ibis Styles brands.	*www.ibishotel.com*

Hotel groups information *continued*

THE INDEPENDENTS HOTEL ASSOCIATION	**The Independents** A consortium of independently owned, mainly two, three and four star hotels across Britain.	*0844 800 9965* *(Calls cost 7p per minute plus your phone company's access charge)* *www.theindependents.co.uk*
IRELAND'S BLUE BOOK	**Ireland's Blue Book** A collection of country houses, historic hotels, castles and restaurants throughout Ireland.	*00 353 1 676 9914* *www.irelands-blue-book.ie*
IRISH COUNTRY HOTELS	**Irish Country Hotels** A collection of family-run hotels, all across Ireland.	*00 353 1 295 8900 (local) 0818 281 281* *www.irishcountryhotels.com*
LAKE DISTRICT HOTELS	**Lake District Hotels** A small collection of hotels situated in some beautiful parts of Lake District countryside and in some Lakeland towns.	*0800 840 1240 www.lakedistricthotels.net*
LEGACY HOTELS	**Legacy Hotels** A small group of three and four star hotels growing its coverage across the UK.	*0844 411 9011* *(Calls cost 7p per minute plus your phone company's access charge)* *www.legacy-hotels.co.uk*
Leisureplex HOLIDAY HOTELS	**Leisureplex** A group of 21 three star hotels located in many popular seaside resorts.	*01257 248000 www.leisureplex.co.uk*
MACDONALD HOTELS & RESORTS	**Macdonald** A large group of predominantly four star hotels, both traditional and modern in style and located across the UK. Many hotels enjoy rural settings and state-of-the-art spa facilities.	*0844 879 9000* *(Calls cost 7p per minute plus your phone company's access charge)* *www.macdonaldhotels.co.uk*
Malmaison	**Malmaison** A growing brand of modern, luxurious city centre hotels that provide deeply comfortable bedrooms, exciting restaurants and carefully selected wine lists.	*0871 943 0350* *(Calls cost 10p per minute plus your phone company's access charge)* *www.malmaison.com*
MANOR HOUSE HOTELS	**Manor House** Located throughout Ireland, this group offers a selection of independent, high quality country and manor house hotels.	*00 353 1 295 8900 (local) 0818 281 281* *www.manorhousehotels.com*
Marriott	**Marriott** This international brand has four and five star hotels in primary locations. Most are modern and have leisure facilities with a focus on activities such as golf.	*00800 1927 1927 www.marriott.co.uk*
MAYBOURNE HOTEL GROUP	**Maybourne Hotels** A hotel group representing the prestigious London five star hotels – The Berkeley, Claridge's and The Connaught.	*020 7107 8800 (Head Office)* *www.maybourne.com*
Mercure HOTELS	**Mercure Hotels** A large group of three and four star hotels throughout England, Scotland and Wales.	*0871 663 0627* *(Calls cost 10p per minute plus your phone company's access charge)* *www.mercure.com*
M GALLERY	**MGallery** A series of upmarket, leisure-based and individually presented hotels. Part of the Accor brand.	*0871 663 0624* *(Calls cost 10p per minute plus your phone company's access charge)* *www.mgallery.com*

THE
RED CARNATION
HOTEL COLLECTION

Red Carnation Hotels are a collection of family-run, award-winning boutique hotels
in the UK, Ireland, South Africa, Switzerland and the USA.
Each hotel is a landmark of history and tradition,
with a peerless reputation for exquisite fine dining and sumptuous surroundings.
We pride ourselves on delivering warm, thoughtful and highly-personalised service.
"No request is too large, No detail too small"

www.RedCarnation.com

Hotel groups information *continued*

MILLENNIUM MILLENNIUM · COPTHORNE	**Millennium & Copthorne** Group with 10 high-quality, four star hotels, and 1 five star, mainly in central London.	*0800 414741 www.millenniumhotels.com*
MORAN H O T E L S	**Moran Hotels** A privately owned group with 2 four star Moran Hotels, and 1 three star Bewley's Hotel. All have strategic locations in the UK and Ireland.	*00 353 1 459 3650 www.moranhotels.com*
NEW FOREST H OTELS	**New Forest Hotels** A collection of properties situated in the New Forest National Park, each with its own distinct character. All have an AA Rosette award for culinary excellence.	*0800 444441 www.newforesthotels.co.uk*
NOVOTEL HOTELS & RESORTS	**Novotel** Part of French group Accor, Novotel provides mainly modern three star hotels and a new generation of four star hotels in key locations throughout the UK.	*0871 663 0626* *(Calls cost 10p per minute plus your phone company's access charge)* *www.novotel.com*
Park Plaza Hotels & Resorts	**Park Plaza Hotels** A European based group increasing its presence in the UK with quality four star hotels in primary locations.	*0800 169 6128 www.parkplaza.com*
PEEL HOTELS PLC	**Peel Hotels** A group of mainly 3 and 4 star hotels located across the UK.	*0845 601 7335* *(Calls cost 7p per minute plus your phone company's access charge)* *www.peelhotels.co.uk*
Premier Inn	**Premier Inns** The largest and fastest growing budget hotel group with over 700 hotels offering quality, modern accommodation in key locations throughout the UK and Ireland. Each hotel is located adjacent to a family restaurant and bar.	*0871 527 8000* *(Calls cost 13p per minute plus your phone company's access charge)* *www.premierinn.com*
PRIDE OF BRITAIN HOTELS	**Pride of Britain** A consortium of privately owned high quality British hotels, often in the country house style, many of which have been awarded Red Stars and AA Rosettes.	*0800 089 3929* *www.prideofbritainhotels.com*
PH	principal hayley	**Principal Hayley** A collection of luxury properties from Victorian grandeur to iconic city centre hotels.	*0844 824 6171* *(Calls cost 7p per minute plus your phone company's access charge)* *www.ph-hotels.com*
QHOTELS	**QHotels** A hotel group with individually styled 4 star establishments located across the UK, in city locations and countryside retreats.	*0845 074 0060* *(Calls cost 7p per minute plus your phone company's access charge)* *www.qhotels.co.uk*
®RAMADA	**Ramada** A large hotel group with many properties throughout the UK in three brands – Ramada, Ramada Hotel & Resort, and Ramada Plaza.	*0808 100 0783 www.ramada.co.uk*
THE RED CARNATION HOTEL COLLECTION	**Red Carnation** A unique collection of prestigious four and five star hotels in Dorset, the Channel Islands and Ireland providing luxurious surroundings and attentive service.	*www.redcarnationhotels.com*
RELAIS & CHATEAUX	**Relais et Chateaux** An international consortium of rural, privately owned hotels, mainly in the country house style.	*00800 2000 0002 www.relaischateaux.com*

AA WALKING GUIDES

The 50 Best Walks of 2–10 Miles by Region and City

- Easy-to-follow directions with clear waypointed maps
- Colour-coded routes – pick from easy strolls through to more challenging walks
- Fascinating background reading for every walk
- Advice for dog owners
- Great for a full day out with recommended sights and attractions plus places to eat and drink

Hotel groups information *continued*

Renaissance One of the Marriott brands, Renaissance is a collection of individual hotels offering comfortable guest rooms, quality cuisine and good levels of service.	00800 1927 1927 www.marriott.co.uk
Richardson Hotels A group of 4 three and four star hotels located in Cornwall and Devon.	www.richardsonhotels.co.uk
Rocco Forte Hotels A small group of luxury hotels spread across Europe. Owned by Sir Rocco Forte, with two hotels in the UK, situated in major city locations.	00800 7666 6667 www.roccofortehotels.com
Scotland's Hotels of Distinction A consortium of independent Scottish hotels in the three and four star range.	www.hotels-of-distinction.com
Sheraton Represented in the UK by a small number of four and five star hotels in London and Scotland.	www.starwoodhotels.com
Small Luxury Hotels of the World Part of an international consortium of mainly privately owned hotels, often in the country house style.	0800 037 1888 www.slh.com
Surya Hotels A privately owned group of six 3 and 4 star hotels in East Anglia and the South East of England	www.suryahotels.co.uk
TA Hotel Collection A privately owned collection of three and four star hotels across Suffolk	01728 452176 www.tahotelcollection.co.uk
The Circle A consortium of independently owned, mainly two and three star hotels, across Britain.	01865 875888 www.circlehotels.co.uk
Thwaites A small group of four star hotels which feature spa facilities and well-equipped bedrooms ideal for both business and leisure guests.	www.shirehotels.com
Warner Leisure Hotels A collection of 3 and 4 star country hotels and villages, exclusively for adults. Renowned for their restaurants, daytime activities and live entertainment.	0330 100 9774 www.warnerleisurehotels.co.uk
Welcome Break Good quality, modern, budget accommodation at motorway services.	01908 299700 www.welcomebreak.co.uk
Z Hotels Modern hotels in city centre locations with out-of-town prices	www.thezhotels.com

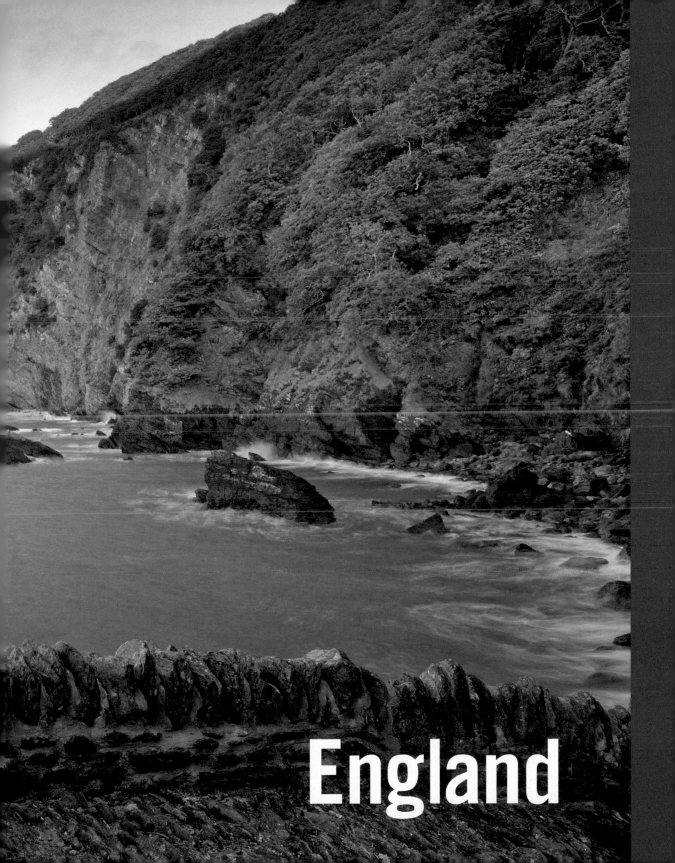

England

A

ABINGDON-ON-THAMES
Oxfordshire

Map 5 SU49

Premier Inn Abingdon

BUDGET HOTEL

tel: 0871 527 8014 *(Calls cost 13p per minute plus your phone company's access charge)*
Marcham Rd OX14 1AD
web: www.premierinn.com
dir: *On A415. Approx 0.5m from A34 at Abingdon South junct Marcham Interchange*

High quality, budget accommodation ideal for both families and business travellers. Spacious, en suite bedrooms feature tea and coffee making facilities, and Freeview TV in most hotels. Internet access and WiFi are available for a small fee. The adjacent family restaurant features a wide and varied menu. See also the Hotel Groups pages.

Rooms 27

ACCRINGTON
Lancashire

Map 18 SD72

Mercure Blackburn Dunkenhalgh Hotel & Spa

★★★★ 73% HOTEL

tel: 01254 398021 **Blackburn Rd, Clayton-le-Moors BB5 5JP**
email: H6617@accor.com **web:** www.mercure.com
dir: *M65 junct 7, left at rdbt, left at lights, hotel 100yds on left*

Set in delightfully tended grounds yet only a stone's throw from the M65, this fine mansion has conference and banqueting facilities that attract the wedding and corporate markets. The state-of-the-art thermal suite allows guests to relax and take life easy. Bedrooms come in a variety of styles, sizes and standards; some are located away from the main hotel building.

Rooms 175 (119 annexe) (36 fmly) (43 GF) 🅿 **Facilities** Spa STV WiFi HL 🕹 Gym Thermal suite Aerobics studio Xmas New Year **Conf** Class 200 Board 100 Thtr 400 **Services** Lift **Parking** 400 **Notes** ⊗ Civ Wed 300

ADDINGHAM
West Yorkshire

Map 19 SE05

Craven Heifer

◎◎ RESTAURANT WITH ROOMS

tel: 01943 830106 **Main St LS29 0PL**
email: info@wellfedpubs.co.uk **web:** www.thecravenheifer.com
dir: *A65 Skipton to Otley road, at rdbt onto B6160 signed Addingham. Craven Heifer at next junct.*

The Craven Heifer is located close to the town of Skipton and boasts themed rooms based on Yorkshire celebrities (e.g. Dame Judi Dench, David Hockney and Henry Moore). The bar is a traditional 'Dalesway' inn with stone and oak floors, open fires, leather seating, real ale and outstanding food. The two AA Rosette cuisine is beautifully complemented by a carefully chosen wine list. A warm and very friendly welcome from the well-informed staff is guaranteed.

Rooms 7

ALCESTER
Warwickshire

Map 10 SP05

Kings Court Hotel

★★★ 78% HOTEL

tel: 01789 763111 **Kings Coughton B49 5QQ**
email: info@kingscourthotel.co.uk **web:** www.kingscourthotel.co.uk
dir: *1m N on A435*

This privately-owned hotel dates back to Tudor times and the bedrooms in the original house have oak beams. Most guests are accommodated in the well-appointed modern wings. The bar and restaurant offer very good dishes from interesting menus. The hotel is licensed to hold civil ceremonies, and the pretty garden is ideal for summer weddings.

Rooms 61 (57 annexe) (2 fmly) (30 GF) 🅿 **S** £68-£90; **D** £70-£100 (incl. bkfst)* **Facilities** FTV WiFi 🕹 Gym Xmas New Year **Conf** Class 60 Board 40 Thtr 100 Del from £99 to £140* **Parking** 100 **Notes** LB Civ Wed 100

ALDEBURGH
Suffolk

Map 13 TM45

Brudenell Hotel

★★★★ 85% ◎◎ HOTEL

tel: 01728 452071 **The Parade IP15 5BU**
email: info@brudenellhotel.co.uk **web:** www.brudenellhotel.co.uk
dir: *A12, A1094. In town, right into High St. Hotel on seafront adjoining Fort Green car park*

Situated at the far end of the town centre just a step away from the beach, this hotel has a contemporary appearance, enhanced by subtle lighting and quality soft furnishings. Many of the bedrooms have superb sea views; they include deluxe rooms with king-sized beds and superior rooms suitable for families. The informal restaurant showcases skilfully prepared dishes that use fresh, seasonal produce, especially local fish, seafood and game.

Rooms 44 (17 fmly) 🅿 **S** £115-£140; **D** £115-£355 (incl. bkfst)* **Facilities** STV WiFi Xmas New Year **Conf** Class 20 Board 20 Thtr 20 Del from £185 to £255* **Services** Lift **Parking** 18 **Notes** LB

The White Lion Hotel

★★★ 88% ◎ HOTEL

tel: 01728 452720 **Market Cross Place IP15 5BJ**
email: info@whitelion.co.uk **web:** www.whitelion.co.uk
dir: *A12 onto A1094, follow signs to Aldeburgh at junct on left. Hotel on right*

A popular 15th-century hotel situated at the quiet end of town overlooking the sea. Bedrooms are pleasantly decorated and thoughtfully equipped, many rooms have lovely sea views. Public areas include two lounges and an elegant restaurant, where locally-caught fish and seafood are served. There is also a modern brasserie.

Rooms 38 **Facilities** STV WiFi 🕹 Xmas New Year **Conf** Class 50 Board 30 Thtr 80 **Parking** 10 **Notes** Civ Wed 90

ALDERLEY EDGE
Cheshire

Map 16 SJ87

Alderley Edge Hotel

★★★★ 78% @@@ HOTEL

tel: 01625 583033 **Macclesfield Rd SK9 7BJ**
email: reservations@alderleyedgehotel.com **web**: www.alderleyedgehotel.com
dir: *From A34 in Alderley Edge onto B5087 towards Macclesfield. Hotel 200yds on right*

This well-furnished hotel, with its charming grounds, was originally a country house built for one of the region's 'cotton kings'. The bedrooms and suites are attractively furnished, offering excellent quality and comfort. The welcoming bar and adjacent lounge lead into the conservatory restaurant where imaginative, memorable food and friendly, attentive service are highlights of any visit.

Rooms 50 (4 fmly) (6 GF) **Facilities** STV WiFi **Conf** Class 40 Board 30 Thtr 120 **Services** Lift **Parking** 90 **Notes** ⊗ Closed 1 Jan RS 25-26 Dec Civ Wed 114

★ **Find out more** about the AA's Hotel rating scheme on page 18

ALDERMINSTER
Warwickshire

Map 10 SP24

INSPECTORS' CHOICE

Ettington Park Hotel

★★★★ @@ COUNTRY HOUSE HOTEL

Hand PICKED HOTELS
BUILT FOR PLEASURE

tel: 01789 450123 & 0845 072 7454
(Calls cost 5p per minute plus your phone company's access charge) **CV37 8BU**
email: ettingtonpark@handpicked.co.uk
web: www.handpickedhotels.co.uk/ettingtonpark
dir: *Off A3400 5m S of Stratford, just outside Alderminster M40 Junct 15/A46 towards Stratford Upon Avon, A439 in town centre, A3400 to Shipston, 0.5m on left*

Set in 40 acres of grounds in the picturesque Stour Valley, Ettington Park offers the best of both worlds - the peace of the countryside and easy access to main roads and motorway networks. Bedrooms are spacious and individually decorated; views include the delightful grounds and gardens, or the historic chapel. Luxurious day rooms extend to the period drawing room, the oak-panelled dining room with inlays of family crests, a range of contemporary meeting rooms and an indoor leisure centre.

Rooms 48 (20 annexe) (5 fmly) (10 GF) **Facilities** STV WiFi HL ⊙ ⌣ ⌣ Clay pigeon shooting Archery Sauna Steam room Xmas New Year **Conf** Class 48 Board 48 Thtr 90 **Services** Lift **Parking** 100 **Notes** ⊗ Civ Wed 96

ALDERSHOT
Hampshire

Map 5 SU85

Potters International Hotel

★★★ 71% HOTEL

tel: 01252 344000 **1 Fleet Rd GU11 2ET**
email: reservations@pottersinthotel.com **web**: www.pottersinthotel.com
dir: *Access via A325 & A321 towards Fleet*

This modern hotel is located within easy reach of Aldershot. Extensive air-conditioned public areas include ample lounge areas, a pub and a more formal restaurant; there are also conference rooms and a very good leisure club. Bedrooms, mostly spacious, are well equipped and have been attractively decorated and furnished.

Rooms 103 (9 fmly) (9 GF) **Facilities** STV WiFi ⊙ Gym Beauty treatment room **Conf** Class 250 Board 100 Thtr 400 **Services** Lift **Parking** 120 **Notes** ⊗

A

ALDERSHOT *continued*

Premier Inn Aldershot

BUDGET HOTEL

tel: 0871 527 8018 *(Calls cost 13p per minute plus your phone company's access charge)*
7 Wellington Av GU11 1SQ
web: www.premierinn.com
dir: *M3 junct 4, A331. A325 through Farnborough. Pass Barons BMW then Queens Rdbt. Adjacent to Willems Park Brewers Fayre*

High quality, budget accommodation ideal for both families and business travellers. Spacious, en suite bedrooms feature tea and coffee making facilities, and Freeview TV in most hotels. Internet access and WiFi are available for a small fee. The adjacent family restaurant features a wide and varied menu. See also the Hotel Groups pages.

Rooms 84

ALDWARK
North Yorkshire **Map 19 SE46**

Aldwark Manor Golf & Spa Hotel

★★★★ 78% ❀ HOTEL

tel: 01347 838146 **YO61 1UF**
email: aldwarkmanor@qhotels.co.uk **web:** www.qhotels.co.uk
dir: *A1/A59 towards Green Hammerton, then B6265 Little Ouseburn. Follow signs for Aldwark Bridge/Manor. A19 through Linton-on-Ouse*

Mature parkland forms the impressive backdrop for this rambling 19th-century mansion, with the River Ure flowing gently through the hotel's own 18-hole golf course. Bedrooms vary - the rooms in the main house are traditional and those in the extension are modern in design. Impressive conference and banqueting facilities and a stylish, very well equipped leisure club are available.

Rooms 53 (6 fmly) ❧ **S** £70-£160; **D** £80-£170 (incl. bkfst)* **Facilities** Spa FTV WiFi ❂ ♨ 18 Putt green Gym Sauna Steam room Xmas New Year **Conf** Class 100 Board 80 Thtr 240 Del from £129 to £175* **Services** Lift **Parking** 150 **Notes** LB Civ Wed 140

Food Allergies

A recent EU regulation makes it easier for those with food allergies to choose safer foods when eating out. 14 allergens are listed in the regulation, and pubs and restaurants must now list any of these used in the dishes they offer.

ALFRISTON
East Sussex **Map 6 TQ50**

Deans Place

★★★ 86% ❀❀ HOTEL

tel: 01323 870248 **Seaford Rd BN26 5TW**
email: mail@deansplacehotel.co.uk **web:** www.deansplacehotel.co.uk
dir: *Exit A27 between Eastbourne & Brighton, signed Alfriston & Drusillas Zoo Park. S through village towards Seaford*

Situated on the southern fringe of the village, this friendly hotel is set in attractive gardens. Bedrooms vary in size and are well appointed with good facilities. A wide range of food is offered including an extensive bar menu and a fine dining option in The Dining Room restaurant.

Rooms 36 (4 fmly) (8 GF) ❧ **S** £80; **D** £90-£160 (incl. bkfst) **Facilities** FTV WiFi ❂ Putt green ⛳ Boules Xmas New Year **Conf** Class 100 Board 60 Thtr 200 **Parking** 100 **Notes** LB Civ Wed 150

ALMONDSBURY
Gloucestershire **Map 4 ST68**

Aztec Hotel & Spa

★★★★ 81% ❀ HOTEL

tel: 01454 201090 **Aztec West BS32 4TS**
email: aztec@shirehotels.com **web:** www.aztechotelbristol.com

(For full entry see Bristol)

ALNWICK

See **Embleton**

ALSAGER
Cheshire   Map 15 SJ75

Best Western Plus Manor House Hotel

★★★ 82% HOTEL

tel: 01270 884000 **Audley Rd ST7 2QQ**
email: res@manorhousealsager.com **web:** www.manorhousealsager.co.uk
dir: *M6 junct 16, A500 towards Stoke-on-Trent. 1st junct signed Audley, left to Alsager, hotel 2m on left*

Manor House Hotel is peacefully located in the village of Alsager, with easy links to the M6 and major road networks. Modern refurbishment and period architecture sit comfortably together to create a stylish interior. Bedrooms are decorated in attractive colour schemes and are well equipped for both business and leisure guests. Complimentary WiFi is available throughout. Public areas encompass Stables bar, a large lobby lounge, and Ostler's restaurant, which is set in the oldest part of the property.

Rooms 57 (4 fmly) (8 GF) ☏ **S** £69-£119; **D** £79-£129 (incl. bkfst)* **Facilities** FTV WiFi ↕ ⚘ **Conf** Class 108 Board 82 Thtr 200 Del from £120 to £140* **Services** Lift **Parking** 150 **Notes** LB ⊗ Civ Wed 150

ALSTON
Cumbria   Map 18 NY74

Lovelady Shield Country House Hotel

★★★ 81% ⚜⚜ COUNTRY HOUSE HOTEL

tel: 01434 381203 & 381305 **CA9 3LF**
email: enquiries@lovelady.co.uk **web:** www.lovelady.co.uk
dir: *2m E, signed off A689 at junct with B6294*

Located in the heart of the Pennines close to England's highest market town, this delightful country house is set in three acres of landscaped gardens. Accommodation is provided in stylish, thoughtfully equipped bedrooms. Carefully prepared meals are served in the elegant dining room and there is a choice of appealing lounges with log fires in the cooler months.

Rooms 10 (1 fmly) ☏ **Facilities** FTV WiFi New Year **Conf** Class 12 Board 12 **Parking** 20 **Notes** LB Civ Wed 100

Alston House

RESTAURANT WITH ROOMS

tel: 01434 382200 **Townfoot CA9 3RN**
email: alstonhouse@fsmail.net **web:** www.alstonhouse.co.uk
dir: *On A686 opposite Spar garage*

Located at the foot of the town, this family-owned restaurant with rooms provides well-equipped, stylish and comfortable accommodation. The kitchen serves both modern and traditional dishes with flair and creativity. Alston House runs a café during the day, serving light meals and afternoon teas.

Rooms 7 (3 fmly)

ALTRINCHAM
Greater Manchester   Map 15 SJ78

Mercure Altrincham Bowden Hotel

★★★ 76% HOTEL

tel: 0161 928 7121 & 941 1866 **Langham Rd, Bowdon WA14 2HT**
email: enquiries@hotels-altrincham.com **web:** www.hotels-altrincham.com
dir: *A556 towards Manchester, into Park Rd at lights, hotel 1m on right*

Situated within easy access of Manchester and the Airport, this hotel offers comfortable and well equipped bedrooms. Public areas include the Café Bar and The Restaurant, both serving a good choice of dishes. A well-equipped leisure centre has an indoor heated pool, spa, sauna and comprehensive air-conditioned gym. There is free WiFi throughout.

Rooms 87 (8 fmly) (13 GF) **Facilities** FTV WiFi ⚘ Gym Sauna Steam room Xmas New Year **Conf** Class 48 Board 50 Thtr 120 **Parking** 125 **Notes** Civ Wed 120

Premier Inn Manchester Altrincham

BUDGET HOTEL

tel: 0871 527 8738 *(Calls cost 13p per minute plus your phone company's access charge)*
Manchester Rd WA14 4PH
web: www.premierinn.com
dir: *From N: M60 junct 7, A56 towards Altrincham. From S: M6 junct 19, A556 then A56 towards Sale*

High quality, budget accommodation ideal for both families and business travellers. Spacious, en suite bedrooms feature tea and coffee making facilities, and Freeview TV in most hotels. Internet access and WiFi are available for a small fee. The adjacent family restaurant features a wide and varied menu. See also the Hotel Groups pages.

Rooms 43

ALVESTON
Gloucestershire   Map 4 ST68

Alveston House Hotel

★★★ 83% ⚘ HOTEL

tel: 01454 415050 **Davids Ln BS35 2LA**
email: info@alvestonhousehotel.co.uk **web:** www.alvestonhousehotel.co.uk
dir: *M5 junct 14 from N or junct 16 from S, on A38*

In a quiet area with easy access to the city and a short drive from both the M4 and M5, this smartly presented hotel provides an impressive combination of good service, friendly hospitality and a relaxed atmosphere. The comfortable bedrooms are well equipped for both business and leisure guests. The restaurant offers carefully prepared fresh food, and the pleasant bar and conservatory area is perfect for enjoying a pre-dinner drink.

Rooms 29 (1 fmly) (6 GF) ☏ **S** £85-£125; **D** £110-£145 (incl. bkfst)* **Facilities** FTV WiFi ↕ Beauty treatments Xmas New Year **Conf** Class 48 Board 50 Thtr 85 Del from £130 to £145* **Parking** 75 **Notes** LB Civ Wed 75

A

AMBERLEY
West Sussex   Map 6 TQ01

INSPECTORS' CHOICE

Amberley Castle

★★★★ ◎◎◎ �‍ COUNTRY HOUSE HOTEL

BROWNSWORD HOTELS

tel: 01798 831992 **BN18 9LT**
email: info@amberleycastle.co.uk web: www.amberleycastle.co.uk
dir: *On B2139, off A29 between Bury & Storrington*

The delightful castle hotel is idyllically set in the Sussex countryside, and boasts 900 years of history. The battlements (complete with mighty portcullis; one of the few in Europe that still works) enclose the hotel. Beyond these walls are acres of stunning parkland that feature formal gardens, koi ponds and a thatched treehouse accessed by a rope bridge. Guests can enjoy the magnificent restaurant where pre-booking is essential. Named after castles in Sussex, each of the sumptuously furnished bedrooms and suites is unique in design. Luxury amenities are provided in all rooms.

Rooms 19 (5 annexe) (5 fmly) (5 GF) �‍ S £175-£535; **D** £200-£670 (incl. bkfst)*
Facilities FTV WiFi �‍ �‍ Putt green �‍ Xmas New Year **Conf** Class 30 Board 30 Thtr 56 **Parking** 40 **Notes** LB �‍ No children 5yrs Civ Wed 56

AMBLESIDE
Cumbria   Map 18 NY30

See also **Elterwater**

HIGHLY RECOMMENDED

Forest Side

★★★★ 86% ◎◎◎ HOTEL

tel: 01539 435250 **Keswick Rd, Grasmere LA22 9RN**
email: info@theforestside.com web: www.theforestside.com
dir: *Leave M6 at junct 36, take 1st exit at rdbt onto A590 to Grasmere. Take 2nd exit at mini-rdbt. Hotel is 0.5m on the right*

Located on the edge of Grasmere village this former mansion house has been lovingly converted into a charming and relaxing hotel. Dinner is a must, with the team working closely with local suppliers and also growing much of their own produce in the walled garden, or foraging the local area. Twenty bedrooms provide stunning views of the hills and countryside beyond.

Rooms 20 (5 fmly) (2 GF) �‍ **D** £299-£549 (incl. bkfst & dinner)* **Facilities** FTV WiFi �‍ �‍ Xmas New Year **Parking** 42 **Notes** LB Civ Wed 60

Waterhead Hotel

★★★★ 78% ◎ TOWN HOUSE HOTEL   English Lakes
Hotels Resorts & Venues

tel: 015394 32566 **Lake Rd LA22 0ER**
email: waterhead@englishlakes.co.uk web: www.englishlakes.co.uk
dir: *A591 to Ambleside. Hotel opposite Waterhead Pier*

With an enviable location opposite the bay, this well-established hotel offers contemporary and comfortable accommodation with CD/DVD players, plasma screens and internet access. There is a bar with a garden terrace overlooking the lake and a stylish restaurant serving classical cuisine with a modern twist. Staff are very attentive and friendly. Guests can enjoy full use of the leisure facilities at a nearby hotel.

Rooms 41 (3 fmly) (7 GF) **Facilities** FTV WiFi ⚛ Free use of leisure facilities at sister hotel (1m) Xmas New Year **Conf** Class 30 Board 26 Thtr 40 **Parking** 43 **Notes** Civ Wed 80

Regent Hotel

★★★ 86% HOTEL

tel: 015394 32254 **Waterhead Bay LA22 0ES**
email: info@regentlakes.co.uk web: www.regentlakes.co.uk
dir: *M6 junct 36, 1m S on A591*

This attractive holiday hotel, situated close to Waterhead Bay, offers a warm welcome. Bedrooms come in a variety of styles, including three suites and five bedrooms in the garden wing. Public areas are contemporary and comfortable; the light, airy restaurant is the setting for hearty, enjoyable meals.

Rooms 32 (7 fmly) (9 GF) ⚛ S £59-£139; **D** £69-£165 (incl. bkfst) **Facilities** FTV WiFi New Year **Parking** 38 **Notes** LB

Rothay Manor

★★★ 85% ◎◎ HOTEL

tel: 015394 33605 **Rothay Bridge LA22 0EH**
email: hotel@rothaymanor.co.uk web: www.rothaymanor.co.uk

Originally built in 1823 for a wealthy Liverpool merchant, Rothay Manor exists today as a welcoming hotel. Perfectly located for touring the Lakes and set in its own stunning grounds, the hotel features 19 individual bedrooms. Public areas include a range of comfortable lounges and the popular restaurant where a range of imaginative dishes are provided. There are a number of dog friendly and accessible bedrooms available.

Rooms 19 (2 fmly) (2 GF) ⚛ S £120-£235; **D** £135-£250 (incl. bkfst)* **Facilities** STV FTV WiFi ⚛ ⚛ Xmas New Year **Conf** Board 18 Thtr 22 **Parking** 50 **Notes** Closed 3-21 Jan

Follow us on twitter
@TheAA_Lifestyle

Best Western Ambleside Salutation Hotel

BW Best Western

★★★ 84% HOTEL

tel: 015394 32244 **Lake Rd LA22 9BX**
email: ambleside@hotelslakedistrict.com **web:** www.hotelslakedistrict.com
dir: *A591 to Ambleside, onto one-way system, Wansfell Rd into Compston Rd. Right at lights into village*

A former coaching inn, this hotel lies in the centre of the town. Bedrooms are tastefully appointed and thoughtfully equipped; many boast balconies and fine views. Inviting public areas include an attractive restaurant and a choice of comfortable lounges for relaxing. For the more energetic there is a swimming pool and small gym, and for relaxation a spa and treatment rooms.

Best Western Ambleside Salutation Hotel

Rooms 54 (12 annexe) (4 fmly) (1 GF) ⌇ **S** £91-£105; **D** £132-£179 (incl. bkfst)*
Facilities Spa WiFi ☜ Gym Sauna Steam room Xmas New Year **Conf** Class 36 Board 26 Thtr 80 **Services** Lift **Parking** 54 **Notes** LB Closed 18-19 Dec

See advert below

A

AMESBURY
Wiltshire
Map 5 SU14

Holiday Inn Salisbury - Stonehenge
★★★★ 75% HOTEL

Holiday Inn

tel: 0345 241 3535 **Midsummer Place, Solstice Park SP4 7SQ**
email: reservations@hisalisbury-stonehenge.co.uk
web: www.hisalisbury-stonehenge.co.uk
dir: Exit A303, follow signs into Solstice Park. Hotel adjacent to service area

This hotel of striking modern design is located on the A303 very close to Stonehenge. All bedrooms have been appointed to the highest standards with unique headboards, air conditioning and broadband connection included in the generous amenities. Fluffy towels and powerful showers are provided in the modern bathrooms. The Solstice Bar and Grill is open from 7am-11pm and offers a range of snacks and meals.

Rooms 103 (24 fmly) (8 GF) ↖ **S** £79-£220; **D** £79-£220* **Facilities** FTV WiFi ↻ Xmas New Year **Conf** Class 20 Board 20 Thtr 25 **Services** Lift Air con **Parking** 168 **Notes** LB

ANDOVER
Hampshire
Map 5 SU34

Esseborne Manor
★★★ 81% ◉◉ HOTEL

tel: 01264 736444 **Hurstbourne Tarrant SP11 0ER**
email: info@esseborne-manor.co.uk **web:** www.esseborne-manor.co.uk
dir: Halfway between Andover & Newbury on A343, 1m N of Hurstbourne Tarrant

Set in two acres of well-tended gardens, this attractive manor house is surrounded by the open countryside of the North Wessex Downs. Bedrooms are delightfully individual and are split between the main house, an adjoining courtyard and separate garden cottage. There's a wonderfully relaxed atmosphere throughout, and public rooms combine elegance with comfort.

Rooms 18 (7 annexe) (5 fmly) (6 GF) ↖ **S** £92-£112; **D** £112-£165 (incl. bkfst)* **Facilities** STV FTV WiFi ⛳ New Year **Conf** Class 40 Board 30 Thtr 60 Del from £148 to £152* **Parking** 50 **Notes** LB Civ Wed 100

Premier Inn Andover
BUDGET HOTEL

Premier Inn

tel: 0871 527 8020 *(Calls cost 13p per minute plus your phone company's access charge)*
West Portway Industrial Estate, Joule Rd SP10 3UX
web: www.premierinn.com
dir: From A303 follow A342/A343 signs. Hotel at rdbt junct of A342 & A343 adjacent to Portway Inn Brewers Fayre

High quality, budget accommodation ideal for both families and business travellers. Spacious, en suite bedrooms feature tea and coffee making facilities, and Freeview TV in most hotels. Internet access and WiFi are available for a small fee. The adjacent family restaurant features a wide and varied menu. See also the Hotel Groups pages.

Rooms 81

ANSTY
Warwickshire
Map 11 SP48

Macdonald Ansty Hall
★★★★ 75% ◉ HOTEL

MACDONALD
HOTELS & RESORTS

tel: 0344 879 9031 & 02476 612222 **Main Rd CV7 9HZ**
email: ansty@macdonald-hotels.co.uk **web:** www.macdonald-hotels.co.uk/anstyhall
dir: M6 junct 2 onto B4065 signed Ansty. Hotel 1.5m on left

Dating back to 1678, this Grade II listed Georgian house is set in eight acres of attractive grounds and woodland. The hotel enjoys a central yet tranquil location. Spacious bedrooms feature a traditional decorative style and a range of extras. Rooms are divided between the main house and the newer annexe.

Rooms 62 (39 annexe) (4 fmly) (22 GF) **Facilities** FTV WiFi ↻ Xmas New Year **Conf** Class 60 Board 60 Thtr 150 Del from £130 to £260* **Services** Lift **Parking** 100 **Notes** Civ Wed 100

APPLEBY-IN-WESTMORLAND
Cumbria
Map 18 NY62

Appleby Manor Hotel & Garden Spa
★★★★ 79% ◉ COUNTRY HOUSE HOTEL

tel: 017683 51571 **Roman Rd CA16 6JB**
email: reception@applebymanor.co.uk **web:** www.applebymanor.co.uk
dir: M6 junct 40, A66 towards Brough. Take Appleby turn, immediately right. 0.5m to hotel

Appleby Manor Hotel and Garden Spa is an imposing country mansion, set in extensive grounds amid stunning Cumbrian scenery. The Dunbobbin family and their experienced staff ensure a warm welcome and attentive service. Comfortable and well-presented bedrooms vary in style, but all cater well for the modern guest; some rooms benefit from having patio areas. The bar offers a wide range of malt whiskies, with the restaurant and bistro offering high-quality, award-winning food. New for 2016 is the luxury Garden Spa boasting treatment rooms, hydrotherapy pool, outdoor hot tubs and thermal rooms.

Rooms 30 (7 annexe) (9 fmly) (10 GF) ↖ **D** £110-£240 (incl. bkfst)* **Facilities** Spa FTV WiFi ↻ ⛲ Putt green Steam room Sauna Salt room Experience shower Hydrotherapy Pool New Year **Conf** Class 25 Board 28 Thtr 38 Del from £145 to £195* **Parking** 51 **Notes** LB ⊗ Closed 24-26 Dec RS 6-13 Jun Civ Wed 60

ARLINGHAM
Gloucestershire
Map 4 SO71

The Old Passage Inn
◉◉ ⍟ RESTAURANT WITH ROOMS

tel: 01452 740547 **Passage Rd GL2 7JR**
email: oldpassage@btconnect.com **web:** www.theoldpassage.com
dir: A38 onto B4071 through Frampton on Severn. 4m to Arlingham, through village to river

Delightfully located on the very edge of the River Severn, this relaxing restaurant with rooms combines high quality food with an air of tranquillity. Bedrooms and bathrooms are decorated in a modern style, and have a collection of welcome extras including a well-stocked mini-bar. The menu offers a wide range of seafood and shellfish dishes including crab, oysters and lobsters from Cornwall, kept alive in seawater tanks. An outdoor terrace is available in warmer months.

Rooms 2

A

ARUNDEL
West Sussex
Map 6 TQ00

Comfort Inn Arundel
★★★ 73% HOTEL

tel: 01903 840840 **Lyminster Rd, Crossbush Services BN17 7QQ**
web: www.comfortinnarundel.com
dir: A27/A284, 1st right into services

A modern, purpose-built hotel ideally situated for exploring the nearby historic town and castle. There is a smart brasserie restaurant and bar, alongside a range of meeting rooms, all air-conditioned, which makes this an ideal venue for business guests. Bedrooms are spacious, smartly decorated and well equipped.

Rooms 53 **Facilities** WiFi ⊳ **Conf** Class 35 Board 35 Thtr 35

Premier Inn Arundel
BUDGET HOTEL

tel: 0871 527 8022 *(Calls cost 13p per minute plus your phone company's access charge)*
Crossbush Ln BN18 9PQ
web: www.premierinn.com
dir: At junct of A27 &A284, 1m E of Arundel

High quality, budget accommodation ideal for both families and business travellers. Spacious, en suite bedrooms feature tea and coffee making facilities, and Freeview TV in most hotels. Internet access and WiFi are available for a small fee. The adjacent family restaurant features a wide and varied menu. See also the Hotel Groups pages.

Rooms 31

The Town House
 RESTAURANT WITH ROOMS

tel: 01903 883847 **65 High St BN18 9AJ**
email: enquiries@thetownhouse.co.uk **web:** www.thetownhouse.co.uk
dir: A27 to Arundel, Into High Street, establishment on left at top of hill

This is an elegant, Grade II listed Regency building overlooking Arundel Castle, just a short walk from the shops and centre of the town. Bedrooms and public areas retain the building's unspoilt character. The ceiling in the dining room is particularly spectacular and originated in Florence in the 16th century.

Rooms 5 (1 fmly)

ASCOT
Berkshire
Map 6 SU96

Coworth Park
★★★★★ 89% ◉◉ COUNTRY HOUSE HOTEL

tel: 01344 876600 & 756784 **Blacknest Rd SL5 7SE**
email: reservations.CPA@dorchestercollection.com **web:** www.coworthpark.com
dir: M25 junct 13 S onto A30 Egham/Bagshot. Past Wentworth Golf Club turn right at lights onto Blacknest Rd (A329) hotel on left

Set in 240 acres of stunning parkland, Coworth Park is part of the luxury Dorchester Collection, sister to The Dorchester in London. The hotel offers luxurious guest rooms and suites, polo grounds, stables and a spa. Children are well cared for too, with a 'Kids Concierge' who can arrange a wide variety of activities for them. The hotel maintains a strong 'green' policy, as does the kitchen team where local quality suppliers are a priority. Casual dining is available in the popular Barn restaurant, which is located in a converted stable block.

Rooms 70 (40 fmly) (27 GF) ⋔ **Facilities** Spa STV FTV WiFi ⊳ ⊛ ♨ ⤙ Gym Polo Equestrian centre Archery Laser clays Falconry Duck herding ♬ Xmas New Year Child facilities **Conf** Class 54 Board 40 Thtr 100 Del from £325 **Services** Lift Air con **Parking** 100 **Notes** ⊗ Civ Wed 250

Macdonald Berystede Hotel & Spa
★★★★ 80% ◉ HOTEL

tel: 01344 623311 & 0344 879 9104 **Bagshot Rd, Sunninghill SL5 9JH**
email: general.berystede@macdonald-hotels.co.uk
web: www.macdonald-hotels.co.uk/berystede
dir: A30, B3020 (Windmill Pub). 1.25m to hotel on left just before junct with A330

This impressive Victorian mansion, close to Ascot Racecourse, offers executive bedrooms that are spacious, comfortable and particularly well equipped. Public rooms include a cosy bar and an elegant restaurant which serves creative dishes. The impressive self-contained conference centre and spa facility appeal to both conference and leisure guests.

Rooms 126 (61 fmly) (33 GF) **Facilities** Spa STV WiFi ⊳ ⊛ ⤙ Gym Leisure complex (thermal & beauty treatments) Outdoor garden spa Xmas New Year **Conf** Class 220 Board 150 Thtr 330 **Services** Lift **Parking** 200 **Notes** Civ Wed 300

ASENBY
North Yorkshire
Map 19 SE37

Crab Manor
◉◉ RESTAURANT WITH ROOMS

tel: 01845 577286 **Dishforth Rd YO7 3QL**
web: www.crabandlobster.co.uk
dir: A1(M) junct 49, on outskirts of village

This stunning, 18th-century Grade II listed Georgian manor is located in the heart of the North Yorkshire Dales. Each bedroom is themed around the world's most famous hotels and has high-quality furnishings, beautiful wallpaper, and thoughtful extras. Scandinavian log cabins are also available in the grounds, which have their own terrace with hot tubs. There is a comfortable lounge bar where guests can relax in the Manor before enjoying dinner next door in the Crab & Lobster Restaurant, which specialises in fresh local seafood. The attractive gardens offer a lovely backdrop.

Rooms 17 (9 annexe) (3 fmly)

ASHBY-DE-LA-ZOUCH
Leicestershire
Map 11 SK31

Premier Inn Ashby De La Zouch
BUDGET HOTEL

tel: 0871 527 8026 *(Calls cost 13p per minute plus your phone company's access charge)*
Flagstaff Island LE65 1DS
web: www.premierinn.com
dir: M1 junct 23a, follow A42 (M42), Tamworth & Birmingham signs. Hotel at rdbt at A42 junct 13. NB for Sat Nav use LE65 1JP

High quality, budget accommodation ideal for both families and business travellers. Spacious, en suite bedrooms feature tea and coffee making facilities, and Freeview TV in most hotels. Internet access and WiFi are available for a small fee. The adjacent family restaurant features a wide and varied menu. See also the Hotel Groups pages.

Rooms 76

A

ASHFORD
Kent

Map 7 TR04

INSPECTORS' CHOICE

Eastwell Manor
★★★★ ◉◉ HOTEL

tel: 01233 213000 & 213020 **Eastwell Park, Boughton Lees TN25 4HR**
email: enquiries@eastwellmanor.co.uk **web:** www.eastwellmanor.co.uk
dir: M20 junct 9, follow Faversham A251 signs. Hotel on left on entering Boughton Lees on A251

Set in 62 acres of landscaped grounds, this lovely hotel dates back to the Norman conquest and boasts a number of interesting features, including rooms with carved wood panelling and huge baronial stone fireplaces. Accommodation is divided between the manor house and the courtyard mews cottages. The luxury Pavilion Spa in the grounds has an all-day brasserie, and award-winning fine dining is offered in the main restaurant.

Rooms 62 (39 annexe) (2 fmly) (15 GF) ❀ **Facilities** Spa FTV WiFi 🐾 ⚄ ⚒ 9 ⚄ Putt green ⚄ Gym Boules 🎵 Xmas New Year **Conf** Class 70 Board 60 Thtr 180 **Services** Lift **Parking** 200 **Notes** ⊗ Civ Wed 135

Ashford International Hotel
★★★★ 81% HOTEL

INSPIRED BY YOU

tel: 01233 219988 **Simone Weil Av TN24 8UX**
email: ashford@qhotels.co.uk **web:** www.qhotels.co.uk
dir: M20 junct 9, exit for Ashford/Canterbury. Left at 1st rdbt, hotel 200mtrs on left

Situated just off the M20 and with easy links to the Eurotunnel, Eurostar and ferry terminals, this hotel has been stunningly appointed. The slick, stylishly presented bedrooms are equipped with the latest amenities. Public areas include the spacious Horizons Wine Bar and Restaurant serving a competitively priced menu, and Quench Sports Bar for relaxing drinks. The Reflections leisure club boasts a pool, fully-equipped gym, spa facilities and treatment rooms.

Rooms 179 (29 fmly) (57 GF) ❀ **S** £91–£141; **D** £103–£153 (incl. bkfst)*
Facilities Spa WiFi 🐾 Gym Aroma steam room Rock sauna Feature shower Ice fountain Xmas New Year **Conf** Class 180 Board 26 Thtr 400 Del from £125 to £159 **Services** Lift Air con **Parking** 400 **Notes** LB Civ Wed 400

Premier Inn Ashford Central
BUDGET HOTEL

tel: 0871 527 8030 *(Calls cost 13p per minute plus your phone company's access charge)*
Hall Av, Orbital Park, Sevington TN24 0GN
web: www.premierinn.com
dir: M20 junct 10 S'bound: 4th exit at rdbt. N'bound: 1st exit onto A2070 signed Brenzett. Hotel on right at next rdbt

High quality, budget accommodation ideal for both families and business travellers. Spacious, en suite bedrooms feature tea and coffee making facilities, and Freeview TV in most hotels. Internet access and WiFi are available for a small fee. The adjacent family restaurant features a wide and varied menu. See also the Hotel Groups pages.

Rooms 60

Premier Inn Ashford (Eureka Leisure Park)
BUDGET HOTEL

tel: 0871 527 8028 *(Calls cost 13p per minute plus your phone company's access charge)*
Eureka Leisure Park TN25 4BN
web: www.premierinn.com
dir: M20 junct 9, take 1st exit on left

Rooms 74

Premier Inn Ashford North
BUDGET HOTEL

tel: 0871 527 8032 *(Calls cost 13p per minute plus your phone company's access charge)*
Maidstone Road (A20), Hothfield Common TN26 1AP
web: www.premierinn.com
dir: M20 junct 9, A20 follow Lenham signs. Hotel between Ashford & Charing

Rooms 60

ASHINGTON
Northumberland

Map 21 NZ28

Premier Inn Ashington
BUDGET HOTEL

tel: 0871 527 8034 *(Calls cost 13p per minute plus your phone company's access charge)*
Queen Elizabeth Country Park, Woodhorn NE63 9AT
web: www.premierinn.com
dir: From A1 follow signs to Morpeth then Woodhorn Colliery Museum/Ashington. Through Ashington. Hotel in Queen Elizabeth II Country Park

High quality, budget accommodation ideal for both families and business travellers. Spacious, en suite bedrooms feature tea and coffee making facilities, and Freeview TV in most hotels. Internet access and WiFi are available for a small fee. The adjacent family restaurant features a wide and varied menu. See also the Hotel Groups pages.

Rooms 61

A

ATTLEBOROUGH
Norfolk
Map 13 TM09

Sherbourne House Hotel

★★★ 77% SMALL HOTEL

tel: 01953 454363 **8 Attleborough Rd NR17 2JX**
email: stay@sherbourne-house.co.uk **web:** www.sherbourne-house.co.uk
dir: A11 from London/Thetford towards Attleborough, through town centre, pass church on right, next left, hotel on right after 500mtrs

Built in 1740 this fine manor house is set among beautifully landscaped gardens and is a short walk from the historic market town of Attleborough. Much of the house has been refurbished and many of the original features sympathetically restored. Bedrooms are spacious and comfortable, and there is a light-filled conservatory lounge for guests. An extensive dinner menu is available in the evenings and freshly prepared breakfasts are served in the charming breakfast room overlooking the gardens. WiFi is available throughout the property and the hotel is ideally placed for visitors to Snetterton motor racing circuit.

Rooms 9 (1 fmly) (1 GF) ↖ **S** £50; **D** £95-£115 (incl. bkfst)* **Facilities** FTV WiFi **Conf** Class 18 Board 22 Thtr 30 **Parking** 20

AUSTWICK
North Yorkshire
Map 18 SD76

The Traddock

◉◉ ▣ RESTAURANT WITH ROOMS

tel: 015242 51224 **Settle LA2 8BY**
email: info@thetraddock.co.uk **web:** www.thetraddock.co.uk
dir: From Skipton take A65 towards Kendal, 3m after Settle turn right signed Austwick, cross hump back bridge, 100yds on left

Situated within the Yorkshire Dales National Park and a peaceful village environment, this fine Georgian country house with well-tended gardens offers a haven of calm and good hospitality. There are two comfortable lounges with real fires and fine furnishings, as well as a cosy bar and an elegant dining room serving fine cuisine. Bedrooms are individually styled with many homely touches.

Rooms 12 (2 fmly)

AXBRIDGE
Somerset
Map 4 ST45

The Oak House

◉◉ RESTAURANT WITH ROOMS

tel: 01934 732444 **The Square BS26 2AP**
email: info@theoakhousesomerset.com **web:** www.theoakhousesomerset.com
dir: M5 junct 22, A38 N, turn right towards Axbridge & Cheddar

This impressive restaurant with rooms is located in the middle of the village and provides a relaxed, high quality experience, whether guests are coming to enjoy the restaurant or to stay in one of the nine bedrooms above. Hospitality and service are delivered in an efficient and helpful manner by a young and enthusiastic team. The kitchen has a serious approach and delivers delightful dishes full of flavour, utilising the best quality produce.

Rooms 9 (2 fmly)

AXMINSTER
Devon
Map 4 SY29

Fairwater Head Hotel

★★★ 79% ◉ HOTEL

tel: 01297 678349 **Hawkchurch EX13 5TX**
email: stay@fairwaterheadhotel.co.uk **web:** www.fairwaterheadhotel.co.uk
dir: From B3165 Crewkerne to Lyme Regis road, follow Hawkchurch signs

This elegant Edwardian country house provides a perfect location for anyone looking for a peaceful break. Surrounded by extensive gardens and rolling countryside, the setting guarantees relaxation. Bedrooms are located both within the main house and the garden wing, and all provide good levels of comfort. Public areas are very appealing and include lounge areas, a bar and an elegant restaurant. Food is a highlight, with excellent local produce prepared with care and skill.

Rooms 16 (4 annexe) (8 GF) ↖ **D** £110-£140 (incl. bkfst)* **Facilities** FTV WiFi Library New Year **Conf** Class 25 Board 20 Thtr 35 Del from £149 to £169* **Parking** 30 **Notes** LB Closed 1-30 Jan

AYLESBURY
Buckinghamshire
Map 11 SP81

Hartwell House Hotel, Restaurant & Spa

★★★★ ◉◉ HOTEL

tel: 01296 747444 **Oxford Rd HP17 8NR**
email: info@hartwell-house.com **web:** www.hartwell-house.com
dir: From S: M40 junct 7, A329 to Thame, then A418 towards Aylesbury. After 6m, through Stone, hotel on left. From N: M40 junct 9 for Bicester. A41 to Aylesbury, A418 to Oxford for 2m. Hotel on right

This beautiful, historic house is set in 90 acres of unspoilt parkland. The grand public rooms are truly magnificent, and feature many fine works of art. The service standards are very high; guests will find that the staff offer attentive and traditional hospitality without stuffiness. There is an elegant, award-winning restaurant where carefully prepared dishes use the best local produce. Bedrooms are spacious, elegant and very comfortable. Most are in the main house, but some, including suites, are in the nearby, renovated coach house, which also houses an excellent spa.

Rooms 46 (16 annexe) (3 fmly) (10 GF) ↖ **S** £155-£200; **D** £200-£300 (incl. bkfst)* **Facilities** Spa STV WiFi ♨ ☒ supervised ⌣ ⌣ Gym Sauna Steam rooms ♫ Xmas New Year **Conf** Class 40 Board 40 Thtr 100 Del from £282 to £354* **Services** Lift **Parking** 91 **Notes** No children 6yrs RS Xmas/New Year Civ Wed 120

A

AYLESBURY *continued*

Premier Inn Aylesbury

BUDGET HOTEL

tel: 0871 527 8036 *(Calls cost 13p per minute plus your phone company's access charge)*
Buckingham Rd HP19 9QL
web: www.premierinn.com
dir: *From Aylesbury on A413 towards Buckingham. Hotel in 1m on left adjacent to lights*

High quality, budget accommodation ideal for both families and business travellers. Spacious, en suite bedrooms feature tea and coffee making facilities, and Freeview TV in most hotels. Internet access and WiFi are available for a small fee. The adjacent family restaurant features a wide and varied menu. See also the Hotel Groups pages.

Rooms 64

AYNHO
Northamptonshire   Map 11 SP53

Cartwright Hotel

★★★ 81% HOTEL

tel: 01869 811885 **1-5 Croughton Rd OX17 3BE**
email: cartwright@oxfordshire-hotels.co.uk **web:** www.oxfordshire-hotels.co.uk
dir: *M40 junct 10, A43, B4100 to Aynho*

This former coaching inn is located between Banbury and Oxford, making it ideally located for visiting the many tourist attractions the area has to offer, including Blenheim Palace and the circuit at Silverstone. The hotel features individually designed bedrooms which range from double to executive, and premiere standards with flat-screen digital TVs and complimentary WiFi. Secure parking is available.

Rooms 21 (12 annexe) (2 fmly) (12 GF) ✿ **S** £120-£130; **D** £130-£140 (incl. bkfst)* **Facilities** FTV WiFi ↳ Xmas New Year **Conf** Class 40 Board 20 Thtr 45 Del from £155 to £165* **Parking** 15 **Notes** LB ⊗

BABBACOMBE
See **Torquay**

Find out more about the NEW Hotel Breakfast Award on page 11

BAGSHOT
Surrey   Map 6 SU96

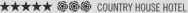

Pennyhill Park, an Exclusive Hotel & Spa

★★★★★ ❀❀❀ COUNTRY HOUSE HOTEL

tel: 01276 471774 & 486150 **London Rd GU19 5EU**
email: enquiries@pennyhillpark.co.uk **web:** www.exclusive.co.uk
dir: *M3 junct 3, follow signs to Camberley. On A30 between Bagshot & Camberley*

This delightful country-house hotel, set in 120 acres of grounds, provides every modern comfort. The stylish bedrooms are individually designed and have impressive bathrooms. Leisure facilities include a jogging trail, a golf course and a state-of-the-art spa with a thermal sequencing experience, ozone treated swimming and hydrotherapy pools, along with a comprehensive range of therapies and treatments. In addition there is a choice of eating options, lounges and bars to relax in.

Rooms 123 (97 annexe) (6 fmly) (26 GF) ✿ **D** £255-£395* **Facilities** Spa STV WiFi ⊛ ↘ ↧ 9 ⌣ Fishing Gym Archery Clay shooting Plunge pool Turkish steam room Rugby pitch Bike hire ♫ Xmas New Year **Conf** Class 144 Board 72 Thtr 200 Del from £290* **Services** Lift **Parking** 500 **Notes** LB Civ Wed 140

Premier Inn Bagshot

BUDGET HOTEL

tel: 0871 527 8040 *(Calls cost 13p per minute plus your phone company's access charge)*
1 London Rd GU19 5HR
web: www.premierinn.com
dir: *On A30 (London Rd) just before junct with A322 (Bracknell Rd). Adjacent to Cricketers Beefeater*

High quality, budget accommodation ideal for both families and business travellers. Spacious, en suite bedrooms feature tea and coffee making facilities, and Freeview TV in most hotels. Internet access and WiFi are available for a small fee. The adjacent family restaurant features a wide and varied menu. See also the Hotel Groups pages.

Rooms 53

B

BAINBRIDGE
North Yorkshire   Map 18 SD99

INSPECTORS' CHOICE

Yorebridge House

◎◎◎ ♍ RESTAURANT WITH ROOMS

tel: 01969 652060 **DL8 3EE**
email: enquiries@yorebridgehouse.co.uk **web:** www.yorebridgehouse.co.uk
dir: *A648 to Bainbridge. Yorebridge House N of centre on right before river*

Yorebridge House is situated by the river on the edge of Bainbridge, in the heart
of the North Yorkshire Dales. In the Victorian era this was a schoolmaster's
house and school, the building now offers luxury boutique-style accommodation.
Each bedroom is individually designed with high-quality furnishings and
thoughtful extras. All rooms have stunning views of the Dales and some have
their own terrace with hot tub. There is a comfortable lounge bar where guests
can relax before enjoying an excellent, three AA Rosette award-winning dinner in
the attractive and elegant dining room.

Rooms 11 (4 annexe) (11 fmly)

BALDOCK SERVICES
Hertfordshire   Map 12 TL23

Days Inn Stevenage North - A1   **WELCOMEBREAK**

AA Advertised

tel: 01462 730598 **Baldock Extra Motorways, A1(M) Junction 10, Radwell
SG7 5TR**
email: stevenage.hotel@welcomebreak.co.uk **web:** www.welcomebreak.co.uk
dir: *A1(M) junct 10 Baldock Extra Services*

This modern, purpose built accommodation offers smartly appointed, well-equipped
bedrooms, with good power showers. There is a choice of adjacent food outlets
where guests may enjoy breakfast, snacks and meals.

Rooms 62 (14 fmly) (30 GF) (8 smoking) **Facilities** STV FTV WiFi ⇗ **Services** Air con
Parking 120

BALSALL COMMON
West Midlands   Map 10 SP27

Nailcote Hall

★★★★ 77% ◎ HOTEL

tel: 024 7646 6174 **Nailcote Ln, Berkswell CV7 7DE**
email: info@nailcotehall.co.uk **web:** www.nailcotehall.co.uk
dir: *On B4101*

This 17th-century house, set in 15 acres of grounds, boasts a 9-hole championship
golf course and Roman bath-style swimming pool amongst its many facilities. The
bedrooms are spacious and elegantly furnished. The eating options are the fine
dining restaurant where smart casual dress is required, or The Piano Bar where
more informal meals are served.

Rooms 40 (19 annexe) (2 fmly) (15 GF) **Facilities** STV FTV WiFi ⓢ supervised ♨ 9 ⌕
Putt green ⛳ Gym ♫ Xmas New Year **Conf** Class 80 Board 44 Thtr 140 **Services** Lift
Parking 200 **Notes** ⊗ Civ Wed 120

Premier Inn Balsall Common (Near NEC)

BUDGET HOTEL

tel: 0871 527 8042 *(Calls cost 13p per minute plus your phone company's access charge)*
Kenilworth Rd CV7 7EX
web: www.premierinn.com
dir: *M42 junct 6, A45 towards Coventry for 0.5m. A452 signed Leamington/Kenilworth.
In 3m hotel on right*

High quality, budget accommodation ideal for both families and business
travellers. Spacious, en suite bedrooms feature tea and coffee making facilities,
and Freeview TV in most hotels. Internet access and WiFi are available for a small
fee. The adjacent family restaurant features a wide and varied menu. See also the
Hotel Groups pages.

Rooms 66

B

Waren House Hotel

★★★ 83% ◎◎ COUNTRY HOUSE HOTEL

tel: 01668 214581 **Waren Mill NE70 7EE**
email: enquiries@warenhousehotel.co.uk **web:** www.warenhousehotel.co.uk
dir: *2m E of A1 turn onto B1342 to Waren Mill, at T-junct turn right, hotel 100yds on right*

This delightful Georgian mansion is set in six acres of woodland and offers a welcoming atmosphere and views of the coast. The individually themed bedrooms and suites include many with large bathrooms. Good, home-cooked, AA Rosette-worthy food is served in the elegant dining room. A comfortable lounge and library are also available.

Rooms 13 (4 annexe) (3 GF) ⌇ **S** £115-£155; **D** £180-£260 (incl. bkfst & dinner)*
Facilities FTV WiFi Xmas New Year **Parking** 20 **Notes** ⊗ No children 14yrs

Victoria Hotel

★★★ 79% HOTEL

tel: 01668 214431 **Front St NE69 7BP**
email: enquiries@thevictoriahotelbamburgh.co.uk
web: www.thevictoriahotelbamburgh.co.uk
dir: *Turn off A1, N of Alnwick onto B1342, follow signs to Bamburgh. Hotel opposite village green*

Set on the delightful village green and overlooked by Bamburgh Castle, this hotel offers bedrooms with high quality furnishings and modern conveniences including LCD TV, a hairdryer, trouser press and complimentary refreshment tray. Bailey's Bar and Restaurant offers locally sourced food on menus served throughout the day. The staff pay great attention to detail and the hotel makes an ideal base from which to tour this beautiful area of Northumberland.

Rooms 38 (3 fmly) (4 GF) ⌇ **S** £35-£65; **D** £75-£185 (incl. bkfst) **Facilities** FTV WiFi Xmas New Year **Conf** Class 20 Board 12 Thtr 25 Del from £65 to £90 **Parking** 20

HIGHLY RECOMMENDED

Best Western Plus Wroxton House Hotel

★★★ 87% ◎◎ HOTEL

tel: 01295 730777 **Wroxton St Mary OX15 6QB**
email: reservations@wroxtonhousehotel.com **web:** www.wroxtonhousehotel.com
dir: *M40 junct 11, A422 signed Banbury & Wroxton. Approx 3m, hotel on right on entering Wroxton*

Dating in part from 1649, this partially thatched hotel is set just off the main road. Bedrooms, either created from cottages or situated in a contemporary wing, are comfortable and well equipped with WiFi and LCD TVs. The public areas are open plan and the low-beamed Restaurant 1649 has a peaceful atmosphere for dining.

Rooms 32 (3 annexe) (5 fmly) (8 GF) ⌇ **S** £62.10-£168; **D** £80.10-£188*
Facilities STV FTV WiFi ↻ New Year **Conf** Class 40 Board 40 Thtr 90 Del from £128 to £142* **Parking** 60 **Notes** LB ⊗ Civ Wed 90

Mercure Banbury Whately Hall Hotel

★★★ 77% HOTEL

tel: 01295 253261 **Banbury Cross OX16 0AN**
email: h6633@accor.com **web:** www.mercure.com
dir: *M40 junct 11, straight over 2 rdbts, left at 3rd, 0.25m to Banbury Cross, hotel on right*

Dating back to 1677, this historic inn boasts many original features such as stone passages, priests' holes and a fine wooden staircase. Spacious public areas include the oak-panelled restaurant, which overlooks the attractive well-tended gardens, a choice of lounges and a traditional bar. Smartly appointed bedrooms vary in size and style but all are thoughtfully equipped.

Rooms 69 (6 fmly) (2 GF) **Facilities** FTV WiFi Xmas New Year **Conf** Class 40 Board 40 Thtr 120 **Services** Lift **Parking** 52 **Notes** ⊗ Civ Wed 120

Premier Inn Banbury (M40 Jct 11)

BUDGET HOTEL

tel: 0871 527 9458 *(Calls cost 13p per minute plus your phone company's access charge)*
Stroud Park, Ermont Way OX16 4AE
web: www.premierinn.com
dir: *M40 junct 11, follow Banbury signs. Keep in left lane, take slip road on left. Hotel in Stroud Park Estate on left*

High quality, budget accommodation ideal for both families and business travellers. Spacious, en suite bedrooms feature tea and coffee making facilities, and Freeview TV in most hotels. Internet access and WiFi are available for a small fee. The adjacent family restaurant features a wide and varied menu. See also the Hotel Groups pages.

Rooms 128

Premier Inn Barking

BUDGET HOTEL

tel: 0871 527 8048 *(Calls cost 13p per minute plus your phone company's access charge)*
Highbridge Rd IG11 7BA
web: www.premierinn.com
dir: *A13 onto A406 signed Barking/Ilford. At Barking, exit at Tesco/A406 slip road. Hotel on left*

High quality, budget accommodation ideal for both families and business travellers. Spacious, en suite bedrooms feature tea and coffee making facilities, and Freeview TV in most hotels. Internet access and WiFi are available for a small fee. The adjacent family restaurant features a wide and varied menu. See also the Hotel Groups pages.

Rooms 88

Ibis Budget London Barking

AA Advertised

tel: 020 8507 8500 **Highbridge Rd IG11 7BA**
email: H3188@accor.com **web:** www.ibishotel.com

Modern, budget hotel offering comfortable accommodation in bright and practical bedrooms. Breakfast is self-service and dinner is available in the restaurant.

Rooms 70 🐾 **Facilities** FTV WiFi **Services** Lift **Parking** 50

Ibis London East Barking

AA Advertised

tel: 020 8477 4100 **Highbridge Rd IG11 7BA**
email: H2042@accor.com **web:** www.ibishotel.com
dir: *Exit Barking from A406 or A13*

Modern, budget hotel offering comfortable accommodation in bright and practical bedrooms. Breakfast is self-service and dinner is available in the restaurant.

Rooms 86 (26 GF) **Facilities** FTV WiFi HL **Services** Lift **Parking** 60

BARLBOROUGH
Derbyshire   **Map 16 SK47**

Ibis Chesterfield North

AA Advertised

tel: 01246 813222 **Tallys End, Chesterfield Rd S43 4TX**
email: H3157@accor.com **web:** www.ibishotel.com
dir: *M1 junct 30. Towards A619, right at rdbt towards Chesterfield. Hotel immediately left*

Modern, budget hotel offering comfortable accommodation in bright and practical bedrooms. Breakfast is self-service and dinner is available in the restaurant.

Rooms 86 (11 fmly) 🐾 **Facilities** FTV WiFi HL **Conf** Board 18 Thtr 35 **Services** Lift **Parking** 60

BARNARD CASTLE
County Durham   **Map 19 NZ01**

The Morritt Country House Hotel & Spa

★★★★ 78% ◉◉ HOTEL

tel: 01833 627232 **Greta Bridge DL12 9SE**
email: relax@themorritt.co.uk **web:** www.themorritt.co.uk
dir: *From M1 (east) exit at junct 57 onto A66 westbound. From M6 (west) exit at junct 40 onto A66 eastbound. Follow signs to Greta Bridge*

In the heart of beautiful Teesdale, this 17th-century former coaching house, with connections to Dickens, is full of character and is a popular meeting place. The bar area has two amazing Dickens murals - one newly created in 2012 to commemorate Dickens' 200th birthday. The hotel prides itself on its traditional values, apparent in the quality of its service, locally-sourced food and individually styled rooms. Guests can enjoy pampering and treatments in the adjoining new spa.

Rooms 26 (6 annexe) **Conf** Class 60 Board 40 Thtr 120

BARNBY MOOR
Nottinghamshire   **Map 16 SK68**

B

Ye Olde Bell Hotel & Restaurant

★★★★ 80% ◉ HOTEL

tel: 01777 705121 **DN22 8QS**
email: enquiries@yeoldebell-hotel.co.uk **web:** www.yeoldebell-hotel.co.uk
dir: *A1(M) south near junct 34, exit Barnby Moor or A1(M) north exit A620 Retford. Hotel on A638 between Retford & Bawtry*

This beautifully refurbished 17th-century hotel is conveniently located just off the A1 between Retford and Doncaster in the rural village of Barnby Moor. Public rooms have a wealth of original character such as traditional log fires and ornate plaster work, and there is an outside terrace also available at the front of the main bar. Restaurant 1650 features elegant wood panelling as well as a striking contemporary bar. The tastefully appointed bedrooms are furnished to a high standard and are attractively co-ordinated. All benefit from modern bathrooms. The hotel also features a stylish hair and beauty treatment salon and a fitness suite. 2017 will see the opening of a new spa facility, the result of a multi-million pound investment. The gardens are a feature and are perfect for weddings or outside entertaining in warmer weather.

Rooms 59 (10 annexe) (5 fmly) (8 GF) 🐾 **Facilities** FTV WiFi ⌀ Gym Hair salon Beauty treatment room Xmas New Year Child facilities **Conf** Class 100 Board 50 Thtr 250 Del from £99 to £145 **Parking** 200 **Notes** ⊗ Civ Wed 250

B

BARNET	Map 6 TQ29
Greater London	

Savoro Restaurant with Rooms

◎ RESTAURANT WITH ROOMS

tel: 020 8449 9888 **206 High St EN5 5SZ**
email: savoro@savoro.co.uk **web:** www.savoro.co.uk
dir: M25 junct 23, A1000. Establishment in crescent behind Hadley Green Jaguar Garage

Set back from the main high street, the traditional frontage of this establishment belies the stylishly contemporary bedrooms within. Several have modern four-poster beds and all have well designed bathrooms. The award-winning restaurant is an additional bonus, serving food which is all freshly prepared in-house, from bread to ice cream.

Rooms 11 (2 fmly)

BARNSLEY	Map 16 SE30
South Yorkshire	

Tankersley Manor

★★★★ 74% HOTEL

INSPIRED BY YOU

tel: 01226 744700 **Church Ln S75 3DQ**
email: tankersleymanor@qhotels.co.uk **web:** www.qhotels.co.uk

(For full entry see Tankersley)

Premier Inn Barnsley Central M1 Jct 37

BUDGET HOTEL

Premier Inn

tel: 0871 527 9204 *(Calls cost 13p per minute plus your phone company's access charge)*
Gateway Plaza, Sackville St S70 2RD
web: www.premierinn.com
dir: M1 junct 37, A628 (Dodworth Rd) signed Barnsley. In approx 1m 2nd exit at rdbt into Shambles St, car park entrance on left

High quality, budget accommodation ideal for both families and business travellers. Spacious, en suite bedrooms feature tea and coffee making facilities, and Freeview TV in most hotels. Internet access and WiFi are available for a small fee. The adjacent family restaurant features a wide and varied menu. See also the Hotel Groups pages.

Rooms 110

BARNSTAPLE	Map 3 SS53
Devon	

The Imperial Hotel

Brend Hotels

★★★★ 75% HOTEL

tel: 01271 345861 **Taw Vale Pde EX32 8NB**
email: reservations@brend-imperial.co.uk **web:** www.brend-imperial.co.uk
dir: M5 junct 27/A361 to Barnstaple. Follow town centre signs, passing Tesco. Straight on at next 2 rdbts. Hotel on right

This smart and attractive hotel is pleasantly located at the centre of Barnstaple and overlooks the River Taw. Staff are friendly and offer attentive service. The comfortable bedrooms are of various sizes; some have balconies and many enjoy river views. Afternoon tea is available in the lounge, and the appetising cuisine is freshly prepared.

Rooms 63 (8 annexe) (9 fmly) (4 GF) ⚡ **S** £80-£95; **D** £100-£260* **Facilities** FTV WiFi ♨ Leisure facilities at sister hotel Xmas New Year **Conf** Class 40 Board 30 Thtr 60 **Services** Lift **Parking** 80 **Notes** LB ⊗ Civ Wed 50

See advert on opposite page

B

The Royal & Fortescue Hotel

★★★ 83% HOTEL

tel: 01271 342289 Boutport St EX31 1HG
email: reservations@royalfortescue.co.uk web: www.royalfortescue.co.uk
dir: From A361 onto Barbican Rd signed town centre, right into Queen St, left into Boutport St, hotel on left

Formerly a coaching inn, this friendly and convivial hotel is conveniently located in the centre of town. Bedrooms vary in size and all are decorated and furnished to a consistently high standard. In addition to the formal restaurant, guests can take snacks in the popular coffee shop or dine more informally in The Bank, a bistro and café bar.

Rooms 49 (4 fmly) (4 GF) ♦ S £60-£115; D £70-£155* Facilities FTV WiFi ♫ Leisure facilities available at sister hotel Xmas New Year Conf Class 25 Board 25 Thtr 25 Services Lift Parking 40 Notes LB ⊗

The Barnstaple Hotel

★★★ 81% HOTEL

tel: 01271 376221 Braunton Rd EX31 1LE
email: reservations@barnstaplehotel.co.uk web: www. barnstaplehotel.co.uk
dir: Outskirts of Barnstaple on A361

This well-established hotel enjoys a convenient location on the edge of town. Bedrooms are spacious and well equipped, many with access to a balcony overlooking the outdoor pool and garden. A wide choice is offered from various menus based on local produce, served in the Brasserie Restaurant. There is an extensive range of leisure and conference facilities.

Rooms 60 (4 fmly) (17 GF) ♦ S £69-£119; D £77-£137* Facilities FTV WiFi ♫ ⊗ ↘ Gym Beauty treatment room Saunas Chill out sanctuary Xmas New Year Child facilities Conf Class 100 Board 50 Thtr 250 Parking 250 Notes LB ⊗ Civ Wed 150

B

BARNSTAPLE *continued*

The Park Hotel

★★★ 78% HOTEL

tel: 01271 372166 **Taw Vale EX32 9AE**
email: reservations@parkhotel.co.uk web: www.parkhotel.co.uk
dir: *A361 to Barnstaple, 0.5m from town centre. Opposite Rock Park*

Enjoying views across the park and within easy walking distance of the town centre, this modern hotel offers a choice of bedrooms in both the main building and the Garden Court, just across the car park. Public rooms are open-plan in style and the friendly staff offer attentive service in a relaxed atmosphere.

Rooms 49 (16 annexe) (3 fmly) (10 GF) ⟐ **S** £60-£100; **D** £75-£115* **Facilities** FTV WiFi ⟐ Leisure facilities available at sister hotel Xmas New Year **Conf** Class 50 Board 30 Thtr 80 **Services** Lift **Parking** 80 **Notes** LB ⊗ Civ Wed 100

Premier Inn Barnstaple

BUDGET HOTEL

tel: 0871 527 8052 *(Calls cost 13p per minute plus your phone company's access charge)*
Whiddon Dr, off Eastern Av EX32 8RY
web: www.premierinn.com
dir: *Exit A361 (North Devon Link Rd) towards Barnstaple. Right at Portmore rdbt*

High quality, budget accommodation ideal for both families and business travellers. Spacious, en suite bedrooms feature tea and coffee making facilities, and Freeview TV in most hotels. Internet access and WiFi are available for a small fee. The adjacent family restaurant features a wide and varied menu. See also the Hotel Groups pages.

Rooms 71

| BARROW-IN-FURNESS | Map 18 SD26 |
| Cumbria | |

Abbey House Hotel

★★★★ 78% ⊚ HOTEL

tel: 01229 838282 & 0844 826 2091
(Calls cost 7p per minute plus your phone company's access charge) **Abbey Rd LA13 0PA**
email: enquiries@abbeyhousehotel.com web: www.abbeyhousehotel.com
dir: *From A590 follow signs for Furness General Hospital & Furness Abbey. Hotel approx 100yds on left*

Set in 14 acres of private gardens and woodland, this red stone building is a local landmark. A recent redevelopment project has seen striking results; a sharp and contemporary style sits well with the original architectural features and charm of the building. Bedrooms are stylish and well equipped. Service is personal and food is a highlight of any stay. Business and function facilities also impress.

Rooms 61 (4 annexe) (6 fmly) (2 GF) ⟐ **Facilities** STV FTV WiFi ⟐ Beauty treatment room Xmas New Year **Conf** Class 120 Board 80 Thtr 300 **Services** Lift **Parking** 100 **Notes** Civ Wed 120

Clarence House Country Hotel & Restaurant

★★★★ 69% ⊚ HOTEL

tel: 01229 462508 **Skelgate, Dalton-in-Furness LA15 8BQ**
email: clarencehsehotel@aol.com web: www.clarencehouse-hotel.co.uk
dir: *A590 through Ulverston & Lindal, 2nd exit at rdbt & 1st exit at next. Follow signs to Dalton, hotel at top of hill on right*

This hotel is located in ornamental grounds with unrestricted countryside views. Bedrooms are individually themed with those in the main hotel being particularly stylish and comfortable. The public rooms are spacious and also furnished to a high standard. The popular conservatory restaurant and contemporary brasserie offer well-prepared dishes from extensive menus. There is a delightful barn conversion that is ideal for weddings.

Rooms 18 (11 annexe) (1 fmly) (5 GF) ⟐ **Facilities** FTV WiFi ⟑ New Year **Conf** Class 40 Board 15 Thtr 100 **Parking** 40 **Notes** LB Closed 24-26 Dec Civ Wed 100

Premier Inn Barrow-in-Furness

BUDGET HOTEL

tel: 0871 527 9470 *(Calls cost 13p per minute plus your phone company's access charge)*
North Rd LA14 2PW
web: www.premierinn.com
dir: *M6 junct 36, A590. In 3m take slip road signed Barrow-in-Furness. Follow signs for Barrow-In-Furness & A590. At rdbt 2nd exit signed Walney Island & A590. Approx 0.5m, hotel on right*

High quality, budget accommodation ideal for both families and business travellers. Spacious, en suite bedrooms feature tea and coffee making facilities, and Freeview TV in most hotels. Internet access and WiFi are available for a small fee. The adjacent family restaurant features a wide and varied menu. See also the Hotel Groups pages.

Rooms 80

| BARTON | Map 18 SD53 |
| Lancashire | |

Barton Grange Hotel

★★★★ 77% HOTEL

tel: 01772 862551 **Garstang Rd PR3 5AA**
email: stay@bartongrangehotel.com web: www.bartongrangehotel.co.uk
dir: *M6 junct 32, follow Garstang (A6) signs for 2.5m. Hotel on right*

Situated close to the M6, this modern, stylish hotel benefits from extensive public areas that include leisure facilities with a swimming pool, sauna and gym. Comfortable, well-appointed bedrooms include executive rooms and family rooms, as well as attractive accommodation in an adjacent cottage. The unique Walled Garden Bistro offers all-day eating.

Rooms 51 (8 annexe) (8 fmly) (4 GF) ⟐ **Facilities** STV WiFi ⟐ ⟑ Gym Sauna ⟑ Xmas New Year **Conf** Class 100 Board 80 Thtr 300 **Services** Lift **Parking** 250 **Notes** ⊗ Civ Wed 300

BARTON-ON-SEA
Hampshire
Map 5 SZ29

Pebble Beach

 RESTAURANT WITH ROOMS

tel: 01425 627777 **Marine Dr BH25 7DZ**
email: mail@pebblebeach-uk.com web: www.pebblebeach-uk.com
dir: *A35 from Southampton onto A337 to New Milton, left into Barton Court Av to clifftop*

Situated on the clifftop, the restaurant at Pebble Beach boasts stunning views towards The Needles. Bedrooms and bathrooms (situated above the restaurant) are well equipped and provide a range of accessories. A freshly cooked breakfast is served in the main restaurant, or outside on the wonderful terrace. Next door, Petit Pebbles delicatessen is a recent addition and well worth a visit.

Rooms 4

BASILDON
Essex
Map 6 TQ78

Premier Inn Basildon (East Mayne)

BUDGET HOTEL

tel: 0871 527 8054 *(Calls cost 13p per minute plus your phone company's access charge)*
Felmores, East Mayne SS13 1BW
web: www.premierinn.com
dir: *M25 junct 29 , A127 towards Southend, take A132 S signed Basildon & Wickford at Neverdon exit. Hotel on left*

High quality, budget accommodation ideal for both families and business travellers. Spacious, en suite bedrooms feature tea and coffee making facilities, and Freeview TV in most hotels. Internet access and WiFi are available for a small fee. The adjacent family restaurant features a wide and varied menu. See also the Hotel Groups pages.

Rooms 74

Premier Inn Basildon (Festival Park)

BUDGET HOTEL

tel: 0871 527 8056 *(Calls cost 13p per minute plus your phone company's access charge)*
Festival Leisure Park, Pipps Hill Road South, Off Cranes Farm Rd SS14 3WB
web: www.premierinn.com
dir: *M25 junct 9, A217 towards Basildon. Take A17. Hotel just off A1235 adjacent to David Lloyd Leisure Club*

Rooms 82

Premier Inn Basildon South

BUDGET HOTEL

tel: 0871 527 8060 *(Calls cost 13p per minute plus your phone company's access charge)*
High Rd, Fobbing, Stanford-Le-Hope SS17 9NR
web: www.premierinn.com
dir: *M2 junct 30/31, A13 towards Southend. 10m to Five Bells Rdbt junct with A176. Right into Fobbing High Rd. Hotel on left*

Rooms 61

BASINGSTOKE
Hampshire
Map 5 SU65

Tylney Hall Hotel

★★★★  HOTEL

tel: 01256 764881 **Ridge Ln RG27 9AZ**
email: sales@tylneyhall.com web: www.tylneyhall.com

(For full entry see Rotherwick)

Oakley Hall Hotel

★★★★ 88% ◉◉ COUNTRY HOUSE HOTEL

tel: 01256 783350 **Rectory Rd, Oakley RG23 7EL**
email: enquiries@oakleyhall-park.com web: www.oakleyhall-park.com
dir: *M3 junct 7, follow Basingstoke signs. In 500yds before lights turn left onto A30 towards Oakley, immediately right onto unclass road towards Oakley. In 3m left at T-junct into Rectory Rd. Left onto B3400. Hotel signed 1st on left*

An impressive drive leads to this country house which benefits from delightful country views across north Hampshire. Built in 1795, it was once owned by the Bramston family who were friends of Jane Austen. An ideal wedding venue, Oakley Hall also has an excellent range of conference facilities, and is a great place to spend a relaxing leisure break. The bedrooms are spacious; many are located in the impressively restored courtyard and are particularly well equipped; there is also the delightful Garden Cottage. The stylish 1795 Bar & Lounge and the Glasshouse Restaurant offer contemporary surroundings in which to relax and enjoy the excellent food and friendly service.

Rooms 47 (18 annexe) (14 fmly) (23 GF) ⚡ S £250–£390; D £250–£390 (incl. bkfst)* **Facilities** FTV WiFi ↕ Clay pigeon shooting Archery In room pamper treatments Xmas New Year **Conf** Class 82 Board 50 Thtr 300 Del from £199 to £279* **Services** Lift Air con **Parking** 100 **Notes** LB ⊗ Civ Wed 100

Audleys Wood Hotel

★★★★ 81% ◉◉ HOTEL

tel: 01256 817555 & 0845 0727 405
(Calls cost 5p per minute plus your phone company's access charge) **Alton Rd RG25 2JT**
email: audleyswood@handpicked.co.uk
web: www.handpickedhotels.co.uk/hotels/audleys-wood-hotel-basingstoke/
dir: *M3 junct 6. From Basingstoke take A339 towards Alton, hotel on right*

A long sweeping drive leads to what was once a Victorian hunting lodge. This traditional country-house hotel offers bedrooms with flat-screen TVs and MP3 player connections. Smart and traditional public areas have log fires, and the dining options include the award-winning Simonds Room and a contemporary conservatory with a small minstrels' gallery.

Rooms 72 (23 fmly) (34 GF) **Facilities** STV FTV WiFi ↕ HL ↙ Xmas New Year **Conf** Class 80 Board 60 Thtr 200 Del from £145 to £180* **Parking** 100 **Notes** ⊗ Civ Wed 100

B

BASINGSTOKE *continued*

The Hampshire Court Hotel

★★★★ 79% HOTEL

INSPIRED BY YOU

tel: 01256 319700 **Centre Dr, Chineham RG24 8FY**
email: hampshirecourt@qhotels.co.uk **web:** www.qhotels.co.uk
dir: *Off A33 Reading Rd, behind Chineham Shopping Centre, via Great Binfields Rd*

This hotel boasts a range of smart, comfortable and stylish bedrooms, and leisure facilities that are unrivalled locally. Facilities include indoor and outdoor tennis courts, two swimming pools, a gym and a number of treatment rooms.

Rooms 90 (6 fmly) Facilities Spa STV WiFi HL Gym Steam room Sauna Exercise studios Xmas New Year **Conf** Class 800 Board 60 Thtr 1500 **Services** Lift **Parking** 220 **Notes** Civ Wed 1500

Apollo Hotel

★★★★ 74% HOTEL

tel: 01256 796700 **Aldermaston Roundabout RG24 9NU**
email: enquiries@apollohotels.com **web:** www.apollohotels.com
dir: *M3 junct 6. Follow ring road N towards Newbury. Follow A340 Aldermaston signs. Hotel on rdbt, 5th exit into Popley Way for access*

This modern hotel provides well-equipped accommodation and spacious public areas, appealing to both the leisure and business guest. Facilities include a smartly appointed leisure club, a business centre, along with a good choice of formal and informal eating in two restaurants; Vespers is the fine dining option.

Rooms 125 (49 GF) **S** £73-£260; **D** £83-£275 (incl. bkfst)* **Facilities** Spa FTV WiFi Gym Sauna Steam room New Year **Conf** Class 196 Board 30 Thtr 255 Del from £130 to £185* **Services** Lift **Parking** 200 **Notes** Civ Wed 150

Premier Inn Basingstoke Central

BUDGET HOTEL

Premier Inn

tel: 0871 527 8062 *(Calls cost 13p per minute plus your phone company's access charge)*
Basingstoke Leisure Park, Worting Rd RG22 6PG
web: www.premierinn.com
dir: *M3 junct 6, A339 towards Newbury. A340 follow brown Leisure Park signs. At next rdbt right onto B3400 (Churchill Way West). Right on next rdbt into Leisure Park. Hotel adjacent to Spruce Goose Beefeater*

High quality, budget accommodation ideal for both families and business travellers. Spacious, en suite bedrooms feature tea and coffee making facilities, and Freeview TV in most hotels. Internet access and WiFi are available for a small fee. The adjacent family restaurant features a wide and varied menu. See also the Hotel Groups pages.

Rooms 99

Premier Inn Basingstoke Town Centre Hotel

BUDGET HOTEL

Premier Inn

tel: 0871 527 9518 *(Calls cost 13p per minute plus your phone company's access charge)*
Victoria St RG21 3BT
web: www.premierinn.com
dir: *M3 junct 6 signed Basingstoke. Then follow A30 & Alton signs. At next rdbt take 3rd exit to Fairfield, left into New Road. Hotel on left after Caston's car park*

Rooms 81

BASLOW
Derbyshire

Map 16 SK27

Cavendish Hotel

★★★★ 80% HOTEL

CLASSIC BRITISH HOTELS

tel: 01246 582311 **Church Ln DE45 1SP**
email: info@cavendish-hotel.net **web:** www.cavendish-hotel.net
dir: *M1 junct 29/A617 W to Chesterfield & A619 to Baslow. Hotel in village centre, off main road*

This stylish property, dating back to the 18th century, is delightfully situated on the outskirts of the Chatsworth Estate. All rooms enjoy far-reaching views across the estate and benefit from the slightly elevated position. Bedrooms are elegantly appointed and offer a host of thoughtful amenities, while bathrooms have been refurbished and have Temple Spa toiletries. Comfortable public areas are furnished with period pieces and paintings from the Duke's extensive art collection. Guests have a choice of dining in either the informal conservatory Garden Room or the elegant Gallery Restaurant. A sun terrace has also been created recently overlooking the croquet lawn and estate beyond.

Rooms 24 (3 fmly) (2 GF) **S** £155-£325; **D** £205-£325* **Facilities** FTV WiFi Putt green Fishing offsite can be arranged Xmas New Year **Conf** Class 8 Board 18 Thtr 25 Del £215* **Parking** 50 **Notes** RS 25 Dec evening Civ Wed 50

INSPECTORS' CHOICE

Fischer's Baslow Hall

★★★ HOTEL

tel: 01246 583259 **Calver Rd DE45 1RR**
email: reservations@fischers-baslowhall.co.uk **web:** www.fischers-baslowhall.co.uk
dir: *On A623 between Baslow & Calver*

Located at the end of a chestnut tree-lined drive on the edge of the Chatsworth Estate, in marvellous gardens, this beautiful Derbyshire manor house offers

B

sumptuous accommodation and facilities. Staff provide very friendly and personally attentive service. There are two styles of bedroom available - traditional, individually-themed rooms in the main house and spacious, more contemporary-styled rooms with Italian marble bathrooms in the Garden House. The cuisine is excellent and may prove the highlight of any stay.

Fischer's Baslow Hall

Rooms 11 (5 annexe) (4 GF) ⚡ **S** £125-£175; **D** £200-£270 (incl. bkfst) **Facilities** FTV WiFi ♫ **Conf** Board 15 Thtr 20 Del £225 **Parking** 40 **Notes** LB ⊗ No children 5yrs Closed 25-26 Dec RS 31 Dec Civ Wed 38

BASSENTHWAITE
Cumbria
Map 18 NY23

INSPECTORS' CHOICE

Armathwaite Hall Hotel and Spa
★★★★ ⊛⊛ COUNTRY HOUSE HOTEL

tel: 017687 76551 **CA12 4RE**
email: reservations@armathwaite-hall.com **web:** www.armathwaite-hall.com
dir: *M6 junct 40/A66 to Keswick rdbt then A591 signed Carlisle. 8m to Castle Inn junct, turn left. Hotel 300yds*

Enjoying fine views over Bassenthwaite Lake, this impressive mansion, dating from the 17th century, is situated amid 400 acres of deer park. The comfortably furnished bedrooms and well-appointed bathrooms are complemented by a choice of public rooms that have many original features. The spa is an outstanding asset to the leisure facilities; it offers an infinity pool, thermal suite, sauna, state-of-the-art gym, treatments, exercise classes and a hot tub overlooking the landscaped gardens.

Rooms 46 (8 fmly) (8 GF) ⚡ **Facilities** Spa STV WiFi ♫ supervised ♨ Fishing ♨ Gym Archery Clay shooting Quad & mountain bikes Falconry Xmas New Year **Conf** Class 50 Board 60 Thtr 200 **Services** Lift **Parking** 100 **Notes** Civ Wed 150

Best Western Plus Castle Inn
BW Best Western PLUS
★★★★ 75% HOTEL

tel: 017687 76401 **CA12 4RG**
email: reservations@castleinncumbria.co.uk **web:** www.castleinncumbria.co.uk
dir: *A591 to Carlisle, pass Bassenthwaite village on right. Hotel on left of T-junct*

Overlooking some of England's highest fells and Bassenthwaite Lake, this fine hotel is ideally situated for exploring Bassenthwaite, Keswick and the Lake District. The accommodation, extensive leisure facilities and friendly service are certainly strong points here. Ritson's Restaurant and Laker's Lounge offer a range of dishes using locally sourced meats from the fells; managed, sustainable fish stocks; and international and seasonal ingredients.

Rooms 42 (4 fmly) (9 GF) ⚡ **Facilities** FTV WiFi ♫ ♨ Putt green Gym Sauna Steam room Xmas New Year **Conf** Class 108 Board 60 Thtr 200 **Parking** 120 **Notes** Civ Wed 180

HIGHLY RECOMMENDED

The Pheasant
★★★ 86% ⊛ HOTEL

tel: 017687 76234 **CA13 9YE**
email: info@the-pheasant.co.uk **web:** www.the-pheasant.co.uk
dir: *Midway between Keswick & Cockermouth, signed from A66*

Enjoying a rural setting, within well-tended gardens, on the western side of Bassenthwaite Lake, this friendly 500-year-old inn is steeped in tradition. The attractive oak-panelled bar has seen few changes over the years, and features log fires and a great selection of malt whiskies. The individually decorated bedrooms are stylish and thoughtfully equipped.

Rooms 15 (2 annexe) (2 GF) ⚡ **Facilities** FTV WiFi ♫ New Year **Parking** 40 **Notes** No children 12yrs Closed 25 Dec

---

Ravenstone Lodge
★★★ 80% ⊛ COUNTRY HOUSE HOTEL

tel: 01768 776629 & 07584 317120 **CA12 4QG**
email: enquiries@ravenstonelodge.co.uk **web:** www.ravenstonelodge.co.uk
dir: *5m N of Keswick on A591*

Close to both Keswick and Bassenthwaite, set in rolling countryside, this small country house hotel offers warm, genuine hospitality along with high quality food. Bedrooms are well equipped and appointed, benefitting from a rolling refurbishment programme. Outside garden seating or the large conservatory offer unrestricted views of the picture postcard location.

Rooms 9 (1 fmly) (2 GF) ⚡ **D** £80-£160 (incl. bkfst)* **Facilities** FTV WiFi ♫ **Parking** 15 **Notes** ⊗

B

BATH
Somerset   Map 4 ST76

See also **Colerne & Hinton Charterhouse**

The Royal Crescent Hotel & Spa
★★★★★ ◎◎◎ HOTEL

tel: 0330 823333 **16 Royal Crescent BA1 2LS**
email: info@royalcrescent.co.uk **web:** www.royalcrescent.co.uk
dir: *From A4, right at lights. 2nd left into Bennett St, into The Circus, 2nd exit into Brock St*

The Royal Crescent Hotel is set in a number of houses in Bath's famous Royal Crescent, and is one of the country's most interesting and historic places to stay. Bedrooms offer a range of suites and sizes, all with individual style and character; many have views across the city, and all are most comfortably appointed. Public rooms make the most of the character of the houses and are styled in keeping with the elegance of the period. The hotel has a superb spa and range of leisure facilities, as well as a number of meeting rooms and private dining venues. The bar and Dower House restaurant offer the very best of contemporary dining and are not to be missed. Ingredients are sourced locally where possible, and elegantly presented by Head Chef David Campbell and his team.

Rooms 45 (8 fmly) (7 GF) ☎ S £265–£1115; D £265–£1115 (incl. bkfst)*
Facilities Spa STV FTV WiFi ⌕ ⌕ ⌕ Gym Xmas New Year **Conf** Class 18 Board 30 Thtr 60 Del from £330 to £1095* **Services** Lift Air con **Parking** 27
Notes Civ Wed 50

The Bath Priory Hotel, Restaurant & Spa
★★★★★ ◎◎◎ HOTEL   BROWNSWORD HOTELS

tel: 01225 331922 **Weston Rd BA1 2XT**
email: info@thebathpriory.co.uk **web:** www.thebathpriory.co.uk
dir: *Adjacent to Victoria Park*

The Bath Priory Hotel is a country house set in four acres of beautiful grounds. It features a luxury spa and an award-winning, multi-AA Rosetted restaurant. The Priory Restaurant is under the direction of Head Chef, Sam Moody. Sam and his team deliver food that is derived from modern European cuisine, and is created from the very finest local produce and seasonal fruit, vegetable and herbs from the property's own garden. Opening onto the leafy gardens, the Mediterranean-style spa features an indoor heated swimming pool with a pool-side sauna and modern steam pod. Luxury beauty treatments are also available by appointment. Luxurious bedrooms have elegant decor and free WiFi access. All rooms feature period furniture and spacious en suite bathrooms with fluffy bathrobes and designer toiletries.

Rooms 33 (6 annexe) (2 fmly) (1 GF) ☎ S £175–£775; D £195–£795 (incl. bkfst)*
Facilities Spa STV FTV WiFi ⌕ ⌕ ⌕ Gym Steam pod Sauna Xmas New Year
Conf Class 24 Board 16 Thtr 24 Del from £270 to £380* **Parking** 40
Notes Civ Wed 70

Macdonald Bath Spa
★★★★★ 87% ◎◎ HOTEL

tel: 0344 879 9106 & 01225 444424 **Sydney Rd BA2 6JF**
email: sales.bathspa@macdonald-hotels.co.uk
web: www.macdonaldhotels.co.uk/bathspa
dir: *A4, left onto A36 at 1st lights. Right at lights after pedestrian crossing left into Sydney Place. Hotel 200yds on right*

A delightful Georgian mansion set amidst seven acres of pretty landscaped grounds, just a short walk from the many and varied delights of the city centre. A timeless elegance pervades the gracious public areas and bedrooms. Facilities include a popular leisure club, a choice of dining options and a number of meeting rooms.

Rooms 129 (3 fmly) (17 GF) ☎ D fr £169* **Facilities** Spa STV FTV WiFi ⌕ HL ⌕ ⌕ ⌕ Gym Thermal suite Outdoor hydro pool Whirlpool Xmas New Year **Conf** Class 100 Board 50 Thtr 130 Del from £173 to £299* **Services** Lift Air con **Parking** 160
Notes LB Civ Wed 130

Bailbrook House Hotel

★★★★ 83% ◉◉ HOTEL

tel: 01225 855100 & 0845 072 7515
(Calls cost 7p per minute plus your phone company's access charge)
Eveleigh Av, London Road West BA1 7JD
email: reception.bailbrook@handpicked.co.uk **web:** www.bailbrookhouse.co.uk
dir: *M4 junct 18/A46, at bottom of long hill take slip road to city centre. At rdbt take 1st exit, London Rd. Hotel 200mtrs on left*

In the last few years, Bailbrook House Hotel has seen a dramatic rebuilding programme, and offers superior accommodation, ideally situated on the edge of Bath, set in attractive grounds with ample parking. It is perfectly placed to avoid parking and driving in the city, but close enough to allow ease of access. Bedrooms are spacious and extremely well appointed. There are two dining options and a range of meeting and conference facilities.

Rooms 94 (81 annexe) (2 fmly) (27 GF) 📶 **Facilities** STV FTV WiFi ⬡ Gym New Year **Conf** Class 72 Board 40 Thtr 160 **Services** Lift Air con **Parking** 120 **Notes** ⊗ Civ Wed 120

Abbey Hotel

★★★★ 76% ◉◉◉ HOTEL

tel: 01225 461603 **1 North Pde BA1 1LF**
email: karenkevelijhan@abbeyhotelbath.co.uk **web:** www.abbeyhotelbath.co.uk
dir: *M4 junct 18/A46 for approx 8m. At rdbt right onto A4 for 2m. Once past Morrissons stay in left lane & turn left at lights. Over bridge & right at lights. Over rdbt & right at lights. Hotel at end of road*

Perfectly located in the heart of Bath, just a two minute stroll from the famous Abbey, this popular hotel offers a relaxing welcome with professional, helpful service in contemporary surroundings. The impressive Brasserie offers an excellent range of the highest quality dishes with something to suit all tastes. In the warmer months, outdoor seating on the front terrace is the ideal location for coffee or lunch.

Rooms 60 (7 fmly) (3 GF) 📶 **Facilities** WiFi ⬡ Xmas New Year **Conf** Class 10 Board 16 Thtr 30 **Services** Lift **Notes** LB Civ Wed 60

Francis Hotel Bath - MGallery

★★★★ 76% HOTEL

tel: 01225 424105 **Queen Square BA1 2HH**
email: h6636@accor.com **web:** www.francishotel.com
dir: *M4 junct 18/A46 to Bath junct. 3rd exit onto A4, right into George St, left into Gay St into Queen Sq. Hotel on left*

This unique and distinctive hotel occupies seven of the original 18th-century townhouses that make up the south side of the centrally located Queen Square, with all of Bath's main attractions within walking distance. In each bedroom, guests can expect a comfortable bed with Egyptian cotton linen, a bathrobe, luxury toiletries, flat screen TV, air-conditioning, a safe, and complimentary WiFi. The Regency-inspired No. 10 Bar and Emily's Tea Room offer welcoming settings for the enjoyment of the hotel's signature cocktails and menus (including an extensive selection of afternoon teas). A short stroll through the hotel takes guests into Raymond Blanc's 'Brasserie Blanc'. There are a number of meeting rooms and private dining venues for any special occasion or gathering.

Rooms 98 (3 GF) 📶 **D** £120-£350 **Facilities** STV WiFi ⬡ HL Xmas **Conf** Class 40 Board 30 Thtr 80 **Services** Lift Air con **Parking** 40 **Notes** LB ⊗ Civ Wed 100

The Queensberry Hotel

★★★ ◉◉◉ HOTEL

tel: 01225 447928 **Russel St BA1 2QF**
email: reservations@thequeensberry.co.uk **web:** www.thequeensberry.co.uk
dir: *100mtrs from the Assembly Rooms*

This charming family-run hotel, situated in a quiet residential street near the city centre, consists of four delightful townhouses. The spacious bedrooms offer deep armchairs, marble bathrooms and a range of modern comforts. Sumptuously furnished sitting rooms add to The Queensberry's appeal and allow access to the very attractive and peaceful walled gardens. The Olive Tree is a stylish restaurant that combines Georgian opulence with contemporary simplicity. Innovative menus are based on best quality ingredients and outstanding cooking. Valet parking proves a useful service.

Rooms 29 (2 fmly) (4 GF) 📶 **D** £99-£425* **Facilities** FTV WiFi ⬡ **Conf** Class 12 Board 25 Thtr 35 **Del** from £200 to £275* **Services** Lift **Parking** 6 **Notes** ⊗

Haringtons Hotel

★★★ 81% METRO HOTEL

tel: 01225 461728 & 445883 **8-10 Queen St BA1 1HE**
email: post@haringtonshotel.co.uk **web:** www.haringtonshotel.co.uk
dir: *A4 into George St, into Milsom St. 1st right into Quiet St, 1st left into Queen St*

Dating back to the 18th century, this hotel is situated in the heart of the city and provides all the expected modern facilities and comforts. Although a full dinner in a restaurant is not offered, the comfortably furnished lounge is light and airy and open throughout the day for light snacks and refreshments. A warm welcome is assured from the proprietors and staff, making this a delightful place to stay.

Rooms 13 (3 fmly) 📶 **S** £79-£148; **D** £79-£168 (incl. bkfst)* **Facilities** STV FTV WiFi **Conf** Class 10 Board 12 Thtr 18 **Parking** 11 **Notes** LB ⊗

BATH *continued*

Premier Inn Bath

BUDGET HOTEL

tel: 0871 527 9454 *(Calls cost 13p per minute plus your phone company's access charge)*
James Street West BA1 2BX
web: www.premierinn.com
dir: *M4 junct 18, A46 towards city centre. In approx 7m 3rd exit A4 towards city centre. 1.5m left into Gay St, through Queen Sq, straight ahead into Charles St. At 2nd lights left into James St West. Hotel 200mtrs on right*

High quality, budget accommodation ideal for both families and business travellers. Spacious, en suite bedrooms feature tea and coffee making facilities, and Freeview TV in most hotels. Internet access and WiFi are available for a small fee. The adjacent family restaurant features a wide and varied menu. See also the Hotel Groups pages.

Rooms 108

Milsoms Bath

RESTAURANT WITH ROOMS

tel: 01225 750128 **24 Milsom St BA1 1DG**
email: bath@milsomshotel.co.uk **web:** www.milsomshotel.co.uk
dir: *M4 junct 18, A46 (Bath), 3m, through Pennsylvania. 3rd exit at rdbt onto A420 (Bristol). 1st left signed Hamswell/Park & Ride, left at junct towards Lansdown. Right at next T-junct. 5th right into George St. 1st left into Milsom St*

Located at the end of the main street in busy, central Bath, this stylish restaurant with rooms offers a range of comfortable, well-equipped accommodation. The ground-floor Loch Fyne Restaurant serves an excellent selection of dishes at both lunch and dinner, with an emphasis on the freshest quality fish and shellfish. A good selection of hot and cold items is also available in the same restaurant at breakfast.

Rooms 9

BATTLE	Map 7 TQ71
East Sussex	

The Powder Mills Hotel

★★★ 82% ◎◎ HOTEL

tel: 01424 775511 **Powdermill Ln TN33 0SP**
email: reservations@thepowdermills.com **web:** www.powdermillshotel.com
dir: *M25 junct 5, A21 towards Hastings. At Johns Cross take A2100 to Battle. Pass Abbey on right, 1st right into Powdermill Ln. 1m, hotel on right*

A delightful 18th-century country-house hotel set amidst 150 acres of landscaped grounds with lakes and woodland. The individually decorated bedrooms are tastefully furnished and thoughtfully equipped; some rooms have sun terraces with lovely views over the lake. Public rooms include a cosy lounge bar, music room, drawing room, library, restaurant and conservatory.

Rooms 49 (19 annexe) (5 GF) ♠ **S** £90-£120; **D** £140-£350 (incl. bkfst)*
Facilities FTV WiFi ⬥ ⚓ ☁ Fishing Jogging trails Woodland walks Clay pigeon shooting Archery Xmas New Year **Conf** Class 50 Board 16 Thtr 250 Del from £170 to £380* **Parking** 101 **Notes** LB Civ Wed 100

Brickwall Hotel

★★★ 79% HOTEL

tel: 01424 870253 & 870339 **The Green, Sedlescombe TN33 0QA**
email: info@brickwallhotel.com **web:** www.brickwallhotel.com
dir: *A21 on B2244 at top of Sedlescombe Green*

This is a well-maintained Tudor house, which is situated in the heart of a pretty village overlooking the green. The spacious public rooms feature a lovely wood-panelled restaurant with a wealth of oak beams, a choice of lounges and a smart bar. Bedrooms are pleasantly decorated and some have garden views.

Rooms 24 (2 fmly) (17 GF) ♠ **S** £60-£75; **D** £80-£125 (incl. bkfst)* **Facilities** FTV WiFi ⬥ ⚓ Xmas New Year **Conf** Class 40 Board 30 Thtr 30 **Parking** 40 **Notes** LB

BEACONSFIELD SERVICES	Map 6 SU99
Buckinghamshire	

Ibis Budget Beaconsfield

AA Advertised

tel: 01494 680929 **M40 Jct 2 Services, Hedgerley Rd, Burtley Wood HP9 2SE**
email: 6598@accor.com **web:** www.ibis.com
dir: *Located within M40 junct 2 services*

Modern, budget hotel offering comfortable accommodation in bright and practical bedrooms. Breakfast is self-service and dinner is available in the restaurant.

Rooms 105 ♠ **Facilities** FTV WiFi HL **Services** Lift

BEAMINSTER	Map 4 ST40
Dorset	

BridgeHouse

★★★ 82% ◎◎ HOTEL

tel: 01308 862200 **3 Prout Bridge DT8 3AY**
email: enquiries@bridge-house.co.uk **web:** www.bridge-house.co.uk
dir: *A3066 to Beaminster, hotel 100yds from town square*

Dating back to the 13th century, this property offers friendly and attentive service. The stylish bedrooms feature finest Italian cotton linens, flat-screen TVs and WiFi. There are five types of room to choose from, including four-poster and coach house rooms. Smartly presented public areas include the Georgian dining room, a cosy bar and an adjacent lounge. There's also a breakfast room and the Beaminster Brasserie with its alfresco eating area under a canopy overlooking the attractive walled garden.

Rooms 13 (4 annexe) (2 fmly) (4 GF) ♠ **S** fr £115; **D** fr £120 (incl. bkfst)*
Facilities FTV WiFi ⬥ Xmas New Year **Conf** Class 14 Board 10 Thtr 24 Del £185* **Parking** 20 **Notes** LB Civ Wed 100

BEANACRE
Wiltshire
Map 4 ST96

Beechfield House

★★★★ ◉ COUNTRY HOUSE HOTEL

tel: 01225 703700 **SN12 7PU**
email: reception@beechfieldhouse.co.uk **web:** www.beechfieldhouse.co.uk
dir: *M4 junct 17, A350 S, bypass Chippenham, towards Melksham. Hotel on left in Beanacre*

This is a charming, privately-owned hotel set within eight acres of beautiful grounds that has its own arboretum. Bedrooms are individually styled and include four-poster rooms, and ground-floor rooms in the coach house. Relaxing public areas are comfortably furnished and there is a beauty salon with a range of pampering treatments available. At dinner there is a very good selection of carefully prepared dishes with an emphasis on seasonal and local produce.

Rooms 24 (7 fmly) (4 GF) **D** £150-£225 (incl. bkfst)* **Facilities** FTV WiFi ⌦ ❧ ⤴ Beauty treatment room Xmas New Year **Conf** Class 60 Board 36 Thtr 80 **Parking** 70 **Notes** LB Civ Wed 70

BEAULIEU
Hampshire
Map 5 SU30

The Montagu Arms Hotel

★★★★ 84% ◉◉◉◉ ⛲ HOTEL

tel: 01590 612324 & 624467 **Palace Ln SO42 7ZL**
email: reservations@montaguarmshotel.co.uk **web:** www.montaguarmshotel.co.uk
dir: *M27 junct 2, follow signs for Beaulieu. In Dibden Purlieu right at rdbt. Hotel on left in Beaulieu*

Situated at the heart of this charming village and surrounded by glorious New Forest scenery, the Montagu Arms dates back to 1742, and still retains the character of a traditional country house. The individually designed bedrooms include some with four-posters. Public rooms include a choice of two dining options: the informal Monty's brasserie serving home-cooked classics, and the stylish, award-winning Terrace Restaurant. Much produce comes from the kitchen garden project which saw a derelict piece of land to the rear transformed to produce organic fruit, vegetables and herbs plus free-range eggs from the hens. In warmer weather there is a sheltered alfresco eating area overlooking the pretty terraced garden. Complimentary use of leisure and spa facilities is available to guests at a sister hotel six miles away.

Rooms 22 (3 fmly) ⇌ **S** £139-£234; **D** £172-£349 (incl. bkfst)* **Facilities** FTV WiFi ⤴ Complimentary use of spa in Brockenhurst Xmas New Year **Conf** Class 45 Board 30 Thtr 60 Del from £175* **Parking** 86 **Notes** LB ⊗ Civ Wed 100

Beaulieu Hotel

★★★ 81% ◉ HOTEL

NEW FOREST HOTELS

tel: 023 8029 3344 & 0800 444441 **Beaulieu Rd SO42 7YQ**
email: beaulieu@newforesthotels.co.uk **web:** www.newforesthotels.co.uk
dir: *M27 junct 1, A337 towards Lyndhurst. Left at lights, through Lyndhurst, right onto B3056, hotel in 3m*

Located in the heart of the beautiful New Forest National Park and close to Beaulieu Road railway station, this popular, small hotel provides an ideal base for exploring the area. Once a coaching inn, the hotel now particularly welcomes families; children will delight in seeing the ponies on the doorstep. Bedrooms, all with free WiFi and flat-screen TVs, range from cosy Keeper rooms to Crown rooms which also have four-posters and iPod docking stations. The relaxing Exbury Restaurant has doors that lead out onto the patio area and the landscaped gardens, and alfresco eating is possible in the summer.

Rooms 35 (4 annexe) (5 fmly) (4 GF) ⇌ **Facilities** FTV WiFi ⌦ HL ⟳ Steam room Xmas New Year **Conf** Class 100 Board 100 Thtr 250 **Services** Lift **Parking** 60 **Notes** Civ Wed 200

B

BEAULIEU *continued*

The Master Builders at Bucklers Hard

★★★ 81% @ HOTEL

tel: 01590 616253 **Buckler's Hard SO42 7XB**
email: enquiries@themasterbuilders.co.uk **web:** www.themasterbuilders.co.uk
dir: *M27 junct 2, follow Beaulieu signs. At T-junct left onto B3056, 1st left to Buckler's Hard. Hotel 2m on left before village*

A tranquil historic riverside is the backdrop for this delightful property. The main house bedrooms are full of historical features and are of individual design, and in addition there are some bedrooms in the newer wing. Public areas include a popular bar and guest lounge, while the grounds are an ideal location for alfresco dining in the summer months. Award-winning cuisine is served in the stylish dining room.

Rooms 26 (18 annexe) (4 fmly) (8 GF) **Facilities** FTV WiFi ⧖ Xmas New Year **Conf** Class 30 Board 20 Thtr 40 **Parking** 40 **Notes** LB Civ Wed 100

BECCLES	**Map 13 TM48**
Suffolk	

Waveney House Hotel

★★★ 81% HOTEL

tel: 01502 712270 **Puddingmoor NR34 9PL**
email: enquiries@waveneyhousehotel.co.uk **web:** www.waveneyhousehotel.co.uk
dir: *From A146 onto Common Lane North, left into Pound Rd, left into Ravensmere, right onto Smallgate, right onto Old Market, continue to Puddingmoor*

Waveney House is an exceptionally well presented, privately-owned hotel situated by the River Waveney on the edge of this busy little market town. The stylish public rooms include a smart lounge bar and a contemporary-style restaurant with views over the river. All of the rooms have individual decor, and second-floor rooms include vaulted oak-beamed rafters. Some also enjoy picturesque River Waveney and Waveney Marsh views, and two bridal suites are available. The bar menu is sure to include something for everyone, and meals can be taken on the Riverside Terrace.

Rooms 12 (3 fmly) ⧖ **Facilities** FTV WiFi Xmas New Year **Conf** Class 100 Board 50 Thtr 160 **Parking** 45 **Notes** ⊗ Civ Wed 80

BEDFORD	**Map 12 TL04**
Bedfordshire	

Barns Hotel

★★★★ 76% @ HOTEL

tel: 01234 270044 **Cardington Rd MK44 3SA**
email: reservations@barnshotelbedford.co.uk **web:** www.barnshotelbedford.co.uk
dir: *M1 junct 13, A421, approx 10m to A603 Sandy/Bedford exit, hotel on right at 2nd rdbt*

A tranquil location on the outskirts of Bedford, friendly staff and well-equipped bedrooms all combine to make this a good choice. Cosy day rooms and two informal bars add to the hotel's appeal, while large windows in the restaurant make the most of the view over the river. The original barn houses the conference and function suite.

Rooms 49 (18 GF) ⧖ **S** fr £68; **D** fr £78* **Facilities** WiFi Free use of local leisure centre (1m) Xmas New Year **Conf** Class 40 Board 40 Thtr 120 Del from £135 to £215* **Parking** 90 **Notes** LB ⊗ Civ Wed 90

The Bedford Swan Hotel

★★★★ 75% @ HOTEL

tel: 01234 346565 **The Embankment MK40 1RW**
email: info@bedfordswanhotel.co.uk **web:** www.bedfordswanhotel.co.uk
dir: *Towards Bedford - A421 or A1M/A428*

This historic hotel successfully combines original features with modern comforts. The bedrooms ooze style and quality, and the needs of the modern traveller are well catered for. The award-winning River Room Restaurant offers a varied choice of freshly prepared dishes. The hotel also offers meeting and function rooms, spa facilities and secure parking.

Rooms 113 (10 fmly) (12 smoking) **Facilities** Spa STV FTV WiFi ⧖ ⊗ Xmas New Year **Conf** Class 40 Board 60 Thtr 250 **Services** Lift Air con **Parking** 80 **Notes** Civ Wed 250

Premier Inn Bedford (Priory Marina)

BUDGET HOTEL

tel: 0871 527 8066 *(Calls cost 13p per minute plus your phone company's access charge)*
Priory Country Park, Barkers Ln MK41 9DJ
web: www.premierinn.com
dir: *M1 junct 13, A421, A6, A428 signed Cambridge. Cross River Ouse, right at next rdbt into Barkers Lane. Follow Priory Country Park signs. Hotel adjacent to Priory Marina Beefeater*

High quality, budget accommodation ideal for both families and business travellers. Spacious, en suite bedrooms feature tea and coffee making facilities, and Freeview TV in most hotels. Internet access and WiFi are available for a small fee. The adjacent family restaurant features a wide and varied menu. See also the Hotel Groups pages.

Rooms 57

Premier Inn Bedford South (A421)

BUDGET HOTEL

tel: 0871 527 9410 *(Calls cost 13p per minute plus your phone company's access charge)*
Marsh Leys, Kempston MK42 7DN
web: www.premierinn.com
dir: *See website for detailed directions*

Rooms 60

BELTON	**Map 11 SK93**
Lincolnshire	

Belton Woods

★★★★ 77% HOTEL

tel: 01476 593200 **NG32 2LN**
web: www.qhotels.co.uk
dir: *A1 to Gonerby Moor Services. B1174 towards Great Gonerby. At top of hill turn left towards Manthorpe/Belton. At T-junct turn left onto A607. Hotel 0.25m on left*

Beautifully located amidst 475 acres of picturesque countryside, this is a destination venue for lovers of sport, especially golf, as well as a relaxing executive retreat for seminars. Comfortable and well-equipped accommodation complements the elegant and spacious public areas, which provide a good choice of drinking, dining and relaxing options.

Rooms 136 (136 fmly) (68 GF) ⧖ **Facilities** Spa STV FTV WiFi ⧖ HL ⊗ supervised ⧖ 45 ⧖ Putt green ⧖ Gym Squash Outdoor activity centre ♫ Xmas New Year **Conf** Class 180 Board 80 Thtr 270 **Services** Lift **Parking** 350 **Notes** Civ Wed 80

BEMBRIDGE
Isle of Wight
Map 5 SZ68

Bembridge Coast Hotel
★★★ 81% HOTEL

WARNER LEISURE HOTELS

tel: 01983 873931 **Fishermans Walk PO35 5TH**
web: www.warnerleisurehotels.co.uk
dir: *A3055 Ryde to Sandown, approx 1.5m, left at lights into Carpenter's Rd to St Helens. At mini-rdb 2nd exit onto A3395 signed Bembridge. In Bembridge follow one-way system to right, left after bakery into Forelands Rd. 1m, left into Lane End Rd. Follow to end, right to hotel entrance*

This hotel occupies a delightfully peaceful location on the east coast of the Isle of Wight in 23-acre grounds. The accommodation is comfortable, and there are a number of rooms with sea views for which a small supplementary charge applies. A full activities itinerary ensures that guests can make the most of what the hotel, and this beautiful island, has to offer. The helpful reservations team can also arrange ferry bookings from the UK mainland. Please note that this is an adults-only (over 21 years) hotel.

Rooms 258 (30 annexe) (76 GF) ⚫ **Facilities** Spa FTV WiFi HL ⓣ supervised Putt green ⚫ Gym Tropicarium Solarium Archery Rifle shooting Crossbow Indoor & outdoor bowls ♫ Xmas New Year **Services** Lift **Parking** 154 **Notes** ⊗ No children 21yrs

BERWICK-UPON-TWEED
Northumberland
Map 21 NT95

Queens Head
★★★ 82% SMALL HOTEL

tel: 01289 307852 **Sandgate TD15 1EP**
email: info@queensheadberwick.co.uk **web:** www.queensheadberwick.co.uk
dir: *A1 towards centre & town hall, into High St. Right at bottom to Hide Hill*

The Queens Head is a small hotel situated in the town centre, close to the old walls of this former garrison town. Bedrooms provide many thoughtful extras as standard. Dining remains a strong aspect with a carte menu that offers an impressive choice of tasty, freshly prepared dishes served in the comfortable lounge or dining room.

Rooms 6 (1 fmly) ⚫ **S** £70-£85; **D** £80-£95 (incl. bkfst) **Facilities** STV FTV WiFi ⚫ **Notes** ⊗ Closed 26 Dec & 1 Jan

BEVERLEY
East Riding of Yorkshire
Map 17 TA03

Best Western Lairgate Hotel
★★★ 72% HOTEL

BW Best Western.

tel: 01482 882141 **30/32 Lairgate HU17 8EP**
email: lairgate@bestwestern.co.uk **web:** www.bestwestern.co.uk
dir: *A63 towards town centre. Hotel 220yds on left, follow one-way system*

Located just off the market square, this pleasing Georgian hotel has been appointed to offer stylish accommodation. Bedrooms are elegant and well equipped, and public rooms include a comfortable lounge, a lounge bar, and restaurant with a popular sun terrace.

Rooms 30 (1 fmly) (8 GF) ⚫ **Facilities** FTV WiFi ♫ New Year **Conf** Class 40 Board 30 Thtr 80 **Parking** 18 **Notes** LB ⊗ Closed 26 Dec & 1 Jan RS 25 Dec

Premier Inn Beverley Town Centre
BUDGET HOTEL

tel: 0871 527 9490 *(Calls cost 13p per minute plus your phone company's access charge)*
Flemingate Centre, Flemingate HU17 0NQ
email: beverleytowncentre.pi@premierinn.com **web:** www.premierinn.com
dir: *From N: From York on A1079, at rdbt onto A1174, follow Flemingate Centre Car Park signs. From S: M62 junct 38, B1230. 7m, left into Wold Rd. 1m, right into Walkington. Left into Coppleflat Ln, to Killingwoldgraves. At rdbt 3rd exit onto A1174, follow Flemingate Centre Car Park signs*

High quality, budget accommodation ideal for both families and business travellers. Spacious, en suite bedrooms feature tea and coffee making facilities, and Freeview TV in most hotels. Internet access and WiFi are available for a small fee. The adjacent family restaurant features a wide and varied menu. See also the Hotel Groups pages.

Rooms 80

BEWDLEY
Worcestershire
Map 10 SO77

Mercure Kidderminster Hotel
★★★★ 71% HOTEL

tel: 01299 406402 & 0844 815 9033
(Calls cost 7p per minute plus your phone company's access charge) **Habberley Rd DY12 1LA**
email: info@mercurekidderminster.co.uk **web:** www.mercurekidderminster.co.uk
dir: *A456 towards Kidderminster to ring road, follow signs to Bewdley. Pass Safari Park then exit A456/Town Centre, take sharp right after 200yds onto B4190, hotel 400yds on right*

This 19th-century property is set in 20 acres of neat landscaped grounds in the Worcestershire countryside, close to West Midland Safari Park. The bedrooms are modern and well equipped; some rooms have great views of the grounds. Public rooms include a choice of lounges and the brasserie restaurant; the property also boasts great leisure facilities that include a coffee shop, hairdressers and a 25 metre swimming pool.

Rooms 44 (9 fmly) (1/ GF) ⚫ **Facilities** FTV WiFi ⚫ ⓣ supervised ⚫ Gym Beauty treatment room Sauna Steam room Spa bath **Conf** Class 150 Board 80 Thtr 450 **Parking** 150 **Notes** ⊗ Civ Wed 350

BEXHILL
East Sussex
Map 6 TQ70

The Cooden Beach Hotel
★★★ 81% HOTEL

tel: 01424 842281 **Cooden Beach TN39 4TT**
email: rooms@thecoodenbeachhotel.co.uk **web:** www.thecoodenbeachhotel.co.uk
dir: *A259 towards Bexhill. Signed at rdbt in Little Common Village. Hotel at end of road in Cooden, just past railway station*

This privately owned hotel is situated in private gardens which have direct access to the beach. With a train station within walking distance the location is perfectly suited for both business and leisure guests. Bedrooms are comfortably appointed, and public areas include a spacious restaurant, lounge, bar and leisure centre with swimming pool.

Rooms 41 (8 annexe) (10 fmly) (4 GF) ⚫ **Facilities** FTV WiFi ⚫ ⓣ Gym Sauna Steam room Spa bath Beauty treatment room Xmas New Year **Conf** Class 40 Board 40 Thtr 150 Del from £135 **Parking** 60 **Notes** Civ Wed 160

BEXLEYHEATH
Greater London   Map 6 TQ47

Premier Inn London Bexleyheath

BUDGET HOTEL

tel: 0871 527 9562 *(Calls cost 13p per minute plus your phone company's access charge)*
51 Albion Rd DA6 7AR
web: www.premierinn.com
dir: *From M25 follow sings for M1 & M11. Take A2(W) exit towards London (SE & C)/ Bexleyheath). Merge onto A2, take A223 signed Bexley/Bexleyheath Town Centre/A220. At rdbt take 1st exit into Bourne Rd, left into Albion Rd (A207). At rdbt 3rd exit, hotel will be on the left*

High quality, budget accommodation ideal for both families and business travellers. Spacious, en suite bedrooms feature tea and coffee making facilities, and Freeview TV in most hotels. Internet access and WiFi are available for a small fee. The adjacent family restaurant features a wide and varied menu. See also the Hotel Groups pages.

Rooms 92

BIBURY
Gloucestershire   Map 5 SP10

Swan Hotel

★★★★ 76% HOTEL

tel: 01285 740695 **GL7 5NW**
email: info@swanhotel.co.uk **web:** www.cotswold-inns-hotels.co.uk
dir: *9m S of Burford A40 onto B4425. 6m N of Cirencester A4179 onto B4425*

This hotel, built in the 17th century as a coaching inn, is set in peaceful and picturesque surroundings. It provides well-equipped and smartly presented accommodation, including four luxury cottage suites set just outside the main hotel. The elegant public areas are comfortable and have feature fireplaces. There is a choice of dining options to suit all tastes.

Rooms 22 (4 annexe) (1 fmly) ☞ **Facilities** FTV WiFi Fishing Xmas New Year **Conf** Class 50 Board 32 Thtr 80 **Services** Lift **Parking** 22 **Notes** Civ Wed 110

BICESTER
Oxfordshire   Map 11 SP52

Premier Inn Bicester

BUDGET HOTEL

tel: 0871 527 9394 *(Calls cost 13p per minute plus your phone company's access charge)*
Oxford Rd OX26 1BT
web: www.premierinn.com
dir: *M40 junct 9, A41 towards Bicester. 1.5m, hotel on left adjacent to Brewers Fayre*

High quality, budget accommodation ideal for both families and business travellers. Spacious, en suite bedrooms feature tea and coffee making facilities, and Freeview TV in most hotels. Internet access and WiFi are available for a small fee. The adjacent family restaurant features a wide and varied menu. See also the Hotel Groups pages.

Rooms 84

BIDEFORD
Devon   Map 3 SS42

The Royal Hotel

★★★ 75% HOTEL

tel: 01237 472005 **Barnstaple St EX39 4AE**
email: reservations@royalbideford.co.uk **web:** www.royalbideford.co.uk
dir: *At eastern end of old Bideford Bridge*

A quiet and relaxing hotel, the Royal is set near the river within a five-minute walk of the busy town centre and the quay. The bright, well maintained public areas retain much of the charm and style of the hotel's 16th-century origins, particularly in the wood-panelled Kingsley Suite. Bedrooms are well equipped and comfortable. Meals and lounge snacks are delicious.

Rooms 32 (2 fmly) (2 GF) ☞ **S** £60-£150; **D** £80-£170* **Facilities** FTV WiFi ॐ Xmas New Year **Conf** Class 100 Board 100 Thtr 100 **Services** Lift **Parking** 70 **Notes** LB ⊗ Civ Wed 130

Durrant House Hotel

★★★ Ⓐ HOTEL

tel: 01237 472361 **Heywood Rd, Northam EX39 3QB**
email: info@durranthousehotel.com **web:** www.durranthousehotel.com
dir: *A39 to Bideford, over New Torridge Bridge, right at rdbt, hotel 500yds on right*

This large hotel offers bedrooms with Italian-marble bathrooms, and all include a hospitality tray, hairdryer, TV, clock radio and an iron with ironing board; superior rooms have wonderful views of the Torridge estuary and Taw Valley, plus rain showers, sofas and luxury toiletries. The fine dining, oak-panelled Olive Tree Restaurant offers dishes based on locally sourced produce.

Rooms 125 (25 fmly) ☞ **S** £35-£75; **D** £70-£170 (incl. bkfst)* **Facilities** Spa STV FTV WiFi HL ॐ Gym Sauna Sun shower Pool table ♬ Xmas New Year **Conf** Class 100 Board 80 Thtr 350 Del from £79.50 to £110* **Services** Lift **Parking** 200 **Notes** Civ Wed 200

BIGBURY-ON-SEA
Devon   Map 3 SX64

Burgh Island Hotel

AA Advertised

tel: 01548 810514 **Burgh Island TQ7 4BG**
email: reception@burghisland.com **web:** www.burghisland.com
dir: *M5/A38 : follow signs to Bigbury on Sea/Burgh Island. Call for parking directions (do not drive over beach)*

Burgh Island Hotel is an iconic Devon landmark, set on its own tidal island, surrounded by golden beaches. Built in 1929, extended in 1932 and now restored to its '30s glamour, this was a regular haunt of Agatha Christie, Noel Coward and

B

other glamourous figures of the time. Where the management can establish a real connection, the bedrooms bear the name of a visiting celebrity guest; Jessie Matthews, Josephine Baker, Malcolm Campbell and so on. All rooms are different in design but similar in quality and style. All have WiFi but strictly no TVs (although there is a TV in the library room). Thoughtful extras in the rooms include Burgh Island bespoke toiletries, chocolates and water. Fresh tea or coffee is brought to the rooms each morning at a guest's preferred time. Food served in the restaurant is mainly locally-sourced, and some comes from the hotel's own polytunnel. The hotel also has a billards room, table tennis, spa treatments, a sea water bathing pool, and a rowing boat is available to borrow.

Rooms 25 (2 annexe) (1 GF) ⚘ **S** £310; **D** £400-£665 (incl. bkfst & dinner)*
Facilities FTV WiFi ⚲ ⚇ ⚇ Beauty treatment room Table tennis 🎵 Xmas New Year
Services Lift **Parking** 22 **Notes** LB ⊗ No children 5yrs Closed 2-19 Jan Civ Wed 70

BILDESTON
Suffolk   Map 13 TL94

The Bildeston Crown

U

tel: 01449 740510 **104-106 High St IP7 7EB**
email: reception@thebildestoncrown.co.uk **web:** www.thebildestoncrown.co.uk
dir: A12 junct 31, B1070 towards Hadleigh. At T-junct left onto A1141, right onto B1115. Hotel 0.5m

Currently the rating for this establishment is not confirmed. This may be due to a change of ownership or because it has only recently joined the AA rating scheme. For further details please see the AA website: theAA.com

Rooms 12 ⚘ **Facilities** STV FTV WiFi Xmas New Year **Conf** Class 25 Board 16 Thtr 40
Services Lift **Parking** 30

BILLINGHAM
County Durham   Map 19 NZ42

INSPECTORS' CHOICE

Wynyard Hall Hotel
★★★★ ◎◎ HOTEL

tel: 01740 644811 **Wynyard TS22 5NF**
email: reception@wynyardhall.co.uk **web:** www.wynyardhall.co.uk
dir: A19, A1027 towards Stockton. At rdbt take B1274 (Junction Rd). At next rdbt take A177 (Durham Rd). Right onto Wynyard Rd signed Wolviston. Left into estate

Drive through the gates, over the lion bridge, and Wynyard Hall will immediately impress with its grandeur and elegance. The opulent public areas are as much a feature of the property as are the grounds and gardens. The individually designed bedrooms and suites are stunning, with a combination of modern and period style furniture. The elegant, award-winning Duke of Wellington restaurant

is also impressive. The Essential Time Treatment Suite offers many relaxing therapies and beauty treatments. As a wedding venue the hall provides the option for a civil ceremony, or a religious service in the chapel, followed by a memorable reception.

Wynyard Hall Hotel

Rooms 24 (4 annexe) (1 fmly) (3 GF) ⚘ **S** £195-£275; **D** £195-£275 (incl. bkfst)*
Facilities Spa FTV WiFi ⚐ Clay pigeon shooting Archery Hawk walk Boot camp Walled garden Farmshop Xmas New Year **Conf** Class 680 Board 100 Thtr 1000 Del from £175 to £250* **Services** Lift **Parking** 500 **Notes** LB ⊗ Civ Wed 150

BILSBORROW
Lancashire   Map 18 SD53

Premier Inn Preston North

BUDGET HOTEL

tel: 0871 527 8912 *(Calls cost 13p per minute plus your phone company's access charge)*
Garstang Rd PR3 0RN
web: www.premierinn.com
dir: 4m from M6 junct 32 on A6 towards Garstang. 7m from Preston

High quality, budget accommodation ideal for both families and business travellers. Spacious, en suite bedrooms feature tea and coffee making facilities, and Freeview TV in most hotels. Internet access and WiFi are available for a small fee. The adjacent family restaurant features a wide and varied menu. See also the Hotel Groups pages.

Rooms 42

BINGLEY
West Yorkshire   Map 19 SE13

Mercure Bradford, Bankfield Hotel
★★★ 75% HOTEL

tel: 01274 519300 & 0844 815 9004
(Calls cost 7p per minute plus your phone company's access charge) **Bradford Rd BD16 1TU**
email: info@mercurebradford.co.uk **web:** www.mercurebradford.co.uk
dir: From M62 junct 26 onto M606, at rdbt follow signs for A650 Skipton/Keighley, hotel 2m from Shipley

This striking gothic style mansion house is set in landscaped gardens and is a short walk from the River Aire. The rural setting is peaceful yet the hotel is also convenient for Bradford and Leeds. The hotel is understandably a popular wedding venue and also caters well for corporate guests with extensive meeting facilities available in a designated conference centre. Free WiFi access is provided throughout the hotel.

Rooms 103 (8 fmly) ⚘ **S** £49-£199; **D** £59-£209* **Facilities** FTV WiFi ⚐
Conf Class 200 Board 80 Thtr 350 Del from £75 to £175* **Services** Lift **Parking** 350
Notes Civ Wed 350

B

BIRCHANGER GREEN MOTORWAY SERVICE AREA (M11) Map 6 TL52
Essex

Days Inn London Stansted Airport - M1

WELCOMEBREAK

AA Advertised

tel: 01279 656477 **Birchanger Services, M11 Motorway, Old Dunmow Rd CM23 5QZ**
email: daysinnlsa@welcomebreak.co.uk **web:** www.welcomebreak.co.uk
dir: *M11 junct 8*

This modern building offers accommodation in smart, spacious and well-equipped bedrooms, suitable for families and business travellers, and all with en suite bathrooms. Continental breakfast is available and other refreshments may be taken at the nearby family restaurant.

Rooms 60 (12 fmly) (29 GF) (8 smoking) **Facilities** FTV WiFi ⌗ **Parking** 60

BIRKENHEAD Map 15 SJ38
Merseyside

The RiverHill Hotel

★★★ 84% SMALL HOTEL

tel: 0151 653 3773 **Talbot Rd, Prenton CH43 2HJ**
email: reception@theriverhill.co.uk **web:** www.theriverhill.co.uk
dir: *M53 junct 3, A552. Left onto B5151 at lights, hotel 0.5m on right*

Pretty lawns and gardens provide the setting for this friendly, privately owned hotel. Its convenient location and attractive grounds make it a popular wedding venue. The comfortable bedrooms are equipped with a wealth of extras; ground floor, family, and four-poster rooms are available. Well-cooked meals and substantial breakfasts are served in the elegant restaurant overlooking the garden.

Rooms 14 (1 fmly) **Facilities** FTV WiFi Free use of local leisure facilities
Conf Class 30 Board 52 Thtr 50 **Parking** 32 **Notes** ⊗ Civ Wed 40

Premier Inn Birkenhead Town Centre

BUDGET HOTEL

tel: 0871 527 9630 *(Calls cost 13p per minute plus your phone company's access charge)*
Conway St CH41 5AP
web: www.premierinn.com
dir: *M53 junct 5, follow Birkenhead, A41 & New Chester Rd signs. Straight on at 3 rdbts. Keep left towards A41/New Ferry Bypass. Keep right, follow signs for Wallasey/All Docks. Under flyover, left into Market St. 1st left into Hamilton St. Hotel on right*

High quality, budget accommodation ideal for both families and business travellers. Spacious, en suite bedrooms feature tea and coffee making facilities, and Freeview TV in most hotels. Internet access and WiFi are available for a small fee. The adjacent family restaurant features a wide and varied menu. See also the Hotel Groups pages.

Rooms 67

Premier Inn Wirral (Greasby)

BUDGET HOTEL

tel: 0871 527 9176 *(Calls cost 13p per minute plus your phone company's access charge)*
Greasby Rd, Greasby, Wirral CH49 2PP
web: www.premierinn.com
dir: *9m from Liverpool city centre. 2m from M53 junct 2. Just off B5139*

Rooms 30

BIRMINGHAM Map 10 SP08
West Midlands

See also Bromsgrove, Lea Marston, Oldbury & Sutton Coldfield (Royal)

Hotel du Vin & Bistro Birmingham

★★★★ 81% ◉ TOWN HOUSE HOTEL

tel: 0121 794 3005 & 0844 736 4250
(Calls cost 5p per minute plus your phone company's access charge) **Church St B3 2NR**
email: info@birmingham.hotelduvin.com **web:** www.hotelduvin.com
dir: *M6 junct 6/A38(M) to city centre, over flyover. Keep left & exit at St Chads Circus signed Jewellery Quarter. At lights & rdbt take 1st exit, follow signs for Colmore Row, opposite cathedral. Right into Church St, across Barwick St. Hotel on right*

The former Birmingham Eye Hospital has become a chic and sophisticated hotel. The stylish, high-ceilinged rooms, all with a wine theme, are luxuriously appointed and feature stunning bathrooms, sumptuous duvets and Egyptian cotton sheets. The Bistro offers relaxed dining and a top-notch wine list, while other attractions include a champagne bar, a wine boutique and a health club.

Rooms 66 ⌂ **Facilities** Spa STV FTV WiFi ⌗ Gym Steam room Sauna Plunge shower Xmas New Year **Conf** Class 40 Board 40 Thtr 84 **Services** Lift Air con
Notes Civ Wed 84

Macdonald Burlington Hotel

★★★★ 76% HOTEL

tel: 0344 879 9019 & 0121 643 9191 **Burlington Arcade, 126 New St B2 4JQ**
email: events.burlington@macdonald-hotels.co.uk
web: www.macdonaldhotels.co.uk/burlington
dir: *M6 junct 6, A38, follow city centre signs*

The Burlington's original Victorian grandeur - the marble and iron staircases and the high ceilings - blend seamlessly with modern facilities. Bedrooms are equipped to a good standard and public areas include a stylish bar and coffee lounge. The Berlioz Restaurant specialises in innovative dishes using fresh produce.

Rooms 114 (6 fmly) ⌂ **Facilities** FTV WiFi ⌗ HL New Year **Conf** Class 200 Board 80 Thtr 500 Del from £130 to £270 **Services** Lift Air con **Notes** Closed 24-26 Dec Civ Wed 400

Novotel Birmingham Centre

NOVOTEL
HOTELS & RESORTS

★★★★ 76% HOTEL

tel: 0121 643 2000 **70 Broad St B1 2HT**
email: h1077@accor.com **web:** www.novotel.com
dir: *M6 junct 6, A38(M) Aston Expressway, A456 towards Kidderminster*

This large, modern, purpose-built hotel benefits from an excellent city centre location, with the bonus of secure parking. Bedrooms are spacious, modern and well equipped especially for business users; four rooms have facilities for less able guests. Public areas include the Garden Brasserie, function rooms and a fitness suite with sauna and steam room.

Rooms 148 (148 fmly) ⌂ **Facilities** WiFi ⌗ Gym Fitness room Cardiovascular equipment Sauna Steam room New Year **Conf** Class 120 Board 90 Thtr 300 **Services** Lift **Parking** 53

B

Malmaison Birmingham

★★★★ 75%  HOTEL

tel: 0121 246 5000 **1 Wharfside St, The Mailbox B1 1RD**
email: birmingham@malmaison.com **web:** www.malmaison.com
dir: *M6 junct 6, A38 towards Birmingham. Hotel within The Mailbox, signed from A38*

The 'Mailbox' development, of which this stylish and contemporary hotel is a part, incorporates the very best in fashionable shopping outlets, an array of restaurants and ample parking. The air-conditioned bedrooms are stylishly decorated and feature comprehensive facilities. Public rooms include a contemporary bar and brasserie which prove a hit with guests and locals alike. Gymtonic, and a Petit Spa offering rejuvenating treatments are also available.

Rooms 192 ✆ **S** £79-£225; **D** £79-£225* **Facilities** **Spa** STV FTV WiFi ⌲ Gym Sauna Steam room ♫ **Conf** Class 40 Board 24 Thtr 150 Del from £165* **Services** Lift Air con **Notes** LB Civ Wed 120

Hallmark Hotel Birmingham Strathallan

★★★★ 72% HOTEL

tel: 0330 028 3410 **225 Hagley Rd, Edgbaston B16 9RY**
email: strathallan@hallmarkhotels.co.uk **web:** www.hallmarkhotels.co.uk
dir: *From A38 follow signs for ICC into Broad St, towards Five Ways island, take underpass to Hagley Rd. Hotel 0.5m*

Located just a few minutes from the city's central attractions and with the benefit of excellent parking, this hotel provides a range of comfortable and well-equipped bedrooms. A modern lounge bar and contemporary restaurant offer a good range of dining options.

Rooms 135 (36 fmly) ✆ **Facilities** STV FTV WiFi ⌲ Gym Xmas New Year **Conf** Class 90 Board 50 Thtr 170 **Services** Lift **Parking** 120 **Notes** ⊗

Best Western Westley Hotel

★★★ 81% HOTEL

 Best Western

tel: 0121 706 4312 **80-90 Westley Rd, Acocks Green B27 7UJ**
email: reservations@westley-hotel.co.uk **web:** www.westley-hotel.co.uk
dir: *A41 signed Birmingham on Solihull by-pass, to Acocks Green. At rdbt, 2nd exit B4146 Westley Rd. Hotel 200yds on left*

Situated in the city suburbs and conveniently located for the NEC and the airport, this friendly hotel provides well-equipped, smartly presented bedrooms. In addition to the main restaurant, there is also a lively bar and brasserie together with a large function room.

Rooms 37 (11 annexe) (3 fmly) (3 GF) **Facilities** STV WiFi ⌲ New Year **Conf** Class 80 Board 50 Thtr 200 **Parking** 150 **Notes** ⊗ Civ Wed 200

The Royal Angus

★★★ 75% HOTEL

THE HOTEL COLLECTION

tel: 0121 606 4500 **St Chad's Queensway B4 6HY**
email: royalangus@thehotelcollection.co.uk **web:** www.thehotelcollection.co.uk
dir: *From M6 junct 6 follow signs for city centre (A38). Left onto A4400 St Chads Queensway. Hotel on left*

The Royal Angus Hotel offers comfortably appointed accommodation within a few minutes' walk of the Bullring Shopping Centre, Grand Central and and Colmore Row. The hotel benefits from numerous conference rooms and free WiFi. Discounted parking is available in the neighbouring car park.

Rooms 133 (5 fmly) ✆ **S** £49-£239; **D** £49-£239* **Facilities** WiFi **Conf** Class 90 Board 35 Thtr 200 Del from £110 to £169* **Services** Lift **Notes** Civ Wed 200

Edgbaston Palace Hotel

★★★ 73% HOTEL

tel: 0121 452 1577 **198-200 Hagley Rd, Edgbaston B16 9PQ**
email: enquiries@edgbastonpalacehotel.com **web:** www.edgbastonpalacehotel.com
dir: *M5 junct 3 N, A456 for 4.3m. Hotel on right*

Dating back to the 19th century, this Grade II listed Victorian property has bedrooms that are modern, well appointed and offer good comfort levels. The hospitality is warm, personal and refreshing. Supervised children under 18 are welcome.

Rooms 48 (21 annexe) (3 fmly) (16 GF) **Facilities** FTV WiFi **Conf** Class 70 Board 60 Thtr 200 **Parking** 70 **Notes** ⊗ Civ Wed

Great Barr Hotel & Conference Centre

★★★ 67% HOTEL

tel: 0121 357 1141 **Pear Tree Dr, Newton Rd, Great Barr B43 6HS**
email: sales@thegreatbarrhotel.com **web:** www.thegreatbarrhotel.com
dir: *M6 junct 7, at Scott Arms x-rds right towards West Bromwich (A4010) Newton Rd. Hotel 1m on right*

This busy hotel, situated in a leafy residential area, is particularly popular with business clients; the hotel has excellent, state-of-the-art training and seminar facilities. There is a traditional oak-panelled bar and formal restaurant, and bedrooms are appointed to a good standard with the expected amenities.

Rooms 92 (6 fmly) ✆ **Facilities** STV WiFi ⌲ **Conf** Class 90 Board 60 Thtr 200 **Parking** 200 **Notes** RS BH (restaurant may close) Civ Wed 200

Holiday Inn Express Birmingham - South A45

BUDGET HOTEL

tel: 0121 289 3333 **1270 Coventry Rd, Yardley B25 8BS**
email: reservations@hiex-birmingham.co.uk
web: www.hiexpressbirminghamsouth.co.uk
dir: *A45 Coventry*

A modern hotel ideal for families and business travellers. Fresh and uncomplicated, the spacious rooms include Sky TV, power shower and tea and coffee-making facilities. Continental buffet breakfast is included in the room rate; other meals may be taken at the nearby family pub or restaurant. See also the Hotel Groups pages.

Rooms 83 ✆ **Conf** Board 16 Thtr 24

Premier Inn Birmingham Broad St Canal Side

BUDGET HOTEL

tel: 0871 527 8078 *(Calls cost 13p per minute plus your phone company's access charge)*
20 Bridge St B1 2JH
web: www.premierinn.com
dir: *M6 junct 6, A38(M) towards city centre. Follow signs for city centre/ICC/A456 (Broad St). Left at Hyatt Hotel, hotel on right at bottom of Bridge St*

High quality, budget accommodation ideal for both families and business travellers. Spacious, en suite bedrooms feature tea and coffee making facilities, and Freeview TV in most hotels. Internet access and WiFi are available for a small fee. The adjacent family restaurant features a wide and varied menu. See also the Hotel Groups pages.

Rooms 85

BIRMINGHAM *continued*

Premier Inn Birmingham Broad Street (Brindley Place)

BUDGET HOTEL

tel: 0871 527 8076 *(Calls cost 13p per minute plus your phone company's access charge)*
80 Broad St B15 1AU
web: www.premierinn.com
dir: *M6 junct 6, A38(M) (Aston Expressway). Follow City Centre, ICC & NIA signs into Broad St. Right into Sheepcote St. 2nd left at rdbt into Essington St. Hotel on left. NB for Sat Nav use B16 8AL*

Rooms 58

Premier Inn Birmingham Central East

BUDGET HOTEL

tel: 0871 527 8080 *(Calls cost 13p per minute plus your phone company's access charge)*
Richard St, Aston, Waterlinks B7 4AA
web: www.premierinn.com
dir: *M6 junct 6, signed city centre. A38(M) signed A4540 (ring road). At rdbt 1st exit 50mtrs left into Richard St, hotel on left, barrier access to car park*

Rooms 100

Premier Inn Birmingham Central (Hagley Road)

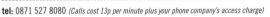

BUDGET HOTEL

tel: 0871 527 8082 *(Calls cost 13p per minute plus your phone company's access charge)*
Hagley Rd B16 9NY
web: www.premierinn.com
dir: *M6 junct 6, A38(M) (Aston Express Way). Follow city centre, ICC & NIA signs, into Broad St. From M5 junct 3, A456 for approx 3m, hotel on left*

Rooms 65

Premier Inn Birmingham City Centre (New Street)

BUDGET HOTEL

tel: 0871 527 9442 *(Calls cost 13p per minute plus your phone company's access charge)*
Birmingham Exchange Buildings, Stephenson Place B2 4NH
web: www.premierinn.com
dir: *M6 junct 6, A38 (Corporation St) keep right at fork. Exit towards New St, merge into Suffolk St Queensway. At rdbt 1st exit into Smallbrook Queensway, left into Hill St, right into Queen's Drive. Multi-storey parking at New St Station, The Pallasades or Bull Ring*

Rooms 140

Premier Inn Birmingham City Centre (Waterloo Street)

BUDGET HOTEL

tel: 0871 527 8074 *(Calls cost 13p per minute plus your phone company's access charge)*
3-6 Waterloo St B2 5PG
web: www.premierinn.com
dir: *M6 junct 6, A38 (Corporation St). Follow West Bromwich/A41 signs. Merge into St Chad's Queensway. 2nd exit for Great Charles St Queensway, becomes Livery St. Left into Waterloo St*

Rooms 152

Premier Inn Birmingham (Great Barr/M6 Jct 7)

BUDGET HOTEL

tel: 0871 527 8072 *(Calls cost 13p per minute plus your phone company's access charge)*
Birmingham Rd, Great Barr B43 7AG
web: www.premierinn.com
dir: *M6 junct 7, A34 towards Walsall. Hotel on left behind Beacon Harvester*

Rooms 33

Premier Inn Birmingham South (Hall Green)

BUDGET HOTEL

tel: 0871 527 8092 *(Calls cost 13p per minute plus your phone company's access charge)*
Stratford Rd, Hall Green B28 9ES
web: www.premierinn.com
dir: *M42 junct 4, A34 towards Shirley signed Birmingham. Straight on at 6 rdbts. At 7th rdbt 4th exit. Hotel on left*

Rooms 52

Premier Inn Birmingham South (Longbridge St)

BUDGET HOTEL

tel: 0871 527 9434 *(Calls cost 13p per minute plus your phone company's access charge)*
2 College St, Longbridge B31 2US
web: www.premierinn.com
dir: *M5 junct 4, A38 towards Birmingham. 3m (pass Morrisons & McDonald's) to rdbt. 1st exit towards A38 (B'ham). Right at 1st lights signed Longbridge train station. 1st right at Sainsburys, hotel on right. NB for Sat Nav use B31 2TW*

Rooms 75

Ibis Birmingham Centre New Street

AA Advertised

tel: 0121 622 6010 **Arcadian Centre, Ladywell Walk B5 4ST**
email: h1459@accor.com **web:** www.ibishotel.com
dir: *From motorways follow city centre signs. Then follow Bullring or Indoor Market signs. Hotel adjacent to market*

Modern, budget hotel offering comfortable accommodation in bright and practical bedrooms. Breakfast is self-service and dinner is available in the restaurant.

Rooms 159 (5 fmly) S fr £49; D fr £49* **Facilities** FTV WiFi **Conf** Class 60 Board 50 Thtr 120 **Services** Lift **Parking** 20

Ibis Budget Birmingham Centre

AA Advertised

tel: 0121 622 7575 **1 Great Colmore St B15 2AP**
email: 5678@accor.com **web:** www.ibishotel.com
dir: *M6 junct 6, A38 City Centre & Bromsgrove. Left at lights signed Birmingham Airport & NEC. 4th exit at rdbt, A38 Bromsgrove. Right at lights back on to A38(M). Hotel 1st on left into Great Colmore St*

Modern, budget hotel offering comfortable accommodation in bright and practical bedrooms. Breakfast is self-service and dinner is available in the restaurant.

Rooms 250 (250 fmly) **Facilities** FTV WiFi **Services** Lift

---

BIRMINGHAM AIRPORT
West Midlands   Map 10 SP18

Novotel Birmingham Airport
★★★★ 73% HOTEL

tel: 0121 782 7000 & 782 4111 **B26 3QL**
email: H1158@accor.com **web:** www.novotel.com
dir: *M42 junct 6, A45 to Birmingham, signed to airport. Hotel opposite main terminal*

This smartly decorated hotel with air conditioning throughout its public areas and bedrooms benefits from being less than a minute's walk from the main terminal of Birmingham International Airport. Spacious bedrooms are comfortable, and modern bathrooms are stylish with powerful showers. The Elements bar and restaurant provides a great atmosphere for meals and a fitness room is available on site. Long-stay car parking packages can be arranged at this location.

Rooms 195 (24 fmly) **Facilities** FTV WiFi Gym Fitness room **Conf** Class 10 Board 20 Thtr 35 **Services** Lift Air con

Ibis Birmingham Airport

AA Advertised

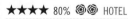

tel: 0121 780 5800 **Ambassador Rd, Bickenhill, Solihull B26 3AW**
email: H6359@accor.com **web:** www.ibishotel.com
dir: *M42 junct 6, A45 follow signs to Birmingham Airport*

Modern, budget hotel offering comfortable accommodation in bright and practical bedrooms. Breakfast is self-service and dinner is available in the restaurant.

Rooms 162 **Facilities** STV FTV WiFi HL **Services** Lift

Ibis Budget Birmingham Airport

AA Advertised

tel: 0121 780 5858 **Ambassador Rd, Birmingham Airport, Solihull B26 3QL**
email: 6365@accor.com **web:** www.ibishotel.com
dir: *Exit M42 at Junction 6 A45 and follow signs for Birmingham Airport. Follow directional signage all the way into the airport bear right at rapid drop off. Then turn left into Ambassador Rd, hotel is located opposite NCP car park number 2*

Modern, budget hotel offering comfortable accommodation in bright and practical bedrooms. Breakfast is self-service and dinner is available in the restaurant.

Rooms 120 **Facilities** WiFi **Services** Lift

BIRMINGHAM (NATIONAL EXHIBITION CENTRE)
West Midlands   Map 10 SP18

Moor Hall Hotel & Spa
★★★★ 80% ◉◉ HOTEL

tel: 0121 308 3751 **Moor Hall Dr, Four Oaks B75 6LN**
email: mail@moorhallhotel.co.uk **web:** www.moorhallhotel.co.uk

(For full entry see Sutton Coldfield)

Nailcote Hall
★★★★ 77% ◉ HOTEL

tel: 024 7646 6174 **Nailcote Ln, Berkswell CV7 7DE**
email: info@nailcotehall.co.uk **web:** www.nailcotehall.co.uk

(For full entry see Balsall Common)

Arden Hotel & Leisure Club
★★★ 75% HOTEL

tel: 01675 443221 **Coventry Rd, Bickenhill B92 0EH**
email: enquiries@ardenhotel.co.uk **web:** www.ardenhotel.co.uk
dir: *M42 junct 6, A45 towards Birmingham. Hotel 0.25m on right, just off Birmingham International railway island*

This smart hotel neighbouring the NEC and Birmingham Airport, offers modern rooms and well-equipped leisure facilities. After dinner in the formal restaurant, the place to relax is the spacious lounge area, or the large snooker room available to resident guests. A buffet breakfast is served in the bright and airy Meeting Place. Free WiFi and on-site parking are also available.

Rooms 216 (6 fmly) (6 GF) (4 smoking) **S** £49-£249; **D** £49-£249 **Facilities** Spa FTV WiFi Gym Beautician Xmas New Year **Conf** Class 40 Board 60 Thtr 200 Del from £99 to £299* **Services** Lift **Parking** 300 **Notes** LB Civ Wed 100

Premier Inn Birmingham NEC/Airport

BUDGET HOTEL

tel: 0871 527 8086 *(Calls cost 13p per minute plus your phone company's access charge)*
Off Bickenhill Parkway, National Exhibition Centre B40 1QA
web: www.premierinn.com
dir: *M42 junct 6 signed NEC. Turn right towards North Way. Follow Premier Inn signs. Hotel on left at 5th rdbt*

High quality, budget accommodation ideal for both families and business travellers. Spacious, en suite bedrooms feature tea and coffee making facilities, and Freeview TV in most hotels. Internet access and WiFi are available for a small fee. The adjacent family restaurant features a wide and varied menu. See also the Hotel Groups pages.

Rooms 247

BISHOP AUCKLAND
County Durham   Map 19 NZ22

Premier Inn Bishop Auckland

BUDGET HOTEL

tel: 0871 527 8096 *(Calls cost 13p per minute plus your phone company's access charge)*
West Auckland Rd DL14 9AP
web: www.premierinn.com
dir: *From S: A1 junct 58, left onto A68 signed Corbridge/Bishop Auckland. At 1st rdbt 2nd exit onto A6072 signed Shildon. Straight on at 4 rdbts, follow Shildon/Bishop Auckland signs. Hotel approx 1m on left*

High quality, budget accommodation ideal for both families and business travellers. Spacious, en suite bedrooms feature tea and coffee making facilities, and Freeview TV in most hotels. Internet access and WiFi are available for a small fee. The adjacent family restaurant features a wide and varied menu. See also the Hotel Groups pages.

Rooms 60

B

BISHOP'S STORTFORD
Hertfordshire   Map 6 TL42

Down Hall Country House Hotel
★★★★ 77% ◉ HOTEL

tel: 01279 731441 **Hatfield Heath CM22 7AS**
email: info@downhall.co.uk **web:** www.downhall.co.uk
dir: *A1060, at Hatfield Heath keep left. Right into lane opposite Hunters Meet restaurant, left at end, follow signs*

Imposing country house hotel set amidst 100 acres of mature grounds in a peaceful location just a short drive from Stansted Airport. Bedrooms are generally quite spacious; each one is pleasantly decorated, tastefully furnished and equipped with modern facilities. Public rooms include a choice of restaurants, a cocktail bar, two lounges and leisure facilities.

Rooms 100 (20 GF) ⋔ **S** £79–£189; **D** £89–£199 (incl. bkfst)* **Facilities** Spa FTV WiFi ⌖ ↯ Gym Giant chess Sauna Steam room Hydrotherapy pool Xmas New Year **Conf** Class 140 Board 68 Thtr 200 Del from £169 to £245* **Services** Lift **Parking** 150 **Notes** Civ Wed 150

The Great Hallingbury Manor Hotel
★★★ 80% HOTEL

tel: 01279 506475 & 0330 333 2868 **Tilekiln Green, Great Hallingbury CM22 7TJ**
email: info@greathallingburymanor.co.uk **web:** www.greathallingburymanor.co.uk
dir: *M11 junct 8 rdbt take exit to B1256, turn immediately right at petrol station. Under bridge, sharp left bend, continue for 500yds. Hotel on left*

This Tudor-style manor is set in lovely landscaped grounds and is surrounded by open countryside. The property is situated close to Stansted Airport, and the major road networks are within easy reach. The interior has a very contemporary feel, and bedrooms are smartly appointed with a range of thoughtful touches; public areas include a choice of lounges, a bar and an open-plan restaurant.

Rooms 45 (22 annexe) (3 fmly) (16 GF) ⋔ **Facilities** FTV WiFi ⌖ Xmas New Year **Conf** Class 80 Board 30 Thtr 170 **Parking** 50 **Notes** Civ Wed 170

Ramada London Stansted Airport - M11
AA Advertised

tel: 01279 213900 **Birchanger Services, M11 Motorway, Old Dunmow Rd CM23 5QZ**
email: ramadalsa@welcomebreak.co.uk **web:** www.welcomebreak.co.uk
dir: *M11 junct 8*

This modern building offers accommodation in smart, spacious and well-equipped bedrooms, suitable for families and business travellers, and all with en suite

bathrooms. There is an attractive lounge area and a dining room where breakfast is served and other refreshments may be taken.

Rooms 76 (15 fmly) (16 GF) (8 smoking) ⋔ **Facilities** FTV WiFi ⌖ **Services** Lift Air con **Parking** 100

BLACKBURN
Lancashire   Map 18 SD62

See also Langho

Premier Inn Blackburn South (M65 Jct 4)
BUDGET HOTEL

tel: 0871 527 8100 *(Calls cost 13p per minute plus your phone company's access charge)*
Off Eccleshill Rd, Riversway Dr, Lower Darwen BB3 0SN
web: www.premierinn.com
dir: *At M65 junct 4*

High quality, budget accommodation ideal for both families and business travellers. Spacious, en suite bedrooms feature tea and coffee making facilities, and Freeview TV in most hotels. Internet access and WiFi are available for a small fee. The adjacent family restaurant features a wide and varied menu. See also the Hotel Groups pages.

Rooms 62

Premier Inn Blackburn Town Centre Hotel
BUDGET HOTEL

tel: 0871 527 9622 *(Calls cost 13p per minute plus your phone company's access charge)*
3 Cathedral Square BB1 1FB
email: blackburntowncentre.pi@premierinn.com **web:** www.premierinn.com
dir: *M6 junct 29, M65 (West) towards Blackburn. At junct 4 follow signs for A666/Blackburn Town Centre, then follow signs for Blackburn Railway Station. On Jubilee St the car park is adjacent to railway station, hotel opposite*

Rooms 60

BLACKPOOL
Lancashire   Map 18 SD33

The Imperial Hotel
★★★★ 73% HOTEL

THE
HOTEL
COLLECTION

tel: 01253 623971 **North Promenade FY1 2HB**
email: imperialblackpool@thehotelcollection.co.uk **web:** www.thehotelcollection.co.uk
dir: *M55 junct 2, A583 (North Shore), follow signs to North Promenade. Hotel on seafront, north of tower*

Enjoying a prime seafront location, this grand Victorian hotel offers smartly appointed, well-equipped bedrooms and spacious, elegant public areas. Facilities include a smart leisure club, a comfortable lounge, the No 10 bar and an attractive split-level restaurant that overlooks the seafront. Conferences and functions are extremely well catered for.

Rooms 180 (16 fmly) ⋔ **D** £60-£250* **Facilities** Spa STV FTV WiFi ⌖ HL ⓑ supervised Gym Xmas New Year **Conf** Class 280 Board 70 Thtr 600 Del from £115 to £145 **Services** Lift **Parking** 150 **Notes** Civ Wed 200

B

Best Western Carlton Hotel Blackpool

 Best Western

★★★ 73% HOTEL

tel: 01253 628966 **282 North Promenade FY1 2EZ**
email: mail@carltonhotelblackpool.co.uk **web:** www.bw-carltonhotel.co.uk
dir: M6 junct 32/M55 - follow signs for North Shore. Between Blackpool Tower & Gynn Sq

Enjoying a prime seafront location, this hotel offers bedrooms that are attractively furnished in modern style. Public areas include a choice of bar lounge and seafront lounges. Well cooked meals are served in the elegant Caesar's restaurant; extensive function facilities are available.

Rooms 58 (7 fmly) **Facilities** FTV WiFi Xmas New Year **Conf** Class 40 Board 40 Thtr 90 **Services** Lift **Parking** 40 **Notes** LB Civ Wed 90

Carousel Hotel

★★★ 72% HOTEL

tel: 01253 402642 **663-671 New South Prom FY4 1RN**
email: carousel.reservations@sleepwellhotels.com **web:** www.sleepwellhotels.com
dir: From M55 follow signs to airport, pass airport to lights. Turn right, hotel 100yds on right

This friendly seafront hotel, close to the Pleasure Beach, offers smart, contemporary accommodation. Bedrooms are comfortably appointed and have a modern, stylish feel to them. An airy restaurant and a spacious bar/lounge both overlook the Promenade. The hotel has good conference and meeting facilities and its own car park.

Rooms 92 (22 fmly) **S** £35-£80; **D** £40-£90 (incl. bkfst)* **Facilities** FTV WiFi Xmas New Year **Conf** Class 30 Board 40 Thtr 100 Del from £60 to £120 **Services** Lift **Parking** 46 **Notes** LB Civ Wed 150

Queens Hotel

Leisureplex
HOLIDAY HOTELS

★★★ 68% HOTEL

tel: 01253 342015 & 336980 **469-471 South Promenade FY4 1AY**
email: queens.blackpool@leisureplex.co.uk **web:** www.leisureplex.co.uk

Queens Hotel is situated on the South Promenade overlooking the Irish Sea, close to the South Pier and Pleasure Beach. The bedrooms are well equipped and some rooms have lovely sea views. The spacious public areas include a choice of lounges, a range of bars, a conservatory and a large dining room as well as a refurbished 300-seat theatre bar.

Rooms 117 (9 fmly) **Facilities** FTV WiFi HL supervised Xmas New Year **Conf** Class 60 Board 60 Thtr 80 **Services** Lift **Parking** 55 **Notes** Closed Jan-Feb

New Guilderoy Hotel

★★ 78% SMALL HOTEL

tel: 01253 351547 **57-59 Holmfield Rd, North Shore FY2 9RU**
email: simon_connelly@yahoo.com **web:** www.new-guilderoy-hotel-blackpool.co.uk
dir: M55 Blackpool. Follow signs North Shore. Located behind The Cliffs Hotel, Queens Promenade

This pleasant, personally-run hotel caters for a wide market and sits in a quiet location, away from the hubbub of the town, yet conveniently close to attractions and the famous promenade. There is a relaxing lounge and a cosy bar with a very good wine list to choose from. Home cooked food is a feature here and menus at both dinner and breakfast offer a good choice.

Rooms 15 (4 fmly) **Facilities** FTV WiFi Xmas New Year **Notes** LB Closed 10 Nov-22 Dec RS 2 Jan-28 Feb

The Viking Hotel

★★ 76% HOTEL

tel: 01253 348411 & 0844 811 5570
(Calls cost 5p per minute plus your phone company's access charge)
479 South Promenade FY4 1AX
email: reservations@choice-hotels.co.uk **web:** www.choicehotels.co.uk
dir: M55 junct 3, follow Pleasure Beach signs

In a prime location at the centre of the South Promenade, this hotel offers comfortable accommodation and a warm welcome. Meals are served in the attractive sea view restaurant and entertainment is available nightly in the renowned 'Talk of the Coast' night club. On-site parking is a boon and leisure facilities at sister hotels are also available free of charge.

Rooms 100 (10 GF) **S** £38-£96; **D** £70-£136 (incl. bkfst & dinner) **Facilities** FTV WiFi Cabaret club Xmas New Year **Services** Lift **Parking** 50 **Notes** LB No children 18yrs

The Claremont Hotel

★★ 74% HOTEL

tel: 01253 293122 & 0844 811 5570
(Calls cost 5p per minute plus your phone company's access charge)
270 North Promenade FY1 1SA
email: reservations@choice-hotels.co.uk **web:** www.choicehotels.co.uk
dir: M55 junct 3 follow sign for promenade. Hotel beyond North Pier

Conveniently situated, the Claremont is a popular family holiday hotel. Bedrooms are bright and attractively decorated, and extensive public areas include a spacious air-conditioned restaurant which offers a good choice of dishes. There is a well equipped, supervised children's play room, and entertainment is provided during the season.

Rooms 143 (50 fmly) **S** £44-£74; **D** £79-£139 (incl. bkfst & dinner) **Facilities** FTV WiFi Beauty treatments Xmas New Year **Services** Lift **Parking** 40 **Notes** LB

The Cliffs Hotel

★★ 74% HOTEL

tel: 01253 595559 & 0844 811 5570
(Calls cost 5p per minute plus your phone company's access charge)
Queens Promenade FY2 9SG
email: reservations@choice-hotels.co.uk **web:** www.choicehotels.co.uk
dir: M55 junct 3, follow Promenade signs. Hotel just after Gynn rdbt

This large, privately owned and extremely popular promenade hotel is within easy reach of the town centre. The well equipped bedrooms, including spacious family rooms, vary in size. Public areas offer an all-day coffee shop, a smart restaurant and a suite of games rooms where kids of all ages are entertained. A modern gym and leisure pool complete the experience.

Rooms 163 (47 fmly) **S** £36-£69; **D** £69-£138 **Facilities** FTV WiFi supervised Gym Beauty treatment rooms Sauna Xmas New Year **Conf** Class 210 Board 50 Thtr 475 Del from £99 to £125 **Services** Lift **Parking** 30 **Notes** Civ Wed 100

B

BLACKPOOL *continued*

The Craig-y-Don Hotel

★★ 68% HOTEL

tel: 01253 624249 **211-213 Central Promenade FY1 5DL**
email: craig-y-donhotel@btconnect.com **web:** www.craig-y-don.com
dir: *On promenade, 2/3m past Blackpool Pleasure Beach*

The Craig-y-Don Hotel has a prime promenade position, and many rooms enjoy sea views. This is very much a holiday hotel which offers great value packages throughout the year. Freshly cooked dinner is available in the spacious dining room. Bedrooms are available in a range of sizes all equipped to a modern standard. The busy bar features cabaret and entertainment most nights.

Rooms 62 (33 fmly) (11 GF) 🐾 **S** £30-£50; **D** £50-£80 (incl. bkfst)* **Facilities** FTV WiFi 🎵 Xmas New Year **Services** Lift **Notes** ⊗ RS Nov-May wknds only

Lyndene Hotel

★★ 🅰 HOTEL

tel: 01253 346779 **303/315 Promenade FY1 6AN**
email: enquiries@lyndenehotel.com **web:** www.lyndenehotel.com

Family run for over 20 years, this hotel is on the promenade and offers bedrooms with LCD flat-screen TVs, safes and hospitality trays; some rooms are on the ground floor. Public rooms include two air-conditioned lounges, two restaurants and an outside seating area and sun terrace. Entertainment is offered every evening.

Rooms 140 (60 fmly) (12 GF) (140 smoking) 🐾 **Facilities** FTV WiFi ⚲ 🎵 Xmas New Year **Services** Lift **Parking** 70 **Notes** ⊗ No children 5yrs

Hotel Ibis Styles Blackpool

BUDGET HOTEL

tel: 01253 752478 **Talbot Square FY1 1ND**
email: H9148@accor.com **web:** www.focushotels.co.uk/hotels
dir: *M55 junct 4, follow signs for A583 Blackpool North Shore, approx 4m to seafront. Property on right opposite North Pier entrance*

Modern, budget hotel offering comfortable accommodation in bright and practical bedrooms. Breakfast is self-service and dinner is available in the restaurant. See also the Hotel Groups pages.

Rooms 90 (4 fmly) 🐾

Premier Inn Blackpool Airport

BUDGET HOTEL

tel: 0871 527 8106 *(Calls cost 13p per minute plus your phone company's access charge)*
Squire Gate Ln FY4 2QS
web: www.premierinn.com
dir: *M55 junct 4, A5230, left at 1st rdbt towards airport. Hotel just before Squires Gate rail station*

High quality, budget accommodation ideal for both families and business travellers. Spacious, en suite bedrooms feature tea and coffee making facilities, and Freeview TV in most hotels. Internet access and WiFi are available for a small fee. The adjacent family restaurant features a wide and varied menu. See also the Hotel Groups pages.

Rooms 39

Premier Inn Blackpool (Bispham)

BUDGET HOTEL

tel: 0871 527 8102 *(Calls cost 13p per minute plus your phone company's access charge)*
Devonshire Rd, Bispham FY2 0AR
web: www.premierinn.com
dir: *M55 junct 4, A583. At 5th lights turn right (Whitegate Drive). Approx. 4.5m onto A587 Devonshire Rd*

Rooms 67

Premier Inn Blackpool Central

BUDGET HOTEL

tel: 0871 527 8108 *(Calls cost 13p per minute plus your phone company's access charge)*
Yeadon Way, South Shore FY1 6BF
web: www.premierinn.com
dir: *M55 junct 4 to Blackpool, straight on at last island onto Yeaden Way. Follow signs for Central Car Park/Coach Area. Left at Total garage*

Rooms 103

Premier Inn Blackpool East (M55 Jct 4)

BUDGET HOTEL

tel: 0871 527 8110 *(Calls cost 13p per minute plus your phone company's access charge)*
Whitehills Park, Preston New Rd FY4 5NZ
web: www.premierinn.com
dir: *Just off M55 junct 4. 1st left off rdbt. Hotel on right*

Rooms 81

B

INSPECTORS' CHOICE

Morston Hall
★★★★ ◉◉◉ HOTEL

tel: 01263 741041 & 740419 **Morston, Holt NR25 7AA**
email: reception@morstonhall.com **web:** www.morstonhall.com
dir: 1m W of Blakeney on A149 - King's Lynn to Cromer road

This delightful 17th-century country house hotel enjoys a tranquil setting amid well-tended gardens. The comfortable public rooms offer a choice of attractive lounges and a sunny conservatory, while the elegant dining room is the perfect setting to enjoy Galton Blackiston's award-winning cuisine. The spacious bedrooms are individually decorated and stylishly furnished with modern opulence.

Rooms 13 (6 annexe) (7 GF) ⚹ **S** £240-£300; **D** £350-£400 (incl. bkfst & dinner)* **Facilities** STV FTV WiFi ⚓ New Year **Conf** Class 20 Board 16 **Parking** 40 **Notes** Closed 1 Jan-last Fri in Jan & 2 days Xmas

The Blakeney Hotel
★★★★ 79% ◉ HOTEL

tel: 01263 740797 **The Quay NR25 7NE**
email: reception@blakeneyhotel.co.uk **web:** www.blakeneyhotel.co.uk
dir: From A148 between Fakenham & Holt, take B1156 to Langham & Blakeney

A traditional, privately-owned hotel situated on the quayside with superb views across the estuary and the salt marshes to Blakeney Point. Public rooms feature an elegant restaurant, ground-floor lounge, a bar and a first-floor sun lounge overlooking the harbour. Bedrooms are smartly decorated and equipped with modern facilities. The leisure area is a real feature with pool, sauna, steam room and mini-gym.

Rooms 64 (16 annexe) (20 fmly) (17 GF) ⚹ **S** £88-£160; **D** £176-£396 (incl. bkfst & dinner) **Facilities** FTV WiFi ⚓ HL ⚙ Gym Billiards Snooker Table tennis Sauna Steam room Spa bath Xmas New Year **Conf** Class 100 Board 100 Thtr 150 Del £150 **Services** Lift **Parking** 60 **Notes** LB

HIGHLY RECOMMENDED

The Lord Crewe Arms Blanchland
★★★ 88% ◉ COUNTRY HOUSE HOTEL

tel: 01434 675469 **The Square DH8 9SP**
email: enquiries@lordcrewearmsblanchland.co.uk
web: www.lordcrewearmsblanchland.co.uk
dir: 10m S of Hexham via B6306

Set in the tranquil and picturesque Northumbrian countryside, "The Crewe" dates back to the 12th century, and was built as the Abbot's Priory. The building has plenty of character from the vaulted crypt bar to the numerous large open log fires. Bedrooms come in three styles: Cosy, Canny, and Champion. The team are naturally friendly with two dining options serving "proper, unpretentious country grub".

Rooms 21 (17 annexe) (6 GF) ⚹ **D** £99-£184 (incl. bkfst)* **Facilities** FTV WiFi ⚘ Fishing ⚓ Xmas New Year **Conf** Class 60 Board 30 Thtr 60 Del £180* **Parking** 25 **Notes** Civ Wed 60

Premier Inn Weston-Super-Mare (Lympsham)

BUDGET HOTEL

tel: 0871 527 9154 *(Calls cost 13p per minute plus your phone company's access charge)*
Bridgwater Rd, Lympsham BS24 OBP
web: www.premierinn.com
dir: M5 junct 22, A38 (Bristol Rd) signed Weston-Super-Mare. At 1st rdbt take 1st exit into Bridgewater Rd (A370). Approx 2m to hotel

High quality, budget accommodation ideal for both families and business travellers. Spacious, en suite bedrooms feature tea and coffee making facilities, and Freeview TV in most hotels. Internet access and WiFi are available for a small fee. The adjacent family restaurant features a wide and varied menu. See also the Hotel Groups pages.

Rooms 45

B

BODMIN
Cornwall   Map 2 SX06

Trehellas House Hotel & Restaurant

★★★ 75% ⊛ SMALL HOTEL

tel: 01208 72700 **Washaway PL30 3AD**
email: enquiries@trehellashouse.co.uk **web:** www.trehellashouse.co.uk
dir: *A389 from Bodmin towards Wadebridge. Hotel on right 0.5m beyond road to Camelford*

This 18th-century former posting inn retains many original features and provides comfortable accommodation. Bedrooms are located in both the main house and adjacent coach house - all provide the same high standards. An interesting choice of cuisine, with an emphasis on locally-sourced ingredients, is offered in the impressive slate-floored restaurant.

Rooms 12 (7 annexe) (2 fmly) (5 GF) **Facilities** FTV WiFi ⤻ Xmas New Year **Conf** Board 20 Thtr 20 **Parking** 32 **Notes** No children 13yrs

Premier Inn Bodmin

BUDGET HOTEL

tel: 0871 527 8112 *(Calls cost 13p per minute plus your phone company's access charge)*
Launceston Rd PL31 2AR
web: www.premierinn.com
dir: *From A30 S'bound exit onto A389, hotel 0.5m on right. N'bound exit onto A38, follow A389 signs. Left at T-junct*

High quality, budget accommodation ideal for both families and business travellers. Spacious, en suite bedrooms feature tea and coffee making facilities, and Freeview TV in most hotels. Internet access and WiFi are available for a small fee. The adjacent family restaurant features a wide and varied menu. See also the Hotel Groups pages.

Rooms 44

BOGNOR REGIS
West Sussex   Map 6 SZ99

The Inglenook

★★★ 73% SMALL HOTEL

tel: 01243 262495 & 265411 **255 Pagham Rd, Nyetimber PO21 3QB**
email: reception@the-inglenook.com **web:** www.the-inglenook.com
dir: *A27 into Vinnetrow Rd, left at Walnut Tree, hotel 2.5m on right*

This 16th-century inn retains much of its original character, including exposed beams throughout. Bedrooms are individually decorated and vary in size. There is a cosy lounge, a well-kept garden and a bar that offers a popular evening menu and convivial atmosphere. The restaurant, overlooking the garden, also serves enjoyable cuisine.

Rooms 18 (1 fmly) (2 GF) ⟁ S £60-£80; **D** £80-£215 (incl. bkfst)* **Facilities** STV FTV WiFi Xmas New Year **Conf** Class 50 Board 50 Thtr 100 Del from £110 to £120* **Parking** 35 **Notes** LB Civ Wed 80

The Royal Norfolk Hotel

★★★ 72% HOTEL   **Leisureplex**
                                          HOLIDAY HOTELS

tel: 01243 826222 **The Esplanade PO21 2LH**
email: royalnorfolk@leisureplex.co.uk **web:** www.leisureplex.co.uk
dir: *From A259 follow Longford Rd through lights to Canada Grove to T-junct. Right, take 2nd exit at rdbt. Hotel on right*

Located on the seafront, but set back behind well-tended lawns and gardens, is this fine Regency hotel. The bedrooms are traditionally furnished and provide

guests with modern comforts. There are sea views from the bar and restaurant, as well as the lounges.

Rooms 60 (4 fmly) (7 GF) ⟁ **S** £39-£72; **D** £62-£125 (incl. bkfst)* **Facilities** FTV WiFi ♫ Xmas New Year **Services** Lift **Parking** 40 **Notes** LB ⊗ Closed 2 Jan-14 Feb

Premier Inn Bognor Regis

BUDGET HOTEL

tel: 0871 527 8114 *(Calls cost 13p per minute plus your phone company's access charge)*
Shripney Rd PO22 9PA
web: www.premierinn.com
dir: *From A27 & A29 rdbt junct follow Bognor Regis signs. Approx 4m, hotel on left*

High quality, budget accommodation ideal for both families and business travellers. Spacious, en suite bedrooms feature tea and coffee making facilities, and Freeview TV in most hotels. Internet access and WiFi are available for a small fee. The adjacent family restaurant features a wide and varied menu. See also the Hotel Groups pages.

Rooms 46

BOLTON
Greater Manchester   Map 15 SD70

Mercure Bolton Georgian House Hotel

★★★ 75% HOTEL

tel: 01942 850900 & 0844 815 9029
(Calls cost 7p per minute plus your phone company's access charge)
Manchester Rd, Blackrod BL6 5RU
email: info@mercurebolton.co.uk **web:** www.mercurebolton.co.uk
dir: *M61 junct 6, follow Blackrod A6027 signs. 200mtrs turn right onto A6 signed Chorley. Hotel 0.5m on right*

This hotel has a pleasant location and very good parking, convenient for corporate or leisure guests alike. Bedrooms are pleasantly appointed, and beds very comfortable. There is a range of meeting rooms and the hotel is popular for weddings. There is a choice of dining venues and a pleasant bar.

Rooms 91 (6 fmly) **Facilities** FTV WiFi ⇄ ⊗ Gym Sauna Beauty treatments Dance studio **Conf** Class 100 Board 40 Thtr 275 **Parking** 250 **Notes** Civ Wed 275

Mercure Bolton Last Drop Village Hotel & Spa

★★★ 74% HOTEL   Mercure
                                          HOTELS

tel: 01204 591131 **Hospital Rd, Bromley Cross BL7 9PZ**
email: h6634@accor.com **web:** www.mercure.com
dir: *3m N of Bolton off B5472*

Mercure Bolton Last Drop Village Hotel & Spa is a collection of 18th-century farmhouses set on cobbled streets with various shops and a local pub. Extensive self-contained conference rooms, a modern health and beauty spa and breathtaking views of the West Pennine Moors make this a popular choice with both corporate and leisure guests. The bedrooms are well equipped and spacious.

Rooms 128 (10 annexe) (29 fmly) (20 GF) ⟁ **Facilities** Spa FTV WiFi ⇄ ⊗ Gym Craft shops Thermal suite Rock sauna Steam bath Bio sauna Hydro pool Xmas New Year **Conf** Class 300 Board 95 Thtr 700 **Services** Lift **Parking** 400 **Notes** Civ Wed 500

THE DEVONSHIRE ARMS
HOTEL & SPA

The Perfect Destination

The Devonshire Arms Hotel & Spa is an elegant and beautiful country retreat set in the stunning Yorkshire Dales. Located just 10 minutes from Skipton town centre, this is an exceptional place to escape for tranquillity and pleasure. Fine food, elegant interiors, luxurious accommodation and a stunning location will make your experience unforgettable.

- Four red star property with 40 bedrooms
- Four AA Rosette Burlington Restaurant
- Located on the 30,000 Bolton Abbey Estate

- The Devonshire Spa provides an oasis of tranquillity
- Complimentary Wi-Fi
- Beautiful private dining & function rooms

The Devonshire Arms Hotel & Spa | Bolton Abbey | North Yorkshire | BD23 6AJ
t: **01756 718111** e: **res@devonshirehotels.co.uk** w: **devonshirehotels.co.uk**

B

BOLTON *continued*

Premier Inn Bolton (Reebok Stadium)

BUDGET HOTEL

tel: 0871 527 8116 *(Calls cost 13p per minute plus your phone company's access charge)*
Arena Approach 3, Horwich BL6 6LB
web: www.premierinn.com
dir: *M61 junct 6, right at rdbt, left at 2nd rdbt*

High quality, budget accommodation ideal for both families and business travellers. Spacious, en suite bedrooms feature tea and coffee making facilities, and Freeview TV in most hotels. Internet access and WiFi are available for a small fee. The adjacent family restaurant features a wide and varied menu. See also the Hotel Groups pages.

Rooms 126

Premier Inn Bolton West

BUDGET HOTEL

tel: 0871 527 8118 *(Calls cost 13p per minute plus your phone company's access charge)*
991 Chorley New Rd, Horwich BL6 4BA
web: www.premierinn.com
dir: *M61 junct 6, follow dual carriageway signed Bolton/Horwich (Reebok Stadium on left). Hotel at 2nd rdbt*

Rooms 60

BOLTON ABBEY   Map 19 SE05
North Yorkshire

The Devonshire Arms Hotel & Spa

★★★★ ⬤ HOTEL

tel: 01756 710441 & 718111   **BD23 6AJ**
email: res@devonshirehotels.co.uk **web:** www.thedevonshirearms.co.uk
dir: *On B6160, 250yds N of junct with A59*

With stunning views of the Wharfedale countryside this beautiful hotel, owned by the Duke and Duchess of Devonshire, dates back to the 17th century. A long tradition of fine hospitality continues to this day, as guests' needs are accommodated in fine style, with attention to detail and friendly, personalised service. Bedrooms are elegantly furnished; those in the old part of the house are particularly spacious and have four-posters and fine antiques. The rest of the hotel is equally elegant, and it is a pleasure to spend time in one of the cosy sitting rooms. The Burlington Restaurant offers accomplished cuisine, while the Brasserie provides a lighter alternative. Both serve fresh and seasonal produce, largely from neighbouring farms, fields and rivers of the estate, as well as the hotel's own kitchen garden.

Rooms 40 (3 fmly) (17 GF) 🐾 **Facilities** Spa STV FTV WiFi ⬆ 🏹 supervised 🎣 Fishing ⛳ Gym Classic cars Falconry Laser pigeon shooting Fly fishing Cricket Xmas New Year **Conf** Class 40 Board 30 Thtr 120 Del £225 **Parking** 150 **Notes** Civ Wed 90

See advert on page 79

BOREHAMWOOD
Hertfordshire   Map 6 TQ19

Premier Inn London Elstree/Borehamwood

BUDGET HOTEL

tel: 0871 527 8654 *(Calls cost 13p per minute plus your phone company's access charge)*
Warwick Rd WD6 1US
web: www.premierinn.com
dir: *Exit A1 signed Borehamwood onto A5135 (Elstree Way). Pass BP Garage, left into Warwick Rd*

High quality, budget accommodation ideal for both families and business travellers. Spacious, en suite bedrooms feature tea and coffee making facilities, and Freeview TV in most hotels. Internet access and WiFi are available for a small fee. The adjacent family restaurant features a wide and varied menu. See also the Hotel Groups pages.

Rooms 124

Ibis London Elstree Borehamwood

AA Advertised

tel: 020 8736 2600 **Elstree Way WD6 1JY**
email: H6186@accor.com **web:** www.ibishotel.com
dir: *M25 junct 23, A1, exit at Borehamwood, take A5135 Elstree Way*

Modern, budget hotel offering comfortable accommodation in bright and practical bedrooms. Breakfast is self-service and dinner is available in the restaurant.

Rooms 122 (16 fmly) (16 GF) **Facilities** WiFi **Services** Lift Air con **Parking** 100 **Notes** LB

BOROUGHBRIDGE
North Yorkshire   Map 19 SE36

Best Western Crown Hotel

★★★ 77% HOTEL

tel: 01423 322328 **Horsefair YO51 9LB**
email: sales@crownboroughbridge.co.uk **web:** www.crownboroughbridge.co.uk
dir: *A1(M) junct 48 towards Boroughbridge. Hotel 1m*

Situated in the centre of town but convenient for the A1(M), The Crown provides a full leisure complex, conference rooms and a secure car park. Bedrooms are well appointed. A wide range of well-prepared dishes can be enjoyed in both the restaurant and bar.

Rooms 37 (3 fmly) (2 GF) **Facilities** FTV WiFi ▷ HL ⚲ supervised Gym Xmas New Year **Conf** Class 80 Board 80 Thtr 150 **Parking** 60 **Notes** ⊗ Civ Wed 120

The Crown Inn

◉◉ ♟ RESTAURANT WITH ROOMS

tel: 01423 322300 **Roecliffe YO51 9LY**
email: info@crowninnroecliffe.co.uk **web:** www.crowninnroecliffe.co.uk
dir: *A1(M) junct 48, follow signs for Boroughbridge. At rdbt exit towards Roecliffe & brown tourist signs*

The Crown is a 16th-century coaching inn providing an excellent combination of traditional charm and modern comforts. Service is friendly and professional and food is a highlight of any stay. The kitchen team use the finest of Yorkshire produce from the best local suppliers to create a weekly-changing seasonal menu. Bedrooms are attractively furnished with stylish en suite bathrooms.

Rooms 4 (1 fmly)

BORROWDALE
Cumbria   Map 18 NY21

See also **Keswick & Rosthwaite**

Lodore Falls Hotel

★★★★ 81% ◉ HOTEL

LAKE DISTRICT HOTELS

tel: 017687 77285 & 0800 840 1246 **CA12 5UX**
email: lodorefalls@lakedistricthotels.net **web:** www.lakedistricthotels.net/lodorefalls
dir: *M6 junct 40, A66 to Keswick, B5289 to Borrowdale. Hotel on left*

This impressive hotel has an enviable location overlooking Derwentwater. The bedrooms, many with lake or fell views, are comfortably equipped; family rooms and suites are also available. The dining room, bar and lounge areas are appointed to a very high standard. One of the treatments in the hotel's Elemis Spa actually makes use of the Lodore Waterfall.

Rooms 69 (11 fmly) **S** fr £115; **D** fr £230 (incl. bkfst) **Facilities** Spa STV FTV WiFi ⚲ ⚲ ⚲ Fishing Gym Sauna Xmas New Year **Conf** Class 90 Board 45 Thtr 200 **Services** Lift **Parking** 103 **Notes** Civ Wed 130

Borrowdale Gates Hotel

★★★★ 78% ◉ COUNTRY HOUSE HOTEL

tel: 017687 77204 & 0845 833 2524
(The only charge for this call will be your phone company's access charge) **CA12 5UQ**
email: hotel@borrowdale-gates.com **web:** www.borrowdale-gates.com
dir: *From A66 follow B5289 for approx 4m. Turn right over bridge, hotel 0.25m beyond village*

This friendly hotel is peacefully located in the Borrowdale Valley, close to the village but in its own three acres of wooded grounds. Public rooms include comfortable lounges and a restaurant with picture postcard views. Bedrooms and their en suites have benefited from investment and refurbishment with very good results.

Rooms 25 (2 fmly) (9 GF) **S** £75-£110; **D** £150-£310 (incl. bkfst)* **Facilities** STV FTV WiFi ▷ Xmas New Year **Services** Lift Air con **Parking** 25 **Notes** LB Closed 5-25 Jan

B

BORROWDALE *continued*

Borrowdale Hotel
★★★★ 75% HOTEL

LAKE DISTRICT ■■■■■ HOTELS

tel: 017687 77224 & 0800 840 1244 **CA12 5UY**
email: borrowdale@lakedistricthotels.net
web: www.lakedistricthotels.net/borrowdalehotel
dir: *3m from Keswick, on B5289 at S end of Lake Derwentwater*

Situated in the beautiful Borrowdale Valley overlooking Derwentwater, this traditionally styled hotel guarantees a friendly welcome. Extensive public areas include a choice of lounges, traditional dining room, lounge bar and popular conservatory which serves more informal meals. Bedrooms vary in style and size, including two that are suitable for less able guests.

Rooms 40 (2 fmly) (4 GF) ⬥ **S** fr £105; **D** fr £136 (incl. bkfst) **Facilities** STV FTV WiFi ⬥ Leisure facilities available at nearby sister hotel Xmas New Year **Conf** Class 30 Board 24 Thtr 80 **Parking** 30

Leathes Head Hotel
★★★ 85% ◉◉ HOTEL

tel: 017687 77247 & 77650 **CA12 5UY**
email: reservations@leatheshead.co.uk **web:** www.leatheshead.co.uk
dir: *3.5m from Keswick on B5289 (Borrowdale road). Hotel on left 0.25m before Grange Bridge*

A fine Edwardian building, with lovely gardens, set in the heart of the unspoilt Borrowdale Valley. The hospitality and customer care are really outstanding here. The bedrooms have commanding views and the award-winning food, including a wonderful Cumbrian breakfast, will not disappoint.

Rooms 11 (2 fmly) (3 GF) ⬥ **D** £150-£265 (incl. bkfst & dinner)* **Facilities** FTV WiFi **Parking** 16 **Notes** No children 15yrs Closed late Nov-mid Feb

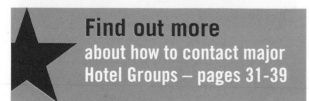

Find out more
about how to contact major Hotel Groups — pages 31-39

BOSCASTLE
Cornwall
Map 2 SX09

The Wellington Hotel
★★★ 78% ◉◉ HOTEL

tel: 01840 250202 **The Harbour PL35 0AQ**
email: info@wellingtonhotelboscastle.com **web:** www.wellingtonhotelboscastle.com
dir: *A30/A395 at Davidstowe follow Boscastle signs. B3266 to village. Right into Old Rd*

This 16th-century coaching inn is very much a landmark in Boscastle and has been providing rest and relaxation for weary travellers for many years. There is character in abundance which adds to its engaging charm and personality. The Long Bar is popular with visitors and locals alike and features a delightful galleried area. The stylish bedrooms come in varying sizes, including the spacious Tower Rooms; all provide contemporary comforts and the expected necessities. In addition to the bar menus, The Waterloo Restaurant is the elegant setting for accomplished cuisine.

Rooms 17 (3 annexe) (3 fmly) ⬥ **S** £50-£65; **D** £95-£135 (incl. bkfst)* **Facilities** FTV WiFi ⬥ Xmas New Year **Conf** Class 40 Board 24 Thtr 50 Del from £95 to £125* **Parking** 14 **Notes** LB

BOSHAM
West Sussex
Map 5 SU80

HIGHLY RECOMMENDED

The Millstream Hotel & Restaurant
★★★ 86% ◉◉ HOTEL

tel: 01243 573234 **Bosham Ln PO18 8HL**
email: info@millstreamhotel.co.uk **web:** www.millstreamhotel.com
dir: *4m W of Chichester on A259, left at Bosham rdbt. After 0.5m right at T-junct signed to church & quay. Hotel 0.5m on right*

Located in the idyllic village of Bosham, this attractive hotel provides comfortable, well-equipped and tastefully decorated bedrooms. Many guests regularly return here for the relaxed atmosphere created by the notably efficient and friendly staff. Public rooms include a cocktail bar that opens onto the garden, and a pleasant award-winning restaurant where varied and freshly prepared cuisine can be enjoyed. Markwick's Brasserie Restaurant is open all day for coffee, snacks, light lunches and dinners.

Rooms 35 (2 annexe) (2 fmly) (9 GF) ⬥ **Facilities** FTV WiFi Painting & Bridge breaks ♫ Xmas New Year **Conf** Class 20 Board 20 Thtr 45 **Parking** 44 **Notes** ⊗ Civ Wed 75

BOSTON
Lincolnshire
Map 12 TF34

White Hart Hotel and Eatery
★★★ 79% HOTEL

tel: 01205 311900 **1-5 High St, Bridge Foot PE21 8SH**
email: whitehartboston@innmail.co.uk **web:** www.whitehartboston.com
dir: *In town centre*

The White Hart Hotel is well appointed and attractive, and is conveniently located in the centre of this market town with great views of the 700-year-old St Botolph's Church, known as the Boston Stump, from its riverside location. The hotel has spacious public areas including the Riverside Restaurant for evening meals, and

B

the lively Courtyard Bar which is open for brunch, lunch and afternoon tea. There is a wonderful outside area for relaxing, eating and drinking. Conferences and weddings are catered for, and off-street parking in a private car park is also available.

Rooms 26 🕿 **S** £79-£119; **D** £89-£129 (incl. bkfst)* **Facilities** FTV WiFi ☼ HL Xmas New Year **Conf** Class 26 Board 26 Thtr 80 Del from £129* **Parking** 45 **Notes** Civ Wed 80

Supreme Inns Boston

★★★ 77% HOTEL

tel: 01205 822804 **Donnington Rd, Bicker Bar Roundabout PE20 3AN**
email: enquiries@supremeinns.co.uk **web:** www.supremeinns.co.uk
dir: At rdbt junct of A52 & A17

Situated south west of Boston and surrounded by the Lincolnshire Fens, this modern, purpose-built hotel offers well equipped bedrooms that have flat-screen TVs and internet access. Food is available in the restaurant or all day in the relaxing bar area. Wedding, private dinner and conference facilities are all available.

Rooms 55 (27 GF) **Facilities** FTV WiFi ☼ Xmas New Year **Conf** Board 30 Thtr 50 **Parking** 65 **Notes** ⊗

Premier Inn Boston

BUDGET HOTEL

tel: 0871 527 8120 (Calls cost 13p per minute plus your phone company's access charge)
Wainfleet Rd PE21 9RW
web: www.premierinn.com
dir: A52, 300yds E of junct with A16 Boston/Grimsby road

High quality, budget accommodation ideal for both families and business travellers. Spacious, en suite bedrooms feature tea and coffee making facilities, and Freeview TV in most hotels. Internet access and WiFi are available for a small fee. The adjacent family restaurant features a wide and varied menu. See also the Hotel Groups pages.

Rooms 73

BOTLEY
Hampshire | Map 5 SU51

Macdonald Botley Park Hotel & Spa

★★★★ 76% COUNTRY HOUSE HOTEL

MACDONALD HOTELS & RESORTS

tel: 01489 780888 & 0344 879 9034 **Winchester Rd, Boorley Green SO32 2UA**
email: general.botleypark@macdonald-hotels.co.uk
web: www.macdonald-hotels.co.uk/botleypark
dir: M27 junct 7, A334 towards Botley. At 1st rdbt left, pass M&S store, over at next 5 mini rdbts. At 6th mini rdbt turn right. In 0.5km hotel on left

This modern and spacious hotel has bedrooms which are comfortably appointed with a good range of extras, and extensive leisure facilities are on offer. Attractive public areas include a relaxing restaurant and the more informal Swing and Divot Bar.

Rooms 130 (30 fmly) (34 GF) 🕿 **Facilities** Spa STV WiFi ☼ ⊗ Gym Squash Dance studio Sauna Steam Room Relaxation lounge Xmas New Year **Conf** Class 180 Board 140 Thtr 450 Del from £140 to £180* **Services** Air con **Parking** 310 **Notes** ⊗ Civ Wed 400

BOURNEMOUTH
Dorset | Map 5 SZ19

See also **Christchurch**

Bournemouth Highcliff Marriott Hotel

★★★★ 80% ◉◉ HOTEL

Marriott.

tel: 01202 557702 **St Michaels Rd, West Cliff BH2 5DU**
email: mhrs.bohbm.ays@marriotthotels.co.uk
web: www.bournemouthhighcliffmarriott.co.uk
dir: A338 into Bournemouth then BIC signs to West Cliff Rd. 2nd right into St Michaels Rd. Hotel at end of road on left

Originally built as a row of coastguard cottages, this establishment has expanded over the years into a very elegant and charming hotel. Impeccably maintained throughout, many of the bedrooms have sea views. An excellent range of leisure, business and conference facilities are offered, as well as private dining and banqueting rooms. The hotel also has direct access to the Bournemouth International Centre.

Rooms 160 (19 annexe) (22 fmly) (4 GF) 🕿 **Facilities** STV FTV WiFi ☼ ⊗ ⊰ ⊱ Gym Beautician Beauty treatment room Xmas New Year **Conf** Class 180 Board 90 Thtr 350 **Services** Lift Air con **Parking** 80 **Notes** ⊗ Civ Wed 120

The Green House

★★★★ 79% ◉◉ TOWN HOUSE HOTEL

tel: 01202 498900 **4 Grove Rd BH1 3AX**
email: reception@thegreenhousehotel.com **web:** www.thegreenhousehotel.com

This hotel has a clear commitment to ecological responsibility which goes beyond just energy efficient lighting; everything has been designed and built to be sympathetic to the environment. The beautifully appointed bedrooms and bathrooms demonstrate the 'green' principle from the locally made 100% wool carpets and solid wood furniture, to the wallpapers and paint that have been used. The ingredients used for the menus are locally sourced and organic.

Rooms 32 (3 fmly) (6 GF) 🕿 **Facilities** FTV WiFi ☼ In room beauty treatments Xmas New Year **Conf** Class 40 Board 40 Thtr 100 **Services** Lift **Parking** 32 **Notes** ⊗ Civ Wed 100

Hotel Miramar

★★★★ 77% HOTEL

tel: 01202 556581 **East Overcliff Dr, East Cliff BH1 3AL**
email: sales@miramar-bournemouth.com **web:** www.miramar-bournemouth.com
dir: From Wessex Way rdbt into St Pauls Rd, right at next rdbt. 3rd exit at next rdbt, 2nd exit at next rdbt into Grove Rd. Hotel car park on right

Conveniently located on the East Cliff, this Edwardian hotel enjoys glorious sea views. The Miramar was a favoured destination of famed author J.R.R. Tolkien, who often stayed here. The bedrooms are comfortable and well equipped, and there are spacious public areas and a choice of lounges. The friendly staff and relaxing environment are also noteworthy.

Rooms 43 (6 fmly) 🕿 **Facilities** FTV WiFi ☼ HL ♫ Xmas New Year **Conf** Class 50 Board 50 Thtr 200 Del from £100 to £150* **Services** Lift **Parking** 90 **Notes** Civ Wed 110

BOURNEMOUTH *continued*

Best Western Plus The Connaught Hotel

Best Western PLUS.

★★★★ 76% ◉◉ HOTEL

tel: 01202 298020 **30 West Hill Rd, West Cliff BH2 5PH**
email: reception@theconnaught.co.uk **web:** www.theconnaught.co.uk
dir: *Follow Town Centre West & BIC signs*

Conveniently located on the West Cliff, close to the BIC, beaches and town centre, this privately-owned hotel offers well equipped, neatly decorated rooms, some with balconies. The hotel boasts a very well-equipped leisure complex with a large pool and gym. Breakfast and dinner offer imaginative dishes made with quality local ingredients.

Rooms 80 (27 annexe) ☌ **S** £65-£90; **D** £80-£150 (incl. bkfst) **Facilities** Spa FTV WiFi ↻ ☜ supervised Gym Beauty treatments Sauna room Steam room ♫ Xmas New Year **Conf** Class 60 Board 35 Thtr 180 Del from £140 to £200* **Services** Lift **Parking** 66 **Notes** ⊗ Civ Wed 130

See advert on opposite page

Park Central Hotel

★★★★ 76% ◉◉ HOTEL

tel: 01202 203600 **Exeter Rd BH2 5AJ**
email: reception@parkcentralhotel.co.uk **web:** www.parkcentralhotel.co.uk
dir: *A338, A35 (St Pauls Rd). At rdbt 3rd exit onto B3066 (Holdenburst Rd). Straight on at 3 rdbts, hotel on right opposite Bournemouth International Centre*

Located opposite Bournemouth International Centre, this modern, contemporary hotel is in a good location and has sea views; bedrooms are comfortable and attractively furnished. The menu features creative modern ideas based on intuitive combinations of well-sourced raw materials featuring, of course a great deal of seafood. A pre-theatre menu is also available, but be sure to book as this can prove very popular.

Rooms 48 (6 fmly) (7 GF) ☌ **S** £49-£170; **D** £69-£190 (incl. bkfst)* **Facilities** FTV WiFi ↻ In room spa ♫ New Year **Services** Lift **Parking** 29 **Notes** ⊗

Hallmark Hotel Bournemouth Carlton

★★★★ 76% ◉ HOTEL

tel: 0330 028 3411 **East Overcliff BH1 3DN**
email: carlton@hallmarkhotels.co.uk **web:** www.hallmarkhotels.co.uk
dir: *From M3, M27 towards Bournemouth on A338, follow signs to East Cliff, hotel on seafront*

Enjoying a prime location on the East Cliff, and with views of the Isle of Wight and Dorset coastline, the Carlton has attractive gardens and pool area. Most of the spacious bedrooms enjoy sea views. Leisure facilities include an indoor and outdoor pool as well as a gym. Guests can enjoy an interesting range of carefully prepared dishes in Frederick's restaurant. The conference and banqueting facilities are varied.

Rooms 76 (17 fmly) (8 GF) ☌ **Facilities** Spa FTV WiFi ☜ ☈ Gym Hair & beauty salon Xmas New Year **Conf** Class 110 Board 50 Thtr 200 **Services** Lift **Parking** 87 **Notes** Civ Wed 200

Hallmark Hotel Bournemouth East Cliff

★★★★ 76% HOTEL

tel: 01202 554545 **East Overcliff Dr BH1 3AN**
email: eastcliff@hallmarkhotels.co.uk **web:** www.hallmarkhotels.co.uk
dir: *From M3, M27 towards Bournemouth on A33 follow signs to East Cliff, hotel on seafront*

Enjoying panoramic views across the bay, this popular hotel offers bedrooms that are modern and contemporary in style; they are appointed to a very high standard, and many have the benefit of balconies and sea views. Stylish public areas include a range of inviting lounges, a spacious restaurant and a selection of conference rooms.

Rooms 67 (15 fmly) (2 GF) (5 smoking) ☌ **Facilities** FTV WiFi ↻ ☈ Full leisure facilities at adjacent Hallmark Carlton Xmas New Year **Conf** Class 60 Board 40 Thtr 150 **Services** Lift **Parking** 45 **Notes** Civ Wed 250

Hermitage Hotel

★★★★ 75% HOTEL

tel: 01202 557363 **Exeter Rd BH2 5AH**
email: info@hermitage-hotel.co.uk **web:** www.hermitage-hotel.co.uk
dir: *A338 Ringwood, follow signs for BIC & pier. Hotel directly opposite*

Occupying an impressive location overlooking the seafront, at the heart of the town centre, the Hermitage offers friendly and attentive service. The majority of the smart bedrooms are comfortably appointed and all are very well equipped; many rooms have sea views. The wood-panelled lounge provides an elegant and tranquil area, as does the restaurant where well-prepared and interesting dishes are served.

Rooms 74 (11 annexe) (9 fmly) (7 GF) S £55.50-£82; **D** £111-£164 (incl. bkfst)*
Facilities FTV WiFi Xmas New Year **Conf** Class 60 Board 60 Thtr 180 **Services** Lift
Parking 58 **Notes**

The Norfolk

★★★★ 74% HOTEL

tel: 01202 551521 **Richmond Hill BH2 6EN**
email: rooms@norfolkroyale-hotel-bournemouth.com **web:** www.peelhotels.co.uk
dir: *A338 into Bournemouth take Richmond Hill exit to A347 Wimborne, turn left at top into Richmond Hill. Hotel on right*

Easily recognisable by its wrought iron balconies, this Edwardian hotel is conveniently located for the centre of the town. Most of the bedrooms are contained in a modern wing at the side of the building, overlooking the pretty landscaped gardens. There is a car park at rear of the hotel.

Rooms 95 (23 fmly) (9 GF) S £76-£168; **D** £121-£213 (incl. bkfst)* **Facilities** STV
FTV WiFi HL Membership of nearby health club Xmas New Year Child
facilities **Conf** Class 50 Board 40 Thtr 150 Del from £130 to £160* **Services** Lift
Parking 95 **Notes** LB Civ Wed 150

Hallmark Hotel Bournemouth West Cliff

★★★★ 69% HOTEL

tel: 0330 028 3413 **Durley Chine Rd, West Cliff BH2 5JS**
email: westcliff@hallmarkhotels.co.uk **web:** www.hallmarkhotels.co.uk
dir: *A338 follow signs to West Cliff & BIC, hotel on right*

This property is conveniently located and offers a friendly atmosphere and attentive service. The comfortable bedrooms are tastefully appointed and are suitable for both business and leisure guests. The restaurant and bar serve a good choice of dishes, and the well-appointed leisure area is popular with both residents and locals alike. There is also a good range of conference facilities and meeting rooms.

Rooms 83 (5 GF) S £59-£150; **D** £75-£190 (incl. bkfst)* **Facilities** Spa FTV WiFi
Gym Sauna Steam room Aromatherapy cave Relaxation room Xmas New Year
Conf Class 80 Board 40 Thtr 250 Del from £85 to £175* **Services** Lift **Parking** 80
Notes LB Civ Wed 200

The Riviera Hotel

★★★ 81% HOTEL

tel: 01202 763653 **Burnaby Rd, Alum Chine BH4 8JF**
email: info@rivierabournemouth.co.uk **web:** www.rivierabournemouth.co.uk
dir: *A338, follow signs to Alum Chine*

The Riviera offers a range of comfortable, well-furnished bedrooms and bathrooms. Welcoming staff provide efficient service delivered in a friendly manner. In addition to a spacious lounge with regular entertainment, there are indoor and outdoor pools, all just a short walk from the beach. Accomplished cuisine is not to be missed.

Rooms 70 (4 annexe) (24 fmly) (7 GF) S £25-£85; **D** £35-£185 **Facilities** FTV WiFi
Gym Games room Sauna Spa bath Treatments available in the Coast Spa
Xmas New Year **Conf** Class 120 Board 50 Thtr 180 Del from £75 to £215
Services Lift **Parking** 45 **Notes** LB Civ Wed 160

BOURNEMOUTH *continued*

Best Western Hotel Royale

BW Best Western.

★★★ 81% HOTEL

tel: 01202 554794 **16 Gervis Rd BH1 3EQ**
email: info@thehotelroyale.com **web:** www.thehotelroyale.com
dir: *M27 junct 1, A31 onto A338 to Bournemouth, follow signs for East Cliff & seafront. Over 2 rdbts into Gervis Rd. Hotel on right*

Located on the East Cliff, just a short walk from the seafront and local shops and amenities, is this privately-owned hotel. Public areas are contemporary in style, and facilities include a small health club and spacious function rooms. Bedrooms are comfortable and well furnished.

Rooms 64 (8 annexe) (22 fmly) (8 GF) 🐾 **Facilities** STV FTV WiFi ⚲ 🕤 Xmas New Year **Conf** Class 60 Board 40 Thtr 100 **Services** Lift **Parking** 80 **Notes** ⊗

Royal Exeter Hotel

★★★ 80% HOTEL

tel: 01202 438000 **Exeter Rd BH2 5AG**
email: enquiries@royalexeterhotel.com **web:** www.royalexeterhotel.com
dir: *Opposite Bournemouth International Centre*

Ideally located opposite the Bournemouth International Centre, and convenient for the beach and town centre, this busy hotel caters for both business and leisure guests. Public areas are smart, and there's a modern open-plan lounge bar and restaurant, together with an exciting adjoining bar complex.

Rooms 54 (13 fmly) (12 smoking) 🐾 **Facilities** FTV WiFi Gym 🎵 **Conf** Class 40 Board 40 Thtr 100 Del from £85 to £125 **Services** Lift **Parking** 50 **Notes** ⊗

See advert on opposite page

Elstead Hotel

★★★ 79% HOTEL

tel: 01202 293071 **Knyveton Rd BH1 3QP**
email: info@the-elstead.co.uk **web:** www.the-elstead.co.uk
dir: *A338 (Wessex Way) to St Pauls rdbt, left & left again*

Ideal as a base for business and leisure travellers, Elstead Hotel is conveniently located for the town centre, seafront and BIC. An impressive range of facilities is offered, including meeting rooms, an indoor leisure centre and comfortable lounges.

Rooms 50 (15 fmly) 🐾 **Facilities** FTV WiFi 🕤 supervised Gym Sauna Steam room Pool & snooker tables Xmas New Year **Conf** Class 70 Board 35 Thtr 80 **Services** Lift **Parking** 40 **Notes** Civ Wed 60

B

Mayfair Hotel

★★★ 78% HOTEL

tel: 01202 551983 **27 Bath Rd BH1 2NW**
email: info@themayfair.com **web:** www.themayfair.com
dir: *Exit A338 at St Pauls Rd (Asda rdbt), right into Holdenhurst Rd, 3rd exit from Lansdowne rdbt*

Occupying a central location in the heart of Bournemouth and within walking distance of both the town centre and the seafront, this hotel offers guests comfortable, modern accommodation. There is a spacious restaurant and bar area, plus a pleasant outdoor patio and function room.

Rooms 40 (6 fmly) (1 GF) **Facilities** WiFi Ballroom dancing programme on request Xmas New Year **Conf** Class 40 Board 30 Thtr 60 **Services** Lift **Parking** 30 **Notes** ⊗ Civ Wed 80

Durley Dean Hotel

★★★ 77% HOTEL

tel: 01202 557711 **West Cliff Rd BH2 5HE**
email: reservations@durleydean.co.uk **web:** www.durleydean.co.uk
dir: *Into Bournemouth, follow signs for Westcliff. Onto Durley Chine Rd South to next rdbt, hotel at 2nd exit on left*

Situated close to the seafront on the West Cliff, Durley Dean is a modern hotel with bedrooms that vary in size and style. The hotel has a restaurant, a comfortable bar and several meeting rooms. Parking is also a bonus. Additional facilities include a new spa with indoor pool, gym, and treatment rooms for a touch of pampering.

Rooms 117 (36 fmly) (6 GF) **Facilities** FTV WiFi ⓢ ⓢ Gym Sauna ♫ Xmas New Year **Conf** Class 40 Board 45 Thtr 150 **Services** Lift **Parking** 30 **Notes** ⊗ Civ Wed 120

Trouville Hotel

★★★ 75% HOTEL

tel: 01202 552262 **Priory Rd BH2 5DH**
email: reception@trouvillehotel.com **web:** www.trouvillehotel.com
dir: *Follow Town Centre West signs. Exit at rdbt signed BIC/West Cliff/Beaches. 2nd exit at next rdbt, left at next rdbt. Hotel on left near end of Priory Rd*

Located near Bournemouth International Centre, the seafront and the shops, this hotel has the advantage of indoor leisure facilities and a large car park. Bedrooms are generally a good size with comfortable furnishings, and there are plenty of family rooms. The air-conditioned restaurant offers a daily changing menu.

Rooms 99 (19 annexe) (21 fmly) (2 GF) ⌂ **Facilities** FTV WiFi ⓢ ⓢ Gym Sauna Beauty treatment room ♫ Xmas New Year **Conf** Class 100 Board 80 Thtr 250 **Services** Lift **Parking** 70 **Notes** Civ Wed 130

Hotel Collingwood

★★★ 74% HOTEL

tel: 01202 557575 **11 Priory Rd, West Cliff BH2 5DF**
email: info@hotel-collingwood.co.uk **web:** www.hotel-collingwood.co.uk
dir: *A338 left at West Cliff sign, over 1st rdbt, left at 2nd rdbt. Hotel 500yds on left*

This privately owned and managed hotel is situated close to the BIC. The bedrooms are airy, with an emphasis on guest comfort. An excellent range of leisure facilities is available, and the public areas are spacious and welcoming. Pinks Restaurant offers carefully prepared cuisine and a fixed-price, five-course dinner.

Rooms 53 (16 fmly) (6 GF) ⌂ **S** £35-£90; **D** £70-£180 (incl. bkfst & dinner)* **Facilities** FTV WiFi ⓢ ⓢ Gym Steam room Sauna Games room Snooker room ♫ Xmas New Year **Conf** Class 40 Board 20 Thtr 80 **Services** Lift **Parking** 55

B

BOURNEMOUTH *continued*

Hotel Piccadilly

★★★ 74% HOTEL

tel: 01202 298024 **25 Bath Rd BH1 2NN**
email: enquiries@hotelpiccadilly.co.uk **web:** www.hotelpiccadilly.co.uk
dir: *From A338 take 1st exit rdbt, signed East Cliff. 3rd exit at next rdbt signed Lansdowne, 3rd exit at next rdbt into Bath Rd*

Hotel Piccadilly offers a friendly welcome to guests, many of whom return on a regular basis, particularly for the superb ballroom-dancing facilities and small-break packages which are a feature here. Bedrooms are smartly decorated, well maintained and comfortable. Dining in the attractive restaurant is always popular, and dishes are freshly prepared and appetising.

Rooms 45 (2 fmly) (5 GF) **S** £35-£55; **D** £70-£110 (incl. bkfst)* **Facilities** FTV WiFi Ballroom Massage/treatment room Xmas New Year **Conf** Class 50 Board 50 Thtr 140 Del from £45 to £75 **Services** Lift **Parking** 45 **Notes** LB ⊗

Marsham Court Hotel

★★★ 74% HOTEL

tel: 01202 552111 & 446644 **Russell Cotes Rd, East Cliff BH1 3AB**
email: reservations@marshamcourthotel.co.uk **web:** www.marshamcourthotel.co.uk
dir: *A338, at St Pauls rdbt follow signs to East Cliff, Pier & Beaches. 3rd exit Holdenhurst Rd, at next rdbt 3rd exit Bath Rd, at next rdbt 2nd exit, hotel car park immediately on right*

This hotel, in a quiet location, is set in attractive gardens with splendid views over the bay; it is just a short stroll from the town, beach and BIC. Bedrooms vary in size but all are comfortably appointed, and some have sea views. The bar and lounge areas lead onto the south-facing terrace, which has an outdoor pool. Impressive conference and banqueting facilities are available.

Rooms 87 (25 fmly) **S** £69-£114; **D** £69-£114* **Facilities** FTV WiFi ⇗ ⅃ Indoor games room Xmas New Year **Conf** Class 120 Board 80 Thtr 230 Del from £103.50 to £133.50* **Services** Lift **Parking** 99 **Notes** ⊗ Civ Wed 180

Devon Towers Hotel

Leisureplex
HOLIDAY HOTELS

★★★ 71% HOTEL

tel: 01202 553863 **58-62 St Michael's Rd, West Cliff BH2 5ED**
email: devontowers@leisureplex.co.uk **web:** www.leisureplex.co.uk
dir: *A338 into Bournemouth, follow signs for BIC. Left into St. Michaels Rd at top of hill. Hotel 100mtrs on left*

Located in a quiet road within walking distance of the West Cliff and shops, this hotel appeals to the budget leisure market. The four-course menus offer plenty of choice and entertainment is featured most evenings. The bar and lobby area provide plenty of space for relaxing.

Rooms 60 (8 GF) **Facilities** FTV WiFi ♫ Xmas New Year **Services** Lift **Parking** 6 **Notes** ⊗ Closed Jan-mid Feb (ex Xmas) RS mid-end Feb, Mar & Nov

Tower House Hotel

★★ 78% HOTEL

tel: 01202 290742 **West Cliff Gardens BH2 5HP**
email: towerhouse.hotel@btconnect.com **web:** www.towerhousehotelbournemouth.com

Tower House Hotel is a popular family-owned and run hotel on the West Cliff. The owners and their staff are friendly and helpful. The bedrooms are comfortable and well maintained, and the hotel provides good off-road parking.

Rooms 32 (12 fmly) (3 GF) **Facilities** FTV WiFi Xmas New Year **Services** Lift **Parking** 30 **Notes** Closed 2-31 Jan

Bourne Hall Hotel

★★ 65% METRO HOTEL

tel: 01202 299715 **14 Priory Rd BH2 5DN**
email: info@bournehall.co.uk **web:** www.bournehall.co.uk

Situated on the West Cliff, this welcoming family-run establishment is ideally located for a relaxing break in Bournemouth. Just a short stroll from the wonderful stretch of golden sands, there is much to explore. Bedrooms are simply furnished and some have the benefit of sea views, while public areas include a spacious bar and lounge with outside terrace area. Breakfast is served in the elegant dining room.

Rooms 47 (7 fmly) (5 GF) **S** £20-£70; **D** £25-£110 (incl. bkfst)* **Facilities** FTV WiFi Xmas New Year **Services** Lift **Parking** 37 **Notes** Closed some wknds

Premier Inn Bournemouth Central

BUDGET HOTEL

tel: 0871 527 8124 *(Calls cost 13p per minute plus your phone company's access charge)*
Westover Rd BH1 2BZ
web: www.premierinn.com
dir: *M27 junct 1, A31. Left at Ashley Heath junct. A338 towards Bournemouth. At rdbt 1st exit. At next rdbt 3rd exit (Holdenhurst Rd). At next rdbt 3rd exit (Bath Rd). At next rdbt 3rd exit onto Bath Hill. At next rdbt into Westover Rd, right into Hinton Rd, hotel on right*

High quality, budget accommodation ideal for both families and business travellers. Spacious, en suite bedrooms feature tea and coffee making facilities, and Freeview TV in most hotels. Internet access and WiFi are available for a small fee. The adjacent family restaurant features a wide and varied menu. See also the Hotel Groups pages.

Rooms 120

Premier Inn Bournemouth East (Lynton Court)

BUDGET HOTEL

tel: 0871 527 8126 *(Calls cost 13p per minute plus your phone company's access charge)*
47 Christchurch Rd, Boscombe BH1 3PA
web: www.premierinn.com
dir: *M27 junct 1, A31, 9m, left at Ashley Heath junct, take A338 signed Bournemouth. At 1st rdbt take 1st exit into Saint Paul's Rd. At 2nd rdbt 1st exit onto Christchurch Rd. Hotel on right*

Rooms 20

Premier Inn Bournemouth Westcliffe

BUDGET HOTEL

tel: 0871 527 8128 *(Calls cost 13p per minute plus your phone company's access charge)*
Poole Rd BH2 5QU
web: www.premierinn.com
dir: *M27 junct 1, A31. At Ashley Heath junction, left. Take A338 signed Bournemouth. At Bournemouth West rdbt 1st exit signed Ring Road, West Cliff. At next rdbt (St Michael's) 3rd exit (signed Westbourne) into Poole Rd. Hotel on right*

Rooms 168

BOURTON-ON-THE-WATER
Gloucestershire   Map 10 SP12

Chester House Hotel

★★★ 79% SMALL HOTEL

tel: 01451 820286 **Victoria St GL54 2BU**
email: info@chesterhousehotel.com **web:** www.chesterhousehotel.com
dir: On A429 between Northleach & Stow-on-the-Wold

Chester House Hotel occupies a secluded but central location in this delightful Cotswold village. Bedrooms, some at ground floor level, are situated in the main house and adjoining coach house. The public areas are stylish, light and airy. Breakfast is taken in the main building whereas dinner is served in the attractive restaurant just a few yards away.

Rooms 22 (10 annexe) (3 fmly) (8 GF) ☞ **D** £99-£140 (incl. bkfst)* **Facilities** FTV WiFi ↳ Beauty therapist New Year **Parking** 18 **Notes** Closed 2 Jan-10 Feb

INSPECTORS' CHOICE

The Dial House

◎◎◎ RESTAURANT WITH ROOMS

tel: 01451 822244 **High St GL54 2AN**
email: info@dialhousehotel.com **web:** www.dialhousehotel.com

With an idyllic location in the middle of the delightful village of Bourton-on-the-Water, this high quality accommodation offers a well judged mix of professional and efficient service with a relaxed and friendly ambience. Bedrooms and bathrooms offer a range of shapes and sizes and all are decorated and maintained to high standards. Off-street car parking and a pleasant garden are provided to the rear of the property. Dinner is a highlight, offering a range of carefully prepared dishes that combine fine English produce with French culinary techniques.

Rooms 14 (5 annexe)

BOWNESS ON WINDERMERE

See **Windermere**

BRACKNELL
Berkshire   Map 5 SU86

Coppid Beech

★★★★ 72% HOTEL

tel: 01344 303333 **John Nike Way RG12 8TF**
email: sales@coppidbeech.com **web:** www.coppidbeech.com
dir: M4 junct 10 take Wokingham/Bracknell onto A329. In 2m take B3408 to Binfield, at lights turn right. Hotel 200yds on right

This chalet designed hotel offers extensive facilities and includes a ski-slope, ice rink, nightclub, health club and Bier Keller. Bedrooms range from suites to standard rooms - all are impressively equipped. A choice of dining is offered; there's a full bistro menu available in the Keller, and for more formal dining.

Rooms 205 (6 fmly) (16 GF) **Facilities** STV WiFi ☜ Gym Beauty treatment room Ice rink Dry ski slope Snow boarding Freestyle park ♫ New Year **Conf** Class 161 Board 24 Thtr 350 **Services** Lift Air con **Parking** 350 **Notes** ⊗ Civ Wed 200

Stirrups Country House Hotel

★★★ 82% HOTEL

tel: 01344 882284 **Maidens Green RG42 6LD**
email: reception@stirrupshotel.co.uk **web:** www.stirrupshotel.co.uk
dir: 3m N on B3022 towards Windsor

Situated in a peaceful location between Maidenhead, Bracknell and Windsor, this hotel has high standards of comfort particularly in the bedrooms; some rooms have a small sitting room area. There is a popular bar, a restaurant, function rooms and delightful grounds.

Rooms 36 (5 annexe) (6 fmly) (5 GF) ☞ **S** £80-£115; **D** £80-£115* **Facilities** FTV WiFi ↳ HL New Year **Conf** Class 50 Board 40 Thtr 100 Del from £160* **Services** Lift **Parking** 100 **Notes** LB ⊗ Civ Wed 100

Premier Inn Bracknell Central

BUDGET HOTEL

tel: 0871 527 8132 (Calls cost 13p per minute plus your phone company's access charge)
Wokingham Rd RG42 1NA
web: www.premierinn.com
dir: M4 junct 10, A329(M) (Bracknell) to lights. 1st left, 3rd exit rdbt by Morrisons to town centre. Left at rdbt, left at next rdbt. Hotel on left

High quality, budget accommodation ideal for both families and business travellers. Spacious, en suite bedrooms feature tea and coffee making facilities, and Freeview TV in most hotels. Internet access and WiFi are available for a small fee. The adjacent family restaurant features a wide and varied menu. See also the Hotel Groups pages.

Rooms 80

Premier Inn Bracknell (Twin Bridges)

BUDGET HOTEL

tel: 0871 527 8130 (Calls cost 13p per minute plus your phone company's access charge)
Downshire Way RG12 7AA
web: www.premierinn.com
dir: M4 junct 10, A329(M) towards Bracknell. Straight on at mini rdbt. At Twin Bridges rdbt take 2nd exit. Hotel on right adjacent to Downshire Arms Beefeater

Rooms 28

BRADFORD
West Yorkshire   Map 19 SE13

See also **Gomersal**

Best Western Plus Cedar Court Hotel

★★★★ 72% HOTEL

tel: 01274 406606 **Mayo Av, Off Rooley Ln BD5 8HW**
email: sales@cedarcourtbradford.co.uk **web:** www.cedarcourthotels.co.uk
dir: M62 junct 26, M606, to end of motorway, take 1st left

This purpose built, modern hotel is conveniently located just off the motorway and close to the city centre and the airport. The hotel boasts extensive function and conference facilities, a well-equipped leisure club and an elegant restaurant. Bedrooms are comfortably appointed for both business and leisure guests.

Rooms 131 (7 fmly) (23 GF) **Facilities** STV FTV WiFi ↳ ☜ Gym Steam room Sauna Solarium New Year **Conf** Class 300 Board 100 Thtr 800 **Services** Lift **Parking** 350 **Notes** ⊗ Civ Wed 550

B

BRADFORD *continued*

Midland Hotel

★★★ 77% HOTEL

tel: 01274 735735 **Forster Square BD1 4HU**
email: info@midland-hotel-bradford.com **web:** www.peelhotels.co.uk
dir: *M62 junct 26, M606, past ASDA, left at rdbt onto A650. Through 2 rdbts & 2 lights. Follow A6181/Haworth signs. Up hill, next left into Manor Row. Hotel 400mtrs*

Ideally situated in the heart of the city, this grand Victorian hotel provides modern, very well equipped accommodation and comfortable, spacious day rooms. Ample parking is available in what was once the city's railway station, and a Victorian walkway linking the hotel to the old platform can still be used today.

Rooms 90 (5 fmly) (4 smoking) ✿ **Facilities** STV FTV WiFi ⮑ HL New Year **Conf** Class 150 Board 100 Thtr 450 **Services** Lift **Parking** 60 **Notes** Civ Wed 450

Best Western Bradford Guide Post Hotel

★★★ 75% HOTEL

tel: 01274 607866 **Common Rd, Low Moor BD12 OST**
email: sue.barnes@guideposthotel.net **web:** www.guideposthotel.net
dir: *From M606 rdbt take 2nd exit. At next rdbt take 1st exit (Cleckheaton Rd). 0.5m, turn right at bollard into Common Rd*

Situated south of the city, this hotel offers attractively styled, modern, comfortable bedrooms. The restaurant offers an extensive range of food using fresh, local produce; lighter snack meals are served in the bar. There is also a choice of well-equipped meeting and function rooms. There is disabled access to the hotel, restaurant and one function room.

Rooms 42 (10 fmly) (13 GF) ✿ **Facilities** FTV WiFi ⮑ Complimentary use of nearby swimming & gym facilities **Conf** Class 80 Board 60 Thtr 120 **Parking** 100 **Notes** Civ Wed 120

Premier Inn Bradford Central

BUDGET HOTEL

tel: 0871 527 9306 *(Calls cost 13p per minute plus your phone company's access charge)*
Vicar Ln BD1 5LD
web: www.premierinn.com
dir: *M62 junct 24, M606, at junct 3 take 4th exit into Rooley Ln (A6177) towards Ring Rd/A650/Leeds/A647. In 1m 1st exit into Wakefield Rd towards City Centre. Follow Wakefield Rd/A650 signs. Straight on at 2 rdbts, right into Vicar Ln*

High quality, budget accommodation ideal for both families and business travellers. Spacious, en suite bedrooms feature tea and coffee making facilities, and Freeview TV in most hotels. Internet access and WiFi are available for a small fee. The adjacent family restaurant features a wide and varied menu. See also the Hotel Groups pages.

Rooms 118

Ibis Budget Bradford

AA Advertised

tel: 01274 724415 **Prince Court, Canal Rd BD1 4SJ**
email: h6364@accor.com **web:** www.ibishotel.com

Modern, budget hotel offering comfortable accommodation in bright and practical bedrooms. Breakfast is self-service and dinner is available in the restaurant.

Rooms 86 ✿ **Facilities** WiFi **Services** Lift Air con **Parking** 86

BRADFORD-ON-AVON	**Map 4 ST86**
Wiltshire	

Widbrook Grange

★★★ 79% COUNTRY HOUSE HOTEL

tel: 01225 864750 & 863173 **Trowbridge Rd BA15 1UH**
email: stay@widbrookgrange.com **web:** www.widbrookgrange.com
dir: *1m SE from Bradford on A363, hotel diagonally opposite Bradford Marina & Arabian Stud*

Widbrook Grange is an impressive Bath-stone country house, offering a quiet retreat a short drive from the bustle of Bath. Spacious bedrooms are located either in the main house or in the converted farm buildings, with some rooms having four-poster beds. Leisure facilities include a small gym and indoor swimming pool with beauty treatments available on request. The brasserie focuses on local seasonal produce at breakfast and dinner.

Rooms 19 (15 annexe) (6 fmly) (13 GF) ✿ **Facilities** FTV WiFi ⮑ ☼ Gym Children's weekend play room Beauty treatments Xmas New Year **Conf** Class 35 Board 25 Thtr 50 **Parking** 50 **Notes** Civ Wed 50

BRAINTREE	**Map 7 TL72**
Essex	

Premier Inn Braintree (A120)

BUDGET HOTEL

tel: 0871 527 8138 *(Calls cost 13p per minute plus your phone company's access charge)*
Cressing Rd, Galley's Corner CM77 8GG
web: www.premierinn.com
dir: *On A120 (Stansted to Braintree link road). Adjacent to Mulberry Tree Brewers Fayre*

High quality, budget accommodation ideal for both families and business travellers. Spacious, en suite bedrooms feature tea and coffee making facilities, and Freeview TV in most hotels. Internet access and WiFi are available for a small fee. The adjacent family restaurant features a wide and varied menu. See also the Hotel Groups pages.

Rooms 60

Premier Inn Braintree (Freeport Village)

BUDGET HOTEL

tel: 0871 527 8140 *(Calls cost 13p per minute plus your phone company's access charge)*
Fowlers Farm, Cressing Rd CM77 8DH
web: www.premierinn.com
dir: *M11 junct 8, follow signs to A120 Colchester & Freeport Shopping Village. At Galley's Corner rdbt, 4th exit, left into Wyevale Garden Centre. Hotel adjacent*

Rooms 48

BRAITHWAITE
Cumbria   Map 18 NY22

INSPECTORS' CHOICE

The Cottage in the Wood
@@@ ♀ RESTAURANT WITH ROOMS

tel: 017687 78409 & 07730 312193 **Whinlatter Pass CA12 5TW**
email: relax@thecottageinthewood.co.uk **web:** www.thecottageinthewood.co.uk
dir: *M6 junct 40, A66 W. After Keswick exit for Braithwaite via Whinlatter Pass (B5292), establishment at top of pass*

This charming property sits on wooded hills with striking views of Skiddaw, and is conveniently placed for Keswick. The owners provide excellent hospitality in a relaxed manner. The award-winning food, freshly prepared and locally sourced, is served in the bright and welcoming conservatory restaurant that has stunning views. The comfortable bedrooms are well appointed and have many useful extras.

Rooms 9

BRAMPTON
Cumbria   Map 21 NY56

INSPECTORS' CHOICE

Farlam Hall Hotel
★★★ ♀ HOTEL

tel: 016977 46234 **Hallbankgate CA8 2NG**
email: farlam@relaischateaux.com **web:** www.farlamhall.co.uk
dir: *On A689 (Brampton to Alston). Hotel 2m on left - not in Farlam village*

This delightful country house has a history dating back to 1428, although the building today is very much the result of alterations carried out in the mid-19th century. The hotel is run by a friendly family team and their enthusiastic staff, and is set in beautifully landscaped Victorian gardens complete with an ornamental lake and stream. Lovingly restored over many years, it provides very high standards of comfort and hospitality. Gracious public rooms are very relaxing, and a lot of thought has gone into the beautiful bedrooms, many of which are simply stunning. Nearby are Hadrian's Wall and the Northern Pennines Area of Outstanding Natural Beauty, which both provide endless opportunities for walking and sightseeing.

Rooms 12 (1 annexe) (2 GF) ⚡ **S** £165-£195; **D** £310-£370 (incl. bkfst & dinner)* **Facilities** FTV WiFi ♨ 🦢 New Year **Conf** Class 24 Board 12 Thtr 24 Del from £185 to £215* **Parking** 25 **Notes** LB No children 5yrs Closed 24-30 Dec & 4-21 Jan Civ Wed 45

BRANCASTER STAITHE
Norfolk   Map 13 TF74

The White Horse
★★★ 83% @@ HOTEL

tel: 01485 210262 **PE31 8BY**
email: reception@whitehorsebrancaster.co.uk **web:** www.whitehorsebrancaster.co.uk
dir: *On A149 (coast road) midway between Hunstanton & Wells-next-the-Sea*

A charming hotel situated on the north Norfolk coast with contemporary bedrooms in two wings, some featuring an interesting cobbled fascia. Each room is attractively decorated and thoughtfully equipped. There is a large bar and a lounge area leading through to the conservatory restaurant, with stunning tidal marshland views across to Scolt Head Island.

Rooms 15 (8 annexe) (4 fmly) (8 GF) ⚡ **S** £65-£180; **D** £100-£230 (incl. bkfst)* **Facilities** FTV WiFi ♨ Holistic therapies in room Xmas New Year **Parking** 60

BRANDON
Warwickshire   Map 11 SP47

Mercure Coventry Brandon Hall Hotel & Spa
★★★★ 76% @ HOTEL   Mercure HOTELS

tel: 024 7654 6000 **Main St CV8 3FW**
email: h6625@accor.com **web:** www.mercure.com
dir: *A45 towards Coventry S. After Peugeot-Citroen garage on left, at island take 5th exit to M1 South/London (back onto A45). After 200yds, immediately after Texaco garage, left into Brandon Ln, hotel after 2.5m*

An impressive tree-lined avenue leads to this 17th-century property which sits in 17 acres of grounds. The hotel provides a peaceful and friendly sanctuary away from the hustle and bustle. Bedrooms provide comfortable facilities and a good range of extras for guest comfort. There is a Spa Naturel with health, beauty and fitness facilities in a separate building.

Rooms 120 (30 annexe) (10 fmly) (50 GF) ⚡ **Facilities** Spa STV WiFi ⊛ Gym Steam room Sauna Xmas New Year **Conf** Class 120 Board 112 Thtr 280 **Services** Lift **Parking** 200 **Notes** Civ Wed 280

BRANKSOME
See **Poole**

BRANSCOMBE
Devon   Map 4 SY18

The Bulstone Hotel
★★ 74% HOTEL

tel: 01297 680446 **High Bulstone EX12 3BL**
email: bulstone@aol.com **web:** www.childfriendlyhotels.com
dir: *A3052 (Exeter to Lyme Regis road) at Branscombe Cross follow brown hotel sign*

Situated in a peaceful location close to the beautiful east Devon coast, this family-friendly hotel is ideally placed for a relaxing break with plenty of attractions within easy reach. All bedrooms consist of a main bedroom and separate children's room, each being practically furnished and equipped. Additional facilities include a playroom, a snug lounge, and the dining room where enjoyable home-cooked meals are offered. There is no charge for children under ten, and children's tea is at 5pm.

Rooms 7 (7 fmly) (4 GF) **S** £50-£70; **D** £90-£120 (incl. bkfst)* **Facilities** FTV WiFi Children's playroom Xmas New Year Child facilities **Conf** Class 25 Board 25 **Parking** 25 **Notes** LB ⊗

B

BRENTFORD
Greater London

Novotel London Brentford

★★★★ 76% HOTEL PLAN 1 C3

NOVOTEL
HOTELS & RESORTS

tel: 020 3693 1800 & 7660 2230 **Great West Rd TW8 0GP**
email: H6995@accor.com **web:** www.novotel.com
dir: *Please call for directions*

Located just 20 minutes from Heathrow with Richmond and Twickenham Stadium just a couple of minutes away, Novotel London Brentford offers stylish public areas throughout, and comfortably appointed rooms ideal for both corporate and leisure guests alike. There are conference facilities on site and a leisure suite on the lower ground. Parking is available on site and South Ealing and Brentford station is less than one mile from the hotel.

Rooms 202 (90 fmly) ✿ **Facilities** FTV WiFi ☌ HL ☒ Gym **Conf** Class 50 Board 30 Thtr 90 **Services** Lift Air con **Parking** 100

Premier Inn London Kew

BUDGET HOTEL PLAN 1 C3

Premier Inn

tel: 0871 527 8670 *(Calls cost 13p per minute plus your phone company's access charge)*
52 High St TW8 0BB
web: www.premierinn.com
dir: *At junct of A4 (M4), A205 & A406, Chiswick rdbt, take A205 towards Kew & Brentford. 200yds right fork onto A315 (High St), for 0.5m. Hotel on left*

High quality, budget accommodation ideal for both families and business travellers. Spacious, en suite bedrooms feature tea and coffee making facilities, and Freeview TV in most hotels. Internet access and WiFi are available for a small fee. The adjacent family restaurant features a wide and varied menu. See also the Hotel Groups pages.

Rooms 141

BRENTWOOD
Essex
Map 6 TQ59

Marygreen Manor Hotel

★★★★ 74% ⑨⑨ HOTEL

CLASSIC BRITISH HOTELS

tel: 01277 225252 **London Rd CM14 4NR**
email: info@marygreenmanor.co.uk **web:** www.marygreenmanor.co.uk
dir: *M25 junct 28, onto A1023 over 2 sets of lights, hotel on right*

This 16th-century house was built by Robert Wright, who named the house 'Manor of Mary Green' after his young bride. Public rooms exude character and have a wealth of original features that include exposed beams, carved panelling and the impressive Tudors Restaurant. Bedrooms are tastefully decorated and thoughtfully equipped.

Rooms 44 (40 annexe) (35 GF) ✿ **S** £107-£160; **D** £107-£160 **Facilities** STV FTV WiFi ☌ **Conf** Class 20 Board 25 Thtr 50 **Parking** 100 **Notes** ⊗ Civ Wed 60

De Rougemont Manor

★★★★ 74% HOTEL

tel: 01277 226418 **Great Warley St CM13 3JP**
email: info@derougemontmanor.co.uk **web:** www.derougemontmanor.co.uk
dir: *M25 junct 29, A127 to Southend then B186 towards Great Warley*

Expect a warm welcome at this family-owned and managed hotel, situated on the outskirts of Brentwood just off the M25. The stylish bedrooms are divided between the main hotel and a bedroom wing; each one is tastefully appointed and well

equipped. Public rooms include a smart lounge bar, restaurant and a choice of seating areas.

Rooms 73 (9 annexe) (6 fmly) (16 GF) ✿ **Facilities** FTV WiFi ☌ ⌇ ⌣ Gym Beauty treatment rooms 3-acre nature reserve Xmas New Year **Conf** Class 66 Board 42 Thtr 260 Del from £130 to £150* **Services** Lift Air con **Parking** 200 **Notes** ⊗ Civ Wed 90

Premier Inn Brentwood

BUDGET HOTEL

Premier Inn

tel: 0871 527 8142 *(Calls cost 13p per minute plus your phone company's access charge)*
Brentwood House, 169 Kings Rd CM14 4EG
web: www.premierinn.com
dir: *From S: M25 junct 28 take A1023 (or from N: at Brook Street rdbt 2nd exit onto A1023). Right at lights into Kings Rd, at rdbt 2nd exit into Kings Rd*

High quality, budget accommodation ideal for both families and business travellers. Spacious, en suite bedrooms feature tea and coffee making facilities, and Freeview TV in most hotels. Internet access and WiFi are available for a small fee. The adjacent family restaurant features a wide and varied menu. See also the Hotel Groups pages.

Rooms 122

BRIDGWATER
Somerset
Map 4 ST23

Walnut Tree Hotel

★★★ 77% HOTEL

tel: 01278 662255 **North Petherton TA6 6QA**
email: reservations@walnuttreehotel.com **web:** www.walnuttreehotel.com
dir: *M5 junct 24. Follow North Petherton signs. 1.3m. Hotel in village centre*

Popular with both business and leisure guests, this 18th-century former coaching inn is conveniently located within easy reach of the M5. The spacious and smartly decorated bedrooms are well furnished to ensure a comfortable and relaxing stay. An extensive selection of dishes is offered in either the restaurant, or the more informal setting of the bistro.

Rooms 30 (3 fmly) (3 GF) ✿ **Facilities** FTV WiFi ☌ Xmas New Year **Conf** Class 60 Board 50 Thtr 100 **Parking** 70 **Notes** ⊗ Civ Wed 100

Apple Tree Hotel

★★★ 73% HOTEL

tel: 01278 733238 **Keenthorne, Nether Stowey TA5 1HZ**
email: reservations@appletreehotel.com **web:** www.appletreehotel.com
dir: *A39 from Bridgwater towards Minehead. Hotel on left, 2m past Cannington*

Once a farm cottage, dating back over 300 years, this popular hotel now provides a perfect base from which to explore the many and varied places of interest in the locale, including the unspoilt beauty of the Quantock Hills. Whether choosing to stay for business or leisure, the warmth of welcome is always the same, with the owners ensuring guests are well looked after. Bedrooms provide all the expected contemporary comforts, with rooms offered in both the main building and adjacent garden rooms. Dinner is served in the conservatory restaurant, perhaps preceded with a relaxing drink in the bar or library lounge.

Rooms 16 (2 fmly) (7 GF) ✿ **Facilities** FTV WiFi ☌ **Conf** Class 12 Board 12 Thtr 20 **Parking** 30 **Notes** ⊗

Premier Inn Bridgwater

BUDGET HOTEL

tel: 0871 527 8148 *(Calls cost 13p per minute plus your phone company's access charge)*
Express Park, Bristol Rd TA6 4RR
web: www.premierinn.com
dir: *M5 junct 23, A38 to Bridgwater. Hotel on right in 2m*

High quality, budget accommodation ideal for both families and business travellers. Spacious, en suite bedrooms feature tea and coffee making facilities, and Freeview TV in most hotels. Internet access and WiFi are available for a small fee. The adjacent family restaurant features a wide and varied menu. See also the Hotel Groups pages.

Rooms 67

BRIDLINGTON
East Riding of Yorkshire   **Map 17 TA16**

Expanse Hotel

★★★ 75% HOTEL

tel: 01262 675347 **North Marine Dr YO15 2LS**
email: reservations@expanse.co.uk **web:** www.expanse.co.uk
dir: *Follow North Beach signs, pass under railway arch for North Marine Drive. Hotel at bottom of hill*

This traditional seaside hotel overlooks the bay and has been in the same family's ownership for many years. Service is relaxed and friendly and the modern bedrooms are well equipped. Comfortable public areas include a conference suite, a choice of bars and an inviting lounge. Complimentary WiFi is available.

Rooms 45 (2 fmly) ⚡ **Facilities** FTV WiFi ▷ ♬ Xmas New Year **Conf** Class 50 Board 50 Thtr 180 **Services** Lift **Parking** 17 **Notes** LB ⊗ Civ Wed 140

BRIGHOUSE
West Yorkshire   **Map 16 SE12**

Premier Inn Huddersfield North

BUDGET HOTEL

tel: 0871 527 8530 *(Calls cost 13p per minute plus your phone company's access charge)*
Wakefield Rd HD6 4HA
web: www.premierinn.com
dir: *M62 junct 25, A644 signed Huddersfield, Dewsbury & Wakefield. Hotel 500mtrs up hill on right*

High quality, budget accommodation ideal for both families and business travellers. Spacious, en suite bedrooms feature tea and coffee making facilities, and Freeview TV in most hotels. Internet access and WiFi are available for a small fee. The adjacent family restaurant features a wide and varied menu. See also the Hotel Groups pages.

Rooms 99

BRIGHTON & HOVE
East Sussex   **Map 6 TQ30**

See also **Steyning**

Mercure Brighton Seafront Hotel

★★★★ 79% HOTEL

tel: 0844 815 9061 *(Calls cost 5p per minute plus your phone company's access charge)*
149 Kings Rd BN1 2PP
email: info@mercurebrighton.co.uk **web:** www.mercurebrighton.co.uk
dir: *A23 follow signs for seafront. Right at Brighton Pier rdbt. Hotel on right, just after West Pier*

Located right on the seafront in the heart of Brighton, this hotel offers uninterrupted sea views from all seafront-facing rooms and public areas. Brighton Pier, the Lanes and Town Centre are just a couple of minutes walk. The Hotel is spacious and offers comfortably appointed accommodation, all with complimentary WiFi access. Plenty of secure off-road parking is available.

Rooms 116 (11 fmly) **Facilities** FTV WiFi ▷ **Conf** Class 80 Board 60 Thtr 180 **Parking** 36 **Notes** ⊗ Civ Wed 180

Hotel du Vin Brighton

Hotel du Vin & Bistro

★★★★ 78% ⊛ TOWN HOUSE HOTEL

tel: 01273 718588 **2-6 Ship St BN1 1AD**
email: info@brighton.hotelduvin.com **web:** www.hotelduvin.com
dir: *From A23 follow seafront/city centre signs. Right at seafront, right into Middle St. Follow to end bear right into Ship St. Hotel on right*

This tastefully converted mock-Tudor building occupies a convenient location in a quiet side street close to the seafront. The individually designed bedrooms have a wine theme, and all are comprehensively equipped. Public areas offer a spacious split-level bar, an atmospheric and locally popular restaurant, plus useful private dining and meeting facilities.

Rooms 49 (2 fmly) (4 GF) **Facilities** STV WiFi ♬ Xmas New Year **Conf** Class 50 Board 60 Thtr 80 **Services** Air con **Notes** Civ Wed 120

The Old Ship Hotel

THE HOTEL COLLECTION

★★★★ 73% HOTEL

tel: 01273 329001 **King's Rd BN1 1NR**
email: oldship@thehotelcollection.co.uk **web:** www.thehotelcollection.co.uk
dir: *A23 to seafront, right at rdbt along Kings Rd. Hotel 200yds on right*

This historic hotel enjoys a stunning seafront location and offers guests elegant surroundings to relax in. Bedrooms are well designed, with modern facilities ensuring comfort. Many original features have been retained, including the Paganini Ballroom. Facilities include a sleek bar, alfresco dining and a variety of conference rooms.

Rooms 154 ⚡ **S** £75-£350; **D** £75-£350* **Facilities** FTV WiFi HL Gym Xmas New Year **Conf** Class 100 Board 35 Thtr 250 Del from £125 to £225* **Services** Lift **Parking** 40 **Notes** LB Civ Wed 150

B

BRIGHTON & HOVE *continued*

Blanch House

★★★ 80% TOWN HOUSE HOTEL

tel: 01273 603504 **17 Atlingworth Sreet BN2 1PL**
email: info@blanchhouse.co.uk **web:** www.blanchhouse.co.uk
dir: *Take A23 to A259, left at the pier/seafront*

Blanch House is located in the heart of Kemp Town with the seafront and town centre just a couple of minutes walk away. Bedrooms are individual in their design and style yet all are comfortable and of a very good quality. The spacious function suite is ideal for private meetings, dinners or weddings. There is a bar (open daily) where guests can enjoy cocktails, champagne and afternoon tea.

Rooms 12 ☙ **S** £95-£225; **D** £105-£235 (incl. bkfst)* **Facilities** FTV WiFi ☙
Conf Class 16 Board 20 Thtr 40 Del from £175 to £200* **Notes** LB ⊗ No children 15yrs Civ Wed 40

Best Western Princes Marine

★★★ 79% HOTEL

tel: 01273 207660 **153 Kingsway BN3 4GR**
email: princesmarine@bestwestern.co.uk **web:** www.princesmarinehotel.co.uk
dir: *Right at Brighton Pier, follow seafront for 2m. Hotel 200yds from King Alfred leisure centre*

This friendly hotel enjoys a seafront location and offers spacious, comfortable bedrooms equipped with a good range of facilities including free WiFi. Ten newly created rooms on the top floor, some with private balconies, offer incredible sea views and tranquillity. There is a stylish restaurant, modern bar and a flexible meeting room. Limited and secure parking is available at the rear.

Rooms 57 (4 fmly) ☙ **S** £39-£200; **D** £49-£250 **Facilities** STV FTV WiFi ☙
Conf Class 40 Board 40 Thtr 70 Del from £100 to £150 **Services** Lift **Parking** 25
Notes LB ⊗

Queens Hotel

★★★ 73% HOTEL

tel: 01273 321222 & 0800 970 7570 **1-3 King's Rd BN1 1NS**
email: info@queenshotelbrighton.com **web:** www.queenshotelbrighton.com
dir: *A23 to Brighton town centre, follow signs for seafront. At Brighton Pier right onto seafront, hotel 500mtrs right hand side*

This hotel has a fantastic location with views of the beach and pier. The modern bedrooms and bathrooms are spacious, and many benefit from uninterrupted sea views. All bedrooms have LCD TVs and free WiFi. There is a spacious bar and restaurant area plus fully equipped spa, gym and swimming pool.

Rooms 94 (28 fmly) **S** £59-£399; **D** £59-£499 (incl. bkfst) **Facilities** Spa FTV WiFi ☙
HL ☙ supervised Gym Beauty salon **Conf** Class 50 Board 50 Thtr 150 Del from £129
to £199 **Services** Lift **Notes** ⊗

The Kings Hotel

★★★ 72% METRO HOTEL

tel: 01273 820854 **139-141 Kings Rd BN1 2NA**
email: info@kingshotelbrighton.co.uk **web:** www.kingshotelbrighton.com
dir: *Follow signs to seafront. At Brighton Pier rdbt take 3rd exit & drive west (seafront on left). Hotel adjacent to West Pier*

Located on the seafront adjacent to West Pier, this Grade II listed, Regency building has been restored to offer contemporary accommodation. Although the hotel does not provide a full dinner service, light snacks are available throughout the day and

evening in the public areas and also in the guests' bedrooms. There is limited parking space which is a bonus in Brighton.

Rooms 96 (5 fmly) (9 GF) ☙ **Facilities** FTV WiFi ☙ **Services** Lift **Parking** 11

Umi Brighton Hotel

★★★ 72% HOTEL

tel: 01273 323221 **64 King's Rd BN1 1NA**
email: reservations@umibrighton.co.uk **web:** www.umibrighton.co.uk
dir: *On A259 adjacent to Brighton Centre*

Umi Hotel is located right in the heart of Brighton on the seafront with just a short walk to the Pier, Station and City Centre. Bedrooms are modern in style and include free WiFi access; all seafront bedrooms benefit from excellent uninterrupted sea views. The little Bay Restaurant has a theatre-style theme and offers a good range of dishes at very affordable prices, both cooked and continental breakfasts are served here daily. There is a Coffee Republic on site.

Rooms 77 (20 fmly) (1 GF) **Facilities** FTV WiFi ☙ HL Free use of leisure centre in Queens Hotel ♫ **Conf** Class 20 Board 20 Thtr 20 Del from £99 to £250*
Services Lift **Notes** Civ Wed 50

Ambassador Brighton

★★ 69% METRO HOTEL

tel: 01273 676869 **22-23 New Steine, Marine Pde BN2 1PD**
email: info@ambassadorbrighton.co.uk **web:** www.ambassadorbrighton.co.uk

At the heart of bustling Kemp Town, overlooking the attractive garden square next to the seaside, this well-established property has a friendly and relaxing atmosphere. Bedrooms are well equipped and vary in size, with the largest having the best views. A small lounge with a separate bar is available.

Rooms 24 (9 fmly) (3 GF) (2 smoking) **S** £55-£85; **D** £79-£125 (incl. bkfst)*
Facilities STV FTV WiFi ☙ HL

Premier Inn Brighton City Centre

BUDGET HOTEL

tel: 0871 527 8150 *(Calls cost 13p per minute plus your phone company's access charge)*
144 North St BN1 1RE
web: www.premierinn.com
dir: *From A23 follow signs for city centre. Right at lights near Royal Pavilion, take road ahead on left (runs adjacent to Pavilion) into Church St, 1st left into New Rd leading North St*

High quality, budget accommodation ideal for both families and business travellers. Spacious, en suite bedrooms feature tea and coffee making facilities, and Freeview TV in most hotels. Internet access and WiFi are available for a small fee. The adjacent family restaurant features a wide and varied menu. See also the Hotel Groups pages.

Rooms 160

The Grand Brighton

AA Advertised ◉◉

tel: 01273 224300 **97-99 King's Rd BN1 2FW**
email: reservations@grandbrighton.co.uk **web:** www.grandbrighton.co.uk/
dir: *On A259 adjacent to Brighton Centre*

Dating back to the mid-19th century, this landmark seafront hotel, with its eye-catching white façade and intricate balconies, is as grand as the name suggests. Bedrooms include a number of deluxe sea view rooms, some with balconies, and

B

suites, also with sea views. The hotel is perhaps best known for its extensive conference and banqueting facilities; there is also an impressive conservatory adjoining the bar.

Rooms 201 (60 fmly) S £82-£380; **D** £92-£400 (incl. bkfst)* **Facilities** Spa FTV WiFi Gym Thermal suite 🎵 Xmas New Year **Conf** Class 450 Board 60 Thtr 800 Del from £180 to £240* **Services** Lift **Parking** 50 **Notes** Civ Wed 800

Ibis Brighton City Centre

AA Advertised

tel: 01273 201000 **88-92 Queens Rd BN1 3XE**
email: h6444@accor.com **web:** www.ibishotel.com

Modern, budget hotel offering comfortable accommodation in bright and practical bedrooms. Breakfast is self-service and dinner is available in the restaurant.

Rooms 140 (25 fmly) (8 GF) **Facilities** FTV WiFi HL **Services** Lift Air con

---

BRISTOL	Map 4 ST57
Bristol	

Aztec Hotel & Spa

★★★★ 81% HOTEL

tel: 01454 201090 **Aztec West BS32 4TS**
email: aztec@shirehotels.com **web:** www.aztechotelbristol.com
dir: Access via M5 junct 16 & M4

Situated close to Cribbs Causeway shopping centre and major motorway links, this stylish hotel offers comfortable, very well-equipped bedrooms and suites. Built in a Nordic style, public rooms boast log fires and vaulted ceilings. Leisure facilities include a popular gym and good size pool. The Quarter Jacks Restaurant Bar & Lounge offers relaxed informal dining with a focus on simply prepared, quality regional foods. The hotel has a spa with a gym, pool, children's pool, whirlpool, sauna, steam room and a range of treatments. Thwaites Hotels is the AA Hotel Group of the Year 2016-17.

Rooms 128 (8 fmly) (29 GF) **S** £110-£200; **D** £110-£200* **Facilities** Spa STV WiFi HL Gym Steam room Sauna Children's splash pool Activity studio New Year **Conf** Class 120 Board 36 Thtr 200 Del from £130 to £200* **Services** Lift **Parking** 240 **Notes** LB Civ Wed 120

DoubleTree by Hilton Bristol City Centre

★★★★ 78% HOTEL

tel: 0117 926 0041 **Redcliffe Way BS1 6NL**
email: sales@focusbristol.co.uk **web:** www.doubletree3.hilton.com
dir: 1m from M32. 400yds from Temple Meads BR station, before church

This large modern hotel is situated in the heart of the city centre and offers spacious public areas and ample parking. Bedrooms are well equipped for both business and leisure guests. Dining options include a relaxed bar and a unique kiln restaurant where a good selection of freshly prepared dishes is available.

Rooms 206 **D** £79-£207* **Facilities** FTV WiFi Gym New Year **Conf** Class 120 Board 75 Thtr 300 Del from £122 to £167* **Services** Lift Air con **Parking** 150 **Notes** Civ Wed 250

Hotel du Vin Bristol

★★★★ 77% TOWN HOUSE HOTEL

tel: 0117 925 5577 & 0844 736 4252
(Calls cost 5p per minute plus your phone company's access charge)
The Sugar House, Narrow Lewins Mead BS1 2NU
email: info.bristol@hotelduvin.com **web:** www.hotelduvin.com
dir: From A4 follow city centre signs. After 400yds pass Rupert St NCP on right. Hotel on opposite carriageway

This hotel is part of one of Britain's most innovative hotel groups, offering high standards of hospitality and accommodation. Housed in a Grade II listed, converted 18th-century sugar refinery, it provides great facilities with a modern, minimalist design. The bedrooms are exceptionally well designed and the bistro offers an excellent menu and wine list.

Rooms 40 (10 fmly) **Facilities** STV FTV WiFi 🎵 New Year **Conf** Class 36 Board 34 Thtr 72 **Services** Lift **Parking** 9 **Notes** Civ Wed 65

Mercure Bristol Holland House Hotel & Spa

★★★★ 77% HOTEL

tel: 0117 968 9900 **Redcliffe Hill BS1 6SQ**
email: h6698@accor.com **web:** www.mercure.com
dir: M4 junct 19 towards city centre, follow signs A4 then A370, take A38 Redcliffe Hill. Hotel opposite St Mary Redcliffe Church

This modern hotel, just a ten-minute walk from Bristol Temple Meads, has striking, contemporary style throughout, and offers some impressive facilities including a spa, a fitness suite and meeting rooms. The hotel has a green-bicycle service for guests. Bedrooms are stylishly designed with large plasma-screen TVs, comfortable beds and free internet access. An impressive new dining area offers a wide range of dishes with a menu to suit all tastes.

Rooms 275 (59 fmly) (44 GF) **S** fr £105; **D** fr £115 (incl. bkfst)* **Facilities** Spa FTV WiFi HL Gym Xmas New Year **Conf** Class 150 Board 80 Thtr 220 **Services** Lift Air con **Parking** 140 **Notes** LB Civ Wed 220

Mercure Bristol North The Grange

★★★★ 76% COUNTRY HOUSE HOTEL

tel: 01454 771420 & 0844 815 9063 *(Calls cost 7p per minute plus your phone company's access charge)* **Northwoods, Winterbourne BS36 1RP**
email: gm.mercurebristolnorthgrange@jupiterhotels.co.uk **web:** www.mercurebristol.co.uk
dir: A38 towards Filton/Bristol. At rdbt 1st exit into Bradley Stoke Way, at lights 1st left into Woodlands Ln, at 2nd rdbt left into Tench Ln. In 1m left at T-junct, hotel 200yds on left

Built in the 19th century and surrounded by 18 acres of attractive grounds, this is a pleasant hotel situated only a short drive from the city centre. The bedrooms are spacious and well equipped with a range of meeting facilities also available. The conservatory bar has a terrace which makes a delightful place to enjoy a drink under the shade of a 200-year-old cedar tree. The hotel is popular as a wedding venue.

Rooms 68 (10 fmly) (22 GF) **Facilities** STV FTV WiFi Xmas New Year **Conf** Class 60 Board 76 Thtr 180 **Parking** 180 **Notes** Civ Wed 180

BRISTOL *continued*

Mercure Brigstow Bristol

★★★★ 74% HOTEL

tel: 0117 929 1030 **5-7 Welsh Back BS1 4SP**
email: H6548@accor.com **web:** www.mercure.com
dir: *From the centre follow Baldwin St then right into Queen Charlotte St*

In a prime position on the river, this handsome, purpose-built hotel is designed and finished with care. The shopping centre and theatres are within easy walking distance. Bedrooms are stylish and extremely well equipped, including plasma TV screens in the bathrooms. There is an integrated state-of-the-art conference and meeting centre, and a smart restaurant and bar overlooking the harbour. Guests have complimentary use of a squash and health club, plus free internet access.

Rooms 116 ⁛ **Facilities** STV FTV WiFi Gym Free access to nearby gym & squash courts New Year **Conf** Class 40 Board 30 Thtr 85 **Services** Lift Air con **Notes** ⊗ Civ Wed 80

Novotel Bristol Centre

★★★★ 74% HOTEL

NOVOTEL
HOTELS & RESORTS

tel: 0117 976 9988 **Victoria St BS1 6HY**
email: H5622@accor.com **web:** www.novotel.com
dir: *At end of M32 follow signs for Temple Meads station to rdbt. Final exit, hotel immediately on right*

This city centre hotel provides smart, contemporary style accommodation. Most of the bedrooms demonstrate the Novotel 'Novation' style with unique swivel desk, internet access, air-conditioning and a host of extras. The hotel is convenient for the mainline railway station and also has its own car park.

Rooms 131 (34 fmly) ⁛ **S** £60–£165; **D** £60–£300 **Facilities** STV FTV WiFi HL Gym Sauna Steam room **Conf** Class 70 Board 35 Thtr 210 Del from £170 to £250 **Services** Lift Air con **Parking** 100 **Notes** LB Civ Wed 100

Best Western Henbury Lodge Hotel

★★★ 80% ⧆⧆ HOTEL

BW **Best Western.**

tel: 0117 950 2615 **Station Rd, Henbury BS10 7QQ**
email: info@henburyhotel.com **web:** www.henburyhotel.com
dir: *M5 junct 17/A4018 towards city centre, 3rd rdbt right into Crow Ln. At end turn right, hotel 200mtrs on right*

This quietly located hotel is popular with both business and leisure guests. Bedrooms, in a wide range of shapes and sizes, are divided between the main

house and a converted stable block; all are comfortably furnished and equipped. The small and friendly team offer a very personal welcome and many guests here are regulars. Dinner and breakfast are taken in the stylish restaurant where high quality local produce is used.

Rooms 22 (10 annexe) (4 fmly) (6 GF) **S** £112–£117; **D** £127–£137 (incl. bkfst)* **Facilities** FTV WiFi ⋈ **Conf** Class 15 Board 20 Thtr 20 Del from £175* **Parking** 22 **Notes** ⊗ Closed 20 Dec-4 Jan

The Avon Gorge Hotel

★★★ 79% ⧆ HOTEL

tel: 0117 973 8955 **Sion Hill, Clifton BS8 4LD**
email: rooms@theavongorge.com **web:** www.theavongorge.com
dir: *From S: M5 junct 19, A369 to Clifton Toll, over suspension bridge, 1st right into Sion Hill. From N: M5 junct 18A, A4 to Bristol, under suspension bridge, follow signs to bridge, exit Sion Hill*

This is a delightful terraced property overlooking the Clifton Suspension Bridge. It offers bedrooms of varying shapes and sizes with either views across the river, or of Clifton Village. Meals can be taken in the contemporary Bridge Café restaurant where a range of carefully prepared, tempting dishes is available. There is a limited amount of free parking space at the rear of the hotel or on-street (no restrictions) in the vicinity.

Rooms 75 (8 fmly) (4 GF) **Facilities** STV WiFi ⋈ Xmas New Year **Conf** Class 40 Board 30 Thtr 100 **Services** Lift **Parking** 25 **Notes** Civ Wed 100

Rodney Hotel

★★★ 68% HOTEL

tel: 0117 973 5422 **4 Rodney Place, Clifton BS8 4HY**
email: rodney@cliftonhotels.com **web:** www.cliftonhotels.com/bristolhotels/rodney
dir: *Off Clifton Down Rd*

With easy access from the M5, this attractive, listed building in Clifton is conveniently close to the city centre. The individually decorated bedrooms provide a useful range of extra facilities for the business traveller; the public areas include a smart bar, and a small restaurant offering enjoyable and carefully prepared dishes. A pleasant rear garden provides additional seating in the summer months.

Rooms 31 (1 fmly) (2 GF) ⁛ **Facilities** FTV WiFi **Conf** Class 20 Board 20 Thtr 30 **Parking** 7 **Notes** Closed 22 Dec-3 Jan RS Sun Civ Wed 40

Clifton Hotel

★★ 72% HOTEL

tel: 0117 973 6882 **St Pauls Rd, Clifton BS8 1LX**
email: clifton@cliftonhotels.com **web:** www.cliftonhotels.com/bristolhotels/clifton
dir: *M32 follow Bristol/Clifton signs, along Park St. Left at lights into St Pauls Rd*

This popular hotel offers a relaxed, friendly service and very well equipped bedrooms. There is a welcoming lounge by the reception, and in summer months drinks and meals can be enjoyed on the terrace. Racks Bar and Restaurant offers an interesting selection of modern dishes in informal surroundings. There is some street parking, but for a small charge, secure garage parking is available.

Rooms 59 (2 fmly) (12 GF) ⁛ **Facilities** STV FTV WiFi **Services** Lift **Parking** 12

B

Premier Inn Bristol Airport (Sidcot)

BUDGET HOTEL

tel: 0871 527 8154 *(Calls cost 13p per minute plus your phone company's access charge)*
Bridgwater Rd, Winscombe BS25 1NN
web: www.premierinn.com
dir: *Between M5 junct 21 & 22 (9m from Bristol Airport), onto A371 towards Banwell, Winscombe to A38. Right at lights, Hotel 300yds on left*

High quality, budget accommodation ideal for both families and business travellers. Spacious, en suite bedrooms feature tea and coffee making facilities, and Freeview TV in most hotels. Internet access and WiFi are available for a small fee. The adjacent family restaurant features a wide and varied menu. See also the Hotel Groups pages.

Rooms 31

Premier Inn Bristol (Alveston)

BUDGET HOTEL

tel: 0871 527 8152 *(Calls cost 13p per minute plus your phone company's access charge)*
Thornbury Rd, Alveston BS35 3LL
web: www.premierinn.com
dir: *Just off M5. From N: exit at junct 14 onto A38 towards Bristol. From S: exit at junct 16 onto A38 towards Gloucester*

Rooms 75

Premier Inn Bristol City Centre (Haymarket)

BUDGET HOTEL

tel: 0871 527 8156 *(Calls cost 13p per minute plus your phone company's access charge)*
The Haymarket BS1 3LR
web: www.premierinn.com
dir: *M4 junct 19, M32 towards city centre. Through 2 sets of lights, at 3rd lights turn right, to rdbt, take 2nd exit. Hotel on left*

Rooms 224

Premier Inn Bristol City Centre King St

BUDGET HOTEL

tel: 0871 527 8158 *(Calls cost 13p per minute plus your phone company's access charge)*
Llandoger Trow, King St BS1 4ER
web: www.premierinn.com
dir: *A38 into city centre. Left onto B4053 Baldwin St. Right into Queen Charlotte St, follow one-way system, bear right at river. Hotel on right*

Rooms 60

Premier Inn Bristol City Centre (Lewins Mead)

BUDGET HOTEL

tel: 0871 527 9594 *(Calls cost 13p per minute plus your phone company's access charge)*
Lewins Mead BS1 2PY
email: BristolCityCentreLewinsMead.PI@premierinn.com **web:** www.premierinn.com
dir: *From N: M4 junct 19, M32 (city centre/Clifton/bus station). 3rd exit at rdbt. 4th left into Lwr Moulden St, hotel on right. From S: M5 junct 19, A369. Keep right, at rdbt 1st exit, merge onto A370. Right into Hotwell Rd. At rdbt 3rd exit to next rdbt. Keep right, left onto A38. Hotel on left*

Rooms 167

Premier Inn Bristol Cribbs Causeway

BUDGET HOTEL

tel: 0871 527 8160 *(Calls cost 13p per minute plus your phone company's access charge)*
Cribbs Causeway, Catbrain Ln BS10 7TQ
web: www.premierinn.com
dir: *M5 junct 17, A4018. 1st left at rdbt into Lysander Rd. Right into Catbrain Hill, leads to Catbrain Lane*

Rooms 177

Premier Inn Bristol East (Emersons Green)

BUDGET HOTEL

tel: 0871 527 8162 *(Calls cost 13p per minute plus your phone company's access charge)*
200/202 Westerleigh Rd, Emersons Green BS16 7AN
web: www.premierinn.com
dir: *M4 junct 19 onto M32 junct 1, left onto A4174 (Avon Ring Rd). Hotel at 3rd rdbt*

Rooms 83

Premier Inn Bristol Filton

BUDGET HOTEL

tel: 0871 527 8164 *(Calls cost 13p per minute plus your phone company's access charge)*
Shield Retail Park, Gloucester Road North, Filton BS34 7BR
web: www.premierinn.com
dir: *M5 junct 16, A38 signed Filton/Patchway. Pass airport & Royal Mail on right. Left at 2nd rdbt, 1st left into retail park*

Rooms 62

Premier Inn Bristol South

BUDGET HOTEL

tel: 0871 527 8166 *(Calls cost 13p per minute plus your phone company's access charge)*
Hengrove Leisure Park, Hengrove Way BS14 0HR
web: www.premierinn.com
dir: *From city centre take A37 to Wells & Shepton Mallet. Right onto A4174. Hotel at 3rd lights*

Rooms 88

Ibis Bristol Centre

AA Advertised

tel: 0117 319 9000 **Explore Ln BS1 5TY**
email: H5547@accor.com **web:** www.ibishotel.com
dir: *Off A4 in harbourside district*

Modern, budget hotel offering comfortable accommodation in bright and practical bedrooms. Breakfast is self-service and dinner is available in the restaurant.

Rooms 182 (2 fmly) **Facilities** STV FTV WiFi ⌖ **Services** Lift

B

BRISTOL continued

Ibis Bristol Temple Meads Quay

AA Advertised

tel: 0117 319 9001 **Avon St BS2 0PS**
email: H6593@accor.com **web:** www.ibishotel.com
dir: M4 junct 19, M32, follow Temple Meads train station signs. Left after underpass

Modern, budget hotel offering comfortable accommodation in bright and practical bedrooms. Breakfast is self-service and dinner is available in the restaurant.

Rooms 141 (7 fmly) Facilities FTV WiFi HL **Conf** Class 12 Board 12 Thtr 12
Services Lift

BRIXHAM	Map 3 SX95
Devon	

Berry Head Hotel

THE INDEPENDENTS
HOTEL ASSOCIATION

★★★ 78% HOTEL

tel: 01803 853225 **Berry Head Rd TQ5 9AJ**
email: stay@berryheadhotel.com **web:** www.berryheadhotel.com
dir: From marina 1m, hotel on left

Set in a stunning cliff-top location, this imposing property dates back to 1809, and has spectacular views across Torbay. Public areas include two comfortable lounges, an outdoor terrace, and a swimming pool, together with a bar serving a range of popular dishes. Many of the bedrooms have the benefit of splendid sea views.

Rooms 32 (7 fmly) **S** £55-£75; **D** £110-£150 (incl. bkfst)* **Facilities** FTV WiFi Petanque Sailing Deep sea fishing Yacht charter Xmas New Year **Conf** Class 250 Board 40 Thtr 300 **Services** Lift **Parking** 100 **Notes** LB Civ Wed 200

Quayside Hotel

★★★ 76% HOTEL

tel: 01803 855751 **41-49 King St TQ5 9TJ**
email: reservations@quaysidehotel.co.uk **web:** www.quaysidehotel.co.uk
dir: A380, at 2nd rdbt at Kingskerwell towards Brixham on A3022

With views over the harbour and bay, this hotel was formerly six cottages, and the public rooms retain a certain cosiness and intimacy. These include the lounge, residents' bar and Ernie Lister's public bar. Freshly-landed fish features on the menus, alongside a number of creative and skilfully prepared dishes, served in the well-appointed restaurant. Good food is also available in the public bar. The owners and their team of local staff provide friendly and attentive service.

Rooms 29 (2 fmly) **S** £65-£170; **D** £98-£180 (incl. bkfst)* **Facilities** FTV WiFi Xmas New Year **Conf** Class 18 Board 18 Thtr 25 **Parking** 30 **Notes** LB

BROADWAY	Map 10 SP03
Worcestershire	

INSPECTORS' CHOICE

Dormy House Hotel

★★★★ HOTEL

tel: 01386 852711 **Willersey Hill WR12 7LF**
email: reservations@dormyhouse.co.uk. **web:** www.dormyhouse.co.uk
dir: 2m E of Broadway off A44, at top of Fish Hill turn for Saintbury/Picnic area. In 0.5m turn left, hotel on left

Dormy House is a converted 17th-century farmhouse set in 400-acre grounds on the Farncombe Estate, with stunning views over Broadway. A few years ago the hotel underwent a multi-million pound refurbishment, part of which was a luxury spa offering a wide range of treatments, a swimming pool, a Veuve Clicquot Champagne nail bar, gym and thermal suite. The best traditions are retained - customer care, real fires, comfortable sofas and afternoon teas. Dinner features an interesting choice of dishes created by a skilled kitchen brigade.

Dormy House Hotel

Rooms 38 (19 annexe) (8 fmly) (19 GF) **S** £195-£510; **D** £195-£510 (incl. bkfst)* **Facilities** Spa STV FTV WiFi Gym Nature & jogging trail Circular walks Champagne nail bar Xmas New Year **Conf** Class 16 Board 16 Thtr 16 Del from £300 to £350* **Parking** 70 **Notes** LB Civ Wed 80

See advert on opposite page

B

The Fish

★★★ 86% ⊛ HOTEL

tel: 01386 858000 & 852711 **Farncombe Estate WR12 7LJ**
email: reception@thefishhotel.co.uk web: www.thefishhotel.co.uk
dir: *Follow A44 to Moreton-in-Marsh then follow signs to Evesham & Broadway. Take Saintbury turn by Broadway Tower, estate on the left*

Part of the 400-acre Farncombe Estate, The Fish benefits from far-reaching views across the Worcestershire countryside. Smartly appointed bedrooms are located on the hillside in former farm houses and converted buildings, within easy reach of The Lodge, where all the hotel's main facilities can be found. Outdoor activities can be arranged in addition to the on-site tennis court and gym.

Rooms 47 (44 GF) **Facilities** FTV WiFi HL Gym Xmas New Year
Conf Class 70 Board 50 Thtr 120 **Services** Air con **Parking** 200

The Broadway Hotel

★★★ 82% ⊛⊛ HOTEL

COTSWOLD INNS & HOTELS

tel: 01386 852401 **The Green, High St WR12 7AA**
email: info@broadwayhotel.info web: www.cotswold-inns-hotels.co.uk
dir: *Follow signs to Evesham, then Broadway. Left onto Leamington Rd, hotel just off village green*

The Broadway Hotel is a half-timbered Cotswold stone property, built in the 15th century as a retreat for the Abbots of Pershore. It combines modern, attractive decor with original charm and character. Bedrooms are tastefully furnished and well equipped while public rooms include a relaxing lounge, cosy bar and charming restaurant; alfresco all-day dining in summer months proves popular.

Rooms 19 (1 fmly) (3 GF) **D** £140-£300 (incl. bkfst)* **Facilities** FTV WiFi Xmas New Year **Parking** 20

Foxhill Manor

Ⓤ

tel: 01386 852711 **Farncombe Estate WR12 7LJ**
email: reservations@foxhillmanor.com web: www.foxhillmanor.com
dir: *Off A44 between Broadway & Moreton-in-Marsh on Fish hill. 1m outside Broadway village*

Currently the rating for this establishment is not confirmed. This may be due to a change of ownership or because it has only recently joined the AA rating scheme. For further details please see the AA website: theAA.com

Rooms 8 (1 fmly) (2 GF) **Facilities** STV FTV WiFi Gym In room treatments **Conf** Class 40 Board 28 Thtr 70 **Services** Air con **Parking** 30 **Notes** No children 12yrs Civ Wed 70

B

BROADWAY *continued*

Russell's

◎◎ ⧠ RESTAURANT WITH ROOMS

tel: 01386 853555 **20 High St WR12 7DT**
email: info@russellsofbroadway.co.uk **web:** www.russellsofbroadway.co.uk
dir: *Opposite village green*

Situated in the centre of picturesque Broadway, this restaurant with rooms makes a great base for exploring local attractions. The superbly appointed bedrooms, each with its own character, have air conditioning and a wide range of extras. The cuisine is a real draw here with skilful use made of freshly-prepared, local produce.

Rooms 7 (3 annexe) (4 fmly)

BROCKENHURST	Map 5 SU30
Hampshire	

INSPECTORS' CHOICE

Rhinefield House Hotel

★★★★ ◎◎ HOTEL

tel: 01590 622922 & 0845 072 7516
(Calls cost 5p per minute plus your phone company's access charge) **Rhinefield Rd SO42 7QB**
email: rhinefieldhouse@handpicked.co.uk
web: www.handpickedhotels.co.uk/rhinefieldhouse
dir: *A35 towards Christchurch. 3m from Lyndhurst turn left to Rhinefield, 1.5m to hotel*

This stunning 19th-century, mock-Elizabethan mansion is set in 40 acres of beautifully landscaped gardens and forest. Bedrooms are spacious and great consideration is given to guest comfort. The elegant and award-winning Armada Restaurant is richly furnished, and features a fireplace carving (nine years in the making) that is worth taking time to admire. If the weather permits, the delightful terrace is just the place for enjoying alfresco eating.

Rhinefield House Hotel

Rooms 50 (10 fmly) (18 GF) **Facilities** Spa STV WiFi ⇘ HL ⊗ ⤸ ⌣ ⩊ Gym Hydrotherapy pool Plunge pool Steam room Sauna Xmas New Year **Conf** Class 72 Board 56 Thtr 160 **Services** Lift **Parking** 100 **Notes** ⊗ Civ Wed 130

See advert on opposite page

HIGHLY RECOMMENDED

Careys Manor Hotel & Senspa

★★★★ 84% ◎◎◎ HOTEL

tel: 01590 624467 & 623551 **Lyndhurst Rd SO42 7RH**
email: stay@careysmanor.com **web:** www.careysmanor.com
dir: *M27 junct 3, M271, A35 to Lyndhurst. A337 towards Brockenhurst. Hotel on left after Beaulieu sign*

This smart property offers a host of facilities that include an Oriental-style spa and leisure suite with an excellent range of unusual treatments, as well as three contrasting restaurants that offer a choice of Thai, French or modern British cuisine. Many of the spacious and well-appointed bedrooms have balconies overlooking the gardens. Extensive function and conference facilities are also available.

Rooms 79 (61 annexe) (31 GF) **Facilities** Spa FTV WiFi ⇘ ⊗ ⩊ Gym Steam room Beauty therapists Hydrotherapy pool Xmas New Year **Conf** Class 70 Board 40 Thtr 120 **Services** Lift **Parking** 180 **Notes** ⊗ No children 16yrs Civ Wed 100

The Balmer Lawn Hotel

★★★★ 80% ◎ HOTEL

tel: 01590 623116 **Lyndhurst Rd SO42 7ZB**
email: info@balmerlawnhotel.com **web:** www.balmerlawnhotel.com
dir: *Just off A337 from Brockenhurst towards Lymington*

Situated in the heart of the New Forest, this peacefully located hotel provides comfortable public rooms and a wide range of bedrooms. A selection of carefully prepared and enjoyable dishes is offered in the spacious restaurant. The extensive function and leisure facilities make this popular with both families and conference delegates.

Rooms 53 (10 fmly) ⧠ **Facilities** Spa FTV WiFi ⊗ ⤸ ⌣ Gym Squash Indoor leisure suite Sauna ⤳ Xmas New Year **Conf** Class 76 Board 48 Thtr 150 Del from £135 to £175* **Services** Lift **Parking** 100 **Notes** Civ Wed 120

INSPECTORS' CHOICE

THE PIG

★★★ ◉◉ ☒ COUNTRY HOUSE HOTEL

tel: 01590 622354 **Beaulieu Rd SO42 7QL**
email: info@thepighotel.com **web:** www.thepighotel.co.uk
dir: At Brockenhurst onto B3055 Beaulieu Road. 1m on left up private road

A delightful country house where the focus is very much on the food, with the chef, gardener and forager working as a team to create menus of seasonal, locally sourced produce; all ingredients are found within a 15-mile radius. The result of such a policy is that menus change daily, and sometimes even more frequently. The stylish dining room is an authentically reproduced Victorian greenhouse, and alfresco eating is possible as there is a wood-fired oven in the courtyard. The bedrooms have eclectic furnishings, good beds and views of either the forest or the garden; two suites with private courtyards are available.

Rooms 31 (15 annexe) (4 fmly) (12 GF) ⚬ **D** £149-£435* **Facilities** STV FTV WiFi ⚬ ⚬ ⚬ Massage treatment rooms Xmas New Year **Conf** Board 14 **Parking** 30 **Notes** ⊗ Civ Wed 60

Cloud Hotel

★★★ 79% SMALL HOTEL

tel: 01590 622165 & 622354 **Meerut Rd SO42 7TD**
email: enquiries@cloudhotel.co.uk **web:** www.cloudhotel.co.uk
dir: M27 junct 1 signed New Forest, A337 through Lyndhurst to Brockenhurst. On entering Brockenhurst 1st right. Hotel 300mtrs

This charming hotel enjoys a peaceful location on the edge of the village. The bedrooms are bright and comfortable with pine furnishings and smart en suite facilities. Public rooms include a selection of cosy lounges, a delightful rear garden with outdoor seating and a restaurant specialising in home-cooked, wholesome English food.

Rooms 18 (1 fmly) (2 GF) ⚬ **Facilities** FTV WiFi ⚬ Xmas **Conf** Class 12 Board 12 Thtr 40 **Parking** 20 **Notes** ⊗ No children 14yrs Closed 27 Dec-11 Jan

Forest Park Hotel

★★★ 71% HOTEL

tel: 01590 622844 **Rhinefield Rd SO42 7ZG**
email: reservations@forestpark-hotel.co.uk **web:** www.forestpark-hotel.co.uk
dir: M27 junct 1, follow signs for A337 Lyndhurst. Follow road for 3m, left at lights onto A35, A337 Lymington Brockenhurst, right into Meerut Road, right at T-junct

Located in the heart of the beautiful New Forest National Park this popular hotel provides an ideal base for exploring this remarkable area. Accommodation offers 38 rooms with garden or forest views, and free WiFi available throughout. The hotel is child friendly; they will delight in seeing the ponies on the doorstep. The recently refurbished restaurant has views of the beautiful landscaped gardens with delicious food to match. The bar offers a more relaxed atmosphere with food served from midday to 9 in the evening.

Rooms 38 (4 fmly) (7 GF) ⚬ **Facilities** FTV WiFi HL ♫ Xmas New Year **Conf** Class 15 Board 20 Thtr 40 **Parking** 38 **Notes** Civ Wed 70

B

BROCKENHURST *continued*

The Cottage Hotel

★★ 72% HOTEL

tel: 01590 622296 **Sway Rd SO42 7SH**
email: enquiries@cottagelodge.co.uk **web:** www.cottagelodge.co.uk
dir: *Exit A337 opposite Careys Manor Hotel into Grigg Ln, 0.25m over x-rds, cottage next to war memorial*

Parts of this attractive small hotel date back over 300 years, and it has been skilfully modernised by the resident owners, to provide a choice of well furnished, bright bedrooms. There is a low-beamed lounge and a licensed restaurant which offers both table d'hôte and a varied à la carte menu. Light refreshments and cream teas are served on the terrace tea garden between Easter and October.

Rooms 15 (3 fmly) (7 GF) ⚓ **Facilities** FTV WiFi ⌕ **Conf** Class 8 Board 8 Thtr 8 **Parking** 15 **Notes** LB ⊗ Closed 1 wk at Xmas

BROMBOROUGH	Map 15 SJ38
Merseyside	

Premier Inn Wirral (Bromborough)

BUDGET HOTEL

tel: 0871 527 9172 *(Calls cost 13p per minute plus your phone company's access charge)*
High St, Bromborough Cross CH62 7EZ
web: www.premierinn.com
dir: *On A41 (New Chester Rd), 2m from M53 junct 5*

High quality, budget accommodation ideal for both families and business travellers. Spacious, en suite bedrooms feature tea and coffee making facilities, and Freeview TV in most hotels. Internet access and WiFi are available for a small fee. The adjacent family restaurant features a wide and varied menu. See also the Hotel Groups pages.

Rooms 32

BROME	Map 13 TM17
Suffolk	

Best Western Brome Grange Hotel

★★★ 78% ◎ HOTEL

tel: 01379 870456 **Norwich Rd, Nr Diss IP23 8AP**
email: info@bromegrangehotel.co.uk **web:** www.bromegrange.co.uk
dir: *Located on the A140 between Ipswich & Norwich in the village of Brome*

Conveniently located between Ipswich and Norfolk the Best Western Brome Hotel offers bedrooms that are spacious, well equipped and attractively presented. The charming cosy bar has lots of character and the restaurant is very popular with locals and residents. A warm welcome is assured and ample secure parking is available for guests.

Rooms 40 (24 annexe) (2 fmly) (24 GF) ⚓ **Facilities** Spa FTV WiFi Gym Xmas New Year **Conf** Class 60 Board 40 Thtr 150 **Services** Lift **Parking** 100 **Notes** Civ Wed 110

BROMLEY
Greater London

Bromley Court Hotel

★★★ 78% HOTEL PLAN 1 H1

tel: 020 8461 8600 & 8461 8627 **Bromley Hill BR1 4JD**
email: enquiries@bromleycourthotel.co.uk **web:** www.bromleycourthotel.co.uk
dir: *N of town centre, off A21. Private drive opposite Volkswagen garage on Bromley Hill*

Set amid three acres of grounds, this smart hotel enjoys a peaceful location, in a residential area on the outskirts of town. Well maintained bedrooms are smartly appointed and thoughtfully equipped. The contemporary-style restaurant offers a good choice of meals in comfortable surroundings. Extensive facilities include a leisure club and a good range of meeting rooms.

Rooms 117 (4 fmly) ⚓ **Facilities** STV FTV WiFi ⌕ Gym Steam room ♫ Xmas New Year **Conf** Class 70 Board 40 Thtr 150 **Services** Lift Air con **Parking** 86 **Notes** ⊗ Civ Wed 180

BROMSGROVE	Map 10 SO97
Worcestershire	

Premier Inn Bromsgrove Central

BUDGET HOTEL

tel: 0871 527 8168 *(Calls cost 13p per minute plus your phone company's access charge)*
Birmingham Rd B61 0BA
web: www.premierinn.com
dir: *M42 junct 1 (S'bound access only) or M5 junct 4 S'bound or M5 junct 5 N'bound onto A38 towards Bromsgrove. Hotel adjacent to Guild Brewers Fayre. NB for Sat Nav use B60 1GJ*

High quality, budget accommodation ideal for both families and business travellers. Spacious, en suite bedrooms feature tea and coffee making facilities, and Freeview TV in most hotels. Internet access and WiFi are available for a small fee. The adjacent family restaurant features a wide and varied menu. See also the Hotel Groups pages.

Rooms 78

Premier Inn Bromsgrove South (Worcester Road)

BUDGET HOTEL

tel: 0871 527 8170 *(Calls cost 13p per minute plus your phone company's access charge)*
Worcester Rd, Upton Warren B61 7ET
web: www.premierinn.com
dir: *M5 junct 5, A38 towards Bromsgrove, 1.2m. Or M42 junct 1, A38 S, cross over A448*

Rooms 27

BROXTON	Map 15 SJ45
Cheshire	

Carden Park Hotel, Golf Resort & Spa

★★★★ 82% ◎ HOTEL

tel: 01829 731000 **Carden Park CH3 9DQ**
email: reservations@cardenpark.co.uk **web:** www.cardenpark.co.uk
dir: *M56 junct 15, M53 Chester. Take A41 signed Whitchurch. 8m. At Broxton rdbt right onto A534 (signed Wrexham). Hotel 1.5m on left*

This impressive Cheshire estate dates back to the 17th century and consists of 1,000 acres of mature parkland. The hotel offers a choice of dining options along

B

with superb leisure facilities that include golf courses, a fully equipped gym, a swimming pool and popular spa. Spacious, thoughtfully equipped bedrooms have excellent business and in-room entertainment facilities.

Rooms 196 (83 annexe) (24 fmly) (68 GF) ⚓ **Facilities** Spa STV FTV WiFi ↻ 🕲 ⚓ 36 ⛳ Putt green Gym Archery Mountain bike Laser clay shooting Sauna Steam room Segway Quad bikes Xmas New Year **Conf** Class 240 Board 125 Thtr 350 **Services** Lift **Parking** 700 **Notes** ⊗ Civ Wed 350

BRYHER
Cornwall (Isles of Scilly)

Map 2 SV81

HIGHLY RECOMMENDED

Hell Bay
★★★★ 83% ◉◉◉ HOTEL

tel: 01720 422947 **TR23 0PR**
email: contactus@hellbay.co.uk **web:** www.hellbay.co.uk
dir: Access by boat from Penzance, plane from Exeter, Newquay or Land's End

Located on the smallest of the inhabited islands of the Scilly Isles on the edge of the Atlantic, this hotel makes a really special destination. The owners have filled the hotel with original works of art by artists who have connections with the islands, and the interior is decorated in cool blues and greens creating an extremely restful environment. The contemporary bedrooms are equally stylish, and many have garden access and stunning sea views. Eating here is a delight, and naturally seafood features strongly on the award-winning, daily-changing menus.

Rooms 25 (25 annexe) (4 fmly) (15 GF) ⚓ **S** £105–£390; **D** £170–£620 (incl. bkfst)* **Facilities** FTV WiFi ↻ ⚒ ⚓ 7 ⛳ ⛲ Gym Beauty treatment room **Conf** Class 36 Board 20 **Notes** LB Closed Nov-Feb

---

BUCKHURST HILL
Essex

Map 6 TQ49

Premier Inn Loughton/Buckhurst Hill

BUDGET HOTEL

tel: 0871 527 8686 (Calls cost 13p per minute plus your phone company's access charge)
High Rd IG9 5HT
web: www.premierinn.com
dir: M25 junct 26 towards Loughton. A121 into Buckhurst Hill (approx 5m), hotel on left

High quality, budget accommodation ideal for both families and business travellers. Spacious, en suite bedrooms feature tea and coffee making facilities, and Freeview TV in most hotels. Internet access and WiFi are available for a small fee. The adjacent family restaurant features a wide and varied menu. See also the Hotel Groups pages.

Rooms 50

BUCKINGHAM
Buckinghamshire

Map 11 SP63

Buckingham Villiers Hotel
★★★★ 73% ◉ HOTEL

tel: 01280 822444 **3 Castle St MK18 1BS**
email: villiers@oxfordshire-hotels.co.uk **web:** www.oxfordshire-hotels.co.uk
dir: M1 junct 13 N or junct 15 S follow signs to Buckingham. Castle St by Old Town Hall

Guests can enjoy a town centre location with a high degree of comfort at this 400-year-old former coaching inn. Relaxing public areas feature flagstone floors,

oak panelling and real fires, while bedrooms are modern, spacious and equipped to a high level. Diners can unwind in the atmospheric bar before taking dinner in the award-winning restaurant.

Rooms 49 (4 fmly) (3 GF) **S** £75–£110; **D** £90–£160 (incl. bkfst)* **Facilities** STV FTV WiFi Xmas New Year **Conf** Class 120 Board 80 Thtr 250 Del from £140 to £165* **Services** Lift **Parking** 52 **Notes** LB ⊗ Civ Wed 180

Best Western Buckingham Hotel

★★★ 75% HOTEL

tel: 01280 822622 **Buckingham Ring Rd MK18 1RY**
email: info@thebuckinghamhotel.co.uk **web:** www.thebuckinghamhotel.co.uk
dir: A421 to Buckingham, take ring road S towards Brackley & Bicester. Hotel on left

A purpose-built hotel, which offers comfortable and spacious rooms with well designed working spaces for business travellers. There are also extensive conference facilities. The open-plan restaurant and bar offer a good range of dishes, and the well-equipped leisure suite is popular with guests.

Rooms 70 (6 fmly) (31 GF) **S** fr £50; **D** fr £85* **Facilities** STV FTV WiFi ↻ 🕲 supervised Gym Sauna Steam room Xmas New Year **Conf** Class 60 Board 60 Thtr 200 Del from £125 to £150* **Parking** 200 **Notes** Civ Wed 120

BUCKLAND (NEAR BROADWAY)
Gloucestershire

Map 10 SP03

INSPECTORS' CHOICE

Buckland Manor
★★★★ ◉◉◉ ⚑ COUNTRY HOUSE HOTEL

tel: 01386 852626 **WR12 7LY**
email: info@bucklandmanor.co.uk **web:** www.bucklandmanor.co.uk
dir: 2m S of Broadway, off B4632

Buckland Manor is a grand 13th-century manor house, surrounded by well-kept and beautiful gardens that feature a stream and waterfall. Everything at this hotel is geared to encourage rest and relaxation. Spacious bedrooms and public areas are furnished with high quality pieces and decorated in keeping with the style of the manor; crackling log fires warm the wonderful lounges. The elegant dining room, with views over the rolling hills, is the perfect place to enjoy dishes that use excellent local produce.

Rooms 15 (1 fmly) (4 GF) ⚓ **S** £205–£590; **D** £225–£610 (incl. bkfst)*
Facilities FTV WiFi ⛳ Putt green ⛲ Xmas New Year **Conf** Board 25 Thtr 30 **Parking** 20 **Notes** ⊗ No children 10yrs Civ Wed 40

B

BUDE
Cornwall   Map 2 SS20

Falcon Hotel
★★★ 80% HOTEL

tel: 01288 352005 **Breakwater Rd EX23 8SD**
email: reservations@falconhotel.com **web:** www.falconhotel.com
dir: M5 South junct 31 to A30 Oakhampton, A386 to Bude then A3079 to A39 right to Bude. Continue down hill, left at rdbt, Hotel on the right after bridge.

Dating back to 1798, this long-established hotel boasts delightful walled gardens, ideal for afternoon teas. Bedrooms offer high standards of comfort and quality; there is also a four-poster room complete with spa bath. A choice of menus is offered in the elegant restaurant and the friendly bar. The hotel has an impressive function room.

Rooms 29 (8 fmly) ⌂ **S** £70; **D** £140 (incl. bkfst)* **Facilities** STV FTV WiFi ⌂ ♫ New Year **Conf** Class 100 Board 50 Thtr 200 **Services** Lift **Parking** 65 **Notes** LB ⊗ Closed 25 Dec Civ Wed 160

BURFORD
Oxfordshire   Map 5 SP21

The Bay Tree Hotel
★★★★ 77% ⊛ HOTEL

COTSWOLD INNS & HOTELS

tel: 01993 822791 **Sheep St OX18 4LW**
email: info@baytreehotel.info **web:** www.cotswold-inns-hotels.co.uk
dir: A40 or A361 to Burford. From High St turn into Sheep St, next to old market square. Hotel on right

The Bay Tree's modern decorative style combines seamlessly with features from this delightful inn's long history. Bedrooms are tastefully furnished and some have four-poster or half-tester beds. Public areas consist of a character bar, a sophisticated airy restaurant, a selection of meeting rooms and an attractive walled garden.

Rooms 21 (13 annexe) (2 fmly) (3 GF) **Facilities** FTV WiFi ⚑ Xmas New Year **Conf** Class 12 Board 25 Thtr 40 **Parking** 50 **Notes** Civ Wed 90

HIGHLY RECOMMENDED

The Lamb Inn
★★★ 87% ⊛⊛⊛ SMALL HOTEL

COTSWOLD INNS & HOTELS

tel: 01993 823155 **Sheep St OX18 4LR**
email: info@lambinn-burford.co.uk
web: www.cotswold-inns-hotels.co.uk/the-lamb-inn
dir: A40 into Burford, downhill, 1st left into Sheep St, hotel last on right

This enchanting old inn is just a short walk from the centre of this delightful Cotswold village. An abundance of character and charm is found in the cosy lounge with log fire, and intimate bar with flagged floors. An elegant restaurant offers locally sourced produce in carefully prepared dishes. Bedrooms, some with original features, are comfortable and well appointed.

Rooms 17 (1 fmly) (4 GF) ⌂ **Facilities** FTV WiFi Xmas New Year

BURGESS HILL
West Sussex   Map 6 TQ31

Premier Inn Burgess Hill
BUDGET HOTEL

Premier Inn

tel: 0871 527 8172 *(Calls cost 13p per minute plus your phone company's access charge)*
Charles Av RH15 9AG
web: www.premierinn.com
dir: M25 junct 7, M23, A23. Left at Burgess Hill follow A2300 signs. At rdbt 2nd exit onto A2300. At next rdbt 4th exit onto A273, straight on at next 2 rdbts, at 3rd rdbt (Tesco) 1st left. Hotel 2nd left

High quality, budget accommodation ideal for both families and business travellers. Spacious, en suite bedrooms feature tea and coffee making facilities, and Freeview TV in most hotels. Internet access and WiFi are available for a small fee. The adjacent family restaurant features a wide and varied menu. See also the Hotel Groups pages.

Rooms 60

BURLEY
Hampshire   Map 5 SU20

Burley Manor
★★★★ 80% ⊛ HOTEL

NEW FOREST HOTELS

tel: 01425 403522 **Ringwood Rd BH24 4BS**
email: burley.manor@newforesthotels.co.uk **web:** www.burleymanor.com
dir: From E - M27 end to A31 for 7m take Burley slip road. follow signs to hotel.From W - A31, 2nd sliproad after Ringwood to Burley. Follow signs to hotel.

Burley Manor is located in the New Forest and enjoys beautiful parkland views. Bedrooms are located in the main Manor House as well as the stables and all have been refurbished to a high standard with quality furnishings and bold use of colours. Drinks can be enjoyed in the comfortable, elegantly furnished lounge and bar; and when weather permits, on the garden patio. In the restaurant, the menu has Mediterranean influences, and some dishes are cooked in the wood-fired oven. There is also the chef's pantry for small private dinners; while the barn is ideal for larger celebrations.

Rooms 40 **S** £70-£250; **D** £109-£289 (incl. bkfst)* **Facilities** WiFi ⚲ **Conf** Class 24 Board 40 Thtr 70 **Notes** No children 13 yrs

Moorhill House Hotel
★★★ 79% ⊛ COUNTRY HOUSE HOTEL

NEW FOREST HOTELS

tel: 01425 403285 & 0800 444 441 **BH24 4AG**
email: moorhill@newforesthotels.co.uk **web:** www.newforesthotels.co.uk
dir: M27, A31, follow signs to Burley, through village, up hill, right opposite school & cricket grounds

Situated deep in the heart of the New Forest and formerly a grand gentleman's residence, this charming hotel offers a relaxed and friendly environment. Bedrooms, which come in varying sizes, are smartly decorated. A range of facilities is provided and guests can relax by walking around the extensive grounds. Both dinner and breakfast offer a choice of interesting and freshly prepared dishes.

Rooms 31 (13 fmly) (3 GF) ⌂ **Facilities** FTV WiFi ⌂ HL ☺ ⚲ Badminton (Apr-Sep) Sauna Xmas New Year **Conf** Class 60 Board 65 Thtr 120 **Parking** 50 **Notes** Civ Wed 90

BURNHAM	Map 6 SU98
Buckinghamshire

Burnham Beeches Hotel

★★★★ 77% ◎◎ HOTEL

tel: 0844 736 8603 *(Calls cost 7p per minute plus your phone company's access charge)*
& 01628 429955 **Grove Rd SL1 8DP**
email: sales.burnhambeeches@corushotels.com
web: www.corushotels.com/burnham-beeches
dir: *M40 junct 2, A355 towards Slough, right at 2nd rdbt, 1st right to Grove Rd*

Set in attractive mature grounds on the fringes of woodland, this extended Georgian manor house has spacious, comfortable and well-equipped bedrooms. Public rooms include a cosy lounge/bar offering all-day snacks and an elegant wood-panelled restaurant that serves interesting cuisine; there are also conference facilities, a fitness centre and pool.

Rooms 82 (22 fmly) (12 GF) ⌇ **S** £100-£180; **D** £110-£200* **Facilities** FTV WiFi ⓧ ⛎ Gym Beauty treatment room Xmas New Year **Conf** Class 80 Board 60 Thtr 150 **Services** Lift **Parking** 150 **Notes** ⊗ Civ Wed 120

BURNLEY	Map 18 SD83
Lancashire

Premier Inn Burnley

BUDGET HOTEL

tel: 0871 527 8174 *(Calls cost 13p per minute plus your phone company's access charge)*
Queen Victoria Rd BB10 3EF
web: www.premierinn.com
dir: *M65 junct 12, 5th exit at rdbt, 1st exit at rdbt, keep in right lane at lights, 2nd exit at next rdbt, 3rd at next rdbt, under bridge, left before football ground*

High quality, budget accommodation ideal for both families and business travellers. Spacious, en suite bedrooms feature tea and coffee making facilities, and Freeview TV in most hotels. Internet access and WiFi are available for a small fee. The adjacent family restaurant features a wide and varied menu. See also the Hotel Groups pages.

Rooms 67

BURNSALL	Map 19 SE06
North Yorkshire

The Devonshire Fell

◎ RESTAURANT WITH ROOMS

tel: 01756 729000 & 718111 **BD23 6BT**
email: manager@devonshirefell.co.uk **web:** www.devonshirefell.co.uk
dir: *On B6160, 6m from Bolton Abbey rdbt, A59 junct*

Located on the edge of the attractive village of Burnsall, The Devonshire Fell is colourful, contemporary and quirky. Originally a gentleman's club it enjoys what may be one of the finest locations in the country. Overlooking the village of Burnsall in the heart of the Dales, the views are quite wonderful. A brasserie-style menu is served in the light and airy conservatory restaurant, with views of the Fells and Dales on the outside and original modern art work within. Intimate and friendly, The Devonshire Fell is a superb choice for those looking to escape from it all. Expect quality surroundings, home comforts and a friendly, warm welcome.

Rooms 16 (2 fmly)

BURRINGTON (NEAR PORTSMOUTH ARMS STATION)	Map 3 SS61
Devon

INSPECTORS' CHOICE

Northcote Manor

★★★ ◎◎ COUNTRY HOUSE HOTEL

tel: 01769 560501 **EX37 9LZ**
email: rest@northcotemanor.co.uk **web:** www.northcotemanor.co.uk
dir: *From A377 opposite Portsmouth Arms, into hotel drive. NB do not enter Burrington village*

A warm and friendly welcome is assured at this beautiful country-house hotel, built in 1716 and surrounded by 20 acres of grounds and woodlands. Guests can enjoy wonderful views over the Taw River Valley while relaxing in the delightful environment created by the attentive staff. A meal in either the intimate, more formal Manor House Restaurant or the Walled Garden Restaurant will prove a highlight; both offer menus of the finest local produce used in well-prepared dishes. Bedrooms, including some suites, are individually styled, spacious and well appointed.

Rooms 16 (2 fmly) (3 GF) ⌇ **Facilities** FTV WiFi ⓢ ⛎ Xmas New Year **Conf** Class 50 Board 30 Thtr 80 **Parking** 50 **Notes** Civ Wed 100

BURTON UPON TRENT	Map 10 SK22
Staffordshire

Mercure Burton Upon Trent Newton Park

★★★★ 73% COUNTRY HOUSE HOTEL

tel: 01283 703568 & 707500 **Newton Solney DE15 0SS**
email: info@mercureburton.co.uk **web:** www.mercureburton.co.uk
dir: *On B5008 past Repton to Newton Solney. Hotel on left*

Standing in eight acres of grounds, this Grade II listed 18th-century Italian-style country manor provides comfort in elegant surroundings. The well-equipped bedrooms are suitable for both business and leisure guests. The oak-panelled restaurant serves a good choice of dishes and overlooks the landscaped gardens. Eight fully-equipped meeting rooms are available.

Rooms 50 (3 fmly) (5 GF) ⌇ **Facilities** STV FTV WiFi ↻ **Conf** Class 70 Board 60 Thtr 100 **Services** Lift **Parking** 100 **Notes** Civ Wed 100

B

BURTON UPON TRENT *continued*

Holiday Inn Express Burton upon Trent

BUDGET HOTEL

tel: 01283 504300 **2nd Av, Centrum 100 DE14 2WF**
email: reservations@exhiburton.co.uk **web:** www.exhiburton.co.uk
dir: *From A38 Branston exit take A5121 signed Town Centre. At McDonalds rdbt, turn left into 2nd Avenue. Hotel on left*

A modern hotel ideal for families and business travellers. Fresh and uncomplicated, the spacious rooms include Sky TV, power shower and tea and coffee-making facilities. Continental buffet breakfast is included in the room rate; other meals may be taken at the nearby family pub or restaurant. See also the Hotel Groups pages.

Rooms 82 (47 fmly) (14 GF) ✆ **S** £50-£130; **D** £50-£130 (incl. bkfst)* **Conf** Class 30 Board 25 Thtr 60 Del from £119 to £139*

Premier Inn Burton upon Trent Central

BUDGET HOTEL

tel: 0871 527 9280 *(Calls cost 13p per minute plus your phone company's access charge)*
Wellington Rd DE14 2WD
web: www.premierinn.com
dir: *Exit A38 at Branston junction onto A5121 to Burton on Trent. Straight on at lights. At rdbt take 3rd exit, hotel on left*

High quality, budget accommodation ideal for both families and business travellers. Spacious, en suite bedrooms feature tea and coffee making facilities, and Freeview TV in most hotels. Internet access and WiFi are available for a small fee. The adjacent family restaurant features a wide and varied menu. See also the Hotel Groups pages.

Rooms 64

Premier Inn Burton upon Trent East

BUDGET HOTEL

tel: 0871 527 8176 *(Calls cost 13p per minute plus your phone company's access charge)*
Ashby Road East DE15 0PU
web: www.premierinn.com
dir: *2m E of Burton upon Trent on A50*

Rooms 32

BURY	Map 15 SD81
Greater Manchester	

Red Hall Hotel

★★★ 81% 🏵 HOTEL

tel: 01706 822476 **Manchester Rd, Walmersley BL9 5NA**
email: info@red-hall.co.uk **web:** www.red-hall.co.uk
dir: *M66 junct 1, A56. Over motorway bridge, hotel approx 300mtrs on right*

Originally a farmhouse, this now much enlarged hotel is located in the picturesque village of Warmersley just off the M66, making it ideal for business and leisure guests alike. Bright bedrooms are comfortable, contemporary, and equipped to a modern standard. The newly revamped 'Oscars' restaurant serves a wide-ranging menu. Meeting and event facilities complete the package.

Rooms 37 (2 fmly) (18 GF) ✆ **Facilities** STV FTV WiFi Xmas New Year **Conf** Class 60 Board 30 Thtr 140 Del from £99* **Services** Lift **Parking** 100 **Notes** Civ Wed 80

Premier Inn Manchester Bury

BUDGET HOTEL

tel: 0871 527 9294 *(Calls cost 13p per minute plus your phone company's access charge)*
5 Knowsley Place, Duke St BL9 0EJ
web: www.premierinn.com
dir: *M66 junct 2, A58 towards Bolton & Bury. At rdbt in Bury centre follow A58 (Angouleme Way). Left in Knowsley St, hotel on left*

High quality, budget accommodation ideal for both families and business travellers. Spacious, en suite bedrooms feature tea and coffee making facilities, and Freeview TV in most hotels. Internet access and WiFi are available for a small fee. The adjacent family restaurant features a wide and varied menu. See also the Hotel Groups pages.

Rooms 115

BURY ST EDMUNDS	Map 13 TL86
Suffolk	

The Angel Hotel

★★★★ 81% 🏵🏵 TOWN HOUSE HOTEL

tel: 01284 714000 **Angel Hill IP33 1LT**
email: staying@theangel.co.uk **web:** www.theangel.co.uk
dir: *From A134, left at rdbt into Northgate St. Continue to lights, right into Mustow St, left into Angel Hill. Hotel on right*

The Angel Hotel is an impressive building situated just a short walk from the town centre. One of the hotel's more notable guests over the last 400 years was Charles Dickens, who is reputed to have written part of *The Pickwick Papers* while in residence. The hotel offers a range of individually designed bedrooms that include a selection of four-poster rooms and a suite.

Rooms 78 (5 fmly) (22 GF) ✆ **S** £110-£160; **D** £120-£270 **Facilities** FTV WiFi **Conf** Class 16 Board 16 Thtr 22 **Services** Lift **Parking** 20 **Notes** LB

Best Western Priory Hotel

★★★ 82% 🏵 HOTEL

tel: 01284 766181 **Mildenhall Rd IP32 6EH**
email: reservations@prioryhotel.co.uk **web:** www.prioryhotel.co.uk
dir: *From A14 (junct 43) take Bury St Edmunds W slip road. Follow signs to Brandon. At mini-rdbt turn right. Hotel 0.5m on left*

Priory Hotel is an 18th-century Grade II listed building set in landscaped grounds on the outskirts of town. The attractively decorated, tastefully furnished and thoughtfully equipped bedrooms are split between the main house and garden wings, which have their own sun terraces. Public rooms feature a smart restaurant, a conservatory dining room and a lounge bar.

Rooms 36 (29 annexe) (1 fmly) (30 GF) ✆ **S** £90-£97; **D** £98-£105 (incl. bkfst)* **Facilities** FTV WiFi Xmas New Year **Conf** Class 24 Board 30 Thtr 75 Del from £120 to £142* **Parking** 60 **Notes** Civ Wed 75

C

The Grange Hotel

★★★ 77% COUNTRY HOUSE HOTEL

tel: 01359 231260 **Barton Rd, Thurston IP31 3PQ**
email: info@grangecountryhousehotel.com **web:** www.grangecountryhousehotel.com
dir: *A14 junct 45 towards Gt Barton, right at T-junct. At x-rds left into Barton Rd to Thurston. At rdbt, left after 0.5m, hotel on right*

The Grange Hotel is a Tudor-style country-house hotel situated on the outskirts of town. The individually decorated bedrooms have co-ordinated fabrics and many thoughtful touches; some rooms have nice views of the gardens. Public areas include a smart lounge bar, two private dining rooms, the Garden Restaurant and banqueting facilities.

Rooms 18 (5 annexe) (1 fmly) (3 GF) ♠ **Facilities** FTV WiFi Beauty treatment room ♫ Xmas New Year **Conf** Class 40 Board 30 Thtr 135 **Parking** 100 **Notes** Civ Wed 150

Premier Inn Bury St Edmunds Town Centre

BUDGET HOTEL

tel: 0871 527 9512 *(Calls cost 13p per minute plus your phone company's access charge)*
Raingate St IP33 2AR
web: www.premierinn.com
dir: *A14 junct 44 signed Bury St Edmunds East/Sudbury A134. At rdbt 3rd exit towards Bury St Edmunds. At next rdbt 2nd exit (Town Centre/A1302). At next rdbt 3rd exit (town centre). At mini rdbt 3rd exit into Westgate St. At Greene King Brewery (one-way system) into Crown St. Hotel at bottom of hill*

High quality, budget accommodation ideal for both families and business travellers. Spacious, en suite bedrooms feature tea and coffee making facilities, and Freeview TV in most hotels. Internet access and WiFi are available for a small fee. The adjacent family restaurant features a wide and varied menu. See also the Hotel Groups pages.

Rooms 75

BUXTON
Derbyshire — Map 16 SK07

Best Western Lee Wood Hotel

★★★★ 74% HOTEL

tel: 01298 23002 **The Park SK17 6TQ**
email: reservations@leewoodhotel.co.uk **web:** www.leewoodhotel.co.uk
dir: *From town centre take A5004 NE, hotel 150mtrs beyond University of Derby - Buxton Campus*

This elegant Georgian hotel offers high standards of comfort and hospitality. The individually furnished bedrooms are generally spacious, with all of the expected modern conveniences. There is a choice of two comfortable lounges and a conservatory restaurant. The quality cooking, good service and fine hospitality are noteworthy.

Rooms 39 (5 annexe) (4 fmly) **Facilities** STV FTV WiFi ♦ Gym Serenity beauty & wellbeing New Year **Conf** Class 65 Board 40 Thtr 120 **Services** Lift **Parking** 50 **Notes** Civ Wed 120

CADNAM
Hampshire — Map 5 SU31

Bartley Lodge Hotel

★★★ 86% HOTEL

tel: 023 8081 2248 & 0800 444441 **Lyndhurst Rd SO40 2NR**
email: bartley@newforesthotels.co.uk **web:** www.newforesthotels.co.uk
dir: *M27 junct 1 at 1st rdbt 1st exit, at 2nd rdbt 3rd exit onto A337. Hotel sign on left*

This 18th-century former hunting lodge is very quietly situated, yet is just minutes from the M27. Bedrooms vary in size but all are well equipped. There is a selection of small lounge areas, a cosy bar and an indoor pool, together with a small fitness suite. The Crystal dining room offers a tempting choice of well prepared dishes.

Rooms 40 (15 fmly) (4 GF) ♠ **Facilities** FTV WiFi ♦ IIL ⊛ ♨ Sauna Xmas New Year **Conf** Class 60 Board 60 Thtr 120 **Services** Lift **Parking** 60 **Notes** Civ Wed 100

CALLOW END
Worcestershire — Map 10 SO84

Stanbrook Abbey

Ⓤ HOTEL

tel: 01905 409300 **Jennet Tree Ln WR2 4QN**
email: mb@stanbrookabbey.com **web:** www.stanbrookabbey.com
dir: *M5 junct 7, A4440 to Powick, B4424 to Callow End, hotel on right*

Currently the rating for this establishment is not confirmed. This may be due to a change of ownership or because it has only recently joined the AA rating scheme. For further details please see the AA website: theAA.com

Rooms 56 (5 annexe) (3 fmly) ♠ **S** £80-£430; **D** £90-£450 (incl. bkfst)*
Facilities FTV WiFi ♦ Putt green ♨ ♫ Xmas New Year **Conf** Class 250 Board 140 Thtr 300 Del from £145 to £230* **Services** Lift **Parking** 260 **Notes** LB ⊗ Civ Wed 280

CAMBER
East Sussex — Map 7 TQ91

The Gallivant

◎◎ RESTAURANT WITH ROOMS

tel: 01797 225057 **New Lydd Rd TN31 7RB**
email: beachbistro@thegallivanthotel.com **web:** www.thegallivanthotel.com

The Gallivant is located right on the edge of Camber Sands and just a short drive from the historic town of Rye. The inn offers modern, coastal-styled accommodation with light airy decor and reconditioned driftwood furniture. Rooms are well equipped and ideal for both business and leisure guests. There's a bar and the award-winning Beach Bistro serves food daily. The large function suite is open year round and is perfect for parties or weddings. The sand dunes and beach are just across the road in front of the inn.

Rooms 20 (4 annexe) (4 fmly)

CAMBERLEY
Surrey   **Map 6 SU86**

See also **Yateley**

Macdonald Frimley Hall Hotel & Spa
★★★★ 80% 🏵🏵 HOTEL

tel: 01276 413100 & 0344 8799110 **Lime Av GU15 2BG**
email: sales.frimleyhall@macdonald-hotels.co.uk
web: www.macdonaldhotels.co.uk/frimleyhall
dir: *M3 junct 3, A321 follow Bagshot signs. Through lights, left onto A30 signed Camberley & Basingstoke. To rdbt, 2nd exit onto A325, take 5th right*

The epitome of classic English elegance, Macdonald Frimley Hall Hotel is an ivy-clad Victorian manor house set in two acres of immaculate grounds in the heart of Surrey. The bedrooms and public areas are smart and have a modern decorative theme. The hotel boasts an impressive health club and spa with treatment rooms, a fully equipped gym and heated indoor swimming pool.

Rooms 98 (15 fmly) 🐾 **Facilities** **Spa** FTV WiFi ⬆ HL ⌚ Gym Technogym Sauna Steam room Relaxation room Xmas New Year **Conf** Class 100 Board 60 Thtr 250 **Parking** 150 **Notes** Civ Wed 220

Lakeside International
★★★ 74% HOTEL

tel: 01252 838000 **Wharf Rd, Frimley Green GU16 6JR**
email: info@lakesideinthotel.com **web:** www.lakesideinternationalhotel.com
dir: *Exit A321 at mini-rdbt turn into Wharf Rd. Lakeside complex on right*

This hotel, geared towards the business market, enjoys a lakeside location with noteworthy views. Bedrooms are modern, comfortable and with a range of facilities. Public areas are spacious and include a residents' lounge, bar, games room, a smart restaurant and an established health and leisure club.

Rooms 98 (1 fmly) (31 GF) 🐾 **Facilities** FTV WiFi ⌚ Gym Squash Sauna Steam room **Conf** Class 100 Board 40 Thtr 120 **Services** Lift **Parking** 250 **Notes** ⊗ Civ Wed 100

Premier Inn Camberley
BUDGET HOTEL

tel: 0871 527 9322 *(Calls cost 13p per minute plus your phone company's access charge)*
Park St GU15 3SG
web: www.premierinn.com
dir: *M3 junct 4, A331 towards Camberley. In 2m, at major junct into right lane, 4th exit signed A30. For parking, in 1m, right into Southern Rd for Atrium Car Park*

High quality, budget accommodation ideal for both families and business travellers. Spacious, en suite bedrooms feature tea and coffee making facilities, and Freeview TV in most hotels. Internet access and WiFi are available for a small fee. The adjacent family restaurant features a wide and varied menu. See also the Hotel Groups pages.

Rooms 95

Premier Inn Sandhurst
BUDGET HOTEL

tel: 0871 527 8958 *(Calls cost 13p per minute plus your phone company's access charge)*
221 Yorktown Rd, College Town, Sandurst GU47 0RT
web: www.premierinn.com
dir: *M3 junct 4, A331 to Camberley. At large rdbt take A321 towards Bracknell. At 3rd lights, hotel on left*

Rooms 54

CAMBORNE
Cornwall   **Map 2 SW63**

Premier Inn Camborne
BUDGET HOTEL

tel: 0871 527 9308 *(Calls cost 13p per minute plus your phone company's access charge)*
Treswithian Rd TR14 7NF
web: www.premierinn.com
dir: *From M5 (S) junct 31, A30 to Bodmin, then to Redruth, follow signs to Camborne. Left onto A3047, to rdbt, 1st exit to hotel*

High quality, budget accommodation ideal for both families and business travellers. Spacious, en suite bedrooms feature tea and coffee making facilities, and Freeview TV in most hotels. Internet access and WiFi are available for a small fee. The adjacent family restaurant features a wide and varied menu. See also the Hotel Groups pages.

Rooms 65

CAMBOURNE
Cambridgeshire   **Map 12 TL35**

The Cambridge Belfry
★★★★ 81% HOTEL

tel: 01954 714600 **Back St CB23 6BW**
email: cambridgebelfry@qhotels.co.uk **web:** www.qhotels.co.uk
dir: *M11 junct 13, A428 towards Bedford, follow signs to Cambourne. Exit at Cambourne, keep left. Left at rdbt, hotel on left*

This exciting hotel, built beside the water, is located at the gateway to Cambourne Village and Business Park. Contemporary in style throughout, the hotel boasts state-of-the-art leisure facilities, including Reflections Spa offering a range of therapies and treatments, and extensive conference and banqueting rooms. Meals are served in the Bridge Restaurant, and original artwork is displayed throughout the hotel.

Rooms 120 (30 GF) 🐾 **Facilities** **Spa** FTV WiFi ⬆ HL ⌚ 🏊 Gym Beauty treatments Fitness classes Xmas New Year **Conf** Class 70 Board 70 Thtr 250 **Services** Lift **Parking** 200 **Notes** Civ Wed 130

C

CAMBRIDGE
Cambridgeshire   Map 12 TL45

Hotel Felix
★★★★ 81% ◉◉ HOTEL

tel: 01223 277977 **Whitehouse Ln, Huntingdon Rd CB3 OLX**
email: help@hotelfelix.co.uk **web:** www.hotelfelix.co.uk
dir: *M11 junct 13. From A1 N, take A14 onto A1307. At 'City of Cambridge' sign left into Whitehouse Ln*

A beautiful Victorian mansion set amidst three acres of landscaped gardens, this property was originally built in 1852 for a surgeon from the famous Addenbrookes Hospital. The contemporary-style bedrooms have carefully chosen furniture and many thoughtful touches, while public rooms feature an open-plan bar, the adjacent Graffiti restaurant and a small quiet lounge.

Rooms 52 (5 fmly) (26 GF) ⟨ **S** £205-£315; **D** £220-£345 (incl. bkfst)* **Facilities** STV WiFi ☼ Xmas New Year **Conf** Class 36 Board 34 Thtr 60 **Services** Lift **Parking** 90 **Notes** LB Civ Wed 60

The Gonville Hotel
★★★★ 80% HOTEL

tel: 01223 366611 & 221111 **Gonville Place CB1 1LY**
email: info@gonvillehotel.co.uk **web:** www.gonvillehotel.co.uk
dir: *M11 junct 11, on A1309 follow city centre signs. At 2nd mini rdbt right into Lensfield Rd, over junct with lights. Hotel 25yds on right*

This is a well-established hotel situated on the inner ring road, a short walk across the green from the city centre. The air-conditioned public areas are cheerfully furnished, and include a lounge bar and brasserie. Bedrooms are well appointed and appealing, offering a good range of facilities for both corporate and leisure guests.

Rooms 84 (2 fmly) (8 GF) ⟨ **S** £99-£150; **D** £115-£270 (incl. bkfst)* **Facilities** FTV WiFi ☼ HL ♫ New Year **Conf** Class 30 Board 30 Thtr 50 **Services** Lift Air con **Parking** 80 **Notes** LB RS 24-29 Dec

The Varsity Hotel & Spa
★★★★ 80% HOTEL

tel: 01223 306030 **Thompson's Ln CB5 8AQ**
email: info@thevarsityhotel.co.uk **web:** www.thevarsityhotel.co.uk
dir: *M11 junct 13, pass Park & Ride, next rdbt 1st left, right at next junct into Bridge St, right into Thompou's Lane*

Situated close to the River Cam and occupying a central location, The Varsity Hotel is a stylish property. The bedrooms are smartly decorated and have all the expected facilities including power showers, CD players and free internet access. The River Bar, to the side of the hotel, has a buzzing atmosphere and offers a range of popular dishes. The hotel has a health club and spa, and a roof top bar.

Rooms 42 (2 fmly) ⟨ **D** £150-£550 (incl. bkfst)* **Facilities** Spa FTV WiFi ☼ Gym Sauna Steam room Valet parking New Year **Conf** Class 40 Board 30 Thtr 60 **Services** Lift Air con **Notes** Civ Wed 60

Best Western Plus Cambridge Quy Mill Hotel   Best Western PLUS
★★★★ 79% ◉◉ HOTEL

tel: 01223 293383 & 378110 **Church Rd, Stow Cum Quy CB25 9AF**
email: info@cambridgequymill.co.uk **web:** www.cambridgequymill.co.uk
dir: *Exit A14 at junct 35, E of Cambridge, onto B1102 for 50yds. Entrance opposite church*

Set in open countryside, this 19th-century former watermill is conveniently situated for access to Cambridge. Bedroom styles differ, yet each room is smartly appointed and brightly decorated; superior, spacious courtyard rooms are noteworthy. Well-designed public areas include several spacious bar/lounges, with a choice of casual and formal eating areas; service is both friendly and helpful. There is a smart leisure club with state-of-the-art equipment, as well as a health spa.

Rooms 51 (30 annexe) (4 fmly) (24 GF) ⟨ **S** £95-£195; **D** £125-£235* **Facilities** Spa FTV WiFi ☼ HL ⊞ Gym Sauna Steam room Wellness suite New Year **Conf** Class 30 Board 24 Thtr 80 Del from £175 to £210* **Parking** 90 **Notes** ⊗ RS 25 Dec Civ Wed 80

Hotel du Vin Cambridge   Hotel du Vin & Bistro
★★★★ 77% ◉ TOWN HOUSE HOTEL

tel: 01223 227330 & 0844 736 4253
(Calls cost 5p per minute plus your phone company's access charge)
15-19 Trumpington St CB2 1QA
email: info.cambridge@hotelduvin.com **web:** www.hotelduvin.com
dir: *M11 junct 11 Cambridge S, pass Trumpington Park & Ride on left. Hotel 2m on right after double rdbt*

This beautiful building, which dates back in part to medieval times, has been transformed to enhance its many quirky architectural features. The bedrooms and suites, some with private terraces, have the company's trademark monsoon showers and Egyptian linen. The French-style bistro has an open kitchen and the bar is set in the unusual labyrinth of vaulted cellar rooms. Other parts of the hotel include a library, a specialist wine-tasting room and a private dining room.

Rooms 41 (3 annexe) (6 GF) ⟨ **Facilities** STV WiFi Xmas New Year **Conf** Class 18 Board 18 Thtr 30 **Services** Lift Air con **Parking** 24

C

C

CAMBRIDGE *continued*

Hallmark Hotel Cambridge

★★★★ 76% HOTEL

tel: 0330 028 3400 **Bar Hill CB23 8EU**
email: cambridge@hallmarkhotels.co.uk **web:** www.hallmarkhotels.co.uk
dir: *M11 junct 13, A14, follow signs for Huntingdon. Take B1050 Bar Hill, hotel 1st exit on rdbt*

The Hallmark Hotel Cambridge is ideally situated in 200 acres of open countryside, just five miles from the university city of Cambridge. Public rooms include a brasserie restaurant and the popular Gallery Bar. The contemporary-style bedrooms are smartly decorated and equipped with a good range of useful facilities. The hotel also has a leisure club, swimming pool and golf course.

Rooms 136 (35 fmly) (68 GF) (4 smoking) **D** fr £95 (incl. dinner)* **Facilities** STV FTV WiFi ☼ HL ⏁ ⚘ 18 ⛳ Putt green Gym Hair & beauty salon Steam room Sauna Xmas New Year **Conf** Class 90 Board 45 Thtr 220 Del from £140* **Services** Lift **Parking** 200 **Notes** LB Civ Wed 200

The Lensfield Hotel

★★★ 80% METRO HOTEL

tel: 01223 355017 **53-57 Lensfield Rd CB2 1EN**
email: reservations@lensfieldhotel.co.uk **web:** www.lensfieldhotel.co.uk
dir: *M11 juncts 11, 12 or 13, follow signs to city centre. Access via Silver St, Trumpington St, left into Lensfield Rd*

Located close to all the city's attractions, this constantly improving hotel provides a range of attractive bedrooms, equipped with thoughtful extras. Comprehensive breakfasts are taken in an elegant dining room, and a comfortable bar and cosy foyer lounge are also available.

Rooms 40 (3 fmly) (4 GF) **Facilities** Spa STV FTV WiFi ☼ HL Gym Thermal suite Fitness suite **Services** Air con **Parking** 5 **Notes** ⊗ Closed last 2 wks in Dec-4 Jan

Arundel House Hotel

★★★ 78% HOTEL

tel: 01223 367701 **Chesterton Rd CB4 3AN**
email: info@arundelhousehotels.co.uk **web:** www.arundelhousehotels.co.uk
dir: *In city centre on A1303*

Overlooking the River Cam and enjoying views of open parkland, this popular and smart hotel was originally a row of townhouses dating from Victorian times.

Bedrooms are attractive and have a special character. The smart public areas feature a conservatory for informal snacks, a spacious bar and an elegant restaurant for more serious dining.

Rooms 103 (22 annexe) (7 fmly) (14 GF) **Facilities** FTV WiFi ☼ New Year **Conf** Class 24 Board 22 Thtr 50 **Parking** 70 **Notes** LB ⊗ Closed 25-26 Dec

Centennial Hotel

★★★ 75% HOTEL

tel: 01223 314652 **63-71 Hills Rd CB2 1PG**
email: reception@centennialhotel.co.uk **web:** www.centennialhotel.co.uk
dir: *M11 junct 11, A1309 to Cambridge. Right into Brooklands Ave to end. Left, hotel 100yds on right*

This friendly hotel is convenient for the railway station and town centre. Well-presented public areas include a welcoming lounge, a relaxing bar and restaurant on the lower-ground level. Bedrooms are generally spacious, well maintained and thoughtfully equipped with a good range of facilities; several rooms are available on the ground floor.

Rooms 39 (1 fmly) (7 GF) ✆ **Facilities** FTV WiFi ☼ **Conf** Class 25 Board 25 Thtr 25 **Parking** 28 **Notes** ⊗ Closed 23 Dec-1 Jan

Ashley Hotel

★★ 79% METRO HOTEL

tel: 01223 350059 & 367701 **74-76 Chesterton Rd CB4 1ER**
email: info@arundelhousehotels.co.uk **web:** www.arundelhousehotels.co.uk
dir: *On city centre ring road*

Expect a warm welcome at this delightful Victorian property situated just a short walk from the River Cam. The smartly decorated bedrooms are generally quite spacious and equipped with a good range of useful extras. Breakfast is served at individual tables in the smart lower ground floor dining room.

Rooms 16 (5 fmly) (5 GF) **Facilities** FTV WiFi ☼ **Parking** 12 **Notes** ⊗ Closed 24-26 Dec

C

Premier Inn Cambridge (A14 Jct 32)

BUDGET HOTEL

tel: 0871 527 8186 *(Calls cost 13p per minute plus your phone company's access charge)*
Ring Fort Rd CB4 2GW
web: www.premierinn.com
dir: *A14 junct 32, follow B1049/city centre signs. At 1st lights left into Kings Hedges Rd, 2nd left into Ring Fort Rd*

High quality, budget accommodation ideal for both families and business travellers. Spacious, en suite bedrooms feature tea and coffee making facilities, and Freeview TV in most hotels. Internet access and WiFi are available for a small fee. The adjacent family restaurant features a wide and varied menu. See also the Hotel Groups pages.

Rooms 154

Premier Inn Cambridge City Centre

BUDGET HOTEL

tel: 0871 527 9396 *(Calls cost 13p per minute plus your phone company's access charge)*
Newmarket Rd CB1 3EP
web: www.premierinn.com
dir: *M11 junct 12, A603, left at mini rdbt then take 2nd exit at next rdbt (continue on A603). Through lights, at rdbt take 3rd exit onto A1134 signed Ring Road, Newmarket & Airport. Hotel on right*

Rooms 120

CAMBRIDGE SERVICES   Map 12 TL36
Cambridgeshire

Days Inn Cambridge - A1

AA Advertised

tel: 01954 267176 **Cambridge Extra Services, Junction A14/M11 CB23 4WU**
email: cambridge.hotel@welcomebreak.co.uk **web:** www.welcomebreak.co.uk
dir: *A14/M11 Cambridge Extra Services*

This modern, purpose built accommodation offers smartly appointed, well-equipped bedrooms, with good power showers. There is a choice of adjacent food outlets where guests may enjoy breakfast, snacks and meals.

Rooms 82 (14 fmly) (40 GF) (19 smoking) **Facilities** FTV WiFi ⌁ **Services** Air con **Parking** 120

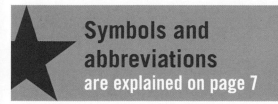

Symbols and abbreviations are explained on page 7

Find your way
with the online AA Route Planner:
www.theaa.com/route-planner

CANNOCK   Map 10 SJ91
Staffordshire

Premier Inn Cannock (Orbital)

BUDGET HOTEL

tel: 0871 527 8190 *(Calls cost 13p per minute plus your phone company's access charge)*
Eastern Way WS11 8XR
web: www.premierinn.com
dir: *N'bound: M6 (Toll) junct 7, A5. At rdbt 1st exit (A5), 4th exit onto A460, 1st exit. S'bound: (no access from M6 Toll). M6 junct 11, A460 signed Cannock. At next 2 rdbts take 3rd exit. At next rdbt 1st exit onto service road. Hotel adjacent to Orbital Brewers Fayre*

High quality, budget accommodation ideal for both families and business travellers. Spacious, en suite bedrooms feature tea and coffee making facilities, and Freeview TV in most hotels. Internet access and WiFi are available for a small fee. The adjacent family restaurant features a wide and varied menu. See also the Hotel Groups pages.

Rooms 21

Premier Inn Cannock South

BUDGET HOTEL

tel: 0871 527 8192 *(Calls cost 13p per minute plus your phone company's access charge)*
Watling St WS11 1SJ
web: www.premierinn.com
dir: *At junct of A5 & A460, 2m from M6 juncts 11 & 12*

Rooms 60

CANTERBURY   Map 7 TR15
Kent

ABode Canterbury
★★★★ 82% ◉◉ HOTEL   **ABode** HOTELS

tel: 01227 766266 & 826678 **High St CT1 2RX**
email: reservations@abodecanterbury.co.uk **web:** www.abodecanterbury.co.uk
dir: *M2 junct 7. Follow Canterbury signs onto ring road. At Wincheap rdbt turn into city. Left into Rosemary Ln, into Stour St. Hotel at end*

ABode Canterbury is a stylish hotel set on Canterbury's main street. A range of well appointed bedrooms and suites are available, many retaining original features, all boasting modern facilities and smart en suites. A choice of dining options and bars include The County Restaurant, a smart Champagne Bar, and the more relaxed and hip Old Brewery Tavern.

Rooms 72 (10 fmly) ⌁ **S** £99-£225; **D** £99-£550* **Facilities** FTV WiFi ⌁ Gym Xmas New Year **Conf** Class 48 Board 20 Thtr 140 Del from £150 to £195 **Services** Lift Air con **Parking** 44 **Notes** LB ⊗ Civ Wed 100

C

CANTERBURY *continued*

Best Western Abbots Barton Hotel

BW Best Western.

★★★ 79% @ HOTEL

tel: 01227 760341 **New Dover Rd CT1 3DU**
email: info@abbotsbartonhotel.com **web:** www.abbotsbartonhotel.com
dir: *Phone for directions*

Abbots Barton Hotel is in a central location, just a 10-minute walk from the city centre, and benefits from two acres of gardens and on-site parking. Bedrooms are comfortably appointed throughout, traditional in style yet with all modern amenities including free WiFi and digital TV. The bar and restaurant are open daily, and there are good function facilities with a private bar and patio - ideal for conferences and weddings.

Rooms 53 (3 fmly) (6 GF) **S** £85-£105; **D** £105-£130 (incl. bkfst)* **Facilities** STV FTV WiFi ⇗ Xmas New Year **Conf** Class 60 Board 60 Thtr 130 Del from £129 to £149* **Services** Lift Air con **Parking** 40 **Notes** LB Civ Wed 80

Castle House

★★★ 73% METRO HOTEL

tel: 01227 761897 **28 Castle St CT1 2PT**
email: info@castlehousehotel.co.uk **web:** www.castlehousehotel.co.uk
dir: *Next to Canterbury Castle*

Conveniently located in the city centre opposite the imposing ruins of the ancient Norman castle; part of the building dates back to the 1730s. Bedrooms are spacious, all with en suite facilities and many useful extras, such as WiFi. There is a walled garden in which to relax during the warmer months.

Rooms 15

Premier Inn Canterbury City Centre

Premier Inn

BUDGET HOTEL

tel: 0871 527 9408 *(Calls cost 13p per minute plus your phone company's access charge)*
New Dover Rd CT1 1UP
web: www.premierinn.com
dir: *M2 junct 7. At Brenley Corner rdbt 4th exit onto A2. Left then merge onto A2050. At London Rd rdbt 2nd exit (A2050). At St Peters rdbt 3rd exit onto A290. At Wincheap rdbt 2nd exit onto A28. At St Georges rdbt 2nd exit onto A257. At lights right (A257). At lights right onto A2050. Hotel in view*

High quality, budget accommodation ideal for both families and business travellers. Spacious, en suite bedrooms feature tea and coffee making facilities, and Freeview TV in most hotels. Internet access and WiFi are available for a small fee. The adjacent family restaurant features a wide and varied menu. See also the Hotel Groups pages.

Rooms 120

CARBIS BAY

See **St Ives (Cornwall)**

CARLISLE
Cumbria

Map 18 NY35

Crown Hotel

★★★★ 76% @ HOTEL

tel: 01228 561888 **Station Rd, Wetheral CA4 8ES**
email: info@crownhotelwetheral.co.uk **web:** www.crownhotelwetheral.co.uk
dir: *M6 junct 42, B6263 to Wetheral, right at village shop, car park at rear of hotel*

Set in the attractive village of Wetheral, with landscaped gardens to the rear, this hotel is well suited for both business and leisure guests, as well as families. There are more than fifty bedrooms in a variety of sizes and styles, and include two apartments in an adjacent house, ideal for longer stays. A choice of dining options is available, with the popular Waltons Bar as an informal alternative to the main Conservatory Restaurant. Weddings and conferences can be catered for, and there are also leisure club facilities which include a swimming pool, jacuzzi, squash court, two gyms, and a sauna.

Rooms 51 (2 annexe) (10 fmly) (3 GF) ⌁ **S** £60-£70; **D** £85-£139 (incl. bkfst)* **Facilities** Spa STV WiFi HL ⊛ supervised Gym Squash Children's splash pool Steam room Beauty room Sauna Dance studio Xmas New Year **Conf** Class 60 Board 65 Thtr 140 Del from £130 to £145* **Parking** 55 **Notes** LB Civ Wed 120

Hallmark Hotel Carlisle

★★★★ 74% HOTEL

tel: 0330 028 3401 **Court Square CA1 1QY**
email: carlisle@hallmarkhotels.co.uk **web:** www.hallmarkhotels.co.uk
dir: M6 junct 43, to city centre, then follow road to left & railway station

This hotel is at the heart of the town, opposite the railway station. Most of the bedrooms have benefited from an investment programme, and the smart ground-floor areas include a popular bar and restaurant. A number of meeting rooms are available and at the rear of the hotel is a small car park.

Rooms 70 (3 fmly) ⋔ **Facilities** FTV WiFi Xmas New Year **Conf** Class 100 Board 30 Thtr 240 **Services** Lift **Parking** 26 **Notes** ⊗ Civ Wed 200

The Crown & Mitre

★★★ 74% HOTEL

PEEL HOTELS PLC

tel: 01228 525491 **4 English St CA3 8HZ**
email: info@crownandmitre-hotel-carlisle.com
web: www.crownandmitre-hotel-carlisle.com
dir: A6 to city centre, pass station on left. Turn left at end of English St, then immediate right onto Blackfriars St

Located in the heart of the city, this Edwardian hotel is close to the cathedral and a few minutes' walk from the castle. Bedrooms vary in size and style, from smart executive rooms to more functional standard rooms. Public rooms include a comfortable lounge area and the lovely bar with its feature stained-glass windows.

Rooms 95 (20 annexe) (4 fmly) ⋔ **Facilities** STV FTV WiFi ⌖ ⊛ Xmas New Year **Conf** Class 250 Board 50 Thtr 100 **Services** Lift **Parking** 42 **Notes** Civ Wed 200

Premier Inn Carlisle Central

BUDGET HOTEL

tel: 0871 527 8210 *(Calls cost 13p per minute plus your phone company's access charge)*
Warwick Rd CA1 2WF
web: www.premierinn.com
dir: M6 junct 43, on A69

High quality, budget accommodation ideal for both families and business travellers. Spacious, en suite bedrooms feature tea and coffee making facilities, and Freeview TV in most hotels. Internet access and WiFi are available for a small fee. The adjacent family restaurant features a wide and varied menu. See also the Hotel Groups pages.

Rooms 65

Premier Inn Carlisle Central North

BUDGET HOTEL

tel: 0871 527 8212 *(Calls cost 13p per minute plus your phone company's access charge)*
Kingstown Rd CA3 0AT
web: www.premierinn.com
dir: M6 junct 44, A7 towards Carlisle, hotel 1m on left

Rooms 49

Premier Inn Carlisle (M6 Jct 42)

BUDGET HOTEL

tel: 0871 527 8206 *(Calls cost 13p per minute plus your phone company's access charge)*
Carleton CA4 0AD
web: www.premierinn.com
dir: Just off M6 junct 42, S of Carlisle

Rooms 80

Premier Inn Carlisle (M6 Jct 44)

BUDGET HOTEL

tel: 0871 527 8208 *(Calls cost 13p per minute plus your phone company's access charge)*
Parkhouse Rd CA3 0JR
web: www.premierinn.com
dir: M6 junct 44, A7 signed Carlisle. Hotel on right at 1st set of lights

Rooms 127

Ibis Carlisle

AA Advertised

tel: 01228 518000 **Portlands, Botchergate CA1 1RP**
email: H3443@accor.com **web:** www.ibishotel.com
dir: M6 junct 42/43 follow signs for city centre. Hotel on Botchergate

Modern, budget hotel offering comfortable accommodation in bright and practical bedrooms. Breakfast is self-service and dinner is available in the restaurant

Rooms 102 (17 fmly) ⋔ **Facilities** STV FTV WiFi ⌖ HL **Services** Lift Air con

CARTMEL	Map 18 SD37
Cumbria	

Aynsome Manor Hotel

★★★ 82% ⊛ COUNTRY HOUSE HOTEL

tel: 015395 36653 **LA11 6HH**
email: aynsomemanor@btconnect.com **web:** www.aynsomemanorhotel.co.uk
dir: M6 junct 36, A590 signed Barrow-in-Furness towards Cartmel. Left at end of road, hotel before village

Dating back, in part, to the early 16th century, this manor house overlooks the fells and the nearby priory. Spacious bedrooms, including some courtyard rooms, are comfortably furnished. Dinner in the elegant restaurant features local produce whenever possible, and there is a choice of lounges to relax in.

Rooms 12 (2 annexe) (2 fmly) ⋔ **S** £75–£110; **D** £80–£130 (incl. bkfst)*
Facilities FTV WiFi New Year **Parking** 20 **Notes** LB Closed 2-31 Jan

C

CARTMEL *continued*

L'Enclume

⊚⊚⊚⊚⊚ RESTAURANT WITH ROOMS

tel: 015395 36362 **Cavendish St LA11 6PZ**
email: info@lenclume.co.uk **web:** www.lenclume.co.uk
dir: *From A590 turn left for Cartmel before Newby Bridge*

L'Enclume is a delightful 13th-century property in the heart of a lovely village, and offers top notch 21st-century cooking that draws foodies from far and wide. Once the village forge (l'enclume is French for 'the anvil') it's now the location for some of Britain's best food, and Simon Rogan's imaginative and adventurous cooking may be sampled in the stylish restaurant. Individually designed, modern, en suite rooms vary in size and style, and are either in the main property or dotted about the village only a few moments' walk from the restaurant.

Rooms 16 (11 annexe) (3 fmly)

CASTLE CARY
Somerset   **Map 4 ST63**

The Pilgrims

⊚⊚ 🍴 RESTAURANT WITH ROOMS

tel: 01963 240600 **Lovington BA7 7PT**
email: jools@thepilgrimsatlovington.co.uk **web:** www.thepilgrimsatlovington.co.uk
dir: *On B3153, 1.5m E of lights on A37 at Lydford*

The Pilgrims describes itself as 'the pub that thinks it's a restaurant', which is pretty accurate. With a real emphasis on fresh, local and carefully prepared produce, both dinner and breakfast are the focus of any stay here. In addition, the resident family proprietors provide a friendly and relaxed atmosphere. Comfortable and well-equipped bedrooms are available in the adjacent converted cider barn.

Rooms 5 (5 annexe)

CASTLE COMBE
Wiltshire   **Map 4 ST87**

The Manor House, an Exclusive Hotel & Golf Club

★★★★★ 84% ⊚⊚⊚ COUNTRY HOUSE HOTEL

tel: 01249 782206 **SN14 7HR**
email: enquiries@manorhouse.co.uk **web:** www.exclusive.co.uk
dir: *M4 junct 17 follow Chippenham signs onto A420 Bristol, then right onto B4039. Through village, right after bridge. Follow brown tourism signs to Castle Combe Racing Circuit*

This delightful hotel is situated in a secluded valley adjacent to a picturesque village, where there have been no new buildings for 300 years. There are 365 acres of grounds to enjoy, complete with an Italian garden and an 18-hole golf course. Bedrooms, some in the main house and some in a row of stone cottages, have been superbly furnished, and public rooms include a number of cosy lounges with roaring fires. Service is a pleasing blend of professionalism and friendliness. The award-winning food utilises top quality local produce.

Rooms 48 (27 annexe) (8 fmly) (13 GF) 🐾 **D** £215-£430 (incl. bkfst)* **Facilities** STV WiFi ↙ 18 ⛳ Putt green Fishing 🦢 Beauty treatment room Jogging track Giant games on lawns Xmas New Year **Conf** Class 50 Board 34 Thtr 100 Del from £165* **Parking** 100 **Notes** LB Civ Wed 110

CASTLE DONINGTON

See **East Midlands Airport**

CASTLEFORD
West Yorkshire   **Map 16 SE42**

Premier Inn Castleford M62 Jct 31

BUDGET HOTEL

tel: 0871 527 8216 *(Calls cost 13p per minute plus your phone company's access charge)*
Pioneer Way WF10 5TG
web: www.premierinn.com
dir: *M62 junct 31, A655 towards Castleford, right at 1st lights, then left*

High quality, budget accommodation ideal for both families and business travellers. Spacious, en suite bedrooms feature tea and coffee making facilities, and Freeview TV in most hotels. Internet access and WiFi are available for a small fee. The adjacent family restaurant features a wide and varied menu. See also the Hotel Groups pages.

Rooms 62

Premier Inn Castleford (Xscape, M62 Jct 32)

BUDGET HOTEL   Premier Inn

tel: 0871 527 8218 *(Calls cost 13p per minute plus your phone company's access charge)*
Colarado Way WF10 4TA
web: www.premierinn.com
dir: *M62 junct 32, follow signs for Xscape. Hotel adjacent to Xscape complex*

Rooms 119

CATTERICK
North Yorkshire   **Map 19 SE29**

Premier Inn Catterick Garrison

BUDGET HOTEL   Premier Inn

tel: 0871 527 9568 *(Calls cost 13p per minute plus your phone company's access charge)*
Princes Gate DL9 3BA
web: www.premierinn.com
dir: *A1 towards Wetherby, right onto A6136 (Catterick Garrison). At 1st rdbt take 1st exit (A6136/Richmond), straight on at 4 mini rdbts. At 5th rdbt 3rd exit, hotel on left*

High quality, budget accommodation ideal for both families and business travellers. Spacious, en suite bedrooms feature tea and coffee making facilities, and Freeview TV in most hotels. Internet access and WiFi are available for a small fee. The adjacent family restaurant features a wide and varied menu. See also the Hotel Groups pages.

Rooms 60

C

CAVENDISH
Suffolk   Map 13 TL84

The George

◎◎ 🍴 RESTAURANT WITH ROOMS

tel: 01787 280248 **The Green CO10 8BA**
email: thegeorgecavendish@gmail.com **web:** www.thecavendishgeorge.co.uk
dir: *A1092 into Cavendish, The George next to village green*

The George is situated in the heart of the pretty village of Cavendish and has five very stylish bedrooms which have retained many of their original features, as well as being very comfortable and spacious. The front-facing rooms overlook the village. The award-winning restaurant is very well appointed and dinner should not be missed. Guests are guaranteed to receive a warm welcome, attentive friendly service and great food.

Rooms 5 (1 fmly)

CHADDESLEY CORBETT
Worcestershire   Map 10 SO87

INSPECTORS' CHOICE

Brockencote Hall Country House Hotel

★★★★ ◎◎◎ 🍴 COUNTRY HOUSE HOTEL

tel: 01562 777876 **DY10 4PY**
email: info@brockencotehall.com **web:** www.brockencotehall.com
dir: *A38 to Bromsgrove, off A448 towards Kidderminster*

Brockencote Hall Hotel is a Victorian country manor house hotel set in 70 acres of beautiful parkland, complete with a scenic lake, tennis courts and dovecote. A fountain adorns the approach, the terrace and gardens have been freshly landscaped, and the private dining rooms, restaurant and public areas are classically decorated in gentle greys, lavenders and damson velvets. Head Chef Adam Brown creates inspired dishes that revolve around the seasons and local suppliers, with a focus on the purity of flavours.

Rooms 21 (4 fmly) (5 GF) 🐾 **S** £115-£335; **D** £135-£365 (incl. bkfst)
Facilities FTV WiFi ⌨ 🏊 Fishing 🚣 Xmas New Year **Conf** Class 35 Board 35 Thtr 80 Del £215 **Parking** 60 **Notes** ⊗ Civ Wed 90

CHAGFORD
Devon   Map 3 SX78

INSPECTORS' CHOICE

Gidleigh Park

★★★★★ 🍴 COUNTRY HOUSE HOTEL

tel: 01647 432367 **TQ13 8HH**
email: info@gidleigh.co.uk **web:** www.gidleigh.co.uk
dir: *From Chagford, right at Lloyds Bank into Mill St. After 150yds fork right. 2m to end*

Built in 1928 as a private residence for an Australian shipping magnate and set in 107 acres of lovingly tended grounds, this world-renowned hotel retains a timeless charm and a very endearing, homely atmosphere. The individually styled bedrooms are sumptuously furnished; some with separate seating areas, some with balconies and many enjoying panoramic views. There are spa suites, a loft suite which is ideal for families, and the stunning thatched Pavilion in the grounds. The latter has two bedrooms, two bathrooms, a lounge and kitchen diner. The spacious public areas feature antique furniture, beautiful flower arrangements and magnificent artwork. All of this is topped off with accomplished cuisine to complete the Gidleigh experience.

Rooms 24 (3 annexe) (4 fmly) (3 GF) 🐾 **Facilities** STV FTV WiFi 🏌 Putt green Fishing 🎳 Bowls Xmas New Year **Conf** Class 22 Board 18 Thtr 22 **Parking** 45

Mill End Hotel

Ⓤ

tel: 01647 432282 **Dartmoor National Park TQ13 8JN**
email: info@millendhotel.com **web:** www.millendhotel.com
dir: *From A30 at Whiddon Down take A382 to Moretonhampstead. In 3.5m hump back bridge at Sandy Park, hotel on right*

Currently the rating for this establishment is not confirmed. This may be due to a change of ownership or because it has only recently joined the AA rating scheme. For further details please see the AA website: theAA.com

Rooms 20 **Conf** Class 20 Board 30 Thtr 30

C

CHANDLER'S CROSS
Hertfordshire   Map 6 TQ09

The Grove
★★★★★ ◉◉◉ HOTEL

tel: 01923 807807 **WD3 4TG**
email: info@thegrove.co.uk **web:** www.thegrove.co.uk
dir: M25 junct 19, A411 towards Watford. Hotel on right

Set amid 300 acres of rolling countryside, much of which is golf course, the hotel combines historic features with cutting-edge, modern design. The spacious bedrooms have the latest in temperature control, lighting technology and flat-screen TVs; many have balconies. Suites in the original mansion are particularly stunning. Championship golf, a world-class spa and three dining options are just a few of the treasures to sample here. The hotel also has extensive crèche facilities. The hotel has three dining options - Collette's with 3 AA Rosettes that offers fine dining, and a more relaxed style in the Glasshouse and Stables restaurants. The walled garden is also well worth exploring.

Rooms 217 (69 fmly) (35 GF) 🐾 **Facilities** Spa STV FTV WiFi ⌕ ⊗ supervised ⟡ supervised ⚓ 18 ⛳ Putt green ⛳ Gym Walk & cycle trails Giant chess Driving range Kids club Games room Xmas New Year **Conf** Class 300 Board 78 Thtr 450 **Services** Lift Air con **Parking** 400 **Notes** ⊗ Civ Wed 450

CHARD
Somerset   Map 4 ST30

Cricket St Thomas Hotel
WARNER LEISURE HOTELS

★★★★ 75% COUNTRY HOUSE HOTEL

tel: 01460 30111 **TA20 4DD**
email: cricket.sales@bourne-leisure.co.uk **web:** www.warnerleisurehotels.co.uk
dir: M5 junct 25, A358 towards Chard, A30 to Crewkerne. Hotel 3m from Chard

This Grade II listed house has an interesting history, including the fact that Lord Nelson and Lady Hamilton were frequent visitors. The hotel is set in splendid parkland, with colourful gardens, lakes, and a unique woodland area. Various holiday packages are available, and there are extensive leisure facilities, as well as live entertainment and various dining venues, including Fenocchi's, with an Italian-themed menu. The bedrooms are spacious and well appointed. Please note that this is an adults-only (over 21 years) hotel.

Rooms 239 (84 GF) 🐾 **Facilities** Spa FTV WiFi HL ⊗ ⛳ Putt green ⛳ Gym Rifle shooting Archery ♫ Xmas New Year **Conf** Class 50 Board 25 Thtr 80 **Services** Lift **Parking** 351 **Notes** ⊗ No children 21yrs Civ Wed 80

Lordleaze Hotel
THE INDEPENDENTS
HOTEL ASSOCIATION

★★★ 77% HOTEL

tel: 01460 61066 **Henderson Dr, Forton Rd TA20 2HW**
email: info@lordleazehotel.com **web:** www.lordleazehotel.com
dir: A358 from Chard, left at St Mary's Church to Forton & Winsham on B3162. Follow signs to hotel

Conveniently and quietly located, this hotel is close to the Devon, Dorset and Somerset borders, and only minutes from Chard. All bedrooms are well equipped and comfortable. The friendly lounge bar has a wood-burning stove and serves tempting bar meals. The conservatory restaurant offers more formal dining.

Rooms 25 (2 fmly) (7 GF) 🐾 S £79-£90; D £125-£135* **Facilities** FTV WiFi Xmas New Year **Conf** Class 60 Board 40 Thtr 180 Del from £130 to £145* **Parking** 55 **Notes** LB Civ Wed 100

CHARMOUTH
Dorset   Map 4 SY39

Fernhill Hotel
★★★ 82% HOTEL

tel: 01297 560492 **Fernhill DT6 6BX**
email: mail@fernhill-hotel.co.uk **web:** www.fernhill-hotel.co.uk
dir: A35 onto A3052 to Lyme Regis. Hotel 0.25m on left

Fernhill is a small, friendly hotel in well-tended grounds on top of a hill. It boasts an outdoor pool and treatment rooms, together with elegant public areas. Each of the comfortable bedrooms is individually styled and many have views of the Char Valley and beyond. The menus are based on seasonal, locally sourced produce.

Rooms 10 (1 fmly) 🐾 **Facilities** FTV WiFi ⌕ ⟡ Fishing Holistic treatment centre Massage baths Xmas **Conf** Class 20 Board 24 Thtr 100 **Parking** 48 **Notes** LB ⊗ Closed 31 Dec-30 Jan Civ Wed 100

C

CHARNOCK RICHARD MOTORWAY SERVICE AREA (M6)   Map 15 SD51
Lancashire

Days Inn Charnock Richard - M6
AA Advertised

tel: 01257 791746 **Welcome Break Service Area PR7 5LR**
email: charnockhotel@welcomebreak.co.uk **web:** www.welcomebreak.co.uk
dir: *Between junct 27 & 28 of M6 N'bound. 500yds from Camelot Theme Park via Mill Lane*

This modern building offers accommodation in smart, spacious and well-equipped bedrooms, suitable for families and business travellers, and all with en suite bathrooms. Continental breakfast is available and other refreshments may be taken at the nearby family restaurant.

Rooms 100 (68 fmly) (32 GF) (20 smoking) **Facilities** FTV WiFi ᐳ **Conf** Class 16 Board 24 Thtr 40 **Parking** 100

CHATHAM   Map 7 TQ76
Kent

Bridgewood Manor
★★★★ 80% HOTEL

QHOTELS
INSPIRED BY YOU

tel: 01634 201333 **Bridgewood Roundabout, Walderslade Woods ME5 9AX**
email: bridgewoodmanor@qhotels.co.uk **web:** www.qhotels.co.uk
dir: *Adjacent to Bridgewood rdbt on A229. Take 3rd exit signed Walderslade & Lordswood. Hotel 50mtrs on left*

Bridgewood Manor is a modern, purpose-built hotel situated on the outskirts of Rochester. Bedrooms are pleasantly decorated, comfortably furnished and equipped with many thoughtful touches. The hotel has an excellent range of leisure and conference facilities. Guests can dine in the informal Terrace Bistro or experience fine dining in the more formal Squires restaurant, where the service is both attentive and friendly.

Rooms 100 (12 fmly) (26 GF) **Facilities** Spa FTV WiFi ⏱ supervised 🏊 Gym Beauty treatments Xmas New Year **Conf** Class 110 Board 80 Thtr 200 **Services** Lift **Parking** 170 **Notes** Civ Wed 130

CHATHILL   Map 21 NU12
Northumberland

Doxford Hall Hotel & Spa
★★★★ ◎◎ COUNTRY HOUSE HOTEL

tel: 01665 589700 **NE67 5DN**
email: info@doxfordhall.com **web:** www.doxfordhall.com
dir: *8m N of Alnwick just off A1, signed Christon Bank & Seahouses. Take B6347 follow signs for hotel*

A beautiful country-house hotel set in a private estate, surrounded by countryside and convenient for visiting nearby historic towns and attractions. Bedrooms are spacious and luxuriously furnished, each named after Northumbrian Castles. The dining room and lounges are very attractive. There is an impressive grand staircase and beautiful wood throughout the hotel. The spa adds to the range of facilities.

Rooms 34 (3 annexe) (1 fmly) (11 GF) ✿ **S** £79-£200; **D** £99-£280 (incl. bkfst)*
Facilities Spa FTV WiFi ᐳ HL ⏱ supervised Gym Sauna Steam room Xmas New Year **Conf** Class 100 Board 22 Thtr 250 Del from £129 to £160* **Services** Lift **Parking** 100 **Notes** Civ Wed 250

CHEADLE   Map 16 SJ88
Greater Manchester

Premier Inn Manchester (Cheadle)
BUDGET HOTEL

tel: 0871 527 8728 *(Calls cost 13p per minute plus your phone company's access charge)*
Royal Crescent SK8 3FE
web: www.premierinn.com
dir: *Exit A34 at Cheadle Royal rdbt behind TGI Friday's*

High quality, budget accommodation ideal for both families and business travellers. Spacious, en suite bedrooms feature tea and coffee making facilities, and Freeview TV in most hotels. Internet access and WiFi are available for a small fee. The adjacent family restaurant features a wide and varied menu. See also the Hotel Groups pages.

Rooms 65

C

CHELMSFORD
Essex
Map 6 TL70

Pontlands Park
★★★ 83% HOTEL

tel: 01245 476444 **West Hanningfield Rd, Great Baddow CM2 8HR**
email: sales@pontlandsparkhotel.co.uk **web:** www.heritageleisure.co.uk
dir: A12, A130 , A1114 to Chelmsford. 1st exit at rdbt, 1st slip road on left. Left towards
Great Baddow, 1st left into West Hanningfield Rd. Hotel 400yds on left

A Victorian country-house hotel situated in a peaceful rural location amid attractive
landscaped grounds. The stylishly furnished bedrooms are generally quite spacious;
each is individually decorated and equipped with modern facilities. The elegant
public rooms include a tastefully furnished sitting room, a cosy lounge bar, smart
conservatory restaurant and an intimate dining room.

Rooms 35 (10 fmly) (11 GF) **Facilities** FTV WiFi 🐾 ⚲ Gym Beauty room
Conf Class 40 Board 40 Thtr 100 **Parking** 100 **Notes** ⊗ Closed 24-26 Dec
Civ Wed 100

County Hotel
★★★ 82% ⚙ HOTEL

tel: 01245 455700 **29 Rainsford Rd CM1 2PZ**
email: sales@countyhotelgroup.co.uk **web:** www.countyhotelgroup.co.uk
dir: From town centre, past rail & bus station. Hotel 300yds left beyond lights

This popular hotel is ideally situated within easy walking distance of the railway
station, bus depot and town centre. Stylish bedrooms offer spacious comfort and
plentiful extras including free WiFi. There are a smart restaurant, bar and lounge as
well as sunny outdoor terraces for making the most of warm weather. The hotel also
has a range of meeting rooms and banqueting facilities.

Rooms 50 🐾 **S** £60-£95; **D** £70-£140* **Facilities** FTV WiFi ⇣ HL Xmas New Year
Conf Class 84 Board 64 Thtr 160 Del from £125 to £175* **Services** Lift **Parking** 80
Notes LB ⊗ Closed 27-30 Dec Civ Wed 80

Best Western Ivy Hill
★★★ 81% HOTEL

tel: 01277 353040 & 355111 **Writtle Rd, Margaretting CM4 OEH**
email: sales@ivyhillhotel.co.uk **web:** www.heritageleisure.co.uk
dir: Just off A12 junct 14. Hotel on left at top of slip road

A smartly appointed hotel conveniently situated just off the A12. The spacious
bedrooms are tastefully decorated, have co-ordinated fabrics and all the expected
facilities. Public rooms include a choice of lounges, a cosy bar, a smart
conservatory and restaurant, as well as a range of conference and banqueting
facilities.

Rooms 31 (5 fmly) (9 GF) **Facilities** FTV WiFi ⇣ **Conf** Class 80 Board 40 Thtr 180
Parking 200 **Notes** ⊗ Closed 24-26 Dec Civ Wed 100

Best Western Atlantic Hotel

★★★ 77% HOTEL

tel: 01245 268168 **New St CM1 1PP**
email: info@atlantichotel.co.uk **web:** www.atlantichotel.co.uk
dir: From Chelmsford rail station, left into Victoria Rd, left at lights into New St, hotel
on right

Ideally situated just a short walk from the railway station with its quick links to
London, this modern, purpose-built hotel has contemporary-style bedrooms
equipped with modern facilities. The open-plan public areas include the Italian
Sapori Ristorante, a lounge bar and a conservatory.

Rooms 59 (3 fmly) (27 GF) 🐾 **S** £70-£145; **D** £70-£145* **Facilities** STV WiFi Gym
Complimentary use of facilities at Absalute Gym **Conf** Class 40 Board 10 Thtr 15
Del from £135 to £170* **Services** Air con **Parking** 60 **Notes** ⊗ Closed 23 Dec-3 Jan

Premier Inn Chelmsford (Boreham)
BUDGET HOTEL

tel: 0871 527 8220 (Calls cost 13p per minute plus your phone company's access charge)
Main Rd, Boreham CM3 3HJ
web: www.premierinn.com
dir: M25 junct 28, A12 to Colchester, B1137 to Boreham

High quality, budget accommodation ideal for both families and business
travellers. Spacious, en suite bedrooms feature tea and coffee making facilities,
and Freeview TV in most hotels. Internet access and WiFi are available for a small
fee. The adjacent family restaurant features a wide and varied menu. See also the
Hotel Groups pages.

Rooms 80

Premier Inn Chelmsford City Centre
BUDGET HOTEL

tel: 0871 527 9534 (Calls cost 13p per minute plus your phone company's access charge)
Victoria Rd CM1 1NY
web: www.premierinn.com
dir: A12 junct 15 (Harlow,Chelmsford/A414). At rdbt take A414 (3 Mile Hill). At next rdbt
take A41114. 1st exit at next rdbt (Moulsham St/B1007), continue into New London Rd.
Left into Parkway. At rdbt 2nd exit into Victoria St. At next rdbt 1st exit into Duke St. At
next rdbt 1st exit into Victoria Rd

Rooms 99

Premier Inn Chelmsford (Springfield)
BUDGET HOTEL

tel: 0871 527 8222 (Calls cost 13p per minute plus your phone company's access charge)
Chelmsford Service Area, Colchester Rd, Springfield CM2 5PY
web: www.premierinn.com
dir: At A12 junct 19, Chelmsford bypass, signed Chelmsford Service Area

Rooms 91

C

CHELTENHAM
Gloucestershire

Map 10 SO92

Ellenborough Park

★★★★★ 86% ⊛⊛⊛ COUNTRY HOUSE HOTEL

tel: 01242 545454 **Southam Rd GL52 3NH**
email: info@ellenboroughpark.com **web:** www.ellenboroughpark.com
dir: *A46 right after 3m onto B4079, merges with A435, 4m, over 3 rdbts, left onto Southam Lane, right onto Old Road, right onto B4632, hotel on right*

Set on the original Cheltenham Racecourse estate, this impressive hotel dates in part from the 16th century and has been beautifully restored. The Nina Campbell-designed bedrooms and suites are spread across the main house and adjacent buildings, and all feature superb beds, a great range of modern amenities, and luxurious bathrooms. The stylish Indian-themed spa has a gym and outdoor heated pool. There are two dining options; the modern Brasserie offers a country house menu, while the elegant, oak-panelled Beaufort dining room is more formal and offers a high standard of classic cuisine.

Rooms 61 (44 annexe) (16 fmly) (19 GF) ⟁ **S** fr £179; **D** fr £199 (incl. bkfst)*
Facilities Spa STV FTV WiFi ⅋ HL ⚲ ⚲ Gym Xmas New Year **Conf** Class 70 Board 40 Thtr 120 **Services** Lift Air con **Parking** 130 **Notes** LB Civ Wed 120

The Greenway Hotel & Spa

★★★★ 80% ⊛⊛ COUNTRY HOUSE HOTEL

tel: 01242 862352 **Shurdington GL51 4UG**
email: info@thegreenway.co.uk **web:** www.thegreenwayhotelandspa.com
dir: *From Cheltenham centre 2.5m S on A46*

This hotel, with a wealth of history, is peacefully located in a delightful setting within easy reach of the many attractions of the Cotswolds and also the M5. The Manor House bedrooms are luxuriously appointed - traditional in style yet with plasma TVs and internet access. The tranquil Coach House rooms, in the converted stable block, have direct access to the beautiful grounds. The attractive dining room overlooks the sunken garden and is the venue for excellent food, proudly served by dedicated and attentive staff.

Rooms 21 (8 annexe) (1 fmly) ⟁ **S** £139-£209; **D** £169-£419 (incl. bkfst)
Facilities Spa FTV WiFi ⚲ ⚲ Gym Xmas New Year **Conf** Board 18 Thtr 50 Del from £189 to £249 **Parking** 30 **Notes** LB Civ Wed 60

The Cheltenham Chase Hotel

★★★★ 80% HOTEL

tel: 01452 519988 **Shurdington Rd, Brockworth GL3 4PB**
email: cheltenhamreservations@qhotels.co.uk **web:** www.qhotels.co.uk
dir: *M5 junct 11a onto A417 Cirencester. 1st exit A46 to Stroud, hotel 500yds on left.*

Conveniently positioned for Cheltenham, Gloucester, and the M5, this hotel is set in landscaped grounds with ample parking. Bedrooms are spacious with attractive colour schemes and excellent facilities; executive rooms and suites benefit from air conditioning. Public areas include an open-plan bar/lounge, Hardy's restaurant, extensive meeting and functions rooms and a well-equipped leisure club.

Rooms 122 (19 fmly) (44 GF) ⟁ **S** £79-£143; **D** £92-£163 (incl. bkfst)*
Facilities Spa STV FTV WiFi ⅋ ⚲ Gym Steam room Sauna Xmas New Year **Conf** Class 160 Board 80 Thtr 350 Del from £125 to £185* **Services** Lift Air con **Parking** 240 **Notes** LB ⊛ Civ Wed 344

Hotel du Vin Cheltenham

★★★★ 78% ⊛ HOTEL

tel: 01242 588450 & 0844 736 4254
(Calls cost 5p per minute plus your phone company's access charge) **Parabola Rd GL50 3AQ**
email: info@cheltenham.hotelduvin.com **web:** www.hotelduvin.com
dir: *M5 junct 11, follow signs for city centre. At rdbt opposite Morgan Estate Agents take 2nd left, 200mtrs to Parabola Rd*

This hotel, in the Montpellier area of the town, has spacious public areas that are packed with stylish features. The pewter-topped bar has comfortable seating and the spacious restaurant has the Hotel du Vin trademark design; alfresco dining is possible on the extensive terrace area. Bedrooms are very comfortable, with Egyptian linen, deep baths and power showers. The spa is the ideal place to relax and unwind. Although parking is limited, it is a definite bonus. Service is friendly and attentive.

Rooms 49 (2 fmly) (5 GF) ⟁ **Facilities** Spa STV WiFi **Conf** Class 24 Board 24 Thtr 30 **Services** Lift Air con **Parking** 26 **Notes** Civ Wed 60

Queen's Hotel Cheltenham - MGallery by Sofitel

★★★★ 78% HOTEL

tel: 01242 514754 **The Promenade GL50 1NN**
email: h6632@accor.com **web:** www.mgallery.com
dir: *Follow town centre signs. Left at Montpellier Walk rdbt. Entrance 500mtrs right*

With its spectacular position at the top of the main promenade, this landmark hotel is an ideal base from which to explore the charms of this Regency spa town and also the Cotswolds. Bedrooms are very comfortable and include two beautiful four-poster rooms. Smart public rooms include the popular Gold Cup bar and a choice of dining options.

Rooms 84 (6 fmly) ⟁ **Facilities** STV WiFi ⅋ HL Xmas New Year **Conf** Class 60 Board 40 Thtr 120 **Services** Lift Air con **Parking** 70 **Notes** Civ Wed 100

C

CHELTENHAM *continued*

The Cheltenham Park

★★★★ 77% HOTEL

tel: 01242 229280 **Cirencester Rd, Charlton Kings GL53 8EA**
web: www.cheltenhampark-hotel.co.uk
dir: *On A435, 2m SE of Cheltenham near Lilley Brook Golf Course*

Located south of Cheltenham, this attractive Georgian property is set in its own landscaped gardens, adjacent to Lilley Brook Golf Course. All the bedrooms, whether premium or standard, are spacious and well equipped for both business and leisure guests. The hotel has an impressive health and leisure club with the latest gym equipment, plus a pool, steam room and beauty salon; extensive meeting facilities are available.

Rooms 152 (119 annexe) **Facilities** Spa WiFi 🕓 supervised Gym Beauty treatment rooms Sauna Steam room Xmas New Year **Conf** Class 180 Board 110 Thtr 320 **Parking** 170 **Notes** Civ Wed 100

George Hotel

★★★ 80% HOTEL

COTSWOLD INNS & HOTELS

tel: 01242 235751 **St Georges Rd GL50 3DZ**
email: hotel@stayatthegeorge.co.uk **web:** www.stayatthegeorge.co.uk
dir: *M5 junct 11 follow town centre signs. At 2nd lights left into Gloucester Rd, past rail station over mini-rdbt. At lights right into St Georges Rd. Hotel 0.75m on left*

A genuinely friendly, privately-owned hotel occupying part of a Regency terrace, just two-minutes walk from the town centre. The contemporary interior is elegant and stylish, and the well-equipped, modern bedrooms offer a relaxing haven; individually designed junior suites and deluxe double rooms are available. Lunch or dinner can be enjoyed in the lively atmosphere of Monty's Brasserie, perhaps followed by an evening in the vibrant cocktail bar which hosts live entertainment on Friday and Saturday evenings.

Rooms 31 (1 GF) 🐾 **S** £120–£200; **D** £130–£210 (incl. bkfst)* **Facilities** STV FTV WiFi Live music at wknds 🎵 **Conf** Class 18 Board 24 Thtr 30 **Parking** 30 **Notes** LB ⊗ Closed 25-26 Dec RS 24 Dec

Cotswold Grange Hotel

Ⓤ

tel: 01242 515119 **Pittville Circus Rd GL52 2QH**
email: info@cotswoldgrange.co.uk **web:** www.cotswoldgrange.co.uk
dir: *From town centre, follow Prestbury signs. Right at 1st rdbt, next rdbt straight over, hotel 100yds on left*

Currently the rating for this establishment is not confirmed. This may be due to a change of ownership or because it has only recently joined the AA rating scheme. For further details please see the AA website: theAA.com

Rooms 20 **Conf** Class 24 Board 28 Thtr 50

Premier Inn Cheltenham Central

BUDGET HOTEL

tel: 0871 527 8224 *(Calls cost 13p per minute plus your phone company's access charge)*
374 Gloucester Rd GL51 7AY
web: www.premierinn.com
dir: *M5 junct 11, A40 (Cheltenham). Follow dual carriageway to end, straight on at 1st rdbt, right at 2nd rdbt*

High quality, budget accommodation ideal for both families and business travellers. Spacious, en suite bedrooms feature tea and coffee making facilities, and Freeview TV in most hotels. Internet access and WiFi are available for a small fee. The adjacent family restaurant features a wide and varied menu. See also the Hotel Groups pages.

Rooms 67

Premier Inn Cheltenham West

BUDGET HOTEL

tel: 0871 527 8226 *(Calls cost 13p per minute plus your phone company's access charge)*
Tewkesbury Rd, Uckington GL51 9SL
web: www.premierinn.com
dir: *M5 junct 10 (S'bound exit only), A4019, hotel in 2m. Or M5 junct 11, A40 towards Cheltenham. At Benhall Rdbt left onto A4103 (Princess Elizabeth Way) follow racecourse signs. At rdbt left onto A4019 signed Tewkesbury/M5 North. Hotel opposite Sainsburys*

Rooms 58

CHESSINGTON	Map 6 TQ16
Greater London	

Premier Inn Chessington

BUDGET HOTEL

tel: 0871 527 8228 *(Calls cost 13p per minute plus your phone company's access charge)*
Leatherhead Rd KT9 2NE
web: www.premierinn.com
dir: *M25 junct 9, A243 towards Kingston-upon-Thames for approx 2m. Hotel adjacent to Chessington World of Adventures*

High quality, budget accommodation ideal for both families and business travellers. Spacious, en suite bedrooms feature tea and coffee making facilities, and Freeview TV in most hotels. Internet access and WiFi are available for a small fee. The adjacent family restaurant features a wide and varied menu. See also the Hotel Groups pages.

Rooms 62

C

CHESTER
Cheshire

Map 15 SJ46

See also **Puddington**

The Chester Grosvenor

★★★★★ ◉◉◉ ♨ HOTEL

tel: 01244 324024 **Eastgate CH1 1LT**
email: reservations@chestergrosvenor.com **web:** www.chestergrosvenor.com
dir: *A56 follow signs for city centre hotels. On Eastgate St next to the Eastgate clock*

Located within the Roman walls of the city, this Grade II listed, half-timbered building is the essence of Englishness. Furnished with fine fabrics and queen or king-size beds, the suites and bedrooms are of the highest standard, each designed with guest comfort as a priority. The eating options are the art deco La Brasserie, a bustling venue awarded 2 AA Rosettes; the Arkle Bar and Lounge for morning coffee, light lunches, afternoon tea and drinks; plus the fine dining restaurant, Simon Radley at The Chester Grosvenor, which offers creative cuisine with flair and style, and has been awarded 4 AA Rosettes. The hotel has a luxury spa and small fitness centre.

Rooms 80 ♠ **Facilities** Spa STV FTV WiFi ♦ HL Gym Thermal suite Relaxation room ♫ New Year **Conf** Class 100 Board 50 Thtr 250 Del from £195* **Services** Lift Air con **Notes** ⊗ Closed 25 Dec RS Sun & Mon Civ Wed 250

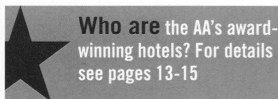

Who are the AA's award-winning hotels? For details see pages 13-15

Grosvenor Pulford Hotel & Spa

★★★★ 80% ◉ HOTEL

tel: 01244 570560 **Wrexham Rd, Pulford CH4 9DG**
email: reservations@grosvenorpulfordhotel.co.uk **web:** www.grosvenorpulfordhotel.co.uk
dir: *M53, A55 at junct signed A483 Chester/Wrexham & North Wales. Left onto B5445, hotel 2m on right*

Set in a rural location, this modern, stylish hotel features a magnificent spa with a large Roman-style swimming pool. Among the range of bedrooms are several executive suites, and others that have spiral staircases leading to the bedroom sections. A smart brasserie restaurant and bar provides a wide range of imaginative dishes in a relaxed atmosphere.

Rooms 73 (10 fmly) (19 GF) ♠ **Facilities** Spa STV FTV WiFi ♦ HL ⊕ ♨ Gym Steam room Sauna Xmas New Year **Conf** Class 100 Board 60 Thtr 220 **Services** Lift **Parking** 200 **Notes** Civ Wed 200

Best Western Premier Hallmark Hotel Chester The Queen

★★★★ 79% ◉◉ HOTEL

tel: 0330 028 3402 **City Rd CH1 3AH**
email: queen@hallmarkhotels.co.uk **web:** www.hallmarkhotels.co.uk
dir: *Follow signs for railway station, hotel opposite*

This hotel is ideally located opposite the railway station and just a couple minutes' walk from the city. Public areas include a restaurant, small gym, waiting room bar, separate lounge and Roman-themed gardens. Bedrooms are generally spacious and reflect the hotel's Victorian heritage.

Rooms 218 (11 fmly) (12 GF) ♠ **Facilities** STV FTV WiFi ♦ HL Gym Beauty treatment room Table tennis ♫ Xmas New Year **Conf** Class 150 Board 60 Thtr 400 **Services** Lift **Parking** 150 **Notes** ⊗ Civ Wed 400

C

CHESTER *continued*

ABode Chester

★★★★ 78% ◉◉ ⊛ HOTEL

ABode
HOTELS

tel: 01244 347000 **Grosvenor Rd CH1 2DJ**
email: generalmanager@abodechester.co.uk **web:** www.abodechester.co.uk

This modern, glass-fronted property sits prominently in the centre of Chester overlooking the Castle and adjacent to the racecourse. Bedrooms are well designed and equipped for the modern traveller with a range of large spacious suites also available. Food is a highlight here, with a range of dining options and bars. The restaurant, on the fifth floor, crowns the top of the building with far-reaching views over Chester Racecourse and beyond. Additional facilities include secure parking, a gym and beauty treatments.

Rooms 84 (7 fmly) **Facilities** FTV WiFi ⇗ Gym ♫ Xmas New Year **Conf** Class 24 Board 36 Thtr 90 Del from £175 to £235* **Services** Lift Air con **Parking** 39 **Notes** ⊗ Civ Wed 60

Macdonald New Blossoms Hotel

★★★★ 75% HOTEL

MACDONALD
HOTELS & RESORTS

tel: 01244 323186 & 0344 8799113 **St John St CH1 1HL**
email: events.blossoms@macdonald-hotels.co.uk
web: www.macdonaldhotels.co.uk/blossoms
dir: M53 junct 12 follow city centre signs for Eastgate, through pedestrian zone, hotel on left

Ideally located to explore the historic city of Chester, this is a modern and contemporary hotel. Bedrooms range from executive to feature four-poster rooms, with many retaining the charm of the original Victorian building. A stylish brasserie restaurant and bar offer an informal dining experience.

Rooms 67 (1 fmly) **Facilities** FTV WiFi ⇘ Xmas New Year **Conf** Class 50 Board 40 Thtr 90 **Services** Lift Air con **Notes** ⊗ Civ Wed 80

Mercure Chester Abbots Well Hotel

★★★★ 74% HOTEL

tel: 0844 815 9001 *(Calls cost 7p per minute plus your phone company's access charge)*
Whitchurch Rd, Christleton CH3 5QL
email: gm.mercurechester@jupiterhotels.co.uk **web:** www.mercurechester.co.uk
dir: A41 Whitchurch, hotel on right in 200mtrs

This smart, modern hotel is located just a short drive from the city centre; with extensive meeting and function facilities, a well-equipped leisure club and ample parking, it is a popular conference venue. Bedrooms vary in size and style but all are well equipped for both business and leisure guests. Food is served in the airy restaurant and also in the large open-plan bar lounge.

Rooms 126 (9 fmly) (58 GF) **Facilities** STV ⇘ ⊛ Gym Treatment room Xmas New Year **Conf** Class 140 Board 100 Thtr 230 **Services** Lift **Parking** 280 **Notes** ⊗ Civ Wed 180

Best Western Hallmark Hotel Chester Westminster

★★★ 82% HOTEL

tel: 0330 028 3424 **City Rd CH1 3AF**
email: westminster@hallmarkhotels.co.uk **web:** www.hallmarkhotels.co.uk
dir: A56, 3m to city centre, left signed rail station. Hotel opposite station, on right

Situated next to the railway station and close to the city centre, the Westminster is an established hotel catering for a wide market. It has an attractive Tudor-style exterior, but bedrooms are modern and well equipped with a few luxurious touches; family rooms are also available. There is a choice of bars and lounges, and the dining room serves a broad range of dishes.

Rooms 75 (5 fmly) (5 GF) **Facilities** FTV WiFi Free gym facilities at sister hotel Xmas New Year **Conf** Class 60 Board 40 Thtr 150 **Services** Lift **Notes** ⊗ Civ Wed 100

Mill Hotel & Spa Destination

★★★ 78% HOTEL

tel: 01244 350035 **Milton St CH1 3NF**
email: reservations@millhotel.com **web:** www.millhotel.com
dir: M53 junct 12, A56, left at 2nd rdbt A5268, 1st left, 2nd left

There have been constant improvements at this stylish conversion of an old corn mill which enjoys an idyllic canalside location close to the city centre. The bedrooms come in a variety of styles, some accessed over the enclosed canal bridge. There are several dining and bar options, and meals are even served on a broad-beam boat that cruises Chester's canal system, to and from the hotel. A well-equipped leisure centre and spa treatments are also provided.

Rooms 132 (49 annexe) (57 fmly) **S** £74-£94; **D** £98-£145 (incl. bkfst)* **Facilities** Spa STV FTV WiFi HL ⊛ supervised Gym Aerobic studio Hairdresser Sauna Steam room Kinesis studio ♫ Xmas New Year **Conf** Class 36 Board 30 Thtr 100 Del from £125 to £155* **Services** Lift **Parking** 120 **Notes** LB ⊗

C

Brookside Hotel

★★★ 75% HOTEL

tel: 01244 381943 & 390898 **Brook Ln CH2 2AN**
email: info@brookside-hotel.co.uk **web:** www.brookside-hotel.co.uk
dir: M53 junct 12, A56 towards Chester, A41. 0.5m left signed Newton (Plas Newton Ln). 0.5m right into Brook Ln. Hotel 0.5m. Or from Chester inner ring road follow A5116/Ellesmere Port/Hospital signs (keep in right lane to take right fork). Immediately left. At mini-rdbt 2nd right

This hotel is conveniently located in a residential area just north of the city centre. The attractive public areas consist of a foyer lounge, a small bar and a split-level restaurant. The homely bedrooms are thoughtfully furnished and some feature four-poster beds.

Rooms 26 (9 fmly) (4 GF) **Facilities** WiFi **Conf** Class 20 Board 12 **Parking** 20 **Notes** ⊗ Closed 20 Dec-3 Jan

Premier Inn Chester Central (North)

BUDGET HOTEL

tel: 0871 527 8230 (Calls cost 13p per minute plus your phone company's access charge)
76 Liverpool Rd CH2 1AU
web: www.premierinn.com
dir: M53 junct 12, A56. At 2nd rdbt right signed A41 to Chester Zoo. At 1st lights left into Heath Rd, leads into Mill Ln. Under small rail bridge. Hotel at end on right

High quality, budget accommodation ideal for both families and business travellers. Spacious, en suite bedrooms feature tea and coffee making facilities, and Freeview TV in most hotels. Internet access and WiFi are available for a small fee. The adjacent family restaurant features a wide and varied menu. See also the Hotel Groups pages.

Rooms 31

Premier Inn Chester Central (South East)

BUDGET HOTEL

tel: 0871 527 8232 (Calls cost 13p per minute plus your phone company's access charge)
Caldy Valley Rd, Boughton CH3 5PR
web: www.premierinn.com
dir: M53 junct 12, A56 to Chester. At 1st lights onto A41 (Whitchurch). At 2nd rdbt rd exit into Caldy Valley Rd (Huntington). Hotel on right

Rooms 93

Premier Inn Chester City Centre

BUDGET HOTEL

tel: 0871 527 8234 (Calls cost 13p per minute plus your phone company's access charge)
20-24 City Rd CH1 3AE
web: www.premierinn.com
dir: M53 junct 12, follow A56/Chester City Centre signs. At rdbt 1st exit onto A5268 (St Oswalds Way) follow railway station signs. At Bar's Rdbt 1st exit. Hotel on right

Rooms 120

CHESTERFIELD
Derbyshire
Map 16 SK37

HIGHLY RECOMMENDED

Casa Hotel

★★★★ 84% ◉◉ HOTEL

tel: 01246 245999 **Lockoford Ln S41 7JB**
email: enquiries@casahotels.co.uk **web:** www.casahotels.co.uk
dir: M1 junct 29 to A617 Chesterfield/A61 Sheffield, 1st exit at rdbt, hotel on left

A luxurious hotel with a contemporary Spanish theme throughout. The stylish bedrooms feature air conditioning, Hypnos beds and bathrooms with rainshowers. Some also have jacuzzi baths and two have balconies with hot tubs. Cocina Restaurant offers appealing menus featuring ingredients from the hotel's own organic farm. The conference and events facilities are excellent and complimentary WiFi is offered.

Rooms 100 (6 fmly) 🐾 **Facilities** STV FTV WiFi ⊹ HL Gym **Conf** Class 140 Board 50 Thtr 280 Del from £150 to £190* **Services** Lift Air con **Parking** 200 **Notes** ⊗ Civ Wed 280

C

CHESTERFIELD *continued*

Peak Edge Hotel at the Red Lion

★★★★ 81% HOTEL

tel: 01246 566142 **Darley Rd, Stone Edge S45 OLW**
email: sleep@peakedgehotel.co.uk **web:** www.peakedgehotel.co.uk
dir: *M1 junct 29, A617 to Chesterfield. At rdbt take 1st exit onto A61, at next rdbt 2nd exit onto Whitecotes Ln, continue onto Matlock Rd (A632) then Darley Rd (B5057)*

The Peak Edge Hotel is set in the heart of the Derbyshire countryside and surrounded by great views on all sides. The modern rooms are spacious, comfortable, and all benefit from high quality bathrooms. The inn has a rustic, 17th-century feel, with stone walls and wooden flooring. The staff are very friendly and well informed. Food is a highlight of any stay, with locally sourced produce put to good use.

Rooms 27 (2 fmly) (15 GF) **Facilities** FTV WiFi Xmas New Year **Conf** Class 120 Board 40 Thtr 140 **Services** Lift Air con **Parking** 70 **Notes** LB Civ Wed 140

Ringwood Hall Hotel

★★★ 86% HOTEL — THE INDEPENDENTS

tel: 01246 280077 **Brimington S43 1DQ**
email: reception@ringwoodhallhotel.com **web:** www.ringwoodhallhotel.com
dir: *M1 junct 30, A619 to Chesterfield through Staveley. Hotel on left*

Ringwood Hall is a beautifully presented Georgian manor house set in 29 acres of peaceful grounds, between the M1 and Chesterfield. The stylish bedrooms include 'Feature Rooms' and three apartments within the grounds. Public areas include comfortable lounges, the Markham Bar and a cocktail lounge. The health and fitness club has a pool, sauna, steam room and gym.

Rooms 74 (10 annexe) (32 fmly) (32 GF) **S** fr £105; **D** fr £110 (incl. bkfst)*
Facilities FTV WiFi Gym Steam room Sauna Xmas New Year **Conf** Class 80 Board 60 Thtr 250 **Parking** 150 **Notes** LB Civ Wed 250

Sandpiper Hotel

★★★ 70% HOTEL — THE INDEPENDENTS

tel: 01246 450550 **Sheffield Rd, Sheepbridge S41 9EH**
email: sue@sandpiperhotel.co.uk **web:** www.sandpiperhotel.co.uk
dir: *M1 junct 29, A617 to Chesterfield then A61 to Sheffield. 1st exit take Dronfield/Unstone sign. Hotel 0.5m on left*

Conveniently situated for both the A61, the M1, and Chesterfield, this modern hotel offers comfortable and well-furnished bedrooms. Public areas are situated in a separate building across the car park, and include a cosy bar and open-plan restaurant, serving a range of interesting and popular dishes.

Rooms 40 (6 fmly) (11 GF) **S** fr £55; **D** fr £55* **Facilities** FTV WiFi New Year **Conf** Class 35 Board 35 Thtr 100 **Services** Lift **Parking** 80 **Notes** Civ Wed 90

Premier Inn Chesterfield North

BUDGET HOTEL

tel: 0871 527 8238 *(Calls cost 13p per minute plus your phone company's access charge)*
Tapton Lock Hill, off Rotherway S41 7NJ
web: www.premierinn.com
dir: *Adjacent to Tesco, at A61 & A619 rdbt, 1m N of city centre*

High quality, budget accommodation ideal for both families and business travellers. Spacious, en suite bedrooms feature tea and coffee making facilities, and Freeview TV in most hotels. Internet access and WiFi are available for a small fee. The adjacent family restaurant features a wide and varied menu. See also the Hotel Groups pages.

Rooms 88

Premier Inn Chesterfield West

BUDGET HOTEL

tel: 0871 527 8240 *(Calls cost 13p per minute plus your phone company's access charge)*
Baslow Rd, Eastmoor S42 7DA
web: www.premierinn.com
dir: *M1 junct 29, A617. At next rdbt 2nd exit. At next rdbt 1st exit into Markham Rd. At next rdbt 2nd exit into Wheatbridge Rd, left into Chatsworth Rd. 2.5m to hotel*

Rooms 25

Ibis Chesterfield Centre

AA Advertised — **ibis**

tel: 01246 221333 **Lordsmill St S41 7RW**
email: h3160@accor.com **web:** www.ibishotel.com
dir: *M1 junct 29/A617 to Chesterfield. 2nd exit at 1st rdbt. Hotel on right at 2nd rdbt*

Modern, budget hotel offering comfortable accommodation in bright and practical bedrooms. Breakfast is self-service and dinner is available in the restaurant.

Rooms 86 (15 fmly) (8 GF) **Facilities** FTV WiFi **Conf** Board 12 Thtr 25 **Services** Lift **Parking** 50

CHESTER-LE-STREET
County Durham — **Map 19 NZ25**

Lumley Castle Hotel

★★★★ 76% HOTEL

tel: 0191 389 1111 **Lumley Castle DH3 4NX**
email: reservations@lumleycastle.com **web:** www.lumleycastle.com
dir: *A1(M) junct 63, follow Chester-le-Street signs. Follow signs for Riverside then Lumley Castle*

Dominating the Country Durham landscape for the past 600 years, Lumley Castle cannot help but impress. The place has a real sense of theatre and as a guest you are left in no doubt that you are in a proper castle. The magnificent state rooms, along with other public areas, are very well presented in accord with all expectations. Bedrooms differ in style, size and type and make good use of all available space. The staff are warm and welcoming, and quality food is served throughout.

Rooms 73 (47 annexe) (9 fmly) (27 GF) **S** fr £69; **D** fr £89 (incl. bkfst)*
Facilities FTV WiFi HL Xmas New Year **Conf** Class 60 Board 50 Thtr 150 Del from £145 to £165* **Services** Lift **Parking** 150 **Notes** Closed 24-26 Dec & 1-2 Jan Civ Wed 144

CHICHESTER
West Sussex — **Map 5 SU80**

The Goodwood Hotel

★★★★ 82% HOTEL

tel: 01243 775537 **PO18 0QB**
email: reservations@goodwood.com **web:** www.goodwood.com/estate/the-goodwood-hotel

(For full entry see Goodwood)

C

Chichester Harbour Hotel

★★★★ 78% HOTEL

tel: 01243 778000 **57 North St PO19 1NH**
email: chichester@harbourhotels.co.uk **web:** www.chichester-harbour-hotel.co.uk
dir: *From A27, onto inner ring road to Northgate. At Northgate rdbt left into North St, hotel on left*

This well-presented Grade II listed, Georgian property occupies a prime position at the top of North Street. The stylish bedrooms have flat-screen TVs, Egyptian cotton linen and high-speed WiFi access. The bar and restaurant are contemporary venues for enjoying meals, and refreshments which are served all day. The hotel is just a few minutes' away from the famous Festival Theatre; and Goodwood, for motorsport and horse racing, is also close by.

Rooms 37 (1 annexe) (2 fmly) **S** £85-£120; **D** £125-£300* **Facilities** FTV WiFi ♪ Xmas New Year **Conf** Class 50 Board 30 Thtr 50 Del from £165 to £300* **Services** Lift **Parking** 35 **Notes** LB ⊗ Civ Wed 70

HIGHLY RECOMMENDED

The Millstream Hotel & Restaurant

★★★ 86% ◉◉ HOTEL

tel: 01243 573234 **Bosham Ln PO18 8HL**
email: info@millstreamhotel.co.uk **web:** www.millstreamhotel.com

(For full entry see Bosham)

Crouchers Country Hotel & Restaurant

★★★ 83% ◉◉ HOTEL

tel. 01243 784995 **Birdham Rd PO20 7EH**
email: crouchers@btconnect.com **web:** www.crouchershotel.com
dir: *From A27 (Chichester bypass) onto A286 towards West Wittering, 2m, hotel on left between Chichester Marina & Dell Quay*

This friendly, family-run hotel, situated in open countryside, is just a short drive from the harbour. The stylish and well-equipped bedrooms are situated in a separate barn, coach house and stable block, and include four-poster rooms and rooms with patios that overlook the fields. The modern oak-beamed restaurant, with country views, serves award-winning cuisine.

Rooms 26 (23 annexe) (2 fmly) (15 GF) **Facilities** STV FTV WiFi Xmas New Year **Conf** Class 80 Board 50 Thtr 80 **Parking** 80 **Notes** Civ Wed 70

Premier Inn Chichester

BUDGET HOTEL

tel: 0871 527 8242 *(Calls cost 13p per minute plus your phone company's access charge)*
Chichester Gate Leisure Park, Terminus Rd PO19 8EL
web: www.premierinn.com
dir: *A27 towards city centre. Follow Terminus Road Industrial Estate signs. Left at 1st lights, left at next lights into Chichester Gate Leisure Park. Hotel on right*

High quality, budget accommodation ideal for both families and business travellers. Spacious, en suite bedrooms feature tea and coffee making facilities, and Freeview TV in most hotels. Internet access and WiFi are available for a small fee. The adjacent family restaurant features a wide and varied menu. See also the Hotel Groups pages.

Rooms 83

CHIEVELEY
Berkshire · Map 5 SU47

Crab & Boar

◉◉ RESTAURANT WITH ROOMS

tel: 01635 247550 **Wantage Rd RG20 8UE**
email: info@crabandboar.com **web:** www.crabandboar.com
dir: *1.5m W of Chieveley on B4494*

Part of The Epicurean Collection, this recently refurbished and renovated former pub has been appointed to a very high standard and bedrooms include a full range of modern amenities. Some ground floor rooms have a small private patio area complete with a luxury private hot tub. The warm and cosy restaurant offers an extensive and award-winning range of dishes, using the best suppliers in the south.

Rooms 14 (5 annexe)

CHILDER THORNTON
Cheshire · Map 15 SJ37

Premier Inn Wirral (Childer Thornton)

BUDGET HOTEL

tel: 0871 527 9174 *(Calls cost 13p per minute plus your phone company's access charge)*
New Chester Rd CH66 1QW
web: www.premierinn.com
dir: *M53 junct 5, A41 towards Chester. Hotel on right, same entrance as Burleydam Garden Centre*

High quality, budget accommodation ideal for both families and business travellers. Spacious, en suite bedrooms feature tea and coffee making facilities, and Freeview TV in most hotels. Internet access and WiFi are available for a small fee. The adjacent family restaurant features a wide and varied menu. See also the Hotel Groups pages.

Rooms 52

CHILGROVE
West Sussex · Map 5 SU81

The White Horse

◉ RESTAURANT WITH ROOMS

tel: 01243 519444 **High St PO18 9HX**
email: info@thewhitehorse.co.uk **web:** www.thewhitehorse.co.uk
dir: *From Chichester take A286 N, turn left onto B2141 to village*

Part of The Epicurean Collection, located on the edge of the South Downs, this spacious property offers stylish and relaxed surroundings. The bar and dining areas have an opulent feel, with lots of quirky touches and interesting features. Guests are welcome to enjoy a pint and relax, or dine from the appealing and wide-ranging menus. The emphasis is on local produce and food is a highlight. Bedrooms offer an attractive blend of traditional and contemporary features, with wooden beams, sheepskin rugs and king-sized beds. Most open out onto the private courtyard and feature either copper baths or large rain showers, with a couple even having hot tubs. AA Funkiest B&B of the Year Award Runner-Up 2016-2017.

Rooms 15

C

CHIPPENHAM
Wiltshire — Map 4 ST97

Best Western Plus Angel Hotel
■■LEGACY
■■HOTELS.

★★★ 80% HOTEL

tel: 01249 652615 **Market Place SN15 3HD**
email: reception@angelhotelchippenham.co.uk **web:** www.angelhotelchippenham.co.uk
dir: *Follow tourist signs for Bowood House. Under railway arch, follow 'Borough Parade Parking' signs. Hotel adjacent to car park*

Several impressive buildings combine to make this smart and comfortable hotel. The well-equipped bedrooms vary from those in the main house where character is the key, to the smart executive-style, courtyard rooms. The lounge and restaurant are bright and modern, and offer an imaginative carte and an all-day menu.

Rooms 50 (35 annexe) (3 fmly) (12 GF) **Facilities** STV FTV WiFi ☖ ☒ Gym
Conf Class 50 Board 50 Thtr 100 **Parking** 50

Premier Inn Chippenham

BUDGET HOTEL

tel: 0871 527 8244 *(Calls cost 13p per minute plus your phone company's access charge)*
Cepen Park, West Cepen Way SN14 6UZ
web: www.premierinn.com
dir: *M4 junct 17, A350 towards Chippenham. Hotel at 1st main rdbt*

High quality, budget accommodation ideal for both families and business travellers. Spacious, en suite bedrooms feature tea and coffee making facilities, and Freeview TV in most hotels. Internet access and WiFi are available for a small fee. The adjacent family restaurant features a wide and varied menu. See also the Hotel Groups pages.

Rooms 130

CHIPPING CAMPDEN
Gloucestershire — Map 10 SP13

HIGHLY RECOMMENDED

Three Ways House

★★★ 86% ◉ HOTEL

tel: 01386 438429 **Chapel Ln, Mickleton GL55 6SB**
email: reception@puddingclub.com **web:** www.threewayshousehotel.com
dir: *In Mickleton centre, on B4632 Stratford-upon-Avon to Broadway road*

Built in 1870, this charming hotel has welcomed guests for over 100 years and is home to the world famous Pudding Club, formed in 1985 to promote traditional English puddings. Individuality is a hallmark here, as reflected in a number of the bedrooms that have been designed around a pudding theme. Public areas are stylish and include the air-conditioned restaurant, lounges and meeting rooms.

Rooms 48 (7 fmly) (14 GF) ☏ **S** £88-£130; **D** £155-£260 (incl. bkfst)*
Facilities FTV WiFi ☖ ♫ Xmas New Year **Conf** Class 40 Board 35 Thtr 100
Del from £140* **Services** Lift **Parking** 37 **Notes** LB Civ Wed 100

The Kings
◉◉ ☕ RESTAURANT WITH ROOMS

tel: 01386 840256 & 841056 **The Square, High St GL55 6AW**
email: info@kingscampden.co.uk **web:** www.kingscampden.co.uk
dir: *In centre of town square*

Located in the centre of this delightful Cotswold town, The Kings effortlessly blends a relaxed and friendly welcome with efficient service. Bedrooms and bathrooms come in a range of shapes and sizes and all are appointed to a high level of quality and comfort. Dining options, whether in the main restaurant or the comfortable bar area, serve a tempting menu to suit all tastes, from light salads and pasta, to meat and fish dishes.

Rooms 19 (5 annexe) (3 fmly)

The Seagrave Arms
◉◉ RESTAURANT WITH ROOMS

tel: 01386 840192 **Friday St, Weston-sub-Edge GL55 6QH**
email: enquiries@seagravearms.com **web:** www.seagravearms.com
dir: *From Moreton-in-Marsh take A44 towards Evesham. Approx 7m right onto B4081 signed Chipping Campden. Becomes Sheep St. At junct with High Street, left into Dyers Ln. 0.5m over Dovers Hill, into Weston-sub-Edge, becomes Church St. Inn on left*

Part of The Epicurean Collection, This Grade II-listed, 400-year-old house is set in the heart of the Cotswolds. It offers modern accommodation in the main house and also rooms around the courtyard. The inn is full of character, serving award-winning seasonal food every day of the week, with occasional specialist nights. Staff are warm and friendly, and the bar offers local ales and good wines. There is ample parking and attractive gardens.

Rooms 8 (3 annexe)

CHIPPING NORTON
Oxfordshire — Map 10 SP32

Wild Thyme Restaurant with Rooms
◉◉ RESTAURANT WITH ROOMS

tel: 01608 645060 **10 New St OX7 5LJ**
email: enquiries@wildthymerestaurant.co.uk **web:** www.wildthymerestaurant.co.uk
dir: *On A44 in town centre off market square*

Set in the bustling Cotswold market town of Chipping Norton, this restaurant with rooms offers three en suite bedrooms that are individually designed, well equipped, and have many thoughtful extras. The restaurant serves exciting Modern British food that is presented with relaxed and friendly service.

Rooms 3

C

CHITTLEHAMHOLT
Devon
Map 3 SS62

Highbullen Hotel, Golf & Country Club

tel: 01769 540561 **EX37 9HD**
email: welcome@highbullen.co.uk **web:** www.highbullen.co.uk
dir: M5 junct 27/A361/B3227 towards South Molton. Towards end of High St bear left onto B3226. Follow road along Mole Valley for 5m then follow brown tourist signs

Currently the rating for this establishment is not confirmed. This may be due to a change of ownership or because it has only recently joined the AA rating scheme. For further details please see the AA website: theAA.com

Rooms 37 **D** £95-£425 (incl. bkfst)* **Facilities** FTV WiFi ☕ ⟲ ♨ 18 ⛳ Fishing 🏊 Gym Sauna Steam room Shooting Pilates retreats Fitness classes **Conf** Class 180 Board 50 Thtr 400 **Notes** Civ Wed 200

CHORLEY
Lancashire
Map 15 SD51

Premier Inn Chorley North
BUDGET HOTEL

tel: 0871 527 8246 *(Calls cost 13p per minute plus your phone company's access charge)*
Malthouse Farm, Moss Ln, Whittle-le-Woods PR6 8AB
web: www.premierinn.com
dir: M61 junct 8 onto A674 (Wheelton), 400yds on left into Moss Ln

High quality, budget accommodation ideal for both families and business travellers. Spacious, en suite bedrooms feature tea and coffee making facilities, and Freeview TV in most hotels. Internet access and WiFi are available for a small fee. The adjacent family restaurant features a wide and varied menu. See also the Hotel Groups pages.

Rooms 80

Premier Inn Chorley South
BUDGET HOTEL

tel: 0871 527 8248 *(Calls cost 13p per minute plus your phone company's access charge)*
Bolton Rd PR7 4AB
web: www.premierinn.com
dir: From N: M61 junct 8, A6 to Chorley. From S: M6 junct 27 follow Standish signs. Left onto A5106 to Chorley, A6 towards Preston. Hotel 0.5m on right

Rooms 29

Find out more about the AA Hotel of the Year for England on page 13

CHRISTCHURCH
Dorset
Map 5 SZ19

Captain's Club Hotel & Spa
★★★★ 83% ◉◉ HOTEL

tel: 01202 475111 **Wick Ferry, Wick Ln BH23 1HU**
email: reservations@captainsclubhotel.com **web:** www.captainsclubhotel.com
dir: B3073 to Christchurch. On Fountain rdbt take 5th exit (Sopers Ln) 2nd left (St Margarets Ave) 1st right onto Wick Ln

The Captain's Club Hotel is situated in the heart of the town on the banks of the River Stour at Christchurch Quay, and only ten minutes from Bournemouth. All bedrooms, including the suites and apartments, have views overlooking the river. Guests can relax in the hydrotherapy pool, enjoy a spa treatment or sample the cuisine in Tides Restaurant.

Rooms 29 (12 fmly) ☕ **Facilities** Spa STV FTV WiFi ☕ Hydrotherapy pool Sauna Dry flotation ♫ **Conf** Class 72 Board 64 Thtr 140 Del from £195 to £245 **Services** Lift Air con **Parking** 41 **Notes** Civ Wed 100

See advert on page 128

C

CHRISTCHURCH *continued*

HIGHLY RECOMMENDED

Christchurch Harbour Hotel

★★★★ 83% HOTEL

tel: 01202 483434 **95 Mudeford BH23 3NT**
email: christchurch@harbourhotels.co.uk web: www.christchurch-harbour-hotel.co.uk
dir: *On A35 to Christchurch onto A337 to Highcliffe. Right at rdbt, hotel 1.5m on left*

Delightfully situated on the side of Mudeford Quay close to sandy beaches, and conveniently located for Bournemouth Airport and the BIC, this hotel boasts an impressive spa and leisure facility. The bedrooms are particularly well appointed and stylishly finished; many have excellent views, and some have balconies. Guests can eat in the award-winning Jetty Restaurant, or the Upper Deck Bar and Restaurant.

Rooms 64 (2 fmly) (14 GF) 🐾 **Facilities Spa** FTV WiFi ↘ 🌀 Gym Steam room Sauna Exercise classes Hydrotherapy pool Xmas New Year **Conf** Class 20 Board 30 Thtr 100 **Services** Lift **Parking** 55 **Notes** ⊗ Civ Wed 100

Premier Inn Christchurch East

BUDGET HOTEL

tel: 0871 527 8250 *(Calls cost 13p per minute plus your phone company's access charge)*
Somerford Rd BH23 3QG
web: www.premierinn.com
dir: *In Christchurch from A35 & B3059 rdbt junct take B3059 Somerford Rd*

High quality, budget accommodation ideal for both families and business travellers. Spacious, en suite bedrooms feature tea and coffee making facilities, and Freeview TV in most hotels. Internet access and WiFi are available for a small fee. The adjacent family restaurant features a wide and varied menu. See also the Hotel Groups pages.

Rooms 124

Premier Inn Christchurch West

BUDGET HOTEL

tel: 0871 527 8252 *(Calls cost 13p per minute plus your phone company's access charge)*
Barrack Rd BH23 2BN
web: www.premierinn.com
dir: *From A338 take A3060 towards Christchurch. Left onto A35. Hotel on right*

Rooms 61

CHURT	Map 5 SU83
Surrey	

Best Western Frensham Pond Hotel

★★★★ 76% HOTEL

tel: 01252 795161 **Bacon Ln GU10 2QB**
email: info@frenshampondhotel.co.uk web: www.bw-frenshampondhotel.co.uk
dir: *A3 onto A287. 4m left at 'Beware Horses' sign. Hotel 0.25m*

This 15th-century house occupies a superb location on the edge of Frensham Pond. Recently refurbished, the bedrooms offer style, comfort and a host of amenities

C

including air conditioning. The annexe rooms have their own patio and private entrance. The contemporary bar and lounge offers a range of snacks while the restaurant offers a more formal menu for both lunch and dinner. Flexible meeting rooms are well equipped to host a range of functions from business meetings to wedding celebrations and private dining. There is a well-equipped fitness room and secure parking. The Spa is due to open by the end of the year.

Rooms 53 (12 annexe) (16 fmly) (27 GF) ⚓ **Facilities** STV FTV WiFi ⌇ Gym Xmas New Year **Conf** Class 45 Board 40 Thtr 120 Del from £120 to £185* **Services** Air con **Parking** 120 **Notes** Civ Wed 130

CIRENCESTER
Gloucestershire
Map 5 SP00

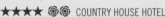

INSPECTORS' CHOICE

Barnsley House

★★★★ ◎◎ COUNTRY HOUSE HOTEL

tel: 01285 740000 **GL7 5EE**
email: info@barnsleyhouse.com **web:** www.barnsleyhouse.com
dir: 4m NE of Cirencester on B4425

This delightful Cotswold country house has been appointed to provide the highest levels of quality, comfort and relaxation. Individually styled bedrooms come in a range of shapes and sizes, from the large character rooms in the main house to the more contemporary-style stable rooms; all rooms have garden views and are packed with guest extras and little luxuries, including plasma TVs in the bathrooms. The delightful gardens, originally designed in the late 1950s by previous owner and award-winning gardener Rosemary Verey and her husband, include a fruit and vegetable area which is the home of much of the produce used in the delicious cuisine on offer in Potager Restaurant. In the grounds is the Garden Spa with treatment rooms, sauna, steam room and an outdoor hydrotherapy pool. The hotel also has a cinema.

Rooms 18 (12 annexe) (10 GF) ⚓ **S** £281-£511; **D** £299-£529 (incl. bkfst)* **Facilities** Spa STV FTV WiFi ⌇ ☂ ⛳ Cinema Bicycles Hydrotherapy pool Relaxation rooms Xmas New Year **Conf** Class 20 Board 18 Thtr 30 Del £360* **Parking** 30 **Notes** ⊗ No children 14yrs Civ Wed 120

Corinium Hotel & Restaurant

★★★ ⚠ SMALL HOTEL

tel: 01285 659711 **12 Gloucester St GL7 2DG**
email: info@coriniumhotel.co.uk **web:** www.coriniumhotel.co.uk
dir: From A417/A419/A429 towards Cirencester. A435 at rdbt. After 500mtrs turn left at lights, then 1st right, car park on left

This delightful 16th-century small hotel is quietly situated just five minutes walk from town, and is an ideal base from which to explore the Cotswolds. The Corinium has a locally renowned restaurant offering Modern British cuisine, as well as a cosy bar full of Cotswold charm. Other benefits include free WiFi throughout the hotel, an attractive secluded garden for alfresco dining, and ample free parking.

Rooms 15 (2 fmly) (2 GF) **S** £65-£80; **D** £85-£130 (incl. bkfst)* **Facilities** FTV WiFi ⌇ **Conf** Class 30 Board 34 Thtr 70 Del from £140 to £160* **Parking** 30 **Notes** LB

CLACTON-ON-SEA
Essex
Map 7 TM11

The Kingscliff Hotel

★★★ 77% HOTEL

tel: 01255 812343 & 0330 333 2992 **55 King's Pde, Holland on Sea CO15 5JB**
email: info@thekingscliffhotel.com **web:** www.thekingscliffhotel.co.uk
dir: A12 junct 29 onto A120, then A133, at Weeley rdbt take 3rd exit, turn onto Marine Parade East & continue onto Kings Parade

The Kingscliff Hotel enjoys a prominent position along the seafront. Bedrooms are all attractively presented, comfortable and very well equipped; some front-facing rooms enjoy wonderful sea views. There is a popular restaurant along with a stylish lounge bar for guests. Secure parking is available and free WiFi is offered throughout the hotel. This is also a very popular wedding and conference venue.

Rooms 30 (2 fmly) (7 GF) ⚓ **Facilities** FTV WiFi ⌇ Xmas New Year **Conf** Class 50 Board 30 Thtr 90 **Parking** 50 **Notes** ⊗ Civ Wed 100

Premier Inn Clacton-on-Sea

BUDGET HOTEL

tel: 0871 527 8254 (Calls cost 13p per minute plus your phone company's access charge)
Crown Green Roundabout, Colchester Rd, Trending CO16 9AA
web: www.premierinn.com
dir: A12, A120 towards Harwich. In 4m take A133 to Clacton-on-Sea. Hotel off Weeley Rdbt

High quality, budget accommodation ideal for both families and business travellers. Spacious, en suite bedrooms feature tea and coffee making facilities, and Freeview TV in most hotels. Internet access and WiFi are available for a small fee. The adjacent family restaurant features a wide and varied menu. See also the Hotel Groups pages.

Rooms 66

Premier Inn Clacton-on-Sea (Seafront) Hotel

BUDGET HOTEL

tel: 0871 527 8254 (Calls cost 13p per minute plus your phone company's access charge)
8 Marine Parade West CO15 1RD
web: www.premierinn.com
dir: From A12 take A120 towards Harwich. 4m, take A133 to Clacton-on-Sea. Hotel accessed from rdbt at Weeley. Adjacent to bowling green

Rooms 66

C

CLAVERDON
Warwickshire   Map 10 SP16

Ardencote
★★★★ 76% ◉ HOTEL

tel: 01926 843111 **The Cumsey, Lye Green Rd, Claverdon CV35 8LT**
email: hotel@ardencote.com **web:** www.ardencote.com
dir: *Phone or see website for directions*

Originally built as a gentleman's residence around 1860, this hotel is set in 83 acres of landscaped grounds. Public rooms include a choice of lounge areas, a cocktail bar and conservatory breakfast room. Main meals are served in the Lodge Restaurant, a separate building with a light contemporary style, which sits beside a small lake; and in the modern Brasserie. An extensive range of leisure, golf and conference facilities are provided and bedrooms are smartly decorated and tastefully furnished.

Rooms 110 (10 fmly) (30 GF) 🐾 **Facilities** Spa STV FTV WiFi 🕸 HL 🕙 ᴿ 🛝 18 🏌
Putt green 🏌 Gym Squash Sauna Steam room Dance studio Relaxation rooms Xmas
New Year **Conf** Class 70 Board 50 Thtr 175 Del from £135 to £155* **Services** Lift
Air con **Parking** 350 **Notes** ⊗ Civ Wed 150

CLEARWELL
Gloucestershire   Map 4 SO50

HIGHLY RECOMMENDED

Tudor Farmhouse Hotel & Restaurant
★★★ ◉◉ HOTEL

tel: 01594 833046 **High St GL16 8JS**
email: info@tudorfarmhousehotel.co.uk **web:** www.tudorfarmhousehotel.co.uk
dir: *A4136 onto B4228, through Coleford, right into Clearwell, hotel on right just before War Memorial Cross*

Dating from the 13th century, this idyllic former farmhouse retains a host of original features including exposed stonework, oak beams, wall panelling and wonderful inglenook fireplaces. Bedrooms have great individuality and style and are located either in the main house or in converted buildings in the grounds. Creative menus offer quality cuisine, served in the intimate, candlelit restaurant.

Rooms 23 (18 annexe) (3 fmly) (10 GF) 🐾 **Facilities** STV FTV WiFi 🕸 HL Xmas New
Year **Conf** Class 20 Board 12 Thtr 30 **Parking** 30 **Notes** Closed 2-5 Jan

CLECKHEATON
West Yorkshire   Map 19 SE12

Premier Inn Bradford South
BUDGET HOTEL

Premier Inn

tel: 0871 527 8136 *(Calls cost 13p per minute plus your phone company's access charge)*
Whitehall Rd, Dye House Dr BD19 6HG
web: www.premierinn.com
dir: *On A58 at intersection with M62 & M606*

High quality, budget accommodation ideal for both families and business travellers. Spacious, en suite bedrooms feature tea and coffee making facilities, and Freeview TV in most hotels. Internet access and WiFi are available for a small fee. The adjacent family restaurant features a wide and varied menu. See also the Hotel Groups pages.

Rooms 60

C

CLEETHORPES
Lincolnshire   Map 17 TA30

Kingsway Hotel

★★★ 80% HOTEL

tel: 01472 601122 **Kingsway DN35 OAE**
email: reception@kingsway-hotel.com **web:** www.kingsway-hotel.com
dir: Exit A180 at Grimsby, to Cleethorpes seafront. Hotel at Kingsway & Queen Parade junct - A1098

This seafront hotel has been in the same family for four generations and continues to provide traditional comfort and friendly service. The lounges are comfortable and good food is served in the pleasant dining room. The bedrooms are bright and nicely furnished - most are comfortably proportioned.

Rooms 46 ₹ **S** £79-£95; **D** £85-£114 (incl. bkfst)* **Facilities** STV FTV WiFi
Conf Board 18 Thtr 22 **Services** Lift **Parking** 50 **Notes** ⊗ No children 5yrs Closed 25-26 Dec

Premier Inn Cleethorpes

BUDGET HOTEL

tel: 0871 527 9470 *(Calls cost 13p per minute plus your phone company's access charge)*
Meridian Point DN35 OPN
web: www.premierinn.com
dir: A180 through Grimsby to Cleethorpes. At 4th rdbt take 2nd exit into Isaac's Hill (A1098). In 0.5m take 2nd exit at rdbt into Alexandra Rd (A1098). At next rdbt take 1st exit into Kingsway. Hotel 1m on right

High quality, budget accommodation ideal for both families and business travellers. Spacious, en suite bedrooms feature tea and coffee making facilities, and Freeview TV in most hotels. Internet access and WiFi are available for a small fee. The adjacent family restaurant features a wide and varied menu. See also the Hotel Groups pages.

Rooms 60

CLITHEROE
Lancashire   Map 18 SD74

The Assheton Arms

⚜ RESTAURANT WITH ROOMS

tel: 01200 441227 **Downham BB7 4BJ**
email: info@asshetonarms.com **web:** www.seafoodpubcompany.com
dir: A59 to Chatburn, then follow Downham signs

This historic Grade II-listed building is located in the conservation village of Downham, with stunning views of the Pendle Hills. The inn is owned by the Seafood Pub Company which means you can expect outstanding seafood. The rooms are spacious with traditional fittings yet maintain a modern feel. The team are young, friendly and guarantee a warm welcome.

Rooms 12 (11 annexe) (4 fmly)

Find out more about the **AA Hotel Group of the Year** see page 17

CLOVELLY
Devon   Map 3 SS32

Red Lion Hotel

★★ 81% HOTEL

tel: 01237 431237 **The Quay EX39 5TF**
email: stay@clovelly.co.uk **web:** www.clovelly.co.uk
dir: Exit A39 at Clovelly Cross onto B3237. Pass visitor centre, 1st left by white rails to harbour

'Idyllic' is the only word that describes the harbour-side setting of this charming 18th-century inn, with the famous fishing village forming a spectacular backdrop. Bedrooms are stylish and enjoy delightful views. The inn's relaxed atmosphere is conducive to relaxation, even when the harbour comes alive with the activities of the local fishermen during the day.

Rooms 17 (6 annexe) (5 fmly) (2 GF) ₹ **S** £103-£120; **D** £156-£190 (incl. bkfst)*
Facilities FTV WiFi Sea fishing Diving, tennis & spa treatments can be arranged Xmas New Year **Parking** 11 **Notes** LB Civ Wed 70

New Inn

★★ 73% HOTEL

tel: 01237 431303 **High St EX39 5TQ**
email: newinn@clovelly.co.uk **web:** www.clovelly.co.uk
dir: At Clovelly Cross, exit A39 onto B3237. Follow down hill for 1.5m. Right at sign 'All vehicles for Clovelly'

Famed for its cobbled descent to the harbour, this fascinating fishing village is a traffic-free zone. Consequently, luggage is conveyed by sledge or donkey to this much-photographed hotel. Carefully renovated bedrooms and public areas are smartly presented with quality, locally-made furnishings. Meals may be taken in the elegant restaurant or the popular Upalong bar.

Rooms 8 (1 fmly) (1 GF) ₹ **Facilities** FTV WiFi Sea fishing Diving & tennis can be arranged Xmas New Year **Notes** Civ Wed 50

C

CLOWNE
Derbyshire   Map 16 SK47

Hotel Van Dyk
★★★★ 76% SMALL HOTEL

tel: 01246 810219 **Worksop Rd S43 4TD**
email: info@hotelvandyk.co.uk **web:** www.vandykhotel.co.uk
dir: *M1 junct 30, 2nd right towards Worksop, 2nd rdbt 1st exit, 3rd rdbt straight over. Through lights, hotel 100yds on right*

A sympathetic renovation has resulted in a small vibrant boutique-style hotel where staff are always on hand to offer friendly and welcoming service. Accommodation is luxurious and equipped with many thoughtful extras. Bowdens Restaurant offers fine dining and makes the ideal setting for a memorable evening; alternatively there's Southgate Grill for those looking for a more casual eating option.

Rooms 15 (4 fmly) ⊘ **Facilities** FTV WiFi Xmas New Year **Conf** Class 50 Board 60 Thtr 150 **Parking** 120 **Notes** ⊗ Civ Wed 120

COBHAM
Surrey   Map 6 TQ16

Premier Inn Cobham
BUDGET HOTEL

tel: 0871 527 8256 *(Calls cost 13p per minute plus your phone company's access charge)*
Portsmouth Rd, Fairmile KT11 1BW
web: www.premierinn.com
dir: *M25 junct 10, A3 towards London, A245 towards Cobham. In Cobham town centre left onto A307 (Portsmouth Rd). Hotel on left*

High quality, budget accommodation ideal for both families and business travellers. Spacious, en suite bedrooms feature tea and coffee making facilities, and Freeview TV in most hotels. Internet access and WiFi are available for a small fee. The adjacent family restaurant features a wide and varied menu. See also the Hotel Groups pages.

Rooms 48

Days Inn Cobham - M25
AA Advertised   **WELCOMEBREAK**

tel: 01932 868958 **Cobham Services, M25 J9/10 Downside KT11 3DB**
email: cobham.hotel@welcomebreak.co.uk **web:** www.welcomebreak.co.uk
dir: *Between junct 9 & 10 at Extra Cobham services on M25. Accessible from both sides of motorway*

This modern building offers accommodation in smart, spacious and well-equipped bedrooms, suitable for families and business travellers, and all with en suite bathrooms. Continental breakfast is available and other refreshments may be taken at the nearby family restaurant.

Rooms 75 (18 fmly) (35 GF) ⊘ **Facilities** FTV WiFi ⇘ HL **Services** Lift Air con **Parking** 200

COCKERMOUTH
Cumbria   Map 18 NY13

The Trout Hotel
★★★★ 80% HOTEL

tel: 01900 823591 **Crown St CA13 0EJ**
email: reservations@trouthotel.co.uk **web:** www.trouthotel.co.uk
dir: *Adjacent to Wordsworth House*

Dating back to 1670, this privately owned hotel has an enviable setting on the banks of the River Derwent. The well-equipped bedrooms, some contained in a wing overlooking the river, are comfortable and mostly spacious. The Terrace Bar & Bistro, serving food all day, has a sheltered patio area. There is also a cosy bar, a choice of lounge areas and an attractive, traditional-style dining room that offers a good choice of set-price dishes. Recent flooding has led to a lot of refurbishment.

Rooms 49 (4 fmly) (15 GF) ⊘ **S** £100-£155; **D** £120-£240 (incl. bkfst)* **Facilities** STV FTV WiFi ⇘ Fishing Xmas New Year **Conf** Class 20 Board 20 Thtr 25 **Parking** 40 **Notes** LB Civ Wed 60

COLCHESTER
Essex   Map 13 TL92

Wivenhoe House Hotel

★★★★ 83% HOTEL

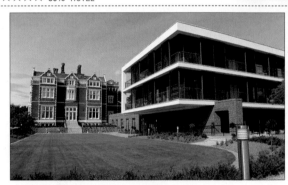

tel: 01206 863666 **Wivenhoe Park CO4 3SQ**
email: info@wivenhoehouse.co.uk **web:** www.wivenhoehouse.co.uk
dir: *From A12 take exit signed Colchester. Follow A133 towards Clacton. Take B1027 for Wivenhoe, right on Boundry Rd, right on Park Rd, signed*

A superb building which forms part of Essex University, the property has been totally refurbished. The bedrooms are split between the main building and the more contemporary extension; each one has been individually decorated, furnished to a very high standard and has modern technology. Public rooms include the Signatures fine dining restaurant and a modern brasserie; there is also a choice of lounges with plush furnishings.

Rooms 40 (6 fmly) ⊘ **S** £95-£140; **D** £95-£140 (incl. bkfst)* **Facilities** STV FTV WiFi ⇘ Xmas New Year **Conf** Class 70 Board 22 Thtr 180 Del from £140* **Services** Lift **Parking** 150 **Notes** LB Civ Wed 180

Stoke by Nayland Hotel, Golf & Spa

★★★★ 77% ◎◎ HOTEL

tel: 01206 262836 & 265835 **Keepers Ln, Leavenheath CO6 4PZ**
email: sales@stokebynayland.com **web:** www.stokebynayland.com
dir: Exit A134 at Leavenheath onto B1068, hotel 0.75m on right

This hotel is situated on the edge of Dedham Vale, an Area of Outstanding Natural Beauty, in 300 acres of undulating countryside with lakes and two golf courses. The spacious bedrooms are attractively decorated and equipped with modern facilities, such as free WiFi available throughout. Public rooms include the Spikes bar, a conservatory, a lounge, a smart restaurant, conference and banqueting suites, and the superb Peake Spa and Fitness Centre that offers extensive facilities including health and beauty treatments.

Rooms 80 (6 fmly) (26 GF) **Facilities** Spa STV FTV WiFi ᐧ ⓢ supervised ⌣ 36 Putt green Fishing Gym Squash Driving range Pro golf tuition ♫ Xmas New Year **Conf** Class 300 Board 60 Thtr 450 **Services** Lift **Parking** 400 **Notes** ⊗ Civ Wed 200

Crowne Plaza Resort Colchester - Five Lakes

★★★★ 74% HOTEL

tel: 01621 868888 **Colchester Rd CM9 8HX**
email: enquiries@cpcolchester.co.uk **web:** www.cpcolchester.co.uk

(For full entry see Tolleshunt Knights)

The North Hill Hotel

★★★ 82% ◎◎ HOTEL

tel: 01206 574001 **51 North Hill CO1 1PY**
email: info@northhillhotel.com **web:** www.northhillhotel.com
dir: Follow directions for town centre, down North Hill, hotel on left

The North Hill Hotel is situated in the centre of this historic town. The contemporary open-plan public areas include a small lounge bar and the Green Room restaurant. The smartly appointed bedrooms are modern and well equipped with large flat-screen TVs and many thoughtful touches.

Rooms 24 (7 annexe) (3 fmly) (4 GF) ᐧ **Facilities** FTV WiFi New Year **Conf** Class 25 Board 20 Thtr 30 **Notes** ⊗

Best Western The Rose & Crown Hotel

★★★ 80% HOTEL

tel: 01206 866677 **East St CO1 2TZ**
email: info@rose-and-crown.com **web:** www.rose-and-crown.com
dir: From A12 follow Rollerworld signs, hotel by level crossing

This delightful 14th-century coaching inn is situated close to the shops and is full of charm and character. Public areas feature a wealth of exposed beams and timbered walls, and includes the contemporary East St Grill. Although the bedrooms vary in size, all are stylishly decorated and equipped with many thoughtful extras suitable for both business and leisure guests; luxury executive rooms are available.

Rooms 39 (3 fmly) (12 GF) **Facilities** WiFi **Conf** Class 50 Board 45 Thtr 100 **Services** Lift **Parking** 50 **Notes** ⊗ Civ Wed 80

Premier Inn Colchester (A12)

BUDGET HOTEL

tel: 0871 527 8260 *(Calls cost 13p per minute plus your phone company's access charge)*
Ipswich Rd CO4 9WP
web: www.premierinn.com
dir: From A12 exit at Colchester Nrth/A1232 junct off towards Colchester. Hotel on right, 200yds from rdbt. NB for Sat Nav use CO4 9TD

High quality, budget accommodation ideal for both families and business travellers. Spacious, en suite bedrooms feature tea and coffee making facilities, and Freeview TV in most hotels. Internet access and WiFi are available for a small fee. The adjacent family restaurant features a wide and varied menu. See also the Hotel Groups pages.

Rooms 104

Premier Inn Colchester Central

BUDGET HOTEL

tel: 0871 527 8258 *(Calls cost 13p per minute plus your phone company's access charge)*
Cowdray Av CO1 1UT
web: www.premierinn.com
dir: From Ipswich A12 junct 29. At rdbt onto A1232 (Ipswich road). At 2nd rdbt 2nd exit onto A133 (Cowdray Ave). Hotel approx 0.5m on right

Rooms 20

Premier Inn Colchester Town Centre

BUDGET HOTEL

tel: 0871 527 9506 **St Peter's St CO1 1HY**
email: ColchesterTownCentre.PI@premierinn.com **web:** www.premierinn.com
dir: A12 to Colchester. Follow Colchester & A133 signs. At rdbt onto A133. At next rdbt 3rd exit signed Westway & A134. At next rdbt 2nd exit onto Middleborough, continue to St Peter's St, hotel on left

Rooms 85

COLEFORD	Map 4 SO51
Gloucestershire	

Bells Hotel & The Forest of Dean Golf Club

★★★ 71% HOTEL

tel: 01594 832583 **Lords Hill GL16 8BE**
email: enquiries@bells-hotel.co.uk **web:** www.bells-hotel.co.uk
dir: 0.25m from Coleford. Off B4228

Set in its own grounds, with an 18-hole golf course, this purpose-built establishment offers a range of facilities. Bedrooms vary in style and space, and a number are on the ground floor. There is a small gym, and a comfortable bar and lounge which is available until late. The hotel's club house, just yards away, has a bar with all-day meals and snacks, a restaurant, a games/TV room and conference and function rooms.

Rooms 53 (12 fmly) (36 GF) (5 smoking) ᐧ **Facilities** FTV WiFi ⌣ 18 Putt green Bowling green Short mat bowling room ♫ Xmas New Year **Conf** Class 250 Board 100 Thtr 350 **Parking** 100 **Notes** ⊗ Civ Wed 150

C

COLERNE
Wiltshire

Map 4 ST87

Lucknam Park Hotel & Spa
★★★★★ @@@ ☻ COUNTRY HOUSE HOTEL

tel: 01225 742777 **SN14 8AZ**
email: reservations@lucknampark.co.uk web: www.lucknampark.co.uk
dir: *M4 junct 17, A350 towards Chippenham, then A420 towards Bristol for 3m. At Ford left to Colerne, 3m, right at x-rds, entrance on right*

Approaching this Palladian mansion along a magnificent mile-long avenue of beech and lime trees, builds a wonderful sense of anticipation. Surrounded by 500 acres of parkland and beautiful gardens, the hotel offers a wealth of choices ranging from pampered relaxation within the indulgent spa, complete with an innovative Well-Being centre; to more energetic equestrian pursuits. Elegant bedrooms and suites are split between the main building and adjacent courtyard, all of which exude quality, individuality and comfort. Dining options range from the informal Brasserie (awarded 2 AA Rosettes), to the formal and very accomplished main restaurant, The Park (with 3 AA Rosettes), where skilled, sincere and engaging staff contribute to a memorable experience. For anyone with a passion for food, the recently opened Cookery School is also worth investigating.

Rooms 42 (18 annexe) (16 GF) ⌖ **S** £360-£1085; **D** £360-£1085 (incl. bkfst)
Facilities Spa STV FTV WiFi ↘ ⊛ ☺ ☺ Gym Cross country course Mountain bikes Equestrian centre Cookery school Xmas New Year **Conf** Class 24 Board 24 Thtr 60 Del from £412 to £812* **Parking** 80 **Notes** LB ⊗ Civ Wed 110

COLTISHALL
Norfolk

Map 13 TG21

Norfolk Mead Hotel
★★★★ 79% @@ COUNTRY HOUSE HOTEL

tel: 01603 737531 **Church Loke NR12 7DN**
email: info@norfolkmead.co.uk web: www.norfolkmead.co.uk
dir: *Coltishall village, go right with petrol station on left, 200 yds church on right, go down driveway*

This beautiful hotel enjoys a peaceful location and is set in its own extensive grounds, while still being a short walk to the pretty village of Coltishall. A major renovation was completed a few years ago; bedrooms are all beautifully designed, and the public areas are very well appointed. Afternoon tea can be enjoyed in the walled garden on finer days and the cosy bar is very comfortable. There is an award-winning restaurant, which benefits from garden and river views.

Rooms 13 (2 annexe) (2 fmly) (1 GF) ⌖ **D** £135-£280 (incl. bkfst) **Facilities** Spa FTV WiFi ↘ ☺ Beauty treatment rooms Xmas New Year **Conf** Class 150 Board 150 Thtr 200 Del from £177.50* **Parking** 40 **Notes** ⊗ Civ Wed 40

CONSETT
County Durham

Map 19 NZ15

Best Western Derwent Manor Hotel
★★★ 79% HOTEL

tel: 01207 592000 & 599767 **Hole Row, Allensford DH8 9BB**
email: reservations@bw-derwentmanor.co.uk web: www.bw-derwentmanorhotel.co.uk

The Best Western Derwent Manor Hotel enjoys an elevated position overlooking the Derwent Valley. Set in 20 acres, the hotel is ideally located within easy distance of both Newcastle and Durham with a wealth of visitor attractions close by. Bedrooms are generous in size and comfortable, and guests have use of a well-appointed gym and pool area as well as a welcoming bar serving food throughout the day. The main restaurant offers a full-on dining experience with local produce used to create a balanced menu.

Rooms 48 (15 fmly) (24 GF) ⌖ **S** £65-£145; **D** £85-£195 (incl. bkfst)* **Facilities** FTV WiFi ↘ ☺ supervised Gym Xmas New Year **Conf** Class 170 Board 80 Thtr 350 Del from £99 to £145* **Services** Lift **Parking** 100 **Notes** LB Civ Wed 300

COPTHORNE
See **Gatwick Airport**

CORBY
Northamptonshire

Map 11 SP88

Premier Inn Corby
BUDGET HOTEL

tel: 0871 527 8264 *(Calls cost 13p per minute plus your phone company's access charge)*
1 Little Colliers Field NN18 8TJ
web: www.premierinn.com
dir: *M1 junct 19, A14 E'bound. Exit at junct 7, left at rdbt onto A43. At next rdbt left onto A6003. Hotel at next rdbt. NB for Sat Nav use NN18 9EX*

High quality, budget accommodation ideal for both families and business travellers. Spacious, en suite bedrooms feature tea and coffee making facilities, and Freeview TV in most hotels. Internet access and WiFi are available for a small fee. The adjacent family restaurant features a wide and varied menu. See also the Hotel Groups pages.

Rooms 71

CORFE CASTLE
Dorset

Map 4 SY98

Mortons House Hotel
★★★ 86% @@ HOTEL

tel: 01929 480988 **49 East St BH20 5EE**
email: stay@mortonshouse.co.uk web: www.mortonshouse.co.uk
dir: *On A351 between Wareham & Swanage*

Set in delightful gardens and grounds with excellent views of Corfe Castle, this impressive building dates back to Tudor times. The oak-panelled drawing room has a roaring log fire in cooler months, and an interesting range of enjoyable cuisine is available in the well-appointed dining room. Bedrooms, many with views of the castle, are comfortable and well equipped.

Rooms 21 (7 annexe) (2 fmly) (7 GF) ⌖ **S** £85-£105; **D** £160-£215 (incl. bkfst)* **Facilities** FTV WiFi HL Xmas New Year **Conf** Class 45 Board 20 Thtr 45 Del from £150* **Parking** 40 **Notes** LB ⊗ Civ Wed 60

C

CORLEY MOTORWAY SERVICE AREA (M6)
Warwickshire
Map 10 SP38

Days Inn Corley - NEC - M6
WELCOMEBREAK

AA Advertised

tel: 01676 543800 **Junction 3-4, M6 North, Corley CV7 8NR**
email: corley.hotel@welcomebreak.co.uk **web:** www.welcomebreak.co.uk
dir: On M6 between juncts 3 & 4 N'bound

This modern building offers accommodation in smart, spacious and well-equipped bedrooms, suitable for families and business travellers, and all with en suite bathrooms. Continental breakfast is available and other refreshments may be taken at the nearby family restaurant.

Rooms 50 (13 fmly) (24 GF) (8 smoking) ᔔ **Facilities** FTV WiFi ᕔ **Parking** 120

CORNHILL-ON-TWEED
Northumberland
Map 21 NT83

HIGHLY RECOMMENDED

Tillmouth Park Country House Hotel
★★★ 87% ◉ COUNTRY HOUSE HOTEL

tel: 01890 882255 **TD12 4UU**
email: reception@tillmouthpark.f9.co.uk **web:** www.tillmouthpark.co.uk
dir: Exit A1(M) at East Ord rdbt at Berwick-upon-Tweed. Take A698 signed Cornhill & Coldstream. Hotel 9m on left

Tillmouth Park is an imposing mansion set in landscaped grounds by the River Till. Gracious public rooms include a stunning galleried lounge with a drawing room adjacent. The quiet, elegant dining room overlooks the gardens, while lunches and early dinners are available in the bistro. Bedrooms retain much traditional character and include several magnificent master rooms.

Rooms 14 (2 annexe) (2 fmly) (2 GF) (4 smoking) **S** £69-£225; **D** £175-£245 (incl. bkfst)* **Facilities** FTV WiFi Game shooting Fishing **Conf** Class 20 Board 20 Thtr 50 Del from £200 to £270* **Parking** 50 **Notes** LB Closed 26 Dec-1 Apr

CORSE LAWN
Gloucestershire
Map 10 SO83

Corse Lawn House Hotel
★★★ 80% ◉◉ HOTEL

tel: 01452 780771 **GL19 4LZ**
email: enquiries@corselawn.com **web:** www.corselawn.com
dir: On B4211 5m SW of Tewkesbury

This gracious Grade II-listed Queen Anne house, in twelve acres of grounds, has been home to the Hine family for more than thirty years. Aided by an enthusiastic and committed team, the family continues to preside over all aspects of the hotel, creating a wonderfully relaxed environment. Bedrooms offer a reassuring mix of comfort and quality, and include four-poster rooms. In both The Restaurant and The Bistro the impressive cuisine is based on excellent produce, much of it locally sourced.

Rooms 18 (3 fmly) (5 GF) ᔔ **S** £60-£100; **D** £99-£180 (incl. bkfst)* **Facilities** STV FTV WiFi ᕔ ᘐ ᕉ ᘻ Badminton Table tennis New Year **Conf** Class 30 Board 25 Thtr 50 Del from £135 to £155* **Parking** 62 **Notes** LB Closed 24-26 Dec Civ Wed 70

CORSHAM
Wiltshire
Map 4 ST87

Guyers House Hotel
★★★★ 76% ◉◉ COUNTRY HOUSE HOTEL

tel: 01249 713399 **Pickwick SN13 0PS**
web: www.guyershouse.com
dir: A4 between Pickwick & Corsham

This privately owned hotel retains the charm and ambiance of a country house. The bedrooms are well appointed in keeping with the style of the house, and equipped with all modern amenities. The award-winning restaurant is the ideal place for an intimate dinner or a family gathering; alfresco dining is possible when the weather is favourable. The gardens are a feature and are open to the public on certain days under the National Garden Scheme. The hotel is conveniently located for easy access to Bath.

Rooms 37 (13 GF) ᔔ **S** £99-£105; **D** £160-£250 (incl. bkfst)* **Facilities** FTV WiFi ᕔ ᘐ ᘻ Gym Xmas **Conf** Class 34 Board 24 Thtr 75 Del from £140* **Parking** 70 **Notes** ⊗ Closed 30 Dec-3 Jan Civ Wed 100

COVENTRY
West Midlands
Map 10 SP37

See also **Meriden & Nuneaton**

Best Western Plus Windmill Village Hotel
Best Western PLUS
★★★★ 77% HOTEL

tel: 024 7640 4040 **Birmingham Rd, Allesley CV5 9AL**
email: reservations@windmillvillagehotel.co.uk **web:** www.windmillvillagehotel.co.uk
dir: A45, close to Coventry City Centre

This modern hotel is conveniently located on the outskirts of Coventry and is a short drive from Birmingham and the NEC. Bedrooms are all very attractively presented and most rooms have views over the hotel's challenging golf course. The leisure facilities are first rate and include a very well-equipped gym and a swimming pool. Business guests are well catered for with a range of conference facilities including business suites, and free WiFi is available throughout the hotel.

Rooms 105 (35 annexe) (10 fmly) (39 GF) ᔔ **Facilities** Spa FTV WiFi ᕔ ⊗ supervised ᘻ 18 Putt green Gym Xmas New Year **Conf** Class 140 Board 60 Thtr 400 **Services** Lift **Parking** 400 **Notes** Civ Wed 100

Novotel Coventry
NOVOTEL
HOTELS & RESORTS
★★★ 78% HOTEL

tel: 024 7636 5000 **Wilsons Ln CV6 6HL**
email: h0506@accor-hotels.com **web:** www.novotel.com
dir: M6 junct 3. Follow signs for B4113 towards Longford & Bedworth. 3rd exit on large rdbt

Novotel Coventry is a modern hotel convenient for Birmingham, Coventry and the motorway network, offering spacious, well-equipped accommodation. The bright brasserie has extended dining hours, alternatively there is an extensive room-service menu. Family rooms and a play area make this a child-friendly hotel, and for adults, there is also a mini-gym and a selection of meeting rooms.

Rooms 98 (25 GF) ᔔ **Facilities** STV WiFi ᕔ Mini gym **Conf** Class 100 Board 40 Thtr 200 **Services** Lift **Parking** 120 **Notes** Civ Wed 50

COVENTRY *continued*

The Chace Hotel

★★★ 72% HOTEL

tel: 024 7630 3398 **Toll Bar End, London Rd CV3 4EQ**
email: thechace@corushotels.com **web:** www.corushotels.com/coventry
dir: *A45 or A46 follow to Toll Bar Rdbt/Coventry Airport, take B4116 to Willenhall, over mini-rdbt, hotel on left*

Conveniently located for ease of access to the motorway network and Coventry Airport, The Chace hotel has a long history as an important residence in Willenhall, and was once the home of Dr Charles Webb Iliffe. Rooms vary in style across the property; all are furnished to a good standard. Public areas boast many original and period features including portraits of the doctor and his wife. A popular restaurant and number of function rooms along with ample free parking are also available.

Rooms 66 (2 fmly) (24 GF) **Facilities** FTV WiFi ⬧ Xmas New Year **Conf** Class 40 Board 56 Thtr 100 Del from £115 to £135 **Parking** 100 **Notes** Civ Wed 100

Premier Inn Coventry City Centre

BUDGET HOTEL

tel: 0871 527 8272 *(Calls cost 13p per minute plus your phone company's access charge)*
Belgrade Plaza, Bond St CV1 4AH
web: www.premierinn.com
dir: *A4053 (ring road) junct 9, follow Belgrade Plaza car park signs. Hotel in same complex*

High quality, budget accommodation ideal for both families and business travellers. Spacious, en suite bedrooms feature tea and coffee making facilities, and Freeview TV in most hotels. Internet access and WiFi are available for a small fee. The adjacent family restaurant features a wide and varied menu. See also the Hotel Groups pages.

Rooms 120

Premier Inn Coventry City Centre (Earlsdon Park)

BUDGET HOTEL

tel: 0871 527 9318 *(Calls cost 13p per minute plus your phone company's access charge)*
Earlsdon Park CV1 3BH
web: www.premierinn.com
dir: *From Coventry ring road follow Ikea signs. Hotel adjacent to Coventry RFC on Butts Rd. Parking in multi storey adjacent*

Rooms 100

Premier Inn Coventry East (Ansty)

BUDGET HOTEL

tel: 0871 527 8274 *(Calls cost 13p per minute plus your phone company's access charge)*
Coombe Fields Rd, Ansty CV7 9JP
web: www.premierinn.com
dir: *M6 junct 2, B4065 towards Ansty. After village right onto B4029 signed Brinklow. Right into Coombe Fields Rd, hotel on right*

Rooms 28

Premier Inn Coventry East (Binley/A46)

BUDGET HOTEL

tel: 0871 527 8268 *(Calls cost 13p per minute plus your phone company's access charge)*
Rugby Rd, Binley Woods CV3 2TA
web: www.premierinn.com
dir: *M6 junct 2 follow Warwick, A46 & M40 signs. Follow 'All traffic' signs, under bridge onto A46. Left at 1st rdbt to Binley. Hotel on right at next rdbt*

Rooms 96

Premier Inn Coventry East (M6 Jct 2)

BUDGET HOTEL

tel: 0871 527 8266 *(Calls cost 13p per minute plus your phone company's access charge)*
Gielgud Way, Cross Point Business Park CV2 2SZ
web: www.premierinn.com
dir: *M6 junct 2 towards Coventry onto A4600 (Hinckley road). At rdbt 1st exit into Parkway, left at next rdbt into Olivier Way. At next rdbt straight on into retail park towards cinema, hotel on right*

Rooms 48

Premier Inn Coventry South (A45)

BUDGET HOTEL

tel: 0871 527 8270 *(Calls cost 13p per minute plus your phone company's access charge)*
Kenpas Highway CV3 6PB
web: www.premierinn.com
dir: *M6 junct 2, A46. Follow A45 towards Birmingham*

Rooms 38

| **COWES**
Isle of Wight | **Map 5 SZ49** |

Best Western New Holmwood Hotel

★★★ 79% HOTEL

tel: 01983 292508 **Queens Rd, Egypt Point PO31 8BW**
email: reception@newholmwoodhotel.co.uk **web:** www.newholmwoodhotel.co.uk
dir: *From A3020 at Northwood Garage lights, left & follow to rdbt. 1st left then sharp right into Baring Rd, 4th left into Egypt Hill. At bottom turn right, hotel on right*

Just by the Esplanade, this hotel has an enviable outlook. Bedrooms are comfortable and very well equipped, and the light and airy, glass-fronted restaurant looks out to sea and serves a range of interesting meals. The sun terrace is delightful in the summer and there is a choice of meeting rooms for all occasions. Parking is available on a first-come, first-serve basis.

Rooms 26 (1 fmly) (9 GF) ⬧ **Facilities** STV FTV WiFi ⬧ Xmas New Year **Conf** Class 60 Board 50 Thtr 100 Del from £121 to £160* **Parking** 20 **Notes** Civ Wed 60

C

CRAMLINGTON
Northumberland

Map 21 NZ27

Premier Inn Newcastle Gosforth/Cramlington

BUDGET HOTEL

tel: 0871 527 8788 *(Calls cost 13p per minute plus your phone company's access charge)*
Moor Farm Roundabout, Off Front St, Annitsford NE23 7QA
web: www.premierinn.com
dir: *At rdbt junct of A19 & A189, S of Cramlington*

High quality, budget accommodation ideal for both families and business travellers. Spacious, en suite bedrooms feature tea and coffee making facilities, and Freeview TV in most hotels. Internet access and WiFi are available for a small fee. The adjacent family restaurant features a wide and varied menu. See also the Hotel Groups pages.

Rooms 79

CRAWLEY

See **Gatwick Airport**

CREWE
Cheshire

Map 15 SJ75

Crewe Hall
★★★★ 81% HOTEL

QHOTELS
INSPIRED BY YOU

tel: 01270 253333 **Weston Rd CW1 6UZ**
email: crewehall@qhotels.co.uk **web:** www.qhotels.co.uk
dir: M6 junct 16, A500 to Crewe. Take A5020. 1st exit at next rdbt to Crewe. Hotel 150yds on right

Standing in 500 acres of mature grounds, this historic hall dates back to the 17th century, yet retains an elaborate interior with Victorian-style architecture. Bedrooms are spacious, well equipped and comfortable with traditionally styled suites in the main hall and modern rooms in the west wing. Afternoon tea is served in The Sheridan Lounge, while The Brasserie Restaurant and Bar is contemporary and has a relaxed atmosphere. The health and beauty spa ensure that the hotel is a popular choice with both corporate and leisure guests.

Rooms 117 (91 annexe) (5 fmly) (35 GF) 🐾 **S** £87-£307; **D** £99-£319 (incl. bkfst)
Facilities Spa STV WiFi ♿ 🎱 ♨ Gym Enclosed events field **Conf** Class 172 Board 96 Thtr 364 Del from £135 to £295 **Services** Lift **Parking** 500 **Notes** LB Civ Wed 180

Hunters Lodge Hotel
★★★ 66% HOTEL

tel: 01270 539100 **Sydney Rd, Sydney CW1 5LU**
email: info@hunterslodge.co.uk **web:** www.hunterslodge.co.uk
dir: M6 junct 16. 1m from Crewe station, off A534

Dating back to the 18th century, the hotel has been extended and modernised over the years. Accommodation, mainly located in adjacent well-equipped bedroom wings, includes family and four-poster rooms. Imaginative dishes are served in the popular bar which also offers open fires and friendly and efficient service.

Rooms 57 (4 fmly) (31 GF) (2 smoking) **Facilities** STV FTV WiFi ♿ Gym **Conf** Class 100 Board 80 Thtr 160 **Parking** 240 **Notes** ⊗ RS Sun eve Civ Wed 130

Premier Inn Crewe Central

BUDGET HOTEL

tel: 0871 527 8276 *(Calls cost 13p per minute plus your phone company's access charge)*
Weston Rd CW1 6FX
web: www.premierinn.com
dir: *M6 junct 16, A500, at rdbt 3rd exit onto A5020 (Old Park Rd). At next rdbt 2nd exit into Western Rd, at next rdbt 3rd exit, hotel on left*

High quality, budget accommodation ideal for both families and business travellers. Spacious, en suite bedrooms feature tea and coffee making facilities, and Freeview TV in most hotels. Internet access and WiFi are available for a small fee. The adjacent family restaurant features a wide and varied menu. See also the Hotel Groups pages.

Rooms 20

Premier Inn Crewe West

BUDGET HOTEL

Premier Inn

tel: 0871 527 8278 *(Calls cost 13p per minute plus your phone company's access charge)*
Coppenhall Ln, Woolstanwood CW2 8SD
web: www.premierinn.com
dir: *At junct of A530 & A532, 9m from M6 junct 16 N'bound*

Rooms 80

CRICK
Northamptonshire

Map 11 SP57

Ibis Rugby

ibis

AA Advertised

tel: 01788 824331 **Parklands NN6 7EX**
email: H3588@accor.com **web:** www.ibishotel.com
dir: *M1 junct 18, follow Daventry/Rugby A5 signs. At rdbt 3rd exit signed DIRFT East. Hotel on right*

Modern, budget hotel offering comfortable accommodation in bright and practical bedrooms. Breakfast is self-service and dinner is available in the restaurant.

Rooms 111 (47 fmly) (12 GF) **Conf** Class 25 Board 25 Thtr 30 **Services** Lift **Parking** 111

CROMER
Norfolk

Map 13 TG24

Sea Marge Hotel
★★★ 81% HOTEL

tel: 01263 579579 **16 High St, Overstrand NR27 0AB**
email: seamarge@mackenziehotels.com **web:** www.mackenziehotels.com
dir: *A140 from Norwich then A149 to Cromer, B1159 to Overstrand. Hotel in village centre*

An elegant Grade II listed Edwardian mansion perched on the clifftop amidst pretty landscaped gardens which lead down to the beach. Bedrooms are tastefully decorated and thoughtfully equipped; many have superb sea views. Public rooms offer a wide choice of areas in which to relax, including Frazer's restaurant and a smart lounge bar.

Rooms 25 (6 annexe) (6 fmly) (3 GF) 🐾 **S** fr £101; **D** fr £162 (incl. bkfst)*
Facilities FTV WiFi ⛳ Xmas New Year **Conf** Class 55 Board 30 Thtr 70 **Services** Lift **Parking** 50 **Notes** LB

CROMER *continued*

The Cliftonville Hotel

★★★ 78% HOTEL

tel: 01263 512543 **Seafront NR27 9AS**
email: reservations@cliftonvillehotel.co.uk **web:** www.cliftonvillehotel.co.uk
dir: *From A149 (coast road) 500yds from town centre, N'bound on clifftop by sunken gardens*

The Cliftonville Hotel is an imposing Edwardian hotel situated on the main coast road with stunning views of the sea. Public areas feature a magnificent staircase, minstrels' gallery, coffee shop, lounge bar, a further residents' lounge, Boltons Bistro and an additional restaurant. The pleasantly decorated bedrooms are generally quite spacious and have lovely sea views.

Rooms 30 (3 fmly) ⬧ **S** £45-£100; **D** £90-£200 (incl. bkfst)* **Facilities** FTV WiFi ⬧ Xmas New Year **Conf** Class 100 Board 60 Thtr 150 Del from £70 to £210* **Services** Lift **Parking** 20 **Notes** LB

Hotel de Paris

★★★ 71% HOTEL

Leisureplex
HOLIDAY HOTELS

tel: 01263 513141 **High St NR27 9HG**
email: deparis.cromer@alfatravel.co.uk **web:** www.leisureplex.co.uk
dir: *Enter Church St (one way) after lights left straight into Jetty St, car park at end on left*

An imposing, traditional-style resort hotel, situated in a prominent position overlooking the pier and beach. The bedrooms are pleasantly decorated and equipped with a good range of useful extras; many rooms have lovely sea views. The spacious public areas include a large lounge bar, restaurant, games room and a further lounge.

Rooms 63 (8 fmly) ⬧ **Facilities** FTV WiFi ♪ Xmas New Year **Services** Lift **Parking** 14 **Notes** ⊗ Closed Jan-Feb RS Mar & Nov-Dec

---

CROOKLANDS   Map 18 SD58
Cumbria

Crooklands Hotel

★★★ 78% HOTEL

tel: 015395 67432 **LA7 7NW**
email: reception@crooklands.com **web:** www.crooklands.com
dir: *M6 junct 36 onto A65. Left at rdbt. Hotel 1.5m on right past garage*

Although only a stone's throw from the M6, this hotel enjoys a peaceful rural location. Housed in a converted 200-year-old farmhouse, the restaurant retains many original features such as the beams and stone walls. Bedrooms are a mix of modern and traditional and vary in size. The hotel is a popular stop-over for both leisure and corporate guests travelling between England and Scotland.

Rooms 30 (1 fmly) (14 GF) ⬧ **Facilities** FTV WiFi New Year **Conf** Class 50 Board 40 Thtr 80 **Services** Lift **Parking** 80 **Notes** ⊗ Closed 24-28 Dec

---

CROYDON   Map 6 TQ36
Greater London

Croydon Park Hotel

★★★★ 73% HOTEL

tel: 020 8680 9200 **7 Altyre Rd CR9 5AA**
email: info@croydonparkhotel.com **web:** www.croydonparkhotel.com
dir: *3 min walk from East Croydon Station*

This hotel is located in the heart of the town centre, a 3-minute walk from East Croydon train station and with easy access to both Gatwick Airport and central London. Bedrooms vary in style, but all are comfortably appointed. The two dining options are Whistlers Bar with a menu available throughout the day, and Oscars Brasserie with a daily buffet and carte menu. Conference and leisure facilities are available.

Rooms 211 (36 fmly) (6 GF) **Facilities** FTV WiFi ⬧ ⬧ Gym Squash Sauna Xmas New Year **Conf** Class 100 Board 30 Thtr 220 **Services** Lift Air con **Parking** 91 **Notes** ⊗ Civ Wed 220

Hallmark Hotel London Croydon Aerodrome

★★★★ 72% HOTEL

tel: 0330 028 3403 **Purley Way CR9 4LT**
email: croydon@hallmarkhotels.co.uk **web:** www.hallmarkhotels.co.uk
dir: *Follow A23 & Central London signs. Hotel on left adjacent to Airport House*

This hotel (formerly the Aerodrome Hotel) sits in a prime location and offers comfortably appointed bedrooms, all with LCD TVs and free WiFi throughout. Public areas are stylish and modern in their design and include a spacious open-plan bar and brasserie. Ideal for both the leisure and corporate market, there are a number of fully-equipped meeting and conference facilities.

Rooms 110 (10 fmly) ⬧ **Facilities** FTV WiFi ⬧ **Conf** Class 60 Board 36 Thtr 170 **Services** Lift **Parking** 79 **Notes** ⊗ Civ Wed 150

Selsdon Park Hotel & Golf Club

★★★★ 72% HOTEL

tel: 020 8657 8811 **Addington Rd, Sanderstead CR2 8YA**
email: selsdonpark.reception@principal-hayley.com **web:** www.principal-hayley.com
dir: *3m SE of Croydon, off A2022*

Surrounded by 200 acres of mature parkland with its own 18-hole golf course, this imposing Jacobean mansion is less than 20 minutes from central London. The hotel's impressive range of conference rooms along with the spectacular views of the North Downs countryside, make this a popular venue for both weddings and meetings. The leisure facilities are impressive.

Rooms 199 (19 fmly) (33 GF) **Facilities** Spa FTV WiFi ⌁ HL ⊛ 🏊 18 Putt green 🏌 Gym Squash Xmas **Conf** Class 250 Board 100 Thtr 350 **Services** Lift **Parking** 300 **Notes** ⊛ Civ Wed 350

Holiday Inn Express London - Croydon

BUDGET HOTEL

tel: 020 8253 1200 **1 Priddys Yard, Off Frith Rd CRO 1TS**
email: gm@exhicroydon.com **web:** www.hiexpress.com/london-croydon
dir: *From A235 into Lower Coombe St, at rdbt 1st exit, at next rdbt 2nd exit onto dual carriageway, right to Centrale Shopping Centre, under car park, follow to right, 1st left*

A modern hotel ideal for families and business travellers. Fresh and uncomplicated, the spacious rooms include Sky TV, power shower and tea and coffee-making facilities. Continental buffet breakfast is included in the room rate; other meals may be taken at the nearby family pub or restaurant. See also the Hotel Groups pages.

Rooms 156 (62 fmly) **Conf** Class 30 Board 30 Thtr 60

Premier Inn Croydon (Purley A23)

BUDGET HOTEL

tel: 0871 527 8282 *(Calls cost 13p per minute plus your phone company's access charge)*
The Colonnades Leisure Park, 619 Purley Way CRO 4RQ
web: www.premierinn.com
dir: *From N: M1, M25, A23 towards Croydon. From S: M25 junct 7, A23 towards Purley Way, 8m, hotel close to junct with Waddon Way*

High quality, budget accommodation ideal for both families and business travellers. Spacious, en suite bedrooms feature tea and coffee making facilities, and Freeview TV in most hotels. Internet access and WiFi are available for a small fee. The adjacent family restaurant features a wide and varied menu. See also the Hotel Groups pages.

Rooms 84

Premier Inn Croydon South (A212)

BUDGET HOTEL

tel: 0871 527 8280 *(Calls cost 13p per minute plus your phone company's access charge)*
104 Coombe Rd CRO 5RB
web: www.premierinn.com
dir: *M25 junct 7, A23 to Purley, A235 to Croydon. Pass Tree House pub on left. Right at lights onto A212*

Rooms 39

Premier Inn Croydon Town Centre Hotel

BUDGET HOTEL

tel: 0871 527 9438 *(Calls cost 13p per minute plus your phone company's access charge)*
Philips House, Lansdowne Rd CRO 2BX
web: www.premierinn.com
dir: *Phone for directions*

Rooms 168

CULLOMPTON
Devon

Map 3 ST00

Padbrook Park

★★★ 79% HOTEL

tel: 01884 836100 **EX15 1RU**
email: info@padbrookpark.co.uk **web:** www.padbrookpark.co.uk
dir: *1m from M5 junct 28, follow brown signs*

This purpose-built hotel is part of a golf and leisure complex located in the Culm Valley, just one mile from the M5. Set in 100 acres of parkland with an 18-hole golf course, Padbrook Park has a friendly, relaxed atmosphere and a contemporary feel. A variety of room types is available, including family, inter-connecting, superior and deluxe rooms.

Rooms 40 (4 fmly) (11 GF) **S** fr £60; **D** fr £75* **Facilities** STV FTV WiFi ⌁ HL 🏌 18 Putt green Fishing Gym 3 rink bowling centre Crazy golf Beauty treatment room ♫ Xmas New Year **Conf** Class 150 Board 50 Thtr 200 **Services** Lift **Parking** 250 **Notes** LB ⊛ Civ Wed 200

DAGENHAM
Greater London

Map 6 TQ48

Premier Inn London Dagenham

BUDGET HOTEL

tel: 0871 527 9364 *(Calls cost 13p per minute plus your phone company's access charge)*
Chequers Corner, 2 New Rd RM9 6YS
web: www.premierinn.com
dir: *M25 junct 30/A13 signed Barking. Continue on A13 through underpass then flyover, following directions to Central London, Barking & Docklands. Left off A13 - Dagenham East. At rdbt 4th exit, then left at traffic signals onto A1306 Dagenham. Continue at traffic signals. Inn on left*

High quality, budget accommodation ideal for both families and business travellers. Spacious, en suite bedrooms feature tea and coffee making facilities, and Freeview TV in most hotels. Internet access and WiFi are available for a small fee. The adjacent family restaurant features a wide and varied menu. See also the Hotel Groups pages.

Rooms 80

D

DARLINGTON
County Durham

Map 19 NZ21

INSPECTORS' CHOICE

Rockliffe Hall
★★★★★ ◉◉◉ HOTEL

tel: 01325 729999 **Rockliffe Park, Hurworth-on-Tees DL2 2DU**
email: enquiries@rockliffehall.com **web:** www.rockliffehall.com
dir: A66 towards Darlington, A167, through Hurworth-on-Tees. In Croft-on-Tees left into Hurworth Rd

This impressive hotel enjoys a peaceful setting on a restored 18th-century estate by the banks of the River Tees. Luxurious, spacious bedrooms, contemporary in style, are split between the original old hall, the new hall and Tiplady Lodge. Dining options include The Orangery, The Clubhouse and The Brasserie. A state-of-the-art spa and championship golf course, with a first-class club house, complete the picture.

Rooms 61 (5 fmly) (17 GF) ☛ **S** £190-£455; **D** £205-£475 (incl. bkfst)*
Facilities Spa STV FTV WiFi ▷ ⑤ ↖ ↧ 18 Putt green Fishing ↘ Gym Nordic walking ♫ Xmas New Year **Conf** Class 100 Board 30 Thtr 180 Del from £245* **Services** Lift Air con **Parking** 200 **Notes** LB Civ Wed 180

Headlam Hall
★★★★ 79% ◉◉ HOTEL

tel: 01325 730238 **Headlam, Gainford DL2 3HA**
email: admin@headlamhall.co.uk **web:** www.headlamhall.co.uk
dir: 2m N of A67 between Piercebridge & Gainford

This impressive Jacobean hall lies in farmland north-east of Piercebridge and has its own 9-hole golf course. The main house retains many historical features, including flagstone floors and a pillared hall. Bedrooms are well proportioned and traditionally styled; a converted coach house contains the more modern rooms. There are extensive conference facilities, and the hotel is popular as a wedding venue. Further facilities include a stunning spa complex with a 14-metre pool, an outdoor hot spa, drench shower, sauna and steam room, as well as a gym with the latest cardio and resistance equipment, and five treatment rooms offering a range of therapies and beauty treatments.

Rooms 38 (22 annexe) (4 fmly) (9 GF) ☛ **S** £100-£160; **D** £130-£190 (incl. bkfst)*
Facilities Spa STV FTV WiFi ▷ ⑤ ↧ 9 ⌗ Putt green Fishing ↘ Gym New Year **Conf** Class 40 Board 40 Thtr 120 Del from £140 to £180* **Services** Lift **Parking** 80 **Notes** LB Closed 24-26 Dec Civ Wed 150

Bannatyne Hotel Darlington
★★★★ 73% HOTEL

tel: 0344 248 3832 **Southend Av DL3 7HZ**
email: enquiries.darlingtonhotel@bannatyne.co.uk **web:** www.bannatyne.co.uk
dir: From S: A1(M) junct 57, A66(M) signed Darlington. 2nd rdbt 2nd exit into Grange Rd. 3rd left into Southend Ave. From N: A1(M) junct 58, A68 signed Darlington, left at 1st rdbt, 2nd rdbt 2nd exit into Carmel Rd N, into Carmel Rd S. Left at 4th rdbt into Grange Rd, 3rd left

This hotel, with excellent parking, is close to the town centre and provides well-equipped accommodation with WiFi in all areas. Public areas include the brasserie-style bar and restaurant, Maxine's, plus good function, conference and wedding facilities. Free use of Bannatyne's Spa and gym (just five minutes away) is also available to guests. Very friendly hospitality is assured from the young and enthusiastic team at this hotel.

Rooms 60 (1 fmly) (11 GF) ☛ **S** £70-£130; **D** £80-£130 (incl. bkfst)* **Facilities** FTV WiFi ▷ Guests have complimentary use of nearby health club Xmas New Year **Conf** Class 60 Board 60 Thtr 120 **Services** Lift **Parking** 60 **Notes** ⊗ Civ Wed 120

Hall Garth Hotel, Golf and Country Club
★★★ 81% HOTEL

tel: 01325 300400 **Coatham Mundeville DL1 3LU**
email: gm@hallgarthdarlington.co.uk **web:** www.hallgarthdarlington.co.uk
dir: A1(M) junct 59, A167 towards Darlington. After 600yds left at top of hill, hotel on right

Peacefully situated in grounds that feature a golf course, this hotel is just a few minutes from the motorway network. The well-equipped bedrooms come in various styles - it's worth asking for one of the trendy, modern rooms. Public rooms include relaxing lounges, a fine-dining restaurant and a separate pub. The extensive leisure and conference facilities are an important focus here.

Rooms 56 (16 annexe) (3 fmly) (1 GF) **Facilities** Spa STV FTV WiFi ▷ ⑤ supervised ↧ 9 Putt green Gym Steam room Beauty salon Sauna Xmas New Year **Conf** Class 160 Board 80 Thtr 250 Del from £115 to £148* **Parking** 150 **Notes** Civ Wed 170

Best Western Walworth Castle Hotel
★★★ 75% HOTEL

tel: 01325 485470 **Walworth DL2 2LY**
email: enquiries@walworthcastle.co.uk **web:** www.bw-walworthcastle.co.uk
dir: A1(M) junct 58 follow signs to Corbridge. Left at The Dog pub. Hotel on left after 2m

This 12th-century castle is privately owned and has been tastefully converted. Accommodation is offered in a range of styles, including an impressive suite and more compact rooms in an adjoining wing. Dinner can be taken in the fine dining Hansards Restaurant or the more relaxed Farmer's Bar. This is a popular venue for conferences and weddings.

Rooms 32 (14 annexe) (4 fmly) (8 GF) ☛ **S** £79-£99; **D** £89-£240 (incl. bkfst) **Facilities** FTV WiFi ▷ ↘ Falconry centre Xmas New Year **Conf** Class 60 Board 40 Thtr 120 Del from £125 to £155 **Parking** 100 **Notes** ⊗ Civ Wed 100

Premier Inn Darlington

BUDGET HOTEL

tel: 0871 527 8286 (Calls cost 13p per minute plus your phone company's access charge)
Morton Park Way, Morton Park DL1 4PJ
web: www.premierinn.com
dir: A1(M) junct 57, A66(M), A66 towards Teeside. At 3rd rdbt left onto B6280. Hotel on right. From N: A1(M) junct 57 onto A167, A1150, A66 towards Darlington, right onto B6280. Hotel on right

High quality, budget accommodation ideal for both families and business travellers. Spacious, en suite bedrooms feature tea and coffee making facilities, and Freeview TV in most hotels. Internet access and WiFi are available for a small fee. The adjacent family restaurant features a wide and varied menu. See also the Hotel Groups pages.

Rooms 79

DARTFORD
Kent — Map 6 TQ57

Rowhill Grange Hotel & Utopia Spa

★★★★ 81% @@ HOTEL

tel: 01322 615136 **Wilmington DA2 7QH**
email: admin@rowhillgrange.co.uk web: www.rowhillgrange.co.uk
dir: M25 junct 3 take B2173 to Swanley, then B258 to Hextable

Set in nine acres of mature woodland this hotel enjoys a tranquil setting, yet is still easily accessible to road networks. Bedrooms are stylishly and individually decorated; many have four-poster or sleigh beds. The elegant lounge is popular for afternoon teas, and the leisure and conference facilities are impressive. There is a smart, conservatory restaurant and also a more informal brasserie.

Rooms 38 (8 annexe) (4 fmly) (3 GF) ► **S** £109-£479; **D** £109-£479* **Facilities** Spa STV FTV WiFi ⓑ ⓧ ⓢ Gym Beauty treatment Hair salon Aerobic studio Japanese therapy pool Xmas New Year **Conf** Class 64 Board 34 Thtr 160 Del from £149* **Services** Lift **Parking** 150 **Notes** LB ⓧ Civ Wed 150

Premier Inn Dartford

BUDGET HOTEL

tel: 0871 527 9328 (Calls cost 13p per minute plus your phone company's access charge)
Halcrow Av DA1 5FX
web: www.premierinn.com
dir: M25 junct 1A , A206 towards Erith. At next rdbt right to Bridge Business Park. At next rdbt left towards Power Station. Hotel 300yds on left

High quality, budget accommodation ideal for both families and business travellers. Spacious, en suite bedrooms feature tea and coffee making facilities, and Freeview TV in most hotels. Internet access and WiFi are available for a small fee. The adjacent family restaurant features a wide and varied menu. See also the Hotel Groups pages.

Rooms 120

DARTMOUTH
Devon — Map 3 SX85

The Dart Marina Hotel

★★★★ 79% @ HOTEL

tel: 01803 832580 & 837120 **Sandquay Rd TQ6 9PH**
email: reservations@dartmarina.com web: www.dartmarina.com
dir: A3122 from Totnes to Dartmouth. Follow road which becomes College Way, before Higher Ferry. Hotel sharp left in Sandquay Rd

Boasting a stunning riverside location with its own marina, this is a very special place to stay. Bedrooms vary in style, all have wonderful views, and some have private balconies where you can sit and soak up the atmosphere. The stylish public areas take full advantage of the waterside setting with opportunities to dine alfresco. The River Restaurant is the venue for accomplished cooking.

Rooms 49 (4 annexe) (4 fmly) (4 GF) ► **S** £115-£155; **D** £180-£440 (incl. bkfst)* **Facilities** Spa FTV WiFi ⓧ Gym Xmas New Year **Services** Lift **Parking** 50 **Notes** LB

Royal Castle Hotel

★★★ 82% @ HOTEL

tel: 01803 833033 **11 The Quay TQ6 9PS**
email: enquiry@royalcastle.co.uk web: www.royalcastle.co.uk
dir: In centre of town, overlooking Inner Harbour

At the edge of the harbour, this imposing 17th-century former coaching inn is filled with charm and character. Bedrooms are well equipped and comfortable, and many have harbour views. A choice of quiet seating areas is offered in addition to both the traditional and contemporary bars. A variety of eating options is available including the main restaurant which has lovely views.

Rooms 24 (3 fmly) ► **Facilities** FTV WiFi ⓑ ♫ Xmas New Year **Conf** Class 30 Board 20 Thtr 50 **Parking** 15 **Notes** Civ Wed 80

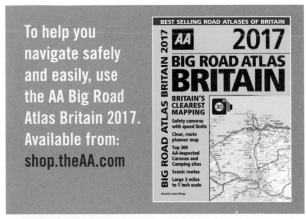

D

INSPECTORS' CHOICE

Fawsley Hall

★★★★ ◉◉ ♨ HOTEL

tel: 01327 892000 & 0845 072 7482 *(Calls cost 5p per minute plus your phone company's access charge)* **Fawsley NN11 3BA**
email: reservations@fawsleyhall.com web: www.fawsleyhall.com
dir: *A361 S of Daventry, between Badby & Charwelton, hotel signed single track lane*

Dating back to the 15th century, this delightful hotel is peacefully located in beautiful gardens designed by 'Capability' Brown. Spacious, individually designed bedrooms and stylish public areas are beautifully furnished with antique and period pieces. The different wings of the house - Tudor, Georgian and Victorian - all have their distinct identity. For a true sense of the past, why not stay in the Queen's Suite, where Elizabeth I slept in 1575. Afternoon tea is served in the impressive Great Hall, and dinner is available in the award-winning fine-dining restaurant, with its original beams and stonework, an impressive inglenook fireplace, and candlelit tables dressed in fine white linen. The hotel has its own cinema and The Grayshot Spa features an ozone pool, treatment rooms and fitness studio.

Rooms 60 (14 annexe) (2 GF) ⚓ **Facilities** Spa STV WiFi ⚐ ⚘ ⚐ Gym Health & beauty treatment rooms Fitness studio 29-seat cinema Xmas New Year **Conf** Class 64 Board 40 Thtr 120 **Parking** 140 **Notes** ⊗ Civ Wed 120

Mercure Daventry Court Hotel

★★★★ 74% HOTEL

tel: 01327 307000 **Sedgemoor Way NN11 0SG**
email: HA010@accor.com web: www.themercure.com/Daventrycourt
dir: *M1 junct 16, A45 to Daventry, at 1st rdbt turn right signed Kilsby/M1(N). Hotel on right in 1m*

This modern, striking hotel overlooking Drayton Water boasts spacious public areas that include a good range of banqueting, meeting and leisure facilities. It is a popular venue for conferences. Bedrooms are suitable for both business and leisure guests.

Rooms 155 (17 fmly) ⚓ **Facilities** Spa FTV WiFi HL ⚐ supervised Gym Steam room Sauna Health & beauty salon New Year **Conf** Class 200 Board 100 Thtr 600 Del from £125 to £145 **Services** Lift **Parking** 350 **Notes** Civ Wed 280

Langstone Cliff Hotel

★★★ 80% HOTEL   THE INDEPENDENTS

tel: 01626 868000 **Dawlish Warren EX7 0NA**
email: reception@langstone-hotel.co.uk web: www.langstone-hotel.co.uk
dir: *1.5m NE off A379 - Exeter Rd to Dawlish Warren*

A family-owned and run hotel, the Langstone Cliff Hotel offers a range of leisure, conference and function facilities. Bedrooms, many with sea views and balconies, are spacious, comfortable and well equipped. The hotel has a number of attractive lounges and a well-stocked bar. Dinner is served, often carvery style, in the restaurant.

Rooms 64 (2 annexe) (52 fmly) (10 GF) ⚓ **S** £49-£130; **D** £69-£150 (incl. bkfst)*
Facilities STV FTV WiFi ⚐ HL ⚐ ⚐ ⚐ Putt green Gym Table tennis Golf practice area Hair & beauty salon Therapy room Ballroom ♫ Xmas New Year Child facilities **Conf** Class 200 Board 80 Thtr 400 Del from £90 to £120* **Services** Lift **Parking** 200 **Notes** LB Civ Wed 400

Dunkerleys Hotel & Restaurant

★★★ 78% ◉◉ HOTEL

tel: 01304 375016 **19 Beach St CT14 7AH**
email: info@dunkerleys.co.uk web: www.dunkerleys.co.uk
dir: *From M20 or M2 follow signs for A258 Deal. Hotel close to Pier*

This hotel is centrally located and on the seafront. Bedrooms are furnished to a high standard with a good range of amenities. The restaurant and bar offer a comfortable and attractive environment in which to relax and to enjoy the cuisine that makes the best use of local ingredients. Service throughout is friendly and attentive.

Rooms 16 (2 fmly) **S** £60-£110; **D** £80-£150 (incl. bkfst)* **Facilities** FTV WiFi Xmas New Year **Notes** LB ⊗ RS Sun eve & Mon

DEDDINGTON
Oxfordshire   Map 11 SP43

Deddington Arms
★★★ 77% HOTEL

tel: 01869 338364 **Horsefair OX15 0SH**
email: deddarms@oxfordshire-hotels.co.uk **web:** www.oxfordshire-hotels.co.uk
dir: *From S: M40 junct 10/A43. 1st rdbt left to Aynho B4100 & left to Deddington B4031.*
From N: M40 junct 11 to hospital & Adderbury on A4260, then to Deddington

This charming and friendly old inn is conveniently located off the market square. The well-equipped bedrooms are comfortably appointed and situated either in the main building or a purpose-built courtyard wing. The bar is full of character, and the delightful restaurant enjoys a well-deserved reputation locally.

Rooms 27 (4 fmly) (10 GF) **S** £70-£120; **D** £75-£180 (incl. bkfst)* **Facilities** FTV WiFi
⤢ Xmas New Year **Conf** Class 20 Board 25 Thtr 40 Del from £130 to £145*
Parking 36 **Notes** LB ⊗

DEDHAM
Essex   Map 13 TM03

INSPECTORS' CHOICE

Maison Talbooth
★★★ ◉◉ COUNTRY HOUSE HOTEL

tel: 01206 322367 **Stratford Rd CO7 6HN**
email: maison@milsomhotels.co.uk **web:** www.milsomhotels.com/maisontalbooth
dir: *A12 towards Ipswich, 1st turn signed Dedham, follow to left bend, turn right.*
Hotel 1m on right

Warm hospitality and quality service are to be expected at this Victorian country-house hotel, which is situated in a peaceful rural location amidst pretty landscaped grounds overlooking the Stour River Valley. Public areas include a comfortable drawing room where guests may take afternoon tea or snacks. Residents are chauffeured to the popular Le Talbooth Restaurant just a mile away for dinner. The spacious bedrooms are individually decorated and tastefully furnished with lovely co-ordinated fabrics and many thoughtful touches.

Rooms 12 (1 fmly) (5 GF) ◑ **D** £220-£425 (incl. bkfst)* **Facilities** Spa STV WiFi
⤢ ⚘ ⚘ Xmas New Year **Conf** Class 20 Board 16 Thtr 30 **Parking** 40 **Notes** LB
Civ Wed 50

milsoms
★★★ 83% ◉ SMALL HOTEL

tel: 01206 322795 **Stratford Rd CO7 6HN**
email: milsoms@milsomhotels.com **web:** www.milsomhotels.com/milsoms
dir: *6m N of Colchester off A12, follow Stratford St Mary/Dedham signs. Turn right over*
A12, hotel on left

Situated in the Dedham Vale, an Area of Outstanding Natural Beauty, milsoms is the perfect base to explore the countryside on the Essex/Suffolk border. This small hotel is styled along the lines of a contemporary 'gastro bar' combining good food served in an informal atmosphere, with stylish and well-appointed accommodation.

Rooms 15 (3 fmly) (4 GF) **D** £140-£190 (incl. bkfst)* **Facilities** STV WiFi Use of spa at nearby sister hotel Maison Talbooth Xmas **Conf** Board 24 Del £175* **Parking** 90
Notes LB

DELPH
Greater Manchester   Map 16 SD90

The Saddleworth Hotel
★★★★ 80% ◉ COUNTRY HOUSE HOTEL

tel: 01457 871888 **Huddersfield Rd OL3 5LX**
email: enquiries@thesaddleworthhotel.co.uk **web:** www.thesaddleworthhotel.co.uk
dir: *M62 junct 21, A640 towards Huddersfield. At Junction Inn take A6052 towards Delph;*
at White Lion left onto unclassified road; in 0.5m left on A62 towards Huddersfield. Hotel
0.5m on right

Situated in nine acres of landscaped gardens and woodlands in the Castleshaw Valley, this lovingly restored 17th-century building, once a coaching station, has stunning views. The hotel offers comfort and opulence together with a team of staff who provide delightful customer care. Antique pieces have been acquired from far and wide, and no expense has been spared to provide guests with the latest up-to-date facilities. The restaurant, with black table linen and crystal glassware, offers an award-winning, fashionably understated, modern European menu.

Rooms 16 (8 annexe) (4 fmly) (4 GF) **Facilities** FTV WiFi ⤢ ⚘ Gym Xmas New Year
Conf Class 40 Board 40 Thtr 150 **Parking** 140 **Notes** ⊗ Civ Wed 250

D

DERBY
Derbyshire

Map 11 SK33

See also **Morley**

Hallmark Hotel Derby Midland
★★★★ 79% HOTEL

tel: 0330 028 3405 **Midland Rd DE1 2SQ**
email: derby@hallmarkhotels.co.uk **web:** www.hallmarkhotels.co.uk
dir: *Opposite rail station*

This early Victorian hotel situated opposite Derby Midland Station provides very comfortable accommodation. The executive rooms are ideal for business travellers as they are equipped with writing desks and high speed internet access. Public rooms include a comfortable lounge and a popular restaurant. Service is skilled, attentive and friendly. There is also a walled garden and private parking.

Rooms 102 (6 fmly) **Facilities** FTV WiFi ♬ Xmas New Year **Conf** Class 50 Board 35 Thtr 150 **Services** Lift **Parking** 70 **Notes** Civ Wed 150

Hallmark Hotel Derby Mickleover Court
★★★★ 76% HOTEL

tel: 0330 028 3404 **Etwall Rd, Mickleover DE3 0XX**
email: mickleover@hallmarkhotels.co.uk **web:** www.hallmarkhotels.co.uk
dir: *A50 towards Derby, exit at junct 5. A516 towards Derby, take exit signed Mickleover*

Located close to Derby, this modern hotel is well suited to both the conference and leisure markets. Bedrooms are spacious, air conditioned, well equipped and include some smart executive rooms and suites. The well presented leisure facilities are amongst the best in the region.

Rooms 99 (20 fmly) (5 smoking) 🐾 **Facilities** STV FTV WiFi ➷ 🏊 Gym Beauty salon Steam room Xmas New Year **Conf** Class 106 Board 45 Thtr 200 **Services** Lift Air con **Parking** 225 **Notes** Civ Wed 200

Hallmark Inn Derby
★★★ 73% METRO HOTEL

tel: 0330 028 3425 **Midland Rd DE1 2SL**
email: derbyinn@hallmarkhotels.co.uk **web:** www.hallmarkhotels.co.uk
dir: *City centre, adj to railway station*

This is a contemporary hotel, offering quality accommodation plus a lounge bar, free WiFi and free parking. Situated just 100 metres from the railway station and not far from the city centre.

Rooms 87 (24 fmly) **Facilities** FTV WiFi **Conf** Class 20 Board 30 Thtr 60 **Services** Lift **Parking** 90 **Notes** ⊗

Premier Inn Derby City Centre
BUDGET HOTEL

tel: 0871 527 9638 **Cathedral Quarter, Full St DE1 3AF**
web: www.premierinn.com
dir: *From N: M1 junct 25, A52. 10m, 2nd exit at rdbt into Eastgate. In 0.6m, exit for Irongate, left into Queens St, left into Full St. From S: From A38 onto A516 (M1 South/Nottingham). 2nd exit at rdbt into Uttoxeter New Rd. 1.4m, 2nd exit at rdbt into Stafford St, right into Cathedral Rd, then Full St*

High quality, budget accommodation ideal for both families and business travellers. Spacious, en suite bedrooms feature tea and coffee making facilities, and Freeview TV in most hotels. Internet access and WiFi are available for a small fee. The adjacent family restaurant features a wide and varied menu. See also the Hotel Groups pages.

Rooms 118

Premier Inn Derby East
BUDGET HOTEL

tel: 0871 527 8292 *(Calls cost 13p per minute plus your phone company's access charge)*
The Wyvern, Stanier Way DE21 6BF
web: www.premierinn.com
dir: *M1 junct 25, A52 towards Derby. After 6.5m exit for Wyvern/Pride Park. 1st exit at rdbt (A52 Nottingham), straight on at next rdbt. Hotel on left*

Rooms 108

Premier Inn Derby North West
BUDGET HOTEL

tel: 0871 527 8294 *(Calls cost 13p per minute plus your phone company's access charge)*
95 Ashbourne Rd, Mackworth DE22 4LZ
web: www.premierinn.com
dir: *Exit M1 junct 25 onto A52 towards Derby. At Pentagon Island straight ahead towards city centre. Follow A52/Ashbourne signs into Mackworth*

Rooms 22

Premier Inn Derby South
BUDGET HOTEL

tel: 0871 527 8296 *(Calls cost 13p per minute plus your phone company's access charge)*
Foresters Leisure Park, Osmaston Park Rd DE23 8AG
web: www.premierinn.com
dir: *M1 junct 24, A6 towards Derby. Left onto A5111 (ring road), hotel in 2m*

Rooms 51

Premier Inn Derby West

BUDGET HOTEL

tel: 0871 527 8298 *(Calls cost 13p per minute plus your phone company's access charge)*
Manor Park Way, Uttoxeter New Rd DE22 3HN
web: www.premierinn.com
dir: *M1 junct 25, A38 W towards Burton upon Trent (approx 15m). Left at island (city hospital), right at lights, 3rd exit at city hospital island*

Rooms 86

DERBY SERVICE AREA (A50)
Derbyshire

Map 11 SK42

Days Inn Donington - A50

AA Advertised

WELCOMEBREAK

tel: 01332 799666 **Welcome Break Services, A50 Westbound DE72 2WA**
email: derby.hotel@welcomebreak.co.uk **web:** www.welcomebreak.co.uk
dir: *M1 junct 24/24a, onto A50 towards Stoke/Derby. Hotel between juncts 1 & 2*

This modern building offers accommodation in smart, spacious and well-equipped bedrooms, suitable for families and business travellers, and all with en suite bathrooms. Continental breakfast is available and other refreshments may be taken at the nearby family restaurant.

Rooms 47 (38 fmly) (17 GF) (9 smoking) **Facilities** FTV WiFi ➪ **Conf** Class 20 Board 40 Thtr 40 **Parking** 80

DEVIZES
Wiltshire

Map 4 SU06

The Peppermill

◎◎ RESTAURANT WITH ROOMS

tel: 01380 710407 **40 Saint John's St SN10 1BL**
email: philip@peppermilldevizes.co.uk **web:** www.peppermilldevizes.co.uk
dir: *Situated in the market place*

Situated in the heart of Devizes, The Peppermill offers seven bedrooms located above the restaurant, in one of the oldest buildings in the town. The en suite bath/shower rooms have underfloor heating, limestone floors and heated mirrors. Hypnos Royal Lansdowne beds, three of which split into twins if needed, have goose-down bedding and Egyptian cotton bed linen to ensure a good night's sleep. The restaurant serves breakfast, lunch and dinner, all offered daily.

Rooms 7

Follow us on Facebook
www.facebook.com/TheAAUK

f Find us on Facebook

DIDCOT
Oxfordshire

Map 5 SU59

Premier Inn Oxford South (Didcot)

BUDGET HOTEL

tel: 0871 527 8868 *(Calls cost 13p per minute plus your phone company's access charge)*
Milton Heights, Milton OX14 4TX
web: www.premierinn.com
dir: *On A4130. Just off A34 at Milton interchange, between Oxford & Newbury*

High quality, budget accommodation ideal for both families and business travellers. Spacious, en suite bedrooms feature tea and coffee making facilities, and Freeview TV in most hotels. Internet access and WiFi are available for a small fee. The adjacent family restaurant features a wide and varied menu. See also the Hotel Groups pages.

Rooms 135

DOGMERSFIELD
Hampshire

Map 5 SU75

INSPECTORS' CHOICE

Four Seasons Hotel Hampshire

★★★★★ ◎◎ ⚘ COUNTRY HOUSE HOTEL

tel: 01252 853000 **Dogmersfield Park, Chalky Ln RG27 8TD**
email: reservations.ham@fourseasons.com **web:** www.fourseasons.com/hampshire
dir: *M3 junct 5 onto A287 Farnham. After 1.5m left for Dogmersfield, hotel 0.6m on left*

This Georgian manor house, set in 500 acres of rolling grounds and English Heritage listed gardens, offers the upmost in luxury and relaxation, just an hour from London. The spacious and stylish bedrooms are particularly well appointed and offer up-to-date technology. Fitness and spa facilities include nearly every conceivable indoor and outdoor activity, in addition to luxurious pampering. An elegant restaurant, a healthy-eating spa café and a trendy bar are popular venues.

Rooms 133 (23 GF) 🐾 **Facilities** Spa STV WiFi 🏊 ♨ Fishing 🚣 Gym Clay pigeon Bikes Canal boat Falconry Horse riding Jogging trails Rope course ♬ Xmas New Year Child facilities **Conf** Class 110 Board 60 Thtr 260 Del from £186 to £210* **Services** Lift Air con **Parking** 165 **Notes** Civ Wed 200

D

DONCASTER
South Yorkshire   Map 16 SE50

Best Western Premier Mount Pleasant Hotel

★★★★ 78% HOTEL

tel: 01302 868696 & 868219 **Great North Rd DN11 0HW**
email: reception@mountpleasant.co.uk **web:** www.mountpleasant.co.uk

(For full entry see Rossington)

Premier Inn Doncaster Central East

BUDGET HOTEL

tel: 0871 527 8304 *(Calls cost 13p per minute plus your phone company's access charge)*
Doncaster Leisure Park, Herten Way DN4 7NW
web: www.premierinn.com
dir: *M18 junct 3, signed Doncaster racecourse. Left into Whiterose Way (B&Q on left). Straight on at rdbt into Wilmington Dr, right at next rdbt into Lakeside Boulevard. At next rdbt 2nd exit. Straight on at next rdbt, hotel ahead*

High quality, budget accommodation ideal for both families and business travellers. Spacious, en suite bedrooms feature tea and coffee making facilities, and Freeview TV in most hotels. Internet access and WiFi are available for a small fee. The adjacent family restaurant features a wide and varied menu. See also the Hotel Groups pages.

Rooms 47

Premier Inn Doncaster Central (High Fishergate)

BUDGET HOTEL

tel: 0871 527 8302 *(Calls cost 13p per minute plus your phone company's access charge)*
High Fishergate DN1 1QZ
web: www.premierinn.com
dir: *Off A630 Church Way*

Rooms 138

Premier Inn Doncaster (Lakeside)

BUDGET HOTEL

tel: 0871 527 8300 *(Calls cost 13p per minute plus your phone company's access charge)*
Wilmington Dr, Doncaster Carr DN4 5PJ
web: www.premierinn.com
dir: *M18 junct 3, A6182. Hotel near junct with access road*

Rooms 66

DORCHESTER
Dorset   Map 4 SY69

The Wessex Royale Hotel

THE INDEPENDENTS
HOTEL ASSOCIATION

★★★ 78% 🏵 HOTEL

tel: 01305 262660 **High West St DT1 1UP**
email: info@wessexroyalehotel.co.uk **web:** www.wessexroyalehotel.co.uk
dir: *From A35 follow town centre signs. Straight on, hotel at top of hill on left*

This centrally situated Georgian townhouse dates from 1756 and successfully combines historic charm with modern comforts. The restaurant is a relaxed venue for enjoying innovative food, and the hotel offers the benefit of a smart conservatory, ideal for functions. Limited courtyard parking is available.

Rooms 27 (2 annexe) (3 fmly) (2 GF) 🐾 **Facilities** STV FTV WiFi ⓘ **Conf** Class 40 Board 40 Thtr 80 **Parking** 11 **Notes** ⊗ Closed 23 Dec-2 Jan

---

Premier Inn Dorchester

BUDGET HOTEL

tel: 0871 527 9376 *(Calls cost 13p per minute plus your phone company's access charge)*
21 Weymouth Avene DT1 1GA
web: www.premierinn.com
dir: *On A35 follow Dorchester & Weymouth signs. At rdbt take B3150 (Stinsford Hill) left into Kings Rd. At rdbt 2nd exit into Prince of Wales Rd (B3144). Left into Weymouth Ave. Left into Brewery Sq*

High quality, budget accommodation ideal for both families and business travellers. Spacious, en suite bedrooms feature tea and coffee making facilities, and Freeview TV in most hotels. Internet access and WiFi are available for a small fee. The adjacent family restaurant features a wide and varied menu. See also the Hotel Groups pages.

Rooms 76

DORCHESTER (ON THAMES)
Oxfordshire   Map 5 SU59

White Hart Hotel

★★★ 74% HOTEL

tel: 01865 340074 **High St OX10 7HN**
email: whitehart@oxfordshire-hotels.co.uk **web:** www.oxfordshire-hotels.co.uk
dir: *M40 junct 6, take B4009 through Watlington & Benson to A4074. Follow signs to Dorchester. Hotel on right*

Period charm and character are plentiful throughout this 17th-century coaching inn, which is situated in the heart of a picturesque village. The spacious bedrooms are individually decorated and thoughtfully equipped. Public rooms include a cosy bar, a choice of lounges and an atmospheric restaurant, complete with vaulted timber ceiling.

Rooms 28 (4 annexe) (2 fmly) (9 GF) 🐾 **Facilities** FTV WiFi ⓘ Xmas New Year **Conf** Class 20 Board 18 Thtr 30 **Parking** 36 **Notes** ⊗

DORKING
Surrey   Map 6 TQ14

Mercure Boxhill Burford Bridge Hotel

★★★★ 80% 🏵 HOTEL

tel: 01306 884561 **Burford Bridge, Box Hill RH5 6BX**
email: h6635@accor.com **web:** www.mercure.com
dir: *M25 junct 9, A245 towards Dorking. Hotel approx 5m on A24*

Steeped in history, this hotel was reputedly where Lord Nelson and Lady Hamilton met for the last time, and it is said that the landscape around the hotel has inspired many poets. The hotel has a contemporary feel throughout. The grounds, running down to the River Mole, are extensive, and there are good transport links to major centres, including London. The elegant Emlyn Restaurant offers a modern award-winning menu.

Rooms 57 (22 fmly) (3 GF) **S** £100-£150; **D** £100-£160* **Facilities** STV FTV WiFi ⓘ ⚲ supervised Xmas New Year **Conf** Class 80 Board 60 Thtr 120 Del from £120 to £200* **Services** Air con **Parking** 130 **Notes** ⊗ Civ Wed 200

Mercure Dorking White Horse Hotel

★★★ 74% HOTEL

tel: 01306 881138 **High St RH4 1BE**
email: h6637@accor.com **web:** www.mercure.com
dir: *M25 junct 9, A24 S towards Dorking. Hotel in town centre*

The hotel was first established as an inn in 1750, although parts of the building date back as far as the 15th century. Its town centre location and Dickensian charm have long made this a popular destination for travellers. There are beamed ceilings, open fires and four-poster beds; more contemporary rooms can be found in the garden wing.

Rooms 78 (41 annexe) (2 fmly) (5 GF) **Facilities** FTV WiFi Discount at local leisure centre Xmas New Year **Conf** Class 30 Board 30 Thtr 50 **Parking** 58 **Notes** LB

DORRIDGE
West Midlands

Map 10 SP17

HIGHLY RECOMMENDED

Hogarths Hotel
★★★★ 84% ◉◉ HOTEL

tel: 01564 779988 **Four Ashes Rd B93 8QE**
email: reception@hogarths.co.uk **web:** www.hogarths.co.uk
dir: M42 junct 4, 1st exit to A3400. Left to Gate Ln. Left onto Four Ashes Rd. Hotel 300 mtrs on left

Hogarths Hotel, with its contemporary interior design and panoramic views of the gardens from the open-plan and airy Brasserie, is a stunning property. The relaxed style of service is in keeping and effective. Bedrooms meet all modern requirements, and many have their own balcony or outside area. The young team deliver high quality and friendly service throughout. The lake area for weddings and conferences events is a stunning attraction in the well-kept and managed gardens.

Rooms 49 (5 annexe) (9 fmly) (15 GF) 🐾 **D** £135-£160 **Facilities** FTV WiFi 🎵 Xmas New Year **Conf** Class 200 Board 60 Thtr 400 **Services** Lift **Parking** 120 **Notes** Civ Wed 120

DOVER
Kent

Map 7 TR34

Best Western Plus Dover Marina Hotel
★★★★ 75% HOTEL   Best Western **PLUS**

tel: 01304 203633 **Dover Waterfront CT17 9BP**
email: reservations@dovermarinahotel.co.uk **web:** www.dovermarinahotel.co.uk
dir: M20 junct 13, A20 to Dover, straight on at 2 rdbts, at 3rd take 2nd exit into Union St. Cross swing bridge, next left into Marine Pde/Waterloo Cres. Hotel 200yds on left

An attractive terraced waterfront hotel overlooking the harbour, offering a wide range of facilities including meeting rooms, health club, hairdresser and beauty treatments. Some of the tastefully decorated bedrooms have balconies, some have broadband access and many of the rooms have superb sea views. Public rooms include a large, open-plan lounge bar and a smart bistro restaurant.

Rooms 81 (5 fmly) 🐾 **Facilities** Spa STV FTV WiFi 🎵 HL Gym Sauna Xmas New Year **Conf** Class 60 Board 50 Thtr 110 Del from £125* **Services** Lift **Notes** ⊗ Civ Wed 100

Ramada Hotel Dover
★★★★ 74% HOTEL   ⓡRAMADA.

tel: 01304 821230 **Singledge Ln, Whitfield CT16 3EL**
email: reservations@ramadadover.co.uk **web:** www.ramadadover.co.uk
dir: From M20 follow signs to A2 towards Canterbury. Turn right after Whitfield rdbt. From A2 towards Dover, turn left before Whitfield rdbt

Ramada Hotel Dover is a modern purpose-built hotel situated in a quiet location between Dover and Canterbury, close to the ferry port and seaside. The open-plan public areas are contemporary in style and include a lounge, a bar and The Olive Tree Restaurant. The stylish bedrooms are simply decorated with co-ordinated soft furnishings and many thoughtful extras.

Rooms 68 (19 fmly) (68 GF) 🐾 **Facilities** FTV WiFi 🎵 HL Gym 🎵 Xmas New Year **Conf** Class 25 Board 20 Thtr 400 **Parking** 110 **Notes** ⊗ Civ Wed 80

DOVER *continued*

Wallett's Court Country House Hotel & Spa

★★★★ 71% HOTEL

tel: 01304 852424 & 0800 035 1628 **West Cliffe, St Margarets-at-Cliffe CT15 6EW**
email: wc@wallettscourt.com **web:** www.wallettscourt.com
dir: From Dover take A258 towards Deal. 1st right to St Margarets-at-Cliffe & West Cliffe, 1m on right opposite West Cliffe church

Wallett's Court is a lovely Jacobean manor situated in a peaceful location on the outskirts of town. Bedrooms in the original house are traditionally furnished whereas the rooms in the courtyard buildings are more modern; all are equipped to a high standard. Public rooms include a smart bar, a lounge and a restaurant that utilises local organic produce. An impressive spa facility is housed in converted barn buildings in the grounds.

Rooms 13 (10 annexe) (2 fmly) (5 GF) ⚓ **S** £75-£125; **D** £135-£225 (incl. bkfst)*
Facilities Spa FTV WiFi 🏊 ⛳ Putt green ♨ Gym Treatment suite Aromatherapy massage Beauty therapy Golf pitching range Xmas New Year **Conf** Class 25 Board 16 Thtr 25 **Parking** 30 **Notes** LB Civ Wed 40

Premier Inn Dover (A20)

BUDGET HOTEL

tel: 0871 527 8310 *(Calls cost 13p per minute plus your phone company's access charge)*
Folkestone Rd CT15 7AB
web: www.premierinn.com
dir: A20 to Dover. Through tunnel, take 2nd exit onto B2011. 1st left at rdbt. In 1m hotel on left

High quality, budget accommodation ideal for both families and business travellers. Spacious, en suite bedrooms feature tea and coffee making facilities, and Freeview TV in most hotels. Internet access and WiFi are available for a small fee. The adjacent family restaurant features a wide and varied menu. See also the Hotel Groups pages.

Rooms 64

Premier Inn Dover Central (Eastern Ferry Terminal)

BUDGET HOTEL

tel: 0871 527 8306 *(Calls cost 13p per minute plus your phone company's access charge)*
Marine Court, Marine Pde CT16 1LW
web: www.premierinn.com
dir: In town centre adjacent to ferry terminal. M20 junct 13 onto A20 for 8.2m

Rooms 100

Premier Inn Dover East

BUDGET HOTEL

tel: 0871 527 8308 *(Calls cost 13p per minute plus your phone company's access charge)*
Jubilee Way, Guston Wood CT15 5FD
web: www.premierinn.com
dir: At rdbt junct of A2 & A258

Rooms 40

The Marquis at Alkham

 RESTAURANT WITH ROOMS

tel: 01304 873410 & 822945 **Alkham Valley Rd, Alkham CT15 7DF**
email: info@themarquisatalkham.co.uk **web:** www.themarquisatalkham.co.uk
dir: A256 from Dover, at rdbt 1st exit into London Rd, left into Alkham Rd, Alkham Valley Rd. Establishment 1.5m after sharp bend

Located between Dover and Folkestone, this contemporary restaurant with rooms offers luxury accommodation with modern features; flat-screen TVs, WiFi, power showers and bathrobes to mention but a few. All the stylish bedrooms are individually designed and have fantastic views of the Kent Downs. The award-winning restaurant, open for lunch and dinner, specialises in modern British cuisine guided by chef Andrew King. Both continental and a choice of cooked breakfasts are offered.

Rooms 10 (3 fmly)

DRIFFIELD (GREAT)	**Map 17 TA05**
East Riding of Yorkshire	

Best Western Bell Hotel

★★★ 81% HOTEL

🅑🅦 Best Western.

tel: 01377 256661 **46 Market Place YO25 6AN**
email: bell@bestwestern.co.uk **web:** www.bw-bellhotel.co.uk
dir: From A164, right at lights. Car park 50yds on left behind black railings

This 250-year-old hotel incorporates the old corn exchange and town hall. It is furnished with antique and period pieces, and contains many items of local historical interest. The bedrooms vary in size, but all offer modern facilities and some have their own sitting rooms. The hotel has a relaxed and very friendly atmosphere. In the separate leisure club there is an impressive range of facilities including a pool, a gym, and a spa which boasts a wide range of treatments and features a hydrotherapy pool, a saunarium, a Rasul chamber and a flotation chamber. Spa packages and pamper days are available.

Rooms 16 (3 GF) ⚓ **Facilities Spa** FTV WiFi ↳ 🏊 Gym Squash Elemis treatments Snooker room 🎵 New Year **Conf** Class 100 Board 40 Thtr 150 **Services** Lift **Parking** 18 **Notes** ⊗ No children 16yrs Closed 25 Dec & 1 Jan RS 24 & 26 Dec Civ Wed 120

DROITWICH SPA	**Map 10 SO86**
Worcestershire	

St Andrews Town Hotel

★★★ 85% HOTEL

tel: 01905 779677 **St Andrews Dr WR9 8AL**
email: enquiries@st-andrewshotel.com **web:** www.st-andrewshotel.com
dir: From N: M5 junct 5, right onto A38, left onto B4065 Bromsgrove Rd, Queen St, B4090 Worcester Rd, right into St Andrews Drive. From S: M5 junct 6, left onto A4538, right onto A38, B4090 Worcester Rd, left into St Andrews Drive after Methodist Church

Ideally located in the heart of Droitwich Spa and only minutes from both the town centre and motorway links, this elegant Georgian hotel is the ideal place to enjoy a comfortable stay in attractively designed bedrooms. Classic British dishes are served in the restaurant, with good use made of locally sourced, seasonal ingredients. The tranquil gardens make an ideal location for weddings and special occasions.

Rooms 31 (4 fmly) (6 GF) ⚓ **S** fr £50; **D** fr £65 (incl. bkfst) **Facilities** FTV WiFi **Conf** Class 50 Board 30 Thtr 150 Del from £134.95 **Parking** 60 **Notes** LB ⊗ Civ Wed 100

DUDLEY	Map 10 SO99
West Midlands	

Premier Inn Dudley Town Centre

BUDGET HOTEL

tel: 0871 527 9420 *(Calls cost 13p per minute plus your phone company's access charge)*
Castlegate Business Park, Castlegate Way DY1 4TA
web: www.premierinn.com
dir: *From N: M5 junct 2, A4123 signed Dudley. At rdbt onto A4123. 4th exit into Wolverhampton Rd (A4123). Left into Birmingham Rd (A461). At rdbt 4th exit into Castlegate Way. At next rdbt 3rd exit*

High quality, budget accommodation ideal for both families and business travellers. Spacious, en suite bedrooms feature tea and coffee making facilities, and Freeview TV in most hotels. Internet access and WiFi are available for a small fee. The adjacent family restaurant features a wide and varied menu. See also the Hotel Groups pages.

Rooms 63

DUMBLETON	Map 10 SP03
Gloucestershire	

Dumbleton Hall Hotel

★★★ 79% COUNTRY HOUSE HOTEL

tel: 01386 881240 **WR11 7TS**
email: dh@pofr.co.uk **web:** www.dumbletonhall.co.uk
dir: *M5 junct 9/A46. 2nd exit at rdbt signed Evesham. Through Beckford for 1m, turn right signed Dumbleton. Hotel at S end of village*

Standing on the site of a 16th-century building also known as Dumbleton Hall, the current mansion, surrounded by 19 acres of landscaped gardens and parkland, was built in the mid-18th century. Panoramic views of the Vale of Evesham can be seen from every window, and the spacious public rooms make this an ideal venue for weddings, conferences or just as a hideaway retreat. The individually designed bedrooms vary in size and layout; one room is adapted for less able guests.

Rooms 34 (9 fmly) **Facilities** WiFi ❧ Xmas New Year **Conf** Class 60 Board 60 Thtr 100 **Services** Lift **Parking** 60 **Notes** Civ Wed 100

DUNSTABLE	Map 11 TL02
Bedfordshire	

Premier Inn Dunstable/Luton

BUDGET HOTEL

tel: 0871 527 8330 *(Calls cost 13p per minute plus your phone company's access charge)*
350 Luton Rd LU5 4LL
web: www.premierinn.com
dir: *M1 junct 11, follow Dunstable signs. At 1st rdbt turn right. Hotel on left on A505*

High quality, budget accommodation ideal for both families and business travellers. Spacious, en suite bedrooms feature tea and coffee making facilities, and Freeview TV in most hotels. Internet access and WiFi are available for a small fee. The adjacent family restaurant features a wide and varied menu. See also the Hotel Groups pages.

Rooms 42

Premier Inn Dunstable South (A5)

BUDGET HOTEL

tel: 0871 527 8332 *(Calls cost 13p per minute plus your phone company's access charge)*
Watling St, Kensworth LU6 3QP
web: www.premierinn.com
dir: *M1 junct 9 towards Dunstable on A5, hotel on right after Packhorse pub*

Rooms 40

D

DUNWICH	Map 13 TM47
Suffolk	

The Ship at Dunwich

★★ 82% ⊛ SMALL HOTEL

tel: 01728 648219 **St James St IP17 3DT**
email: info@shipatdunwich.co.uk **web:** www.shipatdunwich.co.uk
dir: *From N: A12, exit at Blythburgh onto B1125, then left to village. Inn at end of road. From S: A12, turn right to Westleton. Follow signs for Dunwich*

The Ship is a delightful inn situated in the heart of this quiet village, surrounded by nature reserves and heathland, and just a short walk from the beach. Public rooms feature a smart lounge bar with an open fire and real ales on tap. The comfortable bedrooms are traditionally furnished; some rooms have lovely views across the sea or marshes.

Rooms 16 (5 annexe) (4 fmly) (5 GF) **S** £112.50-£135; **D** £112.50-£135 (incl. bkfst)*
Facilities FTV WiFi Xmas New Year **Parking** 15

DURHAM	Map 19 NZ24
County Durham	

HIGHLY RECOMMENDED

Ramside Hall Hotel Golf & Spa

★★★★ 84% ⊛ HOTEL

tel: 0191 386 5282 **Carrville DH1 1TD**
email: mail@ramsidehallhotel.co.uk **web:** www.ramsidehallhotel.co.uk
dir: *A1(M) junct 62, A690 to Sunderland. Straight on at lights. 200mtrs after rail bridge turn right*

With its proximity to the motorway and delightful parkland setting, this establishment combines the best of both worlds - convenience and tranquillity. The hotel boasts two championship golf courses, a choice of lounges, several eating options including the Rib Room, specialising in Steaks; and Fusion, their new Asian-inspired concept. Bedrooms are furnished and decorated to a very high standard and include some stunning suites. A recent addition to the property is an excellent spa and leisure facility.

Rooms 128 (10 fmly) (28 GF) **D** £99-£650 **Facilities** Spa STV FTV WiFi ↩ ⊛ supervised ⊰ supervised ⌗ 36 Putt green Gym Steam room Sauna Hydro pool Golf academy Driving range ♫ Xmas New Year **Conf** Class 160 Board 40 Thtr 500 Del from £119 to £179* **Services** Lift **Parking** 750 **Notes** Civ Wed 500

DURHAM *continued*

Honest Lawyer Hotel
★★★ 81% HOTEL

tel: 0191 378 3780 **Croxdale Bridge, Croxdale DH1 3SP**
email: enquiries@honestlawyerhotel.com **web:** www.honestlawyerhotel.com
dir: *A1(M) junct 61, A688 towards Bishops Auckland. Right at rdbt, continue on A688, right at next rdbt onto A167 towards Durham. In 2.5m hotel on right*

This hotel offers a mixture of smart motel-style bedrooms along with six junior suites in the main building that have four-poster beds. 40" LCD TVs, power showers and complimentary WiFi are provided as standard. Facilities also include a beauty treatment room and a boutique offering ladies fashion, jewellery and gifts. Bailey's Bar & Restaurant, with its open kitchen, offers a seasonally changing menu and friendly service. There is also a terrace and modern event facilities. There are good transportation links to Durham and the motorway.

Rooms 51 (45 annexe) (3 fmly) (45 GF) **Facilities** FTV WiFi ⅃ Xmas New Year **Conf** Class 27 Board 24 Thtr 50 **Services** Air con **Parking** 150

Premier Inn Durham City Centre
BUDGET HOTEL

tel: 0871 527 8338 *(Calls cost 13p per minute plus your phone company's access charge)*
Freemans Place, Walkergate DH1 1SQ
web: www.premierinn.com
dir: *A1(M) junct 62, A690 (Leazes Rd) towards city centre. In Durham follow Watergate signs, under bridge immediately left into Walkergate (one way). Back under A690, hotel on right*

High quality, budget accommodation ideal for both families and business travellers. Spacious, en suite bedrooms feature tea and coffee making facilities, and Freeview TV in most hotels. Internet access and WiFi are available for a small fee. The adjacent family restaurant features a wide and varied menu. See also the Hotel Groups pages.

Rooms 103

Premier Inn Durham East
BUDGET HOTEL

tel: 0871 527 8340 *(Calls cost 13p per minute plus your phone company's access charge)*
Broomside Park, Belmont Industrial Estate DH1 1GG
web: www.premierinn.com
dir: *A1(M) junct 62, A690 W towards Durham. In 1m left. Hotel on left*

Rooms 62

Premier Inn Durham North
BUDGET HOTEL

tel: 0871 527 8342 *(Calls cost 13p per minute plus your phone company's access charge)*
adj. Arnison Retail Centre, Pity Me DH1 5GB
web: www.premierinn.com
dir: *A1 junct 63, A167 to Durham. Straight on at 5 rbts, left at 6th rbt. Hotel on right after 200yds*

Rooms 77

EAST GRINSTEAD
West Sussex   Map 6 TQ33

Premier Inn East Grinstead
BUDGET HOTEL

tel: 0871 527 8348 *(Calls cost 13p per minute plus your phone company's access charge)*
London Rd, Felbridge RH19 2QR
web: www.premierinn.com
dir: *M25 junct 6. Hotel at junction of A22 & A264*

High quality, budget accommodation ideal for both families and business travellers. Spacious, en suite bedrooms feature tea and coffee making facilities, and Freeview TV in most hotels. Internet access and WiFi are available for a small fee. The adjacent family restaurant features a wide and varied menu. See also the Hotel Groups pages.

Rooms 41

EAST HORSLEY
Surrey   Map 6 TQ05

The Thatcher's Hotel
★★★ 78% HOTEL

tel: 01483 284291 & 0330 333 2843 **Guildford Rd KT24 6TB**
email: reception@thatchershotel.co.uk **web:** www.thatchershotel.co.uk/
dir: *M25 junct 10/A3 exit to London/Guildford/Kingston. At rdbt take 3rd exit onto A3 for 0.5m, turn left onto Old Lane, 2.3m turn right onto Hirsham Road, at end turn left*

This Tudor-style property sits within its own garden in the tranquil Surrey countryside, and is the ideal base for visiting Thorpe Park. The hotel offers a choice of comfortable accommodation, meeting rooms for all occasions, free parking and a well-appointed restaurant overlooking the garden. Traditional afternoon tea is served in the Club Bar, together with a range of beverages. Free WiFi is offered throughout the hotel.

Rooms 87 (12 fmly) (20 GF) ⌂ **Facilities** FTV WiFi ♭ Xmas New Year **Conf** Class 70 Board 66 Thtr 170 **Services** Lift **Parking** 140 **Notes** Civ Wed 140

EAST MIDLANDS AIRPORT
Leicestershire   Map 11 SK42

Best Western Premier Yew Lodge Hotel & Spa
★★★★ 77% HOTEL

tel: 01509 672518 **Packington Hill DE74 2DF**
email: info@yewlodgehotel.co.uk **web:** www.yewlodgehotel.co.uk
dir: *M1 junct 24. Follow signs to Loughborough & Kegworth on A6. On entering village, right 1st lights, hotel 400yds on right*

This smart, family-owned hotel is close to both the motorway and airport, yet is peacefully located. Modern, stylish bedrooms and public areas are thoughtfully appointed and smartly presented. The restaurant serves interesting dishes, while lounge service and extensive conference facilities are available. A very well equipped spa and leisure centre complete the picture.

Rooms 114 (22 fmly) ⌂ **Facilities** Spa STV FTV WiFi ♭ HL ⊛ Gym Beauty therapy suite Steam room Sauna Power plate Xmas New Year **Conf** Class 150 Board 84 Thtr 330 **Services** Lift **Parking** 180 **Notes** Civ Wed 260

Premier Inn East Midlands Airport

BUDGET HOTEL

tel: 0871 527 8350 *(Calls cost 13p per minute plus your phone company's access charge)*
Pegasus Business Park, Herald Way DE74 2TQ
web: www.premierinn.com
dir: *From S: M1 junct 23a, A453 signed to airport. From N: M1 junct 24, A456 signed to airport. Hotel on Pegasus Business Park*

High quality, budget accommodation ideal for both families and business travellers. Spacious, en suite bedrooms feature tea and coffee making facilities, and Freeview TV in most hotels. Internet access and WiFi are available for a small fee. The adjacent family restaurant features a wide and varied menu. See also the Hotel Groups pages.

Rooms 80

EASTBOURNE	Map 6 TV69
East Sussex	

The Grand Hotel

★★★★★ 85% ◉◉ HOTEL

tel: 01323 412345 **King Edwards Pde BN21 4EQ**
email: reservations@grandeastbourne.com **web:** www.grandeastbourne.com
dir: *On seafront W of Eastbourne, 1m from railway station*

This famous Victorian hotel offers high standards of service and hospitality, and is in close proximity to both the beach and the South Downs National Park. The extensive public rooms feature a magnificent Great Hall, with marble columns and high ceilings, where guests can relax and enjoy afternoon tea. The spacious bedrooms provide high levels of comfort; many with stunning sea views and a number with private balconies. Guests can choose fine dining in The Mirabelle, or the Garden Restaurant, and there are bars as well as superb spa and leisure facilities.

Rooms 152 (20 fmly) (4 GF) ⟅ **S** £160-£220; **D** £190-£250 (incl. bkfst)*
Facilities Spa STV FTV WiFi ⓑ HL ⊛ supervised ⟆ supervised Putt green Gym Snooker table ♫ Xmas New Year Child facilities **Conf** Class 200 Board 40 Thtr 350 Del from £200 to £300* **Services** Lift **Parking** 80 **Notes** LB Civ Wed 300

Langham Hotel

★★★★ 75% ◉ HOTEL

tel: 01323 731451 **43-49 Royal Pde BN22 7AH**
web: www.langhamhotel.co.uk
dir: *Follow seafront signs. Hotel 0.5m E of pier*

This popular hotel is situated in a prominent position with superb views of the sea and pier. Bedrooms are pleasantly decorated, and equipped with modern facilities. Superior rooms, some with four-poster beds are stylish and offer sea views. The spacious public rooms include the Grand Parade bar, a lounge and a fine dining conservatory restaurant. The hotel has 40 additional secure, charged-for parking spaces within 350 yards on Fridays, Saturdays and Sundays.

Rooms 77 (2 fmly) ⟅ **S** £42-£67; **D** £85-£230 (incl. bkfst)* **Facilities** STV FTV WiFi ⓑ ♫ Xmas New Year **Conf** Class 40 Board 30 Thtr 80 **Services** Lift **Parking** 9 **Notes** ⊗ Civ Wed 120

Hydro Hotel

★★★ 83% HOTEL

tel: 01323 720643 **Mount Rd BN20 7HZ**
email: sales@hydrohotel.com **web:** www.hydrohotel.com
dir: *From pier/seafront, right along Grand Parade. At Grand Hotel follow Hydro Hotel sign. Into South Cliff, 200mtrs*

This well-managed and popular hotel enjoys an elevated position with views of attractive gardens and the sea beyond. The spacious bedrooms are attractive and well equipped. In addition to the comfortable lounges, guests also have access to fitness facilities and a hairdressing salon. Service is both professional and efficient throughout.

Rooms 83 (3 fmly) (3 GF) ⟅ **Facilities** FTV WiFi ⟆ Putt green ⟆ Beauty room Hair salon Xmas New Year **Conf** Class 90 Board 40 Thtr 140 **Services** Lift **Parking** 40 **Notes** LB RS 24-28 & 30-31 Dec Civ Wed 120

Best Western Lansdowne Hotel

★★★ 80% HOTEL

tel: 01323 725174 & 745483 **King Edward's Pde BN21 4EE**
email: enquiries@lansdowne-hotel.co.uk **web:** www.bw-lansdownehotel.co.uk
dir: *At W end of seafront opposite Western Lawns, 1m from railway station*

Enjoying an enviable position at the quieter end of the parade, this hotel overlooks the Western Lawns and Wish Tower, and is just a few minutes' walk from many of the town's attractions. Public rooms include a variety of lounges, a range of meeting rooms, and games rooms. Bedrooms are attractively decorated and many offer sea views. The hotel has a wheelchair lift near the front entrance that operates between the pavement and one of the ground-floor public rooms.

Rooms 102 (10 fmly) ⟅ **S** £70-£90; **D** £114-£164 (incl. bkfst) **Facilities** FTV WiFi ⓑ HL Table tennis Pool table 2 Snooker tables Xmas New Year **Conf** Class 40 Board 40 Thtr 80 Del from £105 to £145 **Services** Lift **Parking** 22 **Notes** LB Civ Wed 60

EASTBOURNE *continued*

The Devonshire Park Hotel

★★★ 80% HOTEL

tel: 01323 728144 **27-29 Carlisle Rd BN21 4JR**
email: info@devonshire-park-hotel.co.uk **web:** www.devonshire-park-hotel.co.uk
dir: *Follow signs to seafront, exit at Wish Tower. Hotel opposite Congress Theatre*

A handsome family-run hotel handily placed for the seafront and theatres. Attractively furnished rooms are spacious and comfortable; many boast king-size beds and all are equipped with WiFi and satellite TV. Guests can relax in the well presented lounges, the cosy bar or, when the weather's fine, on the garden terrace.

Rooms 35 (8 GF) 🐾 **Facilities** STV WiFi Xmas New Year **Services** Lift **Parking** 25 **Notes** LB ⊗ No children 12yrs

New Wilmington Hotel

★★★ 79% HOTEL

tel: 01323 721219 **25-27 Compton St BN21 4DU**
email: info@new-wilmington-hotel.co.uk **web:** www.new-wilmington-hotel.co.uk
dir: *A22 to Eastbourne seafront. Right along promenade to Wish Tower. Right, then left at end of road, hotel 2nd on left*

This friendly, family-run hotel is conveniently located close to the seafront, the Congress Theatre and Winter Gardens. Public rooms are well presented and include a cosy bar, a small comfortable lounge and a spacious restaurant. Bedrooms are comfortably appointed and tastefully decorated; family and superior bedrooms are available.

Rooms 40 (14 fmly) (3 GF) 🐾 **S** £62.50-£72.50; **D** £78-£140 (incl. bkfst)* **Facilities** STV FTV WiFi ♙ 🎵 Xmas New Year **Conf** Class 20 Board 20 Thtr 40 **Services** Lift **Parking** 3 **Notes** LB Closed 3 Jan-mid Feb

The Palm Court

★★★ 72% HOTEL

tel: 01323 725811 **15 Burlington Place BN21 4AR**
email: thepalmcourt@btconnect.com **web:** www.thepalmcourthotel.co.uk
dir: *From pier, W along seafront, Burlington Place 5th right*

This family-run hotel is ideally situated close to the seafront and local theatres. The well appointed public areas include the lounge, spacious bar and stylish restaurant. Bedrooms vary in size but all offer plenty of handy accessories, comfortable furnishings and bright modern bathrooms. Good mobility facilities are provided.

Rooms 38 (5 GF) 🐾 **S** £44-£52; **D** £88-£102 (incl. bkfst) **Facilities** FTV WiFi Xmas New Year **Services** Lift **Notes** LB ⊗

Queens Hotel

★★★ 71% HOTEL

Leisureplex
HOLIDAY HOTELS

tel: 01323 722822 **Marine Pde BN21 3DY**
email: queens.eastbourne@alfatravel.co.uk **web:** www.leisureplex.co.uk
dir: *Follow signs for seafront, hotel opposite pier*

Popular with tour groups, this long-established hotel enjoys a central, prominent seafront location overlooking the pier. Spacious public areas include a choice of lounges, and regular entertainment is also provided. Bedrooms are suitably appointed and equipped.

Rooms 122 (5 fmly) 🐾 **Facilities** FTV WiFi Snooker 🎵 Xmas New Year **Services** Lift **Parking** 50 **Notes** ⊗ Closed Jan (ex New Year) RS Nov, Feb-Mar

The Big Sleep Hotel

★★★ 63% METRO HOTEL

tel: 01323 722676 **Landsdown Ter, King Edward Pde BN21 4EB**
email: bookings.eastbourne@thebigsleephotel.com **web:** www.thebigsleephotel.com

Located on the seafront with front rooms offering relaxing views, The Big Sleep is a new breed of establishment whose ethos is design, comfort and value for money. There is a range of stylish rooms to choose from, and rates include a continental buffet breakfast, with a cooked breakfast available at an extra cost. Free WiFi is available in the recreation room, together with a pool table and other games. Sky Sports is available in all rooms. The lounge offers a limited and well-priced menu. The hotel also offers two contemporary meeting rooms for business meetings. Sister properties can be found in Cheltenham and Cardiff.

Rooms 50 (4 fmly) (4 GF) 🐾 **Facilities** STV FTV WiFi **Conf** Class 24 Board 26 Thtr 40 **Services** Lift

Savoy Court Hotel

★★ 72% HOTEL

tel: 01323 723132 **11-15 Cavendish Place BN21 3EJ**
email: info@savoycourthotel.co.uk **web:** www.savoycourthotel.co.uk
dir: *M25 junct 6, A22 to Eastbourne. Hotel 50mtrs from pier*

Located close to the pier and within easy walking distance of the beaches and open-air bandstand this hotel offers bedrooms that are pleasantly decorated and furnished. The public areas include a cosy lounge and spacious bar/lounge for relaxing at the end of the day.

Rooms 29 (3 fmly) (5 GF) **Facilities** FTV WiFi ♙ Xmas New Year **Conf** Class 40 Board 30 Thtr 60 **Services** Lift **Notes** ⊗

Alexandra Hotel

★★ 71% HOTEL

tel: 01323 720131 **King Edwards Pde BN21 4DR**
email: alexandrahotel@mistral.co.uk **web:** www.alexandrahoteleastbourne.co.uk
dir: *On seafront at junct of Carlisle Rd & King Edward Parade*

Located at the west end of the town, opposite the Wishing Tower, this hotel boasts panoramic views of the sea from many rooms. Bedrooms vary in size but are comfortable with good facilities for guests. A warm welcome is guaranteed at this long-standing, family-run establishment.

Rooms 38 (2 fmly) (3 GF) 🐾 **Facilities** FTV WiFi ♙ 🎵 Xmas New Year **Services** Lift **Notes** ⊗ Closed Jan & Feb RS Mar

Premier Inn Eastbourne

BUDGET HOTEL

tel: 0871 527 8352 *(Calls cost 13p per minute plus your phone company's access charge)*
Willingdon Dr BN23 8AL
web: www.premierinn.com
dir: *From A22 or A27 at Polegate, take bypass signed Eastbourne (A22). Continue to Shinewater rdbt. Left towards Langney. Hotel 0.25m on left*

High quality, budget accommodation ideal for both families and business travellers. Spacious, en suite bedrooms feature tea and coffee making facilities, and Freeview TV in most hotels. Internet access and WiFi are available for a small fee. The adjacent family restaurant features a wide and varied menu. See also the Hotel Groups pages.

Rooms 47

Premier Inn Eastbourne (Polegate)

BUDGET HOTEL

tel: 0871 527 8354 *(Calls cost 13p per minute plus your phone company's access charge)*
Hailsham Rd, Polegate BN26 6QL
web: www.premierinn.com
dir: *At rdbt junct of A22 & A27*

Rooms 56

Premier Inn Eastbourne Town Centre

BUDGET HOTEL

tel: 0871 527 9448 *(Calls cost 13p per minute plus your phone company's access charge)*
Terminus Rd BN21 3DF
web: www.premierinn.com
dir: *From Lewis on A27, A2270, right at lights (Polegate). At next rdbt 1st exit onto A2021 (E'bourne). At rdbt 2nd exit (All other routes). At rdbt 2nd exit onto A2040). At rdbt 1st exit (Upper Ave). At end left into Cavendish Pl (Seafront). At pier right into Grand Parade, next right into Terminus Rd*

Rooms 65

EASTLEIGH
Hampshire   Map 5 SU41

Premier Inn Southampton (Eastleigh)

BUDGET HOTEL

tel: 0871 527 8994 *(Calls cost 13p per minute plus your phone company's access charge)*
Leigh Rd SO50 9YX
web: www.premierinn.com
dir: *M3 junct 13, A335 towards Eastleigh. Hotel on right*

High quality, budget accommodation ideal for both families and business travellers. Spacious, en suite bedrooms feature tea and coffee making facilities, and Freeview TV in most hotels. Internet access and WiFi are available for a small fee. The adjacent family restaurant features a wide and varied menu. See also the Hotel Groups pages.

Rooms 80

EDGEHILL
Warwickshire   Map 11 SP34

Castle at Edgehill

◎◎ RESTAURANT WITH ROOMS

tel: 01295 670255 **Main St OX15 6DJ**
email: enquiries@castleatedgehill.co.uk **web:** www.castleatedgehill.co.uk

Built in 1742 to mark the centenary of the battle of Edgehill, where Charles I raised his standard at the start of the Civil War, the building has a unique history. Sympathetically refurbished in recent years, many of the original features have been restored and the exposed stone walls, along with the wood-panelled restaurant, really add to the character of the building. The Tower bedrooms boast panoramic views from their elevated position and bedrooms are all well-appointed. Dinner is not to be missed in the two AA Rosette award-winning restaurant and breakfast features the best in local produce.

Rooms 4 (2 annexe) (1 fmly)

EDGWARE
Greater London   Map 6 TQ19

Premier Inn London Edgware

BUDGET HOTEL

tel: 0871 527 8652 *(Calls cost 13p per minute plus your phone company's access charge)*
435 Burnt Oak Broadway HA8 5AQ
web: www.premierinn.com
dir: *M1 junct 4, A41, A5 towards Edgware. 3m to hotel*

High quality, budget accommodation ideal for both families and business travellers. Spacious, en suite bedrooms feature tea and coffee making facilities, and Freeview TV in most hotels. Internet access and WiFi are available for a small fee. The adjacent family restaurant features a wide and varied menu. See also the Hotel Groups pages.

Rooms 114

EDMONTON
Greater London   Map 6 TQ39

Premier Inn London Edmonton

BUDGET HOTEL

tel: 0871 527 9404 *(Calls cost 13p per minute plus your phone company's access charge)*
Advent Way, Edmonton N18 3AF
web: www.premierinn.com
dir: *From A406 exit at Cooks Ferry rdbt. 1st exit into Advent Way. Left (remain on Advent Way). Right into Eley Rd. Left into Nobel Rd. 2nd left into Advent Way*

High quality, budget accommodation ideal for both families and business travellers. Spacious, en suite bedrooms feature tea and coffee making facilities, and Freeview TV in most hotels. Internet access and WiFi are available for a small fee. The adjacent family restaurant features a wide and varied menu. See also the Hotel Groups pages.

Rooms 96

E

E

INSPECTORS' CHOICE

Great Fosters

★★★★ ◉◉◉ HOTEL

tel: 01784 433822 **Stroude Rd TW20 9UR**
email: reception@greatfosters.co.uk **web:** www.greatfosters.co.uk
dir: *From A30 Bagshot to Staines, right at lights by Wheatsheaf pub into Christchurch Rd. Straight on at rdbt. Left at lights into Stroude Rd. Hotel 0.75m on right*

This Grade II listed mansion dates back to the 16th century. The main house rooms are very much in keeping with the house's original style but are, of course, up-to-date with modern amenities. The stables and cloisters provide particularly stylish and luxurious accommodation. A stimulating range of award-winning cuisine can be enjoyed in The Tudor Room. The beautiful public rooms, including the Terrace during the summer months, provide the perfect setting for afternoon tea and cocktails. A host of meeting and event facilities provide the setting for a range of individual events.

Rooms 43 (22 annexe) (1 fmly) (13 GF) 🐾 **S** £180–£225; **D** £225–£575
Facilities STV WiFi ⬇ 🏌 ⚓ 🚣 Xmas New Year **Conf** Class 72 Board 50 Thtr 150
Del from £275 to £355 **Parking** 200 **Notes** LB ⊗ Civ Wed 180

the runnymede-on-thames

★★★★ 82% ◉ HOTEL

tel: 01784 220600 **Windsor Rd TW20 0AG**
email: info@therunnymede.co.uk **web:** www.therunnymede.co.uk
dir: *M25 junct 13, onto A308 towards Windsor*

Enjoying a peaceful location beside the River Thames, this large modern hotel, with its excellent range of facilities, balances both leisure and corporate business. The extensive function suites, together with spacious lounges and stylish, well laid-out bedrooms are impressive. Superb spa facilities are available, and the good food and beverage venues offer wonderful river views.

Rooms 180 (19 fmly) 🐾 **S** £200–£260; **D** £220–£280* **Facilities** Spa STV WiFi ⬇ HL 🏊 supervised 🎾 supervised ⚽ Gym Dance studio Boat hire 🎵 Xmas New Year **Conf** Class 180 Board 80 Thtr 300 Del from £249* **Services** Lift Air con **Parking** 300 **Notes** LB Civ Wed 142

Mercure Chester North Woodhey House Hotel

★★★ 74% HOTEL

tel: 0151 339 5121 **Berwick Road West / Welsh Rd, Little Sutton CH66 4PS**
email: enquiries@woodheyhouse-hotel-chester.com **web:** www.mercure.com
dir: *A41 S, right at 2nd set of lights onto A550 towards Queensferry. Hotel 1m on left*

Located in a quiet rural setting, yet within easy reach of the M53, this hotel is an ideal stop-off for both business and leisure guests. All bedrooms are well equipped, and the day rooms are stylishly appointed. They include a bar, restaurant and a very good range of meeting and conference facilities. The hotel also has an indoor pool, gym and steam room.

Rooms 75 (8 fmly) (23 GF) 🐾 **S** £60–£80; **D** £60–£104* **Facilities** FTV WiFi 🏊 Gym Sauna Steam room Xmas New Year **Conf** Class 120 Board 80 Thtr 250 Del from £85 to £150* **Services** Lift **Parking** 150 **Notes** LB Civ Wed 100

HIGHLY RECOMMENDED

Laura Ashley The Manor

★★★★ 83% ◉◉ HOTEL

tel: 020 8327 4700 **Barnet Ln WD6 3RE**
email: elstree@lauraashleyhotels.com
web: www.lauraashleyhotels.com/themanorelstree

This old Tudor house, built circa 1540, is set in ten acres of grounds, and was purchased by Laura Ashley in 2012. It was then refurbished throughout to reflect the rich design heritage of the company. Public rooms include a smart bar with original features, and the panelled Cavendish restaurant. Bedrooms are tastefully decorated and furnished in Laura Ashley-style, and have modern facilities.

Rooms 49 (36 annexe) **Facilities** FTV WiFi Gym Xmas New Year **Conf** Class 30 Board 36 Thtr 80 **Parking** 100 **Notes** LB ⊗ Civ Wed 86

E

ELTERWATER
Cumbria — Map 18 NY30

HIGHLY RECOMMENDED

Langdale Hotel & Spa
★★★★ 83% ◎ COUNTRY HOUSE HOTEL

tel: 015394 38014 & 38012 **The Langdale Estate LA22 9JD**
email: info@langdale.co.uk **web:** www.langdale.co.uk
dir: *In Langdale Valley W of Ambleside*

Founded on the site of an abandoned 19th-century gunpowder works, this thoroughly modern hotel and resort is set in 35 acres of woodland and waterways. Comfortable bedrooms, many with spa baths, vary in size. Extensive public areas include the exceptional new Stove restaurant and bar. The ever improving, luxurious spa and leisure facilities are on hand and there is also a traditional pub run by the hotel just along the main road.

Rooms 56 (51 annexe) (4 fmly) (25 GF) ⬥ **Facilities** Spa STV FTV WiFi ⊗ supervised ⬥ Fishing Gym Steam room Solarium Aerobics studio Health & beauty salon Cycle hire Xmas New Year **Conf** Class 20 Board 18 Thtr 40 Del from £145 to £205* **Parking** 65 **Notes** ⊗ Civ Wed 34

New Dungeon Ghyll Hotel
★★★ 79% HOTEL

tel: 015394 37213 **Ambleside, Great Langdale LA22 9JX**
email: enquiries@dungeon-ghyll.com **web:** www.dungeon-ghyll.com
dir: *From Ambleside follow A593 towards Coniston for 3m, at Skelwith Bridge right onto B5343 towards 'The Langdales'*

This friendly hotel enjoys a tranquil, idyllic position at the head of the valley, set among the impressive peaks of Langdale. Bedrooms vary in size and style, but all the rooms are brightly decorated and smartly furnished. Bar meals are served all day, and dinner can be enjoyed in the restaurant overlooking the landscaped gardens; there is also a cosy lounge/bar.

Rooms 22 (1 fmly) (4 GF) ⬥ **Facilities** FTV WiFi ⊗ Xmas New Year **Parking** 30 **Notes** ⊗ Civ Wed 60

EMBLETON
Northumberland — Map 21 NU22

Dunstanburgh Castle Hotel
★★ 85% HOTEL

tel: 01665 576111 **NE66 3UN**
email: stay@dunstanburghcastlehotel.co.uk **web:** www.dunstanburghcastlehotel.co.uk
dir: *From A1 take B1340 to Denwick through Rennington. Right signed Embleton, over level crossing, left at xrds, 2m to Embleton, hotel on right.*

The focal point of the village, this friendly, family-run hotel has a dining room and grill room that offer different menus, plus a cosy bar and two lounges. In addition to the main bedrooms, a barn conversion houses three stunning suites, each with a lounge and gallery bedroom above.

Rooms 32 (12 annexe) (6 fmly) ⬥ **S** £40-£70; **D** £80-£140 (incl. bkfst)* **Facilities** WiFi **Parking** 33 **Notes** LB Closed Dec-Jan

EMSWORTH
Hampshire — Map 5 SU70

Brookfield Hotel
★★★ 81% HOTEL

tel: 01243 373363 **Havant Rd PO10 7LF**
email: bookings@brookfieldhotel.co.uk **web:** www.brookfieldhotel.co.uk
dir: *From A27 onto A259 towards Emsworth. Hotel 0.5m on left*

This well-established family-run hotel has spacious public areas with popular conference and banqueting facilities. Bedrooms are in a modern style, and comfortably furnished. The popular Hermitage Restaurant offers a seasonally changing menu and an interesting wine list.

Rooms 39 (6 fmly) (12 GF) ⬥ **Facilities** FTV WiFi ⊗ Xmas New Year **Conf** Class 50 Board 50 Thtr 100 **Parking** 80 **Notes** ⊗ Civ Wed 100

36 on the Quay
◎◎◎ RESTAURANT WITH ROOMS

tel: 01243 375592 & 372257 **47 South St PO10 7EG**
web: www.36onthequay.co.uk
dir: *Last building on right in South St, which runs from square in centre of Emsworth*

Occupying a prime position with far-reaching views over the estuary, this 16th-century house is the scene for some accomplished and exciting cuisine. The elegant restaurant occupies centre stage with peaceful pastel shades, local art and crisp napery together with glimpses of the bustling harbour outside. The contemporary bedrooms offer style, comfort and thoughtful extras.

Rooms 7 (2 annexe)

ENFIELD
Greater London — Map 6 TQ39

Royal Chace Hotel
★★★★ 79% ◎ HOTEL

tel: 020 8884 8181 **162 The Ridgeway EN2 8AR**
email: reservations@royalchacehotel.co.uk **web:** www.royal-chace.com
dir: *M25 junct 24, A1005 towards Enfield. Hotel 3m on right*

This professionally-run, privately owned hotel enjoys a peaceful location with open fields to the rear. Public rooms are smartly appointed; the ground-floor Kings Restaurant is particularly appealing with its warm colour schemes and friendly service. Bedrooms are well presented and thoughtfully equipped.

Rooms 92 (5 fmly) (32 GF) ⬥ **Facilities** FTV WiFi ⊗ Gym New Year **Conf** Class 100 Board 40 Thtr 250 **Parking** 200 **Notes** ⊗ RS Sun eve Civ Wed 220

E

ENFIELD *continued*

Premier Inn Enfield

BUDGET HOTEL

tel: 0871 527 8374 *(Calls cost 13p per minute plus your phone company's access charge)*
Innova Park, Corner of Solar Way EN3 7XY
web: www.premierinn.com
dir: *M25 junct 25, A10 towards London, left into Bullsmoor Lane & Mollison Ave. Over rdbt, right at lights into Innova Science Park*

High quality, budget accommodation ideal for both families and business travellers. Spacious, en suite bedrooms feature tea and coffee making facilities, and Freeview TV in most hotels. Internet access and WiFi are available for a small fee. The adjacent family restaurant features a wide and varied menu. See also the Hotel Groups pages.

Rooms 202

EPPING	Map 6 TL40
Essex	

The Bell Hotel

★★★ 75% HOTEL

tel: 01992 573138 **High Rd, Bell Common CM16 4DG**
email: reservations@bellhotelepping.com **web:** www.bellhotelepping.com
dir: *M11 junct 7, B1393 to Epping. Hotel on right past town centre*

This hotel enjoys a convenient location on the outskirts of the town centre, close to the M25 and M1. The nearby tube station allows for quick access to London. There is a range of bedroom styles, all attractively presented and featuring LCD TVs and free WiFi. Public areas include a cosy bar and a popular restaurant, along with well-equipped conference facilities.

Rooms 79 (5 fmly) (38 GF) (10 smoking) **Facilities** FTV WiFi ⌕ Xmas New Year **Conf** Class 50 Board 50 Thtr 85 **Parking** 80 **Notes** ⊗ Civ Wed 60

EPSOM	Map 6 TQ26
Surrey	

Premier Inn Epsom Central

BUDGET HOTEL

tel: 0871 527 8376 *(Calls cost 13p per minute plus your phone company's access charge)*
2-4 St Margarets Dr, off Dorking Rd KT18 7LB
web: www.premierinn.com
dir: *M25 junct 9, A24 towards Epsom, hotel on left, just before town centre*

High quality, budget accommodation ideal for both families and business travellers. Spacious, en suite bedrooms feature tea and coffee making facilities, and Freeview TV in most hotels. Internet access and WiFi are available for a small fee. The adjacent family restaurant features a wide and varied menu. See also the Hotel Groups pages.

Rooms 58

Premier Inn Epsom North

BUDGET HOTEL

tel: 0871 527 8380 *(Calls cost 13p per minute plus your phone company's access charge)*
272 Kingston Rd, Ewell KT19 0SH
web: www.premierinn.com
dir: *M25 junct 8, A217 towards Sutton. A240 towards Ewell. At Beggars Hill rdbt 2nd exit into Kingston Rd*

Rooms 29

ERMINGTON	Map 3 SX65
Devon	

Plantation House

◉◉ ⬗ RESTAURANT WITH ROOMS

tel: 01548 831100 & 830741 **Totnes Rd PL21 9NS**
email: info@plantationhousehotel.co.uk **web:** www.plantationhousehotel.co.uk

Peacefully situated within the picturesque South Hams, this former parish rectory now provides an intimate and relaxing base from which to explore the area. Quality, comfort and individuality are hallmarks throughout, with bedrooms offering impressive standards and a host of thoughtful extras. The stylish bathrooms come equipped with fluffy towels, robes and under-floor heating. A drink beside the crackling log fire is the ideal prelude to dinner, where skill and passion underpin menus focusing upon wonderful local produce. Breakfast is equally enjoyable, with superb eggs provided by the resident hens.

Rooms 8

ESCRICK	Map 16 SE64
North Yorkshire	

The Parsonage Country House Hotel

★★★ 81% ◉ COUNTRY HOUSE HOTEL

tel: 01904 728111 **York Rd YO19 6LF**
email: reservations@parsonagehotel.co.uk **web:** www.parsonagehotel.co.uk
dir: *A64 onto A19 Selby, Follow to Escrick. Hotel by St Helens Church*

This 19th-century, former parsonage has been carefully restored and extended, and is situated in six acres of gardens. Bedrooms are smartly appointed and well equipped for both business and leisure guests. Public areas include an elegant restaurant, conference facilities and a choice of attractive lounges. Cloisters Spa is located in the formal gardens and includes a swimming pool, jacuzzi, sauna, steam room, aromatherapy salt room and an excellent gym. Please note that the Spa and Health Club is for adults aged 18+ only. The Fat Abbot is the newly refurbished gastro pub also located in the grounds offering a more relaxed dining experience.

Rooms 53 (16 annexe) (4 fmly) (9 GF) ⬗ **Facilities** Spa FTV WiFi ⌕ ⊛ Gym Sauna Steam room Aromatherapy room Salt room Xmas New Year **Conf** Class 80 Board 50 Thtr 150 Del from £99 to £140* **Services** Lift **Parking** 120 **Notes** ⊗ Civ Wed 150

E

EVERSHOT
Dorset

Map 4 ST50

INSPECTORS' CHOICE

Summer Lodge Country House Hotel, Restaurant & Spa

THE RED CARNATION HOTEL COLLECTION

★★★★ ◉◉◉ ⚲ COUNTRY HOUSE HOTEL

tel: 01935 482000 & 482030 **Fore St DT2 0JR**
email: summer@relaischateaux.com **web:** www.summerlodgehotel.co.uk
dir: 1m W of A37 halfway between Dorchester & Yeovil

This picturesque hotel is situated in the heart of Dorset and is the ideal retreat; it's worth arriving in time for the excellent afternoon tea. Bedrooms are appointed to a very high standard; each is individually designed, with upholstered walls and a wealth of luxurious facilities. Expect plasma screen TVs, DVD players, radios, air conditioning and WiFi access, plus little touches such as homemade shortbread, fresh fruit and scented candles. The delightful public areas include a sumptuous lounge complete with an open fire, and the elegant restaurant where the cuisine continues to be the high point of any stay.

Rooms 24 (14 annexe) (6 fmly) (3 GF) ⋔ **S** £215-£760; **D** £215 £760 (incl. bkfst)* **Facilities** Spa STV FTV WiFi ⇗ ⊛ ⊛ ⊛ Gym Sauna Xmas New Year **Conf** Class 16 Board 16 Thtr 24 Del from £375 to £575* **Services** Air con **Parking** 41 **Notes** LB Closed 2-25 Jan Civ Wed 30

George Albert Hotel

★★★ 81% ◉ HOTEL

tel: 01935 483430 **Wardon Hill DT2 9PW**
email: enquiries@gahotel.co.uk **web:** www.gahotel.co.uk
dir: On A37 - between Yeovil & Dorchester. Adjacent to Southern Counties Kart Track

Situated mid-way between Dorchester and Yeovil, this hotel has much to offer for both business and leisure guests. The bedrooms offer impressive levels of comfort and many also have wonderful views across the Dorset countryside. Stylish public areas include extensive function rooms, a relaxing lounge, and a choice of dining options. Additional facilities include a karting track and clay-pigeon shooting.

Rooms 39 (3 fmly) ⋔ **Facilities** FTV WiFi ⇗ Clay pigeon Kart track Xmas New Year **Conf** Class 60 Board 90 Thtr 250 **Services** Lift Air con **Parking** 200 **Notes** ⊗ Civ Wed 405

EVESHAM
Worcestershire

Map 10 SP04

Wood Norton Hotel

★★★★ 79% ◉ HOTEL

tel: 01386 765611 **Worcester Rd WR11 4YB**
email: info@thewoodnorton.com **web:** www.thewoodnorton.com
dir: 2m from Evesham on A44, after Chadbury

Equidistant from Worcester, Stratford-Upon-Avon and Cheltenham, this 19th-century former hunting lodge, originally built for European royalty, is ideally located for exploring the Cotswolds. Modern refurbishment and period architecture sit comfortably together, creating a stylish interior. Bedrooms are well equipped for both business and leisure guests, and complimentary WiFi is available throughout. Public areas encompass a stylish bar, guest lounges and an oak-panelled dining room overlooking the gardens.

Rooms 50 (30 annexe) (6 fmly) (12 GF) ⋔ **Facilities** FTV WiFi Xmas New Year **Conf** Class 60 Board 40 Thtr 200 **Services** Lift **Notes** LB ⊗ Civ Wed

Dumbleton Hall Hotel

★★★ 79% COUNTRY HOUSE HOTEL

tel: 01386 881240 **WR11 7TS**
email: dh@pofr.co.uk **web:** www.dumbletonhall.co.uk

(For full entry see Dumbleton)

Premier Inn Evesham

BUDGET HOTEL

Premier Inn

tel: 0871 527 8384 *(Calls cost 13p per minute plus your phone company's access charge)*
Evesham Country Park, A46 Trunk Rd, Twyford WR11 4TP
web: www.premierinn.com
dir: *At rdbt junct of A46(T) & A4184 at N end of Evesham bypass. Adjacent to Evesham Country Park*

High quality, budget accommodation ideal for both families and business travellers. Spacious, en suite bedrooms feature tea and coffee making facilities, and Freeview TV in most hotels. Internet access and WiFi are available for a small fee. The adjacent family restaurant features a wide and varied menu. See also the Hotel Groups pages.

Rooms 108

E

EXETER
Devon

Map 3 SX99

ABode Exeter

★★★★ 81% ◉◉ HOTEL

ABode
HOTELS

tel: 01392 319955 **Cathedral Yard EX1 1HD**
email: reservationsexeter@abodehotels.co.uk **web:** www.abodeexeter.co.uk
dir: M5 junct 30 towards A379. Follow city centre signs. Hotel opposite cathedral behind High St

ABode Exeter enjoys a central location in the heart of the city's Cathedral Yard. Steeped in history, this property, formerly The Royal Clarence, is reported to have been the very first hotel in England. A range of well-appointed bedrooms and suites, many retaining original features, all boast modern facilities and smart en suites. A choice of dining options and bars includes the all-day Cafe Bar & Grill, and the more relaxed Well House Tavern.

Rooms 53 (3 fmly) ☏ **Facilities** STV FTV WiFi ♨ Gym Xmas New Year **Conf** Class 70 Board 50 Thtr 150 **Services** Lift Air con **Notes** ⊗ Civ Wed 70

Mercure Exeter Southgate Hotel & Spa

★★★★ 73% HOTEL

Mercure
HOTELS

tel: 01392 412812 **Southernhay East EX1 1QF**
email: h6624@accor.com **web:** www.mercure.com
dir: M5 junct 30, 3rd exit (Exeter), 2nd left towards city centre, 3rd exit at next rdbt, hotel 2m on right

Centrally located and with excellent parking, The Southgate offers a diverse range of leisure and business facilities. Public areas are pleasantly spacious with comfortable seating in the bar and lounge; there is also a terrace. The bedrooms, in differing sizes, are well equipped and have modern facilities.

Rooms 156 (21 fmly) (23 GF) ☏ **D** £80-£250* **Facilities** FTV WiFi ♨ ☒ supervised Gym Sauna Spa bath New Year **Conf** Class 90 Board 60 Thtr 180 Del from £130 to £160* **Services** Lift **Parking** 101 **Notes** LB ⊗ Civ Wed 100

The Devon Hotel

★★★ 80% HOTEL

Brend Hotels

tel: 01392 259268 **Exeter Bypass, Matford EX2 8XU**
email: reservations@devonhotel.co.uk **web:** www.devonhotel.co.uk
dir: M5 junct 30 follow Marsh Barton Ind Est signs on A379. Hotel on Marsh Barton rdbt

Within easy access of the city centre, the M5 and the city's business parks, this smart Georgian hotel offers modern, comfortable accommodation. The Carriages Bar and Brasserie is popular with guests and locals alike, offering a wide range of dishes as well as a carvery at both lunch and dinner. Service is friendly and attentive, and extensive meeting and business facilities are available.

Rooms 60 (60 annexe) (17 fmly) (21 GF) ☏ **S** £75-£110; **D** £80-£120* **Facilities** FTV WiFi ♨ Gym Xmas New Year **Conf** Class 80 Board 40 Thtr 150 **Parking** 150 **Notes** LB ⊗ Civ Wed 100

Best Western Lord Haldon Country Hotel

BW Best Western.

★★★ 79% HOTEL

tel: 01392 832483 **Dunchideock EX6 7YF**
email: enquiries@lordhaldonhotel.co.uk **web:** www.lordhaldonhotel.co.uk
dir: M5 junct 31, A30, 1st exit, follow signs through Ide to Dunchideock

Set in rural tranquillity, this is an attractive country house where guests are assured of a warm welcome from the professional team of staff. The well-equipped bedrooms are comfortable, and many have stunning views. The daily-changing menu features skilfully cooked dishes, with most of the produce sourced locally.

Rooms 25 (3 fmly) ☏ **Facilities** FTV WiFi ♨ Xmas New Year **Conf** Class 100 Board 40 Thtr 250 **Parking** 120 **Notes** Civ Wed 120

Queens Court Hotel

★★★ 75% ◉ HOTEL

tel: 01392 272709 **6-8 Bystock Ter EX4 4HY**
email: enquiries@queenscourt-hotel.co.uk **web:** www.queenscourt-hotel.co.uk
dir: Exit dual carriageway at junct 30 onto B5132 Topsham Rd, towards city centre. Hotel 200yds from Central Station

Quietly located within walking distance of the city centre, this privately owned hotel is a listed, early Victorian property that provides friendly hospitality. The smart public areas and contemporary bedrooms are tastefully furnished, and the stylish and attractive Olive Tree restaurant offers an award-winning selection of dishes. Rooms are available for conferences, meetings, weddings and parties. Complimentary parking is available in a public car park directly opposite the hotel entrance.

Rooms 19 (1 fmly) (1 GF) ☏ **Facilities** FTV WiFi **Conf** Class 30 Board 35 Thtr 60 **Services** Lift **Notes** ⊗ Closed Xmas & New Year RS 23 Dec-01 Jan Civ Wed 60

E

Gipsy Hill Hotel

THE INDEPENDENTS
HOTEL ASSOCIATION

★★★ 75% HOTEL

tel: 01392 465252 **Gipsy Hill Ln, Monkerton EX1 3RN**
email: stay@gipsyhillhotel.co.uk **web:** www.gipsyhillhotel.co.uk
dir: *M5 junct 29 towards Exeter. Right at 1st rdbt, right again at next rdbt, turn left onto Pinn Lane, right onto Gipsy Hill Lane*

Located on the edge of the city, with easy access to the M5 and the airport, this popular hotel is set in attractive, well-tended gardens and boasts far-reaching country views. The hotel offers a range of conference and function rooms, comfortable bedrooms and modern facilities including free WiFi. An intimate bar and lounge are adjacent to the elegant restaurant. Secure indoor cycle storage is also provided.

Rooms 37 (17 annexe) (4 fmly) (12 GF) 🐾 **S** £49-£79; **D** £59-£89 (incl. bkfst)*
Facilities FTV WiFi ♫ Xmas New Year **Conf** Class 80 Board 80 Thtr 300 Del from £130 to £150* **Parking** 74 **Notes** ⊗ Civ Wed 160

Barton Cross Hotel & Restaurant

★★★ 74% ⊚ HOTEL

tel: 01392 841245 **Huxham, Stoke Canon EX5 4EJ**
email: bartonxhuxham@aol.com **web:** www.thebartoncrosshotel.co.uk
dir: *From A396, 0.5m to Stoke Canon, 3m N of Exeter*

17th-century charm combined with 21st-century luxury sums up the appeal of this lovely country hotel. The bedrooms are spacious, tastefully decorated and well maintained. Public areas include the cosy first-floor lounge and a lounge/bar with warming log fire. The restaurant offers a seasonally changing menu of consistently enjoyable cuisine.

Rooms 9 (2 fmly) (2 GF) (1 smoking) 🐾 **S** £80-£90; **D** £110-£120 (incl. bkfst)
Facilities STV FTV WiFi ♫ Xmas New Year **Conf** Class 20 Board 20 Thtr 20 **Parking** 35
Notes LB

Southernhay House

U ⊚

tel: 01392 435324 & 439000 **36 Southernhay East EX1 1NX**
email: home@southernhayhouse.com **web:** www.southernhayhouse.com
dir: *M5 junct 30 (S), follow signs for city centre, at inner ring road rdbt (Vue Cinema), left to Western Way, 1st right & 1st left. A38 junct 30 (N) as above*

Located in the heart of Exeter and just a short stroll from the Cathedral and city centre shops, this elegant and intimate hotel dates back to the Georgian period. Lovingly restored, the style is an engaging blend of traditional and contemporary with bedrooms offering impressive levels of comfort and individuality. Public areas include a wonderful cocktail bar. Dinner provides an opportunity to sample enjoyable dishes with a focus upon seasonality, freshness and flavour. For further details please see the AA website: theAA.com

Rooms 10 🐾 **S** £150-£260; **D** £150-£260 (incl. bkfst)* **Facilities** FTV WiFi ♫
Conf Board 16 **Notes** LB ⊗ No children 12yrs Civ Wed 28

Premier Inn Exeter Central St Davids

BUDGET HOTEL

tel: 0871 527 9278 *(Calls cost 13p per minute plus your phone company's access charge)*
Bonhay Rd EX4 4BG
web: www.premierinn.com
dir: *M5 junct 31, A30 towards Bodmin & Oakehampton. Exit onto A377 towards Exeter & Crediton. Hotel on left*

High quality, budget accommodation ideal for both families and business travellers. Spacious, en suite bedrooms feature tea and coffee making facilities, and Freeview TV in most hotels. Internet access and WiFi are available for a small fee. The adjacent family restaurant features a wide and varied menu. See also the Hotel Groups pages.

Rooms 102

Premier Inn Exeter City Centre

BUDGET HOTEL

tel: 0871 527 9570 *(Calls cost 13p per minute plus your phone company's access charge)*
2 Southernhay Gardens EX1 1SG
email: ExeterCityCentre.PI@premierinn.com **web:** www.premierinn.com
dir: *M5 junct 29, A3015. Right at lights into Honiton Rd. At Moor Lane rdbt 2nd exit (A3015) then B3183. At next rdbt 1st exit into Western Way (B3212). Right into Barnfield Rd, left then left again into Southernhay Gardens*

Rooms 120

Premier Inn Exeter (Countess Wear)

BUDGET HOTEL

tel: 0871 527 8386 *(Calls cost 13p per minute plus your phone company's access charge)*
398 Topsham Rd EX2 6HE
web: www.premierinn.com
dir: *2m from M5 junct 30/A30 junct 29. Follow signs for Exeter & Dawlish (A379). On dual carriageway take 2nd slip road on left at Countess Wear rdbt. Hotel adjacent to Beefeater*

Rooms 44

Premier Inn Exeter M5 Jct 29

BUDGET HOTEL

tel: 0871 527 9468 *(Calls cost 13p per minute plus your phone company's access charge)*
Fitzroy Rd EX1 3LJ
web: www.premierinn.com
dir: *M5 junct 29, A3015 towards city centre. Straight on at 1st rdbt. 2nd right (at lights) into Fitzroy Rd*

Rooms 102

Chi Restaurant & Bar with Accommodation

RESTAURANT WITH ROOMS

tel: 01626 890213 **Fore St, Kenton EX6 8LD**
email: enquiries@chi-restaurant.co.uk **web:** www.chi-restaurant.co.uk
dir: *5m S of Exeter. M5 junct 30, A379 towards Dawlish, in village centre*

This former pub has been spectacularly transformed into a chic and contemporary bar, allied with a stylish Chinese restaurant. Dishes are beautifully presented with an emphasis on quality produce and authenticity, resulting in a memorable dining experience. Bedrooms are well equipped and all provide good levels of space and comfort, along with modern bathrooms.

Rooms 5 (1 fmly)

E

EXFORD
Somerset
Map 3 SS83

Crown Hotel

★★★ 80% HOTEL

tel: 01643 831554 **Park St TA24 7PP**
email: info@crownhotelexmoor.co.uk **web:** www.crownhotelexmoor.co.uk
dir: *M5 junct 25, follow Taunton signs. Take A358 from Taunton, then B3224 via Wheddon Cross to Exford*

Guest comfort is of utmost importance here at the Crown Hotel. Afternoon tea is served in the lounge beside a roaring fire, and tempting menus in the bar and restaurant are all part of the charm of this old coaching inn, that specialises in breaks for shooting and other country sports. Bedrooms retain a traditional style yet offer a range of modern comforts and facilities. Many have views of the pretty moorland village.

Rooms 16 (3 fmly) ☞ **S** £67.50-£87.50; **D** £115-£175 (incl. bkfst)* **Facilities** FTV WiFi ☕ Xmas New Year **Conf** Board 15 **Parking** 30 **Notes** LB

EXMOUTH
Devon
Map 3 SY08

Cavendish Hotel

Leisureplex
HOLIDAY HOTELS

★★★ 70% HOTEL

tel: 01395 272528 **11 Morton Crescent, The Esplanade EX8 1BE**
email: cavendish.exmouth@alfatravel.co.uk **web:** www.leisureplex.co.uk
dir: *Follow seafront signs, hotel in centre of large crescent*

Situated on the seafront, this terraced hotel attracts many groups from around the country, and is within walking distance of the town centre. The bedrooms are neatly presented, and front-facing rooms are always popular. Entertainment is provided on most evenings during the summer.

Rooms 78 (3 fmly) (21 GF) ☞ **Facilities** FTV WiFi Snooker ♫ Xmas New Year **Services** Lift **Parking** 25 **Notes** ⊗ Closed Dec-Jan (ex Xmas) RS Nov & Feb-Mar

Premier Inn Exmouth Seafront

BUDGET HOTEL

tel: 0871 527 9400 *(Calls cost 13p per minute plus your phone company's access charge)*
The Esplanade EX8 2AZ
web: www.premierinn.com
dir: *M5 junct 30, A376 signed Exeter/Exmouth. At rdbt take A376. At 4th rdbt take 2nd exit into Imperial Rd. After next rdbt, right onto Alexandra Terr. 1st left into Morton Rd, left onto Esplanade. Hotel on left*

High quality, budget accommodation ideal for both families and business travellers. Spacious, en suite bedrooms feature tea and coffee making facilities, and Freeview TV in most hotels. Internet access and WiFi are available for a small fee. The adjacent family restaurant features a wide and varied menu. See also the Hotel Groups pages.

Rooms 60

FALFIELD
Gloucestershire
Map 4 ST69

Best Western The Gables Hotel

Best Western

★★★ 77% HOTEL

tel: 01454 260502 **Bristol Rd GL12 8DL**
email: mail@thegablesbristol.co.uk **web:** www.thegablesbristol.co.uk
dir: *M5 junct 14 N'bound. Left at end of sliproad. Right onto A38, hotel 300yds on right*

Conveniently located just a few minutes from the motorway, this establishment is ideally suited to both business and leisure guests, with easy access to Cheltenham, Gloucester, Bristol and Bath. Bedrooms are spacious and well equipped. Relaxing public areas consist of a light and airy bar, and a restaurant where meals and all-day snacks are available; a more formal restaurant is open for dinner. There is also a range of meeting rooms.

Rooms 46 (4 fmly) (18 GF) **S** £75-£125; **D** £85-£165 (incl. bkfst)* **Facilities** FTV WiFi ☕ New Year **Conf** Class 90 Board 50 Thtr 200 **Parking** 104 **Notes** LB ⊗ Civ Wed 150

F

FALMOUTH
Cornwall

Map 2 SW83

See also **Mawnan Smith**

The Royal Duchy Hotel

★★★★ 79% @@ HOTEL

tel: 01326 313042 **Cliff Rd TR11 4NX**
email: reservations@royalduchy.com **web:** www.royalduchy.com
dir: *On Cliff Rd, along Falmouth seafront*

Staff at this hotel, which looks out over the sea and towards Pendennis Castle, create a very friendly environment. The comfortable lounge and cocktail bar are well appointed and just the place for a light lunch. Leisure facilities include a beauty salon, and meeting rooms are also available. The award-winning Terrace Restaurant serves carefully prepared dishes, and guests can sit on the sea-facing terrace in warmer weather. The bedrooms vary in size and aspect, and many have sea views. Babysitting is happily arranged for families with small children and babies.

Rooms 43 (6 fmly) (1 GF) 🐾 **S** £85-£122; **D** £150-£380 (incl. bkfst)* **Facilities** FTV WiFi ⌂ 🅫 Games room Sauna Hot stone therapy beds Beauty treatment room 🎵 Xmas New Year Child facilities **Conf** Thtr 50 **Services** Lift **Parking** 50 **Notes** LB ⊗ Civ Wed 100

See advert on opposite page

St Michael's Hotel and Spa

★★★★ 77% @@ HOTEL

tel: 01326 312707 **Gyllyngvase Beach, Seafront TR11 4NB**
email: info@stmichaelshotel.co.uk **web:** www.stmichaelshotel.co.uk
dir: *A39 into Falmouth, follow beach signs, at 2nd mini-rdbt into Pennance Rd. Take 2nd left & 2nd left again*

Overlooking the bay, this hotel is in an excellent position and commands lovely views. It is appointed in a fresh, contemporary style that reflects its location by the sea. The Flying Fish restaurant has a great atmosphere and a real buzz about it. The light and bright bedrooms, some with balconies, are well equipped. There are excellent leisure facilities including a fitness and health club together with a spa offering many treatments. The attractive gardens also provide a place to relax and unwind.

Rooms 61 (8 annexe) (7 fmly) (12 GF) 🐾 **Facilities** Spa FTV WiFi ⌂ 🅫 ♨ Gym Sauna Steam room Aqua aerobics Fitness classes Xmas New Year **Conf** Class 150 Board 50 Thtr 200 Del from £146 to £222* **Parking** 60 **Notes** ⊗ Civ Wed 80

The Greenbank Hotel

★★★★ 75% @@ HOTEL

tel: 01326 312440 **Harbourside TR11 2SR**
email: reception@greenbank-hotel.co.uk **web:** www.greenbank-hotel.co.uk
dir: *A39 to Falmouth, left at Ponsharden rdbt onto North Parade. 500yds past Falmouth Marina on the Harbourfront*

Located by the marina, and with its own private quay dating from the 17th century, The Greenbank Hotel has a strong maritime theme throughout. Set at the water's edge, the lounge, restaurant and many bedrooms all benefit from harbour views. The restaurant provides a choice of interesting and enjoyable dishes.

Rooms 60 (6 fmly) 🐾 **S** £69-£119; **D** £109-£279 (incl. bkfst)* **Facilities** FTV WiFi ⌂ Private beach & quay Beauty treatment room Xmas New Year **Conf** Class 30 Board 50 Thtr 120 **Services** Lift **Parking** 68 **Notes** LB Civ Wed 120

Merchants Manor

★★★★ 74% @ HOTEL

tel: 01326 211427 **1 Weston Manor TR11 4AJ**
email: info@merchantsmanor.com **web:** www.merchantsmanor.com

Merchants Manor is an historical country house situated within walking distance of the busy Falmouth town centre and pretty beaches. Beautiful original features have been sympathetically mixed with modern and contemporary style and design. Newly renovated rooms are trendy and comfortable with a keen eye on quality and standards. It's ideal for that special wedding or family celebration with the added benefit of leisure facilities for families, including a good size gym. There is also generous seating in the recently renovated lounge, perfect for a morning coffee or afternoon tea.

Rooms 39 (2 fmly) (11 GF) 🐾 **Facilities** FTV WiFi ⌂ HL 🅫 Gym Sauna In room treatments Xmas New Year **Conf** Class 140 Board 60 Thtr 180 **Parking** 126 **Notes** LB Civ Wed 120

FALMOUTH *continued*

Penmere Manor Hotel

★★★ 80% HOTEL

tel: 01326 211411 **Mongleath Rd TR11 4PN**
email: reservations@penmere.co.uk **web:** www.penmere.co.uk
dir: *Take 2nd exit at Hillhead rdbt, over next rdbt to Union Rd. Follow road and turn left onto Mongleath Rd*

Set in five acres on the outskirts of town, this Georgian manor house was originally built for a ship's captain. Now a family-owned hotel it provides friendly service and a good range of facilities. Bedrooms vary in size and are located in the manor house and the garden wing. Various menus are available in the bar and the smart restaurant. There is a leisure club with an indoor heated pool, jacuzzi, sauna and a well-equipped small gymnasium. The water in the pool is UV filtered.

Rooms 37 (12 fmly) (13 GF) 🛏 **S** £75-£85; **D** £140-£160 (incl. bkfst)* **Facilities** FTV WiFi 🕃 Gym Sauna New Year **Conf** Class 20 Board 30 Thtr 60 Del from £144.50 to £173* **Parking** 50 **Notes** LB Closed 22-27 Dec

Penmorvah Manor

★★★ 78% @ HOTEL

tel: 01326 250277 **Budock Water TR11 5ED**
email: reception@penmorvah.co.uk **web:** www.penmorvah.co.uk
dir: *A39 to Hillhead rdbt, take 2nd exit. Right at Falmouth Football Club, through Budock. Hotel opposite Penjerrick Gardens*

Situated within two miles of central Falmouth, this extended Victorian manor house is a peaceful hideaway, set in six acres of private woodland and gardens. Penmorvah is well positioned for visiting the local gardens, and offers many garden-tour breaks. Dinner features locally sourced, quality ingredients such as Cornish cheeses, meat, fish and game.

Rooms 27 (1 fmly) (10 GF) 🛏 **S** £49-£69; **D** £109-£169 (incl. bkfst)* **Facilities** FTV WiFi ♭ Xmas New Year **Conf** Class 100 Board 40 Thtr 120 Del from £95 to £125* **Parking** 100 **Notes** LB Civ Wed 120

Falmouth Hotel

★★★ 77% @ HOTEL

RICHARDSON HOTELS
Where Memories are Made

tel: 01326 312671 & 0800 019 3121 **Castle Beach TR11 4NZ**
email: reservations@falmouthhotel.com **web:** www.falmouthhotel.com
dir: *A30 to Truro then A390 to Falmouth. Follow signs for beaches, hotel on seafront near Pendennis Castle*

This spectacular beach-front Victorian property affords wonderful sea views from many of its comfortable bedrooms, some of which have their own balconies. Spacious public areas include a number of inviting lounges, a choice of dining options and an impressive range of leisure facilities.

Rooms 71 (16 fmly) 🛏 **Facilities** Spa FTV WiFi ♭ 🕃 Gym Elemis Spa treatment rooms Xmas New Year **Conf** Class 150 Board 100 Thtr 250 **Services** Lift **Parking** 120 **Notes** Civ Wed 250

Madeira Hotel

Leisureplex
HOLIDAY HOTELS

★★★ 70% HOTEL

tel: 01326 313531 **Cliff Rd TR11 4NY**
email: madeira.falmouth@alfatravel.co.uk **web:** www.leisureplex.co.uk
dir: *A39 (Truro to Falmouth), follow tourist 'Hotels' signs to seafront*

This popular hotel offers splendid sea views and a pleasant, convenient location, which is close to the town. Extensive sun lounges are popular haunts from which to enjoy the views, while additional facilities include an oak-panelled cocktail bar. Bedrooms, many with sea views, are available in a range of sizes.

Rooms 50 (8 fmly) (7 GF) **Facilities** FTV ♫ Xmas **Services** Lift **Parking** 11 **Notes** ⊗ Closed Dec-Feb (ex Xmas) RS Nov & Mar

Membly Hall Hotel

★★ 71% HOTEL

tel: 01326 312869 **Sea Front, Cliff Rd TR11 4NT**
email: memblyhallhotel@tiscali.co.uk **web:** www.memblyhallhotel.co.uk
dir: *A39 to Falmouth. Follow seafront & beaches signs*

Located conveniently on the seafront and enjoying splendid views, this family-run hotel offers friendly service. Bedrooms are pleasantly spacious and well equipped. Carefully prepared and enjoyable meals are served in the spacious dining room. Live entertainment is provided on some evenings and there is also a sauna and spa pool.

Rooms 35 (3 fmly) (6 GF) 🛏 **Facilities** FTV WiFi Gym Indoor short bowls Table tennis Pool table Sauna Spa pool ♫ New Year **Conf** Class 130 Board 60 Thtr 150 **Services** Lift **Parking** 30 **Notes** LB ⊗ Closed Xmas week RS Dec-Jan

FAREHAM	Map 5 SU50
Hampshire	

Solent Hotel & Spa

★★★★ 82% @ HOTEL

tel: 01489 880000 **Rookery Av, Whiteley PO15 7AJ**
email: solent@shirehotels.com **web:** www.solenthotel.com
dir: *M27 junct 9, hotel on Solent Business Park*

Close to the M27 with easy access to Portsmouth, the New Forest and other attractions, this smart, purpose-built hotel enjoys a peaceful location. Bedrooms are spacious and very well appointed and there is a well-equipped spa with health and beauty facilities. Thwaites Hotels is the AA Hotel Group of the Year 2016-2017.

Rooms 115 (9 fmly) (39 GF) **S** £113-£200; **D** £113-£200* **Facilities** Spa STV WiFi ♭ HL 🕃 ♨ Gym Steam room Sauna Children's splash pool Activity studio Xmas New Year **Conf** Class 100 Board 80 Thtr 200 Del from £130 to £180* **Services** Lift **Parking** 200 **Notes** LB ⊗ Civ Wed 160

Lysses House Hotel

★★★ 74% HOTEL

tel: 01329 822622 **51 High St PO16 7BQ**
email: lysses@lysses.co.uk **web:** www.lysses.co.uk
dir: M27 junct 11 follow Fareham signs, stay in left lane to Delme rdbt. At rdbt 3rd exit into East St, follow into High St. Hotel at top on right

This attractive Georgian hotel is situated on the edge of the town in a quiet location and provides spacious and well-equipped accommodation. There are conference facilities, and a lounge bar serving a range of snacks together with the Richmond Restaurant that offers imaginative cuisine.

Rooms 21 (2 fmly) (7 GF) ⬅ **S** £70–£97; **D** £102.50–£124.50 (incl. bkfst)*
Facilities FTV WiFi Free entry to gym/pool 5mins walk away **Conf** Class 42 Board 28 Thtr 95 Del from £149.50 to £167.50* **Services** Lift **Parking** 30 **Notes** ⊗ Closed 25 Dec-1 Jan RS 24 Dec & BHs Civ Wed 100

Premier Inn Fareham

BUDGET HOTEL

tel: 0871 527 8396 *(Calls cost 13p per minute plus your phone company's access charge)*
Southampton Rd, Park Gate SO31 6AF
web: www.premierinn.com
dir: M27 junct 9, follow Fareham West, A27 signs. NB for Sat Nav use SO31 6BZ

High quality, budget accommodation ideal for both families and business travellers. Spacious, en suite bedrooms feature tea and coffee making facilities, and Freeview TV in most hotels. Internet access and WiFi are available for a small fee. The adjacent family restaurant features a wide and varied menu. See also the Hotel Groups pages.

Rooms 61

FARINGDON
Oxfordshire

Map 5 SU29

HIGHLY RECOMMENDED

Sudbury House

★★★★ 83% ⍟⍟⍟ HOTEL

tel: 01367 241272 **56 London St SN7 7AA**
email: gm@sudburyhouse.co.uk **web:** www.sudburyhouse.co.uk
dir: M40 junct 9, A34. A420, London St 0.5m on left

Sat in nine acres of well-tended grounds and located on the edge of the Cotswolds, Sudbury House is a great place to relax and unwind. Restaurant 56 offers fine dining while the brasserie, with its open-plan kitchen is more relaxed. Accommodation has a contemporary design and offers great comfort.

Rooms 50 (2 fmly) (10 GF) ⬅ **S** £104–£190; **D** £114–£200* **Facilities** FTV WiFi ⍩ Xmas New Year **Conf** Class 16 Board 30 Thtr 100 Del from £160 to £180* **Services** Lift **Parking** 60 **Notes** LB Civ Wed 180

FARNBOROUGH
Hampshire

Map 5 SU85

INSPECTORS' CHOICE

Aviator

★★★★ ⍟⍟ HOTEL

tel: 01252 555890 **Farnborough Rd GU14 6EL**
email: enquiries@aviatorbytag.com **web:** www.aviatorbytag.com
dir: A325 to Aldershot, 3m, hotel on right

Aviator is a striking property with a modern, sleek interior overlooking Farnborough airfield and located close to the main transport networks. This hotel is suitable for both business and leisure travellers. The bedrooms are well designed and provide complimentary WiFi. Both the Brasserie and the One Eleven source local ingredients for their menus.

Rooms 169 ⬅ **S** £145–£855; **D** £145–£855 **Facilities** STV WiFi ⍩ Gym Exercise studio Therapeutic, holistic & beauty treatments Xmas New Year **Conf** Class 48 Board 38 Thtr 110 Del from £245 **Services** Lift Air con **Parking** 169 **Notes** ⊗ Civ Wed 150

Premier Inn Farnborough

BUDGET HOTEL

tel: 0871 527 8398 *(Calls cost 13p per minute plus your phone company's access charge)*
Ively Rd, Southwood GU14 0JP
web: www.premierinn.com
dir: M3 junct 4a, A327 to Farnborough. Hotel on left at 5th rdbt, Monkey Puzzle Rdbt

High quality, budget accommodation ideal for both families and business travellers. Spacious, en suite bedrooms feature tea and coffee making facilities, and Freeview TV in most hotels. Internet access and WiFi are available for a small fee. The adjacent family restaurant features a wide and varied menu. See also the Hotel Groups pages.

Rooms 82

FARNHAM
Surrey   Map 5 SU84

Best Western Frensham Pond Hotel
 Best Western.

★★★★ 76% HOTEL

tel: 01252 795161 **Bacon Ln GU10 2QB**
email: info@frenshampondhotel.co.uk **web:** www.bw-frenshampondhotel.co.uk

(For full entry see Churt)

Mercure Farnham Bush Hotel
Mercure HOTELS

★★★ 78% HOTEL

tel: 01252 234800 **The Borough GU9 7NN**
email: H6621@accor.com **web:** www.mercure.com
dir: *M3 junct 4, A31, follow town centre signs. At East Street lights turn left, hotel on right*

Dating back to the 17th century, this extended former coaching inn is attractively presented and has a courtyard and a lawned garden. The bedrooms are well appointed, with quality fabrics and good facilities. The public areas include the panelled Oak Lounge, a smart cocktail bar and a conference facility in an adjoining building.

Rooms 94 (3 fmly) (27 GF) **Facilities** FTV WiFi Xmas **Conf** Class 80 Board 30 Thtr 140 **Parking** 70 **Notes** Civ Wed 100

The Farnham Hog's Back Hotel

★★★ 77% HOTEL

tel: 01252 782345 & 0330 333 2841 **Hog's Back, Seale GU10 1EX**
email: res@farnhamhogsbackhotel.co.uk **web:** www.farnhamhogsbackhotel.co.uk
dir: *On A31 Hogs Back Road 15 mins from Farnham & Guildford*

The Farnham Hog's Back Hotel offers a convenient location, plenty of free parking, comfortable rooms with all the required amenities, including free WiFi, and the extensive Active Life Health Club. There is also a choice of two event suites, one of which has its own exclusive entrance, designed to host a range of different occasions such as business meetings, weddings or civil partnerships.

Rooms 96 (17 fmly) (24 GF) **Facilities** Spa WiFi HL Gym Steam room Sauna Xmas New Year **Conf** Class 120 Board 40 Thtr 180 **Parking** 150 **Notes** Civ Wed 150

FAVERSHAM
Kent   Map 7 TR06

Faversham Creek & Red Sails Restaurant

RESTAURANT WITH ROOMS

tel: 01795 533535 & 534689 **Conduit St ME13 7BH**
email: office@favershamcreekhotel.co.uk **web:** www.favershamcreekhotel.co.uk
dir: *M2 junct 6 onto A251. At T-junct left then right into The Mall. Pass railway station, continue on B2041. Left into Quay Ln*

Located in the heart of Faversham and adjacent to the Creek, this restaurant with rooms offers modern accommodation with its own individual style, and rooms named after characters from the Faversham area. Bedrooms are well equipped and ideal for both business and leisure guests alike. There is a courtyard terrace where guests can enjoy lunch or pre-dinner drinks before dining in the award-winning Red Sails Restaurant. Parking is available on site.

Rooms 6 (4 fmly)

FAWKHAM GREEN
Kent   Map 6 TQ56

Brandshatch Place Hotel & Spa
Hand PICKED HOTELS   BUILT FOR PLEASURE

★★★★ 78% ⊛⊛ HOTEL

tel: 01474 875000 & 0845 072 7395 *(Calls cost 5p per minute plus your phone company's access charge)*
Brands Hatch Rd, Fawkham Green DA3 8NQ
email: brandshatchplace@handpicked.co.uk
web: www.handpickedhotels.co.uk/brandshatchplace
dir: *M25 junct 3, A20 West Kingsdown. Left at paddock entrance/Fawkham Green sign. 3rd left signed Fawkham Rd. Hotel 500mtrs on right*

This charming 18th-century Georgian country house close to the famous racing circuit offers stylish and elegant rooms. Bedrooms are appointed to a very high standard, offering impressive facilities and excellent levels of comfort and quality. The hotel also features a comprehensive leisure club with substantial crèche facilities.

Rooms 38 (12 annexe) (1 fmly) (6 GF) **S** £109-£219; **D** £109-£219 (incl. bkfst)*
Facilities Spa STV FTV WiFi Gym Aerobic dance studio Sauna Steam room Spin studio Xmas New Year Child facilities **Conf** Class 60 Board 50 Thtr 160 Del from £125 to £175* **Services** Lift **Parking** 100 **Notes** LB Civ Wed 110

FELIXSTOWE
Suffolk   Map 13 TM33

Best Western Brook Hotel
 Best Western.

★★★ 77% HOTEL

tel: 01394 278441 **Orwell Rd IP11 7PF**
email: welcome@brookhotel.com **web:** www.brookhotel.com

The Brook Hotel is a modern, well furnished building ideally situated in a residential area close to the town centre and the sea. Public areas include a lounge bar, a large open-plan restaurant with a bar area and a residents' lounge. Bedrooms are generally quite spacious; each one is pleasantly decorated and equipped with modern facilities.

Rooms 25 (5 fmly) (3 GF) **Facilities** FTV WiFi Xmas New Year **Conf** Class 60 Board 60 Thtr 100 **Parking** 20 **Notes** Civ Wed 150

Marlborough Hotel

★★ 69% HOTEL

tel: 01394 285621 **Sea Front IP11 2BJ**
email: hsm@marlborough-hotel-felix.com **web:** www.marlborough-hotel-felix.com
dir: *From A14 follow 'Docks' signs. Over Dock rdbt, rail crossing & lights. Left at T-junct. Hotel 400mtrs on left*

Situated on the seafront, overlooking the beach and just a short stroll from the pier and town centre, this traditional resort hotel offers a good range of facilities including the smart Rattan Restaurant, Flying Boat Bar and L'Aperitif lounge. The pleasantly decorated bedrooms come in a variety of styles; some have lovely sea views.

Rooms 48 (1 fmly) **Facilities** STV WiFi Pool table Xmas New Year **Conf** Class 60 Board 40 Thtr 80 **Services** Lift **Parking** 16 **Notes**

F

Premier Inn Felixstowe Town Centre

BUDGET HOTEL

tel: 0871 527 9536 **Undercliffe Rd West IP11 2AN**
web: www.premierinn.com
dir: *A14 towards Felixstowe. At rdbt (Trimley St Mary on right) follow Town Centre (A154) signs. At next rdbt right into Garrison Ln. Hotel on left before Undercliffe Rd*

High quality, budget accommodation ideal for both families and business travellers. Spacious, en suite bedrooms feature tea and coffee making facilities, and Freeview TV in most hotels. Internet access and WiFi are available for a small fee. The adjacent family restaurant features a wide and varied menu. See also the Hotel Groups pages.

FERNDOWN
Dorset
Map 5 SU00

Premier Inn Bournemouth/Ferndown

BUDGET HOTEL

tel: 0871 527 8122 *(Calls cost 13p per minute plus your phone company's access charge)*
Ringwood Rd, Tricketts Cross BH22 9BB
web: www.premierinn.com
dir: *Off A348 just before Tricketts Cross rdbt*

High quality, budget accommodation ideal for both families and business travellers. Spacious, en suite bedrooms feature tea and coffee making facilities, and Freeview TV in most hotels. Internet access and WiFi are available for a small fee. The adjacent family restaurant features a wide and varied menu. See also the Hotel Groups pages.

Rooms 32

FIVEHEAD
Somerset
Map 3 ST32

Langford Fivehead

◉◉ RESTAURANT WITH ROOMS

tel: 01460 282020 **Lower Swell TA3 6PH**
email: rebecca@thelangford.co **web:** www.langfordfivehead.co.uk

Documents indicate that there has been a house on this site since 1255 and the current property retains a significant proportion of a 15th-century hall house. In keeping with the grand character found throughout the building, guests can be assured of the most pleasant of welcomes and helpful, relaxing hospitality and service. Bedrooms offer a range of shapes and styles and are decorated and equipped to very high standards (although deliberately, no TVs in bedrooms). The restaurant is a delight of home-grown and local produce, providing delicious dining at both dinner and breakfast.

Rooms 6

FLAMBOROUGH
East Riding of Yorkshire
Map 17 TA27

North Star Hotel

★★ 81% SMALL HOTEL

tel: 01262 850379 **North Marine Dr YO15 1BL**
email: thenorthstarhotel@live.co.uk **web:** www.thenorthstarhotel.co.uk
dir: *B1229 or B1255 to Flamborough. Follow signs for North Landing along North Marine Dr. Hotel 100yds from sea*

Standing close to the North Landing of Flamborough Head, this family-run hotel overlooks delightful countryside, and provides excellent accommodation and caring hospitality. A good range of fresh local food, especially fish, is available in both the bar and the dining room.

Rooms 7 ☏ **S** fr £55; **D** fr £100 (incl. bkfst)* **Facilities** FTV **Parking** 60 **Notes** LB ⊗ Closed Xmas RS Nov-Etr

FLEET
Hampshire
Map 5 SU85

Premier Inn Fleet

BUDGET HOTEL

tel: 0871 527 9446 *(Calls cost 13p per minute plus your phone company's access charge)*
Waterfront Business Park, 7-11 Fleet Rd GU51 3QT
web: www.premierinn.com
dir: *On A3013*

High quality, budget accommodation ideal for both families and business travellers. Spacious, en suite bedrooms feature tea and coffee making facilities, and Freeview TV in most hotels. Internet access and WiFi are available for a small fee. The adjacent family restaurant features a wide and varied menu. See also the Hotel Groups pages.

Rooms 70

FLEET MOTORWAY SERVICE AREA (M3)
Hampshire
Map 5 SU75

Days Inn Fleet - M3

AA Advertised
WELCOMEBREAK

tel: 01252 815587 **Fleet Services GU51 1AA**
email: fleet.hotel@welcomebreak.co.uk **web:** www.welcomebreak.co.uk
dir: *Between junct 4a & 5 southbound on M3*

This modern building offers accommodation in smart, spacious and well-equipped bedrooms, suitable for families and business travellers, and all with en suite bathrooms. Continental breakfast is available and other refreshments may be taken at the nearby family restaurant.

Rooms 59 (46 fmly) (5 smoking) **Facilities** STV FTV WiFi **Parking** 60

F

FLITWICK
Bedfordshire   Map 11 TL03

Hallmark Hotel Flitwick Manor
★★★★ 75% ◉◉ COUNTRY HOUSE HOTEL

tel: 0330 028 3406 **Church Rd MK45 1AE**
email: flitwick@hallmarkhotels.co.uk **web:** www.hallmarkhotels.co.uk
dir: *M1 junct 12, follow signs for Flitwick, turn left into Church Rd, hotel on left*

With its picturesque setting in acres of gardens and parkland, yet only minutes from the motorway, this lovely Georgian house combines the best of both worlds, being both accessible and peaceful. Bedrooms are individually decorated and furnished with period pieces; some are air conditioned. Cosy and intimate, the lounge and restaurant give the hotel a home-from-home feel.

Rooms 18 (1 fmly) (5 GF) (1 smoking) 🕭 **Facilities** STV FTV WiFi ⌂ 🏊 Putt green 🏌 Xmas New Year **Conf** Class 30 Board 22 Thtr 50 **Parking** 18 **Notes** LB Civ Wed 58

FOLKESTONE
Kent   Map 7 TR23

Best Western Clifton Hotel
★★★ 77% HOTEL   BW Best Western.

tel: 01303 851231 **The Leas CT20 2EB**
email: reservations@thecliftonhotel.com **web:** www.thecliftonhotel.com
dir: *M20 junct 13, 0.25m W of town centre on A259*

This privately-owned Victorian-style hotel occupies a prime location, looking out across the English Channel. The bedrooms are comfortably appointed and most have views of the sea. Public areas include a traditionally furnished lounge, a popular bar serving a good range of beers, and several well-appointed conference rooms.

Rooms 80 (5 fmly) 🕭 **Facilities** FTV WiFi Games room Xmas New Year **Conf** Class 36 Board 32 Thtr 80 **Services** Lift

Silver Stars

The AA Silver Star rating denotes a Hotel that we highly recommend. They have a superior level of quality within their star rating, high standards of hospitality, service and cleanliness.

Find out more about the AA Hotel of the Year for London on page 13

The Southcliff Hotel
★★ 71% METRO HOTEL

tel: 01303 850075 **22-26 The Leas CT20 2DY**
email: sales@thesouthcliff.co.uk **web:** www.thesouthcliff.co.uk
dir: *M20 junct 13, follow signs for The Leas. Left at rdbt onto Sandgate Rd, right onto Shakespeare Terrace, right at end of road, hotel on right*

Located on the town's panoramic promenade with a bird's eye view of the sea, this historical Victorian hotel is perfectly located for cross channel connections and is only minutes from the town centre. The bedrooms are spacious and airy with some boasting balconies and sea views. Enjoy a freshly prepared breakfast in the spacious breakfast room on the lower ground floor or relax in the bar. The front lounge is perfect to peruse newspapers or get stuck in a nice book. Plenty of street parking available.

Rooms 68 🕭 **S** £26.50-£36; **D** £39-£63 (incl. bkfst) **Facilities** FTV WiFi ⌂ **Conf** Class 120 Board 50 Thtr 200 **Services** Lift **Notes** ⊗

Premier Inn Folkestone (Channel Tunnel)
BUDGET HOTEL   Premier Inn

tel: 0871 527 8400 *(Calls cost 13p per minute plus your phone company's access charge)*
Cherry Garden Ln CT19 4AP
web: www.premierinn.com
dir: *M20 junct 13. Follow Folkestone, A20 signs. At lights turn right, hotel on right*

High quality, budget accommodation ideal for both families and business travellers. Spacious, en suite bedrooms feature tea and coffee making facilities, and Freeview TV in most hotels. Internet access and WiFi are available for a small fee. The adjacent family restaurant features a wide and varied menu. See also the Hotel Groups pages.

Rooms 81

Rocksalt Rooms
◉◉ RESTAURANT WITH ROOMS

tel: 01303 212070 **2 Back St CT19 6NN**
email: info@rocksaltfolkestone.co.uk **web:** www.rocksaltfolkestone.co.uk
dir: *M20 junct 13 follow signs to harbour (A259). At harbour left onto Fish Market*

Overlooking the busy harbour, often crowded with small leisure boats, with wonderful sea views, Rocksalt enjoys a great location in Folkestone. Bedrooms are stylish, well appointed with original antique beds and equipped with a host of thoughtful little extras. Continental breakfasts are delivered promptly to the guests' rooms each morning, and dinner is served in the award-winning restaurant that is also blessed with panoramic views.

Rooms 4 (1 fmly)

F

FOREST ROW
East Sussex   Map 6 TQ43

Ashdown Park Hotel & Country Club

★★★★ ◎◎ ♨ HOTEL

tel: 01342 824988 **Wych Cross RH18 5JR**
email: reservations@ashdownpark.com **web:** www.ashdownpark.com
dir: A264 to East Grinstead, then A22 to Eastbourne. 2m S of Forest Row at Wych Cross lights. Left to Hartfield, hotel on right 0.75m

Situated in 186 acres of landscaped gardens and parkland, this impressive country house enjoys a peaceful countryside setting in the heart of the Ashdown Forest. Bedrooms are individually styled and decorated. Public rooms include a restored 18th-century chapel, ideal for exclusive meetings and wedding parties, plus three drawing rooms, a cocktail bar and the award-winning Anderida Restaurant. The extensive indoor and outdoor leisure facilities include the Country Club and Spa plus an 18-hole, par 3 golf course and driving range.

Rooms 106 (12 fmly) (16 GF) ☂ **Facilities** Spa FTV WiFi ⓑ HL ☏ ⚓ 18 ⚑ Putt green ⚑ Gym Aerobics Snooker Clay pigeon Archery Falconry Cycling Xmas New Year **Conf** Class 70 Board 40 Thtr 160 **Parking** 200 **Notes** Civ Wed 150

FOWEY
Cornwall   Map 2 SX15

The Fowey Hotel
★★★★ 77% ◎◎ HOTEL

RICHARDSON HOTELS
Where Memories are Made

tel: 01726 832551 **The Esplanade PL23 1HX**
email: reservations@thefoweyhotel.co.uk **web:** www.thefoweyhotel.co.uk
dir: A30 to Okehampton, continue to Bodmin. Then B3269 to Fowey for 1m, on right bend left junct then right into Dagands Rd. Hotel 200mtrs

This attractive hotel stands proudly above the estuary, with marvellous views of the river from the public areas and the majority of the bedrooms. High standards are evident throughout, augmented by a relaxed and welcoming atmosphere. There is a spacious bar, an elegant restaurant and a smart drawing room. Imaginative dinners make good use of quality local ingredients.

Rooms 37 (2 fmly) ☂ **Facilities** FTV WiFi Xmas New Year **Conf** Class 60 Board 20 Thtr 100 **Services** Lift **Parking** 17 **Notes** Civ Wed 120

Fowey Hall
AA Advertised ◎◎

tel: 01726 833866 **Hanson Dr PL23 1ET**
email: info@foweyhallhotel.co.uk **web:** www.foweyhallhotel.co.uk
dir: M5, A30 turn off at Bodmon, follow signs to Lostwithiel & Fowey

Built in 1899, this listed mansion looks out on to the English Channel. The imaginatively designed bedrooms offer charm, individuality and sumptuous comfort; the Garden Wing rooms add an extra dimension to a stay here. The beautifully appointed public rooms include the wood panelled dining room where accomplished cuisine is served. This is a very family friendly hotel with a crèche, baby sitting and listening services, plus many other facilities for children. The luxury spa includes a swimming pool, treatment rooms and a sun deck with a glorious view.

Rooms 36 (8 annexe) (30 fmly) (10 GF) **Facilities** Spa STV FTV WiFi ⓑ ☏ Free creche for children of 0-8 yrs Xmas New Year Child facilities **Conf** Class 20 Board 20 Thtr 40 **Parking** 40 **Notes** LB Civ Wed 120

FRADDON
Cornwall   Map 2 SW95

Premier Inn Newquay (A30/Fraddon)
BUDGET HOTEL

Premier Inn

tel: 0871 527 8816 *(Calls cost 13p per minute plus your phone company's access charge)*
Penhale Round TR9 6NA
web: www.premierinn.com
dir: On A30, 2m S of Indian Queens

High quality, budget accommodation ideal for both families and business travellers. Spacious, en suite bedrooms feature tea and coffee making facilities, and Freeview TV in most hotels. Internet access and WiFi are available for a small fee. The adjacent family restaurant features a wide and varied menu. See also the Hotel Groups pages.

Rooms 65

F

FRANKBY
Merseyside

Map 15 SJ28

Hillbark Hotel & Spa

★★★★★ 86% ◉◉ HOTEL

tel: 0151 625 2400 **Royden Park CH48 1NP**
email: enquiries@hillbarkhotel.co.uk **web:** www.hillbarkhotel.co.uk
dir: *M53 junct 3, A552 Upton, right onto A551 Arrowe Park Rd. 0.6m at lights left into Arrowe Brook Rd. 0.5m on left*

Originally built in 1891 on Bidston Hill, this Elizabethan-style mansion was actually moved, brick by brick, to its current site in 1931. The house now sits in a 250-acre woodland estate and enjoys delightful views towards the River Dee and to hills in North Wales. Bedrooms are luxuriously furnished and well equipped, while elegant day rooms are richly styled. There is a choice of eating options, including a fine dining restaurant, and guests also have use of a spa.

Rooms 18 (1 fmly) ☞ **S** £160-£680; **D** £180-£700 (incl. bkfst)* **Facilities** Spa STV FTV WiFi ⌕ 🏊 Gym Cinema Library Games room Children's play area 🎵 Xmas New Year **Conf** Class 300 Board 60 Thtr 750 Del from £204 to £318* **Services** Lift **Parking** 160 **Notes** LB ⊗ Civ Wed 500

FRESHWATER
Isle of Wight

Map 5 SZ38

Albion Hotel

★★★ 72% HOTEL

tel: 01983 755755 **PO40 9RA**
email: enquiries@albionhotel.info **web:** www.sandringhamhotel.co.uk/albion

In an idyllic location on the island's southern heritage coast, the Albion Hotel is right on the seafront with stunning views of Freshwater Bay. The bedrooms and bathrooms are spacious and offer guests modern, comfortable accommodation; many rooms have balconies. Breakfast and dinner are served in the traditionally styled restaurant that also enjoys the lovely views.

Rooms 40 **Facilities** ⌖ Xmas **Conf** Class 30 Board 40 Thtr 60 **Parking** 30

FROME
Somerset

Map 4 ST74

Premier Inn Frome

BUDGET HOTEL

tel: 0871 527 8404 *(Calls cost 13p per minute plus your phone company's access charge)*
Commerce Park, Jenson Av BA11 2LD
web: www.premierinn.com
dir: *M4 junct 18, A46 follow Warminster & Frome signs. Hotel off A361 (Frome bypass) in Commerce Park*

High quality, budget accommodation ideal for both families and business travellers. Spacious, en suite bedrooms feature tea and coffee making facilities, and Freeview TV in most hotels. Internet access and WiFi are available for a small fee. The adjacent family restaurant features a wide and varied menu. See also the Hotel Groups pages.

Rooms 119

GARSTANG
Lancashire

Map 18 SD44

Best Western Garstang Country Hotel & Golf Centre

★★★ 79% HOTEL

tel: 01995 600100 **Garstang Rd, Bowgreave PR3 1YE**
email: reception@garstanghotelandgolf.com **web:** www.garstanghotelandgolf.com
dir: *M6 junct 32 take 1st right after Shell garage on A6 onto B6430. 1m, hotel on left*

This smart, purpose-built hotel enjoys a peaceful location alongside its own 18-hole golf course. Comfortable and spacious bedrooms are well equipped for both business and leisure guests, while inviting public areas include quiet lounges, the Kingfisher restaurant and the more informal Brad Beer Brasserie.

Rooms 33 (17 GF) ☞ **Facilities** STV FTV WiFi ⌕ 🏌 18 Putt green Golf driving range Xmas New Year **Conf** Class 150 Board 80 Thtr 250 **Services** Lift **Parking** 172 **Notes** LB ⊗ Civ Wed 200

GATESHEAD
Tyne & Wear

Map 21 NZ26

HIGHLY RECOMMENDED

Eslington Villa Hotel

★★★ 84% ◉ HOTEL

tel: 0191 487 6017 & 420 0666 **8 Station Rd, Low Fell NE9 6DR**
email: home@eslingtonvilla.co.uk **web:** www.eslingtonvilla.co.uk
dir: *From A1(M) exit for Team Valley Trading Estate. Right at 2nd rdbt along Eastern Av. Left at car show room, hotel 100yds on left*

Set in a residential area, this smart hotel combines a bright, contemporary atmosphere with the period style of a fine Victorian villa. The overall ambience is relaxed and inviting. Chunky sofas grace the cocktail lounge, while tempting dishes can be enjoyed in either the classical dining room or modern conservatory overlooking the Team Valley.

Rooms 17 (2 fmly) (3 GF) ☞ **S** £84.50-£94.50; **D** £94.50-£125 (incl. bkfst)* **Facilities** FTV WiFi **Conf** Class 30 Board 25 Thtr 36 Del from £125 to £145* **Parking** 28 **Notes** ⊗ Closed 25-26 Dec & 1 Jan

Ramada Encore Newcastle - Gateshead

★★★ 79% HOTEL

tel: 0191 481 3600 **Hawks Rd, Gateshead Quays NE8 3AD**
web: www.encorenewcastlegateshead.co.uk
dir: *Located Gateshead Quays*

This modern, purpose-built hotel is located at the Gateshead Quays. Bedrooms are well appointed and comfortable, with well-presented en suites. Public areas are open-plan with a relaxed all-day menu serving food in all locations. A small gym and off-road parking are added benefits.

Rooms 200 (75 fmly) ☞ **Facilities** FTV WiFi ⌕ HL Gym **Conf** Class 14 Board 18 Thtr 20 **Services** Lift **Parking** 70 **Notes** ⊗

Premier Inn Newcastle (Metro Centre)

BUDGET HOTEL

tel: 0871 527 8792 *(Calls cost 13p per minute plus your phone company's access charge)*
Derwent Haugh Rd, Swalwell NE16 3BL
web: www.premierinn.com
dir: *From A1 & A694 junct into Derwent Haugh Rd. 1m N of Metro Centre*

High quality, budget accommodation ideal for both families and business travellers. Spacious, en suite bedrooms feature tea and coffee making facilities, and Freeview TV in most hotels. Internet access and WiFi are available for a small fee. The adjacent family restaurant features a wide and varied menu. See also the Hotel Groups pages.

Rooms 72

Premier Inn Newcastle South

BUDGET HOTEL

tel: 0871 527 8806 *(Calls cost 13p per minute plus your phone company's access charge)*
Lobley Hill Rd NE11 9NA
web: www.premierinn.com
dir: *A1 onto A692*

Rooms 42

Premier Inn Newcastle (Team Valley)

BUDGET HOTEL

tel: 0871 527 8794 *(Calls cost 13p per minute plus your phone company's access charge)*
Maingate, Kingsway North, Team Valley NE11 0BE
web: www.premierinn.com
dir: *A1 onto B1426 signed Team Valley (S'bound) or Teams/Consett (N'bound). Take Gateshead exit at rdbt. At bottom of hill straight on at rdbt. Hotel opposite*

Rooms 115

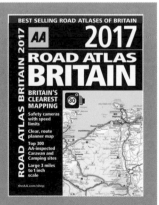

GATWICK AIRPORT (LONDON)
West Sussex

Map 6 TQ24

See also **Dorking, East Grinstead & Reigate**

INSPECTORS' CHOICE

Langshott Manor

★★★★ ⊛⊛⊛ COUNTRY HOUSE HOTEL

tel: 01293 786680 **Langshott Ln RH6 9LN**
email: admin@langshottmanor.com **web:** www.langshottmanor.com
dir: *From A23 take Ladbroke Rd, off Chequers rdbt to Langshott, after 0.75m hotel on right*

On the outskirts of Horley, this charming timber framed Tudor manor house is set amidst beautifully landscaped grounds with an ancient moat. The stylish public areas feature a choice of inviting lounges with polished oak panelling, exposed beams and crackling log fires. Each bedroom - whether in the manor itself or in one of three mews buildings in the grounds - has been designed with flair and imagination. Expect sumptuous furnishings, Egyptian linens, flat-screen TVs and bathrooms with deep baths and power showers. The Mulberry restaurant overlooks a picturesque pond and offers an imaginative menu.

Rooms 22 (15 annexe) (2 fmly) (8 GF) 📶 **S** £99-£159; **D** £99-£319* **Facilities** FTV WiFi ⤵ Xmas New Year **Conf** Class 20 Board 22 Thtr 40 Del from £179* **Parking** 25 **Notes** LB ⊗ Civ Wed 60

Holiday Inn London Gatwick Worth

★★★★ 79% HOTEL

tel: 01293 884806 **Crabbet Park, Turners Hill Rd, Worth RH10 4SS**
email: info@higatwickworth.co.uk **web:** www.higatwickworth.co.uk
dir: *M23 junct 10/A264 Copthorne Way at rdbt last exit towards Three Bridges. 1st left along Old Hollow, right at end of lane then 1st right into Crabbet Park*

This purpose-built hotel is ideally placed for access to Gatwick Airport. The bedrooms are spacious and suitably appointed with good facilities. Public areas consist of a light and airy bar area and a brasserie-style restaurant offering good value meals. Guests have use of the superb leisure club next door.

Rooms 118 (39 fmly) (56 GF) 📶 **Facilities** FTV WiFi ⤵ HL Use of gym & pool next door (chargeable) Xmas New Year **Conf** Class 80 Board 80 Thtr 250 **Services** Lift Air con **Parking** 150 **Notes** ⊗ Civ Wed 60

GATWICK AIRPORT (LONDON) *continued*

Sofitel London Gatwick

★★★★ 78% ◉◉ HOTEL

tel: 01293 567070 & 555000 **North Terminal RH6 OPH**
email: slg@sofitelgatwick.com **web:** www.sofitelgatwick.com
dir: *M23 junct 9, follow to 2nd rdbt. Hotel straight ahead*

One of the closest hotels to the airport, this modern, purpose-built hotel is located only minutes from the terminals. Bedrooms are contemporary and all are air conditioned. Guests have a choice of eating options including a French-style café, a brasserie and an oriental restaurant.

Rooms 518 (19 fmly) **Facilities** FTV WiFi ⚡ Gym **Conf** Class 150 Board 90 Thtr 300 **Services** Lift Air con **Parking** 565 **Notes** ⊗

Hilton London Gatwick Airport Hotel

★★★★ 74% HOTEL

tel: 01293 518080 **South Terminal RH6 0LL**
email: london.gatwick@hilton.com **web:** www.hilton.com
dir: *M23 junct 9 towards Gatwick Airport, then 1st exit at junct 9a & follow the road. Right after 600yds*

Excellent location at Gatwick Airport with a direct covered link directly from the main hotel to the Gatwick South Terminal. This hotel offers a range of facilities including two restaurants, bars, fitness facilities and onsite parking. Bedrooms are modern and comfortably appointed, very quiet rooms offering a good overnight stay for corporate and leisure guests alike.

Rooms 821 (31 fmly) (47 GF) (22 smoking) ⚡ **S** £84-£195; **D** £84-£195* **Facilities** FTV HL Gym **Conf** Class 225 Board 80 Thtr 450 Del from £102 to £185* **Services** Lift Air con **Notes** LB

Stanhill Court Hotel

★★★ 82% HOTEL

tel: 01293 862166 **Stanhill Rd, Charlwood RH6 0EP**
email: enquiries@stanhillcourthotel.co.uk **web:** www.stanhillcourthotel.co.uk
dir: *N of Charlwood towards Newdigate*

This hotel dates back to 1881 and enjoys a secluded location of 35 acres of well-tended grounds with views over the Downs. Bedrooms are individually furnished and decorated, and many have four-poster beds. Public areas include a library, a bright Spanish-style bar and a traditional wood-panelled restaurant. Extensive and varied function facilities make this a popular wedding venue.

Rooms 34 (2 fmly) (1 GF) ⚡ **Facilities** FTV WiFi ⚡ ⚓ Xmas New Year **Conf** Class 100 Board 70 Thtr 300 **Parking** 150 **Notes** ⊗ Civ Wed 300

Premier Inn Gatwick Airport North

BUDGET HOTEL

tel: 0871 527 9354 *(Calls cost 13p per minute plus your phone company's access charge)*
Crossway, Gatwick North Terminal RH6 0PH
web: www.premierinn.com
dir: *M23 junct 9. Follow signs for Gatwick North Terminal, at North Terminal rdbt enter at Arrivals Road (2nd exit), turn right onto Northway (Drop Off point), hotel is on right*

High quality, budget accommodation ideal for both families and business travellers. Spacious, en suite bedrooms feature tea and coffee making facilities, and Freeview TV in most hotels. Internet access and WiFi are available for a small fee. The adjacent family restaurant features a wide and varied menu. See also the Hotel Groups pages.

Rooms 701

Premier Inn Gatwick Airport South

BUDGET HOTEL

tel: 0871 527 8408 *(Calls cost 13p per minute plus your phone company's access charge)*
London Rd, Lowfield Heath RH10 9ST
web: www.premierinn.com
dir: *M23 junct 9a towards North Terminal rdbt. Follow A23 & Crawley signs. Hotel in 2m*

Rooms 105

Premier Inn Gatwick Crawley Town (Goffs Park)

BUDGET HOTEL

tel: 0871 527 8414 *(Calls cost 13p per minute plus your phone company's access charge)*
45 Goffs Park Rd RH11 8AX
web: www.premierinn.com
dir: *M23 junct 11, A23 towards Crawley. At 2nd rdbt take 3rd exit for town centre, then 2nd right into Goffs Park Rd*

Rooms 48

Premier Inn Gatwick Crawley Town West

BUDGET HOTEL

tel: 0871 527 8412 *(Calls cost 13p per minute plus your phone company's access charge)*
Crawley Av, Gossops Green RH10 8BA
web: www.premierinn.com
dir: *M23 junct 11, A23 towards Crawley & Gatwick Airport*

Rooms 83

Premier Inn London Gatwick Airport A23

BUDGET HOTEL

tel: 0871 527 8406 *(Calls cost 13p per minute plus your phone company's access charge)*
Longbridge Way, North Terminal RH6 0NX
web: www.premierinn.com
dir: *M23 junct 9/9A towards North Terminal, at rdbt take 3rd exit, hotel on right*

Rooms 220

Premier Inn London Gatwick Airport East

BUDGET HOTEL

tel: 0871 527 8410 *(Calls cost 13p per minute plus your phone company's access charge)*
Balcombe Rd, Worth RH10 3NL
web: www.premierinn.com
dir: *M23 junct 10, B2036 S towards Crawley*

Rooms 42

Premier Inn London Gatwick Manor Royal

BUDGET HOTEL

tel: 0871 527 9214 *(Calls cost 13p per minute plus your phone company's access charge)*
Crawley Business Quarter, Fleming Way RH10 9DF
web: www.premierinn.com
dir: *M23 junct 10, A2011 (Crawley Ave). At rdbt 4th exit onto A23 (London Rd), at rdbt right into Fleming Way. Hotel 300yds on left*

Rooms 204

Arora Hotel Gatwick

AA Advertised

tel: 01293 597701 & 530000 **Southgate Av, Southgate RH10 6LW**
email: gatwick@arorahotels.com **web:** www.arorahotels.com
dir: *M23 junct 10 then A2011 to Crawley. At 1st rdbt take 2nd exit towards town centre, at 2nd rdbt take 1st exit towards the County Mall. At both sets of lights proceed straight over; the County Mall on right, go straight under railway bridge, hotel on right*

The Arora Hotel Gatwick/Crawley is situated in the heart of Crawley town centre, perfectly placed for easy access to M23/A23 and M25 motorways, direct access to Crawley rain station, and is a short journey from Gatwick Airport by direct bus transfer. Accommodation is stylish and there are excellent meeting, conference, training and banqueting facilities. Meals and drinks can be taken in the Grill restaurant, a traditional pub or the bar. There is also an internet café, a luxurious health and fitness club and on-site car parking facilities.

Rooms 432 (120 annexe) (15 fmly) (24 GF) **S** fr £65, **D** fr £85* **Facilities** FTV WiFi HL Gym Treatment room Xmas **Conf** Class 150 Board 60 Thtr 270 Del from £140* **Services** Lift Air con **Parking** 245 **Notes** Civ Wed 270

Ibis London Gatwick Airport

AA Advertised

tel: 01293 590300 **London Rd, County Oak RH10 9GY**
email: H1889@accor.com **web:** www.ibishotel.com
dir: *M23 junct 10, A2011 towards Crawley. Onto A23 left towards Crawley/Brighton. Hotel on left*

Modern, budget hotel offering comfortable accommodation in bright and practical bedrooms. Breakfast is self-service and dinner is available in the restaurant.

Rooms 141 **Facilities** FTV WiFi HL **Services** Lift **Parking** 70

GERRARDS CROSS
Buckinghamshire
Map 6 TQ08

The Bull Hotel

★★★★ 76% HOTEL

tel: 01753 885995 **Oxford Rd SL9 7PA**
email: bull@sarova.com **web:** www.sarova.com
dir: *M40 junct 2 follow Beaconsfield on A355. After 0.5m 2nd exit at rdbt signed A40 Gerrards Cross for 2m. The Bull is on right*

Dating from the 17th-century, this former inn has been extensively refurbished to provide smart, well-equipped bedrooms. Public areas include the popular bar and Beeches Restaurant, serving a wide variety of dishes to suit all tastes. In addition there is the informal Jack Shrimpton bar offering snacks and bar meals. Attractive gardens and a good range of function rooms make this a popular wedding and events venue.

Rooms 150 (15 fmly) (19 GF) **Facilities** FTV WiFi Use of private leisure facilities Xmas New Year **Conf** Class 108 Board 40 Thtr 180 Del from £175 to £260* **Services** Lift **Parking** 150 **Notes** Civ Wed 114

GILLINGHAM
Kent
Map 7 TQ76

Premier Inn Chatham/Gillingham (Victory Pier)

BUDGET HOTEL

tel: 0871 527 9510 *(Calls cost 13p per minute plus your phone company's access charge)*
Blake Av ME7 1GB
web: www.premierinn.com
dir: *From A289 (Pier Rd) in Gillingham, at lights, into Pegasus Way. 1st left*

High quality, budget accommodation ideal for both families and business travellers. Spacious, en suite bedrooms feature tea and coffee making facilities, and Freeview TV in most hotels. Internet access and WiFi are available for a small fee. The adjacent family restaurant features a wide and varied menu. See also the Hotel Groups pages.

Rooms 80

Premier Inn Gillingham Business Park

BUDGET HOTEL

tel: 0871 527 8416 *(Calls cost 13p per minute plus your phone company's access charge)*
Will Adams Way ME8 6BY
web: www.premierinn.com
dir: *M2 junct 4, A278 to A2. Left at Tesco. Hotel at next rdbt*

Rooms 76

Premier Inn Gillingham/Rainham

BUDGET HOTEL

tel: 0871 527 9268 *(Calls cost 13p per minute plus your phone company's access charge)*
High St, Rainham ME8 7JE
web: www.premierinn.com
dir: *M25 junct 2 (Canterbury/Dover/A2), A2 to M2 (Dover). Exit at junct 4 (Rainham/Medway Tunnel), straight on at 2 rdbts. At 3rd rdbt take 3rd exit (Rainham High St). Hotel on right at 3rd lights*

Rooms 26

GIRTON
Cambridgeshire
Map 12 TL46

Premier Inn Cambridge North (Girton)

BUDGET HOTEL

tel: 0871 527 8188 *(Calls cost 13p per minute plus your phone company's access charge)*
Huntingdon Rd CB3 0DR
web: www.premierinn.com
dir: *A14 junct 31 follow signs towards Cambridge. Pass BP garage, next right. Hotel adjacent to Traveller's Rest Beefeater*

High quality, budget accommodation ideal for both families and business travellers. Spacious, en suite bedrooms feature tea and coffee making facilities, and Freeview TV in most hotels. Internet access and WiFi are available for a small fee. The adjacent family restaurant features a wide and varied menu. See also the Hotel Groups pages.

Rooms 20

G

GISBURN
Lancashire
Map 18 SD84

Stirk House Hotel

★★★ 85% ⊛ HOTEL

tel: 01200 445581 **BB7 4LJ**
email: reservations@stirkhouse.co.uk **web:** www.stirkhouse.co.uk
dir: W of village, on A59. Hotel 0.5m on left

This delightful historic hotel enjoys a peaceful location in its own grounds, amid rolling countryside. Extensive public areas include excellent conference and banqueting facilities, a leisure centre and an elegant restaurant. The stylish bedrooms and suites vary in size and style but all are comfortable and well equipped. Hospitality is warm and friendly, and service attentive.

Rooms 33 (11 annexe) (2 fmly) (10 GF) ⚓ **Facilities** STV WiFi 🌀 Gym Beauty treatment room Aromatherapy Personal training Kick boxing New Year **Conf** Class 150 Board 45 Thtr 200 **Parking** 100 **Notes** Civ Wed 120

GLASTONBURY
Somerset
Map 4 ST53

Premier Inn Glastonbury

BUDGET HOTEL

tel: 0871 527 9398 *(Calls cost 13p per minute plus your phone company's access charge)*
Morland Rd BA6 9FW
web: www.premierinn.com
dir: *From A361 & A39 rdbt junct (SW of Glastonbury) take A39 towards Street. Right at lights into Morlands Enterprise Park. Left at 1st rdbt*

High quality, budget accommodation ideal for both families and business travellers. Spacious, en suite bedrooms feature tea and coffee making facilities, and Freeview TV in most hotels. Internet access and WiFi are available for a small fee. The adjacent family restaurant features a wide and varied menu. See also the Hotel Groups pages.

Rooms 78

GLENRIDDING
Cumbria
Map 18 NY31

Inn on the Lake

LAKE DISTRICT HOTELS

★★★★ 81% ⊛⊛ HOTEL

tel: 017684 82444 & 0800 840 1245 **Lake Ullswater CA11 OPE**
email: innonthelake@lakedistricthotels.net **web:** www.lakedistricthotels.net/innonthelake
dir: *M6 junct 40, A66 to Keswick. At rdbt take A592 to Ullswater Lake. Along lake to Glenridding. Hotel on left on entering village*

In a picturesque lakeside setting, this restored Victorian hotel is a popular leisure destination as well as catering for weddings and conferences. Superb views can be enjoyed from the bedrooms and from the garden terrace where afternoon teas are served during warmer months. There is a popular pub in the grounds, and moorings for yachts are available to guests. Sailing tuition can be arranged.

Rooms 47 (20 fmly) (1 GF) ⚓ **S** fr £115; **D** fr £230 (incl. bkfst) **Facilities** FTV WiFi ⚗ Putt green 🏌 Gym Sauna 9 hole pitch & putt course Xmas New Year **Conf** Class 42 Board 30 Thtr 100 **Services** Lift **Parking** 100 **Notes** Civ Wed 110

Best Western Glenridding Hotel

ⒷⓌ Best Western.

★★★ 79% HOTEL

tel: 01768 482289 **CA11 OPB**
email: glenridding@bestwestern.co.uk **web:** www.bw-glenriddinghotel.co.uk
dir: *N'bound M6 junct 36, A591 Windermere then A592, for 14m. S'bound M6 junct 40, A592 for 13m*

(Please note: Best Western Glenridding Hotel is currently closed due to flooding, but hopes to re-open in Autumn 2016) This friendly hotel benefits from a picturesque location in the village centre, and many rooms have fine views of the lake and fells. Public areas are extensive and include a choice of dining options including Ratchers Restaurant and a café. Leisure facilities are available along with a conference room and a garden function room.

Rooms 36 (7 fmly) (8 GF) **Facilities** STV WiFi ⚗ Spa bath Sauna Snooker Table tennis Xmas New Year **Conf** Class 30 Board 24 Thtr 30 **Services** Lift **Parking** 30 **Notes** Civ Wed 120

GLOSSOP
Derbyshire
Map 16 SK09

Wind in the Willows Hotel

★★ 85% COUNTRY HOUSE HOTEL

tel: 01457 868001 **Derbyshire Level SK13 7PT**
email: info@windinthewillows.co.uk **web:** www.windinthewillows.co.uk
dir: *1m E of Glossop on A57, turn right opposite Royal Oak, hotel 400yds on right*

This impressive house sits in peaceful grounds with lovely views of the Peak District National Park. Individually furnished bedrooms are in keeping with the Victorian style of the house. Beautiful original oak panelling and crackling log fires add to the charm of the lounges and dining room. There is also a conference suite that is perfect for meetings, private dining or special occasions.

Rooms 12 ⚓ **S** fr £75; **D** fr £145 (incl. bkfst) **Facilities** FTV WiFi ⚗ Xmas New Year **Conf** Class 12 Board 16 Thtr 40 **Parking** 16 **Notes** LB ⊗ No children 10yrs

GLOUCESTER
Gloucestershire
Map 10 SO81

Hatton Court

★★★★ 75% ⊛ COUNTRY HOUSE HOTEL

tel: 01452 617412 **Upton Hill, Upton St Leonards GL4 8DE**
email: res@hatton-court.co.uk **web:** www.hatton-court.co.uk
dir: *From Gloucester on B4073 Painswick Rd. Hotel at top of hill on right*

Built in the style of a 17th-century Cotswold manor house and set in seven acres of well-kept gardens, this hotel is popular with both business and leisure guests. It stands at the top of Upton Hill and commands truly spectacular views of the Severn Valley. The bedrooms, including a four-poster room, are comfortable and tastefully furnished with many extra facilities. The elegant Tara Restaurant offers varied menus, and outdoor seating in summer; there is also a bar and foyer lounge.

Rooms 45 (28 annexe) (6 fmly) ⚓ **S** £80-£200; **D** £80-£400 (incl. bkfst) **Facilities** FTV WiFi HL 🏌 Gym Xmas New Year **Conf** Class 100 Board 60 Thtr 200 **Del** from £110 to £160 **Parking** 80 **Notes** LB Civ Wed 120

Hatherley Manor

★★★★ 74% HOTEL

tel: 01452 730217 **Down Hatherley Ln GL2 9QA**
email: reservations@hatherleymanor.com **web:** www.hatherleymanor.com
dir: *A38 into Down Hatherley Lane, signed. Hotel 600yds on left*

Within easy striking distance of the M5, Gloucester, Cheltenham and the Cotswolds, this stylish 17th-century manor, set in attractive grounds, remains popular with both business and leisure guests. Bedrooms are well appointed and offer contemporary comforts. A particularly impressive range of meeting and function rooms is available.

Rooms 50 (5 fmly) (18 GF) ⚞ **Facilities** FTV WiFi ⚑ Xmas New Year **Conf** Class 90 Board 75 Thtr 400 **Parking** 250 **Notes** Civ Wed 300

Hallmark Hotel Gloucester

★★★★ 73% HOTEL

tel: 0330 028 3408 **Matson Ln, Robinswood Hill GL4 6EA**
email: gloucester@hallmarkhotels.co.uk **web:** www.hallmarkhotels.co.uk
dir: *A40 towards Gloucester onto A38. 1st exit at 4th rdbt (Painswick Rd). Right onto Matson Lane*

Ideally located for exploring the Cotswolds and Gloucester, this hotel offers well-appointed bedrooms and relaxing public areas. The large leisure club has a well-equipped gym, squash courts and pool. Complimentary WiFi is available throughout.

Rooms 95 (6 fmly) (21 GF) ⚞ **Facilities Spa** FTV WiFi ⚑ ⚞ supervised Gym Squash Beauty salon Xmas New Year **Conf** Class 150 Board 18 Thtr 220 Del from £119 to £199 **Parking** 150 **Notes** Civ Wed 120

Mercure Gloucester, Bowden Hall Hotel

★★★★ 71% HOTEL

tel: 01452 614121 & 0844 815 9077 *Calls cost 7p per minute plus your phone company's access charge)*
Bondend Ln, Upton St Leonards GL4 8ED
email: info@mercuregloucester.co.uk **web:** www.mercuregloucester.co.uk
dir: *A417/A38/Gloucester. At rdbt take 2nd exit. At 2nd lights left onto Abbeymead Ave/ Metz Way. 1.5m, 3rd left onto Upton Lane, left into Bondend Rd, then left into Bondend Lane. Hotel at end*

Conveniently located a short distance from the M5, the hotel is set in delightful grounds and is an ideal venue for weddings, banquets and meetings, or for a quiet break. Bedrooms are spacious and nicely appointed and many have lovely views of the grounds. Guests can choose to dine in the restaurant or bar.

Rooms 72 (15 fmly) ⚞ **Facilities** FTV WiFi ⚑ HL ♬ Xmas New Year **Conf** Class 70 Board 35 Thtr 180 **Parking** 180 **Notes** Civ Wed 200

Premier Inn Gloucester (Barnwood)

BUDGET HOTEL

tel: 0871 527 8456 *(Calls cost 13p per minute plus your phone company's access charge)*
Barnwood GL4 3HR
web: www.premierinn.com
dir: *M5 junct 11, A40 towards Gloucester. At 1st rdbt A417 towards Cirencester, at next rdbt take 4th exit*

High quality, budget accommodation ideal for both families and business travellers. Spacious, en suite bedrooms feature tea and coffee making facilities, and Freeview TV in most hotels. Internet access and WiFi are available for a small fee. The adjacent family restaurant features a wide and varied menu. See also the Hotel Groups pages.

Rooms 83

Premier Inn Gloucester Business Park

BUDGET HOTEL

tel: 0871 527 8462 *(Calls cost 13p per minute plus your phone company's access charge)*
Gloucester Business Park, Brockworth GL3 4AJ
web: www.premierinn.com
dir: *M5 junct 11a, A417 towards Cirencester. At Brockworth Rdbt follow Gloucester Business Park signs, onto dual carriageway (Valiant Way). At next rdbt left into Delta Way. Hotel adjacent to Tesco*

Rooms 48

Premier Inn Gloucester (Little Witcombe)

BUDGET HOTEL

tel: 0871 527 8458 *(Calls cost 13p per minute plus your phone company's access charge)*
Witcombe GL3 4SS
web: www.premierinn.com
dir: *M5 junct 11a, A417 signed Cirencester. At 1st exit turn right onto A46 towards Stroud & Witcombe. Left at next rdbt by Crosshands pub*

Rooms 39

Premier Inn Gloucester (Longford)

BUDGET HOTEL

tel: 0871 527 8460 *(Calls cost 13p per minute plus your phone company's access charge)*
Tewkesbury Rd, Longford GL2 9BE
web: www.premierinn.com
dir: *M5 junct 11, A40 towards Gloucester & Ross-on-Wye. Hotel on A38 towards Gloucester*

Rooms 60

Premier Inn Gloucester (Twigworth)

BUDGET HOTEL

tel: 0871 527 8464 *(Calls cost 13p per minute plus your phone company's access charge)*
Tewkesbury Rd, Twigworth GL2 9PG
web: www.premierinn.com
dir: *On A38, 1m N from junct with A40*

Rooms 50

Ibis Gloucester

AA Advertised

tel: 01452 623650 **Sawmills End, Corinium Ave A417 GL4 3DG**
email: H6900@accor.com **web:** www.ibishotel.com
dir: *M5 junct 11a, left on A417. At rdbt 2nd exit. At rdbt take A417 Corinium Ave for 0.5 m then left on Sawmills End. Hotel on left*

Modern, budget hotel offering comfortable accommodation in bright and practical bedrooms. Breakfast is self-service and dinner is available in the restaurant.

Rooms 127 (127 fmly) **Facilities** STV FTV WiFi **Services** Lift

G

GLOUCESTER *continued*

The Wharf House Restaurant with Rooms

◉ RESTAURANT WITH ROOMS

tel: 01452 332900 **Over GL2 8DB**
email: enquiries@thewharfhouse.co.uk **web:** www.thewharfhouse.co.uk
dir: *From A40 between Gloucester & Highnam exit at lights for Over. Establishment signed*

The Wharf House was built to replace the old lock cottage and, as the name suggests, it is located at the very edge of the river; it has pleasant views and an outdoor terrace. The bedrooms and bathrooms have been finished to a high standard, and there are plenty of guest extras. Seasonal, local produce can be enjoyed both at breakfast and dinner in the delightful AA Rosetted restaurant.

Rooms 7 (1 fmly)

GOATHLAND
North Yorkshire

Map 19 NZ80

Mallyan Spout Hotel

★★★ 82% ◉ COUNTRY HOUSE HOTEL

tel: 01947 896486 **YO22 5AN**
email: info@mallyanspout.co.uk **web:** www.mallyanspout.co.uk
dir: *A169 Pickering to Whitby. Take Goathland turn, hotel opp St Mary's Church*

This Grade II listed building is set in the charming village of Goathland best known for being the setting of the fictional village of Aidensfield in the popular TV series *Heartbeat*. The popular seaside resort of Whitby is just a short driving distance away. The hotel is privately owned and is full of character and charm. The bedrooms provide comfortable accommodation and the public areas house three lounges, some with open fires and a bar boasting a selection of real ales. The restaurant serves a good mix of modern and traditional dishes.

Rooms 20 (4 fmly) ☞ **Facilities** FTV WiFi New Year **Conf** Class 50 Board 35 Thtr 50 **Parking** 24 **Notes** ⊗ Closed 23-27 Dec Civ Wed 65

GODALMING
Surrey

Map 6 SU94

Premier Inn Godalming

BUDGET HOTEL

tel: 0871 527 8466 *(Calls cost 13p per minute plus your phone company's access charge)*
Guildford Rd GU7 3BX
web: www.premierinn.com
dir: *Exit A3 onto A3000 signed Godalming. 1m to rdbt, turn right into Guildford Rd towards Godalming. Hotel on left in 500yds*

High quality, budget accommodation ideal for both families and business travellers. Spacious, en suite bedrooms feature tea and coffee making facilities, and Freeview TV in most hotels. Internet access and WiFi are available for a small fee. The adjacent family restaurant features a wide and varied menu. See also the Hotel Groups pages.

Rooms 16

GOLANT
Cornwall

Map 2 SX15

Cormorant Hotel & Restaurant

★★★ 81% ◉◉ HOTEL

tel: 01726 833426 **PL23 1LL**
email: relax@cormoranthotel.co.uk **web:** www.cormoranthotel.co.uk
dir: *A390 onto B3269 signed Fowey. In 3m left to Golant, through village to end of road, hotel on right*

This hotel focuses on traditional hospitality, attentive service and good food. All the bedrooms enjoy views of the river, and guests can expect goose and down duvets, flat-screen digital TVs and free WiFi access. Breakfast and lunch may be taken on the terrace which overlooks the river.

Rooms 14 (4 GF) ☞ **S** £65-£160; **D** £80-£180 (incl. bkfst)* **Facilities** FTV WiFi ⤢ ⊗ Xmas New Year **Parking** 20 **Notes** LB ⊗ No children 16yrs

---

GOMERSAL
West Yorkshire

Map 19 SE22

Gomersal Park Hotel

★★★ 80% HOTEL

tel: 01274 869386 **Moor Ln BD19 4LJ**
email: enquiries@gomersalparkhotel.com **web:** www.gomersalparkhotel.com
dir: *A62 to Huddersfield. At junct with A65, by Greyhound Pub right, after 1m take 1st right after Oakwell Hall*

Constructed around a 19th-century house, this stylish, modern hotel enjoys a peaceful location and pleasant grounds. Deep sofas ensure comfort in the open-plan lounge, and the Massimo Italian Restaurant offers a wide choice of freshly prepared meals. The well-equipped bedrooms are contemporary and comfortable. Extensive public areas include a fantastic, newly built leisure spa and a wide variety of air-conditioned conference and function suites.

Rooms 86 (3 fmly) (32 GF) ☞ **Facilities** Spa FTV WiFi ⤢ ⊗ supervised Gym Sauna **Conf** Class 130 Board 60 Thtr 250 **Services** Lift **Parking** 150 **Notes** Civ Wed 200

GOODRINGTON

See **Paignton**

GOODWOOD
West Sussex

Map 6 SU81

The Goodwood Hotel

★★★★ 82% ◉◉ HOTEL

tel: 01243 775537 **PO18 0QB**
email: reservations@goodwood.com **web:** www.goodwood.com/estate/the-goodwood-hotel
dir: *Off A285, 3m NE of Chichester*

Set at the centre of the 12,000-acre Goodwood Estate, this attractive hotel boasts extensive indoor and outdoor leisure facilities, along with a range of meeting rooms plus conference and banqueting facilities. Bedrooms are furnished to a consistently high standard, including individually decorated character rooms located in the old coaching inn; and garden rooms, each with a patio. Eating options include The Richmond Arms which sources produce extensively from the Estate's very own farm; The Richmond Arms Bar, and The Goodwood Bar and Grill. Overnight guests can also choose to dine in The Kennels, a private members' clubhouse.

Rooms 91 (15 fmly) (31 GF) ☞ **S** £125-£490; **D** £135-£500 (incl. bkfst)*
Facilities Spa STV FTV WiFi ⤢ ⊗ ⚐ 18 ⛳ Putt green Gym Golf driving range Sauna Steam room Fitness studio Xmas New Year **Conf** Class 60 Board 40 Thtr 150 Del from £192 to £300* **Parking** 150 **Notes** LB Civ Wed 120

GOOLE
East Riding of Yorkshire · Map 17 SE72

The Lowther Hotel

★★★ 83% @ HOTEL

tel: 01405 767999 **Aire St DN14 5QW**
email: info@lowtherhotel.co.uk **web:** www.lowtherhotel.co.uk
dir: *M62 junct 36, A614, follow town centre signs. At clock tower rdbt right into Aire St. Hotel at end on left*

A beautifully restored, Georgian Grade II* listed building that combines historic features with contemporary design, set in a unique location, overlooking the port. Bedrooms are stylish, well equipped and have free WiFi. Public areas include Bar Absolut and The Burlington Restaurant. The impressive Mural Rooms are perfect for weddings, conferences and meetings. Private parking is also available.

Rooms 12 (3 fmly) ⚏ **S** £56-£65; **D** £75-£85 (incl. bkfst)* **Facilities** FTV WiFi 🎵 Xmas New Year **Conf** Class 40 Board 30 Thtr 100 **Parking** 14 **Notes** LB ⊗ Civ Wed 60

Premier Inn Goole

BUDGET HOTEL

tel: 0871 527 8468 *(Calls cost 13p per minute plus your phone company's access charge)*
Rawcliffe Rd, Airmyn DN14 8JS
web: www.premierinn.com
dir: *M62 junct 36, A614 signed Rawcliffe. Hotel immediately on left*

High quality, budget accommodation ideal for both families and business travellers. Spacious, en suite bedrooms feature tea and coffee making facilities, and Freeview TV in most hotels. Internet access and WiFi are available for a small fee. The adjacent family restaurant features a wide and varied menu. See also the Hotel Groups pages.

Rooms 73

GORDANO SERVICE AREA (M5)
Somerset · Map 4 ST57

Days Inn Bristol West - M5

WELCOMEBREAK

AA Advertised

tel: 01275 373709 & 373624 **BS20 7XG**
email: gordano.hotel@welcomebreak.co.uk **web:** www.welcomebreak.co.uk
dir: *M5 junct 19, follow signs for Gordano Services*

This modern building offers accommodation in smart, spacious and well-equipped bedrooms, suitable for families and business travellers, and all with en suite bathrooms. Continental breakfast is available and other refreshments may be taken at the nearby family restaurant.

Rooms 60 (52 fmly) (29 GF) (8 smoking) **Facilities** FTV WiFi ⅋ **Conf** Board 10 **Parking** 60

GORING
Oxfordshire · Map 5 SU68

The Miller of Mansfield

@@ RESTAURANT WITH ROOMS

tel: 01491 872829 & 07702 853413 **High St RG8 9AW**
email: reservations@millerofmansfield.com **web:** www.millerofmansfield.com
dir: *M4 junct 12, S on A4 towards Newbury. 3rd rdbt onto A340 to Pangbourne. A329 to Streatley, right at lights onto B4009 into Goring*

The frontage of this former coaching inn hides sumptuous rooms furnished in a distinctive and individual style. An award-winning restaurant serves appealing dishes using locally sourced ingredients, and there is a comfortable bar, which serves real ales, fine wines and afternoon tea, a bar menu provides quick bites to eat.

Rooms 13 (2 fmly)

GORLESTON ON SEA
Norfolk · Map 13 TG50

The Pier Hotel

★★★ 85% HOTEL

tel: 01493 662631 **Harbourmouth, South Pier NR31 6PL**
email: bookings@pierhotelgorleston.co.uk **web:** www.pierhotelgorleston.co.uk
dir: *From A47 W of Great Yarmouth take A12 signed Lowestoft. At 3rd rdbt 1st left Beccles Rd, signed Gorleston. At rdbt 2nd left Church Rd. Next rdbt 1st left Baker St. Right into Pier Plain, then Pier Walk to Pier Gdns*

Ideally situated on the seafront this hotel offers smartly appointed bedrooms that are thoughtfully equipped and have a good range of useful extras; some rooms have superb sea views. The public areas include a large restaurant and a conservatory, which leads to a terrace and bar.

Rooms 21 (1 fmly) ⚏ **S** £65-£125; **D** £80-£150 (incl. bkfst) **Facilities** STV FTV WiFi ⅋ New Year **Parking** 25 **Notes** LB ⊗

G

GOSFORTH
Cumbria
Map 18 NY00

Westlakes Hotel
★★★ 86% HOTEL

tel: 019467 25221 **CA20 1HP**
email: info@westlakeshotel.co.uk **web:** www.westlakeshotel.co.uk
dir: *From A595 take B5344 signed Seascale. Hotel entrance 1st right*

Located amid the stunning scenery of the western lakes and within easy striking distance of a whole array of visitor attractions, Westlakes Hotel offers accommodation of a high standard, with many thoughtful extras provided. High quality food is served in the restaurant with relaxed and friendly service led by the hands-on owners and their team. There are excellent walking opportunities from this hotel.

Rooms 10 (4 annexe) (1 GF) 🤙 **S** £75-£100; **D** £75-£140 (incl. bkfst)* **Facilities** FTV WiFi **Conf** Class 30 Board 30 Thtr 50 Del £110* **Parking** 50 **Notes** LB ⊗

GOSPORT
Hampshire
Map 5 SZ69

Premier Inn Gosport
BUDGET HOTEL

tel: 0871 527 9436 *(Calls cost 13p per minute plus your phone company's access charge)*
Fareham Rd PO13 0ZX
web: www.premierinn.com
dir: *M27 junct 11 (W'bound exit), at Wallington rdbt 1st exit onto A27 (Fareham Central Gosport & A32). At Quay St rdbt left onto A32. At rdbt 2nd exit onto A32. Left at one-way system signed Gosport. Right at lights into Forrest Way, left into Holbrook, & Gosport Leisure Centre*

High quality, budget accommodation ideal for both families and business travellers. Spacious, en suite bedrooms feature tea and coffee making facilities, and Freeview TV in most hotels. Internet access and WiFi are available for a small fee. The adjacent family restaurant features a wide and varied menu. See also the Hotel Groups pages.

Rooms 63

GRANGE-OVER-SANDS
Cumbria
Map 18 SD47

Netherwood Hotel
★★★ 77% HOTEL

tel: 015395 32552 **Lindale Rd LA11 6ET**
email: enquiries@netherwood-hotel.co.uk **web:** www.netherwood-hotel.co.uk
dir: *On B5277 before station*

This imposing hotel stands in terraced grounds, enjoys fine views of Morecambe Bay, and is also popular as a conference and wedding venue. Good levels of hospitality and service ensure all guests are well looked after. Bedrooms vary in size but all are well furnished and have smart modern bathrooms. Magnificent woodwork is a feature of the public areas.

Rooms 34 (5 fmly) 🤙 **S** £80-£110; **D** £120-£180 (incl. bkfst)* **Facilities** FTV WiFi ⊛ supervised 🏊 Gym Steam room Fitness centre Xmas New Year **Conf** Class 150 Board 60 Thtr 150 **Services** Lift **Parking** 100 **Notes** LB Civ Wed 200

Cumbria Grand Hotel
★★★ 73% HOTEL

tel: 015395 32331 **LA11 6EN**
email: salescumbria@strathmorehotels.com **web:** www.strathmorehotels.com
dir: *M6 junct 36, A590 & follow Grange-over-Sands signs*

Set within extensive grounds, this large hotel offers fine views over Morecambe Bay and caters well for a mixed market. Public areas are pure nostalgia, and include a grand dining room and fine ballroom. Bedrooms are comfortably equipped and some have views of the bay.

Rooms 122 (10 fmly) (25 GF) 🤙 **Facilities** STV WiFi 🏊 Putt green Snooker & pool table Table tennis 🎵 Xmas New Year **Conf** Class 80 Board 36 Thtr 160 **Services** Lift **Parking** 75

Clare House
★★ ⊛ HOTEL

tel: 015395 33026 & 34253 **Park Rd LA11 7HQ**
email: info@clarehousehotel.co.uk **web:** www.clarehousehotel.co.uk
dir: *A590 onto B5277, through Lindale into Grange, keep left, hotel 0.5m on left past Crown Hill & St Paul's Church*

A warm, genuine welcome awaits guests at this delightful hotel, proudly run by the Read family for over 40 years. Situated in its own secluded gardens, it provides a relaxed haven in which to enjoy the panoramic views across Morecambe Bay. The stylish bedrooms and public areas are comfortable and attractively furnished. Skilfully prepared dinners and hearty breakfasts are served in the elegant dining room.

Rooms 18 (4 GF) 🤙 **Facilities** FTV WiFi 🏊 **Parking** 18 **Notes** ⊗ Closed mid Dec-late Mar

G

GRANTHAM
Lincolnshire   Map 11 SK93

Premier Inn Grantham

BUDGET HOTEL

tel: 0871 527 8470 *(Calls cost 13p per minute plus your phone company's access charge)*
A1/607 Junction, Harlaxton Rd NG31 7UA
web: www.premierinn.com
dir: *A1 onto A607. N'bound: hotel on right. S'bound: under A1, hotel on left*

High quality, budget accommodation ideal for both families and business travellers. Spacious, en suite bedrooms feature tea and coffee making facilities, and Freeview TV in most hotels. Internet access and WiFi are available for a small fee. The adjacent family restaurant features a wide and varied menu. See also the Hotel Groups pages.

Rooms 95

GRASMERE
Cumbria   Map 18 NY30

HIGHLY RECOMMENDED

The Wordsworth Hotel & Spa

★★★★ 81% ◉ HOTEL

tel: 015394 35592 & 35509 **Stock Ln LA22 9SW**
email: enquiry@thewordsworthhotel.co.uk **web:** www.thewordsworthhotel.co.uk
dir: *Off A591. In centre of village adjacent to St Oswald's Church*

This historic hotel ideally situated in the heart of Grasmere provides high levels of style and luxury. The bedrooms are equipped with smart furnishings, comfortable beds with Egyptian cotton linens and quality accessories. Guests can enjoy fine dining in the modernised Signature Restaurant which boasts stylish and elegant decor and for a less formal dining experience, light meals and fine ales are offered in the Dove Bistro. The hotel has a heated swimming pool and the sauna and spa make the ideal place for relaxation.

Rooms 38 (4 fmly) (3 GF) **Facilities** Spa FTV WiFi ⬆ ⊗ ⬇ Sauna Xmas New Year **Conf** Class 80 Board 40 Thtr 120 **Services** Lift **Parking** 40 **Notes** LB Civ Wed 100

Rothay Garden Hotel

★★★★ 84% ◉◉ HOTEL

tel: 015394 35334 **Broadgate LA22 9RJ**
email: stay@rothaygarden.com **web:** www.rothaygarden.com
dir: *A591, opposite Swan Hotel, into Grasmere, 300yds on left*

Situated just on the edge of Grasmere Village in two acres of riverside gardens this stylishly designed hotel offers comfort and luxury. Bedrooms include five Loft Suites which are named after the fells they overlook, while upper floors have their own balconies. The garden spa is the perfect place to relax with steam room, sauna and heated relaxing beds. The chic bar and lounges provide somewhere to unwind before dinner which is served in the Garden Restaurant.

Rooms 30 (3 fmly) (8 GF) **S** £110-£165; **D** £220-£360 (incl. bkfst & dinner)*
Facilities FTV WiFi ⬆ HL Sauna Aromatherapy room Infra red loungers Spa pool Xmas New Year **Parking** 35 **Notes** LB No children 12yrs

The Daffodil Hotel & Spa

★★★★ 83% ◉ HOTEL

tel: 015394 63550 **Keswick Rd LA22 9PR**
email: stay@daffodilhotel.com **web:** www.daffodilhotel.com
dir: *M6 junct 36 then A591, past Windermere & Ambleside. Hotel on left on entering Grasmere*

The Daffodil Hotel provides very high levels of service, comfort and luxury in a beautiful location on the edge of Grasmere, within easy walking distance of the village. Most rooms have either a lake or a valley view, several with private balconies, and are equipped to very high standards.

Rooms 78 (11 fmly) **D** £133-£363 (incl. bkfst)* **Facilities** Spa FTV WiFi ⬆ HL Sauna Steam room Tepidarium Thermal pool Mud rasul room Xmas New Year **Conf** Class 150 Board 32 Thtr 400 Del from £160 to £300* **Services** Lift Air con **Parking** 96 **Notes** LB Civ Wed 200

Oak Bank Hotel

★★★ 83% ◉◉ HOTEL

tel: 015394 35217 **Broadgate LA22 9TA**
email: info@lakedistricthotel.co.uk **web:** www.lakedistricthotel.co.uk
dir: *N'bound: M6 junct 36 onto A591 to Windermere, Ambleside, then Grasmere. S'bound: M6 junct 40 onto A66 to Keswick, A591 to Grasmere*

Privately owned and personally-run by friendly proprietors, Oak Bank is a Victorian house in the charming village of Grasmere. Bedrooms are well-equipped and include one suite with jacuzzi bath. The four Superior View Rooms have fantastic views of the surrounding fells. In colder weather, welcoming log fires burn in the comfortable lounges. The restaurant has a conservatory extension overlooking the garden, and there is also a pleasant bar.

Rooms 13 (1 GF) **S** £92-£120; **D** £98 £181 (incl. bkfst) **Facilities** STV FTV WiFi New Year **Parking** 13 **Notes** LB Closed 2-19 Jan, 18-26 Dec

Macdonald Swan Hotel

★★★ 80% HOTEL

tel: 01539 435742 & 0344 879 9120 **LA22 9RF**
email: sales/oldengland@macdonald-hotels.co.uk **web:** www.macdonaldhotels.co.uk
dir: *M6 junct 36, A591 towards Kendal, A590 to Keswick through Ambleside. Hotel on right on entering village*

Close to Dove Cottage and occupying a prominent position on the edge of the village, this 300-year-old inn is mentioned in Wordsworth's poem, *The Waggoner*. Attractive public areas are spacious and comfortable, and bedrooms are equally stylish. A modern bar and grill menu is available, while the elegant restaurant offers more formal dining.

Rooms 37 (2 fmly) (21 GF) **Facilities** FTV WiFi HL Xmas New Year **Conf** Class 20 Board 30 Thtr 40 **Parking** 45 **Notes** Civ Wed 60

G

GRASSINGTON
North Yorkshire   Map 19 SE06

Grassington House
 RESTAURANT WITH ROOMS

tel: 01756 752406 **5 The Square BD23 5AQ**
email: bookings@grassingtonhouse.co.uk **web:** www.grassingtonhouse.co.uk
dir: *A59 into Grassington, in town square opposite post office*

Located in the square of the popular village of Grassington, this beautifully
converted Georgian house is personally run by owners John and Sue. Delicious food,
individually designed bedrooms and warm hospitality ensure an enjoyable stay.
There is a stylish lounge bar looking out to the square and the restaurant is split
between two rooms; here guests will find the emphasis is on fresh, local ingredients
and attentive, yet friendly service.

Rooms 9 (2 fmly)

GRAVESEND
Kent   Map 6 TQ67

Premier Inn Gravesend (A2/Singlewell)
BUDGET HOTEL

tel: 0871 527 8472 *(Calls cost 13p per minute plus your phone company's access charge)*
Hevercourt Rd, Singlewell DA12 5UQ
web: www.premierinn.com
dir: *At Gravesend East exit on A2*

High quality, budget accommodation ideal for both families and business
travellers. Spacious, en suite bedrooms feature tea and coffee making facilities,
and Freeview TV in most hotels. Internet access and WiFi are available for a small
fee. The adjacent family restaurant features a wide and varied menu. See also the
Hotel Groups pages.

Rooms 31

Premier Inn Gravesend Central
BUDGET HOTEL   Premier Inn

tel: 0871 527 8474 *(Calls cost 13p per minute plus your phone company's access charge)*
Wrotham Rd DA11 7LF
web: www.premierinn.com
dir: *A2 onto A227 towards town centre, 1m to hotel*

Rooms 55

GREAT BIRCHAM
Norfolk   Map 13 TF73

HIGHLY RECOMMENDED

The Kings Head Hotel
★★★ 86% ⊛ HOTEL

tel: 01485 578265 **PE31 6RJ**
email: info@thekingsheadhotel.co.uk **web:** www.thekingsheadhotel.co.uk
dir: *A148 to Hillington through village, 1st left Bircham*

A delightful family-run hotel situated in the heart of this north Norfolk village
close to Royal Sandringham. The property is very contemporary, yet still retains

much of its original character. The spacious bedrooms are tastefully appointed
and equipped with modern facilities. Public rooms inlude a lounge, bar,
restaurant and further dining room.

Rooms 12 ☕ **Facilities** FTV WiFi ⇲ Xmas New Year **Conf** Class 30 Board 20 Thtr 40
Parking 30 **Notes** Civ Wed 80

GREAT CHESTERFORD
Essex   Map 12 TL54

The Crown House
★★★ 78% HOTEL

tel: 01799 530515 & 530257 **CB10 1NY**
email: reservations@crownhousehotel.com **web:** www.crownhousehotel.com
dir: *From N: M11 at junct 9 (from S junct 10) follow signs for Saffron Walden, then Great
Chesterford B1383*

This Georgian coaching inn, situated in a peaceful village close to the M11, has
been sympathetically restored and retains much original character. The bedrooms
are well equipped and individually decorated; some rooms have delightful four-
poster beds. Public rooms include an attractive lounge bar, an elegant oak-panelled
restaurant and an airy conservatory.

Rooms 18 (10 annexe) (1 fmly) (5 GF) ☕ **Facilities** FTV WiFi ⇲ New Year
Conf Class 14 Board 12 Thtr 30 **Parking** 30 **Notes** Closed 27-30 Dec Civ Wed 60

GREAT MILTON
Oxfordshire — Map 5 SP60

Belmond Le Manoir aux Quat' Saisons
★★★★★ ◉◉◉◉◉ HOTEL

tel: 01844 278881 **Church Rd OX44 7PD**
email: manoir.mqs@belmond.com **web:** www.belmond.com/lemanoir
dir: *From A329 2nd right to Great Milton Manor, hotel 200yds on right*

Even though Le Manoir is now very much part of the British scene, its iconic chef patron, Raymond Blanc, still fizzes with new ideas and projects. His first loves are his kitchen and his garden and the vital link between them. The fascinating grounds feature a Japanese tea garden and two acres of vegetables and herbs that supply the kitchen with an almost never-ending supply of top-notch produce. Even the car park has a stunning artichoke sculpture. The kitchen is the epicentre, with outstanding cooking highlighting freshness and seasonality. Bedrooms in this idyllic 'grand house on a small scale' are either in the main house or around an outside courtyard; all offer the highest levels of comfort and quality, have magnificent marble bathrooms and are equipped with a host of thoughtful extra touches. For something really special there is the 15th-century dovecot with a stunning upper-floor bedroom and a bathroom below. La Belle Epoque is the private dining room, ideal for weddings, celebrations and corporate events.

Rooms 32 (23 annexe) (13 GF) ⌇ **D** fr £570 (incl. bkfst)* **Facilities** STV FTV WiFi ⌇ 🍽 Cookery school Water gardens Bikes Spa treatment Xmas New Year **Conf** Class 30 Board 24 Thtr 80 **Parking** 60 **Notes** ⊗ Civ Wed 50

GREAT TOTHAM
Essex — Map 7 TL81

The Bull & Willow Room at Great Totham
◉◉ RESTAURANT WITH ROOMS

tel: 01621 893385 & 894020 **2 Maldon Rd CM9 8NH**
email: reservations@thebullatgreattotham.co.uk
web: www.thebullatgreattotham.co.uk
dir: *Exit A12 at Witham junct to Great Totham*

A 16th-century coaching inn located in the village of Great Totham, The Bull is now a very stylish restaurant with rooms that offers en suite bedrooms with satellite TVs with Freeview; WiFi is available throughout. Guests can enjoy dinner in the gastro-pub or in the award-winning fine dining restaurant, The Willow Room.

Rooms 4 (4 annexe)

GREAT YARMOUTH
Norfolk — Map 13 TG50

Imperial Hotel
★★★★ 75% ◉ HOTEL

THE INDEPENDENTS
HOTEL ASSOCIATION

tel: 01493 842000 **North Dr NR30 1EQ**
email: reservations@imperialhotel.co.uk **web:** www.imperialhotel.co.uk
dir: *Follow signs to seafront, turn left. Hotel opposite Waterways*

This friendly, family-run hotel is situated at the quieter end of the seafront within easy walking distance of the town centre. Bedrooms are attractively decorated with co-ordinated soft furnishings and many thoughtful touches; most rooms have superb sea views. Public areas include the smart Bar Fizz and the Café Cru restaurant.

Rooms 39 (4 fmly) ⌇ **S** £80-£140; **D** £90-£160 (incl. bkfst) **Facilities** FTV WiFi ⌇ New Year **Conf** Class 40 Board 30 Thtr 140 Del from £130 to £170 **Services** Lift **Parking** 40 **Notes** LB Civ Wed 140

The Prom Hotel
★★★ 81% ◉ HOTEL

tel: 01493 842308 **77 Marine Pde NR30 2DH**
email: info@promhotel.co.uk **web:** www.promhotel.co.uk

The Prom Hotel is ideally situated on the seafront close to the bright lights and attractions of Marine Parade. The open-plan public areas include a smart lounge bar with views of the sea, and a relaxed restaurant; guests also have the use of a further quieter lounge bar with plush seating. The modern contemporary bedrooms are smartly appointed and have many thoughtful touches; many rooms have lovely sea views.

Rooms 33 (1 fmly) ⌇ **S** £68-£85; **D** £80-£115 (incl. bkfst) **Facilities** STV FTV WiFi ⌇ Xmas New Year **Conf** Class 40 Board 30 Thtr 50 Del from £119.25 to £149.25 **Services** Lift **Parking** 30 **Notes** LB ⊗ Civ Wed 60

GREAT YARMOUTH continued

Andover House

★★★ 79% ◉◉ ◉ SMALL HOTEL

tel: 01493 843490 **28-30 Camperdown NR30 3JB**
email: bookings@andoverhouse.co.uk **web:** www.andoverhouse.co.uk
dir: *Opposite Wellington Pier turn into Shadingfield Close, right into Kimberley Terrace, follow into Camperdown. Property on left*

This charming Victorian building enjoys a peaceful location on a tree-lined avenue close to the town centre and the beach, making it an ideal base from which to explore the Norfolk Broads. Andover House offers a range of individually styled comfortable bedrooms along with a modern bar and well-appointed lounge areas. The award-winning brasserie-style restaurant offers an extensive choice of imaginative dishes and there is a smart sun terrace available for guests.

Rooms 20 **S** £67-£79; **D** £77-£99 (incl. bkfst)* **Facilities** STV WiFi ⇲ **Conf** Class 20 Board 20 Thtr 36 Del £150* **Notes** LB ⊗ No children 13yrs

The Cliff Hotel

★★★ 79% HOTEL

tel: 01493 662179 **Cliff Hill, Gorleston NR31 6DH**
email: reception@thecliffhotel.co.uk **web:** www.thecliffhotel.co.uk
dir: *A47 Acle new road rdbt 3rd exit, continue A12 3rd rdbt, 1st exit onto Victoria Rd, 3rd right onto Avondale Rd, follow round*

Having undergone a major refurbishment in recent years, the Cliff Hotel offers an extensive choice of stylish, very well appointed bedrooms. Overlooking the harbour and Gorleston Beach, the hotel enjoys a prominent position in the town. Ample secure parking is available and the modern terrace along with the contemporary lounge is very popular with guests.

Rooms 37 (4 fmly) ⋔ **Facilities** FTV WiFi Children's play area ♫ Xmas New Year **Conf** Class 60 Board 45 Thtr 160 **Parking** 30 **Notes** ⊗ Civ Wed 80

Furzedown Hotel

★★★ 79% HOTEL

tel: 01493 844138 **19-20 North Dr NR30 4EW**
email: paul@furzedownhotel.co.uk **web:** www.furzedownhotel.co.uk
dir: *At end of A47 or A12, towards seafront, left, hotel opposite Waterways*

Expect a warm welcome at this family-run hotel situated at the northern end of the seafront overlooking the town's Venetian Waterways. Bedrooms are pleasantly decorated and thoughtfully equipped; many rooms have superb sea views. The stylish public areas include a comfortable lounge bar, a smartly appointed restaurant and a cosy TV room.

Rooms 20 (11 fmly) **Facilities** FTV WiFi New Year **Conf** Class 80 Board 40 Thtr 75 **Parking** 30

Comfort Hotel Great Yarmouth

★★★ 74% HOTEL

tel: 01493 855070 & 850044 **Albert Square NR30 3JH**
email: sales@comfortgreatyarmouth.co.uk **web:** www.comfortgreatyarmouth.co.uk
dir: *From seafront left at Wellington Pier into Kimberley Terr. Left into Albert Sq, hotel on left*

A large hotel situated in the quieter end of town, just off the seafront and within easy walking distance of the town centre. The pleasantly decorated, well-equipped bedrooms are generally quite spacious and include WiFi. Public rooms include a comfortable lounge, a bar and smart brasserie-style restaurant.

Rooms 50 (12 fmly) (3 GF) ⋔ **Facilities** FTV WiFi ⇲ Xmas New Year **Conf** Class 50 Board 30 Thtr 120 **Parking** 15 **Notes** Civ Wed 120

Burlington Palm Hotel

★★★ 73% HOTEL

tel: 01493 844568 **11 North Dr NR30 1EG**
email: enquiries@burlington-hotel.co.uk **web:** www. burlington-hotel.co.uk
dir: *A12 to seafront, left at Marine Lodge. Hotel near tennis courts*

This privately owned hotel is situated at the quiet end of the resort, overlooking the sea. Bedrooms come in a variety of sizes and styles; they are pleasantly decorated and well equipped, and many have lovely sea views. The spacious public rooms include a range of seating areas, a choice of dining rooms, two bars and a heated indoor swimming pool.

Rooms 69 (9 fmly) (1 GF) ⋔ **Facilities** FTV WiFi ⊙ Xmas **Conf** Class 60 Board 30 Thtr 120 **Services** Lift **Parking** 70 **Notes** LB ⊗ Closed 28 Dec-2 Jan

See advert on opposite page

Knights Court Hotel

★★★ 72% HOTEL

tel: 01493 843089 **22 North Dr NR30 4EW**
email: enquiries@knights-court.co.uk **web:** www.knights-court.co.uk
dir: *Within close proximity of A12/A47, Great Yarmouth*

Knights Court Hotel is situated on the sea front at Great Yarmouth and is a small privately-owned hotel. Expect friendly service from Malcolm and the team, who will ensure all guests are welcomed. Bedrooms are comfortable and some offer good views of the sea. High quality ingredients are used at dinner, which is served in the stylish dining room. There is also a cosy lounge bar with thoughtful extras such as a library of books and magazines.

Rooms 20 (6 annexe) (5 fmly) (6 GF) (6 smoking) **Facilities** FTV WiFi ⇲ **Conf** Class 24 Board 24 Thtr 24 **Parking** 15 **Notes** ⊗ Closed 17 Dec-5 Jan

New Beach Hotel

★★★ 71% HOTEL

tel: 01493 332300 **67 Marine Pde NR30 2EJ**
email: newbeach.gtyarmouth@alfatravel.co.uk **web:** www.leisureplex.co.uk
dir: *Follow signs to seafront. Hotel facing Britannia Pier*

This Victorian building is centrally located on the seafront, overlooking Britannia Pier and the sandy beach. Bedrooms are pleasantly decorated and equipped with modern facilities; many have lovely sea views. Dinner is taken in the restaurant which doubles as the ballroom, and guests can also relax in the bar or sunny lounge.

Rooms 94 (8 fmly) ♠ S £28-£49; D £56-£82 (incl. bkfst)* **Facilities** FTV WiFi ♬ Xmas New Year **Services** Lift **Notes** LB ⊗ Closed Jan-Feb RS Mar

The Waverley Hotel

★★★ 68% HOTEL

tel: 01493 853388 **32-34 Princes Rd NR30 2DG**
email: thewaverleyhotel.gy@gmail.com **web:** www.thewaverleyhotelgy.com
dir: *Follow A47 from London to Great Yarmouth or A143 from Haverhill. Hotel opposite Britannia Pier at Princes Rd*

The Waverley is situated in a side road adjacent to the seafront and close to the local amenities. The property has been totally refurbished by the current owner to a very good standard. Public rooms include a large lounge bar, foyer and spacious restaurant. Bedrooms are contemporary in style and have a good range of extra facilities.

Rooms 47 (2 fmly) ♠ **Facilities** FTV WiFi Library ♬ Xmas New Year **Conf** Class 60 Board 60 Thtr 60 **Services** Lift **Notes** ⊗

The Nelson Hotel

★★★ 66% HOTEL

tel: 01493 855551 **1 Marine Pde NR30 3AG**
email: johnrushworth@theukholidaygroup.com **web:** www.grandukhotels.co.uk
dir: *On right of Marine Parade, opposite Sealife Centre*

The Nelson Hotel is ideally situated overlooking the sea, close to the pier and just a short stroll from the town centre and local amenities. It is ideal for both business and leisure guests, and all of the bedrooms are well equipped, while some rooms have lovely sea views. Public areas include a lounge with plush sofas, a bar and a separate dining room.

Rooms 50 (10 fmly) ♠ **Facilities** FTV WiFi ♬ Xmas New Year **Conf** Class 60 Board 60 Thtr 100 **Services** Lift **Notes** ⊗ Closed 2 Jan-end Feb

Premier Inn Great Yarmouth

BUDGET HOTEL

tel: 0871 527 9494 *(Calls cost 13p per minute plus your phone company's access charge)*
Runham Rd NR30 1SH
web: www.premierinn.com
dir: *A12 onto A149, at rdbt left into Runham Rd*

High quality, budget accommodation ideal for both families and business travellers. Spacious, en suite bedrooms feature tea and coffee making facilities, and Freeview TV in most hotels. Internet access and WiFi are available for a small fee. The adjacent family restaurant features a wide and varied menu. See also the Hotel Groups pages.

Rooms 80

G

GREENFORD
Greater London

Premier Inn London Greenford

BUDGET HOTEL PLAN 1 C4

tel: 0871 527 8658 *(Calls cost 13p per minute plus your phone company's access charge)*
Western Av UB6 8TE
web: www.premierinn.com
dir: *From A40 (Western Avenue) E'bound, exit at Perivale. Right, left at 2nd lights. Hotel opposite Hoover Building*

High quality, budget accommodation ideal for both families and business travellers. Spacious, en suite bedrooms feature tea and coffee making facilities, and Freeview TV in most hotels. Internet access and WiFi are available for a small fee. The adjacent family restaurant features a wide and varied menu. See also the Hotel Groups pages.

Rooms 39

GRIMSBY
Lincolnshire
Map 17 TA21

Millfields Hotel

★★★ A HOTEL

THE INDEPENDENTS
HOTEL ASSOCIATION

tel: 01472 356068 **53 Bargate DN34 5AD**
email: info@millfieldshotel.co.uk **web:** www.millfieldshotel.co.uk
dir: *A180, right at KFC rdbt then left at next rdbt. Right at 2nd lights & right onto Bargate, hotel 0.5m on left after Wheatsheaf pub*

Dating from 1879 this hotel is surrounded by its own grounds and caters for both leisure and business guests. The bedrooms are individually designed and there is a four-poster room. The contemporary Orangery Restaurant offers both carte and traditional bar menus. The hotel has extensive leisure facilities.

Rooms 27 (4 annexe) (7 fmly) (13 GF) **Facilities** FTV WiFi Gym Squash Sauna Steam room Hairdresser Beauty salon Aromatherapist **Conf** Class 25 Board 25 Thtr 50 **Parking** 75 **Notes** ⊗ Civ Wed 50

Premier Inn Grimsby

BUDGET HOTEL

tel: 0871 527 8478 *(Calls cost 13p per minute plus your phone company's access charge)*
Europa Park, Appian Way, off Gilbey Rd DN31 2UT
web: www.premierinn.com
dir: *M180 junct 5, A180 towards town centre. At 1st rdbt take 2nd exit. 1st left, left at mini rdbt into Appian Way*

High quality, budget accommodation ideal for both families and business travellers. Spacious, en suite bedrooms feature tea and coffee making facilities, and Freeview TV in most hotels. Internet access and WiFi are available for a small fee. The adjacent family restaurant features a wide and varied menu. See also the Hotel Groups pages.

Rooms 58

GRIMSTON
Norfolk
Map 12 TF72

INSPECTORS' CHOICE

Congham Hall Country House Hotel

★★★ ◉◉ COUNTRY HOUSE HOTEL

tel: 01485 600250 **Lynn Rd PE32 1AH**
email: info@conghamhallhotel.co.uk **web:** www.conghamhallhotel.co.uk
dir: *At A149/A148 junct, NE of King's Lynn, take A148 towards Fakenham for 100yds. Right to Grimston, hotel 2.5m on left*

Congham Hall is an elegant 18th-century Georgian manor set amid 30 acres of mature landscaped grounds and surrounded by parkland. The inviting public rooms provide a range of tastefully furnished areas in which to sit and relax. Imaginative cuisine is served in the Orangery Restaurant which has an intimate atmosphere and panoramic views of the gardens. The bedrooms, tastefully furnished with period pieces, have modern facilities and many thoughtful touches.

Rooms 26 (6 annexe) (12 GF) **S** £135-£325; **D** £135-£325* **Facilities** WiFi ⊛ Putt green ♨ Xmas New Year **Conf** Class 12 Board 28 Thtr 50 Del from £165 to £235* **Parking** 50 **Notes** LB Civ Wed 100

GRINDLEFORD
Derbyshire
Map 16 SK27

The Maynard

★★★ 82% ◉◉ HOTEL

tel: 01433 630321 **Main Rd S32 2HE**
email: info@themaynard.co.uk **web:** www.themaynard.co.uk
dir: *A625 from Sheffield to Castleton. Left into Grindleford on B6521. Hotel on left after Fox House Hotel*

This building, dating back over 100 years, is situated in a beautiful and tranquil location yet within easy reach of Sheffield and the M1. The bedrooms are contemporary in style and offer a wealth of accessories. The Peak District views from the restaurant and garden are stunning.

Rooms 10 (1 fmly) 🐾 **Facilities** FTV WiFi **Conf** Class 60 Board 40 Thtr 120 **Parking** 60 **Notes** Closed 25 Dec Civ Wed 120

GUILDFORD
Surrey
Map 6 SU94

HIGHLY RECOMMENDED

The Mandolay Hotel

★★★★ 83% ◉◉ HOTEL

tel: 01483 303030 **36-40 London Rd GU1 2AE**
email: info@guildford.com **web:** www.guildford.com
dir: *M25 junct 10, follow A3(S) for 7m. Take 3rd exit at 1st rdbt onto London Rd for 1m*

Situated close to the centre of Guildford, The Mandolay Hotel offers 72 comfortable bedrooms. Extensive meeting facilities provide for business visitors with off-street parking available. Free unrestricted WiFi is available throughout the hotel and there are over 900 international TV channels free of charge. A range of dining options, from coffee shop and bar menu to full restaurant service, are on offer.

Rooms 72 (4 fmly) (13 GF) 🐾 **Facilities** STV FTV WiFi ⇗ Xmas New Year **Conf** Class 200 Board 100 Thtr 700 **Services** Lift **Parking** 41 **Notes** ⊗ Civ Wed 500

Premier Inn Guildford Central

BUDGET HOTEL

tel: 0871 527 8482 *(Calls cost 13p per minute plus your phone company's access charge)*
Parkway GU1 1UP
web: www.premierinn.com
dir: *M25 junct 10, follow Portsmouth (A3) signs. Exit for Guildford Centre/Leisure Complex (A322/A320/A25). Turn left, hotel on left*

High quality, budget accommodation ideal for both families and business travellers. Spacious, en suite bedrooms feature tea and coffee making facilities, and Freeview TV in most hotels. Internet access and WiFi are available for a small fee. The adjacent family restaurant features a wide and varied menu. See also the Hotel Groups pages.

Rooms 109

GUISBOROUGH
North Yorkshire
Map 19 NZ61

H

Gisborough Hall

★★★★ 81% ◉◉ HOTEL

MACDONALD HOTELS & RESORTS

tel: 01287 611500 & 0344 879 9149 **Whitby Ln TS14 6PT**
email: general.gisboroughhall@macdonald-hotels.co.uk
web: www.macdonald-hotels.co.uk/Gisborough
dir: *A171, follow signs for Whitby to Waterfall rdbt, 3rd exit into Whitby Ln, hotel 500yds on right*

Dating back to the mid-19th century, this elegant country house provides a pleasing combination of original features and modern facilities. Bedrooms, including four-poster and family rooms, are richly furnished. The elegant Drawing Room is welcoming and has an open fire, while the opulent G Bar & Bistro provides a contemporary alternative. Excellent food is served in Chaloner's Restaurant.

Rooms 71 (2 fmly) (12 GF) 🐾 **Facilities** Spa WiFi ⇗ HL ♨ ♨ Sauna Xmas New Year **Conf** Class 150 Board 32 Thtr 400 **Services** Lift **Parking** 180 **Notes** LB Civ Wed 250

HADLEY WOOD
Greater London
Map 6 TQ29

West Lodge Park Hotel

★★★★ 79% ◉ HOTEL

tel: 020 8216 3900 & 8216 3903 **Cockfosters Rd EN4 0PY**
email: westlodgepark@bealeshotels.co.uk **web:** www.bealeshotels.co.uk
dir: *On A111, 1m S of M25 junct 24*

West Lodge Park Hotel is a stylish country house set in stunning parkland and gardens, yet only 12 miles from central London and a few miles from the M25. Bedrooms are individually decorated in traditional style and offer excellent facilities. Annexe rooms feature air-conditioning and have access to an outdoor patio area. Public rooms include the award-winning Cedar Restaurant, cosy bar area and separate lounge.

Rooms 59 (13 annexe) (4 fmly) (11 GF) 🐾 **S** £66-£120; **D** £94-£170* **Facilities** STV FTV WiFi ⇗ Putt green ♨ Free use of nearby leisure club ♫ Xmas New Year **Conf** Class 30 Board 30 Thtr 64 Del from £185 to £205* **Services** Lift **Parking** 200 **Notes** LB Civ Wed 72

H

HADLOW
Kent

Map 6 TQ65

Hadlow Manor Hotel

★★★ 74% HOTEL

tel: 01732 851442 **Goose Green TN11 0JH**
email: hotel@hadlowmanor.co.uk **web:** www.hadlowmanor.co.uk
dir: On A26 Maidstone to Tonbridge rd. 1m E of Hadlow

This is a friendly, independently owned country-house hotel, ideally situated between Maidstone and Tonbridge. Traditionally styled bedrooms are spacious and attractively furnished with many amenities. Public areas include a sunny restaurant, bar and lounge. The gardens are delightful and there's a seated area ideal for relaxation in warmer weather. Meeting and banqueting facilities are available.

Rooms 29 (2 fmly) (8 GF) **Facilities** STV FTV WiFi Xmas New Year **Conf** Class 90 Board 103 Thtr 200 **Parking** 120 **Notes** ⊗ Civ Wed 200

HAGLEY
Worcestershire

Map 10 SO98

Premier Inn Hagley

BUDGET HOTEL

tel: 0871 527 8484 *(Calls cost 13p per minute plus your phone company's access charge)*
Birmingham Rd DY9 9JS
web: www.premierinn.com
dir: M5 junct 3, A456 towards Kidderminster (dual carriageway). Hotel visible on opposite side of road. At next rdbt double back follow A456 Birmingham signs. Hotel on left

High quality, budget accommodation ideal for both families and business travellers. Spacious, en suite bedrooms feature tea and coffee making facilities, and Freeview TV in most hotels. Internet access and WiFi are available for a small fee. The adjacent family restaurant features a wide and varied menu. See also the Hotel Groups pages.

Rooms 40

HALIFAX
West Yorkshire

Map 19 SE02

Holdsworth House Hotel

★★★★ 75% ⍟⍟ HOTEL

tel: 01422 240024 **Holdsworth Rd, Holmfield HX2 9TG**
email: info@holdsworthhouse.co.uk **web:** www.holdsworthhouse.co.uk
dir: From town centre take A629 towards Keighley. 1.5m right at garage, into Shay Ln. Hotel on right after 1m

This delightful 17th-century Jacobean manor house, set in well-tended gardens, offers individually decorated, thoughtfully equipped bedrooms. Public rooms, adorned with beautiful paintings and antique pieces, include a choice of inviting lounges and superb conference and function facilities. Dinner provides the highlight of any stay and is served in the elegant restaurant by friendly, attentive staff.

Rooms 38 (9 fmly) (20 GF) ☏ **D** £95-£195 (incl. bkfst)* **Facilities** FTV WiFi ⌕ New Year **Conf** Class 75 Board 50 Thtr 150 Del from £195 to £295* **Parking** 60 **Notes** LB Civ Wed 120

Premier Inn Halifax South

BUDGET HOTEL

tel: 0871 527 8486 *(Calls cost 13p per minute plus your phone company's access charge)*
Salterhebble Hill, Huddersfield Rd HX3 0QT
web: www.premierinn.com
dir: Just off M62 junct 24 on A629 towards Halifax

High quality, budget accommodation ideal for both families and business travellers. Spacious, en suite bedrooms feature tea and coffee making facilities, and Freeview TV in most hotels. Internet access and WiFi are available for a small fee. The adjacent family restaurant features a wide and varied menu. See also the Hotel Groups pages.

Rooms 31

Premier Inn Halifax Town Centre

BUDGET HOTEL

tel: 0871 527 9348 *(Calls cost 13p per minute plus your phone company's access charge)*
Broad Street Plaza HX1 1YA
web: www.premierinn.com
dir: Phone for directions

Rooms 100

HAMPTON COURT
Greater London

The Carlton Mitre Hotel

★★★★ 75% HOTEL PLAN 1 B1

tel: 020 8979 9988 & 8783 3505 **Hampton Court Rd KT8 9BN**
email: info@carltonhotels.co.uk **web:** www.carltonhotels.co.uk/mitre
dir: M3 junct 1 follow signs to Sunbury & Hampton Court Palace. At Hampton Court Palace rdbt right, hotel on right

This hotel, dating back in parts to 1655, enjoys an enviable setting on the banks of the River Thames opposite Hampton Court Palace. The riverside restaurant and Edge bar/brasserie command wonderful views as well as spacious terraces for alfresco dining. Bedrooms are spacious and elegant with excellent facilities. Parking is limited.

Rooms 36 (2 fmly) (12 GF) **Facilities** FTV WiFi ⌕ Xmas New Year **Conf** Class 60 Board 40 Thtr 120 **Services** Lift Air con **Parking** 13 **Notes** ⊗ Civ Wed 100

HANDFORTH

See **Manchester Airport**

Find out more about the AA's Hotel rating scheme on page 18

HARROGATE
North Yorkshire

See also **Knaresborough**

Map 19 SE35

INSPECTORS' CHOICE

Rudding Park Hotel, Spa & Golf
★★★★ ◎◎ HOTEL

tel: 01423 871350 **Rudding Park, Follifoot HG3 1JH**
email: reservations@ruddingpark.com **web:** www.ruddingpark.co.uk
dir: *From A61 at rdbt with A658 take York exit, follow signs to Rudding Park*

Set in beautiful parkland, Rudding Park dates from the early 19th century. Interiors are stylishly contemporary and elegant, with luxurious bedrooms; the new Follifoot wing features stunning suites and bedrooms with spas. Carefully prepared meals and Yorkshire tapas are served in the contemporary Clocktower, which has a striking pink chandelier. The stylish bar and conservatory lead to a generous terrace which is perfect for eating alfresco. The grandeur of the mansion house and grounds make this a popular wedding venue. The hotel has an impressive spa, gym, private cinema and extensive conference facilities, plus an adjoining 18-hole, par 72 golf course and driving range.

Rooms 88 (15 fmly) (37 GF) 🐾 **S** fr £147; **D** fr £172 (incl. bkfst & dinner)* **Facilities** Spa STV FTV WiFi ❧ HL ⚓ 18 Putt green Gym Driving range Jogging trail Sauna Hammam 🎵 Xmas New Year **Conf** Class 150 Board 40 Thtr 300 Del from £175 to £285* **Services** Lift **Parking** 350 **Notes** ⊗ Civ Wed 300

West Park Hotel
★★★★ 79% HOTEL

tel: 01423 524471 **West Park HG1 1BJ**
email: enquiries@thewestparkhotel.com **web:** www.thewestparkhotel.com
dir: *A1M junct 47, A59 to Harrogate. 2m straight on A658, 3rd exit at rdbt onto A661 for 2.5m. 1st exit at rdbt onto A6040, 3rd exit next rdbt onto West Park. Hotel 500mtrs on right*

Perfectly situated within a busy area of the popular town of Harrogate this recently refurbished hotel is perfect for the modern day traveller. Bedrooms are equipped with plentiful amounts of accessories and gadgets such as climate control, smart televisions, and Nespresso machines as well as well-stocked hospitality trays. Many bathrooms have separate shower and bath facilities and luxurious toiletries are provided. Meals can be enjoyed in the bustling restaurant and bar area, and outdoor seating is provided for al fresco dining in the summer months.

Rooms 25 (8 fmly) 🐾 **Facilities** FTV WiFi ❧ 🎵 Xmas New Year **Conf** Class 24 Board 30 Thtr 60 Del from £185 to £360* **Services** Lift Air con

---

Nidd Hall Hotel
★★★★ 77% ◎◎ COUNTRY HOUSE HOTEL

WARNER LEISURE HOTELS

tel: 01423 771598 **Nidd HG3 3BN**
web: www.warnerleisurehotels.co.uk
dir: *A59 through Knaresborough, follow signs for Ripley. Hotel on right*

This fine hotel is set in 45 acres of Victorian and Edwardian gardens. Bedrooms are spacious and appointed to a high standard, while public areas are delightful and retain many original features. Leisure and spa facilities are available along with a variety of outdoor activities. This is an adults-only (above 21 years old) hotel.

Rooms 191 (55 GF) 🐾 **Facilities** Spa FTV WiFi HL ⊛ supervised 🦢 Putt green Fishing 🦢 Gym 🎵 Xmas New Year **Conf** Class 40 Board 30 Thtr 60 **Services** Lift **Parking** 200 **Notes** ⊗ No children 21yrs

---

Studley Hotel
★★★★ 77% ◎◎ HOTEL

tel: 01423 560425 **28 Swan Rd HG1 2SE**
email: info@studleyhotel.co.uk **web:** www.studleyhotel.co.uk
dir: *Adjacent to Valley Gardens, opposite Mercer Gallery*

This friendly, well-established hotel, close to the town centre and Valley Gardens, is well known for its Orchid Restaurant, which provides a dynamic and authentic approach to Pacific Rim and Asian cuisine. Bedrooms are modern and come in a variety of styles and sizes, while the stylish bar lounge provides an excellent place for relaxing. A PC is available for guests' use.

Rooms 28 (1 fmly) 🐾 **S** £104-£129; **D** £124-£139 (incl. bkfst)* **Facilities** STV FTV WiFi ❧ Free use of facilities at local Health Club **Conf** Class 15 Board 12 Thtr 15 **Services** Lift **Parking** 15 **Notes** LD ⊛ Closed 25-26 Dec

---

White Hart Hotel
★★★★ 76% ◎◎ HOTEL

tel: 01423 505681 **2 Cold Bath Rd HG2 0NF**
email: reservations@whitehearthotelharrogate.com
web: www.whiteharthotelharrogate.com
dir: *A59 to Harrogate. A661 3rd exit on rdbt to Harrogate. Left at rdbt onto A6040 for 1m. Right onto A61. Bear left down Montpellier Hill*

Set in the heart of Harrogate's antiques quarter, this fine Georgian hotel has free WiFi and luxurious bedrooms, just a few minutes stroll from the town centre, Harrogate International Centre and the famous Valley Gardens. The newly refurbished 'Deluxe' bedrooms have been fully modernised with USB ports and soft tartan furnishings, while the 'Classic' bedrooms retain their older shabby-chic style and antique furniture. All rooms feature flat-screen TVs with Freeview, and en suite bathroom with H2K toiletries. Guests can choose to relax in the residents' lounge or enjoy the atmosphere of The Fat Badger, an adjoining, traditional English pub. The on-site restaurant, The Fat Badger Grill, is the place for breakfast, lunch and dinner. The White Hart Hotel also offers parking for over 80 vehicles.

Rooms 61 🐾 **S** £45-£289; **D** £49-£299* **Facilities** FTV WiFi ❧ Gym Xmas New Year **Conf** Class 40 Board 25 Thtr 80 Del from £153.50* **Services** Lift **Parking** 80 **Notes** ⊗ Civ Wed 80

HARROGATE *continued*

Hotel du Vin & Bistro Harrogate

★★★★ 74% TOWN HOUSE HOTEL

tel: 01423 856800 & 0844 736 4257
(Calls cost 5p per minute plus your phone company's access charge) **Prospect Place HG1 1LB**
email: info@harrogate.hotelduvin.com **web:** www.hotelduvin.com
dir: *A1(M) junct 47, A59 to Harrogate, follow town centre signs to Prince of Wales rdbt, 3rd exit, remain in right lane. Right at lights into Albert St, right into Prospect Place*

This town house was created from eight Georgian-style properties and overlooks The Stray. The spacious, open-plan lobby has seating, a bar and the reception desk. Hidden downstairs is a cosy snug cellar. The French-influenced bistro offers high quality cooking and a great choice of wines. Bedrooms face front and back, and are smart and modern, with excellent 'deluge' showers.

Rooms 48 (4 GF) ⌂ **Facilities** Spa STV FTV WiFi ⇗ New Year **Conf** Class 20 Board 30 Thtr 60 **Services** Lift **Parking** 30 **Notes** Civ Wed 90

Best Western Plus Cedar Court Hotel

★★★★ 74% HOTEL

BW Best Western PLUS.

tel: 01423 858585 & 858595 (Res) **Queens Buildings, Park Pde HG1 5AH**
email: cedarcourt@bestwestern.co.uk **web:** www.cedarcourthotels.co.uk
dir: *From A1(M) follow signs to Harrogate on A661 past Sainsburys. At rdbt left onto A6040. Hotel right after church*

This Grade II listed building was Harrogate's first hotel and enjoys a peaceful location in landscaped grounds, close to the town centre. It provides spacious, well-equipped accommodation. Public areas include a brasserie-style restaurant, a small gym and an open-plan lounge and bar. Functions and conferences are particularly well catered for.

Rooms 100 (8 fmly) (7 GF) **S** £69-£139; **D** £69-£139* **Facilities** FTV WiFi ⇗ Gym Xmas New Year **Conf** Class 80 Board 70 Thtr 320 Del from £134 to £204* **Services** Lift **Parking** 150 **Notes** LB ⊗ Civ Wed 320

The Majestic Hotel

★★★★ 74% HOTEL

THE
HOTEL
COLLECTION

tel: 01423 700300 **Ripon Rd HG1 2HU**
email: majestic@thehotelcollection.co.uk **web:** www.thehotelcollection.co.uk
dir: *M1 onto A1(M) at Wetherby. Take A661 to Harrogate. Hotel in town centre adjacent to Royal Hall & next to Harrogate International Centre*

Popular for conferences and functions, this grand Victorian hotel is set in 12 acres of landscaped grounds that is within walking distance of the town centre. It benefits from spacious public areas, and the comfortable bedrooms, including some spacious suites, come in a variety of sizes.

Rooms 170 (8 fmly) ⌂ **S** £65-£140; **D** £89-£220* **Facilities** Spa FTV WiFi ⇗ HL ⊗ Gym Saunas Xmas New Year **Conf** Class 260 Board 70 Thtr 500 Del from £119 to £150* **Services** Lift **Parking** 250 **Notes** LB Civ Wed 200

Cairn Hotel

★★★ 70% HOTEL

tel: 01423 504005 **Ripon Rd HG1 2JD**
email: salescairn@strathmorehotels.com **web:** www.strathmorehotels.com

This large Victorian hotel is just a short walk from the town centre and also benefits from free on-site parking. Many of the original features have been retained and the spacious foyer lounge and bar areas are perfect for relaxing. Bedrooms are comfortable, with Club Rooms offering extra accessories and luxury touches. Complimentary WiFi is also provided in public areas and there is a fitness room with a mini gym.

Rooms 135 (7 fmly) ⌂ **Facilities** WiFi Gym Xmas New Year **Conf** Class 170 Board 100 Thtr 400 **Services** Lift **Parking** 150 **Notes** LB Civ Wed 150

Premier Inn Harrogate

BUDGET HOTEL

tel: 0871 527 8490 *(Calls cost 13p per minute plus your phone company's access charge)*
Hornbeam Park Av HG2 8RA
web: www.premierinn.com
dir: *A1(M) junct 46 W, A661 to Harrogate. In 2m left at The Woodlands lights. 1.5m left into Hornbeam Park Ave*

High quality, budget accommodation ideal for both families and business travellers. Spacious, en suite bedrooms feature tea and coffee making facilities, and Freeview TV in most hotels. Internet access and WiFi are available for a small fee. The adjacent family restaurant features a wide and varied menu. See also the Hotel Groups pages.

Rooms 68

Premier Inn Harrogate Town Centre

BUDGET HOTEL

tel: 0871 527 9432 *(Calls cost 13p per minute plus your phone company's access charge)*
Springfield Av HG1 2HY
web: www.premierinn.com
dir: *A1 junct 47, follow Ripon/A61 signs. After Ripton follow Harrogate signs. After Cairn Hotel (on right) turn left into Springfield Ave. Hotel on left*

Rooms 107

H

HARROW WEALD
Greater London

Best Western Plus Grim's Dyke Hotel

★★★★ 73% @ HOTEL PLAN 1 B5

tel: 020 8385 3100 & 8954 4227 **Old Redding HA3 6SH**
email: reservations@grimsdyke.com **web:** www.grimsdyke.com
dir: A410 onto A409 north towards Bushey, at top of hill at lights turn left into Old Redding, opposite 'The Viewpoint'

Once home to Sir William Gilbert, this Grade II mansion contains many references to well-known Gilbert and Sullivan productions. The house is set in over 40 acres of beautiful parkland and gardens. Bedrooms in the main house are elegant and traditional, while those in the adjacent lodge are aimed more at the business guest.

Rooms 46 (37 annexe) (4 fmly) (17 GF) 🕻 **Facilities** FTV WiFi 🏌 🐾 Gilbert & Sullivan opera dinner Murder mystery & Sabrage evenings 🎵 Xmas New Year **Conf** Class 60 Board 32 Thtr 90 **Parking** 97 **Notes** LB RS 24-31 Dec Civ Wed 90

HARTLEPOOL
County Durham   Map 19 NZ53

Premier Inn Hartlepool Marina

BUDGET HOTEL

tel: 0871 527 8492 (Calls cost 13p per minute plus your phone company's access charge)
Maritime Av, Hartlepool Marina TS24 0XZ
web: www.premierinn.com
dir: Approx 1m from A689/A179 junct. On marina

High quality, budget accommodation ideal for both families and business travellers. Spacious, en suite bedrooms feature tea and coffee making facilities, and Freeview TV in most hotels. Internet access and WiFi are available for a small fee. The adjacent family restaurant features a wide and varied menu. See also the Hotel Groups pages.

Rooms 98

HARTLEY WINTNEY
Hampshire   Map 5 SU75

The Elvetham Hotel

★★★ 83% HOTEL

tel: 01252 844871 **RG27 8AR**
email: enq@elvethamhotel.co.uk **web:** www.elvethamhotel.co.uk
dir: M3 junct 4A W, junct 5 E or M4 junct 11, A33, B3011. Hotel signed from A323 between Hartley Wintney & Fleet

The Elvetham Hotel is a spectacular 19th-century mansion set in 35 acres of grounds with an arboretum. All bedrooms are individually styled and many have views of the manicured gardens. A popular venue for weddings and conferences, the hotel lends itself to team building events and outdoor pursuits.

Rooms 72 (29 annexe) (10 fmly) (15 GF) 🕻 **S** £90-£110; **D** £125-£200 (incl. bkfst)*
Facilities STV FTV WiFi 🏌 🏊 🐾 Gym Badminton Boules Volleyball New Year
Conf Class 70 Board 48 Thtr 110 Del from £200 to £235 **Parking** 200 **Notes** Closed 24-27 Dec Civ Wed 200

HARTSHEAD MOOR MOTORWAY SERVICE AREA (M62)
West Yorkshire   Map 19 SE12

Days Inn Bradford - M62

WELCOMEBREAK

AA Advertised

tel: 01274 851706 **Hartshead Moor Service Area, Clifton HD6 4JX**
email: hartshead.hotel@welcomebreak.co.uk **web:** www.welcomebreak.co.uk
dir: M62 between junct 25 & 26

This modern building offers accommodation in smart, spacious and well-equipped bedrooms, suitable for families and business travellers, and all with en suite bathrooms. Continental breakfast is available and other refreshments may be taken at the nearby family restaurant.

Rooms 38 (33 fmly) (17 GF) **Facilities** FTV WiFi 🏌 🕻 **Conf** Board 10 **Parking** 100

HARWICH
Essex   Map 13 TM23

The Pier at Harwich

★★★★ 77% @@ SMALL HOTEL

tel: 01255 241212 **The Quay CO12 3HH**
email: pier@milsomhotels.com **web:** www.milsomhotels.com/thepier
dir: From A12 take A120 to Quay. Hotel opposite lifeboat station

Recently re-opened after a major redevelopment, The Pier is situated on the quay, overlooking the ports of Harwich and Felixstowe. The bedrooms are tastefully decorated, thoughtfully equipped, and furnished in a contemporary style; many rooms have superb sea views. The public rooms include the restaurant which is influenced by the best in European cooking, the NAVYÄRD bar and terrace, and a plush residents' lounge.

Rooms 14 (7 annexe) (5 fmly) (1 GF) 🕻 **D** £125-£235 (incl. bkfst)* **Facilities** STV WiFi Day cruises on yachts Golf breaks arranged with nearby course Sea bass fishing Xmas **Conf** Board 16 Del £175* **Services** Lift **Parking** 12 **Notes** LB Civ Wed 50

H

HARROGATE *continued*

Tower Hotel

★★★ 78% HOTEL

tel: 01255 504952 **Dovercourt CO12 3PJ**
email: reception@tower-hotel-harwich.co.uk **web:** www.tower-hotel-harwich.co.uk
dir: *Follow main road into Harwich. Past BP garage on left*

The Tower Hotel is an impressive late 17th-century Italian-style building, with a wealth of ornamental ceiling cornices, beautiful architraves and an impressive balustrade. Bedrooms, many named after prominent people from Harwich's past, are spacious and furnished to a very high standard. Evening meals and breakfast are served in the decorative dining rooms, and Rigby's bar offers tempting meals and a wide range of refreshments.

Rooms 13 (2 fmly) (2 GF) **Facilities** WiFi **Conf** Class 30 Board 30 Thtr 30 **Parking** 30 **Notes** ⊗ Closed 25-26 Dec Civ Wed 70

Premier Inn Harwich

BUDGET HOTEL

tel: 0871 527 8494 *(Calls cost 13p per minute plus your phone company's access charge)*
Parkstone Rd, Dovercourt CO12 4NX
web: www.premierinn.com
dir: *A120 to Harwich, hotel opposite Morrisons. Right at rdbt. Hotel entrance through Lidl car park*

High quality, budget accommodation ideal for both families and business travellers. Spacious, en suite bedrooms feature tea and coffee making facilities, and Freeview TV in most hotels. Internet access and WiFi are available for a small fee. The adjacent family restaurant features a wide and varied menu. See also the Hotel Groups pages.

Rooms 45

HASLEMERE
Surrey

Map 6 SU93

Lythe Hill Hotel & Spa

★★★★ 73% ⍟⍟ HOTEL

tel: 01428 651251 **Petworth Rd GU27 3BQ**
email: lythe@lythehill.co.uk **web:** www.lythehill.co.uk
dir: *From High St onto B2131. Hotel 1.25m on right*

This privately-owned hotel sits in 22 acres of attractive parkland. It has been described as a hamlet of character buildings, each furnished in a style that complements the age of the property; the oldest one dating back to 1475. The restaurant offers interesting, quality dishes, and is also the venue for breakfast and afternoon tea. The bedrooms are split between a number of 15th-century buildings, and vary in size. The stylish Armana spa includes a 16-metre swimming pool, as well as various ESPA treatments and therapies, spa bath, sauna and a fully equipped gym.

Rooms 44 (9 fmly) (19 GF) ⌁ **S** £84.50-£109; **D** £109-£169 (incl. bkfst)*
Facilities Spa FTV WiFi ⍟ ⍟ ⍟ Gym Boules Giant chess ♫ Xmas New Year **Conf** Class 40 Board 30 Thtr 128 **Parking** 120 **Notes** LB Civ Wed 128

HASTINGS & ST LEONARDS
East Sussex

Map 7 TQ80

Bannatyne Spa Hotel Hastings

★★★★ 77% ⍟ HOTEL

tel: 01424 851222 & 0844 248 3836
(Calls cost 7p per minute plus your phone company's access charge) **Battle Rd TN38 8EA**
email: enquiries.hastingshotel@bannatyne.co.uk **web:** www.bannatyne.co.uk
dir: *M25 junct 5, A21 Hastings. At 5th rdbt take 2nd exit Hastings/Filmwell. After 2 rdbts turn right Folkestone/A259/Battle/A2100. Left at A2100/The Ridge Way. At 2nd rdbt right to hotel*

This hotel offers a range of facilities that will appeal to both leisure and business travellers. The well-appointed accommodation is available in a range of types and sizes from small doubles to superior rooms, while the public areas are a tasteful blend of contemporary design and period features. The Conservatory Restaurant has attractive views over the formal garden. There is a spa and health club plus meeting facilities. Free WiFi is available.

Rooms 38 (7 fmly) (4 GF) ⌁ **D** £95-£300 (incl. bkfst)* **Facilities** Spa FTV WiFi ⍟ ⍟ supervised ⍟ Gym Xmas New Year **Conf** Class 300 Board 50 Thtr 425 **Services** Lift **Parking** 150 **Notes** LB ⊗ Civ Wed 300

Best Western Royal Victoria Hotel

★★★ 74% HOTEL

tel: 01424 445544 **Marina, St Leonards-on-Sea TN38 0BD**
email: reception@royalvichotel.co.uk **web:** www.royalvichotel.co.uk
dir: *On A259 (seafront road) 1m W of Hastings pier*

This imposing 18th-century property is situated in a prominent position overlooking the sea. A superb marble staircase leads up from the lobby to the main public areas on the first floor which has panoramic views of the sea. The spacious bedrooms are pleasantly decorated and well equipped, and include duplex and family suites.

Rooms 50 (15 fmly) **Facilities** STV WiFi ⍟ Xmas New Year **Conf** Class 40 Board 40 Thtr 100 **Services** Lift **Parking** 6 **Notes** Civ Wed 50

Premier Inn Hastings

BUDGET HOTEL

tel: 0871 527 8496 *(Calls cost 13p per minute plus your phone company's access charge)*
1 John Macadam Way, St Leonards on Sea TN37 7DB
web: www.premierinn.com
dir: *A21 into Hastings. Hotel on right after junct with A2100 - Battle road*

High quality, budget accommodation ideal for both families and business travellers. Spacious, en suite bedrooms feature tea and coffee making facilities, and Freeview TV in most hotels. Internet access and WiFi are available for a small fee. The adjacent family restaurant features a wide and varied menu. See also the Hotel Groups pages.

Rooms 73

HATFIELD
Hertfordshire   Map 6 TL20

Beales Hotel
★★★★ 78% ⚜ HOTEL

tel: 01707 288500 **Comet Way AL10 9NG**
email: hatfield@bealeshotels.co.uk **web:** www.bealeshotels.co.uk
dir: On A1001 opposite Galleria Shopping Mall - follow signs for Galleria

Beales Hotel is a stunning contemporary property. Within easy access of the M25, its striking exterior incorporates giant glass panels and cedar wood slats. Bedrooms have luxurious beds, flat-screen TVs and smart bathrooms. Public areas include a small bar and attractive restaurant, which opens throughout the day. The hotel is fully air-conditioned and free wired broadband is available in bedrooms, conference and banqueting rooms.

Rooms 53 (3 fmly) (21 GF) ⌁ **Facilities** STV FTV WiFi ⌁ Free use of nearby leisure club Xmas New Year **Conf** Class 124 Board 64 Thtr 300 **Services** Lift Air con **Parking** 126 **Notes** ⊗ RS 27-30 Dec Civ Wed 300

Mercure Hatfield Oak Hotel
★★★ 75% HOTEL

tel: 01707 275701 **Roehyde Way AL10 9AF**
email: enquiries@hotels-hatfield.com **web:** www.hotels-hatfield.com
dir: M25 junct 23 between juncts 2 & 3 of A1(M). Roehyde Way runs parallel to A1(M)

This hotel enjoys an enviable location for both leisure and business guests, as it is within easy reach of major roads and central London. In addition, the University of Hertfordshire is situated nearby. The accommodation has been appointed to a good standard with flat-screen TVs and WiFi, among other facilities. The hotel also caters for conferences and banqueting.

Rooms 76 (5 fmly) (36 GF) ⌁ **Facilities** FTV WiFi ⌁ Xmas New Year **Conf** Class 50 Board 50 Thtr 100 **Parking** 85 **Notes** ⊗ Civ Wed 120

Premier Inn Hatfield
BUDGET HOTEL

tel: 0871 527 8498 (Calls cost 13p per minute plus your phone company's access charge)
Lemsford Rd AL10 ODZ
web: www.premierinn.com
dir: From A1(M) junct 4, A1001 towards Hatfield. At rbt take 2nd exit, 1st right

High quality, budget accommodation ideal for both families and business travellers. Spacious, en suite bedrooms feature tea and coffee making facilities, and Freeview TV in most hotels. Internet access and WiFi are available for a small fee. The adjacent family restaurant features a wide and varied menu. See also the Hotel Groups pages.

Rooms 40

HATHERSAGE
Derbyshire   Map 16 SK28

HIGHLY RECOMMENDED

George Hotel
★★★ 86% ⚜ HOTEL

tel: 01433 650436 **Main Rd S32 1BB**
email: info@george-hotel.net **web:** www.george-hotel.net
dir: In village centre on A6187, SW of Sheffield

The George is a relaxing 500-year-old hostelry in the heart of this picturesque town. The beamed bar lounge has great character and traditional comfort, and the restaurant is light, modern and spacious with original artworks. Upstairs the decor is simpler with lots of light hues; the split-level and four-poster rooms are especially appealing. The quality cuisine is a key feature of the hotel.

Rooms 24 (2 fmly) (5 GF) ⌁ **Facilities** FTV WiFi Xmas New Year **Conf** Class 20 Board 36 Thtr 80 **Parking** 40 **Notes** ⊗ Civ Wed 70

HAVANT
Hampshire   Map 5 SU70

Premier Inn Portsmouth (Havant)
BUDGET HOTEL

tel: 0871 527 8900 (Calls cost 13p per minute plus your phone company's access charge)
65 Bedhampton Hill, Bedhampton PO9 3JN
web: www.premierinn.com
dir: At rdbt just off A3(M) junct 5 towards Bedhampton

High quality, budget accommodation ideal for both families and business travellers. Spacious, en suite bedrooms feature tea and coffee making facilities, and Freeview TV in most hotels. Internet access and WiFi are available for a small fee. The adjacent family restaurant features a wide and varied menu. See also the Hotel Groups pages.

Rooms 59

HAVERHILL
Suffolk   Map 12 TL64

Days Inn Haverhill
BUDGET HOTEL   **DAYS INN**

tel: 01440 716950 **Phoenix Road & Bumpstead Rd, Haverhill Business Park CB9 7AE**
email: info@daysinnhaverhill.co.uk **web:** www.haverhilldaysinn.co.uk
dir: A1017 (Haverhill bypass). Hotel on 5th rdbt

This modern building offers accommodation in smart, spacious and well-equipped bedrooms, suitable for families and business travellers, and all with en suite bathrooms. Continental breakfast is available and other refreshments may be taken at the nearby family restaurant. See also the Hotel Groups pages.

Rooms 80 (8 fmly) (14 GF) ⌁ **Conf** Class 28 Board 24 Thtr 60

H

H

HAWES
North Yorkshire
Map 18 SD88

Simonstone Hall Hotel
★★★ 79% ◎◎ HOTEL

tel: 01969 667255 **Simonstone DL8 3LY**
email: enquiries@simonstonehall.com **web:** www.simonstonehall.com
dir: 1.5m N of Hawes on road signed Muker & Buttertubs

This former hunting lodge provides professional, friendly service and a relaxed atmosphere. There is an inviting drawing room, stylish fine dining restaurant, a bar and a conservatory. The generally spacious bedrooms are elegantly designed to reflect the style of the house, and many offer spectacular views of the countryside.

Rooms 18 (10 fmly) (2 GF) ♦ **Facilities** FTV WiFi Xmas New Year **Conf** Class 20 Board 20 Thtr 50 **Parking** 40 **Notes** Civ Wed 100

HAYDOCK
Merseyside
Map 15 SJ59

Premier Inn Haydock

BUDGET HOTEL

tel: 0871 527 8500 *(Calls cost 13p per minute plus your phone company's access charge)*
Yew Tree Way, Golbourne WA3 3JD
web: www.premierinn.com
dir: M6 junct 23, A580 towards Manchester. Approx 2m. Straight on at major rdbt. Hotel on left

High quality, budget accommodation ideal for both families and business travellers. Spacious, en suite bedrooms feature tea and coffee making facilities, and Freeview TV in most hotels. Internet access and WiFi are available for a small fee. The adjacent family restaurant features a wide and varied menu. See also the Hotel Groups pages.

Rooms 60

HAYLE
Cornwall
Map 2 SW53

Premier Inn Hayle
BUDGET HOTEL

tel: 0871 527 8506 *(Calls cost 13p per minute plus your phone company's access charge)*
Carwin Rise, Loggans TR27 4PN
web: www.premierinn.com
dir: On A30 at Loggans Moor rdbt exit into Carwin Rise. Hotel on right

High quality, budget accommodation ideal for both families and business travellers. Spacious, en suite bedrooms feature tea and coffee making facilities, and Freeview TV in most hotels. Internet access and WiFi are available for a small fee. The adjacent family restaurant features a wide and varied menu. See also the Hotel Groups pages.

Rooms 57

HAYLING ISLAND
Hampshire
Map 5 SU70

Langstone Hotel
★★★★ 75% ◎◎ HOTEL

tel: 023 9246 5011 **Northney Rd PO11 ONQ**
email: info@langstonehotel.co.uk **web:** www.langstonehotel.co.uk
dir: From A27 take A3023 signed Havant/Hayling Island. Over bridge onto Hayling Island, sharp left after bridge

This hotel is located on the north shore of Hayling Island, yet is only minutes from the M27 with easy access to Fareham, Havant and Chichester. All the smartly designed bedrooms, including 45 superior rooms, have views over Langstone harbour. The Brasserie offers a good choice of dishes and overlooks the harbour. A gym, indoor pool, sauna, steam, beauty salon and fitness club are also available.

Rooms 148 (25 fmly) (60 GF) (3 smoking) ♦ **Facilities** Spa FTV WiFi ➹ HL ➲ supervised Gym Sauna Steam room Fitness classes Xmas New Year **Conf** Class 80 Board 50 Thtr 160 **Services** Lift **Parking** 220 **Notes** ⊗ Civ Wed 150

Sinah Warren Hotel

★★★ 81% HOTEL

tel: 023 9246 6421 **Ferry Rd PO11 OBZ**
email: sinahwarren2@bourne-leisure.co.uk **web:** www.warnerleisurehotels.co.uk
dir: A27 at Havant junct, take A3023 to Hayling Island, 2nd exit at rdbt towards Manor Rd, 3rd exit at next rdbt into Ferry Rd. Hotel 1.5m on right

Located in a beautiful part of Hampshire, this hotel offers a great range of leisure facilities and numerous daily in-house and external activities catering for all. The accommodation is spacious, and some rooms have sea views. The packages range from a minimum two-night, half-board stay. Please note that this is an adults-only (over 21 years) hotel.

Rooms 280 (34 annexe) (116 GF) ♦ **Facilities** Spa FTV WiFi HL ➲ ➹ supervised ➳ ➳ Gym ♫ Xmas New Year **Conf** Class 300 Board 250 Thtr 500 **Services** Lift **Parking** 260 **Notes** ⊗ No children 21yrs

HAYWARDS HEATH
West Sussex
Map 6 TQ32

Best Western The Birch Hotel
★★★ 78% HOTEL

tel: 01444 451565 **Lewes Rd RH17 7SF**
email: info@birchhotel.co.uk **web:** www.birchhotel.co.uk
dir: On A272 opposite Princess Royal Hospital & behind Shell Garage

Originally the home of an eminent Harley Street surgeon, this attractive Victorian property has been extended to combine modern facilities with the charm of its original period. Public rooms include the conservatory-style Pavilion Restaurant, along with an open-plan lounge and brasserie-style bar serving a range of light meals.

Rooms 51 (3 fmly) (12 GF) ♦ **S** £82-£105; **D** £89-£115 (incl. bkfst)* **Facilities** STV FTV WiFi ➹ **Conf** Class 30 Board 26 Thtr 50 **Parking** 60 **Notes** Civ Wed 60

HEACHAM
Norfolk

Map 12 TF63

HIGHLY RECOMMENDED

Heacham Manor Hotel

★★★ 86% HOTEL

tel: 01485 536030 & 579800 **Hunstanton Rd PE31 7JX**
email: info@heacham-manor.co.uk **web:** www.heacham-manor.co.uk
dir: On A149 between Heacham & Hunstanton. Near Hunstanton rdbt with water tower

This delightful 16th-century, Grade II listed house has been beautifully restored. The property is approached via a winding driveway through landscaped grounds to the front of the hotel. Public areas include a smart dining room, a sunny conservatory and a cosy bar which leads out onto a terrace. The bedrooms are very stylish and have modern facilities.

Rooms 45 (32 annexe) (10 fmly) (12 GF) **S** £65-£185; **D** £75-£195 (incl. bkfst)* **Facilities** FTV WiFi ⅃ 18 Swimming pools & leisure facilities available at sister resort Xmas New Year **Conf** Class 35 Board 20 Thtr 40 **Parking** 55 **Notes** LB ⊗ Civ Wed 100

HEATHROW AIRPORT (LONDON)
Greater London

See also **Slough & Staines-upon-Thames**

Novotel London Heathrow Airport

★★★★ 77% HOTEL PLAN 1 A3

NOVOTEL
HOTELS & RESORTS

tel: 01895 431431 **Cherry Ln UB7 9HB**
email: H1551-gm@accor.com **web:** www.novotel.com
dir: M4 junct 4, follow Uxbridge signs on A408. Keep left, take 2nd exit off traffic island into Cherry Ln signed West Drayton. Hotel on left

Conveniently located for Heathrow Airport and the motorway network, this modern hotel provides comfortable accommodation. The large, airy indoor atrium creates a sense of space in the public areas, which include an all-day restaurant and bar, meeting rooms, fitness centre and swimming pool. Ample secure parking is available.

Rooms 1/8 (1/8 fmly) (10 GF) **S** £50-£250; **D** £50-£300* **Facilities** FTV WiFi ⅃ HL ⊕ Gym Xmas **Conf** Class 100 Board 90 Thtr 250 **Services** Lift Air con **Parking** 100 **Notes** Civ Wed 160

DoubleTree by Hilton London Heathrow Airport

fOCUShotels
management limited

★★★★ 75% HOTEL PLAN 1 A3

tel: 020 8564 4450 & 8564 4458 **Bath Rd, Cranford TW5 9QE**
email: reservations@doubletree-heathrow.com **web:** www.doubletree3.hilton.com
dir: M4 junct 3 follow signs to Heathrow Terminals 1, 2 & 3. Hotel on right of A4 Bath Rd

This well presented hotel is conveniently situated just three miles from Heathrow Airport. Bedrooms are located in a smart block and all are well appointed for both business and leisure guests; each has a flat-screen TV, climate control and good lighting. Arts Bar and Brasserie lead from a contemporary open-plan reception area. Chargeable car park on site.

Rooms 200 (21 fmly) (38 GF) ⅃ **Facilities** FTV WiFi ⅃ Gym **Conf** Class 35 Board 30 Thtr 70 **Services** Lift Air con **Parking** 65 **Notes** ⊗

Leonardo Heathrow Airport Hotel

★★★★ 74% HOTEL PLAN 1 A3

tel: 020 8990 0000 **Bath Rd UB7 0DP**
email: res.heathrow@leonardo-hotels.com **web:** www.leonardo-hotels.com

The Leonardo Heathrow Hotel is conveniently located on Bath Road just a couple of minutes from the Heathrow Terminals and only 15 minutes by express from Central London. This hotel offers modern accommodation, a good range of meeting and event rooms, a large open-plan bar and restaurant and plenty of parking on site. Free Wifi is available throughout the hotel.

Rooms 230 ⅃ **S** fr £59; **D** fr £59* **Facilities** Spa STV FTV WiFi ⅃ HL Gym Xmas New Year **Conf** Class 60 Board 80 Thtr 120 **Services** Lift Air con **Parking** 180 **Notes** LB

H

HEATHROW AIRPORT (LONDON) *continued*

Best Western Plus Park Grand London Heathrow

★★★★ 73% HOTEL PLAN 1 B3

tel: 020 7479 2266 & 3118 9600 **449 Great West Rd TW5 0BY**
email: john@montcalm.co.uk **web:** www.parkgrandheathrow.co.uk
dir: *From A4 Great Western Rd, turn into Jersey Rd, 3rd exit at rdbt, turn left. Hotel on the left*

This modern hotel is in a convenient location just five miles from London Heathrow Airport and with easy access to Central London. The hotel is modern in style with spacious open-plan public areas including a stylish bar and restaurant. Bedrooms are also modern in style and are very comfortable; all fully air-conditioned and benefiting from digital TV and complimentary WiFi. Parking is available on site.

Rooms 124 (14 fmly) ☀ **Facilities** STV FTV WiFi ⊳ HL Gym **Conf** Class 60 Board 40 Thtr 70 **Services** Lift Air con **Parking** 38 **Notes** ⊗ Civ Wed 80

The Continental Hotel

★★★ 79% HOTEL PLAN 1 B2

tel: 020 8572 3131 & 8538 5883 **29-31 Lampton Rd TW3 1JA**
email: reservations@thecontinental-hotel.com **web:** www.thecontinental-hotel.com
dir: *A4, right onto A3006, left onto A3005 then left onto Lampton Rd*

This hotel enjoys a prime location just a few minutes walk from Hounslow Central Line; central London can be reached in 40 minutes. The bedrooms are air conditioned, and complimentary broadband is available. The bedroom en suites are marble-clad wet rooms with power showers. The on-site Golds Gym has a 21-metre indoor pool, a state-of-the-art fitness centre and beauty treatment rooms.

Rooms 70 (8 fmly) ☀ **D** £70-£150 (incl. bkfst)* **Facilities** Spa STV FTV WiFi ⊳ 🏊 Gym 🎵 Xmas New Year **Services** Lift Air con **Parking** 70 **Notes** LB ⊗

Ramada Hounslow - Heathrow East

★★★ 76% HOTEL PLAN 1 B2

tel: 020 8538 1230 **8-10 Lampton Rd TW3 1JL**
email: gm@ramadahounslow.co.uk **web:** www.ramada.co.uk/hounslow
dir: *A4 Bath Rd, A3006, into Lampton Rd A3005*

A purpose-built hotel situated in the centre of Hounslow, within walking distance of the tube station and with easy access to the motorway network. The accommodation is comfortable and offers a range of amenities. The public areas are light and airy, and parking is available.

Rooms 96 (11 fmly) (4 GF) **Facilities** FTV WiFi 🎵 Xmas New Year **Conf** Class 50 Board 60 Thtr 100 **Services** Lift Air con **Parking** 20 **Notes** ⊗

Premier Inn Hayes Heathrow

BUDGET HOTEL PLAN 1 A4

tel: 0871 527 8504 *(Calls cost 13p per minute plus your phone company's access charge)*
362 Uxbridge Rd UB4 0HF
web: www.premierinn.com
dir: *M4 junct 3, A312 N straight across next rdbt onto dual carriageway, at A4020 junct turn left, hotel 100yds on right*

High quality, budget accommodation ideal for both families and business travellers. Spacious, en suite bedrooms feature tea and coffee making facilities, and Freeview TV in most hotels. Internet access and WiFi are available for a small fee. The adjacent family restaurant features a wide and varied menu. See also the Hotel Groups pages.

Rooms 86

Premier Inn Heathrow Airport (Bath Road)

BUDGET HOTEL PLAN 1 A3

tel: 0871 527 8508 *(Calls cost 13p per minute plus your phone company's access charge)*
15 Bath Rd TW6 2AB
web: www.premierinn.com
dir: *M4 junct 4, follow signs for Heathrow Terminals 1, 2 & 3. Left onto Bath Rd signed A4/London. Hotel on right after 0.5m*

Rooms 594

Premier Inn Heathrow Airport (M4 Jct 4)

BUDGET HOTEL PLAN 1 A3

tel: 0871 527 8510 *(Calls cost 13p per minute plus your phone company's access charge)*
Shepiston Ln, Heathrow Airport UB3 1RW
web: www.premierinn.com
dir: *M4 junct 4 take 3rd exit off rdbt. Hotel on right*

Rooms 134

Premier Inn Heathrow Airport Terminal 5

BUDGET HOTEL PLAN 1 A3

tel: 0871 527 9344 *(Calls cost 13p per minute plus your phone company's access charge)*
Bath Rd, Hillingdon UB7 0EB
web: www.premierinn.com
dir: *M25 junct 14, follow A3113/Heathrow T4 & Cargo signs. At rdbt 1st left onto A3044, at next rdbt 3rd exit signed Longford. Hotel approx 250yds on left*

Rooms 400

Premier Inn London Brentford

BUDGET HOTEL PLAN 1 C3

tel: 0871 527 9560 *(Calls cost 13p per minute plus your phone company's access charge)*
Alfa Laval, Great West Rd, Hounslow TW8 9AD
web: www.premierinn.com
dir: *M4 junct 2, to Chiswick Rdbt. Take 5th exit onto A4 (keep right to next rdbt). Take 1st exit, hotel on right*

Rooms 124

Ibis Budget London Hounslow

AA Advertised PLAN 1 B2

tel: 020 8577 9137 **20-28 Staines Rd TW3 3JS**
email: H6465@accor.com **web:** www.ibishotel.com
dir: *M4 junct 3, take A312 exit, A4 right on Willingham Road, left on Staines Road, hotel on right*

Modern, budget hotel offering comfortable accommodation in bright and practical bedrooms. Breakfast is self-service and dinner is available in the restaurant.

Rooms 148 ☀ **Facilities** STV FTV WiFi HL **Services** Lift **Parking** 27

Ibis London Heathrow Airport

AA Advertised PLAN 1 A3

tel: 020 8759 4888 **112/114 Bath Rd UB3 5AL**
email: H0794@accor.com **web:** www.ibishotel.com/heathrow
dir: *Follow Heathrow Terminals 1, 2 & 3 signs, then onto spur road, exit at sign for A4/ Central London. Hotel 0.5m on left*

Modern, budget hotel offering comfortable accommodation in bright and practical bedrooms. Breakfast is self-service and dinner is available in the restaurant.

Rooms 351 (24 fmly) (39 GF) **Facilities** WiFi **Conf** Class 16 Board 16 Thtr 20 **Services** Lift Air con **Parking** 150

Sofitel London Heathrow

AA Advertised ⓢⓢⓢ PLAN 1 A3

tel: 020 8757 7777 & 8757 7725
Terminal 5, Wentworth Dr, London Heathrow Airport TW6 2GD
email: slh@sofitelheathrow.com **web:** www.sofitelheathrow.com
dir: *M25 junct 14. At rdbt take 2nd exit, after 80mtrs turn left. Hotel on right*

This is the only Heathrow Airport hotel with direct access to Terminal 5 via a covered walkway and Terminals 1, 2, 3 and 4 via courtesy of the Heathrow Express/ Connect rail connection. It is only 21 minutes from Central London by train. Sofitel London Heathrow boasts 605 non-smoking bedrooms including 27 suites, 45 meeting rooms, 2 restaurants, 2 bars and a tea salon as well as private dining options. The hotel also offers a hair salon, a state-of-the-art health spa and gym, as well as on-site car park.

Rooms 605 (38 GF) ⋒ **Facilities** Spa STV FTV WiFi Gym **Conf** Class 820 Board 80 Thtr 1200 **Services** Lift Air con **Parking** 360 **Notes** ⊗ Civ Wed 220

Renaissance London Heathrow Hotel

RENAISSANCE®
LONDON HEATHROW HOTEL

AA Advertised PLAN 1 A3

tel: 020 8897 6363 **Bath Rd TW6 2AQ**
email: rc3@renaissanceheathrow.co.uk **web:** www.renaissancelondonheathrow.co.uk
dir: *M4 junct 4 take spur road towards airport, then 2nd left. At rdbt, 2nd exit signed 'Renaissance Hotel'. Hotel adjacent to Customs House*

This spacious hotel is located on the perimeter of Heathrow Airport with spectacular views of the main runway, and is within easy reach of Windsor, and motorway and rail networks to London. The hotel has excellent conference and leisure facilities.

Rooms 710 (56 GF) ⋒ **S** £69-£299; **D** £69-£299 **Facilities** STV WiFi Gym Steam room Solarium Fitness studio Beauty & massage treatment Personal trainer **Conf** Class 300 Board 80 Thtr 450 Del from £199 to £299 **Services** Lift Air con **Parking** 700 **Notes** LB ⊗

HELLIDON
Northamptonshire
Map 11 SP55

Hellidon Lakes Golf & Spa Hotel

★★★★ 78% HOTEL

tel: 01327 262550 **NN11 6GG**
email: hellidonlakes@qhotels.co.uk **web:** www.qhotels.co.uk
dir: *Off A361 between Daventry & Banbury, signed*

Some 220 acres of beautiful countryside, which include 27 holes of golf and 12 lakes, combine to form a rather spectacular backdrop to this impressive hotel. Bedroom styles vary, from ultra smart, modern rooms through to those in the original wing that offer superb views. There is an extensive range of facilities available, from meeting rooms to a swimming pool, gym and ten-pin bowling. Golfers of all levels can try some of the world's most challenging courses on the indoor golf simulator.

Rooms 110 (5 fmly) ⋒ **Facilities** Spa FTV WiFi HL ⓢ ⌁ 27 Putt green Fishing Gym Beauty therapist Indoor smart golf 10-pin bowling Steam room Coarse fishing lake Xmas New Year **Conf** Class 150 Board 80 Thtr 300 **Services** Lift **Parking** 200 **Notes** Civ Wed 220

HELMSLEY
North Yorkshire
Map 19 SE68

INSPECTORS' CHOICE

Feversham Arms Hotel & Verbena Spa

★★★★ ⑳⑳ HOTEL

tel: 01439 770766 **1-8 High St YO62 5AG**
email: info@fevershamarmshotel.com **web:** www.fevershamarmshotel.com
dir: *A168 signed Thirsk A1, A170 or A64 signed York from A1 to York North, B1363 to Helmsley. Hotel 125mtrs from Market Place*

This long established hotel lies just round the corner from the main square, and under caring ownership proves to be a refined operation, yet without airs and graces. There are several lounge areas and a high-ceilinged conservatory restaurant where menus are created with skill and minimal fuss from good local ingredients. The bedrooms, including four air-conditioned poolside suites (some with wood-burners) and spa suites with balconies or French balconies, all have their own individual character and decor. Expect Egyptian cotton sheets, duck down duvets and Bang and Olufsen TVs with DVD and CD player. The spa offers a comprehensive range of pampering treatments.

Rooms 33 (9 fmly) (8 GF) ⋒ **S** fr £108; **D** fr £120 (incl. bkfst)* **Facilities** Spa STV FTV WiFi Sauna Saunarium Aromatherapy room Monsoon showers Relaxation lounge Xmas New Year **Conf** Class 20 Board 24 Thtr 35 Del from £180 to £380* **Services** Lift **Parking** 50 **Notes** LB Civ Wed 50

HELMSLEY *continued*

Black Swan Hotel
★★★★ 78% HOTEL

tel: 01439 770466 **Market Place YO62 5BJ**
email: enquiries@blackswan-helmsley.co.uk **web:** www.blackswan-helmsley.co.uk
dir: *A1 junct 49, A168, A170 east, hotel 14m from Thirsk*

People have been visiting this establishment for over 200 years and it has become a landmark that dominates the market square. The hotel is renowned for its hospitality and friendliness; many of the staff are long-serving and dedicated. The bedrooms are stylish and include a junior suite and feature rooms. Dinner in the award-winning restaurant is the highlight of any stay. The hotel has a Tearoom and Patisserie that is open daily.

Rooms 45 (4 fmly) **Facilities** STV FTV WiFi Xmas New Year **Conf** Class 30 Board 26 Thtr 50 **Parking** 40 **Notes** Civ Wed 90

The Pheasant Hotel
★★★ ◉◉ COUNTRY HOUSE HOTEL

tel: 01439 771241 **Mill St, Harome YO62 5JG**
email: reservations@thepheasanthotel.com **web:** www.thepheasanthotel.com
dir: *Leave A1(M) at Thirsk, follow A170 E towards Helmsley/Scarborough & then through Helmsley. Right after 0.5m to Harome, follow road for 2.5m*

The Pheasant Hotel sits in a delightful small North Yorkshire village, overlooking the village pond. The public areas are delightful in a very country house style, with ample outside seating areas that are ideal for a delightful afternoon tea. The rooms are spacious, very well appointed and have a luxury feel to them. The small heated pool is easily accessible and the hotel has ample parking. Food is the highlight of the stay with the menu boasting local produce and inventive cooking.

Rooms 16 (2 fmly) (3 GF) **S** £90-£155; **D** £190-£270 (incl. bkfst) **Facilities** FTV WiFi ⓢ ⓢ Xmas New Year **Conf** Class 30 Board 20 Thtr 30 Del from £200 to £300 **Parking** 16 **Notes** Civ Wed 60

HELSTON Cornwall — Map 2 SW62

Premier Inn Helston

BUDGET HOTEL

tel: 0871 527 8512 *(Calls cost 13p per minute plus your phone company's access charge)* **Clodgey Ln TR13 8FZ**
web: www.premierinn.com
dir: *A39 towards Falmouth. Right onto A394 towards Helston, 8m. At rdbt 1st exit (Helston bypass) signed Penzance (A394)/Lizard. Hotel at next rdbt on left. NB for Sat Nav use TR13 0QD*

High quality, budget accommodation ideal for both families and business travellers. Spacious, en suite bedrooms feature tea and coffee making facilities, and Freeview TV in most hotels. Internet access and WiFi are available for a small fee. The adjacent family restaurant features a wide and varied menu. See also the Hotel Groups pages.

Rooms 50

HEMEL HEMPSTEAD Hertfordshire — Map 6 TL00

Aubrey Park Hotel
★★★★ 78% ◉ HOTEL

tel: 01582 792105 **Hemel Hempstead Rd, Redbourn AL3 7AF**
email: reception@aubreypark.co.uk **web:** www.aubreypark.co.uk
dir: *M1 junct 9 follow Hemel Hempstead & St Albans signs for 3m, straight across 2 rdbts onto B487 signed Hemel Hempstead. Hotel on right*

The hotel is conveniently located a short drive from the historic Roman city of St Albans, close to the M1 and the M25, and is an ideal venue for both corporate and leisure guests. Recently refurbished, the hotel is modern with attentive staff, good food, ample parking and extensive, well-equipped meeting areas.

Rooms 137 (10 fmly) (65 GF) **S** £49-£149; **D** £49-£149* **Facilities** FTV WiFi ⓢ Xmas New Year **Conf** Class 96 Board 65 Thtr 200 **Services** Lift **Parking** 129 **Notes** LB Civ Wed 85

The Watermill

★★★ 74% HOTEL

tel: 01442 349955 **London Rd, Bourne End HP1 2RJ**
email: info@hotelwatermill.co.uk **web:** www.hotelwatermill.co.uk
dir: *From M25 & M1 follow signs to Aylesbury on A41, A4251 to Bourne End. Hotel 0.25m on right*

In the heart of the county this modern hotel has been built around an old flour mill on the banks of the River Bulbourne with water meadows adjacent. The thoughtfully equipped, contemporary bedrooms are located in three annexes situated around the complex. A good range of air-conditioned conference and meeting rooms complement the lounge bar and restaurant.

Rooms 71 (71 annexe) (10 fmly) (35 GF) (8 smoking) 🐾 **Facilities** STV FTV WiFi Fishing Xmas New Year **Conf** Class 150 Board 125 Thtr 200 **Parking** 100 **Notes** ⊗ Civ Wed 180

Premier Inn Hemel Hempstead Central

BUDGET HOTEL

tel: 0871 527 8514 *(Calls cost 13p per minute plus your phone company's access charge)*
Moor End Rd HP1 1BT
web: www.premierinn.com
dir: *M1 junct 8, A414, follow town centre signs. Right at 1st mini rdbt, right at 2nd mini rdbt into Seldon Hill Rd, follow Riverside car park signs (footbridge to hotel from floor 3). NB for Sat Nav use HP1 1BT*

High quality, budget accommodation ideal for both families and business travellers. Spacious, en suite bedrooms feature tea and coffee making facilities, and Freeview TV in most hotels. Internet access and WiFi are available for a small fee. The adjacent family restaurant features a wide and varied menu. See also the Hotel Groups pages.

Rooms 114

Premier Inn Hemel Hempstead West

BUDGET HOTEL

tel: 0871 527 8516 *(Calls cost 13p per minute plus your phone company's access charge)*
A41 Service Area, Bourne End HP1 2SB
web: www.premierinn.com
dir: *M25 junct 20, A41 exit at services. Or from M1 junct 8, A414, A41, exit at services*

Rooms 62

Hotel du Vin Henley-on-Thames

★★★★ 76% ⚛ TOWN HOUSE HOTEL

tel: 01491 848400 & 0844 736 4258
(Calls cost 5p per minute plus your phone company's access charge) **New St RG9 2BP**
email: info.henley@hotelduvin.com **web:** www.hotelduvin.com
dir: *M4 junct 8/9 signed High Wycombe, 2nd exit onto A404 in 2m. A4130 to Henley, over bridge, through lights, into Hart St, right into Bell St, right into New St, hotel on right*

Situated just 50 yards from the water's edge, this hotel retains the character and much of the architecture of its former life as a brewery. Food, and naturally wine, take on a strong focus here and guests will find an interesting mix of dishes to choose from; there are three private dining rooms where the fermentation room and old malt house once were; alfresco dining is popular when the weather permits. Bedrooms provide comfort, style and a good range of facilities including power showers. Parking is available and there is a drop-off point in the courtyard.

Rooms 43 (4 fmly) (4 GF) 🐾 **Facilities** STV FTV WiFi ⌕ Xmas New Year **Conf** Class 20 Board 36 Thtr 56 **Services** Air con **Parking** 46 **Notes** Civ Wed 60

Milsoms Henley-on-Thames

RESTAURANT WITH ROOMS

tel: 01491 845780 & 845789 **20 Market Place RG9 2AH**
email: henley@milsomshotel.co.uk **web:** www.milsomshotel.co.uk
dir: *In centre of town, close to town hall*

Seven en suite bedrooms are located in a listed building above the Loch Fyne Restaurant in Henley's Market Place. Each bedroom is individually appointed and equipped to meet the needs of the modern traveller; particular care has been taken to incorporate original features into the contemporary design. The restaurant has a commitment to offer ethically sourced seafood.

Rooms 7 (2 fmly)

See also **Leominster**

Holme Lacy House Hotel

★★★★ 74% COUNTRY HOUSE HOTEL

WARNER LEISURE HOTELS

tel: 01432 870870 **Holme Lacy HR2 6LP**
web: www.warnerleisurehotels.co.uk
dir: *B4399 at Holme Lacy, take lane opposite college. Hotel 500mtrs on right*

This is a grand Grade I listed mansion with a rich history, just a short drive from Hereford, set in twenty acres of superb parkland in the heart of the Wye Valley. The well-appointed bedrooms are comfortable and vary in size and style. There's plenty to do here, with a full daily entertainment programme, an indoor pool, and health and beauty treatments. The three restaurants provide carefully selected menus of quality cuisine. Exclusively for adults (above 21 years old).

Rooms 181 (150 annexe) (53 GF) 🐾 **Facilities** Spa FTV WiFi HL ⊗ ⛳ Putt green Fishing 🏌 Gym Archery Rifle shooting Aquafit Yoga 🎵 Xmas New Year **Services** Lift **Parking** 200 **Notes** ⊗ No children 21yrs

H

H

HEREFORD *continued*

HIGHLY RECOMMENDED

Castle House

★★★ 86% ◉◉ HOTEL

tel: 01432 356321 **Castle St HR1 2NW**
email: info@castlehse.co.uk **web:** www.castlehse.co.uk
dir: *Follow signs to City Centre East. At junct of Commercial Rd & Union St follow brown hotel signs*

Enjoying a prime city centre location, with a terraced garden leading to the castle moat, this delightful Grade II-listed Georgian mansion is the epitome of elegance and sophistication. The character bedrooms are equipped with every luxury to ensure a memorable stay and are complemented perfectly by the well-proportioned and restful lounge and bar. The elegant topiary-themed restaurant is the setting for award-winning modern British cuisine.

Rooms 24 (8 annexe) (4 GF) 🐾 **S** £130-£210; **D** £150-£250 (incl. bkfst)*
Facilities STV FTV WiFi ⇄ Xmas New Year **Services** Lift **Parking** 12 **Notes** LB ⊗ Civ Wed 50

See advert on opposite page

Three Counties Hotel

★★★ 77% HOTEL

tel: 01432 299955 **Belmont Rd HR2 7BP**
email: enquiries@threecountieshotel.co.uk **web:** www.threecountieshotel.co.uk
dir: *On A465 Abergavenny road*

Just a mile west of the city centre, this large, privately owned, modern complex has well-equipped, spacious bedrooms; many are located in separate single-storey buildings around the extensive car park. There is a spacious, comfortable lounge, a traditional bar and an attractive restaurant.

Rooms 60 (32 annexe) (4 fmly) (46 GF) **S** £67-£85; **D** £67-£100* **Facilities** STV FTV WiFi **Conf** Class 200 Board 120 Thtr 450 Del from £110 to £120* **Parking** 250 **Notes** LB Civ Wed 350

Premier Inn Hereford

BUDGET HOTEL

tel: 0871 527 8518 *(Calls cost 13p per minute plus your phone company's access charge)*
Holmer Rd, Holmer HR4 9RS
web: www.premierinn.com
dir: *From N: M5 junct 7, A4103 to Worcester. M50 junct 4, A49 (Leominster road). Hotel 800yds on left*

High quality, budget accommodation ideal for both families and business travellers. Spacious, en suite bedrooms feature tea and coffee making facilities, and Freeview TV in most hotels. Internet access and WiFi are available for a small fee. The adjacent family restaurant features a wide and varied menu. See also the Hotel Groups pages.

Rooms 101

| HERNE BAY | Map 7 TR16 |
| Kent | |

Premier Inn Canterbury North/Herne Bay

BUDGET HOTEL

tel: 0871 527 8520 *(Calls cost 13p per minute plus your phone company's access charge)*
Blacksole Farm, Margate Rd CT6 6LA
web: www.premierinn.com
dir: *From M2 junct 7 follow Canterbury signs, A299 signed Ramsgate/Margate. Exit at Broomfield & Beltinge. Hotel just off rdbt*

High quality, budget accommodation ideal for both families and business travellers. Spacious, en suite bedrooms feature tea and coffee making facilities, and Freeview TV in most hotels. Internet access and WiFi are available for a small fee. The adjacent family restaurant features a wide and varied menu. See also the Hotel Groups pages.

Rooms 50

H

HESWALL
Merseyside

Map 15 SJ28

Premier Inn Wirral (Heswall)

BUDGET HOTEL

tel: 0871 527 9178 *(Calls cost 13p per minute plus your phone company's access charge)*
Chester Rd, Gayton CH60 3SD
web: www.premierinn.com
dir: *M53 junct 4, A5137 signed Heswall. In 3m left at next rdbt, hotel on left*

High quality, budget accommodation ideal for both families and business travellers. Spacious, en suite bedrooms feature tea and coffee making facilities, and Freeview TV in most hotels. Internet access and WiFi are available for a small fee. The adjacent family restaurant features a wide and varied menu. See also the Hotel Groups pages.

Rooms 63

HETHERSETT
Norfolk

Map 13 TG10

Park Farm Hotel

★★★★ 77% @ HOTEL

tel: 01603 810264 **NR9 3DL**
email: enq@parkfarm-hotel.co.uk **web:** www.parkfarm-hotel.co.uk
dir: *5m S of Norwich, exit A11 onto B1172*

Park Farm is an elegant Georgian farmhouse set in landscaped grounds surrounded by open countryside. The property has been owned and run by the Gowing family since 1958. Bedrooms are pleasantly decorated and tastefully furnished; some rooms have patio doors with a sun terrace. Public rooms include a stylish conservatory, a lounge bar, a smart restaurant and superb leisure facilities.

Rooms 53 (16 annexe) (15 fmly) (26 GF) ↟↖ **S** £90-£165; **D** £105-£230 (incl. bkfst)*
Facilities Spa FTV WiFi ⌖ supervised Gym Beauty salon Hairdressing Xmas New Year **Conf** Class 50 Board 50 Thtr 120 Del from £135 to £160* **Parking** 150 **Notes** LB ⊗ Civ Wed 100

HETTON
North Yorkshire

Map 18 SD95

The Angel Inn

@ @ RESTAURANT WITH ROOMS

tel: 01756 730263 **BD23 6LT**
email: info@angelhetton.co.uk **web:** www.angelhetton.co.uk
dir: *B6265 from Skipton towards Grassington. At Rylstone turn left by pond, follow signs to Hetton*

This roadside inn is steeped in history; parts of the building go back more than 500 years. The restaurant and bar are in the main building, which has ivy and green canopies at the front. Food is a highlight of any stay, offering excellent ingredients, skilfully prepared and carefully presented. The large, stylish bedrooms are across the road in a converted barn which has great views of the Dales, private parking and its own wine cave.

Rooms 9

H

HEXHAM
Northumberland

Map 21 NY96

Langley Castle Hotel
★★★★ 82% ◉◉ HOTEL

tel: 01434 688888 **Langley NE47 5LU**
email: manager@langleycastle.com web: www.langleycastle.com
dir: *From A69 S on A686 for 2m. Hotel on right*

Langley is a magnificent 14th-century fortified castle, with its own chapel, set in ten acres of parkland. There is an award-winning restaurant, a comfortable drawing room and a cosy bar. Bedrooms are furnished with period pieces and most feature window seats. Restored buildings in the grounds have been converted into very stylish Castle View bedrooms.

Rooms 27 (18 annexe) (8 fmly) (9 GF) ⚡ **S** £129.50–£219.50; **D** £159–£279 (incl. bkfst)* **Facilities** STV WiFi ⏁ HL Xmas **Conf** Class 60 Board 40 Thtr 120 Del from £175 to £235* **Services** Lift Air con **Parking** 70 **Notes** LB ⊗ Civ Wed 120

Slaley Hall
★★★★ 80% HOTEL

QHOTELS
INSPIRED
BY YOU

tel: 01434 673350 & 0871 222 4688
(Calls cost 10p per minute plus your phone company's access charge) **Slaley NE47 0BX**
web: www.qhotels.co.uk
dir: *A1 from S to A68 link road follow signs for Slaley Hall*

One thousand acres of Northumbrian forest and parkland, two championship golf courses and indoor leisure facilities can all be found here. Spacious bedrooms are fully air conditioned, equipped with a range of extras and the deluxe rooms offer excellent standards. Public rooms include a number of lounges and dining options, including the fine-dining Dukes Grill, informal Claret Jug and the impressive main restaurant that overlooks the golf course.

Rooms 142 (18 fmly) (37 GF) ⚡ **Facilities** Spa FTV WiFi ⏁ supervised ⚓ 36 Putt green Gym Quad bikes Archery Clay pigeon shooting 4x4 driving Xmas New Year **Conf** Class 220 Board 150 Thtr 300 **Services** Lift Air con **Parking** 500 **Notes** Civ Wed 250

Battlesteads
★★★ 85% HOTEL

tel: 01434 230209 **Wark On Tyne NE48 3LS**
email: info@battlesteads.com web: www.battlesteads.com

Battlesteads is located in the peaceful and picturesque village of Wark in the heart of Hadrian's Wall country. Battlesteads has been described as one of the greenest hotels in the country with a host of different eco-friendly systems in place, but it is much more than this. Boasting an observatory to make the best of the area's Dark Skies status, and an award-winning kitchen team sourcing local produce, and even growing their own items for use in the kitchen. Bedrooms are well appointed and presented with quality beds, décor and flooring as standard. The team are warm and friendly, and really do strive to go that extra mile for guests. The log-burning stove in the bar makes it the place to sit while sampling one of a host of real ales available.

Rooms 22 (5 annexe) (2 fmly) (4 GF) ⚡ **Facilities** FTV WiFi ⏁ **Parking** 30 **Notes** Closed 25 Dec Civ Wed 70

Best Western Beaumont Hotel
★★★ 83% HOTEL

BW Best Western.

tel: 01434 602331 **Beaumont St NE46 3LT**
email: reservations@beaumonthotelhexham.co.uk web: www.bw-beaumonthotel.co.uk
dir: *A69 towards town centre*

In a region steeped in history, this family-run hotel is located in the centre of Hexham, overlooking the park and 7th-century abbey. The hotel has two bars, a comfortable reception lounge and a first-floor restaurant. Bedrooms are a mix of traditional and contemporary; the South Wing rooms are spacious with a more contemporary feel and have flat-screen TVs.

Rooms 34 (3 fmly) ⚡ **S** £90–£95; **D** £150–£190 (incl. bkfst) **Facilities** FTV WiFi ⏁ Xmas New Year **Conf** Class 60 Board 40 Thtr 100 **Services** Lift **Parking** 16 **Notes** LB ⊗ Civ Wed 50

HIGHAM
Derbyshire
Map 16 SK35

Santo's Higham Farm Hotel
★★★ 79% HOTEL

tel: 01773 833812 **Main Rd DE55 6EH**
email: reception@santoshighamfarm.co.uk **web:** www.santoshighamfarm.co.uk
dir: *M1 junct 28, A38 towards Derby, then A61 towards Chesterfield. Onto B6013 towards Belper, hotel 300yds on right*

With panoramic views across the rolling Amber Valley, this 15th-century crook barn and farmhouse has been expertly restored and extended. There's an Italian wing and an international wing of themed bedrooms and mini suites. Freshly prepared dishes, especially fish, are available in Guiseppe's restaurant. This hotel makes an ideal romantic hideaway.

Rooms 31 (3 fmly) (7 GF) ⌁ **S** £101-£225; **D** £125-£266 (incl. bkfst)* **Facilities** FTV WiFi ⌁ Xmas New Year **Conf** Class 40 Board 34 Thtr 100 **Parking** 100 **Notes** ⊗ Civ Wcd 100

HIGHBRIDGE
Somerset
Map 4 ST34

Laburnum House Lodge Hotel
★★ 65% HOTEL

tel: 01278 781830 **Sloway Ln, West Huntspill TA9 3RJ**
email: laburnumhh@aol.com **web:** www.laburnumhousehotel.co.uk
dir: *M5 junct 22. W on A38 approx 5m, right at Crossways Inn. 300yds & left into Sloway Ln, 300yds to hotel*

This hotel is in an excellent rural location, set in its own grounds, and offers an impressive range of facilities. The spacious bedrooms are all in individual lodges with their own access, and many are suitable for families. The hotel also offers a range of meeting rooms and leisure facilities. Dogs are welcome here.

Rooms 68 (9 fmly) (68 GF) ⌁ **S** £50-£70; **D** £60-£90* **Facilities** FTV WiFi HL ⊗ ⌁ Gym **Conf** Class 60 Board 40 Thtr 100 Del from £90 to £110* **Parking** 100 **Notes** LB Civ Wed

HIGHCLERE
Hampshire
Map 5 SU45

The Yew Tree
◉◉ RESTAURANT WITH ROOMS

tel: 01635 253360 **Hollington Cross RG20 9SE**
email: info@theyewtree.co.uk **web:** www.theyewtree.co.uk
dir: *1m S of Highclere village*

Part of The Epicurean Collection, Situated in Highclere, this attractive 17th-century country inn has comfortable bedrooms decorated with William Morris print wallpaper and retaining traditional features, giving it an overall cosy feel. Great British cooking can be enjoyed in the attractively-decorated restaurant, where good use is made of high-quality produce and fresh ingredients. The garden, with its own bar and dining areas, is a real bonus feature.

Rooms 8

HIGHCLIFFE
Dorset
Map 5 SZ29

Premier Inn Christchurch/Highcliffe
BUDGET HOTEL

tel: 0871 527 9276 *(Calls cost 13p per minute plus your phone company's access charge)*
266 Lymington Rd BH23 5ET
web: www.premierinn.com
dir: *From A35 (Christchurch rdbt) onto A337 towards New Milton & Lymington. Approx 2m hotel on left*

High quality, budget accommodation ideal for both families and business travellers. Spacious, en suite bedrooms feature tea and coffee making facilities, and Freeview TV in most hotels. Internet access and WiFi are available for a small fee. The adjacent family restaurant features a wide and varied menu. See also the Hotel Groups pages.

Rooms 62

HIGH WYCOMBE
Buckinghamshire
Map 5 SU89

Premier Inn High Wycombe/Beaconsfield
BUDGET HOTEL

tel: 0871 527 8522 *(Calls cost 13p per minute plus your phone company's access charge)*
Thanstead Farm, London Rd, Loudwater HP10 9YL
web: www.premierinn.com
dir: *M40 junct 3, A40 towards High Wycombe*

High quality, budget accommodation ideal for both families and business travellers. Spacious, en suite bedrooms feature tea and coffee making facilities, and Freeview TV in most hotels. Internet access and WiFi are available for a small fee. The adjacent family restaurant features a wide and varied menu. See also the Hotel Groups pages.

Rooms 135

H

HIGH WYCOMBE *continued*

Premier Inn High Wycombe Central

BUDGET HOTEL

tel: 0871 527 9326 *(Calls cost 13p per minute plus your phone company's access charge)*
Arch Way HP13 5HL
web: www.premierinn.com
dir: *M4, junct 8/9, A404M signed Marlow & Wycombe. Exit for High Wycombe, right at rdbt (town centre) via Marlow Hill. Left at 1st mini rdbt, right at next rdbt, left signed Dovecot. Right at next junct into Arch Way, (Sainsburys on left) 1st left, left to hotel. NB for Sat Nav use HP11 2DN*

Rooms 120

HINCKLEY
Leicestershire
Map 11 SP49

Sketchley Grange Hotel

★★★★ 78% HOTEL

focus hotels
management limited

tel: 01455 251133 **Sketchley Ln, Burbage LE10 3HU**
email: info@sketchleygrangehotel.co.uk **web:** www.sketchleygrangehotel.co.uk
dir: *M69 junct 1, B4109 towards Hinckley. Left at 2nd rdbt. Into Sketchley Ln, 1st right, also Sketchley Ln*

Close to motorway connections, this hotel is peacefully set in its own grounds, and enjoys open country views. Extensive leisure facilities include a stylish health and leisure spa. There are modern meeting facilities, a choice of bars, and two dining options, together with comfortable bedrooms furnished with many extras.

Rooms 95 (10 fmly) (7 GF) **Facilities** Spa FTV WiFi ⬚ ⬚ Gym Steam room Sauna Xmas New Year **Conf** Class 150 Board 50 Thtr 280 **Services** Lift **Parking** 300 **Notes** Civ Wed 220

Premier Inn Hinckley

BUDGET HOTEL

tel: 0871 527 8524 *(Calls cost 13p per minute plus your phone company's access charge)*
Coventry Rd LE10 0NB
web: www.premierinn.com
dir: *M69 junct 1, A5 towards Nuneaton. In 2.5m right at rdbt onto B4666 signed Hinckley Town Centre. Hotel on right, entrance via Total petrol station*

High quality, budget accommodation ideal for both families and business travellers. Spacious, en suite bedrooms feature tea and coffee making facilities, and Freeview TV in most hotels. Internet access and WiFi are available for a small fee. The adjacent family restaurant features a wide and varied menu. See also the Hotel Groups pages.

Rooms 91

HINTLESHAM
Suffolk
Map 13 TM04

Hintlesham Hall Hotel

★★★★ ◉◉ HOTEL

CLASSIC BRITISH HOTELS

tel: 01473 652334 **George St IP8 3NS**
email: reservations@hintleshamhall.com **web:** www.hintleshamhall.com
dir: *4m W of Ipswich on A1071 to Hadleigh & Sudbury*

Hospitality and service are key features at this imposing Grade I listed country-house hotel, situated in 175 acres of grounds and landscaped gardens. Originally a manor house dating from the Elizabethan era, the building was extended in the 17th and 18th centuries. It was a Red Cross hospital in World War II and has been a hotel for nearly forty years. Individually decorated bedrooms offer a high degree of comfort; each one is tastefully furnished and equipped with many thoughtful touches. The new Hintlesham Spa has three treatment rooms (including one for couples), a sumptuous relaxation area, nail bar, and enclosed outdoor area with hot tub. The spacious public rooms include a series of comfortable lounges, and an elegant restaurant which serves fine classical cuisine based on top-notch and where practical, local ingredients. WiFi is available throughout. A helicopter landing area is also available.

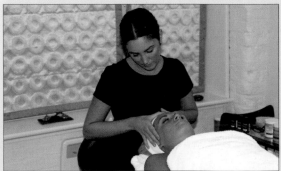

Rooms 32 (10 annexe) (9 GF) **S** £95-£160; **D** £95-£160 **Facilities** Spa FTV WiFi HL ⬚ ⬚ Health & beauty services Clay pigeon shooting ♫ Xmas New Year **Conf** Class 50 Board 32 Thtr 80 **Parking** 60 **Notes** LB Civ Wed 110

HINTON CHARTERHOUSE
Somerset

Map 4 ST75

Homewood Park Hotel & Spa
★★★★ 81% HOTEL

tel: 01225 723731 **Abbey Ln BA2 7TB**
email: info@homewoodpark.co.uk **web:** www.homewoodpark.co.uk
dir: *6m SE of Bath on A36, left at 2nd sign for Freshford*

This hotel has a delightful location in attractive parkland, close to Bath and the Longleat estate. Bedrooms are stylishly and comfortably appointed, and many enjoy splendid countryside views. The spa and leisure facilities are notable, and a meal in the restaurant should not be missed.

Rooms 21 (2 annexe) (3 fmly) (2 GF) **D** £125-£350 (incl. bkfst)* **Facilities** Spa FTV WiFi ✵ Sauna Steam room Nail bar Hydrotherapy pool Xmas New Year **Conf** Class 30 Board 25 Thtr 40 Del from £155 to £260* **Parking** 40 **Notes** LB Civ Wed 120

HITCHIN
Hertfordshire

Map 12 TL12

Needham House Hotel
★★★★ 80%  HOTEL

tel: 01462 417240 **Blakemore End Rd, Little Wymondley SG4 7JJ**
email: reservations@needhamhouse.co.uk **web:** www.needhamhouse.co.uk
dir: *Located 3m from both Hitchin & Stevenage*

Ideally situated just a short drive from the A1(M) the property is set in well-presented grounds and features a spa, gym, open-plan lounge bar, a range of meeting rooms, and a function suite. The hotel has been totally refurbished and reopened in early 2016; the bedrooms are modern and well equipped, some rooms have private terraces.

Rooms 80 **D** fr £50* **Facilities** Spa WiFi Sauna Steam room Relaxation lounge Turkish bath **Notes** ⊗ Civ Wed 150

Premier Inn Hitchin Town Centre
BUDGET HOTEL

tel: 0871 527 9578 *(Calls cost 13p per minute plus your phone company's access charge)*
Portmill Ln SG5 1DJ
web: www.premierinn.com
dir: *A1(M) junct 8, A602 (Hitchin). At 1st rdbt take 4th exit into St Johns Rd, left into Hitchin Hill. At next rdbt 2nd exit into Queen St. 4th left turn into Portmill Ln, hotel on right*

High quality, budget accommodation ideal for both families and business travellers. Spacious, en suite bedrooms feature tea and coffee making facilities, and Freeview TV in most hotels. Internet access and WiFi are available for a small fee. The adjacent family restaurant features a wide and varied menu. See also the Hotel Groups pages.

Rooms 60

HOCKLEY HEATH
West Midlands

Map 10 SP17

Nuthurst Grange Hotel
★★★★ 79% HOTEL

tel: 01564 783972 **Nuthurst Grange Ln B94 5NL**
email: info@nuthurst-grange.co.uk **web:** www.nuthurst-grange.co.uk
dir: *Exit A3400, 0.5m south of Hockley Heath. Turn at sign into Nuthurst Grange Lane*

A stunning avenue is the approach to this country-house hotel, set amid several acres of well-tended gardens and mature grounds, with views over rolling countryside. The spacious bedrooms and bathrooms offer considerable luxury and comfort, and public areas include restful lounges, meeting rooms and a sunny restaurant. The kitchen brigade produces highly imaginative British and French cuisine, complemented by very attentive, professional restaurant service.

Rooms 19 (7 fmly) (2 GF) **Facilities** STV FTV WiFi ✦ **Conf** Class 50 Board 35 Thtr 100 **Parking** 80 **Notes** ⊗ RS 24-26 Dec Civ Wed 100

HOLLINGBOURNE
Kent

Map 7 TQ85

Mercure Maidstone, Great Danes Hotel
★★★★ 71% HOTEL

tel: 0844 815 9045 *(Calls cost 7p per minute plus your phone company's access charge)* **ME17 1RE**
email: info@mercuremaidstone.co.uk **web:** www.mercuremaidstone.co.uk
dir: *M20 junct 8, follow Leeds Castle signs, at 2nd rdbt turn right*

The property is set within 26 acres of private grounds just a few minutes from junction 8 of the M20 and close to the channel ports and Eurotunnel. The smartly appointed bedrooms are well equipped and suitable for business and leisure guests. Public rooms include Art's Bar and Grill as well as an indoor pool, fitness centre and a 9-hole golf course.

Rooms 126 (15 fmly) **Facilities** FTV WiFi ✦ Gym Squash Steam room Beauty treatments **Conf** Class 220 Board 90 Thtr 650 **Parking** 500 **Notes** Civ Wed 650

HOLT
Norfolk

Map 13 TG03

The Pheasant Hotel & Restaurant
★★★★ 81% HOTEL

tel: 01263 588382 & 588540 **Coast Rd, Kelling NR25 7EG**
email: enquiries@pheasanthotelnorfolk.co.uk **web:** www.pheasanthotelnorfolk.co.uk
dir: *On A149 coast road, mid-way between Sheringham & Blakeney*

The Pheasant is a charming country house hotel set in its own extensive grounds, enjoying a peaceful rural location in the small village of Kelling, making it an ideal base from which to explore the beautiful North Norfolk coast and the surrounding villages of Cley and Blakeney. All bedrooms are beautifully presented and most comfortable. Afternoon tea is served on the terrace on warmer days and the lounge bar is cosy.

Rooms 32 (1 fmly) (24 GF) **Facilities** FTV WiFi ✦ Xmas New Year **Conf** Class 50 Thtr 100 **Notes** LB Civ Wed 200

H

HOLT *continued*

The Lawns

 RESTAURANT WITH ROOMS

---

tel: 01263 713390 **26 Station Rd NR25 6BS**
email: info@lawnshotelholt.co.uk **web:** www.lawnshotelholt.co.uk
dir: *A148 (Cromer road). 0.25m from Holt rdbt, turn left, 400yds along Station Rd*

The Lawns is a superb Georgian house situated in the centre of this delightful north Norfolk market town. The open-plan public areas include a large wine bar, a conservatory and a smart restaurant. The spacious bedrooms are tastefully appointed with co-ordinated soft furnishings and have many thoughtful touches.

Rooms 10 (2 annexe)

HONITON
Devon   Map 4 ST10

The Deer Park Country House Hotel

★★★★ 77% COUNTRY HOUSE HOTEL

---

tel: 01404 41266 **Weston EX14 3PG**
email: admin@deerparkcountryhotel.co.uk **web:** www.deerparkcountryhotel.co.uk
dir: *A30, take slip road into Honiton signed Turks Head. Next right then next left into Heathpark Industrial Estate. Hotel approx 1.6m*

This country manor hotel is set in 80 acres of gardens, which includes an alfresco dining area with wood-burning oven and a walled kitchen garden. The hotel is just a short drive from Honiton and has easy access to the A30. The spacious accommodation is located in both the main house and separate, recently refurbished garden rooms; there is even a luxurious treehouse with stunning views across the countryside. Deer Park is ideal for both business and leisure guests, and its picturesque setting makes it ideal for weddings and events. The hotel also boasts the Priory Collection, the largest collection of sporting memorabilia in the country.

Rooms 32 (17 annexe) (2 fmly) (4 GF) ↖ **S** £65-£195; **D** £125-£240 (incl. bkfst)*
Facilities STV FTV WiFi Fishing ⚓ Clay shooting Archery Quad Bikes Segways Xmas New Year **Conf** Class 20 Board 20 Thtr 250 Del from £145 to £165* **Parking** 70
Notes LB Civ Wed 350

Premier Inn Honiton

BUDGET HOTEL

---

tel: 0871 527 9508 *(Calls cost 13p per minute plus your phone company's access charge)*
Turks Head Ln EX14 1BQ
email: Honiton.PI@premierinn.com **web:** www.premierinn.com
dir: *From A30 S'bound, exit at 'Turks Head' junction signed Sidmouth & Cullompton. Turn left, hotel on left. Or from A30 N'bound, follow Honiton & Heathpark signs. Hotel on left*

High quality, budget accommodation ideal for both families and business travellers. Spacious, en suite bedrooms feature tea and coffee making facilities, and Freeview TV in most hotels. Internet access and WiFi are available for a small fee. The adjacent family restaurant features a wide and varied menu. See also the Hotel Groups pages.

Rooms 66

HOPE
Derbyshire   Map 16 SK18

Losehill House Hotel & Spa

★★★★ 78% HOTEL

---

tel: 01433 621219 **Lose Hill Ln, Edale Rd S33 6AF**
email: info@losehillhouse.co.uk **web:** www.losehillhouse.co.uk
dir: *A6187 into Hope. Into Edale Rd opposite church. 1m, left & follow signs to hotel*

Situated down a quiet leafy lane, this hotel occupies a secluded spot in the Peak District National Park. Bedrooms are comfortable and beautifully appointed. The outdoor hot tub, with stunning views over the valley, is a real indulgence; a heated swimming pool, sauna and spa treatments are also on offer. The views from the Orangery Restaurant are a real delight.

Rooms 24 (3 annexe) (4 fmly) (3 GF) ↖ **D** £160-£250 (incl. bkfst)* **Facilities** Spa FTV WiFi ⌚ 🎵 Xmas New Year **Conf** Class 20 Board 15 Thtr 30 **Services** Lift **Parking** 30 **Notes** LB ⊗ Civ Wed 100

HORLEY

Hotels are listed under Gatwick Airport

HORNCASTLE
Lincolnshire   Map 17 TF26

Admiral Rodney Hotel

★★★ 78% HOTEL

---

tel: 01507 523131 **North St LN9 5DX**
email: admiralrodney@innmail.co.uk **web:** www.admiralrodney.com

The Admiral Rodney, a former coaching inn, is located in the picturesque town of Horncastle. Public areas are mostly open plan with a large lounge and bar area to relax in. The spacious bedrooms are well appointed and include up-to-date technology; free WiFi is also available throughout the hotel. A brasserie-style menu is served throughout the day and evening, and guests can eat in either the Courtyard Restaurant or alfresco when the weather's warmer. Large function rooms and extensive parking are all available. The staff are very welcoming.

Rooms 31 (4 fmly) (7 GF) **Facilities** STV FTV WiFi ↕ HL **Conf** Class 60 Board 40 Thtr 140 **Services** Lift **Parking** 60 **Notes** Civ Wed 100

Magpies Restaurant with Rooms

 RESTAURANT WITH ROOMS

---

tel: 01507 527004 **71-73 East St LN9 6AA**
email: info@magpiesrestaurant.co.uk **web:** www.magpiesrestaurant.co.uk
dir: *A158 into Horncastle, continue at lights. On left opposite Trinity Centre*

This quaint and charming property is nestled in the popular market town of Horncastle. The spacious en suite accommodation features three individually appointed rooms. All provide flat-screen TVs, complimentary WiFi, home-made biscuits, mini-bar and luxurious bathrooms. There is a cosy lounge area with wood-burning stove which is perfect for those winter evenings. The two AA Rosette award-winning restaurant provides a good choice of imaginative dishes at both lunch and dinner, and afternoon tea is also served. On-street parking is available nearby.

Rooms 3

HORRINGER
Suffolk   Map 13 TL86

The Ickworth
AA Advertised ◉◉

tel: 01284 735350 **IP29 5QE**
email: info@ickworthhotel.co.uk **web:** www.ickworthhotel.co.uk/
dir: A14 exit for Bury St Edmunds, follow brown signs for Ickworth House, 4th exit at rdbt, cross staggered x-rds. Then onto T-junct, right into village, almost immediately right into Ickworth Estate

The Ickworth is set in 1,800 acres of Suffolk parkland with opportunities for spotting deer, walking, geo-caching, cycling and just generally relaxing. The hotel interior is full of period and contemporary furnishings, marble flooring and modern chandeliers, creating a luxurious and memorable impression. The hotel is also very family-friendly, offering free childcare, a cinema room, adventure playground, lawn games, flexible mealtimes, children's menus, swimming pools, wendy houses, a fairy garden and lots more. The ideal setting for a satisfying family break.

Rooms 51 (23 annexe) (49 fmly) (5 GF) ⌂ **S** £195-£235; **D** £225-£550 (incl. bkfst)*
Facilities Spa FTV WiFi ⌂ ⊕ ♨ ⛴ 1800 Acres of grounds and up to 60 Bikes Xmas New Year Child facilities **Conf** Class 30 Board 24 Thtr 45 **Services** Lift **Parking** 75 **Notes** LB Civ Wed 50

HORSHAM
West Sussex   Map 6 TQ13

Premier Inn Horsham
BUDGET HOTEL

tel: 0871 527 8526 *(Calls cost 13p per minute plus your phone company's access charge)*
57 North St RH12 1RB
web: www.premierinn.com
dir: Opposite railway station, 5m from M23 junct 11

High quality, budget accommodation ideal for both families and business travellers. Spacious, en suite bedrooms feature tea and coffee making facilities, and Freeview TV in most hotels. Internet access and WiFi are available for a small fee. The adjacent family restaurant features a wide and varied menu. See also the Hotel Groups pages.

Rooms 64

HORSLEY
Derbyshire   Map 11 SK34

Horsley Lodge Hotel & Golf Club
★★★ 81% HOTEL

tel: 01332 780838 **Smalley Mill Rd DE21 5BL**
email: reception@horsleylodge.co.uk **web:** www.horsleylodge.co.uk
dir: M1 junct 25 from the S or junct 28 from the N. Off A38 Coxbench/Little Eaton exit

This family-run hotel is full of character. Situated equidistant from Derby and Nottingham, it is ideal for exploring the Peak District. Bedrooms and bathrooms have stylish decor, beautiful fabrics and quality furnishings. Barn Cottage offers even greater luxury and is tucked away not far from the main building. The Brasserie overlooks the 18-hole golf course.

Rooms 14 (3 annexe) (2 fmly) (1 GF) ⌂ **S** fr £89; **D** fr £119 (incl. bkfst)*
Facilities FTV WiFi ⌂ ⌙ 18 Putt green Fishing Golf driving range Xmas New Year **Conf** Class 70 Board 50 Thtr 100 **Parking** 100 **Notes** LB Civ Wed 100

HOUGHTON-LE-SPRING
Tyne & Wear   Map 19 NZ34

Chilton Country Pub & Hotel
★★★ 74% HOTEL

tel: 0191 385 2694 **Black Boy Rd, Chilton Moor, Fencehouses DH4 6PY**
email: reception@chiltoncountrypub.co.uk **web:** www.chiltoncountrypubandhotel.co.uk
dir: A1(M) junct 62, onto A690 towards Sunderland. Left at Rainton Bridge & Fencehouses sign, right at rdbt, next rdbt straight over, next left. At next junct left, hotel on right

This country pub and hotel has been extended from the original farm cottages. Bedrooms are modern and comfortable and some rooms are particularly spacious. This hotel is popular for weddings and functions; there is also a well stocked bar, and a wide range of dishes is served in the Orangery and restaurant.

Rooms 25 (7 fmly) (11 GF) ⌂ **S** £65-£80; **D** £75-£105 (incl. bkfst) **Facilities** STV FTV WiFi ⌂ ♫ Xmas New Year **Conf** Class 50 Board 30 Thtr 150 **Del** from £95 to £150 **Parking** 200 **Notes** LB ⊗ Civ Wed 100

HOVE
See **Brighton & Hove**

HOYLAKE
Merseyside   Map 15 SJ28

Holiday Inn Express Liverpool - Hoylake
BUDGET HOTEL

tel: 0151 632 2073 **The Kings Gap CH47 1HE**
email: info@hiexpresshoylake.com **web:** www.hiexpresshoylake.co.uk
dir: M53 towards Liverpool junct 2, then A551 towards Hoylake, at rdbt turn right onto The King's Gap. Hotel on right

A modern hotel ideal for families and business travellers. Fresh and uncomplicated, the spacious rooms include Sky TV, power shower and tea and coffee-making facilities. Continental buffet breakfast is included in the room rate; other meals may be taken at the nearby family pub or restaurant. See also the Hotel Groups pages.

Rooms 56 (24 fmly) (10 GF) ⌂ **Conf** Class 40 Board 40 Thtr 100

HUCKNALL
Nottinghamshire   Map 16 SK54

Premier Inn Nottingham North West (Hucknall)
BUDGET HOTEL

tel: 0871 527 8852 *(Calls cost 13p per minute plus your phone company's access charge)*
Nottingham Rd NG15 7PY
web: www.premierinn.com
dir: A611, A6002, straight on at 2 rdbts. Hotel 500yds on right

High quality, budget accommodation ideal for both families and business travellers. Spacious, en suite bedrooms feature tea and coffee making facilities, and Freeview TV in most hotels. Internet access and WiFi are available for a small fee. The adjacent family restaurant features a wide and varied menu. See also the Hotel Groups pages.

Rooms 34

H

HUDDERSFIELD
West Yorkshire
Map 16 SE11

Cedar Court Hotel
★★★★ 70% HOTEL

tel: 01422 375431 & 314001 **Ainley Top HD3 3RH**
email: sales@cedar-court-huddersfield.co.uk **web:** www.cedarcourthotels.co.uk
dir: 500yds from M62 junct 24

Sitting adjacent to the M62, this hotel is an ideal location for business travellers and for those touring the West Yorkshire area. Bedrooms are comfortably appointed; there is a busy lounge with snacks available all day, as well as a modern restaurant and a fully equipped leisure centre. In addition, the hotel has extensive meeting and banqueting facilities.

Rooms 113 (6 fmly) (9 GF) **Facilities** STV FTV WiFi ⏳ ⏱ supervised Gym Steam room Sauna Xmas New Year **Conf** Class 150 Board 100 Thtr 500 **Services** Lift **Parking** 250 **Notes** Civ Wed 400

The Huddersfield Central Lodge
★★★ 74% METRO HOTEL

tel: 01484 515551 **11/15 Beast Market HD1 1QF**
email: joe@centrallodge.com **web:** www.centrallodge.com
dir: Off main town centre ring road, take turning for Kirkgate, town centre, 1st right & 1st right again. Hotel on left

This friendly, family-run Metro Hotel offers smart, spacious bedrooms, all en suite. Across a private courtyard from the main building are more rooms, many with kitchenettes. Public rooms include a fully licensed bar and lounge, a 40 square metre conservatory and an outdoor covered and heated smoking area. Large screen TVs are in all of these areas. Many recommended restaurants with a wide variety of cuisine are within a 5 to 10 minute walk from the Central Lodge. On site secure free parking is available to all guests along with free WiFi throughout.

Rooms 23 (4 fmly) (6 smoking) 🐾 **Facilities** FTV WiFi ⏳ **Parking** 50 **Notes** LB

Premier Inn Huddersfield Central
BUDGET HOTEL

tel: 0871 527 8528 (Calls cost 13p per minute plus your phone company's access charge)
St Andrews Way HD1 3AQ
web: www.premierinn.com
dir: Phone or see website for detailed directions

High quality, budget accommodation ideal for both families and business travellers. Spacious, en suite bedrooms feature tea and coffee making facilities, and Freeview TV in most hotels. Internet access and WiFi are available for a small fee. The adjacent family restaurant features a wide and varied menu. See also the Hotel Groups pages.

Rooms 52

Premier Inn Huddersfield West
BUDGET HOTEL

tel: 0871 527 8532 (Calls cost 13p per minute plus your phone company's access charge)
New Hey Rd, Ainley Top HD2 2EA
web: www.premierinn.com
dir: Just off M62 junct 24. From M62 take Brighouse exit from rdbt (A643). 1st left into Grimescar Rd, right into New Hey Rd

Rooms 42

315 Bar and Restaurant
◉◉ RESTAURANT WITH ROOMS

tel: 01484 602613 **315 Wakefield Rd, Lepton HD8 OLX**
email: info@315barandrestaurant.co.uk **web:** www.315barandrestaurant.co.uk
dir: M1 junct 38, A637 towards Huddersfield. At rdbt take A642 towards Huddersfield. Establishment on right in Lepton

In a wonderful setting, 315 Bar and Restaurant is very well presented and benefits from countryside views from the well-appointed dining room and conservatory areas. The interior is modern with open fires that add character and ambiance, while the chef's table gives a real insight into the working of the two AA Rosette award-winning kitchen. Bedrooms are well appointed and modern, and most have feature bathrooms. Staff are friendly and attentive, and there are excellent parking facilities.

Rooms 10 (2 fmly)

HUNGERFORD
Berkshire
Map 5 SU36

Littlecote House Hotel
★★★★ 77% ◉◉ COUNTRY HOUSE HOTEL

WARNER
LEISURE
HOTELS

tel: 01488 682509 **Chilton Foliat RG17 OSU**
email: phil.howden@bourne-leisure.co.uk **web:** www.warnerleisurehotels.co.uk
dir: M4 junct 14, A338, right onto A4, right onto B4192, left into Littlecote Road, hotel 0.5m on right at top of hill

This hotel provides comfortable, spacious accommodation and is located in stunning grounds close to the Cotswolds, only a 10-minute drive from Hungerford. There are traditional-style bedrooms in the ornate Grade I listed Tudor building and more contemporary rooms in the main building. Facilities include a regular programme of entertainment, beauty treatments and a choice of dining locations in either Oliver's Bistro or Pophams Restaurant. This is an adults-only (over 21 years) hotel.

Rooms 208 (19 annexe) (57 GF) 🐾 **Facilities** Spa FTV WiFi HL ⏱ 🏊 Putt green ⛳ Gym ♫ Xmas New Year **Conf** Class 70 Board 30 Thtr 70 **Services** Lift **Notes** No children 21yrs Civ Wed 120

Three Swans Hotel
★★★ 71% HOTEL

tel: 01488 682721 **117 High St RG17 OLZ**
email: info@threeswans.net **web:** www.threeswans.net
dir: M4 junct 14 follow signs to Hungerford. Hotel in High St on left

Centrally located in the bustling market town of Hungerford, this charming former inn, dating back some 700 years, has been renovated in a fresh and airy style. Visitors will still see the original arch under which the horse-drawn carriages once passed. There is a wood-panelled bar, a spacious lounge and attractive rear garden to relax in. The informal restaurant is decorated with artwork by local artists. Bedrooms are well appointed and comfortable.

Rooms 26 (10 annexe) (2 fmly) (5 GF) (3 smoking) 🐾 **Facilities** FTV WiFi Access to local private gym Xmas New Year **Conf** Class 40 Board 30 Thtr 55 **Parking** 30 **Notes** LB

HUNSTANTON
Norfolk — Map 12 TF64

Best Western Le Strange Arms Hotel
BW Best Western.

★★★★ 74% HOTEL

tel: 01485 534411 **Golf Course Rd, Old Hunstanton PE36 6JJ**
email: reception@lestrangearms.co.uk **web:** www.abacushotels.co.uk
dir: Off A149 1m N of Hunstanton. Left at sharp right bend by pitch & putt course

Le Strange Arms is an impressive hotel with superb views from the wide lawns down to the sandy beach and across The Wash. Bedrooms in the main house are individually decorated. Public rooms include the comfortable Oak House and lounge, open for meals from midday, and a conference and banqueting suite. There is a choice of dining options - The Le Strange Bistro, or the Ancient Mariner, a traditional inn adjacent to the hotel, serving good food and real ales.

Rooms 43 (7 annexe) (2 fmly) **Facilities** FTV WiFi Xmas New Year **Conf** Class 150 Board 50 Thtr 180 **Services** Lift **Parking** 80 **Notes** Civ Wed 70

Caley Hall Hotel

★★★ 85% HOTEL

tel: 01485 533486 **Old Hunstanton Rd PE36 6HH**
email: mail@caleyhallhotel.co.uk **web:** www.caleyhallhotel.co.uk
dir: 1m from Hunstanton, on A149

Situated within easy walking distance of the seafront, Caley Hall Hotel offers tastefully decorated bedrooms in a series of converted outbuildings. Each is smartly furnished and thoughtfully equipped. Public rooms feature a large open-plan lounge/bar with plush leather seating, and a restaurant offering an interesting choice of dishes.

Rooms 39 (20 fmly) (30 GF) **S** £59-£145; **D** £79-£155 (incl. bkfst)* **Facilities** STV FTV WiFi New Year **Parking** 50 **Notes** Closed 19-26 Dec & 8-19 Jan

The Neptune Restaurant with Rooms
RESTAURANT WITH ROOMS

tel: 01485 532122 **85 Old Hunstanton Rd, Old Hunstanton PE36 6HZ**
email: reservations@theneptune.co.uk **web:** www.theneptune.co.uk
dir: On A149, past Hunstanton, 200mtrs on left after post office

This charming 18th-century coaching inn, now a restaurant with rooms, is ideally situated for touring the Norfolk coastline. The smartly appointed bedrooms are brightly finished with co-ordinated fabrics and hand-made New England furniture. Public rooms feature white clapboard walls, polished dark wood floors, fresh flowers and Lloyd Loom furniture. Obviously, the food is very much a draw here with the carefully prepared, award-winning cuisine using excellent local produce; from oysters and mussels from Thornham to quinces grown on a neighbouring farm.

Rooms 5

HUNSTRETE
Somerset — Map 4 ST66

INSPECTORS' CHOICE

THE PIG near Bath

★★★ HOTEL

tel: 01761 490490 **Hunstrete House, Pensford BS39 4NS**
email: info@thepignearbath.com **web:** www.thepighotel.com
dir: From Bath take A4 to Bristol. At Globe Inn rdbt 2nd left onto A368 to Wells. 1m after Marksbury turn right for Hunstrete. Hotel next left

A beautiful country house set in delightful grounds with its own deer park, livestock and walled garden, the latter providing the kitchen with much of its excellent produce. Alfresco eating is possible in the warmer months as there is a wood-fired oven in the courtyard. Bedrooms come in an array of shapes and sizes; some located in the main house, some around the courtyard, and others in beautifully converted garden sheds. All are spacious, have high quality fixtures, and come with their own larders and Nespresso machines. There are plenty of comfortable lounges where guests can make themselves at home too. The old dining room can accommodate meetings, and treatments can be taken in the potting shed.

Rooms 29 (5 annexe) (10 GF) **Facilities** FTV WiFi Treatment rooms Xmas New Year **Conf** Board 22 **Parking** 100 **Notes** Civ Wed

HUNTINGDON
Cambridgeshire
Map 12 TL27

HIGHLY RECOMMENDED

The Old Bridge Hotel

★★★ 86% HOTEL

tel: 01480 424300 **1 High St PE29 3TQ**
email: oldbridge@huntsbridge.co.uk **web:** www.huntsbridge.com
dir: *From A14 or A1 follow Huntingdon signs. Hotel visible from inner ring road*

The Old Bridge Hotel is an imposing 18th-century building situated close to shops and amenities. On offer is superb accommodation in stylish and individually decorated bedrooms that include many useful extras. Guests can choose from the same menu whether dining in the open-plan terrace, or the more formal restaurant with its bold colour scheme. There is also an excellent business centre.

Rooms 24 (2 fmly) (2 GF) ⚓ **Facilities** STV FTV WiFi ↳ Fishing Private mooring for boats Xmas New Year **Conf** Class 50 Board 30 Thtr 60 **Services** Air con **Parking** 50 **Notes** Civ Wed 100

Premier Inn Huntingdon (A1/A14)

BUDGET HOTEL

tel: 0871 527 8540 *(Calls cost 13p per minute plus your phone company's access charge)*
Great North Rd, Brampton PE28 4NQ
web: www.premierinn.com
dir: *At junct of A1 & A14. (NB from N do not use junct 14. Take exit for Huntingdon & Brampton). Access to hotel via Services*

High quality, budget accommodation ideal for both families and business travellers. Spacious, en suite bedrooms feature tea and coffee making facilities, and Freeview TV in most hotels. Internet access and WiFi are available for a small fee. The adjacent family restaurant features a wide and varied menu. See also the Hotel Groups pages.

Rooms 104

HYDE
Greater Manchester
Map 16 SJ99

Premier Inn Manchester (Hyde)

BUDGET HOTEL

tel: 0871 527 8712 *(Calls cost 13p per minute plus your phone company's access charge)*
Stockport Rd, Mottram SK14 3AU
web: www.premierinn.com
dir: *At end of M67 between A57 & A560*

High quality, budget accommodation ideal for both families and business travellers. Spacious, en suite bedrooms feature tea and coffee making facilities, and Freeview TV in most hotels. Internet access and WiFi are available for a small fee. The adjacent family restaurant features a wide and varied menu. See also the Hotel Groups pages.

Rooms 83

HYTHE
Kent
Map 7 TR13

Hythe Imperial

★★★★ 75% HOTEL

tel: 01303 267441 **Princes Pde CT21 6AE**
email: h6862@accor.com **web:** www.hytheimperial.co.uk
dir: *M20, junct 11 onto A261. In Hythe follow Folkestone signs. Right into Twiss Rd to hotel*

This imposing seafront hotel is enhanced by impressive grounds including a 13-green golf course, tennis court and extensive gardens. Bedrooms are varied in style but all offer modern facilities, and many enjoy stunning sea views. The elegant restaurant, bar and lounges are traditional in style and retain many original features. The leisure club includes a gym, a squash court, an indoor pool, and a spa offering a range of luxury treatments.

Rooms 100 (11 fmly) (6 GF) ⚓ **Facilities** Spa FTV WiFi ↳ ᠅ ⚓ 13 ⚓ Putt green Gym Squash Aerobic studio Table tennis Sauna Steam room ♫ Xmas New Year **Conf** Class 120 Board 80 Thtr 220 **Services** Lift **Parking** 207 **Notes** Civ Wed 120

Best Western Stade Court

★★★ 74% HOTEL

tel: 01303 268263 **Stade St, West Pde CT21 6DT**
email: stadecourt@bestwestern.co.uk **web:** www.stadecourthotel.co.uk
dir: *M20 junct 11 follow signs for Hythe town centre. Follow brown tourist sign for hotel*

Stade Court is situated right on the seafront with many bedrooms having the benefit of uninterrupted views of the English Channel. The comfortable bedrooms are tastefully decorated and provide free WiFi and in-room beverage-making facilities. Guests can enjoy traditional English or Indian cuisine in the sea-facing restaurant.

Rooms 41 (5 fmly) ⚓ S £35-£65; **D** £45-£85 **Facilities** STV FTV WiFi ↳ Xmas New Year **Conf** Class 20 Board 30 Thtr 40 **Services** Lift **Parking** 11 **Notes** LB Civ Wed 100

ILFORD
Greater London

Premier Inn Ilford

BUDGET HOTEL PLAN 1 H5

tel: 0871 527 8542 *(Calls cost 13p per minute plus your phone company's access charge)*
Redbridge Lane East IG4 5BG
web: www.premierinn.com
dir: *At end of M11 follow London East, A12 & Chelmsford signs onto A12, hotel on left at bottom of slip road*

High quality, budget accommodation ideal for both families and business travellers. Spacious, en suite bedrooms feature tea and coffee making facilities, and Freeview TV in most hotels. Internet access and WiFi are available for a small fee. The adjacent family restaurant features a wide and varied menu. See also the Hotel Groups pages.

Rooms 44

ILFRACOMBE
Devon
Map 3 SS54

Sandy Cove Hotel
★★★ 76% ●● HOTEL

tel: 01271 882 243 **Old Coast Rd, Combe Martin Bay, Berrynarbor EX34 9SR**
email: info@sandycove-hotel.co.uk **web:** www.sandycove-hotel.co.uk
dir: *A339 to Combe Martin, through village towards Ilfracombe for approx 1m. Turn right just over brow of hill marked Sandy Cove*

This hotel enjoys a truly spectacular position, with front-facing bedrooms that benefit from uninterrupted views of the north Devon coastline. In addition, guests can relax on the sea decks or in the terraced garden, and really appreciate the peace and tranquillity. Locally sourced produce is a feature of the menus offered in the dining room, which makes the perfect setting for a romantic dinner or a family gathering.

Rooms 36 (15 fmly) (7 GF) ❧ **Facilities** WiFi ☼ ⓢ ↝ Sauna Steam room Heated relaxation loungers Xmas New Year **Conf** Class 20 Board 30 Thtr 30 **Parking** 45 **Notes** LB Civ Wed 150

Imperial Hotel
Leisureplex
HOLIDAY HOTELS
★★★ 70% HOTEL

tel: 01271 862536 **Wilder Rd EX34 9AL**
email: imperial.ilfracombe@alfatravel.co.uk **web:** www.leisureplex.co.uk
dir: *Opposite Landmark Theatre*

This popular hotel is just a short walk from the shops and harbour, overlooking gardens and the sea. Public areas include the spacious sun lounge, where guests can relax and enjoy the excellent views. Comfortable bedrooms are well equipped, with several having the added bonus of sea views.

Rooms 104 (6 fmly) ❧ **Facilities** FTV WiFi ♬ Xmas New Year **Services** Lift **Parking** 7 **Notes** ⊗ Closed Dec-Feb (ex Xmas/New Year) RS Mar & Nov

The Habit Boutique Rooms
●● RESTAURANT WITH ROOMS

tel: 01271 863272 & 07931 551487 **46-48 Fore St EX34 9DN**
email: info@thehabitboutiquerooms.com **web:** www.thehabitboutiquerooms.com
dir: *Into Ilfracombe on A361, continue to High St until road splits. Take slight left, 100yds on left*

The Habit Boutique Rooms occupy a fully refurbished grand old Victorian building close to Ilfracombe seafront. The eleven renovated rooms, many offering stunning views over the Bristol Channel, are of high quality throughout. There is also an elegant yet relaxed, award-winning, fine dining restaurant; a large bar and lounge area with soaring ceilings extending out on to a large deck; and a fully equipped Pilates studio and beauty treatment rooms. AA Funkiest B&B of the Year Award Runner-Up 2016-2017.

Rooms 11 (4 fmly)

ILKLEY
West Yorkshire
Map 19 SE14

The Craiglands Hotel
★★★ 72% HOTEL

tel: 01943 430001 & 886450 **Cowpasture Rd LS29 8RQ**
email: reservations@craiglands.co.uk **web:** www.craiglands.co.uk
dir: *A65 into Ilkley. Left at T-junct. Past rail station, fork right into Cowpasture Rd. Hotel opposite school*

This grand Victorian hotel is situated close to the town centre. Spacious public areas and a good range of services are ideal for business or leisure. Extensive conference facilities are available along with an elegant restaurant and traditionally styled bar and lounge. Bedrooms, varying in size and style, are comfortably furnished and well equipped.

Rooms 62 (4 fmly) ❧ **Facilities** FTV WiFi ☼ Xmas New Year **Conf** Class 200 Board 100 Thtr 500 **Services** Lift **Parking** 200 **Notes** ⊗ Civ Wed 500

ILSINGTON
Devon
Map 3 SX77

Ilsington Country House Hotel
CLASSIC BRITISH HOTELS
★★★ 88% ●● COUNTRY HOUSE HOTEL

tel: 01364 661452 **Ilsington Village TQ13 9RR**
email: hotel@ilsington.co.uk **web:** www.ilsington.co.uk
dir: *M5 onto A38 to Plymouth. Exit at Bovey Tracey. 3rd exit from rdbt to Ilsington, then 1st right. Hotel in 5m by Post Office*

This friendly, family-owned hotel, offers tranquillity and far-reaching views from its elevated position on the southern slopes of Dartmoor. The stylish suites and bedrooms, some on the ground floor, are individually furnished. The restaurant provides a stunning backdrop for the innovative, daily-changing menus which feature local fish, meat and game. Additional facilities include an indoor pool and the Blue Tiger Inn, where a pint, a bite to eat and convivial conversation can all be enjoyed.

Rooms 25 (4 fmly) (6 GF) ❧ **S** £95-£120; **D** £115-£260 (incl. bkfst) **Facilities** Spa FTV WiFi ⓢ ❧ Gym Steam room Sauna Beauty treatment rooms Hydrotherapy pool Xmas New Year **Conf** Class 60 Board 40 Thtr 100 Del from £145 to £210* **Services** Lift **Parking** 70 **Notes** LB Civ Wed 100

INSTOW
Devon
Map 3 SS43

Commodore Hotel
★★★ 83% HOTEL

tel: 01271 860347 **Marine Pde EX39 4JN**
email: admin@commodore-instow.co.uk **web:** www.commodore-instow.co.uk
dir: *M5 junct 27 follow N Devon link road to Bideford. Right before bridge, hotel in 3m*

Maintaining its links with the local maritime and rural communities, the Commodore provides an interesting place to stay. Situated at the mouth of the Taw and Torridge rivers and overlooking a sandy beach, it offers well-equipped bedrooms, many with balconies. There are five ground-floor suites. Eating options include the restaurant, the Quarterdeck bar, or the terrace in the warmer months.

Rooms 25 (1 fmly) (5 GF) ❧ **S** £75-£105; **D** £85-£248 (incl. bkfst & dinner)* **Facilities** FTV WiFi ☼ Xmas New Year **Parking** 200 **Notes** LB ⊗ No children 3yrs

IPSWICH
Suffolk

Map 13 TM14

Hintlesham Hall Hotel
★★★★ ◉◉ HOTEL

tel: 01473 652334 **George St IP8 3NS**
email: reservations@hintleshamhall.com **web:** www.hintleshamhall.com

(For full entry see Hintlesham)

Salthouse Harbour Hotel
★★★★ ◉◉ TOWN HOUSE HOTEL

tel: 01473 226789 **No 1 Neptune Quay IP4 1AX**
email: frontdesk@salthouseharbour.co.uk **web:** www.salthouseharbour.co.uk
dir: *From A14 junct 56 follow signs for town centre, then Salthouse signs*

Situated just a short walk from the town centre, this waterfront warehouse conversion is a clever mix of contemporary styles and original features. The hotel is stylishly designed throughout with modern art, sculptures, interesting artefacts and striking colours. The spacious bedrooms provide luxurious comfort; some have feature bathrooms and some have balconies. Two air-conditioned penthouse suites, with stunning views, have extras such as state-of-the-art sound systems and telescopes. Award-winning food is served in the busy, ground-floor brasserie, and alfresco eating is possible in warmer weather.

Rooms 70 (6 fmly) ⬧ **D** £129–£319* **Facilities** STV FTV WiFi ⬧ **Services** Lift **Parking** 30 **Notes** LB

milsoms Kesgrave Hall
★★★★ 78% ◉ HOTEL

tel: 01473 333741 **Hall Rd, Kesgrave IP5 2PU**
email: reception@kesgravehall.com **web:** www.milsomhotels.com/kesgravehall
dir: *A12 N of Ipswich, left at Ipswich/Woodbridge rdbt onto A1214. Right after 0.5m into Hall Rd. Hotel 200yds on left*

Kesgrave Hall is a superb 18th-century, Grade II listed Georgian mansion set amidst 38 acres of mature grounds. Appointed in a contemporary style, the large open-plan public areas include a smart bar, a lounge with plush sofas, and a restaurant where guests can watch the chefs in action. Bedrooms are tastefully appointed and thoughtfully equipped.

Rooms 23 (8 annexe) (3 fmly) (8 GF) ⬧ **D** £140–£315 (incl. bkfst)* **Facilities** STV FTV WiFi ⬧ ⬧ Xmas **Conf** Class 200 Board 24 Thtr 600 Del £175* **Parking** 100 **Notes** LB Civ Wed 300

Novotel Ipswich Centre
★★★★ 75% HOTEL

tel: 01473 232400 **Greyfriars Rd IP1 1UP**
email: h0995@accor.com **web:** www.novotel.com
dir: *From A14 towards Felixstowe. Left onto A137, 2m into town centre. Hotel on double rdbt by Stoke Bridge*

This modern, red brick hotel is perfectly placed in the centre of town close to shops, bars and restaurants. The open-plan public areas include a Mediterranean-style restaurant and a bar with a small games area. The bedrooms are smartly appointed and have many thoughtful touches; three rooms are suitable for less mobile guests.

Rooms 101 (8 fmly) ⬧ **Facilities** STV FTV WiFi ⬧ HL Gym Xmas New Year **Conf** Class 100 Board 45 Thtr 180 **Services** Lift Air con **Parking** 53 **Notes** Civ Wed 150

Best Western Claydon Country House Hotel

★★★ 81% ☻ HOTEL

tel: 01473 830382 **16-18 Ipswich Rd, Claydon IP6 OAR**
email: enquiries@hotelsipswich.com **web:** www.hotelsipswich.com
dir: From A14, NW of Ipswich. After 4m take Great Blakenham Rd B1113 to Claydon, hotel on left

A delightful hotel situated just off the A14, within easy driving distance of the town centre. The pleasantly decorated bedrooms are thoughtfully equipped and one room has a lovely four-poster bed. An interesting choice of freshly prepared dishes is available in the smart restaurant, and guests have the use of a relaxing lounge bar.

Rooms 36 (12 GF) ♠ **Facilities** FTV WiFi ⌇ New Year **Conf** Class 50 Board 40 Thtr 80 Del from £120 to £140 **Services** Air con **Parking** 85 **Notes** ⊗ Civ Wed 65

Best Western Gatehouse Hotel

★★★ 77% HOTEL

tel: 01473 741897 **799 Old Norwich Rd IP1 6LH**
email: enquiries@gatehousehotel.com **web:** www.gatehousehotel.com
dir: A14 junct 53, A1156 signed Ipswich, left at lights into Norwich Rd, hotel on left

A Regency-style property set amidst three acres of landscaped grounds, on the outskirts of town in a quiet road just a short drive from the A14. The spacious bedrooms have co-ordinated soft furnishings and many thoughtful touches. Public rooms include a smart lounge bar, an intimate restaurant and a cosy drawing room with plush leather sofas.

Rooms 15 (4 annexe) (1 fmly) (6 GF) ♠ **Facilities** FTV WiFi ⌇ **Parking** 25 **Notes** ⊗

Premier Inn Ipswich (Chantry Park)

BUDGET HOTEL

tel: 0871 527 8548 *(Calls cost 13p per minute plus your phone company's access charge)*
Old Hadleigh Rd IP8 3AR
web: www.premierinn.com
dir: From A12/A14 junct take A1214 to Ipswich town centre. Left at lights by Holiday Inn, left onto A1071. At mini rdbt turn right. Hotel on right

High quality, budget accommodation ideal for both families and business travellers. Spacious, en suite bedrooms feature tea and coffee making facilities, and Freeview TV in most hotels. Internet access and WiFi are available for a small fee. The adjacent family restaurant features a wide and varied menu. See also the Hotel Groups pages.

Rooms 74

Premier Inn Ipswich North

BUDGET HOTEL

tel: 0871 527 8550 *(Calls cost 13p per minute plus your phone company's access charge)*
Paper Mill Ln, Claydon IP6 0BE
web: www.premierinn.com
dir: A14 junct 52. At rdbt exit onto Paper Mill Lane. Hotel 1st left

Rooms 90

Premier Inn Ipswich South

BUDGET HOTEL

tel: 0871 527 8552 *(Calls cost 13p per minute plus your phone company's access charge)*
Bourne Hill, Wherstead IP2 8ND
web: www.premierinn.com
dir: From A14 follow Ipswich Central A137 signs, then Ipswich Central & Docks signs. At bottom of hill at rdbt 2nd exit. Hotel on right

Rooms 40

Premier Inn Ipswich South East

BUDGET HOTEL

tel: 0871 527 8554 *(Calls cost 13p per minute plus your phone company's access charge)*
Augusta Close, Ransomes Euro Park IP3 9SS
web: www.premierinn.com
dir: A14 junct 57, stay in right lane. At rdbt 2nd exit, then 1st left. Hotel adjacent to Swallow Restaurant

Rooms 36

Premier Inn Ipswich Town Centre (Quayside)

BUDGET HOTEL

tel: 0871 527 9388 *(Calls cost 13p per minute plus your phone company's access charge)*
33 Key St IP4 1BZ
web: www.premierinn.com
dir: Phone for directions

Rooms 85

K

KEGWORTH
See **East Midlands Airport**

KEIGHLEY   Map 19 SE04
West Yorkshire

Dalesgate Hotel

★★ 70% HOTEL

tel: 01535 664930 **406 Skipton Rd, Utley BD20 6HP**
email: info@dalesgate.co.uk **web:** www.dalesgate.co.uk
dir: In town centre follow A629 over rdbt onto B6265. Right after 0.75m into St. John's Rd. 1st right into hotel car park

Originally the residence of a local chapel minister, this modern, well-established hotel provides well-equipped, comfortable bedrooms. It also boasts a cosy bar and pleasant restaurant, serving an imaginative range of dishes. A large car park is provided to the rear.

Rooms 20 (2 fmly) (3 GF) **Parking** 25 **Notes** RS 22 Dec-4 Jan

KEIGHLEY continued

Premier Inn Bradford North (Bingley)

BUDGET HOTEL

tel: 0871 527 8134 *(Calls cost 13p per minute plus your phone company's access charge)*
502 Bradford Rd, Sandbeds BD20 5NG
web: www.premierinn.com
dir: *M62 juncts 26 or 27 follow A650/Keighley & Skipton signs. From Bingley Bypass (A650 Cottingley) right at 1st rdbt signed Crossflatts & Micklethwaite. Hotel 50yds on left. NB for Sat Nav use BD20 5NH*

High quality, budget accommodation ideal for both families and business travellers. Spacious, en suite bedrooms feature tea and coffee making facilities, and Freeview TV in most hotels. Internet access and WiFi are available for a small fee. The adjacent family restaurant features a wide and varied menu. See also the Hotel Groups pages.

Rooms 61

| **KENDAL** | **Map 18 SD59** |
| Cumbria | |

See also **Crooklands**

Castle Green Hotel in Kendal

★★★★ 81% ◉◉ HOTEL

tel: 01539 734000 **Castle Green Ln LA9 6RG**
email: reception@castlegreen.co.uk **web:** www.castlegreen.co.uk
dir: *M6 junct 37, A684 towards Kendal. Hotel on right in 5m*

This smart, modern hotel enjoys a peaceful location and is conveniently situated for access to both the town centre and the M6. Stylish bedrooms are thoughtfully equipped for both the business and leisure guest. The Greenhouse Restaurant provides imaginative dishes and boasts a theatre kitchen; alternatively Alexander's Pub serves food all day. The hotel has a fully equipped business centre and leisure club.

Rooms 99 (3 fmly) (25 GF) ✿ **S** £75-£113; **D** £95-£180 (incl. bkfst)* **Facilities** Spa FTV WiFi ⬧ 🕹 Gym Steam room Aerobics Yoga Beauty salon Xmas New Year **Conf** Class 120 Board 100 Thtr 300 Del from £140 to £155* **Services** Lift **Parking** 200 **Notes** LB ⊗ Civ Wed 250

Stonecross Manor Hotel

★★★ 73% HOTEL

tel: 01539 733559 **Milnthorpe Rd LA9 5HP**
email: info@stonecrossmanor.co.uk **web:** www.stonecrossmanor.co.uk
dir: *M6 junct 36, A590, follow signs to Windermere, take exit for Kendal South. Hotel just past 30mph sign on left*

Located on the edge of Kendal, this smart hotel offers a good combination of traditional style and modern facilities. Bedrooms are comfortable, well equipped and some feature four-poster beds. Guests can relax in the lounges or bar and enjoy an extensive choice of home-cooked meals in the pleasant restaurant. Facilities also include a swimming pool.

Rooms 30 (4 fmly) **Facilities** FTV WiFi ⬧ HL 🕹 Xmas New Year **Conf** Class 80 Board 40 Thtr 140 Del from £110 to £120* **Services** Lift **Parking** 55 **Notes** Civ Wed 130

Premier Inn Kendal Central

BUDGET HOTEL

tel: 0871 527 8562 *(Calls cost 13p per minute plus your phone company's access charge)*
Maude St LA9 4QD
web: www.premierinn.com
dir: *M6 junct 36, A591 to Kendal. (NB ignore exit for Kendal South). At Plumbgarm Rdbt take 3rd exit, 0.5m to Kendal. Hotel on right*

High quality, budget accommodation ideal for both families and business travellers. Spacious, en suite bedrooms feature tea and coffee making facilities, and Freeview TV in most hotels. Internet access and WiFi are available for a small fee. The adjacent family restaurant features a wide and varied menu. See also the Hotel Groups pages.

Rooms 92

K

KENILWORTH
Warwickshire   Map 10 SP27

Chesford Grange

QHOTELS
INSPIRED
BY YOU

★★★★ 77% HOTEL

tel: 01926 859331 **Chesford Bridge CV8 2LD**
email: chesfordreservations@qhotels.co.uk **web:** www.qhotels.co.uk
dir: 0.5m SE of junct A46/A452. At rdbt turn right signed Leamington Spa, follow signs to hotel

This much-extended hotel set in 17 acres of private grounds is well situated for Birmingham International Airport, the NEC and major routes. Bedrooms range from traditional style to contemporary rooms featuring state-of-the-art technology. Public areas include a leisure club and extensive conference and banqueting facilities.

Rooms 205 (20 fmly) (43 GF) 🐾 **Facilities** Spa STV WiFi ⌕ ⌕ supervised Gym Steam room Solarium Xmas New Year **Conf** Class 350 Board 50 Thtr 710 **Services** Lift **Parking** 650 **Notes** Civ Wed 700

KENTISBURY
Devon   Map 3 SS64

Kentisbury Grange

★★★★ 81% ◉◉ HOTEL

tel: 01271 882295 **EX31 4NL**
email: reception@kentisburygrange.co.uk **web:** www.kentisburygrange.com
dir: From Barnstaple take A3125. At rdbt take 2nd exit onto A39 to Burrington through Shirwell and Arlington. After Kentisbury Ford, follow signposts for hotel for approx 0.75m.

High quality and comfort are in generous supply at this Victorian country house. Total refurbishment has resulted in an impressive blend of traditional elegance and contemporary luxury. Bedrooms and bathrooms offer those pampering touches which make all the difference, thus ensuring a relaxing and rewarding stay. The Coach House restaurant is the venue for dining, where a skilled kitchen team maximise the benefits of excellent local produce. Surrounded by the stunning North Devon countryside and a short drive from superb beaches, this is a great base from which to explore all the area has to offer.

Rooms 16 (5 annexe) (9 GF) 🐾 **Facilities** FTV WiFi ⌕ Xmas New Year **Conf** Class 12 Board 20 Thtr 30 **Parking** 50 **Notes** ⊗ Civ Wed 50

KENTON
Greater London

Premier Inn London Harrow

Premier Inn

BUDGET HOTEL PLAN 1 C5

tel: 0871 527 8664 (Calls cost 13p per minute plus your phone company's access charge)
Kenton Rd HA3 8AT
web: www.premierinn.com
dir: M1 junct 5, follow Harrow & Kenton signs. Hotel between Harrow & Wembley on A4006 opposite Kenton railway station

High quality, budget accommodation ideal for both families and business travellers. Spacious, en suite bedrooms feature tea and coffee making facilities, and Freeview TV in most hotels. Internet access and WiFi are available for a small fee. The adjacent family restaurant features a wide and varied menu. See also the Hotel Groups pages.

Rooms 119

KESWICK
Cumbria   Map 18 NY22

Inn on the Square
LAKE DISTRICT
HOTELS

★★★★ 79% ◉ HOTEL

tel: 017687 73333 & 0800 8401247 **Main St CA12 5JF**
email: innonthesquare@lakedistricthotels.net **web:** www.innonthesquare.co.uk
dir: A66 to Keswick centre then follow signs to Bell Close car park. Entrance to rear of hotel is at entrance to car park

This luxury hotel opened in 2015 and enjoys a fantastic location as you may expect; on the square in the centre of Keswick. Modern, contemporary and funky design is matched by high levels of comfort. Public areas include the Brossen Steak House and a choice of bars; simply named the Front and Back Bars. Bedrooms are impressive; deeply luxurious beds and furniture feature. Bathrooms are a stunning companion to these. Friendly staff ensure a warm Lakes welcome.

Rooms 34 (1 fmly) 🐾 **S** fr £111; **D** fr £222 (incl. bkfst) **Facilities** STV FTV WiFi ⌕ ♫ Xmas New Year **Services** Lift **Parking** 7

KESWICK *continued*

Dale Head Hall Lakeside Hotel

★★★ 82% COUNTRY HOUSE HOTEL

tel: 017687 72478 **Lake Thirlmere CA12 4TN**
email: onthelakeside@daleheadhall.co.uk **web:** www.daleheadhall.co.uk
dir: *Between Keswick & Grasmere. Exit A591 onto private drive*

Set in attractive, tranquil grounds on the shores of Lake Thirlmere, this historic lakeside residence dates from the 16th century. Comfortable and inviting public areas include a choice of lounges and a traditionally furnished restaurant featuring a daily-changing menu. Most bedrooms are spacious and have views of the lake or surrounding mountains.

Rooms 12 (1 fmly) (2 GF) 🕭 **Facilities** STV FTV WiFi 🎣 Fishing 🎣 Fishing permits Boating Xmas New Year **Conf** Class 20 Board 20 Thtr 20 **Parking** 34 **Notes** LB ⊗ Closed 3-30 Jan Civ Wed 60

Skiddaw Hotel

★★★ 80% HOTEL

LAKE DISTRICT HOTELS

tel: 017687 72071 & 0800 840 1243 **Main St CA12 5BN**
email: skiddawhotel@lakedistricthotels.net **web:** www.lakedistricthotels.net/skiddawhotel
dir: *A66 to Keswick, follow town centre signs. Hotel in market square*

Occupying a central position overlooking the market square, this hotel provides smartly furnished bedrooms that include several family suites and a room with a four-poster bed. In addition to the restaurant, food is served all day in the bar and in the conservatory. There is also a quiet residents' lounge and two conference rooms.

Rooms 43 (7 fmly) 🕭 **S** fr £104; **D** fr £208 (incl. bkfst) **Facilities** STV WiFi Use of leisure facilities at sister hotels (3m) 🎵 Xmas New Year **Conf** Class 60 Board 40 Thtr 90 **Services** Lift **Parking** 35 **Notes** Civ Wed 90

Keswick Country House Hotel

★★★ 79% HOTEL

tel: 0844 811 5580 *(Calls cost 5p per minute plus your phone company's access charge)* & 017687 72020 **Station Rd CA12 4NQ**
email: reservations@choicehotels.co.uk **web:** www.thekeswickhotel.co.uk
dir: *M6 junct 40, A66, 1st slip road into Keswick, then follow signs for leisure pool*

This impressive Victorian hotel is set amid attractive gardens close to the town centre. Eight superior bedrooms are available in the Station Wing, which is accessed through a conservatory. The attractively appointed main house rooms are modern in style and offer a good range of amenities. Public areas include a well-stocked bar, a spacious and relaxing lounge, and a restaurant serving interesting dinners.

Rooms 70 (6 fmly) (4 GF) 🕭 **S** £53-£129; **D** £96-£198 (incl. bkfst & dinner) **Facilities** FTV WiFi Putt green 🎣 Xmas New Year **Conf** Class 70 Board 60 Thtr 110 Del from £105 to £145 **Services** Lift **Parking** 70 **Notes** LB ⊗ Civ Wed 100

Kings Arms Hotel

★★★ 77% HOTEL

LAKE DISTRICT HOTELS

tel: 017687 72083 & 0800 840 1241 **27 Main St CA12 5BL**
email: kingsarms@lakedistricthotels.net **web:** www.lakedistricthotels.net/kingsarms
dir: *M6 junct 40, follow A66 to Keswick then follow signs to town centre*

Located in the heart of Keswick, the Kings Arms Hotel offers modern, tastefully refurbished bedrooms and en suites, alongside intimate public areas and a choice of two restaurants. The bar offers some great local real ales and changing guest beers. The small hands-on team offer friendly and relaxed service.

Rooms 13 🕭 **S** fr £76; **D** fr £96 (incl. bkfst) **Facilities** FTV WiFi Complimentary leisure club membership at sister hotel Xmas **Parking** 13

KETTERING
Northamptonshire

Map 11 SP87

INSPECTORS' CHOICE

Rushton Hall Hotel and Spa

★★★★ ❀❀❀ COUNTRY HOUSE HOTEL

tel: 01536 713001 **Rushton NN14 1RR**
email: enquiries@rushtonhall.com **web:** www.rushtonhall.com
dir: A14 junct 7, A43 to Corby then A6003 to Rushton, turn after bridge

Ruston Hall is an elegant country house hotel set amidst 30 acres of parkland and surrounded by open countryside. The stylish public rooms include a library, a superb open-plan lounge bar with a magnificent vaulted ceiling and plush sofas, and an oak-panelled dining hall, where Adrian Coulthard oversees a very high quality operation. The tastefully appointed bedrooms have co-ordinated fabrics and many thoughtful touches.

Rooms 46 (5 fmly) (2 GF) ↖ **S** £160-£390; **D** £170-£400 (incl. bkfst)*
Facilities Spa FTV WiFi ⇘ 🕃 🦢 🦢 Gym Billiard table Sauna Steam room Xmas New Year **Conf** Class 100 Board 40 Thtr 200 Del from £195 to £225* **Services** Lift **Parking** 140 **Notes** ⊗ Civ Wed 160

Kettering Park Hotel & Spa

★★★★ 81% ❀ HOTEL

tel: 01536 416666 **Kettering Parkway NN15 6XT**
email: kpark@shirehotels.com **web:** www.ketteringparkhotel.com
dir: Exit A14 junct 9 (M1 to A1 link road) hotel in Kettering Venture Park

Expect a warm welcome at this stylish hotel situated just off the A14. The spacious, smartly decorated bedrooms are well equipped and meticulously maintained. Guests can choose from classical or contemporary dishes in the restaurant and lighter meals that are served in the bar. The extensive leisure facilities are impressive. Thwaites Hotels is the AA Hotel Group of the Year 2016-2017.

Rooms 119 (29 fmly) (35 GF) **S** £95-£200; **D** £95-£200* **Facilities** Spa STV FTV WiFi ⇘ HL 🕃 Gym Steam room Sauna Beauty treatment room Children's splash pool Activity studio New Year **Conf** Class 120 Board 40 Thtr 260 Del from £130 to £200* **Services** Lift Air con **Parking** 200 **Notes** LB ⊗ Civ Wed 120

Barton Hall Hotel

★★★ 82% HOTEL

tel: 01536 515505 **Barton Rd, Barton Seagrave NN15 6SG**
email: enquiries@bartonhall.com **web:** www.bartonhall.com
dir: From A14 take junct 10 onto Barton Rd. Hotel on the right approx 0.5m

Barton Hall Hotel offers modern and comfortable accommodation to suit both business and leisure guests. All of the rooms include 40" smart TVs, with complementary WiFi throughout. Dinner can be enjoyed in Vines Brasserie, which serves a traditional menu in a relaxing and friendly environment.

Rooms 29 (3 fmly) (8 GF) ↖ **D** £120-£240 (incl. bkfst)* **Facilities** FTV WiFi ⇘ **Conf** Class 150 Board 60 Thtr 300 Del from £145 to £155 **Parking** 80 **Notes** ⊗ Civ Wed 160

KETTERING continued

Premier Inn Kettering

BUDGET HOTEL

tel: 0871 527 8564 *(Calls cost 13p per minute plus your phone company's access charge)*
Rothwell Rd NN16 8XF
web: www.premierinn.com
dir: *Off A14 junct 7*

High quality, budget accommodation ideal for both families and business travellers. Spacious, en suite bedrooms feature tea and coffee making facilities, and Freeview TV in most hotels. Internet access and WiFi are available for a small fee. The adjacent family restaurant features a wide and varied menu. See also the Hotel Groups pages.

Rooms 83

KIDDERMINSTER	Map 10 SO87
Worcestershire	

Stone Manor Hotel

★★★★ 72% ● HOTEL

tel: 01562 777555 **Stone DY10 4PJ**
email: enquiries@stonemanorhotel.co.uk
web: www.hogarths.co.uk/hogarths-stone-manor
dir: *2.5m from Kidderminster on A448, on right*

This converted and much-extended former manor house set in 25 acres has a history that dates back as far as the Domesday Book. Rooms are comfortably furnished and equipped with modern day essentials, and many of them benefit from far-reaching views across the Worcestershire countryside. This property is well placed for the Midlands motorway network and local attractions, making it a popular venue for both corporate and leisure guests.

Rooms 56 (5 annexe) (2 fmly) (6 GF) ☞ **S** £95-£175; **D** £115-£195* **Facilities** STV WiFi ⊗ ☼ ⚘ Xmas New Year **Conf** Class 40 Board 50 Thtr 100 Del from £145 to £195* **Parking** 400 **Notes** LB Civ Wed 170

The Granary Hotel & Restaurant

★★★ 81% ●● HOTEL

tel: 01562 777535 **Heath Ln, Shenstone DY10 4BS**
email: info@granary-hotel.co.uk **web:** www.granary-hotel.co.uk
dir: *On A450 between Stourbridge & Worcester, 1m from Kidderminster*

This modern hotel offers spacious, well-equipped accommodation with many rooms enjoying views towards Great Witley and the Amberley Hills. Public areas include a bar and a residents' lounge. The attractive, modern restaurant serves dishes created from locally sourced produce that is cooked with flair and imagination. There are also extensive conference facilities, and the hotel is popular as a wedding venue.

Rooms 18 (1 fmly) (18 GF) ☞ **S** £55-£95; **D** £65-£150 (incl. bkfst)* **Facilities** FTV WiFi **Conf** Class 80 Board 70 Thtr 200 Del from £100 to £175* **Parking** 96 **Notes** LB Civ Wed 120

Gainsborough House Hotel

★★★ 79% HOTEL

tel: 01562 820041 **Bewdley Hill DY11 6BS**
email: reservations@gainsboroughhousehotel.com
web: www.gainsboroughhousehotel.com
dir: *Follow A456 to Kidderminster (West Midlands Safari Park) pass hospital, hotel 500yds on left*

This listed Georgian hotel provides a wide range of thoughtfully furnished bedrooms that have smart modern bathrooms. The contemporary decor and furnishing throughout the public areas highlights the many retained period features. A large function suite and several meeting rooms are available.

Rooms 42 (16 fmly) (12 GF) **D** £58-£105* **Facilities** STV FTV WiFi ⊗ Xmas New Year **Conf** Class 70 Board 60 Thtr 250 Del from £95 to £140* **Services** Air con **Parking** 90 **Notes** LB ⊗ Civ Wed 250

Premier Inn Kidderminster

BUDGET HOTEL

tel: 0871 527 9350 *(Calls cost 13p per minute plus your phone company's access charge)*
Slingfield Mill, Weavers Wharf DY10 1AA
web: www.premierinn.com
dir: *M5 junct 3, A456 towards Kidderminster, 5.5m. Straight on at 1st rdbt, left into Lower Mill St. Straight on into Crown Ln*

High quality, budget accommodation ideal for both families and business travellers. Spacious, en suite bedrooms feature tea and coffee making facilities, and Freeview TV in most hotels. Internet access and WiFi are available for a small fee. The adjacent family restaurant features a wide and varied menu. See also the Hotel Groups pages.

Rooms 56

Find out more about **the NEW Hotel Breakfast Award on page 11**

| **KINGHAM** | **Map 10 SP22** |
| Oxfordshire | |

The Wild Rabbit

◉◉◉ ⌖ RESTAURANT WITH ROOMS

tel: 01608 658389 **Church St OX7 6YA**
email: theteam@thewildrabbit.co.uk **web:** www.thewildrabbit.co.uk

Situated in the idyllic Cotswold village of Kingham, this Grade II listed Georgian building has been lovingly restored and now totally refurbished. The rooms are modern and offer up-to-date technology. The public areas are a real feature with a large bar and open-plan restaurant kitchen. An outside dining area has also been added. The food is exceptional, with many French influences evident in the cooking. Service is informal yet professional and very friendly. Ample car parking is available.

Rooms 12 (1 annexe) (1 fmly)

| **KINGSBRIDGE** | **Map 3 SX74** |
| Devon | |

Buckland-Tout-Saints

★★★ 83% ◉◉ COUNTRY HOUSE HOTEL

tel: 01548 853055 **Goveton TQ7 2DS**
email: info@bucklandtoutsaints.co.uk **web:** www.tout-saints.co.uk
dir: Turn off A381 to Goveton. Follow brown tourist signs to St Peter's Church. Hotel 2nd right after church

It is well worth navigating the winding country lanes to dine at this delightful Queen Anne manor house that has been host to many famous guests over the years. Set in over four acres of gardens the hotel is a peaceful retreat. Bedrooms are tastefully furnished and attractively decorated; the majority are very spacious. Local produce is used with care and imagination to create the dishes offered. This is a popular choice for weddings.

Rooms 16 (6 fmly) ⚡ **Facilities** STV WiFi ⊳ ⥾ Xmas New Year **Conf** Class 40 Board 26 Thtr 80 **Parking** 16 **Notes** ⊗ Civ Wed 120

| **KINGSCLERE** | **Map 5 SU55** |
| Hampshire | |

Sandford Springs Hotel and Golf Club

★★★★ 78% HOTEL

tel: 01635 291500 & 291501 **RG26 5RT**
email: info@sandfordsprings.co.uk **web:** www.sandfordsprings.co.uk
dir: M3 junct 6, A339 for 9m, hotel on right; M4 junct 13, A34 to Newbury then A339 for 11m, hotel on left

This modern hotel is located in a lovely country location and offers a super range of facilities with three 9-hole golf courses; the parks, woods and lakes. In addition there are also conference and meeting facilities. The bedrooms are spacious and have good facilities. There is a choice of restaurants, the Dining Room in the hotel and the Kingsclere, which overlooks the golf course, providing all-day dining.

Rooms 40 (4 fmly) (21 GF) ⚡ **Facilities** FTV WiFi ⊳ ⚖ 27 Putt green New Year **Conf** Class 80 Board 40 Thtr 180 Del from £140 to £168 **Services** Lift Air con **Parking** 150 **Notes** ⊗ Civ Wed 100

| **KINGS LANGLEY** | **Map 6 TL00** |
| Hertfordshire | |

Premier Inn Kings Langley

BUDGET HOTEL

tel: 0871 527 8568 *(Calls cost 13p per minute plus your phone company's access charge)*
Hempstead Rd WD4 8BR
web: www.premierinn.com
dir: 1m from M25 junct 20 on A4251 after King's Langley

High quality, budget accommodation ideal for both families and business travellers. Spacious, en suite bedrooms feature tea and coffee making facilities, and Freeview TV in most hotels. Internet access and WiFi are available for a small fee. The adjacent family restaurant features a wide and varied menu. See also the Hotel Groups pages.

Rooms 63

| **KING'S LYNN** | **Map 12 TF62** |
| Norfolk | |

The Duke's Head Hotel

★★★★ 77% ◉ HOTEL

tel: 01553 774996 & 0844 411 9484
(Calls cost 7p per minute plus your phone company's access charge)
5-6 Tuesday Market Place PE30 1JS
email: reception@dukesheadhotel.com **web:** www.dukesheadhotel.com
dir: From A10/A47/A17 enter King's Lynn via South Gates rdbt. Hotel opposite Corn Exchange.

Occupying a central location and overlooking the market square, this hotel is a beautiful property. The bedrooms are smartly decorated, and include wide-screen TVs, free WiFi and bathrooms with walk-in showers. Parking is also available.

Rooms 78 (6 fmly) ⚡ **Facilities** FTV WiFi ⊳ Xmas New Year **Conf** Class 80 Board 100 Thtr 220 **Services** Lift **Parking** 40 **Notes** ⊗ Civ Wed 200

Best Western Plus Knights Hill Hotel and Spa

★★★★ 75% HOTEL

tel: 01553 675566 **Knights Hill Village, South Wootton PE30 3HQ**
email: reception@knightshill.co.uk **web:** www.abacushotels.co.uk
dir: At junct A148 & A149

This hotel village complex is set on a 16th-century site on the outskirts of King's Lynn. The smartly decorated, well-equipped bedrooms are situated in extensions of the original hunting lodge. Public areas have a wealth of historic charm including the Garden Bistro & Bar and the Farmers Arms Inn, which serves good food and real ales. The hotel also has conference and leisure facilities, including the Imagine Spa.

Rooms 79 (12 annexe) (1 fmly) (38 GF) ⚡ **Facilities** Spa STV WiFi ⊳ ⛲ ♨ ⥾ Gym Xmas New Year **Conf** Class 150 Board 30 Thtr 200 **Parking** 350 **Notes** Civ Wed 90

Congham Hall Country House Hotel

★★★ ◉◉ COUNTRY HOUSE HOTEL

tel: 01485 600250 **Lynn Rd PE32 1AH**
email: info@conghamhallhotel.com **web:** www.conghamhallhotel.co.uk

(For full entry see Grimston)

K

K

KING'S LYNN *continued*

Bank House

★★★ 83% HOTEL

tel: 01553 660492 **King's Staithe Square PE30 1RD**
email: info@thebankhouse.co.uk **web:** www.thebankhouse.co.uk
dir: *In King's Lynn Old Town follow quay, through floodgates, hotel on right opposite Custom House*

This Grade II listed, 18th-century town house is situated on the quay side in the heart of King's Lynn's historical quarter. Bedrooms are individually decorated and have high quality fabrics and furnishings along with a range of useful facilities. Public rooms include the Counting House coffee shop, a wine bar and brasserie restaurant, as well as a residents' lounge.

Rooms 12 (5 fmly) ♠ **S** £85-£120; **D** £115-£220 (incl. bkfst)* **Facilities** FTV WiFi ⚡ Xmas New Year **Conf** Class 20 Board 15 Thtr 30 Del from £150* **Notes** LB ⊗

Grange Hotel

★★ 72% HOTEL

tel: 01553 673777 & 671222 **Willow Park, South Wootton Ln PE30 3BP**
email: info@thegrangehotelkingslynn.co.uk **web:** www.thegrangehotelkingslynn.co.uk
dir: *A148 towards King's Lynn for 1.5m. At lights left into Wootton Rd, 400yds, on right into South Wootton Ln. Hotel 1st on left*

Expect a warm welcome at this Edwardian house which is situated in a quiet residential area in its own grounds. Public rooms include a smart lounge bar and a cosy restaurant. The spacious bedrooms are pleasantly decorated and equipped with many thoughtful touches; some are located in an adjacent wing.

Rooms 9 (4 annexe) (2 fmly) (4 GF) **Facilities** WiFi Xmas **Conf** Class 15 Board 12 Thtr 20 **Parking** 15

Premier Inn King's Lynn

BUDGET HOTEL

tel: 0871 527 8570 *(Calls cost 13p per minute plus your phone company's access charge)*
Clenchwarton Rd, West Lynn PE34 3LJ
web: www.premierinn.com
dir: *At junct of A47 & A17*

High quality, budget accommodation ideal for both families and business travellers. Spacious, en suite bedrooms feature tea and coffee making facilities, and Freeview TV in most hotels. Internet access and WiFi are available for a small fee. The adjacent family restaurant features a wide and varied menu. See also the Hotel Groups pages.

Rooms 148

| KINGSTON UPON HULL | Map 17 TA02 |
| East Riding of Yorkshire | |

Best Western Willerby Manor Hotel

★★★ 83% HOTEL

tel: 01482 652616 **Well Ln HU10 6ER**
email: willerbymanor@bestwestern.co.uk **web:** www.willerbymanor.co.uk

(For full entry see Willerby)

Mercure Hull Royal Hotel

★★★ 77% HOTEL

tel: 01482 325087 **170 Ferensway HU1 3UF**
email: reservations@hotels-hull.co.uk **web:** www.hotels-hull.com
dir: *A63 to city centre. Follow signs to railway station, hotel connected*

A railway hotel in Victorian times, this impressive building has been modernised in recent years. The stunning central lounge area is the focal point and there are extensive conference and banqueting facilities, with complimentary parking and WiFi access also provided. The contemporary bedrooms have bold colour schemes with good facilities including flat-screen TVs; many have air conditioning. There is a leisure club adjacent to the hotel.

Rooms 155 (3 fmly) ♠ **Facilities** FTV WiFi Xmas New Year **Conf** Class 150 Board 70 Thtr 400 **Services** Lift **Parking** 84 **Notes** ⊗ Civ Wed 400

Premier Inn Hull City Centre

BUDGET HOTEL

tel: 0871 527 8534 *(Calls cost 13p per minute plus your phone company's access charge)*
Tower St HU9 1TQ
web: www.premierinn.com
dir: *M62, A63 into Hull city centre. At rdbt left onto A1165 (Great Union St), left into Citadel Way. Hotel at end on right*

High quality, budget accommodation ideal for both families and business travellers. Spacious, en suite bedrooms feature tea and coffee making facilities, and Freeview TV in most hotels. Internet access and WiFi are available for a small fee. The adjacent family restaurant features a wide and varied menu. See also the Hotel Groups pages.

Rooms 136

Premier Inn Hull North

BUDGET HOTEL

tel: 0871 527 8536 *(Calls cost 13p per minute plus your phone company's access charge)*
Ashcombe Rd, Kingswood Park HU7 3DD
web: www.premierinn.com
dir: *A63 to town centre, take A1079 N for approx 5m. Right at rdbt onto A1033. Hotel at 2nd rdbt in New Kingswood Park*

Rooms 65

Premier Inn Hull West

BUDGET HOTEL

tel: 0871 527 8538 *(Calls cost 13p per minute plus your phone company's access charge)*
Ferriby Rd, Hessle HU13 0JA
web: www.premierinn.com
dir: *A63 onto A15 to Humber Bridge (Beverley & Hessle Viewpoint). Hotel at 1st rdbt*

Rooms 61

Ibis Hull

AA Advertised

tel: 01482 387500 **Osborne St HU1 2NL**
email: h3479@accor.com **web:** www.ibishotel.com
dir: *M62/A63 straight across at rdbt, follow signs for Princes Quay onto Myton St. Hotel on corner of Osborne St & Ferensway*

Modern, budget hotel offering comfortable accommodation in bright and practical bedrooms. Breakfast is self-service and dinner is available in the restaurant.

Rooms 106 (19 GF) **Facilities** STV WiFi ⚡ **Services** Lift Air con **Parking** 25

KINGSTON UPON THAMES
Greater London

Premier Inn London Kingston upon Thames

BUDGET HOTEL PLAN 1 C1

tel: 0871 527 9586 *(Calls cost 13p per minute plus your phone company's access charge)*
Combined House, 15 Wheatfield Way, Kingston upon Thames KT1 2PA
web: www.premierinn.com
dir: *M25 junct 13, A30 (signed Staines), A308 towards Kingston upon Thames. Pass Bentalls shopping centre, stay in right lane, left at Odeon cinema. On one-way system pass Cattle Market car park on left. Right after car park, left into Eden St. Left into Lady Booth Rd*

High quality, budget accommodation ideal for both families and business travellers. Spacious, en suite bedrooms feature tea and coffee making facilities, and Freeview TV in most hotels. Internet access and WiFi are available for a small fee. The adjacent family restaurant features a wide and varied menu. See also the Hotel Groups pages.

Rooms 160

KINGSWINFORD
West Midlands
Map 10 SO88

Premier Inn Dudley (Kingswinford)

BUDGET HOTEL

tel: 0871 527 8314 *(Calls cost 13p per minute plus your phone company's access charge)*
Dudley Rd DY6 8WT
web: www.premierinn.com
dir: *A4123 to Dudley, A461 follow signs for Russell's Hall Hospital. On A4101 to Kingswinford, hotel opposite Pensnett Trading Estate*

High quality, budget accommodation ideal for both families and business travellers. Spacious, en suite bedrooms feature tea and coffee making facilities, and Freeview TV in most hotels. Internet access and WiFi are available for a small fee. The adjacent family restaurant features a wide and varied menu. See also the Hotel Groups pages.

Rooms 60

KIRKBY LONSDALE
Cumbria
Map 18 SD67

INSPECTORS' CHOICE

Hipping Hall

RESTAURANT WITH ROOMS

tel: 015242 71187 **Cowan Bridge LA6 2JJ**
email: info@hippinghall.com **web:** www.hippinghall.com
dir: *M6 junct 36, A65 through Kirkby Lonsdale towards Skipton. On right after Cowan Bridge*

Close to the market town of Kirkby Lonsdale, Hipping Hall offers spacious bedrooms, designed using soft shades with sumptuous textures and fabrics; the bathrooms use natural stone, slate and limestone to great effect. There are also three spacious cottage suites that create a real hideaway experience. The sitting room, with large, comfortable sofas has a traditional feel. The 3 AA Rosette-worthy restaurant is a 15th-century hall with tapestries and a minstrels' gallery that is as impressive as it is intimate.

Rooms 15 (8 annexe)

The Sun Inn

RESTAURANT WITH ROOMS

tel: 015242 71965 **6 Market St LA6 2AU**
email: email@sun-inn.info **web:** www.sun-inn.info
dir: *From A65 follow signs to town centre. Inn on main street*

The Sun is a 17th-century inn situated in a historic market town, overlooking St Mary's Church. The atmospheric bar features stone walls, wooden beams and log fires with real ales available. Delicious meals are served in the bar or the more formal, modern restaurant. Traditional and modern styles are blended together in the beautifully appointed rooms with excellent en suites.

Rooms 11 (1 fmly)

Plato's

RESTAURANT WITH ROOMS

tel: 015242 74180 **2 Mill Brow LA6 2AT**
email: hello@platoskirkby.co.uk **web:** www.platoskirkbylonsdale.co.uk
dir: *M6 junct 36, A65 Kirkby Lonsdale, after 5m at rdbt take 1st exit, onto one-way system*

Tucked away in the heart of the popular market town, Plato's is steeped in history. Sumptuous bedrooms have a wealth of thoughtful extras, and imaginative food is available in the elegant restaurant with its open-plan kitchen. The lounge bar is more rustic in style with fires to relax by. A warm welcome and professional service is assured. The Pop Shop offers Plato's cuisine to take away.

Rooms 8

KNARESBOROUGH
North Yorkshire
Map 19 SE35

General Tarleton Inn

RESTAURANT WITH ROOMS

tel: 01423 340284 **Boroughbridge Rd, Ferrensby HG5 0PZ**
email: gti@generaltarleton.co.uk **web:** www.generaltarleton.co.uk
dir: *A1(M) junct 48 at Boroughbridge, take A6055 to Knaresborough. 4m on right*

This 18th-century coaching inn is both beautiful and stylish. Though the physical aspects are impressive, the emphasis here is on food with high-quality, skilfully prepared dishes served in the smart bar-brasserie and in the Orangery. There is also a richly furnished cocktail lounge with a galleried private dining room above it. Bedrooms are very comfortable and business guests are also well catered for.

Rooms 13

KNIPTON
Leicestershire
Map 11 SK83

The Manners Arms

RESTAURANT WITH ROOMS

tel: 01476 879222 **Croxton Rd NG32 1RH**
email: info@mannersarms.com **web:** www.mannersarms.com
dir: *From A607 follow signs to Knipton; from A52 follow signs to Belvoir Castle*

Part of the Rutland Estate and built as a hunting lodge for the 6th Duke, The Manners Arms offers thoughtfully furnished bedrooms designed by the present Duchess. Public areas include the intimate Beater's Bar and attractive Red Coats Restaurant, popular for its imaginative menus.

Rooms 10 (1 fmly)

K

KNUTSFORD
Cheshire

Map 15 SJ77

The Mere Golf Resort & Spa
★★★★ 84% HOTEL

tel: 01565 830155 **Chester Rd, Mere WA16 6LJ**
web: www.themereresort.co.uk
dir: *M6 junct 19 or M56 junct 7*

This hotel sits alongside Mere Lake and is close to the picturesque town of Knutsford; there are excellent transport links with Manchester International Airport being only ten minutes away. The resort's historic main Victorian building conveys the classic charm of that era, and offers stylish, luxury accommodation. The championship golf course designed by James Braid is both beautiful and challenging. The spa features an extensive range of treatments and facilities including a Thermal Zone. The staff are professional and very friendly, offering personal service.

Rooms 81 **Conf** Class 350 Board 40 Thtr 700

Cottons Hotel & Spa
★★★★ 79% HOTEL

THWAITES

tel: 01565 650333 **Manchester Rd WA16 0SU**
email: cottons@shirehotels.com **web:** www.shirehotels.co.uk/our-hotels/cottons
dir: *On A50, 1m from M6 junct 19*

The superb leisure facilities and quiet location are great attractions at this hotel, which is just a short distance from Manchester Airport. Bedrooms are smartly appointed in various styles, and executive rooms have very good working areas. The hotel has spacious lounge areas and an excellent leisure centre. Thwaites Hotels is the AA Hotel Group of the Year 2016-2017.

Rooms 139 (14 fmly) (48 GF) ☎ **S** £105-£200; **D** £105-£200* **Facilities** Spa STV WiFi ⇗ ☼ Gym Steam room Activity studio for exercise classes Sauna Children's splash pool Xmas New Year **Conf** Class 100 Board 36 Thtr 200 Del from £130 to £180* **Services** Lift Air con **Parking** 180 **Notes** LB ⊗ Civ Wed 120

Mere Court Hotel & Conference Centre
★★★★ 76% HOTEL

tel: 01565 831000 **Warrington Rd, Mere WA16 0RW**
email: sales@merecourt.co.uk **web:** www.merecourt.co.uk
dir: *A50, 1m W of junct with A556, on right*

This is a smart and attractive hotel, set in extensive, well-tended gardens. The elegant and spacious bedrooms are individually styled and offer a host of thoughtful extras. Conference facilities are particularly impressive and there is a large, self contained, conservatory function suite. Dining is available in the fine dining Arboreum Restaurant.

Rooms 34 (24 fmly) (12 GF) **Facilities** STV FTV WiFi Xmas New Year **Conf** Class 75 Board 50 Thtr 200 **Services** Lift **Parking** 150 **Notes** ⊗ Civ Wed 150

The Longview Hotel
★★ 81% HOTEL

tel: 01565 632119 & 632244 **55 Manchester Rd WA16 0LX**
email: enquiries@longviewhotel.com **web:** www.longviewhotel.com
dir: *M6 junct 19 take A556 W towards Chester. Left at lights onto A5033, 1.5m to rdbt then left. Hotel 200yds on right*

This friendly, personally-run hotel is within a Victorian terrace near the centre of Knutsford, offering high standards of hospitality and attractive public areas including a cellar bar. The restaurant serves a range of dishes. Bedrooms, located either in a superb renovation of a nearby house or within the main building, are individually styled and offer comfortable, modern appointment.

Rooms 32 (19 annexe) (1 fmly) (5 GF) **Facilities** FTV WiFi ⇗ **Conf** Class 20 Board 20 **Parking** 20 **Notes** ⊗ Closed 21 Dec-6 Jan

Premier Inn Knutsford (Bucklow Hill)
BUDGET HOTEL

tel: 0871 527 8572 *(Calls cost 13p per minute plus your phone company's access charge)*
Bucklow Hill WA16 6RD
web: www.premierinn.com
dir: *M6 junct 19, A556 towards Manchester Airport & Stockport*

High quality, budget accommodation ideal for both families and business travellers. Spacious, en suite bedrooms feature tea and coffee making facilities, and Freeview TV in most hotels. Internet access and WiFi are available for a small fee. The adjacent family restaurant features a wide and varied menu. See also the Hotel Groups pages.

Rooms 68

Premier Inn Knutsford (Mere)
BUDGET HOTEL

tel: 0871 527 8574 *(Calls cost 13p per minute plus your phone company's access charge)*
Warrington Rd, Hoo Green, Mere WA16 0PZ
web: www.premierinn.com
dir: *M6 junct 19, A556, follow Manchester signs. At 1st lights left onto A50 towards Warrington. Hotel 1m on right*

Rooms 28

K

Belle Epoque

 RESTAURANT WITH ROOMS

tel: 01565 633060 **60 King St WA16 6DT**
web: www.thebelleepoque.com

This long established fixture on the north west dining scene has welcomed guests for over 40 years. The opulent, boutique styling lives up to its name throughout the bar and restaurant where imaginative French-leaning cuisine is the centrepiece. Accommodation is in seven rooms of varying size. All are equipped to a modern standard.

Rooms 7

LACEBY	Map 17 TA20
Lincolnshire	

Best Western Oaklands Hall Hotel

★★★ 81% HOTEL

tel: 01472 872248 **Barton St DN37 7LF**
email: reception@oaklandshallhotel.co.uk **web:** www.oaklandshallhotel.co.uk
dir: At junct of A46 & A18 at Laceby, on edge of Grimsby

This attractive 19th-century property is located on a private estate in five acres of parkland. It has been refurbished with a contemporary style while retaining beautiful period features. The Comfy Duck restaurant is stylish, and food is a highlight of any stay, with a strong emphasis on local produce. Bedrooms are comfortable and complimentary WiFi is provided.

Rooms 46 (5 fmly) (10 GF) **Facilities** FTV WiFi ♭ TL New Year **Conf** Class 150 Board 50 Thtr 180 Del from £120 to £140* **Parking** 80 **Notes** ⊗ Civ Wed 150

LANCASTER	Map 18 SD46
Lancashire	

Lancaster House

★★★★ 78% HOTEL

tel: 01524 844822 **Green Ln, Ellel LA1 4GJ**
email: lancasterhouse@englishlakes.co.uk **web:** www.englishlakes.co.uk
dir: M6 junct 33 N towards Lancaster. Through Galgate into Green Ln. Hotel before university on right

This modern hotel enjoys a rural setting south of the city and close to the university. The attractive open-plan reception and lounge boast a roaring log fire in colder months. Bedrooms are spacious, and include 19 rooms that are particularly well equipped for business guests. There are leisure facilities with a hot tub and a function suite.

Rooms 99 (29 fmly) (44 GF) **Facilities** Spa STV WiFi ♭ HL ☑ supervised Gym Beauty salon Xmas New Year **Conf** Class 60 Board 48 Thtr 250 **Parking** 120 **Notes** Civ Wed 140

Premier Inn Lancaster

BUDGET HOTEL

tel: 0871 527 8576 *(Calls cost 13p per minute plus your phone company's access charge)*
Lancaster Business Park, Caton Rd LA1 3PE
web: www.premierinn.com
dir: M6 junct 34, A683 towards Lancaster. Hotel 0.25m on left at entrance to Business Park

High quality, budget accommodation ideal for both families and business travellers. Spacious, en suite bedrooms feature tea and coffee making facilities, and Freeview TV in most hotels. Internet access and WiFi are available for a small fee. The adjacent family restaurant features a wide and varied menu. See also the Hotel Groups pages.

Rooms 85

LAND'S END	Map 2 SW32
Cornwall	

The Land's End Hotel

★★★ 78% HOTEL

tel: 01736 871844 **TR19 7AA**
email: reservations@landsendhotel.co.uk **web:** www.landsendhotel.co.uk
dir: *From Penzance take A30, follow Land's End signs. After Sennen 1m to Land's End*

This famous location provides a memorable setting for The Land's End Hotel. Bedrooms, many with stunning views of the Atlantic, are pleasantly decorated and comfortable. Refurbished public areas provide plenty of style and comfort with a relaxing lounge and convivial bar. The restaurant is equally impressive with accomplished cuisine complementing the amazing views out to sea.

Rooms 30 (4 fmly) **Facilities** FTV WiFi Free entry to Land's End Visitor Centre & Attractions Xmas **Conf** Class 50 Board 30 Thtr 100 **Parking** 100 **Notes** ⊗ Civ Wed 120

L

L

LANGHO
Lancashire   Map 18 SD73

AA HOTEL OF THE YEAR
FOR ENGLAND 2016-2017

INSPECTORS' CHOICE

Northcote
★★★★ ◉◉◉◉ ⚘ SMALL HOTEL

tel: 01254 240555 **Northcote Rd BB6 8BE**
email: reception@northcote.com **web:** www.northcote.com
dir: M6 junct 31, 9m to Northcote. Follow Clitheroe A59 signs, Hotel on left before rdbt

This is a gastronomic haven where guests return to sample the delights of its famous kitchen. The outstanding cooking includes Lancashire's finest fare, and fruit and herbs from the hotel's own beautifully laid-out organic gardens. Drinks can be enjoyed in the comfortable, elegantly furnished lounges and bar. Each of the luxury bedrooms has its own identity with sumptuous fabrics and soft furnishings, sophisticated lighting and ultra modern bathrooms; some have a garden patio. New annexe rooms are particularly impressive.

Rooms 26 (8 annexe) (3 fmly) (8 GF) ⚟ **S** £220-£565; **D** £260-£605 (incl. bkfst)*
Facilities STV FTV WiFi ⚓ Xmas New Year **Conf** Class 40 Board 20 Thtr 40 Del £250* **Services** Lift **Parking** 50 **Notes** ⊗ Civ Wed 60

Best Western Mytton Fold Hotel and Golf Club Best Western.
★★★ Ⓐ HOTEL

tel: 01254 240662 & 245392 **Whalley Rd BB6 8AB**
email: reception@myttonfold.co.uk **web:** www.bw-myttonfoldhotel.co.uk
dir: At large rdbt on A59, follow signs for Whalley, exit into Whalley Road. Hotel on right

Set in pretty and well maintained grounds that are a riot of colour in the summer, this hotel has views over the golf course to Pendle Hill beyond. The bedrooms are smart and include two with four-posters. This is a popular wedding venue.

Rooms 43 (12 fmly) (10 GF) ⚟ **Facilities** STV WiFi ⚓ 18 Putt green Xmas **Conf** Class 60 Board 40 Thtr 290 **Services** Lift **Parking** 300 **Notes** LB Closed 1 Jan Civ Wed 250

LASTINGHAM
North Yorkshire   Map 19 SE79

Lastingham Grange Hotel
★★★ 79% HOTEL

tel: 01751 417345 & 417402 **YO62 6TH**
email: reservations@lastinghamgrange.com **web:** www.lastinghamgrange.com
dir: From A170 follow signs for Appleton-le-Moors, continue into Lastingham, pass church on left, right, then left up hill. Hotel on right

A warm welcome and sincere hospitality have been the hallmarks of this hotel for almost 60 years. Antique furniture is plentiful, and the lounge and the dining room both look out onto the terrace and sunken rose garden below. There is a large play area for older children and the moorland views are breathtaking.

Rooms 12 (2 fmly) **S** £120-£150; **D** £175-£210 (incl. bkfst)* **Facilities** FTV WiFi ⚓ Large adventure playground **Parking** 30 **Notes** LB Closed Dec-Feb

LAVENHAM
Suffolk   Map 13 TL94

INSPECTORS' CHOICE

The Swan at Lavenham Hotel and Spa
★★★★ ◉◉ HOTEL

tel: 01787 247477 **High St CO10 9QA**
email: info@theswanatlavenham.co.uk **web:** www.theswanatlavenham.co.uk
dir: From Bury St Edmunds take A134 S, then A1141 to Lavenham

The Swan Hotel and Spa is a delightful collection of listed buildings, dating back to the 14th century, lovingly restored to retain their original charm. Public rooms include comfortable lounge areas, a charming rustic bar, an informal brasserie and a fine-dining restaurant. Bedrooms are tastefully furnished and equipped with many thoughtful touches. The friendly staff are helpful, attentive and offer professional service. Facilities in the newly opened Weavers' House Spa include six treatment rooms offering over 30 treatments, a hot stone sauna, steam room, manicure and pedicure area, a beautiful spa boutique, outdoor terrace and a vitality pool.

Rooms 45 (7 fmly) (9 GF) ⚟ **S** £110; **D** £185-£360 (incl. bkfst)* **Facilities** FTV WiFi ⚓ Steam room Sauna Vitality pool Xmas New Year **Conf** Class 36 Board 30 Thtr 50 Del £165* **Parking** 30 **Notes** Civ Wed 100

Lavenham Great House 'Restaurant With Rooms'

◉◉◉ ⬗ RESTAURANT WITH ROOMS

tel: 01787 247431 **Market Place CO10 9QZ**
email: info@greathouse.co.uk **web:** www.greathouse.co.uk
dir: Exit A1141 into Market Ln, behind cross on Market Place

The 18th-century frontage on Market Place conceals a 15th-century timber-framed building that is now a restaurant with rooms. Lavenham Great House is a little slice of France, offering high-quality rural cuisine served by French staff. The spacious bedrooms are individually decorated and thoughtfully equipped with many useful extras; some rooms have a separate lounge area.

Rooms 5 (1 fmly)

LEA MARSTON
Warwickshire   Map 10 SP29

Lea Marston Hotel & Spa

★★★★ 78% ◉◉ HOTEL

tel: 01675 470468 **Haunch Ln B76 0BY**
email: info@leamarstonhotel.co.uk **web:** www.leamarstonhotel.co.uk
dir: M42 junct 9, A4097 to Kingsbury. Hotel signed 1.5m on right

Excellent access to the motorway network and a good range of sports facilities make this hotel a popular choice for conferences and leisure breaks. Bedrooms are mostly set around an attractive quadrangle and are generously equipped. Diners can choose between the popular Sportsman's Lounge Bar and the elegant Adderley Restaurant.

Rooms 118 (16 fmly) (66 GF) ☏ **Facilities** Spa STV FTV WiFi ⬚ ⬚ ⬚ 9 Putt green Gym Golf driving range Golf simulator Sauna Steam room Rasul Xmas New Year **Conf** Class 50 Board 30 Thtr 140 Del from £130 to £180* **Services** Lift **Parking** 220 **Notes** ⊗ Civ Wed 100

LEAMINGTON SPA (ROYAL)
Warwickshire   Map 10 SP36

Mallory Court Hotel

★★★ ⬗ HOTEL

tel: 01926 330214 **Harbury Ln, Bishop's Tachbrook CV33 9QB**
email: info@mallory.co.uk **web:** www.mallory.co.uk
dir: M40 junct 13 N'bound left, left again towards Bishops Tachbrook, right into Harbury Ln after 0.5m. M40 junct 14 S'bound A452 to Leamington, at 2nd rdbt left into Harbury Ln

Mallory Court Hotel is part of the Eden Hotel Collection and with its tranquil rural setting, this elegant Lutyens-style country house is an idyllic retreat, set in ten acres of landscaped gardens with immaculate lawns and an orchard. Relaxation is easy in the two sumptuous lounges, drawing room or conservatory. Dining is a treat in either the elegant restaurant or the brasserie. Bedrooms in the main house are luxuriously decorated and most have wonderful views. Those in the Knights Suite are more contemporary and have their own access via a smart conference and banqueting facility.

Rooms 43 (23 annexe) (2 fmly) (5 GF) ☏ **S** fr £145; **D** £159-£575 **Facilities** FTV WiFi ⬚ ⬚ ⬚ Gym Xmas New Year **Conf** Class 160 Board 50 Thtr 200 Del from £189 to £240 **Services** Lift **Parking** 120 **Notes** LB ⊗ Civ Wed 160

Best Western Falstaff Hotel

★★★ 73% HOTEL

tel: 01926 312044 **16-20 Warwick New Rd CV32 5JQ**
email: sales@falstaffhotel.com **web:** www.falstaffhotel.com
dir: M40 junct 13 or 14, follow Leamington Spa signs. Over 4 rdbts, under bridge. Left into Princes Dr, right at mini-rdbt

Bedrooms at this hotel come in a variety of sizes and styles and are well equipped, with many thoughtful extras. Snacks can be taken in the relaxing lounge bar, and an interesting selection of English and continental dishes is offered in the restaurant; 24-hour room service is also available. Conference and banqueting facilities are extensive.

Rooms 59 (3 fmly) (16 GF) ☏ **S** £65-£95; **D** £75-£105 (incl. bkfst) **Facilities** FTV WiFi ⬚ Arrangement with local health club Xmas New Year **Conf** Class 30 Board 30 Thtr 70 Del from £125 to £145 **Parking** 40

LEAMINGSTON SPA (ROYAL) *continued*

Premier Inn Leamington Spa Town Centre

BUDGET HOTEL

tel: 0871 527 9380 *(Calls cost 13p per minute plus your phone company's access charge)*
Regency Arcade, The Parade CV32 4BQ
web: www.premierinn.com
dir: *From N: M40 junct 15/A452. Through 4 rdbts. At next rdbt take 4th exit, at final rdbt, take 1st exit A452 (Adelaide Rd). Right onto Dormer Place & left onto St Peters Rd into St Peters car park. Follow directional signage to Premier Inn. From S: M40 junct 13 then follow directions as above*

High quality, budget accommodation ideal for both families and business travellers. Spacious, en suite bedrooms feature tea and coffee making facilities, and Freeview TV in most hotels. Internet access and WiFi are available for a small fee. The adjacent family restaurant features a wide and varied menu. See also the Hotel Groups pages.

Rooms 82

| LEDBURY | Map 10 SO73 |
| Herefordshire | |

Feathers Hotel

★★★ 83% ❀ HOTEL

tel: 01531 635266 & 638950 **High St HR8 1DS**
email: mary@feathers-ledbury.co.uk **web:** www.feathers-ledbury.co.uk
dir: *S from Worcester on A449, E from Hereford on A438, N from Gloucester on A417. Hotel in town centre*

A wealth of authentic features can be found at this historic timber-framed hotel, situated in the middle of town. The comfortably equipped bedrooms are tastefully decorated; there is also Eve's Cottage, in the grounds, and Lanark House, a two-bedroom apartment that is ideal for families and self-catering use. Well-prepared meals can be taken in Fuggles Brasserie with its adjoining bar, and breakfast is served in Quills Restaurant. A swimming pool and gym are available for use by guests.

Rooms 22 (3 annexe) (2 fmly) ☞ **S** £99-£130; **D** £155-£245 (incl. bkfst)*
Facilities STV FTV WiFi ⌖ Gym Steam room New Year **Conf** Class 80 Board 40 Thtr 140 Del £137.50* **Parking** 30 **Notes** LB Civ Wed 100

Leadon House Hotel

★★ 🅰 SMALL HOTEL

tel: 01531 631199 & 07943 551877 **Ross Rd HR8 2LP**
email: leadon.house@btconnect.com **web:** www.leadonhouse.com
dir: *M5 junct 8/M50/A417 exit Ledbury. Left at 1st rdbt then take A449. Hotel 400yds on right by Ledbury Rugby Club*

Enjoy a relaxing break at this family-run hotel, which has been tastefully refurbished in an Edwardian style, offering an idyllic environment and a peaceful night's stay. Many interesting architectural features add to the unique charm and elegance. All rooms are en suite and finished to a high standard, with plenty of attention paid to detail. Also available is the Coach House two bedroom apartment.

Rooms 8 (2 annexe) (1 fmly) (1 GF) **S** £70-£85; **D** £90-£125 (incl. bkfst)*
Facilities FTV WiFi **Parking** 10 **Notes** ⊗ No children 16yrs

Verzon House

⊛⊛ RESTAURANT WITH ROOMS

tel: 01531 670381 **Trumpet HR8 2PZ**
email: info@verzonhouse.com **web:** www.verzonhouse.com
dir: *M50 junct 2 follow signs to Ledbury. Left at rdbt for Hereford. Follow A438 3m then Verzon is on right*

Located on the main road, just a short distance from Ledbury, this delightful restaurant with rooms has been completely refurbished throughout by the new owners. Contemporary styling mixes well with a more traditional country house feel creating a relaxing ambience. Bedrooms offer a range of shapes and sizes, most with glorious views over the countryside towards the Malvern Hills. Dinner and breakfast provide a range of tempting, high-quality dishes all prepared with care and attention.

Rooms 8 (1 fmly)

| LEEDS | Map 19 SE23 |
| West Yorkshire | |

See also **Gomersal & Wakefield**

The New Ellington

★★★★ 83% TOWN HOUSE HOTEL

"bespoke" HOTELS

tel: 0113 204 2150 **23-25 York Place LS1 2EY**
email: info@thenewellington.com **web:** www.thenewellington.com

Near the central railway station and the civic and business quarters, this hotel, with an art deco and a musical theme in part, offers guests modern amenities. Bedrooms are air-conditioned, offer free WiFi, high-quality bed linen and Nespresso coffee machines; some have quiet balconies too. The ground-floor atrium Gin Bar lounge leads to the lower ground floor restaurant that serves a range of interesting dishes. Limited on-site chargeable parking is available on a first-come first-served basis.

Rooms 34 (3 GF) ☞ **S** £110-£395; **D** £110-£395 **Facilities** FTV WiFi ⌖ **Services** Lift Air con **Notes** ⊗ Closed 24-27 Dec

Thorpe Park Hotel & Spa

★★★★ 84% ❀ HOTEL

THWAITES

tel: 0113 264 1000 **Century Way, Thorpe Park LS15 8ZB**
email: thorpepark@shirehotels.com **web:** www.shirehotels.co.uk/our-hotels/thorpe-park
dir: *M1 junct 46, follow signs for Thorpe Park*

Conveniently close to the M1, this hotel offers bedrooms that are modern in both style and facilities. The Terrace and courtyard offer all-day casual dining and refreshments, and the restaurant features a Mediterranean-themed menu. There is also a state-of-the-art spa and leisure facilities. Thwaites Hotels is the AA Hotel Group of the Year 2016-2017.

Rooms 111 (3 fmly) (25 GF) ☞ **S** £106-£200; **D** £106-£200* **Facilities** Spa STV WiFi ⌖ HL ⌖ Gym Activity studio Steam room Sauna New Year **Conf** Class 100 Board 50 Thtr 200 Del from £130 to £180* **Services** Lift Air con **Parking** 200 **Notes** LB ⊗ Civ Wed 150

The Queens
★★★★ 81% HOTEL

tel: 0113 243 1323 **City Square LS1 1PJ**
email: queensreservations@qhotels.co.uk **web:** www.qhotels.co.uk
dir: *M621, M1 & M62 follow signs for city centre & rail station, along Neville St towards City Square. Under rail bridge, at lights left into slip road in front of hotel*

A legacy from the golden age of railways and located in the heart of Leeds, overlooking City Square, this grand Victorian hotel retains much of its original splendour. Public rooms include the spacious lounge bar, a range of conference and function rooms along with the grand ballroom. Bedrooms vary in size but all are very well equipped, and there is a choice of suites available.

Rooms 215 (16 fmly) ⬆ **S** £79-£205; **D** £89-£215 **Facilities** STV WiFi ⬇ New Year **Conf** Class 200 Board 80 Thtr 500 Del from £149 to £209* **Services** Lift Air con **Parking** 55 **Notes** ⊗ Civ Wed 500

Oulton Hall
★★★★ 80% HOTEL

tel: 0113 282 1000 **Rothwell Ln, Oulton LS26 8HN**
email: oultonreception@qhotels.co.uk **web:** www.qhotels.co.uk/oultonhall
dir: *2m from M62 junct 30, follow Rothwell signs, then 'Oulton 1m' sign. 1st exit at next 2 rdbts. Hotel on left. Or 1m from M1 junct 44, follow Castleford & Pontefract sign on A639*

Surrounded by the beautiful Yorkshire Dales, yet only 15 minutes from the city centre, this elegant 19th-century house offers the best of both worlds. Impressive features include stylish, opulent day rooms and delightful formal gardens, which have been restored to their original design. The hotel boasts a choice of dining options, and extensive leisure facilities. Golfers can book preferential tee times at the adjacent golf club.

Rooms 152 **S** £89-£400; **D** £99-£450 (incl. bkfst) **Facilities** Spa STV FTV WiFi IIL ⬇ ⬇ 27 Putt green ⬇ Gym Beauty therapy Sauna Steam room Juice bar Xmas New Year **Conf** Class 160 Board 40 Thtr 350 Del from £130 to £199 **Services** Lift Air con **Parking** 260 **Notes** LB ⊗ Civ Wed 250

Malmaison Leeds
★★★★ 75% ⊚ HOTEL

tel: 0113 398 1000 & 0844 693 0654
(Calls cost 7p per minute plus your phone company's access charge) **1 Swinegate LS1 4AG**
email: leeds@malmaison.com **web:** www.malmaison.com
dir: *M621/M1 junct 3, follow city centre signs. At KPMG building, right into Sovereign Street. Hotel at end on right*

Close to the waterfront, this stylish property offers striking bedrooms with CD players and air conditioning. The popular bar and brasserie feature vaulted ceilings, intimate lighting and offer a choice of a full three-course meal or a substantial snack. Service is both willing and friendly. A small fitness centre and impressive meeting rooms complete the package.

Rooms 100 (4 fmly) ⬆ **Facilities** STV WiFi ⬇ Gym Xmas New Year **Conf** Class 30 Board 30 Thtr 80 **Services** Lift Air con **Notes** Civ Wed 70

The Met
★★★★ 75% HOTEL

tel: 0113 245 0841 **King St LS1 2HQ**
email: metropole.sales@principal-hotels.com **web:** www.principal-hayley.com
dir: *From M1, M62 & M621 follow city centre signs. A65 into Wellington St. At 1st traffic island right into King St, hotel on right*

Said to be the best example of this type of building in the city, this splendid terracotta-fronted hotel is centrally located and convenient for the railway station. All bedrooms are appointed to suit the business traveller, with hi-speed internet access and a working area. The Restaurant and the Tempest Bar make convenient dining options. There are also impressive conference and banqueting facilities. Some parking space is available.

Rooms 120 ⬆ **S** £59-£279; **D** £85-£299* **Facilities** STV FTV WiFi ⬇ Gym Mini gym **Conf** Class 120 Board 100 Thtr 250 Del from £119 to £209* **Services** Lift **Parking** 30 **Notes** LB ⊗ RS 24 Dec-1 Jan Civ Wed 200

Park Plaza Leeds
★★★★ 75% HOTEL

tel: 0113 380 4000 & 0844 415 6720
(Calls cost 7p per minute plus your phone company's access charge) **Boar Ln LS1 5NS**
email: pplinfo@pphe.com **web:** www.parkplaza.com
dir: *Follow signs for city centre*

Chic, stylish, ultra modern, city-centre hotel located just opposite City Square. Chino Latino, located on the first floor, is a fusion Far East and modern Japanese restaurant with a Latino bar. Stylish, air-conditioned bedrooms are spacious and have a range of modern facilities, including high-speed internet connection.

Rooms 187 ⬆ **Facilities** FTV WiFi ⬇ Gym Xmas New Year **Conf** Class 70 Board 60 Thtr 220 **Services** Lift Air con **Parking** 6 **Notes** Civ Wed 120

Novotel Leeds Centre
★★★★ 74% HOTEL

tel: 0113 242 6446 **4 Whitehall, Whitehall Quay LS1 4HR**
email: H3270@accor.com **web:** www.novotel.com
dir: *M621 junct 3, follow signs to rail station. Into Aire St & left at lights*

With a minimalist style, this contemporary hotel provides a quality experience close to the city centre and within walking distance of the train station. Spacious, climate-controlled bedrooms are provided, while public areas are smartly presented. The bar is modern and airy, and Elements Restaurant offers an informal brasserie style. Facilities also include a fitness suite and a sauna. There is complimentary WiFi throughout the hotel.

Rooms 196 (50 fmly) ⬆ **Facilities** STV FTV WiFi ⬇ HL Gym Steam room Sauna **Conf** Class 50 Board 50 Thtr 100 **Services** Lift **Parking** 80

L

LEEDS *continued*

The Cosmopolitan

★★★ 80% HOTEL

PEEL HOTELS PLC

tel: 0113 243 6454 **2 Lower Briggate LS1 4AE**
email: info@cosmopolitan-hotel-leeds.com **web:** www.cosmopolitan-hotel-leeds.com
dir: M621 junct 3. Keep in right lane. Follow until road splits into 4 lanes. Keep right,
right at lights. (ASDA House on left). Left at lights. Over bridge, left, hotel opposite.
Parking in 150mtrs

This smartly presented, Victorian building is located on the south side of the city.
The well-equipped bedrooms offer a choice of standard or executive grades. Staff
are friendly and helpful ensuring a warm and welcoming atmosphere. Discounted
overnight parking is provided in the adjacent 24-hour car park.

Rooms 89 (5 fmly) (14 smoking) ♠ **S** £54-£119; **D** £64-£149* **Facilities** STV FTV
WiFi ↳ Xmas New Year **Conf** Class 45 Board 40 Thtr 120 Del from £95 to £150*
Services Lift

Chevin Country Park Hotel & Spa

★★★ 78% ◉ HOTEL

tel: 01943 467818 **Yorkgate LS21 3NU**
email: chevin@crerarhotels.com **web:** www.crerarhotels.com

(For full entry see Otley)

Mercure Leeds Parkway Hotel

★★★ 74% HOTEL

tel: 0844 815 9020 *(Calls cost 7p per minute plus your phone company's access charge)*
Otley Rd LS16 8AG
email: sales.mercureleedsparkway@jupiterhotels.co.uk **web:** www.mercureleeds.co.uk
dir: From A1 take A58 towards Leeds, then right onto A6120. At A660 turn right towards
Airport/Skipton. Hotel 2m on right

This hotel is conveniently located and caters well for both business and leisure
guests. It is close to Leeds yet has a quiet spot near to the Yorkshire Dales. The
lovely gardens lead on to wildlife walks that can be followed directly into Golden
Acre Park (a beautiful 179 acre park and wildlife sanctuary). The hotel is a popular
wedding venue and also has extensive conference facilities in the adjacent Summit
Centre. A leisure club with indoor pool and fitness centre is also available and the
hotel offers complimentary WiFi.

Rooms 118 (4 fmly) (18 GF) ♠ **Facilities** STV FTV WiFi ↳ ⊛ Gym Beauty facilities
Hair salon Physiotherapy Xmas New Year **Conf** Class 100 Board 65 Thtr 280
Del from £99 to £125* **Services** Lift **Parking** 250 **Notes** Civ Wed 200

Holiday Inn Express Leeds - East

BUDGET HOTEL

tel: 0113 288 0574 **Aberford Rd, Oulton LS26 8EJ**
email: reservations@hiexpressleedseast.co.uk **web:** www.hiexpressleedseast.co.uk
dir: M62 junct 29, E towards Pontefract. Exit at junct 30, A642 signed Rothwell. Hotel
opposite at 1st rdbt

A modern hotel ideal for families and business travellers. Fresh and uncomplicated,
the spacious rooms include Sky TV, power shower and tea and coffee-making
facilities. Continental buffet breakfast is included in the room rate; other meals
may be taken at the nearby family pub or restaurant. See also the Hotel Groups
pages.

Rooms 77 (50 fmly) (32 GF) ♠ **D** £39-£89 (incl. bkfst)* **Conf** Class 20 Board 20
Thtr 25

Premier Inn Leeds/Bradford Airport

BUDGET HOTEL

tel: 0871 527 8578 *(Calls cost 13p per minute plus your phone company's access charge)*
Victoria Av, Yeadon LS19 7AW
web: www.premierinn.com
dir: On A658, near Leeds/Bradford Airport

High quality, budget accommodation ideal for both families and business
travellers. Spacious, en suite bedrooms feature tea and coffee making facilities,
and Freeview TV in most hotels. Internet access and WiFi are available for a small
fee. The adjacent family restaurant features a wide and varied menu. See also the
Hotel Groups pages.

Rooms 76

Premier Inn Leeds City Centre

BUDGET HOTEL

tel: 0871 527 8582 *(Calls cost 13p per minute plus your phone company's access charge)*
Citygate, Wellington St LS3 1LW
web: www.premierinn.com
dir: At A65 & A58 junct

Rooms 140

Premier Inn Leeds City Centre (Leeds Arena)

BUDGET HOTEL

tel: 0871 527 9356 *(Calls cost 13p per minute plus your phone company's access charge)*
Hepworth Point, Claypit Ln LS2 8BQ
web: www.premierinn.com
dir: On foot from Leeds rail station cross road into Park Row, continue into Cookridge St to
Clay Pit Ln. Hotel on left at top of lane

Rooms 131

Premier Inn Leeds City West

BUDGET HOTEL

tel: 0871 527 8584 *(Calls cost 13p per minute plus your phone company's access charge)*
City West One Office Park, Gelderd Rd LS12 6LX
web: www.premierinn.com
dir: M621 junct 1 take ring road towards Leeds. At 1st lights right into Gelderd Rd, right
at rdbt

Rooms 126

Premier Inn Leeds East

BUDGET HOTEL

tel: 0871 527 8586 *(Calls cost 13p per minute plus your phone company's access charge)*
Selby Rd, Whitkirk LS15 7AY
web: www.premierinn.com
dir: M1 junct 46 towards Leeds. At 2nd rdbt follow Temple Newsam signs. Hotel 500mtrs
on right

Rooms 88

L

Premier Inn Leeds South (Birstall)

BUDGET HOTEL

tel: 0871 527 8580 *(Calls cost 13p per minute plus your phone company's access charge)*
Wakefield Rd, Drighlington BD11 1EA
web: www.premierinn.com
dir: *On Drighlington bypass, adjacent to M62 junct 27. Take A650, right to Drighlington, right, hotel on left*

Rooms 60

Ibis Budget Leeds Centre

AA Advertised

tel: 0113 245 0725 **2 The Gateway North, Crown Point Rd LS9 8BZ**
email: H6002@accor.com **web:** www.ibishotel.com
dir: *M1 junct 43, onto M621 (signed Leeds Central). Exit at junct 3, merge onto A653 (signed City Centre). Road becomes A61, at lights left into Crown Point Rd*

Modern, budget hotel offering comfortable accommodation in bright and practical bedrooms. Breakfast is self-service and dinner is available in the restaurant.

Rooms 218 (218 fmly) ⚡ **Facilities** FTV WiFi ↕ HL **Services** Lift

Ibis Leeds Centre

AA Advertised

ibis

tel: 0113 396 9000 **Marlborough St LS1 4PB**
email: H3652@accor.com **web:** www.ibishotel.com
dir: *M1 junct 43 or M62 junct 2 take A643 & follow city centre signs. Left on slip road opposite Yorkshire Post. Hotel opposite TGI Fridays restaurant*

Modern, budget hotel offering comfortable accommodation in bright and practical bedrooms. Breakfast is self-service and dinner is available in the restaurant

Rooms 168 (14 fmly) ⚡ **Facilities** FTV WiFi ↕ HL **Services** Lift

LEEK
Staffordshire   Map 16 SJ95

Premier Inn Leek Town Centre

BUDGET HOTEL

tel: 0871 527 9330 *(Calls cost 13p per minute plus your phone company's access charge)*
Ashbourne Rd ST13 5AS
web: www.premierinn.com
dir: *M6 junct 16, A500. In 6m left at Eturia junction onto A53 signed Leek to the town centre. At lights in town centre turn right onto A523 (Ashbourne Rd). Hotel adjacent to war memorial on left*

High quality, budget accommodation ideal for both families and business travellers. Spacious, en suite bedrooms feature tea and coffee making facilities, and Freeview TV in most hotels. Internet access and WiFi are available for a small fee. The adjacent family restaurant features a wide and varied menu. See also the Hotel Groups pages.

Rooms 63

LEICESTER
Leicestershire   Map 11 SK50

Hotel Maiyango

★★★★ 77% ⓢ SMALL HOTEL

tel: 0116 251 8898 **13-21 St Nicholas Place LE1 4LD**
email: reservations@maiyango.com **web:** www.maiyango.com
dir: *B4114 Narborough Rd to city centre, right onto A47 King Richard III Rd, keep right into St Nicholas Pl*

Hotel Maiyango is a boutique hotel offering a warm welcome and professional service. Access to the public areas is via a discreet foyer adjacent to a Middle Eastern-themed restaurant (under the same ownership), where imaginative food is sure to be a memorable experience. Spacious bedrooms, decorated in minimalist style are enhanced by quality modern art, fine furnishings and superb bathrooms. Parking is available close by.

Rooms 14 ⚡ **D** £79-£139 **Facilities** FTV WiFi ↕ ♫ Xmas New Year **Conf** Class 50 Board 30 Thtr 70 Del from £145 to £155 **Services** Lift Air con **Notes** LB ⊗ Closed 25 Dec RS 1 Jan (closed to new customers)

Mercure Leicester The Grand Hotel

★★★★ 75% HOTEL

tel: 0844 815 9012 *(Calls cost 7p per minute plus your phone company's access charge)*
Granby St LE1 6ES
email: info@mercureleicester.co.uk **web:** www.mercureleicester.co.uk
dir: *A5460 into city. Follow Leicester Central Station signs. Left off St Georges Way, A594 onto Charles St. 1st left onto Northampton St, right onto Granby St. Hotel on left*

Located in the heart of Leicester city centre, this hotel offers well appointed bedrooms and spacious public areas. Conferences and weddings are catered for. On site parking is a plus. Free WiFi is available throughout.

Rooms 104 ⚡ **Facilities** FTV WiFi ↕ Xmas New Year **Conf** Class 200 Board 90 Thtr 350 **Services** Lift **Parking** 120 **Notes** ⊗ Civ Wed 200

Belmont Hotel

★★★ 83% HOTEL

tel: 0116 254 4773 **De Montfort St LE1 7GR**
email: info@belmonthotel.co.uk **web:** www.belmonthotel.co.uk
dir: *From A6 take 1st right after rail station. Hotel 200yds on left*

This well-established hotel, under the same family ownership, has been welcoming guests for over 70 years. It is conveniently situated within easy walking distance of the railway station and city centre though it sits in a quiet leafy residential area. Extensive public rooms are smartly appointed and include the informal Bowie's Bistro, Jamie's Bar with its relaxed atmosphere, and the more formal Cherry Restaurant.

Rooms 74 (7 fmly) (8 GF) (2 smoking) ⚡ **S** £60-£80; **D** £70-£120 (incl. bkfst)*
Facilities FTV WiFi ↕ Gym **Conf** Class 75 Board 65 Thtr 175 **Services** Lift **Parking** 70 **Notes** LB Civ Wed 100

Silver Stars The AA Silver Star rating denotes a Hotel that we highly recommend. They have a superior level of quality within their star rating, high standards of hospitality, service and cleanliness.

LEICESTER *continued*

Premier Inn Leicester (Braunstone)

BUDGET HOTEL

tel: 0871 527 8590 *(Calls cost 13p per minute plus your phone company's access charge)*
Meridian Business Park, Thorpe Astley, Braunstone LE19 1LU
web: www.premierinn.com
dir: *M1 junct 21, follow A563 (outer ring road) signs W to Thorpe Astley. At slip road after Texaco garage. Hotel on left*

High quality, budget accommodation ideal for both families and business travellers. Spacious, en suite bedrooms feature tea and coffee making facilities, and Freeview TV in most hotels. Internet access and WiFi are available for a small fee. The adjacent family restaurant features a wide and varied menu. See also the Hotel Groups pages.

Rooms 75

Premier Inn Leicester Central (A50)

BUDGET HOTEL

tel: 0871 527 8594 *(Calls cost 13p per minute plus your phone company's access charge)*
Heathley Park, Groby Rd LE3 9QE
web: www.premierinn.com
dir: *Off A50, city centre side of County Hall & Glenfield General Hospital*

Rooms 76

Premier Inn Leicester City Centre

BUDGET HOTEL

tel: 0871 527 8596 *(Calls cost 13p per minute plus your phone company's access charge)*
1 St Georges Way LE1 1AA
web: www.premierinn.com
dir: *Phone for detailed directions*

Rooms 135

Premier Inn Leicester (Forest East)

BUDGET HOTEL

tel: 0871 527 8592 *(Calls cost 13p per minute plus your phone company's access charge)*
Hinckley Rd, Leicester Forest East LE3 3GD
web: www.premierinn.com
dir: *M1 junct 21, A5460. At major junct (Holiday Inn on right), left into Braunstone Lane. In 2m left onto A47 towards Hinkley. Hotel 400yds on left*

Rooms 40

Premier Inn Leicester Fosse Park

BUDGET HOTEL

tel: 0871 527 8588 *(Calls cost 13p per minute plus your phone company's access charge)*
Braunstone Lane East LE3 2FW
web: www.premierinn.com
dir: *M1 junct 21, at M69 junct take A5460 towards city. After 1m right at lights to hotel*

Rooms 176

Premier Inn Leicester North West

BUDGET HOTEL

tel: 0871 527 8598 *(Calls cost 13p per minute plus your phone company's access charge)*
Leicester Rd, Glenfield LE3 8HB
web: www.premierinn.com
dir: *M1 junct 21a N'bound, A46. Onto A50 for Glenfield & County Hall. Or M1 junct 22 S'bound onto A50 towards Glenfield. Into County Hall. Hotel on left adjacent to Gynsills*

Rooms 45

Premier Inn Leicester South (Oadby)

BUDGET HOTEL

tel: 0871 527 8600 *(Calls cost 13p per minute plus your phone company's access charge)*
Glen Rise, Oadby LE2 4RG
web: www.premierinn.com
dir: *M1 junct 21, A563 signed South. Right at Leicester racecourse. Follow Market Harborough signs. Dual carriageway, straight on at rdbt. Into single lane, hotel on right*

Rooms 30

Ibis Leicester

AA Advertised

tel: 0116 248 7200 **St Georges Way, Constitution Hill LE1 1PL**
email: H3061@accor.com **web:** www.ibis.com
dir: *From M1/M69 junct 21, follow town centre signs, central ring road A594/railway station, hotel opposite Leicester Mercury*

Modern, budget hotel offering comfortable accommodation in bright and practical bedrooms. Breakfast is self-service and dinner is available in the restaurant.

Rooms 94 (15 fmly) 🐾 **Facilities** FTV WiFi **Services** Lift **Parking** 15

LEICESTER FOREST MOTORWAY SERVICE AREA (M1) Map 11 SK50
Leicestershire

Days Inn Leicester Forest East - M1

AA Advertised

tel: 0116 239 0534 **Leicester Forest East, M1 Junct 21 LE3 3GB**
email: leicester.hotel@welcomebreak.co.uk **web:** www.welcomebreak.co.uk
dir: *On M1 N'bound between junct 21 & 21A*

This modern building offers accommodation in smart, spacious and well-equipped bedrooms, suitable for families and business travellers, and all with en suite bathrooms. Continental breakfast is available, and other refreshments may be taken at the nearby family restaurant.

Rooms 86 (71 fmly) (10 smoking) **Facilities** FTV WiFi ↘ **Conf** Board 10 **Services** Lift **Parking** 100

LEINTWARDINE
Herefordshire   Map 9 SO47

The Lion
RESTAURANT WITH ROOMS

tel: 01547 540203 & 540747 **High St SY7 OJZ**
email: enquiries@thelionleintwardine.co.uk **web:** www.thelionleintwardine.co.uk
dir: *Beside bridge on A4113 (Ludlow to Knighton road) in Leintwardine*

This quiet country restaurant with rooms in the picturesque village of Leintwardine, set beside the River Teme, is just a short distance from Ludlow and Craven Arms. The interior is stylish and all the contemporary bedrooms are en suite. Dining is taken seriously here and the modern, imaginative food uses the freshest local ingredients. The well-stocked bar offers a selection of real ales and lagers and there is a separate drinkers' bar too. The Lion is particularly popular with families as the garden has a secure children's play area, and in warmer months guests can eat alfresco. The friendly staff help to make any visit memorable.

Rooms 8 (1 fmly)

LENHAM
Kent   Map 7 TQ85

INSPECTORS' CHOICE

Chilston Park Hotel
★★★★ HOTEL

HandPICKED HOTELS

tel: 01622 859803 & 0845 072 7426
(Calls cost 5p per minute plus your phone company's access charge) **Sandway ME17 2BE**
email: chilstonpark@handpicked.co.uk
web: www.handpickedhotels.co.uk/chilstonpark
dir: *Exit A20 to Lenham, right into High St, pass station on right, 1st left, over x-roads, hotel 0.25m on left*

This elegant Grade I listed country house is set in 23 acres of immaculately landscaped gardens and parkland. An impressive collection of original paintings and antiques creates a unique environment. The sunken Venetian-style restaurant serves modern British food with French influences. Bedrooms are individual in design, some have four-poster beds and many have garden views.

Rooms 53 (23 annexe) (2 fmly) (3 GF) S £100-£300; D £109-£309 (incl. bkfst)* **Facilities** STV FTV WiFi HL Fishing Xmas New Year **Conf** Class 60 Board 50 Thtr 100 Del from £140 to £165 **Services** Lift **Parking** 100 **Notes** LB Civ Wed 90

LEOMINSTER
Herefordshire   Map 10 SO45

Talbot Hotel
★★★ 73% HOTEL

tel: 01568 616347 **West St HR6 8EP**
email: info@talbothotelleominster.com **web:** www.talbothotelleominster.com
dir: *From A49, A44 or A4112, hotel in town centre*

This charming former coaching inn is located in the town centre and makes an ideal base for exploring the area. Public areas feature original beams and antique furniture, and include an atmospheric bar and elegant restaurant. The bedrooms vary in size, but all are comfortably furnished and equipped. Facilities are available for private functions and conferences.

Rooms 28 (3 fmly) (2 GF) S £59-£68; D £79-£91.50* **Facilities** FTV WiFi **Conf** Class 60 Board 30 Thtr 130 Del £95* **Parking** 26 **Notes**

LEYLAND
Lancashire   Map 15 SD52

Best Western Premier Hallmark Hotel Preston Leyland
★★★★ 76% HOTEL

tel: 0330 028 3420 **Leyland Way PR25 4JX**
email: leyland@hallmarkhotels.co.uk **web:** www.hallmarkhotels.co.uk
dir: *M6 junct 28, left at end of slip road, hotel 100mtrs on left*

This purpose-built hotel enjoys a convenient location, just off the M6, within easy reach of Preston and Blackpool. Spacious public areas include extensive conference and banqueting facilities as well as a smart leisure club.

Rooms 93 (4 fmly) (31 GF) D £59-£149 (incl. bkfst)* **Facilities** FTV WiFi HL supervised Xmas New Year **Conf** Class 100 Board 40 Thtr 220 Del from £125 to £149* **Parking** 150 **Notes** LB Civ Wed 200

L

L

LICHFIELD
Staffordshire

Map 10 SK10

Swinfen Hall Hotel

★★★★ ◉◉◉ HOTEL

tel: 01543 481494 **Swinfen WS14 9RE**
email: info@swinfenhallhotel.co.uk **web:** www.swinfenhallhotel.co.uk
dir: Set back from A38, 2.5m outside Lichfield, towards Birmingham

Dating from 1757, this lavishly decorated mansion has been painstakingly restored by the present owners. It is set in 100 acres of parkland which includes a deer park. Public rooms are particularly stylish, with intricately carved ceilings and impressive oil portraits. Bedrooms on the first floor boast period features and tall sash windows; those on the second floor (the former servants' quarters) are smaller and more contemporary by comparison. Service in the award-winning restaurant is both professional and attentive.

Rooms 17 (5 fmly) 🕭 **Facilities** STV FTV WiFi ⇖ 🏊 Fishing ⬆ Jogging trail 100 acre park New Year **Conf** Class 50 Board 50 Thtr 160 Del from £190* **Parking** 80 **Notes** ⊗ Civ Wed 120

Best Western The George Hotel

★★★ 81% HOTEL

tel: 01543 414822 **12-14 Bird St WS13 6PR**
email: mail@thegeorgelichfield.co.uk **web:** www.thegeorgelichfield.co.uk
dir: From Bowling Green Island on A461 take Lichfield exit. Left at next island into Swan Rd, as road bears left, turn right into Bird St for hotel car park

Situated in the city centre, this privately-owned hotel provides good quality, well-equipped accommodation which includes a room with a four-poster bed. Facilities here include a large ballroom, plus several other rooms for meetings and functions.

Rooms 45 (5 fmly) **S** £50-£109; **D** £60-£130 (incl. bkfst)* **Facilities** FTV WiFi ⇖ HL Gym **Conf** Class 60 Board 40 Thtr 110 Del from £130 to £150* **Services** Lift **Parking** 45 **Notes** LB ⊗ Civ Wed 110

Cathedral Lodge Hotel

★★★ 73% HOTEL

tel: 01543 414500 **62 Beacon St WS13 7AR**
email: enquiries@cathedrallodgehotel.com **web:** www.cathedrallodgehotel.com
dir: From Birmingham, A38 to Lichfield. Hotel in city centre

This hotel is within easy walking distance of the famous cathedral and just a short drive from the NEC, Belfry Golf Course and many other attractions. The accommodation is modern, spacious and comfortable, and each room has a large, flat-screen TV with Sky. There is a large function suite together with conference facilities.

Rooms 36 (2 fmly) (6 smoking) **S** £69.50-£75; **D** £79.50-£85 (incl. bkfst)* **Facilities** FTV WiFi ⇖ Xmas New Year **Conf** Class 80 Board 70 Thtr 80 **Notes** LB ⊗

Premier Inn Lichfield City Centre

BUDGET HOTEL

tel: 0871 527 9440 *(Calls cost 13p per minute plus your phone company's access charge)*
Swan Rd WS13 6QZ
web: www.premierinn.com
dir: From M6 Toll junct T5 take A5148. Take A5206 ramp to Lichfield. At rdbt 1st exit (London Rd/A5206) into Upper St John Street (A51). Left into The Friary. 3rd exit at rdbt (Swan Rd). Hotel on right

High quality, budget accommodation ideal for both families and business travellers. Spacious, en suite bedrooms feature tea and coffee making facilities, and Freeview TV in most hotels. Internet access and WiFi are available for a small fee. The adjacent family restaurant features a wide and varied menu. See also the Hotel Groups pages.

Rooms 79

Premier Inn Lichfield North East (A38)

BUDGET HOTEL

tel: 0871 527 8602 *(Calls cost 13p per minute plus your phone company's access charge)*
Fine Ln, Fradley WS13 8RD
web: www.premierinn.com
dir: On A38, 3 NE of Lichfield

Rooms 30

LIFTON
Devon

Map 3 SX38

Arundell Arms
★★★ 82% ◉◉ HOTEL

tel: 01566 784666 **Fore St PL16 OAA**
email: reservations@arundellarms.co.uk **web:** www.arundellarms.co.uk
dir: *1m off A30, 3m E of Launceston*

This former coaching inn, boasting a long history, sits in the heart of a quiet Devon village, and is internationally famous for its country pursuits such as winter shooting and angling. The bedrooms offer individual style and comfort. Public areas are full of character with a relaxed atmosphere, particularly around the open log fire during colder evenings. Award-winning cuisine is a celebration of local produce.

Rooms 24 (3 annexe) (3 fmly) (4 GF) **Facilities** FTV WiFi ⇘ Fishing Game shooting (in winter) Fly fishing school New Year **Conf** Class 30 Board 40 Thtr 100 **Parking** 70 **Notes** Closed 24-27 Dec

LINCOLN
Lincolnshire

Map 17 SK97

DoubleTree by Hilton Lincoln
★★★★ 76% ◉ HOTEL

tel: 01522 565180 **Brayford Wharf North LN1 1YW**
email: lincoln.reservations@hilton.com **web:** www.lincoln.doubletree.com
dir: *A1, A57 Lincoln Road, right onto Newland, follow signs for Brayford Road. Right onto Lucy Tower St, hotel at end*

DoubleTree by Hilton Lincoln has an excellent location by the waterfront with views across the city centre. It is also located close to the university. Built in 2011, this modern hotel offers comfortable and quiet accommodation with complimentary WiFi throughout, and a fitness centre. Guests can enjoy dinner in the Electric Restaurant on the fifth floor with excellent views overlooking the cathedral.

Rooms 115 (17 fmly) ⌁ **S** fr £75; **D** fr £85* **Facilities** STV FTV WiFi ⇘ HL Gym Xmas New Year **Conf** Class 100 Board 40 Thtr 300 Del from £110 to £210* **Services** Lift Air con **Parking** 40 **Notes** LB Civ Wed 250

HIGHLY RECOMMENDED

Washingborough Hall Hotel
★★★ 87% ◉◉ COUNTRY HOUSE HOTEL

tel: 01522 790340 **Church Hill, Washingborough LN4 1BE**
email: enquiries@washingboroughhall.com **web:** www.washingboroughhall.com
dir: *B1190 into Washingborough. Right at rdbt, hotel 500yds on left*

This Georgian manor stands on the edge of the quiet village of Washingborough and is set in attractive gardens. Public rooms are pleasantly furnished and comfortable, while the restaurant offers interesting menus. Bedrooms are individually designed and most have views out over the grounds to the countryside beyond.

Rooms 14 (2 fmly) ⌁ **S** £85-£95; **D** £135-£175 (incl. bkfst)* **Facilities** FTV WiFi ⇘ ⛵ Bicycles for hire **Conf** Class 30 Board 26 Thtr 50 Del from £175* **Parking** 40 **Notes** Civ Wed 100

The Lincoln Hotel
★★★ 80% HOTEL

tel: 01522 520348 **Eastgate LN2 1PN**
email: reservations@thelincolnhotel.com **web:** www.thelincolnhotel.com
dir: *Adjacent to cathedral*

This privately-owned modern hotel enjoys superb uninterrupted views of Lincoln Cathedral. There are ruins of the Roman wall and Eastgate in the grounds. Bedrooms are contemporary with up-to-the-minute facilities. An airy restaurant and bar, a cellar bar, plus a comfortable lounge are provided. There are substantial conference and meeting facilities.

Rooms 71 (4 fmly) (10 GF) ⌁ **Facilities** FTV WiFi Gym **Conf** Class 50 Board 40 Thtr 120 **Services** Lift **Parking** 120 **Notes** LB ⊗ Civ Wed 150

The White Hart
★★★ 80% HOTEL

tel: 01522 526222 & 563293 **Bailgate LN1 3AR**
email: info@whitehart-lincoln.co.uk **web:** www.whitehart-lincoln.co.uk
dir: *A46 onto B1226, through Newport Arch. Hotel 0.5m on left as road bends left*

Lying in the shadow of Lincoln's magnificent cathedral, this hotel is perfectly positioned for exploring the shops and sights of this medieval city. The attractive bedrooms are furnished and decorated in a traditional style and many have views of the cathedral. Given the hotel's central location, parking is a real benefit.

Rooms 50 (3 fmly) **S** £85-£110; **D** £95-£150 (incl. bkfst)* **Facilities** FTV WiFi ⇘ **Conf** Class 70 Board 50 Thtr 160 Del from £135 to £145* **Services** Lift **Parking** 50 **Notes** Civ Wed 120

Branston Hall Hotel
★★★ 77% ◉ COUNTRY HOUSE HOTEL

tel: 01522 793305 **Branston Park, Branston LN4 1PD**
email: info@branstonhall.com **web:** www.branstonhall.com
dir: *On B1188, 3m SE of Lincoln*

Dating back to 1885 this country house sits in 88 acres of beautiful grounds complete with a lake. There is an elegant restaurant, a spacious bar and a beautiful lounge in addition to impressive conference and leisure facilities. Individually styled bedrooms vary in size and include several with four-poster beds. The hotel is a popular wedding venue.

Rooms 50 (7 annexe) (3 fmly) (4 GF) **Facilities** Spa STV FTV WiFi ⊛ Gym Jogging circuit Xmas New Year **Conf** Class 54 Board 40 Thtr 200 **Services** Lift **Parking** 100 **Notes** ⊗ Civ Wed 160

L

LINCOLN *continued*

Tower Hotel

★★★ 75% HOTEL

tel: 01522 529999 **38 Westgate LN1 3BD**
email: tower.hotel@btclick.com **web:** www.lincolntowerhotel.com
dir: *From A46 follow signs to Lincoln N then to Bailgate area. Through arch, 2nd right*

This hotel faces the Norman castle wall and is in a very convenient location for the city. The relaxed and friendly atmosphere is very noticeable here. There's a modern conservatory bar and a stylish restaurant where contemporary dishes are available throughout the day.

Rooms 15 (1 fmly) ⚲ **S** £70; **D** £95-£105 (incl. bkfst)* **Facilities** STV FTV WiFi **Conf** Class 24 Board 16 Thtr 24 **Notes** Closed 24-27 Dec & 1 Jan

Premier Inn Lincoln (Canwick)

BUDGET HOTEL

tel: 0871 527 8604 *(Calls cost 13p per minute plus your phone company's access charge)*
Lincoln Rd, Canwick Hill LN4 2RF
web: www.premierinn.com
dir: *Approx 1m S of city centre at junction of B1188 & B1131*

High quality, budget accommodation ideal for both families and business travellers. Spacious, en suite bedrooms feature tea and coffee making facilities, and Freeview TV in most hotels. Internet access and WiFi are available for a small fee. The adjacent family restaurant features a wide and varied menu. See also the Hotel Groups pages.

Rooms 98

Premier Inn Lincoln City Centre

BUDGET HOTEL

tel: 0871 527 9418 *(Calls cost 13p per minute plus your phone company's access charge)*
Broadgate LN2 5AQ
web: www.premierinn.com
dir: *From N: from A57 left into Mint St B1003. Right into Broadgate A15. From S: on A46 to A1434/Newark Rd rdbt. Straight on next rdbt into St Catherines A15, straight on at next rdbt. Left into St Swithins Sq. Right into Silver St B1003. Right into Broadgate A15*

Rooms 131

Ibis Lincoln

AA Advertised

tel: 01522 698333 **Runcorn Rd (A46), off Whisby Rd LN6 3QZ**
email: H3161@accor.com **web:** www.ibishotel.com
dir: *Exit A46 ring road into Whisby Rd. 1st left*

Modern, budget hotel offering comfortable accommodation in bright and practical bedrooms. Breakfast is self-service and dinner is available in the restaurant

Rooms 86 (19 fmly) (8 GF) ⚲ **S** fr £38; **D** fr £38* **Facilities** WiFi ⚲ HL **Conf** Class 12 Board 20 Thtr 35 **Services** Lift **Parking** 80

The Old Bakery

◉◉ RESTAURANT WITH ROOMS

tel: 01522 576057 & 07949 035554 **26-28 Burton Rd LN1 3LB**
email: enquiries@theold-bakery.co.uk **web:** www.theold-bakery.co.uk
dir: *Exit A46 at Lincoln North follow signs for cathedral. 3rd exit at 1st rdbt, 1st exit at next rdbt*

Situated close to the castle at the top of the town, this converted bakery offers well-equipped bedrooms and a delightful dining operation. The cooking has gained two AA Rosettes, and uses much local produce. Expect good friendly service from the dedicated staff.

Rooms 3 (1 fmly)

LIPHOOK
Hampshire
Map 5 SU83

Old Thorns Manor Hotel Golf & Country Estate

★★★★ 75% HOTEL

tel: 01428 724555 & 725844 **Griggs Green GU30 7PE**
email: reservations@oldthorns.com **web:** www.oldthorns.com
dir: *At Griggs Green exit A3, hotel 0.5m*

Old Thorns is a modern, relaxed and welcoming hotel, set in 400 acres of the peaceful Hampshire countryside, which includes a championship golf course. The bedrooms are spacious and stylish and offer high levels of comfort. The leisure facilities are extensive and include a health club, wellness centre and spa; in addition there is also a sports bar, champagne and cocktail bar, Kings Restaurant and all-day dining is also available.

Rooms 175 (2 fmly) (64 GF) ⚲ **Facilities** Spa STV FTV WiFi ⚲ ⚲ ⚲ 18 ⚲ Putt green Gym Xmas New Year **Conf** Class 100 Board 30 Thtr 300 **Services** Lift **Parking** 278 **Notes** ⊗ Civ Wed 250

LISKEARD
Cornwall · Map 2 SX26

Premier Inn Liskeard

BUDGET HOTEL

tel: 0871 527 8608 *(Calls cost 13p per minute plus your phone company's access charge)*
Liskeard Retail Park, Haviland Rd PL14 3PR
web: www.premierinn.com
dir: *Off A38, on A390 SW of Liskeard*

High quality, budget accommodation ideal for both families and business travellers. Spacious, en suite bedrooms feature tea and coffee making facilities, and Freeview TV in most hotels. Internet access and WiFi are available for a small fee. The adjacent family restaurant features a wide and varied menu. See also the Hotel Groups pages.

Rooms 51

LITTLEHAMPTON
West Sussex · Map 6 TQ00

Premier Inn Littlehampton

BUDGET HOTEL

tel: 0871 527 8610 *(Calls cost 13p per minute plus your phone company's access charge)*
Roundstone Ln, East Preston BN16 1EB
web: www.premierinn.com
dir: *A2/ onto A280 signed Littlehampton/Rustington & Angmering. At next rdbt follow Littlehampton, Rustington/A259 signs. At next rdbt 1st exit signed East Preston. Hotel on left*

High quality, budget accommodation ideal for both families and business travellers. Spacious, en suite bedrooms feature tea and coffee making facilities, and Freeview TV in most hotels. Internet access and WiFi are available for a small fee. The adjacent family restaurant features a wide and varied menu. See also the Hotel Groups pages.

Rooms 20

LIVERPOOL
Merseyside · Map 15 SJ39

Thornton Hall Hotel and Spa

★★★★ 81% ◉◉◉ HOTEL

tel: 0151 336 3938 & 353 3717 **Neston Rd CH63 1JF**
email: reservations@thorntonhallhotel.com **web:** www.thorntonhallhotel.com

(For full entry see Thornton Hough)

Hope Street Hotel

★★★★ 77% ◉◉ HOTEL

tel: 0151 709 3000 **40 Hope St L1 9DA**
email: sleep@hopestreethotel.co.uk **web:** www.hopestreethotel.co.uk
dir: *Follow Cathedral & University signs on entering city. Telephone for detailed directions*

This stylish property is located in the Georgian quarter and is within easy walking distance of the city's cathedrals, theatres, major shops and attractions. Stylish bedrooms and suites many of which benefit from far reaching views across the city's skyline are appointed with flat-screen TVs, DVD players, internet access and comfy beds with Egyptian cotton sheets; the bathrooms have rain showers and deep tubs. The London Carriage Works Restaurant specialises in local, seasonal produce and the adjacent lounge bar offers lighter all-day dining and wonderful cocktails.

Rooms 89 (16 fmly) (5 GF) ⟡ **S** £90-£200; **D** £90-£200* **Facilities** STV FTV WiFi ⟐ Gym Massage & beauty therapists Xmas New Year **Conf** Class 40 Board 30 Thtr 70 Del from £155 to £255* **Services** Lift Air con **Parking** 10 **Notes** LB Civ Wed 70

Malmaison Liverpool

★★★★ 76% ◉ HOTEL

tel: 0151 229 5000 & 0844 693 0655
(Calls cost 5p per minute plus your phone company's access charge)
7 William Jessop Way, Princes Dock L3 1QZ
email: liverpool@malmaison.com **web:** www.malmaison.com
dir: *A5080 follow signs for Pier Head/Southport/Bootle. Into Baln St to rdbt, 1st exit at rdbt, immediately left onto William Jessop Way*

This is a purpose-built hotel with cutting edge and contemporary style. 'Mal' Liverpool, as its known, has a stunning location, alongside the river and docks, and in the heart of the city's regeneration. Bedrooms are stylish and comfortable and are provided with lots of extra facilities. The public areas are packed with fun and style, and there are a number of meeting rooms as well as private dining, including a chef's table.

Rooms 130 ⟡ **Facilities** STV WiFi Gym **Conf** Class 28 Board 22 Thtr 50 **Services** Lift Air con

Novotel Liverpool Centre

★★★★ 76% HOTEL

tel: 0151 702 5100 **40 Hanover St L1 4LN**
email: h6495@accor.com **web:** www.novotel.com

This attractive and stylish city centre hotel is convenient for Liverpool Echo Arena, Liverpool One shopping centre and the Albert Dock; it is adjacent to a town centre car park. The hotel has a range of conference and leisure facilities which include an indoor heated pool and fitness suite. The restaurant offers a contemporary style menu. The hotel now benefits from a relaxed new bar concept called Rope Walks taking its influence from Liverpool's industrial and shipping history. This open-plan bar has many seating options from high stools, to button-backed benches and soft sofas and arm chairs. The bedrooms are comfortable and stylishly designed.

Rooms 209 (127 fmly) ⟡ **Facilities** FTV WiFi ⟐ ⟨⟩ Gym Steam room **Conf** Class 60 Board 50 Thtr 90 **Services** Lift

Hard Days Night Hotel

★★★★ 74% HOTEL

tel: 0151 236 1964 **Central Buildings, North John St L2 6RR**
email: info@harddaysnighthotel.com **web:** www.harddaysnighthotel.com
dir: *Phone for directions*

In the heart of Liverpool; close to Liverpool One (a shoppers delight) and less than a stone's throw from the iconic Cavern Club, Hard Days Night Hotel is a very tasteful celebration of Beatle Mania. Guests travel from far and wide to stay at this hotel, each attractively furnished modern room is very well equipped, and all benefit from a Beatles-inspired, specially commissioned piece of artwork. Blakes restaurant provides a relaxed and informal dining venue, cocktails are served nightly in the 'Fab Four' bar.

Rooms 110 ⟡ **Facilities** STV WiFi ⟐ HL ⨅ **Conf** Class 40 Board 20 Thtr 120 Del from £150 to £350* **Services** Lift Air con **Notes** ⊗ Civ Wed 60

L

LIVERPOOL *continued*

Best Western Hallmark Hotel Liverpool Alicia

★★★ 79% HOTEL

tel: 0330 028 3416 **3 Aigburth Dr, Sefton Park L17 3AA**
email: alicia@hallmarkhotels.co.uk **web:** www.hallmarkhotels.co.uk
dir: *From end of M62 take A5058 to Sefton Park, then left, follow park around*

This stylish and friendly hotel overlooks Sefton Park and is just a few minutes' drive from both the city centre and John Lennon Airport. Bedrooms are well equipped and comfortable. Day rooms include a striking modern restaurant and bar. Extensive, stylish function facilities make this a popular wedding venue.

Rooms 41 (8 fmly) **Facilities** STV WiFi HL Xmas New Year **Conf** Class 80 Board 40 Thtr 120 **Services** Lift **Parking** 40 **Notes** ⊗ Civ Wed 120

Best Western Hallmark Hotel Liverpool Feathers

★★★ 77% HOTEL

tel: 0330 028 3426 **115-125 Mount Pleasant L3 5TF**
email: feathers@hallmarkhotels.co.uk **web:** www.hallmarkhotels.co.uk
dir: *Located in the city centre*

This stylish and friendly hotel has a prime city centre location close to both cathedrals, universities, and shopping areas. Bedrooms come in a variety of distinctive styles and are well equipped and comfortable. Public rooms include a striking modern restaurant and bar.

Rooms 81 **Facilities** FTV WiFi Xmas New Year **Conf** Board 12 Del from £120 to £150* **Parking** 24 **Notes** Civ Wed

Jurys Inn Liverpool

★★★ 75% HOTEL

tel: 0151 244 3777 **No 31 Keel Wharf L3 4FN**
email: jurysinnliverpool@jurysinns.com **web:** www.jurysinns.com
dir: *Follow City Centre & Albert Dock signs. Hotel at Kings Waterfront adjacent to Albert Dock, opposite BT Convention Centre & Echo Arena*

Located on the Kings Waterfront adjacent to the BT Convention Centre, Echo Arena, Albert Dock complex and a short walk from the very popular shopping district of Liverpool One, this hotel offers contemporary and spacious bedrooms. Guests have a choice of dining options - the Innfusion restaurant and the Inntro bar. There are ten dedicated meeting rooms and WiFi is available throughout. There is ample secure parking nearby.

Rooms 310 (58 fmly) **Facilities** FTV WiFi ↕ HL **Conf** Class 50 Board 40 Thtr 100 **Services** Lift Air con **Notes** ⊗ Civ Wed 100

Premier Inn Liverpool (Aintree)

BUDGET HOTEL

tel: 0871 527 8612 *(Calls cost 13p per minute plus your phone company's access charge)*
Ormskirk Rd, Aintree L9 5AS
web: www.premierinn.com
dir: *M58, A57, A59 towards Liverpool. Pass Aintree Retail Park, left at lights into Aintree Racecourse. Hotel on left*

High quality, budget accommodation ideal for both families and business travellers. Spacious, en suite bedrooms feature tea and coffee making facilities, and Freeview TV in most hotels. Internet access and WiFi are available for a small fee. The adjacent family restaurant features a wide and varied menu. See also the Hotel Groups pages.

Rooms 40

Premier Inn Liverpool Albert Dock

BUDGET HOTEL

tel: 0871 527 8622 *(Calls cost 13p per minute plus your phone company's access charge)*
East Britannia Building, Albert Dock L3 4AD
web: www.premierinn.com
dir: *Follow signs for Liverpool City Centre & Albert Dock*

Rooms 186

Premier Inn Liverpool City Centre

BUDGET HOTEL

tel: 0871 527 8624 *(Calls cost 13p per minute plus your phone company's access charge)*
Vernon St L2 2AY
web: www.premierinn.com
dir: *From M62 follow Liverpool City Centre & Birkenhead Tunnel signs. At rdbt 3rd exit into Dale St, right into Vernon St. Hotel on left*

Rooms 165

Premier Inn Liverpool City Centre (Liverpool One)

BUDGET HOTEL

tel: 0871 527 9382 *(Calls cost 13p per minute plus your phone company's access charge)*
48 Hanover St L1 4AF
web: www.premierinn.com
dir: *A5047 follow signs for city centre. At lights left onto A5048, at next lights right onto A5047. A5038 signed Toxteth, Airport. Right into Renshaw St & right onto Ranelagh St. Hotel on left opposite BBC Radio Merseyside*

Rooms 183

Premier Inn Liverpool John Lennon Airport

BUDGET HOTEL

tel: 0871 527 8626 *(Calls cost 13p per minute plus your phone company's access charge)*
57 Speke Hall Av L24 1YQ
web: www.premierinn.com
dir: *A561 towards Liverpool follow 'Liverpool John Lennon Airport' signs into Seake Hall Ave, at 1st rdbt take 2nd left. Hotel 300mtrs on left*

Rooms 100

Premier Inn Liverpool North

BUDGET HOTEL

tel: 0871 527 8628 *(Calls cost 13p per minute plus your phone company's access charge)*
Northern Perimeter Rd L30 7PT
web: www.premierinn.com
dir: *0.25m from end of M58/M5, on A5207*

Rooms 83

Premier Inn Liverpool (Roby)

BUDGET HOTEL

tel: 0871 527 8616 *(Calls cost 13p per minute plus your phone company's access charge)*
Roby Rd, Huyton L36 4HD
web: www.premierinn.com
dir: *Just off M62 junct 5 on A5080*

Rooms 56

Premier Inn Liverpool (Tarbock)

BUDGET HOTEL

tel: 0871 527 8618 *(Calls cost 13p per minute plus your phone company's access charge)*
Wilson Rd, Tarbock L36 6AD
web: www.premierinn.com
dir: *At M62 & M57 junct. M62 junct 6, take A5080 (Huyton).1st right into Wilson Rd*

Rooms 41

Premier Inn Liverpool (West Derby)

BUDGET HOTEL

tel: 0871 527 8620 *(Calls cost 13p per minute plus your phone company's access charge)*
Queens Dr, West Derby L13 ODL
web: www.premierinn.com
dir: *At end of M62 right under flyover onto A5058 (follow football stadium signs). Hotel 1.5m on left, just past Esso garage*

Rooms 85

Ibis Liverpool Centre Albert Dock

AA Advertised

tel: 0151 706 9800 **27 Wapping L1 8LY**
email: H3140@accor.com **web:** www.ibishotel.com
dir: *From M62 follow Albert Dock signs. Opposite Dock entrance*

Modern, budget hotel offering comfortable accommodation in bright and practical bedrooms. Breakfast is self-service and dinner is available in the restaurant.

Rooms 192 (15 fmly) (45 GF) ﹒ **Facilities** STV WiFi HL **Services** Lift **Parking** 110

Ibis Styles Liverpool Centre Dale Street

AA Advertised

tel: 0151 243 1720 **67 Dale St L2 2HJ**
email: H7601@accor.com **web:** www.ibishotel.com
dir: *M6/M62 towards Liverpool. Continue on to Bowring Park Rd, A5080 and follow to Edge Lane, A5047. Continue along Edge Lane then right on to Commutation Row. Continue onto Churchill Way, A57 then Dale St*

Modern, budget hotel offering comfortable accommodation in bright and practical bedrooms. Breakfast is self-service and dinner is available in the restaurant.

Rooms 123 (123 fmly) **Facilities** FTV WiFi **Services** Lift

The Z Hotel Liverpool

AA Advertised

tel: 0151 556 1770 **2 North John St L2 4SA**
email: liverpool@thezhotels.com **web:** www.thezhotels.com
dir: *M62 junct 7, continue onto Bowring Park Road/A5080, then Edge Lane/A5047. Right onto Low Hill, continue onto Erskine Street, then Churchill Way/A57. Left onto North John St, hotel on right*

Z Liverpool has 92 rooms predominantly over the top three floors, with stunning views over the city. This budget boutique hotel is perfectly located for all the city has to offer. Bedrooms all have en suite wet room, crisp bed linen, 40" TV with Sky channels, and complimentary WiFi. Key local attractions include Albert Dock (home to Tate Liverpool and the Maritime Museum), Pier Head, Mann Island, and the Echo arena.

Rooms 92 ﹒ **Facilities** STV FTV WiFi ﹩ **Services** Lift Air con **Notes** ⊗

LIVERSEDGE
West Yorkshire   Map 16 SE12

Healds Hall Hotel & Restaurant

THE INDEPENDENTS
HOTEL ASSOCIATION

★★★ 79% ⊛ HOTEL

tel: 01924 409112 **Leeds Rd WF15 6JA**
email: enquire@healdshall.co.uk **web:** www.healdshall.co.uk
dir: *On A62 between Leeds & Huddersfield. 50yds on left after lights at Swan Pub*

This 18th-century house, in the heart of West Yorkshire, provides comfortable and well equipped accommodation and excellent hospitality. The hotel has earned a good local reputation for the quality of its food and offers a choice of casual or more formal dining styles, from a wide range of dishes on the various menus.

Rooms 24 (3 fmly) (3 GF) ﹒ **S** £50-£110; **D** £50-£150 (incl. bkfst) **Facilities** FTV WiFi ﹩ **Conf** Class 60 Board 45 Thtr 100 Del from £110 to £160 **Parking** 90 **Notes** LB Closed 1 Jan & BH Mon RS Sun eve Civ Wed 100

LIZARD
Cornwall   Map 2 SW71

Housel Bay Hotel

★★★ 74% ⊛ HOTEL

tel: 01326 290417 & 290917 **Housel Cove TR12 7PG**
email: info@houselbay.com **web:** www.houselbay.com
dir: *A39 or A394 to Helston, then A3083. At Lizard sign turn left, left at school, down lane to hotel*

This long-established hotel has stunning views across the Western Approaches, equally enjoyable from the lounge and many of the bedrooms. Good cuisine is available in the stylish dining room, from where guests might enjoy a stroll to the end of the garden, which leads directly onto the Cornwall coastal path.

Rooms 20 (1 fmly) ﹒ **Facilities** FTV WiFi ﹩ Xmas New Year **Services** Lift **Parking** 35 **Notes** LB ⊗ Closed 2 Jan-1 Feb

L

London

Index of London Hotels

This index shows hotels in London in alphabetical order, followed by their postal district or location and plan or map references. Page numbers precede each entry

Index of London Hotels

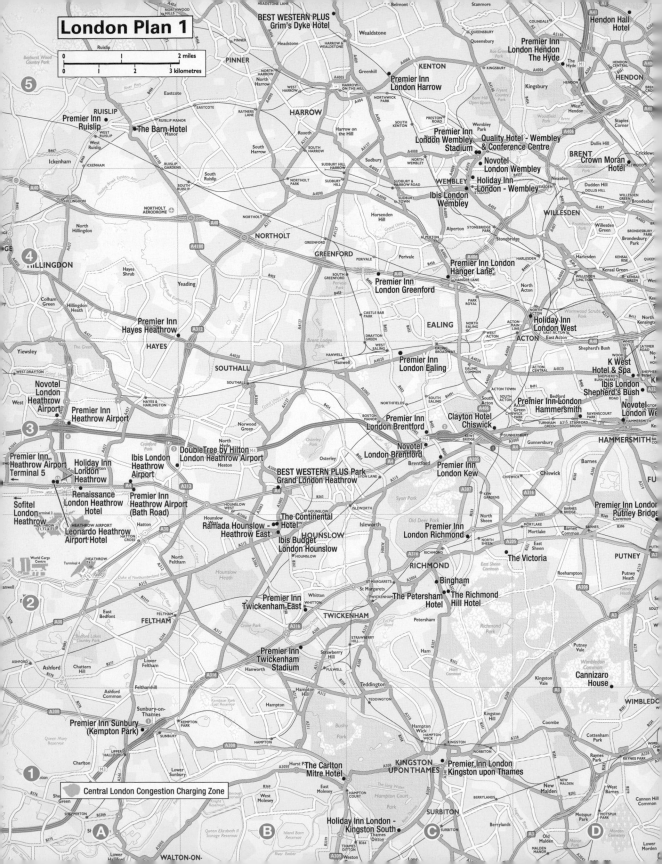

London Plan 1

London Plan 4

Embassy of Slovak

NOTTING HILL GATE

0   250   500 metres
0   250   500 yards

Kensington Gardens

Speke's Monument

Peter Pan Statue

Physical Energy Statue

The Long Water

The Serpentine

Round Pond

Serpentine Bridge

The Serpentine

Police Station

Ranger's Lodge

Hawkesdown House School

Embassy of Russia

Embassy of Lebanon

Romanian Embassy

Kensington Palace

Kensington Palace Green

Sunken Gardens

Bandstand

St Govor's Well

Isis Statue

The Lido

Serpentine Gallery

Diana Princess of Wales Memorial Fountain

Mount Gate

Bowling Green

Tennis Courts

Prince of Wales Gate

Israel Em

Royal Garden Hotel

Fire Station

Kensington & Chelsea Town Hall

St Mary Abbots

St Mary Abbots CE Primary School

KENSINGTON

The Milestone Hotel

High Street Kensington

Heythrop College

Thomas's Day School

St Alban's Grove

Baglioni Hotel London

The Gore

Kensington Gore

Royal College of Art

Royal Albert Hall

Royal Geographical Society

Knightsbridge

KENSINGTON ROAD   A315

Copthorne Tara Hotel London Kensington

Royal College of Music

Imperial College London

Imperial College London

Prince's Gardens

Bromp

Police Station

Pembroke Square

Chantry Square

Imperial College London

Science

Natural History

Darwin Centre

Victoria & Albert

Royal College of Art

The Oratory

The Rembrandt Hotel

The Egerton House Hotel

Police Station

London Lodge Hotel

Superstore

Cromwell

CROMWELL ROAD

Health Centre

Crowne Plaza London-Kensington

Baden Powell House

CROMWELL ROAD

Park International Hotel

Premier Inn London Kensington (Olympia)

CROMWELL ROAD

WEST CROMWELL

Holiday Inn London - Kensington Forum

Millennium Bailey's Hotel London Kensington

Lycée Francais

South Kensington

Marlborough Primary School

Premier Inn London Kensington (Earl's Court)

Millennium Gloucester Hotel London Kensington

South Kensington

Our Lady of Victories RC Primary School

Police Station

K + K Hotel George

BEST WESTERN Burns Hotel

EARL'S COURT STATION

Royal Marsden

Royal Brompton

St Luke's

Twenty Nevern Square Hotel

Earl's Court

OLD BROMPTON ROAD

Royal Brompton

Geans Hampshire School

CHELSEA

St Cuthbert & St Matthias CE Primary School

Bousfield Primary School

Fire Station

Register Office

Earls Court Exhibition Centre

Sports Centre

WEST BROMPTON STATION

St Luke's

Ibis London Earls Court

West Brompton

Brompton Cemetery

Serviie RC Primary School

Chelsea Westminster

Park Walk Primary School

Carlyle's Hou

FULHAM ROAD

KINGS ROAD

Ambulance Station

Fulham Primary School

A   B   C   D   E

London Plan 5

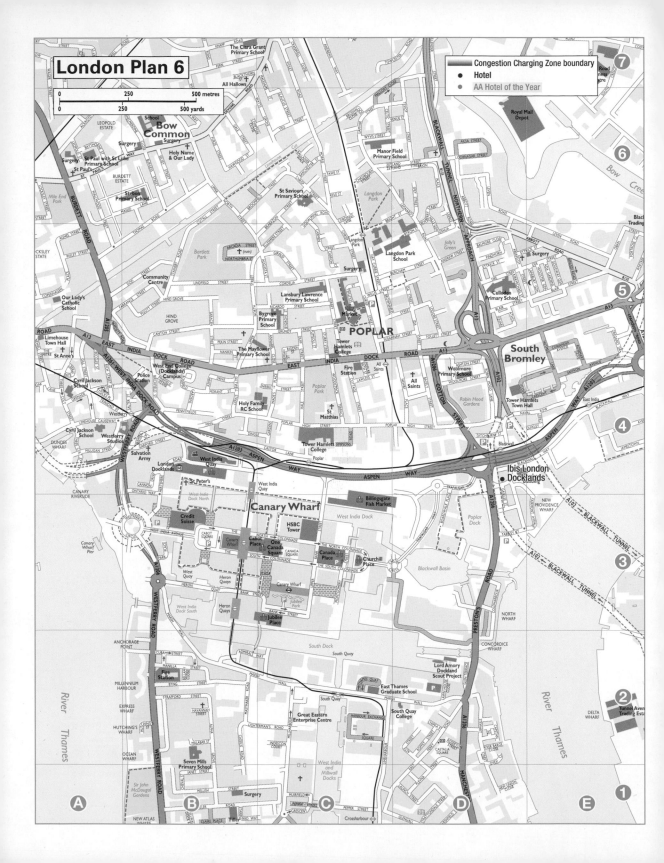

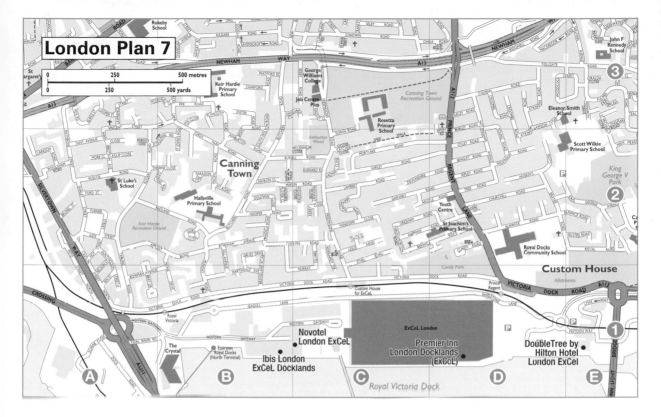

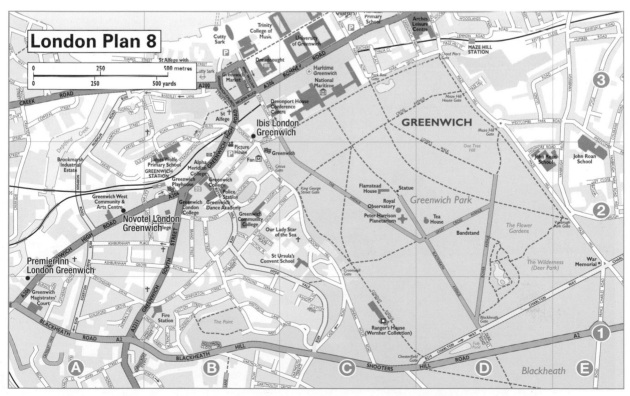

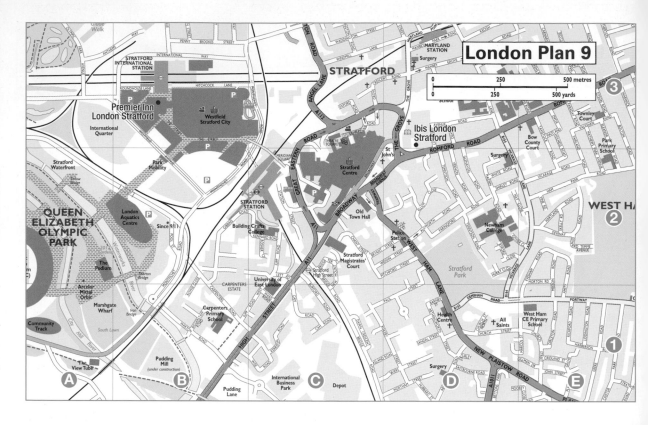

London Plan 9

STRATFORD

WEST HAM

LONDON

Greater London Plans 1-9, pages 240-252. (Small scale maps 6 & 7 at back of book.) Hotels are listed below in postal district order, commencing East, then North, South and West, with a brief indication of the area covered. Detailed plans 2-9 show the locations of AA-appointed hotels within the Central London postal districts. If you do not know the postal district of the hotel you want, please refer to the index preceding the street plans for the entry and map pages. The plan reference for each AA-appointed hotel also appears within its directory entry.

E1 STEPNEY AND EAST OF THE TOWER OF LONDON

hub by Premier Inn London Spitalfields

BUDGET HOTEL PLAN 3 J3

tel: 0333 321 3104 **86 Brick Ln, Spitalfields E1 6RL**
email: Spitalfields.hub@whitbread.com **web:** www.premierinn.com
dir: *Nearest tube stations Aldgate East & Liverpool Street*

High quality, budget accommodation ideal for both families and business travellers. Spacious, en suite bedrooms feature tea and coffee making facilities, and Freeview TV in most hotels. Internet access and WiFi are available for a small fee. The adjacent family restaurant features a wide and varied menu. See also the Hotel Groups pages.

Rooms 189

Premier Inn London City (Aldgate)

BUDGET HOTEL PLAN 3 K2

tel: 0871 527 9526 *(Calls cost 13p per minute plus your phone company's access charge)*
66 Alie St, Aldgate E1 0PX
web: www.premierinn.com
dir: *Exit Aldgate East tube station, S along Leman St. Left into Alie St, hotel on right*

Rooms 250

Premier Inn London City (Tower Hill)

BUDGET HOTEL PLAN 3 J1

tel: 0871 527 8646 *(Calls cost 13p per minute plus your phone company's access charge)*
22-24 Prescott St, Tower Hill E1 8BB
web: www.premierinn.com
dir: *Nearest tube: Tower Hill. 3 mins walk from Docklands Light Rail DLR*

Rooms 165

Ibis London City

AA Advertised PLAN 3 J2

tel: 020 7422 8400 **5 Commercial St E1 6BF**
email: H5011@accor.com **web:** www.ibishotel.com
dir: *M25 junct 30, A13, follow The City signs, then Aldgate signs*

Modern, budget hotel offering comfortable accommodation in bright and practical bedrooms. Breakfast is self-service and dinner is available in the restaurant.

Rooms 348 ↕ **Facilities** STV FTV WiFi ↕ **Services** Lift

E4 CHINGFORD
Map 6 TQ39

Premier Inn Chingford

BUDGET HOTEL

tel: 0871 527 9836 *(Calls cost 13p per minute plus your phone company's access charge)*
Rangers Rd, Chingford E4 7QH
web: www.premierinn.com
dir: *M25 junct 26, A121 (Loughton) At next rdbt 1st exit (A121). At Wake Arms rdbt 2nd exit onto A104 (Woodford). Right onto A1069 (Rangers Rd). 1m, hotel on right*

High quality, budget accommodation ideal for both families and business travellers. Spacious, en suite bedrooms feature tea and coffee making facilities, and Freeview TV in most hotels. Internet access and WiFi are available for a small fee. The adjacent family restaurant features a wide and varied menu. See also the Hotel Groups pages.

Rooms 24

E6 EAST HAM

Premier Inn London Beckton

BUDGET HOTEL PLAN 1 H4

tel: 0871 527 8644 *(Calls cost 13p per minute plus your phone company's access charge)*
1 Woolwich Manor Way, Beckton E6 5NT
web: www.premierinn.com
dir: *A13 onto A117 (Woolwich Manor Way) towards City Airport, hotel on left after 1st rdbt*

High quality, budget accommodation ideal for both families and business travellers. Spacious, en suite bedrooms feature tea and coffee making facilities, and Freeview TV in most hotels. Internet access and WiFi are available for a small fee. The adjacent family restaurant features a wide and varied menu. See also the Hotel Groups pages.

Rooms 124

E8 HACKNEY

Premier Inn London Hackney

BUDGET HOTEL PLAN 1 F4

tel: 0871 527 9582 *(Calls cost 13p per minute plus your phone company's access charge)*
27 Dalston Ln E8 3DF
web: www.premierinn.com
dir: *A406, A10 onto Kinglsand High St, left onto A104, hotel approx 200yds on left*

High quality, budget accommodation ideal for both families and business travellers. Spacious, en suite bedrooms feature tea and coffee making facilities, and Freeview TV in most hotels. Internet access and WiFi are available for a small fee. The adjacent family restaurant features a wide and varied menu. See also the Hotel Groups pages.

Rooms 90

E14 CANARY WHARF & LIMEHOUSE

Ibis London Docklands

AA Advertised PLAN 6 D4

tel: 020 7517 1100 **1 Baffin Way E14 9PE**
email: H2177@accor.com **web:** www.ibishotel.com
dir: *From Tower Bridge follow City Airport and Royal Docks signs, exit for 'Isle of Dogs'. Hotel on 1st left opposite McDonalds*

Modern, budget hotel offering comfortable accommodation in bright and practical bedrooms. Breakfast is self-service and dinner is available in the restaurant.

Rooms 87 (15 GF) **Facilities** STV WiFi ↕ **Services** Lift Air con **Parking** 30

LONDON

E15 STRATFORD

Premier Inn London Stratford

BUDGET HOTEL PLAN 9 B3

tel: 0871 527 9286 *(Calls cost 13p per minute plus your phone company's access charge)*
International Square, Westfield Stratfield City, Montfichet Road, Olympic Park E15 1AZ
web: www.premierinn.com
dir: *From A11 or A12 follow signs for Westfield Shopping City & Stratford International & Car Park A*

High quality, budget accommodation ideal for both families and business travellers. Spacious, en suite bedrooms feature tea and coffee making facilities, and Freeview TV in most hotels. Internet access and WiFi are available for a small fee. The adjacent family restaurant features a wide and varied menu. See also the Hotel Groups pages.

Rooms 267

Ibis London Stratford

AA Advertised PLAN 9 D3

tel: 020 8536 3700 **1A Romford Rd, Stratford E15 4LJ**
email: h3099@accor.com **web:** www.ibishotel.com

Modern, budget hotel offering comfortable accommodation in bright and practical bedrooms. Breakfast is self-service and dinner is available in the restaurant.

Rooms 108 ☎ **Facilities** STV WiFi ⌂ HL **Services** Lift

E16 SILVERTOWN

Novotel London ExCeL

★★★★ 79% HOTEL PLAN 7 C1

tel: 020 7540 9700 **7 Western Gateway, Royal Victoria Docks E16 1AA**
email: H3656@accor.com **web:** www.novotel.com/3656
dir: *M25 junct 30, A13 follow City signs, exit at Canning Town. Follow ExCeL West signs. Hotel adjacent*

This hotel is situated adjacent to the ExCeL exhibition centre and overlooks the Royal Victoria Dock. Design throughout the hotel is contemporary and stylish. Public rooms include a range of meeting rooms, a modern coffee station, indoor leisure facilities and a smart bar and restaurant, both with a terrace overlooking the dock. Bedrooms feature modern decor, a bathroom with separate bath and shower, and an extensive range of extras.

Rooms 257 (176 fmly) ☎ **Facilities** STV FTV WiFi ⌂ HL Gym Sauna Steam room Relaxation room with massage bed **Conf** Class 55 Board 30 Thtr 70 **Services** Lift Air con **Parking** 80 **Notes** Civ Wed 50

DoubleTree by Hilton Hotel London ExCel

★★★★ 78% HOTEL PLAN 7 E1

tel: 020 7540 4820 **Excel 2 Festoon Way, Royal Victoria Dock E16 1RH**
email: reservations@ramadadocklands.co.uk **web:** www.ramadadocklands.co.uk
dir: *Follow signs for ExCeL East & London City Airport. Over Connaught Bridge then immediately left at rdbt*

This hotel benefits from a stunning waterfront location and is close to the events venue, ExCeL, the O2 Arena, Canary Wharf and London City Airport. The accommodation comprises a mix of spacious bedrooms and suites. The relaxed public areas consist of a modern restaurant and informal lounge area. Parking, a fitness room and meeting rooms are available on site. Free WiFi is available.

Rooms 224 (71 fmly) (23 smoking) ☎ **Facilities** FTV WiFi Gym **Conf** Class 20 Board 25 Thtr 30 **Services** Lift Air con **Parking** 60 **Notes** LB Civ Wed 120

Premier Inn London Docklands (ExCeL)

BUDGET HOTEL PLAN 7 D1

tel: 0871 527 8650 *(Calls cost 13p per minute plus your phone company's access charge)*
Excel East, Royal Victoria Dock E16 1SJ
web: www.premierinn.com
dir: *A13 onto A1020. At Connaught rdbt take 2nd exit into Connaught Rd. Hotel on right*

High quality, budget accommodation ideal for both families and business travellers. Spacious, en suite bedrooms feature tea and coffee making facilities, and Freeview TV in most hotels. Internet access and WiFi are available for a small fee. The adjacent family restaurant features a wide and varied menu. See also the Hotel Groups pages.

Rooms 203

Ibis Budget London City Airport

AA Advertised PLAN 1 H3

tel: 020 7474 9106 **North Woolwich Rd, Silvertown E16 2EE**
email: H3578@accor.com **web:** www.ibishotel.com
dir: *From W: M25 junct 30/A13. At rdbt for A406 turn left. From N: M11 junct 1 London, join A406, at rdbt straight on following signs for City Airport then towards Connaught Rd, 1st exit on rdbt*

Modern, budget hotel offering comfortable accommodation in bright and practical bedrooms. Breakfast is self-service and dinner is available in the restaurant.

Rooms 81 (45 fmly) (22 GF) ☎ **Facilities** FTV WiFi HL **Services** Lift **Parking** 40

Ibis London ExCeL Docklands

AA Advertised PLAN 7 B1

tel: 020 7055 2300 **9 Western Gateway, Royal Victoria Docks E16 1AB**
email: H3655@accor.com **web:** www.ibishotel.com
dir: *M25, A13 to London, City Airport, ExCeL East*

Modern, budget hotel offering comfortable accommodation in bright and practical bedrooms. Breakfast is self-service and dinner is available in the restaurant

Rooms 278 ☎ **S** £49-£389; **D** £49-£389* **Facilities** WiFi HL **Services** Lift Air con

EC1 CITY OF LONDON

Malmaison Charterhouse Square

★★★★ 78% ⊛ HOTEL PLAN 3 E3

tel: 020 70123700 **18-21 Charterhouse Square, Clerkenwell EC1M 6AH**
email: reception@malmaison.com **web:** www.malmaison.com
dir: *Exit Barbican Station turn left, take 1st left. Hotel on far left corner of Charterhouse Square*

Situated in a leafy and peaceful square, Malmaison Charterhouse maintains the same focus on quality service and food as the other hotels in the group. The bedrooms, stylishly decorated in calming tones, have all the expected facilities including power showers, CD players and free internet access. The brasserie and bar at the hotel's centre has a buzzing atmosphere and offers traditional French cuisine.

Rooms 97 (5 GF) ☎ **S** £369; **D** £369* **Facilities** STV FTV WiFi ⌂ HL Gym Xmas **Conf** Board 20 Thtr 45 **Services** Lift Air con **Parking** 5

LONDON

The Montcalm London City at The Brewery

AA Advertised PLAN 3 F3

tel: 020 7614 0100 **52 Chiswell St EC1Y 4SB**
email: info@themontcalmlondoncity.co.uk **web:** www.themontcalmlondoncity.co.uk
dir: *From Gatwick M23 N to M25 signed Heathrow Airport/Central London to M4. From Heathrow M4 E 9m*

Situated in the heart of The City is The Montcalm London City at The Brewery. This Grade II listed building has been converted into a luxury hotel, while maintaining many original features. As the name implies, this was formerly the site of Whitbread & Co, Britain's first purpose-built mass production brewery. The last beer brewed here was in 1976, when the site was turned into Whitbread PLC's Head Office. With luxurious suites, deluxe studios and City or Club rooms, The Montcalm London City at The Brewery is ideal for business or leisure.

Rooms 235 ⋔ **Facilities** STV FTV WiFi ⌂ HL Gym Xmas New Year **Conf** Class 40 Board 40 Thtr 60 **Services** Lift Air con **Notes** ⊗ Civ Wed

The Z Hotel Shoreditch

AA Advertised PLAN 3 G5

tel: 020 3551 3700 **136-144 City Rd EC1V 2RL**
email: shoreditch@thezhotels.com **web:** www.thezhotels.com

Z Shoreditch is a newly opened conversion of a former office building, with over one hundred bedrooms. Z Shoreditch is part of The Bower, a new landmark quarter for Old Street comprising offices, restaurants and retail units. As with the others in the Z Hotels chain, bedrooms have en suite wet rooms, crisp bed linen, 40" TV with Sky, and complimentary WiFi.

Rooms 111 ⋔ **Facilities** STV FTV WiFi ⌂ HL **Services** Lift Air con **Notes** ⊗

EC2 MOORGATE

ANdAZ Liverpool Street

★★★★★ 86% HOTEL PLAN 3 H3

tel: 020 7961 1234 **40 Liverpool St EC2M 7QN**
email: guestservices.londonliv@andaz.com **web:** www.london.liverpoolstreet.andaz.com
dir: *On corner of Liverpool St & Bishopsgate, attached to Liverpool St station*

ANdAZ is an exciting and contemporary place to stay - no reception desk here so guests are checked-in by staff with laptops. Bedrooms are stylish, and designed very much with the executive in mind, with iPods and WiFi as well as a mini bar stocked with healthy choices. The dining options are varied and many ; Japanese cuisine in Miyako, 1901 Restaurant and Wine Bar, light snacks available in Catch and Champagne bar and the Eastway brasserie. There are also rooms for private dining and other events.

Rooms 267 ⋔ **Facilities** STV FTV WiFi ⌂ Gym Steam room Beauty treatment rooms New Year **Conf** Class 120 Board 60 Thtr 250 **Services** Lift Air con **Notes** ⊗ Civ Wed 230

EC3 CHEAPSIDE

Novotel London Tower Bridge

★★★★ 78% HOTEL PLAN 3 J1

tel: 020 7265 6000 & 7265 6002 **10 Pepys St EC3N 2NR**
email: H3107@accor.com **web:** www.novotel.com

Located near the Tower of London, this smart hotel is convenient for Docklands, the City, Heathrow and London City airports. Air-conditioned bedrooms are spacious, modern, and offer a great range of facilities. There is a smart bar and restaurant, a small gym, children's play area and extensive meeting and conference facilities.

Rooms 203 (130 fmly) ⋔ **Facilities** STV FTV WiFi ⌂ Gym Steam room Sauna Fitness room ♬ Xmas New Year **Conf** Class 56 Board 25 Thtr 100 **Services** Lift

hub by Premier Inn London Tower Bridge

BUDGET HOTEL PLAN 3 H1

tel: 0333 321 3104 *(Calls cost 13p per minute plus your phone company's access charge)*
28 Great Tower St EC3R 5AT
email: opsmgr.towerbridge.hub@whitbread.com **web:** www.premierinn.com
dir: *Nearest tube stations: Tower Hill & Monument*

High quality, budget accommodation ideal for both families and business travellers. Spacious, en suite bedrooms feature tea and coffee making facilities, and Freeview TV in most hotels. Internet access and WiFi are available for a small fee. The adjacent family restaurant features a wide and varied menu. See also the Hotel Groups pages.

Rooms 112

Premier Inn London City (Monument)

BUDGET HOTEL PLAN 3 H1

tel: 0871 527 9452 *(Calls cost 13p per minute plus your phone company's access charge)*
20 St Mary at Hill EC3R 8EE
web: www.premierinn.com
dir: *Nearest tube stations: Monument & Bank*

Rooms 184

EC4 BLACKFRIARS

Crowne Plaza London - The City

★★★★ 83% HOTEL PLAN 3 E1

CROWNE PLAZA
HOTELS & RESORTS

tel: 020 7438 8000 **19 New Bridge St EC4V 6DB**
email: loncy.info@ihg.com **web:** www.cplondoncityhotel.co.uk
dir: *Opposite Blackfriars station*

With a 1919 façade, and a modern, stylish interior, Crowne Plaza London-The City is located in London's historic Square Mile, near Blackfriars station, minutes away from some of London's most famous attractions such as The London Eye, St Paul's Cathedral and Covent Garden. At the hotel guests can enjoy great dining in two destination restaurants: the celebrated Italian Diciannove or the Chinese Cricket Club offering a mouth-watering range of Sichuan and dim sum specialities with a modern twist. In addition, you can enjoy all-day dining in the comfortable City Lounge, or relax in the stylish champagne bar and cigar terrace, Voltaire.

Rooms 203 (60 fmly) (7 smoking) **D** £120-£800* **Facilities** STV WiFi ⌂ HL Gym ♬ Xmas New Year **Conf** Class 100 Board 50 Thtr 160 Del from £199 to £879* **Services** Lift Air con **Notes** ⊗ Civ Wed 160

Premier Inn London Blackfriars

BUDGET HOTEL PLAN 3 E2

tel: 0871 527 9362 *(Calls cost 13p per minute plus your phone company's access charge)*
1-2 Dorset Rise EC4Y 8EN
web: www.premierinn.com
dir: *Phone for detailed directions*

High quality, budget accommodation ideal for both families and business travellers. Spacious, en suite bedrooms feature tea and coffee making facilities, and Freeview TV in most hotels. Internet access and WiFi are available for a small fee. The adjacent family restaurant features a wide and varied menu. See also the Hotel Groups pages.

Rooms 310

LONDON

EC4 BLACKFRIARS *continued*

The Z Hotel City

AA Advertised PLAN 3 D2

tel: 020 3551 3718 & 3551 3712 **24-28 Fleet St EC4Y 1AA**
email: city@thezhotels.com **web:** www.thezhotels.com/z-city
dir: *Within Temple between Aldwych & Ludgate Circus*

Z City opened in late 2015, and is part of the Z Hotel range. In terms of location, these hotels are unrivalled. Z City is situated in the Temple area, nestled between Aldwych and Ludgate Circus. Immediately behind the hotel is Temple Church, built by the Knights Templar, while opposite is the Royal Courts of Justice. Z City is a designer conversion of a former office building, with 109 bedrooms arranged over lower ground, ground and three upper floors. The bedrooms are functional rather than attractive, yet are carefully considered. Each offers an en suite wet room, crisp bed linen, 48" TV with a full selection of Sky channels, and complimentary WiFi. Some rooms are internal, and therefore windowless.

Rooms 109 (10 fmly) (7 GF) 🐾 **Facilities** STV FTV WiFi HL **Services** Lift Air con **Notes** ⊗

N1 ISLINGTON

Premier Inn London Angel Islington

BUDGET HOTEL PLAN 1 F4

tel: 0871 527 8558 *(Calls cost 13p per minute plus your phone company's access charge)*
Parkfield St, Islington N1 OPS
web: www.premierinn.com
dir: *From A1 (Islington High St) into Berners Rd bear left into Parkfield St. N1 car park opposite hotel*

High quality, budget accommodation ideal for both families and business travellers. Spacious, en suite bedrooms feature tea and coffee making facilities, and Freeview TV in most hotels. Internet access and WiFi are available for a small fee. The adjacent family restaurant features a wide and varied menu. See also the Hotel Groups pages.

Rooms 95

Premier Inn London City (Old Street)

BUDGET HOTEL PLAN 3 G5

tel: 0871 527 9312 *(Calls cost 13p per minute plus your phone company's access charge)*
1 Silicon Way N1 6AT
web: www.premierinn.com
dir: *From Old Street tube station exit 1 (on foot) onto A501 (City Rd). Right into East St. 2nd right into Brunswick Place (Three Crowns pub on corner), 1st left into Corsham St*

Rooms 251

Premier Inn London Kings Cross

BUDGET HOTEL PLAN 3 B6

tel: 0871 527 8672 *(Calls cost 13p per minute plus your phone company's access charge)*
26-30 York Way, Kings Cross N1 9AA
web: www.premierinn.com
dir: *M25 junct 16 onto M40 (becomes A40). Follow City signs, exit at Euston Rd, follow one-way system to York Way*

Rooms 281

N19 HIGHGATE HILL

Premier Inn London Archway

BUDGET HOTEL PLAN 1 E5

tel: 0871 527 9598 **Hamlyn House, Highgate Hill N19 5PA**
email: LondonArchway.PI@premierinn.com **web:** www.premierinn.com
dir: *M1 junct 2, follow Barnet Bypass/Great N Way/A1 signs towards central London. From A406 to A1 junction. Follow Archway Rd until it becomes MacDonald Rd. Hotel on left*

High quality, budget accommodation ideal for both families and business travellers. Spacious, en suite bedrooms feature tea and coffee making facilities, and Freeview TV in most hotels. Internet access and WiFi are available for a small fee. The adjacent family restaurant features a wide and varied menu. See also the Hotel Groups pages.

Rooms 163

NW1 REGENT'S PARK & CAMDEN TOWN

INSPECTORS' CHOICE

The Landmark London

★★★★★ ◎◎ ♨ HOTEL PLAN 2 F3

tel: 020 7631 8000 **222 Marylebone Rd NW1 6JQ**
email: reservations@thelandmark.co.uk **web:** www.landmarklondon.co.uk
dir: *Adjacent to Marylebone Station. Hotel on Marylebone Rd*

Once one of the last truly grand railway hotels, The Landmark boasts a number of stunning features, the most spectacular being the naturally lit central atrium forming the hotel's focal point. When it comes to eating and drinking there are a number of choices, including the Cellars bar for cocktails and upmarket bar meals, the Mirror Bar, and The Gazebo - ideal for a business meeting or a quick snack. The Winter Garden Restaurant has the centre stage in the atrium and is a great place to watch the world go by; and the twotwentytwo restaurant and bar is a relaxing place to meet, eat and drink. The air-conditioned bedrooms are luxurious and have large, stylish bathrooms. There is also a health club that offers a complete wellbeing experience.

Rooms 300 (77 fmly) (52 smoking) 🐾 **Facilities** Spa STV FTV WiFi ♿ ⊗ Gym Beauty treatments & massages ♬ Xmas New Year **Conf** Class 266 Board 50 Thtr 512 **Services** Lift Air con **Parking** 25 **Notes** ⊗ Civ Wed 300

Meliá White House

★★★★ 82% ◎◎ HOTEL PLAN 2 H4

tel: 020 7391 3000 **Albany St, Regents Park NW1 3UP**
email: melia.white.house@melia.com **web:** www.melia-whitehouse.com
dir: *Opposite Gt Portland St underground station & next to Regents Park/Warren Street underground*

Owned by the Spanish Solmelia company, this impressive art deco property is located opposite Great Portland Street tube station. Spacious public areas offer a high degree of comfort and include the newly opened cocktail bar 'Dry Martini by Javier de las Muelas', where guests can enjoy classic cocktails alongside Javier de las Muelas' signature cocktails; the award-winning fine dining Spanish restaurant, L' Albufera; and The Place Restaurant, where tapas-style dishes are served in an informal setting. Stylish bedrooms come in a variety of sizes and styles, but all offer high levels of comfort and are thoughtfully equipped. For longer stays, "The Apartments" are the obvious choice.

Rooms 579 (28 fmly) ♠ **Facilities** STV FTV WiFi ♪ Gym Beauty treatment room ♫ Xmas New Year Child facilities **Conf** Class 80 Board 60 Thtr 140 **Services** Lift Air con **Notes** ⊗

Pullman London St Pancras

★★★★ 79% ◎ HOTEL PLAN 3 A5

tel: 020 7666 9000 & 7666 9010 **100-110 Euston Rd NW1 2AJ**
email: H5309@accor.com **web:** www.accorhotels.com/5309
dir: *Between St Pancras & Euston stations, entrance opposite British Library*

This hotel enjoys a central location adjacent to the British Library and close to some of London's main transport hubs. The style is modern and contemporary throughout. Bedrooms vary in size but are all very well equipped and many have views over the city. Open-plan public areas include a leisure suite and extensive conference facilities including the Shaw Theatre. Free WiFi is available.

Rooms 312 ♠ **Facilities** STV FTV WiFi ♪ HL Gym Sauna Xmas New Year **Conf** Class 220 Board 80 Thtr 446 **Services** Lift Air con **Notes** ⊗

Premier Inn London St Pancras

BUDGET HOTEL PLAN 3 B5

tel: 0871 527 9492 *(Calls cost 13p per minute plus your phone company's access charge)*
Euston House, 81-103 Euston St NW1 2EZ
web: www.premierinn.com
dir: *Nearest tube: London Euston, King's Cross St Pancras*

High quality, budget accommodation ideal for both families and business travellers. Spacious, en suite bedrooms feature tea and coffee making facilities, and Freeview TV in most hotels. Internet access and WiFi are available for a small fee. The adjacent family restaurant features a wide and varied menu. See also the Hotel Groups pages.

Rooms 266

Ibis London Euston St Pancras

AA Advertised PLAN 2 J5

tel: 020 7388 7777 **3 Cardington St NW1 2LW**
email: H0921@accor-hotels.com **web:** www.ibishotel.com
dir: *From Euston Rd or station, right to Melton St & into Cardington St*

Modern, budget hotel offering comfortable accommodation in bright and practical bedrooms. Breakfast is self-service and dinner is available in the restaurant.

Rooms 380 ♠ **Facilities** WiFi HL **Conf** Class 40 Board 40 Thtr 100 **Services** Lift **Parking** 98

NW2 BRENT CROSS & CRICKLEWOOD

Clayton Crown Hotel

★★★★ 76% HOTEL PLAN 1 D5

tel: 020 8452 4175 **142-152 Cricklewood Broadway, Cricklewood NW2 3ED**
web: www.claytonhotels.com
dir: *M1 junct 1 follow signs onto North Circular W A406. Junct with A5 Staples Corner. At rdbt take 1st exit onto A5 to Cricklewood*

This striking hotel is connected by an impressive glass atrium to the popular Crown Pub. Features include excellent function and conference facilities, a leisure club, a choice of stylish lounges and bars and a contemporary restaurant. The air-conditioned bedrooms are appointed to a high standard and include a number of trendy suites.

Rooms 152 (63 fmly) (35 GF) ♠ **Facilities** STV WiFi ♪ 🖐 Gym ♫ Xmas New Year **Conf** Class 150 Board 80 Thtr 300 **Services** Lift Air con **Parking** 39 **Notes** ⊗ Civ Wed 300

NW3 HAMPSTEAD AND SWISS COTTAGE

Premier Inn London Hampstead

BUDGET HOTEL PLAN 1 E4

tel: 0871 527 8662 *(Calls cost 13p per minute plus your phone company's access charge)*
215 Haverstock Hill, Hampstead NW3 4RB
web: www.premierinn.com
dir: *A41 to Swiss Cottage. Before junct take feeder road left into Buckland Cresent into Belsize Ave. Left into Haverstock Hill*

High quality, budget accommodation ideal for both families and business travellers. Spacious, en suite bedrooms feature tea and coffee making facilities, and Freeview TV in most hotels. Internet access and WiFi are available for a small fee. The adjacent family restaurant features a wide and varied menu. See also the Hotel Groups pages.

Rooms 143

NW4 HENDON

Hendon Hall Hotel

★★★★ 78% ◎◎ HOTEL PLAN 1 D5

tel: 020 8457 2500 & 0845 072 7448
(Calls cost 5p per minute plus your phone company's access charge) **Ashley Ln, Hendon NW4 1HF**
email: hendonhall@handpicked.co.uk **web:** www.handpickedhotels.co.uk/hendonhall
dir: *M1 junct 2 follow A406. Right at lights into Parson St, right into Ashley Ln. Hotel on right*

This impressive property was originally built in the 16th century when it was known as Hendon Manor, and is now a stylish hotel boasting smart, well-equipped, comfortable bedrooms with luxury toiletries, free WiFi and well-appointed en suites. Public areas include meeting and conference facilities, a contemporary cocktail bar and a richly decorated restaurant that opens onto a garden terrace. Staff are friendly and attentive.

Rooms 57 ♠ **Facilities** STV FTV WiFi ♪ HL 🖐 Xmas New Year **Conf** Class 130 Board 76 Thtr 200 **Services** Lift Air con **Parking** 70 **Notes** ⊗ Civ Wed 240

LONDON

NW9 KINGSBURY

Premier Inn London Hendon The Hyde

BUDGET HOTEL PLAN 1 D5

tel: 0871 527 9450 *(Calls cost 13p per minute plus your phone company's access charge)*
Hyde House NW9 6LH
web: www.premierinn.com
dir: *M1 junct 4, A41, A5 towards Edgware. Hotel opposite junct of A4006 & Kingsbury*

High quality, budget accommodation ideal for both families and business travellers. Spacious, en suite bedrooms feature tea and coffee making facilities, and Freeview TV in most hotels. Internet access and WiFi are available for a small fee. The adjacent family restaurant features a wide and varied menu. See also the Hotel Groups pages.

Rooms 99

SE1 SOUTHWARK AND WATERLOO

Shangri-La Hotel at The Shard

★★★★★ 86% HOTEL PLAN 5 G6

tel: 020 7234 8000 **31 St Thomas St SE1 9QU**
email: info.slln@shangri-la.com **web:** www.shangri-la.com/london

This hotel in the iconic London Shard is the first foray of the upmarket global brand into the UK and the second into Europe. It won't come as a surprise that every room has a stupendous view, as does the 52nd floor bar, sky pool and, slightly lower down on floor 35, Ting Restaurant. Rooms are fully equipped for business and leisure travellers - free WiFi, air conditioning and ample work space. There are luxurious toiletries in the well-proportioned bathrooms; many with double wash hand basins and heated toilet seats. Full automatic black-out blinds prevent those with vertigo from suffering too much.

Rooms 202 (202 fmly) ⚹ **S** fr £350; **D** fr £350* **Facilities** STV WiFi ⬩ ⬧ Gym Spa treatments available in room or spa residences **Conf** Class 60 Board 50 Thtr 120 **Services** Lift Air con **Parking** 15 **Notes** ⊗ Civ Wed 120

Plaza on the River London

★★★★★ 83% TOWN HOUSE HOTEL PLAN 5 B2

tel: 020 7620 8656 & 0844 854 5295
(Calls cost 7p per minute plus your phone company's access charge)
18 Albert Embankment SE1 7TJ
email: guestrelations@plazaontheriver.co.uk **web:** www.plazaontheriver.co.uk
dir: *From Houses of Parliament turn into Millbank, at rdbt left into Lambeth Bridge. At rdbt 3rd exit into Albert Embankment*

This is a superb modern townhouse overlooking London from the south bank of the Thames, with outstanding views of the capital's landmarks. The bedrooms are large and many are full suites with state-of-the-art technology and kitchen facilities; all are decorated in an elegant modern style. Service includes a full range of in-room dining options; additionally, the bar and restaurant in the adjacent Park Plaza are available to guests.

Rooms 135 (135 fmly) (65 smoking) ⚹ **Facilities** STV FTV WiFi ⬩ HL Gym In room spa Xmas New Year **Conf** Class 405 Board 40 Thtr 700 **Services** Lift Air con **Notes** Civ Wed 400

Park Plaza Westminster Bridge London

★★★★ 81% ◉◉ HOTEL PLAN 5 C5

tel: 020 7620 1110 & 0844 415 6790
(Calls cost 7p per minute plus your phone company's access charge) **SE1 7UT**
email: ppwlres@pphe.com **web:** www.parkplaza.com

A very smart hotel located in the City, close to Waterloo Station, featuring eye-catching, contemporary decor, a state-of-the-art indoor leisure facility and extensive conference and banqueting facilities. There is the awarding-wining Joel brasserie as well as Ichi, the popular sushi bar. The bedrooms are also up-to-the-minute in style and feature a host of extras including a mini bar, a safe and modem points.

Rooms 1019 (575 fmly) ⚹ **Facilities** Spa STV FTV WiFi ⬩ HL ⬧ Gym ♫ Xmas New Year **Conf** Class 800 Board 50 Thtr 2000 **Services** Lift Air con **Notes** LB ⊗ Civ Wed 1400

London Bridge Hotel

★★★★ 81% HOTEL PLAN 5 G6

tel: 020 7855 2200 **8-18 London Bridge St SE1 9SG**
email: sales@londonbridgehotel.com **web:** www.londonbridgehotel.com
dir: *Access through London Bridge Station, past taxi rank, towards Shard into London Bridge St (one way). Hotel on left*

This elegant, independently owned hotel enjoys a prime location on the edge of the City, adjacent to London Bridge station. Smartly appointed, well-equipped bedrooms include a number of spacious deluxe rooms and suites. Free WiFi is available throughout. The Quarter Bar & Lounge is the ideal place for light bites, old favourites and cocktails. The Londinium restaurant offers a seasonal British menu.

Rooms 138 (10 fmly) (5 smoking) **Facilities** STV FTV WiFi ⬩ Gym **Conf** Class 36 Board 36 Thtr 80 **Services** Lift Air con **Notes** ⊗

Park Plaza County Hall London

★★★★ 79%  HOTEL PLAN 5 C5

tel: 020 7021 1800 & 0844 415 6760
(Calls cost 7p per minute plus your phone company's access charge) **1 Addington St SE1 7RY**
email: ppchinfo@pphe.com web: www.parkplazacountyhall.com
dir: *From Houses of Parliament cross Westminster Bridge A302. At rdbt take 4th right at dedicated lights*

This hotel is located just south of Westminster Bridge near Waterloo International Rail Station. A contemporary design-led, air-conditioned establishment, Park Plaza County Hall London features studios and suites, most with kitchenettes and seating areas with flat-screen TV. There are six meeting rooms, an executive lounge, a restaurant and bar, plus a fully-equipped gym with sauna and steam room. WiFi is available.

Rooms 399 (304 fmly) **S** £149–£499; **D** £149-£599* **Facilities** STV FTV WiFi HL Gym Sauna Steam room Beauty therapy room Xmas New Year **Conf** Class 60 Board 40 Thtr 100 **Services** Lift Air con **Notes** LB

Novotel London City South

★★★★ 78% HOTEL PLAN 5 F6

tel: 020 7660 0676 **Southwark Bridge Rd SE1 9HH**
email: H3269@accor.com web: www.novotel.com
dir: *At junct at Thrale St, off Southwark St*

Conveniently located for both business and leisure guests, with The City just across the Thames; other major attractions are also easily accessible. The hotel is contemporary in design with smart, modern bedrooms and spacious public rooms. There are a gym, sauna and steam room on the 6th floor, and limited parking is available at the rear of the hotel.

Rooms 182 (164 fmly) **Facilities** STV FTV WiFi HL Gym Steam room Sauna **Conf** Class 45 Board 40 Thtr 100 **Services** Lift Air con **Parking** 50

Park Plaza Riverbank London

★★★★ 77% HOTEL PLAN 5 C3

tel: 020 7958 8000 & 0844 854 5290
(Calls cost 7p per minute plus your phone company's access charge)
18 Albert Embankment SE1 7SP
email: rppres@pphe.com web: www.parkplazariverbank.com
dir: *From Houses of Parliament turn onto Millbank, at rdbt left onto Lambeth Bridge. At rdbt take 3rd exit onto Albert Embankment*

Situated on the south side of the River Thames, this hotel offers guests the convenience of a central London location and high levels of comfort. Contemporary design coupled with a host of up-to-date facilities, the hotel is home to the Chino Latino brasserie. The air-conditioned bedrooms have flat-screen TVs and large work desks; some rooms and suites have stunning views of the Houses of Parliament. Other facilities include WiFi throughout, high-tech conference rooms, a business centre, and a fitness centre with cardiovascular equipment.

Rooms 521 **Facilities** STV FTV WiFi HL Gym **Conf** Class 405 Board 40 Thtr 700 **Services** Lift Air con **Notes** Civ Wed 400

H10 London Waterloo Hotel

★★★★ 77% HOTEL PLAN 5 E5

tel: 020 7928 4062 **284–302 Waterloo Rd SE1 8RQ**
email: h10.london.waterloo@h10hotels.com web: www.h10hotels.com
dir: *450mtrs from Waterloo Station, 300mtrs from Lambeth North*

This hotel, conveniently situated for the South Bank and Waterloo Station, has a host of features. Bedrooms are stylish and designed with the international traveller in mind. The bar provides a useful internet facility and the stylish restaurant offers fresh and interesting dishes. The staff are friendly and efficient.

Rooms 177 **Facilities** STV FTV WiFi Gym Beauty treatment room Xmas New Year **Conf** Class 45 Board 24 Thtr 70 Del from £140 to £240* **Services** Lift Air con **Notes**

Mercure London Bridge

★★★★ 76% HOTEL PLAN 5 E6

tel: 020 7660 0683 **71–79 Southwark St SE1 0JA**
email: H2814@accor.com web: www.mercure.com
dir: *A200 to London Bridge. Left into Southwark St*

This smart, contemporary hotel forms part of the rejuvenation of the South Bank. With the City of London just over the river and a number of tourist attractions within easy reach, the hotel is well located for business and leisure visitors alike. Facilities include spacious air-cooled bedrooms, a modern bar and the stylish Loft Restaurant.

Rooms 144 (15 fmly) (5 GF) **Facilities** STV FTV WiFi HL Gym Xmas **Conf** Class 40 Board 30 Thtr 60 **Services** Lift Air con

Novotel London Blackfriars

★★★★ 76% HOTEL PLAN 5 E6

tel: 020 7660 0834 **46 Blackfriars Rd SE1 8NZ**
email: H7942@accor.com web: www.novotel.com

This latest generation Novotel is just south of the Thames and was opened in late 2012, utilising the latest in hotel and bedroom technology. There are media hubs in each bedroom, as well as air conditioning and glass walls to the bathroom that "steam-over" in an instant for privacy if desired. There are also a swimming pool, gym and sauna in the basement, and a bar and restaurant on the ground floor.

Rooms 182 (39 fmly) **Facilities** FTV WiFi HL Gym Saunarium **Conf** Class 50 Board 40 Thtr 90 **Services** Lift Air con

Novotel London Waterloo

★★★★ 76% HOTEL PLAN 5 C3

tel: 020 7793 1010 **113 Lambeth Rd SE1 7LS**
email: h1785@accor.com web: www.novotel.com/1785
dir: *Opposite Houses of Parliament on S bank of River Thames*

This hotel is in an excellent location, with Lambeth Palace, the Houses of Parliament and Waterloo Station all within a short walk. The bedrooms are spacious and benefit from air conditioning. Open-plan public areas include the Elements bar and restaurant, and also a children's play area. There's also a fitness room, well-equipped conference facilities and secure parking.

Rooms 187 (80 fmly) **Facilities** STV WiFi HL Gym Steam room Sauna **Conf** Class 24 Board 24 Thtr 40 **Services** Lift Air con **Parking** 40

LONDON

SE1 SOUTHWARK AND WATERLOO *continued*

Days Hotel London Waterloo

BUDGET HOTEL PLAN 5 D4

tel: 020 7922 1331 **54 Kennington Rd SE1 7BJ**
email: book@hotelwaterloo.com **web:** www.hotelwaterloo.com
dir: *On corner of Kennington Rd & Lambeth Rd. Opposite Imperial War Museum*

This modern building offers accommodation in smart, spacious and well-equipped bedrooms, suitable for families and business travellers, and all with en suite bathrooms. Continental breakfast is available and other refreshments may be taken at the nearby family restaurant. See also the Hotel Groups pages.

Rooms 162 (15 fmly) (13 GF) 🐾

Premier Inn London County Hall

BUDGET HOTEL PLAN 5 C5

tel: 0871 527 8648 *(Calls cost 13p per minute plus your phone company's access charge)*
Belvedere Rd, Westminster SE1 7PB
web: www.premierinn.com
dir: *In County Hall building. Nearest tube: Waterloo*

High quality, budget accommodation ideal for both families and business travellers. Spacious, en suite bedrooms feature tea and coffee making facilities, and Freeview TV in most hotels. Internet access and WiFi are available for a small fee. The adjacent family restaurant features a wide and varied menu. See also the Hotel Groups pages.

Rooms 316

Premier Inn London Southwark (Borough Market)

BUDGET HOTEL PLAN 5 F6

tel: 0871 527 8676 *(Calls cost 13p per minute plus your phone company's access charge)*
Bankside, 34 Park St SE1 9EF
web: www.premierinn.com
dir: *A3200 onto A300 (Southwark Bridge Rd), 1st left into Sumner St, right into Park St. From S: M3, A3 follow Central London signs*

Rooms 59

Premier Inn London Southwark (Tate Modern)

BUDGET HOTEL PLAN 5 E6

tel: 0871 527 9332 *(Calls cost 13p per minute plus your phone company's access charge)*
15A Great Suffolk St, Southwark SE1 0FL
web: www.premierinn.com
dir: *Phone for detailed directions*

Rooms 122

Premier Inn London Tower Bridge

BUDGET HOTEL PLAN 5 H5

tel: 0871 527 8678 *(Calls cost 13p per minute plus your phone company's access charge)*
159 Tower Bridge Rd SE1 3LP
web: www.premierinn.com
dir: *S of Tower Bridge on A100*

Rooms 196

Premier Inn London Waterloo

BUDGET HOTEL PLAN 5 C5

tel: 0871 527 9412 *(Calls cost 13p per minute plus your phone company's access charge)*
York Rd, Waterloo SE1 7NJ
web: www.premierinn.com
dir: *Nearest station: Waterloo*

Rooms 234

citizenM London Bankside

AA Advertised PLAN 5 E6

tel: 020 3519 1680 **20 Lavington St SE1 0NZ**
email: supportlba@citizenm.com **web:** www.citizenm.com

Just a short walk from Tate Modern and Shakespeare's Globe, citizenM London Bankside is the height of urban, stylish, business-and-pleasure, boutique accommodation. From the 1 minute check-in promise to the new-media friendly meeting rooms and lobby, this is something different. The bedrooms are stylishly economical, making the most of limited space, with super-sized beds, blackout blinds, free WiFi, ambient mood lighting, a rain shower and a wall-to-wall window above the bed. CanteenM serves breakfast, lunch and dinner, and serves as a 24-hour bar.

Rooms 192 **Facilities** STV FTV WiFi **Services** Lift **Notes** ⊗

Ibis London Blackfriars

AA Advertised PLAN 5 E6

tel: 020 7633 2720 **49 Blackfriars Rd SE1 8NZ**
email: H7943@accor.com **web:** www.ibis.com/7943
dir: *Next to Southwark and Blackfriars underground stations*

Modern, budget hotel offering comfortable accommodation in bright and practical bedrooms. Breakfast is self-service and dinner is available in the restaurant.

Rooms 297 (10 fmly) 🐾 **Facilities** STV FTV WiFi HL **Services** Lift Air con

Ibis Styles London Southwark Rose

AA Advertised PLAN 5 F6

tel: 020 7015 1480 **Southwark Rose, 47 Southwark Bridge Rd SE1 9HH**
email: h7465@accor.com **web:** www.ibishotel.com
dir: *From Westminster Bridge, into Stamford Rd, continue to Southwark St, left into Southwark Bridge Rd*

Conveniently located just south of the River Thames on Southwark Bridge, this modern hotel offers well equipped air-conditioned bedrooms, internet and ample work space. There is a pleasant restaurant, bar lounge and business area on the 6th floor offering breakfast and dinner. The staff are friendly and welcoming. A limited amount of parking is available at the rear of the hotel. See also the Hotel Groups pages.

Rooms 114 (6 fmly) **Conf** Class 50 Board 26 Thtr 60

SE10 GREENWICH

Novotel London Greenwich

★★★★ 77% HOTEL PLAN 8 A2

tel: 020 8312 6800 **173-185 Greenwich High Rd, Greenwich SE10 8JA**
email: H3476@accor.com **web:** www.novotel.com
dir: *Adjacent to Greenwich Station*

This purpose-built hotel is conveniently located for rail and DLR stations, as well as major attractions such as the Royal Maritime Museum and the Royal Observatory. Air-conditioned bedrooms are spacious and equipped with a host of extras, and public areas include a small gym, contemporary lounge bar and restaurant.

Rooms 151 (34 fmly) ⌇ **S** £90-£250; **D** £100-£260* **Facilities** STV FTV WiFi ⌇ HL Gym Steam room Xmas **Conf** Class 40 Board 32 Thtr 92 Del £300* **Services** Lift Air con **Parking** 30

Premier Inn London Greenwich

BUDGET HOTEL PLAN 8 A1

tel: 0871 527 9208 *(Calls cost 13p per minute plus your phone company's access charge)*
43-81 Greenwich High Rd, Greenwich SE10 8JL
web: www.premierinn.com
dir: *Phone for detailed directions*

Rooms 156

Ibis London Greenwich

AA Advertised PLAN 8 B3

tel: 020 8305 1177 **30 Stockwell St, Greenwich SE10 9JN**
email: H0975@accor.com **web:** www.ibishotel.com
dir: *From Waterloo Bridge, Elephant & Castle, A2 to Greenwich*

Modern, budget hotel offering comfortable accommodation in bright and practical bedrooms. Breakfast is self-service and dinner is available in the restaurant.

Rooms 120 (10 fmly) (12 GF) ⌇ **Facilities** WiFi ⌇ **Services** Lift Air con **Parking** 26

SE13 LEWISHAM

Premier Inn London Lewisham

BUDGET HOTEL PLAN 1 G2

tel: 0871 527 9480 *(Calls cost 13p per minute plus your phone company's access charge)*
1-13 Lewisham High St SE13 5AF
email: LondonLewisham.PI@premierinn.com **web:** www.premierinn.com
dir: *From A2 at lights into Lewisham Rd, under rail bridge, inn on left. Or from Lewisham Station (walking), left into Station Rd. At road end, left into Lewisham Rd (A2211). 1st right into Lewisham High St, 1st left into Kings Hall Mews*

Rooms 60

SE15 PECKHAM

Best Western London Peckham Hotel

Best Western.

U PLAN 1 F3

tel: 020 7701 4222 & 7701 5026 **110 Peckham Rd, Peckham SE15 5EU**
email: peckham@eurohotelsgroup.co.uk **web:** www.www.thelondonpeckhamhotel.co.uk
dir: *Phone for directions*

Currently the rating for this establishment is not confirmed. This may be due to a change of ownership or because it has only recently joined the AA rating scheme. For further details please see the AA website: theAA.com

SW1 WESTMINSTER

INSPECTORS' CHOICE

The Berkeley

MAYBOURNE
HOTEL GROUP

★★★★★ ◉◉◉◉◉ ≋ HOTEL PLAN 4 G5

tel: 020 7235 6000 **Wilton Place, Knightsbridge SW1X 7RL**
email: info@the-berkeley.co.uk **web:** www.the-berkeley.co.uk
dir: *300mtrs from Hyde Park Corner along Knightsbridge*

This stylish hotel, just off Knightsbridge, boasts an excellent range of bedrooms, each furnished with care and a host of thoughtful extras. Newer rooms feature trendy, spacious glass and marble bathrooms, and some of the private suites have their own roof terrace. The striking Blue Bar enhances the reception rooms, all of which are adorned with magnificent flower arrangements. Various eating options include the Caramel Room for breakfast, an all-day menu from 11am, and afternoon tea. Marcus Wareing at The Berkeley has attained 5 AA Rosettes for stunning French cuisine, and here guests can also book the chef's table. The health spa offers a range of treatment rooms and includes a stunning open-air, roof-top pool.

Rooms 210 (31 smoking) ⌇ **Facilities** Spa STV FTV WiFi ⌇ HL ⊛ Gym Beauty/ therapy treatments Personal training Xmas New Year **Conf** Class 96 Board 54 Thtr 180 **Services** Lift Air con **Notes** ⊗ Civ Wed 160

LONDON

SW1 WESTMINSTER *continued*

St James's Hotel and Club

★★★★★ ◉◉◉◉ TOWN HOUSE HOTEL PLAN 4 J6

tel: 020 7316 1600 **7-8 Park Place SW1A 1LP**
email: info@stjameshotelandclub.com web: www.stjameshotelandclub.com
dir: *On A4 near Picadilly Circus & St James's St*

Dating back to 1857, this elegant property with its distinctive neo-Gothic exterior is discreetly set in the heart of St James. Inside there is impressive decor created by interior designer Anne Maria Jagdfeld. Air-conditioned bedrooms are appointed to a very high standard and feature luxurious beds alongside a range of modern facilities. Stylish open-plan public areas offer a smart bar/lounge and the fine dining restaurant, Seven Park Place by William Drabble, which serves modern French dishes based on primarily British ingredients.

Rooms 60 (8 fmly) (15 GF) 🐾 **S** £295-£4300; **D** £295-£4300* **Facilities** STV FTV WiFi **Conf** Class 30 Board 25 Thtr 40 Del from £425* **Services** Lift Air con **Notes** LB ⊗ Civ Wed 40

DUKES London

★★★★★ ◉◉◉ HOTEL PLAN 4 J6

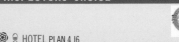

tel: 020 7491 4840 **35 St James's Place SW1A 1NY**
email: bookings@dukeshotel.com web: www.dukeshotel.com
dir: *From Pall Mall into St James's St. 2nd left into St James's Place. Hotel in courtyard on left*

Discreetly tucked away in St James's, Dukes is over 100 years old. Its style is understated, with smart, well-equipped bedrooms and public areas. The

Penthouse Suite has its own balcony with views over Green Park. Facilities include a gym, marble steam room and body-care treatments. The award-winning restaurant, Thirty Six by Nigel Mendham, offers British cuisine based on the very best ingredients. A smart lounge and a sophisticated and buzzing cocktail bar add to guests' enjoyment, and Martinis are a must!

Rooms 90 (40 fmly) (4 GF) 🐾 **Facilities** STV FTV WiFi Gym Steam room Health club Personal training Beauty treatment room Xmas New Year **Conf** Class 30 Board 30 Thtr 70 **Services** Lift Air con **Notes** ⊗ Civ Wed 60

The Goring

★★★★★ ◉◉◉ HOTEL PLAN 4 H4

tel: 020 7396 9000 **Beeston Place SW1W 0JW**
email: reception@thegoring.com web: www.thegoring.com
dir: *Off Lower Grosvenor Place, just prior to Royal Mews*

This icon of British hospitality for over 100 years is centrally located and within walking distance of the Royal Parks and principal shopping areas. Spacious bedrooms and suites, - some contemporary in style with state-of-the-art technology, and others more classically furnished - all boast high levels of comfort and quality. The Duchess of Cambridge stayed in the newly created Royal Suite on the night before her wedding in 2011. Elegant day rooms include the Garden Bar and the drawing room, both popular for afternoon tea and cocktails. The stylish airy restaurant offers a popular menu of contemporary British cuisine, and delightful private dining rooms are available. Guests will experience a personalised service from the attentive and friendly team.

Rooms 69 (9 fmly) 🐾 **S** £335-£615; **D** £380-£710* **Facilities** STV WiFi Free membership of nearby health club Xmas New Year **Conf** Board 20 Thtr 50 **Services** Lift Air con **Parking** 16 **Notes** ⊗ Civ Wed 50

Find out more about the AA Hotel of the Year for London on page 13

INSPECTORS' CHOICE

The Halkin by COMO

★★★★★ ◉◉◉ ⒭ TOWN HOUSE HOTEL PLAN 4 G5

tel: 020 7333 1000 **Halkin St, Belgravia SW1X 7DJ**
email: res.thehalkin@comohotel.com **web:** www.comohotels.com/thehalkin
dir: *Between Belgrave Sq & Grosvenor Place. Via Chapel St into Headfort Place, left into Halkin St*

This smart, contemporary hotel has an enviable and peaceful position just a short stroll from both Hyde Park and the designer shops of Knightsbridge. Service is attentive, friendly and very personalised. The stylish bedrooms and suites are equipped to the highest standard with white marble bathrooms and every conceivable extra. Each floor is discreetly designed following the themes of water, air, fire, earth and sky. There is the airy Halkin Bar that offers all-day eating including an afternoon tea menu, and a stylish restaurant serving award-winning dishes.

Rooms 41 ⒭ **D** £335-£565* **Facilities** STV FTV WiFi ⒭ Gym Complimentary use of spa at sister hotel **Conf** Class 20 Board 26 Thtr 40 **Services** Lift Air con **Notes** LB ⊗

INSPECTORS' CHOICE

Jumeirah Carlton Tower

★★★★★ ◉◉◉ ⒭ HOTEL PLAN 4 F4

tel: 020 7235 1234 **Cadogan Place SW1X 9PY**
email: jctinfo@jumeirah.com **web:** www.jumeirah.com
dir: *A4 towards Knightsbridge, right onto Sloane St. Hotel on left before Cadogan Place*

This impressive hotel enjoys an enviable position in the heart of Knightsbridge, overlooking Cadogan Gardens. The stunningly designed bedrooms, including a

number of suites, vary in size and style. Many have wonderful city views and all have free WiFi. Leisure facilities include a glass-roofed swimming pool, a well-equipped gym and a number of treatment rooms. The renowned Rib Room Bar & Restaurant provides excellent dining, together with the other options of the Club Room, and Chinoiserie.

Jumeirah Carlton Tower

Rooms 216 (76 smoking) ⒭ **D** fr £325* **Facilities** Spa STV FTV WiFi ⒭ ⒭ Gym Golf simulator (50 courses) ♫ **Conf** Class 250 Board 90 Thtr 400 **Services** Lift Air con **Parking** 30 **Notes** ⊗ Civ Wed 400

INSPECTORS' CHOICE

Mandarin Oriental Hyde Park, London

★★★★★ ◉◉◉ ⒭ HOTEL PLAN 4 F5

tel: 020 7235 2000 **66 Knightsbridge SW1X 7LA**
email: molon-reservations@mohg.com **web:** www.mandarinoriental.com/london
dir: *Harrods 400mtrs on right & Harvey Nichols directly opposite hotel*

Situated in fashionable Knightsbridge and overlooking Hyde Park, this iconic venue is a popular destination for highfliers, celebrities and the young and fashionable. Bedrooms, many with park views, are appointed to the highest standards with luxurious features such as the finest Irish linen and goose down pillows. Guests have a choice of dining options - Bar Boulud (with 2 AA Rosettes) offering a contemporary bistro menu of seasonal, rustic French dishes; and Dinner by Heston Blumenthal where the dishes are based on recipes that date back as far as the 14th century, but with Heston's legendary modern twist. The Mandarin Bar serves light snacks and cocktails. The stylish spa is a destination in its own right and offers a range of innovative treatments.

Rooms 189 (84 smoking) ⒭ **S** £355-£960; **Facilities** Spa STV FTV WiFi ⒭ ⒭ Gym Sanarium Steam room Vitality pool Zen colour therapy Relaxation area Xmas New Year **Conf** Class 140 Board 70 Thtr 300 **Services** Lift Air con **Parking** 25 **Notes** ⊗ Civ Wed 250

SW1 WESTMINSTER *continued*

Corinthia Hotel London

★★★★★ ◉◉ HOTEL PLAN 5 B6

tel: 020 7930 8181 **Whitehall Place SW1A 2BD**
email: london@corinthia.com **web:** www.corinthia.com/london
dir: *M4 onto A4, follow Central London signs. Pass Green Park, right into Coventry St, 1st right into Haymarket, left into Pall Mall East, right into Trafalgar Sq, 3rd exit into Whitehall Place*

Steeped in history, this elegant hotel is reputed to be one of London's earliest, having opened in 1885. After a very high quality refurbishment, the hotel has emerged with exceptional style. The team are welcoming and friendly and all requests are skilfully dealt with. Bedrooms, including suites and penthouses, are equipped to very high standards and offer all modern amenities. Eating options are The Northall with British cuisine and The Massimo Restaurant offering Mediterranean seafood. The Bassoon Bar is the place for cocktails and it's worth noting the counter which is actually an elongated piano. Afternoon tea is another highlight served in the stunning lobby lounge. The Espa Spa offers world-class facilities. Valet parking is available.

Rooms 294 (10 fmly) (46 smoking) 🚭 **Facilities** Spa STV WiFi ↕ ⏱ Gym Vitality pool Nail studio Hair salon Relaxation sleep pod Xmas New Year **Conf** Class 120 Board 50 Thtr 250 **Services** Lift Air con **Notes** ⊗ Civ Wed 250

The Stafford London

★★★★★ ◉◉ HOTEL PLAN 4 J6

tel: 020 7493 0111 **16-18 St James's Place SW1A 1NJ**
email: reservations@thestaffordlondon.com **web:** www.thestaffordlondon.com
dir: *Exit Pall Mall into St James's St. 2nd left into St James's Place*

Tucked away in a quiet corner of St James's, this classically styled boutique hotel retains an air of understated luxury. The American Bar is a fabulous venue in its own right, festooned with an eccentric array of celebrity photos, caps and ties. Also, afternoon tea is a long established tradition here. From the pristine, tastefully decorated and air-conditioned bedrooms, to the highly professional, yet friendly service, this exclusive hotel maintains the highest standards. 26 stunning mews suites are available.

Rooms 105 (38 annexe) (8 GF) (2 smoking) 🚭 **Facilities** STV WiFi ↕ Gym Use of fitness club nearby Xmas New Year **Conf** Class 20 Board 24 Thtr 60 **Services** Lift Air con **Notes** ⊗ Civ Wed 44

Taj 51 Buckingham Gate, Suites and Residences

★★★★★ ◉◉ TOWN HOUSE HOTEL PLAN 4 J4

tel: 020 7769 7766 **SW1E 6AF**
email: info.london@tajhotels.com **web:** www.taj51buckinghamgate.co.uk
dir: *From Buckingham Palace onto Buckingham Gate, 100mtrs, hotel on right*

This all-suites hotel is a favourite with those who desire a quiet, sophisticated environment. Each of the suites has its own butler on hand plus a kitchen, and most have large lounge areas furnished in a contemporary style with modern accessories. There are one, two, three and four bedroom suites to choose from, which include the stunning Jaguar Suite and the spectacular brand new Cinema Suite. The hotel has a spa and a well-equipped gym.

Rooms 85 (85 fmly) (3 GF) ☁ **Facilities** Spa STV FTV WiFi ☟ HL Gym Sauna Steam room Xmas New Year **Conf** Class 90 Board 60 Thtr 180 **Services** Lift Air con **Notes** ⊗ Civ Wed 150

INSPECTORS' CHOICE

41

★★★★★ ☷ TOWN HOUSE HOTEL PLAN 4 H4

THE RED CARNATION HOTEL COLLECTION

tel: 020 7300 0041 **41 Buckingham Palace Rd SW1W OPS**
email: book41@rchmail.com **web:** www.41hotel.com
dir: *Opposite Buckingham Palace Mews entrance*

Small, intimate and very private, this stunning town house is located opposite the Royal Mews. Decorated in stylish black and white, bedrooms successfully combine comfort with state-of-the-art technology such as iPod docking stations, interactive TV and free high-speed internet access. Thoughtful touches such as fresh fruit, flowers and scented candles add to the very welcoming atmosphere. The large lounge is the focal point; food and drinks are available as are magazines and newspapers from around the world plus internet access. Attentive personal service and a host of thoughtful extra touches make 41 really special.

Rooms 30 (2 fmly) ☁ S £323-£479; D £347-£539* **Facilities** STV WiFi ☟ Local health club Beauty treatments In-room spa Xmas New Year **Conf** Board 8 **Services** Lift Air con

---

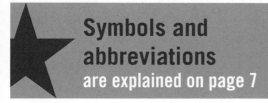

Symbols and abbreviations
are explained on page 7

INSPECTORS' CHOICE

The Lanesborough

★★★★★ ☷ HOTEL PLAN 4 G5

tel: 020 7259 5599 **Hyde Park Corner SW1X 7TA**
email: pmccolgan@lanesborough.com **web:** www.lanesborough.com
dir: *At Hyde Park corner*

The Lanesborough has recently re-opened having benefitted from a huge multi million pound refurbishment; no detail too small and no luxury spared. Set in prestigious Knightsbridge, with panoramic views of Hyde Park, this elegant and luxurious hotel offers nearly a hundred rooms, including almost fifty suites, with a personal butler service for all guests 24 hours a day. Public areas include Celeste Restaurant, The Library Bar and the Withdrawing room. The Garden Room (a lounge for cigar connoisseurs), and the Spa Studio complete these first-class facilities.

Rooms 93 (7 fmly) (G GF) (38 smoking) ☁ **Facilities** Spa STV FTV WiFi ☟ Gym ♫ Xmas New Year **Conf** Class 48 Board 52 Thtr 100 **Services** Lift Air con **Parking** 48 **Notes** Civ Wed 100

The Park Tower Knightsbridge

★★★★★ 86% ◉◉◉ HOTEL PLAN 4 F5

tel: 020 7235 8050 **101 Knightsbridge SW1X 7RN**
web: www.theparktowerknightsbridge.com
dir: *Adjacent to Harvey Nichols*

The hotel sits just a short walk from leafy Hyde Park and some of the most distinguished shops of Knightsbridge. The interiors are luxurious, with handcrafted pieces and marble bathrooms, while the iconic design of the building allows all guests views over Knightsbridge or the park. Relax in the Lounge, where an idyllic tea parlour with afternoon tea is served under magnolia blossom. Dining in Pascal Proyart's One-O-One restaurant is a must for fish lovers.

Rooms 280 ☁ **Facilities** STV FTV WiFi ☟ Gym ♫ **Conf** Class 60 Board 26 Thtr 120 **Services** Lift Air con **Notes** ⊗

SW1 WESTMINSTER *continued*

Sofitel London St James

★★★★★ 86% HOTEL PLAN 4 K6

SOFITEL

tel: 020 7747 2200 **6 Waterloo Place SW1Y 4AN**
email: H3144@sofitel.com **web:** www.sofitelstjames.com
dir: *3 mins walk from Piccadilly Circus & Trafalgar Square*

Located moments away from Trafalgar Square, Sofitel London St James offers a sophisticated yet relaxed welcome, enhanced by a spa; The Balcon, an all-day dining restaurant; and the Rose Lounge, ideal for afternoon tea. With 12 meeting rooms and a private dining room, the hotel can also cater for all manners of functions.

Rooms 183 (102 fmly) **Facilities** Spa STV WiFi Gym So FIT So SPA Xmas New Year **Conf** Class 120 Board 44 Thtr 170 **Services** Lift Air con **Notes** Civ Wed 140

The Royal Horseguards

★★★★★ 82% HOTEL PLAN 5 B6

tel: 0871 376 9033 *(Calls cost 7p per minute plus your phone company's access charge)*
2 Whitehall Court SW1A 2EJ
email: royalhorseguards@guoman.co.uk **web:** www.theroyalhorseguards.com
dir: *Trafalgar Sq to Whitehall, left to Whitehall Pl, turn right*

This majestic hotel in the heart of Whitehall sits beside the Thames and enjoys unrivalled views of the London Eye and the city skyline. Bedrooms, appointed to a high standard, are well equipped and some of the luxurious bathrooms are finished in marble. Impressive public areas and outstanding meeting facilities are also available.

Rooms 282 (7 fmly) **Facilities** STV WiFi Gym Xmas New Year **Conf** Class 180 Board 84 Thtr 240 **Services** Lift Air con **Notes** Civ Wed 228

The Rubens at the Palace

★★★★ 85% HOTEL PLAN 4 H4

THE RED CARNATION
HOTEL COLLECTION

tel: 020 7834 6600 **39 Buckingham Palace Rd SW1W OPS**
email: bookrb@rchmail.com **web:** www.rubenshotel.com
dir: *Opposite Royal Mews, 100mtrs from Buckingham Palace*

This hotel enjoys an enviable location close to Buckingham Palace. Stylish, air-conditioned bedrooms include the pinstripe-walled Savile Row rooms, which follow a tailoring theme, and the opulent Royal rooms, named after different monarchs. Public rooms include The Library fine dining restaurant, and a comfortable stylish cocktail bar and lounge. The team here pride themselves on their warmth and friendliness.

Rooms 161 (14 fmly) **S** £179-£359; **D** £191-£371* **Facilities** STV WiFi Health club & beauty treatment available nearby Xmas New Year **Conf** Class 50 Board 30 Thtr 90 Del from £403.50 to £458.50* **Services** Lift Air con **Notes** Civ Wed 80

St Ermins Hotel

★★★★ 84% HOTEL PLAN 4 K4

tel: 020 7222 7888 & 0800 635 0438
2 Caxton St, St James Park, Westminster SW1H OQW
email: reservations@sterminshotel.co.uk **web:** www.sterminshotel.co.uk
dir: *Just off Victoria St, directly opposite New Scotland Yard*

Located in an enviable London location, the delightful courtyard offers a sanctuary from the hustle and bustle of the city. St Ermins' day rooms are fresh, modern and innovative, with a respectful nod to the hotel's former character. No detail has been overlooked. Food is served in the popular Caxton Grill. Limited valet parking is available by arrangement.

Rooms 331 (18 fmly) (12 GF) **Facilities** STV FTV WiFi HL Gym Xmas New Year **Conf** Class 80 Board 60 Thtr 160 **Services** Lift Air con **Parking** 5 **Notes** Civ Wed 160

Cavendish London

★★★★ 81% HOTEL PLAN 4 J6

tel: 020 7930 2111 **81 Jermyn St SW1Y 6JF**
email: info@thecavendishlondon.com **web:** www.thecavendishlondon.com
dir: *From Piccadilly, pass The Ritz, 1st right into Dukes St before Fortnum & Mason*

This smart, stylish hotel enjoys an enviable location in the prestigious St James's area, just a short walk from Green Park and Piccadilly. Bedrooms have a fresh, contemporary feel, and there are a number of spacious executive rooms, studios and suites. Elegant public areas include a spacious first-floor lounge and well-appointed conference and function facilities. The popular Petrichor restaurant is committed to sourcing sustainable ingredients, especially from British producers. A good value, pre-theatre menu is available.

Rooms 230 (12 fmly) **Facilities** STV WiFi HL **Conf** Class 50 Board 40 Thtr 80 **Services** Lift Air con **Parking** 50 **Notes**

Park Plaza Victoria London

★★★★ 80% ◉◉ HOTEL PLAN 4 J3

Park Plaza
Hotels & Resorts

tel: 020 7769 9999 & 0844 854 5290

(Calls cost 7p per minute plus your phone company's access charge)
239 Vauxhall Bridge Rd SW1V 1EQ
email: info@victoriaparkplaza.com **web:** www.parkplaza.com
dir: *Turn right from Victoria Station*

This smart modern hotel close to Victoria station is well located for all of central London's major attractions. Air-conditioned bedrooms are tastefully appointed and thoughtfully equipped for both business and leisure guests. Airy, stylish public areas include an elegant and popular lounge bar and extensive conference facilities complete with a business centre. The exciting and buzzing Tozi dining space provides small 'cicchetti' dishes highlighting the best Italian produce.

Rooms 299 **Facilities** Spa STV FTV WiFi ↳ HL Gym Sauna Steam room Xmas **Conf** Class 240 Board 45 Thtr 550 **Services** Lift Air con **Parking** 36 **Notes** ⊗ Civ Wed 500

Millennium Hotel London Knightsbridge

★★★★ 77% ◉ HOTEL PLAN 4 F4

MILLENNIUM
HOTELS AND RESORTS
MILLENNIUM • COPTHORNE

tel: 020 7235 4377 **17 Sloane St, Knightsbridge SW1X 9NU**
email: reservations.knightsbridge@millenniumhotels.co.uk
web: www.millenniumhotels.co.uk
dir: *From Knightsbridge tube station towards Sloane St. Hotel 70mtrs on right*

This fashionable hotel boasts an enviable location in Knightsbridge's chic shopping district. Air-conditioned, thoughtfully equipped bedrooms are complemented by a popular lobby lounge and the Tangerine Café Bar that serves food throughout the day. Le Chinois restaurant offers modern Chinese cuisine. Valet parking is available if pre-booked.

Rooms 222 (41 fmly) **Facilities** STV FTV WiFi ↳ Xmas **Conf** Class 80 Board 50 Thtr 120 **Services** Lift Air con **Parking** 11 **Notes** ⊗

Premier Inn London Victoria

BUDGET HOTEL PLAN 4 J3

Premier Inn

tel: 0871 527 8680 *(Calls cost 13p per minute plus your phone company's access charge)*
82-83 Eccleston Square, Victoria SW1V 1PS
web: www.premierinn.com
dir: *From Victoria Station, right into Wilton Rd, 3rd right into Gillingham St, hotel 150mtrs*

High quality, budget accommodation ideal for both families and business travellers. Spacious, en suite bedrooms feature tea and coffee making facilities, and Freeview TV in most hotels. Internet access and WiFi are available for a small fee. The adjacent family restaurant features a wide and varied menu. See also the Hotel Groups pages.

Rooms 110

Jumeirah Lowndes Hotel

AA Advertised PLAN 4 F4

tel: 020 7823 1234 **21 Lowndes St SW1X 9ES**
email: jlhinfo@jumeirah.com **web:** www.jumeirah.com
dir: *M4 onto A4 into London. Left from Brompton Rd into Sloane St. Left into Pont St, Lowndes St next left. Hotel on right*

This chic, contemporary hotel is a smart modern townhouse set in timelessly stylish Belgravia. Guests can enjoy a meal in the international bistro Lowndes Bar & Kitchen, or relax outside on The Terrace with an open-air barbeque. Bedrooms and suites all have a contemporary style with high-spec facilities such as iPads and WiFi. There are also extensive leisure facilities at the nearby Jumeirah Carlton Tower, which includes access to The Peak Health Club & Spa.

Rooms 88 (12 fmly) **Facilities** Spa STV FTV WiFi ↳ ⏱ supervised Gym **Conf** Class 15 Board 16 Thtr 25 **Services** Lift Air con **Notes** ⊗

The Z Hotel Victoria

AA Advertised PLAN 4 H4

Z
HOTELS

tel: 020 3589 3990 **5 Lower Belgrave St SW1W 0NR**
email: victoria@thezhotels.com **web:** www.thezhotels.com
dir: *Near Victoria Station, via Buckingham Palace Rd/A3214*

Z Victoria is the ideal location for Victoria Station, one of the UK's busiest transport interchanges, as well as the Apollo Victoria Theatre, Belgrave Square, Sloane Square and Knightsbridge. The building is a designer conversion of a Victorian townhouse, set in a block of mixed architectural styles. Inside there are just over a hundred rooms, set over eight floors. Each room has an en suite wet room, crisp bed linen, 40" TV with Sky, and complimentary WiFi.

Rooms 106 (8 GF) **Facilities** STV WiFi **Services** Lift Air con **Notes** ⊗

LONDON

SW3 CHELSEA, BROMPTON

The Capital

★★★★★ ⚜⚜⚜ TOWN HOUSE HOTEL PLAN 4 F5

tel: 020 7589 5171 **Basil St, Knightsbridge SW3 1AT**
email: reservations@capitalhotel.co.uk **web:** www.capitalhotel.co.uk
dir: *20yds from Harrods, & Knightsbridge tube station*

Personal service is assured at this small, family-owned hotel set in the heart of Knightsbridge. Beautifully designed bedrooms come in a number of styles, but all rooms feature antique furniture, a marble bathroom and a thoughtful range of extras. Cocktails are a speciality in the delightful, stylish bar, while afternoon tea in the elegant, bijou lounge is a must. The signature restaurant 'Outlaw's at The Capital' provides stunning dishes, featuring the best in British seafood from Nathan Outlaw.

Rooms 49 🐾 **S** £250–£355; **D** £295–£425* **Facilities** STV FTV WiFi ⌂ Xmas New Year **Conf** Class 24 Board 24 Thtr 30 **Services** Lift Air con **Parking** 7 **Notes** ⊗

The Egerton House Hotel

★★★★★ TOWN HOUSE HOTEL PLAN 4 E4

THE
RED CARNATION
HOTEL COLLECTION

tel: 020 7589 2412 **17 Egerton Ter, Knightsbridge SW3 2BX**
email: bookeg@rchmail.com **web:** www.egertonhousehotel.com
dir: *Just off Brompton Rd, between Harrods & Victoria & Albert Museum, opposite Brompton Oratory*

This delightful town house enjoys a prestigious Knightsbridge location, a short walk from Harrods and close to the Victoria & Albert Museum. Air-conditioned

bedrooms and public rooms are appointed to the highest standards, with luxurious furnishings and quality antique pieces; an exceptional range of facilities include iPods, safes, mini bars and flat-screen TVs. Staff offer the highest levels of personalised, attentive service.

Rooms 28 (5 fmly) (2 GF) 🐾 **S** £295–£1600; **D** £295–£1600* **Facilities** STV WiFi Xmas New Year **Conf** Class 12 Board 10 Thtr 14 **Services** Lift Air con **Notes** LB

The Draycott Hotel

★★★★★ 79% TOWN HOUSE HOTEL PLAN 4 F3

tel: 020 7730 6466 **26 Cadogan Gardens SW3 2RP**
email: reservations@draycotthotel.com **web:** www.draycotthotel.com
dir: *From Sloane Sq station towards Peter Jones, keep to left. At Kings Rd take 1st right into Cadogan Gdns, 2nd right, hotel on left corner*

Enjoying a prime location just yards from Sloane Square, this town house provides an ideal base in one of the most fashionable areas of London. Many regular guests regard this as their London residence and staff pride themselves on their hospitality. Beautifully appointed bedrooms include a number of very spacious suites and all are equipped to a high standard. Attractive day rooms, furnished with antique and period pieces, include a choice of lounges, one with access to a lovely sheltered garden.

Rooms 35 (9 fmly) (2 GF) 🐾 **Facilities** STV FTV WiFi Beauty treatments Massage **Services** Lift Air con

INSPECTORS' CHOICE

The Levin

★★★★ TOWN HOUSE HOTEL PLAN 4 F4

tel: 020 7589 6286 **28 Basil St, Knightsbridge SW3 1AS**
email: reservations@thelevinhotel.co.uk **web:** www.thelevinhotel.co.uk
dir: *20yds from Harrods, & Knightsbridge tube station*

This sophisticated town house is the sister property to the adjacent Capital Hotel and enjoys a prime location on the doorstep of Knightsbridge's stylish department and designer stores. Bedrooms and en suites offer stylish elegance alongside a host of up-to-date modern comforts; extra touches include champagne bars, state-of-the-art audio-visual systems, and complimentary WiFi. Guests can enjoy all-day dining in the stylish, popular, lower ground-floor Metro Restaurant.

Rooms 12 (1 GF) **D** £240-£474* **Facilities** STV FTV WiFi ↕ Xmas New Year **Services** Lift Air con **Parking** 7 **Notes** ⊗

The Beaufort

★★★★ 80% TOWN HOUSE HOTEL PLAN 4 F4

tel: 020 7584 5252 **33 Beaufort Gardens SW3 1PP**
email: reservations@thebeaufort.co.uk **web:** www.thebeaufort.co.uk
dir: *100yds past Harrods on left of Brompton Rd*

This friendly, attractive town house enjoys a peaceful location in a tree-lined cul-de-sac just a few minutes' walk from Knightsbridge. Air-conditioned bedrooms are thoughtfully furnished and equipped with CD player, movie channel access, safe, and free WiFi. Guests are offered complimentary drinks and afternoon cream tea with home-made scones and clotted cream. A good continental breakfast is served in bedrooms.

Rooms 29 (3 GF) **S** £160-£230; **D** £200-£300* **Facilities** STV FTV WiFi **Conf** Thtr 10 **Services** Lift Air con **Notes** LB ⊗

SW5 EARL'S COURT

K + K Hotel George

★★★★ 77% HOTEL PLAN 4 A3

tel: 020 7598 8700 & 7598 8707 **1-15 Templeton Place, Earl's Court SW5 9NB**
email: hotelgeorge@kkhotels.co.uk **web:** www.kkhotels.com/george
dir: *Earls Court Rd (A3220), right into Trebovir Rd, right into Templeton Place*

This smart hotel enjoys a central location, just a few minutes' walk from Earls Court and with easy access to London's central attractions. Stylish public areas include a bar/bistro, an executive lounge and meeting facilities, and a restaurant that overlooks the attractive rear garden. Bedrooms are particularly well equipped with a host of useful extras including free, high-speed internet access.

Rooms 154 (38 fmly) (8 GF) ↖ **S** £99-£350; **D** £99-£350 (incl. bkfst)* **Facilities** STV FTV WiFi ↕ HL Gym Wellness area with exercise machines Sauna **Conf** Class 14 Board 18 Thtr 35 Del from £185 to £400 **Services** Lift Air con **Parking** 20

Best Western Burns Hotel

★★★ 75% METRO HOTEL PLAN 4 B3

tel: 020 7373 3151 **18-26 Barkston Gardens, Kensington SW5 0EN**
email: info@burnshotel.co.uk **web:** www.burnshotel.co.uk
dir: *From A4, right to Earls Court Rd (A3220), 2nd left*

This friendly Victorian hotel overlooks a leafy garden in a quiet residential area not far from the Earls Court exhibition centre and tube station. Bedrooms are attractively appointed, with modern facilities. Public areas, although not extensive, are stylish.

Rooms 105 (10 fmly) **Facilities** STV WiFi ↕ **Services** Lift **Notes** ⊗

Premier Inn London Kensington (Earl's Court)

BUDGET HOTEL PLAN 4 B3

tel: 0871 527 8666 *(Calls cost 13p per minute plus your phone company's access charge)*
11 Knaresborough Place, Kensington SW5 0TJ
web: www.premierinn.com
dir: *Just off A4 (Cromwell Rd). Nearest tube: Earls Court*

High quality, budget accommodation ideal for both families and business travellers. Spacious, en suite bedrooms feature tea and coffee making facilities, and Freeview TV in most hotels. Internet access and WiFi are available for a small fee. The adjacent family restaurant features a wide and varied menu. See also the Hotel Groups pages.

Rooms 184

Premier Inn London Kensington (Olympia)

BUDGET HOTEL PLAN 4 A3

tel: 0871 527 8668 *(Calls cost 13p per minute plus your phone company's access charge)*
22-32 West Cromwell Rd, Kensington SW5 9QJ
web: www.premierinn.com
dir: *On N side of West Cromwell Rd, between juncts of Cromwell Rd, Earls Court Rd & Warwick Rd*

Rooms 90

LONDON

SW6 FULHAM

Millennium & Copthorne Hotels at Chelsea FC

★★★★ 79% HOTEL PLAN 1 E3

tel: 020 7565 1400 **Stamford Bridge, Fulham Rd SW6 1HS**
email: reservations@chelseafc.com **web:** www.millenniumhotels.co.uk
dir: *4 mins walk from Fulham Broadway tube station*

A unique destination in a fashionable area of the city. Situated at Chelsea's famous Stamford Bridge ground, the accommodation offered here is very up-to-the-minute. Bedroom facilities include flat-screen LCD TVs, video-on-demand, broadband, WiFi and good-sized desk space; larger Club rooms have additional features. For eating there's a brasserie, the Bridge Bar and sports bar, and for corporate guests a flexible arrangement of meeting and event rooms is available.

Rooms 281 (64 fmly) **Facilities** STV WiFi Stadium & museum tours **Conf** Class 20 Board 25 Thtr 55 Del from £200 to £300* **Services** Lift Air con **Notes** ⊗

Ibis London Earls Court

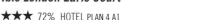

★★★ 72% HOTEL PLAN 4 A1

tel: 020 7610 0880 **47 Lillie Rd SW6 1UD**
email: h5623@accor.com **web:** www.ibishotel.com
dir: *From Hammersmith flyover towards London, keep in right lane, right at Kings pub on Talgarth Rd to join North End Rd. At mini-rdbt turn right. Hotel on left*

Ideally located for access to the Olympia Exhibition Centre, the London Underground, and fashionable Kensington, the Ibis London Earls Court offers a range of well-appointed rooms with superb beds and all modern amenities, including free WiFi. There are also extensive and flexible conference facilities, as well as a choice of dining options: La Table Restaurant with its daily changing self-service buffet and a la carte menu; plus The George & Dragon, a traditional English pub for a more relaxing and authentic experience. Secure, underground parking is also available.

Rooms 504 (20 fmly) **Facilities** FTV WiFi **Conf** Class 750 Board 25 Thtr 1200 **Services** Lift **Parking** 114

Premier Inn London Putney Bridge

BUDGET HOTEL PLAN 1 D2

tel: 0871 527 8674 *(Calls cost 13p per minute plus your phone company's access charge)*
3 Putney Bridge Approach SW6 3JD
web: www.premierinn.com
dir: *Nearest tube: Putney Bridge. Hotel on A219, N of River Thames*

High quality, budget accommodation ideal for both families and business travellers. Spacious, en suite bedrooms feature tea and coffee making facilities, and Freeview TV in most hotels. Internet access and WiFi are available for a small fee. The adjacent family restaurant features a wide and varied menu. See also the Hotel Groups pages.

Rooms 179

SW7 SOUTH KENSINGTON

INSPECTORS' CHOICE

Bulgari Hotel, London

★★★★★ ◉◉◉ HOTEL PLAN 4 F5

tel: 020 7151 1010 & 7151 1082 **171 Knightsbridge SW7 1DW**
email: london@bulgarihotels.co.uk **web:** www.bulgarihotels.com/london
dir: *Almost opposite Hyde Park Knightsbridge*

This striking, contemporary hotel is in the heart of Knightsbridge and becomes the third Bulgari property, after Milan and Bali. Luxury accommodation is stylish and deeply comfortable, complete with Bulgari trunks mini-bar and beverage facility. Bathrooms are equally lavish with deep baths and rain showers. Spacious public areas include a stunning spa complete with a 25 metre swimming pool, separate vitality pool and range of treatment rooms. A unique, hammered silver, oval bar provides the focal point of the bar with a sweeping staircase taking guests down to the Rivea London restaurant which is overseen by Alain Ducasse and his protégé Alexandre Nicolas. Immaculately attired staff offer high standards of service and hospitality.

Rooms 85 (17 smoking) **Facilities** Spa STV WiFi HL Gym The Screening Room cinema Xmas New Year **Conf** Class 80 Board 40 Thtr 100 **Services** Lift Air con **Parking** 6

INSPECTORS' CHOICE

Baglioni Hotel London

★★★★★ ◉ HOTEL PLAN 4 C5

tel: 020 7368 5700 **60 Hyde Park Gate, Kensington Rd, Kensington SW7 5BB**
email: info.london@baglionihotels.com **web:** www.baglionihotels.com
dir: On corner of Hyde Park Gate & De Vere Gardens

Located in the heart of Kensington and overlooking Hyde Park, this small hotel buzzes with Italian style and chic. Bedrooms, mostly suites, are generously sized and designed in bold dark colours; they have espresso machines, interactive plasma-screen TVs and a host of other excellent touches. Service is both professional and friendly, with personal butlers for the bedrooms. Public areas include the main open-plan space with bar, lounge and Osteria 60 restaurant, all merging together with great elan; there is a spa with four treatment rooms and a techno-gym, and a fashionable private club bar downstairs.

Rooms 67 (7 fmly) (30 smoking) ✿ **S** £275-£522; **D** £299-£600* **Facilities** Spa STV FTV WiFi ↕ Gym Steam room ♫ Xmas New Year **Conf** Class 33 Board 34 Thtr 60 Del from £460 to £750* **Services** Lift Air con **Parking** 2 **Notes** Civ Wed 60

Millennium Bailey's Hotel London Kensington

★★★★ 79% ◉ HOTEL PLAN 4 C3

MILLENNIUM
HOTELS AND RESORTS
MILLENNIUM • COPTHORNE

tel: 020 7373 6000 & 7331 6301 **140 Gloucester Rd SW7 4QH**
email: reservations.baileys@millenniumhotels.co.uk **web:** www.thebaileyshotel.co.uk
dir: From A4, at Cromwell Hospital, into Knaresborough Place, to Courtfield Rd to corner of Gloucester Rd, hotel opposite tube station

This elegant hotel has a town house feel and enjoys a prime location. The newly refurbished bedrooms and bathrooms have been completed to a high standard; each floor has a different theme reflecting the history of the building and national heritage. All rooms have been very well equipped and include large TVs, minibars and air-conditioning amongst other things. The public areas include a stylish contemporary and award winning restaurant. Al fresco dining is available during the warmer months. Guests may also use the facilities at the larger sister hotel which is adjacent.

Rooms 212 (27 fmly) ✿ **Facilities** FTV WiFi ↕ HL Xmas New Year **Services** Lift Air con **Parking** 60 **Notes** ⊗

Crowne Plaza London - Kensington

⊛ CROWNE PLAZA HOTELS & RESORTS

★★★★ 78% HOTEL PLAN 4 C3

tel: 020 7373 2222 & 7341 2340 **100 Cromwell Rd SW7 4ER**
email: lonke.reservations@ihg.com **web:** www.cplondonkensingtonhotel.co.uk
dir: Opposite Gloucester Road tube station. From M4 follow Central London signs. At Cromwell Rd hotel is visible on left

A contemporary hotel with a grand Victorian townhouse façade offering newly refurbished accommodation that meet the needs of both leisure and business traveller. The spilt-level Superior Suites are ideal for families and long stays. Facilities include complimentary high-speed WiFi, a state-of-the-art fitness suite, and sauna to name a few. A one-acre landscaped private garden is an oasis of peace and tranquillity. The ground-floor Umami Restaurant offers a real taste of Pan-Asian cooking and a relaxed atmosphere. There are two public car parks in the vicinity.

Rooms 162 (74 fmly) ✿ **Facilities** STV FTV WiFi ↕ Gym **Conf** Class 64 Board 60 Thtr 150 **Services** Lift Air con **Notes** ⊗

The Gore

★★★★ 78% TOWN HOUSE HOTEL PLAN 4 C4

tel: 020 7584 6601 **190 Queen's Gate SW7 5EX**
email: reservations.thegore@starhotels.com **web:** www.gorehotel.com
dir: Adjacent to Royal Albert Hall

Convenient for many of London's attractions including the Royal Albert Hall and close to Gloucester Rd tube station stands this characterful Townhouse. The lounge serves afternoon tea and 190 Queens Gate restaurant and Bar is popular with diners and guests wanting a pre-theatre meal/cocktail. The bedrooms are varied in size from the cosy classics to the more spacious suites, but all are well equipped and are high in quality.

Rooms 50 **Facilities** WiFi **Conf** Class 30 Board 30 Thtr 80 **Notes** ⊗

The Rembrandt Hotel

SAROVA HOTELS

★★★★ 77% HOTEL PLAN 4 E4

tel: 020 7589 8100 **11 Thurloe Place, Knightsbridge SW7 2RS**
email: rembrandt@sarova.com **web:** www.sarova.com
dir: M4 onto A4 Cromwell Rd into central London. Hotel opposite Victoria & Albert Museum

In the heart of South Kensington and Knightsbridge, this attractive hotel has free WiFi and elegant Edwardian architecture. It is opposite the V&A Museum, while tube stations and Harrods are nearby. All of the smartly designed rooms feature flat screen TV, a work desk, tea and coffee making facilities and a mini bar. Enjoy fine dining in the sophisticated Palette restaurant, or relax with a drink in the glamorous 1606 lounge bar. Guests at The Rembrandt have reduced-rate access to Aquilla Health and Fitness, a private health club adjacent to the hotel. This neighbourhood is a great choice for those interested in museums, parks and culture.

Rooms 194 ✿ **S** £169-£485; **D** £179-£495 (incl. bkfst)* **Facilities** Spa STV FTV WiFi ↕ 🏊 Gym **Conf** Class 84 Board 80 Thtr 200 Del from £230 to £580* **Services** Lift Air con **Notes** ⊗ Civ Wed 200

LONDON

SW7 SOUTH KENSINGTON *continued*

Millennium Gloucester Hotel London Kensington

★★★★ 76% HOTEL PLAN 4 C3

tel: 020 7373 6030 **4-18 Harrington Gardens SW7 4LH**
email: reservations.gloucester@millenniumhotels.co.uk
web: www.millenniumhotels.co.uk
dir: *Opposite Gloucester Road underground station*

This spacious, stylish hotel is centrally located, close to The Victoria & Albert Museum and Gloucester Road tube station. Air-conditioned bedrooms are furnished in a variety of contemporary styles, and Clubrooms benefit from a dedicated club lounge with complimentary breakfast and snacks. A wide range of eating options includes Singaporean and Mediterranean cuisine.

Rooms 610 (10 fmly) ☂ **Facilities** STV WiFi ⊿ HL Gym **Conf** Class 300 Board 100 Thtr 500 **Services** Lift Air con **Parking** 110 **Notes** ⊛ Civ Wed 500

Holiday Inn London - Kensington Forum

★★★★ 75% HOTEL PLAN 4 C3

tel: 020 7370 6815 & 0871 942 9100
(Calls cost 13p per minute plus your phone company's access charge) **97 Cromwell Rd SW7 4DN**
email: reservations@hikensington.co.uk **web:** www.hikensingtonforumhotel.co.uk
dir: *From S Circular onto N Circular at Chiswick Flyover. Onto A4 Cromwell Rd to Gloucester Rd*

This hotel is ideally situated within a few minutes' walk from the Gloucester Road underground station and close to many of London's attractions, such as the Natural History Museum, Science Museum, Kensington High Street and the West End. The bedrooms and bathrooms are well appointed and vary in size. The ground-floor areas include a gym and a stylish business lounge.

Rooms 906 (26 fmly) **S** £129-£309; **D** £139-£339 (incl. bkfst) **Facilities** STV FTV WiFi ⊿ HL Gym Fitness room Xmas New Year **Conf** Class 150 Board 50 Thtr 300 Del from £170 to £305 **Services** Lift Air con **Parking** 76 **Notes** ⊛ Civ Wed 250

Park International Hotel

★★★★ 73% HOTEL PLAN 4 D3

tel: 020 7370 5711 **117-129 Cromwell Rd SW7 4DS**
email: reservations@parkinternationalhotel.com **web:** www.parkinternationalhotel.com

The Park International Hotel is within easy reach of all major attractions in Kensington and Chelsea. The hotel offers a range of newly designed rooms to meet the needs of the modern traveller, and the Heritage Suites are individually styled for that extra bit of opulence. Afternoon tea is served in the Checkmate Bar, cocktails in the Piano Bar, and breakfast in the Orchid Room. The menu offers a blend of carefully chosen Thai and Modern British dishes.

Rooms 172 (22 fmly) (15 GF) ☂ **Facilities** STV FTV WiFi ⊿ HL Gym ♫ Xmas New Year **Conf** Class 20 Board 18 Thtr 30 **Services** Lift Air con **Notes** ⊛

SW10 WEST BROMPTON

The Chelsea Harbour Hotel

★★★★★ 83% HOTEL PLAN 1 E3

tel: 020 7823 3000 **Chelsea Harbour SW10 OXG**
email: reservations.chelseaharbour@millenniumhotels.com
web: www.thechelseaharbourhotel.co.uk
dir: *A4 to Earls Court Rd S towards river. Right into Kings Rd, left into Lots Rd*

Against the picturesque backdrop of Chelsea Harbour's small marina, this modern hotel offers spacious, comfortable accommodation. All rooms are suites, which are superbly equipped; many enjoy splendid views of the marina. In addition, there are also several luxurious penthouse suites. Public areas include a modern bar and restaurant, excellent leisure facilities (including a spa) and extensive meeting and function rooms.

Rooms 158 (158 fmly) ☂ **S** £211.20-£350; **D** £211.20-£350 **Facilities** Spa STV FTV WiFi ⊿ ☂ Gym Sauna Steam room Relaxation lounge Hair salon Xmas New Year **Conf** Class 250 Board 50 Thtr 500 Del from £300 to £455 **Services** Lift Air con **Parking** 2000 **Notes** LB ⊛ Civ Wed 450

SW14 EAST SHEEN

The Victoria

⊛⊛ RESTAURANT WITH ROOMS PLAN 1 C2

tel: 020 8876 4238 **10 West Temple Sheen SW14 7RT**
email: bookings@thevictoria.net **web:** www.thevictoria.net
dir: *Off Upper Richmond Rd West into Derby Rd, then into West Temple Sheen*

The Victoria is in a quiet residential area close to Richmond Park. The bedrooms are refreshingly stylish and thoughtfully equipped. The public areas consist of a small contemporary seating area, a modern bar, and an award-winning restaurant that serves imaginative and well sourced dishes. Alfresco dining is also an option.

Rooms 7 (2 fmly)

SW18 WANDSWORTH

Premier Inn London Wandsworth

BUDGET HOTEL PLAN 1 E2

tel: 0871 527 9486 *(Calls cost 13p per minute plus your phone company's access charge)* **45 Garratt Ln SW18 4AD**
web: www.premierinn.com
dir: *From A3 (Wandsworth High St) at lights into Garratt Ln. Hotel on left*

High quality, budget accommodation ideal for both families and business travellers. Spacious, en suite bedrooms feature tea and coffee making facilities, and Freeview TV in most hotels. Internet access and WiFi are available for a small fee. The adjacent family restaurant features a wide and varied menu. See also the Hotel Groups pages.

Rooms 120

SW19 WIMBLEDON

Hotel du Vin at Cannizaro House

★★★★ 78% COUNTRY HOUSE HOTEL PLAN 1 D2

tel: 020 8879 1464 **West Side, Wimbledon Common SW19 4UE**
email: reservations@hotelduvin.com **web:** www.hotelduvin.com
dir: *From A3 follow A219 signed Wimbledon into Parkside, right into Cannizaro Rd, sharp right into West Side*

This unique, 18th-century house located opposite Wimbledon Common and set within 34 acres of Cannizaro Park, offers a tranquil setting, just a short distance from Central London. The hotel has undergone a complete refurbishment with a large stylish bar and dining options including the main restaurant, and the Orangery which enjoys excellent views of the terrace and common. Bedrooms are spacious and stylish with feature walls, high quality furnishings and a good range of amenities including coffee machines, WiFi and Sky TV. Function facilities are available and there is complimentary parking.

Rooms 48 (5 fmly) (5 GF) **Facilities** STV FTV WiFi ⌲ 🌙 In room beauty & spa treatments **Conf** Class 50 Board 40 Thtr 120 **Services** Lift **Parking** 95
Notes Civ Wed 200

Holiday Inn Express Wimbledon South

BUDGET HOTEL PLAN 1 E1

tel: 020 8545 7300 **Miller's Meadhouse, 200 High St, Colliers Wood SW19 2BH**
email: reservations@exhiwimbledon.co.uk **web:** www.exhiwimbledon.co.uk
dir: *A238 Kingston Rd, at lights into Merton High St, signed Colliers Wood. Hotel directly opposite Colliers Wood underground station*

A modern hotel ideal for families and business travellers. Fresh and uncomplicated, the spacious rooms include Sky TV, power shower and tea and coffee-making facilities. Continental buffet breakfast is included in the room rate; other meals may be taken at the nearby family pub or restaurant. See also the Hotel Groups pages.

Rooms 139 (92 fmly) (12 GF) **Conf** Class 12 Board 12 Thtr 20

Premier Inn London Wimbledon South

BUDGET HOTEL PLAN 1 E1

tel: 0871 527 8684 *(Calls cost 13p per minute plus your phone company's access charge)*
27 Chapter Way, Off Merantun Way, Wimbledon SW19 2RF
web: www.premierinn.com
dir: *M25 junct 10, A3 towards London. Exit A298 (Wimbledon) onto A238. Right onto A219, left onto A24 (Merantun Way). At rdbt 3rd exit signed Merton Abbey Mills*

Rooms 134

W1 WEST END

The Connaught

★★★★★ 🍷 HOTEL PLAN 2 G1

MAYBOURNE
HOTEL GROUP

tel: 020 7499 7070 **Carlos Place W1K 2AL**
email: info@the-connaught.co.uk **web:** www.the-connaught.com
dir: *Between Grosvenor Sq & Berkeley Sq*

This iconic hotel is truly spectacular, with stunning interior design. There are sumptuous day rooms and stylish bedrooms with state-of-the-art facilities and marble en suites with deep tubs, TV screens and power showers. Butlers are available at the touch of a button and guests are pampered by friendly, attentive staff offering intuitive service. There is a choice of bars and restaurants including the Espelette bistro, and the award-winning cuisine of Hélène Darroze which is imaginative, inspired and truly memorable. The excellent Aman Spa at the hotel offers health and beauty treatments, a swimming pool and fitness centre.

Rooms 121 (17 smoking) **Facilities** Spa STV FTV WiFi ⌲ Gym **Conf** Class 70 Board 60 Thtr 120 **Services** Lift Air con **Notes** ⊗ Civ Wed 200

LONDON

W1 WEST END *continued*

INSPECTORS' CHOICE

Claridge's

MAYBOURNE HOTEL GROUP

★★★★★ ◎◎◎◎ ⚑ HOTEL PLAN 2 H1

tel: 020 7629 8860 **Brook St W1K 4HR**
email: info@claridges.co.uk web: www.claridges.co.uk
dir: *1st turn after Green Park tube station to Berkeley Sq & 4th exit into Davies St. 3rd right into Brook St*

Once renowned as the resort of kings and princes, Claridge's today continues to set the standards by which other hotels are judged. The sumptuous, air-conditioned bedrooms are elegantly themed to reflect the Victorian or art deco architecture of the building. Fera at Claridge's, overseen by chef Simon Rogan, is now well established, and like the stylish cocktail bar, is a hit with residents and non-residents alike. Service throughout is punctilious and thoroughly professional.

Rooms 197 (144 fmly) 🐾 **Facilities** Spa STV WiFi Gym Beauty & health treatments Use of sister hotel's swimming pool 🎵 Xmas New Year **Conf** Class 130 Board 60 Thtr 250 **Services** Lift Air con **Notes** ⊗ Civ Wed 200

INSPECTORS' CHOICE

45 Park Lane

★★★★★ ◎◎◎ HOTEL PLAN 4 G6

tel: 020 7493 4545 **45 Park Ln W1K 1PN**
email: reservations.45L@dorchestercollection.com web: www.45parklane.com
dir: *Park Lane, near The Dorchester*

This hotel offers luxurious and contemporary interiors. The bedrooms, including ten suites, all have a view of Hyde Park; the Penthouse Suite has its own roof

terrace. A striking central staircase leads to a mezzanine featuring Bar 45, a library and a private media room. Other public areas include a lounge area and CUT at 45 Park Lane, a modern American steak restaurant.

Rooms 46 🐾 **Facilities** STV WiFi ↘ HL Gym 🎵 **Services** Lift Air con **Parking** 12 **Notes** ⊗

INSPECTORS' CHOICE

The Ritz London

★★★★★ ◎◎◎ ⚑ HOTEL PLAN 4 J6

tel: 020 7493 8181 **150 Piccadilly W1J 9BR**
email: enquire@theritzlondon.com web: www.theritzlondon.com
dir: *From Hyde Park Corner E on Piccadilly. Hotel on right after Green Park*

This renowned, stylish hotel offers guests the ultimate in sophistication while still managing to retain all its former historic glory. Bedrooms and suites are exquisitely furnished in Louis XVI style, with fine marble bathrooms and every imaginable comfort. The Ritz London offers complimentary high-speed WiFi. Elegant reception rooms include the Palm Court with its legendary afternoon teas, the beautiful fashionable Rivoli Bar and the sumptuous Ritz Restaurant, complete with gold chandeliers and extraordinary trompe-l'oeil decoration.

Rooms 136 (65 fmly) (24 smoking) 🐾 **S** £320-£875; **D** £320-£875* **Facilities** STV FTV WiFi ↘ Gym The Ritz Club & Casino The Ritz Salon 🎵 Xmas New Year **Conf** Class 40 Board 30 Thtr 70 **Services** Lift Air con **Parking** 10 **Notes** ⊗ Civ Wed 60

Food Allergies

A recent EU regulation makes it easier for those with food allergies to choose safer foods when eating out. 14 allergens are listed in the regulation, and pubs and restaurants must now list any of these used in the dishes they offer.

Athenaeum Hotel & Apartments

★★★★★ ⬤⬤ HOTEL PLAN 4 H6

tel: 020 7499 3464 **116 Piccadilly W1J 7BJ**
email: info@athenaeumhotel.com **web:** www.athenaeumhotel.com
dir: *On Piccadilly, overlooking Green Park*

With a discreet address in Mayfair, this well-loved hotel offers bedrooms appointed to the highest levels of comfort; all include Bose iPod speakers, a pillow menu and WiFi, and several boast views over Green Park. The hotel also has suites, and for the ultimate luxury there's a roof-top suite with a private balcony. The hotel has a whisky bar, the Garden Lounge for award-winning afternoon teas, and even a pudding parlour open in the evenings. The stylish restaurant serves British cuisine which appeals to all ages. A range of spacious and well-appointed apartments can be found in a row of Edwardian townhouses adjacent to the hotel. There is an extensive range of beauty treatments available along with conference and meeting facilities.

Rooms 164 (18 fmly) (12 GF) ⬤ **D** fr £256* **Facilities** STV FTV WiFi Gym Beauty treatment room Steam rooms Sauna Free bike hire Xmas New Year Child facilities **Conf** Class 35 Board 36 Thtr 70 Del from £330 **Services** Lift Air con **Notes** LB Civ Wed 80

Brown's Hotel

ROCCO FORTE HOTELS

★★★★★ ⬤⬤ HOTEL PLAN 2 J1

ℛℱ

tel: 020 7493 6020 **Albemarle St, Mayfair W1S 4BP**
email: reservations.browns@roccofortehotels.com **web:** www.roccofortehotels.com
dir: *A short walk from Green Park, Bond St, Piccadilly & Buckingham Palace*

Brown's is a London hospitality icon that maintains its charm through the successful balance of traditional and contemporary. Bedrooms are luxurious, furnished to the highest standard and come with all the modern comforts expected of such a grand Mayfair hotel. The hotel has 29 suites including two Royal Suites and two Presidential Suites. The elegant, yet informal, HIX Mayfair serves a traditional selection of popular British dishes that are created with great skill, and it is also home to a collection of works by leading British artists. The English Tea Room proves a great meeting place for afternoon tea.

Rooms 117 (12 smoking) ⬤ **Facilities** Spa STV WiFi ⬤ Gym ♫ Xmas New Year **Conf** Class 30 Board 30 Thtr 70 **Services** Lift Air con **Parking** 4 **Notes** ⊗ Civ Wed 70

The Dorchester

★★★★★ ⬤⬤ ⬤ HOTEL PLAN 4 G6

tel: 020 7629 8888 **Park Ln W1K 1QA**
email: reservations.TDL@dorchestercollection.com **web:** www.thedorchester.com
dir: *Halfway along Park Ln between Hyde Park Corner & Marble Arch*

One of London's finest, The Dorchester remains one of the best-loved hotels in the country and always delivers. The spacious bedrooms and suites are beautifully appointed and feature fabulous marble bathrooms. Leading off from the foyer, The Promenade is the perfect setting for afternoon tea or drinks. In the evening guests can relax to the sound of live jazz, while enjoying a cocktail in the stylish bar. Dining options include the sophisticated Chinese restaurant, China Tang; Alain Ducasse at The Dorchester from the world-renowned French chef of the same name; and of course, The Grill.

Rooms 250 ⬤ **Facilities** Spa STV FTV WiFi ⬤ HL Gym Steam rooms Fitness suite ♫ Xmas New Year **Conf** Class 300 Board 42 Thtr 500 **Services** Lift Air con **Notes** ⊗ Civ Wed 432

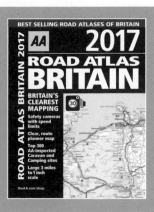

W1 WEST END *continued*

INSPECTORS' CHOICE

Four Seasons Hotel London at Park Lane

★★★★★ ◉◉ ♨ HOTEL PLAN 4 G6

tel: 020 7499 0888 **Hamilton Place, Park Ln W1J 7DR**
email: reservations@fourseasons.com **web:** www.fourseasons.com/london
dir: *From Piccadilly into Old Park Ln, into Hamilton Place*

This long-established popular hotel is discreetly located near Hyde Park Corner, in the heart of Mayfair. It successfully combines modern efficiencies with traditional luxury. Guest care is consistently of the highest order, even down to the smallest detail of the personalised wake-up call. The bedrooms are elegant and spacious, and the unique conservatory rooms are particularly special. Spacious public areas include extensive conference and banqueting facilities, Lane's bar and fine-dining restaurant, and an elegant lounge where wonderful afternoon teas are served.

Rooms 193 (49 smoking) ♠ **Facilities** Spa STV FTV WiFi ⇘ Gym Fitness Centre ♫ Xmas New Year **Conf** Class 174 Board 108 Thtr 375 **Services** Lift Air con **Parking** 10 **Notes** Civ Wed 350

Hyatt Regency London - The Churchill

★★★★★ 88% ◉◉◉ HOTEL PLAN 2 F2

tel: 020 7486 5800 **30 Portman Square W1H 7BH**
email: london.churchill@hyatt.com **web:** www.london.churchill.hyatt.com
dir: *From Marble Arch rdbt, follow signs for Oxford Circus into Oxford St. Left after 2nd lights into Portman St. Hotel on left*

This smart hotel enjoys a central location overlooking Portman Square. Excellent conference and in-room facilities, plus a fitness room make this the ideal choice for both corporate and leisure guests. To set the style, guests are greeted by stunning floral displays in the sophisticated lobby. The Montagu restaurant offers contemporary dining, plus the option to sit at the Chef's Table for a front row seat to watch all the action in the kitchen.

Rooms 434 ♠ **Facilities** STV FTV WiFi ⇘ ≋ Gym Jogging track ♫ Xmas New Year **Conf** Class 160 Board 68 Thtr 250 **Services** Lift Air con **Parking** 48 **Notes** ⊗ Civ Wed 250

Metropolitan London

★★★★★ 87% ◉◉ HOTEL PLAN 4 G6

tel: 020 7447 1000 **Old Park Ln W1K 1LB**
email: res.met.lon@comohotels.com **web:** www.comohotels.com/metropolitanlondon
dir: *On corner of Old Park Ln & Hertford St*

Overlooking Hyde Park this hotel is located within easy reach of the fashionable stores of Knightsbridge and Mayfair. The hotel's contemporary style allows freedom and space to relax. Understated luxury is the key here with bedrooms enjoying great natural light. There is also a Shambhala Spa, steam room and fully equipped gym. For those seeking a culinary experience, Nobu offers innovative Japanese cuisine with an upbeat atmosphere.

Rooms 144 (23 smoking) ♠ **Facilities** Spa STV FTV WiFi ⇘ Gym Steam rooms ♫ **Conf** Class 25 Board 30 Thtr 80 **Services** Lift Air con **Parking** 8 **Notes** Civ Wed 80

AA HOTEL OF THE YEAR
FOR LONDON 2016-2017

The Beaumont

★★★★★ 87% ◉ ♨ HOTEL PLAN 2 G1

tel: 020 7499 1001 **8 Balderton St, Mayfair W1K 6TF**
email: info@thebeaumont.com **web:** www.thebeaumont.com
dir: *M1 junct 1/A41/A501, Oxford St onto North Audley St. 1st left onto North Row, 1st right onto Balderton St*

A recent addition to the London 5-star scene, The Beaumont is a beautifully renovated hotel in the Mayfair area, just a stone's throw from Oxford Street and many of London's attractions. This is the first hotel of restaurateurs, Chris Corbin and Jeremy King. The Art décor-style bedrooms vary in size and are deeply comfortable, with marble bathrooms and up-to-the-minute technology. The Art décor theme is continued into the public areas, which include the popular Colony Grill Room restaurant, American bar and residents' club lounge. A unique aspect of the hotel is ROOM, a monumental mixture of installation space, sculpture, and architecture by Antony Gormley. From the outside, ROOM looks like a crouching figure, perched on one part of the original building; inside is an unusual suite of rooms. Sculpture you can sleep in. The hotel also has a small spa, meeting room, gym and hair salon. A courtesy car is also available subject to availability.

Rooms 73 (9 fmly) ♠ S £395-£580; D £395-£580 (incl. bkfst)* **Facilities** Spa STV FTV WiFi ⇘ HL Gym Sauna Steam room Hamman Xmas **Conf** Board 18 Thtr 40 **Services** Lift Air con **Parking** 3 **Notes** LB

The Langham, London

★★★★★ 86% ◉◉ HOTEL PLAN 2 H3

tel: 020 7636 1000 **Portland Place W1B 1JA**
email: tllon.info@langhamhotels.com **web:** www.langhamlondon.com
dir: *N of Regent St, left opposite All Soul's Church*

This hotel has a grand entrance which leads into restored interior elegance. Dating back to 1865 the building displays a contemporary, luxurious style. Situated near Regent Street it is ideally located for both theatreland and the principal shopping areas. Bedrooms are delightfully appointed and many have excellent views. The Landau restaurant and Artesian bar offer high standards of service, delivered by a friendly team. Palm Court is a great place for afternoon tea or a glass of champagne. There is also an extensive health club complete with a 16-metre pool.

Rooms 380 (9 fmly) (15 smoking) ♠ **Facilities** Spa STV WiFi ⇘ HL ◉ supervised Gym Health club Sauna Steam room Vitality Pool ♫ Xmas New Year **Conf** Class 148 Board 80 Thtr 300 **Services** Lift Air con **Notes** ⊗ Civ Wed 280

The Westbury Hotel

★★★★★ 85% ◉◉◉◉ HOTEL PLAN 2 H1

tel: 020 7629 7755 **Bond St W1S 2YF**
email: reservations@westburymayfair.com **web:** www.westburymayfair.com
dir: *From Oxford Circus S down Regent St, right onto Conduit St, hotel at junct of Conduit St & Bond St*

A well-known London favourite with an international clientele, The Westbury Hotel is located in the heart of the Capital's finest shopping district, neighbour to the world's most exclusive fashion brands, restaurants and nightlife destinations. The standards of accommodation are very high throughout with newly renovated bedrooms and suites offering stunning panoramic views of picturesque Mayfair. Foodies and cocktail fanatics will find plenty to enjoy in-house at Four AA Rosetted restaurant Alyn Williams at The Westbury, Tsukiji Sushi Restaurant, and the award-winning Polo Bar. Private dining is also available.

Rooms 246 (80 fmly) **Facilities** STV FTV WiFi ⇘ Gym Fitness centre Steam room Sauna Xmas New Year **Conf** Class 170 Board 36 Thtr 250 **Services** Lift Air con **Notes** ⊗ Civ Wed 80

Grosvenor House, A JW Marriott Hotel

★★★★★ 85% ◉ HOTEL PLAN 2 G1

GROSVENOR HOUSE
A JW MARRIOTT HOTEL
LONDON

tel: 020 7499 6363 & 7399 8400 **Park Ln W1K 7TN**
email: grosvenor.house@marriotthotels.com **web:** www.londongrosvenorhouse.co.uk
dir: *Centrally located on Park Ln, between Hyde Park Corner & Oxford St*

This quintessentially British hotel, overlooking Hyde Park offers luxurious accommodation, warm hospitality and exemplary service that epitomises the fine hotel culture of London. The property boasts the largest ballroom in Europe, and there is a steakhouse and a cocktail bar. The Park Room and The Library make perfect settings for afternoon tea.

Rooms 496 (10 fmly) (65 smoking) **Facilities** STV WiFi ⇘ Gym Fitness centre ♫ Xmas New Year **Conf** Class 800 Board 140 Thtr 1500 **Services** Lift Air con **Parking** 48 **Notes** ⊗ Civ Wed 1500

Hotel Café Royal

★★★★★ 84% ◉◉ HOTEL PLAN 2 J1

tel: 020 7406 3333 & 7406 3322 **68 Regent St W1B 4DY**
email: enquiries@hotelcaferoyal.com **web:** www.hotelcaferoyal.com
dir: *Please phone for directions*

This impressive and imposing hotel has an enviable location in Piccadilly. Public rooms are impressive and successfully blend modern and classic styles well. There is the popular café, the opulent Oscar Wilde bar for that traditional afternoon tea and the Ten Room for all day dining. The Green bar specialises in cocktails and there is even a members club. The contemporary bedrooms are appointed to an extremely high standard, have marble bathrooms and are amply proportioned. The spa has a luxurious feel where guest can swim, use the gym or enjoy a range of treatments.

Rooms 160 (111 fmly) **Facilities** Spa STV FTV WiFi ⇘ HL ⊛ Gym ♫ Xmas New Year **Conf** Class 60 Board 57 Thtr 160 **Services** Lift Air con **Notes** Civ Wed 120

W1 WEST END *continued*

The London Edition

★★★★★ 84% ◎◎ HOTEL PLAN 2 J2

tel: 020 7781 0000 & 7908 7900 **10 Berners St W1T 3NP**
email: reservations.london@editionhotels.com **web:** www.editionhotels.com/london
dir: *Located in Fitzrouia on the edges of London's Soho neighborhood, Central London*

The London Edition is the latest from the EDITION portfolio, transforming this landmark building with innovation and truly great design. Excellent dining is provided in the Berners Tavern, under direction of award-winning chef Jason Atherton. The reservations-only Punch Room is a great place to unwind, with a traditional punch bowl. Service is personal and friendly with a modern twist, ensuring a flawless and memorable guest experience. A dynamic fusion of past and present makes the best use of space with stunning public areas and artwork. Bedrooms are finished in either light oak or dark walnut creating a cosy, cabin like feel; akin to that of a private yacht.

Rooms 173 (12 fmly) ☛ **Facilities** STV FTV WiFi ⇲ Gym ♪ **Conf** Class 36 Board 14 Thtr 60 **Services** Lift Air con **Notes** ⊗

The Arch London

★★★★★ 83% ◎ HOTEL PLAN 2 F2

tel: 020 7724 4700 **50 Great Cumberland Place W1H 7FD**
email: info@thearchlondon.com **web:** www.thearchlondon.com
dir: *200yds from Marble Arch*

Convenient for many of London's attractions and close to Marble Arch Tube station stands this luxurious hotel. The Martini Library serves afternoon tea, along with light-bites all day, and Hunter 486 offers relaxed dining for both lunch and dinner. Cocktails can be taken in Le Salon de Champagne. Bedrooms are varied in size from the cosy standards to the more spacious suites, but all are well equipped and are high in quality. There is also a well equipped gym for guest use.

Rooms 82 (8 fmly) (8 GF) ☛ **S** £252-£420; **D** £282-£450* **Facilities** STV FTV WiFi ⇲ Gym Xmas New Year **Conf** Class 30 Board 20 Thtr 30 Del from £350 to £650* **Services** Lift Air con **Parking** 4 **Notes** LB

London Hilton on Park Lane

★★★★★ 83% ◎ HOTEL PLAN 4 G6

tel: 020 7493 8000 **22 Park Ln W1K 1BE**
email: reservations.parklane@hilton.com **web:** www.parklanehilton.com
dir: *From N: M1/A41 towards central London & West End. W along Oxford St, into Park Lane. From S: A23 for central London & West End, cross Vauxhall Bridge (A202) & into Park Lane*

Located in the heart of Park Lane, this landmark hotel offers a luxury environment overlooking Hyde Park and the City. A dedicated team of staff is available to meet their guests' every need. Bedrooms are designed with quality appointments and luxury fabrics. Several eating options are available - from the renowned Galvin at Windows to the all-day dining of Podium, which also serves a splendid afternoon tea.

Rooms 453 (52 smoking) ☛ **Facilities** Spa STV FTV WiFi ⇲ Gym ♪ Xmas New Year **Conf** Class 600 Board 60 Thtr 1100 **Services** Lift Air con **Parking** 242 **Notes** ⊗ Civ Wed 1000

The Montcalm

★★★★★ 83% HOTEL PLAN 2 F2

tel: 020 7402 4288 **Great Cumberland Place W1H 7TW**
email: reservations@montcalm.co.uk **web:** www.montcalm.co.uk
dir: *2 mins' walk N from Marble Arch station*

The Montcalm is ideally situated in the heart of London, just a short walk from Marble Arch, Oxford Street, Park Lane, Mayfair, Hyde Park and Theatreland. The elegantly decorated bedrooms are tastefully appointed and have many thoughtful touches. Public areas include a contemporary lounge bar and The Crescent restaurant which serves modern European cuisine. The hotel has a range of private rooms and conference suites, as well as spa, sauna, steam room, gym and exercise pool.

Rooms 143 (17 fmly) (7 GF) ☛ **Facilities** Spa STV WiFi ⊛ Gym **Conf** Class 250 Board 250 Thtr 500 **Services** Lift Air con **Notes** ⊗ Civ Wed 60

Le Meridien Piccadilly

★★★★★ 80% ◎ HOTEL PLAN 2 J1

tel: 020 7734 8000 **21 Piccadilly W1J 0BH**
email: reservations.piccadilly@lemeridien.com **web:** www.lemeridien.com/piccadilly
dir: *100mtrs from Piccadilly Circus*

Situated in the heart of Piccadilly, this well established hotel is ideally located for the West End and Theatreland. The well-equipped, air-conditioned bedrooms, varying in shape and size, are modern and contemporary in style. Public areas include extensive leisure facilities, with a state-of-the-art gym, pool and sauna, the trendy Longitude 0° 8' cocktail bar, and the popular Terrace Restaurant which overlooks Piccadilly.

Rooms 280 (12 fmly) ☛ **Facilities** Spa STV WiFi ⇲ ⊛ supervised Gym Squash ♪ Xmas New Year **Conf** Class 160 Board 80 Thtr 250 **Services** Lift Air con **Notes** ⊗ Civ Wed 200

LONDON

The Chesterfield Mayfair

★★★★ @@ HOTEL PLAN 4 H6

tel: 020 7491 2622 **35 Charles St, Mayfair W1J 5EB**
email: bookch@rchmail.com web: www.chesterfieldmayfair.com
dir: *Hyde Park Corner along Piccadilly, left into Half Moon St. At end left & 1st right into Queens St, then right into Charles St*

Quiet elegance and an atmosphere of exclusivity characterise this stylish Mayfair hotel where attentive, friendly service is paramount. The bedrooms, each with a marble-clad bathroom, have contemporary styles - perhaps with floral fabric walls, an African theme or with Savile Row stripes. In addition to these deluxe bedrooms there are 13 individually designed suites: some with four-poster beds and some with jacuzzis. The Butler's Restaurant is the fine dining option, and The Conservatory, with views over the garden, is just the place for cocktails, light lunches and afternoon teas. The hotel is air-conditioned throughout.

Rooms 107 ☎ S £195-£390; D £220-£1470* Facilities STV FTV WiFi ☼ ♫
Conf Class 45 Board 45 Thtr 100 Del from £310 to £515* Services Lift Air con
Notes LB Civ Wed 120

The Mandeville Hotel

★★★★ 83% @ HOTEL PLAN 2 G2

tel: 020 7935 5599 **Mandeville Place W1U 2BE**
email: sales@mandeville.co.uk web: www.mandeville.co.uk
dir: *3 mins walk from Bond St tube station*

This is a stylish and attractive boutique-style hotel with a very contemporary feel. Bedrooms are high in quality, are air conditioned and large, and have very comfortable beds. One of the suites, The Penthouse, has a patio with views over

London. The Reform Social & Grill Restaurant offers award-winning modern British cuisine, and the cocktail bar is always popular.

Rooms 142 (6 fmly) ☎ S £136-£276; D £160-£300 Facilities STV FTV WiFi ☼ Xmas
New Year Conf Class 20 Board 20 Thtr 40 Services Lift Air con Notes ⊗

Millennium Hotel London Mayfair

★★★★ 79% @@@ HOTEL PLAN 2 G1

tel: 020 7629 9400 **Grosvenor Square W1K 2HP**
email: reservations@millenniumhotels.co.uk web: www.millenniumhotels.co.uk
dir: *S side of Grosvenor Square, 5 mins walk from Oxford St & Bond St stations*

This hotel benefits from a prestigious location in the heart of Mayfair, close to Bond Street. Smart bedrooms are generally spacious and club-floor rooms have exclusive use of their own lounge with complimentary refreshments. A choice of bars and dining options is available along with conference facilities and a fitness room.

Rooms 336 ☎ Facilities STV FTV WiFi ☼ HL Gym Fitness suite ♫ Xmas New Year
Conf Class 250 Board 70 Thtr 500 Del from £160* Services Lift Air con Notes ⊗
Civ Wed 250

DoubleTree by Hilton Hotel, Marble Arch

★★★★ 78% HOTEL PLAN 2 F2

tel: 020 7935 2361 **4 Bryanston St W1H 7BY**
email: lonma.res@hilton.com web: www.londonmarblearch.doubletreebyhilton.com
dir: *Walking distance from Oxford St, Marble Arch & Hyde Park*

This hotel is a well located, historic property. The bedrooms, including executive and deluxe club floor rooms, vary in size but all are smartly equipped, boast bright trendy soft furnishings and are air conditioned; the en suites are equally modern and stylish. The public areas include the Indigo Bar & Lounge, and Fire & Spice Bar & Kitchen. The hotel offers free WiFi throughout.

Rooms 122 (12 fmly) (5 GF) ☎ Facilities STV FTV WiFi ☼ HL Gym Conf Class 60
Board 50 Thtr 130 Services Lift Air con Notes LB ⊗

Park Plaza Sherlock Holmes

★★★★ 76% HOTEL PLAN 2 F3

tel: 020 7486 6161 & 0844 415 6740
(Calls cost 7p per minute plus your phone company's access charge) **108 Baker St W1U 6LJ**
email: info@sherlockholmeshotel.com web: www.sherlockholmeshotel.com
dir: *From Marylebone Flyover into Marylebone Rd. At Baker St turn right for hotel on left*

Chic and modern, this boutique-style hotel is near a number of London underground and rail stations. Public rooms include a popular bar, sited just inside the main entrance, and Sherlock's Grill, where the mesquite-wood burning stove is a feature of the cooking. The hotel also features an indoor health suite and a relaxing lounge.

Rooms 119 (20 fmly) ☎ Facilities STV WiFi ☼ Gym Beauty treatment room Xmas
Conf Class 35 Board 30 Thtr 80 Services Lift Air con Notes ⊗ Civ Wed 80

The Z Hotel Soho

AA Advertised PLAN 3 A2

tel: 020 3551 3701 & 3551 3700 **17 Moor St W1D 5AP**
email: soho@thezhotels.com web: www.thezhotels.com

Z Soho offers a Central London stay for an out-of-town price. This designer conversion of twelve Georgian townhouses combines classic architectural proportions with contemporary style. The rooms are gathered around a central courtyard, set between Charing Cross Road and Old Compton Street. Bedrooms have an en suite wet room, crisp bed linen, 40" TV with Sky, and complimentary WiFi.

Rooms 85 ☎ Facilities STV FTV WiFi ☼ HL Services Lift Air con Notes ⊗

W2 BAYSWATER, PADDINGTON

Lancaster London

★★★★ 85% ◉◉ HOTEL PLAN 2 D1

tel: 020 7551 6000 **Lancaster Ter W2 2TY**
email: book@lancasterlondon.com **web:** www.lancasterlondon.com
dir: *Adjacent to Lancaster Gate tube station, 1m from Paddington Heathrow Express, 1m from A40, opposite Hyde Park*

Located adjacent to Hyde Park, this large hotel offers a wide range of facilities. There are many room types; higher floors have excellent panoramic views of the city and park, and the suites are truly impressive. The hotel also offers two contrasting award-winning restaurants - the contemporary Island Restaurant & Bar, and Nipa restaurant with authentic Thai cuisine. There are spacious state-of-the-art, flexible conference and banqueting facilities, a 24-hour business centre and secure parking. This is an environmentally conscious hotel which has instigated many initiatives including a honey farm on the roof.

Rooms 416 (40 fmly) (28 smoking) ♠ **Facilities** STV FTV WiFi ♨ Gym Xmas New Year **Conf** Class 550 Board 46 Thtr 1000 **Services** Lift Air con **Parking** 12 **Notes** LB ⊗ Civ Wed 1000

Novotel London Paddington

★★★★ 75% HOTEL PLAN 2 C3

tel: 020 7266 6000 **3 Kingdom St, Paddington W2 6BD**
email: h6455@accor.com **web:** www.novotel.com
dir: *Easy access from Westway A40 & Bishops Bridge Rd A4206*

Located in the Paddington Central area, this hotel is easily accessible by road, and is only a few minutes walk from Paddington Station. Ideal for business or leisure guests. The facilities include the Elements Restaurant, a bar, conference facilities, a swimming pool, sauna, plus steam and fitness rooms. An NCP car park is a 5-minute walk away.

Rooms 206 (24 fmly) **Facilities** STV WiFi ♨ ☒ Gym Steam room Sauna **Conf** Class 70 Board 40 Thtr 150 Del from £339 to £469* **Services** Lift

Hotel Indigo

★★★★ 74% HOTEL PLAN 2 D2

tel: 020 7706 4444 **16 London St, Paddington W2 1HL**
email: malcolm@lth-hotels.com **web:** www.indigopaddington.com

This smart hotel is located within a stone's throw of Paddington Station. Contemporary and stylish, bedrooms vary in size but are equipped with all modern extras; they boast high quality comfy beds, ensuring a great night's sleep, and en suites with power showers and quality toiletries. Delightful public areas include a restaurant, bar and a coffee shop offering tempting cakes. The latest addition of a cosy and tranquil seating area at the back of the property can be accessed from the first floor's corridor. Parking is available at the nearby public car park.

Rooms 64 ♠ **Facilities** STV FTV WiFi HL Gym **Services** Lift Air con **Notes** ⊗

Lancaster Gate Hotel

★★★ 78% HOTEL PLAN 2 C1

tel: 020 7479 2500 & 7262 5090 **66 Lancaster Gate W2 3NA**
email: info@lghhydepark.co.uk **web:** www.lancastergatehotelhydepark.co.uk
dir: *Just off Bayswater Rd*

This hotel offers a convenient location between Oxford Street and Knightsbridge and is also close to Hyde Park and Kensington Gardens. Bedrooms are well equipped with broadband and safes, as well as TVs with a wide range of channels. There is a

comfortable bar and stylish restaurant, and the hotel also has a range of meeting rooms.

Rooms 188 (7 fmly) (13 GF) (5 smoking) **Facilities** STV FTV WiFi Off site leisure facilities available **Conf** Class 24 Board 28 Thtr 50 **Services** Lift Air con **Notes** No children 18yrs

Mitre House Hotel

★★ 74% METRO HOTEL PLAN 2 D2

tel: 020 7723 8040 & 7402 5695 **178-184 Sussex Gardens, Hyde Park W2 1TU**
email: reservations@mitrehousehotel.com **web:** www.mitrehousehotel.com
dir: *Parallel to Bayswater Rd & one block from Paddington Station*

This family-run hotel continues to offers a warm welcome and attentive service. It is ideally located, close to Paddington station and near the West End and major attractions. Bedrooms include a number of family suites and there is a lounge bar. Limited parking is available.

Rooms 69 (7 fmly) (7 GF) (69 smoking) **Facilities** STV WiFi **Services** Lift **Parking** 20 **Notes** ⊗

W3 ACTON

Holiday Inn London West

★★★ 82% HOTEL PLAN 1 D4

tel: 020 8753 0800 **4 Portal Way, Gypsy Corner / A40 W3 6RT**
email: enquiries@hilondonwest.co.uk **web:** www.hilondonwest.co.uk
dir: *Located just off the A40*

The Holiday Inn London West is the perfect base for visiting central London, Wembley Stadium and the Westfield Shopping Centre. The Park Royal Business Park is also just a stone's throw away. Having undergone a multi-million pound refurbishment, the hotel now offers newly created Executive Rooms, alongside standard rooms which offer all the modern comforts. The open-plan public areas are perfect for a variety of events, from one-to-one business meetings to family occasions and larger parties. The hotel also offers limited secure parking and a fitness studio on the top floor.

Rooms 225 (48 annexe) (51 fmly) ♠ **S** £89-£189; **D** £99-£199* **Facilities** STV FTV WiFi ♨ HL Gym Xmas **Conf** Class 25 Board 25 Thtr 90 Del from £189 to £289* **Services** Lift Air con **Parking** 60 **Notes** LB ⊗ Civ Wed 100

W4 CHISWICK

Clayton Hotel Chiswick

★★★★ 75% HOTEL PLAN 1 C3

tel: 020 8996 5200 **626 Chiswick High Rd W4 5RY**
email: info.chiswick@claytonhotels.com **web:** www.claytonhotelchiswick.com
dir: *Located 0.2m from Chiswick rbdt/London M4*

This stylish, modern hotel is conveniently located for Heathrow and central London, with Gunnersby tube station just a few minutes' walk away. Airy, spacious public areas include a modern restaurant, a popular bar and excellent meeting facilities. Fully air-conditioned bedrooms are stylish and extremely well appointed with broadband, laptop safes and flat-screen TVs. All boast spacious, modern bathrooms, many with walk-in rain showers.

Rooms 227 (10 fmly) (9 GF) ♠ **S** £99-£299; **D** £99-£299* **Facilities** STV FTV WiFi ♨ Gym Xmas New Year **Conf** Class 45 Board 40 Thtr 300 **Services** Lift Air con **Parking** 100 **Notes** LB ⊗ Civ Wed 300

LONDON

W5 EALING

Premier Inn London Ealing

BUDGET HOTEL PLAN 1 C3

tel: 0871 527 9368 *(Calls cost 13p per minute plus your phone company's access charge)*
22-24 Uxbridge Rd, Ealing W5 2SR
web: www.premierinn.com
dir: *M4 junct 1, A406 (signed North Circular & M1). Left onto A4020 (signed Ealing & Southall). Hotel on right after Ealing Broadway tube station*

High quality, budget accommodation ideal for both families and business travellers. Spacious, en suite bedrooms feature tea and coffee making facilities, and Freeview TV in most hotels. Internet access and WiFi are available for a small fee. The adjacent family restaurant features a wide and varied menu. See also the Hotel Groups pages.

Rooms 165

Premier Inn London Hanger Lane

BUDGET HOTEL PLAN 1 C4

tel: 0871 527 8346 *(Calls cost 13p per minute plus your phone company's access charge)*
1-6 Ritz Pde, Ealing W5 3RA
web: www.premierinn.com
dir: *M4 junct 2, A4 follow North Circular/A406 signs, for 0.5m. Take A406 for approx 2.5m. Right into Ashbourne Rd, immediately left into Ashbourne Parade, right into Ritz Parade. Hotel on right*

Rooms 167

W6 HAMMERSMITH

Novotel London West

★★★★ 76% ◉ HOTEL PLAN 1 D3

tel: 020 8741 1555 **1 Shortlands W6 8DR**
email: H0737@accor.com **web:** www.novotellondonwest.co.uk
dir: *M4 (A4) & A316 junct at Hogarth rdbt. Along Great West Rd, left for Hammersmith before flyover. On Hammersmith Bridge Rd to rdbt, take 5th exit. 1st left into Shortlands, 1st left to hotel main entrance*

A Hammersmith landmark, this substantial hotel is a popular base for both business and leisure travellers. Spacious, air-conditioned bedrooms have a good range of extras and many have additional beds, making them suitable for families. The comfort of the bedrooms is complemented by a choice of dining options; the Aroma Restaurant offers a daily changing buffet style cuisine, the award-winning Artisan Grill with its a la carte menu of the highest quality meats and fish simply prepared, or the Lounge Bar for a more informal experience with a menu showcasing old favourites and light dishes. The hotel also has its own car park, business centre and shop, and boasts one of the largest convention centres in Europe.

Rooms 630 (148 fmly) **Facilities** STV WiFi Gym ♫ **Conf** Class 540 Board 75 Thtr 1000 **Services** Lift Air con **Parking** 240 **Notes** Civ Wed 1000

Premier Inn London Hammersmith

BUDGET HOTEL PLAN 1 D3

tel: 0871 527 8660 *(Calls cost 13p per minute plus your phone company's access charge)*
255 King St, Hammersmith W6 9LU
web: www.premierinn.com
dir: *From central London on A4 to Hammersmith, follow A315 towards Chiswick*

High quality, budget accommodation ideal for both families and business travellers. Spacious, en suite bedrooms feature tea and coffee making facilities,

and Freeview TV in most hotels. Internet access and WiFi are available for a small fee. The adjacent family restaurant features a wide and varied menu. See also the Hotel Groups pages.

Rooms 119

W8 KENSINGTON

INSPECTORS' CHOICE

Royal Garden Hotel

★★★★★ ◉◉◉ HOTEL PLAN 4 B5

tel: 020 7937 8000 **2-24 Kensington High St W8 4PT**
email: reservations@royalgardenhotel.co.uk **web:** www.royalgardenhotel.co.uk
dir: *Adjacent to Kensington Palace*

This landmark hotel, just a short walk from the Royal Albert Hall, has airy, stylish public rooms that include the Park Terrace Restaurant, Lounge and Bar; Bertie's cocktail bar and the contemporary 10th-floor Min Jiang Restaurant. The latter offers authentic Chinese cuisine and enjoys breathtaking views of the city. The stylish and contemporary bedrooms are equipped with up-to-date facilities and include a number of spacious, air conditioned rooms and suites with super views over Kensington Gardens. All rooms have iPod docking stations, flat-screen TVs and triple-glazed windows as standard.

Rooms 394 (59 fmly) (35 smoking) ✆ **Facilities** Spa STV FTV WiFi ☼ HL Gym Health club Therapy Suites ♫ Xmas New Year **Conf** Class 320 Board 100 Thtr 550 **Services** Lift Air con **Parking** 200 **Notes** ⊗ Civ Wed 400

See advert on page 282

W8 KENSINGTON *continued*

The Milestone Hotel

★★★★★ ⊛⊛ 🏆 HOTEL PLAN 4 B5

tel: 020 7917 1000 **1 Kensington Court W8 5DL**
email: bookms@rchmail.com **web:** www.milestonehotel.com
dir: *From Warwick Rd right into Kensington High St. Hotel 400yds past Kensington tube station. Adjacent to Kensington Palace*

This delightful town house enjoys a wonderful location opposite Kensington Palace and is near some seriously elegant shops. The individually themed bedrooms include a selection of stunning suites that are equipped with every conceivable extra - fruit, cookies, chocolates, complimentary newspapers and even the next day's weather forecast. Up-to-the-minute technology includes high speed WiFi and interactive TV. Public areas include the luxurious Park Lounge where afternoon tea is served, the delightful split-level Stables Bar, a conservatory, the sumptuous Cheneston's restaurant and a fully equipped small gym, resistance pool and spa treatment room.

Rooms 62 (9 fmly) (1 GF) (5 smoking) 🐾 **S** £354-£714; **D** £384-£744*
Facilities STV FTV WiFi ⬇ HL ⊛ Gym Beauty treatment room ♫ Xmas New Year
Conf Class 20 Board 20 Thtr 50 Del from £469 to £515* **Services** Lift Air con
Parking 1 **Notes** LB

See advert on opposite page

Copthorne Tara Hotel London Kensington

★★★★ 77% HOTEL PLAN 4 B4

tel: 020 7937 7211 & 7872 2000 **Scarsdale Place, Wrights Ln W8 5SR**
email: reservations.tara@millenniumhotels.co.uk **web:** www.millenniumhotels.co.uk
dir: *From Kensington High St into Wrights Ln. NB for Sat Nav use W8 5SY*

This expansive hotel is ideally placed for Kensington High Street shops and tube station. Smart public areas include a trendy coffee shop, a gym, a stylish brasserie and bar, plus extensive conference facilities. Bedrooms include several well-equipped rooms for less mobile guests, in addition to a number of Connoisseur rooms that have the use of a club lounge as one of its many complimentary facilities.

Rooms 833 (3 fmly) 🐾 **Facilities** FTV WiFi ⬇ HL Fitness room Xmas New Year
Conf Class 160 Board 90 Thtr 280 **Services** Lift Air con **Parking** 126 **Notes** ⊗
Civ Wed 280

London Lodge Hotel

★★★ 78% TOWN HOUSE HOTEL PLAN 4 A3

tel: 020 7244 8444 **134-136 Lexham Gardens, Kensington W8 6JE**
email: info@londonlodgehotel.com **web:** www. londonlodgehotel.com
dir: *Located in the heart of Kensington, close to Olympia exhibition centre. At junct of A4 & Cromwell Rd*

The London Lodge Hotel is made out of two beautiful Victorian town houses; sympathetically converted to form a home away from home. The hotel is located in a quiet residential area of Kensington, close to public transport and within walking distance of major attractions. All rooms are nicely appointed and offer all modern facilities.

Rooms 28 (1 fmly) (6 GF) **S** £89.50-£179; **D** £109-£299 (incl. bkfst) **Facilities** FTV WiFi ⓑ **Conf** Class 15 Board 10 Thtr 25 Del from £120 to £299* **Services** Lift Air con **Notes** LB ⊗

K West Hotel & Spa

★★★★ 80% HOTEL PLAN 1 D3

tel: 020 8008 6600 **Richmond Way W14 0AX**
email: info@k-west.co.uk **web:** www.k-west.co.uk
dir: *From A40(M) take Shepherd's Bush exit. At Holland Park rdbt 3rd exit. 1st left & left again. Hotel straight ahead*

This stylish, contemporary hotel is conveniently located for Notting Hill, the exhibition halls and the BBC; Bond Street is only a 10-minute tube journey away. Funky, minimalist public areas include a trendy lobby bar and mezzanine-style restaurant. Spacious bedrooms and suites are extremely well appointed and offer luxurious bedding and a host of thoughtful extras such as CD and DVD players. WiFi is available throughout. The spa offers a comprehensive range of health, beauty and relaxation treatments.

Rooms 220 (31 GF) ⓕ **Facilities** Spa STV FTV WiFi ⓑ Gym Hydrotherapy pool Sauna Steam room Snow room Solarium ♫ New Year **Conf** Class 20 Board 25 Thtr 55 **Services** Lift Air con **Parking** 100 **Notes** ⊗

Ibis London Shepherd's Bush

ibis

AA Advertised PLAN 1 D3

tel: 020 7348 2020 **3-5 Rockley Rd W14 0DJ**
email: H7813@accor.com **web:** www.ibis.com/7813
dir: *Walking distance from Shepherd's Bush Market & Shepherd's Bush Central Tube Station*

Modern, budget hotel offering comfortable accommodation in bright and practical bedrooms. Breakfast is self-service and dinner is available in the restaurant.

Rooms 128 ⓕ **Facilities** FTV WiFi HL **Services** Lift

LONDON

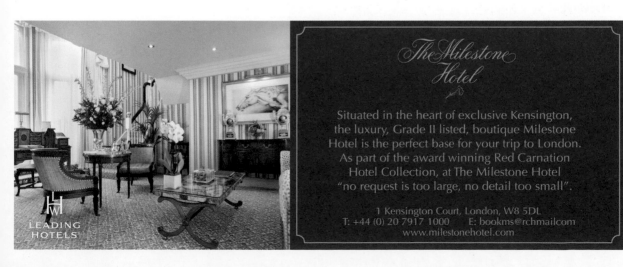

WC1 BLOOMSBURY, HOLBORN

INSPECTORS' CHOICE

Rosewood London

★★★★★ ⓐⓐ HOTEL PLAN 3 C3

tel: 020 7781 8888 **252 High Holborn WC1V 7EN**
email: london@rosewoodhotels.com **web:** www.rosewoodhotels.com/london
dir: *200mtrs E from Holborn underground station*

Situated in the heart of Holborn, this impressive hotel was originally built in 1912, and designed by H. Percy Monckton in a flamboyant Edwardian style. Interior design by Tony Chi is striking, stylish, and unconventional in parts, and so combines a London residential feel which is wholly sympathetic to its many heritage features. Spacious public areas include the very popular Scarfes Bar, Holborn Dining Room and the elegant Mirror Room salon, complete with stunning flower displays, where afternoon tea is served. Modern contemporary accommodation is luxurious with many super touches, and includes an impressive range of suites.

Rooms 306 (24 fmly) (10 smoking) ☁ **Facilities** Spa STV FTV WiFi ↕ Gym Amethyst steam rooms Sauna Relaxation lounge ♫ Xmas New Year **Conf** Class 255 Board 82 Thtr 370 **Services** Lift Air con **Parking** 10 **Notes** Civ Wed 340

HIGHLY RECOMMENDED

The Montague on the Gardens

★★★★ 86% ⓐ HOTEL PLAN 3 B3

THE
RED CARNATION
HOTEL COLLECTION

tel: 020 7637 1001 **15 Montague St, Bloomsbury WC1B 5BJ**
email: bookmt@rchmail.com **web:** www.montaguehotel.com
dir: *Just off Russell Square, adjacent to British Museum*

This stylish hotel is situated right next to the British Museum. A special feature is the alfresco terrace overlooking a delightful garden. Other public rooms include the Blue Door Bistro and Chef's Table, a bar, a lounge and a conservatory where traditional afternoon teas are served. The bedrooms are beautifully appointed and range from split-level suites to more compact rooms.

Rooms 100 (10 fmly) (19 GF) ☁ **S** £180-£348; **D** £204-£372* **Facilities** STV WiFi ↕ HL Gym ♫ Xmas New Year **Conf** Class 50 Board 50 Thtr 120 Del from £263 to £472* **Services** Lift Air con **Notes** LB Civ Wed 90

Hotel Russell

★★★★ 76% HOTEL PLAN 3 B4

tel: 020 7837 6470 **Russell Square WC1B 5BE**
email: russell.reservations@principal-hayley.com **web:** www.principal-hayley.com
dir: *From A501 into Woburn Place. Hotel 500mtrs on left*

This landmark Grade II, Victorian hotel is located on Russell Square, within walking distance of the West End and theatre district. Many bedrooms are stylish and state-of-the-art in design, while others are more traditional. Spacious public areas include the impressive foyer with a restored mosaic floor, a choice of lounges and an elegant restaurant.

Rooms 373 (2 fmly) ☁ **Facilities** STV FTV WiFi HL **Conf** Class 200 Board 75 Thtr 450 **Services** Lift Air con **Notes** ⊗ Civ Wed 300

Holiday Inn London Kings Cross/Bloomsbury

★★★★ 73% HOTEL PLAN 3 C5

tel: 020 7833 3900 & 7698 4030 **1 Kings Cross Rd WC1X 9HX**
email: sales@holidayinnlondon.com **web:** www.holidayinn.co.uk
dir: *On corner of King Cross Rd & Calthorpe St*

Conveniently located for Kings Cross station and The City, this modern hotel offers smart, spacious air-conditioned accommodation with a wide range of facilities. There are versatile meeting rooms, a bar, a well-equipped fitness centre and a choice of restaurants including one serving Indian cuisine.

Rooms 405 (163 fmly) (126 smoking) ☁ **Facilities** Spa STV FTV WiFi HL ⓧ Gym **Conf** Class 120 Board 30 Thtr 220 **Services** Lift Air con **Parking** 14 **Notes** ⊗

Bedford Hotel

★★★ 74% HOTEL PLAN 3 B3

tel: 020 7636 7822 & 7692 3620 **83-93 Southampton Row WC1B 4HD**
email: info@imperialhotels.co.uk **web:** www.imperialhotels.co.uk

Just off Russell Square, this intimate hotel is ideal for visits to the British Museum and Covent Garden. The bedrooms are well equipped with all the expected facilities including modem points if requested. The ground floor has a lounge, a bar and restaurant plus there's a delightful secret rear garden. The underground car park is a bonus.

Rooms 184 (1 fmly) **S** £95; **D** £127 (incl. bkfst)* **Facilities** FTV WiFi Xmas New Year **Conf** Board 12 Del from £165* **Services** Lift **Parking** 50 **Notes** LB ⊗

Premier Inn London Euston

BUDGET HOTEL PLAN 3 A5

tel: 0871 527 8656 *(Calls cost 13p per minute plus your phone company's access charge)*
1 Duke's Rd, Euston WC1H 9PJ
web: www.premierinn.com
dir: *On corner of Euston Road & Duke's Road, between Kings Cross/St Pancras & Euston stations*

High quality, budget accommodation ideal for both families and business travellers. Spacious, en suite bedrooms feature tea and coffee making facilities, and Freeview TV in most hotels. Internet access and WiFi are available for a small fee. The adjacent family restaurant features a wide and varied menu. See also the Hotel Groups pages.

Rooms 265

Premier Inn London Holborn

BUDGET HOTEL PLAN 3 C3

tel: 0871 527 9496 *(Calls cost 13p per minute plus your phone company's access charge)*
27 Red Lion St WC1R 4PS
web: www.premierinn.com
dir: *Nearest tube: Holburn & Chancery Lane*

Rooms 150

WC2 SOHO, STRAND

INSPECTORS' CHOICE

The Savoy

★★★★★ HOTEL PLAN 3 C1

tel: 020 7836 4343 **Strand WC2R OEU**
email: savoy@fairmont.com **web:** www.fairmont.com/savoy
dir: *Halfway along The Strand between Trafalgar Sq & Aldwych & steps from Covent Garden*

The Savoy has been at the forefront of the London hotel scene since it opened in 1889. The hotel was lovingly restored in 2010, with much of its art deco and Edwardian heritage kept intact. The bedrooms, including an extensive range of stunning suites, vary in style and size, and many overlook the River Thames. The Savoy Grill and American Bar remain as well-loved favourites; Kaspar's offers informal yet luxury all-day dining; the Thames Foyer is renowned for its afternoon teas; and the Beaufort Bar offers cocktails that push the boundaries of mixology. Immaculately presented staff offer excellent standards of hospitality and service.

Rooms 267 (5 fmly) (10 smoking) **Facilities** Spa STV FTV WiFi supervised Gym Fitness gallery Health & beauty treatments Personal training Xmas New Year **Conf** Class 300 Board 60 Thtr 500 **Services** Lift Air con **Parking** 20 **Notes** Civ Wed 300

Premier Inn London Leicester Square

BUDGET HOTEL PLAN 3 A1

tel: 0871 527 9334 *(Calls cost 13p per minute plus your phone company's access charge)*
1 Leicester Place, Leicester Square WC2H 7BP
web: www.premierinn.com
dir: *Nearest tube station: Leicester Sq. From Cranbourne St into Leicester Sq. Hotel on right (Leicester Pl). Car parks: China Town & Witcombe St, approx 10 mins walk*

High quality, budget accommodation ideal for both families and business travellers. Spacious, en suite bedrooms feature tea and coffee making facilities, and Freeview TV in most hotels. Internet access and WiFi are available for a small fee. The adjacent family restaurant features a wide and varied menu. See also the Hotel Groups pages.

Rooms 83

The Z Hotel Piccadilly

AA Advertised PLAN 3 A1

tel: 020 3551 3720 **2 Orange St WC2H 7DF**
email: piccadilly@thezhotels.com **web:** www.thezhotels.com

Z Piccadilly is just a short walk from Piccadilly Circus, and offers a West End location for an out-of-town price. This is a converted office building, with 112 bedrooms arranged over lower ground, ground and five upper floors. Each room has an en suite wet room, crisp bed linen, 48" TV with Sky, and complimentary WiFi.

Rooms 112 (10 GF) **Facilities** STV FTV WiFi **Services** Lift Air con **Notes**

LONDON GATEWAY MOTORWAY SERVICE AREA (M1)   Map 6 TQ19
Greater London

Ramada London North - M1

AA Advertised

tel: 020 8906 7000 **Welcome Break Services Area, M1 junct 2-4 NW7 3HU**
email: ramadaln@welcomebreak.co.uk **web:** www.welcomebreak.co.uk
dir: *On M1 between junct 2/4 N'bound & S'bound*

This modern building offers accommodation in smart, spacious and well-equipped bedrooms, suitable for families and business travellers, and all with en suite bathrooms. Continental breakfast is available and other refreshments may be taken at the nearby family restaurant.

Rooms 200 (190 fmly) (80 GF) (20 smoking) **Facilities** FTV WiFi Gym **Conf** Class 30 Board 50 Thtr 70 **Services** Lift Air con **Parking** 160 **Notes** Civ Wed 80

LONGHORSLEY   Map 21 NZ19
Northumberland

Macdonald Linden Hall, Golf & Country Club

★★★★ 78% HOTEL

tel: 01670 500000 & 0344 879 9084 **NE65 8XF**
email: lindenhall@macdonald.hotels.co.uk **web:** www.macdonaldhotels.co.uk
dir: *N'bound on A1 take A697 towards Coldstream. Hotel 1m N of Longhorsley*

This impressive Georgian mansion lies in 400 acres of parkland and offers extensive indoor and outdoor leisure facilities including a golf course. The Dobson Restaurant provides a fine dining experience, or guests can eat in the more informal Linden Tree pub. The good-sized bedrooms have a restrained modern style. The team of staff are enthusiastic and professional.

Rooms 50 (3 fmly) (16 GF) **Facilities** Spa STV FTV WiFi supervised 18 Putt green Gym Steam room Sauna Xmas New Year **Conf** Class 120 Board 50 Thtr 300 **Services** Lift **Parking** 300 **Notes** Civ Wed 120

LONG MELFORD
Suffolk   Map 13 TL84

Long Melford Swan
@@@@ RESTAURANT WITH ROOMS

tel: 01787 464545 **Hall St CO10 9JQ**
email: info@longmelfordswan.co.uk **web:** www.longmelfordswan.co.uk
dir: *From A134 into Long Melford, on main road through village*

Located in the very heart of Long Melford, bedrooms have all been completely refurbished with stylish decor and modern fixtures, home-made refreshments on arrival, turn-down service and feature bathrooms. All of the rooms are located just next door in Melford House, adjacent to the main bar and restaurant. This family-run business offers an excellent restaurant with attentive service and a large alfresco dining area in the walled garden. Lunch and dinner are served daily, and a range of cooked and continental dishes are offered for breakfast in the restaurant.

Rooms 6 (4 annexe)

LOOE
Cornwall   Map 2 SX25

Trelaske Hotel & Restaurant
★★★ 83% @@@@ HOTEL

tel: 01503 262159 **Polperro Rd PL13 2JS**
email: info@trelaske.co.uk **web:** www.trelaske.co.uk
dir: *B252 signed Looe. Over Looe bridge signed Polperro. 1.9m, hotel signed on left, turn right*

This small and welcoming hotel offers comfortable accommodation, professional and friendly service plus award-winning food. Set in its own very well-tended and pretty grounds, it is only two miles from Polperro and Looe.

Rooms 7 (4 annexe) (2 fmly) (2 GF) ⌂ **S** £95-£120; **D** £120-£130 (incl. bkfst)
Facilities FTV WiFi **Conf** Class 30 Board 40 Thtr 100 Del from £140 to £160
Parking 50 **Notes** LB Closed 20 Dec-28 Feb

Hannafore Point Hotel   THE INDEPENDENTS
                                              HOTEL ASSOCIATION
★★★ 75% HOTEL

tel: 01503 263273 **Marine Dr, West Looe PL13 2DG**
email: stay@hannaforepointhotel.com **web:** www.hannaforepointhotel.com
dir: *A38, left onto A385 to Looe. Over bridge turn left. Hotel 0.5m on left*

With panoramic coastal views of St George's Island around to Rame Head, this popular hotel provides a warm welcome. The wonderful view is certainly a feature of the spacious restaurant and bar, creating a scenic backdrop for both dinners and breakfasts. Additional facilities include a heated indoor pool and a gym.

Rooms 37 (5 fmly) ⌂ **Facilities** Spa FTV WiFi ⌂ ⌂ Gym Steam room Sauna Hydro pool & shower ♪ Xmas New Year **Conf** Class 80 Board 40 Thtr 120 **Services** Lift **Parking** 32 **Notes** Civ Wed 150

LOUGHBOROUGH
Leicestershire   Map 11 SK51

Quorn Country Hotel
★★★★ 78% @ HOTEL

tel: 01509 415050 & 415061 **Charnwood House, 66 Leicester Rd LE12 8BB**
email: reservations@quorncountryhotel.co.uk **web:** www.primahotels.co.uk/quorn

(For full entry see Quorn)

Burleigh Court Hotel and Conference Centre
★★★★ Ⓐ HOTEL

tel: 01509 211515 & 633033 **Off Ashby Rd LE11 3TD**
email: info@welcometoimago.com **web:** www.burleigh-court.co.uk
dir: *M1 junct 23 then A512 Ashby Road to Loughborough. At 1st rdbt right into Holywell Way, signed Burleigh Court & Holywell Park. Obtain visitors badge from gatehouse then turn left at next rdbt & enter Loughborough University Campus using West Entrance. Hotel car park on 2nd right*

Set in the grounds of Loughborough University, with modern design, clean lines, and bright, airy public areas, Burleigh Court is an ideal choice for anyone planning a conference in the East Midlands, or visiting the Uni. Accommodation ranges from luxury suites and executive rooms to high quality economy lodge rooms. The restaurant and bar provide a wide choice of cuisine, made with locally-sourced produce. Guests can enjoy extensive spa facilities, with a well-equipped gym, a swimming pool, a whirlpool spa, a steam room, and a sauna. Conference facilities are also extensive, and offer a wide range of packages and options.

Rooms 225 (40 annexe) (8 fmly) (79 GF) ⌂ **S** £46-£80; **D** £67-£123* **Facilities** Spa FTV WiFi ⌂ HL ⌂ Gym **Conf** Class 90 Board 56 Thtr 200 **Services** Lift **Parking** 189 **Notes** LB ⊗ Closed 25-30 Dec Civ Wed 200

Link Hotel
★★★ 83% HOTEL

tel: 01509 211800 **New Ashby Rd LE11 4EX**
email: info@linkhotel.co.uk **web:** www.linkhotelloughborough.co.uk
dir: *M1 junct 23, follow A512 signed Loughborough. Continue on A512, turn left onto slip road to reach hotel*

Ideally located, close to Loughborough University, and only half a mile away from J23 on the M1, this hotel offers modern and stylish accommodation, with warm hospitality at the forefront. A modern restaurant, bar and lounge area are available. A small gym is also on site.

Rooms 94 (12 fmly) (47 GF) ⌂ **Facilities** FTV WiFi ⌂ Gym Xmas New Year **Conf** Class 40 Board 30 Thtr 180 **Services** Air con **Parking** 164 **Notes** ⊗ Civ Wed 154

L

Premier Inn Loughborough

BUDGET HOTEL

tel: 0871 527 9314 *(Calls cost 13p per minute plus your phone company's access charge)*
Southfields Rd LE11 9SA
web: www.premierinn.com
dir: M1 junct 23, A512 towards Loughborough. Left into Greenclose Ln. Right onto A6, Right into Southfield Rd, hotel on left

High quality, budget accommodation ideal for both families and business travellers. Spacious, en suite bedrooms feature tea and coffee making facilities, and Freeview TV in most hotels. Internet access and WiFi are available for a small fee. The adjacent family restaurant features a wide and varied menu. See also the Hotel Groups pages.

Rooms 112

LOUTH
Lincolnshire   Map 17 TF38

Brackenborough Hotel

★★★ 88% ⊛ HOTEL

tel: 01507 609169 **Cordeaux Corner, Brackenborough LN11 0SZ**
email: reception@brackenborough.co.uk **web:** www.oakridgehotels.co.uk
dir: On A16, Louth to Grimsby road, 1m from Louth

In an idyllic setting amid well-tended gardens, this hotel offers attractive bedrooms, each individually decorated with co-ordinated furnishings and many extras. The award-winning bistro offers informal dining and the menu is based on locally sourced produce. The hotel specialises in weddings, events and private functions and has excellent conference facilities. Free WiFi is available. Guests have free access to state-of-the-art leisure facilities (less than half a mile away) that includes a swimming pool, tennis courts and a gym.

Rooms 24 (2 fmly) (6 GF) ⚡ **S** £96-£104; **D** £124-£132 (incl. bkfst)* **Facilities** FTV WiFi ⍾ Gym ♫ Xmas New Year **Conf** Class 150 Board 50 Thtr 300 **Services** Air con **Parking** 90 **Notes** ⊗ Civ Wed 220

Best Western Kenwick Park Hotel

BW Best Western.

★★★ 77% HOTEL

tel: 01507 608806 **Kenwick Park Estate LN11 8NR**
email: enquiries@kenwick-park.co.uk **web:** www.kenwick-park.co.uk
dir: A16 from Grimsby, then A157 Mablethorpe/Manby Rd. Hotel 400mtrs down hill on right

This elegant Georgian house is situated on the 320-acre Kenwick Park estate, overlooking its own golf course. Bedrooms are spacious and comfortable, and provide modern facilities. Public areas include a restaurant and a conservatory bar that overlook the grounds. There is also an extensive leisure centre and state-of-the-art conference and banqueting facilities.

Rooms 34 (5 annexe) (10 fmly) (11 GF) **Facilities** Spa FTV WiFi ⌿ 18 ⛳ Putt green Gym Health & beauty centre Xmas New Year **Conf** Class 40 Board 90 Thtr 250 Del from £127 to £150 **Parking** 100 **Notes** Civ Wed 200

LOWER BARTLE
Lancashire   Map 18 SD43

Bartle Hall Hotel

★★★★ 75% HOTEL

tel: 01772 690506 **Lea Ln PR4 0HA**
email: info@bartlehall.co.uk **web:** www.bartlehall.co.uk
dir: M6 junct 32 into Tom Benson Way, follow signs for Woodplumpton/Bartle Hall

Ideally situated between Preston and Blackpool, Bartle Hall is within easy access of the M6 and the Lake District. Set in its own extensive grounds the hotel offers comfortable, well-equipped and renovated accommodation. The restaurant cuisine uses local produce and there is a large comfortable bar and lounge. There are also extensive conference facilities, and the hotel is a popular wedding venue.

Rooms 15 (2 annexe) (3 fmly) (2 GF) ⚡ **Facilities** FTV WiFi ⍾ HL Xmas New Year **Conf** Class 50 Board 40 Thtr 200 Del from £130 to £160* **Parking** 150 **Notes** Civ Wed 130

LOWER BEEDING
West Sussex   Map 6 TQ22

INSPECTORS' CHOICE

South Lodge, an Exclusive Hotel

★★★★★ ⊛⊛ ♀ COUNTRY HOUSE HOTEL

EXCLUSIVE HOTELS

tel: 01403 891711 **Brighton Rd RH13 6PS**
email: enquiries@southlodgehotel.co.uk **web:** www.exclusive.co.uk
dir: A23, onto B2110. Right, through Handcross to A281 junct. Left, hotel on right

This impeccably presented 19th-century lodge with stunning views of the rolling South Downs is an ideal retreat. There is the traditional and elegant Camellia Restaurant; as well as a more innovative take on the chef's table concept - a mini-restaurant within the kitchen itself. Guests can take a tour of the restored Victorian wine cellar, either with a sommelier or on their own. The elegant lounge is popular for afternoon teas. Bedrooms are individually designed with character and quality throughout. The conference facilities are impressive.

Rooms 89 (11 fmly) (19 GF) ⚡ **D** £195-£360 (incl. bkfst)* **Facilities** STV WiFi ⍾ ⌿ 36 ⛳ Putt green Fishing ♣ Gym Mountain bikes Archery Clay pigeon shooting Wine tasting Xmas New Year **Conf** Class 100 Board 50 Thtr 180 Del from £240 to £390* **Services** Lift **Parking** 200 **Notes** LB Civ Wed 130

Silver Stars

The AA Silver Star rating denotes a Hotel that we highly recommend. They have a superior level of quality within their star rating, high standards of hospitality, service and cleanliness.

L

LOWER SLAUGHTER
Gloucestershire

Map 10 SP12

The Slaughters Manor House

★★★★ ◉◉◉ COUNTRY HOUSE HOTEL

Andrew BROWNSWORD HOTELS

tel: 01451 820456 **GL54 2HP**
email: info@slaughtersmanor.co.uk **web:** www.slaughtersmanor.co.uk
dir: *Exit A429 signed 'The Slaughters'. Manor 0.5m on right on entering village*

The Slaughters Manor House, reopened in March 2016 after three months of refurbishment, with a new, sophisticated countryside concept unveiled throughout the entire ground floor. Offering a contemporary interpretation of countryside life, the manor boasts well defined rooms, including a snug, billiards room, library and lounge, and not forgetting the bar in partnership with the Sipsmith distillery. These alluring rooms are unified by the use of natural materials, finishes and objects, and a simple colour palette. The restaurant at The Slaughters Manor House is run by Nik Chappell, executive chef.

Rooms 19 (8 annexe) (5 fmly) (4 GF) 🐾 **Facilities** STV FTV WiFi ⚲ ☕ ⚑ Xmas New Year **Conf** Class 40 Board 30 Thtr 70 **Parking** 20 **Notes** Civ Wed 74

LOWESTOFT
Suffolk

Map 13 TM59

Ivy House Country Hotel

★★★ 83% ◉◉ HOTEL

tel: 01502 501353 & 588144 **Ivy Ln, Beccles Rd, Oulton Broad NR33 8HY**
email: aa@ivyhousecountryhotel.co.uk **web:** www.ivyhousecountryhotel.co.uk
dir: *On A146 SW of Oulton Broad turn into Ivy Ln beside Esso petrol station. Over railway bridge, follow private drive*

A peacefully located, family-run hotel set in three acres of mature landscaped grounds and just a short walk from Oulton Broad. Public rooms include an 18th-century thatched barn restaurant where an interesting choice of dishes is served. The attractively decorated bedrooms are housed in garden wings, and many have lovely views of the grounds to the countryside beyond.

Rooms 20 (10 annexe) (1 fmly) (17 GF) 🐾 **Facilities** FTV WiFi ⚲ Xmas New Year **Conf** Class 250 Board 100 Thtr 250 **Parking** 300 **Notes** Civ Wed 250

Premier Inn Lowestoft

BUDGET HOTEL

Premier Inn

tel: 0871 527 8688 *(Calls cost 13p per minute plus your phone company's access charge)*
249 Yarmouth Rd NR32 4AA
web: www.premierinn.com
dir: *On A12, 2m N of Lowestoft*

High quality, budget accommodation ideal for both families and business travellers. Spacious, en suite bedrooms feature tea and coffee making facilities, and Freeview TV in most hotels. Internet access and WiFi are available for a small fee. The adjacent family restaurant features a wide and varied menu. See also the Hotel Groups pages.

Rooms 99

LUDLOW
Shropshire

Map 10 SO57

Fishmore Hall

★★★ ◉◉◉ SMALL HOTEL

tel: 01584 875148 **Fishmore Rd SY8 3DP**
email: reception@fishmorehall.co.uk **web:** www.fishmorehall.co.uk
dir: *A49 into Henley Rd. 1st right, Weyman Rd, at bottom of hill right into Fishmore Rd*

Located in a rural area within easy reach of the town centre, this Palladian-style Georgian house has been sympathetically renovated and extended to provide high standards of comfort and facilities. The contemporary interior highlights many period features, and public areas include a comfortable lounge and restaurant, the setting for award-winning imaginative cooking.

Rooms 15 (1 GF) 🐾 **Facilities** FTV WiFi ⚲ ☕ Treatment cabin offering beauty treatments & massage Xmas New Year **Conf** Class 60 Board 40 Thtr 130 **Services** Lift **Parking** 48 **Notes** LB Civ Wed 130

Overton Grange Hotel and Restaurant

★★★ 86% ◉ HOTEL

tel: 01584 873500 & 0845 476 1000 *(Calls cost 7p per minute plus your phone company's access charge)* **Old Hereford Rd SY8 4AD**
email: info@overtongrangehotel.com **web:** www.overtongrangehotel.com
dir: *A49, B4361 to Ludlow. Hotel 200yds on left*

This is a traditional country-house hotel with stylish, comfortable bedrooms, and high standards of guest care. Food is an important part of what the hotel has to offer and the restaurant serves classically based, French-style cuisine, using locally sourced produce whenever possible. Meeting and conference rooms are available.

Rooms 14 ☏ **S** £99-£199; **D** £99-£199 (incl. bkfst)* **Facilities** FTV WiFi ⓢ Beauty treatment rooms Xmas **Conf** Class 50 Board 30 Thtr 100 **Parking** 45 **Notes** LB ⊗ No children 7yrs

The Feathers Hotel

★★★ 82% ◉ HOTEL

tel: 01584 875261 **The Bull Ring SY8 1AA**
email: enquiries@feathersatludlow.co.uk **web:** www.feathersatludlow.co.uk
dir: *From A49 follow town centre signs to ccntrc. Hotel on left*

Famous for the carved woodwork outside and in, this picture-postcard 17th-century hotel is one of the town's best-known landmarks and is in an excellent location. Bedrooms are traditional both in style and decor. The public areas have retained much of the traditional charm, and the first-floor lounge is particularly stunning. Modern British menus are offered in the smart restaurant which has wooden beams and exposed brickwork.

Rooms 40 (3 fmly) ☏ **S** £95-£145; **D** £135-£215 (incl. bkfst)* **Facilities** STV FTV WiFi ↻ Xmas New Year **Conf** Class 40 Board 40 Thtr 80 Del £145* **Services** Lift **Parking** 33 **Notes** LB

Dinham Hall Hotel

★★★ 81% ◉◉ HOTEL

tel: 01584 876464 **By The Castle SY8 1EJ**
email: info@dinhamhall.com **web:** www.dinhamhall.com
dir: *In town centre, opposite castle*

Built in 1792, this lovely house stands in attractive gardens immediately opposite Ludlow Castle, and it has a well-deserved reputation for warm hospitality. The well-equipped bedrooms include two in a converted cottage, and some rooms have four-poster beds. The comfortable public rooms are elegantly appointed. Dishes served in the brasserie-style restaurant are based on good, seasonal produce.

Rooms 13 (2 annexe) (2 fmly) (2 GF) **S** £99-£149; **D** £99-£199 (incl. bkfst) **Facilities** FTV WiFi Xmas New Year **Conf** Class 20 Board 26 Thtr 40 **Parking** 16 **Notes** LB No children 7yrs

Old Downton Lodge

◉◉◉ RESTAURANT WITH ROOMS

tel: 01568 771826 & 07977 475881 **Downton on the Rock SY8 2HU**
email: bookings@olddowntonlodge.com **web:** www.olddowntonlodge.com
dir: *From Ludlow onto A49 towards Shrewsbury, 1st left onto A4113. After 1.9m turn left signed Downton, 3m on single track road. Turn right, signed*

Originally a farm, this high-end establishment has bags of character, and is a stylish, comfortable and tranquil place to stay. Bedrooms are spacious and very well appointed, with comfortable beds and luxurious bathrooms. Old Downton Lodge is within easy reach of Ludlow's many attractions, and is in a peaceful location with good parking, pleasant grounds, ideal for walks and country pursuits. There is an honesty bar and excellent wine list. Breakfast should not be missed, and the three AA Rosette-worthy dinner is a highlight, with an imaginative five- or seven-course tasting menu using local, seasonal and foraged produce, served every Tuesday to Saturday evening.

Rooms 9

The Clive Bar & Restaurant with Rooms

◉ ⛨ RESTAURANT WITH ROOMS

tel: 01584 856565 & 856665 **Bromfield SY8 2JR**
email: info@theclive.co.uk **web:** www.theclive.co.uk
dir: *2m N of Ludlow on A49 in Bromfield*

The Clive is just two miles from the busy town of Ludlow and is a convenient base for visiting the local attractions or for business. Based at the Ludlow Food Centre, good use is made of food made on site or from the company farms, ensuring local seasonal produce at every meal. The bedrooms, located in an annexe, are spacious and very well equipped; some are suitable for families and many are on the ground-floor level. Meals are available in the well-known Clive Restaurant or in the bar areas. The property also has a small meeting room.

Rooms 14 (14 annexe) (1 fmly)

The Cliffe at Dinham

RESTAURANT WITH ROOMS

tel: 01584 872063 & 876975 **Halton Ln, Dinham SY8 2JE**
email: info@thecliffeatdinham.co.uk **web:** www.thecliffeatdinham.co.uk

This former gentleman's residence is a short stroll from the River Teme, with magnificent views of Ludlow Castle, just a short walk from the vibrant centre of Ludlow. The Cliffe has recently been refurbished, with a successful blend of the existing Victorian features and a more contemporary style. The rooms are comfortable and well equipped. Relaxed dining from locally sourced ingredients is offered in the attractive dining room, and there is a pleasant terraced area overlooking the gardens.

Rooms 13 (2 annexe) (3 fmly)

L

LUTON
Bedfordshire

Map 6 TL02

Luton Hoo Hotel, Golf and Spa
★★★★★ 87% HOTEL

tel: 01582 734437 & 698888 **The Mansion House LU1 3TQ**
email: reservations@lutonhoo.com **web:** www.lutonhoo.com
dir: M1 junct 10 towards Harpenden & St Albans. Hotel approx 1m on left

A luxury hotel in more than 1,000 acres of 'Capability' Brown designed parkland and formal gardens, with an 18-hole, par 73 golf course and the River Lea meandering through. The centrepiece is the Grade I listed Mansion House that has architectural influences by many famous architects including Robert Adams. There are three sumptuous lounges where guests can enjoy afternoon tea and pre-dinner drinks, and two eating options - The Wernher Restaurant and the Adams Brasserie. The spacious bedrooms and impressive suites combine historic character with modern amenities. The Robert Adams Club House is the perfect place for relaxation, with the brasserie, a spa, golf, pool and gym together with two bars, and Warren Weir, at the foot of the estate, on the river bank is an exclusive retreat for weddings and meetings.

Rooms 228 (50 fmly) (65 GF) 🐾 **D** £320–£1200 (incl. bkfst) **Facilities** Spa FTV WiFi ❧ HL 🎱 ⚓ 18 🏌 Putt green Fishing 🎣 Gym Bird watching Clay pigeon shooting Archery Falconry Cycling Snooker 🎵 Xmas New Year **Conf** Class 220 Board 60 Thtr 388 Del from £270 to £415 **Services** Lift **Parking** 316 **Notes** Civ Wed 380

Icon Hotel
★★★ 83% HOTEL

tel: 01582 722123 **15 Stuart St LU1 2SA**
email: reservations@iconhotelluton.com **web:** www.iconhotelluton.com
dir: M1 junct 10 & 10A, A1081 signed Luton, left follow Luton Retail Park & station signs. Left at next rdbt, left at next rdbt onto A505 Park Viaduct. Straight on at next rdbt, left into Hastings St

This modern, purpose-built hotel occupies a prominent position close to the town centre and is a short drive from the international airport. The contemporary, open-plan bar is very comfortable and Capello's Restaurant offers a modern Mediterranean menu. The bedrooms are attractively presented and feature the latest technology along with large LCD TVs and complimentary WiFi. There is a range of business suites and a well-equipped gym.

Rooms 60 (7 fmly) (5 GF) 🐾 **Facilities** FTV WiFi ❧ Gym Therapy treatments by prior arrangement 🎵 Xmas New Year **Conf** Class 30 Board 25 Thtr 60 **Services** Lift Air con **Parking** 18 **Notes** ⊗

Premier Inn Luton Town Centre
BUDGET HOTEL

tel: 0871 527 9542 *(Calls cost 13p per minute plus your phone company's access charge)*
Regent St LU1 5FA
web: www.premierinn.com
dir: M1 junct 10 (S'bound), A1081 (Luton Airport). At 1st rdbt left onto London Rd (A1081). Into Castle St, left into Windsor St. 1st right into Chapel St. 1st left into Regent St. Hotel on left

High quality, budget accommodation ideal for both families and business travellers. Spacious, en suite bedrooms feature tea and coffee making facilities, and Freeview TV in most hotels. Internet access and WiFi are available for a small fee. The adjacent family restaurant features a wide and varied menu. See also the Hotel Groups pages.

Rooms 120

LUTON AIRPORT
Bedfordshire

Map 6 TL12

Premier Inn Luton Airport
BUDGET HOTEL

tel: 0871 527 8690 *(Calls cost 13p per minute plus your phone company's access charge)*
Osborne Rd LU1 3HJ
web: www.premierinn.com
dir: M1 junct 10, A1081 follow signs for Luton, at 3rd rdbt left into Gypsy Lane, left at next rdbt

High quality, budget accommodation ideal for both families and business travellers. Spacious, en suite bedrooms feature tea and coffee making facilities, and Freeview TV in most hotels. Internet access and WiFi are available for a small fee. The adjacent family restaurant features a wide and varied menu. See also the Hotel Groups pages.

Rooms 134

Ibis London Luton Airport

AA Advertised

tel: 01582 424488 **Spittlesea Rd LU2 9NH**
email: H1040@accor.com **web:** www.ibishotel.com
dir: M1 junct 10, follow signs to Luton Airport. Hotel 600mtrs from airport

Modern, budget hotel offering comfortable accommodation in bright and practical bedrooms. Breakfast is self-service and dinner is available in the restaurant.

Rooms 162 (8 fmly) ⟲ **Facilities** FTV WiFi ⌁ **Conf** Class 18 Board 30 Thtr 60 **Services** Lift **Parking** 75

LYME REGIS
Dorset **Map 4 SY39**

Royal Lion Hotel

★★★ 75% HOTEL

tel: 01297 445622 **Broad St DT7 3QF**
email: enquiries@royallionhotel.com **web:** www.royallionhotel.com
dir: From W on A35 take A3052, or from E take B3165 to Lyme Regis. Hotel in town centre, opposite The Fossil Shop

This 17th-century, former coaching inn is full of character and charm, and is just a short walk from the seafront. Bedrooms vary in size; those in the newer wing are more spacious and some have balconies, sea views or a private terrace. In addition to the elegant dining room and guest lounges, a heated pool, jacuzzi, sauna and small gym are available. A good selection of enjoyable, well-prepared dishes is offered in either the bar or main restaurant. There is a car park at the rear.

Rooms 33 (8 fmly) (4 GF) ⟲ **S** £66–£75; **D** £116–£170 (incl. bkfst)* **Facilities** FTV WiFi ⌖ Sauna Games room Snooker tables Table tennis Xmas New Year **Conf** Class 20 Board 20 Thtr 50 **Parking** 33 **Notes** LB

LYMINGTON
Hampshire **Map 5 SZ39**

Macdonald Elmers Court Hotel & Resort

★★★★ 76% HOTEL

tel: 0344 879 9060 **South Baddesley Rd SO41 5ZB**
email: elmerscourt@macdonald-hotels.co.uk **web:** www.macdonaldhotels.co.uk
dir: M27 junct 1, through Lyndhurst, Brockenhurst to Lymington, hotel 200yds right after Lymington ferry terminal

Originally known as The Elms, this Tudor manor house dates back to the 1820s. Ideally located at the edge of the New Forest and overlooking The Solent with views towards the Isle of Wight, the hotel offers suites and self-catering accommodation in the grounds, along with a host of leisure facilities.

Rooms 42 (42 annexe) (8 fmly) (22 GF) ⟲ **Facilities** Spa FTV WiFi ⌖ ↳ supervised ☒ Putt green ⌇ Gym Squash Steam room Aerobics classes Sauna Table tennis Xmas New Year **Conf** Class 70 Board 40 Thtr 120 **Parking** 100 **Notes** ⊗ Civ Wed 120

Stanwell House Hotel

★★★ 88% ◉◉ HOTEL

tel: 01590 677123 **14-15 High St SO41 9AA**
email: enquiries@stanwellhouse.com **web:** www.stanwellhouse.com
dir: M27 junct 1, follow signs to Lyndhurst then Lymington

Stanwell House Hotel is a privately owned Georgian building situated on the wide high street only a few minutes from the marina, and a short drive from the New Forest. Styling itself as a boutique hotel, the bedrooms are individually designed; there are Terrace rooms with garden access, four-poster rooms, and Georgian rooms in the older part of the building. The four suites include two with their own roof terrace. Dining options include the informal bistro and the intimate Seafood Restaurant. Service is friendly and attentive. A meeting room is available.

Rooms 29 (7 fmly) (7 GF) ⟲ **D** £145-£295 (incl. bkfst)* **Facilities** FTV WiFi ⌁ Xmas New Year **Conf** Class 35 Board 30 Thtr 70 Del from £175 to £245* **Parking** 12 **Notes** LB Civ Wed 100

Premier Inn Lymington (New Forest Hordle)

BUDGET HOTEL

tel: 0871 527 8692 (Calls cost 13p per minute plus your phone company's access charge)
Silver St, Hordle SO41 0FN
web: www.premierinn.com
dir: M27 junct 1, A337, 3.5m, left into High St (A35) right into Gosport Ln. Left into Clay Hill (A337), Right into Grigg Ln (B3055), Approx 8m, left into Barrows Ln, right into Silver St

High quality, budget accommodation ideal for both families and business travellers. Spacious, en suite bedrooms feature tea and coffee making facilities, and Freeview TV in most hotels. Internet access and WiFi are available for a small fee. The adjacent family restaurant features a wide and varied menu. See also the Hotel Groups pages.

Rooms 20

L

LYNDHURST	Map 5 SU30
Hampshire	

Lime Wood

★★★★★ ⑧⑧⑧ COUNTRY HOUSE HOTEL

tel: 023 8028 7177 **Beaulieu Rd SO43 7FZ**
email: info@limewood.co.uk web: www.limewood.co.uk
dir: Exit A35 onto B3056 towards Beaulieu, hotel 1m on right

This meticulously restored country house situated deep in the New Forest, provides a wealth of facilities and much opulence. The hotel prides itself on its relaxed, friendly and attentive service, and has lots to interest and captivate. The luxurious bedrooms are notable; some are in the pavilion and some in the main house. A major attraction at Lime Wood is the restaurant, Hartnett Holder & Co which is headed up by Luke Holder and, as you'd expect, Angela Hartnett. The Herb House spa offers a hydrotherapy pool and many other excellent facilities along with a gym and steam room.

Rooms 32 (16 annexe) (7 fmly) (5 GF) ⚡ **S** £275–£1050; **D** £275–£1050
Facilities Spa STV FTV WiFi ⬇ ⌖ Gym Xmas New Year **Conf** Board 30 Thtr 50
Del from £385 to £505* **Services** Lift **Parking** 60 **Notes** LB Civ Wed 60

See advert on opposite page

Best Western Forest Lodge Hotel

★★★ 83% ⑧⑧ HOTEL

NEW FOREST HOTELS

tel: 023 8028 3677 & 0800 444 441 **Pikes Hill, Romsey Rd SO43 7AS**
email: forest@newforesthotels.co.uk web: www.newforesthotels.co.uk
dir: M27 junct 1, A337 towards Lyndhurst. In village, with police station & courts on right, take 1st right into Pikes Hill

Situated on the edge of Lyndhurst, this hotel is set well back from the main road. The smart, contemporary bedrooms include four-poster rooms and family rooms; children are very welcome here. The eating options are the Forest Restaurant and the fine-dining Glasshouse Restaurant. There is an indoor swimming pool and Nordic sauna.

Rooms 36 (11 fmly) (10 GF) ⚡ **Facilities** FTV WiFi ⬇ HL ⌖ Xmas New Year
Conf Class 70 Board 60 Thtr 120 **Parking** 50 **Notes** Civ Wed 90

Ormonde House Hotel

★★★ 72% METRO HOTEL

tel: 023 8028 2806 **Southampton Rd SO43 7BT**
email: enquiries@ormondehouse.co.uk web: www.ormondehouse.co.uk
dir: M27/M271/A35 E through Ashurst, hotel on right on entering Lyndhurst

Ormonde House is located on the edge of Lyndhurst village in the heart of the New Forest, and provides comfortable en suite accommodation, with breakfast served in the dining room and conservatory. It is dog friendly with ample off-street parking. The ideal location for all New Forest activities and attractions.

Rooms 21 (4 annexe) (2 fmly) (7 GF) ⚡ **S** £65–£125; **D** £75–£145 (incl. bkfst)*
Facilities FTV WiFi New Year **Parking** 21 **Notes** LB Closed 13-27 Dec

LYNMOUTH	Map 3 SS74
Devon	

Rising Sun Hotel

★★ 81% ⑧ HOTEL

tel: 01598 753223 **Harbourside EX35 6EG**
email: reception@risingsunlynmouth.co.uk web: www.risingsunlynmouth.co.uk
dir: M5 junct 23, A39 to Minehead. Hotel on harbour

The Rising Sun is a delightful thatched establishment, once a smugglers' inn, that sits on the harbour front. Popular with locals and guests alike, there is the option of eating in either the convivial bar or the restaurant; a comfortable, quiet lounge is also available. Bedrooms, located in the inn and adjoining cottages, are individually designed and have modern facilities.

Rooms 14 (1 fmly) (1 GF) **Facilities** Xmas

HARTNETT HOLDER & CO

LOCAL INGREDIENTS, ITALIAN HEART

Angela Hartnett & Luke Holder do the cooking
at Lime Wood's Harnett Holder & Co.

Well-crafted, locally sourced Italian dishes
in the heart of the New Forest!

hhandco.co.uk
023 8028 7177

L

LYTHAM ST ANNES
Lancashire   Map 18 SD32

Clifton Arms Hotel

★★★★ 79% ⊛⊛ HOTEL

---

tel: 01253 739898 **West Beach, Lytham FY8 5QJ**
email: welcome@cliftonarms-lytham.com **web:** www.cliftonarmslytham.com
dir: On A584 along seafront

This well established hotel occupies a prime position overlooking Lytham Green and the Ribble Estuary beyond. Bedrooms vary in size and are appointed to a high standard; front-facing rooms are particularly spacious and enjoy splendid views. There is an elegant restaurant, a stylish open-plan lounge and cocktail bar, as well as function and conference facilities.

Rooms 48 (2 fmly) ↰ **S** £88-£108; **D** £155-£185 (incl. bkfst)* **Facilities** STV FTV WiFi ↳ Xmas New Year **Conf** Class 100 Board 60 Thtr 150 Del from £130 to £160* **Services** Lift **Parking** 40 **Notes** LB ⊗ Civ Wed 100

Bedford Hotel

★★★ 82% ⊛ HOTEL

---

tel: 01253 724636 **307-313 Clifton Drive South FY8 1HN**
email: reservations@bedford-hotel.com **web:** www.bedford-hotel.com
dir: From M55 follow signs for airport to last lights. Left through 2 sets of lights. Hotel 300yds on left

This popular family-run hotel is close to the town centre and the seafront. Bedrooms vary in size and style and include superior and club class rooms. Newer bedrooms are particularly elegant and tastefully appointed. Spacious public areas include a choice of lounges, a coffee shop, fitness facilities and an impressive function suite. The Restaurant offers imaginative dishes, skilfully prepared.

Rooms 44 (6 GF) ↰ **Facilities** FTV WiFi ↳ Gym Hydrotherapy spa bath Xmas New Year **Conf** Class 140 Board 60 Thtr 200 **Services** Lift **Parking** 25 **Notes** ⊗

Best Western Glendower Hotel

★★★ 81% ⊛ HOTEL

BW **Best Western.**

---

tel: 01253 723241 **North Promenade FY8 2NQ**
email: recp@theglendowerhotel.co.uk **web:** www.glendowerhotel.co.uk
dir: M55 follow airport signs. Left at Promenade to St Annes. Hotel 500yds from pier

Located on the seafront and with easy access to the town centre, this popular, friendly hotel offers comfortably furnished, well-equipped accommodation. Bedrooms vary in size and style, and include four-poster rooms and very popular family suites. Public areas feature a choice of smart, comfortable lounges, a bright, modern leisure club and function facilities.

Rooms 61 (17 fmly) ↰ **S** £50-£95; **D** £65-£165 (incl. bkfst)* **Facilities** FTV WiFi ↳ Gym Snooker room Table tennis room ♫ Xmas New Year **Conf** Class 120 Board 50 Thtr 150 **Services** Lift **Parking** 45 **Notes** LB Civ Wed 150

MACCLESFIELD
Cheshire   Map 16 SJ97

The Shrigley Hall Hotel, Golf & Country Club

★★★★ 76% ⊛ HOTEL

THE HOTEL COLLECTION

---

tel: 01625 575757 **Shrigley Park, Pott Shrigley SK10 5SB**
email: shrigleyhall@thehotelcollection.co.uk **web:** www.thehotelcollection.co.uk
dir: Exit A523 at Legh Arms towards Pott Shrigley. Hotel 2m on left before village

Originally built in 1825, Shrigley Hall is an impressive hotel set in 262 acres of mature parkland, commanding stunning views of the countryside. Features include a championship golf course. The public areas are spacious, combining traditional and contemporary decor, and include a well-equipped gym. There is a wide choice of bedroom sizes and styles.

Rooms 148 (11 fmly) ↰ **Facilities** Spa STV WiFi ⊗ supervised ↟ 18 ⛳ Putt green Fishing Gym Beauty salon Hydro centre ♫ Xmas New Year **Conf** Class 110 Board 42 Thtr 180 Del from £125 to £150 **Services** Lift **Parking** 300 **Notes** Civ Wed 150

Premier Inn Macclesfield North

BUDGET HOTEL

Premier Inn

---

tel: 0871 527 8694 (Calls cost 13p per minute plus your phone company's access charge)
Tytherington Business Park, Springwood Way, Tytherington SK10 2XA
web: www.premierinn.com
dir: On A523 in Tytherington Business Park

High quality, budget accommodation ideal for both families and business travellers. Spacious, en suite bedrooms feature tea and coffee making facilities, and Freeview TV in most hotels. Internet access and WiFi are available for a small fee. The adjacent family restaurant features a wide and varied menu. See also the Hotel Groups pages.

Rooms 55

Premier Inn Macclesfield South West

BUDGET HOTEL

Premier Inn

---

tel: 0871 527 8696 (Calls cost 13p per minute plus your phone company's access charge)
Congleton Rd, Gawsworth SK11 7XD
web: www.premierinn.com
dir: M6 junct 17, A534 towards Congleton, A536 towards Macclesfield to Gawsworth. Hotel on left

Rooms 28

MAIDENCOMBE

See **Torquay**

MAIDENHEAD
Berkshire   Map 6 SU88

Fredrick's Hotel and Spa
★★★★ 77% ◉◉ HOTEL

tel: 01628 581000 **Shoppenhangers Rd SL6 2PZ**
email: reservations@fredricks-hotel.co.uk **web:** www.fredricks-hotel.co.uk
dir: M4 junct 8/9, 1st exit off M404 signed Cox Green. Hotel on right, 300 yds after garage

Set in attractive grounds on the fringes of Maidenhead, this stylish hotel has comfortable and well-equipped bedrooms. Public rooms include the Wintergarden restaurant, which serves afternoon tea as well as varied bar menus; and Fredrick's Restaurant which has a wide selection for lunch and dinner. There are also conference facilities, a fitness room, pool and spa. Fredrick's is a very popular venue for weddings.

Rooms 37 (5 fmly) (14 GF) ♠ **S** £109-£169; **D** £129-£189 (incl. bkfst)* **Facilities** Spa FTV WiFi ⤵ ⊗ ⫟ Gym Xmas New Year **Conf** Class 65 Board 46 Thtr 100 Del from £209 to £279* **Parking** 80 **Notes** LB ⊗ Civ Wed 150

Premier Inn Maidenhead Town Centre
BUDGET HOTEL

tel: 0871 527 9520 (Calls cost 13p per minute plus your phone company's access charge)
Kidwells Park Dr SL6 8AQ
email: maidenheadtowncentre.pi@premierinn.com **web:** www.premierinn.com
dir: From A308(M) towards Maidenhead. 1st exit at next rdbt onto A308. 2nd exit signed Braywick Rd/A308. 1st exit at next rdbt into Bad Godesberg Way. 3rd exit at next rdbt into Market St, right into West St, right into Kidwells Park Dr, hotel on right

High quality, budget accommodation ideal for both families and business travellers. Spacious, en suite bedrooms feature tea and coffee making facilities, and Freeview TV in most hotels. Internet access and WiFi are available for a small fee. The adjacent family restaurant features a wide and varied menu. See also the Hotel Groups pages.

Rooms 124

MAIDSTONE
Kent   Map 7 TQ75

Grange Moor Hotel
★★★ ⚑ HOTEL

tel: 01622 677623 **4-8 St Michael's Rd ME16 8BS**
email: reservations@grangemoor.co.uk **web:** www.grangemoor.co.uk
dir: From town centre towards A26 Tonbridge rd. Hotel 0.25m on left, just after church

Grange Moor Hotel is easily recognised in summer by its colourful hanging baskets. On offer are 50 well-appointed bedrooms that have TV, radio alarm clock, hairdryer, and tea- and coffee-making facilities. There is a guest lounge area and a Tudor-style bar and restaurant.

Rooms 50 (11 annexe) (5 fmly) (7 GF) ♠ **Facilities** FTV WiFi **Conf** Class 60 Board 40 Thtr 100 **Parking** 75 **Notes** ⊗ Closed 23-30 Dec Civ Wed 75

Premier Inn Maidstone (A26/Wateringbury)
BUDGET HOTEL

tel: 0871 527 8706 (Calls cost 13p per minute plus your phone company's access charge)
103 Tonbridge Rd, Wateringbury ME18 5NS
web: www.premierinn.com
dir: M25 junct 3 onto M20. Exit at junct 4 onto A228 towards West Malling. A26 towards Maidstone, approx 3m

High quality, budget accommodation ideal for both families and business travellers. Spacious, en suite bedrooms feature tea and coffee making facilities, and Freeview TV in most hotels. Internet access and WiFi are available for a small fee. The adjacent family restaurant features a wide and varied menu. See also the Hotel Groups pages.

Rooms 39

Premier Inn Maidstone (Allington)
BUDGET HOTEL

tel: 0871 527 8698 (Calls cost 13p per minute plus your phone company's access charge)
London Rd ME16 0HG
web: www.premierinn.com
dir: M20 junct 5, 0.5m on London Rd towards Maidstone

Rooms 65

Premier Inn Maidstone (Leybourne)
BUDGET HOTEL

tel: 0871 527 8702 (Calls cost 13p per minute plus your phone company's access charge)
Castle Way, Leybourne, West Malling ME19 5TR
web: www.premierinn.com
dir: M20 junct 4, A228, hotel on left

Rooms 40

Premier Inn Maidstone (Sandling)
BUDGET HOTEL

tel: 0871 527 8704 (Calls cost 13p per minute plus your phone company's access charge)
Allington Lock, Sandling ME14 3AS
web: www.premierinn.com
dir: M20 junct 6, follow Museum of Kent Life signs

Rooms 40

Premier Inn Maidstone Town Centre
BUDGET HOTEL

tel: 0871 527 9392 (Calls cost 13p per minute plus your phone company's access charge)
5-11 London Rd ME16 8HR
web: www.premierinn.com
dir: M20 junct 5, A20 signed Maidstone (West) & Aylesford. At next rdbt 1st exit (Maidstone). Straight on at next rdbt

Rooms 99

M

MALMESBURY Wiltshire   Map 4 ST98

Whatley Manor Hotel and Spa

★★★★★ ◉◉◉◉ ☕ HOTEL

tel: 01666 822888 **Easton Grey SN16 0RB**
email: reservations@whatleymanor.com **web:** www.whatleymanor.com
dir: *M4 junct 17, follow signs to Malmesbury, continue over 2 rdbts. Follow B4040 & signs for Sherston, hotel 2m on left*

Sitting in 12 acres of beautiful countryside, this impressive country house provides the most luxurious surroundings. Spacious bedrooms, most with views over the attractive gardens, are individually decorated with splendid features such as Bang & Olufsen sound and vision systems, and unique works of art. Several eating options are available: Le Mazot, a Swiss-style brasserie; The Dining Room that serves classical French cuisine with a contemporary twist, via a choice of tasting menus; plus the Kitchen Garden Terrace for alfresco breakfasts, lunches and dinners. Guests might even like to take a hamper and a picnic rug and find a quiet spot in the grounds. The old Loggia Barn is ideal for wedding ceremonies, and the Aquarius Spa is magnificent.

Rooms 23 (4 GF) 🛏 **D** £335-£915 (incl. bkfst)* **Facilities** Spa STV FTV WiFi ◟ Fishing Gym Cinema Hydro pool (indoor/outdoor) Xmas New Year **Conf** Class 20 Board 24 Thtr 60 Del from £325 to £355* **Services** Lift **Parking** 100 **Notes** LB No children 12yrs Closed 1st wk of Jan Civ Wed 100

Best Western Mayfield House Hotel

★★★ 75% HOTEL

tel: 01666 577409 **Crudwell SN16 9EW**
email: reception@mayfieldhousehotel.co.uk **web:** www.mayfieldhousehotel.co.uk
dir: *M4 junct 17, A429 to Cirencester. 2m N of Malmesbury on left in Crudwell village*

This popular hotel is in an ideal location for exploring the many attractions that Wiltshire and The Cotswolds have to offer. Bedrooms come in a range of shapes and sizes, and include some on the ground-floor level in a cottage adjacent to the main building. In addition to outdoor seating, guests can relax with a drink in the comfortable lounge area, where orders are taken for the carefully prepared dinner to follow.

Rooms 28 (8 annexe) (4 fmly) (8 GF) 🛏 **Facilities** FTV WiFi ◟ ☃ Xmas New Year **Conf** Class 30 Board 25 Thtr 40 **Parking** 50 **Notes** LB

MALTON North Yorkshire   Map 19 SE77

The Talbot Hotel

★★★★ 82% ◉◉ HOTEL

tel: 01653 639096 **Yorkersgate YO17 7AJ**
email: info@talbotmalton.co.uk **web:** www.talbotmalton.co.uk
dir: *From York take A64, exit at Malton sign. Hotel on right*

This hotel is owned by the Fitzwilliam Estate and is set in its own beautifully landscaped grounds close to the historic market town. The interior features individually decorated bedrooms, including two luxurious suites. Each of the guest rooms has its own distinct personality. The restaurant has elegant furniture, crisp white linen and fine silver cutlery, while the Brasserie offers a more relaxed setting. Elegant public areas can be found throughout this stunning hotel.

Rooms 26 (3 GF) 🛏 **S** £145-£325; **D** £145-£325 (incl. bkfst)* **Facilities** FTV WiFi HL Xmas New Year **Conf** Class 30 Board 24 Thtr 60 Del from £195* **Parking** 35 **Notes** Civ Wed 60

MALVERN Worcestershire   Map 10 SO74

The Malvern

★★★★ 74% ◉ HOTEL

tel: 01684 898290 **Grovewood Rd WR14 1GD**
email: enquiries@themalvernspa.com **web:** www.themalvernspa.com
dir: *A4440 to Malvern. Over 2 rdbts, at 3rd rdbt turn left. 6m, left at rdbt, over 1st rdbt, hotel on right*

This modern, friendly hotel is set on the outskirts of the famous spa town. The bedrooms are contemporary with sumptuous beds, and many guest extras are provided; the bathrooms have quality fixtures and fittings. There is a brasserie restaurant which offers quality seasonal menus that include healthy options and vegetarian dishes. The Malvern Spa, designed exclusively for adults, includes a hydrotherapy pool which goes from inside to outside, heat experiences, a range of saunas, crystal steam room, salt grotto, and adventure showers, along with a host of treatments. There is also a 50-station gym with state-of-the-art equipment. There is ample parking around the hotel.

Rooms 33 🛏 **S** £113-£163; **D** £122-£172 (incl. bkfst)* **Facilities** Spa FTV WiFi ◟ ⊕ ☃ Gym Exercise classes Xmas New Year **Services** Lift Air con **Parking** 82 **Notes** LB ⊗ No children 18yrs

The Abbey Hotel

★★★★ 74% HOTEL

SAROVA HOTELS

tel: 01684 892332 & 897897 **Abbey Rd WR14 3ET**
email: abbey@sarova.co.uk **web:** www.sarova.com
dir: *In Great Malvern town centre, opposite theatres*

This large, impressive, ivy-clad hotel stands in the centre of Great Malvern, at the foot of the Malvern Hills, next to the Abbey and close to the theatre. It provides well-equipped modern accommodation equally suitable for business guests and tourists. Facilities include a good range of function rooms making the hotel a popular venue for meetings and events.

Rooms 103 (11 fmly) (23 GF) **S** £100-£195; **D** £110-£205 (incl. bkfst)* **Facilities** STV FTV WiFi ⊳ Xmas New Year **Conf** Class 120 Board 40 Thtr 300 Del from £195* **Services** Lift **Parking** 85 **Notes** LB Civ Wed 300

The Cottage in the Wood

★★★ 82% ⑳⑳ HOTEL

tel: 01684 588860 **Holywell Rd, Malvern Wells WR14 4LG**
email: reception@cottageinthewood.co.uk **web:** www.cottageinthewood.co.uk
dir: *On Ledbury side of Great Malvern on A449 Worcester - Ledbury road*

Set high on the hillside with stunning, far reaching views across the Worcestershire countryside, The Cottage in The Wood offers traditional rooms in the main house, as well as more cosy rooms in Beech Cottage. Also on offer is The Pinnacles; of the three this is the most recent addition and has larger room sizes and semi-private terraces or balconies. The main house has a very well-stocked bar, a cosy fire in winter and a large terrace which is ideal for sunny days. Dinner is not to be missed and involves innovative dishes utilising produce from within the three counties where possible.

Rooms 30 (23 annexe) (10 GF) ✿ **Facilities** FTV WiFi ⊳ HL Xmas New Year **Conf** Class 14 Board 14 Thtr 20 **Parking** 45

The Cotford Hotel & L'Amuse Bouche Restaurant

★★★ 81% ⑳⑳ HOTEL

tel: 01684 572427 **51 Graham Rd WR14 2HU**
email: reservations@cotfordhotel.co.uk **web:** www.cotfordhotel.co.uk
dir: *From Worcester follow signs to Malvern on A449. Left into Graham Rd signed town centre, hotel on right*

This delightful house, built in 1851, reputedly for the Bishop of Worcester, stands in attractive gardens with stunning views of The Malverns. Bedrooms have been authentically renovated, retaining many of the original features and with a good selection of welcome extras. Food, service and hospitality are all major strengths.

The Cotford Hotel & L'Amuse Bouche Restaurant

Rooms 15 (3 fmly) (1 GF) ✿ **S** £69.50-£89; **D** £130-£145 (incl. bkfst)* **Facilities** STV FTV WiFi ⊳ 🍴 **Conf** Class 26 Board 12 Thtr 26 **Parking** 15 **Notes** LB

See advert on page 298

Mount Pleasant Hotel

★★★ 72% HOTEL

tel: 01684 561837 **Belle Vue Ter WR14 4PZ**
email: reception@mountpleasanthotel.co.uk **web:** www.mountpleasanthotel.co.uk
dir: *On A449, in town centre opposite Priory Church*

Mount Pleasant is an attractive Georgian house in the town centre that occupies an elevated position, and overlooks Priory Church and the picturesque Severn Plain. It is family-run, with a relaxed atmosphere; offers spacious, fully equipped bedrooms, and the Spring Bar and Restaurant that serves home-made classic British cuisine as well as tea, coffee, cakes and biscuits. In winter guests can sit beside real log fires, and in warmer months the garden makes a delightful place to relax.

Rooms 14 (1 fmly) ✿ **Facilities** FTV WiFi Xmas New Year **Conf** Class 40 Board 50 Thtr 90 **Parking** 20 **Notes** ⊗

Holdfast Cottage Hotel

★★ 82% HOTEL

tel: 01684 310288 **Marlbank Rd, Welland WR13 6NA**
email: enquiries@holdfast-cottage.co.uk **web:** www.holdfast-cottage.co.uk
dir: *M50 junct 1, follow Upton Three Counties/A38 signs, onto A4104 to Welland*

At the base of the Malvern Hills this delightful wisteria-covered hotel sits in attractive manicured grounds. Charming public areas include an intimate bar, a log fire-enhanced lounge and an elegant dining room. Bedrooms vary in size but all are comfortable and well appointed. Fresh local and seasonal produce are the basis for the cuisine.

Rooms 8 (1 fmly) **S** £60; **D** £80-£99 (incl. bkfst)* **Facilities** FTV WiFi ⊳ Xmas New Year **Parking** 16 **Notes** LB ⊗ Civ Wed 50

M

MALVERN continued

The Great Malvern Hotel

★★ 76% HOTEL

tel: 01684 563411 **Graham Rd WR14 2HN**
email: sutton@great-malvern-hotel.co.uk **web:** www.great-malvern-hotel.co.uk
dir: *From Worcester on A449, left after fire station into Graham Rd. Hotel at end on right*

Close to the town centre this privately owned and managed hotel is ideally situated for many of Malvern's attractions. The accommodation is spacious and well equipped. Public areas include quiet lounge areas, and a cosy bar which is popular with locals.

Rooms 13 (1 fmly) **S** £60-£75; **D** £80-£100 (incl. bkfst)* **Facilities** STV FTV WiFi ♘ 🎵 **Conf** Class 20 Board 20 Thtr 20 **Services** Lift **Parking** 9

Premier Inn Malvern

BUDGET HOTEL

tel: 0871 527 9406 *(Calls cost 13p per minute plus your phone company's access charge)*
Townsend Way WR14 1GD
web: www.premierinn.com
dir: *M5 junct 7, A44 (1st exit from S; 3rd exit from N). At rdbt 1st exit onto A440. 1st exit at 3rd rdbt onto A449 (Malvern Rd). At next rdbt 1st exit into Townsend Way (B4208). At next rdbt 2nd exit into Grove Wood Rd*

High quality, budget accommodation ideal for both families and business travellers. Spacious, en suite bedrooms feature tea and coffee making facilities, and Freeview TV in most hotels. Internet access and WiFi are available for a small fee. The adjacent family restaurant features a wide and varied menu. See also the Hotel Groups pages.

Rooms 66

See also **Manchester Airport & Sale**

Hotel Gotham

★★★★★ 84% 🏵🏵 HOTEL

tel: 0161 4130000 **100 King St M2 4WU**
email: reservations@hotelgotham.co.uk **web:** www.bespokehotels.com/hotelgotham

A new addition to the Manchester scene, Hotel Gotham is a beautifully renovated former bank designed by Edwin Lutyens, with Art decor themes throughout. The Brass Club is a popular cocktail bar with balcony's overlooking the city and Honey, the hotel's restaurant offers guests innovative cooking. Bedrooms and bathrooms are spacious, stylish and there are subtle references to the hotels former life everywhere.

Rooms 60 (8 fmly) ⟋ **S** £145-£1000; **D** £155-£1000 (incl. bkfst)* **Facilities** WiFi ♘ 🎵 Xmas New Year **Conf** Class 14 Board 14 Thtr 20 Del from £225 to £450* **Services** Lift Air con **Parking** 40 **Notes** LB

The Lowry Hotel

★★★★★ 83% HOTEL

tel: 0161 827 4000 **50 Dearmans Place, Chapel Wharf, Salford M3 5LH**
email: enquiries@thelowryhotel.com **web:** www.thelowryhotel.com
dir: *M6 junct 19, A556/M56/A5103 for 4.5m. At rdbt take A57(M) to lights, right onto Water St. Left to New Quay St/Trinity Way. At 1st lights right into Chapel St for hotel*

This modern, contemporary hotel, set beside the River Irwell in the centre of the city, offers spacious bedrooms equipped to meet the needs of business and leisure visitors alike. Many of the rooms look out over the river, as do the sumptuous suites. The River Room restaurant produces good brasserie cooking. Extensive business and function facilities are available, together with a spa to provide extra pampering.

Rooms 165 ⟋ **S** £119-£699; **D** £119-£699* **Facilities** Spa STV FTV WiFi ♘ Gym Sauna Relaxation rooms 🎵 Xmas New Year **Conf** Class 250 Board 38 Thtr 400 **Services** Lift Air con **Parking** 88 **Notes** LB Civ Wed 200

M

HIGHLY RECOMMENDED

The Midland

★★★★ 86% ❀❀❀❀ HOTEL

tel: 0161 236 3333 **Peter St M60 2DS**
email: midlandsales@qhotels.co.uk **web:** www.qhotels.co.uk
dir: *M602 junct 3, follow Manchester Central Convention Complex signs, hotel opposite*

This much-loved, centrally located, well-established Edwardian-style hotel (Grade II listed) offers stylish, thoughtfully equipped bedrooms that have a contemporary feel. Elegant public areas are equally impressive and facilities include extensive function and meeting rooms. Eating options include the Octogan Lounge and the award-winning classical French restaurant, the Wyvern.

Rooms 312 (13 fmly) ➮ **S** £139-£599; **D** £139-£599 **Facilities** Spa STV FTV WiFi ⬇ HL ⌚ Gym Hair & beauty salon ♫ **Conf** Class 300 Board 120 Thtr 600 **Del** from £179 to £239* **Services** Lift Air con **Notes** ⊗ Civ Wed 600

ABode Manchester

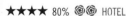

★★★★ 80% ❀❀ HOTEL

tel: 0161 247 7744 **107 Piccadilly M1 2DB**
email: gm@abodemanchester.co.uk **web:** www.abodemanchester.co.uk
dir: *M62/M602 follow signs for city centre/Piccadilly*

Located in the heart of Piccadilly, this Grade II listed former wholesale textile warehouse has embraced its industrial heritage. Exposed steel beams and structural iron columns together with an ornate wrought iron and walnut staircase are striking features. Beds are low and comfortable, while feature walls, a tuck box filled with regional food and drink, and complimentary WiFi can be found in all rooms. A choice of dining options includes a fine-dining restaurant, Café Bow for more relaxed informal dining, and a Champagne bar in the basement.

Rooms 61 **Facilities** STV WiFi ⬇ Xmas New Year **Conf** Class 16 Board 26 Thtr 30 **Services** Lift Air con **Notes** ⊗ RS 25 Dec-2 Jan

Macdonald Manchester Hotel

★★★★ 79% ◉ HOTEL

tel: 0161 272 3200 & 0344 879 9088 **London Rd M1 2PG**
email: general.manchester@macdonald-hotels.co.uk **web:** www.macdonaldhotels.co.uk
dir: *Opposite Piccadilly Station*

Ideally situated just a short walk from Piccadilly Station, this hotel provides a handy location for both business and leisure travellers. Stylish, modern rooms have plasma TVs and iPod docking stations, and the bathrooms offer walk-in power showers and luxury baths. The first-floor restaurant serves skilfully prepared dinners and hearty breakfasts. Staff throughout are cheerful and keen to please.

Rooms 338 (14 fmly) ➮ **Facilities** Spa FTV WiFi ⬇ HL Gym Sauna New Year **Conf** Class 150 Board 80 Thtr 250 **Services** Lift Air con **Parking** 85 **Notes** ⊗ Civ Wed 200

Holiday Inn Manchester - MediaCityUK

★★★★ 76% HOTEL

tel: 0161 813 1040 **Media City UK, Salford M50 2HT**
web: www.holidayinn.com/mediacity
dir: *M602 junct 2 onto A576 to Salford Quays signed MediaCityUK*

Located in the heart of the exciting media district on Salford Quays, this hotel is adjacent to the main production studios and only minutes from Old Trafford and The Lowry Centre. The stylish Hub Bar features TV-themed murals. Food is served from Marco Pierre Whites' New York Italian on the mezzanine floor. Bedrooms are well equipped with safes and mini-bars, and many have views of the Manchester Shipping Canal. There's complimentary WiFi throughout, and a mini-gym is available to guests.

Rooms 218 (10 fmly) ➮ **S** £99-£169; **D** £99-£169* **Facilities** STV FTV WiFi ⬇ HL Gym Xmas New Year **Conf** Class 25 Board 30 Thtr 44 Del from £135 to £185* **Services** Lift Air con **Parking** 5000 **Notes** LB Civ Wed 70

Novotel Manchester Centre

★★★★ 76% HOTEL

tel: 0161 235 2200 **21 Dickinson St M1 4LX**
email: H3145@accor.com **web:** www.novotel.com
dir: *From Oxford St into Portland St, left into Dickinson St. Hotel on right*

This smart, modern property enjoys a central location convenient for theatres, shops, China Town and Manchester's business district. Spacious bedrooms are thoughtfully equipped and brightly decorated. Open-plan, contemporary public areas include an all-day restaurant and a stylish bar. Extensive conference and meeting facilities are available.

Rooms 164 (15 fmly) ➮ **Facilities** STV FTV WiFi ⬇ HL Gym Steam room Sauna Aromatherapy **Conf** Class 50 Board 36 Thtr 90 Del from £119 to £199* **Services** Lift Air con

Hotel Football

★★★★ 75% HOTEL

tel: 0161 751 0430 **99 Sir Matt Busby Way M16 0SZ**
email: info@hotelfootball.com **web:** www.hotelfootball.com
dir: *Follow A56 unitl Sir Matt Busby Way. Hotel opposite Manchester Utd football stadium*

Hotel Football is a stylish contemporary hotel offering comfortable accommodation with relaxed and friendly service. All day dining is available in Café Football where dishes are themed around footballers, managers and match day treats. The hotel also offers a gym and five-a-side football pitch on the top floor.

Rooms 133 ➮ **Facilities** STV FTV WiFi ⬇ HL Gym ♫ Xmas New Year **Conf** Class 250 Board 40 Thtr 350 **Services** Lift Air con **Notes** ⊗ Civ Wed 300

MANCHESTER *continued*

Malmaison Manchester

★★★★ 74% ⓦ HOTEL

tel: 0161 278 1000 & 0844 693 0657
(Calls cost 5p per minute plus your phone company's access charge) **Piccadilly M1 3AQ**
email: manchester@malmaison.com **web:** www.malmaison.com
dir: *Follow city centre signs, then signs to Piccadilly station. Hotel at bottom of station approach*

Stylish and chic, Malmaison Manchester offers the best of contemporary hotel-keeping in a relaxed and comfortable environment. Converted from a former warehouse, it offers a range of bright meeting rooms, a gym and treatment rooms. The Smoak Bar & Grill is impressive and understandably popular. Air-conditioned suites combine comfort with stunning design. Expect the unusual in some of the rooms, for instance the Cinema Suites have a private screening room with 52" screen and surround-sound.

Rooms 167 ☈ **Facilities** **Spa** STV WiFi ⅃ HL Gym Sauna Relaxation area Solarium Massage chairs Xmas New Year **Conf** Class 40 Board 30 Thtr 100 **Services** Lift Air con **Notes** Civ Wed 100

Arora Hotel

★★★★ 74% HOTEL

tel: 0161 236 8999 **18-24 Princess St M1 4LG**
email: manchesterreservations@arorahotels.com **web:** www.manchester.arorahotels.com
dir: *Phone for detailed directions*

Conveniently located close to the city centre and ideal for both shopping and Theatres, the Arora provides comfortable accommodation. The hotel also has meeting room facilities, a small gym and a contemporary dining room in 24 Bar and Grill.

Rooms 141 (32 fmly) (15 GF) ☈ **Facilities** FTV WiFi ⅃ Gym **Conf** Class 40 Board 45 Thtr 100 Del from £165 to £195* **Services** Lift Air con **Notes** ⊗ Civ Wed 60

The Palace Hotel

★★★★ 73% HOTEL

tel: 0161 288 1111 **Oxford St M60 7HA**
email: richard.morrell@principal-hayley.com **web:** www.principal-hayley.com
dir: *Opposite Manchester Oxford Road rail station*

Formerly the offices of the Refuge Life Assurance Company, this impressive neo-Gothic building occupies a central location. There is a vast lobby, spacious open-plan bar lounge and restaurant, and extensive conference and function facilities. Bedrooms vary in size and style but are all spacious and well equipped.

Rooms 275 (59 fmly) ☈ **Facilities** STV WiFi **Conf** Class 650 Board 200 Thtr 1000 **Services** Lift **Notes** ⊗ Civ Wed 600

Mercure Manchester Piccadilly Hotel

★★★★ 72% HOTEL

tel: 0844 815 9024 *(Calls cost 5p per minute plus your phone company's access charge)*
Portland St M1 4PH
email: info@mercuremanchester.co.uk **web:** www.jupiterhotels.co.uk
dir: *Opposite Piccadilly Gardens*

Overlooking Piccadilly Gardens and views of the city, this hotel is located within the heart of Manchester. Bedrooms and bathrooms are tastefully appointed, with a range of rooms for both leisure and business guests. Contemporary dining can be enjoyed within the Brasserie and popular bar areas. A range of spacious meetings

and events space is also available. Free WiFi across the hotel is a plus. Parking is available.

Rooms 280 ☈ **Facilities** FTV WiFi ⅃ **Conf** Class 320 Board 60 Thtr 800 **Services** Lift Air con **Parking** 80 **Notes** ⊗ Civ Wed 800

Best Western Hallmark Hotel Manchester Willow Bank

★★★ 77% HOTEL

tel: 0330 028 3427 **340-342 Wilmslow Rd, Fallowfield M14 6AF**
email: willowbank@hallmarkhotels.co.uk **web:** www.hallmarkhotels.co.uk
dir: *M60 junct 5, A5103, left onto B5093. Hotel 2.5m on left*

This popular hotel is conveniently located three miles from the city centre, close to the universities. Bedrooms vary in size and style but all are appointed to impressively high standards; they are well equipped and many rooms benefit from CD players and PlayStations. Spacious, elegant public areas include a bar, a restaurant and meeting rooms.

Rooms 116 (4 fmly) **Facilities** FTV WiFi Xmas New Year **Conf** Class 50 Board 60 Thtr 120 **Parking** 100 **Notes** Civ Wed 125

Novotel Manchester West

★★★ 75% HOTEL

tel: 0161 799 3535 **Worsley Brow M28 2YA**
email: H0907@accor.com **web:** www.novotel.com

(For full entry see Worsley)

Chancellors Hotel & Conference Centre

★★★ 72% HOTEL

tel: 0161 907 7414 **Moseley Rd, Fallowfield M14 6NN**
email: chancellors@manchester.ac.uk **web:** www.chancellorshotel.co.uk
dir: *Phone for detailed directions*

A Grade II listed manor house set in five acres of landscaped gardens hidden in the heart of Fallowfield, well located for the city's shopping, business and commercial centres. Bedrooms offer modern facilities and the cuisine is enjoyable. WiFi and secure parking are available.

Rooms 70 (4 fmly) (16 GF) **Facilities** FTV WiFi ⅃ HL **Conf** Class 100 Board 50 Thtr 125 **Services** Lift **Parking** 70 **Notes** LB ⊗ Closed 25 Dec Civ Wed 125

Holiday Inn Express Manchester - Oxford Road

BUDGET HOTEL

tel: 0161 238 6660 **2 Oxford Rd M1 5QA**
email: info@hiemanchester.co.uk **web:** www.hiemanchester.co.uk
dir: *From A57(M) follow signs for Peters Fields & A5103, into Cambridge St. 2nd right into Hulme St, ahead onto Charles St. Opp BBC building*

A modern hotel ideal for families and business travellers. Fresh and uncomplicated, the spacious rooms include power shower and tea and coffee-making facilities. Continental buffet breakfast is included in the room rate; other meals may be taken at the nearby family pub or restaurant. The hotel is within walking distance of The Arndale shopping centre, Manchester Art Gallery, The Palace Theatre and Manchester Metropolitan University. It also has easy access to the Trafford Centre and both the Old Trafford and City of Manchester stadiums. See also the Hotel Groups pages.

Rooms 147

M

Premier Inn Manchester Central

BUDGET HOTEL

tel: 0871 527 8742 *(Calls cost 13p per minute plus your phone company's access charge)*
Bishopsgate, 7-11 Lower Mosley St M2 3DW
web: www.premierinn.com
dir: *M56 to end, A5103 towards city. Right at 2nd lights. At next lights left into Oxford Rd, left at junct of St Peters Sq. Hotel on left*

High quality, budget accommodation ideal for both families and business travellers. Spacious, en suite bedrooms feature tea and coffee making facilities, and Freeview TV in most hotels. Internet access and WiFi are available for a small fee. The adjacent family restaurant features a wide and varied menu. See also the Hotel Groups pages.

Rooms 197

Premier Inn Manchester City Centre (Arena/Printworks)

BUDGET HOTEL

tel: 0871 527 8744 *(Calls cost 13p per minute plus your phone company's access charge)*
North Tower, Victoria Bridge St, Salford M3 5AS
web: www.premierinn.com
dir: *M602 to city centre, A57(M) towards GMEX. 2nd exit follow A56 city centre signs. Left before MEN arena onto A6, 1st left*

Rooms 170

Premier Inn Manchester City Centre (Piccadilly)

BUDGET HOTEL

tel: 0871 527 9390 *(Calls cost 13p per minute plus your phone company's access charge)*
72 Dale St M1 2HR
web: www.premierinn.com
dir: *Phone for detailed directions*

Rooms 193

Premier Inn Manchester City Centre (Portland Street)

BUDGET HOTEL

tel: 0871 527 8746 *(Calls cost 13p per minute plus your phone company's access charge)*
The Circus, 112-114 Portland St M1 4WB
web: www.premierinn.com
dir: *M6 junct 19, A556. M56, exit junct 3 onto A5103 to Medlock St, right into Whitworth St, left into Oxford St, right into Portland St*

Rooms 232

Premier Inn Manchester (Deansgate Locks)

BUDGET HOTEL

tel: 0871 527 8740 *(Calls cost 13p per minute plus your phone company's access charge)*
Medlock St M15 5FJ
web: www.premierinn.com
dir: *M60 junct 24, A57(M) (Mancunian Way) towards city centre. Hotel adjacent, on A5103 Medlock St*

Rooms 199

Premier Inn Manchester (Denton)

BUDGET HOTEL

tel: 0871 527 8708 *(Calls cost 13p per minute plus your phone company's access charge)*
Alphagate Dr, Manchester Rd South, Denton M34 3SH
web: www.premierinn.com
dir: *M60 junct 24, A57 signed Denton. 1st right at lights, right at next lights, hotel on left*

Rooms 58

Premier Inn Manchester (Heaton Park)

BUDGET HOTEL

tel: 0871 527 8710 *(Calls cost 13p per minute plus your phone company's access charge)*
Middleton Rd, Crumpsall M8 4NB
web: www.premierinn.com
dir: *M60 junct 19, A576 towards Manchester, through 2 sets of lights. Hotel on left*

Rooms 45

Premier Inn Manchester Old Trafford

BUDGET HOTEL

tel: 0871 527 8750 *(Calls cost 13p per minute plus your phone company's access charge)*
Waters Reach, Trafford Park M17 1WS
web: www.premierinn.com
dir: *M6 junct 19, A556 towards Altrincham. Follow Stretford & Manchester City Centre signs (road becomes A56). Follow Manchester United Football Stadium signs. At stadium left at lights. Into Sir Matt Busby Way, after 1st lights hotel on right*

Rooms 172

Premier Inn Manchester (Salford Quays)

BUDGET HOTEL

tel: 0871 527 8718 *(Calls cost 13p per minute plus your phone company's access charge)*
11 The Quays, Salford Quays, Salford M50 3SQ
web: www.premierinn.com
dir: *M602 junct 3, A5063, on Salford Quays*

Rooms 80

Premier Inn Manchester Trafford Centre North

BUDGET HOTEL

tel: 0871 527 8752 *(Calls cost 13p per minute plus your phone company's access charge)*
18-20 Trafford Boulevard, Urmston M41 7JE
web: www.premierinn.com
dir: *M6, onto M62 at junct 21a, towards Manchester. M62 junct 1, M60 towards south. M60 junct 10, take B5214. Hotel on left just before Ellesmere Circle*

Rooms 62

Premier Inn Manchester Trafford Centre South

BUDGET HOTEL

tel: 0871 527 8754 *(Calls cost 13p per minute plus your phone company's access charge)*
Wilderspool Wood, Trafford Centre M17 8WW
web: www.premierinn.com
dir: *M6 onto M62 junct 21a towards Manchester. Or M62 junct 1 onto M60 S. Or M60 junct 10, B5124 towards Trafford Park. At 1st rdbt take last exit for Trafford Centre parking. At 2nd rdbt straight on. Hotel on left*

Rooms 60

MANCHESTER *continued*

Premier Inn Manchester Trafford Centre West

BUDGET HOTEL

tel: 0871 527 8756 *(Calls cost 13p per minute plus your phone company's access charge)*
Old Park Ln M17 8PG
web: www.premierinn.com
dir: *M60 junct 10 towards The Trafford Centre*

Rooms 234

Premier Inn Manchester (West Didsbury)

BUDGET HOTEL

tel: 0871 527 8722 *(Calls cost 13p per minute plus your phone company's access charge)*
Christies Field Office Park, Derwent Ave, Didsbury M21 7QS
web: www.premierinn.com
dir: *M60 junct 5, A5103 (Princess Parkway) towards Manchester on A5103. Hotel approx 1m*

Rooms 81

Ibis Budget Manchester Centre Pollard Street

AA Advertised

tel: 0161 272 2020 **2 Pollard St M4 7DB**
email: H6943@accor.com **web:** www.ibishotel.com
dir: *From S & W: Follow A57(M)/A635/A665. Right onto A662/Pollard St. From E: Follow A57, right onto A6010/Pottery Lane, then left onto A662*

Modern, budget hotel offering comfortable accommodation in bright and practical bedrooms. Breakfast is self-service and dinner is available in the restaurant.

Rooms 150 (150 fmly) **Facilities** FTV WiFi **Services** Lift

Ibis Budget Manchester Salford Quays

AA Advertised

tel: 0161 848 0898 **19 Trafford Rd, Salford M5 3AW**
email: H6003@accor.com **web:** www.ibis.com
dir: *M60 junct 12 onto M602. At junct 3 follow A5063 Salford Quays onto Trafford Road. Hotel within 100mtrs of Salford Quays metro stop. From M56 take A5013 Manchester, join M60 toward Stretford until junct 12, follow as above*

Modern, budget hotel offering comfortable accommodation in bright and practical bedrooms. Breakfast is self-service and dinner is available in the restaurant.

Rooms 210 (210 fmly) **S** £33-£159; **D** £33-£159* **Facilities** FTV WiFi **Services** Lift **Parking** 40

Ibis Manchester Centre Portland Street

AA Advertised

tel: 0161 619 9000 **96 Portland St M1 4JY**
email: H3142@accor.com **web:** www.ibishotel.com
dir: *In city centre, between Princess St & Oxford St*

Modern, budget hotel offering comfortable accommodation in bright and practical bedrooms. Breakfast is self-service and dinner is available in the restaurant.

Rooms 127 (16 fmly) **Facilities** FTV WiFi HL **Services** Lift

Ibis Manchester Centre Princess Street

AA Advertised

tel: 0161 272 5000 **Charles St, Princess St M1 7DL**
email: H3143@accor.com **web:** www.ibishotel.com
dir: *M62, M602 towards Manchester Centre, follow signs for UMIST/A34*

Modern, budget hotel offering comfortable accommodation in bright and practical bedrooms. Breakfast is self-service and dinner is available in the restaurant.

Rooms 126 **Facilities** STV FTV WiFi HL **Services** Lift

MANCHESTER AIRPORT	Map 15 SJ88
Greater Manchester	

See also **Altrincham**

The Stanneylands

★★★★ 78% ◉◉ HOTEL

tel: 01625 525225 **Stanneylands Rd SK9 4EY**
email: reservations@stanneylands.co.uk **web:** www.stanneylandshotel.co.uk
dir: *From M56 at airport exit, follow signs to Wilmslow. Left towards Handforth. Left at lights into Stanneylands Rd, hotel on left*

This traditional country house hotel, just three miles from Manchester Airport, offers well-equipped bedrooms that include suites, prestige and executive rooms together with delightful, comfortable day rooms. The cuisine in the restaurant is of a high standard, and ranges from traditional favourites to more imaginative modern dishes. There is also the contemporary Calico café bar in a conservatory setting offering all-day menus, including afternoon tea, and live music played on the baby grand piano. The hotel makes an ideal wedding venue, and the staff throughout are friendly and obliging.

Rooms 55 (2 fmly) (10 GF) **S** £70-£120; **D** £70-£120* **Facilities** STV FTV WiFi Beauty treatment room ♫ Xmas New Year **Conf** Class 50 Board 40 Thtr 120 Del from £130 to £165* **Services** Lift **Parking** 108 **Notes** LB ⊗ Civ Wed 100

Best Western Plus Pinewood on Wilmslow

★★★★ 77% ◉ HOTEL

tel: 01625 529211 **180 Wilmslow Rd SK9 3LF**
email: pinewood.res@pinewood-hotel.co.uk **web:** www.pinewood-hotel.co.uk
dir: *Phone for detailed directions*

This stylish hotel is conveniently situated for the M60, Trafford Park, Trafford Centre and Manchester Airport. Bedrooms provide very good quality accommodation; many have now been totally refurbished and all come with WiFi. New modern public areas and Brasserie are a real delight and are open every night with a choice of menu. Ample car parking is available.

Rooms 89 (3 fmly) **Facilities** FTV WiFi HL Use of nearby Total Fitness Club Xmas New Year **Conf** Class 60 Board 60 Thtr 120 **Services** Lift **Parking** 120 **Notes** ⊗ Civ Wed 120

Hallmark Hotel Manchester Airport

★★★★ 77% HOTEL

tel: 0330 028 3419 **Stanley Rd SK9 3LD**
email: manchester@hallmarkhotels.co.uk **web:** www.hallmarkhotels.co.uk
dir: *M60 junct 3/A34 signed Cheadle/Wilmslow. Right at 3rd rdbt into Stanley Rd (B5094). Hotel on left*

Ideally located for Manchester Airport and just a few miles from both the Trafford Centre and the city's many shops, the Hallmark Hotel offers well appointed bedrooms. Guests can relax and unwind in the hotel's 20-metre pool, jacuzzi and steam rooms. The brasserie is open for both lunch and dinner, and offers a range of international dishes.

Rooms 88 (12 fmly) (12 GF) **Facilities** Spa FTV WiFi ↕ 🔧 Gym Steam room Sauna Hair salon New Year **Conf** Class 250 Board 60 Thtr 500 **Services** Lift **Notes** ⊗ Civ Wed 300

Crowne Plaza Manchester Airport

★★★★ 75% HOTEL

CROWNE PLAZA
HOTELS & RESORTS

tel: 0871 942 9055 *(Calls cost 10p per minute plus your phone company's access charge)*
Ringway Rd M90 3NS
email: reservations@cpmanchesterairport.co.uk
web: www.cpmanchesterairporthotel.co.uk
dir: *M56 junct 5 signed Manchester Airport. At airport, follow signs to Terminal 1 & 3. Hotel adjacent to Terminal 3. Long stay car park on left*

Located by Terminal 3 this smart, modern hotel offers well-equipped, comfortable bedrooms, all with air-conditioning and effective double-glazing. A choice of dining options and bars is available, and the hotel has spacious leisure facilities and ample on-site parking. The hospitality is friendly, with several long-serving staff members who greet regular customers as friends.

Rooms 299 (35 fmly) (53 GF) **Facilities** STV WiFi ↕ HL Gym Saunas **Conf** Class 25 Board 20 Thtr 30 **Services** Lift Air con **Parking** 300 **Notes** ⊗

Premier Inn Manchester Airport Hotel (M56 Jct 6 South)

BUDGET HOTEL

tel: 0871 527 8726 *(Calls cost 13p per minute plus your phone company's access charge)*
Runger Ln, Wilmslow Rd M90 5DL
web: www.premierinn.com
dir: *M56 junct 6, follow Wilmslow & Hale signs. Merge onto M56 signed Warrington, Macclesfield & Hale. Left into Runger Ln signed Freight Terminal*

High quality, budget accommodation ideal for both families and business travellers. Spacious, en suite bedrooms feature tea and coffee making facilities, and Freeview TV in most hotels. Internet access and WiFi are available for a small fee. The adjacent family restaurant features a wide and varied menu. See also the Hotel Groups pages.

Rooms 195

Premier Inn Manchester Airport (M56 Jct 6) Runger Lane North

BUDGET HOTEL

tel: 0871 527 8730 *(Calls cost 13p per minute plus your phone company's access charge)*
Runger Ln, Wilmslow Rd M90 5DL
web: www.premierinn.com
dir: *M56 junct 6, follow Airport signs. 2nd exit at rdbt. Hotel on left. Through Travelodge car park. Hotel on right*

Rooms 165

Premier Inn Manchester (Handforth)

BUDGET HOTEL

tel: 0871 527 8732 *(Calls cost 13p per minute plus your phone company's access charge)*
30 Wilmslow Rd SK9 3EW
web: www.premierinn.com
dir: *M56 junct 6, A538 towards Wilmslow. At main junct into town centre bear left. In 2m hotel at top of hill on right just after Wilmslow Garden Centre*

Rooms 35

Premier Inn Manchester (Wilmslow)

BUDGET HOTEL

tel: 0871 527 8736 *(Calls cost 13p per minute plus your phone company's access charge)*
Racecourse Rd, Wilmslow SK9 5LR
web: www.premierinn.com
dir: *M6 junct 19 to Knutsford, follow Wilmslow signs. Left at 1st & 2nd lights towards Wilmslow. Through Mobberley, left just before Bird in Hand pub. At T-junct, right. Hotel 150yds on right*

Rooms 37

MARAZION	Map 2 SW53
Cornwall	

Mount Haven Hotel & Restaurant

★★★ 85% ⑳⑳ HOTEL

tel: 01736 710249 **Turnpike Rd TR17 0DQ**
email: reception@mounthaven.co.uk **web:** www.mounthaven.co.uk
dir: *From A30 towards Penzance. At rdbt take exit for Helston onto A394. Next rdbt right into Marazion, hotel on left*

This hotel enjoys spectacular views across the sea towards St Michaels Mount. All rooms have spacious balconies from where the views can be enjoyed - sunrises and sunsets can be spectacular. Bedrooms are contemporarily styled and have comfortable beds and exotic fabrics. Dining is a highlight with the freshest local seafood and fish used to create interesting menus. A range of holistic therapies is available, and the attentive and friendly service helps make a relaxing and enchanting environment throughout.

Rooms 18 (1 fmly) (6 GF) 🐾 **S** £90–£210; **D** £130–£240 (incl. bkfst)* **Facilities** FTV WiFi ↕ Aromatherapy Reflexology Massage Reiki Hot rocks Beauty treatment room **Parking** 32 **Notes** Closed 18 Dec-8 Feb

MARGATE	Map 7 TR37
Kent	

Sands Hotel

★★★★ 78% ⑳⑳ TOWN HOUSE HOTEL

tel: 01843 228228 **16 Marine Dr CT9 1DH**
email: info@sandshotelmargate.co.uk **web:** www.sandshotelmargate.co.uk
dir: *From London M2, A299 to A28 to Margate*

Located in the centre of Margate, The Sands Hotel benefits from uninterrupted sea views. The Bay Restaurant and Bar which is open for breakfast, lunch, afternoon tea and dinner also has great views, and hotel guests can enjoy the private roof terrace at the very top of the hotel. Bedrooms and bathrooms are all contemporary in style having all been completely refurbished within the last few years, and many benefit from having their own private balconies.

Rooms 20 (6 fmly) 🐾 **Facilities** STV FTV WiFi ↕ HL 🎵 Xmas New Year **Conf** Class 55 Board 30 Thtr 80 Del from £175 to £240* **Services** Lift Air con **Notes** ⊗ Civ Wed 80

Premier Inn Margate

BUDGET HOTEL

tel: 0871 527 8762 *(Calls cost 13p per minute plus your phone company's access charge)*
Station Green, Station Rd CT9 5AF
web: www.premierinn.com
dir: *M2, A299, A28 to Margate seafront. Hotel adjacent to Margate station*

High quality, budget accommodation ideal for both families and business travellers. Spacious, en suite bedrooms feature tea and coffee making facilities, and Freeview TV in most hotels. Internet access and WiFi are available for a small fee. The adjacent family restaurant features a wide and varied menu. See also the Hotel Groups pages.

Rooms 64

M

M

MARKET DRAYTON
Shropshire   Map 15 SJ63

INSPECTORS' CHOICE

Goldstone Hall
★★★ ◉◉ HOTEL

tel: 01630 661202 **Goldstone Rd TF9 2NA**
email: enquiries@goldstonehall.com **web:** www.goldstonehall.com
dir: *4m S of Market Drayton, 4m N of Newport. Hotel signed from A529 & A41*

Situated in extensive grounds, this sympathetically refurbished period property is a family-run hotel. It provides traditionally furnished, well-equipped accommodation with outstanding en suite bathrooms and lots of thoughtful extras. Public rooms are extensive and include a choice of lounges, a snooker room and a conservatory. The kitchen has a well deserved reputation for good food that utilises home-grown produce, and a warm welcome is assured.

Rooms 12 (2 GF) ⌁ **S** £90-£115; **D** £150-£180 (incl. bkfst)* **Facilities** STV FTV WiFi ⌁ ✿ Snooker table New Year **Conf** Class 30 Board 30 Thtr 50 Del from £160* **Parking** 60 **Notes** LB ⊗ Civ Wed 100

MARKET HARBOROUGH
Leicestershire   Map 11 SP78

Three Swans Hotel
★★★ 80% HOTEL

tel: 01858 466644 **21 High St LE16 7NJ**
email: threeswans@innmail.co.uk **web:** www.threeswans.co.uk
dir: *M1 junct 20, A304 to Market Harborough. Through town centre on A6 from Leicester, hotel on right*

Public areas in this former coaching inn include an elegant fine dining restaurant and cocktail bar, a smart foyer lounge and popular public bar areas. Bedroom styles and sizes vary, but are very well appointed and equipped. Those in the wing are particularly impressive, offering high quality and spacious accommodation.

Rooms 59 (46 annexe) (10 fmly) (20 GF) ⌁ **S** £89-£139; **D** £109-£149*
Facilities STV FTV WiFi ⌁ Xmas New Year **Conf** Class 90 Board 50 Thtr 250 Del from £145 to £165* **Services** Lift **Parking** 70 **Notes** Civ Wed 140

Premier Inn Market Harborough
BUDGET HOTEL

tel: 0871 527 8764 *(Calls cost 13p per minute plus your phone company's access charge)*
Melton Rd, East Langton LE16 7TG
web: www.premierinn.com
dir: *On A6, N of Market Harborough. Hotel on rdbt junct of A6 & B6047*

High quality, budget accommodation ideal for both families and business travellers. Spacious, en suite bedrooms feature tea and coffee making facilities, and Freeview TV in most hotels. Internet access and WiFi are available for a small fee. The adjacent family restaurant features a wide and varied menu. See also the Hotel Groups pages.

Rooms 40

MARKET RASEN
Lincolnshire   Map 17 TF18

The Advocate Arms
◉◉ RESTAURANT WITH ROOMS

tel: 01673 842364 **2 Queen St LN8 3EH**
email: info@advocatearms.co.uk **web:** www.advocatearms.co.uk
dir: *In town centre*

Appointed to a high standard, this 18th-century property is located in the heart of Market Rasen and combines historic character with contemporary design. The operation centres around the stylish restaurant where service is friendly yet professional and the food is a highlight. The attractive bedrooms are very well equipped and feature luxury bathrooms.

Rooms 10 (2 fmly)

MARLOW
Buckinghamshire
Map 5 SU88

INSPECTORS' CHOICE

Macdonald Compleat Angler

★★★★ ◎◎◎ ♥ HOTEL

MACDONALD
HOTELS & RESORTS

tel: 01628 484444 **Marlow Bridge SL7 1RG**
email: compleatangler@macdonald-hotels.co.uk
web: www.macdonaldhotels.co.uk/compleatangler
dir: *M4 junct 8/9 or M40 junct 4, A404(M) to rdbt, Risham exit, 1m to Marlow Bridge, hotel on right*

This well established hotel enjoys an idyllic location overlooking the River Thames and the delightful Marlow weir. The bedrooms, which differ in size and style, are all individually decorated and are equipped with flat-screen satellite TVs, high-speed internet and air-conditioning. Some rooms have balconies with views of the weir and some have four-posters. The Riverside Restaurant provides outstanding and award-winning cuisine. In summer guests can use two boats that the hotel has moored on the river and fishing is, of course, a popular activity - a ghillie can accompany guests if arranged in advance. Staff throughout are keen to please and nothing is too much trouble.

Rooms 64 (6 fmly) (6 GF) **S** £150-£290; **D** £165-£350 (incl. bkfst)* **Facilities** FTV WiFi ⊿ HL Fishing Fly & coarse fishing River trips (Apr-Sep) Xmas New Year **Conf** Class 65 Board 36 Thtr 150 Del from £275 to £380* **Services** Lift **Parking** 100 **Notes** LB Civ Wed 120

HIGHLY RECOMMENDED

Danesfield House Hotel & Spa

★★★★ 86% ◎◎ HOTEL

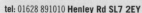

tel: 01628 891010 **Henley Rd SL7 2EY**
email: reservations@danesfieldhouse.co.uk **web:** www.danesfieldhouse.co.uk
dir: *2m from Marlow on A4155 towards Henley*

Set in 65 acres of elevated grounds just 45 minutes from central London and 30 minutes from Heathrow, this hotel enjoys spectacular views across the River Thames. Impressive public rooms include the cathedral-like Great Hall, an impressive spa, and The Orangery for informal dining. The beautiful Oak Room restaurant is also an ideal setting to enjoy superb, imaginative fine dining. Some bedrooms have balconies and stunning views. Nothing is too much trouble for the team of committed staff.

Rooms 78 (3 fmly) (27 GF) ♥ **S** £209-£1100; **D** £234-£1299 (incl. bkfst) **Facilities** Spa STV FTV WiFi ⊿ ⊛ ♨ Putt green ⤵ Gym Jogging trail Steam room Hydrotherapy room Sauna Xmas New Year **Conf** Class 60 Board 50 Thtr 100 **Services** Lift **Parking** 100 **Notes** LB Civ Wed 120

Crowne Plaza Marlow

★★★★ 81% ◎ HOTEL

tel: 01628 496800 **Field House Ln SL7 1GJ**
email: enquiries@cpmarlow.co.uk **web:** www.cpmarlow.co.uk
dir: *A404 exit to Marlow, left at mini rdbt, left into Field House Lane*

This hotel is in the Thames Valley not far from Windsor, Henley-on-Thames and the motorway. The public areas are air conditioned and include the Agua Café and Bar and Glaze Restaurant. Leisure facilities include an up-to-the-minute gym and large pool. The bedrooms, including six contemporary suites, enjoy plenty of natural light and have excellent workstations; the Club Rooms have European and US power points

Rooms 168 (47 fmly) (56 GF) (11 smoking) ♥ **Facilities** Spa STV FTV WiFi HL ⊛ ⤵ Gym Sauna Steam room Dance studio Xmas New Year **Conf** Class 180 Board 30 Thtr 450 **Services** Lift Air con **Parking** 300 **Notes** ⊗ Civ Wed 300

Premier Inn Marlow

BUDGET HOTEL

Premier Inn

tel: 0871 527 8766 *(Calls cost 13p per minute plus your phone company's access charge)*
The Causeway SL7 2AA
web: www.premierinn.com
dir: *M40 junct 4, A404 signed Marlow/Maidenhead. Left, follow A4155 signs to Marlow. At 3rd rdbt 1st exit into High St, signed Bisham. Straight on at mini rdbt. Hotel on left*

High quality, budget accommodation ideal for both families and business travellers. Spacious, en suite bedrooms feature tea and coffee making facilities, and Freeview TV in most hotels. Internet access and WiFi are available for a small fee. The adjacent family restaurant features a wide and varied menu. See also the Hotel Groups pages.

Rooms 17

MARSTON
Lincolnshire
Map 11 SK84

Ramada Resort Grantham

★★★ 71% HOTEL

tel: 01400 250909 **Toll Bar Rd NG32 2HT**
email: reservations@ramadaresortgrantham.co.uk
web: www.ramadaresortgrantham.co.uk
dir: *From A1 N: left to Marston adjacent to petrol station. From A1 S: 1st right after Allington/Belton exit*

Located in the countryside one mile from the A1, this sympathetically renovated and extended former period barn provides a range of thoughtfully furnished bedrooms, ideal for both business and leisure customers. Imaginative food is offered in the attractive beamed restaurant, and extensive leisure facilities include a swimming pool, sauna, steam room and a well-equipped gym.

Rooms 103 (11 fmly) (46 GF) ♥ **Facilities** Spa STV FTV WiFi ⊿ HL ⊛ Gym Sauna Steam room Solarium Xmas New Year **Conf** Class 180 Board 100 Thtr 300 **Services** Lift **Parking** 280 **Notes** Civ Wed 250

MASHAM
North Yorkshire
Map 19 SE28

INSPECTORS' CHOICE

Swinton Park
★★★★ ◎◎◎ HOTEL

tel: 01765 680900 **Swinton HG4 4JH**
email: reservations@swintonpark.com **web:** www.swintonpark.com
dir: *Phone for detailed directions*

Although extended during the Victorian and Edwardian eras, the original part of this welcoming castle dates from the 17th century. Bedrooms are luxuriously furnished and come with a host of thoughtful extras. Samuel's restaurant (built by the current owner's great-great-great grandfather) is very elegant and serves imaginative dishes using local produce. The majority of the food is sourced from the 20,000-acre Swinton Estate, as the hotel, winner of several green awards, is committed to keeping the 'food miles' to a minimum. The gardens, including a four-acre walled garden, have been gradually restored. The Deerhouse is the venue for the hotel's alfresco food festivals, summer BBQs and weddings.

Rooms 31 (6 fmly) ⬥ **Facilities** Spa FTV WiFi ⬥ ⬥ 9 Putt green Fishing ⬥ Gym Shooting Falconry Pony trekking Cookery school Xmas New Year **Conf** Class 60 Board 40 Thtr 110 **Services** Lift **Parking** 50 **Notes** Civ Wed 120

MATFEN
Northumberland
Map 21 NZ07

Matfen Hall
★★★★ 81% ◎◎ HOTEL

tel: 01661 886500 & 855708 **NE20 ORH**
email: info@matfenhall.com **web:** www.matfenhall.com
dir: *A69 onto B6318. Hotel just before village*

Matfen Hall is a luxurious and elegant stately home set in 300 acres of beautiful Northumbrian countryside. The hotel offers individually decorated bedrooms in both traditional and contemporary styles, while the impressive public rooms include the Library Restaurant, the Print Room, and the Conservatory Bar, all surrounding the Great Hall, which is perfect for weddings and private dining. The golf estate includes a 27-hole course, a par 3 course and a driving range. Relax in the stylish spa, leisure and conference facilities.

Rooms 53 (11 fmly) ⬥ **Facilities** Spa STV FTV WiFi ⬥ HL ⬥ supervised ⬥ 27 Putt green Gym Sauna Steam room Salt grotto Ice fountain Aerobics Driving range Golf academy Xmas New Year **Conf** Class 46 Board 40 Thtr 120 **Services** Lift **Parking** 150 **Notes** Civ Wed 120

MAWGAN PORTH
Cornwall
Map 2 SW86

The Scarlet Hotel
★★★★ 82% ◎◎ HOTEL

tel: 01637 861800 **Tredragon Rd TR8 4DQ**
email: stay@scarlethotel.co.uk **web:** www.scarlethotel.co.uk
dir: *A39, A30 towards Truro. At Trekenning rdbt take A3059, follow Newquay Airport signs. Right after garage signed St Mawgan & Airport. Right after airport, at T-junct signed Padstow B3276. At Mawgan Porth left. Hotel 250yds*

Built as an eco hotel, this strikingly modern property has a stunning cliff-top location with magnificent views, and offers something a little different. The very stylish and well-equipped bedrooms are categorised in five types: Just Right, Generous, Unique, Spacious and Indulgent. The Ayurvedic spa is exceptional and encompasses the rejuvenation of the whole body and mind; relaxation is the key here. Cuisine is equally important, and in tune with the hotel's environment policies, daily-changing menus feature fresh, seasonal and local produce. The team of 'hosts' offer a high level of hospitality and service.

Rooms 37 (5 GF) ⬥ **S** £220-£440; **D** £240-£460 (incl. bkfst)* **Facilities** Spa FTV WiFi ⬥ ⬥ ⬥ Yoga room Meditation room ⬥ Xmas New Year **Conf** Board 16 **Services** Lift **Parking** 37 **Notes** LB No children 16yrs Closed 3-28 Jan Civ Wed 74

Bedruthan Hotel and Spa

★★★★ 78% HOTEL

tel: 01637 861200 & 860860 **TR8 4BU**
email: stay@bedruthan.com **web:** www.bedruthan.com
dir: *From A39 or A30 follow signs to Newquay Airport. Pass airport, right at T-junct to Mawgan Porth. Hotel at top of hill on left*

Bedruthan Hotel and Spa enjoys stunning views over Mawgan Porth Bay from the public rooms and the majority of the bedrooms. This is a very child-friendly hotel. Children's clubs for various ages are provided in addition to children's dining areas and appropriate meals and times. An homage to architecture of the 1970s, with a comfortable, contemporary feel, this hotel also has conference facilities. A choice of dining options is available with the relaxed vibe of the Wild Café, or alternatively The Herring which offers a creative and innovative menu, utilising excellent Cornish produce.

Rooms 101 (60 fmly) (1 GF) **Facilities** Spa FTV WiFi Gym Sauna Steam room Hydro pool Pool table Snooker room Outooor spa garden New Year Child facilities **Conf** Class 60 Board 40 Thtr 200 Del from £104.50* **Services** Lift **Parking** 100 **Notes** Closed 2-27 Jan Civ Wed 150

MAWNAN SMITH	Map 2 SW72
Cornwall	

Budock Vean - The Hotel on the River

★★★★ 78% COUNTRY HOUSE HOTEL

tel: 01326 252100 & 250288 **TR11 5LG**
email: relax@budockvean.co.uk **web:** www.budockvean.co.uk
dir: *From A39 follow tourist signs to Trebah Gardens. 0.5m to hotel*

Set in 65 acres of attractive, well-tended grounds, this peaceful hotel offers an impressive range of facilities. It is convenient for visiting the Helford River estuary and many local gardens, or simply as a tranquil venue for a leisure break. The bedrooms are spacious and come in a choice of styles; some overlook the grounds and the golf course.

Rooms 57 (2 fmly) **S** £60-£141; **D** £120-£282 (incl. bkfst)* **Facilities** Spa FTV WiFi 9 Putt green Private river boat & foreshore Kayaking Xmas New Year **Conf** Class 30 Board 20 Thtr 60 **Services** Lift **Parking** 100 **Notes** LB Closed 3 wks Jan Civ Wed 60

Meudon Hotel

★★★★ 74% COUNTRY HOUSE HOTEL

tel: 01326 250541 **TR11 5HT**
email: wecare@meudon.co.uk **web:** www.meudon.co.uk
dir: *From Truro A39 towards Falmouth at Hillhead - Anchor & Cannons rdbt, follow signs to Mabe then Mawnan Smith, left at Red Lion, hotel on right*

This charming late Victorian mansion is a relaxing place to stay, with friendly hospitality and attentive service. It sits in impressive 9-acre gardens that lead down to a private beach. The spacious and comfortable bedrooms are situated in a more modern building. The cuisine features the best of local Cornish produce and is served in the conservatory restaurant.

Rooms 29 (2 fmly) (15 GF) **S** £99; **D** £130-£255 (incl. bkfst)* **Facilities** FTV WiFi Fishing Private beach Hair salon Beauty treatment room Xmas **Conf** Class 30 Board 30 Thtr 30 Del £200* **Services** Lift **Parking** 50 **Notes** LB Closed 28 Dec-Jan

Trelawne Hotel

★★★ 82% HOTEL

tel: 01326 250226 **Maenporth Rd TR11 5HT**
email: info@trelawnehotel.co.uk **web:** www.trelawnehotel.co.uk
dir: *A39 to Falmouth, right at Hillhead rdbt signed Maenporth. Past beach, up hill, hotel on left*

This hotel is surrounded by attractive lawns and gardens, and enjoys superb coastal views. An informal atmosphere prevails, and many guests return year after year. Bedrooms, many with sea views, are of varying sizes, but all are well equipped. Dinner features quality local produce used in imaginative dishes.

Rooms 11 (2 fmly) (4 GF) **S** £65-£90; **D** £80-£160 (incl. bkfst)* **Facilities** FTV WiFi Xmas **Parking** 16 **Notes** LB RS Jan-Feb

MELBOURN	Map 12 TL34
Cambridgeshire	

The Sheene Mill

RESTAURANT WITH ROOMS

tel: 01763 261393 **39 Station Rd SG8 6DX**
email: reservations@sheenemill.com **web:** www.sheenemill.com
dir: *M11 junct 10 onto A505 towards Royston. Right to Melbourn, pass church on right, on left before old bridge*

This 16th century watermill is ideally situated just off the A10, a short drive from both Cambridge and Royston. The bedrooms are individually decorated and well equipped; some rooms overlook the mill pond and terrace. Public rooms include a comfortable lounge, a bar, conservatory and a delightful restaurant overlooking the pond.

Rooms 9 (3 fmly)

MELKSHAM	Map 4 ST96
Wiltshire	

Shaw Country Hotel

★★ 76% SMALL HOTEL

tel: 01225 702836 & 790321 **Bath Rd, Shaw SN12 8EF**
email: info@shawcountryhotel.com **web:** www.shawcountryhotel.com
dir: *1m from Melksham, 9m from Bath on A365*

Located within easy reach of both Bath and the M4, this relaxed and friendly hotel sits in its own gardens and includes a patio area ideal for enjoying a drink during the summer months. The house boasts very well-appointed bedrooms, a comfortable lounge and bar, and the Mulberry Restaurant, where a wide selection of innovative dishes make up both carte and set menus. A spacious function room is a useful addition.

Rooms 13 (2 fmly) **S** £65-£73; **D** £90-£95 (incl. bkfst) **Facilities** FTV WiFi **Conf** Class 40 Board 20 Thtr 60 **Parking** 30 **Notes** LB Closed 26-28 Dec & 1 Jan Civ Wed 70

MELTON MOWBRAY	Map 11 SK71
Leicestershire	

INSPECTORS' CHOICE

Stapleford Park

★★★★ ◎◎ COUNTRY HOUSE HOTEL

tel: 01572 787000 **Stapleford LE14 2EF**
email: reservations@stapleford.co.uk web: www.staplefordpark.com
dir: *1m SW of B676, 4m E of Melton Mowbray & 9m W of Colsterworth*

This stunning mansion, dating back to the 14th century, sits in over 500 acres of beautiful grounds. Spacious, sumptuous public rooms include a choice of lounges and an elegant restaurant. An additional brasserie-style restaurant is located in the golf complex. The hotel also boasts a spa with health and beauty treatments and gym, plus horse riding and many other country pursuits. Bedrooms are individually styled and furnished to a high standard. Attentive service is delivered with a relaxed yet professional style. Dinner, in the impressive dining room, is a highlight of any stay.

Rooms 55 (7 annexe) (10 fmly) ⚲ **Facilities** Spa STV FTV WiFi ↕ ⊛ ⅃ 18 ⚲ Putt green Fishing ⚲ Gym Archery Croquet Falconry Horse riding Petanque Shooting Billiards ♫ Xmas New Year **Conf** Class 140 Board 80 Thtr 200 **Services** Lift **Parking** 120 **Notes** Civ Wed 160

Quorn Lodge Hotel

★★★ 71% HOTEL

tel: 01664 566660 **46 Asfordby Rd LE13 0HR**
email: quornlodge@aol.com web: www.quornlodge.co.uk
dir: *From town centre take A6006. Hotel 300yds from junct of A606/A607 on right*

Centrally located, this smart, privately-owned and managed hotel offers a comfortable and welcoming atmosphere. Bedrooms are individually decorated and thoughtfully designed. The public rooms consist of a bright restaurant overlooking the garden, a cosy lounge bar and a modern function suite. High standards are maintained throughout and parking is a bonus.

Rooms 21 (4 fmly) (3 GF) ⚲ **Facilities** STV FTV WiFi ↕ Gym **Conf** Class 70 Board 80 Thtr 100 **Parking** 38 **Notes** LB ⊗ Civ Wed 80

Scalford Hall Hotel

★★★ 70% HOTEL

tel: 01664 444654 **Melton Rd LE14 4UB**
email: reception@scalfordhall.co.uk web: www.scalfordhall.co.uk
dir: *A6006 towards Melton Mowbray. Left at 2nd lights into Scalford Rd, hotel 3m on left*

Scalford Hall Hotel is located just five minutes away from the market town of Melton Mowbray. It is a good venue for weddings, galas, and team building events, and the pavilion can host up to 600 guests. Accommodation is comfortable, and in summer months guests can relax in the attractively landscaped gardens.

Rooms 79 (52 annexe) (3 fmly) (16 GF) ⚲ **Facilities** FTV WiFi ↕ HL ⚲ Gym Xmas New Year **Conf** Class 350 Board 50 Thtr 600 **Parking** 200 **Notes** Civ Wed 600

Premier Inn Melton Mowbray

BUDGET HOTEL

tel: 0871 527 9584 *(Calls cost 13p per minute plus your phone company's access charge)*
5 Norman Way LE13 1JE
web: www.premierinn.com
dir: *On A607, N of town centre*

High quality, budget accommodation ideal for both families and business travellers. Spacious, en suite bedrooms feature tea and coffee making facilities, and Freeview TV in most hotels. Internet access and WiFi are available for a small fee. The adjacent family restaurant features a wide and varied menu. See also the Hotel Groups pages.

Rooms 55

MEMBURY MOTORWAY SERVICE AREA (M4)	Map 5 SU37
Berkshire	

Days Inn Membury - M4

AA Advertised

WELCOMEBREAK

tel: 01488 72336 **Membury Service Area RG17 7TZ**
email: membury.hotel@welcomebreak.co.uk web: www.welcomebreak.co.uk
dir: *M4 between junct 14 & 15*

This modern building offers accommodation in smart, spacious and well-equipped bedrooms, suitable for families and business travellers, and all with en suite bathrooms. Continental breakfast is available and other refreshments may be taken at the nearby family restaurant.

Rooms 38 (32 fmly) (17 GF) (5 smoking) **Facilities** FTV WiFi ↕ Game zone amusements **Conf** Board 10 **Parking** 200

MERIDEN
West Midlands
Map 10 SP28

Forest of Arden, A Marriott Hotel & Country Club

★★★★ 77% ● HOTEL

tel: 01676 522335 **Maxstoke Ln CV7 7HR**
web: www.marriottforestofarden.co.uk
dir: M42 junct 6 onto A45 towards Coventry, over Stonebridge flyover. After 0.75m left into Shepherds Ln. Left at T-junct. Hotel 1.5m on left

The ancient oaks, rolling hills and natural lakes of the 10,000 acre Forest of Arden estate provide an idyllic backdrop for this modern hotel and country club. The hotel boasts an excellent range of leisure facilities and is regarded as one of the finest golfing destinations in the UK. Bedrooms provide every modern convenience and a full range of facilities.

Rooms 214 (65 GF) ◗ **Facilities** Spa WiFi ⊕ ₤ 18 ⌢ Putt green Fishing ◡ Gym Floodlit golf academy New Year **Conf** Class 180 Board 40 Thtr 300 **Services** Lift **Parking** 300 **Notes** ⊗ Civ Wed 250

Best Western Plus Manor NEC Birmingham

Best Western PLUS

★★★★ 76% ●● HOTEL

tel: 01676 522735 **Main Rd CV7 7NH**
email: reservations@manorhotelmeriden.co.uk **web:** www.manorhotelmeriden.co.uk
dir: M42 junct 6, A45 towards Coventry then A452 signed Leamington. At rdbt take B4102 signed Meriden, hotel on left

This sympathetically extended Georgian manor in the heart of a sleepy village is just a few minutes away from the M6, M42 and National Exhibition Centre. The Regency Restaurant offers modern dishes, while Houston's serves lighter meals and snacks. The bedrooms are smart and well equipped.

Rooms 112 (15 fmly) (20 GF) ◗ **Facilities** FTV WiFi ⌀ Xmas New Year **Conf** Class 150 Board 60 Thtr 250 **Services** Lift **Parking** 190 **Notes** Civ Wed 200

MEVAGISSEY
Cornwall
Map 2 SX04

Tremarne Hotel

★★★ 84% HOTEL

tel: 01726 842213 **Polkirt PL26 6UY**
email: info@tremarne-hotel.co.uk **web:** www.tremarne-hotel.co.uk
dir: A30 from Exeter, take A390 at St Austell then B3273 to Mevagissey. Follow Portmellon signs through Mevagissey. At top of Polkirt Hill 1st right into Higherwell Park. Hotel drive facing

A very popular destination, set in landscaped gardens with a swimming pool, Tremarne Hotel enjoys superb views towards Mevagissey. The friendliness of Michael, Fitz and the team cannot be bettered. The hotel offers comfortable, individually styled bedrooms that either have views of the sea or the countryside. Guests can expect good service and freshly-cooked food on a daily-changing menu.

Rooms 13 **S** £72-£98; **D** £90-£170 (incl. bkfst)* **Facilities** FTV WiFi ⌀ ⌃ Xmas New Year **Parking** 15 **Notes** LB ⊗

Trevalsa Court Hotel

★★★ 80% ●● HOTEL

tel: 01726 842468 **School Hill, Polstreath PL26 6TH**
email: stay@trevalsa-hotel.co.uk **web:** www.trevalsa-hotel.co.uk
dir: From St Austell take B3273 to Mevagissey. Pass sign to Pentewan. At top of hill left at x-rds. Hotel signed

Very well located above the town of Mevagissey, with easy access to nearby attractions, this establishment is an Arts & Crafts style property appointed to a high standard throughout with lots of original features. Bedrooms, many with sea views, are comfortable and well presented; there is also a stylish guests' sitting room with views across the bay.

Rooms 14 (1 annexe) (1 fmly) (4 GF) ◗ **S** £65-£115; **D** £120-£260 (incl. bkfst)* **Facilities** FTV WiFi ⌀ **Parking** 20 **Notes** LB Closed Dec & Jan

MEXBOROUGH
South Yorkshire
Map 16 SE40

Best Western Plus Pastures Hotel

Best Western PLUS

★★★ 82% HOTEL

tel: 01709 577707 **Pastures Rd S64 0JJ**
email: info@pastureshotel.co.uk **web:** www.pastureshotel.co.uk
dir: 0.5m from town centre on A6023, left by CLS Mot, signed Denaby Ings & Cadeby. Hotel on right

This private hotel is in a rural setting beside a working canal with views of Conisbrough Castle in the distance, and is convenient for Doncaster or the Dearne Valley with its nature reserves and leisure centre. Guests can dine in the Pastures Lodge pub and family restaurant situated opposite the hotel, or in Reeds restaurant in the hotel. Bedrooms, in a modern, purpose-built block, are quiet, comfortable and equipped with many modern facilities including flat-screen smart TV and in-room safe.

Rooms 60 (5 fmly) (28 GF) ◗ **S** fr £67; **D** fr £79 (incl. bkfst)* **Facilities** STV WiFi ⌀ Xmas New Year **Conf** Class 170 Board 100 Thtr 250 Del from £115* **Services** Lift **Parking** 179 **Notes** ⊗ Civ Wed 200

MICHAELWOOD MOTORWAY SERVICE AREA (M5)
Gloucestershire
Map 4 ST79

Days Inn Michaelwood - M5

WELCOMEBREAK

AA Advertised

tel: 01454 261513 **Michaelwood Service Area, Lower Wick GL11 6DD**
email: michaelwood.hotel@welcomebreak.co.uk **web:** www.welcomebreak.co.uk
dir: M5 N'bound between junct 13 & 14

This modern building offers accommodation in smart, spacious and well-equipped bedrooms, suitable for families and business travellers, and all with en suite bathrooms. Continental breakfast is available and other refreshments may be taken at the nearby family restaurant.

Rooms 38 (15 fmly) (7 smoking) **Facilities** FTV WiFi ⌀ **Conf** Board 10 **Parking** 40

M

M

MIDDLESBROUGH
North Yorkshire   Map 19 NZ41

Premier Inn Middlesbrough Central South

BUDGET HOTEL

tel: 0871 527 8770 *(Calls cost 13p per minute plus your phone company's access charge)*
Marton Way TS4 3BS
web: www.premierinn.com
dir: *Off A172 opposite South Cleveland Hospital complex*

High quality, budget accommodation ideal for both families and business travellers. Spacious, en suite bedrooms feature tea and coffee making facilities, and Freeview TV in most hotels. Internet access and WiFi are available for a small fee. The adjacent family restaurant features a wide and varied menu. See also the Hotel Groups pages.

Rooms 74

MIDDLETON-IN-TEESDALE
County Durham   Map 18 NY92

The Teesdale Hotel

★★ 71% HOTEL

tel: 01833 640264 **Market Place DL12 0QG**
email: enquiries@teesdalehotel.co.uk **web:** www.teesdalehotel.co.uk
dir: *From Barnard Castle take B6278, follow signs for Middleton-in-Teesdale & Highforce. Hotel in town centre*

Located in the heart of this popular village, The Teesdale Hotel is a family-run establishment that offers a relaxed and friendly atmosphere. Bedrooms and bathrooms are well equipped and offer a good standard of quality and comfort. Public areas include a residents' lounge on the first floor, a spacious restaurant and a lounge bar which is popular with locals.

Rooms 14 (1 fmly) 🐾 **Facilities** WiFi **Conf** Class 20 Board 20 Thtr 40 **Parking** 20

MIDDLETON STONEY
Oxfordshire   Map 11 SP52

Best Western The Jersey Arms

★★ 76% HOTEL

tel: 01869 343234 & 343270 **OX25 4AD**
email: jerseyarms@bestwestern.co.uk **web:** www.jerseyarms.com
dir: *3m from A34, on B430, 10m N of Oxford, between junct 9 & 10 of M40*

With a history dating back to the 13th century, the Jersey Arms combines old-fashioned charm with contemporary style and elegance. The individually designed bedrooms are well equipped and comfortable. The lounge has an open fire, and the smart and spacious restaurant provides a calm atmosphere in which to enjoy the popular cuisine.

Rooms 20 (14 annexe) (3 fmly) (9 GF) **S** £65-£85; **D** £110-£145 (incl. bkfst)*
Facilities FTV WiFi ⌂ **Conf** Class 20 Board 20 Thtr 20 Del from £100 to £150*
Parking 55 **Notes** ⊗

MIDDLETON TYAS
North Yorkshire   Map 19 NZ20

INSPECTORS' CHOICE

The Coach House

◉◉ RESTAURANT WITH ROOMS

tel: 01325 377977 **Middleton Lodge DL10 6NJ**
email: info@middletonlodge.co.uk **web:** www.middletonlodge.co.uk

Nestled within a 200-acre estate, surrounded by tall trees and winding footpaths, this picturesque setting really sets the tone for your stay. Bedrooms are annexed in a courtyard style setting and are furnished to a luxurious standard. Traditional features such as exposed beams and high ceilings are coupled with a wide range of modern accessories such as flat-screen TV, Nespresso machines and complimentary WiFi. An interesting range of meals are served in the modern restaurant, alongside a selection of cocktails. Beauty treatments are also available to book. Weddings and private functions can also be booked in the main house, Middleton Lodge.

Rooms 9

MIDSOMER NORTON
Somerset   Map 4 ST65

Best Western Plus Centurion Hotel

★★★★ 79% ◉ HOTEL

tel: 01761 417711 & 412214 **Charlton Ln BA3 4BD**
email: enquiries@centurionhotel.co.uk **web:** www.centurionhotel.co.uk
dir: *Just off A367, 10m S of Bath. Once in Radstock follow signs at mini rdbt for Shepton Mallet/Wells, follow for 2m, left at small rdbt*

Centurion Hotel is located just nine miles from Bath in a peaceful area with surrounding grounds and a nine-hole golf course. Bedrooms and bathrooms have been recently completely refurbished and offer good levels of quality and comfort. In addition to the relaxing public areas a range of leisure facilities are available, including gym, swimming pool and the new Green Apple spa. Dinner may be taken in the relaxed Jays bar or the more stylish Cubros Restaurant with the option of dining in the conservatory area.

Rooms 45 (2 fmly) (18 GF) 🐾 **S** £87.50-£97.50; **D** £100-£132.50 (incl. bkfst)*
Facilities Spa FTV WiFi ⌂ ⊛ ⅃ 9 Putt green Gym Sauna Steam room New Year
Conf Class 50 Board 50 Thtr 180 Del from £133.30* **Parking** 100 **Notes** LB ⊗
Closed 24-26 Dec Civ Wed 110

MILTON COMMON
Oxfordshire   Map 5 SP60

The Oxfordshire

★★★★ 80% ◉ HOTEL

tel: 01844 278300 **Rycote Ln OX9 2PU**
email: gm@theoxfordshire.com **web:** www.theoxfordshire.com
dir: *M40 junct 7 N'bound (junct 8 S'bound), A329 towards Thame*

Located within easy reach of the M40, this hotel is at the championship golf course, The Oxfordshire, in the heart of the beautiful Chilterns. The accommodation offers impressive levels of comfort and quality, and all rooms are air-conditioned and have access onto a balcony. The Tempus Spa includes a 15-metre pool, modern gym and three treatment rooms. This resort makes an ideal location for a relaxing break, especially for golf enthusiasts.

Rooms 50 (18 GF) **Facilities** Spa FTV WiFi ⌂ ⊛ ⅃ 18 Putt green Gym Sauna Steam room New Year **Conf** Class 66 Board 54 Thtr 180 **Services** Lift Air con **Parking** 150 **Notes** ⊗ Civ Wed

The Oxford Belfry

★★★★ 79% HOTEL

tel: 01844 279381 **OX9 2JW**
email: oxfordbelfry@qhotels.co.uk **web:** www.qhotels.co.uk
dir: M40 junct 7 onto A329 to Thame. Left onto A40, hotel 300yds on right

This modern hotel has a relatively rural location and enjoys lovely views of the countryside to the rear. The hotel is built around two very attractive courtyards and has a number of lounges and conference rooms, as well as indoor leisure facilities and outdoor tennis courts. Bedrooms are large and feature a range of extras.

Rooms 154 (20 fmly) (66 GF) ↰ **S** £107-£167; **D** £119-£179 **Facilities** Spa FTV WiFi ↳ HL 🕐 ♨ Gym Steam room Sauna Xmas New Year **Conf** Class 180 Board 100 Thtr 450 Del from £145 to £180 **Services** Lift **Parking** 350 **Notes** ⊗ Civ Wed 300

MILTON KEYNES	Map 11 SP83
Buckinghamshire	

Mercure Milton Keynes Abbey Hill

★★★★ 74% HOTEL

tel: 01908 561666 **The Approach, Monks Way, Two Mile Ash MK8 8LY**
email: h8876@accor.com **web:** www.mercure-milton-keynes-abbey-hill.com
dir: M1 junct 14/A509, 3rd exit at rdbt onto London Road. 1st exit at rdbt onto A422, straight across 7 rdbts, 3rd exit onto Monks Way, left to the Approach

Mercure Milton Keynes Abbey Hill Hotel is located close to Central Milton Keynes Train Station and within easy access to the M1 and Luton Airport. The hotel has bedrooms with a modern and contemporary design, and provides a relaxing setting for meetings and events. Guests can enjoy a selection of freshly cooked meals in the bar and restaurant. Free car parking and WiFi available.

Rooms 92 (14 fmly) (44 GF) ↰ **D** £39-£230 **Facilities** STV FTV WiFi ↳ HL Putt green Gym Xmas New Year **Conf** Class 120 Board 80 Thtr 250 Del from £150 to £200* **Services** Air con **Parking** 120 **Notes** LB ⊗ Civ Wed 120

Mercure Milton Keynes Parkside Hotel

★★★★ 73% ⊛ HOTEL

tel: 01908 661919 **Newport Rd, Woughton on the Green MK6 3LR**
email: H6627@accor.com **web:** www.mercure.com
dir: M1 junct 14, A509 towards Milton Keynes. 2nd exit on H6 follow signs to Woughton on the Green

Set in a peaceful rural location, The Merure Milton Keynes Parkside Hotel is just a few minutes' drive from the town centre. The spacious rooms are modern, attractively decorated and well equipped. Public areas are tastefully appointed and the popular restaurant offers an interesting choice of dishes. The hotel also has a range of conference/function facilities and plenty of parking.

Rooms 49 (10 annexe) (2 fmly) (20 GF) ↰ **Facilities** STV FTV WiFi ↳ HL Free entry to health & fitness club (approx 2m) Xmas New Year **Conf** Class 60 Board 50 Thtr 150 Del from £99 to £149* **Services** Air con **Parking** 75 **Notes** ⊗ Civ Wed 120

Novotel Milton Keynes

★★★ 75% HOTEL

tel: 01908 322212 **Saxon St, Layburn Court, Heelands MK13 7RA**
email: H3272@accor.com **web:** www.novotel.com
dir: M1 junct 14, follow Childsway signs towards city centre. Right into Saxon Way, straight across all rdbts, hotel on left

Contemporary in style, this purpose-built hotel is situated on the outskirts of the town, just a few minutes' drive from the centre and mainline railway station.

Bedrooms provide ample workspace and a good range of facilities for the modern traveller, and public rooms include a children's play area and indoor leisure centre.

Rooms 124 (40 fmly) (33 GF) ↰ **Facilities** FTV WiFi ↳ 🕐 Gym Steam room Sauna **Conf** Class 75 Board 40 Thtr 120 **Services** Lift **Parking** 130 **Notes** Civ Wed 100

Premier Inn Milton Keynes Central

BUDGET HOTEL

tel: 0871 527 8774 *(Calls cost 13p per minute plus your phone company's access charge)*
Secklow Gate West MK9 3BZ
web: www.premierinn.com
dir: M1 junct 14 follow H6 route over 6 rdbts, at 7th (South Secklow) turn right, hotel on left

High quality, budget accommodation ideal for both families and business travellers. Spacious, en suite bedrooms feature tea and coffee making facilities, and Freeview TV in most hotels. Internet access and WiFi are available for a small fee. The adjacent family restaurant features a wide and varied menu. See also the Hotel Groups pages.

Rooms 38

Premier Inn Milton Keynes East (Willen Lake)

BUDGET HOTEL

tel: 0871 527 8778 *(Calls cost 13p per minute plus your phone company's access charge)*
Brickhill St, Willen Lake MK15 9HQ
web: www.premierinn.com
dir: M1 junct 14, H6 (Childsway). Right at 3rd rdbt into Brickhill St. Right at 1st mini rdbt, hotel 1st left

Rooms 41

Premier Inn Milton Keynes South

BUDGET HOTEL

tel: 0871 527 8780 *(Calls cost 13p per minute plus your phone company's access charge)*
Lakeside Grove, Bletcham Way, Caldecotte MK7 8HP
web: www.premierinn.com
dir: M1 junct 14, towards Milton Keynes on H6 (Childs Way). Straight on at 2 rdbts. Left at 3rd onto V10 (Brickhill St). Straight on at 5 rdbts, at 6th right onto H10 Bletcham Way

Rooms 61

Premier Inn Milton Keynes South West (Furzton Lake)

BUDGET HOTEL

tel: 0871 527 8776 *(Calls cost 13p per minute plus your phone company's access charge)*
Shirwell Crescent, Furzton MK4 1GA
web: www.premierinn.com
dir: M1 junct 14, A509 to Milton Keynes. Straight on at 8 rdbts, at 9th rdbt (North Grafton) left onto V6. Right at next onto H7. Over The Bowl rdbt, hotel on left

Rooms 120

M

M

MINEHEAD
Somerset
Map 3 SS94

Channel House Hotel

★★★ 81% SMALL HOTEL

tel: 01643 703229 **Church Path TA24 5QG**
email: channelhouse@btconnect.com **web:** www.channelhouse.co.uk
dir: *From A39 right at rdbt to seafront, left onto promenade. 1st right, 1st left into Blenheim Gdns, 1st right into Northfield Rd*

This family-run hotel offers relaxing surroundings, yet is only a short walk from the town centre. The South West Coastal Path starts from the hotel's two-acre gardens. Many of the exceptionally well-equipped bedrooms benefit from wonderful views, and imaginative menus are created from the best local produce. Channel House Hotel is totally non-smoking.

Rooms 8 ⌂ **Facilities** FTV WiFi **Services** Air con **Parking** 10 **Notes** LB ⊗ No children 15yrs Closed Nov & 29 Dec-15 Mar

Northfield Hotel

★★★ 78% HOTEL

tel: 01643 705155 **Northfield Rd TA24 5PU**
email: res@nfhotel.co.uk **web:** www.northfield-hotel.co.uk
dir: *M5 junct 23, follow A38 to Bridgwater then A39 to Minehead*

Dating back to the Edwardian era, this hotel was originally a private house. From its elevated position, it enjoys lovely views out over the town and the Bristol Channel. The peaceful setting makes it an ideal location for exploring both locally and further afield, with the stunning expanse of Exmoor just a short drive away. Bedrooms offer good levels of comfort and quality, likewise the spacious and elegant public areas with a choice of lounges available. The attractive wood-panelled dining room is the venue for enjoyable cuisine with a range of dishes to suit all tastes. Additional facilities include a lovely garden and indoor swimming pool.

Rooms 30 (4 fmly) (4 GF) ⌂ **S** £65-£155; **D** £100-£185 (incl. bkfst)* **Facilities** FTV WiFi ⊕ Putt green Gym Xmas **Conf** Class 30 Board 20 Thtr 40 Del from £100 to £200 **Services** Lift **Parking** 30 **Notes** LB

MINSTER
Kent
Map 7 TR36

Premier Inn Ramsgate

BUDGET HOTEL

tel: 0871 527 9270 *(Calls cost 13p per minute plus your phone company's access charge)*
Tothill St CT12 4HY
web: www.premierinn.com
dir: *M25 onto A2 (signed Dover) merge onto M2 (signed Canterbury). Onto A299 (signed Margate/Ramsgate). Hotel at Minster rdbt*

High quality, budget accommodation ideal for both families and business travellers. Spacious, en suite bedrooms feature tea and coffee making facilities, and Freeview TV in most hotels. Internet access and WiFi are available for a small fee. The adjacent family restaurant features a wide and varied menu. See also the Hotel Groups pages.

Rooms 71

MONK FRYSTON
North Yorkshire
Map 19 SE52

Monk Fryston Hall Hotel

★★★ 80% COUNTRY HOUSE HOTEL

tel: 01977 682369 **LS25 5DU**
email: reception@monkfrystonhallhotel.co.uk **web:** www.monkfrystonhallhotel.co.uk
dir: *A1(M) junct 42, A63 towards Selby. Monk Fryston 2m, hotel on left*

This delightful 16th-century mansion house enjoys a peaceful location in 30 acres of grounds, yet is only minutes' drive from the A1. Many original features have been retained and the public rooms are furnished with antique and period pieces. Bedrooms are individually styled and thoughtfully equipped for both business and leisure guests.

Rooms 29 (2 fmly) (5 GF) ⌂ **S** £69-£109; **D** £79-£189 (incl. bkfst)* **Facilities** FTV WiFi ⌂ ⌂ Xmas New Year **Conf** Class 30 Board 25 Thtr 100 Del from £109 to £199* **Parking** 80 **Notes** LB Civ Wed 150

MORECAMBE
Lancashire
Map 18 SD46

The Midland

English Lakes
Hotels Resorts & Venues

★★★★ 74% ⊛ HOTEL

tel: 01524 424000 **Marine Road West LA4 4BU**
email: themidland@englishlakes.co.uk **web:** www.englishlakes.co.uk/hotels/midland
dir: *A589 towards Morecambe, follow seafront signs, left on B5321 Lancaster Rd, then Easton Rd, left into Central Drive. Right at rdbt on seafront. Left to hotel entrance*

This art deco hotel sits on the seafront and commands stunning views across Morecambe Bay to the mountains of the Lake District. Stylish and modern accommodation is provided in the well-appointed bedrooms. Spa facilities are available on site, and guests can use the leisure club at the nearby sister hotel.

Rooms 44 (16 fmly) ⌂ **Facilities** FTV WiFi ⌂ Xmas New Year **Conf** Class 30 Board 48 Thtr 140 **Services** Lift **Parking** 70 **Notes** Civ Wed 140

Lothersdale Hotel

★★★ 79% HOTEL

tel: 01524 416404 **320-323 Marine Rd LA4 5AA**
email: hello@bfhotels.com **web:** www.bfhotels.com
dir: *M6 junct 34 follow signs for Morecambe & Heysham. Straight over 3 rdbts following sign for Promenade. At seafront turn left, hotel 0.5m on left*

Located in a central position on Morecambe's promenade, the Lothersdale Hotel offers enviable views across the bay and the Lakeland hills beyond. There are two dining options, Aspects Bistro and Aspects 320 tapas bar. Conference and function rooms are available, with car parking located to the rear of the hotel. Free WiFi is provided too.

Rooms 42 (1 fmly) (5 GF) ⌂ **S** £37-£55; **D** £55-£165 (incl. bkfst) **Facilities** FTV WiFi New Year **Conf** Class 100 Board 60 Thtr 120 Del from £75 to £129 **Services** Lift **Parking** 20 **Notes** LB ⊗ Closed 22 -27 Dec Civ Wed 110

Clarendon Hotel

★★★ 74% HOTEL

tel: 01524 410180 **76 Marine Road West, West End Promenade LA4 4EP**
email: clarendon@mitchellshotels.co.uk **web:** www.mitchells.co.uk
dir: *M6 junct 34 follow Morecambe signs. At rdbt (Toby Carvery on corner) 1st exit to Westgate, follow to seafront. Right at lights, hotel 3rd block*

This traditional seafront hotel offers views over Morecambe Bay, modern facilities and convenient parking. An extensive fish and grill menu is offered in the contemporary Waterfront Restaurant and guests can relax in the comfortable lounge bar. Davy Jones Locker in the basement has a more traditional pub atmosphere and offers cask ales and regular live entertainment.

Rooms 29 (3 fmly) ⁿ **Facilities** STV WiFi HL Xmas New Year **Conf** Class 40 Board 40 Thtr 90 **Services** Lift **Parking** 22 **Notes** Civ Wed 60

MORETONHAMPSTEAD
Devon
Map 3 SX78

The White Hart Hotel

★★★ 81% HOTEL

tel: 01647 440500 **The Square TQ13 8NQ**
email: enquiries@whitehartdartmoor.co.uk **web:** www.whitehartdartmoor.co.uk
dir: *A30 towards Okehampton. At Whiddon Down take A382 for Moretonhampstead*

Dating back to the 1700s, this former coaching inn is located on the edge of Dartmoor. A relaxed and friendly atmosphere prevails, with the staff providing attentive service. Comfortable bedrooms have a blend of traditional and contemporary styles with thoughtful extras provided. Dining is in either the brasserie restaurant or more informally in the bar, where quality cuisine is served.

Rooms 28 (8 annexe) (3 fmly) (4 GF) ⁿ **S** £50-£70; **D** £80-£110 (incl. bkfst)*
Facilities FTV WiFi Xmas New Year **Conf** Class 30 Board 20 Thtr 50 **Notes** LB Civ Wed 60

Bovey Castle

Ⓤ

tel: 01647 445000 & 445007 **Dartmoor National Park, North Bovey TQ13 8RE**
email: info@boveycastle.com **web:** www.boveycastle.com
dir: *M5 junct 31 signed A30 Okehampton, stay on A30 until Whitton Down. Follow signs to Morehampton A382, stay on A382 until rdbt, turn right for Postbridge & Princetown B3212. Stay on B3212 for approx 1.5m. Bovey Castle is on left*

This country manor has a fascinating history and is set in 400 acres. It became known as Bovey Castle in 2003, and since then has been restored to its former glory, offering guests elegance, charm and a chance to 'get away from it all'. A number of country pursuits are available at the property, including a championship golf course. Each bedroom is unique in design and range from classic or castle rooms to state room and grand state rooms. In addition, within the grounds there are lodges, each with three en suite bedrooms. The spa has a superb pool and many therapeutic treatments.

Rooms 60 (14 annexe) (9 fmly) (2 GF) ⁿ **S** £139-£199; **D** £179-£719 (incl. bkfst)*
Facilities Spa STV FTV WiFi ⚡ 18 ⛳ Putt green Fishing Gym Falconry Archery Clay pigeon Shooting Table tennis Cider & gin making Xmas New Year Child facilities **Conf** Class 64 Board 50 Thtr 120 Del from £259* **Services** Lift **Parking** 60 **Notes** LB Civ Wed 150

MORETON-IN-MARSH
Gloucestershire
Map 10 SP23

COTSWOLD INNS & HOTELS

Manor House Hotel

★★★★ 81% ◉◉ HOTEL

tel: 01608 650501 **High St GL56 OLJ**
email: info@manorhousehotel.info **web:** www.cotswold-inns-hotels.co.uk
dir: *Off A429 at south end of town. Take East St off High St, hotel car park 3rd right*

Dating back to the 16th century, this charming Cotswold coaching inn retains much of its original character, with stone walls, impressive fireplaces and a relaxed, country-house atmosphere. Bedrooms vary in size and reflect the individuality of the building; all are well equipped and some are particularly opulent. Comfortable public areas include a popular bar, a brasserie and the stylish Mulberry Restaurant where an opportunity to enjoy an evening meal should not be missed.

Rooms 35 (1 annexe) (3 fmly) (1 GF) ⁿ **Facilities** FTV WiFi Xmas New Year **Conf** Class 48 Board 54 Thtr 120 **Services** Lift **Parking** 24 **Notes** Civ Wed 120

White Hart Royal Hotel

★★★ 80% ◉ HOTEL

tel: 01608 650731 **High St GL56 OBA**
email: whr@bulldogmail.co.uk **web:** www.whitehartroyal.co.uk
dir: *On High St at junct with Oxford Rd*

This historic hotel has been providing accommodation for hundreds of years and today offers high standards of quality and comfort. Public areas are full of character, and the bedrooms, in a wide range of shapes and sizes, include several very spacious and luxurious rooms situated adjacent to the main building. A varied range of well prepared dishes is available throughout the day and evening in the main bar and the relaxing restaurant.

Rooms 28 (8 annexe) (2 fmly) (9 GF) ⁿ **Facilities** FTV WiFi HL Xmas New Year **Conf** Class 40 Board 20 Thtr 55 **Parking** 6 **Notes** Civ Wed 50

Redesdale Arms

★★★ 79% ◉ HOTEL

tel: 01608 650308 **High St GL56 0AW**
web: www.redesdalearms.com
dir: *On A429, 0.5m from rail station*

This fine old inn has played a central role in the town for centuries. Traditional features combine successfully with contemporary comforts; bedrooms are located in the main building and in an annexe. Guests can choose from an imaginative menu in either the stylish restaurant or the conservatory.

Rooms 34 (26 annexe) (6 fmly) (16 GF) ⁿ **S** £100-£140; **D** £130-£170 (incl. bkfst)*
Facilities STV FTV WiFi Xmas New Year **Parking** 17 **Notes** ⊗

M

MORLEY
Derbyshire

Map 11 SK34

The Morley Hayes Hotel
★★★★ 79% ◎◎ HOTEL

tel: 01332 780480 & 782005 Main Rd DE7 6DG
email: hotel@morleyhayes.com web: www.morleyhayes.com
dir: 4m N of Derby on A608

Located in rolling countryside this modern golfing destination provides extremely comfortable, stylish bedrooms with wide-ranging facilities, plasma TVs, and state-of-the-art bathrooms; the plush suites are particularly eye-catching. Creative cuisine is offered in the Dovecote Restaurant, and both Roosters and the Spikes sports bar provide informal eating options.

Rooms 32 (4 fmly) (15 GF) 🐾 Facilities STV FTV WiFi ↕ HL ⌇ 27 Putt green Golf driving range Conf Class 50 Board 40 Thtr 120 Services Lift Air con Parking 245 Notes LB ⊗ Civ Wed 90

MORPETH
Northumberland

Map 21 NZ28

Eshott Hall
★★★★ 77% ◎◎ COUNTRY HOUSE HOTEL

tel: 01670 787454 Eshott NE65 9EN
email: info@eshotthall.co.uk web: www.eshotthall.co.uk
dir: A1 Northbound from Morpeth 5m. A1 Southbound from Alnwick 15m

Eshott Hall dates back to the 16th century and is set behind walled gardens in the heart of Northumberland, just a few miles from the A1. Bedrooms are extremely comfortable and very well appointed, in keeping with the style and character of the house. Award-winning food uses the best from the local larder with public areas offering a real 'wow' factor.

Rooms 17 (6 annexe) (3 fmly) (3 GF) 🐾 S £69.50-£135; D £99-£185 (incl. bkfst)* Facilities FTV WiFi ⌇ ≋ Conf Class 70 Board 50 Thtr 120 Parking 75 Notes RS Oct-Mar Civ Wed 80

MOTTRAM ST ANDREW
Cheshire

Map 16 SJ87

Mottram Hall
★★★★ 79% HOTEL

QHOTELS
INSPIRED
BY YOU

tel: 01625 828135 Wilmslow Rd SK10 4QT
email: mottramevents@qhotels.co.uk web: www.qhotels.co.uk
dir: M6 junct 18 from S, M6 junct 20 from N, M56 junct 6, A538 Prestbury

Set in 272 acres of some of Cheshire's most beautiful parkland, this 18th-century Georgian country house is certainly an idyllic retreat. The hotel boasts extensive leisure facilities, including a championship golf course, swimming pool, gym and spa. Bedrooms are well equipped and elegantly furnished, and include a number of four-poster rooms and suites.

Rooms 120 (37 fmly) (28 GF) 🐾 S £97-£237; D £109-£249 (incl. bkfst)* Facilities Spa WiFi ↕ ⊛ supervised ⌇ 18 ⌇ Putt green Fishing Gym FA approved football pitch Xmas New Year Conf Class 120 Board 60 Thtr 180 Del from £139 to £189* Services Lift Parking 300 Notes LB ⊗ Civ Wed 160

MUCH WENLOCK
Shropshire

Map 10 SO69

Raven Hotel
★★★ 78% ◎◎ HOTEL

tel: 01952 727251 30 Barrow St TF13 6EN
email: enquiry@ravenhotel.com web: www.ravenhotel.com
dir: M54 junct 4 or 5, take A442 S, then A4169 to Much Wenlock

This town-centre hotel spreads across several historic buildings with a 17th-century coaching inn at its centre. The accommodation is well furnished and equipped to offer modern comfort; some ground-floor rooms are available. Public areas feature an interesting collection of prints and memorabilia connected with the modern-day Olympic Games - an idea which was, interestingly, born in Much Wenlock.

Rooms 20 (13 annexe) (5 GF) Facilities FTV WiFi ↕ New Year Conf Board 16 Thtr 16 Parking 30 Notes ⊗ Closed 25-26 Dec

Gaskell Arms
★★★ 75% SMALL HOTEL

tel: 01952 727212 Bourton Rd TF13 6AQ
email: maxine@gaskellarms.co.uk web: www.gaskellarms.co.uk
dir: M6 junct 10A onto M54, exit at junct 4, follow signs for Ironbridge/Much Wenlock & A4169

This 17th-century former coaching inn has exposed beams and log fires in the public areas, and much original charm and character is retained throughout. In addition to the lounge bar and restaurant offering a wide range of meals and snacks, there is a small bar which is popular with locals. Well-equipped bedrooms, some located in stylishly renovated stables, provide good standards of comfort.

Rooms 14 (3 fmly) (5 GF) Facilities FTV WiFi ↕ Conf Class 30 Board 20 Thtr 30 Parking 40 Notes LB ⊗

MUDEFORD
See Christchurch

Silver Stars

The AA Silver Star rating denotes a Hotel that we highly recommend. They have a superior level of quality within their star rating, high standards of hospitality, service and cleanliness.

M

MULLION
Cornwall
Map 2 SW61

HIGHLY RECOMMENDED

Mullion Cove Hotel
★★★ 88% ◉◉ HOTEL

tel: 01326 240328 **TR12 7EP**
email: enquiries@mullion-cove.co.uk **web:** www.mullion-cove.co.uk
dir: A3083 towards The Lizard. Through Mullion towards Mullion Cove. Hotel in approx 1m

Built at the turn of the last century and set high above the working harbour of Mullion, this hotel has spectacular views of the rugged coastline; seaward facing rooms are always popular. The elegant restaurant offers some carefully prepared dishes using local produce, while an alternative option is to eat less formally in the stylish bistro. After dinner, guests might like to relax in one of the charming lounges.

Rooms 30 (3 fmly) (3 GF) ☎ **S** fr £110; **D** £146-£366 (incl. bkfst & dinner)*
Facilities FTV WiFi ⚷ Xmas New Year **Conf** Class 20 Board 30 Thtr 50
Del from £199 to £299* **Services** Lift **Parking** 60 **Notes** LB

Polurrian Bay Hotel

AA Advertised ◉

tel: 01326 240421 **TR12 7EN**
email: info@polurrianhotel.com **web:** www.polurrianhotel.com
dir: A394 to Helston. Follow The Lizard & Mullion signs onto A3083. Approx 5m, right onto B3296 to Mullion. Follow one-way system to T-junct, left signed Mullion Cove. 0.5m right, follow hotel sign

Polurrian Bay Hotel boasts a stunning cliff-top position with spectacular views across St Mount's Bay. It is very much a family-friendly establishment with a range of facilities available. Small children can be entertained in the crèche, while the spa provides some rest and relaxation for mum and dad. Bedrooms provide impressive levels of comfort and quality, and many also enjoy wonderful sea views. Public areas include the Vista, a wonderful area in which to relax and take in the breathtaking scenery while enjoying a light lunch.

Rooms 41 (12 fmly) (8 GF) ☎ **Facilities** Spa FTV WiFi ⇲ ⚷ ⚹ ⚲ Gym Xmas New Year Child facilities **Conf** Class 12 Board 30 Thtr 90 **Notes** LB Civ Wed 80

NAILSWORTH
Gloucestershire
Map 4 ST89

Wild Garlic Restaurant and Rooms

◉◉ ⚑ RESTAURANT WITH ROOMS

tel: 01453 832615 **3 Cossack Square GL6 0DB**
email: info@wild-garlic.co.uk **web:** www.wild-garlic.co.uk
dir: M4 junct 18, A46 towards Stroud. Enter Nailsworth, left at rdbt, immediately left. Establishment opposite Britannia pub

Situated in a quiet corner of charming Nailsworth, this restaurant with rooms offers a delightful combination of welcoming, relaxed hospitality and serious cuisine. The spacious and well-equipped bedrooms are situated above the award-winning restaurant. The small and friendly team of staff ensure guests are very well looked after throughout their stay.

Rooms 3 (2 fmly)

N

NANTWICH
Cheshire

Map 15 SJ65

INSPECTORS' CHOICE

Rookery Hall Hotel & Spa
★★★★ ◉◉ ⬤ HOTEL

tel: 01270 610016 & 0845 072 7533
(Calls cost 5p per minute plus your phone company's access charge)
Main Rd, Worleston CW5 6DQ
email: rookeryhall@handpicked.co.uk **web:** www.handpickedhotels.co.uk/rookeryhall
dir: *From A51 N of Nantwich take B5074 Winsford, signed Rookery Hall. Hotel 1.5m on right*

This fine 19th-century mansion is set in 38 acres of gardens, pasture and parkland. Bedrooms are spacious and appointed to a high standard with wide-screen plasma TVs and DVD players; many rooms have separate walk-in showers as well as deep tubs. Public areas are delightful and retain many original features. There is an extensive, state-of-the art spa and leisure complex.

Rooms 70 (39 annexe) (6 fmly) (23 GF) ⬤ **Facilities** Spa STV FTV WiFi ⬇ HL ⬤ ⬤ Gym Sauna Crystal steam room Hydrotherapy pool Xmas New Year **Conf** Class 90 Board 46 Thtr 200 **Services** Lift **Parking** 120 **Notes** ⊗ Civ Wed 160

Alvaston Hall Hotel
★★★ 82% HOTEL

WARNER
LEISURE
HOTELS
We're all grown up

tel: 01270 624341 **Middlewich Rd CW5 6PD**
web: www.warnerleisurehotels.co.uk

Alvaston Hall is a Grade-II listed Victorian property located in the delightful Cheshire countryside and set in extensive grounds. A variety of very well equipped bedrooms are available; some have spacious seating areas and some have outdoor terraces. Outdoor and indoor leisure facilities include a 9-hole golf course, hair and beauty treatments, and a great range of entertainment and activities including an impressive new cabaret facility. Please note that this is an adults-only (over 21 years) hotel.

Rooms 245 (15 annexe) (101 GF) ⬤ **Facilities** Spa FTV WiFi HL ⬤ supervised ⬇ 9 Putt green ⬤ Gym Archery Bowling green ♫ Xmas New Year **Services** Lift **Parking** 300 **Notes** ⊗ No children 21yrs

Premier Inn Crewe/Nantwich

Premier Inn

BUDGET HOTEL

tel: 0871 527 8782 *(Calls cost 13p per minute plus your phone company's access charge)*
221 Crewe Rd CW5 6NE
web: www.premierinn.com
dir: *M6 junct 16, A500 towards Chester, A534 towards Nantwich. Hotel approx 100yds on right*

High quality, budget accommodation ideal for both families and business travellers. Spacious, en suite bedrooms feature tea and coffee making facilities, and Freeview TV in most hotels. Internet access and WiFi are available for a small fee. The adjacent family restaurant features a wide and varied menu. See also the Hotel Groups pages.

Rooms 37

NEAR SAWREY
Cumbria

Map 18 SD39

Sawrey House Hotel
★★★ 82% COUNTRY HOUSE HOTEL

tel: 015394 36387 **LA22 0LF**
email: enquiries@sawreyhouse.com **web:** www.sawreyhouse.com
dir: *Exit M6 junct 36, follow signs to Barrow in Furness. Hotel at Newby Bridge*

Sawrey House Hotel was built in 1830 for a vicar who was to become the headmaster of the nearby Hawkshead Grammar School. It's ideally located in the peaceful village of Near Sawrey, next to Beatrix Potter's Hill Top home. The car ferry is just over two miles away, and due to being off the beaten track the area enjoys an abundance of unspoilt walks. The award-winning restaurant offers imaginative dishes using the best quality produce that Cumbria can provide.

Rooms 11 (2 GF) ⬤ **Facilities** FTV WiFi ⬇ ⬤ New Year **Parking** 19 **Notes** LB ⊗ No children 12yrs Civ Wed 40

NEW ALRESFORD
Hampshire

Map 5 SU53

Swan Hotel
★★★ 78% HOTEL

THE INDEPENDENTS
HOTEL ASSOCIATION

tel: 01962 732302 & 734427 **11 West St SO24 9AD**
email: swanhotel@btinternet.com **web:** www.swanhotelalresford.com
dir: *Exit A31 onto B3047*

This former coaching inn dates back to the 18th century and remains a busy and popular destination for travellers and locals alike. Bedrooms are situated in both the main building and the more modern wing. The lounge bar and adjacent restaurant are open all day; for more traditional dining there is another restaurant which overlooks the busy village street.

Rooms 23 (12 annexe) (3 fmly) (5 GF) ⬤ **S** £70-£80; **D** £100-£150 (incl. bkfst)*
Facilities FTV WiFi ⬇ New Year **Conf** Class 60 Board 40 Thtr 90 Del from £105 to £115* **Parking** 25 **Notes** RS 25 Dec

NEWARK-ON-TRENT
Nottinghamshire   Map 17 SK75

Premier Inn Newark
BUDGET HOTEL

tel: 0871 527 8784 *(Calls cost 13p per minute plus your phone company's access charge)*
Lincoln Rd NG24 2DB
web: www.premierinn.com
dir: *At junct of A1 & A46 & A17, follow B6166 signs*

High quality, budget accommodation ideal for both families and business travellers. Spacious, en suite bedrooms feature tea and coffee making facilities, and Freeview TV in most hotels. Internet access and WiFi are available for a small fee. The adjacent family restaurant features a wide and varied menu. See also the Hotel Groups pages.

Rooms 70

NEWBURY
Berkshire   Map 5 SU46

See also **Andover**

INSPECTORS' CHOICE

The Vineyard
★★★★★ ⚫⚫⚫ 🍴 HOTEL

tel: 01635 528770 **Stockcross RG20 8JU**
email: general@the-vineyard.co.uk **web:** www.the-vineyard.co.uk
dir: *From M4 junct 13, A34 towards Newbury, exit at 3rd junct for Speen. Right at rdbt then right again at 2nd rdbt*

A haven of style in the Berkshire countryside, this hotel prides itself on a superb art collection, which can be seen throughout the building. Bedrooms come in a variety of styles, including many split-level suites that are exceptionally well equipped. Comfortable lounges lead into the stylish restaurant, which has an impressive selection of wines from California and around the world; the cellar holds over 30,000 wines including bottles from the award-winning estate of owner Sir Peter Michael. The welcome throughout the hotel is warm and sincere, the service professional yet relaxed.

Rooms 49 (18 GF) S £175-£675; D £175-£675* **Facilities** Spa STV WiFi Gym Xmas New Year **Conf** Class 70 Board 30 Thtr 140 Del from £250* **Services** Lift Air con **Parking** 100 **Notes** LB Civ Wed 100

HIGHLY RECOMMENDED

Donnington Valley Hotel & Spa
★★★★ 84% ⚫⚫ HOTEL

tel: 01635 551199 **Old Oxford Rd, Donnington RG14 3AG**
email: general@donningtonvalley.co.uk **web:** www.donningtonvalley.co.uk
dir: *M4 junct 13, A34 signed Newbury. Take exit signed Donnington/Services, at rdbt 2nd exit signed Donnington. Left at next rdbt. Hotel 2m on right*

In its own grounds complete with an 18-hole golf course, this stylish hotel boasts excellent facilities for both corporate and leisure guests; from the state-of-the-art spa offering excellent treatments, to an extensive range of meeting and function rooms. Air-conditioned bedrooms are stylish, spacious and particularly well equipped with fridges, lap-top safes and internet access. The Wine Press restaurant offers imaginative food complemented by a superb wine list.

Rooms 111 (4 fmly) (36 GF) S £76.50-£208; D £165-£251 (incl. bkfst)* **Facilities** Spa STV WiFi 18 Putt green Gym Aromatherapy Sauna Steam room Studio Xmas New Year **Conf** Class 50 Board 65 Thtr 160 Del from £130* **Services** Lift Air con **Parking** 150 **Notes** Civ Wed 85

Regency Park Hotel
★★★★ 78% ⚫ HOTEL

tel: 01635 871555 **Bowling Green Rd, Thatcham RG18 3RP**
email: info@regencyparkhotel.co.uk **web:** www.regencyparkhotel.co.uk
dir: *From Newbury take A4 signed Thatcham & Reading. 2nd rdbt exit signed Cold Ash. Hotel 1m on left*

This smart, stylish hotel is ideal for both business and leisure guests. Spacious, well-equipped bedrooms include a number of contemporary, tasteful executive rooms. Smart, airy public areas include a state-of-the-art spa and leisure club, plus the Watermark Restaurant which offers appealing cuisine.

Rooms 108 (10 fmly) (9 GF) **Facilities** Spa STV FTV WiFi HL Gym Beauty treatments Sauna Steam room Xmas New Year **Conf** Class 80 Board 70 Thtr 200 **Services** Lift **Parking** 200 **Notes** Civ Wed 100

N

NEWBURY continued

Mercure Newbury Elcot Park

★★★★ 74% HOTEL

tel: 0844 815 9060 (Calls cost 7p per minute plus your phone company's access charge)
Elcot RG20 8NJ
email: gm.mercurenewburyelcotpark@jupiterhotels.co.uk
web: www.mercurenewbury.co.uk
dir: M4 junct 13, A338 to Hungerford, A4 to Newbury. Hotel 4m from Hungerford

Enjoying a peaceful location within easy reach of both the A4 and M4, this country-house hotel is set in 16 acres of gardens and woodland. Bedrooms are comfortably appointed and include some located in an adjacent mews. Public areas include the Orangery Restaurant which enjoys views over the Kennet Valley and a range of conference rooms.

Rooms 73 (17 annexe) (6 fmly) (25 GF) Facilities FTV WiFi ⌖ ⌕ ⌔ Gym New Year Conf Class 60 Board 50 Thtr 140 Services Lift Parking 120 Notes Civ Wed 140

Best Western West Grange Hotel

★★★ 79% HOTEL

tel: 01635 273074 Cox's Ln, Bath Rd, Midgham RG7 5UP
email: reservations@westgrangehotel.co.uk web: www.westgrangehotel.co.uk
dir: M4 junct 12, A4 Bath Rd, follow Newbury signs. Through Woolhampton, hotel on right in approx 2m

Conveniently situated between Reading and Newbury this modern hotel has well-appointed, spacious bedrooms; executive rooms are beautifully presented and have a host of additional features. The contemporary open-plan lounge and restaurant area serves an extensive choice of British cuisine. There is a range of business suites along with a larger conference room. Gardens are a real feature and the central courtyard is popular with guests.

Rooms 62 (1 fmly) (21 GF) S £55-£150; D £65-£180* Facilities FTV WiFi ⌖ Xmas New Year Conf Class 25 Board 30 Thtr 50 Del from £180 to £250* Services Lift Parking 50 Notes ⊗

The Chequers Hotel

★★★ 75% HOTEL

tel: 01635 38000 6-8 Oxford St RG14 1JB
email: info@chequershotelnewbury.co.uk web: www.chequershotelnewbury.co.uk
dir: M4 junct 13, A34 S, A339 to Newbury. At 2nd rdbt right to town centre. At clock tower rdbt right, hotel on right

Situated just at the top of the main shopping street in Newbury and convenient for fast road connections, this 18th-century former coaching inn retains original features along with contemporary touches. The bedrooms come in a range of sizes and JP's Bistro is a popular eaterie. The hotel has ample parking which is a definite advantage in this town.

Rooms 56 (2 fmly) (6 GF) Facilities FTV WiFi ⌖ Conf Class 36 Board 40 Thtr 120 Parking 60 Notes ⊗ Civ Wed 80

Donnington Grove Country Club

★★★ 74% HOTEL

tel: 01635 581000 Grove Rd, Donnington RG14 2LA
email: enquiries@donnington-grove.com web: www.donnington-grove.com

Situated on the outskirts of Newbury, overlooked by historic Donnington Castle, this hotel offers comfortable bedrooms in a number of types. Once a splendid manor house, accommodation has been tastefully added to meet the needs of the leisure and business traveller. The estate comprises some 550 acres featuring a popular championship golf course designed by Dave Thomas in 1991.

Rooms 39 (27 GF) S £97-£147; D £107-£157* Facilities FTV WiFi ⌖ ⌔ 18 Putt green Fishing New Year Conf Class 30 Board 36 Thtr 100 Del from £145 to £175* Services Lift Parking 90 Notes LB ⊗ Civ Wed 100

NEWBY BRIDGE	Map 18 SD38
Cumbria	

HIGHLY RECOMMENDED

Lakeside Hotel Lake Windermere

★★★★ 86% ⑱⑱ HOTEL

tel: 015395 30001 Lakeside LA12 8AT
email: sales@lakesidehotel.co.uk web: www.lakesidehotel.co.uk
dir: M6 junct 36, A590 to Barrow, follow signs to Newby Bridge. Right over bridge, hotel 1m on right

This impressive hotel enjoys an enviable location on the southern edge of Lake Windermere and has easy access to the Lakeside & Haverthwaite Steam Railway, and the ferry terminal. Bedrooms are individually styled, and many enjoy delightful lake views. Spacious lounges and a choice of restaurants are available. The state-of-the-art spa is exclusive to residents and provides a range of treatment suites. Staff throughout are friendly and nothing is too much trouble.

Rooms 74 (8 fmly) (8 GF) S £139-£169; D £169-£289 (incl. bkfst)* Facilities Spa STV WiFi ⌔ Fishing Gym Private jetty Rowing boats ♫ Xmas New Year Conf Class 50 Board 40 Thtr 100 Services Lift Parking 200 Notes ⊗ Civ Wed 70

The Swan Hotel & Spa

★★★★ 78% HOTEL

tel: 015395 31681 LA12 8NB
email: enquiries@swanhotel.com web: www.swanhotel.com
dir: M6 junct 36, A591, merge onto A590. At rdbts follow A590, left at Newby Bridge rdbt, 1st right for hotel

Newly re-opened after recent flooding, the Swan Hotel is set in idyllic surroundings. This hotel offers something to suit every taste, from a gym and spa therapies for adults to a dedicated children's lounge. The well-equipped bedrooms are thoroughly modern, but each has a vintage touch. Good quality meals are served in the River Room; in good weather guests can eat on the riverside terrace.

Rooms 51 (8 fmly) (14 GF) Facilities Spa FTV WiFi ⌔ Gym Sauna Steam room Xmas New Year Conf Class 60 Board 40 Thtr 100 Services Lift Air con Parking 100 Notes ⊗ Civ Wed 100

Whitewater Hotel

★★★★ 72% ⑱ HOTEL

tel: 015395 31133 The Lakeland Village LA12 8PX
email: enquiries@whitewater-hotel.co.uk web: www.whitewater-hotel.co.uk
dir: M6 junct 36, follow signs for A590 Barrow, 1m, through Newby Bridge. Right at sign for Lakeland Village, hotel on left

This tasteful conversion of an old mill on the River Leven is close to the southern end of Lake Windermere. Bedrooms, many with lovely river views, are spacious and comfortable. Public areas include a luxurious, well-equipped spa, squash courts,

N

and a choice of comfortable lounges. The Dolly Blue bar overlooks the river and is a vibrant informal alternative to the fine dining restaurant.

Rooms 38 (10 fmly) (2 GF) ⌁ **Facilities** Spa STV FTV WiFi ⌂ ⊙ supervised ⌕ Gym Squash Table tennis Xmas New Year **Conf** Class 32 Board 40 Thtr 80 **Services** Lift **Parking** 50 **Notes** ⊗ Civ Wed 110

NEWCASTLE-UNDER-LYME	Map 10 SJ84
Staffordshire	

Premier Inn Newcastle-under-Lyme

BUDGET HOTEL

tel: 0871 527 8808 *(Calls cost 13p per minute plus your phone company's access charge)*
Talke Rd, Chesterton ST5 7AL
web: www.premierinn.com
dir: *M6 junct 12, A500, A34 to Newcastle-under-Lyme. Hotel 0.5m on right*

High quality, budget accommodation ideal for both families and business travellers. Spacious, en suite bedrooms feature tea and coffee making facilities, and Freeview TV in most hotels. Internet access and WiFi are available for a small fee. The adjacent family restaurant features a wide and varied menu. See also the Hotel Groups pages.

Rooms 83

NEWCASTLE UPON TYNE	Map 21 NZ26
Tyne & Wear	

Jesmond Dene House

★★★★ ◉◉◉ HOTEL

tel: 0191 212 3000 **Jesmond Dene Rd NE2 2EY**
email: info@jesmonddenehouse.co.uk **web:** www.jesmonddenehouse.co.uk
dir: *A167 N to A184. Right, right again into Jesmond Dene Rd, hotel on left*

This grand house, overlooking the wooded valley of Jesmond Dene, yet just five minutes from the centre of town, has been sympathetically converted into a stylish, contemporary hotel destination. The bedrooms are beautifully designed and boast flat-screen TVs, sumptuous beds with Egyptian cotton linen, digital radios, well-stocked mini bars, free broadband, desk space and safes. Equally eye-catching bathrooms with underfloor heating are equipped with high quality bespoke amenities. The stylish restaurant is the venue for innovative cooking which will prove a highlight of any stay.

Rooms 40 (8 annexe) (1 fmly) (4 GF) ⌁ **S** £130-£275; **D** £152-£402 (incl. bkfst)*
Facilities STV FTV WiFi ⌂ HL **Conf** Class 40 Board 40 Thtr 120 Del from £180 to £255* **Services** Lift **Parking** 64 **Notes** LB ⊗ Civ Wed 100

Hotel du Vin Newcastle

★★★★ 79% ◉ TOWN HOUSE HOTEL

tel: 0191 229 2200 **Allan House, City Rd NE1 2BE**
email: reception.newcastle@hotelduvin.com **web:** www.hotelduvin.com
dir: *A1 junct 65 onto A184 Gateshead/Newcastle, Quayside to City Rd*

The former maintenance depot of the Tyne Tees Shipping Company, this is a landmark building on the Tyne, which has been transformed into a modern and stylish hotel. Bedrooms are well equipped and deeply comfortable with all the Hotel du Vin trademark items such as Egyptian cotton sheets, plasma TVs, DVD players and monsoon showers. Guests can dine in the bistro, or alfresco if the weather allows in the courtyard.

Rooms 42 (6 GF) ⌁ **Facilities** STV WiFi HL **Conf** Board 20 Thtr 26 **Services** Lift Air con **Parking** 10 **Notes** Civ Wed 40

Malmaison Newcastle

★★★★ 78% ◉ HOTEL

tel: 0191 389 8627 & 0844 693 0658 *(Calls cost 5p per minute plus your phone company's access charge)* **104 Quayside NE1 3DX**
email: newcastle@malmaison.com **web:** www.malmaison.com
dir: *Follow signs for city centre, then for Quayside/Law Courts. Hotel 100yds past Law Courts*

Overlooking the river and the Millennium Bridge, the hotel has a prime position in the very popular quayside district. Bedrooms have striking decor, CD/DVD players, mini-bars and a number of individual touches. Food and drink are an integral part of the operation here, with a stylish brasserie-style restaurant, plus the Café Mal, a deli-style café next door to the main entrance.

Rooms 122 (10 fmly) ⌁ **Facilities** Spa STV FTV WiFi Gym **Conf** Class 50 Board 30 Thtr 80 **Services** Lift Air con **Parking** 50 **Notes** Civ Wed 80

Holiday Inn Newcastle Jesmond

★★★★ 77% HOTEL

tel: 0191 281 5511 & 07854 590612 **Jesmond Rd NE2 1PR**
web: www.hinewcastle.co.uk

Holiday Inn Newcastle Jesmond is located next to the Metro Station and benefits from off-road parking. The interior is modern, and there is a vibrant restaurant and bar operation. This is a great location for enjoying the café culture of Jesmond or the upbeat pace of the city centre.

Rooms 116 ⌁ **Facilities** STV FTV WiFi ⌂ HL Gym ♫ New Year **Conf** Class 160 Board 46 Thtr 250 **Services** Lift Air con **Parking** 80 **Notes** ⊗ Civ Wed

The Vermont Hotel

★★★★ 77% HOTEL

tel: 0191 233 1010 **Castle Garth NE1 1RQ**
email: info@vermonthotel.co.uk **web:** www.vermont-hotel.com

This iconic building offers some great views of the city. Centrally located and benefiting from some off-road car parking, The Vermont Hotel is accessible from both the Quayside and from the castle.

Rooms 101 ⌁ **Facilities** FTV WiFi ⌂ Gym Sauna Steam room ♫ Xmas New Year **Conf** Class 80 Board 60 Thtr 220 **Services** Lift **Parking** 100 **Notes** ⊗ Civ Wed 220

N

NEWCASTLE UPON TYNE *continued*

HIGHLY RECOMMENDED

Eslington Villa Hotel

★★★ 84% 🏵 HOTEL

tel: 0191 487 6017 & 420 0666 **8 Station Rd, Low Fell NE9 6DR**
email: home@eslingtonvilla.co.uk **web:** www.eslingtonvilla.co.uk

(For full entry see Gateshead)

Horton Grange Country House Hotel

★★★ 81% HOTEL

tel: 01661 860686 **Berwick Hill, Ponteland NE13 6BU**
email: info@hortongrange.co.uk **web:** www.hortongrange.co.uk
dir: *A1/A19 junct at Seaton Burn take 1st exit at 1st rdbt, after 1m, left signed Ponteland/ Dinnington. Hotel on right approx 2m*

Horton Grange is a Grade II listed building set in its own grounds just a short distance from Newcastle Airport and Ponteland. The main house has traditionally styled executive bedrooms, and in addition there are four contemporary garden rooms that are elegant and spacious. All bedrooms have flat-screen TVs, digital radios and broadband access. Food is served in the light and airy restaurant and the lounge, both of which overlook the gardens.

Rooms 9 (4 annexe) (1 fmly) (4 GF) 🛇 **S** £54-£99; **D** £64-£129 (incl. bkfst)*
Facilities FTV WiFi Xmas New Year **Conf** Class 40 Board 30 Thtr 120 Del from £119 to £179* **Parking** 50 **Notes** LB 🛇 Civ Wed 120

The Caledonian Hotel, Newcastle

★★★ 79% HOTEL

tel: 0191 281 7881 **64 Osborne Rd, Jesmond NE2 2AT**
email: info@caledonian-hotel-newcastle.com **web:** www.peelhotels.co.uk
dir: *From A1 follow signs to Newcastle City, cross Tyne Bridge to Tynemouth. Left at lights at Osborne Rd, hotel on right*

This hotel is located in the Jesmond area of the city, and offers comfortable bedrooms that are well equipped. The public areas include the trendy Billabong Bar and Bistro which serves food all day, and the terrace where a cosmopolitan atmosphere prevails. Alfresco dining is available.

Rooms 90 (6 fmly) (7 GF) (7 smoking) 🛇 **Facilities** WiFi Xmas New Year **Conf** Class 50 Board 50 Thtr 100 **Services** Lift **Parking** 35 **Notes** 🛇 Civ Wed 70

Best Western New Kent Hotel

★★★ Ⓐ HOTEL

tel: 0191 281 7711 **127 Osborne Rd NE2 2TB**
email: reservations@newkenthotel.co.uk **web:** www.newkenthotel.co.uk
dir: *On B1600, opposite St Georges Church*

This popular business hotel offers relaxed service and typical Geordie hospitality. The bright modern bedrooms are well equipped and the modern bar is an ideal meeting place. A range of generous, good value dishes is served in the restaurant, which doubles as a wedding venue.

Rooms 32 (4 fmly) **Facilities** STV FTV WiFi 🛇 Xmas New Year **Conf** Class 30 Board 40 Thtr 60 **Parking** 22 **Notes** LB Civ Wed 90

Premier Inn Newcastle Central

BUDGET HOTEL

tel: 0871 527 8802 *(Calls cost 13p per minute plus your phone company's access charge)*
New Bridge Street West NE1 8BS
web: www.premierinn.com
dir: *Follow Gateshead & Newcastle signs on A167(M), over Tyne Bridge. A193 signed Wallsend & city centre, left to Carliol Square, hotel on corner*

High quality, budget accommodation ideal for both families and business travellers. Spacious, en suite bedrooms feature tea and coffee making facilities, and Freeview TV in most hotels. Internet access and WiFi are available for a small fee. The adjacent family restaurant features a wide and varied menu. See also the Hotel Groups pages.

Rooms 186

Premier Inn Newcastle City Centre (Millennium Bridge)

BUDGET HOTEL

tel: 0871 527 8800 *(Calls cost 13p per minute plus your phone company's access charge)*
City Rd, Quayside NE1 2AN
web: www.premierinn.com
dir: *At corner of City Rd (A186) & Crawhall Rd*

Rooms 82

Premier Inn Newcastle (Holystone)

BUDGET HOTEL

tel: 0871 527 8790 *(Calls cost 13p per minute plus your phone company's access charge)*
The Stonebrook, Edmund Rd, Holystone NE27 0UN
web: www.premierinn.com
dir: *3m N of Tyne Tunnel. From A19 take A191 signed Gosforth. Hotel on left*

Rooms 80

Premier Inn Newcastle Quayside

BUDGET HOTEL

tel: 0871 527 8804 *(Calls cost 13p per minute plus your phone company's access charge)*
The Quayside NE1 3AE
web: www.premierinn.com
dir: *S'bound: A1, A167(M), A186 signed Walker & Wallsend follow B1600 Quayside signs. N'bound: A1, A184, A189 (cross river). 1st exit, follow B1600 Quayside signs. Hotel at foot of Tyne Bridge in Exchange building*

Rooms 152

NEWCASTLE UPON TYNE AIRPORT   Map 21 NZ17
Tyne & Wear

Novotel Newcastle Airport

★★★ 79% HOTEL

tel: 028 4345 2800 **Ponteland Rd, Kenton NE3 3HZ**
email: H1118@accor.com **web:** www.novotel.com
dir: *A1(M) airport junct onto A696, take Kingston Park exit*

This modern, well-proportioned hotel lies just off the bypass and is a five minute drive from the airport. The hotel has a scheduled shuttle service and flight information screens for air passengers. Bedrooms are spacious with a range of extras. The Elements Restaurant offers a flexible dining option and is open until late. There is a contemporary lounge bar and also a small leisure centre for the more energetic guests. Secure parking is available.

Rooms 126 (36 fmly) **Facilities** FTV WiFi Gym Sauna Xmas New Year
Conf Class 150 Board 100 Thtr 200 **Services** Lift **Parking** 200 **Notes** Civ Wed 200

Premier Inn Newcastle Airport

BUDGET HOTEL

tel: 0871 527 8796 *(Calls cost 13p per minute plus your phone company's access charge)*
Newcastle Int Airport, Ponteland Rd, Prestwick NE20 9DB
web: www.premierinn.com
dir: *A1 onto A696, follow Airport signs. At rdbt take turn immediately after airport exit*

High quality, budget accommodation ideal for both families and business travellers. Spacious, en suite bedrooms feature tea and coffee making facilities, and Freeview TV in most hotels. Internet access and WiFi are available for a small fee. The adjacent family restaurant features a wide and varied menu. See also the Hotel Groups pages.

Rooms 88

Premier Inn Newcastle Airport (South)

BUDGET HOTEL

tel: 0871 527 8798 *(Calls cost 13p per minute plus your phone company's access charge)*
Callerton Lane Ends, Woolsington NE13 8DF
web: www.premierinn.com
dir: *Just off A696 on B6918, 0.3m from airport*

Rooms 53

NEWENT
Gloucestershire — Map 10 SO72

Three Choirs Vineyards

RESTAURANT WITH ROOMS

tel: 01531 890223 **GL18 1LS**
email: info@threechoirs.com **web:** www.three-choirs-vineyards.co.uk
dir: *On B4215 N of Newent, follow brown tourist signs*

This thriving vineyard continues to go from strength to strength and provides a wonderfully different place to stay. The restaurant, which overlooks the 100-acre estate, enjoys a popular following thanks to well-executed dishes that make good use of local produce. Spacious, high quality bedrooms are equipped with many extras, and each opens onto a private patio area which has lovely views.

Rooms 11 (11 annexe) (1 fmly)

NEWHAVEN
East Sussex — Map 6 TQ40

Premier Inn Newhaven

BUDGET HOTEL

tel: 0871 527 8810 *(Calls cost 13p per minute plus your phone company's access charge)*
Avis Rd BN9 0AG
web: www.premierinn.com
dir: *From A26 (New Rd) through Drove Industrial Estate, left after underpass. Hotel in same complex as Sainsbury's*

High quality, budget accommodation ideal for both families and business travellers. Spacious, en suite bedrooms feature tea and coffee making facilities,

and Freeview TV in most hotels. Internet access and WiFi are available for a small fee. The adjacent family restaurant features a wide and varied menu. See also the Hotel Groups pages.

Rooms 83

NEWMARKET
Suffolk — Map 12 TL66

INSPECTORS' CHOICE

Bedford Lodge Hotel & Spa
★★★★ HOTEL

tel: 01638 663175 **Bury Rd CB8 7BX**
email: info@bedfordlodgehotel.co.uk **web:** www.bedfordlodgehotel.co.uk
dir: *From town centre take A1304 towards Bury St Edmunds, hotel 0.5m on left*

Bedford Lodge Hotel is an imposing 18th-century Georgian hunting lodge with more modern additions, set in three acres of secluded landscaped gardens. Public rooms feature the AA Rosette-worthy Squires restaurant, Roxana Bar and a small lounge. The hotel also features superb leisure facilities including The Edge Health and Fitness Club, as well as self-contained conference and banqueting suites. Contemporary bedrooms have a light, airy feel, and each is tastefully furnished and well equipped.

Rooms 77 (6 fmly) (21 GF) (3 smoking) **Facilities** Spa STV FTV WiFi Gym Steam room Sauna Hydrotherapy pool Rasul Dry floatation New Year
Conf Class 80 Board 50 Thtr 180 **Services** Lift Air con **Parking** 120 **Notes**
RS Sat lunch Civ Wed 150

N

NEWMARKET *continued*

Tuddenham Mill

★★★★ 81% ⊛⊛ HOTEL

tel: 01638 713552 **High St, Tuddenham St Mary IP28 6SQ**
email: info@tuddenhammill.co.uk **web:** www.tuddenhammill.co.uk
dir: *M11 junct 9, merge A14. Left lane junct 38 towards Thetford/Norwich. Signed Tuddenham*

Tuddenham Mill is a beautifully converted old watermill set amidst landscaped grounds between Newmarket and Bury St Edmunds. The contemporary style bedrooms are situated in separate buildings adjacent to the main building, and each one is tastefully appointed with co-ordinated fabrics and soft furnishings. The public areas have a wealth of original features such as the water wheel and exposed beams; they include a lounge bar, a smart restaurant, a meeting room and choice of terraces.

Rooms 15 (12 annexe) (8 GF) ⦁ **S** £395; **D** £395 (incl. bkfst)* **Facilities** STV FTV WiFi ⦁ Putt green Xmas New Year **Conf** Class 16 Board 16 Thtr 40 Del from £150* **Parking** 40 **Notes** LB Civ Wed 60

Best Western Heath Court Hotel

★★★ 79% HOTEL

tel: 01638 667171 **Moulton Rd CB8 8DY**
email: quality@heathcourthotel.com **web:** www.heathcourthotel.com

Heath Court Hotel enjoys a very convenient location close to the town centre and overlooks the Newmarket gallops. Bedrooms are all well-equipped and spacious, and free WiFi is available throughout the hotel, which has recently been refurbished. Ample secure parking is available and there is a popular restaurant and bar.

Rooms 43 (2 fmly) **S** £60-£95; **D** £79-£213 (incl. bkfst)* **Facilities** STV FTV WiFi ⦁ New Year **Conf** Class 45 Board 40 Thtr 130 Del from £100 to £115* **Services** Lift **Parking** 60 **Notes** LB Civ Wed 120

Premier Inn Newmarket

BUDGET HOTEL

tel: 0871 527 9296 *(Calls cost 13p per minute plus your phone company's access charge)*
Fred Archer Way CB8 7XN
web: www.premierinn.com
dir: *A14 junct 37, A142 (Fordham Rd). 2.3m, straight on at 2 rdbts. At end of Fordham Rd, into right lane, turn right. Hotel on right*

High quality, budget accommodation ideal for both families and business travellers. Spacious, en suite bedrooms feature tea and coffee making facilities, and Freeview TV in most hotels. Internet access and WiFi are available for a small fee. The adjacent family restaurant features a wide and varied menu. See also the Hotel Groups pages.

Rooms 75

NEW MILTON
Hampshire

Map 5 SZ29

Chewton Glen Hotel & Spa

★★★★★ ⊛⊛ ☗ COUNTRY HOUSE HOTEL

tel: 01425 275341 **Christchurch Rd BH25 6QS**
email: reservations@chewtonglen.com **web:** www.chewtonglen.com
dir: *A35 from Lyndhurst for 10m, left at staggered junct. Follow tourist sign for hotel through Walkford, take 2nd left*

Chewton has had a revitalisation in recent years; the eco-friendly tree-houses point the hotel in a fresh and exciting direction. The extensive grounds include, - in addition to activities like golf and croquet, - a walled garden, which provides for the hotel kitchen, and is a feature in its own right. Bedrooms are luxurious and delightfully appointed, while public areas are stylish and comfortable, the perfect place for traditional afternoon tea. Cuisine as ever, is at the forefront, and the Vetiver restaurant has something for every diner.

Rooms 70 (12 annexe) (43 fmly) (11 GF) ⦁ **D** £325-£1495* **Facilities** Spa STV FTV WiFi ⦁ ⦁ ⦁ ⦁ 9 ⦁ Putt green ⦁ Gym Hydrotherapy spa Dance studio Cycling & jogging trail Clay shooting Archery ♫ Xmas New Year Child facilities **Conf** Class 70 Board 40 Thtr 150 Del from £275* **Services** Air con **Parking** 150 **Notes** ⊗ Civ Wed 140

NEWPORT	Map 5 SZ58
Isle of Wight	

Premier Inn Isle of Wight (Newport)

BUDGET HOTEL

tel: 0871 527 8556 *(Calls cost 13p per minute plus your phone company's access charge)*
Seaclose, Fairlee Rd PO30 2DN
web: www.premierinn.com
dir: *From Newport take A3054 signed Ryde. In 0.75m at Seaclose lights, turn left. Hotel adjacent to council offices*

High quality, budget accommodation ideal for both families and business travellers. Spacious, en suite bedrooms feature tea and coffee making facilities, and Freeview TV in most hotels. Internet access and WiFi are available for a small fee. The adjacent family restaurant features a wide and varied menu. See also the Hotel Groups pages.

Rooms 68

NEWPORT	Map 15 SJ71
Shropshire	

Premier Inn Newport/Telford

BUDGET HOTEL

tel: 0871 527 8808 *(Calls cost 13p per minute plus your phone company's access charge)*
Stafford Rd TF10 9BY
web: www.premierinn.com
dir: *From A41 E of Newport take A518 towards Stafford. Hotel on right adjacent to Mere Park Garden Centre*

High quality, budget accommodation ideal for both families and business travellers. Spacious, en suite bedrooms feature tea and coffee making facilities, and Freeview TV in most hotels. Internet access and WiFi are available for a small fee. The adjacent family restaurant features a wide and varied menu. See also the Hotel Groups pages.

Rooms 50

NEWPORT PAGNELL MOTORWAY SERVICE AREA (M1)	Map 11 SP84
Buckinghamshire	

Days Inn Milton Keynes

WELCOMEBREAK

AA Advertised

tel: 01908 610878 **Newport Pagnell Services, M1 Junct 14/15 MK16 9DS**
email: miltonkeynes.hotelmanager@welcomebreak.co.uk
web: www.welcomebreak.co.uk/hotels/milton-keynes
dir: *M1 Northbound junct 14/15. Hotel is located in Welcome Break services off Little Linford Lane*

This modern building offers accommodation in smart, spacious and well-equipped bedrooms, suitable for families and business travellers, and all with en suite bathrooms. Continental breakfast is available and other refreshments may be taken at the nearby family restaurant.

Rooms 87 (14 fmly) (25 GF) (4 smoking) **Facilities** STV FTV WiFi **Conf** Class 12 Board 16 Thtr 40 **Parking** 90

NEWQUAY	Map 2 SW86
Cornwall	

Headland Hotel

★★★★ 83% @ HOTEL

tel: 01637 872211 **Fistral Beach TR7 1EW**
email: reception@headlandhotel.co.uk **web:** www.headlandhotel.co.uk
dir: *A30 onto A392 at Indian Queens, approaching Newquay follow signs for Fistral Beach, hotel adjacent*

This Victorian hotel enjoys a stunning location overlooking the sea on three sides, so views can be enjoyed from most of the windows. Bedrooms are comfortable and spacious. The grand public areas, with impressive floral displays, include various lounges and as a complement to the formal dining room, The Terrace offers a relaxed alternative. Recent additions include the spa, gym and leisure facilities including relaxation pool, steam room, aromatherapy showers and sauna. Self-catering cottages are available, and guests staying in these are welcome to use the hotel facilities.

Rooms 96 (30 fmly) **S** £80 £400, **D** £100-£500 (incl. bkfst)* **Facilities** Spa STV FTV WiFi 🏊 🎾 👤 9 🏌 Putt green 🏋 Gym Pitch & putt Fitness centre Spa & wellness centre 🎵 Xmas New Year **Conf** Class 120 Board 40 Thtr 250 **Services** Lift **Parking** 300 **Notes** Civ Wed 250

N

NEWQUAY *continued*

Atlantic Hotel

★★★★ 79% ⬤ HOTEL

tel: 01637 872244 **Dane Rd TR7 1EN**
email: info@atlantichotelnewquay.co.uk **web:** www.atlantichotelnewquay.co.uk
dir: *A30 onto A392 to Indian Queens, approaching Newquay. Follow signs for Fistral Beach, hotel on hill overlooking sea & harbour*

Glamour, grandeur and a warm welcome await at the Atlantic Hotel. Set in ten acres of private headland, this stunning art-deco hotel offers sweeping views of the Atlantic Ocean. Each room is unique, comfortably furnished and comes with a glorious sea view. Diners can enjoy a range of contemporary dishes that offer the best local seafood and seasonal produce, in the relaxed, elegant atmosphere at Silks Bistro and Champagne Bar. The south-facing terrace, sun-trap pool and spa treatment room offer a range of spaces to relax and indulge. Just a short stroll from Newquay, and the South West Coast Path, the Atlantic Hotel is the perfect base for exploring the dramatic north Cornwall coast.

Rooms 57 (4 annexe) (10 fmly) ☏ **Facilities** STV FTV WiFi ☺ ☜ ☆ Surf school Steam room Sauna ♬ Xmas New Year **Conf** Class 350 Board 150 Thtr 350 Del from £125 to £185 **Services** Lift **Parking** 57 **Notes** Civ Wed 360

Best Western Hotel Bristol

★★★ 80% HOTEL   **Best Western**

tel: 01637 875181 **Narrowcliff TR7 2PQ**
email: info@hotelbristol.co.uk **web:** www.hotelbristol.co.uk
dir: *A30 onto A392, then A3058. Hotel 2.5m on left*

This hotel is conveniently situated, and many of the bedrooms enjoy fine sea views. Staff are friendly and provide a professional and attentive service. There is a range

of comfortable lounges, ideal for relaxing prior to eating in the elegant dining room. There are also leisure and conference facilities.

Rooms 74 (23 fmly) ☏ **S** £83-£133; **D** £136-£226 (incl. bkfst)* **Facilities** FTV WiFi HL ☜ Table tennis Xmas New Year Child facilities **Conf** Class 80 Board 30 Thtr 200 **Services** Lift **Parking** 105 **Notes** LB Closed 4-15 Jan Civ Wed 300

Trebarwith Hotel

★★★ 80% HOTEL

tel: 01637 872288 & 0800 387520 **Trebarwith Crescent TR7 1BZ**
email: enquiry@trebarwith-hotel.co.uk **web:** www.trebarwith-hotel.co.uk
dir: *From A3058 into Mount Wise Rd. 3rd right into Marcus Hill, across East St into Trebarwith Cres. Hotel at end*

With breathtaking views of the rugged coastline and a path leading to the beach, this friendly, family-run hotel is set in its own grounds close to the town centre. The public rooms include a lounge, ballroom, restaurant and cinema. The comfortable bedrooms include four-poster and family rooms, and many benefit from the sea views.

Rooms 41 (8 fmly) (1 GF) ☏ **Facilities** FTV WiFi ☺ ☜ Fishing Video theatre Games room Surf school Padi/SSI scuba diving centre ♬ **Conf** Class 30 Board 18 Thtr 45 **Parking** 41 **Notes** ⊗ Closed Nov-5 Apr

The Legacy Hotel Victoria

★★★ 75% HOTEL   ◼◼ **LEGACY HOTELS**

tel: 0844 411 9025 *(Calls cost 7p per minute plus your phone company's access charge)*
& 0330 333 2825 **East St TR7 1DB**
email: bookings@hotel-victoria.co.uk **web:** www.legacy-hotels.co.uk
dir: *A30 towards Bodmin following signs to Newquay. Hotel next to Newquay's main post office*

Standing on the cliffs, overlooking Newquay Bay, the hotel is situated at the centre of this vibrant town. The spacious lounges and bar areas all benefit from glorious views. Varied menus, using the best of local produce, are offered in the restaurant. Bedrooms vary from spacious superior rooms and suites to standard inland-facing rooms. Berties pub, a nightclub, and indoor leisure facilities are also available.

Rooms 71 (23 fmly) (1 GF) ☏ **Facilities** FTV WiFi ☜ Gym Beauty treatment room Sauna Steam room **Conf** Class 130 Board 50 Thtr 200 **Services** Lift **Parking** 50 **Notes** Civ Wed 150

Kilbirnie Hotel

★★★ 71% HOTEL

tel: 01637 875155 **Narrowcliff TR7 2RS**
email: info@kilbirniehotel.co.uk **web:** www.kilbirniehotel.co.uk
dir: *On A392*

With delightful views over the open space known as The Barrowfields and beyond to the sea, this privately-run hotel offers an impressive range of facilities. The reception rooms are spacious and comfortable, and during summer months become the venue for a programme of entertainment. Bedrooms vary in size and style, and some enjoy fine sea views.

Rooms 66 (6 fmly) (8 GF) ☏ **S** £30-£60; **D** £60-£120* **Facilities** FTV WiFi ☜ Gym Fitness room Snooker room Sauna Xmas New Year **Conf** Class 50 Board 25 Thtr 100 **Services** Lift Air con **Parking** 58 **Notes** Closed 2-31 Jan

Eliot Hotel

Leisureplex
HOLIDAY HOTELS

★★★ 68% HOTEL

tel: 01637 878177 **Edgcumbe Av TR7 2NH**
email: eliot.newquay@alfatravel.co.uk **web:** www.leisureplex.co.uk
dir: A30 onto A392 towards Quintrell Downs. Right at rdbt onto A3058. 4m to Newquay, left at amusements onto Edgcumbe Ave. Hotel on left

Located in a quiet residential area just a short walk from the beaches and the varied attractions of the town, this long-established hotel offers comfortable accommodation. Entertainment is provided most nights throughout the season and guests can relax in the spacious public areas.

Rooms 76 (10 fmly) ✿ **S** £50; **D** £84 (incl. bkfst)* **Facilities** FTV WiFi ⌇ Pool table Table tennis ♫ Xmas New Year **Services** Lift **Parking** 20 **Notes** ⊗ Closed Dec-Jan (ex Xmas/New Year) RS Feb-Mar

Hotel California

★★★ 67% HOTEL

tel: 01637 879292 & 872798 **Pentire Crescent TR7 1PU**
email: info@hotel-california.co.uk **web:** www.hotel-california.co.uk
dir: A392 to Newquay, follow signs for Pentire Hotels & Guest Houses

This hotel is tucked away in a delightful location, close to Fistral Beach and adjacent to the River Gannel. Many bedrooms have views across the river towards the sea, and some have balconies. There is an impressive range of leisure facilities, including ten-pin bowling and both indoor and outdoor pools. The cuisine is enjoyable and menus offer a range of interesting dishes.

Rooms 70 (27 fmly) (13 GF) **Facilities** FTV WiFi HL ⌇ Squash 4-lane American bowling alley Hairdresser Snooker & pool room Sauna Solarium ♫ Xmas New Year **Conf** Class 100 Board 30 Thtr 100 **Services** Lift **Parking** 60 **Notes** Closed 3-25 Jan Civ Wed 150

Priory Lodge Hotel

★★ 78% HOTEL

tel: 0163/ 874111 **30 Mount Wise TR7 2BN**
email: fionapocklington@tiscali.co.uk **web:** www.priorylodgehotel.co.uk
dir: From lights in town centre onto Berry Rd, right onto B3282 Mount Wise, 0.5m on right

This hotel enjoys a central location close to the town centre, the harbour and the local beaches. Secure parking is available at the hotel along with a range of leisure facilities including a heated pool, sauna, games room and hot tub. Attractively decorated bedrooms vary in size and style - many have sea views over Towan Beach.

Rooms 28 (6 annexe) (13 fmly) (1 GF) **S** £40-£50; **D** £80-£95 (incl. bkfst)* **Facilities** FTV WiFi ⌇ ♫ **Parking** 30 **Notes** ⊗ Closed Dec-end Mar

Premier Inn Newquay (Quintrell Downs)

Premier Inn

BUDGET HOTEL

tel: 0871 527 8818 (Calls cost 13p per minute plus your phone company's access charge)
Quintrell Downs TR8 4LE
web: www.premierinn.com
dir: From A30 take A39. At rdbt 2nd exit signed Newquay A392. 4m, in Quintrell Downs take 1st exit at rdbt. Hotel on left

High quality, budget accommodation ideal for both families and business travellers. Spacious, en suite bedrooms feature tea and coffee making facilities, and Freeview TV in most hotels. Internet access and WiFi are available for a small fee. The adjacent family restaurant features a wide and varied menu. See also the Hotel Groups pages.

Rooms 74

Lewinnick Lodge

RESTAURANT WITH ROOMS

tel: 01637 878117 **Pentire Headland TR7 1QD**
email: thelodge@hospitalitycornwall.com
web: www.hospitalitycornwall.com/lewinnicklodge
dir: From A392, at rdbt exit into Pentire Rd then Pentire Ave. Turn right to Lewinnick Lodge

Set above the cliffs of Pentire Headland, looking out across the mighty Atlantic, guests are guaranteed amazing coastal views here at Lewinnick Lodge. The bedrooms were designed by Guy Bostock and are modern, spacious, and offer many thoughtful extras; some have open-plan bathrooms. Modern British food (with an emphasis on fresh fish) is served all day.

Rooms 11 (1 fmly)

NEWTON ABBOT	Map 3 SX87
Devon	

See also Ilsington

Best Western Passage House Hotel

BW Best Western.

★★★ 75% HOTEL

tel: 01626 355515 **Hackney Ln, Kingsteignton TQ12 3QH**
email: mail@passagehousegroup.co.uk **web:** www.passagehousegroup.co.uk/hotel
dir: A380 onto A381, follow racecourse signs

With memorable views of the Teign Estuary, this popular hotel provides spacious, well-equipped bedrooms. An impressive range of leisure and meeting facilities is offered and a conservatory provides a pleasant extension to the bar and lounge. A choice of eating options is available, either in the main restaurant, or the adjacent Passage House Inn for less formal dining.

Rooms 90 (52 annexe) (64 fmly) (26 GF) **Facilities** Spa WiFi ⌇ ⊙ supervised Gym **Conf** Class 50 Board 40 Thtr 120 **Services** Lift **Parking** 300 **Notes** ⊗ RS 24-27 Dec Civ Wed 75

Premier Inn Newton Abbot

Premier Inn

BUDGET HOTEL

tel: 0871 527 9300 (Calls cost 13p per minute plus your phone company's access charge)
Newton Abbott Racecourse, Newton Rd TQ12 3AF
web: www.premierinn.com
dir: A380 exit at Ware Barton signed A383/Ashburton, follow brown signs for Newton Abbot Racecourse through Kingsteignton. Then follow Officials Entrance sign to hotel

High quality, budget accommodation ideal for both families and business travellers. Spacious, en suite bedrooms feature tea and coffee making facilities, and Freeview TV in most hotels. Internet access and WiFi are available for a small fee. The adjacent family restaurant features a wide and varied menu. See also the Hotel Groups pages.

Rooms 84

N

NEWTON AYCLIFFE
County Durham — Map 19 NZ22

Premier Inn Durham (Newton Aycliffe)

BUDGET HOTEL

tel: 0871 527 8336 *(Calls cost 13p per minute plus your phone company's access charge)*
Ricknall Ln, Great North Rd DL5 6JG
web: www.premierinn.com
dir: On A167 E of Newton Aycliffe, 3m from A1(M)

High quality, budget accommodation ideal for both families and business travellers. Spacious, en suite bedrooms feature tea and coffee making facilities, and Freeview TV in most hotels. Internet access and WiFi are available for a small fee. The adjacent family restaurant features a wide and varied menu. See also the Hotel Groups pages.

Rooms 44

NORMAN CROSS
Cambridgeshire — Map 12 TL19

Premier Inn Peterborough (A1(M) Jct 16)

BUDGET HOTEL

tel: 0871 527 8870 *(Calls cost 13p per minute plus your phone company's access charge)*
Norman Cross, A1(M) Junction 16 PE7 3TB
web: www.premierinn.com
dir: A1(M) junct 16, A15 towards Yaxley, hotel in 100yds

High quality, budget accommodation ideal for both families and business travellers. Spacious, en suite bedrooms feature tea and coffee making facilities, and Freeview TV in most hotels. Internet access and WiFi are available for a small fee. The adjacent family restaurant features a wide and varied menu. See also the Hotel Groups pages.

Rooms 99

NORMANTON
Rutland — Map 11 SK90

Best Western Normanton Park Hotel

★★★ 71% HOTEL

tel: 01780 720315 **Oakham LE15 8RP**
email: info@normantonpark.co.uk **web:** www.bw-normantonparkhotel.co.uk
dir: From A1 follow A606 towards Oakham, 5m. Turn left, 1.5m. Hotel on right

This hotel offers some of Rutland Water's best views over the south shore. The comfortable bedrooms are located in the main house and the courtyard. Public rooms include a conservatory dining room overlooking the water, and a cosy lounge is available for guests to relax in.

Rooms 30 (7 annexe) (6 fmly) (11 GF) ⌇ **S** £80-£110; **D** £95-£140 (incl. bkfst)* **Facilities** FTV WiFi ↕ Xmas New Year **Conf** Class 60 Board 80 Thtr 200 Del from £90 to £145* **Parking** 100 **Notes** Civ Wed 80

NORTHAMPTON
Northamptonshire — Map 11 SP76

Westone Manor Hotel

★★★ 70% HOTEL

tel: 01604 410796 & 739955 **Ashley Way, Weston Favell NN3 3EA**
email: enquiries@hotels-northampton.com **web:** www.hotels-northampton.com
dir: A43 Kettering for 0.5m. Then A4500 for Town Centre/Earls Barton/Weston Favell. Left at lights onto A4500 for 100yds. 1st right at sign Westone Manor Hotel Northampton, over small rdbt, hotel on left

Built in 1914 as the home of the local shoe manufacturer William Sears, this property has since been expanded, and now offers comfortable accommodation to the rear. A lounge, bar, and conservatory restaurant are available. Free WiFi is available throughout the hotel.

Rooms 69 (38 annexe) (2 fmly) (19 GF) **S** £55-£60; **D** £60-£75* **Facilities** FTV WiFi Xmas New Year **Conf** Class 60 Board 60 Thtr 120 Del from £90 to £180 **Services** Lift **Parking** 70 **Notes** ⊗ Civ Wed 120

Premier Inn Northampton Bedford Road/A428

BUDGET HOTEL

tel: 0871 527 8822 *(Calls cost 13p per minute plus your phone company's access charge)*
The Lakes, Bedford Rd NN4 7YD
web: www.premierinn.com
dir: M1 junct 15, follow A508 (A45) signs to Northampton. A428 at rdbt take 4th exit (signed Bedford). Left at next rdbt. Hotel on right

High quality, budget accommodation ideal for both families and business travellers. Spacious, en suite bedrooms feature tea and coffee making facilities, and Freeview TV in most hotels. Internet access and WiFi are available for a small fee. The adjacent family restaurant features a wide and varied menu. See also the Hotel Groups pages.

Rooms 44

Premier Inn Northampton Great Billing/A45

BUDGET HOTEL

tel: 0871 527 8824 *(Calls cost 13p per minute plus your phone company's access charge)*
Crow Ln, Great Billing NN3 9DA
web: www.premierinn.com
dir: M1 junct 15, A508, A45 follow Billing Aquadrome signs

Rooms 60

Premier Inn Northampton South (Wootton)

BUDGET HOTEL

tel: 0871 527 8826 *(Calls cost 13p per minute plus your phone company's access charge)*
Newport Pagnell Road West, Wootton NN4 7JJ
web: www.premierinn.com
dir: M1 junct 15, A508 towards Northampton, exit at junct with A45. At rdbt take B526. Hotel on right

Rooms 70

Premier Inn Northampton Town Centre

BUDGET HOTEL

tel: 0871 527 9590 *(Calls cost 13p per minute plus your phone company's access charge)*
St. Johns St NN1 1FA
email: NorthamptonTownCentre.PI@premierinn.com **web:** www.premierinn.com
dir: *From N: M1 junct 16, A45, signed Northampton West. At rdbt onto A4 (Northampton). Pass Northampton Rugby Ground on right. At Northampton Rail Station turn right at lights, (stay in left lane) 2nd exit at rdbt left at 2nd*

Rooms 104

Premier Inn Northampton West (Harpole)

BUDGET HOTEL

tel: 0871 527 8828 *(Calls cost 13p per minute plus your phone company's access charge)*
Harpole Turn, Weedon Rd, Harpole NN7 4DD
web: www.premierinn.com
dir: *M1 junct 16, A45 towards Northampton. In 1m left into Harpole Turn. Hotel on left*

Rooms 75

Ibis Northampton Centre

AA Advertised

tel: 01604 608900 **Sol Central, Marefair NN1 1SR**
email: H3657@accor.com **web:** www.ibishotel.com
dir: *M1 junct 15/15a & city centre towards railway station*

Modern, budget hotel offering comfortable accommodation in bright and practical bedrooms. Breakfast is self-service and dinner is available in the restaurant.

Rooms 151 (14 fmly) **Facilities** WiFi **Services** Lift

NORTH FERRIBY
East Riding of Yorkshire
Map 17 SE92

Hallmark Hotel Hull

★★★★ 74% HOTEL

tel: 0330 028 3414 **Ferriby High Rd HU14 3LG**
email: hull@hallmarkhotels.co.uk **web:** www.hallmarkhotels.co.uk
dir: *M62 onto A63 towards Hull. Exit at Humber Bridge signage. Follow North Ferriby signs, hotel 0.5m on left*

This property is situated just outside Hull city centre, with breathtaking views of the Humber Bridge. Service is attentive with a friendly atmosphere. The comfortable bedrooms are tastefully appointed and are suitable for both business and leisure guests. The restaurant and bar serve a good choice of dishes. Conference facilities are available along with free WiFi and private parking.

Rooms 95 (3 fmly) (16 GF) **Facilities** STV FTV WiFi Xmas New Year **Conf** Class 85 Board 86 Thtr 200 **Parking** 150 **Notes** Civ Wed 200

NORTH KILWORTH
Leicestershire
Map 11 SP68

INSPECTORS' CHOICE

Kilworth House Hotel & Theatre

★★★★ ◎◎ HOTEL

tel: 01858 880058 **Lutterworth Rd LE17 6JE**
email: info@kilworthhouse.co.uk **web:** www.kilworthhouse.co.uk
dir: *A4304 towards Market Harborough, after Walcote, hotel 1.5m on right*

Kilworth House Hotel is a restored Victorian country house located in 38 acres of private grounds offering state-of-the-art conference rooms. The gracious public areas feature many period pieces and original art works. The bedrooms are very comfortable and well equipped, and the large Orangery is now used for informal dining, while the opulent Wordsworth Restaurant has a more formal air. Close to the lake an open-air theatre which seats 540 has been built; professional productions are performed, and picnics can be arranged, or dinner back at the hotel is also an option.

Rooms 44 (2 fmly) (13 GF) **D** £145-£390 (incl. bkfst)* **Facilities** Spa FTV WiFi Fishing Gym Beauty therapy rooms Xmas New Year **Conf** Class 30 Board 30 Thtr 80 Del from £205 to £254* **Services** Lift **Parking** 140 **Notes** LB Civ Wed 180

NORTH SHIELDS
Tyne & Wear
Map 21 NZ36

Premier Inn North Shields (Ferry Terminal)

BUDGET HOTEL

tel: 0871 527 8818 *(Calls cost 13p per minute plus your phone company's access charge)*
Coble Dene Rd NE29 6DL
web: www.premierinn.com
dir: *From all directions follow signs for Royal Quays (Outlet Centre) & International Ferry Terminal. From A187 take Coble Dene Rd. At 3rd rdbt right, 1st right at mini rdbt*

High quality, budget accommodation ideal for both families and business travellers. Spacious, en suite bedrooms feature tea and coffee making facilities, and Freeview TV in most hotels. Internet access and WiFi are available for a small fee. The adjacent family restaurant features a wide and varied menu. See also the Hotel Groups pages.

Rooms 74

NORTH WALSHAM
Norfolk   Map 13 TG23

Beechwood Hotel
★★★ 88% ◉◉ HOTEL

tel: 01692 403231 **20 Cromer Rd NR28 0HD**
email: info@beechwood-hotel.co.uk **web:** www.beechwood-hotel.co.uk
dir: B1150 from Norwich. At North Walsham left at 1st lights, then right at next

Beechwood Hotel offers a friendly and informal atmosphere, comfortable and well-appointed bedrooms, and a creative head chef sourcing produce from local farms and Cromer fishermen. Near to a Heritage coastline, the Norfolk Broads and the cathedral city of Norwich, this is a great place for a short break.

Rooms 18 (4 GF) ↑ **S** £70-£96; **D** £100-£175 (incl. bkfst)* **Facilities** FTV WiFi ↳ ⊌ New Year **Conf** Class 20 Board 20 Thtr 20 **Parking** 20 **Notes** LB

NORTHWICH
Cheshire   Map 15 SJ67

Premier Inn Northwich (Sandiway)
BUDGET HOTEL

tel: 0871 527 8830 *(Calls cost 13p per minute plus your phone company's access charge)*
520 Chester Rd, Sandiway CW8 2DN
web: www.premierinn.com
dir: M6 junct 19, A556 towards Chester. Hotel in 11m

High quality, budget accommodation ideal for both families and business travellers. Spacious, en suite bedrooms feature tea and coffee making facilities, and Freeview TV in most hotels. Internet access and WiFi are available for a small fee. The adjacent family restaurant features a wide and varied menu. See also the Hotel Groups pages.

Rooms 42

Premier Inn Northwich South
BUDGET HOTEL

tel: 0871 527 8832 *(Calls cost 13p per minute plus your phone company's access charge)*
London Rd, Leftwich CW9 8EG
web: www.premierinn.com
dir: Just off M6 junct 19. Follow A556 towards Chester. Right at sign for Northwich & Davenham

Rooms 43

NORWICH
Norfolk   Map 13 TG20

Maids Head Hotel
★★★★ 81% ◉◉ HOTEL

tel: 01603 209955 **Tombland NR3 1LB**
email: reservations@maidsheadhotel.co.uk **web:** www.maidsheadhotel.co.uk
dir: In city centre. Telephone or see website for detailed directions

The Maids Head Hotel is an impressive 13th-century building situated close to the impressive Norman cathedral, and within easy walking distance of the city centre. The bedrooms are pleasantly decorated and thoughtfully equipped; some rooms have original oak beams. The spacious public rooms include a Jacobean bar, a range of seating areas and the Courtyard Restaurant.

Rooms 84 (10 fmly) ↑ **Facilities** FTV WiFi ↳ Beauty treatment room Use of nearby gym Xmas New Year **Conf** Class 30 Board 50 Thtr 100 **Services** Lift **Parking** 83 **Notes** ⊗ Civ Wed 100

St Giles House Hotel
★★★★ 81% ◉◉ HOTEL

tel: 01603 275180 **41-45 St Giles St NR2 1JR**
email: reception@stgileshousehotel.com **web:** www.stgileshousehotel.com
dir: A11 into central Norwich. Left at rdbt (Chapelfield Shopping Centre). 3rd exit at next rdbt. Left onto St Giles St. Hotel on left

St Giles House Hotel is a stylish 19th-century, Grade II listed building situated in the heart of the city. The property has a wealth of magnificent original features such as wood-panelling, ornamental plasterwork and marble floors. Public areas include an open-plan lounge bar/restaurant, a smart lounge with plush sofas and a Parisian-style terrace. The spacious, contemporary bedrooms are individually designed and have many thoughtful touches.

Rooms 24 (3 GF) ↑ **Facilities** Spa FTV WiFi Xmas New Year **Conf** Class 20 Board 24 Thtr 45 **Services** Lift **Parking** 30 **Notes** ⊗ Civ Wed 60

Park Farm Hotel
★★★★ 77% ◉ HOTEL

tel: 01603 810264 **NR9 3DL**
email: enq@parkfarm-hotel.co.uk **web:** www.parkfarm-hotel.co.uk

(For full entry see Hethersett)

Dunston Hall
★★★★ 77% HOTEL

tel: 01508 470444 **Ipswich Rd NR14 8PQ**
web: www.qhotels.co.uk
dir: From A47 take A140 (Ipswich road). 0.25m, hotel on left

Dunston Hall is an imposing Grade II listed building set amidst 170 acres of landscaped grounds just a short drive from the city centre. The spacious bedrooms are smartly decorated, tastefully furnished and equipped to a high standard. The attractively appointed public rooms offer a wide choice of areas in which to relax, and the hotel also boasts a superb range of leisure facilities including an 18-hole PGA golf course, floodlit tennis courts and a football pitch.

Rooms 169 (16 fmly) (16 GF) (2 smoking) **Facilities** Spa WiFi ⊗ ↻ 18 Putt green Gym Floodlit driving range Xmas New Year **Conf** Class 140 Board 80 Thtr 300 **Services** Lift **Parking** 500 **Notes** Civ Wed 90

Mercure Norwich Hotel
★★★★ 75% HOTEL

tel: 0844 815 9036 *(Calls cost 5p per minute plus your phone company's access charge)*
121-131 Boundary Rd NR3 2BA
email: info@mercurenorwich.co.uk **web:** www.mercurenorwich.co.uk
dir: Approx 2m from airport on A140 Norwich ring road

This purpose-built property is situated on the outer ring road within easy striking distance of the city centre. Bedrooms are spacious and well equipped with modern facilities. Public rooms include an open-plan lounge bar and a smart restaurant. The hotel has leisure facilities, meeting rooms and a banqueting suite.

Rooms 107 **Facilities** FTV WiFi ↳ ↻ Gym Sauna Steam room **Conf** Class 160 Board 80 Thtr 400 **Parking** 225 **Notes** ⊗ Civ Wed 400

Best Western Annesley House Hotel

★★★ 87% ◉◉ HOTEL

tel: 01603 624553 **6 Newmarket Rd NR2 2LA**
email: annesleyhouse@bestwestern.co.uk **web:** www.bw-annesleyhouse.co.uk
dir: On A11, 0.5m before city centre

This delightful Georgian property is set in three acres of landscaped gardens close to the city centre. Bedrooms are split between three separate houses, two of which are linked by a glass walkway. Each is attractively decorated, tastefully furnished and thoughtfully equipped. Public rooms include a comfortable lounge/bar and a smart conservatory restaurant which overlooks the gardens.

Rooms 30 (12 annexe) (1 fmly) (9 GF) 🐾 **Facilities** FTV WiFi ↳ **Parking** 28
Notes ⊗ Closed 24 Dec-28 Jan

Stower Grange

★★★ 80% ◉ COUNTRY HOUSE HOTEL

tel: 01603 860210 **40 School Rd, Drayton NR8 6EF**
email: enquiries@stowergrange.co.uk **web:** www.stowergrange.co.uk
dir: Norwich ring road N to Asda supermarket. Take A1067 (Fakenham Rd) at Drayton, right at lights into School Rd. Hotel 150yds on right

Expect a warm welcome at this 17th-century, ivy-clad property situated in a peaceful residential area close to the city centre and airport. The individually decorated bedrooms are generally quite spacious; each is tastefully furnished and equipped with many thoughtful touches. Public rooms include a smart open-plan lounge bar and an elegant restaurant.

Rooms 11 (1 fmly) 🐾 **S** £80-£90; **D** £110-£150 (incl. bkfst)* **Facilities** FTV WiFi ↳
New Year **Conf** Class 45 Board 30 Thtr 100 Del £155* **Parking** 40 **Notes** LB
Civ Wed 100

Best Western Brook Hotel Norwich

★★★ 73% HOTEL

tel: 01603 741161 **2 Barnard Rd, Bowthorpe NR5 9JB**
email: welcome@brookhotelnorwich.com **web:** www.brookhotelnorwich.com
dir: A47 towards Swaffham then A1074. Over double rdbt, to next rdbt, hotel on last exit

Brook Hotel Norwich is a modern, purpose-built hotel situated to the west of the city centre, just off the A47. The open-plan public areas include a lounge bar with TV, a foyer with plush sofas and a large dining room. The spacious bedrooms are equipped for both leisure and business guest alike.

Rooms 81 (13 fmly) (40 GF) **S** £70-£140; **D** £80-£150 (incl. bkfst)* **Facilities** FTV
WiFi Gym Xmas New Year **Conf** Class 90 Board 60 Thtr 200 **Services** Air con
Parking 100 **Notes** Civ Wed 200

Premier Inn Norwich Airport

BUDGET HOTEL

tel: 0871 527 8836 *(Calls cost 13p per minute plus your phone company's access charge)*
Delft Way NR6 6BB
web: www.premierinn.com
dir: From Norwich take A140 signed Cromer & Airport. Right at lights into Amsterdam Way. At mini-rdbt turn right. Hotel on right

High quality, budget accommodation ideal for both families and business travellers. Spacious, en suite bedrooms feature tea and coffee making facilities, and Freeview TV in most hotels. Internet access and WiFi are available for a small fee. The adjacent family restaurant features a wide and varied menu. See also the Hotel Groups pages.

Rooms 80

Premier Inn Norwich (Broadlands Park)

BUDGET HOTEL

tel: 0871 527 8838 *(Calls cost 13p per minute plus your phone company's access charge)*
Broadlands Business Park, Old Chapel Way NR7 0WG
web: www.premierinn.com
dir: A47 onto A1042, 3m E of city centre

Rooms 92

Premier Inn Norwich City Centre (Duke Street)

BUDGET HOTEL

tel: 0871 527 8840 *(Calls cost 13p per minute plus your phone company's access charge)*
Duke St NR3 3AP
web: www.premierinn.com
dir: From A1074, straight on at lights (Toys'R'Us) into St Benedict's St (or from A147, A140, A11) right at lights. At next lights into Duke St. Car park in St Andrews multi-storey on right - free to guests

Rooms 117

Premier Inn Norwich Nelson City Centre

BUDGET HOTEL

tel: 0871 527 8842 *(Calls cost 13p per minute plus your phone company's access charge)*
Prince of Wales Rd NR1 1DX
web: www.premierinn.com
dir: Follow city centre, football ground & railway station signs. Hotel opposite station

Rooms 159

Premier Inn Norwich (Showground A47)

BUDGET HOTEL

tel: 0871 527 8834 *(Calls cost 13p per minute plus your phone company's access charge)*
Longwater Interchange, Dereham Rd, New Costessey NR5 0TP
web: www.premierinn.com
dir: A47 towards Dereham, take A1074 to City Centre. At rdbt 2nd exit, hotel on right. From N: A47 through Dereham. Straight on at 1st rdbt, at 2nd rdbt take 3rd exit. Hotel on left

Rooms 62

N

NORWICH *continued*

Brasteds

 RESTAURANT WITH ROOMS

tel: 01508 491112 **Manor Farm Barns, Fox Rd, Framingham Pigot NR14 7PZ**
email: enquiries@brasteds.co.uk **web:** www.brasteds.co.uk
dir: *A11 onto A47 towards Great Yarmouth, then A146. 0.5m, right into Fox Rd, 0.5m on left*

Brasteds is a lovely detached property set in 20 acres of mature, landscaped parkland on the outskirts of Norwich. The tastefully appointed bedrooms have beautiful soft furnishings and fabrics along with comfortable seating and many thoughtful touches. Public rooms include a cosy snug with plush sofas, and a smart dining room where breakfast is served. Dinner is available in Brasteds Restaurant, which can be found in an adjacent building.

Rooms 6 (1 fmly)

The Old Rectory

RESTAURANT WITH ROOMS

tel: 01603 700772 **103 Yarmouth Rd, Thorpe St Andrew NR7 0HF**
email: enquiries@oldrectorynorwich.com **web:** www.oldrectorynorwich.com
dir: *From A47 southern bypass onto A1042 towards Norwich N & E. Left at slip road onto A1042. Follow signs to "All routes" & Thorpe St Andrew, at mini rdbt left onto A1242. Straight on at lights, entrance on right*

This delightful Grade II listed Georgian property is ideally located in a peaceful area overlooking the River Yare, just a few minutes' drive from the city centre. Spacious bedrooms are individually designed with carefully chosen soft fabrics, plush furniture and many thoughtful touches; many of the rooms overlook the swimming pool and landscaped gardens. Accomplished cooking is offered via an interesting daily-changing menu, which features skilfully prepared local produce.

Rooms 8 (3 annexe)

Find out more about the AA's Hotel rating scheme on page 18

NOTTINGHAM
Nottinghamshire

Map 11 SK53

Hart's Hotel

★★★★ 83% HOTEL

tel: 0115 988 1900 **Standard Hill, Park Row NG1 6GN**
email: reception@hartshotel.co.uk **web:** www.hartsnottingham.co.uk
dir: *At junct of Park Row & Ropewalk*

This outstanding modern building stands on the site of the ramparts of the medieval castle, overlooking the city. Many of the bedrooms enjoy splendid views; all are well appointed and stylish. The Park Bar is the focal point of the public areas. Service is professional and caring and fine dining is offered at nearby Hart's Restaurant. Secure parking and private gardens are an added bonus.

Rooms 32 (1 fmly) (7 GF) **D** £134-£274* **Facilities** STV FTV WiFi Small unsupervised exercise room Beauty treatments Use of local tennis club Xmas New Year **Conf** Class 75 Board 30 Thtr 100 Del from £190* **Services** Lift **Parking** 16 **Notes** LB Civ Wed 100

The Nottingham Belfry

★★★★ 79% HOTEL

QHOTELS
INSPIRED BY YOU

tel: 0115 973 9393 **Mellor's Way, Off Woodhouse Way NG8 6PY**
email: nottinghambelfry@qhotels.co.uk **web:** www.qhotels.co.uk
dir: *From M1 junct 26 take A610 towards Nottingham. A6002 to Stapleford/Strelley. 0.75m, last exit at rdbt, hotel on right*

Set conveniently close to the motorway links, yet not far from the city centre attractions, this modern hotel has a stylish and impressive interior. Bedrooms and bathrooms are spaciously appointed and very comfortable. There are two restaurants and two bars that offer interesting and satisfying cuisine. Staff are friendly and helpful.

Rooms 120 (20 fmly) (36 GF) **Facilities** Spa STV FTV WiFi HL Gym Sauna Steam room Aerobic studio Xmas New Year **Conf** Class 360 Board 60 Thtr 700 **Services** Lift **Parking** 250 **Notes** Civ Wed 500

N

Park Plaza Nottingham

★★★★ 74% ◎◎ HOTEL

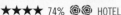

tel: 0115 947 7200 & 0844 415 6730 *(Calls cost 7p per minute plus your phone company's access charge)* **41 Maid Marian Way NG1 6GD**
email: ppnsales@pphe.com **web:** www.parkplaza.com/nottinghamuk
dir: *A6200 Derby Rd into Wollaton St. 2nd exit into Maid Marian Way. Hotel on left*

This modern hotel is located in the centre of the city within walking distance of retail, commercial and tourist attractions. Bedrooms are spacious and comfortable, with many extras, including laptop safes and air conditioning. Service is discreetly attentive in the foyer lounge and the Chino Latino restaurant, where Pan-Asian cooking is a feature.

Rooms 178 (10 fmly) ♐ **Facilities** STV FTV WiFi ♘ Gym Complimentary fitness suite **Conf** Class 100 Board 54 Thtr 200 **Services** Lift Air con **Parking** 30 **Notes** ⊗ Civ Wed 180

Best Western Bestwood Lodge

★★★ 72% HOTEL

tel: 0115 920 3011 **Bestwood Country Park, Arnold NG5 8NE**
email: enquiries@bestwoodlodgehotel.co.uk **web:** www.bw-bestwoodlodge.co.uk
dir: *From Nottingham take A60, left at lights into Oxclose Ln, right at next lights into Queens Bower Rd. 1st right. Keep right at fork in road*

Set in 700 acres of parkland, this Victorian building, once a hunting lodge, has stunning architecture that includes Gothic features and high vaulted ceilings. Bedrooms include all the modern comforts, suitable for both business and leisure guests, and the popular restaurant serves an extensive menu.

Rooms 39 (5 fmly) **Facilities** FTV WiFi ♨ Guided walks Xmas **Conf** Class 65 Board 50 Thtr 200 **Parking** 120 **Notes** RS 25 Dec & 1 Jan Civ Wed 80

The Strathdon

★★ 72% HOTEL

tel. 0115 941 8501 **Derby Rd NG1 5FT**
email: info@strathdon-hotel-nottingham.com **web:** www.peelhotels.co.uk
dir: *From M1 follow city centre signs. At Canning Circus into one-way system into Wollaton St, keep right, next right to hotel*

This city-centre hotel has modern facilities and is very convenient for all city attractions. A popular themed bar has a large-screen TV and serves an extensive range of popular fresh food, while more formal dining is available in Bobbins Restaurant on certain evenings.

Rooms 68 (4 fmly) (16 smoking) **Facilities** FTV WiFi ♘ Xmas New Year **Conf** Class 60 Board 40 Thtr 150 **Services** Lift **Notes** Civ Wed 85

Premier Inn Nottingham Arena (London Rd)

BUDGET HOTEL

tel: 0871 527 8848 *(Calls cost 13p per minute plus your phone company's access charge)*
Island Site, London Rd NG2 4UU
web: www.premierinn.com
dir: *M1 junct 25, A52 into city centre. Follow signs for A60 to Loughborough. Hotel adjacent to BBC building*

High quality, budget accommodation ideal for both families and business travellers. Spacious, en suite bedrooms feature tea and coffee making facilities, and Freeview TV in most hotels. Internet access and WiFi are available for a small fee. The adjacent family restaurant features a wide and varied menu. See also the Hotel Groups pages.

Rooms 87

Premier Inn Nottingham Castle Marina

BUDGET HOTEL

tel: 0871 527 8844 *(Calls cost 13p per minute plus your phone company's access charge)*
Castle Marina Park, Castle Bridge Rd NG7 1GX
web: www.premierinn.com
dir: *M1 junct 24, A453. Follow ring road & signs for Queen's Drive Industrial Estate. After Homebase left into Castle Bridge Rd, opposite Pizza Hut restaurant. Hotel adjacent to Boathouse Beefeater*

Rooms 61

Premier Inn Nottingham City Centre Chapel Bar

BUDGET HOTEL

tel: 0871 527 9658 *(Calls cost 13p per minute plus your phone company's access charge)*
7 Chapel Quarter, Chapel Bar NG1 6JS
web: www.premierinn.com
dir: *M1 junct 26, follow Nottingham City Centre signs. Into Maid Marian Way (A6008). 1st right into Friar Ln*

Rooms 60

Premier Inn Nottingham City Centre (Goldsmith Street)

BUDGET HOTEL

tel: 0871 527 8846 *(Calls cost 13p per minute plus your phone company's access charge)*
Goldsmith St NG1 5LT
web: www.premierinn.com
dir: *A610 to city centre. Follow signs for Nottingham Trent University into Talbot St. 1st left into Clarendon St. Right at lights. Hotel on right*

Rooms 161

Premier Inn Nottingham North (Daybrook)

BUDGET HOTEL

tel: 0871 527 8850 *(Calls cost 13p per minute plus your phone company's access charge)*
101 Mansfield Rd, Daybrook NG5 6BH
web: www.premierinn.com
dir: *M1 junct 26, A610 towards Nottingham. Left onto A6514. Left onto A60 towards Mansfield. Hotel 0.25m on left*

Rooms 64

Premier Inn Nottingham South

BUDGET HOTEL

tel: 0871 527 8854 *(Calls cost 13p per minute plus your phone company's access charge)*
Loughborough Rd, Ruddington NG11 6LS
web: www.premierinn.com
dir: *M1 junct 24, follow A453 signs to Nottingham, A52 to Grantham. Hotel at 1st rdbt on left*

Rooms 60

NOTTINGHAM *continued*

Premier Inn Nottingham West

BUDGET HOTEL

tel: 0871 527 8856 *(Calls cost 13p per minute plus your phone company's access charge)*
The Phoenix Centre, Millennium Way West NG8 6AS
web: www.premierinn.com
dir: *M1 junct 26, 1m on A610 towards Nottingham*

Rooms 99

Ibis Nottingham Centre

AA Advertised

tel: 0115 985 3600 **16 Fletcher Gate NG1 2FS**
email: h6160@accor.com **web:** www.ibishotel.com
dir: *In Lace Market area of city centre*

Modern, budget hotel offering comfortable accommodation in bright and practical bedrooms. Breakfast is self-service and dinner is available in the restaurant.

Rooms 142 (33 fmly) ⌃ **Facilities** STV FTV WiFi ⌂ **Services** Lift

NUNEATON
Warwickshire — Map 11 SP39

Best Western Weston Hall Hotel

★★★ 74% HOTEL

tel: 024 7631 2989 **Weston Ln, Bulkington CV12 9RU**
email: info@westonhallhotel.co.uk **web:** www.bw-westonhallhotel.co.uk
dir: *M6 junct 2, B4065 through Ansty. Left in Shilton, from Bulkington follow Nuneaton signs, into Weston Ln at 30mph sign*

This Grade II listed hotel, with origins dating back to the reign of Elizabeth I, sits within seven acres of peaceful grounds. The original three-gabled building retains many original features, such as the carved wooden fireplace in the library. Friendly service is provided; and the bedrooms, that vary in size, are thoughtfully equipped.

Rooms 38 (1 fmly) (14 GF) **Facilities** FTV WiFi ⌔ New Year **Conf** Class 100 Board 60 Thtr 200 **Parking** 250 **Notes** Civ Wed 200

Premier Inn Nuneaton/Coventry

BUDGET HOTEL

tel: 0871 527 8858 *(Calls cost 13p per minute plus your phone company's access charge)*
Coventry Rd CV10 7PJ
web: www.premierinn.com
dir: *M6 junct 3, A444 towards Nuneaton. Hotel on B4113 on right, just off Griff Rdbt towards Bedworth*

High quality, budget accommodation ideal for both families and business travellers. Spacious, en suite bedrooms feature tea and coffee making facilities, and Freeview TV in most hotels. Internet access and WiFi are available for a small fee. The adjacent family restaurant features a wide and varied menu. See also the Hotel Groups pages.

Rooms 50

OAKHAM
Rutland — Map 11 SK80

INSPECTORS' CHOICE

Hambleton Hall

★★★★ ⍟⍟⍟⍟ ≋ COUNTRY HOUSE HOTEL

tel: 01572 756991 **Hambleton LE15 8TH**
email: hotel@hambletonhall.com **web:** www.hambletonhall.com
dir: *3m E off A606*

Established over 30 years ago by Tim and Stefa Hart this delightful country house enjoys tranquil and spectacular views over Rutland Water. The beautifully manicured grounds are a delight to walk in. The bedrooms in the main house are stylish, individually decorated, and equipped with a range of thoughtful extras. A two-bedroom folly, with its own sitting and breakfast room, is only a short walk away. Day rooms include a cosy bar and a sumptuous drawing room, both featuring open fires. The elegant restaurant serves very accomplished, award-winning cuisine with menus highlighting locally sourced, seasonal produce - some of which is grown in the hotel's own grounds.

Rooms 17 (2 annexe) ⌃ **S** fr £195; **D** £270-£440 (incl. bkfst)* **Facilities** STV FTV WiFi ⌂ ⌲ ⌕ ⌘ Private access to lake Xmas New Year **Conf** Board 24 Thtr 40 Del from £300 to £330* **Services** Lift **Parking** 40 **Notes** LB Civ Wed 60

Barnsdale Lodge Hotel

★★★ 78% ⍟ HOTEL

tel: 01572 724678 **The Avenue, Rutland Water, North Shore LE15 8AH**
email: enquiries@barnsdalelodge.co.uk **web:** www.barnsdalelodge.co.uk
dir: *A1 onto A606. Hotel 5m on right, 2m E of Oakham*

A popular and interesting hotel converted from a farmstead overlooking Rutland Water. The public areas are dominated by a successful food operation with a good range of appealing meals on offer for either formal or informal dining. Bedrooms are comfortably appointed with excellent beds enhanced by contemporary soft furnishings and thoughtful extras.

Barnsdale Lodge Hotel

Rooms 45 (2 tmly) (17 GF) 🐾 **S** £80–£95; **D** £97.50–£152 (incl. bkfst)* **Facilities** FTV WiFi 🏊 Fishing 🚣 Archery Beauty treatment room Golf Sailing Shooting Hair salon Xmas New Year **Conf** Class 120 Board 76 Thtr 330 Del from £112.50* **Parking** 250 **Notes** Civ Wed 200

OKEHAMPTON
Devon

Map 3 SX59

Manor House Hotel

★★★ 70% HOTEL

tel: 01837 53053 **Fowley Cross EX20 4NA**
email: reception@manorhousehotel.co.uk **web:** www.manorhousehotel.co.uk
dir: *Exit A30 at Sourton Cross flyover, right onto A386. Hotel 1.5m on right*

Enjoying views to Dartmoor in the distance, this hotel specialises in short breaks and is set in 17 acres of grounds, close to the A30. The superb range of sporting and craft facilities has been enhanced by an impressive swimming pool and relaxation spa; golf is also offered at the adjacent sister hotel. Bedrooms, many located on the ground floor, are comfortable and well equipped.

Rooms 204 (92 fmly) (93 GF) 🐾 **Facilities** Spa FTV WiFi 🏊 🐾 ⚓ 99 🏌 Putt green Fishing 🚣 Gym Squash Craft centre Indoor bowls Shooting ranges Indoor tennis Exercise classes Xmas New Year **Parking** 204 **Notes** ⊗

Ashbury Hotel

★★★ 68% HOTEL

tel: 01837 55453 **Higher Maddaford, Southcott EX20 4NL**
email: reception@manorhousehotel.co.uk **web:** www.ashburygolfhotel.co.uk
dir: *Exit A30 at Sourton Cross onto A386. Left onto A3079 to Bude at Fowley Cross. After 1m right to Ashbury. Hotel 0.5m on right*

With no less than five courses and a clubhouse with lounge, bar and dining facilities, The Ashbury is a golfers' paradise. The majority of the well-equipped bedrooms are located in the farmhouse and the courtyard-style development around the putting green. Guests can enjoy the many on-site leisure facilities or join the activities available at the nearby sister hotel.

Rooms 222 (115 fmly) (89 GF) 🐾 **Facilities** Spa FTV WiFi 🏊 🐾 ⚓ 99 🏌 Putt green Fishing Gym Badminton Shooting ranges Ten-pin bowling Indoor bowls 5-a-side Craft centre New Year **Conf** Class 60 Board 40 Thtr 250 **Parking** 200 **Notes** ⊗

OLDBURY
West Midlands

Map 10 SO98

Premier Inn Birmingham Oldbury M5 Jct 2

BUDGET HOTEL

tel: 0871 527 8090 *(Calls cost 13p per minute plus your phone company's access charge)*
Wolverhampton Rd B69 2BH
web: www.premierinn.com
dir: *M5 junct 2, A4123 (Wolverhampton Rd) N towards Dudley*

High quality, budget accommodation ideal for both families and business travellers. Spacious, en suite bedrooms feature tea and coffee making facilities, and Freeview TV in most hotels. Internet access and WiFi are available for a small fee. The adjacent family restaurant features a wide and varied menu. See also the Hotel Groups pages.

Rooms 60

OLDHAM
Greater Manchester

Map 16 SD90

Best Western Hotel Smokies Park

★★★ 79% HOTEL

tel: 0161 785 5000 **Ashton Rd, Bardsley OL8 3HX**
email: sales@smokies.co.uk **web:** www.smokies.co.uk
dir: *On A627 between Oldham & Ashton-under-Lyne*

This modern, stylish hotel offers smart, comfortable bedrooms and suites. A wide range of Italian and English dishes is offered in the Mediterranean-style restaurant and there is a welcoming lounge bar with live entertainment at weekends. Also available are a small yet well equipped, residents-only fitness centre and extensive function facilities.

Rooms 73 (10 fmly) (22 GF) 🐾 **Facilities** FTV WiFi 🏊 Gym Xmas New Year **Conf** Class 100 Board 40 Thtr 400 Del £135 **Services** Lift **Parking** 120 **Notes** ⊗ RS 25 Dec-3 Jan Civ Wed 400

Premier Inn Oldham (Broadway)

BUDGET HOTEL

tel: 0871 527 8860 *(Calls cost 13p per minute plus your phone company's access charge)*
Broadway/Hollinwood Av, Chadderton OL9 8DW
web: www.premierinn.com
dir: *M60 (anti-clockwise) junct 21, signed Manchester city centre. Take A663, hotel 400yds on left*

High quality, budget accommodation ideal for both families and business travellers. Spacious, en suite bedrooms feature tea and coffee making facilities, and Freeview TV in most hotels. Internet access and WiFi are available for a small fee. The adjacent family restaurant features a wide and varied menu. See also the Hotel Groups pages.

Rooms 58

Premier Inn Oldham Central

BUDGET HOTEL

tel: 0871 527 8862 *(Calls cost 13p per minute plus your phone company's access charge)*
Westwood Park, Chadderton Way, Chadderton OL1 2NA
web: www.premierinn.com
dir: *M62 junct 20, A627(M) to Oldham. Take A627 (Chadderton Way). Hotel on left opposite B&Q Depot*

Rooms 58

O

OLD HARLOW
Essex
Map 6 TL41

Premier Inn Harlow
BUDGET HOTEL

tel: 0871 527 8488 *(Calls cost 13p per minute plus your phone company's access charge)*
Cambridge Rd CM20 2EP
web: www.premierinn.com
dir: *M11 junct 7, A414, A1184 Sawbridgeworth to Bishop's Stortford road*

High quality, budget accommodation ideal for both families and business travellers. Spacious, en suite bedrooms feature tea and coffee making facilities, and Freeview TV in most hotels. Internet access and WiFi are available for a small fee. The adjacent family restaurant features a wide and varied menu. See also the Hotel Groups pages.

Rooms 81

OLDSTEAD
North Yorkshire
Map 19 SE57

INSPECTORS' CHOICE

The Black Swan at Oldstead
@@@@ ⚲ RESTAURANT WITH ROOMS

tel: 01347 868387 **YO61 4BL**
email: enquiries@blackswanoldstead.co.uk **web:** www.blackswanoldstead.co.uk
dir: *Exit A19, 3m S Thirsk for Coxwold, left in Coxwold, left at Byland Abbey for Oldstead*

The Black Swan is set amidst the stunning scenery of the North York Moors National Park, and parts of the building date back to the 16th century. Well appointed, very comfortable bedrooms and bathrooms provide the perfect get-away. Open fires, a traditional bar and a restaurant, serving award-winning food, are the icing on the cake for this little gem of a property.

Rooms 9 (5 annexe)

OLLERTON
Nottinghamshire
Map 16 SK66

Thoresby Hall Hotel
★★★★ 81% @@ COUNTRY HOUSE HOTEL

WARNER LEISURE HOTELS

tel: 01623 821000 **Thoresby Park NG22 9WH**
email: reception.thoresbyhall@bourne-leisure.co.uk **web:** www.warnerleisurehotels.co.uk

Thoresby Hall is a magnificent Grade I Victorian country house, set in acres of rolling parklands on the edge of Sherwood Forest. Guests can choose to relax in the spa, stroll around the beautiful gardens or just sit and relax in the Great Hall. Bedrooms vary in style and size. This is an adults only (over 21 years) hotel.

Rooms 221 (168 annexe) (72 GF) ⚓ **Facilities** Spa FTV WiFi HL ⚙ supervised ⚲ Putt green Fishing ⚲ Gym Rifle shooting Archery Outdoor bowls Fencing Laser clay Yoga Tai chi ♫ Xmas New Year **Conf** Class 200 Board 30 Thtr 400 **Services** Lift **Parking** 240 **Notes** ⊗ No children 21yrs

ORFORD
Suffolk
Map 13 TM45

The Crown & Castle
★★★ 87% @@ HOTEL

tel: 01394 450205 **IP12 2LJ**
email: info@crownandcastle.co.uk **web:** www.crownandcastle.co.uk
dir: *Turn right from B1084 on entering village, towards castle*

The Crown & Castle is a delightful inn situated adjacent to the Norman castle keep. Contemporary style bedrooms are spilt between the main house and the garden wing; the latter are more spacious and have patios with access to the garden. The restaurant has an informal atmosphere with polished tables and local artwork, and a menu that features quality, locally sourced produce.

Rooms 21 (14 annexe) (2 fmly) (13 GF) ⚓ **D** £130-£260 (incl. bkfst)* **Facilities** FTV WiFi ⚲ HL Xmas New Year **Parking** 17 **Notes** LB No children 8yrs

ORMSKIRK
Lancashire
Map 15 SD40

Premier Inn Southport (Ormskirk)
BUDGET HOTEL

tel: 0871 527 9010 *(Calls cost 13p per minute plus your phone company's access charge)*
544 Southport Rd, Scarisbrick L40 9RG
web: www.premierinn.com
dir: *From Southport follow Ormskirk/A570 signs. Hotel on right off A570 Southport Rd at 1st lights, entrance just after lights*

High quality, budget accommodation ideal for both families and business travellers. Spacious, en suite bedrooms feature tea and coffee making facilities, and Freeview TV in most hotels. Internet access and WiFi are available for a small fee. The adjacent family restaurant features a wide and varied menu. See also the Hotel Groups pages.

Rooms 20

ORSETT
Essex
Map 6 TQ68

Orsett Hall Hotel, Restaurant & Spa
★★★★ 76% COUNTRY HOUSE HOTEL

tel: 01375 891402 **Prince Charles Av RM16 3HS**
email: reception@orsetthall.co.uk **web:** www.orsetthall.co.uk
dir: *M25 junct 29, A127 Southend, A128 Hotel 3m on right*

This beautiful country house hotel, conveniently located for the M25, is set in 12 acres of landscaped gardens, and has individually designed, luxurious bedrooms. The award-winning Garden restaurant is a fabulous dining venue and the stylish modern bar is popular with guests for afternoon tea. Orsett Hall has a first rate spa, and a very well equipped gym along with a range of business suites. Free WiFi is available throughout.

Rooms 56 (24 annexe) (2 fmly) (14 GF) ⚓ **Facilities** Spa FTV WiFi ⚲ Gym Hair salon ♫ Xmas New Year **Conf** Class 200 Board 50 Thtr 450 Del from £160* **Services** Lift Air con **Parking** 250 **Notes** ⊗ Civ Wed 400

O

OSMOTHERLEY
North Yorkshire
Map 19 SE49

The Cleveland Tontine

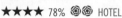 RESTAURANT WITH ROOMS

tel: 01609 882671 **Staddlebridge DL6 3JB**
email: bookings@theclevelandtontine.co.uk **web:** www.theclevelandtontine.co.uk
dir: *Just off A172 junct on A19 Nbound*

This iconic destination restaurant with rooms is a stunning place. Contemporary public areas sit alongside a traditional restaurant with open fires, tiled flooring and great food. Afternoon tea can be taken in the conservatory overlooking the gardens. Bedrooms are individually designed, with modern furniture and feature bathrooms. The service is friendly and relaxed, there is ample parking and major road links are close by.

Rooms 7 (4 fmly)

OSWESTRY
Shropshire
Map 15 SJ22

Wynnstay Hotel

★★★★ 78% HOTEL

tel: 01691 655261 **Church St SY11 2SZ**
email: info@wynnstayhotel.com **web:** www.wynnstayhotel.com
dir: *B4083 to town, fork left at Honda Garage, right at lights. Hotel opposite church*

This Georgian property was once a coaching inn and posting house and surrounds a unique 200-year-old bowling green. Elegant public areas include a health, leisure and beauty centre, which is housed in a former coach house. Well-equipped bedrooms are individually styled and include several suites, four-poster rooms and a self-catering apartment. The Four Seasons Restaurant has a well-deserved reputation for its food, and the adjacent Wilsons café/bar is a stylish, informal alternative.

Rooms 34 (5 fmly) **Facilities** Spa FTV WiFi ⊕ supervised Gym Crown bowling green Beauty suite ♫ New Year **Conf** Class 150 Board 50 Thtr 290 **Parking** 80 **Notes** ⊗ Civ Wed 90

HIGHLY RECOMMENDED

Pen-y-Dyffryn Country Hotel

★★★ 86% COUNTRY HOUSE HOTEL

WELSH RAREBITS
Hotels of Distinction

tel: 01691 653700 **Rhydycroesau SY10 7JD**
email: stay@peny.co.uk **web:** www.peny.co.uk
dir: *A5 into town centre. Follow signs to Llansilin on B4580, hotel 3m W of Oswestry before Rhydycroesau*

Peacefully situated in five acres of grounds, this charming old house dates back to around 1840, when it was built as a rectory. The tastefully appointed public rooms have real fires, lit in colder weather, and the accommodation includes several mini-cottages, each with its own patio. Many guests are attracted to this hotel for the excellent food and attentive, friendly service.

Rooms 12 (4 annexe) (1 fmly) (1 GF) **S** £79-£99; **D** £136-£198 (incl. bkfst)*
Facilities STV FTV WiFi ♭ Guided walks In room treatments available New Year **Parking** 18 **Notes** LB No children 3yrs Closed 18 Dec-19 Jan (ex New Year)

Sweeney Hall Hotel

★★★ 75% COUNTRY HOUSE HOTEL

tel: 01691 652450 **Morda SY10 9EU**
email: enquiries@sweeneyhall.co.uk **web:** www.sweeneyhall.co.uk
dir: *From A5 on outskirts of Oswestry, take A483 towards Welshpool, hotel 2m on left*

This Grade I Listed, friendly family-owned hotel was built in 1805 although previous settlements on this site date back to the 16th century. It was used as a refuge for the Protestant Dissenters and has been sympathetically converted. Sweeney Hall is set amidst several acres of mature parkland with views over the surrounding countryside. Located with easy access to the larger centres of Oswestry and Shrewsbury, it makes an ideal base for exploring the Shropshire countryside. A welcoming log fire is lit on arrival in the colder months and the smart terrace area is ideal for whiling away a summers' evening. Bedrooms are spacious and well equipped. The comfortable restaurant is open for breakfast, lunch and dinner, with Sunday Lunch a popular favourite.

Rooms 11 (1 annexe) (4 fmly) **S** £65-£85; **D** £105-£140 (incl. bkfst) **Facilities** FTV WiFi New Year **Conf** Class 20 Board 24 Thtr 72 **Parking** 100 **Notes** Civ Wed 72

Lion Quays Hotel & Spa

Ⓤ HOTEL

tel: 01691 684300 **Weston Rhyn SY11 3EN**
email: info@lionquays.com **web:** www.lionquays.com
dir: *On A5, 3m N of Oswestry*

Currently the rating for this establishment is not confirmed. This may be due to a change of ownership or because it has only recently joined the AA rating scheme. For further details please see the AA website: theAA.com

Rooms 82 (3 fmly) (25 GF) **Facilities** Spa FTV WiFi ♭ ⊕ ≗ Gym Xmas New Year **Conf** Thtr 400 **Services** Lift **Parking** 300 **Notes** Civ Wed 400

Premier Inn Oswestry

BUDGET HOTEL

tel: 0871 527 8864 *(Calls cost 13p per minute plus your phone company's access charge)*
SY10 8NN
web: www.premierinn.com
dir: *From rdbt junct of A483 & A5 (SE of Oswestry) take A5 signed Oswestry B4579. Hotel 500yds*

High quality, budget accommodation ideal for both families and business travellers. Spacious, en suite bedrooms feature tea and coffee making facilities, and Freeview TV in most hotels. Internet access and WiFi are available for a small fee. The adjacent family restaurant features a wide and varied menu. See also the Hotel Groups pages.

Rooms 59

O

OSWESTRY *continued*

Sebastians

◎◎ ⏰ RESTAURANT WITH ROOMS

tel: 01691 655444 **45 Willow St SY11 1AQ**
email: sebastians.rest@virgin.net **web:** www.sebastians-hotel.co.uk
dir: *From town centre, take turn signed Selattyn into Willow St. 400yds from junct on left opposite Willow Street Gallery*

Sebastians is an intrinsic part of the leisure scene in Oswestry and has built up a loyal local following. Meals feature French influences, with a multi-choice set menu as well as a simpler market menu. Rooms are set around the pretty terrace courtyard, and provide very comfortable accommodation with all the comforts of home.

Rooms 6 (4 annexe) (2 fmly)

OTLEY   Map 19 SE24
West Yorkshire

Chevin Country Park Hotel & Spa

★★★ 78% ◎ HOTEL

tel: 01943 467818 **Yorkgate LS21 3NU**
email: chevin@crerarhotels.com **web:** www.crerarhotels.com
dir: *From Leeds/Bradford Airport rdbt take A658 N towards Harrogate, 0.75m to lights. Left, 2nd left into Yorkgate. Hotel 0.5m on left*

Chevin Country Park Hotel & Spa is peacefully located in its own woodland yet is convenient for major road links and the airport. Bedrooms are split between the original main building and chalet-style accommodation in the extensive grounds. Public areas include a bar and several lounges. The Lakeside Restaurant provides views over the small lake, and good leisure facilities are available.

Rooms 49 (30 annexe) (7 fmly) (45 GF) **S** £80-£100; **D** £110-£140 (incl. bkfst)*
Facilities Spa FTV WiFi ⓑ ⌀ Fishing Gym Steam room Xmas New Year
Conf Class 90 Board 50 Thtr 120 **Parking** 100 **Notes** LB Civ Wed 100

Food Allergies

A recent EU regulation makes it easier for those with food allergies to choose safer foods when eating out. 14 allergens are listed in the regulation, and pubs and restaurants must now list any of these used in the dishes they offer.

OTTERSHAW   Map 6 TQ06
Surrey

HIGHLY RECOMMENDED

Foxhills

★★★★ 83% ◎◎ HOTEL

tel: 01932 872050 & 704500 **Stonehill Rd KT16 OEL**
email: reservations@foxhills.co.uk **web:** www.foxhills.co.uk
dir: *M25 junct 11, A320 to Woking. 2nd rdbt last exit into Chobham Rd. Right into Foxhills Rd, left into Stonehill Rd*

Foxhills is a welcome retreat, set in a 400-acre Surrey estate just 25 minutes from Waterloo and Heathrow, with easy access to major road networks including the M25. The entire resort is bursting with things to do, including golf, tennis, three pools and impressive indoor leisure facilities. At the heart of the estate and just a short walk from the spacious well appointed bedrooms, stands the 19th-century Manor House, home to the popular and spacious Manor Lounge & Bar.

Rooms 70 (8 fmly) (39 GF) ⌀ **S** £145-£260; **D** £145-£260 (incl. bkfst)
Facilities Spa STV FTV WiFi ⓑ ⓩ ⟶ ⌀ 45 ⌀ Putt green ⌀ Gym Squash
Children's adventure playground Country pursuits Off-road course Hairdresser ♫
Xmas New Year **Conf** Class 60 Board 30 Thtr 150 Del from £270 to £500
Parking 500 **Notes** ⊗ Civ Wed 90

OUNDLE   Map 11 TL08
Northamptonshire

The Talbot Hotel

★★★ 80% ◎ HOTEL

tel: 01832 273621 **New St PE8 4EA**
email: talbot@bulldogmail.co.uk **web:** www.thetalbot-oundle.com
dir: *A605 Northampton/Oundle at rdbt exit Oundle A427 - Station Rd turn onto New St*

This Grade I listed property is steeped in history and is reputed to house the staircase that Mary Queen of Scots walked down to her execution in 1587. Following extensive refurbishment, the hotel offers an open-plan eatery and coffee shop for relaxed dining. Accommodation offers a mix of traditional and contemporary, but all provide up-to-date amenities for guest comfort.

Rooms 34 (2 fmly) (12 GF) ⌀ **S** £69-£129; **D** £79-£149 (incl. bkfst)* **Facilities** FTV
WiFi Xmas New Year **Conf** Class 50 Board 30 Thtr 100 Del from £145 to £165*
Parking 30 **Notes** LB Civ Wed 80

OXFORD Oxfordshire	**Map 5 SP50**

Belmond Le Manoir aux Quat' Saisons

★★★★★ ◉◉◉◉◉ HOTEL

tel: 01844 278881 **Church Rd OX44 7PD**
email: manoir.mqs@belmond.com **web:** www.belmond.com/lemanoir

(For full entry see Great Milton)

Macdonald Randolph Hotel

★★★★★ 81% HOTEL

tel: 01865 256400 **Beaumont St OX1 2LN**
email: randolph@macdonald-hotels.co.uk **web:** www.macdonaldhotels.co.uk/Randolph
dir: *M40 junct 8, A40 signed Oxford/Cheltenham, 5m, at lights to ring road rdbt. Right signed Kidlington/North Oxford. At next rdbt left towards city centre - A4165/ Banbury rd. Through Summertown to lights at end of St Giles. Hotel on right*

Superbly located near the city centre, The Randolph boasts impressive neo-Gothic architecture and tasteful decor. The spacious and traditional restaurant, complete with picture windows, is the ideal place to watch the world go by while enjoying freshly prepared, modern dishes. Bedrooms include a mix of classical and contemporary wing rooms, which have been appointed to a high standard. Parking is a real bonus.

Rooms 151 **Facilities** Spa STV FTV WiFi Gym Beauty treatment rooms Thermal suite Mini gym Xmas New Year **Conf** Class 130 Board 60 Thtr 300 **Services** Lift **Parking** 45 **Notes** Civ Wed 120

Oxford Thames Four Pillars Hotel

★★★★ 80% ◉ HOTEL

tel: 0800 374692 & 01865 334444 **Henley Rd, Sandford-on-Thames OX4 4GX**
email: thames@four-pillars.co.uk **web:** www.oxfordthameshotel.co.uk
dir: *M40 junct 8 towards Oxford, then take A40 to Oxford, follow ring road. Left at rdbt towards Cowley. At rdbt with lights turn left to Littlemore, hotel approx 1m on right*

Set in 30 acres of beautiful grounds beside the river, this mellow stone property provides a quiet retreat, yet is close to the city. The spacious and traditional River Room Restaurant has superb views of the hotel's own boat moored on the river. The gardens can be enjoyed from the patios or balconies in the newer bedroom wings. Public rooms include a beamed bar and lounge area with minstrels' gallery, and Jerome's Leisure Club. The hotel is popular as a wedding venue.

Rooms 104 (5 fmly) (49 GF) **Facilities** Spa FTV WiFi Gym Steam room Sauna Xmas New Year **Conf** Class 80 Board 40 Thtr 120 **Parking** 130 **Notes** Civ Wed 150

Oxford Spires Four Pillars Hotel

★★★★ 78% HOTEL

tel: 0800 374692 & 01865 324324 **Abingdon Rd OX1 4PS**
email: spires@four-pillars.co.uk **web:** www.four-pillars.co.uk/spires
dir: *From M40 junct 8 towards Oxford. Left towards Cowley. At 3rd rdbt follow city centre signs. Hotel in 1m. From A34 Hincksey Hill junct towards Oxford. Left at 1st rdbt. Hotel in 1m*

This purpose-built hotel is surrounded by extensive parkland, yet is only a short walk from the city centre. Bedrooms are attractively furnished, well equipped and

include several apartments. Public areas include a spacious restaurant, open-plan bar/lounge, leisure club and extensive conference facilities.

Rooms 181 (10 annexe) (1 fmly) (54 GF) **Facilities** Spa FTV WiFi Gym Steam room Sauna Xmas New Year **Conf** Class 96 Board 76 Thtr 266 Del from £125 to £195* **Services** Lift **Parking** 160 **Notes** Civ Wed 200

Malmaison Oxford

★★★★ 77% ◉ HOTEL

tel: 01865 268400 & 689944 **Oxford Castle, 3 New Rd OX1 1AY**
email: oxford@malmaison.com **web:** www.malmaison.com
dir: *M40 junct 9, A34 N to Botley interchange. Follow city centre & rail station signs. At rail station take the 2nd exit at rdbt, then 1st exit into Park End St. Straight on at next lights, hotel 2nd left*

Once the city's prison, this is definitely a hotel with a difference. Many of the rooms are actually converted from the old cells. Not to worry though as there have been many improvements in facilities, services and decor since the prisoners left 20 years ago. Exceedingly comfortable beds and luxury bathrooms are just two of the changes. The hotel has a popular brasserie with quality and value much in evidence. Limited parking space is available.

Rooms 95 (5 GF) **S** £145-£560; **D** £145-£560* **Facilities** STV FTV WiFi Xmas New Year **Conf** Class 40 Board 40 Thtr 80 Del from £200 to £280* **Services** Lift **Parking** 30 **Notes** LB Civ Wed 80

Mercure Oxford Eastgate Hotel

★★★★ 77% HOTEL

tel: 01865 248332 **73 High St OX1 4BE**
email: h6668@accor.com **web:** www.mercure.com
dir: *A40 follow signs to Headington & Oxford city centre, over Magdalen Bridge, stay in left lane, through lights, left into Merton St, entrance to car park on left*

Totally refurbished in 2015 the Mercure Eastgate Hotel has a range of beautifully presented bedrooms and stylish public areas. This 17th-century building enjoys a great location in the centre of historic Oxford and occupies a site at the city's East Gate. The stylish Marco's New York Italian Restaurant at the hotel is very popular and afternoon tea served in the comfortable lounge is another favourite with guests. Secure car parking is available at the hotel.

Rooms 64 (3 fmly) (4 GF) **Facilities** WiFi Xmas New Year **Services** Lift Air con **Parking** 40 **Notes** ⊗

Cotswold Lodge Hotel

★★★★ 75% ◉ HOTEL

tel: 01865 512121 **66a Banbury Rd OX2 6JP**
email: info@cotswoldlodgehotel.co.uk **web:** www.cotswoldlodgehotel.co.uk
dir: *A40 Oxford ring rd onto A4165 Banbury rd signed city centre/Summertown. Hotel 2m on left*

This Victorian property is located close to the centre of Oxford and offers smart, comfortable accommodation. Stylish bedrooms and suites are attractively presented and some have balconies. The public areas have an elegant country-house feel. The hotel is popular with business guests and caters for conferences and banquets.

Rooms 49 (14 GF) **S** £65-£155; **D** £95-£185 (incl. bkfst)* **Facilities** STV FTV WiFi Xmas New Year **Conf** Class 45 Board 40 Thtr 100 Del from £135 to £155 **Parking** 40 **Notes** LB ⊗ Civ Wed 100

O

OXFORD *continued*

Hawkwell House

★★★★ 74% HOTEL

tel: 01865 749988 **Church Way, Iffley Village OX4 4DZ**
email: reservations@hawkwellhouse.co.uk **web:** www.hawkwellhouse.co.uk
dir: *A34 follow signs to Cowley. At Littlemore rdbt A4158 exit into Iffley Rd. After lights left to Iffley*

Set in a peaceful residential location, Hawkwell House is just a few minutes' drive from the Oxford ring road. The spacious rooms are modern, attractively decorated and well equipped. Public areas are tastefully appointed and the conservatory-style restaurant offers an interesting choice of dishes. The hotel also has a range of conference and function facilities.

Rooms 77 (15 annexe) (10 fmly) (15 GF) ⚡ **Facilities** STV FTV WiFi ⛲ Xmas New Year **Conf** Class 100 Board 80 Thtr 200 **Services** Lift **Parking** 120 **Notes** ⊗ Civ Wed 150

Manor House Hotel

★★ 75% METRO HOTEL

tel: 01865 727627 & 458177 **250 Iffley Rd OX4 1SE**
email: manorhousehotel@hotmail.com **web:** www.manorhouseoxford.com
dir: *On A4158, 1m from city centre*

This family-run establishment is easily accessible from the city centre and all major road links. The hotel provides informal, friendly and attentive service. The comfortably furnished bedrooms are well equipped. The hotel has a bar but there is a selection of restaurants and popular pubs within easy walking distance. Limited private parking is available.

Rooms 8 (2 fmly) ⚡ **S** £89; **D** £110 (incl. bkfst)* **Facilities** STV FTV WiFi ⛲ **Parking** 6 **Notes** ⊗ Closed 20 Dec-20 Jan

Bath Place Hotel

★★ 69% METRO HOTEL

tel: 01865 791812 **4-5 Bath Place, Holywell St OX1 3SU**
email: info@bathplace.co.uk **web:** www.bathplace.co.uk
dir: *On S side of Holywell St, parallel to High St*

The hotel has been created from a group of 17th-century cottages originally built by Flemish weavers who were permitted to settle outside the city walls. This lovely hotel is very much at the heart of the city today and offers individually designed bedrooms, including some with four-posters.

Rooms 16 (3 fmly) (5 GF) ⚡ **S** £95-£110; **D** £128-£165 (incl. bkfst)* **Facilities** FTV WiFi **Parking** 16

Premier Inn Oxford

BUDGET HOTEL

tel: 0871 527 8866 *(Calls cost 13p per minute plus your phone company's access charge)*
Oxford Business Park, Garsington Rd OX4 2JZ
web: www.premierinn.com
dir: *On Oxford Business Park, just off A4142 & B480 junct*

High quality, budget accommodation ideal for both families and business travellers. Spacious, en suite bedrooms feature tea and coffee making facilities, and Freeview TV in most hotels. Internet access and WiFi are available for a small fee. The adjacent family restaurant features a wide and varied menu. See also the Hotel Groups pages.

Rooms 143

OXFORD MOTORWAY SERVICE AREA (M40)   **Map 5 SP60**
Oxfordshire

Ramada Oxford

WELCOME**BREAK**

AA Advertised

tel: 01865 877000 **M40 junct 8a, Waterstock OX33 1LJ**
email: oxford.hotel@welcomebreak.co.uk **web:** www.welcomebreak.co.uk
dir: *M40 junct 8a, at Welcome Break service area*

This modern building offers accommodation in smart, spacious and well-equipped bedrooms, suitable for families and business travellers, and all with en suite bathrooms. Continental breakfast is available and other refreshments may be taken at the nearby family restaurant.

Rooms 59 (56 fmly) (25 GF) (10 smoking) **Facilities** FTV WiFi ⛲ **Parking** 100

PADSTOW   **Map 2 SW97**
Cornwall

HIGHLY RECOMMENDED

Treglos Hotel

★★★★ 82% ⊛ HOTEL

tel: 01841 520727 **Constantine Bay PL28 8JH**
email: stay@treglos-hotel.com **web:** www.treglos-hotel.com
dir: *From Oakhampton A30, follow A39 towards Wadebridge, then B3274 to Padstow. After 2m turn left to St Merryn. After 3m, at St Merryn x-rd/s turn left. Take next right to Treglos. After 1m turn right after Constantine Bay Stores. Hotel is on left*

This long-established hotel is situated on the edge of the stunning Cornish coast with breathtaking views. The atmosphere is all about sophistication and elegance. Bedrooms are soundly appointed and well equipped, and there is a contemporary dining room with enjoyable cuisine and wonderful views over the coast. Guests will find a superb bar and lounges to relax and unwind in. On-site parking is a bonus.

Rooms 42 ⚡ **S** £75-£118; **D** £150-£237 (incl. bkfst)* **Facilities** Spa FTV WiFi ⛲ ⛲ ♨ 18 Putt green Beauty treatments Infrared cabin Games room Childrens playground 🎵 **Services** Lift **Parking** 40 **Notes** LB Closed Dec-Feb

The Metropole

★★★★ 73% ⊛ HOTEL

R
RICHARDSON HOTELS
Where Memories are Made

tel: 01841 532486 **Station Rd PL28 8DB**
email: reservations@the-metropole.co.uk **web:** www.the-metropole.co.uk
dir: *M5/A30 pass Launceston, follow Wadebridge & N Cornwall signs. Take A39, follow Padstow signs*

This long-established hotel first opened its doors to guests back in 1904, and it still retains an air of the sophistication and elegance of a bygone age. Bedrooms are soundly appointed and well equipped; dining options include The Brasserie@ The Met, and the main restaurant with its enjoyable cuisine and wonderful views over the Camel estuary.

Rooms 58 (3 fmly) (2 GF) ⚡ **S** £90-£160; **D** £109-£269 (incl. bkfst)* **Facilities** Spa FTV WiFi ⛲ Xmas New Year **Conf** Class 20 Board 20 Thtr 40 **Services** Lift **Parking** 36 **Notes** LB Civ Wed 110

The Old Ship Hotel

★★ 82% HOTEL

tel: 01841 532357 **Mill Square PL28 8AE**
email: stay@oldshiphotel-padstow.co.uk **web**: www.oldshiphotel-padstow.co.uk
dir: *From M5 take A30 to Bodmin then A389 to Padstow, follow brown tourist signs to car park*

This attractive inn is situated in the heart of the old town's quaint and winding streets, just a short walk from the harbour. A warm welcome is assured, accommodation is pleasant and comfortable, and public areas offer plenty of character. Freshly-caught fish features on both the bar and restaurant menus. On-site parking is a bonus.

Rooms 14 (4 fmly) ♠ S £45-£55; **D** £70-£120 (incl. bkfst) **Facilities** STV FTV WiFi 🎵 Xmas New Year **Parking** 20 **Notes** LB

The Seafood Restaurant

◉◉◉ 🍷 RESTAURANT WITH ROOMS

tel: 01841 532700 **Riverside PL28 8BY**
email: reservations@rickstein.com **web**: www.rickstein.com
dir: *Into town centre, down hill (Station Rd), follow signs to harbour car park, opposite car park*

Food lovers continue to beat a well-trodden path to this famous restaurant. Situated on the edge of the harbour, just a stone's throw from the shops, The Seafood Restaurant offers chic and comfortable bedrooms that boast numerous thoughtful extras; some have views of the estuary and a couple have private balconies with stunning sea views. Service is relaxed and friendly; booking is essential for both accommodation and a table in the restaurant.

Rooms 22 (6 annexe) (12 fmly)

St Petrocs & Bistro

◉ RESTAURANT WITH ROOMS

tel: 01841 532700 **4 New St PL28 8EA**
email: reservations@rickstein.com **web**: www.rickstein.com
dir: *A39 onto A389, follow signs to Padstow town centre*

One of the oldest buildings in town, this charming establishment is just up the hill from the picturesque harbour. Style, comfort and individuality are all great strengths here, particularly so in the impressively equipped bedrooms. Breakfast, lunch and dinner all reflect a serious approach to cuisine, and the popular restaurant has a relaxed, bistro style. Comfortable lounges, a reading room and lovely gardens complete the picture.

Rooms 10 (2 fmly)

Padstow Townhouse

◉◉◉ RESTAURANT WITH ROOMS

tel: 01841 550950 **16/18 High St PL28 8BB**
web: www.paul-ainsworth.co.uk

This cosy 18th-century townhouse offers six individually styled suites, providing all home comforts as well as some little luxuries. Every room has its own 40" curved TV complete with Apple TV, as well free WiFi. Breakfast is served in Rojano's in the Square, and guests are welcome to dine there or at Paul Ainsworth at No.6 restaurant.

Rooms 6

PAIGNTON Map 3 SX86
Devon

Redcliffe Hotel

★★★ 81% HOTEL

tel: 01803 526397 **Marine Dr TQ3 2NL**
email: redclfe@aol.com **web**: www.redcliffehotel.co.uk
dir: *On seafront at Torquay end of Paignton Green*

Set at the water's edge in three acres of well-tended grounds, this popular hotel enjoys uninterrupted views across Tor Bay. On offer is a diverse range of facilities including a leisure complex, beauty treatments and lots of outdoor family activities in the summer. Bedrooms are pleasantly appointed and comfortably furnished, while public areas offer ample space for rest and relaxation.

Rooms 69 (8 fmly) (3 GF) ♠ S £60-£74; **D** £120-£148 (incl. bkfst)* **Facilities** Spa FTV WiFi ♨ 🏊 supervised ⚓ Putt green Fishing Gym Table tennis Carpet bowls Xmas New Year **Conf** Class 50 Board 50 Thtr 150 Del from £75 to £85* **Services** Lift **Parking** 80 **Notes** LB ⊗ Civ Wed 150

The Queens Hotel

★★★ 79% HOTEL

tel: 01803 551048 **2-6 Queens Rd TQ4 6AT**
email: gm@queenspaignton.com **web**: www.queenspaignton.com

This popular hotel enjoys a central location close to the town centre, and within walking distance of the local beaches. Secure parking is available at the hotel along with a range of leisure facilities including a heated pool. Attractively decorated bedrooms vary in size, offering good levels of quality and comfort. Wholesome traditional food is served in the spacious dining room.

Rooms 76 (5 fmly) (6 GF) ♠ S fr £46; **D** fr £92 (incl. bkfst & dinner)* **Facilities** FTV WiFi 🏊 Free use of gym at sister hotel 🎵 Xmas New Year **Services** Lift **Parking** 36 **Notes** LB ⊗

Premier Inn Paignton Seafront (Goodrington Sands)

BUDGET HOTEL

tel: 0871 527 9206 *(Calls cost 13p per minute plus your phone company's access charge)*
Tanners Rd, Goodrington TQ4 6LP
web: www.premierinn.com
dir: *From Newton Abbot take A380 S. Left into A3022 (Totnes Rd), right at Hayes Rd into Penwill Way, right at B3199 into Dartmouth Rd, at lights left into Tanners Rd*

High quality, budget accommodation ideal for both families and business travellers. Spacious, en suite bedrooms feature tea and coffee making facilities, and Freeview TV in most hotels. Internet access and WiFi are available for a small fee. The adjacent family restaurant features a wide and varied menu. See also the Hotel Groups pages.

Rooms 33

Premier Inn Paignton South (Brixham Road)

BUDGET HOTEL

tel: 0871 527 9324 *(Calls cost 13p per minute plus your phone company's access charge)*
White Rock, Long Road South TQ4 7AZ
web: www.premierinn.com
dir: *From A3022 (Brixham Rd) between Tweenaway & Galmpton Warborough, right into Long Rd*

Rooms 61

P

PALTERTON
Derbyshire
Map 16 SK46

Twin Oaks Hotel
★★★ 74% HOTEL

tel: 01246 855455 **Church Ln S44 6UZ**
email: book@twinoakshotel.co.uk **web:** www.twinoakshotel.co.uk
dir: M1 junct 29, take Palterton turn, hotel 100mtrs down road on left

This hotel began life as a picturesque row of colliery cottages, but it has been meticulously redesigned and configured to meet the expectations of the modern business or leisure traveller. The bedrooms provide contemporary accommodation and the attractive public areas include a brasserie and bistro providing a range of dining options. The hotel is a popular wedding destination and enjoys very good transport links as it is near the M1.

Rooms 36 (4 annexe) (4 fmly) (19 GF) **S** £80-£110; **D** £80-£110* **Facilities** FTV WiFi ↳ **Conf** Class 25 Board 25 Thtr 40 **Parking** 80 **Notes** ⊗ Civ Wed 80

PATTERDALE
Cumbria
Map 18 NY31

Patterdale Hotel
★★ 78% HOTEL

tel: 0844 811 5580 *(Calls cost 5p per minute plus your phone company's access charge)*
& 017684 82231 **CA11 0NN**
email: reservations@choice-hotels.co.uk **web:** www.patterdalehotel.co.uk
dir: M6 junct 40, A592 towards Ullswater. 10m to Patterdale

Patterdale is a real tourist destination and this hotel makes a good base for those taking part in the many activity pursuits available in this area. The hotel enjoys delightful views of the valley and fells, being located at the southern end of Ullswater. The modern bedrooms vary in style. In busier periods accommodation is let for a minimum period of two nights.

Rooms 56 (15 fmly) (6 GF) ↳ **S** £40-£68; **D** £78-£130 (incl. bkfst & dinner)
Facilities FTV WiFi Xmas New Year **Services** Lift **Parking** 30 **Notes** LB ⊗

PECKFORTON
Cheshire
Map 15 SJ55

INSPECTORS' CHOICE

Peckforton Castle
★★★★ ⍟⍟⍟ HOTEL

tel: 01829 260930 **Stone House Ln CW6 9TN**
email: info@peckfortoncastle.co.uk **web:** www.peckfortoncastle.co.uk
dir: A49. At Beeston Castle pub right signed Peckforton Castle. Approx 2m, entrance on right

Built in the mid-19th century by parliamentarian and landowner Lord John Tollemache, and now lovingly cared for by The Naylor Family, this Grade I medieval-style castle has been sympathetically renovated to provide high standards of comfort without losing its original charm and character. Bedrooms and public areas retain many period features, and dining in the 1851 Restaurant is a memorable experience. Head Chef, Mark Ellis is passionate about using only the finest ingredients, sourced locally where possible. There are a host of excellent outdoor leisure activities; falconry and off-road Land Rover courses to name just two. The Tranquility Spa caters for those seeking a more serene experience.

Rooms 48 (7 fmly) (2 GF) ⌁ **Facilities** Spa FTV WiFi HL ⍤ Falconry Outdoor pursuits Land Rover experience Abseiling Beauty salon Xmas New Year **Conf** Class 80 Board 40 Thtr 180 **Services** Lift **Parking** 400 **Notes** ⊗ Civ Wed 165

PENDLEBURY
Greater Manchester
Map 15 SD70

Premier Inn Manchester (Swinton)
BUDGET HOTEL

Premier Inn

tel: 0871 527 8720 *(Calls cost 13p per minute plus your phone company's access charge)*
219 Bolton Rd M27 8TG
web: www.premierinn.com
dir: M60 junct 13 towards A572, at rdbt take 3rd exit towards Swinton. At next rdbt take A572. In 2m right onto A580. After 2nd lights A666 Kearsley, 1st left at rdbt. Pass fire station on right, 1st right

High quality, budget accommodation ideal for both families and business travellers. Spacious, en suite bedrooms feature tea and coffee making facilities, and Freeview TV in most hotels. Internet access and WiFi are available for a small fee. The adjacent family restaurant features a wide and varied menu. See also the Hotel Groups pages.

Rooms 31

PENRITH
Cumbria
Map 18 NY53

See also **Glenridding & Shap**

North Lakes Hotel & Spa

★★★★ 79% HOTEL

tel: 01768 868111 **Ullswater Rd CA11 8QT**
email: nlakes@shirehotels.com **web:** www.northlakeshotel.com
dir: *M6 junct 40 at junct with A66*

With a great location, it's no wonder that this modern hotel is perpetually busy. Amenities include a good range of meeting and function rooms and excellent health and leisure facilities including a full spa. Themed public areas have a contemporary, Scandinavian country style and offer plenty of space and comfort. High standards of service are provided by a friendly team of staff. Thwaites Hotels is the AA Hotel Group of the Year 2016-2017.

Rooms 84 (6 fmly) (22 GF) **S** £100-£200; **D** £100-£200* **Facilities** Spa STV WiFi 🏊 ⓣ Gym Children's splash pool Steam room Activity & wellness studios Sauna New Year **Conf** Class 140 Board 30 Thtr 200 Del from £130 to £200* **Services** Lift **Parking** 150 **Notes** LB ⊗ Civ Wed 200

HIGHLY RECOMMENDED

Temple Sowerby House Hotel & Restaurant

★★★ 87% ◉◉ COUNTRY HOUSE HOTEL

tel: 017683 61578 **CA10 1RZ**
email: stay@templesowerby.com **web:** www.templesowerby.com

(For full entry see Temple Sowerby)

The George Hotel

LAKE DISTRICT HOTELS

★★★ 83% HOTEL

tel: 01768 862696 & 0800 840 1242 **Devonshire St CA11 7SU**
email: georgehotel@lakedistricthotels.net **web:** www.lakedistricthotels.net/georgehotel
dir: *M6 junct 40, 1m to town centre. From A6/A66 to Penrith*

This inviting and popular hotel was once visited by 'Bonnie' Prince Charlie. Extended over the years, it currently offers well equipped bedrooms, and spacious public areas that retain a timeless charm. There is a choice of lounge areas that are ideal for morning coffee and afternoon tea.

Rooms 35 (4 fmly) **S** fr £85; **D** fr £172 (incl. bkfst) **Facilities** FTV WiFi ⓣ Xmas New Year **Conf** Class 80 Board 50 Thtr 120 **Parking** 40 **Notes** Civ Wed 120

PENZANCE
Cornwall
Map 2 SW43

Hotel Penzance

★★★★ 78% ◉◉ TOWN HOUSE HOTEL

tel: 01736 363117 **Britons Hill TR18 3AE**
email: reception@hotelpenzance.com **web:** www.hotelpenzance.com
dir: *From A30, left at last rdbt for town centre. 3rd right onto Britons Hill. Hotel on right*

This Edwardian house has been tastefully redesigned, particularly in the contemporary Bay Restaurant. The focus on style is not only limited to the decor, but is also apparent in the award-winning cuisine that is based on fresh Cornish produce. Bedrooms have been appointed to modern standards and are particularly well equipped; many have views across Mounts Bay.

Rooms 25 (2 GF) ⓣ **S** £69-£114; **D** £99-£220 (incl. bkfst)* **Facilities** FTV WiFi ⓣ Xmas New Year **Conf** Class 50 Board 25 Thtr 80 Del from £135 to £155* **Parking** 12

Queens Hotel

★★★ 74% HOTEL

tel: 01736 362371 **The Promenade TR18 4HG**
email: enquiries@queens-hotel.com **web:** www.queens-hotel.com
dir: *A30 to Penzance, follow signs for seafront pass harbour onto promenade, hotel on right*

With views across Mount's Bay towards Newlyn, this impressive Victorian hotel has a long and distinguished history. Comfortable public areas are filled with interesting pictures and artefacts, and in the dining room guests can choose from the daily-changing menu. Bedrooms, many with sea views, vary in style and size.

Rooms 70 (10 fmly) ⓣ **S** £75-£110; **D** £150-£220 (incl. bkfst)* **Facilities** FTV WiFi ⓣ Hair & beauty salon Xmas New Year **Conf** Class 200 Board 120 Thtr 200 Del from £99 to £175* **Services** Lift **Parking** 50 **Notes** LB Civ Wed 250

PETERBOROUGH
Cambridgeshire
Map 12 TL19

Bull Hotel

PEEL HOTELS PLC

★★★★ 78% ◉ HOTEL

tel: 01733 561364 **Westgate PE1 1RB**
email: rooms@bull-hotel-peterborough.com **web:** www.peelhotels.co.uk
dir: *From A1 follow city centre signs. Hotel opposite Queensgate shopping centre. Car park on Broadway adjacent to library*

This pleasant city-centre hotel offers well-equipped, modern accommodation, which includes several wings of deluxe bedrooms. Public rooms include a popular bar and a brasserie-style restaurant serving a flexible range of dishes, with further informal dining available in the lounge. There is a good range of meeting rooms and conference facilities.

Rooms 118 (2 fmly) (5 GF) ⓣ **S** £63-£135; **D** £73-£145 **Facilities** STV WiFi Xmas New Year **Conf** Class 120 Board 40 Thtr 200 Del from £125 to £250 **Parking** 100 **Notes** ⊗ Civ Wed 200

PETERBOROUGH *continued*

Best Western Plus Orton Hall Hotel & Spa

★★★★ 72% 🌐 HOTEL

tel: 01733 391111 **The Village, Orton Longueville PE2 7DN**
email: reception@ortonhall.co.uk **web:** www.abacushotels.co.uk
dir: *Off A605 E, opposite Orton Mere*

Orton Hall is an impressive country-house hotel set in 20 acres of woodland on the outskirts of town and with easy access to the A1. The spacious and relaxing public areas include the baronial Great Room and the Orton Suite for banqueting and meetings, and the oak-panelled, award-winning Huntly Restaurant. The on-site pub, Ramblewood Inn, is an alternative, informal dining option.

Rooms 70 (2 fmly) (15 GF) 🐾 **S** £60-£180; **D** £70-£190* **Facilities** Spa FTV WiFi ⬦ ⊗ Gym Sauna Steam room Xmas New Year **Conf** Class 70 Board 60 Thtr 160 Del from £115 to £150* **Parking** 200 **Notes** LB Civ Wed 150

Bell Inn Hotel

★★★ 82% 🌐 HOTEL

tel: 01733 241066 **Great North Rd PE7 3RA**
email: reception@thebellstilton.co.uk **web:** www.thebellstilton.co.uk

(For full entry see Stilton)

Premier Inn Peterborough (Ferry Meadows)

BUDGET HOTEL

tel: 0871 527 8872 *(Calls cost 13p per minute plus your phone company's access charge)*
Ham Ln, Orton Meadows, Nene Park PE2 5UU
web: www.premierinn.com
dir: *A1(M) S junct 16, A15 through Yaxley, left at rdbt. A1(M) N junct 17, A1139 junct 3 right to Yaxley, right at 2nd rdbt*

High quality, budget accommodation ideal for both families and business travellers. Spacious, en suite bedrooms feature tea and coffee making facilities, and Freeview TV in most hotels. Internet access and WiFi are available for a small fee. The adjacent family restaurant features a wide and varied menu. See also the Hotel Groups pages.

Rooms 40

Premier Inn Peterborough (Hampton)

BUDGET HOTEL

tel: 0871 527 8874 *(Calls cost 13p per minute plus your phone company's access charge)*
Ashbourne Rd, off London Rd, Hampton PE7 8BT
web: www.premierinn.com
dir: *A1(M) S junct 16, A15 through Yaxley, hotel on left at 1st rdbt. Or A1(M) N junct 17, A1139, 2nd exit junct 3 follow Yaxley signs. Hotel on right at 2nd rdbt*

Rooms 143

Premier Inn Peterborough North

BUDGET HOTEL

tel: 0871 527 8876 *(Calls cost 13p per minute plus your phone company's access charge)*
1023 Lincoln Rd, Walton PE4 6AH
web: www.premierinn.com
dir: *A1, A47 towards Peterborough. In 7m exit at junct 17 signed city centre. At rdbt (bottom of slip road) straight on signed city centre. At next rdbt left onto dual carriageway. At next rdbt double back, follow signs for city centre. Hotel in 200mtrs*

Rooms 68

Days Inn Peterborough - A1

AA Advertised

tel: 01733 371540 **Peterborough Extra Services, A1 Junction 17, Great North Road, Haddon PE7 3UQ**
email: peterborough.hotel@welcomebreak.co.uk
web: www.welcomebreak.co.uk
dir: *A1(M) junct 17*

This modern, purpose-built accommodation offers smartly appointed, particularly well-equipped bedrooms with good power showers. There is a choice of adjacent food outlets where guests can enjoy breakfast, snacks and meals.

Rooms 82 (16 fmly) (40 GF) (11 smoking) 🐾 **Facilities** FTV WiFi ⬦ **Services** Air con **Parking** 120

PETERSFIELD	Map 5 SU72
Hampshire	

Langrish House

★★★ 80% 🌐🌐 HOTEL

tel: 01730 266941 **Langrish GU32 1RN**
email: frontdesk@langrishhouse.co.uk **web:** www.langrishhouse.co.uk
dir: *A3 onto A272 towards Winchester. Hotel signed, 2.5m on left*

Langrish House has been in the same family for seven generations. It is located in an extremely peaceful area just a few minutes' drive from Petersfield, halfway between Guildford and Portsmouth. Bedrooms are comfortable and well equipped with stunning views across the gardens to the hills. Guests can eat in the intimate Frederick's Restaurant with views over the lawn, or in the Old Vaults which have an interesting history dating back to 1644. The hotel is licensed for civil ceremonies and various themed events take place throughout the year.

Rooms 13 (1 fmly) (3 GF) 🐾 **Facilities** FTV WiFi ⬦ Xmas New Year **Conf** Class 18 Board 25 Thtr 60 **Parking** 80 **Notes** Closed early Jan Civ Wed 80

Premier Inn Petersfield

BUDGET HOTEL

tel: 0871 527 8878 *(Calls cost 13p per minute plus your phone company's access charge)*
Winchester Rd GU32 3BS
web: www.premierinn.com
dir: *At junct of A3 & A272 W'bound signed Services*

High quality, budget accommodation ideal for both families and business travellers. Spacious, en suite bedrooms feature tea and coffee making facilities, and Freeview TV in most hotels. Internet access and WiFi are available for a small fee. The adjacent family restaurant features a wide and varied menu. See also the Hotel Groups pages.

Rooms 50

P

PICKERING	Map 19 SE78
North Yorkshire	

The White Swan Inn

★★★ 83% ◉◉ HOTEL

tel: 01751 472288 **Market Place YO18 7AA**
email: welcome@white-swan.co.uk **web:** www.white-swan.co.uk
dir: *In town, between church & steam railway station*

This 16th-century coaching inn offers well-equipped, comfortable bedrooms, including suites, either of a more traditional style in the main building or modern in the annexe. Service is friendly and attentive. Good food is served in the attractive restaurant, in the cosy bar and in the lounge, where a log fire burns in cooler months. A private dining room is also available. The comprehensive wine list focuses on many fine vintages.

Rooms 21 (9 annexe) (3 fmly) (8 GF) ⋒ **Facilities** FTV WiFi Xmas New Year **Conf** Class 18 Board 25 Thtr 35 **Parking** 45 **Notes** LB

Best Western Forest & Vale Hotel

BW Best Western.

★★★ 82% HOTEL

tel: 01751 472722 **Malton Rd YO18 7DL**
email: forestvale@bestwestern.co.uk **web:** www.bw-forestandvalehotel.co.uk
dir: *On A169 towards York at rdbt on outskirts of Pickering*

This lovely 18th-century manor house hotel makes an excellent base from which to explore the east coast resorts and the North Yorkshire Moors National Park, one of England's most beautiful areas. A dedicated approach to upgrading means that the hotel is particularly well maintained, inside and out. In addition to standard bedrooms there are more spacious deluxe, superior and executive rooms; they are more traditional in the main house while the ones in the wing are contemporary; one has a four-poster bed.

Rooms 22 (5 annexe) (7 fmly) (5 GF) ⋒ **S** £100-£150; **D** £100-£150* **Facilities** FTV WiFi ⇣ **Conf** Class 40 Board 30 Thtr 100 **Parking** 40 **Notes** LB ⊗ Closed 23-28 Dec Civ Wed 90

The Beansheaf Hotel

★★★ 67% HOTEL

tel: 01653 668614 **Malton Rd YO17 6UE**
email: enquiries@beansheafhotel.com **web:** www.beansheafhotel.com
dir: *On A169 between Malton & Pickering at the Flamingo Land turning*

This modern hotel is conveniently located on the A169 between Pickering and Malton. It is close to the A64 and ideal for exploring the North York Moors or visiting Flamingo Land. Leisure and business guests are equally well catered for with complimentary WiFi provided and there are dedicated meeting rooms. A range of bedrooms are available including singles, doubles, twins and family rooms. Ground floor rooms are also available. A wide range of homemade meals are served in the bar and restaurant.

Rooms 18 (8 GF) ⋒ **Facilities** FTV WiFi ⇣ **Conf** Class 50 Board 25 Thtr 60 **Parking** 35

PLYMOUTH	Map 3 SX45
Devon	

Langdon Court Hotel & Restaurant

★★★★ 77% ◉◉ COUNTRY HOUSE HOTEL

tel: 01752 862358 **Adams Ln, Down Thomas PL9 ODY**
email: enquiries@langdoncourt.com **web:** www.langdoncourt.com
dir: *From Plymouth follow Kingsbridge signs Elberton rdbt. Signs to Langdon Court*

Langdon Court Hotel has a super location, set in seven acres of grounds and away from the traffic and hubbub of the city; a Grade II listed building, this Tudor Mansion in steeped in history and is very stylish. There are some excellent gardens and the hotel management are developing their own vineyard. Bedrooms are stylishly appointed, and comfortably furnished. The restaurant and bar areas offer enjoyable dining featuring fresh and local produce.

Rooms 18 (3 fmly) ⋒ **S** £129-£169; **D** £169-£229 (incl. bkfst)^ **Facilities** STV FTV WiFi ⇣ Fishing Xmas New Year **Conf** Class 20 Board 20 Thtr 60 Del from £159 to £189 **Parking** 60 **Notes** ⊗ Civ Wed 100

Best Western Duke of Cornwall Hotel

BW Best Western.

★★★ 83% ◉ HOTEL

tel: 01752 275850 & 275855 **Millbay Rd PL1 3LG**
email: enquiries@thedukeofcornwall.co.uk **web:** www.thedukeofcornwall.co.uk
dir: *Follow city centre, then Plymouth Pavilions Conference & Leisure Centre signs. Hotel opposite Plymouth Pavilions*

A historic landmark, this city centre hotel is conveniently located. The spacious public areas include a popular bar, comfortable lounge and multi-functional ballroom. Bedrooms, many with far-reaching views, are individually styled and comfortably appointed. The range of dining options includes meals in the bar, or the elegant dining room for a more formal atmosphere.

Rooms 71 (4 fmly) ⋒ **S** £60-£119; **D** £65-£140 (incl. bkfst) **Facilities** STV FTV WiFi ⇣ Xmas New Year **Conf** Class 125 Board 84 Thtr 300 **Services** Lift **Parking** 25 **Notes** LB Civ Wed 300

Invicta Hotel

★★★ 79% HOTEL

tel: 01752 664997 **11-12 Osborne Place, Lockyer St, The Hoe PL1 2PU**
email: invictahotel@btconnect.com **web:** www.invictahotel.co.uk
dir: *A38 to Plymouth, follow city centre signs, then signs to The Hoe & Barbican. Hotel opposite Hoe Park on Lockyer St at junct with Citadel Rd*

Just a short stroll from the city centre, this elegant Victorian establishment stands opposite the famous bowling green. The atmosphere is relaxed and friendly and bedrooms are neatly presented, well-equipped and attractively decorated. Eating options include meals in the bar or in the more formal setting of the dining room.

Rooms 23 (4 fmly) (1 GF) ⋒ **S** £65-£85; **D** £100-£135 (incl. bkfst)* **Facilities** FTV WiFi ⇣ **Conf** Class 30 Board 45 Thtr 45 Del from £150 to £250* **Parking** 14 **Notes** LB Closed 25-26 Dec

P

PLYMOUTH *continued*

Boringdon Hall Hotel

tel: 01752 344455 **Boringdon Hill, Plympton PL7 4DP**
email: info@boringdonhall.co.uk
dir: *A38 at Marsh Mills rdbt follow Plympton signs to small island. Left over bridge and follow tourist signs*

Currently the rating for this establishment is not confirmed. This may be due to a change of ownership or because it has only recently joined the AA rating scheme. For further details please see the AA website: theAA.com

Rooms 40 **Conf** Class 40 Board 50 Thtr 120

Premier Inn Plymouth Centre (Sutton Harbour)

BUDGET HOTEL

tel: 0871 527 8882 *(Calls cost 13p per minute plus your phone company's access charge)*
Sutton Rd, Shepherds Wharf PL4 0HX
web: www.premierinn.com
dir: *A38, A374 towards Plymouth. Follow Coxside & National Marine Aquarium signs. Right at lights after leisure park. Hotel adjacent to Lockyers Quay. NB there are 2 Premier Inns on this site, this hotel is the larger*

High quality, budget accommodation ideal for both families and business travellers. Spacious, en suite bedrooms feature tea and coffee making facilities, and Freeview TV in most hotels. Internet access and WiFi are available for a small fee. The adjacent family restaurant features a wide and varied menu. See also the Hotel Groups pages.

Rooms 107

Premier Inn Plymouth City Centre (Lockyers Quay)

BUDGET HOTEL

tel: 0871 527 8880 *(Calls cost 13p per minute plus your phone company's access charge)*
1 Lockyers Quay, Coxside PL4 0DX
web: www.premierinn.com
dir: *From A38 (Marsh Mills rdbt) take A374 into Plymouth. Follow Coxside & National Marine Aquarium signs*

Rooms 62

Premier Inn Plymouth East

BUDGET HOTEL

tel: 0871 527 8884 *(Calls cost 13p per minute plus your phone company's access charge)*
300 Plymouth Rd, Crabtree PL3 6RW
web: www.premierinn.com
dir: *From E: Exit A38 at Marsh Mill junct. Straight on at rdbt, exit slip road 100mtrs on left. From W: Exit A38 at Plympton junct, at rdbt exit slip road adjacent to A38*

Rooms 81

POCKLINGTON Map 17 SE84
East Riding of Yorkshire

Feathers Hotel

★★ 72% HOTEL

tel: 01759 303155 **56 Market Place Y042 2AH**
email: info@thefeathers-hotel.co.uk web: www.thefeathers-hotel.co.uk
dir: *From York, B1246 signed Pocklington. Hotel just off A1079*

This busy, traditional inn provides comfortable, well-equipped and spacious accommodation. Public areas are smartly presented. Enjoyable meals are served in the bar and the conservatory restaurant; the wide choice of dishes makes excellent use of local and seasonal produce.

Rooms 16 (10 annexe) (2 fmly) (10 GF) ✆ **S** £60; **D** £75 (incl. bkfst)* **Facilities** FTV WiFi **Parking** 25 **Notes** ⊗

POLPERRO Map 2 SX25
Cornwall

HIGHLY RECOMMENDED

Talland Bay Hotel

★★★ 87% ◉◉ COUNTRY HOUSE HOTEL

tel: 01503 272667 **Porthallow PL13 2JB**
email: info@tallandbayhotel.co.uk web: www.tallandbayhotel.co.uk
dir: *From Looe over bridge towards Polperro on A387, 2nd turn to hotel*

This hotel has the benefit of a wonderful location with far-reaching views, situated in its own extensive gardens that run down almost to the cliff edge. The bedrooms come in a range of styles - classic twins and doubles, and rooms and suites with sea views. There is also cottage accommodation, and one is particularly suitable for families or those with dogs. The public areas of the hotel are impressive and stylish. Eating options include a Brasserie and the Terrace Restaurant, where guests will find accomplished cooking, with an emphasis on carefully prepared local produce.

Rooms 23 (2 fmly) (5 GF) ✆ **S** £110–£270; **D** £120–£280 (incl. bkfst)* **Facilities** FTV WiFi ⇘ ⚘ Xmas New Year **Conf** Class 20 Board 20 Thtr 20 **Parking** 23 **Notes** Civ Wed 60

PONTEFRACT Map 16 SE42
West Yorkshire

Wentbridge House Hotel

★★★★ 82% ◉◉ HOTEL

tel: 01977 620444 **The Great North Rd, Wentbridge WF8 3JJ**
email: info@wentbridgehouse.co.uk web: www.wentbridgehouse.co.uk
dir: *M62 junct 33 onto A1 S, hotel in 4m*

This well-established hotel sits in 20 acres of landscaped gardens, offering spacious, well-equipped bedrooms and a choice of dining styles. Service in the Fleur de Lys restaurant is polished and friendly, and a varied menu offers a good choice of interesting dishes. The Brasserie has a more relaxed style of modern dining.

Rooms 41 (4 annexe) (4 fmly) (4 GF) ✆ **S** £110–£200; **D** £140–£230 (incl. bkfst)* **Facilities** FTV WiFi Xmas New Year **Conf** Class 100 Board 60 Thtr 130 Del from £110 to £150* **Services** Lift **Parking** 100 **Notes** LB ⊗ Civ Wed 130

Premier Inn Pontefract North
BUDGET HOTEL

tel: 0871 527 8886 *(Calls cost 13p per minute plus your phone company's access charge)*
Pontefract Rd, Knottingley WF11 OBU
web: www.premierinn.com
dir: *M62 junct 33 onto A1 N. Exit at Pontefract junct (A645) to T-junct, right towards Pontefract. Hotel on right*

High quality, budget accommodation ideal for both families and business travellers. Spacious, en suite bedrooms feature tea and coffee making facilities, and Freeview TV in most hotels. Internet access and WiFi are available for a small fee. The adjacent family restaurant features a wide and varied menu. See also the Hotel Groups pages.

Rooms 68

POOLE
Dorset   Map 4 SZ09

Harbour Heights Hotel
★★★★ 76% @@ HOTEL

tel: 0800 484 0048 & 01202 707272 **73 Haven Rd, Sandbanks BH13 7LW**
email: reception@harbourheights.net web: www.fjbhotels.co.uk/harbourheights
dir: *Follow signs for Sandbanks, hotel on left after Canford Cliffs*

Enjoying stunning panoramic outlooks across the Sandbanks Peninsula and Poole Harbour, The Harbour Heights is an unassuming yet stylish and innovative boutique hotel. Attention to detail is very apparent, as state-of-the-art facilities blend with traditional comforts. The Harbar Brasserie is at the heart of Harbour Heights, offering excellent cuisine complemented by a fine and diverse wine cellar. The south-facing sun deck is the perfect setting for watching the cross-channel ferries come and go.

Rooms 38 **D** £80-£220 (incl. bkfst)* **Facilities** STV FTV WiFi Spa bath in all rooms Xmas New Year **Conf** Class 36 Board 22 Thtr 70 **Services** Lift Air con **Parking** 50 **Notes** LB Civ Wed 120

Hotel du Vin Poole
★★★★ 76% @ HOTEL

tel: 01202 785578 & 0844 748 9265 *(Calls cost 5p per minute plus your phone company's access charge)* **Mansion House, Thames St BH15 1JN**
email: info.poole@hotelduvin.com web: www.hotelduvin.com
dir: *A31 to Poole, follow channel ferry signs. Left at Poole bridge onto Poole Quay, 1st left into Thames St. Hotel opposite St James Church*

Offering a fresh approach to the well-established company style, this property boasts some delightful rooms packed with comfort and all the expected Hotel du Vin features. Situated near the harbour the hotel offers nautically-themed bedrooms and suites that have plasma TVs, DVD players and bathrooms with power showers. The public rooms are light, open spaces, and as with the other hotels in this group, the bar and restaurant form centre stage.

Rooms 38 (4 GF) **Facilities** STV WiFi Xmas New Year **Conf** Class 20 Board 20 Thtr 60 **Services** Air con **Parking** 8 **Notes** Civ Wed 100

The Haven
★★★★ 75% @@ HOTEL

tel: 01202 707333 & 0800 484 0048 **161 Banks Rd, Sandbanks BH13 7QL**
email: reservations@fjbhotels.co.uk web: www.fjbcollection.co.uk
dir: *B3965 towards Poole Bay, left onto the Peninsula. Hotel 1.5m on left adjacent to Swanage Toll Ferry*

Enjoying an enviable location at the water's edge with views of Poole Bay, this well established hotel was once the home of radio pioneer, Guglielmo Marconi. A friendly team of staff provide good levels of customer care. Bedrooms vary in size and style; many have balconies and wonderful sea or harbour views. The leisure facilities are noteworthy - the Harmony at the Haven is where guests can find spa treatments, a fully equipped gym, indoor and outdoor heated pools and an all-weather tennis court. The hotel is a popular venue for conferences and weddings.

Rooms 84 (3 fmly) **S** £54-£149; **D** £84-£279 (incl. bkfst) **Facilities** Spa FTV WiFi supervised supervised Gym Dance studio Health & Beauty suite Sauna Steam room Xmas New Year **Conf** Class 70 Board 50 Thtr 160 Del from £139 to £272 **Services** Lift **Parking** 160 **Notes** Civ Wed 80

The Sandbanks
★★★★ 73% HOTEL

tel: 01202 707377 & 0800 484 0048 **15 Banks Rd, Sandbanks BH13 7PS**
email: reservations@fjbhotels.co.uk web: www.fjbhotels.co.uk
dir: *A338 from Bournemouth onto Wessex Way, to Liverpool Victoria rdbt. Left, then 2nd exit onto B3965. Follow beach signs. Hotel on left*

Set on the delightful Sandbanks Peninsula, this well-loved hotel has direct access to the seven-mile Blue Flag beach and enjoys stunning views across Poole Harbour and the sea. Most of the spacious bedrooms have sea views; some are air conditioned. There is an extensive range of leisure facilities, including an on-site watersports academy. The Sandbanks is a family-friendly hotel.

Rooms 108 (31 fmly) **Facilities** STV FTV WiFi supervised Gym Sailing Mountain bikes Children's play area Watersports academy Xmas New Year **Conf** Class 50 Board 80 Thtr 150 **Services** Lift **Parking** 120 **Notes** Civ Wed 100

Premier Inn Poole Centre (Holes Bay)
BUDGET HOTEL

tel: 0871 527 8892 *(Calls cost 13p per minute plus your phone company's access charge)*
Holes Bay Rd BH15 2BD
web: www.premierinn.com
dir: *S of A35 & A349 on A350 (dual carriageway). Follow Poole Channel Ferry signs*

High quality, budget accommodation ideal for both families and business travellers. Spacious, en suite bedrooms feature tea and coffee making facilities, and Freeview TV in most hotels. Internet access and WiFi are available for a small fee. The adjacent family restaurant features a wide and varied menu. See also the Hotel Groups pages.

Rooms 146

Premier Inn Poole North
BUDGET HOTEL

tel: 0871 527 8894 *(Calls cost 13p per minute plus your phone company's access charge)*
Cabot Ln BH17 7DA
web: www.premierinn.com
dir: *Follow Poole/Channel Ferries signs. At Darby's Corner rdbt take 2nd exit. At 2nd lights right into Cabot Ln. Hotel on right*

Rooms 126

POOLE *continued*

Milsoms Poole

RESTAURANT WITH ROOMS

tel: 01202 609000 **47 Haven Rd, Canford Cliffs BH13 7LH**
email: poole@milsomshotel.co.uk **web:** www.milsomshotel.co.uk

Milsoms Poole is located in the Canford Cliffs area, moments from some of the country's best beaches and the picturesque Purbeck Hills. Comfortable and stylish en suite accommodation is situated above the popular seafood Loch Fyne Restaurant. The friendly and helpful team provide a warm welcome. Limited on-site parking is available.

Rooms 8

PORLOCK	Map 3 SS84
Somerset	

The Oaks Hotel

★★★ @ HOTEL

tel: 01643 862265 **TA24 8ES**
email: info@oakshotel.co.uk **web:** www.oakshotel.co.uk
dir: *From E of A39, enter village (road narrows to single track) then follow hotel sign. From W: down Porlock Hill, through village, hotel sign on right*

A relaxing atmosphere is found at this charming Edwardian house, located near to the setting of R D Blackmore's novel, *Lorna Doone*. Quietly located and set in attractive grounds, the hotel enjoys elevated views across the village towards the sea. Bedrooms are thoughtfully furnished and comfortable, and the public rooms include a charming bar and a peaceful drawing room. In the dining room, guests can choose from the daily-changing menu, which features fresh, quality local produce.

Rooms 8 ⑊ **S** fr £175; **D** £240-£260 (incl. bkfst & dinner) **Facilities** FTV WiFi ⌲
Parking 12 **Notes** LB ⊗ No children 8yrs Closed Nov-Mar

PORTHLEVEN	Map 2 SW62
Cornwall	

Kota Restaurant with Rooms

@@ RESTAURANT WITH ROOMS

tel: 01326 562407 **Harbour Head TR13 9JA**
email: kota@btconnect.com **web:** www.kotarestaurant.co.uk
dir: *B3304 from Helston into Porthleven. Kota on harbour opposite slipway*

Overlooking the water, this 300-year-old building is the home of Kota Restaurant ('kota' being the Maori word for 'shellfish'). The bedrooms are approached from a granite stairway to the side of the building. The family room is spacious and has the benefit of harbour views, while the smaller, double room is at the rear of the property. The enthusiastic young owners ensure guests enjoy their stay here, and a meal in the two AA Rosette award-winning restaurant should not be missed. Food and drink is also served in the Kota Kai Bar & Kitchen. Breakfast features the best local produce.

Rooms 2 (2 annexe) (1 fmly)

PORTISHEAD	Map 4 ST47
Somerset	

Premier Inn Portishead

BUDGET HOTEL

tel: 0871 527 8898 *(Calls cost 13p per minute plus your phone company's access charge)*
Wyndham Way BS20 7GA
web: www.premierinn.com
dir: *M5 junct 19, A369 towards Portishead. Over 1st rdbt, hotel at next rdbt*

High quality, budget accommodation ideal for both families and business travellers. Spacious, en suite bedrooms feature tea and coffee making facilities, and Freeview TV in most hotels. Internet access and WiFi are available for a small fee. The adjacent family restaurant features a wide and varied menu. See also the Hotel Groups pages.

Rooms 95

Find out more about the AA's awards for food excellence on page 19

PORTSCATHO
Cornwall   Map 2 SW83

INSPECTORS' CHOICE

Driftwood
★★★ ◉◉◉ HOTEL

tel: 01872 580644 **Rosevine TR2 5EW**
email: info@driftwoodhotel.co.uk **web:** www.driftwoodhotel.co.uk
dir: *A390 towards St Mawes. On A3078 turn left to Rosevine at Trewithian*

Poised on the cliff side with panoramic views, this contemporary hotel has a peaceful and secluded location. A warm welcome is guaranteed, and professional standards of service are provided in an effortless and relaxed manner. Cuisine is at the heart of any stay, with quality local produce used in a sympathetic and highly skilled manner. The extremely comfortable and elegant bedrooms are decorated in soft shades reminiscent of the seashore. There is a sheltered terraced garden that has a large deck for sunbathing.

Rooms 15 (1 annexe) (3 fmly) (3 GF) **S** £170–£245; **D** £200–£285 (incl. bkfst)*
Facilities FTV WiFi ↳ Private beach Beauty treatments on request **Parking** 20
Notes ⊗ Closed 5 Dec–3 Feb

PORTSMOUTH & SOUTHSEA
Hampshire   Map 5 SU60

Portsmouth Marriott Hotel
★★★★ 78% HOTEL

tel: 023 9238 3151 **Southampton Rd PO6 4SH**
web: www.portsmouthmarriott.co.uk
dir: *M27 junct 12, keep left off slip road, exit Cosham. Hotel on left at lights*

Close to the motorway and ferry port, this hotel is well suited for business travellers. The comfortable and well laid-out bedrooms provide a comprehensive range of facilities including up-to-date workstations. The leisure club offers a pool, a gym, and a health and beauty salon.

Rooms 174 (77 fmly) ⬤ **Facilities** STV FTV WiFi ↳ HL ⊛ supervised Gym Exercise studio Beauty salon & treatment room Xmas New Year **Conf** Class 180 Board 30 Thtr 350 **Services** Lift Air con **Parking** 196 **Notes** Civ Wed 350

Best Western Royal Beach Hotel
★★★ 79% HOTEL

tel: 023 9273 1281 **South Pde, Southsea PO4 0RN**
email: enquiries@royalbeachhotel.co.uk **web:** www.royalbeachhotel.co.uk
dir: *M27 to M275, follow signs to seafront. Hotel on seafront*

This former Victorian seafront hotel is a smart and comfortable venue suitable for leisure and business guests alike. Bedrooms and public areas are well presented and generally spacious, and the smart Coast Bar is an ideal venue for a relaxing drink.

Rooms 124 (12 fmly) ⬤ **Facilities** STV FTV WiFi ↳ Xmas New Year **Conf** Class 180 Board 40 Thtr 280 **Services** Lift **Parking** 50 **Notes** Civ Wed 85

The Farmhouse & Innlodge Hotel
★★★ 74% HOTEL

OldEngl‍sh

tel: 023 9265 0510 **Burrfields Rd PO3 5HH**
email: farmhouse.portsmouth@greeneking.co.uk **web:** www.oldenglish.co.uk
dir: *A3(M)/M27 onto A27. Take Southsea exit, follow A2030. 3rd lights right into Burrfields Rd. Hotel 2nd car park on left*

Located on the eastern fringe of the city, this purpose-built hotel is conveniently situated for all major routes. The spacious, modern bedrooms are well equipped and include ground floor and family rooms. The Farmhouse Hungry Horse Pub offers a wide range of eating options, and there is an ActionZone adventure area.

Rooms 74 (6 fmly) (33 GF) **Facilities** FTV WiFi Pony club for children Pool tables ♫ New Year **Conf** Class 64 Board 40 Thtr 150 **Parking** 200 **Notes** ⊛ Civ Wed 120

Premier Inn Portsmouth City Centre
BUDGET HOTEL

tel: 0871 527 9522 *(Calls cost 13p per minute plus your phone company's access charge)*
1 Isambard Brunel Rd PO1 2TR
email: portsmouthcitycentre.pi@premierinn.com **web:** www.premierinn.com
dir: *M275 onto A3 (Portsmouth (W)/Isle of Wight Ferries). At rdbt 2nd left (City Centre/Seafront/Historic Waterfront). At next rdt 2nd left into Marketway. After next rdbt left signed Station into Unicorn Rd. At 2nd rdbt right into Isambard Brunel Rd Under rail bridge, hotel on left*

High quality, budget accommodation ideal for both families and business travellers. Spacious, en suite bedrooms feature tea and coffee making facilities, and Freeview TV in most hotels. Internet access and WiFi are available for a small fee. The adjacent family restaurant features a wide and varied menu. See also the Hotel Groups pages.

Rooms 84

Premier Inn Portsmouth (Horndean)
BUDGET HOTEL

tel: 0871 527 8902 *(Calls cost 13p per minute plus your phone company's access charge)*
2 Havant Rd PO8 ODT
web: www.premierinn.com
dir: *A3(M) junct 2, take B2149 signed Emsworth, Horndean. At rdbt left onto B2149, follow Horndean signs. At next rdbt left onto A3 towards Waterlooville. Hotel on left behind Red Lion*

Rooms 25

P

PORTSMOUTH & SOUTHSEA *continued*

Premier Inn Portsmouth (Port Solent)

BUDGET HOTEL

tel: 0871 527 8906 *(Calls cost 13p per minute plus your phone company's access charge)*
Binnacle Way PO6 4FB
web: www.premierinn.com
dir: *M27 junct 12, left at lights onto Southampton Rd. Left after 200mtrs at lights onto Compass Rd. At mini-rdbt right onto Binnacle Way, hotel on right*

Rooms 108

Premier Inn Portsmouth (Port Solent East)

BUDGET HOTEL

tel: 0871 527 8904 *(Calls cost 13p per minute plus your phone company's access charge)*
1 Southampton Rd, North Harbour PO6 4SA
web: www.premierinn.com
dir: *M27 junct 12, A3, left onto A27. Hotel on left*

Rooms 64

Premier Inn Southsea

BUDGET HOTEL

tel: 0871 527 9014 *(Calls cost 13p per minute plus your phone company's access charge)*
Long Curtain Rd, Southsea PO5 3AA
web: www.premierinn.com
dir: *M1 junct 24, A453. Follow ring road & Queen's Drive Industrial Estate signs. After Homebase left into Castle Bridge Rd, hotel opposite Pizza Hut restaurant*

Rooms 48

Ibis Budget Portsmouth

AA Advertised

tel: 023 9273 6386 **Fratton Way PO4 8SL**
email: H6462@accor.com **web:** www.ibishotel.com
dir: *M27 junct 12 onto M275 then follow signs for City Centre. Left at rdbt, follow signs to Central South Sea & Portsmouth FC*

Modern, budget hotel offering comfortable accommodation in bright and practical bedrooms. Breakfast is self-service and dinner is available in the restaurant.

Rooms 120 **Facilities** FTV WiFi **Services** Lift

Ibis Portsmouth Centre

AA Advertised

tel: 023 9264 0000 **Winston Churchill Av PO1 2LX**
email: h1461@accor.com **web:** www.ibis.com
dir: *M27 junct 12 onto M275. Follow signs for city centre, Sealife Centre & Guildhall. Right at rdbt into Winston Churchill Ave*

Modern, budget hotel offering comfortable accommodation in bright and practical bedrooms. Breakfast is self-service and dinner is available in the restaurant.

Rooms 144 **Facilities** FTV WiFi **Conf** Board 12 **Services** Lift **Parking** 60

PORT SUNLIGHT
Merseyside
Map 15 SJ38

HIGHLY RECOMMENDED

Leverhulme Hotel

★★★★ 83% ◉◉ HOTEL

tel: 0151 644 6655 & 644 5555 **Central Rd CH62 5EZ**
email: enquiries@leverhulmehotel.co.uk **web:** www.leverhulmehotel.co.uk
dir: *From Chester: M53 junct 5, A41 Birkenhead, in approx 4m left into Bolton Rd, on at rdbt, 0.1m right into Church Drive. 0.2m hotel on right. From Liverpool: A41 Chester, 2.7m, 3rd exit at 3rd rdbt into Bolton Rd then follow directions as above*

Built in 1907, this Grade II listed, former cottage hospital is set in the picturesque garden village of Port Sunlight, which was created by Lord Leverhulme for his soap-factory workers in the late 19th century. Following an extensive restoration project, this art deco hotel has stylish bedrooms, appointed to a very high standard; all have impressive facilities including bathrooms with separate showers and LCD TVs; the suites have roof-top terraces and hot tubs. The hotel also features a range of day rooms and an ultra-modern, award-winning restaurant.

Rooms 23 (8 annexe) (1 fmly) (8 GF) **S** £114-£490; **D** £150-£510 (incl. bkfst)*
Facilities STV FTV WiFi HL Gym Games room Children's play area Xmas New Year Child facilities **Conf** Class 140 Board 30 Thtr 300 Del £198* **Parking** 70
Notes LB Civ Wed 240

PRESTON
Lancashire
Map 18 SD52

See also **Garstang**

Barton Grange Hotel

★★★★ 77% HOTEL

tel: 01772 862551 **Garstang Rd PR3 5AA**
email: stay@bartongrangehotel.com **web:** www.bartongrangehotel.co.uk

(For full entry see Barton)

Macdonald Tickled Trout

★★★★ 74% HOTEL

tel: 01772 877091 & 0344 879 9053 **Preston New Rd, Samlesbury PR5 0UJ**
email: general.tickledtrout@macdonald-hotels.co.uk **web:** www.macdonaldhotels.co.uk
dir: *M6 junct 31, A59 towards Preston*

On the banks of the River Ribble, this hotel is conveniently located for the motorway, making it a popular venue for both business and leisure guests. Smartly appointed bedrooms are all tastefully decorated and equipped with a thoughtful range of extras. The hotel boasts a stylish wing of meeting rooms.

Rooms 98 (6 fmly) (10 GF) **Facilities** FTV WiFi Fishing Xmas New Year **Conf** Class 35 Board 20 Thtr 100 **Services** Lift **Parking** 180 **Notes** Civ Wed 90

P

The Legacy Preston International Hotel

★★★ 75% HOTEL

tel: 0844 411 9028 *(Calls cost 7p per minute plus your phone company's access charge)*
& 0330 333 2828 **Marsh Ln PR1 2YF**
email: res-prestoninternational@legacy-hotels.co.uk **web:** www.legacy-hotels.co.uk
dir: M6 junct 31 or 32, A59 ring rd. Hotel in approx 3.5m on one way system

This hotel is ideally located close to the town centre and the M6 making it a popular choice with both business and leisure guests. The contemporary bedrooms are very comfortable and well equipped, and free WiFi is available. The public areas include a light-filled lounge, and the menu in the restaurant offers a wide choice to suit most tastes. The hotel has secure parking.

Rooms 75 (12 fmly) **Facilities** FTV WiFi **Conf** Class 20 Board 20 Thtr 30 **Services** Lift **Parking** 40 **Notes** ⊗

The Park Hotel

★★★ 75% SMALL HOTEL

tel: 01772 726250 & 728096 **209 Tulketh Rd, Ashton-On-Ribble PR2 1ES**
email: info@parkhotelpreston.co.uk **web:** www.parkhotelpreston.co.uk
dir: A59 then A5085 Blackpool Road 2.4m, left into Tulketh Road, A5072, hotel 200yds on right

This Edwardian mansion house provides quality and comfort in keeping with its history. Original features including tall ceilings, tiled floors and stained glass windows are a real bonus. The main bedrooms and bathrooms are spacious and well equipped. Public areas include the homely bar for pre-dinner drinks and the well appointed dining room. Ample off-road car parking is available.

Rooms 18 (10 annexe) (1 fmly) (8 GF) **Facilities** FTV WiFi **Conf** Class 15 Board 15 Thtr 20 **Parking** 14 **Notes** ⊗ RS 20 Dec-5 Jan

Premier Inn Preston Central

BUDGET HOTEL

tel: 0871 527 8908 *(Calls cost 13p per minute plus your phone company's access charge)*
Fox St PR1 2AB
web: www.premierinn.com
dir: Off Ridgway (A59). Telephone for detailed directions

High quality, budget accommodation ideal for both families and business travellers. Spacious, en suite bedrooms feature tea and coffee making facilities, and Freeview TV in most hotels. Internet access and WiFi are available for a small fee. The adjacent family restaurant features a wide and varied menu. See also the Hotel Groups pages.

Rooms 140

Premier Inn Preston East

BUDGET HOTEL

tel: 0871 527 8910 *(Calls cost 13p per minute plus your phone company's access charge)*
Bluebell Way, Preston East Link Rd, Fulwood PR2 5PZ
web: www.premierinn.com
dir: M6 junct 31a, follow ring road under motorway, hotel on left. NB no exit for S'bound traffic - exit at M6 junct 31, join M6 N'bound, exit at junct 31a

Rooms 67

Premier Inn Preston South (Craven Drive)

BUDGET HOTEL

tel: 0871 527 8914 *(Calls cost 13p per minute plus your phone company's access charge)*
Lostock Ln, Bamber Bridge PR5 6BZ
web: www.premierinn.com
dir: M6 junct 29, A582 (Lostock Ln). Straight on at 1st lights, into left lane, hotel on left adjacent to B&Q

Rooms 75

Premier Inn Preston South (Cuerden Way)

BUDGET HOTEL

tel: 0871 527 8916 *(Calls cost 13p per minute plus your phone company's access charge)*
Lostock Ln, Bamber Bridge PR5 6BA
web: www.premierinn.com
dir: Off M65 junct 1 (0.5m from M6 junct 29) close to rdbt junct of A582 & A6

Rooms 42

Premier Inn Preston West

BUDGET HOTEL

tel: 0871 527 8918 *(Calls cost 13p per minute plus your phone company's access charge)*
Blackpool Rd, Lea PR4 0XB
web: www.premierinn.com
dir: Off A583, opposite Texaco garage

Rooms 38

Ibis Preston North

AA Advertised

tel: 01772 861800 **Garstang Rd, Broughton PR3 5JE**
email: H3162@accor.com **web:** www.ibishotel.com
dir: M6 junct 32, then M55 junct 1. Left lane onto A6. Left at slip road, left again at mini-rdbt. 2nd turn, hotel on right past pub

Modern, budget hotel offering comfortable accommodation in bright and practical bedrooms. Breakfast is self-service and dinner is available in the restaurant.

Rooms 82 (27 fmly) (16 GF) **Facilities** STV FTV WiFi HL **Conf** Class 16 Board 12 Thtr 35 **Services** Lift **Parking** 100

PRESTWICH Map 15 SD80
Greater Manchester

Premier Inn Manchester (Prestwich)

BUDGET HOTEL

tel: 0871 527 8714 *(Calls cost 13p per minute plus your phone company's access charge)*
Bury New Rd M25 3AJ
web: www.premierinn.com
dir: M60 junct 17, A56 signed Manchester City Centre, Prestwich & Whitefield. Hotel on left

High quality, budget accommodation ideal for both families and business travellers. Spacious, en suite bedrooms feature tea and coffee making facilities, and Freeview TV in most hotels. Internet access and WiFi are available for a small fee. The adjacent family restaurant features a wide and varied menu. See also the Hotel Groups pages.

Rooms 83

PUDDINGTON
Cheshire

Map 15 SJ37

Macdonald Craxton Wood Hotel
★★★★ 76% ◎◎ HOTEL

tel: 0151 347 4000 & 0344 879 9038 **Parkgate Rd, Ledsham CH66 9PB**
email: craxton@macdonald-hotels.co.uk **web:** www.macdonaldhotels.co.uk
dir: *From M6 take M56 towards N Wales, then A5117/A540 to Hoylake. Hotel on left 200yds past lights*

Set in extensive grounds, this hotel offers a variety of spacious and comfortable rooms, well equipped with modern amenities. The restaurant features a range of dishes including signature grills and locally sourced ingredients. An extensive spa facility and a choice of function suites complete the package.

Rooms 72 (8 fmly) (30 GF) ↝ **Facilities** Spa FTV WiFi ↳ HL ⓣ Gym Sauna Steam room Thermal Spa incl Rasul Xmas New Year **Conf** Class 200 Board 160 Thtr 300 **Services** Lift **Parking** 220 **Notes** ⊗ Civ Wed 350

Premier Inn Wirral (Two Mills)
BUDGET HOTEL

tel: 0871 527 9180 *(Calls cost 13p per minute plus your phone company's access charge)*
Parkgate Rd, Two Mills CH66 9PD
web: www.premierinn.com
dir: *5m from M56 junct 16 & M53 junct 5. On x-rds of A550 & A540*

High quality, budget accommodation ideal for both families and business travellers. Spacious, en suite bedrooms feature tea and coffee making facilities, and Freeview TV in most hotels. Internet access and WiFi are available for a small fee. The adjacent family restaurant features a wide and varied menu. See also the Hotel Groups pages.

Rooms 31

PURTON
Wiltshire

Map 5 SU08

The Pear Tree at Purton
★★★ 82% ◎◎ HOTEL

tel: 01793 772100 **Church End SN5 4ED**
email: stay@peartreepurton.co.uk **web:** www.peartreepurton.co.uk
dir: *M4 junct 16 follow signs to Purton, at Hartford House Stores turn right. Hotel 0.25m on left*

The Pear Tree is a charming 15th-century, former vicarage set amidst extensive landscaped gardens in a peaceful location in the Vale of the White Horse, near the Saxon village of Purton. The resident proprietors and staff provide efficient, dedicated service and friendly hospitality. The spacious bedrooms are individually decorated and have a good range of thoughtful extras such as fresh fruit, sherry and shortbread. Fresh ingredients feature on the award-winning menus.

Rooms 17 (2 fmly) (6 GF) ↝ **S** £109-£119; **D** £109-£149 (incl. bkfst)* **Facilities** FTV WiFi ↳ ⬇ Outdoor giant chess & jenga Vineyard New Year **Conf** Class 30 Board 30 Thtr 60 Del from £179.50 to £229 **Parking** 60 **Notes** LB Closed 26 Dec Civ Wed 50

QUORN
Leicestershire

Map 11 SK51

Quorn Country Hotel
★★★★ 78% ◎ HOTEL

tel: 01509 415050 & 415061 **Charnwood House, 66 Leicester Rd LE12 8BB**
email: reservations@quorncountryhotel.co.uk **web:** www.primahotels.co.uk/quorn
dir: *M1 junct 23 onto A512 into Loughborough. Follow A6 signs. At 1st rdbt towards Quorn, through lights, hotel 500yds from 2nd rdbt*

Professional service is one of the key strengths of this pleasing hotel, which sits beside the river in four acres of landscaped gardens and grounds. The smart modern conference centre and function suites are popular for both corporate functions and weddings. Public rooms include a smart comfortable lounge and bar, and guests have the choice of two dining options: the formal Shires restaurant and the informal conservatory-style Orangery.

Rooms 36 (2 fmly) (11 GF) **Facilities** WiFi ↳ Fishing New Year **Conf** Class 162 Board 40 Thtr 300 **Services** Lift **Parking** 100 **Notes** ⊗ Civ Wed 200

RADLETT
Hertfordshire

Map 6 TL10

Premier Inn St Albans/Bricket Wood
BUDGET HOTEL

tel: 0871 527 9016 *(Calls cost 13p per minute plus your phone company's access charge)*
Smug Oak Ln, Bricketwood AL2 3PN
web: www.premierinn.com
dir: *M1 junct 6 (or M25 junct 21a) follow Watford signs, left at lights signed M1/Bricket Wood. 2nd left into Mount Pleasant Ln, straight on at 2 mini rdbts, right at The Gate pub. Hotel at end*

High quality, budget accommodation ideal for both families and business travellers. Spacious, en suite bedrooms feature tea and coffee making facilities, and Freeview TV in most hotels. Internet access and WiFi are available for a small fee. The adjacent family restaurant features a wide and varied menu. See also the Hotel Groups pages.

Rooms 56

RAINHAM
Greater London

Map 6 TQ58

Premier Inn Rainham
BUDGET HOTEL

tel: 0871 527 8920 *(Calls cost 13p per minute plus your phone company's access charge)*
New Rd, Wennington RM13 9ED
web: www.premierinn.com
dir: *M25 junct 30/31, A13 for Dagenham/Rainham, A1306 towards Wennington, Aveley & Rainham. Hotel 0.5m on right*

High quality, budget accommodation ideal for both families and business travellers. Spacious, en suite bedrooms feature tea and coffee making facilities, and Freeview TV in most hotels. Internet access and WiFi are available for a small fee. The adjacent family restaurant features a wide and varied menu. See also the Hotel Groups pages.

Rooms 82

RAINHILL
Merseyside   Map 15 SJ49

Premier Inn Liverpool (Rainhill)

BUDGET HOTEL

tel: 0871 527 8614 *(Calls cost 13p per minute plus your phone company's access charge)*
804 Warrington Rd L35 6PE
web: www.premierinn.com
dir: *Just off M62 junct 7, A57 towards Rainhill*

High quality, budget accommodation ideal for both families and business travellers. Spacious, en suite bedrooms feature tea and coffee making facilities, and Freeview TV in most hotels. Internet access and WiFi are available for a small fee. The adjacent family restaurant features a wide and varied menu. See also the Hotel Groups pages.

Rooms 34

RAMSGATE
Kent   Map 7 TR36

The Pegwell Bay Hotel

★★★ 79% HOTEL

tel: 01843 599590 **81 Pegwell Rd, Pegwell CT11 0NJ**
email: pegwellbay.reception@thorleytaverns.co.uk **web:** www.pegwellbayhotel.co.uk
dir: *Phone for detailed directions*

Boasting stunning views over the Channel, this historic cliff-top hotel is suitable for guests staying either on business or for leisure. Spacious, comfortable bedrooms are well equipped and include WiFi. A modern lounge, majestic dining room and traditional pub offer a variety of options for eating and for relaxation.

Rooms 42 (5 fmly) (5 GF) **Facilities** FTV WiFi Xmas New Year **Conf** Class 65 Board 65 Thtr 100 **Services** Lift **Parking** 80 **Notes** ⊗ Civ Wed 70

Comfort Inn Ramsgate

★★★ 72% HOTEL

tel: 01843 592345 **Victoria Pde, East Cliff CT11 8DT**
email: reservations@comfortinnramsgate.co.uk **web:** www.comfortinnramsgate.co.uk
dir: *From M2 take A299 signed Ramsgate, B2054 to Victoria Parade, follow sign to harbour and carry on past the harbour up Maleria Walk*

This Victorian hotel stands on the seafront, close to the ferry terminal and the town. Bedrooms, some with balconies, are generously sized and well equipped. Guests can relax in the modern bar and lounge or be pampered in the beauty treatment room. The popular restaurant serves a particularly wide choice of dishes ranging from traditional British cuisine to Indian favourites.

Rooms 44 (8 fmly) ✎ **S** £45-£65; **D** £59-£149 (incl. bkfst) **Facilities** STV FTV WiFi ⇘ Gym Beauty salon Sauna Xmas New Year **Conf** Class 30 Board 30 Thtr 70 Del from £65 to £105 **Services** Lift Air con **Parking** 10 **Notes** LB ⊗

The Oak Hotel

★★ 84% HOTEL

tel: 01843 583686 & 581582 **66 Harbour Pde CT11 8LN**
email: oak.reception@thorleytaverns.co.uk **web:** www.oakhotel.co.uk
dir: *Follow road around harbour, right into Harbour Parade*

Located within easy reach of the railway station, ferry terminal and the town centre's shops, this unpretentious hotel enjoys spectacular views of the marina and harbour. The comfortable bedrooms are attractively presented and very well equipped. The Restaurant Sixty-Six, Caffe Roma and The Lounge Bar offer a variety of dining options along with a selection of wines, beers and spirits.

Rooms 34 (9 fmly) ✎ **Facilities** FTV WiFi **Conf** Class 60 Board 50 Thtr 100 **Notes** ⊗

Holiday Inn Express Ramsgate

BUDGET HOTEL

tel: 01843 820250 **Tothill St CT12 4AU**
email: reservations.ramsgate@holidayinnexpress.org.uk **web:** www.hiexramsgate.co.uk
dir: *On A299, off rdbt junct with B2048*

A modern hotel ideal for families and business travellers. Fresh and uncomplicated, the spacious rooms include Sky TV, power shower and tea and coffee-making facilities. Continental buffet breakfast is included in the room rate; other meals may be taken at the nearby family pub or restaurant. See also the Hotel Groups pages.

Rooms 105 (70 fmly) (33 GF) ✎ **Conf** Class 16 Board 16 Thtr 30

RAVENGLASS
Cumbria   Map 18 SD09

HIGHLY RECOMMENDED

The Pennington Hotel

★★★ 85% ◉ HOTEL

tel: 01229 717222 & 0845 450 6445
(Calls cost 7p per minute plus your phone company's access charge) **CA18 1SD**
email: info@penningtonhotels.com **web:** www.penningtonhotels.com
dir: *In village centre*

This hotel has a very relaxed atmosphere throughout and the public areas are open-plan with high quality fabrics and artwork. Bedrooms are modern in design and have high spec fixtures and fittings in the bathrooms. Honest cooking, based on local and fine quality ingredients, is offered on the seasonal menus. Staff show exceptional customer awareness and provide very attentive and friendly service.

Rooms 21 (3 annexe) (6 fmly) (5 GF) ✎ **Facilities** FTV WiFi ⇘ Xmas New Year **Conf** Class 40 Board 40 Thtr 80 **Parking** 53 **Notes** LB

RAVENSCAR
North Yorkshire   Map 19 NZ90

Raven Hall Country House Hotel

★★★ 79% HOTEL

tel: 01723 870353 **YO13 0ET**
email: enquiries@ravenhall.co.uk **web:** www.ravenhall.co.uk
dir: *A171 towards Whitby. At Cloughton turn right onto unclassified road to Ravenscar*

This impressive cliff-top mansion enjoys breathtaking views over Robin Hood's Bay. Extensive well-kept grounds include tennis courts, putting green, swimming pools and historic battlements. The bedrooms vary in size but all are comfortably equipped, and many offer panoramic views. There are also eight environmentally-friendly Finnish lodges that have been furnished to a high standard.

Rooms 63 (8 annexe) (23 fmly) (5 GF) ✎ **S** £47.50-£70; **D** £95-£140 (incl. bkfst) **Facilities** FTV WiFi ⊛ ⚓ 9 ⚘ Putt green ⚑ Bowls Table tennis Xmas New Year **Conf** Class 80 Board 40 Thtr 100 Del from £95 to £135 **Services** Lift **Parking** 200 **Notes** Civ Wed 100

R

RAYLEIGH
Essex
Map 7 TQ89

Premier Inn Basildon (Rayleigh)

BUDGET HOTEL

tel: 0871 527 8058 *(Calls cost 13p per minute plus your phone company's access charge)*
Rayleigh Weir, Arterial Road (A127) SS6 7XJ
web: www.premierinn.com
dir: *M25 junct 29, A127 towards Southend. Approx 13m exit at Rayleigh Weir junct onto A129 to Rayleigh. Straight on at 2 lights, 1st left. NB for Sat Nav use SS6 7XJ*

High quality, budget accommodation ideal for both families and business travellers. Spacious, en suite bedrooms feature tea and coffee making facilities, and Freeview TV in most hotels. Internet access and WiFi are available for a small fee. The adjacent family restaurant features a wide and varied menu. See also the Hotel Groups pages.

Rooms 50

READING
Berkshire
Map 5 SU77

Holiday Inn Reading M4 Jct 10

★★★★ 82% ◉◉ HOTEL

tel: 0118 944 0444 **Wharfedale Rd, Winnersh Triangle RG41 5TS**
email: reservations@hireadinghotel.com **web:** www.hireadinghotel.com
dir: *M4 junct 10/A329(M) towards Reading (E), 1st exit signed Winnersh/Woodley/A329, left at lights into Wharfedale Rd. Hotel on left*

Situated in the Winnersh Triangle within close proximity of the M4, Reading, Bracknell and Wokingham, this hotel offers a range of air-conditioned, contemporary and stylish bedrooms, eight state-of-the-art meeting rooms and the Esprit Spa & Wellness with extensive leisure facilities including a 19-metre indoor pool and Dermalogica Spa. The Caprice Restaurant offers relaxed dining throughout the day. Complimentary underground parking is provided.

Rooms 174 (23 fmly) ⁋ **S** £55–£189; **D** £55–£189 (incl. bkfst) **Facilities** Spa FTV WiFi ☉ HL ☒ Gym Sauna Steam room ♪♪ Xmas New Year **Conf** Class 160 Board 64 Thtr 260 Del from £120 to £249 **Services** Lift Air con **Parking** 120 **Notes** LB Civ Wed 260

Millennium Madejski Hotel Reading
MILLENNIUM
HOTELS AND RESORTS
MILLENNIUM · COPTHORNE

★★★★ 80% ◉◉ HOTEL

tel: 0118 925 3500 **Madejski Stadium RG2 OFL**
email: reservations.reading@millenniumhotels.co.uk **web:** www.millenniumhotels.co.uk
dir: *M4 junct 11 onto A33, follow signs for Madejski Stadium Complex*

A stylish hotel, that features an atrium lobby with specially commissioned water sculpture, is part of the Madejski stadium complex, home to both Reading FC and the London Irish rugby team. Bedrooms are appointed with spacious workstations and plenty of amenities; there is also a choice of suites and a club floor with its own lounge. The hotel also has a fine dining restaurant.

Rooms 201 (39 fmly) ⁋ **Facilities** Spa STV WiFi ☉ ☒ supervised Gym **Conf** Class 36 Board 30 Thtr 66 **Services** Lift Air con **Parking** 250 **Notes** RS Xmas & New Year

Novotel Reading Centre
NOVOTEL
HOTELS & RESORTS

★★★★ 78% HOTEL

tel: 0118 952 2600 **25b Friar St RG1 1DP**
email: h5432@accor.com **web:** www.novotel.com
dir: *M4 junct 11 or A33 towards Reading, left for Garrard St car park, at rdbt 3rd exit on Friar St*

This attractive and stylish city centre hotel is convenient for Reading's business and shopping centre; it is adjacent to a town centre car park, and has a range of conference facilities and excellent leisure options. The restaurant offers a contemporary style menu and a good wine list too. Bedrooms are comfortable and stylishly designed.

Rooms 178 (154 fmly) **Facilities** FTV WiFi HL ☒ Gym Steam room Sauna **Conf** Class 50 Board 36 Thtr 90 **Services** Lift **Parking** 15

Malmaison Reading
Malmaison
hotels that dare to be different

★★★★ 74% ◉ HOTEL

tel: 0844 693 0660 *(Calls cost 5p per minute plus your phone company's access charge)*
& 0118 956 2300 Great Western House, 18-20 Station Rd RG1 1JX
email: reading@malmaison.com **web:** www.malmaison.com
dir: *Opposite rail station*

This historic hotel has been transformed into the funky Malmaison style which reflects its proximity and long-standing relationship with the railway. Public areas feature rail memorabilia and excellent pictures, and include a Café Mal and a meeting room. Bedrooms here have all the amenities a modern executive would expect, plus comfort and quality in abundance. Dining is interesting too, with a menu that features home-grown and local produce accompanied by an impressive wine list.

Rooms 75 (6 fmly) (4 GF) ⁋ **Facilities** FTV WiFi ☉ HL Xmas New Year **Conf** Class 18 Board 22 Thtr 30 **Services** Lift Air con **Notes** ☒ Civ Wed 20

Best Western Calcot Hotel

★★★ 77% HOTEL

tel: 0118 941 6423 **98 Bath Rd, Calcot RG31 7QN**
email: enquiries@calcothotel.net **web:** www.calcothotel.co.uk
dir: *M4 junct 12, A4 towards Reading, hotel in 0.5m*

This hotel is conveniently located in a residential area just off the motorway. Bedrooms are well equipped with good business facilities, such as data ports and

R

good workspace. There are attractive public rooms and function suites, and the informal restaurant offers enjoyable food in welcoming surroundings.

Rooms 78 (3 fmly) (6 GF) 🐾 **S** £40-£95; **D** £55-£125 **Facilities** FTV WiFi 🎵 New Year **Conf** Class 35 Board 35 Thtr 120 Del from £125 to £155 **Parking** 130 **Notes** Closed 24-30 Dec RS 2 Dec-6 Jan Civ Wed 200

Premier Inn Reading (Caversham Bridge)

BUDGET HOTEL

tel: 0871 527 8922 *(Calls cost 13p per minute plus your phone company's access charge)*
Richfield Av RG1 8EQ
web: www.premierinn.com
dir: *M4 junct 11, A33 to Reading. A329 towards Caversham. Left at TGI Friday's. Left at Crowne Plaza. Hotel 200yds on right*

High quality, budget accommodation ideal for both families and business travellers. Spacious, en suite bedrooms feature tea and coffee making facilities, and Freeview TV in most hotels. Internet access and WiFi are available for a small fee. The adjacent family restaurant features a wide and varied menu. See also the Hotel Groups pages.

Rooms 75

Premier Inn Reading Central

BUDGET HOTEL

tel: 0871 527 8924 *(Calls cost 13p per minute plus your phone company's access charge)*
Letcombe St RG1 2HN
web: www.premierinn.com
dir: *M4 junct 11, A33 towards town centre, straight on at 3 rdbts (approx 3.5m). Right onto A329 signed The Oracle, Riverside Shopping Centre. Branch immediately left, hotel opposite The Oracle shopping centre*

Rooms 151

Premier Inn Reading South

BUDGET HOTEL

tel: 0871 527 8926 *(Calls cost 13p per minute plus your phone company's access charge)*
Goring Ln, Grazeley Green RG7 1LS
web: www.premierinn.com
dir: *M4 junct 11, A33 towards Basingstoke. At rdbt take exit towards Burghfield & Mortimer. 3rd right into Grazeley Green. Under rail bridge turn left. Hotel on left*

Rooms 44

Ibis Reading Centre

AA Advertised

tel: 0118 953 3500 **25A Friar St RG1 1DP**
email: H5431@accor.com **web:** www.ibishotel.com
dir: *A329 into Friar St. Hotel near central railway station. Access by car in Garrard St*

Modern, budget hotel offering comfortable accommodation in bright and practical bedrooms. Breakfast is self-service and dinner is available in the restaurant.

Rooms 182 🐾 **Facilities** FTV WiFi ➷ **Services** Lift

The French Horn

◎◎ RESTAURANT WITH ROOMS

tel: 0118 969 2204 **Sonning RG4 6TN**
email: info@thefrenchhorn.co.uk **web:** www.thefrenchhorn.co.uk
dir: *From A4 into Sonning, follow B478 through village over bridge, on right, car park on left*

This long-established Thames-side establishment has a lovely village setting and retains the traditions of classic hospitality. The restaurant is a particular attraction and has been awarded two AA Rosettes. Bedrooms, including four cottage suites, are spacious and comfortable; many offer stunning views over the river. A private boardroom is available for corporate guests.

Rooms 20 (8 annexe)

REDDITCH Map 10 SP06
Worcestershire

The Abbey Hotel

★★★★ 77% HOTEL

tel: 01527 406600 **Hither Green Ln, Dagnell End Rd, Bordesley B98 9BE**
email: info@theabbeyhotel.co.uk **web:** www.theabbeyhotel.co.uk
dir: *M42 junct 2, A441 to Redditch. End of carriageway turn left A441, Dagnell End Rd on left. Hotel 600yds on right*

With convenient access to the motorway and a proximity to many attractions, this modern hotel is popular with both business and leisure travellers. Bedrooms are well equipped and attractively decorated; the executive corner rooms are especially spacious. Facilities include an 18-hole golf course, pro shop, large indoor pool and extensive conference facilities.

Rooms 99 (20 fmly) (23 GF) 🐾 **Facilities** Spa FTV WiFi ➷ 🕒 ⚓ 18 Putt green Gym Flood lit golf driving range Xmas New Year **Conf** Class 60 Board 30 Thtr 170 **Services** Lift **Parking** 200 **Notes** ⊗ Civ Wed 100

Holiday Inn Express Birmingham - Redditch

BUDGET HOTEL

tel: 01527 584658 **2 Hewell Rd, Enfield B97 6AE**
email: reservations@express.gb.com **web:** www.hieredditchhotel.com
dir: *M42 junct 2. 1st exit from rdbt to A44. 1st exit from rdbt to Bordesleigh. 4th exit from rdbt to Middelhouse Lane. Left at lights into B/ham Rd. 1st right into Clive Road. 1st exit from rdbt to Hewell Rd. 1st right into Gloucester Close*

This modern town centre hotel, adjacent to the station, is ideal for families and business travellers. The spacious tranquil rooms include flat-screen TVs with Freeview channels, and bathrooms with power showers. Complimentary hot buffet breakfast and free WiFi are included in the room rate. Freshly prepared meals are served in the GR Restaurant daily from 6pm-10pm. There are two air-conditioned meeting rooms, with natural light, available. See also the Hotel Groups pages.

Rooms 100 (75 fmly) (10 GF) 🐾 **D** £45-£79 (incl. bkfst)* **Conf** Class 26 Board 20 Thtr 50 Del from £109 to £129*

R

REDDITCH *continued*

Premier Inn Redditch North (A441)

BUDGET HOTEL

tel: 0871 527 9372 *(Calls cost 13p per minute plus your phone company's access charge)*
Bordesley Ln B97 6AQ
web: www.premierinn.com
dir: *M42 junct 3, A435 (Alcester road). In 3m take A4023 towards Redditch & Bromsgrove. Exit 1st rdbt towards Birmingham (A441). At next rdbt 3rd exit onto Alvechurch Highway (A441). At next rdbt 4th exit into Millrace Rd, left into Bordesley Ln. NB for Sat Nav use B97 6RR*

High quality, budget accommodation ideal for both families and business travellers. Spacious, en suite bedrooms feature tea and coffee making facilities, and Freeview TV in most hotels. Internet access and WiFi are available for a small fee. The adjacent family restaurant features a wide and varied menu. See also the Hotel Groups pages.

Rooms 80

Premier Inn Redditch West (A448)

BUDGET HOTEL

tel: 0871 527 8928 *(Calls cost 13p per minute plus your phone company's access charge)*
Birchfield Rd B97 6PX
web: www.premierinn.com
dir: *M5 junct 4, A38 towards Bromsgrove. At rdbt take A448 to Redditch. 1st exit for Webheath. At next rdbt 3rd exit, 1st right into Birchfield Rd*

Rooms 33

REDHILL	Map 6 TQ25
Surrey	

HIGHLY RECOMMENDED

Nutfield Priory Hotel & Spa

★★★★ 83% HOTEL

tel: 01737 824400 & 0845 072 7485
(Calls cost 5p per minute plus your phone company's access charge) **Nutfield RH1 4EL**
email: nutfieldpriory@handpicked.co.uk
web: www.handpickedhotels.co.uk/nutfieldpriory
dir: *M25 junct 6, follow Redhill signs via Godstone on A25. Hotel 1m on left after Nutfield Village. Or M25 junct 8, A25 through Reigate & Redhill. Hotel on right 1.5m after rail bridge*

This Victorian country house dates back to 1872 and is set in 40 acres of grounds with stunning views over the Surrey countryside. The hotel offers a range of individually appointed bedrooms, including 15 feature bedrooms located in the oldest part of the house. All are equipped with an excellent range of facilities. The public areas include the impressive grand hall, the award-winning Cloisters Restaurant, the library, and a cosy lounge bar area. The Nutfield Priory Health Club and Spa is the place to relax and unwind. The hotel also offers a choice of private rooms for weddings, events and business meetings. Additionally, this magnificent country house can be hired for exclusive use.

Rooms 60 (4 fmly) ⚡ **Facilities** Spa STV FTV WiFi ♨ HL ⚄ Gym Squash Steam room Beauty therapy Aerobic & Step classes Saunas Xmas New Year **Conf** Class 50 Board 42 Thtr 90 **Services** Lift Air con **Parking** 130 **Notes** ⊗ Civ Wed 90

Premier Inn Redhill Reigate

BUDGET HOTEL

tel: 0871 527 8930 *(Calls cost 13p per minute plus your phone company's access charge)*
Brighton Rd, Salfords RH1 5BT
web: www.premierinn.com
dir: *On A23, 2m S of Redhill; 3m N of Gatwick Airport*

High quality, budget accommodation ideal for both families and business travellers. Spacious, en suite bedrooms feature tea and coffee making facilities, and Freeview TV in most hotels. Internet access and WiFi are available for a small fee. The adjacent family restaurant features a wide and varied menu. See also the Hotel Groups pages.

Rooms 48

REDRUTH	Map 2 SW64
Cornwall	

Penventon Park Hotel

★★★ 79% HOTEL

tel: 01209 203000 **TR15 1TE**
email: enquiries@penventon.com **web:** www.penventon.co.uk
dir: *Exit A30 at Redruth. Follow signs for Redruth West, hotel 1m S*

Set in attractive parkland, this Georgian mansion is ideal for both business and leisure guests, and is well placed for visiting the glorious Cornish coastal areas. The smart bedrooms include 20 garden suites with patio doors that give access to a decking area and the garden beyond. The menus offer a wide choice of Cornish, British, Italian and French dishes. Leisure facilities include a pool, fitness suite, and health spa with beauty and holistic therapies, as well as function rooms and bars.

Rooms 63 (8 fmly) (23 GF) ⚡ **S** £59-£72; **D** £79-£139 (incl. bkfst)* **Facilities** Spa FTV WiFi ♨ ⚄ supervised Gym Sauna Solarium Personal trainer ♫ Xmas New Year **Conf** Class 100 Board 60 Thtr 200 Del from £107 to £173* **Parking** 100 **Notes** Civ Wed 150

REDWORTH	Map 19 NZ22
County Durham	

The Redworth Hall Hotel

THE HOTEL COLLECTION

★★★★ 78% COUNTRY HOUSE HOTEL

tel: 01388 770600 **DL5 6NL**
email: redworthhall@thehotelcollection.co.uk **web:** www.thehotelcollection.co.uk
dir: *From A1(M) junct 58, A68 signed Corbridge. Follow hotel signs*

This imposing Georgian building includes a health club with state-of-the-art equipment and impressive conference facilities, making this hotel a popular destination for business travellers. There are several spacious lounges to relax in along with the Conservatory Restaurant. Bedrooms are very comfortable and well equipped.

Rooms 143 (12 fmly) ⚡ **Facilities** STV WiFi ♨ HL ⚄ ⚲ ⚄ Gym Bodysense Health & Leisure Club Xmas New Year **Conf** Class 144 Board 90 Thtr 300 **Services** Lift **Parking** 300 **Notes** Civ Wed 240

REIGATE
Surrey

Map 6 TQ25

Best Western Reigate Manor Hotel

 Best Western.

★★★ 78% HOTEL

tel: 01737 240125 **Reigate Hill RH2 9PF**
email: hotel@reigatemanor.co.uk **web:** www.reigatemanor.co.uk
dir: On A217, 1m S of M25 junct 8

On the slopes of Reigate Hill, the hotel is ideally located for access to the town and for motorway links. A range of public rooms is provided along with a variety of function rooms. Bedrooms are either traditional in style in the old house or of contemporary design in the wing.

Rooms 50 (1 fmly) **Facilities** FTV WiFi ⇩ **Conf** Class 80 Board 50 Thtr 200 **Parking** 130 **Notes** ⊗ Civ Wed 200

RENISHAW
Derbyshire

Map 16 SK47

Sitwell Arms Hotel

★★★ 72% HOTEL

tel: 01246 435226 **Station Rd S21 3WF**
email: info@sitwellarms.com **web:** www.sitwellarms.co.uk
dir: On A6135 to Sheffield, W of M1 junct 30

Parts of this attractive stone building date from the 18th century when it was a coaching inn. It has been extended to provide spacious comfortable bedrooms with modern facilities. A wide range of meals is served in the Wild Boar Restaurant, there is also a cocktail bar, informal lounge bar and a smart beer garden with patio and children's play area. The hotel has a gym and a hair and beauty salon.

Rooms 31 (8 fmly) (9 GF) **Facilities** FTV WiFi Gym Fitness studio Hair & beauty salon Xmas New Year **Conf** Class 60 Board 60 Thtr 160 **Services** Lift **Parking** 150 **Notes** ⊗ Civ Wed 150

RETFORD
Nottinghamshire

Map 17 SK78

Ye Olde Bell Hotel & Restaurant

★★★★ 80% ⊛ HOTEL

tel: 01777 705121 **DN22 8QS**
email: enquiries@yeoldebell-hotel.co.uk **web:** www.yeoldebell-hotel.co.uk

(For full entry see Barnby Moor)

Best Western Plus West Retford Hotel

Best Western PLUS

★★★ 80% HOTEL

tel: 01777 706333 **24 North Rd DN22 7XG**
email: reservations@westretfordhotel.co.uk **web:** www.westretfordhotel.co.uk
dir: From A1 take A620 to Ranby/Retford. Left at rdbt into North Rd A638. Hotel on right

Stylishly appointed throughout, and set in very attractive gardens close to the town centre, this 18th-century manor house offers a good range of well-equipped meeting rooms. The spacious, well-laid out bedrooms and suites are located in separate buildings and all offer modern facilities and comforts.

Rooms 63 (15 fmly) (32 GF) ⟰ S £72-£112; **D** £79-£119 (incl. bkfst) **Facilities** FTV WiFi ⇩ Xmas New Year **Conf** Class 80 Board 40 Thtr 150 Del from £110 to £140 **Parking** 150 **Notes** LB ⊗ Civ Wed 150

Blacksmiths

⊛⊛ RESTAURANT WITH ROOMS

tel: 01777 818171 **Town St, Clayworth DN22 9AD**
email: will@blacksmithsclayworth.com **web:** www.blacksmithsclayworth.com
dir: From A631, 2.4m to Clayworth

Blacksmiths is a modern restaurant with annexed accommodation, situated in the quiet village of Clayworth, and a short drive from Retford. Meals in the restaurant are one of the many highlights of the stay, as are the hearty breakfasts which can be delivered as room-service. Bedrooms are a new addition for 2016 and have been finished to an excellent standard. Modern gadgets and accessories are provided such as climate control, large widescreen TVs, and WiFi. Thoughtful extras such as fluffy bathrobes and luxurious toiletries add to the experience. A warm welcome is guaranteed at this owner-run establishment.

Rooms 3 (1 fmly)

RICCALL
North Yorkshire

Map 16 SE63

Per Bacco at The Park View

RESTAURANT WITH ROOMS

tel: 01757 249146 **20 Main St Y019 6PX**
email: gianlucasechi@hotmail.co.uk **web:** www.per-bacco.co.uk
dir: A19 from Selby, left for Riccall by water tower, house 100yds on right

This spacious detached property is located in a quiet residential area and is convenient for York. The ground floor has been converted into an authentic Italian restaurant and there is a wide choice of fresh, home-made dishes, all in a friendly atmosphere. The restaurant is the main part of the business but there is also a range of comfortable en suite bedrooms. Ample parking is available.

Rooms 4 (2 fmly)

RICHMOND
North Yorkshire

Map 19 NZ10

The Frenchgate Restaurant and Hotel

★★★★ 73% ⊛⊛ TOWN HOUSE HOTEL

tel: 01748 822087 & 07921 136362 **59-61 Frenchgate DL10 7AE**
email: info@thefrenchgate.co.uk **web:** www.thefrenchgate.co.uk
dir: From A1 Scotch Corner to Richmond on A6108. After lights, 1st left into Lile Close, leading to Flints Terr for hotel car park. Or for front entrance continue to 1st rdbt, left into Dundas St. At T-junct left into Frenchgate

This sympathetic conversion of an 18th-century town house building offers an impressive level of contemporary, quality accommodation. Modern artworks by local artists adorn the walls of the house. The intimate dining room serves award-winning evening meals and memorable breakfasts. Personal, attentive and friendly staff are on hand to ensure a relaxing stay. Some off-road parking is available.

Rooms 9 (3 fmly) (1 GF) ⟰ **S** £88-£198; **D** £118-£250 (incl. bkfst)* **Facilities** FTV WiFi ⇩ Xmas New Year **Conf** Class 24 Board 20 Thtr 20 Del from £149 to £197* **Parking** 12 **Notes** LB ⊗ Civ Wed 150

R

RICHMOND (UPON THAMES)
Greater London

The Petersham Hotel

★★★★ 80% ◎ ◎ HOTEL PLAN 1 C2

tel: 020 8940 7471 & 8939 1010 **Nightingale Ln TW10 6UZ**
email: enq@petershamhotel.co.uk **web:** www.petershamhotel.co.uk
dir: *From Richmond Bridge rdbt A316 follow Ham & Petersham signs. Hotel in Nightingale Ln on left off Petersham Rd*

Managed by the same family for over 25 years, this attractive hotel is located on a hill overlooking water meadows and a sweep of the River Thames. Bedrooms and suites are comfortably furnished, while public areas combine elegance and some fine architectural features. High quality produce features in dishes offered in the restaurant that looks out over the Thames below.

Rooms 58 (6 fmly) (3 GF) 🐾 **S** £65-£140; **D** £99-£450* **Facilities** STV FTV WiFi 🏃
Xmas New Year **Conf** Board 25 Thtr 35 Del from £265 to £299* **Services** Lift
Parking 60 **Notes** LB ⊗ Civ Wed 40

Richmond Hill Hotel

★★★★ 75% HOTEL PLAN 1 C2

tel: 020 8940 2247 **Richmond Hill TW10 6RW**
email: info.richmond@kewgreen.co.uk **web:** www.richmondhill-hotel.co.uk
dir: *1m from Richamond Station at the top of Richmond Hill*

This attractive Georgian manor is situated on Richmond Hill, enjoying elevated views over the Thames, and the town and the park are within walking distance. Bedrooms vary in size and style but all are comfortable and contemporary in style. There is a well-designed heath club, and extensive conference and banqueting facilities.

Rooms 142 (1 fmly) (15 GF) 🐾 **Facilities** Spa STV FTV WiFi ⓢ Gym Steam room
Health & beauty suite Sauna Xmas New Year **Conf** Class 80 Board 50 Thtr 180
Services Lift Air con **Parking** 97 **Notes** ⊗ Civ Wed 182

HIGHLY RECOMMENDED

Bingham

★★★ 85% ◎ ◎ ◎ ⌾ TOWN HOUSE HOTEL PLAN 1 C2

tel: 020 8940 0902 **61-63 Petersham Rd TW10 6UT**
email: info@thebingham.co.uk **web:** www.thebingham.co.uk
dir: *On A307*

This Georgian building, dating back to 1740, overlooks the River Thames and is within easy reach of the town centre, Kew Gardens and Hampton Court. The contemporary bedrooms feature bespoke art deco style furniture and up-to-the-minute facilities such as WiFi, a digital music library, flat-screen TVs and 'rain

dance' showers. Public rooms have views of the pretty garden and river. Guests can choose from a selection of meals that range from light snacks to two or three-course dinners.

Bingham

Rooms 15 (2 fmly) 🐾 **Facilities** FTV WiFi 🏃 In room beauty treatments Xmas New Year **Conf** Class 70 Board 40 Thtr 100 **Services** Lift Air con **Parking** 8 **Notes** ⊗ RS Sunday eve Civ Wed 90

Premier Inn London Richmond

BUDGET HOTEL PLAN 1 C2

tel: 0871 527 9346 *(Calls cost 13p per minute plus your phone company's access charge)*
136-138 Lower Mortlake Rd, Richmond TW9 2JZ
web: www.premierinn.com
dir: *Phone for directions*

High quality, budget accommodation ideal for both families and business travellers. Spacious, en suite bedrooms feature tea and coffee making facilities, and Freeview TV in most hotels. Internet access and WiFi are available for a small fee. The adjacent family restaurant features a wide and varied menu. See also the Hotel Groups pages.

Rooms 92

RIPLEY
Derbyshire

Map 16 SK35

Premier Inn Ripley

BUDGET HOTEL

tel: 0871 527 8935 *(Calls cost 13p per minute plus your phone company's access charge)*
Nottingham Rd DE5 3QP
web: www.premierinn.com
dir: *From S: M1 junct 26, A610 towards Ripley. Hotel off rdbt adjacent to Butterley Park. From N: M1 junct 28, A38, A610 towards Nottingham. Hotel on right at rdbt*

High quality, budget accommodation ideal for both families and business travellers. Spacious, en suite bedrooms feature tea and coffee making facilities, and Freeview TV in most hotels. Internet access and WiFi are available for a small fee. The adjacent family restaurant features a wide and varied menu. See also the Hotel Groups pages.

Rooms 78

RISLEY
Derbyshire   Map 11 SK43

Risley Hall Hotel & Spa

★★★ 74% HOTEL

tel: 0115 939 9000 **Derby Rd DE72 3SS**
email: reservations@risleyhall.co.uk **web:** www.risleyhall.co.uk
dir: M1 junct 25, follow signs for Risley, then brown signs for Risley Hall

This 16th-century house is set in extensive gardens, and much of the house has been sympathetically restored. Spacious bedrooms are very comfortable, and the hotel has a popular spa and leisure facilities. There's also a charming bar and a stylish restaurant that serves the best in local produce.

Rooms 35 (19 annexe) (7 fmly) (8 GF) ♠ **Facilities** Spa FTV WiFi ⌕ ⊛ Gym New Year **Conf** Class 40 Board 26 Thtr 90 **Services** Lift **Parking** 100 **Notes** ⊗ Civ Wed 110

ROCHDALE
Greater Manchester   Map 16 SD81

Mercure Manchester Norton Grange Hotel & Spa

★★★★ 74% HOTEL

tel: 01706 630788 & 0161 619 9004 **Manchester Rd, Castleton OL11 2XZ**
email: h6631@accor.com **web:** www.mercure.com
dir: M62 junct 20, follow A664/Castleton signs. Right at next 2 rdbts. Hotel 0.5m on left

Standing in nine acres of grounds and mature gardens, this Victorian house provides comfort in elegant surroundings. The well-equipped bedrooms provide a host of extras for both the business and leisure guest. Public areas include the Pickwick bistro and smart Grange Restaurant, both offering a good choice of dishes. There is also an impressive leisure centre.

Rooms 81 (17 fmly) (10 GF) ♠ **Facilities** Spa STV WiFi ⊛ Gym Leisure centre Indoor/Outdoor hydrotherapy pool Thermal suite Rock sauna Xmas New Year **Conf** Class 120 Board 70 Thtr 220 **Services** Lift **Parking** 150 **Notes** Civ Wed 150

Premier Inn Rochdale

BUDGET HOTEL

tel: 0871 527 8936 *(Calls cost 13p per minute plus your phone company's access charge)*
Newhey Rd, Milnrow OL16 4JF
web: www.premierinn.com
dir: M62 junct 21, at rdbt right towards Shaw, under motorway bridge, & 1st left

High quality, budget accommodation ideal for both families and business travellers. Spacious, en suite bedrooms feature tea and coffee making facilities, and Freeview TV in most hotels. Internet access and WiFi are available for a small fee. The adjacent family restaurant features a wide and varied menu. See also the Hotel Groups pages.

Rooms 79

ROCHESTER
Kent   Map 6 TQ76

Premier Inn Rochester

BUDGET HOTEL

tel: 0871 527 8938 *(Calls cost 13p per minute plus your phone company's access charge)*
Medway Valley Leisure Park, Chariot Way, Strood ME2 2SS
web: www.premierinn.com
dir: M2 junct 2, follow Rochester & West Malling signs. At rdbt onto A228 signed Rochester & Strood. At next rdbt 2nd exit into Roman Way signed Medway Valley Park. At next rdbt 1st exit into Chariot Way, hotel in 100mtrs

High quality, budget accommodation ideal for both families and business travellers. Spacious, en suite bedrooms feature tea and coffee making facilities, and Freeview TV in most hotels. Internet access and WiFi are available for a small fee. The adjacent family restaurant features a wide and varied menu. See also the Hotel Groups pages.

Rooms 121

ROMALDKIRK
County Durham   Map 19 NY92

INSPECTORS' CHOICE

The Rose & Crown

★★★ ◉◉ HOTEL

tel: 01833 650213 **DL12 9EB**
email: hotel@rose-and-crown.co.uk **web:** www.rose-and-crown.co.uk
dir: 6m NW from Barnard Castle on B6277

This charming 18th-century country inn is located in the heart of the village, overlooking fine dale scenery. The attractively furnished bedrooms, including suites, are split between the main house and the rear courtyard. Guests might like to have a drink in the cosy bar with its log fire, after returning from a long walk. Good local produce features extensively on the menus that can be enjoyed in the oak-panelled restaurant, or in the brasserie and bar. Service is both friendly and attentive.

Rooms 14 (7 annexe) (2 fmly) (5 GF) ♠ **Facilities** FTV WiFi ⌕ Spa & golf available at nearby Headlam Hall New Year **Conf** Board 12 **Parking** 20 **Notes** Closed 23-27 Dec

ROMFORD
Greater London   Map 6 TQ58

Premier Inn Romford Central

BUDGET HOTEL

tel: 0871 527 8940 *(Calls cost 13p per minute plus your phone company's access charge)*
Mercury Gardens RM1 3EN
web: www.premierinn.com
dir: M25 junct 28, A12 to Gallows Corner. Take A118 to next rdbt, turn left

High quality, budget accommodation ideal for both families and business travellers. Spacious, en suite bedrooms feature tea and coffee making facilities, and Freeview TV in most hotels. Internet access and WiFi are available for a small fee. The adjacent family restaurant features a wide and varied menu. See also the Hotel Groups pages.

Rooms 103

R

ROMFORD *continued*

Premier Inn Romford West

BUDGET HOTEL

tel: 0871 527 8942 *(Calls cost 13p per minute plus your phone company's access charge)*
Whalebone Lane North, Chadwell Heath RM6 6QU
web: www.premierinn.com
dir: *6m from M25 junct 28 on A12 at junct with A1112*

Rooms 44

ROMSEY	Map 5 SU32
Hampshire	

The White Horse Hotel & Brasserie

★★★★ 76% ◎◎ HOTEL

tel: 01794 512431 **19 Market Place SO51 8ZJ**
email: the whitehorsesales@twhromsey.com **web:** www.thewhitehorseromsey.co.uk
dir: *M27 junct 3, follow signs for Romsey, right at Broadlands. In town centre*

This family-friendly hotel is located overlooking the market square of this historic town. The White Horse is a traditional, former coaching inn, and provides very comfortable and very stylish, individually designed bedrooms, including Loft Suites and a Penthouse. Public areas boast relaxing day rooms and an elegant contemporary bar. The Brasserie offers award-winning cuisine, with alfresco dining a possibility during the warmer summer months. Public car parks can be found close by, although the property does operate a valet parking service.

Rooms 31 (4 fmly) ⌒ **S** £95-£105; **D** £115-£295 **Facilities** FTV WiFi ⇘ Xmas New Year **Conf** Class 40 Board 45 Thtr 60 Del from £145 to £160 **Notes** LB Civ Wed 65

See advert on opposite page

Potters Heron Hotel

★★★ 80% HOTEL

tel: 023 8027 7800 **Winchester Rd, Ampfield SO51 9ZF**
email: thepottersheron@pebblehotels.com **web:** www.potters-heron.co.uk
dir: *M3 junct 12 follow Chandler's Ford signs. 2nd exit at 3rd rdbt follow Ampfield signs, over x-rds. Hotel on left in 1m*

This distinctive thatched hotel retains many original features. In a convenient location with access to Winchester, Southampton and the M3, Potters Heron Hotel has modern accommodation and stylish, spacious public areas. Most of the bedrooms have their own balcony or terrace. The pub and restaurant both offer an interesting range of dishes that will suit a variety of tastes.

Rooms 53 (1 fmly) (29 GF) ⌒ **Facilities** WiFi ⇘ Xmas New Year **Conf** Class 40 Board 30 Thtr 100 **Services** Lift **Parking** 120 **Notes** ⊗ Civ Wed 100

Premier Inn Southampton West

BUDGET HOTEL

tel: 0871 527 9004 *(Calls cost 13p per minute plus your phone company's access charge)*
Romsey Rd, Ower SO51 6ZJ
web: www.premierinn.com
dir: *Just off M27 junct 2. Take A36 towards Salisbury. Follow brown tourist signs 'Vine Inn'*

High quality, budget accommodation ideal for both families and business travellers. Spacious, en suite bedrooms feature tea and coffee making facilities, and Freeview TV in most hotels. Internet access and WiFi are available for a small fee. The adjacent family restaurant features a wide and varied menu. See also the Hotel Groups pages.

Rooms 83

ROSSINGTON	Map 16 SK69
South Yorkshire	

Best Western Premier Mount Pleasant Hotel

PREMIER | BEST WESTERN

★★★★ 78% HOTEL

tel: 01302 868696 & 868219 **Great North Rd DN11 OHW**
email: reception@mountpleasant.co.uk **web:** www.mountpleasant.co.uk
dir: *On A638 Great North Road, between Bawtry & Doncaster*

This charming 18th-century house stands in 100 acres of wooded parkland between Doncaster and Bawtry, near Robin Hood Airport. Spacious public areas include well furnished lounges and the elegant Garden Restaurant. There are also a health and wellbeing centre, modern conference facilities and beautiful grounds, ideal for weddings. Bedrooms are individually designed; some have four-poster beds and the spa suites are even more impressive with luxurious bathrooms.

Rooms 68 (22 fmly) (33 GF) ⌒ **S** £79-£129; **D** £99-£259 (incl. bkfst)* **Facilities** Spa STV WiFi ⇘ Beauty salon **Conf** Class 70 Board 70 Thtr 200 Del from £119 to £145* **Services** Lift **Parking** 140 **Notes** LB ⊗ Closed 25 Dec RS 24 Dec Civ Wed 180

R

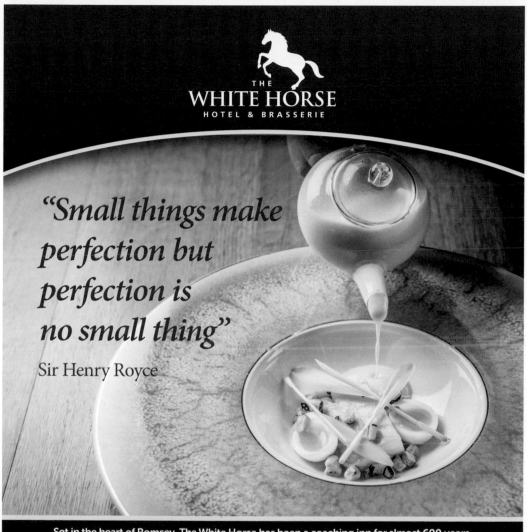

THE
WHITE HORSE
HOTEL & BRASSERIE

"Small things make
perfection but
perfection is
no small thing"

Sir Henry Royce

Set in the heart of Romsey, The White Horse has been a coaching inn for almost 600 years.
The 2 AA rosette awarded Brasserie & Grill is a wonderful place to enjoy every occasion from a
romantic dinner for two to a robust family lunch, during the summer months the courtyard
offers a perfect retreat for al fresco dining. A stay here with us is a time to unwind – relax in one
of our individually designed bedrooms, enjoy a cocktail in our delightful bar or even sample one
of our delicious afternoon teas in the historic Tudor or Palmerston lounges. The hotel is also
fully licensed for wedding ceremonies and offers the most romantic and intimate venue for
your wedding day. **Historic charm meets modern classic chic.**

Market Place, Romsey, Hampshire SO51 8ZJ
T 01794 512431   **F** 01794 517485   **E** thewhitehorse@twhromsey.com
www.thewhitehorseromsey.com

R

ROSS-ON-WYE
Herefordshire   Map 10 SO52

Chase Hotel
★★★ 83% HOTEL

tel: 01989 763161 & 760644 **Gloucester Rd HR9 5LH**
email: res@chasehotel.co.uk **web:** www.chasehotel.co.uk
dir: *M50 junct 4, 1st left exit towards rdbt, left at rdbt towards A40, across next rdbt, right at 3rd rdbt towards town centre, hotel 0.5m on left*

This attractive Georgian mansion sits in its own landscaped grounds and is only a short walk from the town centre. Bedrooms, including two four-poster rooms, vary in size and character; all rooms are appointed to impressive standards. There is a light and spacious bar, and also Harry's restaurant which offers an excellent selection of enjoyable dishes.

Rooms 38 (2 fmly) **S** £69-£190; **D** £79-£210 (incl. bkfst)* **Facilities** STV FTV WiFi ↳ New Year **Conf** Class 100 Board 80 Thtr 300 **Parking** 75 **Notes** LB ⊗ Closed 24-27 Dec Civ Wed 150

Glewstone Court Country House Hotel
★★★ 80% COUNTRY HOUSE HOTEL

tel: 01989 770367 **Glewstone HR9 6AW**
email: info@glewstonecourt.com **web:** www.glewstonecourt.com
dir: *From Ross-on-Wye market place follow A40/A49 Monmouth/Hereford signs, over Wilton Bridge to rdbt, left onto A40 towards Monmouth, in 1m right for hotel*

This charming hotel enjoys an elevated position with views over Ross-on-Wye, and is set in well-tended gardens. The owners ensure guests are well looked after from the moment of arrival. Bedrooms come in a variety of sizes and are tastefully furnished and well equipped. An excellent choice of dishes utilising high quality ingredients should not be missed at dinner.

Rooms 8 (2 fmly) **S** £64-£174; **D** £79-£189 (incl. bkfst)* **Facilities** FTV WiFi ↳ ⤳ New Year **Conf** Class 50 Board 24 Thtr 50 Del from £131 to £241* **Parking** 20 **Notes** Closed 2-18 Jan Civ Wed 70

King's Head Hotel
★★★ 76% HOTEL

tel: 01989 763174 **8 High St HR9 5HL**
email: enquiries@kingshead.co.uk **web:** www.kingshead.co.uk
dir: *In town centre, past market building on right*

This establishment dates back to the 14th century and has a wealth of charm and character. Bedrooms are well equipped and comfortable with thoughtful guest extras provided; both four-poster and family rooms are available. The restaurant offers menus and a specials board that reflect a varied selection of local produce including fresh fish, free range beef and lamb. There is also a well-stocked bar serving hand-pulled, real ales.

Rooms 15 (1 fmly) **S** £65; **D** £85-£110 (incl. bkfst)* **Facilities** FTV WiFi **Parking** 15 **Notes** LB

Premier Inn Ross-on-Wye
BUDGET HOTEL

tel: 0871 527 8944 *(Calls cost 13p per minute plus your phone company's access charge)*
Ledbury Rd HR9 7QJ
web: www.premierinn.com
dir: *M50 junct 4, 1m from town centre*

High quality, budget accommodation ideal for both families and business travellers. Spacious, en suite bedrooms feature tea and coffee making facilities, and Freeview TV in most hotels. Internet access and WiFi are available for a small fee. The adjacent family restaurant features a wide and varied menu. See also the Hotel Groups pages.

Rooms 59

Wilton Court Restaurant with Rooms
 RESTAURANT WITH ROOMS

tel: 01989 562569 **Wilton Ln HR9 6AQ**
email: info@wiltoncourthotel.com **web:** www.wiltoncourthotel.com
dir: *M50 junct 4, A40 towards Monmouth at 3rd rdbt left signed Ross-on-Wye, 1st right, on right*

Dating back to the 16th century, Wilton Court has great charm and a wealth of character. Standing on the banks of the River Wye, just a short walk from the town centre, there is a genuinely relaxed, friendly and unhurried atmosphere created by hosts Roger and Helen Wynn and their reliable team. Bedrooms are tastefully furnished and well equipped, while public areas include a comfortable lounge, traditional bar and pleasant restaurant with a conservatory extension overlooking the garden. High standards of food, using fresh, locally sourced ingredients, are offered.

Rooms 11 (1 fmly)

ROSTHWAITE
Cumbria   Map 18 NY21

See also **Borrowdale**

Scafell Hotel
★★★ 81% HOTEL

tel: 017687 77208 **CA12 5XB**
email: info@scafell.co.uk **web:** www.scafell.co.uk
dir: *M6 junct 40 to Keswick on A66. Take B5289 to Rosthwaite*

Scafell Hotel is a friendly establishment, which enjoys a peaceful location, and is popular with walkers. Bedrooms have been tastefully appointed in a warm country house style with a contemporary twist; some have traditional antique furniture. Public areas include a residents' cocktail bar, lounge and spacious restaurant as well as the popular Riverside Inn, offering all-day menus in summer months.

Rooms 23 (3 fmly) (8 GF) **S** £60-£115; **D** £120-£230 (incl. bkfst)* **Facilities** FTV WiFi Guided walks Xmas New Year **Parking** 50 **Notes** LB Civ Wed 75

ROTHERHAM
South Yorkshire
Map 16 SK49

Hellaby Hall Hotel
★★★★ 75% HOTEL

tel: 01709 702701 **Old Hellaby Ln, Hellaby S66 8SN**
email: reservations@hellabyhallhotel.co.uk web: www.hellabyhallhotel.co.uk
dir: *0.5m off M18 junct 1, onto A631 towards Maltby. Hotel in Hellaby - NB use S66 8EX postcode for Sat Nav*

This 17th-century house was built to a Flemish design with high, beamed ceilings, staircases which lead off to private meeting rooms and a series of oak-panelled lounges. Bedrooms are elegant and well equipped, and guests can dine in the formal Attic Restaurant. There are extensive leisure facilities and conference areas, and the hotel holds a licence for civil weddings.

Rooms 89 (6 fmly) (17 GF) **Facilities** Spa FTV WiFi ⊳ ⊛ Gym Beauty salon Exercise studio Spinning bike studio Xmas New Year **Conf** Class 300 Board 150 Thtr 500 **Services** Lift **Parking** 250 **Notes** ⊛ Civ Wed 250

Carlton Park Hotel
★★★ 79% HOTEL

tel: 01709 849955 **102/104 Moorgate Rd S60 2BG**
email: reservations@carltonparkhotel.com web: www.carltonparkhotel.com
dir: *M1 junct 33, onto A631, then A618. Hotel 800yds past District General Hospital*

This modern hotel is situated in a pleasant residential area of the town, close to the hospital, yet within minutes of the M1. Bedrooms and bathrooms offer very modern facilities; three have separate sitting rooms. The restaurant and bar provide a lively atmosphere and there is a pool and leisure centre.

Rooms 80 (20 fmly) (16 GF) **S** fr £60; **D** fr £70 (incl. bkfst)* **Facilities** STV FTV WiFi ⊳ ⊛ Gym ↕ **Conf** Class 120 Board 60 Thtr 300 **Services** Lift **Parking** 120 **Notes** ⊛ Civ Wed 150

Premier Inn Rotherham East (M18/M1)
BUDGET HOTEL

tel: 0871 527 8946 *(Calls cost 13p per minute plus your phone company's access charge)*
Bawtry Rd S65 3JB
web: www.premierinn.com
dir: *On A631 towards Wickersley, between M18 junct 1 & M1 junct 33*

High quality, budget accommodation ideal for both families and business travellers. Spacious, en suite bedrooms feature tea and coffee making facilities, and Freeview TV in most hotels. Internet access and WiFi are available for a small fee. The adjacent family restaurant features a wide and varied menu. See also the Hotel Groups pages.

Rooms 61

Ibis Rotherham East

AA Advertised

tel: 01709 730333 **Moorhead Way, Bramley S66 1YY**
email: H3163@accor.com web: www.ibishotel.com
dir: *M18 junct 1, left at rdbt, left at 1st lights. Hotel adjacent to supermarket*

Modern, budget hotel offering comfortable accommodation in bright and practical bedrooms. Breakfast is self-service and dinner is available in the restaurant.

Rooms 86 (22 fmly) (8 GF) ⚓ **Facilities** STV WiFi **Conf** Class 20 Board 20 Thtr 30 **Services** Lift **Parking** 90

ROTHERWICK
Hampshire
Map 5 SU75

INSPECTORS' CHOICE

Tylney Hall Hotel
★★★★ ⊛⊛ ♔ HOTEL

tel: 01256 764881 **Ridge Ln RG27 9AZ**
email: sales@tylneyhall.com web: www.tylneyhall.com
dir: *M3 junct 5, A287 to Basingstoke, over junct with A30, over rail bridge, towards Newnham. Right at Newnham Green. Hotel 1m on left*

Tylney Hall is a grand Victorian country house set in 66 acres of beautiful parkland. The hotel offers high standards of comfort in relaxed yet elegant surroundings, featuring magnificently restored water gardens, originally laid out by the famous gardener, Gertrude Jekyll. Spacious public rooms include Italian and Wedgwood styled drawing rooms and the panelled Oak Room Restaurant that offers cuisine based on locally sourced ingredients. The spacious bedrooms are traditionally furnished and offer individual style and high degrees of comfort. The excellent leisure facilities include indoor and outdoor swimming pools, tennis courts, jogging trails, croquet lawns and a spa.

Rooms 112 (77 annexe) (1 fmly) (40 GF) ⚓ **Facilities** Spa STV FTV WiFi ⊳ ⊛ ⟋ ♨ ♒ Gym Clay pigeon shooting Archery Falconry Balloon rides Laser shooting Jogging trail Xmas New Year **Conf** Class 70 Board 40 Thtr 120 **Parking** 120 **Notes** Civ Wed 120

ROWDE
Wiltshire   Map 4 ST96

The George & Dragon
◎◎ RESTAURANT WITH ROOMS

tel: 01380 723053 **High St SN10 2PN**
email: thegandd@tiscali.co.uk **web:** www.thegeorgeanddragonrowde.co.uk
dir: 1.5m from Devizes on A350 towards Chippenham

The George & Dragon dates back to the 14th century when it was a meeting house. Exposed beams, wooden floors, antique rugs and open fires create a warm atmosphere in the bar and restaurant. Bedrooms and bathrooms are very well decorated and equipped with some welcome extras. Dining in the bar or restaurant should not be missed, as local produce and fresh fish deliveries from Cornwall are offered on the daily-changing blackboard menu.

Rooms 3 (1 fmly)

ROWSLEY
Derbyshire   Map 16 SK26

INSPECTORS' CHOICE

The Peacock at Rowsley
★★★ ◎◎◎ HOTEL

tel: 01629 733518 **Bakewell Rd DE4 2EB**
email: reception@thepeacockatrowsley.com **web:** www.thepeacockatrowsley.com
dir: A6,3m before Bakewell, 6m from Matlock towards Bakewell

Set in the beautiful Peak District National Park, and owned by Lord and Lady Manners of Haddon Hall, this hotel combines stylish contemporary design with original period and antique features. Bedrooms are individually designed and boast DVD players, complimentary WiFi and smart marble bathrooms. One bedroom has a delightful four-poster bed. Imaginative cuisine, using local,

seasonal produce, is a highlight. Guests are warmly welcomed and service is attentive. Fly fishing is popular in this area and the hotel has its own fishing rights on seven miles of the Rivers Wye and Derwent.

Rooms 15 (6 fmly) ⚑♨ **S** £115-£167.50; **D** £190-£290 (incl. bkfst)* **Facilities** WiFi ⇗ Fishing 🏊 Free use of Woodlands Fitness Centre Free membership to Bakewell Golf Club 🎵 New Year **Conf** Class 8 Board 16 **Del** £220* **Parking** 25 **Notes** LB No children 10yrs Civ Wed 20

See advert on opposite page

RUBERY
West Midlands   Map 10 SO97

Premier Inn Birmingham South (Rubery)
BUDGET HOTEL

tel: 0871 527 8094 *(Calls cost 13p per minute plus your phone company's access charge)*
Birmingham Great Park, Ashbrook Dr, Parkway B45 9FP
web: www.premierinn.com
dir: M5 junct 4, A38 towards Birmingham. Left at lights before Morrisons signed Great Park. Right at rdbt. Right at next rdbt, hotel on right

High quality, budget accommodation ideal for both families and business travellers. Spacious, en suite bedrooms feature tea and coffee making facilities, and Freeview TV in most hotels. Internet access and WiFi are available for a small fee. The adjacent family restaurant features a wide and varied menu. See also the Hotel Groups pages.

Rooms 62

RUGBY
Warwickshire   Map 11 SP57

Brownsover Hall Hotel
★★★ 80% ◎ HOTEL

tel: 01788 546100 & 555362 **Brownsover Ln, Old Brownsover CV21 1HU**
email: reservations@brownsoverhall.co.uk **web:** www.brownsoverhall.co.uk
dir: M6 junct 1, A426 to Rugby. After 0.5m at rdbt follow Brownsover signs, right into Brownsover Rd, right again into Brownsover Ln. Hotel 250yds on left

Brownsover Hall is a Grade II listed, Victorian Gothic building designed by Sir Gilbert Scott, set in seven acres of wooded parkland. Bedrooms vary in size and style, including spacious and contemporary rooms in the converted stable block. The former chapel makes a stylish restaurant, and for a less formal meal or a relaxing drink, the Whittle Bar is popular.

Rooms 47 (20 annexe) (3 fmly) (11 GF) **Facilities** STV FTV WiFi ⇗ Xmas New Year **Conf** Class 36 Board 40 Thtr 70 **Parking** 100 **Notes** ⊗ Civ Wed 56

Premier Inn Rugby North M6 Jct 1
BUDGET HOTEL

tel: 0871 527 8948 *(Calls cost 13p per minute plus your phone company's access charge)*
Central Park Dr, Central Park CV23 0WE
web: www.premierinn.com
dir: M6 junct 1, S'bound onto A426. Hotel approx 1m on left at rdbt

High quality, budget accommodation ideal for both families and business travellers. Spacious, en suite bedrooms feature tea and coffee making facilities, and Freeview TV in most hotels. Internet access and WiFi are available for a small fee. The adjacent family restaurant features a wide and varied menu. See also the Hotel Groups pages.

Rooms 82

Premier Inn Rugby North (Newbold)

BUDGET HOTEL

tel: 0871 527 8950 *(Calls cost 13p per minute plus your phone company's access charge)*
Brownsover Rd CV21 1HL
web: www.premierinn.com
dir: *M6 junct 1, A426 follow Rugby signs. Straight on at 2 rdbts. At 3rd rdbt, hotel on right. NB for Sat Nav use CV21 1NX*

Rooms 50

RUGELEY
Staffordshire   Map 10 SK01

Premier Inn Rugeley

BUDGET HOTEL

tel: 0871 527 9272 *(Calls cost 13p per minute plus your phone company's access charge)*
Tower Business Park WS15 2HJ
web: www.premierinn.com
dir: *M6 junct 14, A5013 towards Stafford. At rdbt 2nd exit onto A34. Take A513 signed Rugeley. At rdbt take 2nd exit onto A51. Left into Wolsley Rd, left into Powerstation Rd. Hotel off rdbt. NB for Sat Nav use WS15 1PR*

High quality, budget accommodation ideal for both families and business travellers. Spacious, en suite bedrooms feature tea and coffee making facilities, and Freeview TV in most hotels. Internet access and WiFi are available for a small fee. The adjacent family restaurant features a wide and varied menu. See also the Hotel Groups pages.

Rooms 50

RUISLIP
Greater London

The Barn Hotel

★★★ 80% ◉◉ HOTEL PLAN 1 A5

tel: 01895 636057 **West End Rd HA4 6JB**
email: info@thebarnhotel.co.uk web: www.thebarnhotel.co.uk
dir: *A40 onto A4180 (Polish War Memorial) exit to Ruislip. 2m to hotel entrance at mini-rdbt before Ruislip tube station*

A mix of old and new, with parts dating back to the 17th century, this impressive property sits in three acres of gardens. Bedrooms vary in style, from contemporary to traditional with oak beams; all are comfortable and well appointed. The public areas provide a high level of quality and luxury.

Rooms 73 (3 fmly) (33 GF) (20 smoking) Facilities FTV WiFi Xmas New Year Conf Class 50 Board 30 Thtr 80 Del from £185 to £265* Parking 42 Notes ⊗ Civ Wed 64

Premier Inn Ruislip

BUDGET HOTEL PLAN 1 A5

tel: 0871 527 8952 *(Calls cost 13p per minute plus your phone company's access charge)*
Ickenham Rd HA4 7DR
web: www.premierinn.com
dir: *From Ruislip High St into Ickenham Rd (B466). At mini rdbt 1st exit, The Orchard on left*

High quality, budget accommodation ideal for both families and business travellers. Spacious, en suite bedrooms feature tea and coffee making facilities, and Freeview TV in most hotels. Internet access and WiFi are available for a small fee. The adjacent family restaurant features a wide and varied menu. See also the Hotel Groups pages.

Rooms 20

The Peacock at Rowsley

The Peacock at Rowsley is a cosy yet smart hotel located in the heart of the Peak District National Park. The hotel is part of the Haddon Estate and enjoys close links with Haddon Hall where *The Peacock* owners Lord and Lady Edward Manners reside. With individually styled bedrooms and a luxurious suite, this independent hotel offers guests exceptional service, food and comfort.

The Peacock at Rowsley, Derbyshire DE4 2EB · Tel: 01629 733518 · Fax: 01629 732671
Website: www.thepeacockatrowsley.com ·Email: reception@thepeacockatrowsley.com

RUNCORN
Cheshire   Map 15 SJ58

Premier Inn Runcorn

BUDGET HOTEL

tel: 0871 527 8954 *(Calls cost 13p per minute plus your phone company's access charge)*
Chester Rd, Preston Brook WA7 3BB
web: www.premierinn.com
dir: *1m from M56 junct 11, at Preston Brook*

High quality, budget accommodation ideal for both families and business travellers. Spacious, en suite bedrooms feature tea and coffee making facilities, and Freeview TV in most hotels. Internet access and WiFi are available for a small fee. The adjacent family restaurant features a wide and varied menu. See also the Hotel Groups pages.

Rooms 61

RUSPER
West Sussex   Map 6 TQ23

Ghyll Manor

★★★ 83% ◉ COUNTRY HOUSE HOTEL

tel: 0330 123 0371 & 01293 871571 **High St RH12 4PX**
email: enquiries@ghyllmanor.co.uk **web:** www.ghyllmanor.co.uk
dir: *A24 onto A264. Exit at Faygate, follow signs for Rusper, 2m to village*

Located in the quiet village of Rusper, this traditional mansion house is set in 45 acres of idyllic, peaceful grounds. Accommodation is in either the main house or a range of courtyard-style cottages. A pre-dinner drink can be taken beside the fire, followed by an imaginative meal in the charming restaurant.

Rooms 29 (20 annexe) (7 fmly) (21 GF) ⟑ **Facilities** FTV WiFi ⮂ ⛴ Xmas New Year **Conf** Class 60 Board 40 Thtr 120 Del from £174 to £186* **Parking** 50 **Notes** ⊗ Civ Wed 120

RYDE
Isle of Wight   Map 5 SZ59

Lakeside Park Hotel

★★★★ 76% HOTEL

tel: 01983 882266 **High St PO33 4LJ**
email: reception@lakesideparkhotel.com **web:** www.lakesideparkhotel.com
dir: *A3054 towards Newport. Hotel on left after crossing Wotton Bridge*

This hotel has picturesque views of the tidal lake and surrounding countryside. Bedrooms are well appointed with modern amenities and stylish design. Public areas feature a comfortable open-plan bar and lounge, and two restaurants that showcase the best of island produce. Sizable conference and banqueting facilities are available, while the leisure area includes an indoor pool and spa therapy.

Rooms 44 (2 fmly) (16 GF) ⟑ **D** £150-£190 (incl. bkfst)* **Facilities** Spa FTV WiFi ⓢ Sauna Steam room Relaxation room **Conf** Class 60 Board 40 Thtr 150 **Services** Lift Air con **Parking** 140 **Notes** LB ⊗ Civ Wed 120

Yelf's Hotel

★★★ 73% HOTEL

tel: 01983 564062 **Union St PO33 2LG**
email: manager@yelfshotel.com **web:** www.yelfshotel.com
dir: *From Esplanade into Union St. Hotel on right*

This former coaching inn has smart public areas including a busy bar, a separate lounge and an attractive dining room. Bedrooms are comfortably furnished and well

equipped; some are located in an adjoining wing and some in an annexe. A conservatory lounge bar and stylish terrace are ideal for relaxing.

Rooms 40 (9 annexe) (5 fmly) (3 GF) (3 smoking) ⟑ **Facilities** STV FTV WiFi Spa & treatments at sister hotel nearby **Conf** Class 30 Board 50 Thtr 100 **Services** Lift **Parking** 23 **Notes** ⊗ Civ Wed 100

Appley Manor Hotel

★★ 76% HOTEL

tel: 01983 564777 **Appley Rd PO33 1PH**
email: appleymanor@live.co.uk **web:** www.appley-manor.co.uk
dir: *A3055 onto B3330. Hotel 0.25m on left*

Appley Manor is a Victorian manor house, with a long and interesting history, located only five minutes from the town and set in peaceful surroundings. There is a choice of spacious and well-furnished bedrooms, all with comfortable beds, flat screen TVs and free WiFi access. The Manor Inn is a more recent addition, and can be accessed via an internal passageway, and offers and all day menu to cater for a variety of tastes. It is also suitable for a range of events. A choice of breakfasts is served in the formal dining room in the manor house. Parking is plentiful and secure.

Rooms 12 (2 fmly) **S** £55-£65; **D** £66-£80* **Facilities** FTV WiFi **Conf** Class 40 Board 30 Thtr 40 Del from £100 to £120* **Parking** 60 **Notes** ⊗

RYE
East Sussex   Map 7 TQ92

Mermaid Inn

★★★ 82% ◉◉ HOTEL

tel: 01797 223065 & 223788 **Mermaid St TN31 7EY**
email: info@mermaidinn.com **web:** www.mermaidinn.com
dir: *A259, follow signs to town centre, then into Mermaid St*

Situated near the top of a cobbled side street, this famous smugglers' inn is steeped in history, dating back to 1450 with 12th-century cellars. The charming interior has many architectural features such as attractive stone work. The bedrooms vary in size and style but all are tastefully furnished; there are no less than eight four-posters, and the Elizabethan and Dr Syn's Bedchambers are particularly noteworthy. Delightful public rooms include a choice of lounges, cosy bar and smart restaurant.

Rooms 31 (5 fmly) ⟑ **S** £90; **D** £150-£220 (incl. bkfst)* **Facilities** FTV WiFi ⮂ Xmas New Year **Conf** Class 40 Board 30 Thtr 50 Del £260 **Parking** 25 **Notes** LB ⊗

The Hope Anchor Hotel

★★★ 80% SMALL HOTEL

tel: 01797 222216 **Watchbell St TN31 7HA**
email: info@thehopeanchor.co.uk **web:** www.thehopeanchor.co.uk
dir: *From A268, Quayside, right into Wish Ward, into Mermaid St, right into West St, right into Watchbell St, hotel at end*

This historic inn sits high above the town with enviable views out over the harbour and Romney Marsh, and is accessible via delightful cobbled streets. There is a relaxed and friendly atmosphere within the cosy public rooms, while the attractively furnished bedrooms are well equipped and many enjoy good views over the marshes.

Rooms 16 (3 fmly) (1 GF) ↸ **S** £75-£140; **D** £110-£160 (incl. bkfst) **Facilities** FTV WiFi Xmas New Year **Conf** Class 30 Board 20 Thtr 40 Del from £130* **Parking** 12 **Notes** LB

Rye Lodge Hotel

★★★ 74% METRO HOTEL

tel: 01797 223838 & 226688 **Hilders Cliff TN31 7LD**
email: info@ryelodge.co.uk **web:** www.ryelodge.co.uk
dir: *On one-way system follow town centre signs, through Landgate arch, hotel 100yds on right*

Standing in an elevated position, Rye Lodge has panoramic views across Romney Marshes and the Rother Estuary. Traditionally styled bedrooms come in a variety of sizes; they are attractively decorated and thoughtfully equipped. Public rooms feature indoor leisure facilities and the Terrace Room Restaurant where home-made dishes are offered. Lunch and afternoon tea are served on the flower-filled outdoor terrace in warmer months.

Rooms 19 (5 GF) ↸ **S** £75-£200; **D** £105-£200 **Facilities** STV FTV WiFi ☼ HL ☕ Sauna Beauty treatment room **Parking** 20 **Notes** LB

ST AGNES	Map 2 SW75
Cornwall	

Rose-in-Vale Country House Hotel

★★★★ 76% COUNTRY HOUSE HOTEL

tel: 01872 552202 **Mithian TR5 0QD**
email: reception@roseinvalehotel.co.uk **web:** www.roseinvalehotel.co.uk
dir: *A30 S towards Redruth. At Chiverton Cross at rdbt take B3277 signed St Agnes. In 500mtrs follow tourist sign for Rose-in-Vale. Into Mithian, right at Miners Arms, down hill. Hotel on left*

Peacefully located in a wooded valley, this Georgian manor house has a wonderfully relaxed atmosphere and abundant charm. Guests are assured of a warm welcome. Accommodation varies in size and style; several rooms are situated on the ground floor. An imaginative fixed-price menu featuring local produce is served in the spacious restaurant.

Rooms 23 (3 annexe) (1 fmly) (6 GF) ↸ **Facilities** FTV WiFi ☼ ☞ ⛄ ♫ Xmas New Year **Conf** Class 50 Board 40 Thtr 75 **Services** Lift **Parking** 50 **Notes** LB No children 12yrs Closed 4 Jan-1 Feb Civ Wed 80

Beacon Country House Hotel

★★★ 76% SMALL HOTEL

tel: 01872 552318 **Goonvrea Rd TR5 0NW**
email: info@beaconhotel.co.uk **web:** www.beaconhotel.co.uk
dir: *A30 onto B3277 to St Agnes. At rdbt left into Goonvrea Rd. Hotel 0.75m on right*

Set in a quiet and attractive area away from the busy village, this family-run, relaxed hotel has splendid views over the countryside and along the coast to St Ives. Hospitality and customer care are great strengths, with guests assured of a very warm and friendly stay. Bedrooms are comfortable and well equipped, and many benefit from glorious views.

Rooms 11 (2 fmly) (2 GF) ↸ **S** £75-£150; **D** £100-£185 (incl. bkfst)* **Facilities** FTV WiFi ☼ Xmas New Year **Conf** Class 20 Board 20 Del from £100 to £200* **Parking** 12 **Notes** LB ⊗ No children 8yrs Closed 4-31 Jan & Nov

Rosemundy House Hotel

★★★ 71% HOTEL

tel: 01872 552101 **Rosemundy Hill TR5 0UF**
email: info@rosemundy.co.uk **web:** www.rosemundy.co.uk
dir: *A30 to St Agnes, approx 3m. On entering village 1st right signed Rosemundy, hotel at foot of hill*

This elegant Georgian house has been carefully restored and extended to provide comfortable bedrooms and spacious, inviting public areas. The hotel is set in well-maintained gardens complete with an outdoor pool which is available in warmer months. There is a choice of relaxing lounges and a cosy bar.

Rooms 46 (3 fmly) (9 GF) ↸ **Facilities** FTV WiFi ☼ Putt green ⛄ ♫ Xmas New Year **Conf** Board 80 **Parking** 50 **Notes** ⊗ No children 5yrs Closed 12-23 Dec & 2 Jan-12 Feb

ST ALBANS	Map 6 TL10
Hertfordshire	

Sopwell House

★★★★ 81% ☺ HOTEL

tel: 01727 864477 **Cottonmill Ln, Sopwell AL1 2HQ**
email: enquiries@sopwellhouse.co.uk **web:** www.sopwellhouse.co.uk
dir: *M25 junct 21a, 1st exit rdbt to A405. A414 towards St Albans/Hatfield. Slip road Shenley, mini rdbt left*

This fine country hotel is situated in 12 acres of beautifully landscaped gardens and the house overlooks the hotel's golf course. Sopwell House was once the country home of Lord Mountbatten, and offers bedrooms that are all very well appointed, as well as impressive leisure facilities. Afternoon tea is served in the comfortable lounges and there is a choice of restaurants for dinner.

Rooms 128 (16 annexe) (28 fmly) (7 GF) ↸ **Facilities** Spa STV FTV WiFi ☼ ☕ Gym Sauna Steam room Dance studio Xmas New Year **Conf** Class 180 Board 110 Thtr 450 Del from £250* **Services** Lift Air con **Parking** 250 **Notes** ⊗ Civ Wed 380

S

ST ALBANS *continued*

St Michael's Manor

★★★★ 79% HOTEL

tel: 01727 864444 **Fishpool St AL3 4RY**
email: reservations@stmichaelsmanor.com **web:** www.stmichaelsmanor.com
dir: *From St Albans Abbey follow Fishpool Street towards St Michael's village. Hotel 0.5m on left*

Hidden from the street, adjacent to listed buildings, mills and ancient inns, this hotel, with a history dating back 500 years, is set in five acres of beautiful landscaped grounds. Inside there is a real sense of luxury, the high standard of decor and attentive service is complemented by award-winning food; the elegant restaurant overlooks the gardens and lake. Bedrooms are individually styled and have satellite TVs, DVDs and free internet access.

Rooms 30 (8 annexe) (3 fmly) (4 GF) ✆ **S** £110-£140; **D** £150-£340 (incl. bkfst)*
Facilities STV FTV WiFi ⌀ ☃ Xmas New Year **Conf** Class 20 Board 22 Thtr 30
Del from £220 to £285 **Services** Air con **Parking** 80 **Notes** LB ⊗ Civ Wed 140

Ardmore House Hotel

THE INDEPENDENTS
HOTEL ASSOCIATION

★★★ 🅰 HOTEL

tel: 01727 859313 **54 Lemsford Rd AL1 3PR**
email: info@ardmorehousehotel.co.uk **web:** www.ardmorehousehotel.co.uk
dir: *A1081 signed St Albans, through 3 sets of lights & 2 mini rdbts. Right at 3rd mini rdbt, turn right into Alma Rd, through 2 sets of lights. Hotel on right in 800yds*

Located in immaculate surroundings close to the town centre and cathedral, this extended Edwardian house and annexe provides a range of facilities much appreciated by a loyal commercial clientele. The practically furnished bedrooms offer a good range of facilities and the extensive public areas include a spacious conservatory dining room.

Rooms 40 (4 annexe) (5 fmly) (5 GF) ✆ **S** £71.50-£75; **D** £83.50-£160 (incl. bkfst)*
Facilities STV FTV WiFi ⌀ **Conf** Class 50 Board 50 Thtr 130 Del from £152 **Parking** 40
Notes ⊗ Civ Wed 150

Premier Inn Luton South M1 Jct 9

BUDGET HOTEL

tel: 0871 527 8334 *(Calls cost 13p per minute plus your phone company's access charge)*
London Rd, Flamstead AL3 8HT
web: www.premierinn.com
dir: *M1 junct 9, A5 towards Dunstable*

High quality, budget accommodation ideal for both families and business travellers. Spacious, en suite bedrooms feature tea and coffee making facilities, and Freeview TV in most hotels. Internet access and WiFi are available for a small fee. The adjacent family restaurant features a wide and varied menu. See also the Hotel Groups pages.

Rooms 76

Premier Inn St Albans City Centre

BUDGET HOTEL

tel: 0871 527 9464 *(Calls cost 13p per minute plus your phone company's access charge)*
1 Adelaide St AL3 5BH
web: www.premierinn.com
dir: *M25 junct 21A, A405 signed St Albans/London/M1 South. At junct 9 onto A5 towards St Albans. At rdbt 1st exit into Dunstable Rd towards St Albans Redbourn. At rdbt 2nd exit onto A5183. At rdbt 1st exit into St Albans Rd. In 3m take 2nd exit into Redbourn Rd. Right into Drovers Way, hotel on left*

Rooms 123

ST ANNES

See **Lytham St Annes**

ST AUSTELL
Cornwall

Map 2 SX05

Carlyon Bay Hotel

Brend Hotels

★★★★ 80% ◉ HOTEL

tel: 01726 812304 **Sea Rd, Carlyon Bay PL25 3RD**
email: reservations@carlyonbay.com **web:** www.carlyonbay.com
dir: *From St Austell, follow signs for Charlestown. Carlyon Bay signed on left, hotel at end of Sea Rd*

Built in the 1920s, this long-established hotel sits on the cliff top in 250 acres of grounds which include indoor and outdoor pools, a golf course and a spa. Bedrooms are well maintained, and many have marvellous views across St Austell Bay. A good choice of comfortable lounges is available, while facilities for families include kids' clubs and entertainment.

Rooms 86 (14 fmly) ⟋ **S** £85–£160; **D** £140–£440* **Facilities** Spa FTV WiFi ⇘ ⟲ ⤳ ⚘ 18 ⚐ Putt green Gym Hydrotherapy spa pool Hot stone beds ♫ Xmas New Year Child facilities **Conf** Thtr 150 **Services** Lift **Parking** 100 **Notes** LB ⊗ Civ Wed 100

See advert below

The Cornwall Hotel, Spa & Estate

★★★★ 74% ⊛ COUNTRY HOUSE HOTEL

tel: 01726 874050 & 874051 **Pentewan Rd, Tregorrick PL26 7AB**
email: enquiries@thecornwall.com **web:** www.thecornwall.com
dir: *A391 to St Austell then B3273 towards Mevagissey. Hotel approx 0.5m on right*

Set in 43 acres of wooded parkland, this renovated manor house offers guests a real retreat. The restored White House has suites and traditionally styled bedrooms, and adjoining are the contemporary Woodland rooms ranging across standard, family, accessible, and also deluxe which have private balcony areas overlooking the Pentewan Valley. There are superb leisure facilities including the spa with luxury treatments, an infinity pool and state-of-the-art fitness centre. There is a choice of eating options - The Arboretum, the more informal Acorns, and the Drawing Room and Parkland Terrace for afternoon tea and cocktails respectively. This is an ideal base for visiting The Eden Project, The Lost Gardens of Heligan and south Cornwall fishing villages.

Rooms 65 (4 fmly) **S** £60–£250; **D** £75–£265* **Facilities** Spa STV FTV WiFi ⇘ HL ⊛ ⚐ ⚘ Gym Xmas New Year **Conf** Class 30 Board 20 Thtr 40 Del from £130 to £295* **Services** Lift **Parking** 200 **Notes** ⊗ Civ Wed 60

Boscundle Manor

★★★ 84% ⊛⊛ HOTEL

tel: 01726 813557 **Boscundle PL25 3RL**
email: reservations@boscundlemanor.co.uk **web:** www.boscundlemanor.co.uk
dir: *M5 to Exeter then A30 until Bodmin. A391 to St Austell. Turn Left onto A390 then left towards Tregrehan. Hotel drive is 300mtrs on left*

A charming and delightful family-run manor house full of charm, located on the edge of Boscundle, set within five acres of its own private, well maintained and beautiful grounds and gardens. Friendly and attentive staff are eager to ensure guests have a relaxing and enjoyable stay. Accommodation is warm, comfortable and inviting, with a stylish and contemporary feel, yet still cosy. Food is of a high quality, with a good selection of wines and beers to match. Additional seating is offered in the relaxing lounge with open fireplaces; or maybe take a dip in the well-equipped indoor swimming pool, which is part of the excellent leisure facilities.

Rooms 14 (4 annexe) (4 fmly) **Facilities** WiFi ⇘ ⊛ ⚘ Beauty treatments Xmas New Year **Notes** Civ Wed 150

The Pier House

★★★ 78% HOTEL

tel: 01726 67955 **Harbour Front, Charlestown PL25 3NJ**
email: pierhouse@btconnect.com **web:** www.pierhousehotel.com
dir: *A390 to St Austell, at Mt Charles rdbt left into Charlestown Rd*

This genuinely friendly hotel boasts a wonderful harbour location. The unspoilt working port has been the setting for many film and television productions. Most bedrooms have sea views, and the hotel's convivial Harbourside Inn is popular with locals and tourists alike. Locally caught fish features on the varied and interesting restaurant menu.

Rooms 28 (2 annexe) (3 fmly) (2 GF) ⟋ **Facilities** STV WiFi **Parking** 50 **Notes** ⊗ Closed 24-25 Dec

Porth Avallen Hotel

★★★ 75% HOTEL

tel: 01726 812802 **Sea Rd, Carlyon Bay PL25 3SG**
email: info@porthavallen.co.uk **web:** www.porthavallen.co.uk
dir: *A30 onto A391 to St Austell. Right onto A390. Left at lights, follow brown signs, left at rdbt, right into Sea Rd*

This traditional hotel boasts panoramic views over the rugged Cornish coastline. It offers smartly appointed public areas and well-presented bedrooms, many with sea views. There is an oak-panelled lounge and conservatory; both are ideal for relaxation. Extensive dining options, including the stylish Reflections Restaurant, invite guests to choose from fixed-price, carte and all-day brasserie menus. The Olive Garden, inspired by the Mediterranean, is a lovely place to eat alfresco.

Rooms 28 (3 fmly) (3 GF) ⟋ **S** £65–£78; **D** £90–£125 (incl. bkfst)* **Facilities** FTV WiFi ⇘ Xmas New Year **Conf** Class 100 Board 80 Thtr 160 Del from £150 to £300* **Parking** 60 **Notes** ⊗ Civ Wed 160

S

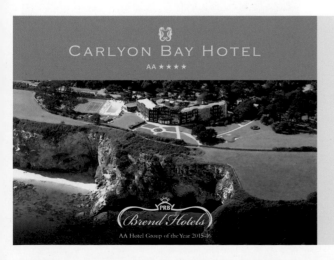

ST AUSTELL *continued*

Premier Inn St Austell

BUDGET HOTEL

tel: 0871 527 9018 *(Calls cost 13p per minute plus your phone company's access charge)*
St Austell Enterprise Park, Treverbyn Rd PL25 4EL
web: www.premierinn.com
dir: *A30 onto A391 signed St Austell. Through Bugle. Continue on A391 at rdbt. Continue to follow St Austell signs. 1st exit at Carclaze rdbt. Hotel at St Austell Enterprise Park*

High quality, budget accommodation ideal for both families and business travellers. Spacious, en suite bedrooms feature tea and coffee making facilities, and Freeview TV in most hotels. Internet access and WiFi are available for a small fee. The adjacent family restaurant features a wide and varied menu. See also the Hotel Groups pages.

Rooms 77

| **ST HELENS** | Map 15 SJ59 |
| Merseyside | |

Premier Inn St Helens (A580/East Lancs)

BUDGET HOTEL

tel: 0871 527 9020 *(Calls cost 13p per minute plus your phone company's access charge)*
Garswood Old Rd, East Lancs Rd WA11 7LX
web: www.premierinn.com
dir: *3m from M6 junct 23, on A580 towards Liverpool*

High quality, budget accommodation ideal for both families and business travellers. Spacious, en suite bedrooms feature tea and coffee making facilities, and Freeview TV in most hotels. Internet access and WiFi are available for a small fee. The adjacent family restaurant features a wide and varied menu. See also the Hotel Groups pages.

Rooms 44

Premier Inn St Helens South

BUDGET HOTEL

tel: 0871 527 9022 *(Calls cost 13p per minute plus your phone company's access charge)*
Eurolink, Lea Green WA9 4TT
web: www.premierinn.com
dir: *M62 junct 7, A570 towards St Helens*

Rooms 40

| **ST IVES** | Map 2 SW54 |
| Cornwall | |

Carbis Bay Hotel

★★★★ 77% HOTEL

tel: 01736 795311 **Carbis Bay TR26 2NP**
email: info@carbisbayhotel.co.uk **web:** www.carbisbayhotel.co.uk
dir: *A3074, through Lelant. 1m, at Carbis Bay 30yds before lights, right into Porthrepta Rd to hotel*

In a peaceful location with access to its own white-sand beach, this hotel offers comfortable accommodation. The attractive public areas feature a smart bar and lounge, and a sun lounge overlooking the sea. Bedrooms, many with fine views, are well equipped. Interesting cuisine and particularly enjoyable breakfasts are offered. A small complex of luxury, self-catering apartments is available.

Rooms 47 (16 fmly) (3 GF) ♙ **Facilities** Spa WiFi ↖ Fishing Private beach ♫ Xmas New Year Child facilities **Conf** Class 80 Board 60 Thtr 120 **Parking** 200 **Notes** ⊗ Civ Wed 150

St Ives Harbour Hotel

★★★★ 73% HOTEL

tel: 01736 795221 **The Terrace TR26 2BN**
email: stives@harbourhotels.co.uk **web:** www.stives-harbour-hotel.co.uk
dir: *On A3074*

This friendly hotel enjoys an enviable location with spectacular views of St Ives Bay. Extensive leisure facilities, a versatile function suite and a number of elegant and stylish lounges are available. The majority of bedrooms are appointed to a very high standard, and many rooms have spectacular sea views, as does the restaurant which looks out over the bay and golden sands below.

Rooms 46 (6 fmly) ♙ **Facilities** Spa FTV WiFi ⊛ Gym Steam room Sauna Xmas New Year **Conf** Class 20 Board 35 Thtr 130 **Services** Lift **Parking** 60 **Notes** Civ Wed 160

The Garrack

★★★ 81% ❀ HOTEL

tel: 01736 796199 **Burthallan Ln TR26 3AA**
email: garrackhotel@btconnect.com **web:** www.garrack.com
dir: *Exit A30 for St Ives. From B3311 follow brown signs for Tate Gallery, then Garrack signs*

The Garrack Hotel is set in two acres of gardens on a hill-top location with thirty miles of coastal views. Bedrooms in the original house are in keeping with the original granite architecture, whereas those in the sea-facing lower ground floor wing are in more modern style. Dinner and breakfast are served in the restaurant which faces the stunning grounds and gardens, with views of the beautiful Cornish coast line thrown in. The small leisure centre is in a separate building to the hotel, consisting of an indoor swimming pool with sauna. Location is ideal for families and walkers wanting to explore Cornwall.

Rooms 19 (4 fmly) (3 GF) ♙ **S** £65-£150; **D** £75-£190 (incl. bkfst)* **Facilities** FTV WiFi HL ⊛ Sauna **Conf** Class 10 Board 20 **Parking** 20

Tregenna Castle Hotel

★★★ 79% HOTEL

tel: 01736 795254 **TR26 2DE**
email: hotel@tregenna-castle.co.uk **web:** www.tregenna-castle.co.uk
dir: *A30 from Exeter to Penzance, at Lelant take A3074 to St Ives, through Carbis Bay, main entrance signed on left*

Sitting at the top of town in beautiful landscaped sub-tropical gardens with woodland walks, this popular hotel boasts spectacular views of St Ives. Many leisure facilities are available, including indoor and outdoor pools, a gym and a sauna. Families are particularly welcome. The individually designed bedrooms are generally spacious. There are two restaurants, the Trelawny Room and the Godrevy Room, while a brasserie provides lighter options in a less formal atmosphere.

Rooms 81 (37 fmly) (16 GF) 🐾 **Facilities** Spa STV FTV WiFi HL ⊗ ⦂ supervised ⦿ 18 ⦿ Putt green ⦿ Gym Squash Sauna Steam room Badminton court ♫ Xmas New Year **Conf** Class 150 Board 30 Thtr 250 **Services** Lift **Parking** 200 **Notes** ⊗ Civ Wed 160

Chy-an-Albany Hotel

★★★ 75% HOTEL

tel: 01736 796759 **Albany Ter TR26 2BS**
email: info@chyanalbanyhotel.com **web:** www.chyanalbanyhotel.com
dir: *A30 onto A3074 signed St Ives, hotel on left just before junct*

Conveniently located, this pleasant hotel enjoys splendid sea views. The comfortable bedrooms come in a variety of sizes; some featuring balconies which make it easy to enjoy those sea views. The friendly staff and the relaxing environment mean that some guests return on a regular basis. Freshly prepared and appetising cuisine is served in the dining room, and a bar menu is also available.

Rooms 39 (10 fmly) 🐾 **Facilities** FTV WiFi **Conf** Class 30 Board 30 Thtr 50 **Services** Lift **Parking** 33 **Notes** ⊗ Civ Wed 70

Cottage Hotel

★★★ 70% HOTEL

Leisureplex
HOLIDAY HOTELS

tel: 01736 795252 **Boskerris Rd, Carbis Bay TR26 2PE**
email: cottage@leisureplex.co.uk **web:** www.leisureplex.co.uk
dir: *From A30 take A3074 to Carbis Bay. Right into Porthreptor Rd Just before rail bridge, left through railway car park Into hotel car park*

Set in quiet, lush gardens, this pleasant hotel offers friendly and attentive service. Smart bedrooms are pleasantly spacious and many rooms enjoy splendid views. Public areas are varied and include a snooker room, a comfortable lounge and a spacious dining room with sea views over the beach and Carbis Bay.

Rooms 80 (18 fmly) (2 GF) 🐾 **Facilities** FTV WiFi ⦂ Snooker ♫ Xmas New Year **Services** Lift **Parking** 20 **Notes** ⊗ Closed Dec-Feb (ex Xmas/New Year) RS Nov & Mar

The Queens

★★ 85% ⊗ HOTEL

tel: 01736 796468 **2 High St TR26 1RR**
email: info@queenshotelstives.com **web:** www.queenshotelstives.com
dir: *A3074 to town centre Hotel is located opp Boots the chemist*

Handily located in the centre of town, just a short stroll from the harbor, this is an ideal location for exploring the charms of St Ives. The bedrooms offer style and comfort with local Cornish artwork and lovely comfy beds. Bathrooms are also light, bright and modern. The relaxing bar and lounge is the venue for enjoyable award-winning cuisine with excellent local produce utilized in simple yet delicious dishes.

Rooms 10 S £59-£159; D £59-£159 (incl. bkfst)* **Facilities** FTV WiFi **Notes** ⊗

ST LEONARDS-ON-SEA
See **Hastings & St Leonards**

ST MARY CHURCH
See **Torquay**

ST MELLION
Cornwall

Map 3 SX36

St Mellion International Resort

★★★★ 79% ⊗⊗ HOTEL

tel: 01579 351351 **PL12 6SD**
email: stmellion@crown-golf.co.uk **web:** www.st-mellion.co.uk
dir: *From M5, A30 towards Plymouth & Saltash. St Mellion off A38 on A388 towards Callington & Launceston*

Set in 450 acres of Cornish countryside, this impressive golfing and leisure complex has much to offer. A vast range of leisure facilities are provided, including three pools, spa facilities and a health club. In addition, the hotel also boasts a choice of championship golf courses. The Jack Nicklaus signature course has hosted many PGA tour events. The bedrooms provide contemporary comforts and many have views across the course. Public areas are equally stylish with a choice of dining options including An Boesti, a fine-dining restaurant overlooking the 18th green.

Rooms 80 (20 fmly) (18 GF) 🐾 **Facilities** Spa FTV WiFi ⦂ ⊗ supervised ⦿ 36 ⦿ Putt green Gym Studio classes Lawn bowls Xmas New Year **Conf** Class 200 Board 80 Thtr 400 **Services** Lift Air con **Parking** 450 **Notes** ⊗ Civ Wed 300

S

ST NEOTS	Map 12 TL16
Cambridgeshire	

The George Hotel & Brasserie

★★★ 88% ◉◉ HOTEL

tel: 01480 812300 **High St, Buckden PE19 5XA**
email: mail@thegeorgebuckden.com **web:** www.thegeorgebuckden.com
dir: 2m S of A1 & A14 junct at Buckden

The George Hotel is ideally situated in the heart of this historic town centre and is just a short drive from the A1. Public rooms feature a bustling ground-floor brasserie, which offers casual dining throughout the day and evening; there is also an informal lounge bar with an open fire and comfy seating. Bedrooms are stylish, tastefully appointed and thoughtfully equipped.

Rooms 12 (1 fmly) ⚑ **S** £75-£95; **D** £100-£150 (incl. bkfst)* **Facilities** STV WiFi ⌂ **Conf** Class 30 Board 28 Thtr 50 Del £180* **Services** Lift **Parking** 25 **Notes** LB ⊗ Civ Wed 60

Premier Inn St Neots (A1/Wyboston)

BUDGET HOTEL

tel: 0871 527 9024 *(Calls cost 13p per minute plus your phone company's access charge)*
Great North Rd, Eaton Socon PE19 8EN
web: www.premierinn.com
dir: Just off A1 at rdbt of A428 & B1428 before St Neots. 1m from St Neots rail station

High quality, budget accommodation ideal for both families and business travellers. Spacious, en suite bedrooms feature tea and coffee making facilities, and Freeview TV in most hotels. Internet access and WiFi are available for a small fee. The adjacent family restaurant features a wide and varied menu. See also the Hotel Groups pages.

Rooms 67

Premier Inn St Neots (Colmworth Park)

BUDGET HOTEL

tel: 0871 527 9026 *(Calls cost 13p per minute plus your phone company's access charge)*
2 Marlborough Rd, Colmworth Business Park PE19 8YP
web: www.premierinn.com
dir: From A1 N'bound: A428 towards Cambridge. 2nd exit at rdbt onto A4128 signed St Neots. Hotel on right. From A1 S'bound: follow A428 Cambridge signs. At rdbt 1st exit onto A4128 signed St Neots, hotel on right

Rooms 71

SALCOMBE	Map 3 SX73
Devon	

Soar Mill Cove Hotel

★★★★ 84% ◉◉ HOTEL

tel: 01548 561566 **Soar Mill Cove, Malborough TQ7 3DS**
email: info@soarmillcove.co.uk **web:** www.soarmillcove.co.uk
dir: 3m W of town off A381 at Malborough. Follow Soar signs

Situated amid spectacular scenery with dramatic sea views, this hotel is ideal for a relaxing stay. Family-run, with a committed team, keen standards of hospitality and service are upheld. Bedrooms are well equipped and many have private terraces. There are different seating areas where, if guests wish, impressive cream teas can be enjoyed, and for the more active, there's a choice of swimming pools. Local produce and seafood are used to good effect in the restaurant.

Rooms 22 (5 fmly) (21 GF) ⚑ **S** £100-£200; **D** £199-£269 (incl. bkfst)* **Facilities** Spa FTV WiFi ⌧ ♨ Gym Table tennis Games room Leisure complex ♫ Xmas **Conf** Class 50 Board 50 Thtr 100 **Parking** 30 **Notes** Closed 2 Jan-8 Feb Civ Wed 150

Salcombe Harbour Hotel

★★★★ 83% ◉ HOTEL

tel: 01548 844444 **Cliff Rd TQ8 8JH**
email: salcombe@harbourhotels.co.uk **web:** www.salcombe-harbour-hotel.co.uk
dir: From A38 Exeter - Plymouth dual carriageway take A384 to Totnes then follow A381 to Kingsbridge & onto Salcombe. On entering Salcombe carry along Main Rd, do not take town signs. Follow road down hill into Bennett Rd. Hotel is 0.25m on right

Situated on the side of the estuary in Salcombe stands this beautiful hotel. There are stunning views, convenient parking and a beautiful spa and leisure facility. The bedrooms are particularly well appointed and stylishly finished; many have excellent views, and some have balconies. Guests can eat in the Jetty Restaurant; outside when the weather allows, which services popular food and local seafood. There is also a function room, spacious bar/lounge and cinema.

Rooms 50 (6 fmly) (6 GF) **D** £204-£424 (incl. bkfst) **Facilities** Spa FTV WiFi ⌂ HL ⌧ Gym Sauna Steam room Xmas New Year **Conf** Class 120 Board 40 Thtr 120 Del from £205 to £425 **Services** Lift **Parking** 50 **Notes** LB Civ Wed 120

Thurlestone Hotel

★★★★ 83% ◉ HOTEL

tel: 01548 560382 **TQ7 3NN**
email: enquiries@thurlestone.co.uk **web:** www.thurlestone.co.uk

(For full entry see Thurlestone)

SALE
Greater Manchester

Map 15 SJ79

Premier Inn Manchester (Sale)

BUDGET HOTEL

tel: 0871 527 8716 *(Calls cost 13p per minute plus your phone company's access charge)*
Carrington Ln, Ashton-upon-Mersey M33 5BL
web: www.premierinn.com
dir: *M60 junct 8, A6144(M) towards Carrington. Left at 1st lights, hotel on left*

High quality, budget accommodation ideal for both families and business travellers. Spacious, en suite bedrooms feature tea and coffee making facilities, and Freeview TV in most hotels. Internet access and WiFi are available for a small fee. The adjacent family restaurant features a wide and varied menu. See also the Hotel Groups pages.

Rooms 61

SALFORD
Greater Manchester

Map 15 SJ89

Premier Inn Manchester Salford Spinningfields

BUDGET HOTEL

tel: 0871 527 9550 *(Calls cost 13p per minute plus your phone company's access charge)*
Irwell St M3 5EN
web: www.premierinn.com
dir: *Sbnd: M60 junct 5, A5103 (city centre). 5m, at rdbt 1st exit (Mancunian Way (A57(M)). Right (A6042), into right lane, right into Irwell St. Nbnd: M60 junct 12, M602 (city centre). A57(M) into Mancunian Way. 1.5m, left onto A6042. Right at lights into Irwell St*

High quality, budget accommodation ideal for both families and business travellers. Spacious, en suite bedrooms feature tea and coffee making facilities, and Freeview TV in most hotels. Internet access and WiFi are available for a small fee. The adjacent family restaurant features a wide and varied menu. See also the Hotel Groups pages.

Rooms 143

SALISBURY
Wiltshire

Map 5 SU12

Milford Hall Hotel

★★★★ 75% ◉ HOTEL

tel: 01722 417411 & 424116 **206 Castle St SP1 3TE**
email: reception@milfordhallhotel.com web: www.milfordhallhotel.com
dir: *Near junct of Castle St, A36 ring road & A345 Amesbury Road*

This hotel offers high standards of accommodation and is within easy walking distance of the city centre. There are two categories of bedroom - traditional rooms in the original Georgian house, and spacious, modern rooms in a purpose-built extension; all are extremely well equipped. Meals are served in the smart brasserie where a varied choice of dishes is provided. Additional facilities include the newly opened Lime Tree Spa, offering a range of treatments, relaxation areas and a gym.

Rooms 45 (2 fmly) (22 GF) ⋒ **Facilities** Spa FTV WiFi Gym Xmas New Year **Conf** Class 90 Board 60 Thtr 200 **Parking** 60 **Notes** ⊗ Civ Wed 120

Mercure Salisbury White Hart Hotel

★★★★ 75% HOTEL

tel: 01722 327476 **St John St SP1 2SD**
email: H6616@accor.com web: www.mercure.com
dir: *M3 juncts 7/8, A303 to A343 for Salisbury then A30. Follow city centre signs on ring road, into Exeter St, leading into St John St. Car park at rear on Brown St*

There has been a hotel on this site since the 16th century, and this building dates from the 17th. Bedrooms vary in style, from contemporary to traditional, but all boast a comprehensive range of facilities. The bar and lounge areas are popular with guests and locals alike for morning coffees and afternoon teas.

Rooms 68 (6 fmly) ⋒ **Facilities** STV WiFi Xmas New Year **Conf** Class 40 Board 40 Thtr 100 **Parking** 60 **Notes** Civ Wed 100

The Legacy Rose & Crown Hotel

★★★★ 73% HOTEL

tel: 0844 411 9046 *(Calls cost 7p per minute plus your phone company's access charge)*
& 0330 333 2846 **Harnham Rd SP2 8JQ**
email: res-roseandcrown@legacy-hotels.co.uk web: www.legacy-hotels.co.uk
dir: *M3 junct 8, A303 & follow Salisbury Ring Road or M27 junct 2, A36 to Salisbury. A338 towards Harnham then Harnham Rd. Hotel on right*

This 13th-century coaching inn, situated beside the river, enjoys picturesque views of Salisbury Cathedral, especially from the Pavilion Restaurant which provides a good range of dishes. Many original features are still retained in the heavy oak-beamed bars. All bedrooms and bathrooms are beautifully appointed. Excellent conference and banqueting facilities are available.

Rooms 34 (5 fmly) (7 GF) ⋒ **Facilities** FTV WiFi Xmas New Year **Conf** Class 30 Board 26 Thtr 90 **Parking** 60 **Notes** ⊗ Civ Wed 100

Best Western Red Lion Hotel

★★★ 78% HOTEL

tel: 01722 323334 **4 Milford St SP1 2AN**
email: reception@the-redlion.co.uk web: www.the-redlion.co.uk
dir: *In city centre close to Guildhall Square*

This 750-year-old hotel is full of character, with a mix of bedrooms, some very stylish refurbished examples, while others are individually designed including one with a medieval fireplace dating back to 1220. The public areas include a bar and a lounge. The elegant Vine Restaurant also serves an interesting mix of modern and traditional dishes.

Rooms 60 (1 fmly) (1 GF) ⋒ **Facilities** FTV WiFi ⌕ Xmas New Year **Conf** Class 40 Board 40 Thtr 110 **Services** Lift **Parking** 7 **Notes** ⊗ Civ Wed 110

Grasmere House Hotel

THE INDEPENDENTS

★★★ 74% HOTEL

tel: 01722 338388 **Harnham Rd SP2 8JN**
email: info@grasmerehotel.com web: www.grasmerehotel.com
dir: *On A3094 on S side of Salisbury adjacent to Harnham church*

This popular hotel, dating from 1896, has gardens that overlook the water meadows and the cathedral. The attractive bedrooms vary in size; all offer excellent quality and comfort, while some rooms are specially equipped for less mobile guests. In summer there is the option of dining on the pleasant outdoor terrace.

Rooms 38 (31 annexe) (16 fmly) (9 GF) ⋒ **Facilities** STV FTV WiFi ⌕ Fishing ⅏ Xmas New Year **Conf** Class 45 Board 45 Thtr 110 **Parking** 64 **Notes** Civ Wed 120

S

SALISBURY *continued*

Premier Inn Salisbury

BUDGET HOTEL

tel: 0871 527 8956 *(Calls cost 13p per minute plus your phone company's access charge)*
Pearce Way, Bishopsdown SP1 3YU
web: www.premierinn.com
dir: *From Salisbury take A30 towards Marlborough. 1m. Hotel off Hampton Park at rdbt*

High quality, budget accommodation ideal for both families and business travellers. Spacious, en suite bedrooms feature tea and coffee making facilities, and Freeview TV in most hotels. Internet access and WiFi are available for a small fee. The adjacent family restaurant features a wide and varied menu. See also the Hotel Groups pages.

Rooms 78

SALTASH	Map 3 SX45
Cornwall	

China Fleet Country Club

★★★ 82% HOTEL

tel: 01752 848668 & 854661 **PL12 6LJ**
email: sales@china-fleet.co.uk **web:** www.china-fleet.co.uk
dir: *A38 towards Plymouth/Saltash. Cross Tamar Bridge, take slip road before tunnel. Right at lights, 1st right follow signs, 0.5m*

Set in 180 acres of stunning Cornish countryside overlooking the beautiful Tamar estuary, this hotel has easy access to Plymouth and the countryside. It offers an extensive range of leisure facilities including an impressive golf course. The one and two-bedroom apartments are located in annexe buildings; each has a kitchen, lounge and flexible sleeping arrangements. The dining options include a brasserie, a coffee shop and an award-winning Farm House Restaurant which offers interesting and imaginative choices.

Rooms 41 (40 fmly) (22 GF) ↟ **S** £78–£98; **D** £78–£98* **Facilities** Spa FTV WiFi ↝ ⊛ supervised ↧ 18 ⚘ Putt green Gym Squash Floodlit driving range Health & beauty suite Hairdresser Badminton Waterslide Xmas New Year **Conf** Class 100 Board 60 Thtr 300 Del £110* **Services** Lift **Parking** 400 **Notes** ⊗ Civ Wed 300

SANDBANKS	

See **Poole**

SANDIWAY	Map 15 SJ67
Cheshire	

Nunsmere Hall Hotel

★★★★ ⊛⊛ COUNTRY HOUSE HOTEL

tel: 01606 889100 **Tarporley Rd, Oakmere CW8 2ES**
email: reception@nunsmere.co.uk **web:** www.nunsmere.co.uk
dir: *M6 junct 18, A54 to Chester, at x-rds with A49 turn left towards Tarporley, hotel 2m on left*

In an idyllic and peaceful setting of well-kept grounds, including a 60-acre lake, this delightful house dates back to 1900. Spacious bedrooms are individually styled, tastefully appointed to a very high standard, and thoughtfully equipped. Guests can relax in the elegant lounges, the library or the oak-panelled bar. Dining in the Crystal Restaurant is a highlight and both a traditional carte and a gourmet menu are offered.

Rooms 36 (8 fmly) (2 GF) ↟ **Facilities** FTV WiFi ↝ ⥻ Xmas New Year **Conf** Class 50 Board 40 Thtr 100 **Services** Lift **Parking** 200 **Notes** ⊗ Civ Wed 120

SANDOWN	Map 5 SZ58
Isle of Wight	

Bayshore Hotel

★★★ 71% HOTEL

Leisureplex HOLIDAY HOTELS

tel: 01983 403154 **12-16 Pier St PO36 8JX**
email: bayshore.sandown@alfatravel.co.uk **web:** www.leisureplex.co.uk
dir: *From Broadway into Melville St, follow Tourist Information Office signs. Across High St, right opposite pier. Hotel on right*

This large hotel is located on the seafront opposite the pier and offers extensive public rooms where live entertainment is provided in season. There is a range of bedrooms to meet a variety of needs, all are well-equipped; front rooms also offer incredible sea views and are priced differently. The team is very friendly and helpful. Free WiFi is provided in the public areas.

Rooms 78 (18 fmly) ↟ **Facilities** FTV WiFi ⥻ Xmas New Year **Services** Lift **Notes** ⊗ Closed Dec-Feb (ex Xmas/New Year) RS Mar & Nov

Sandringham Hotel

★★ 78% HOTEL

tel: 01983 406655 **Esplanade PO36 8AH**
email: info@sandringhamhotel.co.uk **web:** www.sandringhamhotel.co.uk

With a prime seafront location and splendid views, this is one of the largest hotels on the island. Comfortable public areas include a spacious lounge and a heated indoor swimming pool and jacuzzi. Bedrooms vary in size and many sea-facing rooms have a balcony. Regular entertainment is provided in the ballroom.

Rooms 110 (39 fmly) (6 GF) **Facilities** ⊛ ♫ **Xmas Services** Lift **Parking** 82 **Notes** ⊗

Wight Bay Hotel

★★ 76% HOTEL

tel: 01983 402518 **2 Royal St PO36 8LP**
email: booking@wightbayhotel.com **web:** www.wightbayhotel.com
dir: At top of High St, beyond Post Office

Guests return year after year to this friendly and welcoming family-run hotel. It is located near to the High Street and just a short stroll from the beach, pier and shops. Bedrooms, including several at ground floor level, are very well furnished and comfortably equipped. Enjoyable home-cooked meals are served in the spacious dining room.

Rooms 43 (6 fmly) (11 GF) ♠ **Facilities** FTV WiFi ♫ **Xmas New Year Parking** 30 **Notes** ⊗

Premier Inn Isle of Wight Sandown

BUDGET HOTEL

tel: 0871 527 9558 **Merrie Gardens, Newport Rd PO36 9PE**
web: www.premierinn.com
dir: From Fishbourne Ferry Terminal right onto B3731, right onto A3054. Next left into Station Rd. 2m to rdbt. 1st exit into Briddlesford Rd, at next rdbt into Downend Rd. 4m, left onto A3056. 2nd exit at rdbt. At next rdbt 2nd exit into Whitcross Ln

High quality, budget accommodation ideal for both families and business travellers. Spacious, en suite bedrooms feature tea and coffee making facilities, and Freeview TV in most hotels. Internet access and WiFi are available for a small fee. The adjacent family restaurant features a wide and varied menu. See also the Hotel Groups pages.

SANDWICH	**Map 7 TR35**
Kent	

The Lodge at Prince's

★★★ 86% ⊛⊛ HOTEL

tel: 01304 611118 **Prince's Dr, Sandwich Bay CT13 9QB**
email: info@princesgolfclub.co.uk **web:** www.princesgolfclub.co.uk
dir: M2 onto A299 Thanet Way to Manston Airport, A256 to Sandwich, follow sign to golf course

Opened in 2012, and created from the remains of the old clubhouse, The Lodge at Prince's is in the most sought-after locations of the south east coast. There is a choice of bedrooms within three adjoining house, and most rooms offer enviable views of the golf course or the Bay of Sandwich. All rooms have been carefully designed and offer a range of practical amenities including club storage. Award-winning cuisine is served in The Brasserie on the Bay.

Rooms 38 (24 annexe) (1 fmly) (12 GF) ♠ **Facilities** FTV WiFi ♦ HL ↕ 27 Putt green Gym **Xmas New Year Conf** Class 60 Board 50 Thtr 120 Del from £130 to £175 **Services** Lift **Parking** 50

SAUNTON	**Map 3 SS43**
Devon	

Saunton Sands Hotel

★★★★ 81% ⊛ HOTEL *Brend Hotels*

tel: 01271 890212 **EX33 1LQ**
email: reservations@sauntonsands.com **web:** www.sauntonsands.com
dir: Exit A361 at Braunton, signed Croyde B3231, hotel 2m on left

Stunning sea views and direct access to five miles of sandy beach are just two of the highlights at this popular hotel. The majority of sea-facing rooms have balconies, and splendid views can be enjoyed from all of the public areas, which include comfortable lounges. In addition to the dining room, in summer an outside grill has tables on the terrace overlooking the sea. Alternatively, The Sands café/bar, an informal eating option, is a successful innovation located on the beach.

Rooms 92 (39 fmly) ♠ **S** £80-£155; **D** £160-£350 (incl. bkfst)* **Facilities** Spa STV FTV WiFi ♦ ⊛ ↘ ⚲ Putt green Gym Squash Sauna Sun shower Snooker room ♫ **Xmas New Year Child facilities Conf** Class 180 Board 50 Thtr 200 **Services** Lift **Parking** 140 **Notes** LB ⊗ Civ Wed 200

See advert on page 374

S

SCARBOROUGH
North Yorkshire

Map 17 TA08

Crown Spa Hotel

★★★★ 79% HOTEL

tel: 01723 357400 **Esplanade YO11 2AG**
email: info@crownspahotel.com **web:** www.crownspahotel.com
dir: *On A64 follow town centre signs to lights opposite railway station, turn right over Valley Bridge, 1st left, right into Belmont Rd to cliff top*

This well-known hotel has an enviable position overlooking the harbour and South Bay, and most of the front-facing bedrooms have excellent views. All the bedrooms, including suites, are contemporary and have the latest amenities including feature bathrooms. An extensive range of treatments are available in the outstanding spa.

Rooms 115 (42 fmly) ⚡ **S** £53–£150; **D** £63–£250* **Facilities** Spa FTV WiFi ⇩ HL ⛱ Gym Fitness classes Massage Sauna Steam room Xmas New Year **Conf** Class 100 Board 80 Thtr 260 Del from £115 to £225* **Services** Lift **Parking** 17 **Notes** ⊗ Civ Wed 260

Palm Court Hotel

★★★ 83% ⊛ HOTEL

tel: 01723 368161 **St Nicholas Cliff YO11 2ES**
email: info@palmcourt-scarborough.co.uk **web:** www.palmcourtscarborough.co.uk
dir: *Follow signs for town centre & town hall, hotel before town hall on right*

The public rooms are spacious and comfortable at this modern, town centre hotel. Traditional cooking is provided in the attractive restaurant and staff are friendly and helpful. Bedrooms are quite delightfully furnished and well equipped. Extra facilities include a swimming pool and free, covered parking.

Rooms 40 (11 fmly) ⚡ **Facilities** FTV WiFi ⛱ Xmas New Year **Conf** Class 70 Board 60 Thtr 80 Del from £99 to £135 **Services** Lift **Parking** 40 **Notes** ⊗ Civ Wed 80

Red Lea Hotel

★★★ 74% HOTEL

tel: 01723 362431 **Prince of Wales Ter YO11 2AJ**
email: info@redleahotel.co.uk **web:** www.redleahotel.co.uk
dir: *Follow South Cliff signs. Prince of Wales Terrace is off Esplanade opposite cliff lift*

This friendly, family-run hotel is situated close to the cliff lift. Bedrooms are well equipped and comfortably furnished, and many at the front have picturesque views of the coast. There are two large lounges and a spacious dining room where good-value, traditional food is served.

Rooms 66 (7 fmly) ⚡ **Facilities** FTV WiFi ⛱ Xmas New Year **Conf** Class 25 Board 25 Thtr 40 **Services** Lift **Notes** ⊗

The Cumberland

★★★ 70% HOTEL

Leisureplex
HOLIDAY HOTELS

tel: 01723 361826 **Belmont Rd YO11 2AB**
email: cumberland.scarborough@leisureplex.co.uk **web:** www.leisureplex.co.uk
dir: *A64 onto B1437, left at A165 towards town centre. Right into Ramshill Rd, right into Belmont Rd*

On the South Cliff, convenient for the spa complex, beach and town centre shops, this hotel offers comfortably appointed bedrooms; each floor can be accessed by lift. Entertainment is provided most evenings and the meals are carefully prepared.

Rooms 86 (6 fmly) ⚡ **S** £39–£52; **D** £62–£88 (incl. bkfst)* **Facilities** FTV WiFi ♫ Xmas New Year **Services** Lift **Notes** LB ⊗ Closed Jan RS Nov-Dec & Feb

Esplanade Hotel

★★★ 70% HOTEL

tel: 01723 360382 **Belmont Rd YO11 2AA**
email: enquiries@theesplanade.co.uk **web:** www.theesplanade.co.uk
dir: *From town centre over Valley Bridge, left then immediately right into Belmont Rd, hotel 100mtrs on right*

This large hotel enjoys a superb position overlooking South Bay and the harbour. Both the terrace, leading from the lounge bar, and the restaurant, with its striking oriel window, benefit from magnificent views. Bedrooms are comfortably furnished and are well equipped. Touring groups are also well catered for.

Rooms 70 (7 fmly) ⚡ **Facilities** FTV WiFi Xmas New Year **Conf** Class 100 Board 30 Thtr 120 Del from £60 to £92* **Services** Lift **Parking** 15 **Notes** Closed 2-6 Jan

Park Manor Hotel

★★ 78% HOTEL

tel: 01723 372090 **Northstead Manor Dr YO12 6BB**
email: info@parkmanor.co.uk **web:** www.parkmanor.co.uk
dir: *Off A165, adjacent to Peasholm Park*

Enjoying a peaceful residential setting with sea views, this smartly presented, friendly hotel provides the seaside tourist with a wide range of facilities. Bedrooms vary in size and style but all are smartly furnished and well equipped. There are a spacious lounge, smart restaurant, games room and indoor pool plus a steam room for relaxation.

Rooms 41 (6 fmly) (1 GF) ✆ **S** £41.50-£51.50; **D** £76-£113* **Facilities** FTV WiFi ⊛ Pool table Spa bath Steam room Table tennis New Year **Conf** Class 20 Board 20 Thtr 30 Del from £75 to £95* **Services** Lift **Parking** 20 **Notes** LB ⊗ Closed 26 Dec RS 25 Dec

Premier Inn Scarborough

BUDGET HOTEL

tel: 0871 527 9292 *(Calls cost 13p per minute plus your phone company's access charge)*
Falconer Rd YO11 2EN
web: www.premierinn.com
dir: *From A64 into Seamer Rd, follow rail station signs. Right into Valley Bridge Rd. At 1st lights follow Town Hall signs into Somerset St (towards Brunswick shopping centre). At lights follow Town Hall signs into Falconers Rd*

High quality, budget accommodation ideal for both families and business travellers. Spacious, en suite bedrooms feature tea and coffee making facilities, and Freeview TV in most hotels. Internet access and WiFi are available for a small fee. The adjacent family restaurant features a wide and varied menu. See also the Hotel Groups pages.

Rooms 74

SCUNTHORPE
Lincolnshire
Map 17 SE81

Forest Pines Hotel & Golf Resort

★★★★ 81% ⊛ HOTEL

QHOTELS
INSPIRED BY YOU

tel: 01652 650770 **Ermine St, Broughton DN20 0AQ**
email: forestpines@qhotels.co.uk **web:** www.qhotels.co.uk
dir: *200yds from M180 junct 4, on Brigg-Scunthorpe rdbt*

This smart hotel provides a comprehensive range of leisure facilities. Extensive conference rooms, a modern health and beauty spa, and a championship golf course ensure that it is a popular choice with both corporate and leisure guests. The well-equipped bedrooms are modern, spacious, and appointed to a good standard. Extensive public areas include a choice of dining options, with fine dining available in The Eighteen57 fish restaurant, and more informal eating in the Grill Bar.

Rooms 188 (66 fmly) (65 GF) ✆ **Facilities** Spa STV FTV WiFi HL ⊛ ♿ 27 Putt green Gym Mountain bikes Jogging track Xmas New Year **Conf** Class 170 Board 96 Thtr 370 **Services** Lift **Parking** 400 **Notes** Civ Wed 250

Premier Inn Scunthorpe

BUDGET HOTEL

tel: 0871 527 8960 *(Calls cost 13p per minute plus your phone company's access charge)*
Lakeside Retail Park, Lakeside Parkway DN16 3UA
web: www.premierinn.com
dir: *M180 junct 4, A18 towards Scunthorpe. At Morrisons rdbt left onto Lakeside Retail Park, hotel behind Morrisons petrol station*

High quality, budget accommodation ideal for both families and business travellers. Spacious, en suite bedrooms feature tea and coffee making facilities, and Freeview TV in most hotels. Internet access and WiFi are available for a small fee. The adjacent family restaurant features a wide and varied menu. See also the Hotel Groups pages.

Rooms 81

San Pietro Restaurant Rooms

⊛⊛ RESTAURANT WITH ROOMS

tel: 01724 277774 **11 High Street East DN15 6UH**
email: info@sanpietro.uk.com **web:** www.sanpietro.uk.com
dir: *3m from M180, follow signs for Scunthorpe town centre & railway station, left into Brigg Rd/Station Rd. Near windmill*

This family-run restaurant with rooms was purpose-built, and offers comfortable modern accommodation. Bedrooms and bathrooms provide a range of additional extras such as mini-bars, home-made cakes, complimentary WiFi and smart TVs. Dinner and breakfast are served in the annexe Ristorante. Dinner menus have an Italian influence and provide a range of choice including a chef's tasting menu as well as a full à la carte offering. Continental breakfasts are included, with a choice to upgrade to a hearty cooked breakfast. San Pietro was the AA Funkiest Bed and Breakfast of the Year 2015-2016.

Rooms 14

SEAHAM
County Durham
Map 19 NZ44

Seaham Hall

★★★★★ 85% ⊛⊛ HOTEL

tel: 0191 516 1400 **Lord Byron's Walk SR7 7AG**
email: hotel@seaham-hall.com **web:** www.seaham-hall.co.uk
dir: *From A19 take B1404 to Seaham. At lights straight over level crossing. Hotel approx 0.25m on right*

Seaham Hall benefits from a wonderful coastal location. Its interior is sumptuously furnished, with all rooms boasting the highest quality fixtures, fittings and furniture. Many have feature bathrooms, and the garden rooms have their own patio and garden areas. Public rooms boast quality and luxury throughout. The hotel boasts an award-winning Serenity Spa where you can unwind in the pool and hydrotherapy facilities, not forgetting the outside hot tubs; or book a treatment with one of the dedicated team of therapists. Seaham is home to two award-winning restaurants and Ross Stovold, the Head Chef, has created imaginative menus with an emphasis and commitment to the finest quality ingredients. Whether you choose the relaxed Pan-Asian Ozone restaurant in the Serenity Spa or the opulent setting of Byron's Bar & Grill set in the main hall, you can be sure of excellent dining.

Rooms 20 (4 GF) ✆ **S** £195-£795; **D** £195-£795 (incl. bkfst)* **Facilities** Spa STV FTV WiFi ♿ HL ⊛ Putt green ⛳ Gym Games Room Sports lounge Xmas New Year **Conf** Class 48 Board 40 Thtr 100 Del from £225 to £265* **Services** Lift Air con **Parking** 120 **Notes** ⊗ Civ Wed 100

S

SEAHOUSES
Northumberland   Map 21 NU23

The Links Hotel

★★ 85% SMALL HOTEL

tel: 01665 720062 **8 King St NE68 7XP**
email: linkshotel@hotmail.com **web:** www.linkshotel-seahouses.co.uk
dir: Off A1 at Browleside & follow signs along country road

This family-owned small hotel is in the heart of Seahouses. The restaurant is popular with residents and locals alike, offering relaxed and informal dining with quality home cooking and generous portions. Bedrooms are well presented and equipped and some off-road parking is available.

Rooms 16 (6 annexe) (1 fmly) (2 GF) ⬆ **S** £45-£52; **D** £70-£84 (incl. bkfst)*
Facilities STV FTV WiFi ♨ Xmas New Year **Parking** 16

SEASCALE
Cumbria   Map 18 NY00

Sella Park House Hotel

★★★★ 74% ⚛ COUNTRY HOUSE HOTEL

tel: 0845 450 6445 *(Calls cost 7p per minute plus your phone company's access charge)*
& 01946 841601 **Calderbridge CA20 1DW**
email: info@penningtonhotels.com **web:** www.penningtonhotels.com
dir: From A595 at Calderbridge, follow sign for North Gate. Hotel 0.5m on left

This property, which some believe dates back to the 13th century, is set in six acres of mature grounds which lead down to the River Calder. The individually designed bedrooms are very well appointed and have many extras; public areas are comfortable and welcoming. Food in the Priory Restaurant is a highlight with local produce at the heart of each menu selection.

Rooms 16 (5 annexe) (2 GF) ⬆ **S** £90-£110; **D** £90-£130 (incl. bkfst)* **Facilities** FTV WiFi ♨ HL Fishing Xmas New Year **Conf** Class 20 Board 30 Thtr 40 Del from £140 to £180 **Parking** 30 **Notes** LB Civ Wed 150

SEAVIEW
Isle of Wight   Map 5 SZ69

Seaview Hotel

★★★ 81% ⚛ HOTEL

tel: 01983 612711 **High St PO34 5EX**
email: reception@seaviewhotel.co.uk **web:** www.seaviewhotel.co.uk
dir: Please phone for directions

There is an enduring appeal about Seaview, a quiet seaside village where time has reassuringly stood still and the pace of life is unhurried. The hotel is just a few steps from the water's edge, a perfect place to relax and unwind with welcoming staff making every effort to ensure a rewarding experience. A choice of dining options is offered, with fish being a speciality; there is also the Pump Bar, a traditional pub situated in the heart of the hotel. A variety of bedroom styles are offered, both in the main hotel and within separate adjacent buildings, all of which provide contemporary comforts.

Rooms 20 (7 annexe) (6 fmly) (6 GF) ⬆ **Facilities** FTV WiFi New Year **Conf** Class 16 Board 20 Thtr 16 **Services** Lift **Parking** 10 **Notes** Closed 23-27 Dec

SEDGEFIELD
County Durham   Map 19 NZ32

Best Western Plus Hardwick Hall Hotel

Best Western PLUS

★★★★ 79% HOTEL

tel: 01740 620253 **TS21 2EH**
email: info@hardwickhallhotel.co.uk **web:** www.hardwickhallhotel.co.uk
dir: Exit A1(M) junct 60 towards Sedgefield, left at 1st rdbt, hotel 400mtrs on left

Set in extensive parkland, this 18th-century house suits both leisure and corporate guests. It is a top conference and function venue offering an impressive meeting and banqueting complex. Luxurious accommodation includes contemporary rooms, and some with antique furnishings. All are appointed to the same high standard, many have feature bathrooms, and some have stunning views over the lake. Both the modern lounge bar and cellar bistro have a relaxed atmosphere.

Rooms 51 (6 fmly) (12 GF) ⬆ **S** £65-£169; **D** £75-£169* **Facilities** STV FTV WiFi ♨ Xmas New Year **Conf** Class 100 Board 80 Thtr 700 Del from £132* **Services** Lift **Parking** 300 **Notes** LB ⊗ Civ Wed 450

SEDGEMOOR MOTORWAY SERVICE AREA (M5)
Somerset   Map 4 ST35

Days Inn Sedgemoor - M5

WELCOMEBREAK

AA Advertised

tel: 01934 750831 **Sedgemoor BS24 0JL**
email: sedgemoor.hotel@welcomebreak.co.uk **web:** www.welcomebreak.co.uk
dir: M5 Northbound junct 21/22

This modern building offers accommodation in smart, spacious and well-equipped bedrooms, suitable for families and business travellers, and all with en suite bathrooms. Continental breakfast is available and other refreshments may be taken at the nearby family restaurant.

Rooms 40 (22 fmly) (19 GF) (8 smoking) **Facilities** WiFi ♨ **Parking** 40

SEVENOAKS
Kent   Map 6 TQ55

Best Western Donnington Manor Hotel

Best Western.

★★★★ 76% HOTEL

tel: 01732 462681 **London Rd, Dunton Green TN13 2TD**
email: mail@donningtonmanor.com **web:** www.bw-donningtonmanor.co.uk
dir: M25 junct 4, follow signs for Bromley/Orpington to rdbt. Left onto A224 (Dunton Green), left at 2nd rdbt. Left at Rose & Crown, hotel 300yds on right

Donnington Manor has been completely refurbished in the last year. Bedrooms are modern in style throughout offering comfortable accommodations well equipped with free WiFi. There is a range of function rooms ideal for conferences and weddings. Guests can enjoy dinner in the Osteria Chartwell Italian Restaurant and breakfast is served here daily also. Plenty of parking on site and close proximity to the M25, Sevenoaks and Brands Hatch.

Rooms 63 (17 GF) ⬆ **Facilities** STV FTV WiFi ♨ Gym **Conf** Class 70 Board 50 Thtr 120 Del from £105 to £145 **Services** Lift Air con **Parking** 80 **Notes** ⊗ Civ Wed 120

SHAFTESBURY
Dorset
Map 4 ST82

Best Western The Royal Chase Hotel
★★★ 72% HOTEL

Best Western.

tel: 01747 853355 **Royal Chase Roundabout SP7 8DB**
email: reception@theroyalchasehotel.co.uk **web:** www.theroyalchasehotel.co.uk
dir: *A303 to A350 signed Blandford Forum. Avoid town centre, follow road to 3rd rdbt*

Equally suitable for both leisure and business guests, this well-known local landmark is situated close to the famous Gold Hill. Both Standard and Crown bedrooms offer good levels of comfort and quality. In addition to the fixed-price menu in the Byzant Restaurant, guests have the option of eating more informally in the convivial bar.

Rooms 32 (13 fmly) (6 GF) ⋒ **S** £65-£95; **D** £75-£160* **Facilities** FTV WiFi ⌕ ⓧ Turkish steam room Spa pool Xmas New Year **Conf** Class 90 Board 50 Thtr 180 Del £139 **Parking** 100 **Notes** LB Civ Wed 80

La Fleur de Lys Restaurant with Rooms
◉◉ RESTAURANT WITH ROOMS

tel: 01747 853717 **Bleke St SP7 8AW**
email: info@lafleurdelys.co.uk **web:** www.lafleurdelys.co.uk
dir: *From junct of A30 & A350, 0.25m towards town centre*

Located just a few minutes' walk from the famous Gold Hill, this light and airy restaurant with rooms combines efficient service with a relaxed and friendly atmosphere. Bedrooms, which are suitable for both business and leisure guests, vary in size but all are well equipped, comfortable and tastefully furnished. A relaxing guest lounge and courtyard are available for afternoon tea or pre-dinner drinks.

Rooms 8 (2 fmly)

SHANKLIN
Isle of Wight
Map 5 SZ58

Channel View Hotel
★★★ 79% HOTEL

tel: 01983 862309 **Hope Rd PO37 6EH**
email: enquiries@channelviewhotel.co.uk **web:** www.channelviewhotel.co.uk
dir: *Exit A3055 at Esplanade & Beach sign. Hotel 250mtrs on left*

With an elevated cliff-top location overlooking Shanklin Bay, several rooms at this hotel enjoy pleasant views and all are very well decorated and furnished. The hotel is family run, and guests can enjoy efficient service, regular evening entertainment, a heated indoor swimming pool and holistic therapy.

Rooms 56 (15 fmly) ⋒ **S** £47-£64; **D** £94-£128 (incl. bkfst) **Facilities** FTV WiFi ⌕ ⓧ Holistic therapies Aromatherapy ♫ **Services** Lift **Parking** 32 **Notes** Closed Jan-Feb

Shanklin Hotel
★★★ 74% HOTEL

Leisureplex
HOLIDAY HOTELS

tel: 01983 862286 **Clarendon Rd PO37 6DP**
email: shanklin@leisureplex.co.uk **web:** www.leisureplex.co.uk
dir: *From Fishbourne ferry take A3054/A3056/A3055 south towards Shanklin. Left into Clarendon Rd*

The Shanklin Hotel enjoys an enviable location with views over Sandown Bay and beyond. The accommodation is well configured and well appointed; a choice of beds is offered to meet the needs of a varied clientele. Entertainment is provided most evenings. The hotel also offers an indoor pool, game facilities, free WiFi in the public areas, and secure parking.

Rooms 89 (3 fmly) (2 GF) ⋒ **Facilities** FTV WiFi ⌕ ♫ Xmas New Year **Services** Lift **Parking** 32 **Notes** ⊗ Closed 2 Jan-16 Feb RS Feb-Mar & Nov-Dec

Auckland Hotel
★★ 72% HOTEL

tel: 01983 862960 **10 Queens Rd PO37 6AN**
email: aucklandhotel@tiscali.co.uk **web:** www.theaucklandhotel.co.uk

This family-run hotel is located in the heart of Shanklin. Bedrooms are spacious and traditional in style, and all front rooms benefit from balconies with views of Sandown Beach. There is a spacious bar which is often the venue for evening entertainment, and a restaurant where both dinner and breakfast are served daily. The hotel has ample off-road parking and is within just a short walk of the Cliff Lift, providing easy access to the seafront.

Rooms 30 **S** £40-£55; **D** £65-£95 (incl. bkfst)* **Facilities** FTV WiFi ♫ **Parking** 16 **Notes** LB ⊗ Closed Dec-Feb

Malton House Hotel
★★ 71% HOTEL

tel: 01983 865007 **8 Park Rd PO37 6AY**
email: couvoussis@maltonhouse.freeserve.co.uk **web:** www.maltonhouse.co.uk
dir: *Up hill from Hope Rd lights then 3rd left*

Malton House is a well-kept Victorian hotel set in its own gardens in a quiet area, conveniently located for cliff-top walks and the public lift down to the promenade. The bedrooms are comfortable and public rooms include a small lounge, a separate bar and a dining room where traditional home-made meals are served.

Rooms 12 (3 fmly) (2 GF) **S** £36-£40; **D** £64-£72 (incl. bkfst)* **Facilities** WiFi **Parking** 12 **Notes** ⊗ No children 3yrs Closed Oct-Apr

SHAP
Cumbria
Map 18 NY51

Best Western Shap Wells Hotel
★★★ 75% HOTEL

Best Western.

tel: 01931 716628 **CA10 3QU**
email: reservations@shapwellshotel.com **web:** www.bw-shapwellshotel.co.uk
dir: *Between A6 & B6261, 4m S of Shap*

This hotel occupies a wonderful secluded position amid trees and waterfalls. Extensive public areas include function and meeting rooms, a well-stocked bar, a choice of lounges and a spacious restaurant. Bedrooms vary in size and style but all are equipped with the expected facilities.

Rooms 99 (8 annexe) (10 fmly) (10 GF) ⋒ **S** £29-£109; **D** £39-£139 **Facilities** FTV WiFi ⌕ Games room Cardiovascular gym ♫ Xmas New Year **Conf** Class 150 Board 60 Thtr 400 Del from £75 to £150 **Services** Lift **Parking** 200 **Notes** LB Closed 2-24 Jan Civ Wed 150

S

SHEFFIELD
South Yorkshire

Map 16 SK38

Whitley Hall Hotel

★★★★ 79% ◉◉ HOTEL

tel: 0114 245 4444 & 246 0456 **Elliott Ln, Grenoside S35 8NR**
email: reservations@whitleyhall.com **web:** www.whitleyhall.com
dir: A61 past football ground, 2m, right just before Norfolk Arms, left at bottom of hill.
Hotel on left

This 16th-century house stands in 20 acres of landscaped grounds and gardens.
Public rooms are full of character and interesting architectural features, and
command the best views of the gardens. The individually styled bedrooms are
furnished in keeping with the country house setting, as are the oak-panelled
restaurant and bar.

Rooms 32 (3 annexe) (2 fmly) (8 GF) ↟ **S** £90-£130; **D** £100-£160 (incl. dinner)*
Facilities STV FTV WiFi ↘ **Conf** Class 50 Board 34 Thtr 70 Del from £156 to £161*
Services Lift **Parking** 100 **Notes** ⊗ Civ Wed 100

Mercure Sheffield St Paul's Hotel & Spa

★★★★ 79% HOTEL

tel: 0114 278 2000 **119 Norfolk St S1 2JE**
email: h6628@accor.com **web:** www.mercure.com
dir: M1 junct 33, 4th exit at rdbt, left at 1st lights, right at 2nd in front of Crucible
Theatre

This modern, luxury hotel enjoys a central location close to key attractions in the
city. Open-plan public areas are situated in a steel and glass atrium and include a
popular Champagne bar, the Yard Restaurant and Zucca, an Italian Bistro.
Bedrooms are superbly presented and richly furnished. The Vital health and beauty
treatment centre provides a fabulous thermal suite.

Rooms 163 (40 fmly) **Facilities** Spa WiFi ⊛ Sauna Steam room Snail shower Ice
fountain Fitness classes Xmas New Year **Conf** Class 400 Board 30 Thtr 600
Services Lift Air con **Notes** ⊗ Civ Wed 350

Copthorne Hotel Sheffield

★★★★ 77% HOTEL

tel: 0114 252 5480 & 252 5482 **Sheffield United Football Club, Bramhall Ln
S2 4SU**
email: reservations.sheffield@millenniumhotels.co.uk
web: www.millenniumhotels.co.uk/copthornesheffield
dir: M1 junct 33/A57. At Park Square rdbt follow A61 Chesterfield Rd. Follow brown signs
for Bramall Lane

This modern and stylish hotel is situated in the centre of Sheffield. Right next to the
home of Sheffield United FC, it offers contemporary public areas and an award-
winning restaurant on the ground floor. A well-equipped gym is situated on the first
floor. Bedrooms are spacious and comfortable. Ample parking is a plus in this
central location.

Rooms 158 (29 fmly) ↟ **Facilities** STV FTV WiFi ↘ HL Gym **Conf** Class 150 Board 24
Thtr 250 **Services** Lift Air con **Parking** 250 **Notes** ⊗

Mercure Sheffield Parkway Hotel

★★★★ 74% HOTEL

tel: 0114 261 5690 & 0845 485 4528
(Calls cost 7p per minute plus your phone company's access charge)
Brittania Way, Catcliffe S60 5BD
email: info@mercuresheffieldparkway.com **web:** www.mercuresheffieldparkway.com
dir: M1 junct 33, just off A630 Parkway, 4m from city centre

Modern property situated just a short drive from the city centre; the smartly
appointed bedrooms are equipped with modern facilities and are ideally suited for
the business or leisure guest. The open-plan public areas feature a bar and
Brasserie 59, where a good choice of home-made dishes is available.

Rooms 78 (12 fmly) ↟ **Facilities** FTV WiFi ↘ Gym Xmas New Year **Conf** Class 80
Board 40 Thtr 120 Del from £125 to £210 **Services** Lift Air con **Parking** 100
Notes Civ Wed 100

Kenwood Hall

★★★★ 73% HOTEL

tel: 0114 258 3811 **Kenwood Rd S7 1NQ**
web: www.principal-hayley.com
dir: A61 (Barnsley ring road) into St Mary's Rd. Straight over rdbt, left into London Rd,
right at lights. 2nd exit at 2nd rdbt, hotel ahead

Kenwood Hall is a smart, modern hotel peacefully located in a residential suburb a
few miles from the city centre. The stylishly decorated bedrooms are spacious, quiet
and well equipped. The hotel also has a wide range of leisure and meeting
facilities, and secure parking is located in extensive landscaped gardens.

Rooms 114 (8 fmly) **Facilities** STV WiFi ⊛ Fishing Gym Steam room Sauna Solarium
Beauty treatment rooms New Year **Conf** Class 100 Board 60 Thtr 250 **Services** Lift
Parking 150 **Notes** Civ Wed 260

Novotel Sheffield Centre

★★★★ 73% HOTEL

tel: 0114 278 1781 **50 Arundel Gate S1 2PR**
email: h1348@accor.com **web:** www.novotel.com
dir: Between Registry Office & Crucible/Lyceum Theatres, follow signs to Town Hall/
Theatres & Hallam University

In the heart of the city centre, this hotel has stylish public areas including a very
modern restaurant, indoor swimming pool and a range of meeting rooms. Spacious
bedrooms are suitable for family occupation, and the Novation rooms are ideal for
business users.

Rooms 144 (134 fmly) ↟ **Facilities** STV FTV WiFi ⊛ Gym Steam room Xmas
Conf Class 180 Board 100 Thtr 220 **Services** Lift Air con **Parking** 60
Notes Civ Wed 180

Best Western Plus Aston Hall Hotel

★★★ 83% HOTEL

tel: 0114 287 2309 **Worksop Rd, Aston S26 2EE**
email: reservations@astonhallhotel.co.uk **web:** www.astonhallhotel.co.uk
dir: M1 junct 31, follow A57 to Sheffield & follow signs to hotel

Originally built as a manor house and set in spacious grounds with open views across the countryside to the south of the city, this hotel is well located for the M1, Meadowhall, the city, or touring. Extensive conference and banqueting facilities along with picturesque grounds make it an ideal wedding venue. Bedrooms are comfortable and well equipped.

Rooms 52 (6 annexe) (13 GF) ⋒ **Facilities** FTV WiFi ⋫ Gym Xmas New Year **Conf** Class 200 Board 60 Thtr 300 **Services** Lift **Parking** 90 **Notes** ⊗ Civ Wed 300

Best Western Plus Mosborough Hall Hotel

★★★ 82% HOTEL

tel: 0114 248 4353 **High St, Mosborough S20 5EA**
email: hotel@mosboroughhall.co.uk **web:** www.mosboroughhall.co.uk
dir: M1 junct 30, A6135 towards Sheffield. Follow Eckington/Mosborough signs 2m. Sharp bend at top of hill, hotel on right

This 16th-century, Grade II listed manor house is set in gardens not far from the M1 and is convenient for the city centre. The bedrooms offer very high quality and good amenities; some are very spacious. There is a galleried lounge and conservatory bar, and freshly prepared dishes are served in the traditional style dining room.

Rooms 44 (17 GF) ⋒ **Facilities** FTV WiFi ⋫ Spa & beauty treatments Xmas New Year **Conf** Class 125 Board 70 Thtr 220 **Parking** 100 **Notes** Civ Wed 250

Best Western Cutlers Hotel

★★★ 75% METRO HOTEL

tel: 0114 273 9939 **Theatreland George St S1 2PF**
email: enquiries@cutlershotel.co.uk **web:** www.cutlershotel.co.uk
dir: M1 junct 33. At Park Sq follow signs to City Centre & Theatres. At top of Commercial St, left into Arundel Gate. Into right lane, at lights right into Norfolk St, 2nd right into George St. Hotel 50mtrs on left

A modern hotel situated in the city centre with close links to the Crucible theatre and many other city centre attractions. Bedrooms are comfortable and well appointed. Room service and bar snacks are available 24-hours and a small bar dining menu is available on weekdays. Parking is free in a nearby NCP when booking direct with the hotel.

Rooms 45 (2 fmly) **Facilities** STV FTV WiFi **Services** Lift

Premier Inn Sheffield (Arena)

BUDGET HOTEL

tel: 0871 527 8964 (Calls cost 13p per minute plus your phone company's access charge)
Attercliffe Common Rd S9 2LU
web: www.premierinn.com
dir: M1 junct 34, follow signs to city centre. Hotel opposite Arena

High quality, budget accommodation ideal for both families and business travellers. Spacious, en suite bedrooms feature tea and coffee making facilities, and Freeview TV in most hotels. Internet access and WiFi are available for a small fee. The adjacent family restaurant features a wide and varied menu. See also the Hotel Groups pages.

Rooms 95

Premier Inn Sheffield City Centre Angel St

BUDGET HOTEL

tel: 0871 527 8970 (Calls cost 13p per minute plus your phone company's access charge)
Angel St, (Corner of Bank Street) S3 8LN
web: www.premierinn.com
dir: M1 junct 33, follow city centre, A630, A57 signs. At Park Square rdbt 4th exit (A61 Barnsley). Left at 4th lights into Snig Hill, right at lights into Bank St

Rooms 160

Premier Inn Sheffield City Centre (St Mary's Gate)

BUDGET HOTEL

tel: 0871 527 8972 (Calls cost 13p per minute plus your phone company's access charge)
Young St, St Marys Gate S1 4LA
web: www.premierinn.com
dir: M1 junct 33, A630, A57 follow Sheffield City Centre signs. At Park Square rdbt 3rd exit signed A61/Chesterfield. At Granville Square right onto A61 signed Ring Rd. Keep in left lane. At rdbt 3rd exit signed A621. Left into Cumberland St. Left into South Lane. Right into Young St

Rooms 122

Premier Inn Sheffield (Meadowhall)

BUDGET HOTEL

tel: 0871 527 8966 (Calls cost 13p per minute plus your phone company's access charge)
Sheffield Rd, Meadowhall S9 2YL
web: www.premierinn.com
dir: On A61/8 approx 6m from city centre

Rooms 103

Ibis Budget Sheffield Arena

AA Advertised

tel: 0114 243 4109 **298 Attercliffe Common S9 2AG**
email: H6176@accor.com **web:** www.ibishotel.com
dir: M1 junct 33, follow signs for Sheffield City Centre. Park Square rdbt after approx 7m. Take 5th exit (Ponds Forge)

Modern, budget hotel offering comfortable accommodation in bright and practical bedrooms. Breakfast is self-service and dinner is available in the restaurant.

Rooms 95 **Facilities** FTV WiFi **Services** Lift **Notes** ⊗

Ibis Sheffield City

AA Advertised

tel: 0114 241 9600 **Shude Hill S1 2AR**
email: H2891@accor.com **web:** www.ibishotel.com
dir: M1 junct 33, follow signs to Sheffield City Centre A630/A57, at rdbt take 5th exit, signed Ponds Forge, for hotel

Modern, budget hotel offering comfortable accommodation in bright and practical bedrooms. Breakfast is self-service and dinner is available in the restaurant.

Rooms 95 (15 fmly) (3 GF) ⋒ **Facilities** STV WiFi ⋫ **Services** Lift

S

SHEPTON MALLET
Somerset

Map 4 ST64

Charlton House Spa Hotel
★★★★ 80% ◉◉ HOTEL

tel: 0344 248 3830 **Charlton Rd BA4 4PR**
email: gm.charltonhousehotel@bannatyne.co.uk **web:** www.bannatyne.co.uk
dir: On A361 towards Frome, 1m from town centre

A peaceful location with grounds and relaxing spa facilities is just part of the charm of this interesting hotel. Individually designed bedrooms include larger suites and a luxurious lodge in the garden. Guests can relax in the 'shabby chic' lounges or bar area, or in the warmer months there's plenty of outdoor seating. Dinner in the stylish restaurant offers a selection of carefully prepared, high quality dishes. The spa offers a wide range of facilities including treatment rooms, hydrotherapy pool, crystal room, sauna and a fitness studio. The hotel is a popular wedding venue.

Rooms 28 (6 annexe) (3 fmly) (12 GF) ♠ **D** £85-£400 (incl. bkfst)* **Facilities** Spa FTV WiFi ☜ ☊ Gym Sauna Steam room Laconium Experience showers Xmas New Year **Conf** Class 50 Board 25 Thtr 100 Del from £170 to £279* **Parking** 70 **Notes** LB ⊗ Civ Wed 120

SHERBORNE
Dorset

Map 4 ST61

Eastbury Hotel
★★★ 80% ◉◉ HOTEL

tel: 01935 813131 **Long St DT9 3BY**
email: enquiries@theeastburyhotel.co.uk **web:** www.theeastburyhotel.co.uk
dir: From A30 W'bound, left into North Rd, then St Swithin's, left at bottom, hotel 800yds on right

Much of the building's original Georgian charm and elegance is maintained at this smart, comfortable hotel. Just five minutes' stroll from the abbey and close to the town centre, the Eastbury's friendly and attentive staff ensure a relaxed and enjoyable stay. Award-winning cuisine is served in the attractive dining room, overlooking the walled garden, with an alfresco bistro option also available.

Rooms 23 (1 fmly) (3 GF) ♠ **S** £80-£85; **D** £145-£155* **Facilities** FTV WiFi ☟ ☜ New Year **Conf** Class 40 Board 28 Thtr 80 Del £122* **Parking** 30 **Notes** LB Civ Wed 80

Best Western The Grange at Oborne
BW Best Western.
★★★ 79% HOTEL

tel: 01935 813463 **Oborne DT9 4LA**
email: reception@thegrange.co.uk **web:** www.thegrangeatoborne.co.uk
dir: Exit A30, follow signs through village

Set in beautiful gardens in a quiet hamlet, this 200-year-old, family-run hotel has a wealth of charm and character. It offers friendly hospitality together with attentive service. Bedrooms are comfortable and tastefully appointed, public areas are elegantly furnished, and the popular restaurant offers a good selection of dishes.

Rooms 18 (3 fmly) (2 GF) ♠ **S** £89-£169; **D** £99-£179 (incl. bkfst) **Facilities** STV WiFi ☟ Xmas New Year **Conf** Class 40 Board 30 Thtr 80 Del from £147 to £187 **Parking** 45 **Notes** ⊗ Civ Wed 120

SHERINGHAM
Norfolk

Map 13 TG14

Dales Country House Hotel
★★★★ 81% ◉◉ HOTEL

tel: 01263 824555 **Lodge Hill, Upper Sheringham NR26 8TJ**
email: dales@mackenziehotels.com **web:** www.mackenziehotels.com
dir: From Sheringham take B1157 to Upper Sheringham. Through village, hotel on left

Dales Country House is a superb Grade II listed building situated in extensive landscaped grounds on the edge of Sheringham Park. The attractive public rooms are full of original character; they include a choice of lounges as well as an intimate restaurant and a cosy lounge bar. The spacious bedrooms are individually decorated with co-ordinated soft furnishings and many thoughtful touches.

Rooms 21 (5 GF) ♠ **S** fr £107; **D** fr £174 (incl. bkfst)* **Facilities** WiFi ☊ ☜ Giant garden chess & jenga Xmas New Year **Conf** Class 20 Board 27 Thtr 40 **Services** Lift **Parking** 50 **Notes** LB No children 14yrs

SHIFNAL
Shropshire

Map 10 SJ70

Park House Hotel
★★★★ 76% ◉ HOTEL

tel: 01952 460128 **Park St TF11 9BA**
email: reception@parkhousehotel.net **web:** www.parkhousehotel.net
dir: M54 junct 4, A464 (Wolverhampton road) for approx 2m, under railway bridge, hotel 100yds on left

Park House Hotel was created from what were originally two country houses of very different architectural styles. Located on the edge of this historic market town, it offers guests easy access to motorway networks, as well as a choice of banqueting and meeting rooms, plus leisure facilities. Butlers Bar and Restaurant is the setting for imaginative food. Service is friendly and attentive.

Rooms 54 (16 annexe) (4 fmly) (8 GF) (4 smoking) ♠ **Facilities** STV FTV WiFi ☟ ☜ Gym Steam room Sauna Xmas New Year **Conf** Class 80 Board 40 Thtr 160 **Services** Lift **Parking** 90 **Notes** LB Civ Wed 200

SHIPLEY
West Yorkshire

Map 19 SE13

Ibis Bradford Shipley
ibis
AA Advertised

tel: 01274 589333 **Quayside, Salts Mill Rd BD18 3ST**
email: H3158@accor.com **web:** www.ibishotel.com
dir: Follow tourist signs for Salts Mill. Follow A650 signs through Bradford for approx 5m to Shipley

Modern, budget hotel offering comfortable accommodation in bright and practical bedrooms. Breakfast is self-service and dinner is available in the restaurant.

Rooms 78 (20 fmly) (22 GF) ♠ **Facilities** FTV WiFi Free use of gym next door New Year **Conf** Class 16 Board 18 Thtr 20 **Services** Lift **Parking** 100

SHREWSBURY
Shropshire

Map 15 SJ41

Albright Hussey Manor Hotel & Restaurant

★★★★ 77% HOTEL

tel: 01939 290571 & 290523 **Ellesmere Rd, Broad Oak SY4 3AF**
email: info@albrighthussey.co.uk **web:** www.albrighthussey.co.uk
dir: 2.5m N of Shrewsbury on A528, follow signs for Ellesmere

The estate was mentioned in the Domesday Book, but the current manor house is Tudor, dating from around 1524, and is approached over a moat. This Grade II listed, partly black-and-white timbered building maintains an abundance of original features including huge open fireplaces, oak-panelling and beams. The bedrooms, including four-poster rooms, are situated in either the sumptuously appointed main house or in the more modern wing. There's an intimate, award-winning restaurant and a comfortable cocktail bar and lounge.

Rooms 26 (4 fmly) (8 GF) ⚡ **Facilities** FTV WiFi ⚑ Xmas New Year **Conf** Class 180 Board 80 Thtr 250 Del from £125 to £155 **Parking** 100 **Notes** Civ Wed 180

Prince Rupert Hotel

★★★★ 76% HOTEL

tel: 01743 499955 **Butcher Row SY1 1UQ**
email: reservations@prince-rupert-hotel.co.uk **web:** www.princeruperthotel.co.uk
dir: Follow town centre signs, over English Bridge & Wyle Cop Hill. Right into Fish St, hotel 200yds

Parts of this popular town centre hotel date back to medieval times and many bedrooms have exposed beams and other original features. Luxury suites, family rooms and rooms with four-poster beds are all available. As an alternative to the main Royalist Restaurant, diners have a less formal option in Chambers, a popular brasserie. The Camellias Tea Rooms are adjacent, providing snacks and afternoon teas. The hotel's valet parking service is also commendable.

Rooms 70 ⚡ **S** £90-£100; **D** £135-£220 (incl. bkfst) **Facilities** FTV WiFi ⚑ Gym Weight training Steam shower Sauna Snooker room Hair salon Xmas New Year **Conf** Class 80 Board 40 Thtr 120 Del from £140 to £160 **Services** Lift **Parking** 70 **Notes** LB ⊗

Mercure Shrewsbury Albrighton Hall Hotel & Spa

★★★★ 75% COUNTRY HOUSE HOTEL

fOCUShotels
management limited

tel: 01939 291000 **Albrighton SY4 3AG**
email: H6629@accor.com **web:** www.mercureshrewsbury.co.uk
dir: From S: M6 junct 10a to M54 to end. From N: M6 junct 12 to M5 then M54. Follow signs Harlescott & Ellesmere to A528

Dating back to 1630, this former ancestral home is set in 15 acres of attractive gardens. The bedrooms are generally spacious and the stable rooms are particularly popular. Elegant public rooms have rich oak panelling and there is a modern, well-equipped health and fitness centre.

Rooms 87 (24 annexe) (11 fmly) (21 GF) **Facilities** Spa STV WiFi ⊗ ⚑ Gym Thermal suite Relaxation room Spray tan Exercise classes Xmas New Year **Conf** Class 100 Board 80 Thtr 250 Del from £130 to £145* **Services** Lift **Parking** 200 **Notes** ⊗ Civ Wed 250

Lion & Pheasant Hotel

★★★ 81% ◉◉ TOWN HOUSE HOTEL

tel: 01743 770345 **49-50 Wyle Cop SY1 1XJ**
email: info@lionandpheasant.co.uk **web:** www.lionandpheasant.co.uk
dir: From S & E: pass abbey, cross river on English Bridge to Wyle Cop, hotel on left. From N & W: follow Town Centre signs on one-way system to Wyle Cop. Hotel at bottom of hill on right

This 16th-century property stands on Wyle Cop, part of the historic centre of Shrewsbury. The interior decor is minimalist and uses natural materials such as limed oak, linens and silks. The bedrooms are of a high standard and include twin, double and family rooms. Award-winning food is offered in the first-floor restaurant and also in the ground-floor bar area.

Rooms 22 (2 fmly) ⚡ **Facilities** FTV WiFi ⚑ **Conf** Class 30 Board 30 Thtr 30 **Parking** 15 **Notes** ⊗ Closed 25-26 Dec

Abbots Mead Hotel

★★ 75% METRO HOTEL

tel: 01743 235281 **9 St Julian's Friars SY1 1XL**
email: res@abbotsmeadhotel.co.uk **web:** www.abbotsmeadhotel.co.uk
dir: From S into town, 2nd left after English Bridge

This well maintained Georgian town house is located in a quiet cul-de-sac, near the English Bridge and close to both the River Severn and town centre with its many restaurants. Bedrooms are compact, neatly decorated and well equipped. Two lounges are available in addition to an attractive dining room, the setting for breakfasts, and dinner parties by prior arrangement.

Rooms 16 (2 fmly) **S** £55-£65; **D** £78-£85 (incl. bkfst)* **Facilities** WiFi **Parking** 10 **Notes** Closed certain days at Xmas

Premier Inn Shrewsbury (Harmers Hill)

BUDGET HOTEL

tel: 0871 527 8974 (Calls cost 13p per minute plus your phone company's access charge)
Wem Rd, Harmer Hill SY4 3DS
web: www.premierinn.com
dir: M54 junct 7, A5 signed Telford for approx 7m, at rdbt take A49, approx 3m. At next 2 rdbts 2nd exit, at next rdbt 4th exit signed Ellesmere & A528. In approx 3m hotel on left

High quality, budget accommodation ideal for both families and business travellers. Spacious, en suite bedrooms feature tea and coffee making facilities, and Freeview TV in most hotels. Internet access and WiFi are available for a small fee. The adjacent family restaurant features a wide and varied menu. See also the Hotel Groups pages.

Rooms 20

Premier Inn Shrewsbury Town Centre

BUDGET HOTEL

tel: 0871 527 9402 (Calls cost 13p per minute plus your phone company's access charge)
Smithfield Rd SY1 1QB
web: www.premierinn.com
dir: Phone for directions

Rooms 136

SHREWSBURY *continued*

Drapers Hall

◉◉ ☷ RESTAURANT WITH ROOMS

tel: 01743 344679 **10 Saint Mary's Place SY1 1DZ**
email: goodfood@drapershallrestaurant.co.uk **web:** www.drapershallrestaurant.co.uk
dir: *From A5191 (Saint Mary's St) on one-way system into St Mary's Place*

Drapers Hall is a 16th-century, timber-framed property situated in the heart of the market town of Shrewsbury. Rooms differ in size, and all offer high levels of comfort and style, including two spacious suites. Modern bathrooms have a high quality finish and are well equipped for the modern traveller. The original beams and wood panels are complemented by striking art work and large gilt mirrors. A smart modern bar area successfully blends with the original architectural features, and has a great vibe. Accomplished cooking from Nigel Huxley can be enjoyed in a relaxing dining environment. Parking is available on request.

Rooms 6 (2 fmly)

Porter House SY1

◉ RESTAURANT WITH ROOMS

tel: 01743 358870 & 761220 **15 Saint Mary's St SY1 1EQ**
email: hello@porterhousesy1.co.uk **web:** www.porterhousesy1.co.uk
dir: *Follow one-way system around town, opposite St Mary's church*

This fine property is located in the heart of the town. The name comes from a cut of steak, which is relevant to the style of cuisine here, with a real emphasis on locally sourced, good quality steaks and grills, served in the award-winning vibrant restaurant or bar. The four individually designed bedrooms, including a suite, are very comfortable and have spacious and contemporary bathrooms. Breakfast offers a quality range of dishes. Secure parking is available in a nearby public car park.

Rooms 4 (1 fmly)

SIDCUP	Map 6 TQ47
Greater London	

Premier Inn London Sidcup Hotel

BUDGET HOTEL

tel: 0871 527 9640 **101-108 Station Rd, Sidcup DA15 7BS**
web: www.premierinn.com
dir: *From Sidcup station left into Station Rd, under rail bridge. Hotel on right at lights*

High quality, budget accommodation ideal for both families and business travellers. Spacious, en suite bedrooms feature tea and coffee making facilities, and Freeview TV in most hotels. Internet access and WiFi are available for a small fee. The adjacent family restaurant features a wide and varied menu. See also the Hotel Groups pages.

Rooms 100

SIDLESHAM	Map 5 SZ89
West Sussex	

The Crab & Lobster

◉◉ ☷ RESTAURANT WITH ROOMS

tel: 01243 641233 **Mill Ln PO20 7NB**
email: enquiries@crab-lobster.co.uk **web:** www.crab-lobster.co.uk
dir: *A27 onto B2145 signed Selsey. 1st left after garage at Sidlesham into Rookery Ln to Crab & Lobster*

Hidden away on the south coast near Pagham Harbour and only a short drive from Chichester is the stylish Crab & Lobster. Bedrooms are superbly appointed, and

bathrooms are a feature with luxury toiletries and powerful 'raindrop' showers. Guests can enjoy lunch or dinner in the smart restaurant where the menu offers a range of locally caught fresh fish together with other regionally-sourced, seasonal produce.

Rooms 4

SIDMOUTH	Map 3 SY18
Devon	

HIGHLY RECOMMENDED

Hotel Riviera

★★★★ 83% ◉◉ HOTEL

tel: 01395 515201 **The Esplanade EX10 8AY**
email: enquiries@hotelriviera.co.uk **web:** www.hotelriviera.co.uk
dir: *M5 junct 30 & follow A3052*

Overlooking the sea and close to the town centre, the Riviera is a fine example of Regency architecture. The large number of guests that become regular visitors here are testament to the high standards of service and hospitality offered. The front-facing bedrooms benefit from wonderful sea views, and the daily-changing menu places an emphasis on fresh, local produce.

Rooms 26 (6 fmly) ⌁ **S** £109-£215; **D** £198-£410 (incl. bkfst & dinner)*
Facilities FTV WiFi ⬇ ♫ Xmas New Year **Conf** Class 60 Board 30 Thtr 85
Services Lift **Parking** 26 **Notes** LB

See advert on opposite page

The Victoria Hotel

★★★★ 83% HOTEL

tel: 01395 512651 **The Esplanade EX10 8RY**
email: reservations@victoriahotel.co.uk **web:** www. victoriahotel.co.uk
dir: *On seafront*

This imposing building, with manicured gardens, is situated overlooking the town. Wonderful sea views can be enjoyed from many of the comfortable

bedrooms and elegant lounges. With indoor and outdoor leisure facilities, the hotel caters to a year-round clientele. Carefully prepared meals are served in the restaurant. Staff provide a professional and friendly service.

The Victoria Hotel

Rooms 62 (6 fmly) ⬈ **S** £150-£410; **D** £195-£410* **Facilities** FTV WiFi ⬇ ⓧ ↝ ➂ Putt green Hot stone relaxation beds Spa bath Sauna Beauty treatment room Games room ♫ Xmas New Year Child facilities **Conf** Thtr 60 **Services** Lift **Parking** 100 **Notes** LB ⊗

See advert on page 385

S

SIDMOUTH *continued*

The Belmont Hotel

★★★★ 81% HOTEL

Brend Hotels

tel: 01395 512555 **The Esplanade EX10 8RX**
email: reservations@belmont-hotel.co.uk **web:** www.belmont-hotel.co.uk
dir: *On seafront*

Prominently positioned on the seafront just a few minutes' walk from the town centre, this traditional hotel has many returning guests. A choice of comfortable lounges provides ample space for relaxation, and the air-conditioned restaurant has a pianist playing most evenings. Bedrooms are attractively furnished and many have fine views over the esplanade. Leisure facilities are available at the adjacent sister hotel, The Victoria.

Rooms 50 (1 fmly) (2 GF) ✿ **S** £150-£190; **D** £170-£265* **Facilities** STV WiFi ♨ Putt green Leisure facilities available at sister hotel ♫ Xmas New Year **Conf** Thtr 50 **Services** Lift **Parking** 45 **Notes** LB ⊗ Civ Wed 110

See advert on opposite page

Sidmouth Harbour Hotel

★★★ 81% HOTEL

tel: 01395 513252 **Manor Rd EX10 8RU**
email: stay@westcliffhotel.co.uk **web:** www.sidmouth-harbour-hotel.co.uk
dir: *Exit A3052 to Sidmouth then to seafront & esplanade, turn right, hotel directly ahead*

This charming hotel is ideally located within walking distance of Sidmouth's elegant promenade and beaches. The spacious lounges and the cocktail bar open onto a terrace which leads to the pool and croquet lawn. Bedrooms, several with balconies and glorious sea views, are spacious and comfortable, while the restaurant offers a choice of well-prepared dishes.

Rooms 40 (1 fmly) (5 GF) ✿ **Facilities** FTV WiFi ⚜ Putt green Xmas New Year **Conf** Class 20 Board 15 Thtr 30 **Services** Lift **Parking** 40 **Notes** Civ Wed 80

Bedford Hotel

★★★ 80% HOTEL

tel: 01395 513047 **Esplanade EX10 8NR**
email: info@bedfordhotelsidmouth.co.uk **web:** www.bedfordhotelsidmouth.co.uk
dir: *M5 junct 30, A3052 & to Sidmouth. Hotel at centre of Esplanade*

Situated on the seafront, this long established, family-run hotel provides a warm welcome and relaxing atmosphere. Bedrooms are well appointed and many have the added bonus of wonderful sea views. Public areas combine character and comfort with a choice of lounges in which to relax. In addition to the hotel dining room, Pyne's bar and restaurant offers an interesting range of dishes in a convivial environment.

Rooms 40 (3 fmly) (1 GF) ✿ **Facilities** FTV WiFi ♨ Xmas New Year **Services** Lift **Parking** 6

Royal Glen Hotel

★★★ 78% HOTEL

tel: 01395 513221 & 578124 **Glen Rd EX10 8RW**
email: info@royalglenhotel.co.uk **web:** www.royalglenhotel.co.uk
dir: *A303 to Honiton, A375 to Sidford, follow seafront signs, right onto esplanade, right at end into Glen Rd*

This historic 17th-century, Grade I listed hotel has been owned by the same family for several generations. The comfortable bedrooms are furnished in period style. Guests may use the well-maintained gardens and a heated indoor pool, and can enjoy well-prepared food in the elegant dining room.

Rooms 32 (3 fmly) (3 GF) ✿ **S** £48-£82; **D** £96-£184 (incl. bkfst)* **Facilities** FTV WiFi ⊛ Gym Massage & aromatherapy room **Services** Lift **Parking** 22 **Notes** LB Closed Dec-21 Feb

The Royal York & Faulkner Hotel

★★★ 76% HOTEL

tel: 01395 513043 & 0800 220714 **The Esplanade EX10 8AZ**
email: stay@royalyorkhotel.co.uk **web:** www.royalyorkhotel.co.uk
dir: *M5 junct 30 take A3052, 10m to Sidmouth, hotel in centre of Esplanade*

This seafront hotel, owned and run by the same family for over 60 years, maintains its Regency charm and grandeur. The attractive bedrooms vary in size, and many have balconies and sea views. Public rooms are spacious, and traditional dining is offered, alongside Blinis Café-Bar, which is more contemporary in style and offers coffees, lunch and afternoon tea. The spa facilities include a hydrotherapy pool, steam room, sauna and a variety of treatments.

Rooms 72 (2 annexe) (8 fmly) (5 GF) ✿ **S** £59.50-£101; **D** £119-£223 (incl. bkfst & dinner)* **Facilities** Spa FTV WiFi ♨ HL Hydrotherapy pool Steam room Sauna Complimentary use of nearby indoor pool ♫ Xmas New Year **Services** Lift **Parking** 20 **Notes** LB Closed Jan

Mount Pleasant Hotel

★★ 83% HOTEL

tel: 01395 514694 **Salcombe Rd EX10 8JA**
web: www.mountpleasant-hotel.co.uk
dir: *Exit A3052 at Sidford x-rds, in 1.25m turn left into Salcombe Rd, opposite Radway Cinema. Hotel on right after bridge*

Quietly located within almost an acre of gardens, this modernised Georgian hotel is minutes from the town centre and seafront. Bedrooms and public areas provide good levels of comfort and high quality furnishings. Guests return on a regular basis, especially to experience the friendly, relaxed atmosphere. The light and airy restaurant overlooks the pleasant garden and offers a daily-changing menu of traditional, yet imaginative home-cooked dishes.

Rooms 17 (1 fmly) (3 GF) **S** £70.50-£87; **D** £141-£174 (incl. bkfst & dinner)* **Facilities** Putt green **Parking** 20 **Notes** ⊗ No children 8yrs Closed Dec-Feb

S

SIDMOUTH *continued*

The Salty Monk

◉◉ ☒ RESTAURANT WITH ROOMS

tel: 01395 513174 **Church St, Sidford EX10 9QP**
email: saltymonk@btconnect.com **web:** www.saltymonk.co.uk
dir: *On A3052 opposite church in Sidford*

Set in the village of Sidford, this attractive property dates from the 16th century. There's plenty of style and appeal here and each bedroom has a unique identity. Bathrooms are equally special with multi-jet showers, spa baths and cosseting robes and towels. The output from the kitchen is impressive with excellent local produce very much in evidence, served in the elegant surroundings of the restaurant. A mini-spa facility is available.

Rooms 6 (1 annexe)

SILVERSTONE	Map 11 SP64
Northamptonshire	

Premier Inn Silverstone

BUDGET HOTEL

tel: 0871 527 8976 *(Calls cost 13p per minute plus your phone company's access charge)*
Brackley Hatch, Syresham NN13 5TX
web: www.premierinn.com
dir: *On A43 near Silverstone*

High quality, budget accommodation ideal for both families and business travellers. Spacious, en suite bedrooms feature tea and coffee making facilities, and Freeview TV in most hotels. Internet access and WiFi are available for a small fee. The adjacent family restaurant features a wide and varied menu. See also the Hotel Groups pages.

Rooms 79

SITTINGBOURNE	Map 7 TQ96
Kent	

HIGHLY RECOMMENDED

Hempstead House Country Hotel

★★★ 86% ◉ HOTEL

tel: 01795 428020 **London Rd, Bapchild ME9 9PP**
email: info@hempsteadhouse.co.uk **web:** www.hempsteadhouse.co.uk
dir: *1.5m from town centre on A2 towards Canterbury*

Expect a warm welcome at this charming detached Victorian property, situated amidst four acres of mature landscaped gardens. Bedrooms are attractively decorated with lovely co-ordinated fabrics, and are tastefully furnished and equipped with many thoughtful touches. Public rooms feature a choice of elegant lounges as well as a superb conservatory dining room. In summer guests can eat on the terraces. There is a spa and fitness studio.

Rooms 34 (7 fmly) (1 GF) ⚘ **Facilities** Spa STV FTV WiFi ⏲ ⛵ Gym Fitness studio Steam room Sauna Hydrotherapy pool Xmas New Year **Conf** Class 150 Board 100 Thtr 150 **Services** Lift **Parking** 200 **Notes** Civ Wed 150

Premier Inn Sittingbourne Kent

BUDGET HOTEL

tel: 0871 527 8978 *(Calls cost 13p per minute plus your phone company's access charge)*
Bobbing Corner, Sheppy Way, Bobbing ME9 8RZ
web: www.premierinn.com
dir: *M2 junct 5, A249 towards Sheerness, approx 2m. Take 1st slip road after A2 underpass. At rdbt take 1st exit, hotel on left*

High quality, budget accommodation ideal for both families and business travellers. Spacious, en suite bedrooms feature tea and coffee making facilities, and Freeview TV in most hotels. Internet access and WiFi are available for a small fee. The adjacent family restaurant features a wide and varied menu. See also the Hotel Groups pages.

Rooms 62

SKEGNESS	Map 17 TF56
Lincolnshire	

Best Western The Vine Hotel

★★★ 79% HOTEL

ⓑⓦ Best Western.

tel: 01754 763018 & 610611 **Vine Rd, Seacroft PE25 3DB**
email: info@thevinehotel.com **web:** www.bw-vinehotel.co.uk
dir: *A52 to Skegness, S towards Gibraltar Point, right into Drummond Rd, 0.5m, right into Vine Rd*

With its long history this traditional hotel is something of a local landmark. The smartly decorated bedrooms are well equipped and comfortably appointed. Public areas include two character bars that serve excellent local beers. Freshly prepared dishes are offered in the bar and the restaurant; service is both friendly and helpful.

Rooms 25 (3 fmly) **Facilities** FTV WiFi Xmas New Year **Conf** Class 25 Board 30 Thtr 100 **Parking** 50 **Notes** ⊗ Civ Wed 100

Best Western North Shore Hotel & Golf Course

★★★ 73% HOTEL

ⓑⓦ Best Western.

tel: 01754 763298 **North Shore Rd PE25 1DN**
email: info@northshorehotel.co.uk **web:** www.northshorehotel.co.uk
dir: *1m N of town centre on A52, turn right into North Shore Rd*

This hotel enjoys an enviable position on the beachfront, adjacent to its own championship golf course and only ten minutes from the town centre. Spacious public areas include a terrace bar serving informal meals and real ales, a formal restaurant and impressive function rooms. Bedrooms are smartly decorated and thoughtfully equipped.

Rooms 34 (3 annexe) (4 fmly) (3 GF) ⚘ **Facilities** FTV WiFi ⚓ 18 Putt green Xmas New Year **Conf** Class 60 Board 60 Thtr 220 **Parking** 100 **Notes** ⊗ Civ Wed 180

S

The Coniston Hotel Country Estate and Spa

★★★★ 78% HOTEL

tel: 01756 748080 **Coniston Cold BD23 4EA**
email: info@theconistonhotel.com **web:** www.theconistonhotel.com
dir: On A65, 7m NW of Skipton, 8m from Settle

This privately owned hotel set in 1,400 acres of prime country estate is a haven for both leisure and corporate guests. All bedrooms and bathrooms are appointed to a very high standard; the bedroom wing offers large rooms with balconies. The reception, bar and restaurant have style and elegance, and the stunning spa adds to the impressive list of activities for guests.

Rooms 71 (13 fmly) (35 GF) ♠ **S** £130–£147; **D** £146–£162 (incl. bkfst)
Facilities Spa STV FTV WiFi ♙ ☯ ⚲ Fishing Gym Clay pigeon shooting Falconry 4 x
4 off-road experience Fly fishing Archery ♬ Xmas New Year **Conf** Class 80 Board 50
Thtr 200 Del from £139 to £169 **Services** Lift **Parking** 170 **Notes** LB Civ Wed 120

Premier Inn Skipton North (Gargrave)

BUDGET HOTEL

tel: 0871 527 8980 *(Calls cost 13p per minute plus your phone company's access charge)*
Hellifield Rd, Gargrave BD23 3NB
web: www.premierinn.com
dir: NW of Skipton at rdbt junct of A59 & A65, take A65 signed Kendal, Settle & Gargrave.
3.5m. Through Gargrave. Hotel on left

High quality, budget accommodation ideal for both families and business travellers. Spacious, en suite bedrooms feature tea and coffee making facilities, and Freeview TV in most hotels. Internet access and WiFi are available for a small fee. The adjacent family restaurant features a wide and varied menu. See also the Hotel Groups pages.

Rooms 40

Hilton London Heathrow Airport Terminal 5

★★★★ 82% ◉ HOTEL

tel: 01753 686860 **Poyle Rd, Colnbrook SL3 0FF**
email: heathrowairportterminal5.info@hilton.com **web:** www.hilton.com/heathrowt5

Hilton London Heathrow Airport Terminal 5, is located just one mile from Terminal 5 with easy access to the M25. Bedrooms offer practical and modern amenities such as soundproof windows and high quality comfortable beds, so that guests will enjoy a peaceful night sleep. A complimentary shuttle service is available to businesses in Stockley Park and Bedfront Lakes. It is an ideal venue for conferences, meetings and banqueting events for up to 1,000 guests. There are two restaurants; The Gallery offering traditional British dishes, or Mr Todiwala's which offers Pan-Indian cuisine. Guests can relax in the luxury onsite Spa and 24 Fitness Centre.

Rooms 350 (4 fmly) ♠ **Facilities** Spa STV FTV WiFi ♙ Gym **Conf** Class 430 Board 78
Thtr 1400 **Services** Lift Air con **Parking** 486 **Notes** ⊗ Civ Wed 1170

Premier Inn Slough

BUDGET HOTEL

tel: 0871 527 8982 *(Calls cost 13p per minute plus your phone company's access charge)*
76 Uxbridge Rd SL1 1SU
web: www.premierinn.com
dir: 2m from M4 junct 5, 3m from junct 6. Just off A4

High quality, budget accommodation ideal for both families and business travellers. Spacious, en suite bedrooms feature tea and coffee making facilities, and Freeview TV in most hotels. Internet access and WiFi are available for a small fee. The adjacent family restaurant features a wide and varied menu. See also the Hotel Groups pages.

Rooms 129

See also **Dorridge**

The St Johns Hotel

★★★★ 73% HOTEL

tel: 0121 711 3000 & 712 7601 **651 Warwick Rd B91 1AT**
email: enquiries.stjohns@principal-hayley.com **web:** www.principal-hayley.com
dir: M42 junct 5, A41 (Solihull Bypass) signed Solihull. At lights left into Load Ln (signed Solihull Town Centre). At next rdbt 3rd exit onto B425 (Warwick Rd). Hotel on right

With its town centre location, this modern hotel is conveniently situated for the NEC, Birmingham and many local attractions. Bedrooms are air conditioned, attractively decorated and equipped with a comprehensive range of extras. The hotel provides extensive conference facilities, an indoor leisure facility and extensive parking.

Rooms 180 (1 fmly) (9 GF) ♠ **Facilities** STV FTV WiFi HL ☯ Gym Sauna Steam room
Nail treatment room Massage parlour Xmas New Year **Conf** Class 350 Board 40
Thtr 700 **Services** Lift Air con **Parking** 300 **Notes** Civ Wed 350

The Regency Hotel

★★★ 74% HOTEL

tel: 0121 745 6119 **Stratford Rd, Shirley B90 4EB**
email: solihull@corushotels.com **web:** www.corushotels.com/solihull
dir: M42 junct 4 onto A34 for Shirley, cross 1st 3 rdbts, then double back along dual carriageway, hotel on left

This much extended property is ideally located for access to the motorway network and Solihull's Touchwood centre. Rooms vary in style and size across the hotel; each is simply furnished and offers a good standard of comfort. The Circle health and fitness club is well equipped and includes an indoor pool. Ample free parking and WiFi available.

Rooms 111 (7 fmly) (13 GF) **Facilities** FTV WiFi ♙ ☯ supervised Gym Steam room
Sauna Xmas New Year **Conf** Class 80 Board 60 Thtr 180 **Services** Lift **Parking** 240
Notes LB Civ Wed 100

SOLIHULL *continued*

Premier Inn Solihull (Hockley Heath, M42)

BUDGET HOTEL

tel: 0871 527 8984 *(Calls cost 13p per minute plus your phone company's access charge)*
Stratford Rd, Hockley Heath B94 6NX
web: www.premierinn.com
dir: *On A3400, 2m S of M42 junct 4*

High quality, budget accommodation ideal for both families and business travellers. Spacious, en suite bedrooms feature tea and coffee making facilities, and Freeview TV in most hotels. Internet access and WiFi are available for a small fee. The adjacent family restaurant features a wide and varied menu. See also the Hotel Groups pages.

Rooms 78

Premier Inn Solihull (Shirley)

BUDGET HOTEL

tel: 0871 527 8988 *(Calls cost 13p per minute plus your phone company's access charge)*
Stratford Rd, Shirley B90 3AG
web: www.premierinn.com
dir: *M42 junct 4 follow signs for Birmingham. Hotel in Shirley town centre on A34*

Rooms 43

Premier Inn Solihull South (M42)

BUDGET HOTEL

tel: 0871 527 8986 *(Calls cost 13p per minute plus your phone company's access charge)*
Stratford Rd, Shirley B90 4EP
web: www.premierinn.com
dir: *M42 junct 4, A34 N. Hotel in 1m*

Rooms 51

Premier Inn Solihull Town Centre

BUDGET HOTEL

tel: 0871 527 9366 *(Calls cost 13p per minute plus your phone company's access charge)*
Station Rd B91 3RX
web: www.premierinn.com
dir: *M42 junct 5. At rdbt, take 3rd exit onto A41. At lights, turn left onto Lode Lane. At rdbt, take 2nd exit & continue down Lode Lane. At rdbt take 1st exit onto Station Road*

Rooms 115

Find out more about the AA Hotel of the Year for England on page 13

Hampton Manor

 RESTAURANT WITH ROOMS

tel: 01675 446080 **Shadowbrook Ln, Hampton-in-Arden B92 0EN**
email: info@hamptonmanor.com **web:** www.hamptonmanor.com
dir: *M42 junct 6 follow signs for A45 (Birmingham). At 1st rdbt, 1st exit onto B4438 (Catherine de Barnes Ln). Left into Shadowbrook Ln*

Hampton Manor is set in 45 acres of mature woodland, only minutes from Birmingham's major air, rail and road links and the NEC. The manor offers luxurious accommodation with a contemporary and sophisticated style while still maintaining many of its original features and heritage. The bedrooms are all beautifully and uniquely designed and boast sumptuous beds. Fine dining can be enjoyed at Peel's restaurant, which is a fabulous venue for innovative cooking, and will prove the highlight of any stay.

Rooms 15 (3 fmly)

SOUTHAMPTON   Map 5 SU41
Hampshire

See also **Botley**

Botleigh Grange Hotel

★★★★ 76% HOTEL

tel: 01489 787700 & 776969 **Grange Rd, Hedge End SO30 2GA**
email: enquiries@botleighgrange.com **web:** www.botleighgrange.com
dir: *M27 junct 7, A334 to Botley, hotel 1m on left*

This impressive mansion, situated close to the M27, displays good quality throughout. The bedrooms are spacious with a good range of facilities. Public areas include a large conference room and a pleasant terrace with views overlooking the gardens and lake. The restaurant offers interesting menus using fresh, local produce.

Rooms 56 (10 fmly) (9 GF) **Facilities** Spa STV FTV WiFi ⬥ ☜ Fishing Sauna Steam room Relaxation room Monsoon showers Xmas New Year **Conf** Class 120 Board 40 Thtr 500 **Services** Lift **Parking** 300 **Notes** Civ Wed 180

Novotel Southampton

★★★★ 76% HOTEL

NOVOTEL
HOTELS & RESORTS

tel: 023 8033 0550 **1 West Quay Rd SO15 1RA**
email: H1073@accor.com **web:** www.novotel.com
dir: *M27 junct 3, follow city centre/A33 signs. In 1m take right lane for West Quay & Dock Gates 4-10. Hotel entrance on left. Turn at lights by McDonalds, left at rdbt, hotel straight ahead*

Novotel Southampton is a modern, purpose-built hotel situated close to the city centre, railway station, ferry terminal and major road networks. The brightly decorated bedrooms are ideal for families and business guests; four rooms have facilities for the less mobile. The open-plan public areas include the Garden Brasserie, a bar and a leisure complex.

Rooms 121 (50 fmly) ⬧ **Facilities** STV FTV WiFi ⬥ ☜ Gym Sauna **Conf** Class 250 Board 150 Thtr 450 **Services** Lift **Parking** 300 **Notes** Civ Wed 300

Mercure Southampton Centre Dolphin Hotel

★★★★ 72% 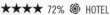 HOTEL

tel: 023 8038 6460 **34-35 High St SO14 2HN**
email: H7876@accor.com **web:** www.mercure.com
dir: *From A33 follow signs for Docks, Old Town & Isle of Wight ferry. At ferry terminal right into High Street, hotel 400yds on left*

Originally a coaching inn, this hotel enjoys a central location set almost in the heart of the town, yet close to the ferry terminals. The bedrooms are appointed to a high standard, and public areas include a traditional bar, popular restaurant and two meeting rooms. Parking at the rear of the hotel is an added bonus.

Rooms 99 (9 annexe) (6 fmly) (27 GF) ⌇ **Facilities** FTV WiFi Xmas New Year **Conf** Class 50 Board 40 Thtr 120 **Services** Lift **Parking** 80 **Notes** Civ Wed 120

Best Western Chilworth Manor

★★★ 78% 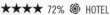 HOTEL

tel: 023 8076 7333 **Chilworth SO16 7PT**
email: sales@chilworth-manor.co.uk **web:** www.bw-chilworthmanor.co.uk
dir: *1m from M3/M27 junct on A27 Romsey Rd N from Southampton. Pass Chilworth Arms on left, in 200mtrs turn left at Southampton Science Park sign. Hotel immediately right*

Set in 12 acres of delightful grounds, this attractive Edwardian manor house is conveniently located for Southampton and also the New Forest National Park. Bedrooms are located in both the main house and an adjoining wing. The hotel is particularly popular as both a conference and a wedding venue.

Rooms 97 (1 fmly) (23 GF) ⌇ **Facilities** Spa FTV WiFi ↯ ⚙ Gym Trail walking Giant chess Petanque Conservation area Xmas New Year **Conf** Class 60 Board 40 Thtr 150 **Services** Lift **Parking** 200 **Notes** ⊗ Civ Wed 105

The Elizabeth House Hotel

★★ 81% HOTEL

tel: 023 8022 4327 **42-44 The Avenue SO17 1XP**
email: mail@elizabethhousehotel.com **web:** www.elizabethhousehotel.com
dir: *On A33, hotel on left after Southampton Common, before main lights*

This hotel is conveniently situated close to the city centre, so provides an ideal base for both business and leisure guests. The bedrooms are well equipped and are attractively furnished with comfort in mind. There is a cosy and atmospheric bistro in the cellar where evening meals are served, and an attractive and versatile function room is also available. Complimentary parking is provided for guests.

Rooms 27 (7 annexe) (9 fmly) (8 GF) ⌇ **S** £75-£84.50; **D** £85-£94.50 (incl. bkfst)* **Facilities** FTV WiFi ↯ **Conf** Class 24 Board 24 Thtr 40 Del £112.50* **Parking** 31

Holiday Inn Express Southampton M27 Jct 7

BUDGET HOTEL

tel: 023 8060 6060 **Botley Rd, West End SO30 3XA**
email: reservations@expressbyholidayinn.uk.net **web:** www.hiesouthamptonhotel.com
dir: *M27 junct 7, follow brown Ageas Bowl signs. Hotel 1m from junct 7 at entrance to The Ageas Bowl on corner Marshall Drive & Botley Rd*

Set in landscaped gardens this hotel, adjacent to the Ageas Bowl, is conveniently located for Southampton Airport, Cruise Terminal and Docks and has ample free parking. There is an air-conditioned conservatory restaurant serving freshly prepared evening meals and complimentary hot breakfast, as well as a fully licensed bar and lounge area with a 42" plasma TV. The hotel offers free WiFi

throughout. Leisure facilities are available at the adjacent Virgin Active Leisure Centre for an additional fee. There are 5 air conditioned meeting rooms for up to 52 delegates. See also the Hotel Groups pages.

Rooms 176 (129 fmly) (38 GF) ⌇ **D** £59-£109 (incl. bkfst)* **Conf** Class 26 Board 20 Thtr 52 Del from £119 to £159*

Premier Inn Southampton Airport

BUDGET HOTEL

tel: 0871 527 8998 *(Calls cost 13p per minute plus your phone company's access charge)*
Mitchell Way SO18 2XU
web: www.premierinn.com
dir: *M27 junct 5, A335 towards Eastleigh. Right at rdbt into Wide Lane. 1st exit at next rdbt into Mitchell Way*

High quality, budget accommodation ideal for both families and business travellers. Spacious, en suite bedrooms feature tea and coffee making facilities, and Freeview TV in most hotels. Internet access and WiFi are available for a small fee. The adjacent family restaurant features a wide and varied menu. See also the Hotel Groups pages.

Rooms 121

Premier Inn Southampton City Centre

BUDGET HOTEL

tel: 0871 527 9266 *(Calls cost 13p per minute plus your phone company's access charge)*
6 Dials, New Rd SO14 0YN
web: www.premierinn.com
dir: *M27 junct 5, A335 signed City Centre. At Charlotte Place rdbt take 3rd exit into East Park Terrace, 1st left into New Rd. Hotel on right*

Rooms 172

Premier Inn Southampton North

BUDGET HOTEL

tel: 0871 527 9002 *(Calls cost 13p per minute plus your phone company's access charge)*
Romsey Rd, Nursling SO16 0XJ
web: www.premierinn.com
dir: *M27 junct 3, M271 towards Romsey. At next rdbt take 3rd exit towards Southampton (A3057). Hotel 1.5m on right*

Rooms 80

Premier Inn Southampton West Quay

BUDGET HOTEL

tel: 0871 527 9298 *(Calls cost 13p per minute plus your phone company's access charge)*
Harbour Pde SO15 1ST
web: www.premierinn.com
dir: *M27 junct 3, follow M271(S)/Southampton/The Docks signs, onto M271, at Redbridge rdbt onto A35 follow Southampton/The Docks/A3024 signs. Merge onto A35 (Redbridge Rd), continue onto Millbrook Flyover/A3024, right at West Quay Rd/A3057, left after Ikea into Harbour Parade*

Rooms 155

S

SOUTHAMPTON *continued*

Ibis Budget Southampton Centre

AA Advertised

tel: 023 8022 7705 **Western Esplanade, 3 West Quay Rd SO15 1RA**
email: H6209@accor.com **web:** www.ibishotel.com
dir: *In heart of city centre, opposite Southampton Central station. Ferry port is 500mtrs from hotel*

Modern, budget hotel offering comfortable accommodation in bright and practical bedrooms. Breakfast is self-service and dinner is available in the restaurant.

Rooms 124 (16 GF) ☏ **Facilities** FTV WiFi HL **Services** Lift **Parking** 120

Ibis Southampton Centre

AA Advertised

tel: 023 8063 4463 **West Quay Rd, Western Esplanade SO15 1RA**
email: H1039@accor.com **web:** www.ibishotel.com
dir: *M27 junct 3, M271, left to city centre (A35), follow Old Town Waterfront to 4th lights, left, left again, hotel opposite station*

Modern, budget hotel offering comfortable accommodation in bright and practical bedrooms. Breakfast is self-service and dinner is available in the restaurant.

Rooms 93 **Facilities** WiFi **Conf** Class 50 Board 40 Thtr 80 **Services** Lift Air con **Parking** 261

Ennio's Restaurant & Boutique Rooms

🍴 RESTAURANT WITH ROOMS

tel: 023 8022 1159 & 07748 966113 **Town Quay Rd SO14 3AS**
email: info@ennios.co.uk **web:** www.ennios.co.uk
dir: *Opposite Red Funnel Ferry terminal*

This fine property, lovingly converted from a former Victorian warehouse, offers luxurious accommodation on Southampton's waterfront. All rooms are en suite and are furnished to a very high standard, including mini-bars and over-sized showers. Downstairs, the popular Ennio's Restaurant and bar is the ideal setting in which to dine, offering an authentic Italian atmosphere and a wonderful selection of dishes. There is limited parking available to the rear of the building.

Rooms 10

Cave Castle Hotel & Country Club

★★★ 79% HOTEL

tel: 01430 422245 **Church Hill HU15 2EU**
email: info@cavecastlehotel.com **web:** www.cavecastlehotel.com
dir: *In village, opposite school*

This beautiful Victorian manor retains original turrets, stone features and much charm, together with modern comforts and style. It stands in 150 acres of meadow and parkland that provide a peaceful setting. Bedrooms are a careful mix of traditional and contemporary styles. Public areas include a well-equipped leisure complex and pool.

Rooms 70 (5 fmly) (14 GF) ☏ **Facilities** Spa FTV WiFi ⌨ ⛳ supervised ⚓ 18 Putt green Fishing Gym New Year **Conf** Class 150 Board 100 Thtr 250 **Services** Lift **Parking** 100 **Notes** ⊗ Civ Wed 150

Cotswold Water Park Four Pillars Hotel

★★★★ 80% HOTEL

tel: 0800 374692 & 01285 864000 **Lake 6 Spine Road East GL7 5FP**
email: waterpark@four-pillars.co.uk **web:** www.cotswoldwaterparkhotel.co.uk
dir: *Off A419, 3m from Cirencester. NB for Sav Nav use GL7 5TL*

This impressive hotel has well-appointed bedrooms and suites, conference facilities for up to 800 delegates, a spa with an 11-metre pool, a gym, a hydro pool, and treatment rooms. An excellent range of dining options is available, and a large car park is provided.

Rooms 328 (58 fmly) (126 GF) ☏ **Facilities** Spa FTV WiFi ⌨ ⛳ Fishing Gym Beauty treatment rooms & therapies Steam room Sauna Xmas New Year **Conf** Class 350 Board 68 Thtr 500 **Services** Lift **Parking** 500 **Notes** ⊗ Civ Wed 370

The Roslin Beach Hotel

★★★★ 82% 🏮 HOTEL

tel: 01702 586375 **Thorpe Esplanade, Thorpe Bay SS1 3BG**
email: info@roslinhotel.com **web:** www.roslinhotel.com
dir: *A127, follow Southend-on-Sea signs. Hotel between Walton Rd & Clieveden Rd on seafront*

This friendly hotel is situated at the quiet end of the esplanade, overlooking the beach and sea. The spacious bedrooms are pleasantly decorated and thoughtfully equipped; some rooms have superb sea views. Public rooms include a large lounge bar, the Mulberry Restaurant and a smart conservatory which overlooks the sea.

Rooms 62 (5 fmly) (11 GF) ☏ **S** £60-£90; **D** £90-£240 (incl. bkfst)* **Facilities** Spa FTV WiFi Gym Xmas New Year **Conf** Class 65 Board 45 Thtr 90 Del from £150 to £300* **Parking** 48 **Notes** LB Civ Wed 100

Holiday Inn Southend

★★★ 73% 🏮 HOTEL

tel: 01702 543001 **77 Eastwoodbury Crescent SS2 6XG**
email: reservations@hisouthend.com **web:** www.hisouthend.com
dir: *M25 junct 29, A127 follow signs to London Southend Airport. Hotel 2mins away*

Built in 2012, Holiday Inn Southend offers a range of modern, well-appointed, stylish bedrooms. The public areas look very smart and have an open-plan contemporary image, and lounges are fitted out with designer furniture and seating. The award-winning 1935 Restaurant is situated on the fifth floor and overlooks the main runway of Southend airport. There are a range of conference facilities and business suites available along with secure parking for guests.

Rooms 129 (17 fmly) ☏ **S** £64-£179; **D** £64-£179 **Facilities** STV FTV WiFi HL Gym Xmas New Year **Conf** Class 50 Board 40 Thtr 140 Del from £129 to £189* **Services** Lift Air con **Parking** 250 **Notes** LB Civ Wed 140

Premier Inn Southend Airport

BUDGET HOTEL

tel: 0871 527 9008 *(Calls cost 13p per minute plus your phone company's access charge)*
Thanet Grange SS2 6GB
web: www.premierinn.com
dir: *At A127 & B1013 junct*

High quality, budget accommodation ideal for both families and business travellers. Spacious, en suite bedrooms feature tea and coffee making facilities, and Freeview TV in most hotels. Internet access and WiFi are available for a small fee. The adjacent family restaurant features a wide and varied menu. See also the Hotel Groups pages.

Rooms 80

Premier Inn Southend on Sea (Eastern Esplanade)

BUDGET HOTEL

tel: 0871 527 9504 *(Calls cost 13p per minute plus your phone company's access charge)*
Eastern Esplanade SS99 1YY
web: www.premierinn.com
dir: *A127 to Southend rail station. At lights, left onto A13 (signed Shoeburyness). At rdbt 3rd exit (signed Seafront). At end of road, left onto Eastern Esplanade (B1016). Hotel on left*

Rooms 81

Premier Inn Southend-on-Sea (Thorpe Bay)

BUDGET HOTEL

tel: 0871 527 9006 *(Calls cost 13p per minute plus your phone company's access charge)*
213 Eastern Esplanade SS1 3AD
web: www.premierinn.com
dir: *Follow signs for A1159 (A13) Shoebury onto dual carriageway. At rdbt, follow signs for Thorpe Bay & seafront, at seafront turn right. Hotel on right*

Rooms 43

SOUTH MIMMS SERVICE AREA (M25)   Map 6 TL20
Hertfordshire

Premier Inn South Mimms/Potters Bar

BUDGET HOTEL

tel: 0871 527 8990 *(Calls cost 13p per minute plus your phone company's access charge)*
Swanland Rd EN6 3NH
web: www.premierinn.com
dir: *M25 junct 23 & A1 take services exit off main rdbt then 1st left & follow hotel signs*

High quality, budget accommodation ideal for both families and business travellers. Spacious, en suite bedrooms feature tea and coffee making facilities, and Freeview TV in most hotels. Internet access and WiFi are available for a small fee. The adjacent family restaurant features a wide and varied menu. See also the Hotel Groups pages.

Rooms 142

Days Inn South Mimms - M25

AA Advertised

tel: 01707 665440 **Bignells Corner, Potters Bar EN6 3QQ**
email: south.mimms.hotel@welcomebreak.co.uk **web:** www.welcomebreak.co.uk
dir: *M25 junct 23, at rdbt follow signs*

This modern building offers accommodation in smart, spacious and well-equipped bedrooms, suitable for families and business travellers, and all with en suite bathrooms. Continental breakfast is available and other refreshments may be taken at the nearby family restaurant.

Rooms 75 (37 fmly) (23 GF) (10 smoking) **Facilities** FTV WiFi ♺ **Services** Lift
Parking 100

SOUTH NORMANTON   Map 16 SK45
Derbyshire

The Derbyshire Hotel

★★★★ 75% HOTEL

tel: 01773 812000 **Carter Lane East DE55 2EH**
email: reservations.derbyshire@principal-hayley.com **web:** www.principal-hayley.com
dir: *M1 junct 28, E on A38 to Mansfield*

Conveniently located by the motorway, this hotel offers comfortable accommodation and a relaxed informal atmosphere through the lounge bar and restaurant. The conference and meeting rooms are appointed to a smart modern standard; delegates also have use of on-site sauna, jacuzzi and steam room in the spa.

Rooms 157 (10 fmly) (61 GF) ⭑ **Facilities** Spa FTV WiFi ♺ ⟨🏊⟩ Gym Steam room Sauna New Year **Conf** Class 120 Board 25 Thtr 250 **Parking** 220 **Notes** Civ Wed 150

Premier Inn Mansfield

BUDGET HOTEL

tel: 0871 527 8758 *(Calls cost 13p per minute plus your phone company's access charge)*
Carter Lane East DE55 2EH
web: www.premierinn.com
dir: *M1 junct 28, A38 signed Mansfield. Entrance 200yds on left*

High quality, budget accommodation ideal for both families and business travellers. Spacious, en suite bedrooms feature tea and coffee making facilities, and Freeview TV in most hotels. Internet access and WiFi are available for a small fee. The adjacent family restaurant features a wide and varied menu. See also the Hotel Groups pages.

Rooms 120

SOUTHPORT   Map 15 SD31
Merseyside

Vincent Hotel

★★★★ 82% ⚛ TOWN HOUSE HOTEL

tel: 01704 883800 **98 Lord St PR8 1JR**
email: manager@thevincenthotel.com **web:** www.thevincenthotel.com
dir: *M58 junct 3, follow signs to Ormskirk & Southport*

This stylish, boutique property occupies a prime location on Southport's famous boulevard. Bedrooms, some with views of the beach, are appointed to a high standard with oversized beds, extremely well stocked mini-bars and stylish en suites with deep tubs. Public areas include a trendy cocktail bar, and an all-day dining concept. The friendly staff offer a professional and personalised service.

Rooms 59 (2 fmly) ⭑ **S** £93-£208; **D** £93-£208* **Facilities** Spa STV FTV WiFi ♺ Gym
Conf Class 96 Board 50 Thtr 196 Del from £130 to £145* **Services** Lift Air con
Parking 50 **Notes** ⊗ Civ Wed 150

S

SOUTHPORT *continued*

Best Western Royal Clifton Hotel & Spa

★★★ 75% HOTEL

tel: 01704 533771 **Promenade PR8 1RB**
email: sales@royalclifton.co.uk **web:** www.royalclifton.co.uk
dir: *Adjacent to Marine Lake*

This grand, traditional hotel benefits from a prime location on the promenade. Bedrooms range in size and style, but all are comfortable and thoughtfully equipped. Public areas include the lively Bar C, the elegant Pavilion Restaurant and a modern, well-equipped leisure club. Extensive conference and banqueting facilities make this hotel a popular function venue.

Rooms 120 (23 fmly) (6 GF) ♠ **Facilities** Spa FTV WiFi ⊳ HL ⊛ Gym Hair & beauty Sauna Steam room Aromatherapy ♫ Xmas New Year **Conf** Class 100 Board 65 Thtr 250 **Services** Lift **Parking** 60 **Notes** ⊗ Civ Wed 150

Premier Inn Southport Central

BUDGET HOTEL

tel: 0871 527 9012 *(Calls cost 13p per minute plus your phone company's access charge)*
Marine Dr PR8 1RY
web: www.premierinn.com
dir: *From Southport follow Promenade & Marine Drive signs. Hotel at junct of Marine Parade & Marine Drive*

High quality, budget accommodation ideal for both families and business travellers. Spacious, en suite bedrooms feature tea and coffee making facilities, and Freeview TV in most hotels. Internet access and WiFi are available for a small fee. The adjacent family restaurant features a wide and varied menu. See also the Hotel Groups pages.

Rooms 94

SOUTHSEA

See **Portsmouth & Southsea**

SOUTH SHIELDS
Tyne & Wear   Map 21 NZ36

Best Western The Sea Hotel

BW Best Western.

★★★ 75% HOTEL

tel: 0191 4270999 **Sea Rd NE33 2LD**
email: info@seahotel.co.uk **web:** www.seahotel.co.uk
dir: *A1(M), past Washington Services onto A194. Then A183 through town centre along Ocean Rd. Hotel on seafront*

Dating from the 1930s, this long-established business hotel overlooks the boating lake and the Tyne estuary. Bedrooms are generally spacious and well equipped and include five annexe rooms with wheelchair access. A range of generously portioned meals is served in both the bar and restaurant.

Rooms 37 (5 annexe) (5 fmly) (5 GF) ♠ **Facilities** FTV WiFi ⊳ New Year **Conf** Class 100 Board 50 Thtr 200 Del from £99 to £119* **Parking** 70 **Notes** RS 26 Dec

Premier Inn South Shields (Port of Tyne)

BUDGET HOTEL

tel: 0871 527 8992 *(Calls cost 13p per minute plus your phone company's access charge)*
Hobson Av, Newcastle Rd NE34 9PQ
web: www.premierinn.com
dir: *A1(M) onto A194(M). 2nd exit at rdbt into Leam Lane (A194). At next rdbt 2nd exit, next rdbt 3rd exit, next rdbt 2nd exit (A194), next rdbt 2nd exit. Hotel on left adjacent to Taybarns*

High quality, budget accommodation ideal for both families and business travellers. Spacious, en suite bedrooms feature tea and coffee making facilities, and Freeview TV in most hotels. Internet access and WiFi are available for a small fee. The adjacent family restaurant features a wide and varied menu. See also the Hotel Groups pages.

Rooms 66

SOUTHWOLD
Suffolk   Map 13 TM57

Swan Hotel

★★★★ 78% ◉◉ HOTEL

tel: 01502 722186 **High St, Market Place IP18 6EG**
email: swan.hotel@adnams.co.uk **web:** www.adnams.co.uk
dir: *A1095 to Southwold. Hotel in town centre. Parking via archway to left of building*

The Swan Hotel is a charming 17th-century coaching inn situated in the heart of this bustling town centre overlooking the market place. Public rooms feature an elegant restaurant, a comfortable drawing room, a cosy bar and a lounge where guests can enjoy afternoon tea. The spacious bedrooms are attractively decorated, tastefully furnished and thoughtfully equipped.

Rooms 42 (17 annexe) (11 fmly) (17 GF) ♠ **Facilities** FTV WiFi HL Beauty treatment room Xmas New Year **Conf** Class 40 Board 30 Thtr 80 **Services** Lift **Parking** 32 **Notes** Civ Wed 60

S

Sutherland House

◎◎ RESTAURANT WITH ROOMS

tel: 01502 724544 **56 High St IP18 6DN**
email: enquiries@sutherlandhouse.co.uk **web:** www.sutherlandhouse.co.uk
dir: A1095 into Southwold, on High St on left after Victoria St

Situated in the heart of the bustling town centre, this delightful 16th-century house has a wealth of character - oak beams, exposed brickwork, open fireplaces and two superb ornate plasterwork ceilings. The stylish bedrooms are tastefully decorated using co-ordinated fabrics and include many thoughtful touches. Public rooms feature a large open-plan contemporary restaurant, which has been awarded two AA Rosettes. There's a modern British menu created with care, and the food miles are listed alongside each dish.

Rooms 4 (1 fmly)

SPALDING
Lincolnshire   Map 12 TF22

Woodlands Hotel

★★★ 75% SMALL HOTEL

tel: 01775 769933 **80 Pinchbeck Rd PE11 1QF**
email: reservations@woodlandshotelspalding.com
web: www.woodlandshotelspalding.com
dir: 10mins walk from city centre

A delightful Victorian house ideally situated just a short walk from the town centre. The public areas have many original features; they include the Oakleaf dining room, the Silver Birch meeting room and the Willows bar. The smartly decorated bedrooms have lovely co-ordinated soft furnishings and many thoughtful touches.

Rooms 17 (5 GF) ✆ **S** £65-£70; **D** £80-£100 (incl. bkfst)* **Facilities** FTV WiFi ⌂ HL **Conf** Class 30 Board 30 Thtr 60 Del from £100 to £130 **Parking** 30 **Notes** ⊗ Civ Wed 65

SPENNYMOOR
County Durham   Map 19 NZ23

Best Western Whitworth Hall Hotel

 Best Western.

★★★ 81% HOTEL

tel: 01388 811772 **Whitworth Hall Country Park DL16 7QX**
email: enquiries@whitworthhall.co.uk **web:** www.whitworthhall.co.uk
dir: A688 to Spennymoor, then Bishop Auckland. At rdbt right to Middlestone Moor. Left at lights, hotel on right

This hotel, peacefully situated in its own grounds in the centre of the deer park, offers comfortable accommodation. Spacious bedrooms, some with excellent views, have stylish and elegant decor. Public areas include a choice of restaurants and bars, a bright conservatory and well-equipped function and conference rooms.

Rooms 29 (2 fmly) (17 GF) **S** £75-£160; **D** £65-£175 (incl. bkfst) **Facilities** FTV WiFi ⌂ Fishing **Conf** Class 40 Board 30 Thtr 100 Del from £105 to £175 **Parking** 100 **Notes** LB ⊗ Civ Wed 100

STAFFORD
Staffordshire   Map 10 SJ92

The Moat House

★★★★ 80% ◎◎ HOTEL

tel: 01785 712217 **Lower Penkridge Rd, Acton Trussell ST17 0RJ**
email: info@moathouse.co.uk **web:** www.moathouse.co.uk
dir: M6 junct 13 onto A449 through Acton Trussell. Hotel on right on exiting village

This 17th-century timbered building, with an idyllic canal-side setting, has been skilfully extended. Bedrooms are stylishly furnished, well equipped and comfortable. The bar offers a range of snacks and the restaurant boasts a popular fine dining option where the head chef displays his skills using top quality produce.

Rooms 41 (4 fmly) (15 GF) ✆ **S** £80-£150; **D** £100-£170 (incl. bkfst)* **Facilities** FTV WiFi New Year **Conf** Class 60 Board 50 Thtr 200 Del from £150 to £175* **Services** Lift **Parking** 200 **Notes** ⊗ Closed 25 Dec Civ Wed 150

Best Western Tillington Hall Hotel

 Best Western.

★★★ 75% HOTEL

tel: 01785 253531 **Eccleshall Rd ST16 1JJ**
email: reservations@tillingtonhall.co.uk **web:** www.tillingtonhall.co.uk
dir: M6 junct 14, A5013 towards Stafford. Hotel 0.5m on left

Located close to the M6, this modern hotel is ideal for both business and leisure guests. There is a spacious restaurant, relaxing coffee lounge and smart bar, alongside a range of function rooms for meetings and events, including the new Garden Suite. Complimentary WiFi access is available.

Rooms 91 (4 fmly) (25 GF) ✆ **S** £55-£115; **D** £65-£125 (incl. bkfst) **Facilities** STV FTV WiFi HL Xmas New Year **Conf** Class 150 Board 75 Thtr 300 Del from £85 to £195 **Services** Lift **Parking** 200 **Notes** LB ⊗ Civ Wed 300

Premier Inn Stafford North (Hurricane)

BUDGET HOTEL

tel: 0871 527 9030 *(Calls cost 13p per minute plus your phone company's access charge)*
1 Hurrican Close ST16 1GZ
web: www.premierinn.com
dir: M6 junct 14, A34 towards Stafford. Hotel approx 2m NW of town centre

High quality, budget accommodation ideal for both families and business travellers. Spacious, en suite bedrooms feature tea and coffee making facilities, and Freeview TV in most hotels. Internet access and WiFi are available for a small fee. The adjacent family restaurant features a wide and varied menu. See also the Hotel Groups pages.

Rooms 102

Premier Inn Stafford North (Spitfire)

BUDGET HOTEL

tel: 0871 527 9032 *(Calls cost 13p per minute plus your phone company's access charge)*
1 Spitfire Close ST16 1GX
web: www.premierinn.com
dir: M6 junct 14, A34 N. Hotel approx 1m on left

Rooms 87

S

STAINES-UPON-THAMES
Surrey

Map 6 TQ07

Mercure London Staines Upon Thames
★★★ 78% HOTEL

tel: 01784 464433 **Thames St TW18 4SJ**
email: h6620@accor.com **web:** www.mercure.com
dir: M25 junct 13. Follow A30/town centre signs (bus station on right). Hotel straight ahead

Located on the banks of the River Thames in a bustling town, this hotel is well positioned for both business and leisure travellers. Meals are served in the Riverside Restaurant, and snacks are available in the spacious lounge/bar; weather permitting the terrace provides a good place for a drink on a summer evening. On-site parking is an additional bonus.

Rooms 88 (17 fmly) (31 GF) **S** fr £82; **D** fr £82* **Facilities** STV FTV WiFi Moorings Xmas New Year **Conf** Class 40 Board 20 Thtr 40 **Parking** 40 **Notes** LB

STALHAM
Norfolk

Map 13 TG32

The Ingham Swan
RESTAURANT WITH ROOMS

tel: 01692 581099 **Sea Palling Rd, Ingham NR12 9AB**
email: info@theinghamswan.co.uk **web:** www.theinghamswan.co.uk
dir: From A149 Stalham, into Old Market Rd towards Upper Staithe Rd/Lower Staithe Rd. At rdbt 1st exit, 2nd exit at next rdbt into Ingham Rd. Continue to Town Rd

The Swan is a charming 14th-century former coaching inn that has been sympathetically restored and enjoys a peaceful rural location in the heart of Norfolk. Stylish, very well equipped bedrooms are most comfortable and the eye-catching original features really add to the presentation. The award-winning restaurant serves the best of Norfolk produce and there is a small bar area for pre-dinner drinks. Secure parking is available along with free WiFi for guests.

Rooms 4 (4 annexe) (2 fmly)

STALLINGBOROUGH
Lincolnshire

Map 17 TA11

Stallingborough Grange Hotel
★★★ 73% HOTEL

tel: 01469 561302 **Riby Rd DN41 8BU**
email: reception@stallingboroughgrange.co.uk **web:** www.stallingboroughgrange.co.uk
dir: From A180 take Stallingborough interchange, through village. At rdbt take 2nd exit onto A1173, hotel 1m on left

Dating back to the 18th century, this independent hotel is not short of character and charm. Bedrooms are furnished with a traditional appeal although modern accessories such as free WiFi are provided. The spacious restaurant offers an interesting choice of meals, alongside the bar area where more relaxed dishes can be enjoyed. Gym facilities are available and ample car parking is provided. The location is convenient with ports such as Grimsby a short distance away.

Rooms 42 (9 GF) **Facilities** STV FTV WiFi HL Gym Xmas New Year **Conf** Class 30 Board 28 Thtr 60 Del £145* **Parking** 80 **Notes** ⊗ Civ Wed 70

STAMFORD
Lincolnshire

Map 11 TF00

The William Cecil
★★★★ 81% ⊛⊛ HOTEL

tel: 01780 750070 **High St, St Martins PE9 2LJ**
email: enquiries@thewilliamcecil.co.uk **web:** www.thewilliamcecil.co.uk
dir: Exit A1 signed Stamford & Burghley Park. Hotel 1st building on right on entering town

This lovely refurbished property is situated on the edge of town within the Burghley Estate. The stylish bedrooms are spacious, individually decorated and have lots of extra little touches. The public rooms include a lounge bar with plush seating and a panelled restaurant. A smart terrace is available for alfresco dining when the weather permits.

Rooms 27 (2 fmly) (5 GF) **Facilities** FTV WiFi Xmas New Year **Conf** Class 60 Board 40 Thtr 120 **Parking** 60 **Notes** Civ Wed 120

The George of Stamford
★★★★ 80% ⊛ HOTEL

tel: 01780 750750 & 750700 (res) **71 St Martins PE9 2LB**
email: reservations@georgehotelofstamford.com **web:** www.georgehotelofstamford.com
dir: A1, 15m N of Peterborough onto B1081, hotel 1m on left

Steeped in hundreds of years of history, this delightful coaching inn provides spacious public areas that include a choice of dining options, inviting lounges, and a business centre. A highlight is afternoon tea, taken in the colourful courtyard when the weather permits. Bedrooms are stylishly appointed and range from traditional to contemporary in design.

Rooms 45 **S** £120; **D** £195–£290 (incl. bkfst)* **Facilities** STV FTV WiFi Complimentary membership to local gym Xmas New Year **Conf** Class 25 Board 25 Thtr 50 Del from £160 to £190* **Parking** 110 **Notes** LB Civ Wed 50

Crown Hotel
★★★ 82% HOTEL

tel: 01780 763136 **All Saints Place PE9 2AG**
email: reservations@thecrownhotelstamford.co.uk
web: www.kneadpubs.co.uk/our-pubs/the-crown-hotel
dir: A1 onto A43, through town to Red Lion Sq, hotel behind All Saints Church

This small, privately owned hotel where hospitality is spontaneous and sincere, is ideally situated in the town centre. Unpretentious British food is served in the modern dining areas and the spacious bar is popular with locals. Bedrooms are appointed to a very high standard being quite contemporary in style and very well equipped; some have four-poster beds. Additional 'superior' rooms are located in a renovated Georgian town house just a short walk up the street.

Rooms 28 (10 annexe) (1 fmly) (1 GF) **Facilities** FTV WiFi Xmas New Year **Conf** Class 12 Board 12 Thtr 20 **Parking** 21

Candlesticks

RESTAURANT WITH ROOMS

tel: 01780 764033 **1 Church Ln PE9 2JU**
email: info@candlestickshotel.co.uk **web:** www.candlestickshotel.co.uk
dir: B1081 into Stamford. Left onto A43. Right into Worthorpe Rd, right into Church Ln

Candlesticks is a 17th-century property situated in a quiet lane in the oldest part of Stamford, just a short walk from the centre of town. The bedrooms are pleasantly decorated and equipped with a good range of useful extras. Public rooms feature Candlesticks restaurant and a cosy bar.

Rooms 8

STANDISH	Map 15 SD51
Greater Manchester	

Premier Inn Wigan North (M6 Jct 27)

BUDGET HOTEL

tel: 0871 527 9166 *(Calls cost 13p per minute plus your phone company's access charge)*
Almond Brook Rd WN6 0SS
web: www.premierinn.com
dir: M6 junct 27 follow signs for Standish. Left at T-junct, then 1st right

High quality, budget accommodation ideal for both families and business travellers. Spacious, en suite bedrooms feature tea and coffee making facilities, and Freeview TV in most hotels. Internet access and WiFi are available for a small fee. The adjacent family restaurant features a wide and varied menu. See also the Hotel Groups pages

Rooms 36

STANSTED AIRPORT	Map 6 TL52
Essex	

See also **Birchanger Green Motorway Service Area (M11)**

Premier Inn Stansted Airport

BUDGET HOTEL

tel: 0871 527 9352 *(Calls cost 13p per minute plus your phone company's access charge)*
Thremhall Av, Stansted Airport CM24 1PY
web: www.premierinn.com
dir: M11 junct 8/8a, follow signs Stansted Airport Terminal. Main rdbt 3rd exit follow signs mid-stay car park. Adjacent BP Petrol Station

High quality, budget accommodation ideal for both families and business travellers. Spacious, en suite bedrooms feature tea and coffee making facilities, and Freeview TV in most hotels. Internet access and WiFi are available for a small fee. The adjacent family restaurant features a wide and varied menu. See also the Hotel Groups pages.

Rooms 303

STEVENAGE	Map 12 TL22
Hertfordshire	

Holiday Inn Stevenage

★★★★ 73% HOTEL

tel: 01438 722727 & 346060 **St George's Way SG1 1HS**
email: reservations@histevenage.com **web:** www.histevenage.com
dir: A1(M) junct 7 take A602 to Stevenage, across 1st rdbt, 1st exit at 2nd rdbt, 2nd exit at next rdbt along St George's Way. Hotel 100yds on right

Holiday Inn Stevenage is situated in the heart of the town centre and just 25 minutes from central London by train. Bedrooms are air conditioned and well equipped; ideal for business and leisure. Public areas are smart, capacious and stylish, and as well as a comfortable bar and restaurant, there is a mini gym. Parking is limited.

Rooms 140 (12 fmly) **Facilities** STV FTV WiFi ▷ HL Gym Xmas New Year **Conf** Class 200 Board 200 Thtr 400 **Services** Lift Air con **Parking** 23 **Notes** Civ Wed 400

Novotel Stevenage

★★★ 80% HOTEL

tel: 01438 346100 & 346250 **Knebworth Park SG1 2AX**
email: H0992@accor.com **web:** www.novotel.com
dir: A1(M) junct 7, at entrance to Knebworth Park

Ideally situated just off the A1(M) is this purpose-built hotel, which is a popular business and conference venue. Bedrooms are pleasantly decorated and equipped with a good range of useful extras. Public rooms include a large open-plan lounge bar serving a range of snacks, and a smartly appointed restaurant.

Rooms 101 (20 fmly) (30 GF) **Facilities** STV WiFi ▷ Use of local health club New Year **Conf** Class 80 Board 70 Thtr 150 **Services** Lift **Parking** 120 **Notes** Civ Wed 120

Roebuck Inn

★★★ 76% HOTEL

tel: 01438 365445 & 365653 **London Rd, Broadwater SG2 8DS**
email: book@roebuckinn.com **web:** www.roebuckinn.com
dir: A1(M) junct 7, right towards Stevenage. At 2nd rdbt take 2nd exit signed Roebuck-London/Knebworth/B197. Hotel in 1.5m

Suitable for both the business and leisure traveller, this hotel provides spacious contemporary accommodation in well-equipped bedrooms. The older part of the building, where there is a restaurant and a cosy public bar with log fire and real ales, dates back to the 15th century.

Rooms 26 (8 fmly) (13 GF) **Facilities** STV FTV WiFi ▷ Xmas New Year **Conf** Class 20 Board 30 Thtr 50 Del from £125* **Parking** 50 **Notes** ⊗

Premier Inn Stevenage

BUDGET HOTEL

tel: 0871 527 9036 *(Calls cost 13p per minute plus your phone company's access charge)*
Corey's Mill Ln SG1 4AA
web: www.premierinn.com
dir: A1(M) junct 8, at intersection with A602 - Hitchin Rd & Corey's Mill Lane

High quality, budget accommodation ideal for both families and business travellers. Spacious, en suite bedrooms feature tea and coffee making facilities, and Freeview TV in most hotels. Internet access and WiFi are available for a small fee. The adjacent family restaurant features a wide and varied menu. See also the Hotel Groups pages.

Rooms 56

Premier Inn Stevenage Central

BUDGET HOTEL

tel: 0871 527 9034 *(Calls cost 13p per minute plus your phone company's access charge)*
Six Hills Way, Horizon Technology Park SG1 2DD
web: www.premierinn.com
dir: A1(M) junct 7, follow Stevenage signs. Left into Gunnels Wood Rd. (NB do not use underpass). Left at next rdbt. Hotel in Horizon Technology Park on left

Rooms 115

S

STEYNING
West Sussex   Map 6 TQ11

Best Western Old Tollgate Hotel & Restaurant   BW Best Western
★★★ 78% HOTEL

tel: 01903 879494 **The Street, Bramber BN44 3WE**
email: info@oldtollgatehotel.com web: www.oldtollgatehotel.com
dir: *From A283 at Steyning rdbt to Bramber. Hotel 200yds on right*

As its name suggests, this well-presented hotel is built on the site of the old toll house. The spacious bedrooms are smartly designed and are furnished to a high standard; eight rooms are air conditioned and have smart power showers. Open for both lunch and dinner, the popular carvery-style restaurant offers an extensive choice of dishes.

Rooms 38 (28 annexe) (5 fmly) (14 GF) 🐾 **Facilities** STV WiFi ⏣ HL New Year **Conf** Class 32 Board 24 Thtr 50 **Services** Lift **Parking** 60 **Notes** ⊗ Civ Wed 70

STILTON
Cambridgeshire   Map 12 TL18

Bell Inn Hotel
★★★ 82% ◉ HOTEL

tel: 01733 241066 **Great North Rd PE7 3RA**
email: reception@thebellstilton.co.uk web: www.thebellstilton.co.uk
dir: *A1(M) junct 16, follow Stilton signs. Hotel in village centre*

This delightful inn is steeped in history and retains many original features, with imaginative food served in both the character village bar/brasserie and the elegant beamed first-floor restaurant; refreshments can be enjoyed in the attractive courtyard and rear gardens when weather permits. Individually designed bedrooms are stylish and equipped to a high standard.

Rooms 22 (3 annexe) (1 fmly) (3 GF) 🐾 **S** £85-£125; **D** £110-£145 (incl. bkfst)* **Facilities** STV FTV WiFi ⏣ **Conf** Class 46 Board 50 Thtr 130 Del from £130* **Parking** 30 **Notes** ⊗ Closed 25 Dec (pm) RS 26 Dec (pm) & 1 Jan (pm) Civ Wed 130

STOCK
Essex   Map 6 TQ69

Greenwoods Hotel & Spa
★★★★ 78% HOTEL

tel: 01277 829990 & 829205 **Stock Rd CM4 9BE**
email: info@greenwoodshotel.co.uk web: www.greenwoodshotel.co.uk
dir: *A12 junct 16 take B1007 signed Billericay. Hotel on right on entering village*

Greenwoods is a beautiful 17th-century, Grade II listed manor house set in extensive landscaped gardens. All bedrooms are tastefully appointed, with marble bathrooms and a wide range of extras; the premier rooms have spa baths and antique beds. The spa facilities are impressive offering the latest beauty treatments, together with saunas, a jacuzzi, steam rooms, a monsoon shower and a 20-metre pool.

Rooms 39 (6 GF) 🐾 **Facilities** Spa STV FTV WiFi ⏣ 🔾 Gym Steam room Sauna Monsoon shower Relaxation suite New Year **Conf** Class 70 Board 52 Thtr 110 Del from £99 to £150* **Services** Lift **Parking** 100 **Notes** ⊗ No children 16yrs Closed 26 Dec & 1 Jan Civ Wed 65

S

STOCKBRIDGE
Hampshire — Map 5 SU33

The Greyhound on the Test
◉◉ ☆ RESTAURANT WITH ROOMS

tel: 01264 810833 **31 High St SO20 6EY**
email: info@thegreyhoundonthetest.co.uk **web:** www.thegreyhoundonthetest.co.uk
dir: 9m NW of Winchester, 8m S of Andover. Off A303

This charming restaurant with rooms has the River Test at its rear and serves great food. In addition, the luxury bedrooms are generally spacious, beautifully styled and come with a host of extras. Bathrooms are modern and come with high quality towels and toiletries. There is also ample parking and well-kept grounds.

Rooms 10

STOCKPORT
Greater Manchester — Map 16 SJ89

See also **Manchester Airport**

Alma Lodge Hotel
★★★ 75% HOTEL

tel: 0161 483 4431 **149 Buxton Rd SK2 6EL**
email: reception@almalodgehotel.com **web:** www.almalodgehotel.com
dir: M60 junct 1 at rdbt take 2nd exit under rail viaduct at lights opposite. At Debenhams turn right onto A6. Hotel approx 1.5m on left

Alma Lodge is a large hotel located on the main road close to the town, offering modern and well-equipped bedrooms. It is family-owned and run and serves a good range of quality Italian cooking in Luigi's restaurant. Good function rooms and free internet access are also available.

Rooms 52 (32 annexe) (2 fmly) **Facilities** FTV WiFi **Conf** Class 100 Board 60 Thtr 250 Del £135 **Parking** 120 **Notes** ⊗ RS BHs Civ Wed 200

The Wycliffe Hotel
★★★ 75% HOTEL

tel: 0161 477 5395 **74 Edgeley Rd, Edgeley SK3 9NQ**
email: reception@wycliffe-hotel.com **web:** www.wycliffe-hotel.com
dir: M60 junct 2, follow A560 Stockport signs, right at 1st lights, hotel 0.5m on left

The Wycliffe is a family-run hotel close to the town centre and convenient for Manchester Airport. The contemporary bedrooms are very well maintained and equipped, with king-size beds and LCD flat-screen TVs. Complimentary WiFi is provided throughout the hotel. There is a well-stocked bar and a popular restaurant where the menu has an Italian feel. There is also a large car park.

Rooms 14 (3 fmly) (2 GF) **S** £71; **D** £91 (incl. bkfst)* **Facilities** FTV WiFi
Conf Class 20 Board 20 Thtr 30 **Parking** 46 **Notes** ⊗ Closed 25-27 Dec RS BHs

Premier Inn Manchester Airport Heald Green
BUDGET HOTEL

tel: 0871 527 8734 *(Calls cost 13p per minute plus your phone company's access charge)*
Finney Ln, Heald Green SK8 3QH
web: www.premierinn.com
dir: M56 junct 5 follow signs to Terminal 1, at rdbt take 2nd exit, at next rdbt follow Cheadle signs. Left at lights, right at next lights

High quality, budget accommodation ideal for both families and business travellers. Spacious, en suite bedrooms feature tea and coffee making facilities, and Freeview TV in most hotels. Internet access and WiFi are available for a small fee. The adjacent family restaurant features a wide and varied menu. See also the Hotel Groups pages.

Rooms 67

Premier Inn Stockport Central
BUDGET HOTEL

tel: 0871 527 9040 *(Calls cost 13p per minute plus your phone company's access charge)*
Churchgate SK1 1YG
web: www.premierinn.com
dir: M60 junct 27, A626 towards Marple. Right at Spring Gardens

Rooms 46

Premier Inn Stockport South
BUDGET HOTEL

tel: 0871 527 9042 *(Calls cost 13p per minute plus your phone company's access charge)*
Buxton Rd, Heaviley SK2 6NB
web: www.premierinn.com
dir: On A6, 1.5m from town centre

Rooms 42

S

STOCKTON-ON-TEES
County Durham   Map 19 NZ41

Premier Inn Stockton-on-Tees/Hartlepool

BUDGET HOTEL

tel: 0871 527 9044 *(Calls cost 13p per minute plus your phone company's access charge)*
Coal Ln, Wolviston TS22 5PZ
web: www.premierinn.com
dir: *A1(M) junct 60, A689, follow Teeside then Hartlepool signs. Hotel on left at A89 & A19 junct*

High quality, budget accommodation ideal for both families and business travellers. Spacious, en suite bedrooms feature tea and coffee making facilities, and Freeview TV in most hotels. Internet access and WiFi are available for a small fee. The adjacent family restaurant features a wide and varied menu. See also the Hotel Groups pages.

Rooms 78

Premier Inn Stockton-on-Tees/Middlesbrough

BUDGET HOTEL

tel: 0871 527 9048 *(Calls cost 13p per minute plus your phone company's access charge)*
Whitewater Way, Thornaby TS17 6QB
web: www.premierinn.com
dir: *A19, A66 towards Stockton & Darlington. Take 1st exit signed Teeside Park/Teesdale. Right at lights over viaduct bridge rdbt & Tees Barrage*

Rooms 110

Premier Inn Stockton-on-Tees West

BUDGET HOTEL

tel: 0871 527 9046 *(Calls cost 13p per minute plus your phone company's access charge)*
Yarm Rd TS18 3RT
web: www.premierinn.com
dir: *A1(M) junct 60, A689 towards Teeside. Follow Hartlepool signs. Hotel on left at A689 & A19 interchange*

Rooms 87

STOKE-BY-NAYLAND
Suffolk   Map 13 TL93

HIGHLY RECOMMENDED

The Crown

★★★ 87% ◉◉ SMALL HOTEL

tel: 01206 262001 & 262346 **CO6 4SE**
email: reservations@crowninn.net web: www.crowninn.net
dir: *Follow Stoke-by-Nayland signs from A12 & A134. Hotel in village off B1068 towards Higham*

Situated in a picturesque village, The Crown, with an award-winning restaurant, has a reputation for making everyone feel welcome. It offers quiet, individually decorated rooms that look out over the countryside. Ground floor rooms, including three with a terrace, are of a contemporary design while upstairs rooms are in a country-house style; each room has WiFi, DVDs and luxury toiletries.

Rooms 11 (1 fmly) (8 GF) **Facilities** FTV WiFi New Year **Conf** Board 12 **Parking** 49 **Notes** Closed 25-26 Dec

STOKE D'ABERNON
Surrey   Map 6 TQ15

Woodlands Park Hotel

★★★★ 82% ◉◉ HOTEL

tel: 01372 843933 & 0845 072 7581
(Calls cost 5p per minute plus your phone company's access charge) **Woodlands Ln KT11 3QB**
email: woodlandspark@handpicked.co.uk
web: www.handpickedhotels.co.uk/woodlandspark
dir: *A3 exit at Cobham. Through town centre & Stoke D'Abernon, left at garden centre into Woodlands Lane, hotel 0.5m on right*

Originally built for the Bryant family, of the matchmaking firm Bryant & May, this lovely Victorian mansion enjoys an attractive parkland setting in ten and a half acres of Surrey countryside. Bedrooms in the wing are contemporary in style while those in the main house are more traditionally decorated. The hotel boasts two dining options, Benson's Brasserie and the Oak Room Restaurant.

Rooms 57 (4 fmly) **Facilities** FTV WiFi HL Xmas New Year **Conf** Class 20 Board 50 Thtr 150 **Services** Lift Air con **Parking** 150 **Notes** Civ Wed 200

STOKE-ON-TRENT
Staffordshire   Map 10 SJ84

Best Western Plus Stoke-on-Trent Moat House

★★★★ 73% HOTEL

tel: 01782 609988 **Etruria Hall, Festival Way, Festival Park ST1 5BQ**
email: reservations.stoke@qmh-hotels.com web: www.bw-stokeontrentmoathouse.co.uk
dir: *M6 junct 15 (or junct 16), A500, follow A53 & Festival Park signs. Keep in left lane, take 1st slip road on left. Left at island, hotel opposite at next island*

This large, modern hotel is located in Stoke's Festival Park, which adjoins Etruria Hall, the former home of Josiah Wedgwood. Bedrooms are spacious and well equipped, and include family rooms, suites and executive rooms. Public areas include a spacious lounge bar and restaurant as well as a business centre, extensive conference facilities and a leisure club.

Rooms 147 **Facilities** Spa FTV WiFi supervised Gym **Conf** Class 400 Board 40 Thtr 650 **Services** Lift Air con **Parking** 250 **Notes** LB Civ Wed 400

Premier Inn Stoke-on-Trent (Hanley)

BUDGET HOTEL

tel: 0871 527 9476 *(Calls cost 13p per minute plus your phone company's access charge)*
Etruria Rd, Hanley ST1 5NH
web: www.premierinn.com
dir: *M6 junct 15, A500. 4.3m, take 5th slip road for A53 (City Centre, Hanley). At rdbt take 4th exit signed Etruria & A53. Keep in left lane until passing flyover entrance. At rdbt take 3rd exit, hotel on right*

High quality, budget accommodation ideal for both families and business travellers. Spacious, en suite bedrooms feature tea and coffee making facilities, and Freeview TV in most hotels. Internet access and WiFi are available for a small fee. The adjacent family restaurant features a wide and varied menu. See also the Hotel Groups pages.

Rooms 96

Premier Inn Stoke/Trentham Gardens

BUDGET HOTEL

tel: 0871 527 9050 *(Calls cost 13p per minute plus your phone company's access charge)*
Stone Rd, Trentham ST4 8JG
web: www.premierinn.com
dir: *M6 junct 15, A500, follow Trentham signs. At rdbt 3rd exit onto A34, 2m to hotel on right in Trentham Gardens*

Rooms 119

Weathervane

BUDGET HOTEL

tel: 01782 388799 **Lysander Rd ST3 7WA**
email: 5305@greenking.co.uk **web:** www.oldenglish.co.uk

A few minutes from the A50 and convenient for both the city and industrial areas, this popular, modern pub and restaurant, under the 'Hungry Horse' brand, provides hearty, well-cooked food at reasonable prices. Adjacent bedrooms are furnished for both commercial and leisure customers. See also the Hotel Groups pages.

Rooms 39 (8 fmly) (18 GF) **Conf** Class 20 Board 20 Thtr 20

STOKE POGES
Buckinghamshire
Map 6 SU98

INSPECTORS' CHOICE

Stoke Park
★★★★★ ◎◎◎ HOTEL

tel: 01753 717171 **Park Rd SL2 4PG**
email: info@stokepark.com **web:** www.stokepark.com
dir: *M4 junct 6, A355 towards Slough, B416 Park Rd. Hotel 1.25m on right*

Located within 300 acres of beautiful parkland created by 'Capability' Brown and Humphry Repton, this hotel offers outstanding leisure and sporting facilities. Inside the stunning mansion house, designed by George III's architect, the public areas display lavish opulence throughout and the bedrooms have a luxurious and classic feel. In contrast, the Pavilion features more contemporary bedrooms and public areas; as well as extensive state-of-the-art health and beauty facilities. The hotel has a championship golf course, tennis courts, and three restaurants, including the award-winning Humphry's and the more informal Italian brasserie, San Marco. There are bars, lounges and meeting rooms as well.

Stoke Park

Rooms 49 (28 annexe) (6 fmly) D £180–£1800* **Facilities** Spa STV FTV WiFi ⓢ ⚓ 27 ⛳ Putt green Fishing ⌘ Gym Indoor golf Games room Hot Activity studios Nail bar Spa boutique Garden lounge New Year **Conf** Class 30 Board 34 Thtr 80 Del £492* **Services** Lift **Parking** 460 **Notes** LB ⊗ Closed 24-26 Dec Civ Wed 146

STON EASTON
Somerset
Map 4 ST65

INSPECTORS' CHOICE

Ston Easton Park Hotel
★★★★ ◎◎ COUNTRY HOUSE HOTEL

tel: 01761 241631 **BA3 4DF**
email: reception@stoneaston.co.uk **web:** www.stoneaston.co.uk
dir: *On A37*

Surrounded by The Mendips, this outstanding Palladian mansion lies in extensive parklands that were landscaped by Humphrey Repton. The architecture and decorative features are stunning. The state rooms include one of England's earliest surviving Print Rooms, and the Palladian Saloon is considered one of Somerset's finest rooms. There is even an Edwardian kitchen that guests might like to take a look at. The helpful and attentive team provide a very efficient service, and the award-winning cuisine uses organic produce from the hotel's own kitchen garden. The bedrooms and bathrooms are all appointed to an excellent standard.

Rooms 23 (3 annexe) (2 fmly) (1 GF) **Facilities** FTV WiFi ⓢ ⌘ Archery Clay pigeon shooting Quad bikes Hot air ballooning Xmas New Year **Conf** Class 60 Board 30 Thtr 100 **Parking** 120 **Notes** Civ Wed 120

S

STOURBRIDGE
West Midlands   Map 10 SO88

Premier Inn Stourbridge Town Centre

BUDGET HOTEL

tel: 0871 527 9482 *(Calls cost 13p per minute plus your phone company's access charge)*
Birmingham St DY8 1JR
web: www.premierinn.com
dir: *On A458*

High quality, budget accommodation ideal for both families and business travellers. Spacious, en suite bedrooms feature tea and coffee making facilities, and Freeview TV in most hotels. Internet access and WiFi are available for a small fee. The adjacent family restaurant features a wide and varied menu. See also the Hotel Groups pages.

Rooms 80

STOURPORT-ON-SEVERN
Worcestershire   Map 10 SO87

Hallmark Hotel Stourport Manor

★★★★ 76% HOTEL

tel: 0330 028 3421 **35 Hartlebury Rd DY13 9JA**
email: stourport@hallmarkhotels.co.uk **web:** www.hallmarkhotels.co.uk
dir: *M5 junct 6, A449 towards Kidderminster, B4193 towards Stourport. Hotel on right*

Once the home of Prime Minister Sir Stanley Baldwin, this much extended country house is set in attractive grounds. A number of bedrooms and suites are located in the original building, although the majority are in a more modern, purpose-built section. Spacious public areas include a range of lounges, a popular restaurant, a leisure club and conference facilities.

Rooms 68 (33 fmly) (31 GF) ⚓ **Facilities** FTV WiFi ⤵ ⚲ supervised ⌣ Putt green Gym Squash Xmas New Year **Conf** Class 110 Board 100 Thtr 400 **Parking** 300 **Notes** Civ Wed 300

STOW-ON-THE-WOLD
Gloucestershire   Map 10 SP12

Wyck Hill House Hotel & Spa

★★★★ 76% ◎◎ HOTEL

tel: 01451 831936 **Burford Rd GL54 1HY**
email: info@wyckhillhousehotel.co.uk **web:** www.wyckhillhousehotel.co.uk
dir: *Exit A429. Hotel 1m on right*

This charming 18th-century house enjoys superb views across the Windrush Valley and is ideally positioned for a relaxing weekend exploring the Cotswolds. The spacious and thoughtfully equipped bedrooms provide high standards of comfort and quality, located both in the main house and also the original coach house. Elegant public rooms include a cosy bar, library, and the magnificent front hall with crackling log fire. The imaginative cuisine makes extensive use of local produce.

Rooms 60 (22 annexe) (4 GF) ⚓ **S** £95-£265; **D** £95-£265 (incl. bkfst)*
Facilities Spa FTV WiFi Sauna Steam room Xmas New Year **Conf** Class 50 Board 50 Thtr 150 Del from £145 to £165* **Services** Lift **Parking** 100 **Notes** LB ⊗ Civ Wed 120

Stow Lodge Hotel

★★★ 78% SMALL HOTEL

tel: 01451 830485 **The Square GL54 1AB**
email: enquiries@stowlodge.co.uk **web:** www.stowlodge.co.uk
dir: *In town centre*

Situated in smart grounds, this family-run hotel has direct access to the market square and provides high standards of customer care. Bedrooms are offered both within the main building and in the converted coach house, all of which provide similar standards of homely comfort. Extensive menus and an interesting wine list make for an enjoyable dining experience.

Rooms 21 (10 annexe) (1 fmly) ⚓ **S** £75-£140; **D** £99-£170 (incl. bkfst)*
Facilities WiFi **Parking** 30 **Notes** LB ⊗ No children 5yrs Closed Xmas-end Jan

Old Stocks Inn

◎ 🍴 RESTAURANT WITH ROOMS

tel: 01451 830666 **The Square GL54 1AP**
email: info@oldstocksinn.com **web:** www.oldstocksinn.com
dir: *From A429 turn into Market Sq, located opposite Town Hall*

The Old Stocks has been lovingly restored, and offers a mix of modern facilities and 17th-century charm. Bedrooms are well designed and make good use of space; there are some unique features in the 'great' rooms. Cuisine is at the heart of the operation, with a café, restaurant and bar making up the impressive ground floor. Award-winning breakfasts are served in the restaurant, whilst lunch and dinner also offer award-winning dining.

Rooms 16 (3 annexe) (4 fmly)

STRATFORD-UPON-AVON
Warwickshire   Map 10 SP25

INSPECTORS' CHOICE

Ettington Park Hotel

★★★★ ◎◎ COUNTRY HOUSE HOTEL

tel: 01789 450123 & 0845 072 7454
(Calls cost 5p per minute plus your phone company's access charge) **CV37 8BU**
email: ettingtonpark@handpicked.co.uk
web: www.handpickedhotels.co.uk/ettingtonpark

(For full entry see Alderminster)

HIGHLY RECOMMENDED

The Welcombe Hotel Spa & Golf Club
★★★★ 85% ◎◎ HOTEL
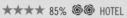

tel: 0330 028 3422 **Warwick Rd CV37 ONR**
email: welcombe@hallmarkhotels.co.uk **web:** www.hallmarkhotels.co.uk
dir: M40 junct 15, A46 towards Stratford-upon-Avon, at rdbt follow signs for A439. Hotel 3m on right

This Jacobean manor house is set in 157 acres of landscaped parkland. Public rooms are impressive, especially the lounge with its wood panelling and ornate marble fireplace, and the gentleman's club-style bar. Bedrooms in the original building are stylish and gracefully proportioned; those in the garden wing are comfortable and thoughtfully equipped. The spa development incorporates advanced, luxurious facilities and treatments.

Rooms 85 (12 fmly) (11 GF) ☔ **Facilities** Spa STV FTV WiFi ⊌ ⊗ ⊀ ⚲ 18 ⛳ Putt green Gym Xmas New Year **Conf** Class 65 Board 40 Thtr 200 Del from £160 to £220* **Parking** 200 **Notes** Civ Wed 120

HIGHLY RECOMMENDED

The Arden Hotel
★★★★ 84% ◎◎ HOTEL
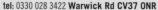

tel: 01789 298682 **Waterside CV37 6BA**
email: enquiries@theardenhotelstratford.com **web:** www.theardenhotelstratford.com
dir: M40 junct 15 follow signs to town centre. At Barclays Bank rdbt left onto High St, 2nd left onto Chapel Lane (Nash's House on left). Hotel car park on right in 40yds

This property is on the same road as the world famous Royal Shakespeare and Swan theatres, and just a short walk from the town centre. The bedrooms and bathrooms have been tastefully designed and have quality fixtures and fittings. The dedicated team provide polite and professional service. Award-winning cuisine is served in the popular restaurant. Ample secure parking is available.

Rooms 45 (6 fmly) (1 GF) ☔ **S** £127.50–£260; **D** £155–£420 (incl. bkfst)* **Facilities** FTV WiFi Xmas New Year **Conf** Class 18 Board 28 Thtr 40 Del from £175 to £190* **Services** Air con **Parking** 50 **Notes** ⊗ Civ Wed 90

Macdonald Alveston Manor
★★★★ 81% ◎ HOTEL

tel: 01789 205478 & 0344 879 9138 **Clopton Bridge CV37 7HP**
email: sales.alvestonmanor@macdonald-hotels.co.uk **web:** www.macdonaldhotels.co.uk
dir: On rdbt, S of Clopton Bridge

A striking red-brick and timbered façade, well-tended grounds, and a giant cedar tree all contribute to the charm of this well-established hotel, just five minutes from Stratford. The bedrooms vary in size and character, and the coach house conversion offers an impressive mix of full and junior suites. The superb leisure complex offers a 20-metre swimming pool, steam room, sauna, a high-tech gym and a host of beauty treatments.

Rooms 113 (8 fmly) (45 GF) **S** £80–£160; **D** £100–£250* **Facilities** Spa FTV WiFi ⊌ ⊗ supervised Gym Techno-gym Beauty treatments Sauna Steam room Xmas New Year **Conf** Class 80 Board 40 Thtr 140 Del from £135 to £175* **Services** Air con **Parking** 150 **Notes** LB Civ Wed 110

The Stratford
★★★★ 80% ◎ HOTEL

tel: 01789 271000 & 271007 **Arden St CV37 6QQ**
email: thestratfordreservations.co.uk **web:** www.qhotels.co.uk
dir: A439 into Stratford. In town follow A3400/Birmingham, at lights left into Arden St, hotel 150yds on right

Situated adjacent to the hospital, within walking distance of the town centre, The Stratford is an eye-catching, contemporary hotel with a red-brick façade. It offers modern, well-equipped and spacious bedrooms. The open-plan public areas include a comfortable lounge, a small, atmospheric bar and a spacious restaurant with exposed beams.

Rooms 102 (7 fmly) (14 GF) ☔ **Facilities** FTV WiFi ⊌ HL Gym Free use of Stratford Manor's leisure facilities Xmas New Year **Conf** Class 66 Board 54 Thtr 132 **Services** Lift Air con **Parking** 92 **Notes** ⊗ Civ Wed 132

Stratford Manor
★★★★ 80% HOTEL

tel: 01789 731173 **Warwick Rd CV37 OPY**
email: stratfordmanor@qhotels.co.uk **web:** www.qhotels.co.uk
dir: M40 junct 15, A46 signed Stratford. At 2nd rdbt take A439 signed Stratford Town Centre. Hotel 1m on left. Or from Stratford centre take A439 signed Warwick & M40. Hotel 3m on right

Just outside Stratford, this hotel is set against a rural backdrop with lovely gardens and ample parking. Public areas include a stylish lounge bar and a contemporary restaurant. Service is both professional and helpful. Bedrooms are smartly appointed, spacious and have generously sized beds and a range of useful facilities. The leisure centre boasts a large indoor pool.

Rooms 104 (8 fmly) (24 GF) ☔ **Facilities** Spa FTV WiFi ⊌ HL ⊗ Gym Sauna Steam room Xmas New Year **Conf** Class 120 Board 100 Thtr 350 **Services** Lift **Parking** 220 **Notes** Civ Wed 150

The Billesley Manor Hotel
★★★★ 77% ◎ HOTEL

tel: 01789 279955 **Billesley, Alcester B49 6NF**
email: billesleymanor@thehotelcollection.co.uk **web:** www.thehotelcollection.co.uk
dir: A46 towards Evesham. Over 3 rdbts, right for Billesley after 2m

This 16th-century manor is set in peaceful grounds and parkland with a delightful yew topiary garden and fountain. The spacious bedrooms and suites, most in traditional country-house style, are thoughtfully designed and well equipped. Conference facilities and some of the bedrooms are found in the cedar barns. Public areas retain many original features, such as oak panelling, fireplaces and exposed stone.

Rooms 72 (29 annexe) (5 GF) ☔ **Facilities** Spa WiFi ⊗ supervised ⊌ Gym Steam room Beauty treatments Yoga studio Xmas New Year **Conf** Class 60 Board 50 Thtr 100 **Parking** 100 **Notes** Civ Wed 75

S

STRATFORD-UPON-AVON *continued*

Macdonald Swan's Nest Hotel

★★★★ 77% HOTEL

tel: 01789 266804 & 0344 879 9140 **Bridgefoot CV37 7LT**
email: sales.swansnest@macdonald-hotels.co.uk
web: www.macdonald-hotels.co.uk/swansnest
dir: *A439 towards Stratford, follow one-way system, left over bridge (A3400), hotel on right*

Dating back to the 17th century, this hotel is said to be one of the earliest brick-built houses in Stratford. It occupies a prime position on the banks of the River Avon and is ideally situated for exploring the town. Bedrooms and bathrooms are appointed to a high standard with some thoughtful guest extras provided.

Rooms 68 (2 fmly) (25 GF) ⚑ **D** £168-£198* **Facilities** FTV WiFi ↘ Use of facilities at Macdonald Alveston Manor New Year **Conf** Class 70 Board 56 Thtr 150 Del from £135 to £165* **Parking** 80 **Notes** Civ Wed 150

The Falcon Hotel

★★★★ 76% ⊛ HOTEL

tel: 01789 279953 **Chapel St CV37 6HA**
email: reception.falcon@sjhotels.co.uk **web:** www.sjhotels.co.uk/hotels/falcon
dir: *M40 junct 15, A46, A439 Warwick Rd. Left onto Bridgeway, slight right, left onto Bridge St, left on High St, hotel on right*

The Falcon Hotel is a Grade II listed property positioned in the heart of historic Stratford-upon-Avon. It offers a blend of Tudor period features and modern day comforts. Bedrooms are equipped to a good standard and public areas are made homely by open fires in colder months. Will's Place Restaurant serves a wide range of award-winning seasonal dishes. Secluded courtyard garden, secure on-site parking and free WiFi available.

Rooms 83 (11 annexe) (6 fmly) (3 GF) **Facilities** FTV WiFi Xmas New Year **Conf** Class 80 Board 40 Thtr 160 **Services** Lift **Parking** 100 **Notes** Civ Wed 140

Mercure Stratford-upon-Avon Shakespeare Hotel

★★★★ 73% ⊛ HOTEL

tel: 01789 294997 **Chapel St CV37 6ER**
email: h6630@accor.com **web:** www.mercure.com
dir: *M40 junct 15. Follow signs for Stratford town centre on A439. Follow one-way system into Bridge St. Left at rdbt, hotel 200yds on left opposite HSBC bank*

Dating back to the early 17th century, The Shakespeare is one of the oldest hotels in this historic town. The hotel name represents one of the earliest exploitations of Stratford as the birthplace of one of the world's leading playwrights. With exposed beams and open fires, the public rooms retain an ambience reminiscent of this era. Bedrooms are appointed to a good standard and remain in keeping with the style of the property.

Rooms 78 (11 annexe) (3 GF) ⚑ **Facilities** WiFi Xmas New Year **Conf** Class 45 Board 40 Thtr 90 **Services** Lift **Parking** 31 **Notes** Civ Wed 100

Best Western Grosvenor Hotel

 Best Western.

★★★ 78% HOTEL

tel: 01789 269213 & 414030 **Warwick Rd CV37 6YT**
email: gm@bwgh.co.uk **web:** www.bwgh.co.uk
dir: *M40 junct 15, follow Stratford signs to A439 Warwick Rd. Hotel 6m, on one-way system*

This hotel is a short distance from the town centre and many historic attractions. Bedroom styles and sizes vary, and the friendly staff offer an efficient service. Refreshments are served in the lounge all day, and room service is available. The Garden Room restaurant offers a choice of dishes from set price and carte menus.

Rooms 73 (16 fmly) (25 GF) **S** £79-£99; **D** £85-£145 **Facilities** FTV WiFi ↘ Xmas New Year **Conf** Class 45 Board 50 Thtr 100 **Parking** 46 **Notes** LB ⊗ Civ Wed 100

Premier Inn Stratford-upon-Avon Central

BUDGET HOTEL

tel: 0871 527 9282 *(Calls cost 13p per minute plus your phone company's access charge)* **Payton Rd CV37 6UQ**
web: www.premierinn.com
dir: *A439, A4300 signed Stratford-upon-Avon. Hotel on left*

High quality, budget accommodation ideal for both families and business travellers. Spacious, en suite bedrooms feature tea and coffee making facilities, and Freeview TV in most hotels. Internet access and WiFi are available for a small fee. The adjacent family restaurant features a wide and varied menu. See also the Hotel Groups pages.

Rooms 87

Premier Inn Stratford-upon-Avon Waterways

BUDGET HOTEL

tel: 0871 527 9316 *(Calls cost 13p per minute plus your phone company's access charge)* **The Waterways, Birmingham Rd CV37 0AZ**
web: www.premierinn.com
dir: *A3400 (Birmingham Rd) towards town centre, pass large retail park on left. Straight over mini rdbt, approx 150yds. Hotel on right*

Rooms 130

STREET	Map 4 ST43
Somerset	

Wessex Hotel

★★★ 68% HOTEL

tel: 01458 443383 **High St BA16 0EF**
email: info@wessexhotel.com **web:** www.wessexhotel.com
dir: *From A303, onto B3151 to Somerton. Then 7m, pass lights by Millfield School. Left at mini-rdbt*

The Wessex Hotel is centrally located in this popular town, with easy access to all the shops and attractions. The bedrooms and bathrooms vary slightly in size but all provide good levels of quality and comfort. A wide range of snacks and refreshments is available throughout the day, including a regular carvery at dinner. Entertainment is often offered in the main season.

Rooms 51 (9 fmly) ⚑ **S** £55-£70; **D** £70-£100 (incl. bkfst)* **Facilities** FTV WiFi HL ♫ Xmas New Year **Conf** Class 120 Board 80 Thtr 400 **Services** Lift **Parking** 70

STROUD
Gloucestershire

Map 4 SO80

The Bear of Rodborough

★★★ 83% ⓐ HOTEL

COTSWOLD INNS & HOTELS

tel: 01453 878522 **Rodborough Common GL5 5DE**
email: info@bearofrodborough.info **web:** www.cotswold-inns-hotels.co.uk
dir: M5 junct 13, A419 to Stroud. Follow signs to Rodborough. Up hill, left at top at T-junct. Hotel on right

This popular 17th-century coaching inn is situated high above Stroud in acres of National Trust parkland. Character abounds in the lounges and cocktail bar, and in the Box Tree Restaurant where the cuisine utilises fresh local produce. Bedrooms offer equal measures of comfort and style with plenty of extra touches. There is also a traditional and well-patronised public bar.

Rooms 46 (18 annexe) (2 fmly) **Facilities** FTV WiFi Xmas New Year **Conf** Class 35 Board 30 Thtr 60 **Parking** 70 **Notes** Civ Wed 70

Burleigh Court Hotel

★★★ 82% ⓐⓐ HOTEL

tel: 01453 883804 **Burleigh, Minchinhampton GL5 2PF**
email: burleighcourt@aol.com **web:** www.burleighcourthotel.co.uk
dir: From Stroud A419 towards Cirencester. Right after 2.5m signed Burleigh & Minchinhampton. Left after 500yds signed Burleigh Court. Hotel 300yds on right

Dating back to the 18th century, this former gentleman's manor house is in a secluded and elevated, though accessible, position with some wonderful countryside views. Public rooms are elegantly styled and include an oak-panelled bar for pre-dinner drinks beside a crackling fire. Combining comfort and quality, no two bedrooms are alike; some are in an adjoining coach house.

Rooms 18 (7 annexe) (2 fmly) (3 GF) ⓣ **S** £110-£130; **D** £175-£240 (incl. bkfst)*
Facilities WiFi ⓣ ⓢ New Year **Conf** Class 30 Board 30 Thtr 50 Del from £180 to £240* **Parking** 40 **Notes** LB Closed 24-26 Dec Civ Wed 50

Premier Inn Stroud

BUDGET HOTEL

Premier Inn

tel: 0871 527 9052 (Calls cost 13p per minute plus your phone company's access charge)
Stratford Lodge, Stratford Rd GL5 4AF
web: www.premierinn.com
dir: M5 junct 13, A419 to town centre, follow Leisure Centre signs. Hotel adjacent to Tesco superstore

High quality, budget accommodation ideal for both families and business travellers. Spacious, en suite bedrooms feature tea and coffee making facilities, and Freeview TV in most hotels. Internet access and WiFi are available for a small fee. The adjacent family restaurant features a wide and varied menu. See also the Hotel Groups pages.

Rooms 32

STUDLAND
Dorset

Map 5 SZ08

THE PIG on the Beach

★★★ ⓐⓐ HOTEL

tel: 01929 450288 **The Manor House, Manor Rd BH19 3AU**
email: info@thepigonthebeach.com **web:** www.thepighotel.com
dir: A338 from Bournemouth, follow signs to Sandbanks ferry, cross on ferry, then 3m to Studland

This former summer house has a dramatic coastal location set within beautiful grounds. It has its own livestock and there is a walled garden, which provides much of the produce for the popular restaurant; an authentically reproduced greenhouse. Alfresco eating is possible in the warmer months as there is a wood-fired oven in the grounds. Bedrooms come in an array of shapes and sizes, located in the main house and there are some feature rooms in outbuildings. All are generally spacious, have high quality fixtures and come with their own larders and Nespresso machines. There are plenty of comfortable lounges where guests can make themselves at home too. Treatments can be taken in the two attractively converted shepherds huts and there's a room just perfect for private dining within the grounds.

Rooms 23 (3 annexe) (6 GF) ⓣ **Facilities** STV FTV WiFi ⓣ Treatment rooms Beach hut Round house Xmas New Year **Parking** 30 **Notes** ⊗ Civ Wed 60

SUDBURY
Suffolk

Map 13 TL84

The Mill Hotel

★★★ 82% HOTEL

tel: 01787 375544 & 0330 333 2996 **Walnut Tree Ln CO10 1BD**
email: info@themillhotelsudbury.co.uk **web:** www.themillhotelsudbury.co.uk
dir: A12 direction Harwich from London, exit junct 27 onto A134, 2nd exit into A133, rdbt 1st exit onto A134, straight over 7 rdbts, 2nd exit onto Newton Road, A131, turn right

Situated on the banks of the River Stour in the Suffolk countryside, close to the town of Sudbury, The Mill Hotel features an original working water mill which is a main feature in the bar/restaurant. The modern bedrooms are well equipped; many rooms have lovely views of the meadow and surrounding countryside. Public rooms include a lounge bar and a restaurant with an outdoor terrace.

Rooms 62 (10 annexe) (4 fmly) (12 GF) ⓣ **Facilities** FTV WiFi ⓣ Xmas New Year **Conf** Class 56 Board 40 Thtr 80 **Parking** 45 **Notes** Civ Wed 80

S

SUDBURY *continued*

The Case Restaurant with Rooms

RESTAURANT WITH ROOMS

tel: 01787 210483 **Further St, Assington CO10 5LD**
email: restaurant@thecaserestaurantwithrooms.co.uk
web: www.thecaserestaurantwithrooms.co.uk
dir: *Exit A12 at Colchester onto A134 to Sudbury. 7m, establishment on left*

The Case Restaurant with Rooms offers dining in comfortable surroundings, along with luxurious accommodation in bedrooms that all enjoy independent access. Some bathrooms come complete with corner jacuzzi, while internet access comes as standard. In the restaurant, local produce is used in all dishes, and bread and delicious desserts are made fresh every day.

Rooms 7 (2 fmly)

SUNBURY
Surrey

Premier Inn Sunbury (Kempton Park)

BUDGET HOTEL PLAN 1 A1

tel: 0871 527 9054 *(Calls cost 13p per minute plus your phone company's access charge)*
Staines Road West, Sunbury Cross TW16 7AT
web: www.premierinn.com
dir: *M25 junct 12, onto M3 signed London & Richmond. Exit at junct 1, take 1st exit at rdbt into Staines Road West (A308). 1st left into Crossways. Hotel on right*

High quality, budget accommodation ideal for both families and business travellers. Spacious, en suite bedrooms feature tea and coffee making facilities, and Freeview TV in most hotels. Internet access and WiFi are available for a small fee. The adjacent family restaurant features a wide and varied menu. See also the Hotel Groups pages.

Rooms 109

SUNDERLAND
Tyne & Wear   Map 19 NZ35

Best Western Roker Hotel

★★★ 81% HOTEL

tel: 0191 567 1786 **Roker Ter, Roker SR6 9ND**
email: reception@rokerhotel.co.uk **web:** www.rokerhotel.co.uk
dir: *Follow A1231 from A9, E to Sunderland, then A1290 to Church St N. Left onto A183 for 0.9m. Hotel is located left, coast to the right*

This modern hotel offers stunning views of the coastline. Well-equipped bedrooms come in a variety of sizes, several have feature bathrooms. Functions, conferences and weddings are all well catered for with a variety of rooms and spaces available. The late-opening R Bar serves food all day with real ales from a local micro-brewery. The Italian Farmhouse Ristorante also provides lunch and dinner, while Let There Be Crumbs is a wonderful teashop operation overlooking the seafront.

Rooms 43 (4 fmly) **Facilities** FTV WiFi ♫ Xmas New Year **Conf** Class 150 Board 100 Thtr 300 **Services** Lift **Parking** 150 **Notes** ⊗ Civ Wed 350

Quality Hotel

U

tel: 0191 519 1999 **Witney Way, Boldon NE35 9PE**
email: gm@hotels-sunderland.com
dir: *From Tyne Tunnel (A19), 2.5m S take 1st exit to rdbt with A184*

Currently the rating for this establishment is not confirmed. This may be due to a change of ownership or because it has only recently joined the AA rating scheme. For further details please see the AA website: theAA.com

Conf Class 100 Board 100 Thtr 230

Premier Inn Sunderland A19/A1231

BUDGET HOTEL

tel: 0871 527 9058 *(Calls cost 13p per minute plus your phone company's access charge)*
Wessington Way, Castletown SR5 3HR
web: www.premierinn.com
dir: *From A19 take A1231 towards Sunderland. Hotel 100yds*

High quality, budget accommodation ideal for both families and business travellers. Spacious, en suite bedrooms feature tea and coffee making facilities, and Freeview TV in most hotels. Internet access and WiFi are available for a small fee. The adjacent family restaurant features a wide and varied menu. See also the Hotel Groups pages.

Rooms 91

Premier Inn Sunderland City Centre

BUDGET HOTEL

tel: 0871 527 9482 *(Calls cost 13p per minute plus your phone company's access charge)*
1-3 Hind St SR1 3QD
web: www.premierinn.com
dir: *From S: A1, A23 towards Sunderland. At 1st rdbt, right. Right at 6th rdbt, hotel on right. From N: A1, A6900, A19. Approx 1m, take A1231 towards Sunderland. Right at rdbt. Right at 4th rdbt. Hotel on right*

Rooms 125

Premier Inn Sunderland North West

BUDGET HOTEL

tel: 0871 527 9056 *(Calls cost 13p per minute plus your phone company's access charge)*
Timber Beach Rd, off Wessington Way, Castletown SR5 3XG
web: www.premierinn.com
dir: *A1(M) junct 65, A1231 towards Sunderland, cross over A19*

Rooms 63

SURBITON
Greater London

Holiday Inn London - Kingston South

★★★★ 77% HOTEL PLAN 1 C1

tel: 020 8786 6565 & 0131 523 1030 **Kingston Tower, Portsmouth Rd KT6 5QQ**
email: enquiries@hikingston.co.uk **web:** www.hikingston.co.uk
dir: *M25 junct 10, A3, left onto A243, 3rd exit at rdbt. At lights left onto A307*

This hotel occupies a convenient location overlooking the River Thames just outside Kingston-upon-Thames and close to Surbiton. Many front-facing bedrooms have beautiful river views; all are comfortable and stylish. The public areas include a

S

small, well-equipped fitness room. Complimentary parking and WiFi are also available.

Rooms 116 (2 fmly) 🐾 **S** £69-£299; **D** £84-£314 **Facilities** FTV WiFi ♨ HL Mini gym Discounted price for guests at nearby gym & pool Xmas New Year **Conf** Class 125 Board 60 Thtr 250 **Services** Lift Air con **Parking** 120 **Notes** ⊗ Civ Wed 210

SUTTON   Map 6 TQ26
Greater London

Holiday Inn London - Sutton

★★★ 79% HOTEL

tel: 020 8234 1100 & 8234 1104 **Gibson Rd SM1 2RF**
email: sales-sutton@ihg.com **web:** www.hilondonsuttonhotel.co.uk
dir: M25 junct 8, A217, B2230. Pass rail station, follow one-way system in right lane. At lights, right then immediately left, left into Gibson Rd

Well located for many famous attractions such as Chessington World of Adventure, the All-England Tennis Club at Wimbledon and Epsom Racecourse, this hotel offers air-conditioned bedrooms ranging from standard to executive, a variety of conference rooms, and leisure facilities with a swimming pool.

Rooms 119 (39 fmly) **Facilities** Spa STV FTV WiFi ♨ HL ⊕ supervised Gym Xmas New Year **Conf** Class 100 Board 70 Thtr 180 **Services** Lift Air con **Parking** 115 **Notes** ⊗ Civ Wed 160

SUTTON COLDFIELD (ROYAL)   Map 10 SP19
West Midlands

INSPECTORS' CHOICE

New Hall Hotel & Spa

★★★★ ◎◎ HOTEL

tel: 0121 378 2442 & 0845 072 7577
(Calls cost 5p per minute plus your phone company's access charge) **Walmley Rd B76 1QX**
email: newhall@handpicked.co.uk **web:** www.handpickedhotels.co.uk/newhall
dir: M42 junct 9, A4097, 2m to rdbt, take 2nd exit signed Walmley. Take 2nd exit from next 5 rdbts follow Sutton Coldfield signs. At 6th rdbt take 3rd exit follow Sutton Coldfield signs. Hotel on left

Situated in 26 acres of beautiful grounds, this hotel is reputed to be the oldest inhabited, moated house in the country. The house's medieval charm and character combine well with 21st-century guest facilities. Executive and luxury suites are available. Public areas, with their fine panelling and mullioned stained-glass windows include the magnificent Great Chamber.

Rooms 60 (14 fmly) (25 GF) 🐾 **S** £112-£156; **D** £112-£156 (incl. bkfst)*
Facilities Spa STV FTV WiFi ⊕ supervised ⚓ 9 ⛳ Gym Steam room Pitch & putt Outdoor trim trail Xmas New Year **Conf** Class 75 Board 35 Thtr 150 Del from £158 to £192* **Parking** 80 **Notes** ⊗ Civ Wed 75

Moor Hall Hotel & Spa

★★★★ 80% ◎◎ HOTEL

tel: 0121 308 3751 **Moor Hall Dr, Four Oaks B75 6LN**
email: mail@moorhallhotel.co.uk **web:** www.moorhallhotel.co.uk
dir: A38 onto A453 towards Sutton Coldfield, right at lights into Weeford Rd. Hotel 150yds on left

Although only a short distance from the city centre this hotel enjoys a peaceful setting, overlooking extensive grounds and an adjacent golf course. Bedrooms are well equipped and executive rooms are particularly spacious. Public rooms include the formal 2 AA Rosette Oak Room Restaurant, and the informal Country Kitchen which offers a carvery and blackboard specials. The hotel also has a well-equipped spa with pool, sauna, steam room, jacuzzi and treatment rooms. Free WiFi available in all rooms and throughout the hotel.

Rooms 83 (5 fmly) (33 GF) 🐾 **S** £65-£140; **D** £80-£165 (incl. bkfst)* **Facilities** Spa FTV WiFi ♨ HL ⊕ Gym Aerobics studio Sauna Steam room **Conf** Class 120 Board 45 Thtr 250 Del from £145 to £180* **Services** Lift **Parking** 170 **Notes** LB ⊗ Civ Wed 180

Ramada Birmingham, Sutton Coldfield

★★★ 75% HOTEL

tel: 0121 351 3111 **Penns Ln, Walmley B76 1LH**
email: enquiries@ramadasuttonhotel.co.uk **web:** www.ramadasuttonhotel.co.uk
dir: From S: M6 junct 5 A452, 3rd rdbt right into Eachelhurst Rd, left at lights into Penns Lane. From N/W: M6 junct 6, Sutton Coldfield A5127, follow signs, 2m on at lights (Macdonalds), 4th right into Penns Lane

This hotel offers comfortable bedrooms which are fully equipped with a range of thoughtful accessories. The public areas provide a leisure facility with a well-equipped gym, alongside a smart lounge bar and function rooms.

Rooms 170 (23 annexe) (26 fmly) (48 GF) 🐾 **S** £59-£94; **D** £59-£94* **Facilities** Spa FTV WiFi ♨ ⊕ Fishing Gym Squash Sauna Steam room Studio Hair salon Weights studio Spin studio Training room Xmas New Year **Conf** Class 200 Board 80 Thtr 600 Del from £109 to £149* **Services** Lift **Parking** 500 **Notes** LB Civ Wed 200

Premier Inn Birmingham North (Sutton Coldfield)

BUDGET HOTEL

tel: 0871 527 8088 *(Calls cost 13p per minute plus your phone company's access charge)*
Whitehouse Common Rd B75 6HD
web: www.premierinn.com
dir: M42 junct 9, A446 towards Lichfield, then A453 to Sutton Coldfield. Left into Whitehouse Common Rd, hotel on left

High quality, budget accommodation ideal for both families and business travellers. Spacious, en suite bedrooms feature tea and coffee making facilities, and Freeview TV in most hotels. Internet access and WiFi are available for a small fee. The adjacent family restaurant features a wide and varied menu. See also the Hotel Groups pages.

Rooms 57

S

SUTTON SCOTNEY
Hampshire
Map 5 SU43

Norton Park

QHOTELS
INSPIRED BY YOU

★★★★ 79% HOTEL

tel: 01962 763000 **SO21 3NB**
email: nortonpark@qhotels.co.uk **web:** www.qhotels.co.uk
dir: *From A303 & A34 junct follow signs to Sutton Scotney. Hotel on Micheldever Station Rd (old A30), 1m from Sutton Scotney*

Set in 54 acres of beautiful parkland in the heart of Hampshire, Norton Park offers both business and leisure guests a great range of amenities. Dating from the 16th century, the hotel is complemented by extensive buildings housing the bedrooms, and public areas which include a superb leisure club and numerous conference facilities. Ample parking is available.

Rooms 175 (11 fmly) (80 GF) 🐾 **Facilities** Spa WiFi ⑤ supervised 🏊 Gym Steam room Sauna Experience shower Ice fountain Xmas New Year **Conf** Class 250 Board 80 Thtr 340 **Services** Lift **Parking** 220 **Notes** Civ Wed 340

SWAFFHAM
Norfolk
Map 13 TF80

Best Western George Hotel

BW Best Western.

★★★ 73% HOTEL

tel: 01760 721238 **Station St PE37 7LJ**
email: georgehotel@bestwestern.co.uk **web:** www.georgehotelswaffham.co.uk
dir: *From the S: M11 junct 9, merge onto A11, continue on A14 exit 38, join A11, at rdbt 2nd exit A1065. From the N: A1, A17, A47*

Located in the centre of historic Swaffham and originally a 16th-century coaching inn, the hotel now offers a range of bedroom styles and sizes. Meals are served every day in The Green Room restaurant, or in the bar for a more informal dining experience. A suitable base for those exploring the North Norfolk Coast.

Rooms 28 (2 fmly) (8 GF) 🐾 **S** £55-£75; **D** £65-£95 (incl. bkfst)* **Facilities** FTV WiFi ↳ **Conf** Class 60 Board 50 Thtr 160 Del from £100 to £160* **Parking** 50 **Notes** LB RS 24-26 Dec

SWANAGE
Dorset
Map 5 SZ07

The Pines Hotel

★★★ 80% HOTEL

tel: 01929 425211 **Burlington Rd BH19 1LT**
email: reservations@pineshotel.co.uk **web:** www.pineshotel.co.uk
dir: *A351 to seafront, left then 2nd right. Hotel at end of road*

Enjoying a peaceful location with spectacular views over the cliffs and sea, The Pines is a pleasant place to stay. Many of the comfortable bedrooms have sea views. Guests can take tea in the lounge, enjoy appetising bar snacks in the attractive bar, and dine on interesting cuisine in the restaurant.

Rooms 50 (26 fmly) (6 GF) 🐾 **S** £77; **D** £154-£212 (incl. bkfst)* **Facilities** FTV WiFi ↳ 🎵 Xmas New Year **Conf** Class 80 Board 80 Thtr 80 Del from £99* **Services** Lift **Parking** 60 **Notes** LB

See advert on opposite page

Purbeck House Hotel

★★★ 74% HOTEL

tel: 01929 422872 **91 High St BH19 2LZ**
email: reservations@purbeckhousehotel.co.uk **web:** www.purbeckhousehotel.co.uk
dir: *A351 to Swanage via Wareham, right into Shore Rd, into Institute Rd, right into High St*

Originally built in 1875 as a private residence for George Burt, this family-run hotel has plenty of history, including wonderful mosaic floors, original servant's bells and ornate ceilings. Bedrooms are varied in style, but all offer the expected comforts, with rooms located both within the main house and in Louisa Lodge, which is just a short stroll through the wonderful Victorian gardens. Impressive cuisine is well worth sampling, served within the grandeur of the former chapel. Generous parking is provided, and Purbeck House is just a short walk from the seafront and town centre.

Rooms 38 **Conf** Class 36 Board 25 Thtr 100 **Parking** 57 **Notes** Closed 23-29 Dec Civ Wed 120

SWANLEY
Kent
Map 6 TQ56

Premier Inn Swanley

BUDGET HOTEL

tel: 0871 527 9288 *(Calls cost 13p per minute plus your phone company's access charge)*
London Rd BR8 7QD
web: www.premierinn.com
dir: *M25 junct 3, B2173 towards Swanley. At rdbt 2nd exit onto B258 (High St). At next rdbt 4th exit into Swanley Ln, 1st exit into Bartholomew Way, at next rdbt 3rd exit into London Rd*

High quality, budget accommodation ideal for both families and business travellers. Spacious, en suite bedrooms feature tea and coffee making facilities, and Freeview TV in most hotels. Internet access and WiFi are available for a small fee. The adjacent family restaurant features a wide and varied menu. See also the Hotel Groups pages.

Rooms 62

S

SWINDON
Wiltshire

Map 5 SU18

Best Western Plus Blunsdon House Hotel

★★★★ 75% HOTEL

tel: 01793 721701 **Blunsdon SN26 7AS**
email: reservations@blunsdonhouse.co.uk **web:** www.blunsdonhouse.co.uk
dir: *M4 junct 15, A419 towards Cirencester. Exit at Blundsdon/Swindon, follow brown hotel signs*

Located just to the north of Swindon, Blunsdon House is set in 30 acres of well-kept grounds, and offers extensive leisure facilities and spacious day rooms. The hotel has a choice of eating and drinking options, including the spacious Carrie's Bar and the contemporary Flame Charcoal Grill and Lunchtime Carvery. Bedrooms are comfortably furnished, and include family rooms with bunk beds and the modern, spacious Pavilion rooms.

Rooms 108 (17 fmly) (27 GF) Facilities **Spa** STV FTV WiFi HL 9 Putt green Gym Beauty therapy Woodland walk Spin studio Xmas New Year
Conf Class 200 Board 55 Thtr 300 Del from £169 to £279* **Services** Lift **Parking** 300
Notes Civ Wed 200

The Pear Tree at Purton

★★★ 82% HOTEL

tel: 01793 772100 **Church End SN5 4ED**
email: stay@peartreepurton.co.uk **web:** www.peartreepurton.co.uk

(For full entry see Purton)

Chiseldon House Hotel

★★★ 80% HOTEL

tel: 01793 741010 **New Rd, Chiseldon SN4 0NE**
email: welcome@chiseldonhouse.com **web:** www.chiseldonhouse.com
dir: *M4 junct 15, A346 signed Marlborough. In 0.5m right onto B4500, 0.25m, hotel on right*

Conveniently located for access to the M4, Chiseldon House is in a quiet location and has a relaxed ambience. Bedrooms include a number of larger rooms but all are comfortably furnished. The award-winning restaurant offers a selection of carefully prepared dishes utilising high quality produce. Guests are welcome to enjoy the pleasant garden with outdoor seating.

Rooms 21 (4 fmly) Facilities FTV WiFi **Conf** Class 20 Board 32 Thtr 65 **Parking** 50 **Notes** Civ Wed 100

Stanton House Hotel

★★★ 77% HOTEL

tel: 01793 861779 & 0843 507 1388
(Calls cost 7p per minute plus your phone company's access charge)
The Avenue, Stanton Fitzwarren SN6 7SD
email: reception@stantonhouse.co.uk **web:** www.stantonhouse.co.uk
dir: *A419 onto A361 towards Highworth, left towards Stanton Fitzwarren about 600yds, hotel on left*

Extensive grounds and superb gardens surround this Cotswold-stone manor house, and the park and Stanton Lake are accessible for some great walks. Smart, well-maintained bedrooms have been equipped with modern comforts. Public areas include a conservatory, a bar and two eating options - The Rosemary Restaurant offering a wide choice of Japanese and European dishes, and the Mt Fuji Restaurant specialising in authentic Japanese food in traditional surroundings. The friendly, multi-lingual staff create a relaxing atmosphere for guests.

Rooms 78 (27 GF) Facilities STV WiFi Xmas New Year **Conf** Class 70 Board 40 Thtr 110 **Services** Lift **Parking** 110 **Notes** Civ Wed 110

Premier Inn Swindon Central

BUDGET HOTEL

tel: 0871 527 9064 *(Calls cost 13p per minute plus your phone company's access charge)*
Kembrey Business Park, Kembrey St SN2 8YS
web: www.premierinn.com
dir: *M4 junct 15, A419 (Swindon bypass) towards Cirencester. In 6m at Turnpike Rdbt 1st left. Hotel on left in 2m*

High quality, budget accommodation ideal for both families and business travellers. Spacious, en suite bedrooms feature tea and coffee making facilities, and Freeview TV in most hotels. Internet access and WiFi are available for a small fee. The adjacent family restaurant features a wide and varied menu. See also the Hotel Groups pages.

Rooms 50

Premier Inn Swindon North

BUDGET HOTEL

tel: 0871 527 9066 *(Calls cost 13p per minute plus your phone company's access charge)*
Broad Bush, Blunsdon SN26 8DJ
web: www.premierinn.com
dir: *N of Swindon. 5m from M4 junct 15. At junct of A419 & B4019*

Rooms 62

Premier Inn Swindon West

BUDGET HOTEL

tel: 0871 527 9068 *(Calls cost 13p per minute plus your phone company's access charge)*
Great Western Way SN5 8UY
web: www.premierinn.com
dir: *M4 junct 16, A3102 to Lydiard Fields. Past Hilton, entrance on left. NB for Sat Nav use SN5 8UB*

Rooms 89

TADWORTH
Surrey

Map 6 TQ25

Premier Inn Epsom South

BUDGET HOTEL

tel: 0871 527 8382 *(Calls cost 13p per minute plus your phone company's access charge)*
Brighton Rd, Burgh Heath KT20 6BW
web: www.premierinn.com
dir: *Just off M25 junct 8 on A217 towards Sutton*

High quality, budget accommodation ideal for both families and business travellers. Spacious, en suite bedrooms feature tea and coffee making facilities, and Freeview TV in most hotels. Internet access and WiFi are available for a small fee. The adjacent family restaurant features a wide and varied menu. See also the Hotel Groups pages.

Rooms 78

S

TAMWORTH Staffordshire	Map 10 SK20

Premier Inn Tamworth Central

BUDGET HOTEL

tel: 0871 527 9070 *(Calls cost 13p per minute plus your phone company's access charge)*
Bonehill Rd, Bitterscote B78 3HQ
web: www.premierinn.com
dir: *M42 junct 10, A5 towards Tamworth. Left in 3m onto A51 signed Tamworth. Straight on at 1st rdbt. At next rdbt 3rd exit. Hotel adjacent to Ladybridge Beefeater*

High quality, budget accommodation ideal for both families and business travellers. Spacious, en suite bedrooms feature tea and coffee making facilities, and Freeview TV in most hotels. Internet access and WiFi are available for a small fee. The adjacent family restaurant features a wide and varied menu. See also the Hotel Groups pages.

Rooms 74

Premier Inn Tamworth South

BUDGET HOTEL

tel: 0871 527 9072 *(Calls cost 13p per minute plus your phone company's access charge)*
Watling St, Wilnecote B77 5PN
web: www.premierinn.com
dir: *M42 junct 10, A5 towards Tamworth. Left in 200yds signed Wilnecote/B5404. Left at next rdbt, hotel on left*

Rooms 32

TANKERSLEY South Yorkshire	Map 16 SK39

Tankersley Manor

★★★★ 74% HOTEL

tel: 01226 744700 **Church Ln S75 3DQ**
email: tankersleymanor@qhotels.co.uk **web:** www.qhotels.co.uk
dir: *M1 junct 36, A61 Sheffield Rd*

High on the moors with views over the countryside, this 17th-century residence is well located for major cities, tourist attractions and motorway links. Where appropriate, bedrooms retain original features such as exposed beams or Yorkshire-stone window sills. The hotel has a bar and brasserie which has old beams and open fires. A well-equipped leisure centre is also available.

Rooms 98 (10 fmly) (16 GF) ⚓ **Facilities** Spa STV FTV WiFi ♨ ⟳ Gym Swimming lessons Beauty treatments New Year **Conf** Class 200 Board 100 Thtr 400 **Services** Lift **Parking** 350 **Notes** Civ Wed 250

Premier Inn Sheffield/Barnsley M1 Jct 36

BUDGET HOTEL

tel: 0871 527 8968 *(Calls cost 13p per minute plus your phone company's access charge)*
Maple Rd S75 3DL
web: www.premierinn.com
dir: *M1 junct 35A (N'bound exit only), A616 for 2m. From M1 junct 36, A61 towards Sheffield*

High quality, budget accommodation ideal for both families and business travellers. Spacious, en suite bedrooms feature tea and coffee making facilities, and Freeview TV in most hotels. Internet access and WiFi are available for a small fee. The adjacent family restaurant features a wide and varied menu. See also the Hotel Groups pages.

Rooms 62

TAPLOW Buckinghamshire	Map 6 SU98

INSPECTORS' CHOICE

Cliveden

★★★★★ ⊛⊛⊛ ⚓ COUNTRY HOUSE HOTEL

tel: 01628 668561 **Cliveden Estate SL6 OJF**
email: info@clivedenhouse.co.uk **web:** www.clivedenhouse.co.uk
dir: *M4 junct 7, A4 towards Maidenhead, 1.5m, onto B476 towards Taplow, 2.5m, hotel on left*

Cliveden is a wonderful stately home that stands at the top of a gravelled boulevard. After a major refurbishment, Cliveden has been restored to its former glory, and is welcoming guests in luxury and style. Visitors are treated as house-guests and staff recapture a tradition of fine hospitality. Bedrooms have individual quality and style, and reception rooms retain a timeless elegance. Restaurant André Garrett at Cliveden has been awarded 3 AA Rosettes for its outstanding cuisine; guests can also dine at the Astor Grill, housed the old stable block.

Rooms 48 (1 annexe) (19 fmly) (13 GF) ⚓ **Facilities** Spa STV FTV WiFi ☜ ⤳ ⛳ ⟳ Gym Squash 2 vintage boats Xmas New Year **Conf** Class 48 Board 40 Thtr 120 Del from £295* **Services** Lift **Parking** 60 **Notes** Civ Wed 120

T

TAPLOW *continued*

Taplow House Hotel

★★★★ 74% HOTEL

tel: 01628 670056 **Berry Hill SL6 0DA**
email: reception@taplowhouse.com **web:** www.taplowhouse.com
dir: *Exit A4 onto Berry Hill, hotel 0.5m on right*

This elegant Georgian manor is set amid beautiful gardens and has been skilfully restored. Character public rooms are pleasing and include a number of air-conditioned conference rooms and an elegant restaurant. Comfortable bedrooms are individually decorated and furnished to a high standard.

Rooms 32 (5 fmly) (2 GF) ⬆ **Facilities** STV FTV WiFi ⬆ ⬆ **Conf** Class 50 Board 42 Thtr 100 Del from £155 to £290* **Services** Air con **Parking** 100 **Notes** ⊗ Civ Wed 100

TARPORLEY	Map 15 SJ56
Cheshire	

Macdonald Portal Hotel Golf & Spa

★★★★ 78% ⬤ HOTEL

tel: 01829 734100 & 0344 879 9082 **Cobblers Cross Ln CW6 0DJ**
email: general.portal@macdonaldhotels.co.uk
web: www.macdonaldhotels.co.uk/theportal
dir: *M6 junct 18, A54 towards Middlewich/Winsford. Left onto A49, through Cotebrook. In approx 1m follow signs for hotel*

This hotel is located in beautiful rolling countryside and provides a luxury base for both the leisure and business guest. The spacious and well-equipped bedrooms have bathrooms with baths and power showers. Extensive leisure facilities include a superb spa, state-of-the-art fitness equipment, three golf courses and a golf academy. The Ranulf Restaurant delivers skilfully prepared, innovative cooking, as well as an excellent breakfast. Staff throughout are very friendly and nothing is too much trouble.

Rooms 85 (29 GF) ⬆ **Facilities** Spa STV FTV WiFi ⬆ HL ⬆ ⬆ 45 Putt green Gym Golf academy Outdoor pursuits New Year **Conf** Class 180 Board 60 Thtr 250 **Services** Lift **Parking** 250 **Notes** Civ Wed 250

TAUNTON	Map 4 ST22
Somerset	

The Mount Somerset Hotel & Spa

★★★★ 83% ⬤⬤ ⬤ COUNTRY HOUSE HOTEL

tel: 01823 442500 **Lower Henlade TA3 5NB**
email: info@mountsomersethotel.co.uk **web:** www.mountsomersethotel.co.uk
dir: *M5 junct 25, A358 towards Chard/Ilminster, at Henlade right into Stoke Rd, left at T-junct at end, then right into drive*

From its elevated and rural position, this impressive Regency house has wonderful views over Taunton Vale. There are impressive quality and comfort levels throughout in the stylish bedrooms and bathrooms. The elegant public rooms combine style and flair with an engaging and intimate atmosphere. In addition to the daily-changing, fixed-price menu, a carefully selected seasonal carte is available in the restaurant.

Rooms 19 (1 fmly) ⬆ **Facilities** Spa FTV WiFi ⬆ Gym Hydrotherapy pool Sauna Steam room Experience showers Xmas New Year **Conf** Class 60 Board 35 Thtr 70 **Services** Lift **Parking** 100 **Notes** Civ Wed 80

Taunton House Hotel

★★★ 74% METRO HOTEL

tel: 01823 272083 **14 Billetfield TA1 3NN**
email: info@tauntonhousehotel.co.uk **web:** www.tauntonhousehotel.co.uk

Centrally and conveniently located, this elegant establishment dates back to the 1850s and retains many original features such as stained-glass windows and a wonderful oak staircase. Bedrooms provide impressive levels of comfort and quality with well-equipped, modern bathrooms. Public areas reflect the same high standards that are a hallmark throughout this hotel.

Rooms 17 (4 fmly) (6 GF) (2 smoking) ⬆ **S** £65-£95; **D** £70-£105 (incl. bkfst)* **Facilities** FTV WiFi ⬆ **Parking** 17 **Notes** ⊗

Corner House Hotel

★★★ 73% HOTEL

tel: 01823 284683 **Park St TA1 4DQ**
email: res@corner-house.co.uk **web:** www.corner-house.co.uk
dir: *0.3m from town centre. Hotel on junct of Park St & A38 - Wellington Rd*

The unusual Victorian façade of the Corner House, with its turrets and stained-glass windows, belies the wealth of modern innovation, quality and style to be found inside. The contemporary bedrooms have state-of-the-art facilities including flat-screen TVs, ample working space, and fridges with complimentary water and fresh milk. The smart public areas include the convivial bar and the relaxed and enjoyable 'Wine & Sausage' eating rooms. Free WiFi is available throughout.

Rooms 45 (10 annexe) (4 fmly) (5 GF) ⬆ **S** £44-£109; **D** £49-£159* **Facilities** FTV WiFi ⬆ Xmas New Year **Conf** Class 32 Board 26 Thtr 45 Del from £129.50 to £159.50* **Parking** 30 **Notes** ⊗

Premier Inn Taunton Central (North)

BUDGET HOTEL

tel: 0871 527 9076 *(Calls cost 13p per minute plus your phone company's access charge)*
Massingham Park, Priorswood Rd TA2 7RX
web: www.premierinn.com
dir: *M5 junct 25, A358 into Taunton, at 2nd rdbt right onto Obridge Viaduct. Hotel at next rdbt*

High quality, budget accommodation ideal for both families and business travellers. Spacious, en suite bedrooms feature tea and coffee making facilities, and Freeview TV in most hotels. Internet access and WiFi are available for a small fee. The adjacent family restaurant features a wide and varied menu. See also the Hotel Groups pages.

Rooms 40

Premier Inn Taunton East

BUDGET HOTEL

tel: 0871 527 9080 *(Calls cost 13p per minute plus your phone company's access charge)*
81 Bridgwater Rd TA1 2DU
web: www.premierinn.com
dir: *M5 junct 25 follow signs to Taunton. Straight on at 1st rdbt, keep left at Creech Castle lights, hotel 200yds on right*

Rooms 60

Premier Inn Taunton (Ruishton)

BUDGET HOTEL

tel: 0871 527 9074 *(Calls cost 13p per minute plus your phone company's access charge)*
Ruishton Ln, Ruishton TA3 5LU
web: www.premierinn.com
dir: *Just off M5 junct 25 on A38*

Rooms 59

TAVISTOCK
Devon   Map 3 SX47

The Horn of Plenty

★★★★ 79% HOTEL

tel: 01822 832528 **Gulworthy PL19 8JD**
email: enquiries@thehornofplenty.co.uk **web:** www.thehornofplenty.co.uk
dir: *From Tavistock take A390 W for 3m. Right at Gulworthy Cross. In 400yds turn left, hotel in 400yds on right*

With stunning views over the Tamar Valley, The Horn of Plenty maintains its reputation as one of Britain's best country-house hotels. Bedrooms are well equipped and have many thoughtful extras. The garden rooms offer impressive levels of both quality and comfort, while award-winning cuisine is served with accomplished skill and a passion for local produce.

Rooms 16 (12 annexe) (3 fmly) (8 GF) **S** £100-£235; **D** £110-£245 (incl. bkfst)*
Facilities FTV WiFi 🌊 Falconry Xmas New Year **Conf** Class 22 Board 16 Thtr 40 **Parking** 35 **Notes** LB Civ Wed 90

Bedford Hotel

★★★ 80% 🏵 HOTEL

tel: 01822 613221 **1 Plymouth Rd PL19 8BB**
email: reception@bedford-hotel.co.uk **web:** www.bedford-hotel.co.uk
dir: *M5 junct 31, A30 Launceston/Okehampton. Then A386 to Tavistock, follow town centre signs. Hotel opposite church*

Built on the site of a Benedictine abbey, this impressive castellated building has been welcoming visitors for over 200 years. Very much a local landmark, the hotel offers comfortable and relaxing public areas, all reflecting charm and character throughout. Bedrooms are traditionally styled with contemporary comforts, while the Woburn Restaurant provides a refined setting for enjoyable cuisine.

Rooms 31 (2 fmly) (5 GF)  **S** £70; **D** £140 (incl. bkfst)* **Facilities** FTV WiFi ↕ Xmas New Year **Conf** Class 100 Board 60 Thtr 160 **Services** Lift **Parking** 52 **Notes** LB Civ Wed 120

TEIGNMOUTH
Devon   Map 3 SX97

Cliffden Hotel

★★★ 73% HOTEL

tel: 01626 770052 **Dawlish Rd TQ14 8TE**
email: cliffden.hotel@visionhotels.co.uk **web:** www.visionhotels.co.uk
dir: *M5 junct 31, A380, B3192 to Teignmouth. Down hill on Exeter Rd to lights, left to rdbt (station on left). Left, follow Dawlish signs. Up hill. Hotel next right*

While this hotel mainly caters for visually impaired guests, their families, friends and guide dogs, it offers a warm welcome to all. This establishment is a listed Victorian building set in six acres of delightful gardens overlooking a small valley. Bedrooms are comfortable, very spacious and thoughtfully equipped. There are also leisure facilities and, of course, special provision for guide dogs.

Rooms 4/ (8 fmly) (10 GF) **S** £40-£80; **D** £75-£160 (incl. bkfst)* **Facilities** FTV WiFi 🕙 supervised 🎵 Xmas New Year **Conf** Class 30 Board 30 Thtr 50 **Services** Lift **Parking** 25 **Notes** Civ Wed 50

TELFORD
Shropshire   Map 10 SJ60

Telford Hotel & Golf Resort

★★★★ 79% HOTEL

QHOTELS
INSPIRED BY YOU

tel: 01952 429977 **Great Hay Dr, Sutton Heights TF7 4DT**
email: telford@qhotels.co.uk **web:** www.qhotels.co.uk
dir: *M54 junct 4, A442. Follow signs for Telford Golf Club*

Set on the edge of Telford with panoramic views of the famous Ironbridge Gorge, this hotel offers excellent standards. Smart bedrooms are complemented by spacious public areas, large conference facilities, a spa with treatment rooms, a golf course and a driving range. Ample parking is available.

Rooms 114 (8 fmly) (50 GF) 🐾 **Facilities** Spa STV WiFi ↕ 🕙 ⚓ 18 Putt green Gym Xmas New Year **Conf** Class 220 Board 100 Thtr 350 **Services** Lift **Parking** 200 **Notes** Civ Wed 250

Hadley Park House

★★★ 83% 🏵 HOTEL

tel: 01952 677269 **Hadley Park TF1 6QJ**
email: info@hadleypark.co.uk **web:** www.hadleypark.co.uk
dir: *Off Hadley Park Island exit A442 to Whitchurch*

Located in Telford, but close to Ironbridge, this elegant Georgian mansion is situated in three acres of its own grounds. Bedrooms are spacious and well equipped. There is a comfortable bar and lounge, and meals are served in the attractive conservatory-style restaurant.

Rooms 22 (6 fmly) (5 GF) 🐾 **Facilities** STV FTV WiFi ↕ Xmas New Year **Conf** Class 60 Board 40 Thtr 200 **Parking** 60 **Notes** ⊗ Civ Wed 200

T

TELFORD *continued*

Best Western Valley Hotel

★★★ 82% HOTEL

tel: 01952 432247 **Ironbridge TF8 7DW**
email: info@thevalleyhotel.co.uk **web:** www.thevalleyhotel.co.uk
dir: *M6, M54 junct 6 onto A5223 to Ironbridge*

This privately owned hotel is situated in attractive gardens, close to the famous Iron Bridge. It was once the home of the Maws family who manufactured ceramic tiles, and fine examples of their craft are found throughout the house. Bedrooms vary in size and are split between the main house and a mews development; imaginative meals are served in the attractive Chez Maws restaurant.

Rooms 44 (3 fmly) (6 GF) ☞ **Facilities** FTV WiFi ☆ **Conf** Class 80 Board 60 Thtr 150 **Services** Lift **Parking** 70 **Notes** ⊗ Closed 24 Dec-2 Jan RS 25 Dec Civ Wed 150

Mercure Telford Madeley Court Hotel

★★★ 77% HOTEL

tel: 01952 680068 **Castlefields Way, Madeley TF7 5DW**
email: enquiries@hotels-telford.com **web:** www.hotels-telford.com
dir: *A464 to Telford then A442, A4169 to Castlefields rdbt, 1st exit onto B4373. Hotel 200yds on left*

This beautifully restored 16th-century manor house is set in extensive grounds and gardens. Bedrooms vary between character rooms and the newer annexe rooms. Public areas consist of two wood-panelled lounges, a lakeside bar and at the centre of the original manor house, The Priory restaurant. The 16th-century Grade I listed mill house makes a lovely location for wedding receptions.

Rooms 49 (49 annexe) (4 fmly) (21 GF) **Facilities** FTV WiFi Xmas New Year **Conf** Class 150 Board 50 Thtr 175 **Parking** 150 **Notes** Civ Wed 175

Premier Inn Telford Central

BUDGET HOTEL

tel: 0871 527 9082 *(Calls cost 13p per minute plus your phone company's access charge)*
Euston Way TF3 4LY
web: www.premierinn.com
dir: *M54 junct 5 follow Central Railway Station signs. Hotel at 2nd exit off rdbt signed railway station*

High quality, budget accommodation ideal for both families and business travellers. Spacious, en suite bedrooms feature tea and coffee making facilities, and Freeview TV in most hotels. Internet access and WiFi are available for a small fee. The adjacent family restaurant features a wide and varied menu. See also the Hotel Groups pages.

Rooms 89

Premier Inn Telford International Centre

BUDGET HOTEL

tel: 0871 527 9500 *(Calls cost 13p per minute plus your phone company's access charge)*
Southwater Square, Saint Quentin Gate TF3 4EJ
web: www.premierinn.com
dir: *M6 junct, M54. Exit at junct 5, take 2nd exit at 1st rdbt into Forge Gate. Merge into middle lane of one-way system. At next rdbt take 3rd exit into Grange Central. Right into St. Quentin Gate*

Rooms 85

Premier Inn Telford North

BUDGET HOTEL

tel: 0871 527 9084 *(Calls cost 13p per minute plus your phone company's access charge)*
Donnington Wood Way, Donnington TF2 8LE
web: www.premierinn.com
dir: *From Telford M54 junct 4, B5060 (Redhill Way) signed Donnington. At rdbt straight on (becomes Donnington Wood Way then School Rd). At mini rdbt take 1st left into Wellington Rd. Hotel adjacent to McDonalds & Shell garage*

Rooms 20

TELFORD SERVICE AREA (M54)	Map 10 SJ70
Shropshire	

Days Inn Telford - M54

WELCOME**BREAK**

AA Advertised

tel: 01952 238400 **Telford Services, Priorslee Rd TF11 8TG**
email: telford.hotel@welcomebreak.co.uk **web:** www.welcomebreak.co.uk
dir: *At M54 junct 4*

This modern building offers accommodation in smart, spacious and well-equipped bedrooms, suitable for families and business travellers, and all with en suite bathrooms. Continental breakfast is available, and other refreshments may be taken at the nearby family restaurant.

Rooms 48 (45 fmly) (21 GF) (9 smoking) **S** £40-£80; **D** £40-£110* **Facilities** FTV WiFi ☆ **Conf** Board 8 **Parking** 100

TEMPLE SOWERBY	Map 18 NY62
Cumbria	

HIGHLY RECOMMENDED

Temple Sowerby House Hotel & Restaurant

★★★ 87% ◉◉ COUNTRY HOUSE HOTEL

tel: 017683 61578 **CA10 1RZ**
email: stay@templesowerby.com **web:** www.templesowerby.com
dir: *7m from M6 junct 40, midway between Penrith & Appleby, in village centre*

Temple Sowerby House Hotel is set in the heart of the Eden Valley, ideal for exploring the northern Lake District and Pennine Fells. Bedrooms are comfortable and stylish, most feature ultra-modern bathrooms, and there is a choice of pleasant lounges. The restaurant, with picture windows overlooking the beautiful walled garden, is a splendid place to enjoy the award-winning cuisine. Staff throughout are friendly and keen to please.

Rooms 12 (4 annexe) (2 GF) ☞ **S** £105-£120; **D** £145-£170 (incl. bkfst)* **Facilities** FTV WiFi ☆ ☕ New Year **Conf** Class 20 Board 20 Thtr 30 Del from £170 to £190* **Parking** 15 **Notes** LB ⊗ No children 12yrs Closed 20-29 Dec Civ Wed 40

TENTERDEN	Map 7 TQ83
Kent	

Little Silver Country Hotel

★★★ 80% HOTEL

tel: 01233 850321 **Ashford Rd, St Michael's TN30 6SP**
email: enquiries@little-silver.co.uk **web:** www.little-silver.co.uk
dir: *M20 junct 8, A274 signed Tenterden*

Located just outside the charming town of Tenterden and within easy reach of many local Kent attractions, this charming hotel is ideal for leisure and business guests as well as being a popular wedding venue. Bedrooms are spaciously appointed and well equipped; many boast spa baths. There are a spacious lounge, small bar and a modern restaurant that overlooks beautifully tended gardens.

Rooms 16 (1 fmly) (6 GF) ⚓ **Facilities** FTV WiFi ♫ Xmas **Conf** Class 50 Board 25 Thtr 75 Del £123.50* **Parking** 70 **Notes** ⊗ Civ Wed 120

London Beach Country Hotel, Spa & Golf Club

★★★ 75% HOTEL

tel: 01580 766279 **Ashford Rd TN30 6HX**
email: enquiries@londonbeach.com **web:** www.londonbeach.com
dir: M20 junct 9, A28 follow signs to Tenterden (10m). Hotel on right 1m before Tenterden

A modern purpose-built hotel situated in mature grounds on the outskirts of Tenterden. The spacious bedrooms are smartly decorated with co-ordinated soft furnishings, and most rooms have balconies with superb views over the golf course. The open-plan public rooms feature a brasserie-style restaurant, where a good choice of dishes is served.

Rooms 26 (2 fmly) (3 smoking) ⚓ **Facilities** Spa FTV WiFi ♫ ⊗ ♨ 9 Putt green Fishing Gym Driving range Health club Xmas New Year **Conf** Class 75 Board 40 Thtr 100 **Services** Lift **Parking** 100 **Notes** ⊗ Civ Wed 100

TETBURY	**Map 4 ST89**
Gloucestershire	

INSPECTORS' CHOICE

Calcot Manor

★★★★ ◉◉ HOTEL

tel: 01666 890391 **Calcot GL8 8YJ**
email: reception@calcot.co **web:** www.calcot.co
dir: 3m W of Tetbury at A4135 & A46 junct

Cistercian monks built the ancient barns and stables around which this lovely English farmhouse is set. No two rooms are identical, and each is beautifully decorated and equipped with modern comforts. Sumptuous sitting rooms, with crackling log fires in the winter, look out over immaculate gardens. There are two dining options: the elegant conservatory restaurant and the informal Gumstool Inn. There are also ample function rooms. The health and leisure spa includes an indoor pool, high-tech gym, massage tables, complementary therapies and much more. For children, a supervised crèche and 'playzone' are a great attraction.

Rooms 35 (23 annexe) (13 fmly) (17 GF) ⚓ **S** £224-£454; **D** £249-£479 (incl. bkfst)* **Facilities** Spa STV WiFi ♫ ⊗ ⊹ ♨ ♨ Gym Clay pigeon shooting Archery Cycling Running track Segways Disc golf Xmas New Year Child facilities **Conf** Class 70 Board 35 Thtr 120 Del from £300* **Parking** 150 **Notes** Civ Wed 100

Hare & Hounds Hotel

★★★★ 78% ◉◉ HOTEL

tel: 01666 881000 **Westonbirt GL8 8QL**
email: reception@hareandhoundshotel.com **web:** www.cotswold-inns-hotels.co.uk
dir: 2.5m SW of Tetbury on A433

This popular hotel, set in extensive grounds, is situated close to Westonbirt Arboretum and has remained under the same ownership for over 50 years. The stylish bedrooms are individually designed; those in the main house are more traditional and the cottage rooms are contemporary. The public rooms include an informal bar and light, airy lounges - one with a log fire lit in colder months. Guests can eat either in the bar or the attractive Beaufort Restaurant.

Rooms 42 (21 annexe) (8 fmly) (13 GF) ⚓ **Facilities** FTV WiFi ⊗ ♨ Beauty treatment room Xmas New Year **Conf** Class 80 Board 40 Thtr 120 **Parking** 85 **Notes** Civ Wed 200

HIGHLY RECOMMENDED

The Close Hotel

★★★ 88% ◉◉ HOTEL

tel: 01666 502272 **8 Long St GL8 8AQ**
email: info@theclose-hotel.com **web:** www.cotswold-inns-hotels.co.uk
dir: M4 junct 17 onto A429 or M5 junct 14 onto B4509, follow Tetbury signs

Even with its town centre location, the Close Hotel retains a country-house feel that has made this a favourite with many for years. Bedrooms are striking and well equipped, with thoughtful touches such as home-made biscuits and bottled water. The public rooms provide a choice of relaxing areas with log fires lit in the winter. In the summer, guests can enjoy the terrace in the attractive walled garden.

Rooms 18 ⚓ **Facilities** FTV WiFi Xmas New Year **Conf** Board 22 Thtr 50 **Parking** 10

The Priory Inn

★★★ 78% SMALL HOTEL

tel: 01666 502251 **London Rd GL8 8JJ**
email: info@theprioryinn.co.uk **web:** www.theprioryinn.co.uk
dir: On A433 (Cirencester to Tetbury road). Hotel 200yds from Market Square

A warm welcome is assured at this attractive inn where friendly service is a high priority. Public areas and bedrooms have a contemporary style that mixes well with more traditional features, such as an open fireplace in the cosy bar dining room. Cuisine, using locally sourced produce, is offered on a menu that should suit all tastes.

Rooms 14 (1 fmly) (4 GF) **S** £59-£135; **D** £79-£135 (incl. bkfst)* **Facilities** FTV WiFi ♫ **Conf** Class 28 Board 28 Thtr 30 Del £129* **Parking** 35 **Notes** ⊗

Snooty Fox

★★★ 78% SMALL HOTEL

tel: 01666 502436 **Market Place GL8 8DD**
email: res@snooty-fox.co.uk **web:** www.snooty-fox.co.uk
dir: In town centre

Centrally situated, this 16th-century coaching inn retains original features and is a popular venue for weekend breaks. The relaxed and friendly atmosphere, the high standard of accommodation, and the food offered in the bar and restaurant, are all very good reasons why many guests return here time and again.

Rooms 12 **S** £50-£200; **D** £50-£200 (incl. bkfst)* **Facilities** FTV WiFi ♫ Xmas New Year **Conf** Class 12 Board 16 Thtr 24 Del from £105 to £145* **Notes** LB

T

TEWKESBURY
Gloucestershire   Map 10 SO83

Premier Inn Tewkesbury

BUDGET HOTEL

tel: 0871 527 9088 *(Calls cost 13p per minute plus your phone company's access charge)*
Shannon Way, Ashchurch GL20 8ND
web: www.premierinn.com
dir: *M5 junct 9, A438 towards Tewkesbury, hotel 400yds on right*

High quality, budget accommodation ideal for both families and business travellers. Spacious, en suite bedrooms feature tea and coffee making facilities, and Freeview TV in most hotels. Internet access and WiFi are available for a small fee. The adjacent family restaurant features a wide and varied menu. See also the Hotel Groups pages.

Rooms 59

THETFORD
Norfolk   Map 13 TL88

Premier Inn Thetford

BUDGET HOTEL

tel: 0871 527 9090 *(Calls cost 13p per minute plus your phone company's access charge)*
Lynn Wood, Maine St IP24 3PG
web: www.premierinn.com
dir: *From A11 N follow Thetford signs. At 3rd rdbt 1st exit for town centre into Brandon Rd. 1st exit into Maine St*

High quality, budget accommodation ideal for both families and business travellers. Spacious, en suite bedrooms feature tea and coffee making facilities, and Freeview TV in most hotels. Internet access and WiFi are available for a small fee. The adjacent family restaurant features a wide and varied menu. See also the Hotel Groups pages.

Rooms 70

THORNBURY
Gloucestershire   Map 4 ST69

INSPECTORS' CHOICE

Thornbury Castle

★★★ ◎◎ COUNTRY HOUSE HOTEL

tel: 01454 281182 **Castle St BS35 1HH**
email: info@thornburycastle.co.uk **web:** www.thornburycastle.co.uk
dir: *On A38 N'bound from Bristol take 1st turn to Thornbury. At end of High St left into Castle St, follow brown sign, entrance to Castle on left behind St Mary's Church*

History fans may be interested to learn that Henry VIII ordered the first owner of this castle to be beheaded! Guests today have the opportunity of sleeping in historical surroundings fitted out with all the modern amenities. Most rooms have four-poster or coronet beds and real fires, and guests can even choose to sleep in the Duke's Bedchamber where King Henry and Anne Boleyn once slept, or in the Tower Suite that has reputedly the widest four-poster bed in England. Tranquil lounges enjoy views over the wonderful gardens, while elegant, wood-panelled dining rooms make memorable settings for a leisurely award-winning meal. Activities include falconry and archery and the castle has its own vineyard. Thornbury is, of course, a popular wedding venue.

Rooms 27 (3 fmly) (4 GF) **Facilities** STV FTV WiFi Archery Helicopter rides Clay pigeon shooting Massage treatment Xmas New Year **Conf** Class 40 Board 30 Thtr 70 **Parking** 50 **Notes** Civ Wed 70

THORNTON HOUGH
Merseyside   Map 15 SJ38

Thornton Hall Hotel and Spa

★★★★ 81% ◎◎◎ HOTEL

tel: 0151 336 3938 & 353 3717 **Neston Rd CH63 1JF**
email: reservations@thorntonhallhotel.com **web:** www.thorntonhallhotel.com
dir: *M53 junct 4, B5151/Neston onto B5136 to Thornton Hough, signed*

Dating back to the mid 1800s, this country-house hotel has been extended, restored and updated. An impressive leisure spa boasting excellent facilities and a separate clinical retreat is a key feature. A choice of eateries is available including the Lawn Restaurant. Bedrooms vary in style and include character rooms in the main house and more contemporary rooms in the garden wings. Delightful grounds and extensive banqueting facilities make this a popular wedding and conference venue.

Rooms 62 (12 fmly) (28 GF) **S** £169; **D** £179 (incl. bkfst)* **Facilities** Spa STV FTV WiFi Gym Outdoor spa pools Steam room Snow cave Aerobics studio **Conf** Class 225 Board 80 Thtr 650 Del £121* **Parking** 250 **Notes** Civ Wed 500

THORPE
Derbyshire
Map 16 SK15

The Izaak Walton Hotel
★★★ 81% HOTEL

tel: 01335 350981 & 350555 **Dovedale DE6 2AY**
email: reception@izaakwaltonhotel.com **web:** www.izaakwaltonhotel.com
dir: A515 onto B5054 to Thorpe, over cattle grid & 2 small bridges, 1st right, sharp left

Often it is claimed that a property is in an idyllic location; this could not be truer than for the Izaak Walton Hotel. The 17th-century property named after the author of The Compleat Angler is nestled in the picturesque Dove Valley, dwarfed by the surrounding peaks known as 'Thorpe Cloud' and 'Bunster Hill', on the Derbyshire/ Staffordshire border. Bedrooms are attractively furnished and comfortably appointed. There are a number of small private sittings rooms and an oak-beamed bar in which to relax. Meals are served in the Haddon Restaurant or Dovedale Bar.

Rooms 38 (3 annexe) (6 fmly) (/ GF) **Facilities** WiFi Fishing Xmas New Year **Conf** Class 80 Board 40 Thtr 100 Del from £130 to £150* **Parking** 40 **Notes** Civ Wed 120

THORPENESS
Suffolk
Map 13 TM45

Thorpeness Hotel
★★★ 85% HOTEL

tel: 01728 452176 **Lakeside Av IP16 4NH**
email: info@thorpeness.co.uk **web:** www.thorpeness.co.uk
dir: A1094 towards Aldeburgh, take coast road N for 2m

Thorpeness Golf Club & Hotel is ideally situated in an unspoilt, tranquil setting close to Aldeburgh and Snape Maltings. The extensive public rooms include a choice of lounges, a restaurant overlooking the golf course, a small bar, a snooker room, clubhouse and meeting rooms. The spacious bedrooms are pleasantly decorated, tastefully furnished and equipped with modern facilities. A James Braid 18-hole heathland golf course, and tennis courts, are available.

Rooms 36 (36 annexe) (10 fmly) (10 GF) **Facilities** WiFi HL 18 Putt green Fishing Cycle hire Rowing boat hire Birdwatching Xmas New Year **Conf** Class 30 Board 24 Thtr 130 **Parking** 80 **Notes** Civ Wed 130

THURLASTON
Warwickshire
Map 11 SP47

Draycote Hotel
★★★ 75% HOTEL

tel: 01788 521800 **London Rd CV23 9LF**
email: mail@draycotehotel.co.uk **web:** www.draycotehotel.co.uk
dir: M1 junct 17 onto M45, A45. Hotel 500mtrs on left

Located in the picturesque Warwickshire countryside and within easy reach of motorway networks, this hotel offers modern, comfortable and well-equipped accommodation with a relaxed and friendly welcome. The hotel has a challenging golf course.

Rooms 49 (2 fmly) (24 GF) **Facilities** FTV WiFi 18 Putt green Golf driving range Chipping green Xmas New Year **Conf** Class 78 Board 30 Thtr 250 Del from £110 to £155 **Parking** 150 **Notes** Civ Wed 170

THURLESTONE
Devon
Map 3 SX64

HIGHLY RECOMMENDED

Thurlestone Hotel
★★★★ 83% HOTEL

tel: 01548 560382 **TQ7 3NN**
email: enquiries@thurlestone.co.uk **web:** www.thurlestone.co.uk
dir: A38, A384 into Totnes, A381 towards Kingsbridge, A379 towards Churchstow, onto B3197. Into lane signed to Thurlestone

This perennially popular hotel has been in the same family-ownership since 1896 and continues to go from strength to strength. A vast range of facilities is available for all the family including indoor and outdoor pools, a golf course and a beauty salon. Bedrooms are equipped to ensure a comfortable stay with many having wonderful views of the south Devon coast. The range of eating options includes the elegant and stylish restaurant with its stunning views.

Rooms 65 (23 fmly) **S** £80-£525; **D** £210-£555 (incl. bkfst)* **Facilities** Spa STV FTV WiFi supervised 9 Putt green Gym Squash Badminton Table tennis Games & Snooker room Toddler room Beauty treatment room Xmas New Year Child facilities **Conf** Class 100 Board 40 Thtr 150 Del from £195 to £595* **Services** Lift **Parking** 121 **Notes** LB Closed 1st 2 wks Jan Civ Wed 160

THURSFORD
Norfolk
Map 13 TF93

The Old Forge Seafood Restaurant
 RESTAURANT WITH ROOMS

tel: 01328 878345 **Fakenham Rd NR21 0BD**
email: sarah.goldspink@btconnect.com **web:** www.seafoodnorthnorfolk.co.uk
dir: On A148 (Fakenham to Holt road)

Expect a warm welcome at this delightfully relaxed restaurant with rooms. The open-plan public areas include a lounge bar with comfy sofas, and an intimate restaurant with pine tables. Bedrooms are pleasantly decorated and equipped with a good range of useful facilities.

Rooms 3

TICEHURST
East Sussex
Map 6 TQ63

Dale Hill Hotel & Golf Club
★★★★ 79% HOTEL

tel: 01580 200112 **TN5 7DQ**
email: info@dalehill.co.uk **web:** www.dalehill.co.uk
dir: M25 junct 5, A21. 5m after Lamberhurst, right at lights onto B2087 to Flimwell. Hotel 1m on left

This modern hotel is situated just a short drive from the village. Extensive public rooms include a lounge bar, a conservatory brasserie, a formal restaurant and the Spike Bar, which is mainly frequented by golf club members and has a lively atmosphere. The hotel also has two superb 18-hole golf courses, a swimming pool and gym.

Rooms 35 (8 fmly) (23 GF) **S** £69-£170; **D** £79-£180 (incl. bkfst)* **Facilities** FTV WiFi 36 Putt green Gym Covered driving range Pool table Xmas New Year **Conf** Class 50 Board 50 Thtr 120 Del from £109 to £129* **Services** Lift **Parking** 220 **Notes** LB Civ Wed 150

T

TINTAGEL
Cornwall

Map 2 SX08

Atlantic View Hotel

★★ 81% SMALL HOTEL

tel: 01840 770221 **Treknow PL34 OEJ**
email: atlantic-view@eclipse.co.uk **web:** www.atlanticviewhoteltintagel.co.uk
dir: B3263 to Tregatta, turn left into Treknow, hotel on road to Trebarwith Strand Beach

Conveniently located for all the attractions of Tintagel, this family-run hotel has a wonderfully relaxed and welcoming atmosphere. Public areas include a bar, comfortable lounge, TV/games room and heated swimming pool. Bedrooms are generally spacious and some have the added advantage of distant sea views.

Rooms 9 (1 fmly) ⌇ **S** £76–£78; **D** £108–£112 (incl. bkfst)* **Facilities** FTV WiFi ⊗ Pool table **Parking** 10 **Notes** LB ⊗ Closed Nov-Feb RS Mar

TITCHWELL
Norfolk

Map 13 TF74

HIGHLY RECOMMENDED

Titchwell Manor Hotel

★★★ 86% ⊚⊚⊚ HOTEL

tel: 01485 210221 **PE31 8BB**
email: eric@titchwellmanor.com **web:** www.titchwellmanor.com
dir: On A149 coast rd, between Brancaster & Thornham

Titchwell Manor Hotel is a friendly, family-run hotel ideally placed for touring the north Norfolk coastline. The tastefully appointed bedrooms are very comfortable; some in the adjacent annexe offer ground floor access. Smart public rooms include a lounge area, relaxed informal bar and the delightful Conservatory Restaurant, overlooking the walled garden. Head Chef Eric Snaith produces imaginative menus that feature quality local produce and fresh fish.

Rooms 27 (19 annexe) (4 fmly) (16 GF) ⌇ **S** £50–£150; **D** £80–£230 (incl. bkfst)* **Facilities** FTV WiFi Xmas New Year **Conf** Class 50 Board 30 Thtr 30 **Parking** 50 **Notes** Civ Wed 90

TOLLARD ROYAL
Wiltshire

Map 4 ST91

King John Inn

⊚⊚ RESTAURANT WITH ROOMS

tel: 01725 516207 **SP5 5PS**
email: info@kingjohninn.co.uk **web:** www.kingjohninn.co.uk
dir: From A354 or A350 onto B3081

Part of The Epicurean Collection, The King John Inn is a traditional style country inn located in a country village. It has a Victorian-style garden pavilion serving seasonal classics such as chargrilled lobster and pigeon sala. The recently added Dove Cottage offers three more en suite bedrooms to go with the five rooms at the inn. All have feature bathrooms. Food and wine is a real feature here with local ingredients much in evidence, alongside excellent levels of hospitality and customer care. Ample parking for residents.

Rooms 8 (3 annexe)

TOLLESHUNT KNIGHTS
Essex

Map 7 TL91

Crowne Plaza Resort Colchester - Five Lakes

★★★★ 74% HOTEL

tel: 01621 868888 **Colchester Rd CM9 8HX**
email: enquiries@cpcolchester.co.uk **web:** www.cpcolchester.co.uk
dir: Exit A12 at Kelvedon, follow brown signs through Tiptree to hotel

This hotel is set amidst 320 acres of open countryside, featuring two golf courses. The spacious bedrooms are furnished to a high standard and have excellent facilities. The public rooms offer a high degree of comfort and include five bars, two restaurants and a large lounge. The property also boasts extensive leisure facilities.

Rooms 194 (80 annexe) (4 fmly) (40 GF) ⌇ **S** £89–£129; **D** £89–£129 **Facilities** Spa STV FTV WiFi ⊗ ↨ 36 ⌂ Putt green Gym Squash Sauna Steam room Badminton Aerobics Studio Nail lounge Relaxation room Xmas New Year **Conf** Class 700 Board 60 Thtr 2000 Del from £129 to £169 **Services** Lift **Parking** 550 **Notes** LB ⊗ Civ Wed 250

TONBRIDGE
Kent

Map 6 TQ54

Best Western Rose & Crown Hotel

BW Best Western.

★★★ 79% HOTEL

tel: 01732 357966 **125 High St TN9 1DD**
email: rose.crown@bestwestern.co.uk **web:** www.roseandcrowntonbridge.co.uk

A 15th-century coaching inn situated in the heart of this bustling town centre. The public areas are light and airy yet still retain much original character such as oak beams and Jacobean panelling. Food is served throughout the day in the Oak Room Bar & Grill. Bedrooms are stylishly decorated, spacious and well presented; amenities include free WiFi.

Rooms 56 (3 fmly) (10 GF) ⌇ **Facilities** FTV WiFi ↨ **Conf** Class 60 Board 60 Thtr 80 **Parking** 43 **Notes** ⊗ Closed 27 Dec-5 Jan RS 24-26 Dec

T

Premier Inn Tonbridge

BUDGET HOTEL

tel: 0871 527 9096 *(Calls cost 13p per minute plus your phone company's access charge)*
Pembury Rd TN11 0NA
web: www.premierinn.com
dir: *11m from M25 junct 5. Follow A21 towards Hastings, pass A26 (Tunbridge Wells) junct. Exit at next junct, 1st exit at rdbt*

High quality, budget accommodation ideal for both families and business travellers. Spacious, en suite bedrooms feature tea and coffee making facilities, and Freeview TV in most hotels. Internet access and WiFi are available for a small fee. The adjacent family restaurant features a wide and varied menu. See also the Hotel Groups pages.

Rooms 40

Premier Inn Tonbridge North

BUDGET HOTEL

tel: 0871 527 9098 *(Calls cost 13p per minute plus your phone company's access charge)*
Hilden Manor, London Rd TN10 3AN
web: www.premierinn.com
dir: *From A21 follow Seven Oaks & Hildenborough signs. At rdbt take 2nd exit onto B245 signed Hildenborough. In 2m hotel on right*

Rooms 41

TORBAY

See **Brixham, Paignton & Torquay**

TORQUAY
Devon

Map 3 SX96

The Imperial Hotel

★★★★ 82% ⊛ HOTEL

tel: 01803 294301 **Park Hill Rd TQ1 2DG**
email: imperialtorquay@thehotelcollection.co.uk **web:** www.thehotelcollection.co.uk
dir: *A380 towards seafront. Turn left to harbour, right at clocktower. Hotel 300yds on right*

This hotel has an enviable location with extensive views of the coastline. Traditional in style, the public areas are elegant and offer a choice of dining options including the Regatta Restaurant, with its stunning views over the bay. Bedrooms are spacious, most with private balconies, and the hotel has an extensive range of indoor and outdoor leisure facilities.

Rooms 152 (14 fmly) ✿ **Facilities** Spa STV WiFi 🕲 ✇ supervised ⌇ Gym Beauty salon Sauna Steam room Xmas New Year **Conf** Class 200 Board 30 Thtr 350 Del from £103 to £160* **Services** Lift **Parking** 140 **Notes** Civ Wed 250

Grand Hotel

★★★★ 77% ⊛ HOTEL

RICHARDSON HOTELS
Where Memories are Made

tel: 01803 296677 **Sea Front TQ2 6NT**
email: reservations@grandtorquay.co.uk **web:** www.grandtorquay.co.uk
dir: *A380 to Torquay. At seafront turn right, then 1st right. Hotel on corner, entrance 1st on left*

Within level walking distance of the town, this large Edwardian hotel overlooks the bay and offers modern facilities. Many of the bedrooms, some with balconies, enjoy the best of the views, but all are very well equipped. The Compass Bar also benefits from the stunning views, and offers an informal alternative to the 1881 Restaurant.

Rooms 132 (32 fmly) (3 GF) ✿ **Facilities** FTV WiFi ▷ 🕲 ✇ supervised Gym ESPA Spa, Indoor & Outdoor heated pools Xmas New Year **Conf** Class 150 Board 60 Thtr 250 **Services** Lift **Parking** 57 **Notes** Civ Wed 250

Palace Hotel

★★★★ 72% HOTEL

tel: 01803 200200 **Babbacombe Rd TQ1 3TG**
email: info@palacetorquay.co.uk **web:** www.palacetorquay.co.uk
dir: *Towards harbour, left by clocktower into Babbacombe Rd, hotel on right after 1m*

Set in 25 acres of stunning, beautifully tended wooded grounds, the Palace offers a tranquil environment. Suitable for business and leisure, the hotel boasts a huge range of well-presented indoor and outdoor facilities. Much of the original charm and grandeur is still in evidence, particularly in the dining room. Many of the bedrooms enjoy views of the magnificent gardens.

Rooms 141 (7 fmly) **Facilities** WiFi 🕲 ✇ 9 ⌇ Putt green ⌇ Gym Squash Table tennis Snooker Childrens' play area Xmas New Year **Conf** Class 800 Board 40 Thtr 1000 **Services** Lift **Parking** 140 **Notes** ⊗ Civ Wed

The Headland Hotel

★★★ 83% ⊛ HOTEL

tel: 01803 295666 **Daddyhole Rd TQ1 2EF**
email: info@headlandtorquay.com **web:** www.headlandtorquay.com
dir: *A380 to Torquay sea front, left then far side of harbour, up hill, 500mtrs & turn right*

This hotel has a delightful location set apart from the bustle of town, but within easy walking distance of the numerous attractions. With its splendid grounds and an elevated view of the bay, the hotel has an enviable position. Bedrooms are very comfortably appointed, many with sea views. Cuisine is a highlight, and the friendly team offer attentive service.

Rooms 78 (16 fmly) (7 GF) ✿ **S** £47-£70; **D** £94-£200 (incl. bkfst & dinner)*
Facilities FTV WiFi 🕲 ⌇ Gym Sauna Steam room ♫ Xmas New Year **Conf** Class 50 Board 40 Thtr 150 **Services** Lift **Parking** 42 **Notes** LB ⊗ Civ Wed 150

Corbyn Head Hotel

★★★ 79% ⊛ HOTEL

tel: 01803 213611 **Torbay Rd, Sea Front TQ2 6RH**
email: info@corbynhead.com **web:** www.corbynhead.com
dir: *Follow signs to Torquay seafront, turn right on seafront. Hotel on right with green canopies*

This hotel occupies a prime position overlooking Torbay, and offers well-equipped bedrooms, many with sea views and some with balconies. The staff are friendly and welcoming, and a well-stocked bar and comfortable lounge are available. Guests can enjoy fine dining in the Harbour View Restaurant, with attentive service assured.

Rooms 45 (4 fmly) (9 GF) **S** £70-£80; **D** £140-£160 (incl. bkfst)* **Facilities** FTV WiFi Squash Use of leisure facilities at sister hotel ♫ Xmas New Year **Conf** Class 30 Board 30 Thtr 80 **Parking** 50 **Notes** LB Civ Wed 85

T

TORQUAY *continued*

Livermead House Hotel

★★★ 76% HOTEL

tel: 01803 294361 & 294363 **Torbay Rd TQ2 6QJ**
email: info@livermead.com **web:** www.livermead.com
dir: *From seafront turn right, follow A379 towards Paignton & Livermead, hotel opposite Institute Beach*

Having a splendid waterfront location, this hotel dates back to the 1820s, and is where Charles Kingsley is said to have written *The Water Babies*. Bedrooms vary in size and style; excellent public rooms are popular for private parties and meetings, and a range of leisure facilities is provided. Enjoyable cuisine is served in the impressive restaurant.

Rooms 67 (6 fmly) (1 GF) **⌂ Facilities** FTV WiFi ⤳ Gym Squash Sauna Games room ♫ Xmas **Conf** Class 175 Board 80 Thtr 250 **Services** Lift **Parking** 131 **Notes** Civ Wed 250

Best Western Livermead Cliff Hotel

BW Best Western.

★★★ 74% HOTEL

tel: 01803 299666 **Torbay Rd TQ2 6RQ**
email: info@livermeadcliff.co.uk **web:** www.livermeadcliff.co.uk
dir: *A379, A3022 to Torquay, towards seafront, turn right towards Paignton. Hotel 600yds on seaward side*

Situated at the water's edge, this long-established hotel offers friendly service and traditional hospitality. The splendid views can be enjoyed from the lounge, bar and dining room. Alternatively, guests can take advantage of refreshment on the wonderful terrace and enjoy one of the best outlooks in the bay. Bedrooms, many with sea views and some with balconies, are comfortable and well equipped; a range of room sizes is available.

Rooms 65 (17 fmly) ⌂ **Facilities** FTV WiFi Fishing Use of facilities at sister hotel Xmas New Year **Conf** Class 60 Board 40 Thtr 120 **Services** Lift **Parking** 80 **Notes** Civ Wed 200

Abbey Lawn Hotel

★★★ 72% HOTEL

tel: 01803 299199 & 203181 **Scarborough Rd TQ2 5UQ**
email: nburfitt@holdsworthhotels.co.uk
web: www.holdsworthhotels.co.uk/the-abbey-lawn

Conveniently located for both the seafront and town centre, this is an ideal base for visiting the attractions of the 'English Riviera'. Many of the bedrooms, including the four-poster suite, benefit from lovely sea views. Facilities include a health club with extensive leisure activities, plus indoor and outdoor pools. Traditional cuisine is served in the elegant restaurant, and evening entertainment is a regular feature in the ballroom.

Rooms 57 (3 fmly) **Facilities** ⊛ ⤳ Gym ♫ Xmas New Year **Services** Lift **Parking** 20 **Notes** ⊗ Closed Jan

Anchorage Hotel

★★★ 71% HOTEL

tel: 01803 326175 **Cary Park, Aveland Rd, Babbacombe TQ1 3PT**
email: enquiries@anchoragehotel.co.uk **web:** www.anchoragehotel.co.uk

Quietly located in a residential area and providing a friendly welcome, this family-run establishment enjoys a great deal of repeat business. Bedrooms come in a range of sizes but all rooms are neatly presented. Evening entertainment is provided regularly in the large and comfortable lounge.

Rooms 56 (5 fmly) (17 GF) **Facilities** FTV WiFi ⤳ ♫ Xmas New Year **Services** Lift **Parking** 26 **Notes** LB

Regina Hotel

★★★ 59% HOTEL

Leisureplex
HOLIDAY HOTELS

tel: 01803 292904 **Victoria Pde TQ1 2BE**
email: regina@leisureplex.co.uk **web:** www.leisureplex.co.uk
dir: *Into Torquay, follow harbour signs, hotel on outer corner of harbour*

This hotel enjoys a pleasant and convenient location right on the harbourside, a short stroll from the town's attractions. Bedrooms, some with harbour views, vary in size. Entertainment is provided on most nights and there is a choice of bars.

Rooms 68 (5 fmly) **Facilities** FTV ♫ Xmas New Year **Services** Lift **Parking** 6 **Notes** ⊗ Closed Jan & part Feb RS Nov-Dec (ex Xmas) & Feb-Mar

Ashley Court Hotel

★★ 64% HOTEL

tel: 01803 292417 **107 Abbey Rd TQ2 5NP**
email: reception@ashleycourt.co.uk **web:** www.ashleycourt.co.uk
dir: *A380 to seafront, left to Shedden Hill to lights, hotel opposite*

Located close to the town centre and within easy strolling distance of the seafront, this hotel offers a warm welcome to guests. Bedrooms are pleasantly appointed and some have sea views. The outdoor pool and patio are popular with guests wishing to soak up some sunshine. Live entertainment is provided every night throughout the season.

Rooms 83 (12 fmly) (8 GF) (14 smoking) ⌂ **Facilities** ⤳ Games room ♫ Xmas New Year **Services** Lift **Parking** 42 **Notes** ⊗ Closed 3 Jan-1 Feb

Premier Inn Torquay

BUDGET HOTEL

tel: 0871 527 9102 *(Calls cost 13p per minute plus your phone company's access charge)*
Seafront, Belgrave Rd TQ2 5HE
web: www.premierinn.com
dir: *On A380 into Torquay, continue to lights (Torre Station on right). Right into Avenue Road to Kings Drive. Left at seafront, hotel at lights*

High quality, budget accommodation ideal for both families and business travellers. Spacious, en suite bedrooms feature tea and coffee making facilities, and Freeview TV in most hotels. Internet access and WiFi are available for a small fee. The adjacent family restaurant features a wide and varied menu. See also the Hotel Groups pages.

Rooms 143

Orestone Manor

 ☺☺ ⚲ RESTAURANT WITH ROOMS

tel: 01803 328098 **Rockhouse Ln, Maidencombe TQ1 4SX**
email: info@orestonemanor.com **web:** www.orestonemanor.com
dir: *N of Torquay on A379, on sharp bend in village of Maidencombe*

Set in an fabulous location overlooking the bay, Orestone Manor has a long history of providing fine food and very comfortable accommodation, coupled with friendly, attentive service. Log fires burn in cooler months, and there is a conservatory, a bar and a sitting room for guests to enjoy. AA Rosettes have been awarded for the uncomplicated modern cuisine which is based on quality local produce.

Rooms 14 (3 annexe) (6 fmly)

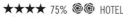

TRING	
Hertfordshire	Map 6 SP91

Pendley Manor Hotel

★★★★ 75% ☺☺ HOTEL

tel: 01442 891891 **Cow Ln HP23 5QY**
email: info@pendley-manor.co.uk **web:** www.pendley-manor.co.uk
dir: *M25 junct 20, A41 Tring exit. At rdbt follow Berkhamsted/London signs. 1st left signed Tring Station & Pendley Manor*

Pendley Manor Hotel is an impressive Victorian mansion set in extensive and mature landscaped grounds where peacocks roam. The spacious bedrooms are situated in both the manor house and the wing, and offer a useful range of facilities. Public areas include a cosy bar, a conservatory lounge and an intimate restaurant as well as a leisure centre.

Rooms 72 (17 fmly) (17 GF) **Facilities** Spa FTV WiFi ↳ ☏ ⚲ Gym Steam room Dance Studio Sauna Snooker room **Conf** Class 80 Board 80 Thtr 250 **Services** Lift **Parking** 150 **Notes** ⊗ Civ Wed 160

Premier Inn Tring

BUDGET HOTEL

tel: 0871 527 9104 *(Calls cost 13p per minute plus your phone company's access charge)*
Tring Hill HP23 4LD
web: www.premierinn.com
dir: *M25 junct 20, A41 towards Aylesbury, at end of Hemel Hempstead/Tring bypass straight on at rdbt, hotel approx 100yds on right*

High quality, budget accommodation ideal for both families and business travellers. Spacious, en suite bedrooms feature tea and coffee making facilities, and Freeview TV in most hotels. Internet access and WiFi are available for a small fee. The adjacent family restaurant features a wide and varied menu. See also the Hotel Groups pages.

Rooms 42

TROWBRIDGE	
Wiltshire	Map 4 ST85

Premier Inn Trowbridge

BUDGET HOTEL

tel: 0871 527 9444 *(Calls cost 13p per minute plus your phone company's access charge)*
St Stephens Place BA14 8AH
web: www.premierinn.com
dir: *M4 junct 17, A429 (Chippenham). A350 (Warminster & Poole). 12m. After Seminton rdbt, at 2nd lights right into West Ashton Rd (Trowbridge). At 1st mini rdbt 2nd exit, at 2nd mini rdbt into County Way. At major rdbt 5th exit into Castle St. At mini rdbt 3rd exit, hotel on right*

High quality, budget accommodation ideal for both families and business travellers. Spacious, en suite bedrooms feature tea and coffee making facilities, and Freeview TV in most hotels. Internet access and WiFi are available for a small fee. The adjacent family restaurant features a wide and varied menu. See also the Hotel Groups pages.

Rooms 80

TRURO	
Cornwall	Map 2 SW84

The Alverton Hotel

★★★★ 76% ☺ HOTEL

tel: 01872 276633 **Tregolls Rd TR1 1ZQ**
email: stay@thealverton.co.uk **web:** www.thealverton.co.uk
dir: *From A30 at Carland Cross take A39 to Truro. At lights right onto A39 (Tregolls Rd) signed Truro/Falmouth*

The Alverton Hotel is a beautiful Grade II listed building which was previously a convent. The bedrooms are smartly decorated, and there is a comfortable lounge/cocktail bar, as well as an attractive restaurant that serves popular meals using locally-sourced produce. Parking is available.

Rooms 33 (4 fmly) (3 GF) **Facilities** FTV WiFi ↳ Xmas New Year **Conf** Class 50 Board 30 Thtr 140 **Parking** 71 **Notes** Civ Wed 90

T

TRURO *continued*

Mannings Hotel

★★★ 87% HOTEL

tel: 01872 270345 **Lemon St TR1 2QB**
email: reception@manningshotels.co.uk **web:** www.manningshotels.co.uk
dir: *A30 to Carland Cross then Truro. Follow brown signs to hotel in city centre*

This popular hotel is located in the heart of Truro and offers an engaging blend of traditional and contemporary. Public areas have a stylish atmosphere with the bar and restaurant proving popular with locals and residents alike. A wide choice of appetising dishes is available, including ethnic, classic and vegetarian as well as daily specials. Bedrooms are pleasantly appointed.

Rooms 43 (9 annexe) (4 fmly) (3 GF) ✿ **S** £65-£85; **D** £85-£115 (incl. bkfst)*
Facilities FTV WiFi **Parking** 43 **Notes** LB ⊗ Closed 25-26 Dec

Premier Inn Truro

BUDGET HOTEL

tel: 0871 527 9106 *(Calls cost 13p per minute plus your phone company's access charge)*
Old Carnon Hill, Carnon Downs TR3 6JT
web: www.premierinn.com
dir: *On A39 (Truro to Falmouth road), 3m SW of Truro*

High quality, budget accommodation ideal for both families and business travellers. Spacious, en suite bedrooms feature tea and coffee making facilities, and Freeview TV in most hotels. Internet access and WiFi are available for a small fee. The adjacent family restaurant features a wide and varied menu. See also the Hotel Groups pages.

Rooms 86

| TUNBRIDGE WELLS (ROYAL) Kent | Map 6 TQ53 |

The Spa Hotel

★★★★ 81% ⊛⊛ HOTEL

tel: 01892 520331 **Mount Ephraim TN4 8XJ**
email: reservations@spahotel.co.uk **web:** www.spahotel.co.uk
dir: *A21 to A26, follow A264 East Grinstead signs, hotel on right*

Set in 14 acres of beautifully tended grounds, this imposing 18th-century mansion offers spacious, modern bedrooms that are stylishly decorated and thoughtfully equipped. The public rooms include the Chandelier Restaurant, a champagne bar and the Orangery which complements the traditional lounge. There are extensive meeting and health club facilities, and a spa offering treatment rooms. It is also licensed for civil wedding ceremonies.

Rooms 70 (4 fmly) (1 GF) ✿ **S** £88.95-£129; **D** £116.90-£198 (incl. bkfst)*
Facilities Spa STV FTV WiFi ⊙ ⊗ ⚹ Gym Xmas New Year **Conf** Class 90 Board 90 Thtr 300 **Services** Lift **Parking** 150 **Notes** LB ⊗ Civ Wed 150

Hotel du Vin Tunbridge Wells

★★★★ 75% ⊛ TOWN HOUSE HOTEL

tel: 01892 232 0749 **Crescent Rd TN1 2LY**
email: reception.tunbridgewells@hotelduvin.com **web:** www.hotelduvin.com
dir: *Follow town centre, to main junct of Mount Pleasant Rd & Crescent Rd/Church Rd. Hotel 150yds on right just past Phillips House*

This impressive Grade II listed building dates from 1762, and as a princess, Queen Victoria often stayed here. The spacious bedrooms are available in a range of sizes, beautifully and individually appointed, and equipped with a host of thoughtful extras. Public rooms include a bistro-style restaurant, two elegant lounges and a small bar.

Rooms 34 ✿ **Facilities** STV WiFi Boules **Conf** Class 40 Board 25 Thtr 60 **Services** Lift **Parking** 30 **Notes** Civ Wed 84

Mercure Tunbridge Wells

★★★★ 70% HOTEL

tel: 01892 823567 & 0844 815 9074 *(Calls cost 7p per minute plus your phone company's access charge)* **8 Tonbridge Rd, Pembury TN2 4QL**
email: sales.mercuretunbridgewells@jupiterhotels.co.uk
web: www.mercuretunbridgewells.co.uk
dir: *M25 junct 5, A21 S. Left at 1st rdbt signed Pembury Hospital. Hotel on left, 400yds past hospital*

Built in the style of a traditional Kentish oast house, this well presented hotel is conveniently located just off the A21 with easy access to the M25. Bedrooms are comfortably appointed for both business and leisure guests. Public areas include a leisure club and a range of meeting rooms.

Rooms 84 (12 fmly) (40 GF) ✿ **Facilities** STV FTV WiFi ⇘ HL ⊙ Steam room Sauna Beauty treatment room Xmas New Year **Conf** Class 80 Board 50 Thtr 150 Del from £115 to £175* **Parking** 100 **Notes** Civ Wed 180

Russell Hotel

★★ 65% METRO HOTEL

tel: 01892 544833 **80 London Rd TN1 1DZ**
email: sales@russell-hotel.com **web:** www.russell-hotel.com
dir: *From Tunbridge Wells A26 junct with Lime Hill Road turn*

This detached Victorian property is situated just a short walk from the centre of town. The generously proportioned bedrooms in the main house are pleasantly decorated and well equipped. In addition, there are several smartly appointed, self-contained suites in an adjacent building. The public rooms include a lounge and cosy bar.

Rooms 26 (5 annexe) (5 fmly) (1 GF) **Facilities** FTV WiFi **Conf** Class 10 Board 10 Thtr 10 **Parking** 14 **Notes** ⊗

TURNERS HILL
West Sussex   Map 6 TQ33

Alexander House Hotel & Utopia Spa

★★★★★ 87% HOTEL

tel: 01342 714914 **East St RH10 4QD**
email: admin@alexanderhouse.co.uk **web:** www.alexanderhouse.co.uk
dir: *6m from M23 junct 10, on B2110 between Turners Hill & East Grinstead*

Set in 175 acres of parkland and landscaped gardens, this delightful country house hotel dates back to the 17th century. Most of the bedrooms are very spacious and all have luxurious bathrooms; the rooms in the most recent wing are particularly stunning. The Utopia Spa has a state-of-the-art pool and gym, as well as specialised treatments.

Rooms 58 (20 annexe) (13 fmly) (10 GF) **Facilities** Spa FTV WiFi Gym Clay shooting Archery Mountain bikes Pony trekking Xmas New Year **Conf** Class 70 Board 40 Thtr 150 **Services** Lift **Parking** 100 **Notes** Civ Wed 100

TWICKENHAM
Greater London

Premier Inn Twickenham East

BUDGET HOTEL PLAN 1 B2

tel: 0871 527 9108 *(Calls cost 13p per minute plus your phone company's access charge)*
Corner Sixth Cross, Staines Rd TW2 5PE
web: www.premierinn.com
dir: *M25 junct 12 onto M3, follow Central London signs, at end of M3 becomes A316. Straight on at 1st rdbt. Hotel 500yds on left*

High quality, budget accommodation ideal for both families and business travellers. Spacious, en suite bedrooms feature tea and coffee making facilities, and Freeview TV in most hotels. Internet access and WiFi are available for a small fee. The adjacent family restaurant features a wide and varied menu. See also the Hotel Groups pages.

Rooms 17

Premier Inn Twickenham Stadium
BUDGET HOTEL PLAN 1 B2

tel: 0871 527 9110 *(Calls cost 13p per minute plus your phone company's access charge)*
Chertsey Rd, Whitton TW2 6LS
web: www.premierinn.com
dir: *From M3 onto A316, then A305 signed Twickenham. At Hospital Bridge Rdbt 3rd exit into Hospital Bridge Rd. Take B358 signed Teddington. Becomes Sixth Cross Rd. Hotel on left*

Rooms 39

TWO BRIDGES
Devon   Map 3 SX67

Two Bridges Hotel
★★★ 78% ◉◉ HOTEL

tel: 01822 892300 **PL20 6SW**
email: enquiries@twobridges.co.uk **web:** www.twobridges.co.uk
dir: *At junct of B3212 & B3357*

This wonderfully relaxing hotel is set in the heart of the Dartmoor National Park, in a beautiful riverside location. Three standards of comfortable rooms provide every modern convenience, and include four-poster rooms. There is a choice of lounges, and fine dining is available in the restaurant, where menus feature local game and other seasonal produce.

Rooms 32 (2 fmly) (10 GF) **Facilities** STV WiFi Fishing Xmas New Year **Conf** Class 60 Board 40 Thtr 130 **Parking** 100 **Notes** LB Closed 7-14 Sep Civ Wed 130

TYNEMOUTH
Tyne & Wear   Map 21 NZ36

Grand Hotel
★★★ 83% HOTEL

tel: 0191 293 6666 **Grand Pde NE30 4ER**
email: reservations@grandhotel-uk.com **web:** www.grandhotel-uk.com
dir: *A1058 for Tynemouth. At coast rdbt turn right. Hotel on right approx 0.5m*

This grand Victorian building offers stunning views of the coast. Bedrooms come in a variety of styles and are well equipped, tastefully decorated and have impressive bathrooms. In addition to the restaurant there are two bars. The elegant and imposing staircase is a focal point, and is a favourite spot for the bride and groom to have their photograph taken after their wedding here.

Rooms 46 (6 annexe) (14 fmly) **Facilities** STV FTV WiFi Xmas New Year **Conf** Class 40 Board 40 Thtr 130 **Services** Lift **Parking** 16 **Notes** RS Sun evening Civ Wed 120

UCKFIELD
East Sussex   Map 6 TQ42

INSPECTORS' CHOICE

Buxted Park Hotel
★★★★ ◉◉ HOTEL

tel: 01825 733333 & 0845 072 7412 *(Calls cost 5p per minute plus your phone company's access charge)* **Buxted TN22 4AY**
email: buxtedpark@handpicked.co.uk **web:** www.handpickedhotels.co.uk/buxtedpark
dir: *From A26 Uckfield bypass take A272 signed Buxted. Through lights, hotel 1m on right*

Buxted Park Hotel is an attractive Grade II listed Georgian mansion dating back to the 17th century, set amidst 300 acres of beautiful countryside and landscaped gardens. The stylish, thoughtfully equipped bedrooms are split between the main house and the modern Garden Wing. An interesting choice of dishes is served in the restaurant.

Rooms 44 (7 fmly) (16 GF) **S** £99-£199; **D** £99-£423 (incl. bkfst)*
Facilities STV WiFi HL Fishing Gym Orienteering Walking trail Snooker room Xmas New Year **Conf** Class 80 Board 42 Thtr 180 Del from £140 to £165*
Services Lift **Parking** 100 **Notes** LB Civ Wed 120

UCKFIELD *continued*

East Sussex National Golf Resort & Spa

★★★★ 81% @@ HOTEL

tel: 01825 880088 **Little Horsted TN22 5ES**
email: reception@eastsussexnational.co.uk **web:** www.eastsussexnational.co.uk
dir: *M25 junct 6, A22 signed East Grinstead & Eastbourne. Straight on at rdbt junct of A22 & A26 (Little Horsted). At next rdbt right to hotel*

This modern hotel is located in a lovely country location and offers a super range of facilities with two golf courses and an impressive leisure suite. In addition there are also conference and meeting facilities. The bedrooms are spacious and have good facilities; all have delightful views across the golf course to the countryside beyond. The cuisine is enjoyable; particularly at breakfast, which is served in the restaurant that overlooks the course.

Rooms 104 (3 fmly) (36 GF) 🐾 **Facilities** Spa STV FTV WiFi ↻ HL ⊗ ⚓ 36 ⚑ Putt green ⚑ Gym Academy of Golf Xmas New Year **Conf** Class 200 Board 50 Thtr 450 **Services** Lift Air con **Parking** 500 **Notes** ⊗ Civ Wed 250

Horsted Place

★★★ @@ ⚑ HOTEL

tel: 01825 750581 **Little Horsted TN22 5TS**
email: hotel@horstedplace.co.uk **web:** www.horstedplace.co.uk
dir: *From Uckfield 2m S on A26 towards Lewes*

This property is one of Britain's finest examples of Gothic revivalist architecture, and much of the 1850s building was designed by Augustus Pugin. The hotel is situated in extensive landscaped grounds, with a tennis court and croquet lawn, and is adjacent to the East Sussex National Golf Club. The spacious bedrooms, in a range of both sizes and designs, are attractively decorated, tastefully furnished, and equipped with many thoughtful touches such as flowers and books. Most bedrooms also have a separate sitting area. Formal dining can be enjoyed in the elegant dining room (no children after 7pm) where the menus are based on quality seasonal produce. Pre-dinner drinks and after-dinner coffees can be enjoyed either in the Drawing Room or on the terrace overlooking the garden.

Rooms 20 (3 annexe) (5 fmly) (2 GF) 🐾 **S** £145-£375; **D** £145-£375 (incl. bkfst)* **Facilities** STV FTV WiFi ⚓ 36 ⚑ ⚑ Free use of gym & indoor pool at nearby hotel ♫ Xmas **Conf** Class 50 Board 40 Thtr 80 Del from £170* **Services** Lift **Parking** 32 **Notes** LB ⊗ No children 7yrs Closed 1-7 Jan Civ Wed 100

Best Western Plus Ullesthorpe Court Hotel & Golf Club

BW Best Western PLUS

★★★★ 77% HOTEL

tel: 01455 209023 **Frolesworth Rd LE17 5BZ**
email: bookings@ullesthorpecourt.co.uk **web:** www.bw-ullesthorpecourt.co.uk
dir: *M1 junct 20 towards Lutterworth. Follow brown tourist signs*

Complete with its own golf club, this impressively equipped hotel is within easy reach of the motorway network, NEC and Birmingham airport. Public areas include both formal and informal eating options and extensive conference and leisure facilities. Spacious bedrooms are thoughtfully equipped for both the business and leisure guest, and a four-poster room is available.

Rooms 72 (3 fmly) (16 GF) 🐾 **Facilities** Spa FTV WiFi ↻ ⊗ supervised ⚓ 18 ⚑ Putt green Gym Beauty room Steam room Sauna Snooker room New Year **Conf** Class 48 Board 30 Thtr 80 **Services** Lift **Parking** 280 **Notes** ⊗ RS 25-26 Dec Civ Wed 120

See **Glenridding & Patterdale**

Lords of the Manor

★★★★ @@@ COUNTRY HOUSE HOTEL

tel: 01451 820243 **GL54 2JD**
email: reservations@lordsofthemanor.com **web:** www.lordsofthemanor.com
dir: *2m W of A429. Exit A40 onto A429, take 'The Slaughters' turn. Through Lower Slaughter for 1m to Upper Slaughter. Hotel on right*

This wonderfully welcoming 17th-century manor house hotel sits in eight acres of gardens and parkland surrounded by Cotswold countryside. A relaxed atmosphere, underpinned by professional and attentive service is the hallmark here, so that guests are often reluctant to leave. The hotel has elegant public rooms that overlook the immaculate lawns, and the restaurant is the venue for consistently impressive cuisine. Bedrooms have much character and charm, combined with the extra touches expected of a hotel of this stature.

Rooms 26 (4 fmly) (9 GF) 🐾 **S** £150-£510; **D** £195-£510 (incl. bkfst)* **Facilities** FTV WiFi Fishing ⚑ Xmas New Year **Conf** Class 20 Board 20 Thtr 30 Del from £275 to £375* **Parking** 40 **Notes** LB Civ Wed 80

UPPINGHAM
Rutland   Map 11 SP89

The Lake Isle
◉◉ ☗ RESTAURANT WITH ROOMS

tel: 01572 822951 **16 High Street East LE15 9PZ**
email: info@lakeisle.co.uk **web:** www.lakeisle.co.uk
dir: From A47, turn left at 2nd lights, 100yds on right

This attractive town house centres around a delightful restaurant and small elegant bar. There is also an inviting first-floor guest lounge, and the bedrooms are extremely well appointed and thoughtfully equipped; spacious split-level cottage suites situated in a quiet courtyard are also available. The imaginative cooking and an extremely impressive wine list are highlights here.

Rooms 12 (3 annexe) (1 fmly)

UPTON UPON SEVERN
Worcestershire   Map 10 SO84

White Lion Hotel
★★★ 75% ◉ HOTEL

tel: 01684 592551 **21 High St WR8 OHJ**
email: reservations@whitelionhotel.biz **web:** www.whitelionhotel.biz
dir: A422, A38 towards Tewkesbury. In 8m take B4104, after 1m cross bridge, turn left to hotel, past bend on left

Famed for being the inn depicted in Henry Fielding's novel *Tom Jones*, this 16th-century hotel is a reminder of 'Old England' with features such as exposed beams and wall timbers still remaining. The quality furnishing and the decor throughout enhance its character; the bedrooms are smart and include one four-poster room.

Rooms 13 (2 annexe) (2 fmly) (2 GF) ⌥ **S** £70-£95; **D** £99-£125 (incl. bkfst)*
Facilities FTV WiFi **Parking** 14 **Notes** LB Closed 1 Jan RS 25 Dec

UTTOXETER
Staffordshire   Map 10 SK03

Premier Inn Uttoxeter
BUDGET HOTEL

tel: 0871 527 9112 *(Calls cost 13p per minute plus your phone company's access charge)*
Derby Rd ST14 5AA
web: www.premierinn.com
dir: At junct of A50 & B5030 on outskirts of Uttoxeter, 7m S of Alton Towers Theme Park

High quality, budget accommodation ideal for both families and business travellers. Spacious, en suite bedrooms feature tea and coffee making facilities, and Freeview TV in most hotels. Internet access and WiFi are available for a small fee. The adjacent family restaurant features a wide and varied menu. See also the Hotel Groups pages.

Rooms 75

UXBRIDGE
Greater London   Map 6 TQ08
See also **also Ruislip**

Lancaster Hotel & Spa
★★★ 81% HOTEL

tel: 01895 268006 **Brunel University, Kingston Ln UB8 3PH**
email: lancaster-suite@brunel.ac.uk **web:** www.brunelcommercial.london
dir: Follow signs for Brunel University. Hotel is situated inside the university grounds

The Lancaster Hotel & Spa is conveniently located within the grounds of Brunel University London and is the ideal location for visiting the university or for professionals on business. The complex has been fully refurbished to a very high standard and offers a range of rooms to meet all budgets. The public areas include a comfortable lounge with a well-stocked bar and a nice terrace for the summer months. Freshly prepared dishes are served in the restaurant adjacent to the lounge area. Multifunctional meeting rooms are available. Parking is offered on site, and the area is patrolled 24 hours a day.

Rooms 70 ⌥ **Facilities** FTV WiFi ⊰ Sports facilities, shops & bank **Conf** Board 16
Services Lift **Parking** 50 **Notes** ⊗ RS 25 Dec

U

UXBRIDGE *continued*

Premier Inn London Uxbridge

BUDGET HOTEL

tel: 0871 527 9574 **Phase 500, Riverside Way UB8 2UX**
email: LondonUxbridge.Beefeatergm@whitbread.com **web:** www.premierinn.com
dir: *M40 junct 1 follow A412/Uxbridge/A4020 signs. At Denham Rdbt 1st exit then 2nd exit into Oxford Rd. 3rd exit at rdbt, left into Cross St. Right into Cowley Rd, right into Trumper Way. Left into New Windsor St, right into Riverside Way*

High quality, budget accommodation ideal for both families and business travellers. Spacious, en suite bedrooms feature tea and coffee making facilities, and Freeview TV in most hotels. Internet access and WiFi are available for a small fee. The adjacent family restaurant features a wide and varied menu. See also the Hotel Groups pages.

Rooms 80

VENTNOR	Map 5 SZ57
Isle of Wight	

The Royal Hotel

★★★★ 80% ◉◉ HOTEL

tel: 01983 852186 **Belgrave Rd PO38 1JJ**
email: enquiries@royalhoteliow.co.uk **web:** www.royalhoteliow.co.uk
dir: *A3055 into Ventnor follow one-way system, after lights left into Belgrave Rd. Hotel on right*

This smart hotel enjoys a central yet peaceful location in its own gardens, complete with an outdoor pool. Spacious, elegant public areas include a bright conservatory, bar and lounge. Bedrooms, appointed to a high standard, vary in size and style. Staff are friendly and efficient, particularly in the smart restaurant, where modern British cuisine is offered.

Rooms 52 (9 fmly) ↟ **S** £95-£125; **D** £190-£290 (incl. bkfst)* **Facilities** FTV WiFi ↝
↝ Beauty treatment room Xmas New Year **Conf** Class 40 Board 24 Thtr 100
Del from £165 to £275* **Services** Lift **Parking** 50 **Notes** LB ⊗ Civ Wed 120

Eversley Hotel

★★★ 72% METRO HOTEL

tel: 01983 852244 & 852462 **Park Av PO38 1LB**
email: eversleyhotel@yahoo.co.uk **web:** www.eversleyhotel.uk.com
dir: *On A3055 W of Ventnor, next to Ventnor Park*

Located west of Ventnor, this family-run Metro hotel enjoys a quiet location and has some rooms with garden and pool views. Bedrooms are generally of a good size and meet the needs of leisure and business travellers alike. The spacious restaurant is

sometimes used for local functions, and there is a bar where light meals are served, as well as a television room, a lounge area, and a card room. Further facilities include a jacuzzi and gym.

Rooms 28 (6 fmly) (2 GF) ↟ **S** £45-£75; **D** £79-£130 (incl. bkfst) **Facilities** STV FTV WiFi ↝ Gym Xmas New Year **Conf** Class 60 Board 20 **Parking** 23 **Notes** Closed 30 Nov-22 Dec & 2 Jan-1 Mar

VERYAN	Map 2 SW93
Cornwall	

The Nare

★★★★ ◉◉ COUNTRY HOUSE HOTEL

tel: 01872 501111 **Carne Beach TR2 5PF**
email: stay@narehotel.co.uk **web:** www.narehotel.co.uk
dir: *A3078 from Tregony, approx 1.5m. Left at Veryan sign, through village towards sea & hotel*

The only 4 AA Red Star hotel in Cornwall, The Nare offers a relaxed, country-house atmosphere in a spectacular coastal setting. The elegantly designed bedrooms, many with balconies, have fresh flowers, carefully chosen artwork and antiques that contribute to their engaging individuality. A choice of dining options is available, from light snacks to superb local seafood.

Rooms 37 (7 fmly) (7 GF) ↟ **S** £150-£290; **D** £290-£835 (incl. bkfst)*
Facilities Spa FTV WiFi ⊗ ↝ ⊛ ⊌ Gym Health & beauty clinic Sauna Steam room Hotel sailing boat Shooting Xmas New Year **Services** Lift **Parking** 80
Notes LB

WADDESDON	Map 11 SP71
Buckinghamshire	

The Five Arrows

◉◉ ⊛ RESTAURANT WITH ROOMS

tel: 01296 651727 **High St HP18 OJE**
email: reservations@thefivearrows.co.uk **web:** www.waddesdon.org.uk/fivearrows
dir: *On A41 in Waddesdon. Into Baker St for car park*

This Grade II listed building with its elaborate Elizabethan-style chimney stacks stands at the gates of Waddesdon Manor and was named after the Rothschild family emblem. Individually styled en suite bedrooms are comfortable and well appointed. Friendly staff are on hand to offer a warm welcome. Alfresco dining is possible in the warmer months.

Rooms 16 (8 annexe) (2 fmly)

WAKEFIELD
West Yorkshire

Map 16 SE32

See also **Liversedge**

Waterton Park Hotel
★★★★ 81% @ HOTEL

tel: 01924 257911 & 249800 **Walton Hall, The Balk, Walton WF2 6PW**
email: info@watertonparkhotel.co.uk **web:** www.watertonparkhotel.co.uk
dir: *3m SE off B6378. Exit M1 junct 39 towards Wakefield. At 3rd rdbt right for Crofton. At 2nd lights right & follow signs*

This Georgian mansion, built on an island in the centre of a 26-acre lake is in a truly idyllic setting. The main house contains many feature bedrooms, and the annexe houses more spacious rooms, all equally well equipped with modern facilities; most of the bedrooms have views over the lake or the 18-hole golf course. The delightful beamed restaurant, two bars and leisure club are located in the old hall, and there is a licence for civil weddings. The newly-built spa is located in the annexed section of the hotel.

Rooms 63 (41 annexe) (5 fmly) (21 GF) 🐾 **Facilities** Spa STV FTV WiFi ☾ ☜ supervised Fishing Gym Steam room Sauna New Year **Conf** Class 80 Board 80 Thtr 150 **Services** Lift **Parking** 200 **Notes** ⊗ Civ Wed 130

Cedar Court Hotel Wakefield
★★★★ 74% HOTEL

tel: 01924 276310 **Denby Dale Rd WF4 3QZ**
email: sales@cedarcourthotels.co.uk **web:** www.cedarcourthotels.co.uk
dir: *Adjacent to M1 junct 39*

This hotel enjoys a convenient location just off the M1. Traditionally styled bedrooms offer a good range of facilities while open-plan public areas include a busy bar and restaurant operation. Conferences and functions are extremely well catered for and a modern leisure club completes the picture.

Rooms 149 (2 fmly) (74 GF) 🐾 **Facilities** FTV WiFi ☾ ☜ supervised Gym Sauna Steam room Beauty treatment room Xmas New Year **Conf** Class 140 Board 80 Thtr 500 Del from £110 to £135* **Services** Lift **Parking** 350 **Notes** Civ Wed 250

Best Western Hotel St Pierre
★★★ 73% HOTEL

tel: 01924 255596 **733 Barnsley Rd, Newmillerdam WF2 6QG**
email: enq@hotelstpierre.co.uk **web:** www.bw-hotelstpierre.co.uk
dir: *M1 junct 39, A636 to Wakefield, right at 2nd rdbt into Asdale Rd to lights. Right onto A61 towards Barnsley. Hotel just after lake on left*

Located in the award-winning village of Newmillerdam this property provides comfortable modern accommodation. All bedrooms are well appointed with quality accessories and complimentary WiFi. The restaurant menu provides a good range of choice and a more relaxed bar menu is also available. An ample amount of on-site parking is available.

Rooms 54 (1 fmly) (4 GF) 🐾 **D** £40-£75* **Facilities** FTV WiFi ☾ New Year **Conf** Class 60 Board 60 Thtr 100 Del from £98 to £128* **Services** Lift **Parking** 74 **Notes** LB ⊗ Civ Wed 100

Premier Inn Wakefield Central
BUDGET HOTEL

tel: 0871 527 9114 *(Calls cost 13p per minute plus your phone company's access charge)*
Thornes Park, Denby Dale Rd WF2 8DY
web: www.premierinn.com
dir: *M1 junct 41, A650 towards Wakefield. Approx 1.5m. Hotel on right*

High quality, budget accommodation ideal for both families and business travellers. Spacious, en suite bedrooms feature tea and coffee making facilities, and Freeview TV in most hotels. Internet access and WiFi are available for a small fee. The adjacent family restaurant features a wide and varied menu. See also the Hotel Groups pages.

Rooms 42

Premier Inn Wakefield City North
BUDGET HOTEL

tel: 0871 527 9116 *(Calls cost 13p per minute plus your phone company's access charge)*
Paragon Business Park, Herriot Way WF1 2UJ
web: www.premierinn.com
dir: *M1 junct 41, A650 (Bradford Rd) for approx 1.5m towards Wakefield centre. Hotel on right adjacent to Bannatynes Health Club*

Rooms 47

Premier Inn Wakefield South M1 Jct 39
BUDGET HOTEL

tel: 0871 527 9118 *(Calls cost 13p per minute plus your phone company's access charge)*
Calder Park, Denby Dale Rd WF4 3BB
web: www.premierinn.com
dir: *M1 junct 39, A636 towards Wakefield. At 1st rdbt 1st exit into Calder Park. Hotel on right*

Rooms 75

Ramada Hotel Wakefield
AA Advertised

tel: 01924 274200 **Silkwood Business Park, M1 junct 40 WF5 9TJ**
email: wakefield.hotel@welcomebreak.co.uk
web: www.welcomebreak.co.uk/hotels/days-hotel-wakefield
dir: *M1 junct 40, follow signs to Wakefield, hotel 400yds on left*

This modern building offers accommodation in smart, spacious and well-equipped bedrooms, suitable for families and business travellers, and all with en suite bathrooms. Continental breakfast is available and other refreshments may be taken at the nearby family restaurant.

Rooms 99 🐾 **Facilities** FTV WiFi ☾ Gym **Conf** Class 15 Board 15 Thtr 25 **Services** Lift **Parking** 80 **Notes** LB ⊗

W

WALLASEY
Merseyside
Map 15 SJ29

Grove House Hotel

★★★ 83% SMALL HOTEL

tel: 0151 639 3947 & 630 4558 **Grove Rd CH45 3HF**
email: reception@thegrovehouse.co.uk **web:** www.thegrovehouse.co.uk
dir: M53 junct 1, A554 (Wallasey New Brighton), right after church into Harrison Drive, left after Windsors Garage into Grove Rd

Ideally situated for Liverpool and the M53, this friendly hotel offers attractive and comfortable bedrooms, which come with a wealth of extras. Well-cooked meals are served in the elegant panelled dining room. Weddings and conferences also catered for.

Rooms 14 (7 fmly) S £59; **D** £79-£99* **Facilities** FTV WiFi **Conf** Class 30 Board 50 Thtr 50 Del from £99 to £109* **Parking** 28 **Notes** ⊗ RS BHs Civ Wed 50

WALLINGFORD
Oxfordshire
Map 5 SU68

The George

★★★ 74% HOTEL

tel: 01491 836665 **High St OX10 0BS**
email: info@george-hotel-wallingford.com **web:** www.peelhotels.co.uk
dir: E side of A329, N end of Wallingford

Old world charm and modern facilities merge seamlessly in this former coaching inn. Bedrooms in the main house have character in abundance. Those in the wing have a more contemporary style, but all are well equipped and attractively decorated. Diners can choose between the restaurant and bistro, or relax in the cosy bar.

Rooms 39 (1 fmly) (9 GF) **Facilities** STV WiFi Xmas New Year **Conf** Class 60 Board 50 Thtr 150 **Parking** 40 **Notes** LB ⊗ Civ Wed 100

WALSALL
West Midlands
Map 10 SP09

Fairlawns Hotel & Spa

★★★★ 78% ⊛⊛ HOTEL

tel: 01922 455122 **178 Little Aston Rd, Aldridge WS9 0NU**
email: reception@fairlawns.co.uk **web:** www.fairlawns.co.uk
dir: Exit A452 towards Aldridge at x-rds with A454. Hotel 600yds on right

In a rural location with immaculate landscaped grounds, this constantly improving hotel offers a wide range of facilities and modern, comfortable bedrooms. Family rooms, one with a four-poster bed, and suites are also available. The Fairlawns Restaurant serves a wide range of award-winning seasonal dishes. The extensive, comprehensively equipped leisure complex is mainly for adult use as there is restricted availability to young people.

Rooms 58 (8 fmly) (1 GF) (3 smoking) S £80-£180; **D** £90-£190* **Facilities** Spa STV FTV WiFi ⟳ ⟲ supervised ⟳ ⟲ Gym Dance studio Beauty salon Bathing suite Floatation suite Sauna Aromatherapy room New Year **Conf** Class 40 Board 30 Thtr 80 **Services** Lift **Parking** 150 **Notes** LB RS 24 Dec-2 Jan Civ Wed 100

Best Western Baron's Court Hotel

★★★ 75% HOTEL

tel: 01543 452020 **Walsall Rd, Walsall Wood WS9 9AH**
email: henry@talashhotels.com **web:** www.bwbaronscourthotel.com
dir: 3.5m out of Walsall town centre, just N of Birmingham, close to M6 Toll

This hotel prides itself on warm hospitality and is conveniently situated for business guests visiting this area. The lounge, bar and restaurant are modern and thoughtfully designed. Conference facilities are available, along with ample car parking.

Rooms 94 (10 fmly) **Facilities** FTV WiFi ⟲ Xmas New Year **Conf** Class 64 Board 45 Thtr 110 **Services** Lift **Parking** 123 **Notes** Civ Wed 120

Holiday Inn Express Birmingham Walsall

BUDGET HOTEL

tel: 01922 705250 **Tempus Ten, Tempus Dr WS2 8TJ**
email: admin@hiexwalsall.com **web:** www.hiexpress.co.uk
dir: M6 junct 10/A454 to Walsall. Right at 1st lights, hotel 200mtrs on right

A modern hotel ideal for families and business travellers. Fresh and uncomplicated, the spacious rooms include Sky TV, power shower and tea and coffee-making facilities. Continental buffet breakfast is included in the room rate; other meals may be taken at the nearby family pub or restaurant. See also the Hotel Groups pages.

Rooms 120 (77 fmly) (30 GF) **Conf** Class 45 Board 36 Thtr 60 Del from £75*

Premier Inn Walsall M6 Jct 10

BUDGET HOTEL

tel: 0871 527 9120 *(Calls cost 13p per minute plus your phone company's access charge)*
Bentley Green, Bentley Road North WS2 0WB
web: www.premierinn.com
dir: M6 junct 10, A454 signed Wolverhampton. 2nd exit (Ansons junct). Left at rdbt, 1st left at next rdbt, hotel on right

High quality, budget accommodation ideal for both families and business travellers. Spacious, en suite bedrooms feature tea and coffee making facilities, and Freeview TV in most hotels. Internet access and WiFi are available for a small fee. The adjacent family restaurant features a wide and varied menu. See also the Hotel Groups pages.

Rooms 60

Premier Inn Walsall Town Centre

BUDGET HOTEL

tel: 0871 527 9374 *(Calls cost 13p per minute plus your phone company's access charge)*
Waterfront, Wolverhampton St WS2 8LR
web: www.premierinn.com
dir: M6 junct 10/A454 Wolverhampton Road to Walsall. Continue on A454. Follow signs for Crown Wharf Shopping Centre. Hotel on right on Wolverhampton St

Rooms 100

WALTHAM ABBEY
Essex   Map 6 TL30

Premier Inn Waltham Abbey

BUDGET HOTEL

tel: 0871 527 9122 *(Calls cost 13p per minute plus your phone company's access charge)*
Sewardstone Rd EN9 3QF
web: www.premierinn.com
dir: *M25 junct 26, A121 towards Waltham Abbey. Left onto A112, hotel 0.5m on left*

High quality, budget accommodation ideal for both families and business travellers. Spacious, en suite bedrooms feature tea and coffee making facilities, and Freeview TV in most hotels. Internet access and WiFi are available for a small fee. The adjacent family restaurant features a wide and varied menu. See also the Hotel Groups pages.

Rooms 99

WANSFORD
Cambridgeshire   Map 12 TL09

The Haycock Hotel

★★★ 87% ● HOTEL

tel: 01780 782223 & 781124 **London Rd PE8 6JA**
email: sales@thehaycock.co.uk **web:** www.macdonaldhotels.co.uk/haycock
dir: *A1 junct to A47 Leicester*

The Haycock Hotel is a charming 17th-century coaching inn set in attractive landscaped grounds in a peaceful village location. The smartly decorated bedrooms are tastefully furnished and thoughtfully equipped. Public rooms include a choice of restaurants, a lounge bar, a cocktail bar and a stylish lounge. The hotel has a staffed business centre, and banqueting facilities are also available.

Rooms 48 (1 fmly) (14 GF) **Facilities** FTV WiFi ↕ Beauty treatment room New Year **Conf** Class 100 Board 45 Thtr 300 **Parking** 300 **Notes** Civ Wed 200

WANTAGE
Oxfordshire   Map 5 SU38

La Fontana Restaurant with Accommodation

RESTAURANT WITH ROOMS

tel: 01235 868287 & 07836 730048 **Oxford Rd, East Hanney OX12 0HP**
email: anna@la-fontana.co.uk **web:** www.la-fontana.co.uk
dir: *A338 from Wantage towards Oxford. Restaurant on right in East Hanney*

Guests are guaranteed a warm welcome at this family-run Italian restaurant located on the outskirts of the busy town of Wantage. The stylish bedrooms are individually designed, well equipped and very comfortable. Dinner should not be missed - the menu features a wide range of regional Italian specialities.

Rooms 15 (3 annexe) (1 fmly)

WARMINSTER
Wiltshire   Map 4 ST84

The Bishopstrow Hotel & Spa

★★★★ 80% ● HOTEL

tel: 01985 212312 **Borenam Rd BA12 9HH**
web: www.bishopstrow.co.uk
dir: *From rdbt on A36 take B3414 towards Warminster. Follow brown hotel signs*

The Bishopstrow Hotel is set in 27 acres of delightful grounds which include modern spa facilities, tennis courts and country walks. Bedrooms are comfortable and stylish, and all are well appointed. Public areas offer several day rooms, and retain the style of the original house. Cuisine is a feature here, and menus offer fresh and local produce.

Rooms 32 (2 annexe) (26 fmly) (9 GF) **S** £99-£495; **D** £160-£535 (incl. bkfst & dinner)* **Facilities** Spa STV FTV WiFi ↕ ↘ ↙ Fishing Gym Thermal rooms Relaxation room Dual treatment room Xmas New Year **Conf** Class 40 Board 36 Thtr 60 Del from £180 to £216* **Parking** 70 **Notes** LB Civ Wed 82

WARRINGTON
Cheshire   Map 15 SJ68

The Park Royal

★★★★ 80% HOTEL

tel: 01925 730706 **Stretton Rd, Stretton WA4 4NS**
email: parkroyalreservations@qhotels.co.uk **web:** www.qhotels.co.uk
dir: *M56 junct 10, A49 to Warrington, at lights turn right to Appleton Thorn, 1st right into Spark Hall Close, hotel on left*

This modern hotel enjoys a peaceful setting, yet is conveniently located just minutes from the M56. The bedrooms are contemporary, well furnished and attractively co-ordinated. Spacious, stylish public areas include extensive conference and function facilities and a comprehensive leisure centre complete with outdoor tennis courts and a spa. Complimentary WiFi is also provided.

Rooms 146 (31 fmly) (31 GF) **Facilities** Spa FTV WiFi ↕ ↙ Gym Dance studio Sauna Xmas New Year **Conf** Class 180 Board 90 Thtr 400 **Services** Lift **Parking** 400 **Notes** Civ Wed 300

Best Western Hallmark Hotel Warrington Fir Grove

★★★ 81% ● HOTEL

tel: 0330 028 3423 **Knutsford Old Rd WA4 2LD**
email: firgrove@hallmarkhotels.co.uk **web:** www.hallmarkhotels.co.uk
dir: *M6 junct 20, follow signs for A50 to Warrington for 2.4m, before swing bridge over canal, turn right & right again*

Situated in a quiet residential area, this hotel is convenient for both the town centre and the motorway network. Comfortable, smart bedrooms, including spacious executive rooms, offer some excellent extra facilities such as iPod docking stations. Public areas include a smart lounge/bar, a neatly appointed restaurant, and excellent function and meeting facilities.

Rooms 52 (3 fmly) (20 GF) **Facilities** STV FTV WiFi ↕ Xmas New Year **Conf** Class 150 Board 50 Thtr 300 Del from £149 to £199* **Parking** 100 **Notes** Civ Wed 180

W

WARRINGTON *continued*

Premier Inn Warrington A49/M62 Jct 9
BUDGET HOTEL

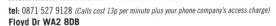

tel: 0871 527 9132 *(Calls cost 13p per minute plus your phone company's access charge)*
Winwick Rd WA2 8RN
web: www.premierinn.com
dir: *M62 junct 9 towards Warrington, hotel 100yds*

High quality, budget accommodation ideal for both families and business travellers. Spacious, en suite bedrooms feature tea and coffee making facilities, and Freeview TV in most hotels. Internet access and WiFi are available for a small fee. The adjacent family restaurant features a wide and varied menu. See also the Hotel Groups pages.

Rooms 40

Premier Inn Warrington Central North
BUDGET HOTEL

tel: 0871 527 9128 *(Calls cost 13p per minute plus your phone company's access charge)*
Floyd Dr WA2 8DB
web: www.premierinn.com
dir: *M62 junct 9, A49 signed Warrington. At next rdbt follow Town Centre signs. Straight on at next rdbt, left into Warrington Collegiate Camp*

Rooms 75

Premier Inn Warrington Centre
BUDGET HOTEL

tel: 0871 527 9126 *(Calls cost 13p per minute plus your phone company's access charge)*
1430 Centre Park, Park Boulevard WA1 1PR
web: www.premierinn.com
dir: *Take A49 to Brian Beven Island Rdbt, into Park Boulevard (Centre Park). Over bridge. Hotel on right*

Rooms 42

Premier Inn Warrington (M6 Jct 21)
BUDGET HOTEL

tel: 0871 527 9124 *(Calls cost 13p per minute plus your phone company's access charge)*
Manchester Rd, Woolston WA1 4GB
web: www.premierinn.com
dir: *Just off M6 junct 21 on A57 to Warrington*

Rooms 105

Premier Inn Warrington North East
BUDGET HOTEL

tel: 0871 527 9130 *(Calls cost 13p per minute plus your phone company's access charge)*
Golborne Rd, Winwick WA2 8LF
web: www.premierinn.com
dir: *M6 junct 22, A573 towards Newton-le-Willows. Dual carriageway to end, take 3rd exit at rdbt. Hotel adjacent to church*

Rooms 42

Premier Inn Warrington South
BUDGET HOTEL

tel: 0871 527 9134 *(Calls cost 13p per minute plus your phone company's access charge)*
Tarporley Rd, Stretton WA4 4NB
web: www.premierinn.com
dir: *Just off M56 junct 10. Follow A49 to Warrington, left at 1st lights*

Rooms 29

WARWICK
Warwickshire
Map 10 SP26

See also **Leamington Spa (Royal) & Wroxall**

Chesford Grange
★★★★ 77% HOTEL

tel: 01926 859331 **Chesford Bridge CV8 2LD**
email: chesfordreservations@qhotels.co.uk **web:** www.qhotels.co.uk

(For full entry see Kenilworth)

Ardencote
★★★★ 76% ⊛ HOTEL

tel: 01926 843111 **The Cumsey, Lye Green Rd, Claverdon CV35 8LT**
email: hotel@ardencote.com **web:** www.ardencote.com

(For full entry see Claverdon)

Premier Inn Warwick
BUDGET HOTEL

tel: 0871 527 9320 *(Calls cost 13p per minute plus your phone company's access charge)*
Opus 40, Birmingham Rd CV34 5JL
web: www.premierinn.com
dir: *M40 junct 15, A46 (Warwick bypass) towards Warwick. Follow A425 signs. From A425 1st left into industrial estate (Opus 40). Hotel 200yds, opposite IBM office*

High quality, budget accommodation ideal for both families and business travellers. Spacious, en suite bedrooms feature tea and coffee making facilities, and Freeview TV in most hotels. Internet access and WiFi are available for a small fee. The adjacent family restaurant features a wide and varied menu. See also the Hotel Groups pages.

Rooms 124

WARWICK MOTORWAY SERVICE AREA (M40)
Warwickshire
Map 11 SP35

Days Inn Warwick North - M40
AA Advertised

tel: 01926 651681
Warwick Services, M40 Northbound Junction 12-13, Banbury Rd CV35 0AA
email: warwick.north.hotel@welcomebreak.co.uk **web:** www.welcomebreak.co.uk
dir: *M40 northbound between junct 12 & 13*

This modern building offers accommodation in smart, spacious and well-equipped bedrooms, suitable for families and business travellers, and all with en suite bathrooms. Continental breakfast is available and other refreshments may be taken at the nearby family restaurant.

Rooms 54 (45 fmly) (8 smoking) **Facilities** FTV WiFi ♨ **Conf** Board 30 **Parking** 100

Days Inn Warwick South - M40

AA Advertised

tel: 01926 652081 **Warwick Services, M40 Southbound, Banbury Rd CV35 0AA**
email: warwick.south.hotel@welcomebreak.co.uk **web:** www.welcomebreak.co.uk
dir: *M40 southbound between junct 14 & 12*

This modern building offers accommodation in smart, spacious and well-equipped bedrooms, suitable for families and business travellers, and all with en suite bathrooms. Continental breakfast is available and other refreshments may be taken at the nearby family restaurant.

Rooms 40 (30 fmly) (19 GF) (4 smoking) **Facilities** FTV WiFi ⅃ **Parking** 500

WASHINGTON	Map 19 NZ35
Tyne & Wear	

Mercure George Washington Hotel, Golf & Spa

U

tel: 0191 402 9988 **Stone Cellar Rd, High Usworth NE37 1PH**
email: reservations@georgewashington.co.uk **web:** www.georgewashington.co.uk
dir: *A1(M) junct 65 onto A194(M). Take A195 signed Washington North. Take last exit from rdbt for Washington then right at mini-rdbt. Hotel 0.5m on right*

Currently the rating for this establishment is not confirmed. This may be due to a change of ownership or because it has only recently joined the AA rating scheme. For further details please see the AA website: theAA.com

Rooms 103

Premier Inn Newcastle (Washington)

BUDGET HOTEL

tel: 0871 527 9136 *(Calls cost 13p per minute plus your phone company's access charge)*
Emerson Rd NE37 1LB
web: www.premierinn.com
dir: *A1(M) junct 64, A195, follow Emerson signs. Left at rdbt, hotel 250yds left*

High quality, budget accommodation ideal for both families and business travellers. Spacious, en suite bedrooms feature tea and coffee making facilities, and Freeview TV in most hotels. Internet access and WiFi are available for a small fee. The adjacent family restaurant features a wide and varied menu. See also the Hotel Groups pages.

Rooms 74

WATERMILLOCK	Map 18 NY42
Cumbria	

Rampsbeck Hotel

★★★★ ◉◉ ♨ HOTEL

tel: 017684 86442 **CA11 0LP**
email: enquiries@rampsbeck.co.uk **web:** www.rampsbeck.co.uk
dir: *M6 junct 40, A592 to Ullswater, at T-junct with lake opp, turn right, hotel 1.5m*

Please note: Rampsbeck Hotel will be closed for major refurbishment from September 2016 to May 2017. This fine country house lies in 18 acres of parkland on the shores of Lake Ullswater, and is furnished with many period and antique pieces. There are three delightful lounges, an elegant restaurant and a traditional bar. Bedrooms come in three grades; the most spacious of which are

spectacular and overlook the lake. Service is attentive and the award-winning cuisine a real highlight.

Rooms 19 (1 fmly) (1 GF) ☊ **S** £110-£200; **D** £170-£350 (incl. bkfst)*
Facilities FTV WiFi ⅃ Xmas New Year **Conf** Class 10 Board 15 Thtr 15 **Parking** 25
Notes LB Closed 12th Sep 2016-May 2017 Civ Wed 65

Macdonald Leeming House

★★★★ 78% ◉◉ HOTEL

tel: 01768 486674 & 0344 879 9142 **CA11 0JJ**
email: leeminghouse@macdonald-hotels.co.uk **web:** www.macdonaldhotels.co.uk
dir: *M6 junct 40, A66 to Keswick. At rdbt take A592 (Ullswater). 5m to T-junct, right (A592). Hotel on left*

This hotel enjoys a superb location, being set in 20 acres of mature wooded gardens in the Lake District National Park, and overlooking Ullswater and the towering fells. Many rooms offer views of the lake and the rugged mountains beyond, with more than half having their own balcony. Public rooms include three sumptuous lounges, a cosy bar and library.

Rooms 41 (1 fmly) (10 GF) **Facilities** WiFi Fishing ⅃ Xmas New Year **Conf** Class 40 Board 30 Thtr 80 **Parking** 50 **Notes** Civ Wed 80

WATFORD	Map 6 TQ19
Hertfordshire	

Mercure London Watford Hotel

★★★★ 71% HOTEL

tel: 020 8901 0000 & 0844 815 9056
(Calls cost 7p per minute plus your phone company's access charge)
A41, Watford Bypass WD25 8JH
email: info@mercurewatford.co.uk **web:** www.mercurewatford.co.uk
dir: *M1 junct 5, A41 S to London. Straight on at island, hotel 1m on left*

This hotel is situated on the outskirts of London close to the M1, M25, A1(M) motorways, and Luton and London Heathrow airports. The bedrooms are smartly appointed and equipped with modern facilities including WiFi and satellite TV. Public rooms include The Brasserie restaurant and bar; guests also have the use of the leisure facilities with a heated pool.

Rooms 218 (3 fmly) **Facilities** WiFi ⅃ ⅃ ♨ Gym Sauna Steam room Beauty treatment room **Conf** Class 120 Board 58 Thtr 200 **Parking** 300 **Notes** ⊗ Civ Wed 200

Best Western White House

★★★ 72% HOTEL

tel: 01923 237316 **Upton Rd WD18 0JF**
email: info@whitehousehotel.co.uk **web:** www.bw-whitehousehotel.co.uk
dir: *From centre ring road, exit left into Upton Rd, hotel on left*

This popular commercial hotel is situated within easy walking distance of the town centre. Bedrooms are pleasantly decorated and offer a good range of facilities that include interactive TV with internet. The public areas are open plan; they include a comfortable lounge/bar, cosy snug and an attractive conservatory restaurant with a sunny open terrace for summer dining. Functions suites are also available.

Rooms 57 (3 fmly) (8 GF) **Facilities** FTV WiFi HL **Services** Lift **Parking** 40 **Notes** ⊗ RS 25 Dec-2 Jan

W

WATFORD *continued*

Premier Inn Watford Central

BUDGET HOTEL

tel: 0871 527 9140 *(Calls cost 13p per minute plus your phone company's access charge)*
Timms Meadow, Water Ln WD17 2NJ
web: www.premierinn.com
dir: *M1 junct 5, A41 into town centre. At rdbt take 3rd exit, stay in left lane through lights. Take 1st left into Water Ln. Hotel on left*

High quality, budget accommodation ideal for both families and business travellers. Spacious, en suite bedrooms feature tea and coffee making facilities, and Freeview TV in most hotels. Internet access and WiFi are available for a small fee. The adjacent family restaurant features a wide and varied menu. See also the Hotel Groups pages.

Rooms 105

Premier Inn Watford (Croxley Green)

BUDGET HOTEL

tel: 0871 527 9138 *(Calls cost 13p per minute plus your phone company's access charge)*
2 Ascot Rd WD18 8AD
web: www.premierinn.com
dir: *M25 junct 18, A404 signed Watford/Rickmansworth, left at 1st rdbt signed A412 Watford. Follow Croxley Green Business Park/Watford signs, at 4th rdbt, 3rd exit. M1 junct 5, A41 towards Watford, follow Watford West & Rickmansworth A412 signs. Then Croxley Green Business Park signs*

Rooms 126

Premier Inn Watford North

BUDGET HOTEL

tel: 0871 527 9142 *(Calls cost 13p per minute plus your phone company's access charge)*
859 St Albans Rd, Garston WD25 0LH
web: www.premierinn.com
dir: *M1 junct 6, A405 towards Watford. At 2nd lights onto A412 (St Albans Rd). Into TGI Friday's car park. Hotel directly behind*

Rooms 60

WATTON
Norfolk　　　　　　　　　　　　　　　　Map 13 TF90

Broom Hall Country Hotel

★★★ 78% COUNTRY HOUSE HOTEL

tel: 01953 882125 **Richmond Rd, Saham Toney IP25 7EX**
email: enquiries@broomhallhotel.co.uk **web:** www.broomhallhotel.co.uk
dir: *From A11 at Thetford onto A1075 to Watton, B1108 towards Swaffham, in 0.5m at rdbt turn right to Saham Toney, hotel 0.5m on left. From A47 take A1075, left onto B1108*

A delightful Victorian country house situated down a private drive and set in mature landscaped gardens surrounded by parkland. The well-equipped bedrooms are split between the main house and an adjacent building. Public rooms include a relaxing lounge, a brasserie restaurant, a lounge bar, a conservatory and a smart restaurant. There is an indoor swimming pool.

Rooms 15 (4 annexe) (3 fmly) (4 GF) ✆ **S** £78-£90; **D** £85-£165 (incl. bkfst)
Facilities Spa FTV WiFi ⇃ ⊕ Massage Beauty treatments **Conf** Class 30 Board 22 Thtr 80 Del from £110 to £160 **Parking** 30 **Notes** LB Closed 24 Dec-4 Jan Civ Wed 70

WELLINGBOROUGH
Northamptonshire　　　　　　　　　　　Map 11 SP86

Premier Inn Wellingborough

BUDGET HOTEL

tel: 0871 527 9144 *(Calls cost 13p per minute plus your phone company's access charge)*
London Rd NN8 2DP
web: www.premierinn.com
dir: *0.5m from town centre on A5193, near Dennington Industrial Estate*

High quality, budget accommodation ideal for both families and business travellers. Spacious, en suite bedrooms feature tea and coffee making facilities, and Freeview TV in most hotels. Internet access and WiFi are available for a small fee. The adjacent family restaurant features a wide and varied menu. See also the Hotel Groups pages.

Rooms 64

Ibis Wellingborough

AA Advertised

tel: 01933 228333 **Enstone Court NN8 2DR**
email: H3164@accor.com **web:** www.ibishotel.com
dir: *At junct of A45 & A509 towards Kettering, SW outskirts of Wellingborough*

Modern, budget hotel offering comfortable accommodation in bright and practical bedrooms. Breakfast is self-service and dinner is available in the restaurant.

Rooms 78 (19 fmly) (22 GF) ✆ **Facilities** FTV WiFi HL **Conf** Thtr 20 **Services** Lift **Parking** 74

WELLS
Somerset　　　　　　　　　　　　　　　　Map 4 ST54

Best Western Plus Swan Hotel

★★★ 86% ◉◉ HOTEL

tel: 01749 836300 **Sadler St BA5 2RX**
email: info@swanhotelwells.co.uk **web:** www.swanhotelwells.co.uk
dir: *A39, A371, on entering Wells follow signs for Hotels & Deliveries. Hotel on right opposite cathedral*

Situated in the shadow of Wells Cathedral, this privately-owned hotel enjoys a truly stunning location, and its owners extend a genuinely friendly welcome. Full of character and with a rich history, the hotel has been restored and extended to provide high levels of quality and comfort. Guests can choose between the larger, period bedrooms in the main building or the more contemporary coach house rooms. Dinner in the oak-panelled restaurant should not be missed.

Rooms 48 (3 fmly) (4 GF) ✆ **D** £82-£114 (incl. bkfst)* **Facilities** FTV WiFi Gym In room treatments **Conf** Class 45 Board 40 Thtr 120 Del £140* **Parking** 30 **Notes** LB ⊗ Civ Wed 90

W

Ancient Gate House Hotel

★★ 78% @ HOTEL

tel: 01749 672029 **20 Sadler St BA5 2SE**
email: info@ancientgatehouse.co.uk **web:** www.ancientgatehouse.co.uk
dir: *1st hotel on left on cathedral green*

Guests are treated to good old-fashioned hospitality and a friendly informal atmosphere at this charming hotel which is full of character. Bedrooms, many with unrivalled cathedral views and four-poster beds, are smartly appointed and stylishly co-ordinated. The Rugantino Restaurant remains popular, offering a mix of traditional and contemporary Italian dishes.

Rooms 9 ⋔ **Facilities** FTV WiFi Xmas New Year **Notes** Closed 27-29 Dec

---

WELWYN GARDEN CITY
Hertfordshire   Map 6 TL21

Tewin Bury Farm Hotel

★★★★ 81% @@ HOTEL

tel: 01438 717793 **Hertford Road (B1000) AL6 0JB**
email: reservations@tewinbury.co.uk **web:** www.tewinbury.co.uk
dir: *From N: A1(M) junct 6, 1st exit signed A1000, at next rdbt 1st exit towards Digswell. 0.1m straight on at rdbt. 1m on B100. Hotel on left*

Situated not far from the A1(M) and within easy reach of Stevenage and Knebworth House, this delightful country-house hotel is part of a thriving farm. Stylish, well-equipped bedrooms of varying sizes are perfectly suited for both leisure and business guests. An award-winning restaurant and meeting rooms are all part of this family-run establishment.

Rooms 36 (20 annexe) (4 fmly) (26 GF) ⋔ **D** £99-£145 (incl. bkfst)* **Facilities** FTV WiFi ᨏ Fishing Cycling Xmas New Year **Conf** Class 300 Board 40 Thtr 500 **Services** Lift **Parking** 400 **Notes** LB ⊗ Civ Wed 300

Best Western Homestead Court Hotel

★★★ 78% HOTEL

tel: 01707 324336 **Homestead Ln AL7 4LX**
email: enquiries@homesteadcourt.co.uk **web:** www.bw-homesteadcourt.co.uk
dir: *Exit A1000, left at lights at Bushall Hotel. Right at rdbt into Howlands, 2nd left at Hollybush public house into Hollybush Ln. 2nd right at War Memorial into Homestead Ln*

This family-run hotel enjoys a quiet location and is a short drive from the centre of Welwyn Garden City and the major road network. Bedrooms are all attractively presented and very well equipped. Free WiFi is available throughout the hotel and there is an extensive choice on the restaurant menu. Ample secure parking is provided and the cosy lounge is a popular casual dining venue.

Rooms 79 (9 annexe) (6 fmly) (5 GF) ⋔ **S** £59-£104; **D** £65-£119* **Facilities** STV FTV WiFi ᨏ HL **Conf** Class 200 Board 80 Thtr 300 Del from £135 to £165* **Services** Lift **Parking** 75 **Notes** ⊗ Civ Wed 250

Premier Inn Welwyn Garden City

BUDGET HOTEL

tel: 0871 527 9146 *(Calls cost 13p per minute plus your phone company's access charge)*
Stanborough Rd AL8 6DQ
web: www.premierinn.com
dir: *A1(M) junct 4, A6129*

High quality, budget accommodation ideal for both families and business travellers. Spacious, en suite bedrooms feature tea and coffee making facilities, and Freeview TV in most hotels. Internet access and WiFi are available for a small fee. The adjacent family restaurant features a wide and varied menu. See also the Hotel Groups pages.

Rooms 120

WEMBLEY
Greater London

Novotel London Wembley

★★★★ 75% HOTEL PLAN 1 C5

tel: 020 8069 1200 & 8069 1203 **5 Olympic Way, Wembley HA9 0NP**
email: h9389@accor.com **web:** www.novotel.com

Located on Olympic Way, Novotel London Wembley offers proximity to Wembley Stadium and Arena. Wembley Park Underground is only a short walk and connects directly to the Eurostar Terminal and Central London. Facilities include free WiFi throughout the hotel, Freeview TV channels in every bedroom, and a fitness centre with panoramic views. The Elements restaurant and bar offers a tempting international menu and drinks.

Rooms 235 (27 fmly) ⋔ **Facilities** FTV WiFi HL Gym **Conf** Class 60 Board 40 Thtr 120 **Services** Lift Air con **Parking** 19

Holiday Inn London - Wembley

★★★★ 73% HOTEL PLAN 1 C4

tel: 020 8902 8839 **Empire Way HA9 8DS**
email: info@hiwembley.co.uk **web:** www.hiwembley.co.uk
dir: *Within easy reach of North Circular, M1, M4 & M40*

This large hotel is ideally situated for the arena, stadium and conference centre. It has a range of modern public areas and well equipped meeting rooms.

Rooms 336 (42 fmly) ⋔ **Facilities** STV WiFi ᨏ HL Ⓖ Gym Steam room Sauna Beauty treatment room **Conf** Class 160 Board 80 Thtr 500 **Services** Lift Air con **Parking** 250 **Notes** ⊗ Civ Wed 500

Quality Hotel London - Wembley & Conference Centre

★★★ 72% HOTEL PLAN 1 C5

tel: 020 8733 9000 **Empire Way HA9 0NH**
email: sales@hotels-wembley.com **web:** www.qualityhotelwembley.co.uk
dir: *M1 junct 6, A406, right onto A404. Right onto Empire Way, after rdbt at lights. Hotel on right*

Conveniently situated within walking distance of both the Arena and conference centres this modern hotel offers smart, comfortable, spacious bedrooms; many are air conditioned. All rooms offer an excellent range of amenities. Air-conditioned public areas include a large restaurant serving a wide range of contemporary dishes.

Rooms 165 (70 fmly) (3 GF) (48 smoking) **Facilities** STV FTV WiFi ᨏ **Conf** Class 90 Board 90 Thtr 150 **Services** Lift Air con **Parking** 65 **Notes** ⊗

W

WEMBLEY continued

Premier Inn London Wembley Stadium

BUDGET HOTEL PLAN 1 C5

tel: 0871 527 8682 *(Calls cost 13p per minute plus your phone company's access charge)*
151 Wembley Park Dr HA9 8HQ
web: www.premierinn.com
dir: *A406 (North Circular) take A404 towards Wembley. 2m right into Wembley Hill Rd, keep right into Empire Way (B4565), pass Wembley Arena on right, keep right around petrol station. Hotel 200yds on left*

High quality, budget accommodation ideal for both families and business travellers. Spacious, en suite bedrooms feature tea and coffee making facilities, and Freeview TV in most hotels. Internet access and WiFi are available for a small fee. The adjacent family restaurant features a wide and varied menu. See also the Hotel Groups pages.

Rooms 154

Ibis London Wembley

AA Advertised PLAN 1 C4

tel: 020 8453 5100 **Southway HA9 6BA**
email: H3141@accor.com **web:** www.ibishotel.com
dir: *From Hanger Lane on A40, take A406 N, exit at Wembley. A404 to lights junct with Wembley Hill Rd, right, 1st right into Southway. Hotel 75mtrs on left*

Modern, budget hotel offering comfortable accommodation in bright and practical bedrooms. Breakfast is self-service and dinner is available in the restaurant.

Rooms 210 (44 fmly) ⌁ **Facilities** STV FTV WiFi **Services** Lift **Parking** 44

WEST AUCKLAND	Map 19 NZ12
County Durham	

The Manor House Hotel

★★★ 78% HOTEL

tel: 01388 834834 **The Green DL14 9HW**
email: enquiries@manorhousehotel.net **web:** www.manorhousehotel.net
dir: *A1(M) junct 58, A68 to West Auckland. At T-junct left, hotel 150yds on right*

This historic manor house, dating back to the 14th century, is full of character. Welcoming log fires await guests on cooler evenings. Comfortable bedrooms are individual in style, tastefully furnished and well equipped. The brasserie and Juniper's restaurant both offer an interesting selection of freshly prepared dishes. Well-equipped leisure facilities are available and the Beauty Rooms offer a range of beauty and holistic treatments, with spa packages also available.

Rooms 35 (11 annexe) (6 fmly) (3 GF) ⌁ **S** £40-£90; **D** £40-£150 (incl. bkfst) **Facilities** Spa FTV WiFi ⌁ Gym Steam room Sauna Xmas New Year **Conf** Class 80 Board 50 Thtr 100 **Parking** 150 **Notes** LB Civ Wed 120

WEST BROMWICH	Map 10 SP09
West Midlands	

Premier Inn West Bromwich

BUDGET HOTEL

tel: 0871 527 9148 *(Calls cost 13p per minute plus your phone company's access charge)*
New Gas St B70 ONP
web: www.premierinn.com
dir: *M5 junct 1, A41 (Expressway) towards Wolverhampton. At 3rd rdbt, hotel on right*

High quality, budget accommodation ideal for both families and business travellers. Spacious, en suite bedrooms feature tea and coffee making facilities, and Freeview TV in most hotels. Internet access and WiFi are available for a small fee. The adjacent family restaurant features a wide and varied menu. See also the Hotel Groups pages.

Rooms 62

Premier Inn West Bromwich Central

BUDGET HOTEL

tel: 0871 527 9150 *(Calls cost 13p per minute plus your phone company's access charge)*
144 High St B70 6JJ
web: www.premierinn.com
dir: *M5 junct 1 towards town centre, hotel 2m*

Rooms 85

WEST DRAYTON	
Hotels are listed under Heathrow Airport	

WEST HOATHLY	Map 6 TV33
West Sussex	

Gravetye Manor Hotel

★★★★ ⍟⍟⍟ ⚲ COUNTRY HOUSE HOTEL

tel: 01342 810567 **Vowels Ln RH19 4LJ**
email: info@gravetyemanor.co.uk **web:** www.gravetyemanor.co.uk
dir: *B2028 to Haywards Heath. 1m after Turners Hill fork left towards Sharpthorne, 1st left into Vowels Lane*

Gravetye Manor is a beautiful Elizabethan mansion, built in 1598 and enjoying a tranquil setting. One of the first country house hotels in Britain, it remains an excellent example of its type. Bedrooms and bathrooms have been sympathetically refurbished with style and luxurious finishing touches. The day rooms, each with oak panelling, fresh flower arrangements and open fires, create a relaxing atmosphere. Cuisine is excellent and makes use of local

W

suppliers and producers. Guests should take time to explore the impressive gardens and grounds; a perfect spot for afternoon tea.

Gravetye Manor Hotel

Rooms 17 D £260-£525 (incl. bkfst)* **Facilities** STV WiFi Fishing Deer stalking Xmas New Year **Conf** Board 15 Del from £320 to £395* **Parking** 30 **Notes** No children 7yrs Civ Wed 60

WEST THURROCK
Essex
Map 6 TQ57

Premier Inn Thurrock East

BUDGET HOTEL

tel: 0871 527 9092 *(Calls cost 13p per minute plus your phone company's access charge)*
Fleming Rd, Unicorn Estate, Chafford Hundred RM16 6YJ
web: www.premierinn.com
dir: *From A13 follow Lakeside Shopping Centre signs. Right at 1st rdbt, straight on at next rdbt, then 1st slip road. Left at next rdbt*

High quality, budget accommodation ideal for both families and business travellers. Spacious, en suite bedrooms feature tea and coffee making facilities, and Freeview TV in most hotels. Internet access and WiFi are available for a small fee. The adjacent family restaurant features a wide and varied menu. See also the Hotel Groups pages.

Rooms 104

Premier Inn Thurrock West

BUDGET HOTEL

tel: 0871 527 9094 *(Calls cost 13p per minute plus your phone company's access charge)*
Stonehouse Ln RM19 1NS
web: www.premierinn.com
dir: *From N: M25 junct 31, A1090 to Purfleet. (NB do not cross Dartford Bridge or follow signs for Lakeside). From S: M25 junct 31. On approach to Dartford Tunnel, bear far left signed Dagenham. After tunnel, hotel at top of slip road*

Rooms 161

Ibis London Thurrock

AA Advertised

tel: 01708 686000 **Weston Av RM20 3JQ**
email: H2176@accor.com **web:** www.ibishotel.com
dir: *M25 junct 31 to West Thurrock Services, right at 1st & 2nd rdbts, left at 3rd rdbt. Hotel on right in 500yds*

Modern, budget hotel offering comfortable accommodation in bright and practical bedrooms. Breakfast is self-service and dinner is available in the restaurant.

Rooms 102 (18 GF) **Facilities** STV WiFi **Services** Lift Air con **Parking** 156

WEST WITTON
North Yorkshire
Map 19 SE08

The Wensleydale Heifer

RESTAURANT WITH ROOMS

tel: 01969 622322 **Main St DL8 4LS**
email: info@wensleydaleheifer.co.uk **web:** www.wensleydaleheifer.co.uk
dir: *A1 to Leeming Bar junct, A684 towards Bedale for approx 10m to Leyburn, then towards Hawes 3.5m to West Witton*

Describing itself as 'boutique style', this 17th-century former coaching inn is very much of the 21st century. The bedrooms, with Egyptian cotton linen and Molton Brown toiletries as standard, are each designed with an interesting theme - for example, Black Sheep, Night at the Movies, True Romantics and Shooters, and for chocolate lovers, there's a bedroom where you can eat as much chocolate as you like! The food is very much the focus here in both the informal fish bar and the contemporary style restaurant. The kitchen prides itself on sourcing the freshest fish and locally reared meats.

Rooms 13 (4 annexe) (2 fmly)

WESTLETON
Suffolk
Map 13 TM46

The Westleton Crown

★★★ 80% HOTEL

tel: 01728 648777 **The Street IP17 3AD**
email: info@westletoncrown.co.uk **web:** www.westletoncrown.co.uk
dir: *A12 N, turn right for Westleton just after Yoxford. Hotel opposite on entering Westleton*

The Westleton Crown is a charming coaching inn situated in a peaceful village location just a few minutes from the A12. Public rooms include a smart, award-winning restaurant, comfortable lounge, and busy bar with exposed beams and open fireplaces. The stylish bedrooms are tastefully decorated and equipped with many thoughtful little extras.

Rooms 34 (22 annexe) (5 fmly) (13 GF) **S** £90-£100; **D** £95-£215 (incl. bkfst)* **Facilities** FTV WiFi Xmas New Year **Parking** 34 **Notes** Civ Wed 90

WESTON-ON-THE-GREEN
Oxfordshire
Map 11 SP51

The Manor At Weston-On-The-Green

★★★★ 83% COUNTRY HOUSE HOTEL

tel: 01869 350621 **Northampton Rd OX25 3QL**
email: house@themanorweston.co.uk **web:** www.themanorweston.com

The Manor is an outstanding country house hotel, offering traditional values and outstanding quality. The gardens are a real delight and taking afternoon tea here is a must. The hotel has been carefully restored and refurbished to a very high standard. Bedrooms are classic in design, but still enjoy all modern day accessories. Dinner in the feature restaurant with its wood panelled walls and gallery area is a highlight of any stay. Professional staff guarantee a seamless experience.

Rooms 25 **S** £110-£300; **D** £120-£400 (incl. bkfst)* **Facilities** FTV WiFi Xmas New Year Child facilities **Conf** Board 20 Thtr 100 Del from £165* **Parking** 60 **Notes** Civ Wed 120

W

WESTON-SUPER-MARE
Somerset   Map 4 ST36

The Royal Hotel
★★★ 78% HOTEL

tel: 01934 423100 **1 South Pde BS23 1JP**
email: reservations@royalhotelweston.com **web:** www.royalhotelweston.com
dir: *M5 junct 21, follow signs to seafront. Hotel next to Winter Gardens Pavillion*

The Royal, which opened in 1810, was the first hotel in Weston and occupies a prime seafront position. It is a grand building and many of the bedrooms, including some with sea views, are spacious and comfortable; family apartments are also available. Public areas include a choice of bars and a restaurant which offers a range of dishes to meet all tastes. Entertainment is provided during the season.

Rooms 44 (3 annexe) (8 fmly) ⚫ **S** £78-£88; **D** £110-£154 (incl. bkfst) **Facilities** FTV WiFi ⬚ HL Beauty treatment room Hair salon Solarium ♫ Xmas New Year
Conf Class 100 Board 60 Thtr 200 Del from £135 to £165 **Services** Lift **Parking** 152
Notes LB ⊗ Civ Wed 200

See advert on opposite page

Beachlands Hotel
★★★ 77% HOTEL

tel: 01934 621401 **17 Uphill Road North BS23 4NG**
email: info@beachlandshotel.com **web:** www.beachlandshotel.com
dir: *M5 junct 21, follow signs for hospital. At hospital rdbt follow signs for beach, hotel 300yds before beach*

This popular hotel is very close to the 18-hole links course and a short walk from the seafront. Elegant public areas include a bar, a choice of lounges and a bright dining room. Bedrooms vary slightly in size, but all are well equipped for both the business and leisure guest. There is the added bonus of a 10-metre indoor pool and a sauna.

Rooms 21 (6 fmly) (11 GF) ⚫ **Facilities** FTV WiFi ⬚ Sauna Beauty treatment room New Year **Conf** Class 20 Board 30 Thtr 60 Del from £120 to £160 **Parking** 28
Notes ⊗ Closed 24-27 Dec Civ Wed 110

Lauriston Hotel
★★★ 70% HOTEL

tel: 01934 620758 **6-12 Knightstone Rd BS23 2AN**
email: lauriston.hotel@actionforblindpeople.org.uk **web:** www.visionhotels.co.uk
dir: *1st right after Winter Gardens, hotel entrance adjacent to Grand Pier*

A friendly welcome is assured at the Lauriston, a pleasant hotel located right on the seafront, just a few minutes' stroll from the pier. The hotel welcomes everyone but caters especially for the visually impaired, their families, friends and guide dogs. There are comfortable and well-appointed bedrooms; and special facilities for guide dogs are, of course, available.

Rooms 37 (2 fmly) (8 GF) ⚫ **Facilities** STV FTV WiFi ⬚ HL ♫ Xmas New Year
Conf Class 12 Board 10 Thtr 18 **Services** Lift **Parking** 16 **Notes** LB Civ Wed 60

Anchor Head Hotel
★★★ 64% HOTEL   **Leisureplex** HOLIDAY HOTELS

tel: 01934 620880 **19 Claremont Crescent, Birnbeck Rd BS23 2EE**
email: anchor.weston@alfatravel.co.uk **web:** www.leisureplex.co.uk
dir: *M5 junct 21, A370 to seafront, right, past Grand Pier towards Brimbeck Pier. Hotel at end of terrace on left*

Enjoying a very pleasant location with views across the bay, the Anchor Head offers a varied choice of comfortable lounges and a relaxing outdoor patio area. Bedrooms and bathrooms are traditionally furnished and include several ground-floor rooms. Dinner and breakfast are served in the spacious dining room that also benefits from sea views.

Rooms 52 (1 fmly) (5 GF) ⚫ **Facilities** FTV ♫ Xmas New Year **Services** Lift **Notes** ⊗ Closed Dec-Feb (ex Xmas/New Year) RS Mar & Nov

Premier Inn Weston-Super-Mare East (A370)
BUDGET HOTEL   **Premier Inn**

tel: 0871 527 9156 *(Calls cost 13p per minute plus your phone company's access charge)*
Hutton Moor Rd BS22 8LY
web: www.premierinn.com
dir: *M5 junct 21, A370 towards Weston-Super-Mare. After 3rd rbt right at lights into Hutton Moor Leisure Centre. Left, into car park*

High quality, budget accommodation ideal for both families and business travellers. Spacious, en suite bedrooms feature tea and coffee making facilities, and Freeview TV in most hotels. Internet access and WiFi are available for a small fee. The adjacent family restaurant features a wide and varied menu. See also the Hotel Groups pages.

Rooms 88

Premier Inn Weston-Super-Mare (Seafront)
BUDGET HOTEL   **Premier Inn**

tel: 0871 527 9378 *(Calls cost 13p per minute plus your phone company's access charge)*
Dolphin Square, Beach Rd BS23 1TT
web: www.premierinn.com
dir: *M5 junct 21, A370 towards Weston-Super-Mare town centre. At double mini rdbt 2nd exit, 1st exit into Oxford St. At end, left into Beach Rd. Left into Carlton St. Hotel on left*

Rooms 112

W

W

WETHERBY
West Yorkshire   Map 16 SE44

INSPECTORS' CHOICE

Wood Hall Hotel & Spa
★★★★ ◉◉ ❦ HOTEL

tel: 01937 587271 & 0845 072 7564 *(Calls cost 5p per minute plus your phone company's access charge)* **Trip Ln, Linton LS22 4JA**
email: woodhall@handpicked.co.uk **web:** www.handpickedhotels.co.uk/woodhall
dir: *From Wetherby take Harrogate road N (A661) for 0.5m, left to Sicklinghall & Linton. Cross bridge, left to Linton & Wood Hall. Turn right opposite Windmill Inn, 1.25m to hotel*

A long sweeping drive leads to this delightful Georgian house situated in 100 acres of parkland. Spacious bedrooms are appointed to an impressive standard and feature comprehensive facilities, including large plasma-screen TVs. Public rooms reflect the same elegance and include a smart drawing room and dining room, both with fantastic views.

Rooms 44 (30 annexe) (5 fmly) ❦ **Facilities** Spa STV FTV WiFi ❧ HL ✆ Fishing Gym Steam room Xmas New Year **Conf** Class 70 Board 40 Thtr 100 Del from £165 to £205* **Services** Lift **Parking** 200 **Notes** ⊗ Civ Wed 100

Bridge Hotel & Spa
★★★★ 79% HOTEL

tel: 01937 580115 **Walshford LS22 5HS**
email: info@bridgewetherby.co.uk **web:** www.bridgewetherby.co.uk
dir: *From N exit A1(M) at junct 47 York or S junct 46 Wetherby Race Centre, 1st left Walshford, follow brown tourist signs*

The Bridge Hotel is located hotel close to the A1, with spacious public areas and a good range of services, making this an ideal venue for business or leisure. The stylish bedrooms are comfortable and well equipped. There is a choice of bars and a large open-plan restaurant. Conference and banqueting suites are also available.

Rooms 30 (2 fmly) (10 GF) **S** £70-£140; **D** £80-£160 (incl. bkfst)* **Facilities** Spa FTV WiFi ❧ Gym Xmas New Year **Conf** Class 50 Board 50 Thtr 200 Del from £120 to £160* **Parking** 150 **Notes** LB Civ Wed 150

Mercure Wetherby Hotel
★★★ 74% HOTEL

tel: 01937 545000 & 0844 815 9067
(Calls cost 7p per minute plus your phone company's access charge) **Leeds Rd LS22 5HE**
email: info@mercurewetherby.co.uk **web:** www.mercurewetherby.co.uk
dir: *A1/A659, then follow A168. Hotel on rdbt*

This modern hotel is well located for motorway access and as well as being close to the historic market town of Wetherby, it is also convenient for Leeds, Harrogate and York. Leeds Bradford Airport is just eight miles away. There is a spacious restaurant and adjacent bar. The Brasserie menu features bistro dishes and daily Chef's specials. Extensive conference facilities are provided with 13 naturally lit meeting rooms available. Complimentary WiFi access is another highlight.

Rooms 103 **Facilities** FTV WiFi ❧ New Year **Conf** Class 60 Board 50 Thtr 150 **Services** Lift **Parking** 167 **Notes** ⊗ Civ Wed 100

Days Inn Wetherby
BUDGET HOTEL

tel: 01937 547557 **Junction 46 A1(M), Kirk Deighton LS22 5GT**
email: reservations@daysinnwetherby.co.uk **web:** www.daysinnwetherby.co.uk
dir: *A1(M) junct 46 at Moto Service Area*

This modern building offers accommodation in smart, spacious and well-equipped bedrooms, suitable for families and business travellers, and all with en suite bathrooms. Continental breakfast is available and other refreshments may be taken at the nearby family restaurant. See also the Hotel Groups pages.

Rooms 129 (33 fmly) (35 GF) ❦ **Conf** Class 20 Board 20 Thtr 30

WEYBRIDGE
Surrey   Map 6 TQ06

HIGHLY RECOMMENDED

Brooklands Hotel
★★★★ 83% ◉◉ HOTEL

tel: 01932 335700 **Brooklands Dr KT13 0SL**
email: info@brooklandshotelsurrey.com **web:** www.brooklandshotelsurrey.com
dir: *Phone for detailed directions*

Overlooking the historic motoring racing circuit, this hotel has stunning design that reflects art deco style of the Mercedes Benz racetrack's heyday in the 1920 and 30s. The bedrooms are notably spacious and very comfortable with many contemporary facilities; all have floor-to-ceiling windows, and many come with balconies overlooking the racetrack. There is a wealth of public areas including leisure and meeting rooms as well as a spa. The contemporary 1907 Restaurant, Bar and Grill offers imaginative menus.

Rooms 131 (5 fmly) ❦ **Facilities** Spa STV FTV WiFi ❧ Gym Xmas New Year **Conf** Class 86 Board 90 Thtr 174 **Services** Lift Air con **Parking** 120 **Notes** ⊗ Civ Wed 174

Oatlands Park Hotel

★★★★ 80% HOTEL

tel: 01932 847242 **146 Oatlands Dr KT13 9HB**
email: info@oatlandsparkhotel.com **web:** www.oatlandsparkhotel.com
dir: *Through High St to Monument Hill mini rdbt. Left into Oatlands Drive. Hotel 500yds on left*

Once a palace for Henry VIII, this impressive building sits in extensive grounds encompassing tennis courts, a gym and a 9-hole golf course. The spacious lounge and bar create a wonderful first impression with tall marble pillars and plush comfortable seating. Most of the bedrooms are very spacious, and all are well equipped.

Rooms 144 (24 fmly) (30 GF) S £130-£205; **D** £140-£215 **Facilities** STV FTV WiFi ᐃ HL ✦ 9 ♨ Putt green 🏌 Gym Jogging course Fitness suite ♫ Xmas New Year **Conf** Class 170 Board 90 Thtr 400 Del from £185 to £250 **Services** Lift Air con **Parking** 208 **Notes** LB ⊗ Civ Wed 370

Best Western Ship Hotel

BW Best Western.

★★★ 78% HOTEL

tel: 01932 848364 **Monument Green KT13 8BQ**
email: reservations@desboroughhotels.com **web:** www.shiphotel.co.uk
dir: *M25 junct 11, at 3rd rdbt left into High St. Hotel 300yds on left*

This former coaching inn has retained much of its period charm and is now a comfortable and welcoming hotel. Bedrooms, some overlooking a delightful courtyard, are spacious and cheerfully decorated. Public areas include a lounge and cocktail bar, restaurant and a popular pub. The high street location and private parking are a bonus.

Rooms 76 (2 fmly) **Facilities** FTV WiFi ᐃ Xmas New Year **Conf** Class 70 Board 60 Thtr 180 **Services** Lift **Parking** 65 **Notes** ⊗ Civ Wed 120

| WEYMOUTH | Map 4 SY67 |
| Dorset | |

Best Western Hotel Rembrandt

BW Best Western.

★★★ 75% HOTEL

tel: 01305 764000 **12-18 Dorchester Rd DT4 7JU**
email: reception@hotelrembrandt.co.uk **web:** www.hotelrembrandt.co.uk
dir: *On A354 from Dorchester, turn left at Manor rdbt & proceed for 0.75m*

Only a short distance from the seafront and the town centre, this hotel is ideal for visiting local attractions. Facilities include a spa, gym and heated pool; a bar and extensive meeting rooms. The restaurant offers an impressive carvery and carte menu, which proves popular with locals and residents alike.

Rooms 78 (27 fmly) (5 GF) S £50-£120; **D** £80-£205 (incl. bkfst)* **Facilities** STV FTV WiFi ᐃ 🏊 Gym Steam room Sauna Beautician Beauty treatment room **Conf** Class 100 Board 60 Thtr 200 Del from £125 to £135* **Services** Lift **Parking** 70 **Notes** LB ⊗ Civ Wed 150

Hotel Rex

★★★ 73% HOTEL

tel: 01305 760400 **29 The Esplanade DT4 8DN**
email: rex@kingshotels.co.uk **web:** www.kingshotels.co.uk
dir: *On seafront opposite Alexandra Gardens*

Originally built as the summer residence for the Duke of Clarence, this hotel benefits from a seafront location with stunning views across Weymouth Bay. Bedrooms, including several sea-facing rooms, are well equipped. A wide range of imaginative dishes is served in the popular and attractive restaurant.

Rooms 31 (2 fmly) S £50-£65; **D** £80-£125 (incl. bkfst)* **Facilities** FTV WiFi New Year **Conf** Class 30 Board 25 Thtr 40 Del from £80 to £100 **Services** Lift **Parking** 9 **Notes** ⊗ Closed Xmas

Crown Hotel

★★ 76% HOTEL

tel: 01305 760800 **51-53 St Thomas St DT4 8EQ**
email: crown@kingshotels.co.uk **web:** www.kingshotels.co.uk
dir: *From Dorchester, A354 to Weymouth. Follow Back Water on left & cross 2nd bridge*

This popular hotel is conveniently located adjacent to the old harbour and is ideal for shopping, local attractions and transportation links, including the ferry. Public areas include an extensive bar, ballroom, and comfortable residents' lounge on the first floor. Themed events, such as mock cruises, are a speciality.

Rooms 86 (15 fmly) S £35-£50; **D** £60-£100 (incl. bkfst)* **Facilities** WiFi New Year **Services** Lift **Parking** 11 **Notes** ⊗ Closed Xmas

Fairhaven Hotel

★★ 75% HOTEL

tel: 01305 760200 **37 The Esplanade DT4 8DH**
email: fairhaven@kingshotels.co.uk **web:** www.kingshotels.co.uk
dir: *On right just before Alexandra Gardens*

Fairhaven Hotel is a popular sea-facing, family-run hotel with a friendly young team of staff. Bedrooms are comfortable and well maintained, and there are two bars, one with panoramic views of the bay. Entertainment is provided most nights during the season.

Rooms 81 (21 fmly) (1 GF) S £35-£50; **D** £60-£120 (incl. bkfst)* **Facilities** WiFi ♫ **Services** Lift **Parking** 14 **Notes** ⊗ Closed Nov-1 Mar

Hotel Central

★★ 72% HOTEL

tel: 01305 760700 **17-19 Maiden St DT4 8BB**
email: central@kingshotels.co.uk **web:** www.kingshotels.co.uk
dir: *In town centre*

Well located for the town, the beach and the ferries to the Channel Islands, and with off-road parking, this privately-owned hotel has friendly staff and comfortable bedrooms. Three rooms are designed for guests with limited mobility. The pleasant dining room offers a varied menu, and live entertainment is provided during the season.

Rooms 28 (5 fmly) (4 GF) **D** fr £60* **Facilities** ♫ **Services** Lift **Parking** 14 **Notes** ⊗ Closed mid Dec-1 Mar

W

WEYMOUTH *continued*

Premier Inn Weymouth

BUDGET HOTEL

tel: 0871 527 9384 *(Calls cost 13p per minute plus your phone company's access charge)*
Gateway Business Park, Mercury Rd DT3 5HJ
web: www.premierinn.com
dir: *M27 junct 1, A31 towards Bournemouth, A35 towards Dorchester. 1st exit at rdbt onto A354 (Weymouth road). At 3rd rdbt take 1st exit into Dorchester Rd. Left into Mercery Rd*

High quality, budget accommodation ideal for both families and business travellers. Spacious, en suite bedrooms feature tea and coffee making facilities, and Freeview TV in most hotels. Internet access and WiFi are available for a small fee. The adjacent family restaurant features a wide and varied menu. See also the Hotel Groups pages.

Rooms 60

Premier Inn Weymouth Seafront

BUDGET HOTEL

tel: 0871 527 9158 *(Calls cost 13p per minute plus your phone company's access charge)*
Lodmoor Country Park, Preston Beach Rd, Green Hill DT4 7SX
web: www.premierinn.com
dir: *Follow signs to Weymouth then brown route signs to Lodmoor Country Park (height restriction 9' 4" at barrier). Hotel adjacent to Lodmoor Brewers Fayre. NB for Sat Nav use DT4 7SL*

Rooms 106

Moonfleet Manor Hotel

AA Advertised

tel: 01305 786948 **Fleet Rd DT3 4ED**
email: info@moonfleetmanorhotel.co.uk **web:** www.moonfleetmanor.co.uk
dir: *Take Fleet Rd just off B1357 at Chickerell. Hotel at end of road*

This enchanting hideaway, where children are especially welcome, is peacefully located at the end of the village of Fleet and enjoys a wonderful sea-facing position. The hotel is furnished with a great deal of style, individuality and panache, particularly in the sumptuous lounges. Bedrooms are equally special with a range of sizes; all are well-equipped and many overlook Chesil Beach. Accomplished cuisine makes use of quality local produce and is served in the elegant restaurant. A host of additional facilities are also offered for all the family, including an indoor pool.

Rooms 36 (6 annexe) (21 fmly) (3 GF) **Facilities** FTV WiFi 🌊 🏊 Squash Indoor play area Creche Xmas New Year **Conf** Class 36 Board 30 Thtr 70 **Services** Lift **Parking** 48 **Notes** Civ Wed 100

Saxonville Hotel

★★★ 78% HOTEL

tel: 01947 602631 **Ladysmith Av, Argyle Rd YO21 3HX**
email: newtons@saxonville.co.uk **web:** www.saxonville.co.uk
dir: *A174 to North Promenade. Turn inland at large four-towered building visible on West Cliff, into Argyle Rd, then 1st right*

The friendly service is noteworthy at this long-established holiday hotel. Well maintained throughout, it offers comfortable bedrooms and inviting public areas that include a well-proportioned restaurant where quality dinners are served.

Rooms 23 (2 fmly) (1 GF) **S** £53.50-£98.50; **D** £107-£167 (incl. bkfst)*
Facilities WiFi **Conf** Class 40 Board 40 Thtr 100 Del from £85 to £110* **Parking** 20 **Notes** ⊗ Closed Dec-Jan

The Cliffemount Hotel

U

tel: 01947 840103 **Bank Top Ln, Runswick Bay TS13 5HU**
email: info@cliffemounthotel.co.uk **web:** www.cliffemounthotel.co.uk
dir: *Exit A174, 8m N of Whitby, 1m to end*

Currently the rating for this establishment is not confirmed. This may be due to a change of ownership or because it has only recently joined the AA rating scheme. For further details please see the AA website: theAA.com

Conf Class 25 Board 16 Thtr 25

Estbek House

 RESTAURANT WITH ROOMS

tel: 01947 893424 **East Row, Sandsend YO21 3SU**
email: info@estbekhouse.co.uk **web:** www.estbekhouse.co.uk
dir: *From Whitby take A174. In Sandsend, left into East Row*

The speciality seafood restaurant on the first floor is the focus of this listed building in a small coastal village north west of Whitby. The seasonal menu is based on fresh, local ingredients, and is overseen by Tim the chef, who has guided his team to two AA Rosettes. There is also a small bar and breakfast room, and four individually appointed bedrooms offering high levels of comfort.

Rooms 4

WHITCHURCH	Map 15 SJ54
Shropshire	

Macdonald Hill Valley Spa, Hotel & Golf

★★★★ 78% HOTEL

tel: 01948 660700 & 0344 879 9049 **Tarporley Rd SY13 4JH**
email: general.hillvalley@macdonald-hotels.co.uk
web: www.macdonald-hotels.co.uk/hillvalley
dir: 2nd exit off A41 towards Whitchurch

Located in rural surroundings on the town's outskirts, this modern hotel is surrounded by two golf courses, and a very well equipped leisure spa is also available. Spacious bedrooms, with country views, are furnished in minimalist style and public areas include a choice of bar lounges and extensive conference facilities.

Rooms 80 (15 fmly) (2/ GF) **Facilities** Spa SIV FTV WiFi ⌁ ⌁ ⌁ 36 Putt green Gym Mud Rasul Xmas New Year **Conf** Class 150 Board 150 Thtr 300 **Services** Lift **Parking** 300 **Notes** Civ Wed 300

WHITEHAVEN	Map 18 NX91
Cumbria	

Premier Inn Whitehaven

BUDGET HOTEL

tel: 0871 527 9160 *(Calls cost 13p per minute plus your phone company's access charge)*
Howgate CA28 6PL
web: www.premierinn.com
dir: On A595 just outside Whitehaven

High quality, budget accommodation ideal for both families and business travellers. Spacious, en suite bedrooms feature tea and coffee making facilities, and Freeview TV in most hotels. Internet access and WiFi are available for a small fee. The adjacent family restaurant features a wide and varied menu. See also the Hotel Groups pages.

Rooms 75

WHITLEY BAY	Map 21 NZ37
Tyne & Wear	

The Royal Hotel

★★★ 77% HOTEL

tel: 0191 252 4777 **13-17 East Pde NE26 1AP**
email: info@royalhotelwhitleybay.co.uk **web:** www.royalhotelwhitleybay.co.uk
dir: From Whitley Bay Metro station left onto Station Square, bear right onto Victoria Terrace, right onto North Parade then right & right again, then left

Overlooking the sea front, this refurbished hotel offers warm hospitality from a friendly team. Bedrooms are well appointed, and the recently opened Noir Drinks Lounge adds a new dimension to the operation. Tapas are served in this area with the option to take dinner in the Italian restaurant next door. Limited off-road car parking is available to the front of the hotel.

Rooms 37 **Facilities** FTV WiFi ⌁ ⌁ **Parking** 10 **Notes** ⊗ Closed 23 Dec-2 Jan

WHITSTABLE	Map 7 TR16
Kent	

Crescent Turner Hotel

★★★ 80% HOTEL

tel: 01227 263506 **Wraik Hill CT5 3BY**
email: info@crescentturner.co.uk **web:** www.crescentturner.co.uk
dir: A299 exit for Whitstable

Located just a couple of miles from Whitstable on Wraik Hill, the Crescent Turner Hotel benefits from fantastic countryside and sea views. Bedrooms are all individual and stylish with contemporary furnishings; many benefit from those extensive views across to Whitstable. There is a bar and restaurant onsite open daily for breakfast, lunch and dinner.

Rooms 17 (2 fmly) (5 GF) **S** £60-£79; **D** £99-£150 (incl. bkfst)* **Facilities** FTV WiFi ⌁ Xmas New Year **Conf** Class 32 Board 30 Thtr 40 Del from £165 to £225* **Parking** 30 **Notes** LB ⊗ Civ Wed 56

Premier Inn Whitstable

BUDGET HOTEL

tel: 0871 527 9162 *(Calls cost 13p per minute plus your phone company's access charge)*
Thanet Way CT5 3DB
web: www.premierinn.com
dir: 2m W of town centre on B2205

High quality, budget accommodation ideal for both families and business travellers. Spacious, en suite bedrooms feature tea and coffee making facilities, and Freeview TV in most hotels. Internet access and WiFi are available for a small fee. The adjacent family restaurant features a wide and varied menu. See also the Hotel Groups pages.

Rooms 73

W

WHITTLEBURY
Northamptonshire   Map 11 SP64

Whittlebury Hall
★★★★ 80% ◉◉ HOTEL

tel: 01327 857857 **NN12 8QH**
email: reservations@whittleburyhall.co.uk **web:** www.whittleburyhall.co.uk
dir: *A43, A413 towards Buckingham, through Whittlebury, turn for hotel on right, signed*

Whittlebury Hall is a purpose-built, Georgian-style country house hotel with excellent spa and leisure facilities and pedestrian access to the Silverstone circuit. Grand public areas feature F1 racing memorabilia, and the accommodation includes some lavishly appointed suites. Food is a strength, with a choice of various dining options. Particularly noteworthy are the afternoon teas in the spacious, comfortable lounge and the fine dining in Murray's Restaurant.

Rooms 212 (4 fmly) (13 smoking) **Facilities** Spa FTV WiFi ⇕ ⊗ Gym Beauty treatments Relaxation room Hair studio Heat & Ice experience Leisure club ♫ Xmas New Year **Conf** Class 175 Board 40 Thtr 500 **Services** Lift **Parking** 450 **Notes** ⊗

WIDNES
Cheshire   Map 15 SJ58

Premier Inn Widnes
BUDGET HOTEL

tel: 0871 527 9306 *(Calls cost 13p per minute plus your phone company's access charge)*
Venture Fields WA8 0GY
web: www.premierinn.com
dir: *M62 junct 7. At Rainhill Stoops rdbt 2nd exit onto A557 (Widnes). Left into Earle Rd (Widnes Waterfront), into Venture Field Leisure Entertainment complex. Hotel on left*

High quality, budget accommodation ideal for both families and business travellers. Spacious, en suite bedrooms feature tea and coffee making facilities, and Freeview TV in most hotels. Internet access and WiFi are available for a small fee. The adjacent family restaurant features a wide and varied menu. See also the Hotel Groups pages.

Rooms 60

WIGAN
Greater Manchester   Map 15 SD50

Macdonald Kilhey Court Hotel
★★★★ 76% HOTEL

tel: 0344 879 9045 & 01257 472100 **Chorley Rd, Standish WN1 2XN**
email: general.kilheycourt@macdonald-hotels.co.uk
web: www.macdonaldhotels.co.uk/kilheycourt
dir: *M6 junct 27, A5209 Standish, over at lights, past church on right, left at rdbt 1st exit, hotel on right 350yds. M61 junct 6, signed Wigan & Haigh Hall. 3m & right at rdbt 2nd exit. Hotel 0.5m on right*

Macdonald Kilhey Court Hotel is peacefully located in its own grounds yet is convenient for the motorway network. Bedrooms are divided between the Victorian house and the modern extension, while public areas have original features, and the split-level restaurant has views over the Worthington Lakes. There are eleven meeting rooms, ideal for exhibitions, and extensive landscaped grounds available for weddings. Facilities also include an indoor pool and spa.

Rooms 62 (18 fmly) (8 GF) ⋔ **Facilities** Spa FTV WiFi ⇕ HL ⊗ Gym Aerobics classes Beauty treatments Xmas New Year **Conf** Class 180 Board 60 Thtr 400 **Services** Lift **Parking** 300 **Notes** Civ Wed 300

Wrightington Hotel & Country Club
★★★★ 75% ◉ HOTEL

tel: 01257 425803 **Moss Ln, Wrightington WN6 9PB**
email: info@wrightingtonhotel.co.uk **web:** www.wrightingtonhotel.co.uk
dir: *M6 junct 27, 0.25m W, hotel on right after church*

Situated in open countryside close to the M6, this privately-owned hotel offers friendly hospitality. Accommodation is well equipped and spacious, and public areas include an extensive leisure complex complete with hair salon, boutique and sports injury lab. Bennetts Restaurant, Blazers bar and extensive, fully air-conditioned banqueting facilities appeal to a broad market, with weddings a key focus.

Rooms 73 (6 fmly) (36 GF) ⋔ **Facilities** Spa STV FTV WiFi ⊗ Gym Squash Hairdressing salon Sports injury clinic New Year **Conf** Class 50 Board 40 Thtr 150 **Services** Lift **Parking** 240 **Notes** LB Civ Wed 100

Mercure Wigan Oak Hotel
★★★ 78% HOTEL

tel: 01942 826888 **Orchard St WN1 3SS**
email: enquiries@hotels-wigan.com **web:** www.hotels-wigan.com
dir: *From S: M6 junct 25, A49 signed Wigan then B5238, right after Grand Arcade Shopping. From N: M6 junct 27, A5209, right onto A49, left at lights, hotel opposite Tesco*

This modern and stylish hotel is situated in the centre of Wigan; easily accessed from the M6 and M61 and well positioned for public transport. The bedrooms are both comfortable and well equipped, and public rooms include the restaurant, conservatory and popular bar. There is free WiFi throughout, and conference and events facilities are available. Ample parking is a plus in this central location.

Rooms 88 (7 fmly) (16 GF) ⋔ **S** £65-£125; **D** £65-£125* **Facilities** FTV WiFi ⇕ New Year **Conf** Class 80 Board 40 Thtr 160 Del from £90 to £125* **Services** Lift **Parking** 100 **Notes** LB Civ Wed 50

Premier Inn Wigan M6 Jct 25
BUDGET HOTEL

tel: 0871 527 9164 *(Calls cost 13p per minute plus your phone company's access charge)*
Warrington Rd, Marus Bridge WN3 6XB
web: www.premierinn.com
dir: *M6 junct 25 (N'bound). At rdbt left, hotel on left*

High quality, budget accommodation ideal for both families and business travellers. Spacious, en suite bedrooms feature tea and coffee making facilities, and Freeview TV in most hotels. Internet access and WiFi are available for a small fee. The adjacent family restaurant features a wide and varied menu. See also the Hotel Groups pages.

Rooms 40

Premier Inn Wigan Town Centre
BUDGET HOTEL

tel: 0871 527 9502 *(Calls cost 13p per minute plus your phone company's access charge)*
Harrogate St WN1 1BL
web: www.premierinn.com
dir: *Nbound: M6 junct 25, A49 (Warrington Rd). 3rd exit at next rdbt into Poolstock Ln (B5238). Left into Chapel Ln, continue into River Way (A49). At lights left into King St, then into Rodney St. Stay in right lane, through lights into Harrogate St*

Rooms 83

W

Premier Inn Wigan West (M6 Jct 26)

BUDGET HOTEL

tel: 0871 527 9168 *(Calls cost 13p per minute plus your phone company's access charge)*
Orrell Rd, Orrell WN5 8HQ
web: www.premierinn.com
dir: *M6 junct 26 follow signs for Upholland & Orrell. At 1st lights turn left. Hotel on right behind Priory Wood Beefeater*

Rooms 40

WILLERBY
East Riding of Yorkshire   **Map 17 TA03**

Mercure Hull Grange Park Hotel

★★★★ 73% HOTEL

tel: 01482 672801 & 0844 815 9037 *(Calls cost 7p per minute plus your phone company's access charge)* **Grange Park Ln HU10 6EA**
email: info@mercurehull.co.uk **web:** www.mercurehull.co.uk
dir: *A164 to Beverley signed Willerby Shopping Park. Left at rdbt into Grange Park Lane, hotel at end*

Originally a 19th-century manor house, this modern hotel provides comfortable accommodation tucked away in 12 acres of landscaped gardens. The location is peaceful yet convenient for the historic market town of Beverley. Hull city centre is only five miles away. Extensive meeting rooms are in a self contained conference centre with complimentary WiFi throughout. The hotel also boasts a health club with indoor swimming pool.

Rooms 100 (4 fmly) **Facilities** FTV WiFi ⑤ ⑤ Gym Sauna Steam room **Conf Class** 260 Board 80 Thtr 550 Del from £95 to £115* **Parking** 600 **Notes** ⊗ Civ Wed 550

Best Western Willerby Manor Hotel

★★★ 83% ⑤ HOTEL

tel: 01482 652616 **Well Ln HU10 6ER**
email: willerbymanor@bestwestern.co.uk **web:** www.willerbymanor.co.uk
dir: *Exit A63, signed Humber Bridge. Right at rdbt by Waitrose. At next rdbt hotel signed*

Set in a quiet residential area, amid well-tended gardens, this hotel was originally a private mansion; it has now been thoughtfully extended to provide very comfortable bedrooms, equipped with many useful extras. There are extensive leisure facilities and a wide choice of meals offered in the contemporary Figs Brasserie which has an impressive heated outdoor area.

Rooms 63 (6 fmly) (20 GF) ⑤ **S** £67-£120; **D** £108-£140 (incl. bkfst)* **Facilities** STV FTV WiFi HL ⑤ supervised ⑤ Gym Steam room Beauty treatment room Aerobic classes New Year **Conf Class** 200 Board 100 Thtr 500 Del £175* **Parking** 300 **Notes** LB Closed 24-26 Dec Civ Wed 150

WILMINGTON
East Sussex   **Map 6 TQ50**

Crossways

⑥⑥ RESTAURANT WITH ROOMS

tel: 01323 482455 **Lewes Rd BN26 5SG**
email: stay@crosswayshotel.co.uk **web:** www.crosswayshotel.co.uk
dir: *On A27 between Lewes & Polegate, 2m E of Alfriston rdbt*

Proprietors David Stott and Clive James have been welcoming guests to this elegant restaurant with rooms for over 25 years. Crossways sits amid stunning gardens and attractively tended grounds. The well-presented bedrooms are tastefully decorated and provide an abundance of thoughtful amenities including free WiFi. Guest comfort is paramount and the warm hospitality ensures guests often return.

Rooms 7

WILMSLOW

See **Manchester Airport**

WIMBORNE MINSTER
Dorset   **Map 5 SZ09**

Les Bouviers Restaurant with Rooms

⑥⑥ RESTAURANT WITH ROOMS

tel: 01202 889555 **Arrowsmith Rd, Canford Magna BH21 3BD**
email: info@lesbouviers.co.uk **web:** www.lesbouviers.co.uk
dir: *A31 onto A349. Left in 0.6m. In approx 1m right into Arrowsmith Rd. Establishment approx 100yds on right*

Les Bouviers is an excellent restaurant with rooms in a great location, set in five and a half acres of grounds. Food is obviously a highlight of any stay here, as is the friendly, attentive service. Chef patron Leonard James Coward's team turn out impressive cooking, which has been recognised with two AA Rosettes. The bedrooms are extremely well equipped and the beds are supremely comfortable. Cream teas can be taken on the terrace.

Rooms 6 (4 fmly)

WINCANTON
Somerset   **Map 4 ST72**

Holbrook House

★★★ 85% ⑥⑥ COUNTRY HOUSE HOTEL

tel: 01963 824466 & 828844 **Holbrook BA9 8BS**
email: enquiries@holbrookhouse.co.uk **web:** www.holbrookhouse.co.uk
dir: *From A303 at Wincanton left onto A371 towards Castle Cary & Shepton Mallet*

This handsome country house offers a unique blend of quality and comfort combined with a friendly atmosphere. Set in 17 acres of peaceful gardens and wooded grounds, Holbrook House makes a perfect retreat. The restaurant provides a selection of innovative dishes prepared with enthusiasm and served by a team of caring staff.

Rooms 21 (5 annexe) (2 fmly) (5 GF) ⑤ **S** £95-£180; **D** £95-£180 (incl. bkfst)* **Facilities** Spa FTV WiFi ⑤ ⑤ ⑤ ⑤ Gym Exercise classes Sauna Steam room Fitness suite ♫ Xmas New Year **Conf Class** 100 Board 55 Thtr 200 Del £160* **Parking** 100 **Notes** LB Civ Wed 250

W

WINCHESTER
Hampshire

Map 5 SU42

Lainston House, an Exclusive Hotel

★★★★★ 87%  HOTEL

tel: 01962 776088 **Woodman Ln, Sparsholt SO21 2LT**
email: enquiries@lainstonhouse.co.uk **web:** www.exclusive.co.uk
dir: 2m NW off B3049 towards Stockbridge

This graceful example of a William and Mary house enjoys a countryside location amidst mature grounds and gardens. Staff provide good levels of courtesy and care with a polished, professional service. Bedrooms are tastefully appointed and include some spectacular, spacious rooms with stylish handmade beds and stunning bathrooms. Public rooms include a cocktail bar built entirely from a single cedar and stocked with an impressive range of rare drinks and cigars.

Rooms 49 (6 fmly) (18 GF) ✆ **S** £180-£540; **D** £195-£555 (incl. bkfst)* **Facilities** STV FTV WiFi ↻ ⌇ Fishing ⛳ Gym Archery Clay pigeon shooting Cycling Hot air ballooning Falconer Cookery school ♫ Xmas New Year **Conf** Class 80 Board 40 Thtr 166 **Parking** 200 **Notes** LB Civ Wed 200

Holiday Inn Winchester

★★★★ 78% ◉◉ HOTEL

Holiday Inn

tel: 01962 670700 **Telegraph Way, Morn Hill SO21 1HZ**
email: info@hiwinchester.co.uk **web:** www.hiwinchester.co.uk
dir: M3 junct 9, A31 signed Alton, A272 & Petersfield. 1st exit at rdbt onto A31, 1.6m, take 1st exit into Alresford Rd, left into Telegraph Way

Located a few miles from the historic city of Winchester and within easy reach of the south's transport links, this modern, purpose-built property is presented to a high standard. Bedrooms are spacious and well-equipped for both the business and leisure guest. Enjoyable cuisine is served in the restaurant and there is a very good range of freshly prepared dishes to choose from. Conference facilities and ample parking are available.

Rooms 141 (7 fmly) (60 GF) ✆ **Facilities** STV FTV WiFi ↻ HL Gym Xmas New Year **Conf** Class 110 Board 120 Thtr 250 **Services** Lift Air con **Parking** 167 **Notes** ⊗ Civ Wed 200

Hotel du Vin Winchester

★★★★ 76% ◉ TOWN HOUSE HOTEL

Hotel du Vin & Bistro

tel: 01962 841414 **14 Southgate St SO23 9EF**
email: info@winchester.hotelduvin.com **web:** www.hotelduvin.com
dir: M3 junct 11 towards Winchester, follow signs. Hotel in approx 2m on left just past cinema

Continuing to set high standards, this inviting hotel is best known for its high profile bistro. The individually designed bedrooms have all the Hotel du Vin signature touches including fine Egyptian cotton linen, power showers and WiFi. The bistro serves imaginative yet simply-cooked dishes from a seasonal, daily-changing menu.

Rooms 24 (4 annexe) (4 GF) ✆ **S** £149-£349; **D** £179-£379* **Facilities** STV WiFi ↻ Xmas New Year **Conf** Class 30 Board 20 Thtr 40 Del from £210 to £250* **Services** Air con **Parking** 35 **Notes** LB Civ Wed 60

Mercure Winchester Wessex Hotel

★★★★ 74% HOTEL

Mercure HOTELS

tel: 01962 861611 **Paternoster Row SO23 9LQ**
email: H6619@accor.com **web:** www.mercure.com
dir: M3 junct 10, 2nd exit at rdbt signed Winchester/B3330. Right at lights, left at 2nd rdbt. Over small bridge, straight on at next rdbt into Broadway. Past Guildhall, 1st left into Colebrook St. Hotel 50yds on right

Occupying an enviable location in the centre of this historic city and adjacent to the spectacular cathedral, Mercure Winchester Wessex Hotel is quietly situated on a side street. Inside, the atmosphere is restful and welcoming, with public areas and some bedrooms enjoying unrivalled views of the hotel's centuries-old neighbour.

Rooms 94 (6 fmly) **S** £80-£160; **D** £80-£160* **Facilities** STV WiFi Xmas New Year **Conf** Class 25 Board 40 Thtr 100 Del from £120 to £170* **Services** Lift **Parking** 30 **Notes** LB Civ Wed 120

Marwell Hotel

★★★ 80% ◉◉ HOTEL

tel: 01962 777681 **Thompsons Ln, Colden Common, Marwell SO21 1JY**
email: info@marwellhotel.co.uk **web:** www.marwellhotel.co.uk
dir: B3354 through Twyford. 1st exit at rdbt B3354, left onto B2177 signed Bishop Waltham. Left into Thompsons Ln after 1m, hotel on left

Taking its theme from the adjacent zoo, this unusual hotel is based on the famous TreeTops safari lodge in Kenya. The well-equipped bedrooms, split between four lodges, convey a safari style, while the smart public areas include an airy lobby bar and an *Out of Africa* themed restaurant. There is also a selection of meeting and leisure facilities.

Rooms 67 (10 fmly) (37 GF) **S** £64-£120; **D** £79-£140 (incl. bkfst)* **Facilities** STV WiFi ↻ ⊛ ♨ 45 Putt green Sauna Spa pool Running machine New Year **Conf** Class 60 Board 60 Thtr 200 Del from £118 to £145* **Parking** 120 **Notes** LB Civ Wed 200

Premier Inn Winchester

BUDGET HOTEL

tel: 0871 527 9424 *(Calls cost 13p per minute plus your phone company's access charge)*
Caledonia House, Winnal Manor Rd SO23 0RS
web: www.premierinn.com
dir: M3 junct 9, A272 to Winchester. At rdbt 3rd exit into Easton Ln. Hotel on left at next rdbt

High quality, budget accommodation ideal for both families and business travellers. Spacious, en suite bedrooms feature tea and coffee making facilities, and Freeview TV in most hotels. Internet access and WiFi are available for a small fee. The adjacent family restaurant features a wide and varied menu. See also the Hotel Groups pages.

Rooms 101

W

Days Inn Winchester

WELCOMEBREAK

AA Advertised

tel: 01962 791135
**Winchester Moto Service Area, M3 S, junct 14/15, Shroner Wood
SO21 1PP**
email: winchester.hotel@welcomebreak.co.uk **web:** www.welcomebreak.co.uk
dir: *M3 Southbound (between juncts 8 & 9), there is no access from M3 Northbound*

This modern building offers accommodation in smart, spacious and well-equipped bedrooms, suitable for families and business travellers, and all with en suite bathrooms. Continental breakfast is available and other refreshments may be taken at the nearby family restaurant.

Rooms 40 (14 fmly) (20 GF) **Facilities** FTV WiFi **Conf** Class 20 Thtr 20 **Parking** 40
Notes Closed 24-26 Dec

Gilpin Hotel & Lake House

★★★★★ 85% ◉◉◉ ⬛ HOTEL

tel: 015394 88818 **Crook Rd LA23 3NE**
email: hotel@thegilpin.co.uk **web:** www.thegilpin.co.uk
dir: *M6 junct 36, A590, A591 to rdbt N of Kendal, onto B5284, hotel 5m on right*

This smart Victorian residence is set in delightful gardens leading to the fells, and is just a short drive from the lake. The individually designed bedrooms are stylish and a number benefit from private terraces; all are spacious and thoughtfully equipped, and each has a private sitting room. In addition there are luxury Garden Suites that lead onto private gardens with cedar-wood hot tubs. The welcoming atmosphere is notable and the attractive day rooms are perfect for relaxing, perhaps beside a real fire. Eating in any of the quartet of dining rooms is a must. The Lake House situated a mile from the main hotel offers an additional six suites, spa and stunning lakeside views.

Rooms 26 (12 annexe) (1 fmly) (12 GF) 🐾 **Facilities** WiFi ⬥ ⬥ Spa treatments Private spa facilities for Lake House guests Xmas New Year **Parking** 40 **Notes** ⊗ No children 7yrs Civ Wed 25

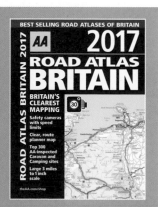
Linthwaite House Hotel & Restaurant

★★★★ COUNTRY HOUSE HOTEL

tel: 015394 88600 **Crook Rd LA23 3JA**
email: stay@linthwaite.com **web:** www.linthwaite.com
dir: *A591 towards The Lakes for 8m to large rdbt, take 1st exit B5284, 6m, hotel on left. 1m past Windermere golf club*

Linthwaite House is set in 14 acres of hilltop grounds and enjoys stunning views over Lake Windermere. Inviting public rooms include an attractive conservatory and adjoining lounge, and an elegant restaurant which occupies three rooms and offers menus based on the finest local ingredients. Bedrooms, which are individually decorated, combine contemporary furnishings with classical styles; all are thoughtfully equipped and include CD players, radios and free WiFi. There is also a Garden Suite and the luxurious Loft Suite which even has a retractable roof and telescope for star gazing. Service and hospitality are attentive and friendly.

Rooms 30 (1 fmly) (7 GF) 🐾 **D** £123-£562 (incl. bkfst)* **Facilities** STV FTV WiFi ⬥ Putt green Fishing ⬥ Beauty treatments Massage Access to nearby spa with pool & gym Xmas New Year **Conf** Class 22 Board 25 Thtr 54 Del from £180 to £300* **Parking** 40 **Notes** LB Civ Wed 64

W

WINDERMERE *continued*

Holbeck Ghyll Country House Hotel

★★★★ COUNTRY HOUSE HOTEL

tel: 015394 32375 **Holbeck Ln LA23 1LU**
email: stay@holbeckghyll.com web: www.holbeckghyll.com
dir: *3m N of Windermere on A591, right into Holbeck Lane signed Troutbeck, hotel 0.5m on left*

Holbeck Ghyll sits high up overlooking the majestic Lake Windermere surrounded by well maintained grounds. The original house was bought in 1888 by Lord Lonsdale, the first president of the AA, who used it as a hunting lodge. Guests today will find that this is a delightful place where the service is professional and attentive. There are beautifully designed, spacious bedrooms situated in the main house and also in lodges in the grounds; each has lake views and some have patios. There are also The Shieling and Miss Potter suites. Each bedroom has Egyptian cotton linens, fresh flowers, LCD satellite TV, CD/ DVD players, bathrobes and a decanter of damson gin. The restaurant impresses with its award-winning cuisine. The hotel also has a health spa, gym and boutique store.

Rooms 30 (17 annexe) (5 fmly) (12 GF) 🐾 S £139-£475; D £159-£525 (incl. bkfst) **Facilities** Spa FTV WiFi ⓑ 🏊 🏄 Sauna Steam room Beauty massage Xmas New Year **Conf** Class 40 Board 30 Thtr 60 Del from £249 to £649 **Parking** 34 **Notes** LB Civ Wed 60

See advert on opposite page

Macdonald Old England Hotel & Spa

★★★★ 83% HOTEL

tel: 0344 879 9144 & 015394 87890 **23 Church St, Bowness LA23 3DF**
email: sales.oldengland@macdonald-hotels.co.uk web: www.macdonaldhotels.co.uk
dir: *Through Windermere to Bowness, straight across at mini-rdbt. Hotel behind church on right*

This hotel stands right on the shore of England's largest lake and boasts superb views, especially through the floor-to-ceiling windows in the Vinand Restaurant. There are several bedroom types; standard, executive and suites; some rooms have been designed for wheelchairs users. The spa has a 20-metre pool, a gym, sauna and steam room.

Rooms 106 (6 fmly) (14 GF) 🐾 **Facilities** Spa STV WiFi ⓑ supervised Gym Private jetties Rock sauna Aromatherapy shower Steam room Ice room Xmas New Year **Conf** Class 60 Board 25 Thtr 150 **Services** Lift **Parking** 90 **Notes** ⊗ Civ Wed 100

Low Wood Bay

★★★★ 81% HOTEL

tel: 015394 33338 **LA23 1LP**
email: lowwoodbay@englishlakes.co.uk web: www.englishlakes.co.uk
dir: *M6 junct 36, A590, A591 to Windermere, then 3m towards Ambleside, hotel on right*

Benefiting from a lakeside location, this hotel offers an excellent range of leisure and conference facilities. Bedrooms, many with panoramic lake views, are attractively furnished, and include a number of larger executive rooms and suites. There is a choice of bars, a spacious restaurant and the more informal Cafe del Lago. The poolside bar offers internet access.

Rooms 111 (13 fmly) (21 GF) 🐾 **Facilities** Spa FTV WiFi ⓑ ⓑ supervised Fishing 🚣 Gym Squash Watersports centre offering water skiing & canoeing Marina Beauty salon Xmas New Year **Conf** Class 180 Board 150 Thtr 340 **Services** Lift **Parking** 200 **Notes** LB Civ Wed 280

Laura Ashley The Belsfield Hotel

★★★★ 80% HOTEL

tel: 015394 42448 **Kendal Rd LA23 3EL**
email: belsfield@lauraashleyhotels.com web: www.lauraashleyhotels.com
dir: *M6 junct 36, A591 Windermere, follow signs for Bowness. At mini rdbt bear left & take 1st left (Kendal Rd). Hotel 200yds on right*

Set in six acres of land and affording some of the finest views of Lake Windermere from its elevated position, the hotel offers comfortable accommodation. A number of rooms and the restaurant have lake views, and the bistro offers a more informal dining option. Relax and take afternoon tea in the elegant drawing room or library.

Rooms 62 (5 fmly) (10 GF) 🐾 S £159-£259; D £159-£259 (incl. bkfst)* **Facilities** FTV WiFi ⓑ 🏌 Putt green Gym Xmas New Year **Conf** Class 60 Board 30 Thtr 100 Del from £199 to £259 **Services** Lift **Parking** 68 **Notes** ⊗ Civ Wed 130

HOLBECK GHYLL

MOMENTS TO SAVOUR

W

Holbeck Ghyll Country House Hotel,
Holbeck Lane, Windermere, Cumbria LA23 1LU
+44 (0)1539 432 375 www.holbeckghyll.com stay@holbeckghyll.com

[f] /holbeck.ghyll [t] @holbeckghyll

WINDERMERE *continued*

Lindeth Howe Country House Hotel & Restaurant

★★★★ 79% ◎◎ COUNTRY HOUSE HOTEL

tel: 015394 45759 **Lindeth Dr, Longtail Hill LA23 3JF**
email: hotel@lindeth-howe.co.uk **web:** www.lindeth-howe.co.uk
dir: *Exit A592, 1m S of Bowness onto B5284 Longtail Hill signed Kendal & Lancaster, hotel last driveway on right*

Historic photographs commemorate the fact that this delightful house was once the family home of Beatrix Potter. Secluded in landscaped grounds, it enjoys views across the valley and Lake Windermere. Public rooms are plentiful and inviting, with the restaurant being the perfect setting for modern country-house cooking. Deluxe and superior bedrooms are spacious and smartly appointed.

Rooms 34 (3 fmly) (2 GF) **Facilities** FTV WiFi Gym Sauna Fitness room Xmas New Year **Conf** Class 20 Board 18 Thtr 30 **Parking** 50 **Notes** Closed 4-16 Jan Civ Wed 100

Storrs Hall Hotel

★★★★ 78% HOTEL

tel: 015394 47111 **Storrs Park LA23 3LG**
email: enquiries@storrshall.com **web:** www.storrshall.com
dir: *On A592, 2m S of Bowness, on Newby Bridge road*

Set in 17 acres of landscaped grounds by the lakeside, this imposing Georgian mansion is delightful. There are numerous lounges to relax in, furnished with fine art and antiques. Individually styled bedrooms are generally spacious and boast impressive bathrooms. The elegant restaurant offers fine views across the lawn to the lake and fells beyond.

Rooms 30 **Facilities** FTV WiFi Fishing In room beauty treatments Xmas New Year **Conf** Class 35 Board 24 Thtr 50 **Parking** 50 **Notes** LB Civ Wed 94

Beech Hill Hotel & Spa

★★★★ 76% HOTEL

tel: 015394 42137 **Newby Bridge Rd LA23 3LR**
email: reservations@beechhillhotel.co.uk **web:** www.beechhillhotel.co.uk
dir: *M6 junct 36, A591 to Windermere. Left onto A592 towards Newby Bridge. Hotel 4m from Bowness-on-Windermere*

Located on the edge of Lake Windermere, the panoramic views across the lake to the Cumbrian fells beyond are impressive. The bedrooms are well appointed and some have balconies overlooking the lake. The open areas, for enjoying coffee or drinks, prove very popular in the summer, and there are cosy lounges with log fires, a fine restaurant, leisure facilities and landscaped gardens. High standards of service can be expected from the attentive, informative and very friendly staff.

Rooms 57 (5 fmly) (4 GF) **Facilities** Spa FTV WiFi Fishing Sauna Steam room Xmas New Year **Parking** 70 **Notes** Civ Wed 130

Merewood Country House Hotel

★★★★ 75% ◎ COUNTRY HOUSE HOTEL

tel: 015394 46484 **Ambleside Rd, Ecclerigg LA23 1LH**
email: info@merewoodhotel.co.uk **web:** www.lakedistrictcountryhotels.co.uk
dir: *M6 junct 36, follow A591 for 15m past Windermere, hotel on right*

A country house in the traditional Lakeland mould, Merewood provides a relaxed environment for guests and polished service to match. The bar and lounges overlook Windermere and the Cumbrian mountains beyond. Bedrooms vary in size with some superb feature rooms. Food is a further notable aspect here with dinner a highlight of any stay. Weddings and functions are ably catered for.

Rooms 20 (2 fmly) **D** £139-£189 (incl. bkfst)* **Facilities** FTV WiFi Xmas New Year **Conf** Class 45 Board 50 Thtr 150 Del from £121 to £192* **Parking** 100 **Notes** LB Civ Wed 122

The Samling

★★★ ◎◎◎ HOTEL

tel: 015394 31922 **Ambleside Rd LA23 1LR**
email: info@thesamlinghotel.co.uk **web:** www.thesamlinghotel.co.uk
dir: *M6 junct 36, A591 through Windermere towards Ambleside. 2m. 300yds past Low Wood Water Sports Centre just after sharp bend turn right into hotel entrance*

This stylish house, built in the late 1700s, is situated in 67 acres of grounds and enjoys an elevated position overlooking Lake Windermere. The spacious, beautifully furnished bedrooms and suites, some in adjacent buildings, are thoughtfully equipped and all have superb bathrooms. Public rooms include a sumptuous drawing room, a small library and an elegant dining room.

Rooms 11 (6 annexe) (6 fmly) (6 GF) **Facilities** STV FTV WiFi Xmas New Year **Conf** Board 14 Thtr 30 Del from £300 to £590* **Parking** 20 **Notes** Civ Wed 50

W

HIGHLY RECOMMENDED

Cedar Manor Hotel & Restaurant

★★★ 88% ❀❀ SMALL HOTEL

tel: 015394 43192 & 42986 **Ambleside Rd LA23 1AX**
email: info@cedarmanor.co.uk web: www.cedarmanor.co.uk
dir: *From A591 follow signs to Windermere. Hotel on left just beyond St Mary's Church*

Built in 1854 as a country retreat, this lovely old house enjoys a peaceful location that is within easy walking distance of the town centre. Bedrooms, some on the ground floor, are attractive and well equipped, with a luxurious annexe suite available for longer stays or romantic getaways. There is a comfortable lounge bar where guests can relax before enjoying dinner in the well-appointed dining room.

Rooms 10 (1 annexe) (1 fmly) (3 GF) ✿ **S** £115-£395; **D** £135-£425 (incl. bkfst)*
Facilities FTV WiFi New Year **Conf** Board 10 Del from £129 to £179* **Parking** 11 **Notes** LB ⊗ Closed 3-21 Jan

HIGHLY RECOMMENDED

Miller Howe Hotel

★★★ 87% ❀❀ ⚲ COUNTRY HOUSE HOTEL

tel: 015394 42536 & 45664 **Rayrigg Rd LA23 1EY**
email: info@millerhowe.com web: www.millerhowe.com
dir: *M6 junct 36, A591 past Windermere, left at rdbt towards Bowness*

This long established hotel enjoys a lakeside setting amidst delightful landscaped gardens. The bright and welcoming day rooms include sumptuous lounges, a conservatory and an opulently decorated restaurant. Imaginative dinners make use of fresh, local produce where possible and there is an extensive, well-balanced wine list. Stylish bedrooms, many with fabulous lake views, include well-equipped cottage rooms and a number with whirlpool baths.

Rooms 15 (3 annexe) (1 GF) ✿ **Facilities** FTV WiFi ⬳ HL Xmas New Year **Parking** 35 **Notes** Civ Wed 75

The Ryebeck

★★★ 86% ❀❀ COUNTRY HOUSE HOTEL

tel: 015394 88195 **Lyth Valley Rd LA23 3JP**
email: info@ryebeck.com web: www.ryebeck.com
dir: *M6 junct 46, follow A591. Right at Plumgarth's rdbt and follow Crooked to end. Left, hotel 300yds on right*

The Ryebeck sits majestically above the shores of Lake Windermere. Set in its own extensive, well-maintained gardens, the hotel enjoys an enviable position providing picture postcard views. Originally built in 1904 as a private home the property has enjoyed a number of different uses before being lovingly transformed into the hotel we see today. Award-winning food, luxurious bedrooms, en suites and warm Lakeland hospitality are just a few of the many reasons to visit The Ryebeck. If this is not enough the views from many of the public areas will be the icing on the cake. Just minutes' drive from the Lake and ferry but within easy access of the M6 guests can enjoy the location of the Lakes without necessarily joining the crush in the town.

Rooms 26 (2 annexe) (7 GF) ✿ **S** £85-£135; **D** £195-£365 (incl. bkfst & dinner)*
Facilities FTV WiFi Xmas New Year **Parking** 30 **Notes** No children 2yrs Civ Wed 82

Hillthwaite

★★★ 82% HOTEL

tel: 015394 43636 & 46691 **Thornbarrow Rd LA23 2DF**
email: reception@hillthwaite.com web: www.hillthwaite.com
dir: *M6 junct 36, A591 Windermere, follow lane road through village A5074, left opposite Goodley Dale School, approx 0.5m from A591*

The family-owned Hillthwaite hotel, set in three acres of landscaped gardens between Windermere and Bowness, is one of the area's highest hotels, overlooking Lake Windermere with magnificent panoramic views over to Langdale Pikes, Crinkle Crags and Coniston Old Man. Individually designed rooms are maintained to a high standard, some with splendid four-poster beds and jacuzzi baths, and most with lake or fell views. Public rooms on the ground floor include a comfortable lounge with well-stocked bar, a feature conservatory and impressive restaurant with stunning views of the South Lakes skyline. Leisure facilities include a heated swimming pool, steam room and sauna.

Rooms 34 (4 annexe) (4 fmly) (3 GF) ✿ **S** £70-£105; **D** £125-£305 (incl. bkfst)*
Facilities FTV WiFi ⊛ Sauna Steam room New Year **Parking** 30 **Notes** Civ Wed 50

Briery Wood Country House Hotel

★★★ 79% ❀ COUNTRY HOUSE HOTEL

tel: 015394 33316 **Ambleside Rd, Ecclerigg LA23 1ES**
email: info@brierywood.co.uk web: www.lakedistrictcountryhotels.co.uk
dir: *M6 junct 36, follow A591 for 15m past Windermere, hotel on right (do not use postcode for Sat Nav)*

This small country house hideaway is part of a small group all nestled on the banks of Windermere. Sited in its own well-tended grounds, Briery Wood is a charming white house that boasts 23 individually-styled bedrooms and a warren of public rooms. Cuisine is a highlight at dinner, though not overly-formal, and the warm welcome and rapport from the team is also noteworthy.

Rooms 23 (4 fmly) (11 GF) **S** £79-£129; **D** £89-£155 (incl. bkfst)* **Facilities** FTV WiFi ⬳ Xmas New Year **Conf** Class 30 Board 30 Thtr 80 Del from £126 to £156* **Parking** 40 **Notes** Civ Wed 113

Windermere Manor Hotel

★★★ 79% HOTEL

tel: 01539 445801 **Rayrigg Rd LA23 1ES**
email: windermere@visionhotels.co.uk web: www.visionhotels.co.uk
dir: *A591 towards Ambleside. At mini-rdbt turn left, hotel 1st on left*

Set above the shores of Lake Windermere in wooded landscaped gardens, this former manor house has been restored to its original splendour. The bedrooms and suites are smart and well appointed. The attractive dining room has an unusual barrel-vaulted wooden roof and serves delicious home cooking. The hotel extends a warm welcome to everyone but caters especially for the visually impaired, their families, friends and guide dogs. Special facilities for guide dogs are provided.

Rooms 35 (7 annexe) (2 fmly) (10 GF) ✿ **Facilities** FTV WiFi HL ⊛ supervised Xmas New Year **Conf** Class 30 Board 15 Thtr 40 **Services** Lift **Parking** 28 **Notes** LB

W

WINDERMERE *continued*

Craig Manor

★★★ 77% HOTEL

tel: 015394 88877 **Lake Rd LA23 2JF**
email: info@craigmanor.co.uk **web:** www.craigmanor.co.uk
dir: *A590, then A591 into Windermere, left at Windermere Hotel, through village, pass Magistrates Court/Police Station, hotel on right*

Situated in the heart of the Lake District, Craig Manor has a relaxed and friendly atmosphere with professional staff providing attentive service. Bedrooms are comfortable and well equipped, and some rooms offer stunning views across the lake. The attractive and elegant lake-facing restaurant serves an excellent choice of quality dishes. The large car park is a further benefit in this popular tourist resort.

Rooms 26 ↝ S £63-£135; **D** £72-£144 (incl. bkfst) **Facilities** FTV WiFi ↘ **Parking** 39 **Notes** LB

WINDSOR	Map 6 SU97
Berkshire	

Macdonald Windsor Hotel

★★★★ HOTEL

MACDONALD
HOTELS & RESORTS

tel: 01753 483100 & 0344 879 9101 **23 High St SL4 1LH**
email: gm.windsor@macdonald-hotels.co.uk
web: www.macdonaldhotels.co.uk/windsor
dir: *M4 junct 6 A355, take A332, rdbt 1st exit signed town centre. In 0.7m turn left into Bachelors Acre*

Just across the street from Windsor Castle, this hotel is an ideal base for visiting that, and all the other famous attractions of the town. It has well-appointed contemporary, designer-led bedrooms, some overlooking the castle, that are decorated in soft shades to create a calm atmosphere, and include flat-screen TVs and Bose iPod docks. The Scottish Steakhouse@Caleys restaurant offers a relaxed and informal dining venue, and 24-hour room service is also available. There is complimentary WiFi in the bedrooms and the conference rooms. The hotel has excellent wedding facilities.

Rooms 120 (4 fmly) ↝ **D** £130-£450* **Facilities** FTV WiFi ↘ HL ♬ **Conf** Class 80 Board 35 Thtr 100 Del from £202.80 to £358.80* **Services** Lift Air con **Parking** 42 **Notes** LB Civ Wed 100

The Oakley Court

★★★★ 83% ◉◉ HOTEL

tel: 01753 609988 & 609900 **Windsor Rd, Water Oakley SL4 5UR**
email: reservations@oakleycourt.co.uk **web:** www.oakleycourt.co.uk
dir: *M4 junct 6, A355, then A332 towards Windsor, right onto A308 towards Maidenhead. Pass racecourse, hotel 2.5m on right*

Built in 1859 this splendid Victorian Gothic mansion is enviably situated in extensive grounds that lead down to the Thames. All bedrooms are spacious, beautifully furnished and many enjoy river views. Extensive public areas include a range of comfortable lounges and the Oakleaf Restaurant. The comprehensive leisure facilities include a fully equipped gym, indoor swimming pool, jacuzzi, sauna, steam room, tennis court, and 9-hole golf course

Rooms 118 (108 annexe) (6 fmly) (42 GF) **D** £169-£399* **Facilities** FTV WiFi ↘ HL ⓢ ⚓ 9 ⛳ Putt green ⛳ Gym Boating Sauna Steam room Snooker Bicycles Xmas New Year **Conf** Class 90 Board 50 Thtr 170 **Services** Air con **Parking** 200 **Notes** LB Civ Wed 170

Castle Hotel Windsor MGallery by Sofitel

★★★★ 82% ◉ HOTEL

tel: 01753 851577 **18 High St SL4 1LJ**
email: h6618@accor.com **web:** www.castlehotelwindsor.com
dir: *M4 junct 6/M25 junct 15, follow signs to Windsor town centre & castle. Hotel at top of hill opposite Guildhall*

This is one of the oldest hotels in Windsor, beginning life as a coaching inn in the 16th century. Located opposite Windsor Castle, it is an ideal base from which to explore the town and its royal connections. Stylish bedrooms are thoughtfully equipped and include four-poster and executive rooms. Public areas are spacious and tastefully decorated.

Rooms 108 (70 annexe) (5 fmly) (3 GF) ↝ **Facilities** STV FTV WiFi ↘ Xmas New Year **Conf** Class 150 Board 50 Thtr 400 **Services** Lift Air con **Parking** 133 **Notes** ⊗ Civ Wed 300

Christopher Hotel

★★★ 80% HOTEL

tel: 01753 852359 **110 High St, Eton SL4 6AN**
email: reservations@thechristopher.co.uk **web:** www.thechristopher.co.uk
dir: *M4 junct 5 Slough E, Colnbrook Datchet Eton, B470. At rdbt 2nd exit for Datchet. Right at mini rdbt, Eton, left into Eton Rd, 3rd rdbt. Left, hotel on right*

This hotel benefits from an ideal location in Eton, being only a short stroll across the pedestrian bridge from historic Windsor Castle and the many other attractions the town has to offer. The hotel has comfortable and smartly decorated accommodation, and a wide range of dishes is available in the informal bar and grill. A stylish room is available for private dining or for meetings.

Rooms 34 (23 annexe) (10 fmly) (22 GF) ↝ **Facilities** FTV WiFi ↘ Xmas New Year **Conf** Board 10 Thtr 30 **Parking** 19 **Notes** LB

W

WINTERINGHAM
Lincolnshire   Map 17 SE92

Winteringham Fields
◉◉◉◉ RESTAURANT WITH ROOMS

tel: 01724 733096 **1 Silver St DN15 9ND**
email: reception@winteringhamfields.co.uk **web:** www.winteringhamfields.co.uk
dir: *In village centre at x-rds*

This highly regarded restaurant with rooms, located deep in the countryside at Winteringham village, is six miles west of the Humber Bridge. Public rooms and bedrooms, some of which are housed in renovated barns and cottages, are delightfully luxurious. There is an abundance of charm, and period features are combined with rich furnishings and fabrics. The award-winning food is a highlight of any stay and guests can expect highly skilled dishes, excellent quality and stunning presentation.

Rooms 15 (11 annexe) (6 fmly)

WISBECH
Cambridgeshire   Map 12 TF40

Crown Lodge Hotel
★★★ 83% ◉ HOTEL   THE INDEPENDENTS HOTEL ASSOCIATION

tel: 01945 773391 & 772206 **Downham Rd, Outwell PE14 8SE**
email: office@thecrownlodgehotel.co.uk **web:** www.thecrownlodgehotel.co.uk
dir: *On A1122, approx 5m from Wisbech*

Crown Lodge Hotel is a friendly, privately-owned hotel situated in a peaceful location on the banks of Well Creek, a short drive from Wisbech. The bedrooms are pleasantly decorated, with co-ordinated fabrics and modern facilities. The public areas are very stylish; they include a lounge bar, brasserie restaurant and a large seating area with plush leather sofas.

Rooms 10 (1 fmly) (10 GF) 🅿 **Facilities** FTV WiFi ⭘ Squash **Conf** Class 60 Board 40 Thtr 80 **Services** Air con **Parking** 55 **Notes** Closed 25-26 Dec & 1 Jan

WISHAW
Warwickshire   Map 10 SP19

The Belfry
★★★★ 83% ◉ HOTEL

tel: 0844 980 0600
(Calls cost 7p per minute plus your phone company's access charge) & 01675 477047
Lichfield Rd B76 9PR
email: enquiries@thebelfry.com **web:** www.thebelfry.com
dir: *M42 junct 9, A446 towards Lichfield, hotel 1m on right*

The Belfry is ideally situated within easy striking distance of the M6, Birmingham and Birmingham Airport. The property is set in 550 acres of countryside and features three golf courses, including the Ryder Cup course, The Brabazon. The facilities include the Ryder Grill, the Brabazon Bar, Leisure Café, Sam's, a Starbucks, a spa, leisure facilities and a golf shop. The bedrooms are modern and well equipped; many of the rooms have views of the surrounding countryside.

Rooms 319 (4 fmly) (98 GF) 🅿 **Facilities** Spa FTV WiFi ⭘ HL ⭘ ⚎ 54 ⭘ Putt green Gym Squash Ryder legends mini golf Children's playground Xmas New Year **Conf** Class 435 Thtr 830 **Services** Lift **Parking** 1000 **Notes** Civ Wed 300

WITNEY
Oxfordshire   Map 5 SP31

Oxford Witney Four Pillars Hotel

★★★★ 78% HOTEL

tel: 0800 374692 & 01993 779777 **Ducklington Ln OX28 4TJ**
email: witney@four-pillars.co.uk **web:** www.four-pillars.co.uk/witney
dir: *M40 junct 9, A34 to A40, exit A415 Witney/Abingdon. Hotel on left, 2nd exit for Witney*

This attractive modern hotel is close to Oxford and Burford and offers spacious, well-equipped bedrooms. The cosy Spinners Bar has comfortable seating areas and the popular Weavers Restaurant offers a good range of dishes. Other amenities include extensive function and leisure facilities, complete with indoor swimming pool.

Rooms 87 (14 fmly) (21 GF) 🅿 **Facilities** FTV WiFi ⭘ ⭘ Gym Steam room Sauna Xmas New Year **Conf** Class 76 Board 44 Thtr 150 **Parking** 120 **Notes** ⊗ Civ Wed 150

Premier Inn Witney
BUDGET HOTEL

tel: 0871 527 9488 *(Calls cost 13p per minute plus your phone company's access charge)*
Beech House, Ducklington Ln OX28 4JF
web: www.premierinn.com
dir: *M40 junct 8 or junct 9 follow Oxford signs, A40 towards Cheltenham. Take A415 (Witney & Abingdon). At bottom of slip road follow Witney signs. Straight on at lights, hotel on right*

High quality, budget accommodation ideal for both families and business travellers. Spacious, en suite bedrooms feature tea and coffee making facilities, and Freeview TV in most hotels. Internet access and WiFi are available for a small fee. The adjacent family restaurant features a wide and varied menu. See also the Hotel Groups pages.

Rooms 57

W

WOBURN
Bedfordshire   Map 11 SP93

The Woburn Hotel
★★★★ 77% ◉◉ HOTEL

tel: 01525 290441 **George St MK17 9PX**
email: info@thewoburnhotel.co.uk **web:** www.thewoburnhotel.co.uk
dir: *M1 junct 13, towards Woburn. In Woburn left at T-junct, hotel in village*

This inn provides a high standard of accommodation. Bedrooms are divided between the original house, a modern extension and some stunning cottage suites. Public areas include the beamed, club-style Tavistock Bar, a range of meeting rooms and an attractive restaurant with interesting dishes on offer.

Rooms 55 (7 annexe) (4 fmly) (25 GF) ☞ **S** £90.50-£152.50; **D** £105-£305 (incl. bkfst)* **Facilities** FTV WiFi ⅃ 54 Putt green Concessionary rate to access Woburn Safari Park & Woburn Abbey Xmas New Year **Conf** Class 30 Board 35 Thtr 60 Del from £165 to £195* **Parking** 80 **Notes** LB ⊗ Civ Wed 60

WOKING
Surrey   Map 6 TQ05

DoubleTree by Hilton Woking
★★★★ 72% HOTEL

tel: 01483 221010 **Victoria Way GU21 8EW**
email: info@dtwoking.com **web:** www.dtwoking.com
dir: *M25 junct 11, A320 to Woking. Follow signs to town centre through 4 rdbts*

Located in the heart of Woking town centre, this newly refurbished hotel offers comfortable accommodation. Bedrooms have been enhanced to provide modern amenities for both business and leisure travellers. Public areas include a spacious lounge bar and restaurant. A number of up-to-date conference and meeting rooms are available. Secure parking available on site.

Rooms 170 (34 fmly) **Facilities** FTV WiFi ↓ Gym Xmas New Year **Conf** Class 100 Board 35 Thtr 300 **Services** Lift Air con **Parking** 45 **Notes** ⊗ Civ Wed 55

Premier Inn Woking Town Centre
BUDGET HOTEL

tel: 0871 527 9462 *(Calls cost 13p per minute plus your phone company's access charge)*
Eurobet House, Church Street West GU21 6HT
web: www.premierinn.com
dir: *See website for detailed directions*

High quality, budget accommodation ideal for both families and business travellers. Spacious, en suite bedrooms feature tea and coffee making facilities, and Freeview TV in most hotels. Internet access and WiFi are available for a small fee. The adjacent family restaurant features a wide and varied menu. See also the Hotel Groups pages.

Rooms 105

Premier Inn Woking West (A324)
BUDGET HOTEL

tel: 0871 527 9182 *(Calls cost 13p per minute plus your phone company's access charge)*
Bridge Barn Ln, Horsell GU21 6NL
web: www.premierinn.com
dir: *From A324 at rdbt into Parley Drive. Left at next rdbt into Goldsworth Rd*

Rooms 56

WOKINGHAM
Berkshire   Map 5 SU86

Cantley House Hotel
★★★ 78% ◉◉ COUNTRY HOUSE HOTEL

tel: 0118 989 5100 **Milton Rd RG40 1JY**
email: reception@cantleyhotel.co.uk **web:** www.cantleyhotel.co.uk
dir: *M4 junct 10, A329(M) to A329 towards Wokingham, then A321, hotel signed*

Cantley House Hotel is located within acres of Berkshire parkland. This Victorian mansion features a number of conference and meeting rooms, benefiting from traditional features. Bedrooms vary from the comfortable cosy doubles to a number of impressively sized suites and executive rooms. The award-winning Milton's restaurant is housed in a beautifully converted 17th-century barn with its own secluded courtyard garden.

Rooms 36 (20 GF) ☞ **S** £75-£99; **D** £85-£145 (incl. bkfst) **Facilities** FTV WiFi ↓ 🦡 ☝ Hairdresser Massage treatments ♫ Xmas New Year **Conf** Class 50 Board 50 Thtr 80 Del from £139 to £249 **Parking** 100 **Notes** LB Civ Wed 150

WOLVERHAMPTON
West Midlands   Map 10 SO99

Novotel Wolverhampton
★★★ 81% HOTEL   NOVOTEL
HOTELS & RESORTS

tel: 01902 871100 **Union St WV1 3JN**
email: H1188@accor.com **web:** www.novotel.com
dir: *6m from M6 junct 10. A454 to Wolverhampton. Hotel on main ring road*

This large, modern, purpose-built hotel stands close to the town centre. It provides spacious, smartly presented and well-equipped bedrooms, all of which contain convertible bed settees for family occupancy. In addition to the open-plan lounge and bar area, there is an attractive brasserie-style restaurant, which overlooks an attractive patio garden.

Rooms 132 (9 fmly) ☞ **S** £50-£119; **D** £60-£119* **Facilities** FTV WiFi ↓ **Conf** Class 100 Board 80 Thtr 200 Del from £99 to £149* **Services** Lift **Parking** 120 **Notes** RS 23 Dec-4 Jan Civ Wed 170

The Mount Hotel and Conference Centre
★★★ 75% ◉ HOTEL

tel: 01902 752055 **Mount Rd, Tettenhall Wood WV6 8HL**
email: sales@themount.co.uk **web:** www.themount.co.uk
dir: *M54 junct 5, follow A41 down to Yew Tree Lane which becomes Mount Road, left at lights*

This historic hotel is peacefully located on the outskirts of the city. Modern refurbishment and period architecture sit comfortably together, creating a stylish interior. Bedrooms are contemporary, with attractive colour schemes and equipment suitable for both business and leisure guests. Complimentary WiFi is available throughout. Public areas encompass a stylish bar and lounge, Drawing Room restaurant overlooking terrace and gardens, and extensive meeting and function rooms including the impressive Great Hall.

Rooms 65 (10 annexe) (20 fmly) (31 GF) ☞ **Facilities** FTV WiFi ↓ Gym Xmas New Year **Conf** Class 50 Board 80 Thtr 180 **Parking** 100 **Notes** ⊗ Civ Wed 140

Holiday Inn Garden Court Wolverhampton

★★★ 74% HOTEL

tel: 01902 390004 **Dunstall Park, Gorse Brook Rd WV6 OPE**
email: holidayinn@wolverhampton-racecourse.com **web:** www.holidayinn.co.uk
dir: *Off A449, 1.5m from city centre. Follow brown sign for Dunstall Park. Adjacent to Wolverhampton Racecourse*

The Holiday Inn Wolverhampton forms an integral part of Wolverhampton Racecourse. Well-appointed, air-conditioned bedrooms have views across the course and stables. Open-plan public areas are modern and bright, with outdoor seating available during summer months. Free WiFi and ample parking available.

Rooms 54 **Facilities** STV WiFi Gym Private location within Wolverhampton Racecourse Outdoor playground **Conf** Class 260 Thtr 600 **Services** Lift **Parking** 1500 **Notes** ⊗

Mercure Wolverhampton Goldthorn Hotel

★★★ 74% HOTEL

tel: 01902 429216 **126 Penn Rd WV3 OER**
email: enquiries@hotels-wolverhampton.com **web:** www.hotels-wolverhampton.com
dir: *A454 then A449 signed Kidderminster. Hotel 1m on right*

This hotel is situated just on the outskirts of the old town and offers easy access to major motorway networks. The bedrooms are comfortable and well equipped; free WiFi is available throughout the hotel. The leisure facilities include a health club with a swimming pool, gym, steam room and sauna. There is also free on-site parking.

Rooms 74 (16 annexe) (12 fmly) (4 GF) **S** £40-£50, **D** £58-£150* **Facilities** FTV WiFi ↻ Gym Sauna Steam room **Conf** Class 70 Board 40 Thtr 140 Del from £100 to £135* **Parking** 100 **Notes** LB Civ Wed 100

Quality Hotel Wolverhampton

★★★ 70% HOTEL

tel: 01902 424433 **Tettenhall Rd WV1 4SW**
email: rcccption@qualityhotelwolverhampton.com
web: www.qualityhotelwolverhampton.com
dir: *A41 junct 3, 1st exit at rdbt. Follow signs for Tettenhall. In Tettenhall Rd, hotel on left*

This hotel is located a short walk from the city centre and the railway station, with convenient access to the motorway networks. Bedrooms provide modern comfort with contemporary decor. Complimentary WiFi is available throughout the hotel. The Americano steakhouse and bar offers American-style dishes, with exotic meats a speciality. There are seven air-conditioned conference and banqueting suites.

Rooms 60 (3 fmly) **Facilities** STV FTV WiFi ↻ Xmas New Year **Conf** Class 300 Board 60 Thtr 500 **Services** Lift **Parking** 120 **Notes** ⊗ Civ Wed 500

Premier Inn Wolverhampton City Centre

BUDGET HOTEL

tel: 0871 527 9186 *(Calls cost 13p per minute plus your phone company's access charge)*
Broad Gauge Way WV10 0BA
web: www.premierinn.com
dir: *M6 junct 10, A454 signed Wolverhampton for approx 2m. Right into Neachalls Ln (signed Wednesfield). 0.75m. At rdbt 1st exit onto A4124 (Wednesfield Way). 1st exit at next rdbt. 2nd exit at 3rd rdbt. At 2nd lights left into Sun St. 1st right, hotel at end of road*

High quality, budget accommodation ideal for both families and business travellers. Spacious, en suite bedrooms feature tea and coffee making facilities, and Freeview TV in most hotels. Internet access and WiFi are available for a small fee. The adjacent family restaurant features a wide and varied menu. See also the Hotel Groups pages.

Rooms 109

Premier Inn Wolverhampton North

BUDGET HOTEL

tel: 0871 527 9184 *(Calls cost 13p per minute plus your phone company's access charge)*
Greenfield Ln, Stafford Rd WV10 6TA
web: www.premierinn.com
dir: *M54 junct 2. Hotel at lights in approx 100yds*

Rooms 80

WOMBWELL
South Yorkshire   Map 16 SE40

Premier Inn Barnsley (Dearne Valley)

BUDGET HOTEL

tel: 0871 527 8050 *(Calls cost 13p per minute plus your phone company's access charge)*
Meadow Gate, Dearne Valley S73 0UN
web: www.premierinn.com
dir: *M1 junct 36 E'bound, A6195 towards Doncaster (5m). Hotel at rdbt adjacent to Meadows Brewers Fayre*

High quality, budget accommodation ideal for both families and business travellers. Spacious, en suite bedrooms feature tea and coffee making facilities, and Freeview TV in most hotels. Internet access and WiFi are available for a small fee. The adjacent family restaurant features a wide and varied menu. See also the Hotel Groups pages.

Rooms 63

WOOBURN
Buckinghamshire   Map 6 SU98

Chequers Inn

★★★ 81% ◉◉ HOTEL

tel: 01628 529575 **Kiln Ln, Wooburn HP10 0JQ**
email: info@chequers-inn.com **web:** www.chequers-inn.com
dir: *M40 junct 2, A40 through Beaconsfield Old Town towards High Wycombe. 2m from town left into Broad Ln. Inn 2.5m*

This 17th-century inn enjoys a peaceful, rural location beside the common. Bedrooms feature stripped-pine furniture, co-ordinated fabrics and an excellent range of extra facilities. The bar has a massive oak post, beams and flagstone floors, while the restaurant overlooks a pretty patio.

Rooms 18 (8 GF) ⌂ **S** fr £99.50; **D** £107.50-£170* **Facilities** FTV WiFi **Conf** Class 30 Board 20 Thtr 50 Del from £155* **Parking** 60 **Notes** ⊗

WOODALL MOTORWAY SERVICE AREA (M1)
South Yorkshire   Map 16 SK48

Days Inn Sheffield - M1

AA Advertised

tel: 0114 248 7992 **Woodall Service Area S26 7XR**
email: woodall.hotel@welcomebreak.co.uk **web:** www.welcomebreak.co.uk
dir: *M1, between juncts 30 & 31 S'bound, at Woodall Services*

This modern building offers accommodation in smart, spacious and well-equipped bedrooms, suitable for families and business travellers, and all with en suite bathrooms. Continental breakfast is available and other refreshments may be taken at the nearby family restaurant.

Rooms 38 (32 fmly) (16 GF) (6 smoking) **Facilities** FTV WiFi ↻ **Conf** Board 10 **Parking** 40

W

WOODBRIDGE
Suffolk
Map 13 TM24

Seckford Hall Hotel
★★★★ 78% ◉◉ HOTEL

tel: 01394 385678 **IP13 6NU**
email: reception@seckford.co.uk **web:** www.seckford.co.uk
dir: *Signed on A12. NB do not follow signs for town centre*

Seckford Hall is an elegant Tudor manor house set amid landscaped grounds just off the A12. It is reputed that Queen Elizabeth I visited this property, and it retains much of its original character. Public rooms include a superb panelled lounge, a cosy bar and an intimate restaurant. The spacious bedrooms are attractively decorated, tastefully furnished and thoughtfully equipped.

Rooms 32 (10 annexe) (4 fmly) (7 GF) 🐾 **Facilities** Spa WiFi ⤵ 🕐 Putt green Fishing Gym Beauty salon Xmas New Year **Conf** Class 46 Board 40 Thtr 120 **Parking** 100 **Notes** Civ Wed 120

The Crown at Woodbridge
★★★ 85% ◉◉ HOTEL

tel: 01394 384242 **The Thoroughfare IP12 1AD**
email: info@thecrownatwoodbridge.co.uk **web:** www.thecrownatwoodbridge.co.uk
dir: *A12 follow signs for Woodbridge onto B1438. 1.25m from rdbt left into Quay St. Hotel on right approx 100yds*

This 17th-century property offers contemporary-style accommodation throughout. The open-plan public areas are tastefully appointed and include a large lounge bar, a restaurant and a private dining room. The stylish bedrooms are tastefully appointed and equipped with modern facilities.

Rooms 10 (2 fmly) 🐾 **S** £100-£190; **D** £110-£200 (incl. bkfst)* **Facilities** STV WiFi **Conf** Class 8 Board 12 Thtr 15 **Parking** 40 **Notes** ⊗

WOODBURY
Devon
Map 3 SY08

Woodbury Park Hotel and Golf Club
★★★★ 76% HOTEL

tel: 01395 233382 **Woodbury Castle EX5 1JJ**
email: enquiries@woodburypark.co.uk **web:** www.woodburypark.co.uk
dir: *M5 junct 30, A376 then A3052 towards Sidmouth, onto B3180, hotel signed*

Situated in 500 acres of beautiful, unspoilt countryside, yet within easy reach of Exeter and the M5, this hotel offers smart, well-equipped and immaculately presented accommodation together with a host of sporting and banqueting facilities. There is a choice of golf courses, a Bodyzone beauty centre and enjoyable dining in the Atrium Restaurant.

Rooms 60 (4 annexe) (4 fmly) (28 GF) 🐾 **Facilities** Spa STV FTV WiFi ⤵ 🕐 ♨ 27 ⛳ Putt green Fishing Gym Squash Beauty salon Football pitch Driving range Fitness studio Cinema suite Xmas New Year **Conf** Class 100 Board 40 Thtr 250 **Services** Lift **Parking** 400 **Notes** ⊗ Civ Wed 150

WOODFORD BRIDGE
Greater London
Map 6 TQ49

Hallmark Hotel London Chigwell Prince Regent
★★★★ 74% HOTEL

tel: 0330 028 3418 **Manor Rd IG8 8AE**
email: princeregent@hallmarkhotels.co.uk **web:** www.hallmarkhotels.co.uk
dir: *From A113 (Chigwell Rd) S of Chigwell into B173 (Manor Rd)*

Situated on the edge of Woodford Bridge and Chigwell, this hotel with delightful rear gardens, offers easy access into London as well as to the M11 and M25. There is a good range of spacious, well-equipped bedrooms. Extensive conference and banqueting facilities are particularly well appointed, and are very suitable for weddings or business events.

Rooms 61 (4 fmly) (15 GF) (6 smoking) 🐾 **Facilities** STV FTV WiFi ⤵ Xmas New Year **Conf** Class 180 Board 80 Thtr 400 **Services** Lift **Parking** 225 **Notes** LB Civ Wed 350

W

WOODFORD GREEN
Greater London   Map 6 TQ49

Best Western Plus Epping Forest
Best Western PLUS

★★★ 74% HOTEL

tel: 020 8787 9988 **30 Oak Hill IG8 9NY**
email: enquiries@eppingforesthotel.co.uk **web:** www.bestwestern.co.uk
dir: M25 junct 27 take M11 S/bound, at end of M11 follow A406 towards west end, stay in left hand lane & take the 1st exit to Woodford, at rdbt take 3rd exit, turn left at petrol station, hotel 150 yds on right

Recently refurbished, this hotel enjoys a very good location on the outskirts of London in Epping Forest. Contemporary open-plan public areas are all attractively presented and the stylish bar is very well appointed and comfortable. There is a real relaxed feel about the hotel and the woodland setting has a real impact. Spacious bedrooms look very smart with some eye-catching bold colours used in their design. Free WiFi is available throughout the hotel and secure parking is available.

Rooms 99 (18 fmly) (24 GF) **Facilities** FTV WiFi Xmas New Year **Services** Lift **Parking** 68 **Notes** ⊗ Civ Wed 200

WOODHALL SPA
Lincolnshire   Map 17 TF16

Petwood

★★★ 78% HOTEL

tel: 01526 352411 **Stixwould Rd LN10 6QG**
email: reception@petwood.co.uk **web:** www.petwood.co.uk
dir: From Sleaford take A153 signed Skegness. At Tattershall turn left on B1192. Hotel is signed from village

This lovely Edwardian house, set in 30 acres of gardens and woodlands, is adjacent to Woodhall Golf Course. Built in 1905, the house was used by 617 Squadron, the famous Dambusters, as an officers' mess during World War II. Bedrooms and public areas are spacious and comfortable, and retain many original features. Weddings and conferences are well catered for in modern facilities.

Rooms 53 (3 GF) ⊛ **S** £75-£85; **D** £95-£185 (incl. bkfst)* **Facilities** FTV WiFi HL Putt green ♨ ♫ Xmas New Year **Conf** Class 100 Board 50 Thtr 250 Del from £152* **Services** Lift **Parking** 140 **Notes** LB Civ Wed 200

See advert on opposite page

WOODLANDS
Hampshire   Map 5 SU31

Woodlands Lodge Hotel

★★★ 79% ⊛ HOTEL

tel: 023 8029 2257 **Bartley Rd, Woodlands SO40 7GN**
email: reception@woodlands-lodge.co.uk **web:** www.woodlands-lodge.co.uk
dir: M27 junct 2, left at rdbt towards Fawley. 2nd rdbt right towards Cadnam. 1st left at White Horse pub onto Woodlands Rd, over cattle grid

An 18th-century former hunting lodge, this hotel is set in four acres of impressive and well-tended grounds on the edge of the New Forest. Well-equipped bedrooms come in varying sizes and styles and a number of bathrooms have a jacuzzi bath. Public areas include a pleasant lounge and intimate cocktail bar.

Rooms 17 (3 fmly) (3 GF) ⊛ **S** £59-£129; **D** £69-£129 (incl. bkfst)* **Facilities** FTV WiFi ♨ Xmas New Year **Conf** Class 20 Board 20 Thtr 65 **Parking** 60 **Notes** Civ Wed 100

WOODSTOCK
Oxfordshire   Map 11 SP41

Macdonald Bear Hotel

★★★★ 78% ⊛⊛ HOTEL

MACDONALD
HOTELS & RESORTS

tel: 01993 811124 & 0344 879 9143 **Park St OX20 1SZ**
email: general.bear@macdonald-hotels.co.uk **web:** www.macdonaldhotels.co.uk
dir: M40 junct 9 follow signs for Oxford & Blenheim Palace. A44 to town centre, hotel on left

With its ivy-clad façade, oak beams and open fireplaces, this 13th-century coaching inn exudes charm and cosiness. The bedrooms are decorated in a modern style that remains in keeping with the historic character of the building. Public rooms include a variety of function rooms, an intimate bar area and an attractive restaurant where attentive service and good food are offered.

Rooms 54 (18 annexe) (1 fmly) (8 GF) ⊛ **Facilities** FTV WiFi Xmas New Year **Conf** Class 12 Board 24 Thtr 40 Del from £145 to £210* **Parking** 40

The Feathers Hotel

★★★★ 77% ⊛⊛ TOWN HOUSE HOTEL

PRIDE OF BRITAIN HOTELS

tel: 01993 812291 **Market St OX20 1SX**
email: reception@feathers.co.uk **web:** www.feathers.co.uk
dir: From A44 Oxford to Woodstock, 1st left after lights. Hotel on left

This intimate and unique hotel enjoys a town centre location with easy access to nearby Blenheim Palace. Public areas are elegant and full of traditional character from the cosy drawing room to the atmospheric restaurant. Individually styled bedrooms are appointed to a high standard and are furnished with attractive period and reproduction furniture.

Rooms 21 (5 annexe) (4 fmly) (2 GF) ⊛ **Facilities** FTV WiFi ♨ Xmas New Year **Conf** Class 18 Board 20 Thtr 40 Del from £216 to £296*

W

WOOKEY HOLE
Somerset   Map 4 ST54

Wookey Hole Hotel

★★ 74% HOTEL

tel: 01749 672243 **BA5 1BB**
email: witch@wookey.co.uk **web:** www.wookey.co.uk

This impressive, modern hotel is located in the heart of the pretty village, famous for its magnificent cave system and just a couple of miles from the historic cathedral city of Wells. The bedrooms are contemporary, spacious and comfortable, with both family and connecting rooms available. Additional facilities include a bar and restaurant. There is ample parking provision.

Rooms 58 (37 fmly) (27 GF) ⌇ S £39.99-£99.99; **D** £39.99-£99.99 **Facilities** FTV WiFi ⇣ 9 hole adventure golf course Xmas New Year **Conf** Class 100 Board 100 Thtr 400 Del from £60 to £150* **Services** Lift **Parking** 800 **Notes** LB ⊗ Civ Wed 120

WOOLACOMBE
Devon   Map 3 SS44

Watersmeet Hotel

★★★★ 78% ◉◉ HOTEL

tel: 01271 870333 **Mortehoe EX34 7EB**
email: info@watersmeethotel.co.uk **web:** www.watersmeethotel.co.uk
dir: B3343 into Woolacombe, right onto esplanade, hotel 0.75m on left

With magnificent views, and steps leading directly to the beach, this popular hotel offers guests attentive service and a relaxing atmosphere. Bedrooms benefit from the wonderful sea views and some have private balconies. Diners in the attractive tiered restaurant can admire the beautiful sunsets while enjoying an innovative

range of dishes offered on the fixed-price menu. Both indoor and outdoor pools are available.

Rooms 25 (4 fmly) (3 GF) ⌇ **S** £105-£195; **D** £120-£310 (incl. bkfst)* **Facilities** FTV WiFi ⓢ ⌇ ⌇ Steam room ♫ Xmas New Year **Conf** Board 20 Thtr 20 **Services** Lift **Parking** 38 **Notes** LB ⊗ Civ Wed 60

The Woolacombe Bay Hotel

★★★★ 77% HOTEL

tel: 01271 870388 **South St EX34 7BN**
email: enquiries@woolacombebayhotel.co.uk **web:** www.woolacombebayhotel.co.uk
dir: A361 onto B3343 to Woolacombe. Hotel in centre

Overlooking one of the finest beaches in England, this privately-owned hotel offers a warm welcome. Public areas are spacious and comfortable, and many of the stylishly furnished and well-equipped bedrooms have balconies with splendid views over the bay. New bathroom suites certainly add to the feeling of luxury. In addition to the elegant surroundings of Doyle's Restaurant, The Bay Brasserie is available as an informal alternative. Extensive leisure facilities are also provided, including a health club, a spa and a very stylish lido.

Rooms 64 (26 fmly) (2 GF) ⌇ **Facilities** Spa FTV WiFi ⓢ ⌇ ⌇ 9 ⌇ Gym Squash Paddling pool Table tennis Snooker Steam room Sauna Xmas New Year Child facilities **Conf** Class 100 Board 50 Thtr 150 **Services** Lift **Parking** 150 **Notes** ⊗ Closed 2 Jan-10 Feb Civ Wed 180

WORCESTER
Worcestershire   Map 10 SO85

Premier Inn Worcester City Centre

BUDGET HOTEL

tel: 0871 527 9456 *(Calls cost 13p per minute plus your phone company's access charge)*
Cricket Ground, New Rd WR2 4QQ
web: www.premierinn.com
dir: *M5 junct 7 (Worcester South), A44 signed Worcester City Centre. At next rdbt 2nd exit (A44 & Worcester City Centre) keep in left lane. At Worcester Cathedral continue on A44, straight on at 3 sets of lights*

High quality, budget accommodation ideal for both families and business travellers. Spacious, en suite bedrooms feature tea and coffee making facilities, and Freeview TV in most hotels. Internet access and WiFi are available for a small fee. The adjacent family restaurant features a wide and varied menu. See also the Hotel Groups pages.

Rooms 120

Premier Inn Worcester (M5 Jct 6)

BUDGET HOTEL

tel: 0871 527 9188 *(Calls cost 13p per minute plus your phone company's access charge)*
Wainwright Way, Warndon WR4 9FA
web: www.premierinn.com
dir: *M5 junct 6. At entrance of Warndon commercial development area*

Rooms 87

WORKINGTON
Cumbria   Map 18 NY02

Washington Central Hotel

★★★★ 73% HOTEL

tel: 01900 65772 **Washington St CA14 3AY**
email: info@washingtoncentralhotel.com
web: www.washingtoncentralhotelworkington.com
dir: *M6 junct 40, A66 to Workington. Left at lights, hotel on right*

Enjoying a prominent town centre location, this modern hotel boasts memorably
hospitable staff. The well-maintained and comfortable bedrooms are equipped with
a range of thoughtful extras. Public areas include numerous lounges, a spacious
bar, Caesars leisure club, a smart restaurant and a popular coffee shop. The
comprehensive conference facilities are ideal for meetings and weddings.

Rooms 57 (12 fmly) ⚑ **S** £100-£125; **D** £150-£180 (incl. bkfst)* **Facilities** FTV WiFi ⌕
⌕ supervised Gym Sauna Steam room New Year **Conf** Class 200 Board 100
Thtr 300 Del £150 **Services** Lift **Parking** 23 **Notes** LB ⊗ Civ Wed 300

WORKSOP
Nottinghamshire   Map 16 SK57

Best Western Lion Hotel

★★★ 80% HOTEL

Best Western

tel: 01909 477925 **112 Bridge St S80 1HT**
email: reception@thelionworksop.co.uk **web:** www.bw-lionhotel.co.uk
dir: *A57 to town centre, turn right at Sainsburys, follow to Norfolk Arms, turn left*

This former coaching inn lies on the edge of the main shopping precinct, with a car
park to the rear. It has been extended to offer modern accommodation that includes
excellent executive rooms. A wide range of interesting dishes is offered in both the
restaurant and bar.

Rooms 46 (3 fmly) (7 GF) ⚑ **S** £52-£82; **D** £56-£86 **Facilities** STV FTV WiFi ⌕ Xmas
New Year **Conf** Class 80 Board 70 Thtr 160 Del from £115 to £135 **Services** Lift
Parking 50 **Notes** LB Civ Wed 150

WORSLEY
Greater Manchester   Map 15 SD70

Novotel Manchester West

★★★ 75% HOTEL

NOVOTEL
HOTELS & RESORTS

tel: 0161 799 3535 **Worsley Brow M28 2YA**
email: H0907@accor.com **web:** www.novotel.com
dir: *Adjacent to M60 junct 13*

Well placed for access to the Peak District and the Lake District, as well as
Manchester, this modern hotel successfully caters for both families and business
guests. The spacious bedrooms have sofa beds and a large work area; the hotel has
an outdoor swimming pool, children's play area and secure parking.

Rooms 119 (10 fmly) (41 GF) ⚑ **Facilities** STV FTV WiFi HL Gym Xmas New Year
Conf Class 130 Board 60 Thtr 220 **Services** Lift **Parking** 95 **Notes** Civ Wed 140

WORTHING
West Sussex   Map 6 TQ10

Ardington Hotel

★★★ 82% HOTEL

tel: 01903 230451 **Steyne Gardens BN11 3DZ**
email: reservations@ardingtonhotel.co.uk **web:** www.ardingtonhotel.co.uk
dir: *A27 to Lancing, to seafront. Follow signs for Worthing. Left at church into Steyne
Gardens*

Overlooking Steyne Gardens adjacent to the seafront, this popular hotel offers well-
appointed bedrooms with a good range of facilities. There's a stylishly modern
lounge/bar with ample seating, where a light menu is available throughout the day.
The popular restaurant offers local seafood and a choice of modern dishes. WiFi is
available in the lounge/bar.

Rooms 45 (4 fmly) (12 GF) **Facilities** STV FTV WiFi **Conf** Class 60 Board 35 Thtr 140
Notes Closed 25 Dec-4 Jan

Premier Inn Worthing Seafront

BUDGET HOTEL

tel: 0871 527 9556 *(Calls cost 13p per minute plus your phone company's access charge)*
127 Marine Pde BN11 3FN
email: WorthingSeafront.PI@premierinn.com **web:** www.premierinn.com
dir: *From A24 & A27 Grove Lodge rdbt follow A24/South signs. At 4th rdbt 1st exit, follow
seafront signs. At seafront, right into Marine Parade, pass pier, hotel approx 1m on right*

High quality, budget accommodation ideal for both families and business
travellers. Spacious, en suite bedrooms feature tea and coffee making facilities,
and Freeview TV in most hotels. Internet access and WiFi are available for a small
fee. The adjacent family restaurant features a wide and varied menu. See also the
Hotel Groups pages.

Rooms 81

W

W

WOTTON-UNDER-EDGE
Gloucestershire

Map 4 ST79

Tortworth Court Four Pillars Hotel
★★★★ 78% HOTEL

tel: 0800 374692 & 01454 263000 **Tortworth GL12 8HH**
email: tortworth@four-pillars.co.uk **web:** www.four-pillars.co.uk/tortworth
dir: M5 junct 14, B4509 towards Wotton. 1st right into Tortworth Rd, next right, hotel 0.5m on right

Set in 30 acres of parkland, this Gothic mansion displays original features cleverly combined with contemporary additions. Elegant public rooms include a choice of dining options, one housed within the library, with another in the atrium. Bedrooms are well equipped, and additional facilities include a host of conference rooms and a leisure centre

Rooms 190 (25 fmly) (74 GF) **Facilities** Spa FTV WiFi ⊗ ⤵ Gym Steam room Sauna Xmas New Year **Conf** Class 200 Board 80 Thtr 400 **Services** Lift **Parking** 200 **Notes** ⊗ Civ Wed 400

WREA GREEN
Lancashire

Map 18 SD33

HIGHLY RECOMMENDED

The Spa Hotel at Ribby Hall Village
★★★★ 83% ◉◉ HOTEL

tel: 01772 671111 & 0800 085 1717 **Ribby Hall Village, Ribby Rd PR4 2PR**
email: enquiries@ribbyhall.co.uk **web:** www.ribbyhall.co.uk/spa-hotel
dir: M55 junct 33 follow A585 towards Kirkham & brown tourist signs for Ribby Hall Village. Straight across 3 rdbts. Ribby Hall Village 200yds on left

Set in one hundred acres of rolling countryside, Ribby Hall is a tranquil and relaxing place to stay. The luxurious bedrooms are comfortable and come in a range of sizes. The spa is the focus of the property, offering hotel guests a wide selection of treatments and the signature aqua-thermal journey. Food is another obvious highlight whether in the new Orangery restaurant or in another of the nine outlets within the village.

Rooms 38 (10 GF) ⚓ **Facilities** Spa STV FTV WiFi ⊳ ⚹ 9 ⤵ Fishing Gym Squash Aqua thermal journey Champagne bar Cycling Woodland trail Xmas New Year **Services** Lift Air con **Parking** 124 **Notes** ⊗ No children 18yrs

Find out more
about how to contact major Hotel Groups – pages 31-39

The Villa Country House Hotel
★★★★ 72% ◉ COUNTRY HOUSE HOTEL

tel: 01772 804040 **Moss Side Ln PR4 2PE**
email: info@thevilla.co.uk **web:** www.thevilla.co.uk
dir: M55 junct 3 follow signs to Kirkham at Wrea Green follow signs to Lytham

Dating back to the 19th century this former gentlemen's residence is packed full of original character and charm. Situated within the peaceful, picturesque village of Wrea Green but convenient for the motorway, it is the ideal location for a relaxing stay for both business and leisure guests. Rooms are thoughtfully appointed for the modern day traveller but still retain some of their original charm. An interesting range of dishes can be tried in the restaurant or alternatively more relaxed options are available in the bar. Ample amounts of car parking is available. Weddings, conferences and special events are well catered for.

Rooms 31 (2 fmly) (10 GF) ⚓ **S** £75-£240; **D** £80-£250 (incl. bkfst)* **Facilities** FTV WiFi Xmas New Year **Conf** Class 100 Board 40 Thtr 300 Del from £165* **Services** Lift **Parking** 120 **Notes** LB Civ Wed 300

WROTHAM
Kent

Map 6 TQ65

Premier Inn Sevenoaks/Maidstone

BUDGET HOTEL

tel: 0871 527 8962 (Calls cost 13p per minute plus your phone company's access charge)
London Rd, Wrotham Heath TN15 7RX
web: www.premierinn.com
dir: M26 junct 2a, A20 S. At lights left onto A20 towards West Malling. Hotel on right.

High quality, budget accommodation ideal for both families and business travellers. Spacious, en suite bedrooms feature tea and coffee making facilities, and Freeview TV in most hotels. Internet access and WiFi are available for a small fee. The adjacent family restaurant features a wide and varied menu. See also the Hotel Groups pages.

Rooms 59

WROXALL
Warwickshire   Map 10 SP27

Wroxall Abbey Hotel & Estate
★★★★ 73% HOTEL

tel: 01926 484470 **Birmingham Rd CV35 7NB**
email: reservation@wroxall.com **web:** www.wroxall.com
dir: *Between Solihull & Warwick on A4141*

Situated in 27 acres of open parkland, yet only 10 miles from the NEC and Birmingham International Airport, this hotel is a magnificent Victorian mansion. Some of the individually designed bedrooms have traditional decor but there are some modern loft rooms as well; some rooms have four-posters. Sonnets Restaurant, with its impressive fireplace and oak panelling, makes the ideal setting for fine dining.

Rooms 72 (24 annexe) (10 GF) 🐾 **Facilities** Spa FTV WiFi 🏊 Fishing 🚵 Gym Xmas New Year **Conf** Class 80 Board 60 Thtr 160 **Services** Lift **Parking** 200 **Notes** ⊗ No children 12yrs Civ Wed 171

WYBOSTON
Bedfordshire   Map 12 TL15

Wyboston Lakes Hotel
Ⓤ

tel: 0333 700 7667 & 01480 479300 **Wyboston Lakes, Great North Rd MK44 3BA**
email: reservations@wybostonlakes.co.uk **web:** www.wybostonlakes.co.uk
dir: *From A1 & A428 junct, follow brown Cambridge signs. Wyboston Lakes & hotel on right, marked by flags*

Currently the rating for this establishment is not confirmed. This may be due to a change of ownership or because it has only recently joined the AA rating scheme. For further details please see the AA website: theAA.com

Rooms 103 (103 annexe) (4 fmly) (50 GF) 🐾 **Facilities** Spa FTV WiFi ⬇ HL ⓣ supervised 🎾 ⚓ 18 Putt green Fishing Gym Golf driving range Nature reserve Watersports New Year **Conf** Class 120 Board 68 Thtr 270 **Services** Lift **Parking** 200 **Notes** ⊗ RS Xmas & 1 Jan Civ Wed 250

YARCOMBE
Devon   Map 4 ST20

The Belfry at Yarcombe
RESTAURANT WITH ROOMS

tel: 01404 861234 **EX14 9BD**
email: stay@thebelfryatyarcombe.co.uk **web:** www.thebelfrycountryhotel.com
dir: *On A30, in village of Yarcombe opposite church*

Built in the late 1860s and originally the village school, The Belfry at Yarcombe now offers bright and clean accommodation. Six comfortable en suite rooms are on offer along with a pleasant guest lounge and south-facing terrace, views across the village and valley are a highlight. Breakfast is served in the restaurant, where dinner is also available Thursday through Saturday. WiFi and off-street parking available.

Rooms 6

YARM
North Yorkshire   Map 19 NZ41

INSPECTORS' CHOICE

Crathorne Hall Hotel
★★★★ ◉◉ HOTEL   Hand PICKED HOTELS BUILT FOR PLEASURE

tel: 01642 700398 & 0845 072 7440
(Calls cost 5p per minute plus your phone company's access charge) **Crathorne TS15 0AR**
email: crathornehall@handpicked.co.uk
web: www.handpickedhotels.co.uk/crathorne-hall
dir: *From A19 take slip road signed Teesside Airport & Kirklevington, right signed Crathorne to hotel*

This splendid Edwardian hall sits in its own landscaped grounds and enjoys fine views of the Leven Valley and rolling Cleveland Hills. The impressively equipped bedrooms and delightful public areas offer sumptuous levels of comfort, with elegant antique furnishings that complement the hotel's architectural style. All bedrooms and suites offer large flat-screen TVs and free broadband among their many facilities. The elegant Leven Restaurant is a traditional setting for fine dining; there's also the Drawing Room for lighter food options. Weather permitting, alfresco eating is available on the terrace, and afternoon tea is always popular. Conference and banqueting facilities are available.

Rooms 37 (10 fmly) 🐾 **S** £105-£155; **D** £110-£185* **Facilities** STV FTV WiFi ⬇ HL 🚶 Jogging track Clay pigeon shooting Xmas **Conf** Class 75 Board 60 Thtr 120 Del from £145 to £185* **Services** Lift **Parking** 88 **Notes** LB ⊗ Civ Wed 90

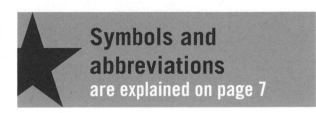

★ **Symbols and abbreviations** are explained on page 7

Y

YARM *continued*

INSPECTORS' CHOICE

Judges Country House Hotel

★★★★ COUNTRY HOUSE HOTEL

tel: 01642 789000 **Kirklevington Hall TS15 9LW**
email: enquiries@judgeshotel.co.uk **web:** www.judgeshotel.co.uk
dir: *1.5m from A19. At A67 junct, follow Yarm road, hotel on left*

Formerly a lodging for local circuit judges, this gracious mansion lies in landscaped grounds through which a stream runs. Stylish bedrooms are individually decorated and come with plenty of extras; four-poster bedrooms and suites are available. Meals are offered in The Conservatory restaurant, and private dining for a small number of guests is available in the wine cellar. Judges is a popular wedding venue. The genuinely caring and attentive service from the staff is truly memorable.

Rooms 21 (3 fmly) (5 GF) 🐾 **S** £110; **D** £125-£215 (incl. bkfst)* **Facilities** FTV WiFi ♨ 🚲 Gym Mountain bikes Nature trails Xmas New Year **Conf** Class 50 Board 38 Thtr 80 Del from £225 to £265* **Parking** 102 **Notes** LB ⊗ Civ Wed 200

YARMOUTH   Map 5 SZ38
Isle of Wight

INSPECTORS' CHOICE

The George Hotel

★★★ ◉◉ HOTEL

tel: 01983 760331 **Quay St PO41 OPE**
email: info@thegeorge.co.uk **web:** www.thegeorge.co.uk
dir: *Between castle & pier*

This delightful 17th-century hotel enjoys a wonderful location at the water's edge, adjacent to the castle and the quay. Public areas include Isla's fine dining restaurant, where organic and local produce are utilised; The Conservatory, for informal dining; a cosy bar and an inviting lounge. Individually styled bedrooms, with many thoughtful extras, are beautifully appointed; some benefit from spacious balconies. The hotel's motor yacht is available for guests to hire.

Rooms 17 (1 GF) 🐾 **S** £110-£315; **D** £150-£375 (incl. bkfst)* **Facilities** STV WiFi ⇲ Sailing from Yarmouth Mountain biking Xmas New Year **Conf** Class 18 Board 18 Thtr 20 Del from £165 to £195* **Notes** LB ⊗ Closed 5-22 Jan Civ Wed 120

Norton Grange Coastal Village

WARNER LEISURE HOTELS

AA Advertised

tel: 01983 760 323 **PO41 OSD**
web: www.warnerleisurehotels.co.uk
dir: *From Yarmouth Ferry Terminal leaving Yarmouth harbour, turn right at rdbt, follow road across Yarmouth bridge A3054. After approx 0.5m hotel on right after bend*

Sitting pretty in one of the UK's sunniest spots just five minutes from Yarmouth ferry port, with access to scenic coastal walks, this friendly chalet village is a favourite for sunseekers. A wide range of leisure activities is on offer, and there is nightly entertainment on the popular half-board breaks. This is an adults only (over 21 years) hotel.

Rooms 208 🐾 **Facilities** FTV WiFi ☉ supervised Putt green ⛳ Gym ♫ Xmas New Year **Parking** 208 **Notes** ⊗ No children 21yrs Closed Jan-Feb

YATELEY
Hampshire — Map 5 SU86

Casa Hotel & Marco Pierre White Restaurant
★★★ 79% @ HOTEL

tel: 01252 873275 **Handford Ln GU46 6BT**
email: reservations@casadeicesari.co.uk **web:** www.thecasahoteluk.com
dir: *M3 junct 4a, follow signs for town centre. Hotel signed*

This delightful hotel where a warm welcome is guaranteed is ideally located for transport networks. It boasts rooms with quality and comfort, and the Marco Pierre White, Wheeler's of St James's Restaurant, which is very popular locally, serves an extensive traditional menu.

Rooms 63 (2 fmly) (15 GF) (33 smoking) **Facilities** FTV WiFi ♄ Xmas New Year **Conf** Class 60 Board 60 Thtr 180 **Services** Lift **Parking** 80 **Notes** ⊗ Civ Wed 120

YATTON
Somerset — Map 4 ST46

Bridge Inn
BUDGET HOTEL

tel: 01934 839100 & 839101 **North End Rd BS49 4AU**
email: bridge.yatton@newbridgeinns.co.uk **web:** www.hungryhorse.co.uk
dir: *M5 junct 20, B3133 to Yatton. 1st left at rdbt, 1st left at 2nd rdbt. Hotel 2.5m on right*

This establishment offers spacious, well-equipped bedrooms, and the bar/restaurant serves a variety of dishes throughout the day in a relaxed and informal environment. Breakfast is a self-service buffet plus a full English breakfast served at the table. There is also a playzone area for children. See also the Hotel Groups pages.

Rooms 40 (6 fmly) (20 GF) **Conf** Class 30 Board 50 Thtr 100

YAXLEY
Suffolk — Map 13 TM17

The Auberge
@@ ⬥ RESTAURANT WITH ROOMS

tel: 01379 783604 **Ipswich Rd IP23 8BZ**
email: aubmail@the-auberge.co.uk **web:** www.the-auberge.co.uk
dir: *On A140 between Norwich & Ipswich at x-rds with B1117*

A warm welcome awaits at The Auberge, a charming 15th-century property, which was once a rural pub but is now a smart restaurant with rooms. The restaurant has gained two AA Rosettes for the good use of fresh, quality produce in well-crafted dishes. The public areas have a wealth of character, such as exposed brickwork and beams, and the grounds are particularly well kept and attractive. The spacious bedrooms are tastefully appointed and have many thoughtful touches; one bedroom has a four-poster.

Rooms 11 (11 annexe) (2 fmly)

YELVERTON
Devon — Map 3 SX56

Moorland Garden Hotel
★★★★ 76% @ HOTEL

tel: 01822 852245 **Yelverton PL20 6DA**
email: stay@moorlandgardenhotel.co.uk **web:** www.moorlandgardenhotel.co.uk
dir: *A38 from Exeter to Plymouth, then A386 towards Tavistock. 5m onto open moorland, hotel 1m on left*

This hotel has a great location for either the city or Dartmoor, and sits in delightful gardens. Bedrooms are spacious, all with garden views and some with impressive balconies. There is a choice of dining as well as a range of meeting and function rooms. Pleasant Devon cream teas are served in the garden in warmer months.

Rooms 44 (5 fmly) (17 GF) ↟ **Facilities** FTV WiFi ♄ HL Reduced fees for residents at golf club Xmas New Year **Conf** Class 60 Board 50 Thtr 170 **Parking** 75 **Notes** Civ Wed 160

YEOVIL
Somerset — Map 4 ST51

The Yeovil Court Hotel & Restaurant
★★★ 79% @@ HOTEL

tel: 01935 863746 **West Coker Rd BA20 2HE**
email: unwind@yeovilhotel.com **web:** www.yeovilhotel.com
dir: *2.5m W of town centre on A30*

This comfortable, family-run hotel offers a very relaxed atmosphere. Bedrooms are well equipped and neatly presented; some are located in an adjacent building. Public areas consist of a smart lounge, a popular bar and an attractive restaurant. Menus combine an interesting selection that includes lighter options, and dishes suited to special occasion dining.

Rooms 30 (12 annexe) (3 fmly) (8 GF) ↟ **Facilities** FTV WiFi ♄ **Conf** Class 18 Board 30 Thtr 50 **Parking** 65 **Notes** RS Sat lunch, 25 Dec eve & 26 Dec Civ Wed 70

Premier Inn Yeovil
BUDGET HOTEL

tel: 0871 527 9192 *(Calls cost 13p per minute plus your phone company's access charge)*
Alvington Ln, Brympton BA22 8UX
web: www.premierinn.com
dir: *M5 junct 25, A358, A303 follow Yeovil signs. At rdbt onto A3088. At next rdbt 1st left, at next rdbt turn left. Hotel on left*

High quality, budget accommodation ideal for both families and business travellers. Spacious, en suite bedrooms feature tea and coffee making facilities, and Freeview TV in most hotels. Internet access and WiFi are available for a small fee. The adjacent family restaurant features a wide and varied menu. See also the Hotel Groups pages.

Rooms 20

YEOVIL *continued*

Premier Inn Yeovil Town Centre

BUDGET HOTEL

tel: 0871 527 9426 *(Calls cost 13p per minute plus your phone company's access charge)*
Key Market House, Middle St BA20 1LT
web: www.premierinn.com
dir: *From N: A37 to end, take A30 (Reckleford). Keep right, take 1st right. Into Sherborne Rd left into Newton Rd. Left into S Western Terr, join Old Station Rd. Hotel on right. From S: A30, at rdbt into Brunswick St. Then Park St, Taunusstein Way, Summer House Terr, Old Station Rd*

Rooms 80

INSPECTORS' CHOICE

Little Barwick House

RESTAURANT WITH ROOMS

tel: 01935 423902 **Barwick Village BA22 9TD**
email: littlebarwick@hotmail.com **web:** www.littlebarwickhouse.co.uk
dir: *From Yeovil A37 towards Dorchester, left at 1st rdbt, 1st left, 0.25m on left*

Situated in a quiet hamlet in three and half acres of gardens and grounds, this listed Georgian dower house is an ideal retreat for those seeking peaceful surroundings and good food. Just one of the highlights of a stay here is a meal in the restaurant, where good use is made of local ingredients. Each of the bedrooms has its own character, and a range of thoughtful extras such as fresh flowers, bottled water and magazines is provided.

Rooms 6

YORK
North Yorkshire   Map 16 SE65

See also **Aldwark & Escrick**

The Grand Hotel & Spa, York

★★★★★ 86% HOTEL

tel: 01904 380038 **Station Rise YO1 6HT**
email: info@thegrandyork.co.uk **web:** www.thegrandyork.co.uk
dir: *In city centre, near station*

Located in the heart of the city, this majestic Edwardian building, built in 1906, has been transformed into a luxury hotel. Spacious, air-conditioned accommodation offers deeply comfortable rooms with luxurious bathrooms. Public areas are equally impressive with a range of delightful lounges, a modern spa in the former vaults and excellent meeting rooms. The Hudson's offers a high standard of dining with modern and classic dishes on offer, all delivered with both flair and a touch of fun. Afternoon tea is presented on a silver stand in a relaxing, tranquil environment. Valet parking is a great asset given the hotel's central location.

Rooms 107 (14 GF) **S** fr £128; **D** fr £128* **Facilities** Spa STV FTV WiFi Gym Sauna Steam room Xmas New Year **Conf** Class 60 Board 50 Thtr 120 Del from £213 to £383* **Services** Lift Air con **Notes** Civ Wed 120

Middlethorpe Hall & Spa

★★★★ HOTEL

tel: 01904 641241 **Bishopthorpe Rd, Middlethorpe YO23 2GB**
email: info@middlethorpe.com **web:** www.middlethorpe.com
dir: *A1/A64 follow York West A1036 signs, then Bishopthorpe, Middlethorpe racecourse signs*

This fine house, dating from the reign of William and Mary, sits in acres of beautifully landscaped gardens. The bedrooms vary in size but all are comfortably furnished; some are located in the main house, and others are in a cottage and converted courtyard stables. Public areas include a small spa and a stately drawing room where afternoon tea is quite an event. The delightful panelled restaurant is a perfect setting for enjoying the imaginative cuisine.

Rooms 29 (19 annexe) (2 fmly) (10 GF) **S** £143-£205; **D** £205-£514 (incl. bkfst)* **Facilities** Spa FTV WiFi Gym Xmas New Year **Conf** Class 30 Board 25 Thtr 56 **Services** Lift **Parking** 71 **Notes** LB No children 6yrs RS 25 & 31 Dec Civ Wed 56

Hotel du Vin & Bistro York

★★★★ 79% HOTEL

tel: 01904 557350 & 0844 748 9268
(Calls cost 7p per minute plus your phone company's access charge) **89 The Mount YO24 1AX**
email: info.york@hotelduvin.com **web:** www.hotelduvin.com
dir: *A1036 towards city centre, 6m. Hotel on right through lights*

This Hotel du Vin offers luxury and quality that will cosset even the most discerning guest. Bedrooms are decadent in design and the bathrooms have huge monsoon showers and feature baths. Dinner in the bistro provides a memorable highlight thanks to exciting menus and a superb wine list. Staff throughout are naturally friendly, nothing is too much trouble.

Rooms 44 (3 fmly) (14 GF) **Facilities** STV FTV WiFi **Conf** Class 10 Board 22 Thtr 60 **Services** Lift Air con **Parking** 18 **Notes** Civ Wed 80

The Grange Hotel

★★★★ 78% ◉◉ HOTEL

tel: 01904 644744 **1 Clifton YO30 6AA**
email: info@grangehotel.co.uk **web:** www.grangehotel.co.uk
dir: *On A19 York/Thirsk rd, approx 500yds from city centre*

This bustling Regency town house is just a few minutes' walk from the centre of York. A professional service is efficiently delivered by caring staff in a very friendly and helpful manner. Public rooms are comfortable and have been stylishly furnished; these include two dining options, the popular and informal Cellar Bar, and main hotel restaurant The Ivy Brasserie, which offers fine dining in a lavishly decorated environment. The individually designed bedrooms are comfortably appointed and have been thoughtfully equipped.

Rooms 41 (1 fmly) (11 GF) ⊛ **Facilities** STV FTV WiFi ↻ Use of nearby health club (chargeable) Xmas New Year **Conf** Class 24 Board 24 Thtr 40 Del from £165* **Services** Lift **Parking** 26 **Notes** ⊗ Civ Wed 90

The Royal York Hotel & Events Centre

★★★★ 77% HOTEL

tel: 01904 653681 **Station Rd YO24 1AA**
email: royalyork.reservations@principal-hayley.com **web:** www.hotelroyalyork.co.uk
dir: *Adjacent to railway station*

Situated in three acres of landscaped grounds in the very heart of the city, this Victorian railway hotel has views over the city and York Minster. Contemporary bedrooms are divided between those in the main hotel and the air-conditioned garden mews. There is also a leisure complex and state-of-the-art conference centre.

Rooms 158 (35 annexe) (1 fmly) ⊛ **Facilities** FTV WiFi ↻ Gym Steam room Weights room Xmas New Year **Conf** Class 250 Board 80 Thtr 410 **Services** Lift **Parking** 90 **Notes** ⊗ Civ Wed 160

York Marriott Hotel

★★★★ 77% HOTEL

tel: 01904 701000 **Tadcaster Rd YO24 1QQ**
email: mhrs.qqyyk.dos@marriott.com **web:** www.yorkmarriott.co.uk
dir: *From A64 at York 'West' onto A1036, follow signs to city centre. Approx 1.5m, hotel on right after church and lights*

Overlooking the racecourse and Knavesmire Parkland, this hotel offers modern accommodation, including family rooms, all with comfort cooling. Within the hotel, guests enjoy the use of extensive leisure facilities including indoor pool, putting green and tennis court. For those wishing to explore the historic and cultural attractions, the city is less than a mile away.

Rooms 151 (45 fmly) (27 GF) ⊛ **S** £79-£349; **D** £89-£359 (incl. bkfst) **Facilities** Spa STV FTV WiFi ↻ HL ↻ ⌇ Gym Beauty treatments Xmas New Year **Conf** Class 90 Board 40 Thtr 190 Del from £129 to £199 **Services** Lift Air con **Parking** 140 **Notes** ⊗ Civ Wed 140

Best Western Plus Dean Court Hotel

★★★★ 76% ◉◉ HOTEL

tel: 01904 625082 **Duncombe Place YO1 7EF**
email: sales@deancourt-york.co.uk **web:** www.deancourt-york.co.uk
dir: *In city centre opposite York Minster*

This smart hotel enjoys a central location overlooking The Minster, and guests will find the service is particularly friendly and efficient. Bedrooms are stylishly appointed and vary in size. Public areas are elegant in a contemporary style and include the popular D.C.H. restaurant which enjoys wonderful views of the cathedral, and The Court café-bistro and bar where a more informal, all-day menu is offered. Valet parking is available.

Rooms 37 (4 fmly) ⊛ **Facilities** STV FTV WiFi ↻ Xmas New Year **Conf** Class 12 Board 32 Thtr 50 Del from £185* **Services** Lift **Parking** 30 **Notes** ⊗

Marmadukes Town House Hotel

★★★★ 75% ◉◉◉ TOWN HOUSE HOTEL

tel: 01904 640101 **4-5 St Peters Grove, Bootham YO30 6AQ**
email: reservations@marmadukestownhousehotelyork.com
web: www.marmadukestownhousehotelyork.com
dir: *A1036 signed York for approx 6m past train station then signed Inner Ring Rd. Over Lendal bridge, at lights left onto A19 Bootham Bar for 0.4m, right into St Peters Grove*

Set in secluded gardens, this Georgian hotel has free WiFi and luxurious rooms with handmade beds. Marmadukes Town House Hotel is just a 10-minute walk from York Minster, the Shambles and the Theatre Royal. The rooms are individually decorated with antique furniture and Egyptian linens, and all have tea- and coffee-making facilities, flatscreen TV/DVD player and stylish bathrooms with designer toiletries. Guests can relax in the elegant lounge bar or leafy garden. There is also a sun lounge with antique sofas, where traditional full English breakfasts are served daily.

Rooms 21 (11 annexe) (2 fmly) (3 GF) ⊛ **S** £45-£159; **D** £49-£419 (incl. bkfst) **Facilities** FTV WiFi **Conf** Class 25 Board 25 Thtr 50 **Parking** 14 **Notes** ⊗ Civ Wed 50

Novotel York Centre

★★★★ 75% HOTEL

tel: 01904 611660 **Fishergate YO10 4FD**
email: H0949@accor.com **web:** www.novotel.com
dir: *A19 north to city centre, hotel set back on left*

Set just outside the ancient city walls, this modern, family-friendly hotel is conveniently located for visitors to the city. Bedrooms feature bathrooms with a separate toilet room, plus excellent desk space and sofa beds. Four rooms are equipped for less able guests. The hotel's facilities include indoor and outdoor children's play areas and an indoor pool.

Rooms 124 (124 fmly) **Facilities** FTV WiFi ↻ HL ↻ Xmas New Year **Conf** Class 100 Board 120 Thtr 210 **Services** Lift **Parking** 140

YORK *continued*

Best Western Monkbar Hotel

★★★★ 73% HOTEL

Best Western.

tel: 01904 638086 **Monkbar YO31 7JA**
email: sales@monkbarhotel.co.uk **web:** www.monkbarhotel.co.uk
dir: *A64 onto A1079 to city, turn right at city walls, take middle lane at lights. Hotel on right*

This smart hotel enjoys a prominent position adjacent to the city walls, and is just a few minutes' walk from York Minster. A recent refurbishment and extension programme has led to improvements in both rooms and conference facilities. Monkbar offers individually-styled bedrooms that are well equipped for both business and leisure guests. Spacious public areas include comfortable lounges, a traditional Yorkshire bar, an airy restaurant and new state-of-the-art meeting and training facilities.

Rooms 125 (2 GF) 🐾 **Facilities** FTV WiFi ⬇ Xmas New Year **Conf** Class 100 Board 60 Thtr 250 **Services** Lift **Notes** ⊗ Civ Wed 150

Mercure York Fairfield Hotel

★★★★ 73% COUNTRY HOUSE HOTEL

tel: 01904 670222 & 0844 815 9038
(Calls cost 7p per minute plus your phone company's access charge) **Shipton Rd, Skelton YO30 1XW**
email: gm.mercureyorkfairfieldmanor@jupiterhotels.co.uk **web:** www.mercureyork.co.uk
dir: *Exit A1237 onto A19, hotel 0.5m on left*

This stylish Georgian mansion stands in six acres of private grounds on the outskirts of the city. The contemporary bedrooms, styled in reds or blues, have broadband access and flat-screen TVs; some rooms have garden and courtyard views. The suites have either four-poster or king-size beds and a separate seating area. Kilby's Restaurant serves bistro food, and 24-hour room service is available. There are good conference facilities.

Rooms 89 (20 fmly) (24 GF) 🐾 **Facilities** WiFi ⬇ HL Use of nearby health club Xmas New Year **Conf** Class 60 Board 60 Thtr 180 **Services** Lift **Parking** 120 **Notes** ⊗ Civ Wed 180

The Churchill Hotel

★★★ 85% ◉◉ HOTEL

tel: 01904 644456 **65 Bootham YO30 7DQ**
email: info@churchillhotel.com **web:** www.churchillhotel.com
dir: *On A19 (Bootham), W from York Minster, hotel 250yds on right*

The Churchill Hotel is a late Georgian manor house set in its own grounds, just a short walk from the Minster and other attractions. Period features and interesting artefacts relating to Winston Churchill are incorporated into smart contemporary design and up-to-date technology. Public areas include the Piano Bar & Restaurant, where innovative menus feature high quality, local produce.

Rooms 32 (4 fmly) (5 GF) **Facilities** WiFi ♬ Xmas New Year **Conf** Class 50 Board 30 Thtr 100 **Services** Lift **Parking** 40 **Notes** Civ Wed 70

The Parsonage Country House Hotel

★★★ 81% ◉ COUNTRY HOUSE HOTEL

tel: 01904 728111 **York Rd YO19 6LF**
email: reservations@parsonagehotel.co.uk **web:** www.parsonagehotel.co.uk

(For full entry see Escrick)

Best Western Kilima Hotel

★★★ 81% HOTEL

Best Western.

tel: 01904 625787 **129 Holgate Rd YO24 4AZ**
email: sales@kilima.co.uk **web:** www.bestwestern.co.uk
dir: *On A59, 1m from York city ctr*

This establishment, a former rectory, is conveniently situated within easy walking distance of the city centre. There is a relaxed and friendly atmosphere with professional, friendly staff providing attentive service. Bedrooms are comfortable and well equipped. There is an indoor pool, a fitness centre and a Turkish steam room.

Rooms 26 (10 fmly) (10 GF) **Facilities** FTV WiFi ⬇ ❄ Gym Leisure complex Steam room Fitness suite Xmas **Conf** Board 14 **Parking** 26 **Notes** LB ⊗

Park Inn by Radisson York City Centre

★★★ 81% HOTEL

tel: 01904 459988 **North St YO1 6JF**
email: reservations.york@rezidorparkinn.com **web:** www.parkinn.co.uk/hotel-york
dir: *In York city centre, less than 1m from train station*

Boasting spectacular views over the River Ouse in the heart of York, this hotel is just minutes away from all the attractions of this historic, walled city. There are impressive conference rooms and leisure facilities, and the RBG Lounge Bar, overlooking the river, serves a wide-ranging menu throughout the day. Private parking is available.

Rooms 200 **Facilities** FTV WiFi **Conf** Class 150 Board 75 Thtr 400 **Services** Lift Air con

Mount Royale

★★★ 80% ◉◉ HOTEL

tel: 01904 628856 **The Mount YO24 1GU**
email: reservations@mountroyale.co.uk **web:** www.mountroyale.co.uk
dir: *W on A1036, 0.5m after racecourse. Hotel on right after lights*

This friendly hotel, a listed building from the 1830s, offers comfortable bedrooms in a variety of styles, several leading onto the delightful gardens. Public rooms include a lounge, a meeting room and a cosy bar; the hotel has an outdoor pool, a sauna and a hot tub plus a beauty therapist. There is a separate restaurant called Oxo's on The Mount, and a cocktail lounge overlooking the gardens. Limited car parking is also available.

Rooms 24 (3 fmly) (6 GF) 🐾 **S** £95-£165; **D** £125-£265 (incl. bkfst)* **Facilities** FTV WiFi ❄ supervised Sauna Steam room Xmas New Year **Conf** Board 25 Thtr 35 **Parking** 24 **Notes** LB

Best Western York Pavilion Hotel

★★★ 78% HOTEL

tel: 01904 622099 & 239900 **45 Main St, Fulford YO10 4PJ**
email: reservations@yorkpavilionhotel.com **web:** www.yorkpavilionhotel.com
dir: Exit A64, York ring rd at A19 junct towards York. Hotel 0.5m on right opposite
Pavilion Court

York Pavilion Hotel is an attractive Georgian hotel situated in its own grounds. All
the bedrooms are individually designed to a high specification; some are in the old
house and some in the converted stables set around a garden terrace. There is a
comfortable lounge, a conference centre and an inviting brasserie-style restaurant
with a regularly changing menu.

Rooms 62 (5 annexe) (4 fmly) (11 GF) ⚓ **S** £105-£130; **D** £105-£170 (incl. bkfst)*
Facilities FTV WiFi ⇣ Xmas New Year **Conf** Class 80 Board 50 Thtr 150 Del from £125
to £165* **Parking** 45 **Notes** LB ⊗ Civ Wed 120

Middletons Hotel

★★★ 74% HOTEL

tel: 01904 611570 **Skeldergate YO1 6DS**
email: reception@middletonsyork.co.uk **web:** www.middletonsyork.co.uk
dir: From A64 Leeds, A1036 towards city centre. Right at City Walls lights, keep left, 1st
left before bridge, then 1st left into Cromwell Rd. Hotel on right

This hotel has been created from several listed buildings and is very well located in
the centre of York. Bedrooms are comfortably equipped. Among its amenities is a
bar-lounge and a dining room where a satisfying range of food is served. An
extensive fitness club is also available along with private parking.

Rooms 56 (19 annexe) (15 fmly) (17 GF) ⚓ **S** £55-£164; **D** £69-£165 (incl. bkfst)*
Facilities FTV WiFi ⇣ ⊗ Gym Fitness centre Beauty treatments Massage
Conf Class 36 Board 36 Thtr 60 **Parking** 40 **Notes** LB Civ Wed 60

Premier Inn York City (Blossom St North)

BUDGET HOTEL

tel: 0871 527 9196 (Calls cost 13p per minute plus your phone company's access charge)
20 Blossom St YO24 1AJ
web: www.premierinn.com
dir: 12m from A1 junct 47, off A59

High quality, budget accommodation ideal for both families and business
travellers. Spacious, en suite bedrooms feature tea and coffee making facilities,
and Freeview TV in most hotels. Internet access and WiFi are available for a small
fee. The adjacent family restaurant features a wide and varied menu. See also the
Hotel Groups pages.

Rooms 102

Premier Inn York City (Blossom St South)

BUDGET HOTEL

tel: 0871 527 9194 (Calls cost 13p per minute plus your phone company's access charge)
28-40 Blossom St YO24 1AJ
web: www.premierinn.com
dir: From S, E & W: A64, A1036 (signed York West). From N: A1 (or A19), A59, follow city
centre signs. At lights left onto A1036. Hotel on left just after cinema. NB no drop-off
point, parking at NCP, Queens St

Rooms 91

Premier Inn York North (Maritime Park)

BUDGET HOTEL

tel: 0871 527 9198 (Calls cost 13p per minute plus your phone company's access charge)
Shipton Rd YO30 5PA
web: www.premierinn.com
dir: From A1237 (ring road), A19 (Shipton Road South) signed York Centre. Hotel on right
in Clifton Park

Rooms 49

Premier Inn York North West (Ring Road)

BUDGET HOTEL

tel: 0871 527 9200 (Calls cost 13p per minute plus your phone company's access charge)
White Rose Close, York Business Park, Nether Poppleton YO26 6RL
web: www.premierinn.com
dir: On A1237 between A19 Thirsk road & A59 Harrogate road

Rooms 82

Premier Inn York South West (A64)

BUDGET HOTEL

tel: 0871 527 9202 (Calls cost 13p per minute plus your phone company's access charge)
Bilbrough Top, Colton YO23 3PP
web: www.premierinn.com
dir: On A64 between Tadcaster & York

Rooms 62

Ibis York Centre

AA Advertised

tel: 01904 658301 **77 The Mount YO24 1BN**
email: H6390@accor.com **web:** www.ibishotel.com
dir: A64/A1036 follow signs to city centre, hotel on right

Modern, budget hotel offering comfortable accommodation in bright and practical
bedrooms. Breakfast is self-service and dinner is available in the restaurant.

Rooms 91 (11 fmly) (3 GF) ⚓ **Facilities** WiFi HL **Conf** Class 16 Board 16 Thtr 24
Services Lift **Parking** 27

ISLE OF MAN

DOUGLAS Map 24 SC37

Admiral House Hotel

★★★ 74% HOTEL

tel: 01624 629551 **12 Loch Promenade IM1 2LX**
email: enquiries@admiralhouse.com **web:** www.admiralhouse.com
dir: Located 2 mins from Douglas Ferry Terminal. 20 mins from airport

Admiral House Hotel is a grand Victorian building with stunning views over Douglas
Bay. Spacious bedrooms and public areas combine period features with
contemporary style. The JAR restaurant is a highlight, offering excellent food, a
stylish setting and professional service. There is also a modern champagne and
cocktail bar, and IGI's Café serves snacks and light meals throughout the day.
Complimentary WiFi is provided throughout.

Rooms 23 (3 fmly) ⚓ **Facilities** FTV WiFi ⇣ Xmas New Year **Services** Lift **Notes** ⊗
Closed 25 Dec & 1 Jan

Channel Islands

GUERNSEY

CASTEL
Map 24

Cobo Bay Hotel

★★★ 85% ◉◉ HOTEL

tel: 01481 257102 **Coast Rd, Cobo GY5 7HB**
email: reservations@cobobayhotel.com **web:** www.cobobayhotel.com
dir: *From airport turn right, follow road to W coast at L'Eree. Turn right onto coast road for 3m to Cobo Bay. Hotel on right*

As the name implies, this popular hotel is situated on the seafront overlooking Cobo Bay. The well-equipped bedrooms are pleasantly decorated; many of the front rooms have balconies and there is a secluded sun terrace to the rear. Public rooms include the Chesterfield Bar with its leather sofas and armchairs, and a welcoming award-winning restaurant and terrace with stunning views of the bay.

Rooms 34 (4 fmly) **Facilities** STV FTV WiFi Sauna Steam room **Conf** Class 30 Board 30 Thtr 100 **Services** Lift **Parking** 8 **Notes** ⊗ Closed 4 Jan-Feb

Le Friquet Hotel

★★★ 79% HOTEL

tel: 01481 256509 **Rue du Friquet GY5 7ST**
email: stay@lefriquethotel.co.uk **web:** www.lefriquethotel.com

Le Friquet (French for 'sparrow') is located in a quiet setting with extensive grounds, an outdoor swimming pool and plenty of private parking. The Hotel offers traditional and comfortably appointed accommodations, all well equipped with a good range of amenities, including WiFi throughout. Guests can enjoy alfresco dining on the terrace or in the main Lobster and Grill Restaurant which is contemporary in style and the only hotel in Guernsey with a live lobster tank. Great hospitality and service can be expected from the friendly team.

Le Friquet Hotel

Rooms 33 (1 fmly) (3 GF) **S** £61.50-£85; **D** £93-£136 (incl. bkfst)* **Facilities** STV FTV WiFi Xmas New Year **Services** Air con **Parking** 40 **Notes** ⊗

FOREST
Map 24

Le Chene Hotel

★★ 76% HOTEL

tel: 01481 235566 **Forest Rd GY8 0AH**
email: info@lechene.co.uk **web:** www.lechene.co.uk
dir: *Between airport & St Peter Port. From airport left to St Peter Port. Hotel on right after 1st lights*

This Victorian manor house is well located for guests wishing to explore Guernsey's spectacular south coast. The building has been skilfully extended to house a range of well-equipped, modern bedrooms. There is a swimming pool, a cosy cellar bar and a varied range of enjoyable freshly-cooked dishes at dinner.

Rooms 26 (2 fmly) (1 GF) (1 smoking) **Facilities** WiFi Library Outdoor sauna **Parking** 20 **Notes** LB ⊗ Closed Oct-Mar

ST MARTIN

Map 24

Bella Luce Hotel, Restaurant & Spa

★★★★ ◎◎ SMALL HOTEL

tel: 01481 238764 **La Fosse GY4 6EB**
email: wakeup@bellalucehotel.com **web:** www.bellalucehotel.com
dir: *From airport, turn left to St Martin. At 3rd set of lights continue 30yds, turn right, straight on to hotel*

This delightful hotel is both contemporary and luxurious; the stylish bedrooms have comfortable beds and designer furnishings, superb bathrooms and up-to-the-minute technology. Public rooms have many interesting features and lots of soft settees and nooks and crannies where guests can relax. The restaurant offers the best produce Guernsey can provide, and chef has a keen sense of adventure. Staff are friendly and attentive, and make sure guests feel welcome.

Rooms 23 (4 fmly) (2 GF) **S** £110-£165; **D** £120-£175 (incl. bkfst)* **Facilities** Spa STV FTV WiFi ⇄ ⤚ ♨ 18 Fishing Gym Sauna ♫ Xmas New Year **Conf** Class 18 Board 25 Thtr 40 **Services** Air con **Parking** 33 **Notes** LB ⊗ Closed 1st 2 wks Jan

La Barbarie Hotel

★★★ 82% ◎ HOTEL

tel: 01481 235217 **Saints Rd, Saints Bay GY4 6ES**
email: reservations@labarbariehotel.com **web:** www.labarbariehotel.com
dir: *At lights in St Martin take road to Saints Bay. Hotel on right at end of Saints Rd*

This former priory dates back to the 17th century and retains much charm and style. Staff help to create a very friendly and attentive atmosphere, and the modern facilities offer guests a relaxing stay. Excellent choices and fresh local ingredients form the basis of the interesting menus in the attractive restaurant and bar.

Rooms 35 (8 GF) ⇄ **S** £90-£142; **D** £98-£169 (incl. bkfst)* **Facilities** STV WiFi ⤚ **Parking** 50 **Notes** LB ⊗ Closed Nov-Feb

Hotel Jerbourg

★★★ 79% ◎ HOTEL

tel: 01481 238826 **Jerbourg Point GY4 6BJ**
email: stay@hoteljerbourg.com **web:** www.hoteljerbourg.com
dir: *From airport turn left to St Martin, right at filter, straight on at lights, hotel at end of road on right*

This hotel boasts excellent sea views from its cliff-top location. Public areas are smartly appointed and include an extensive bar/lounge and bright conservatory-style restaurant. In addition to the fairly extensive carte, a daily-changing menu is available. Bedrooms are well presented and comfortable, and the luxury bay rooms are generally more spacious.

Rooms 32 (4 fmly) (5 GF) **Facilities** FTV WiFi ⤚ Petanque Xmas New Year **Parking** 50 **Notes** LB ⊗ Closed 5 Jan-1 Mar

La Villette Hotel & Leisure Suite

★★★ 79% HOTEL

tel: 01481 235292 **GY4 6QG**
email: reservations@lavillettehotel.co.uk **web:** www.lavillettehotel.co.uk
dir: *Turn left from airport. Follow road past La Trelade Hotel. Take next right, hotel on left*

Set in spacious grounds, this peacefully located, family-run hotel has a friendly atmosphere. The well-equipped bedrooms are spacious and comfortable. Live music is a regular feature in the large bar, while in the separate restaurant a fixed-price menu is provided. Residents have use of the excellent indoor leisure facilities, and there are also beauty treatments and a hairdressing salon.

Rooms 35 (3 fmly) (14 GF) **Facilities** FTV WiFi supervised Gym Steam room Leisure suite Beauty salon Hairdresser Petanque Xmas New Year **Conf** Board 40 Thtr 80 **Services** Lift **Parking** 50 **Notes** ⊗

Saints Bay Hotel

★★★ 76% HOTEL

tel: 01481 238888 **Icart Rd GY4 6JG**
email: info@saintsbayhotel.com **web:** www.saintsbayhotel.com
dir: *From St Martin take Saints Rd into Icart Rd*

Ideally situated in an elevated position near Icart Point headland and above the fishing harbour at Saints Bay, this hotel has superb views. The spacious public rooms include a smart lounge bar, a first-floor lounge and a smart conservatory restaurant that overlooks the swimming pool. Bedrooms are pleasantly decorated and thoughtfully equipped.

Rooms 35 (1 fmly) (13 GF) **Facilities** FTV WiFi Xmas New Year **Parking** 15 **Notes** ⊗

ST PETER PORT	Map 24

The Old Government House Hotel & Spa

★★★★★ 81% ◎ ⬱ HOTEL

RED CARNATION
HOTEL COLLECTION

tel: 01481 724921 **St Ann's Place GY1 2NU**
email: ogh@theoghhotel.com **web:** www.theoghhotel.com
dir: *At junct of St Julian's Ave & St Anns Place*

Affectionately known as the OGH, this is one of the island's leading hotels. Located in the heart of St Peter Port, it is the perfect base from which to explore Guernsey and the other islands of the Bailiwick. Bedrooms vary in size but all are comfortable, and offer high quality accommodation. There is an indulgent health club and spa, and the eating options are the OGH Brasserie, and the award-winning Governor's that offers local produce with a French twist.

Rooms 62 (3 annexe) (6 fmly) **S** £188-£545; **D** £188-£545 (incl. bkfst)*
Facilities Spa STV WiFi HL Gym Steam room Sauna Relaxation room Xmas New Year **Conf** Class 69 Board 66 Thtr 200 Del from £290.50 to £647.50*
Services Lift Air con **Parking** 20

The Duke of Richmond Hotel

★★★★ 80% HOTEL

THE
RED CARNATION
HOTEL COLLECTION

tel: 01481 726221 **Cambridge Park GY1 1UY**
email: manager@dukeofrichmond.com **web:** www.dukeofrichmond.com
dir: *On corner of Cambridge Park & L'Hyvreuse Ave, opposite leisure centre*

Peacefully located in a mainly residential area overlooking Cambridge Park, this hotel has comfortable, well-appointed bedrooms that vary in size. Public areas include a spacious lounge, a terrace and the unique Sausmarez Bar, with its nautical theme. The smartly uniformed team of staff provide professional standards of service.

Rooms 73 (11 fmly) **S** £152-£428; **D** £152-£428 (incl. bkfst)* **Facilities** STV WiFi HL Xmas New Year **Conf** Class 80 Board 40 Thtr 300 Del from £244.50 to £520.50* **Services** Lift Air con **Parking** 5

St Pierre Park Hotel

★★★★ 77% ⬱ HOTEL

Hand PICKED
HOTELS
BUILT FOR PLEASURE

tel: 01481 728282 **Rohais GY1 1FD**
email: reservations.stpierrepark@handpicked.co.uk **web:** www.handpickedhotels.co.uk
dir: *From harbour straight over rdbt, up hill through 3 sets of lights. Right at filter, to lights. Straight ahead, hotel 100mtrs on left*

Peacefully located on the outskirts of town in 45 acres of grounds, this well established hotel also features a 9-hole golf course. Most of the bedrooms overlook the pleasant gardens and have either a balcony or a terrace. Public areas include a choice of restaurants and a stylish bar which opens onto a spacious terrace, overlooking an elegant water feature.

Rooms 131 (5 fmly) (17 GF) **Facilities** Spa STV FTV WiFi HL 9 Putt green Gym Exercise studio with classes Children's playground Crazy golf Xmas **Conf** Class 120 Board 70 Thtr 200 Del from £135 to £205* **Services** Lift **Parking** 150 **Notes** ⊗

Best Western Hotel de Havelet

★★★ 82% ◎ HOTEL

Best Western.

tel: 01481 722199 **Havelet GY1 1BA**
email: stay@dehaveletguernsey.com **web:** www.dehaveletguernsey.com
dir: *From airport follow signs for St Peter Port through St. Martins. At bottom of 'Val de Terres' hill turn left at top of hill, hotel on right*

This extended Georgian hotel looks over the harbour to Castle Cornet. Many of the well-equipped bedrooms are set around a pretty colonial-style courtyard. Day rooms in the original building have period elegance; the restaurant and bar are on the other side of the car park in converted stables.

Rooms 34 (4 fmly) (9 GF) **Facilities** FTV WiFi Sauna Steam room Xmas New Year **Conf** Class 20 Board 18 Thtr 30 **Parking** 40 **Notes** ⊗

ST PETER PORT *continued*

Les Rocquettes Hotel

★★★ 82% HOTEL

tel: 01481 722146 **Les Gravees GY1 1RN**
email: stay@lesrocquettesguernsey.com **web:** www.lesrocquettesguernsey.com
dir: *From ferry terminal take 2nd exit at rdbt, through 5 sets of lights. After 5th lights into Les Gravees. Hotel on right opposite church*

This late 18th-century country mansion is in a good location close to St Peter Port and Beau Sejour. Bedrooms come in three grades - Deluxe, Superior and Standard, but all have plenty of useful facilities. Guests can eat in Oaks restaurant and bar. The hotel has attractive lounge areas on three levels; there is a health suite with a gym and swimming pool with an integrated children's pool.

Rooms 51 (5 fmly) ✎ **S** £60-£100; **D** £100-£160 (incl. bkfst)* **Facilities** FTV WiFi ⓑ ⓣ supervised Gym Beauty treatment room Sauna Steam room Whirlpool Xmas New Year **Conf** Class 60 Board 60 Thtr 100 Del from £125 to £180* **Services** Lift **Parking** 60 **Notes** LB ⊗

Duke of Normandie Hotel

★★★ 81% HOTEL

tel: 01481 721431 **Lefebvre St GY1 2JP**
email: enquiries@dukeofnormandie.com **web:** www.dukeofnormandie.com
dir: *From harbour rdbt St Julians Ave, 3rd left into Anns Place, continue to right, up hill, then left into Lefebvre St, archway entrance on right*

The Duke of Normandie is an 18th-century hotel situated close to the high street and just a short stroll from the harbour. Bedrooms vary in style and include some that have their own access from the courtyard. Public areas feature a smart brasserie, a contemporary lounge-lobby area and a busy bar with beams and an open fireplace.

Rooms 37 (17 annexe) (8 GF) ✎ **S** £39-£89; **D** £90-£159 (incl. bkfst) **Facilities** STV WiFi ⓑ **Parking** 10 **Notes** LB ⊗

Best Western Moores Hotel

★★★ 79% HOTEL

🅑🅦 Best Western.

tel: 01481 724452 **Pollet GY1 1WH**
email: stay@mooresguernsey.com **web:** www.mooresguernsey.com
dir: *Left at airport, follow signs to St Peter Port. Fort Road to seafront, straight on, turn left before rdbt, to hotel*

This elegant granite town house is situated in the heart of St Peter Port among its shops and amenities. Public rooms feature a smart conservatory restaurant which leads out onto a first-floor terrace for alfresco dining; there is also a choice of lounges and bars as well as a patisserie. Bedrooms are pleasantly decorated and thoughtfully equipped.

Rooms 49 (3 annexe) (8 fmly) ✎ **S** £55-£80; **D** £110-£180 (incl. bkfst)* **Facilities** FTV WiFi ⓑ Gym Sauna Xmas New Year **Conf** Class 20 Board 18 Thtr 40 Del from £140 to £200* **Services** Lift **Notes** LB ⊗

ST SAVIOUR   Map 24

The Farmhouse Hotel

★★★★ 82% ◉ SMALL HOTEL

tel: 01481 264181 **Route Des Bas Courtils GY7 9YF**
email: enquiries@thefarmhouse.gg **web:** www.thefarmhouse.gg
dir: *From airport turn left. Approx 1m left at lights. 100mtrs, left, around airport runway perimeter. 1m, left at staggered junct. Hotel in 100mtrs on right. For directions from harbour please see hotel website or contact hotel*

This hotel provides spacious accommodation with amazingly comfortable beds and state-of-the-art bathrooms with under-floor heating. Guests can choose from various stylish dining options including alfresco eating in the warmer months. The outdoor swimming pool is available to guests in the summer and there are lots of countryside walks to enjoy.

Rooms 14 (7 fmly) ✎ **Facilities** STV WiFi ⓣ ♨ **Conf** Class 130 Board 30 Thtr 150 **Services** Air con **Parking** 80 **Notes** ⊗

VALE   Map 24

Peninsula Hotel

★★★ 80% HOTEL

tel: 01481 248400 **Les Dicqs GY6 8JP**
email: peninsula@guernsey.net **web:** www.peninsulahotelguernsey.com
dir: *On coast road at Grand Havre Bay*

Adjacent to the sandy beach and set in five acres of grounds, this modern hotel provides comfortable accommodation. Bedrooms have an additional sofa bed to suit families and good workspace for the business traveller. Both fixed-price and carte menus are served in the restaurant, or guests can eat informally in the bar.

Rooms 99 (99 fmly) (27 GF) ✎ **Facilities** STV WiFi ⓣ Putt green Petanque Children's playground Table Tennis Xmas New Year **Conf** Class 100 Board 105 Thtr 250 **Services** Lift **Parking** 120 **Notes** ⊗ Closed Jan

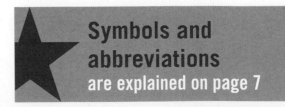

Symbols and abbreviations are explained on page 7

HERM

HERM
Map 24

White House Hotel
★★★ 86% @@ HOTEL

tel: 01481 750075 **GY1 3HR**
email: hotel@herm.com **web:** www.herm.com
dir: *Transport to island by catamaran ferry from St Peter Port, Guernsey*

Enjoying a unique island setting, this attractive hotel is just 20 minutes from Guernsey by sea. Set in well-tended gardens, the hotel offers neatly decorated bedrooms, located in either the main house or adjacent cottages; the majority of rooms have sea views. Guests can relax in one of several lounges, enjoy a drink in one of two bars and choose from two dining options.

Rooms 40 (23 annexe) (23 fmly) (7 GF) **Facilities** WiFi ⚓ ⚲ ⚲ Fishing trips Yacht & motor boat charters **Conf** Board 10 Thtr 50 **Notes** LB ⊗ Closed Nov-Mar

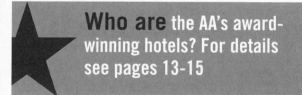

Who are the AA's award-winning hotels? For details see pages 13-15

JERSEY

GOREY
Map 24

The Moorings Hotel & Restaurant
★★★ 83% @@ HOTEL

tel: 01534 853633 **Gorey Pier JE3 6EW**
email: reservations@themooringshotel.com **web:** www.themooringshotel.com
dir: *At foot of Mont Orgueil Castle*

Enjoying an enviable position by the harbour, the heart of this hotel is the restaurant where a selection of menus offers an extensive choice of dishes. Other public areas include a bar, coffee shop and a comfortable first-floor residents' lounge. Bedrooms at the front have a fine view of the harbour; three have access to a balcony. A small sun terrace at the back of the hotel is also available to guests.

Rooms 15 ⚓ **Facilities** FTV WiFi ⚲ Xmas New Year **Conf** Class 20 Board 20 Thtr 20 **Notes** LB ⊗

The Dolphin Hotel and Restaurant
★★ 79% HOTEL

tel: 01534 853370 **Gorey Pier JE3 6EW**
email: dolphinhoteljersey@outlook.com **web:** www.dolphinhoteljersey.com
dir: *At foot of Mont Orgueil Castle*

Located on the main harbour at Gorey, many bedrooms at this popular hotel enjoy views over the sea and beaches. The relaxed and friendly style is apparent from the moment of arrival, and the busy restaurant and bar are popular with locals and tourists alike. Outdoor seating is available in season, and fresh fish and seafood are included on the menu.

Rooms 16 **S** £47.50-£61; **D** £95-£122 (incl. bkfst)* **Facilities** STV WiFi ⚲ 🎵 Xmas New Year **Conf** Class 20 Board 20 Thtr 20 **Notes** ⊗

ROZEL
Map 24

Château la Chaire
★★★★ 82% @@ HOTEL

tel: 01534 863354 **Rozel Bay JE3 6AJ**
email: res@chateau-la-chaire.co.uk **web:** www.chateau-la-chaire.co.uk
dir: *From St Helier on B38 turn left in village by Rozel Bay Inn, hotel 100yds on right*

Built as a gentleman's residence in 1843, Château la Chaire is a haven of peace and tranquillity, set in a secluded wooded valley. Picturesque Rozel Harbour is within easy walking distance, and the house is surrounded by terraced gardens and woods. The helpful staff deliver high standards of guest care, and imaginative menus, making the best use of local produce, are served in the oak-panelled dining room, the conservatory, or on the terrace when the weather permits. Bedroom and suite styles and sizes vary, but all are beautifully appointed and include many nice touches such as towelling robes, slippers, flowers and DVD players. Free WiFi is available throughout the hotel.

Rooms 14 (2 fmly) (1 GF) ⚓ **S** £95-£125; **D** £120-£340 (incl. bkfst)* **Facilities** FTV WiFi ⚲ Xmas New Year **Conf** Class 20 Board 20 Thtr 20 **Parking** 30 **Notes** LB ⊗ No children 7yrs Civ Wed 60

ST BRELADE

Map 24

INSPECTORS' CHOICE

The Atlantic Hotel

★★★★ ◉◉◉◉ 🍴 HOTEL

tel: 01534 744101 **Le Mont de la Pulente JE3 8HE**
email: info@theatlantichotel.com **web:** www.theatlantichotel.com
dir: *From Petit Port turn right into Rue de la Sergente, right again, hotel signed*

Adjoining the manicured fairways of La Moye championship golf course, this hotel enjoys a peaceful setting with breathtaking views over St Ouen's Bay. Stylish bedrooms look onto the course or the sea, and offer a blend of high quality and reassuring comfort. An air of understated luxury is apparent throughout, and the attentive service achieves the perfect balance of friendliness and professionalism. The Ocean restaurant's very talented chef, Mark Jordan, uses the best island produce to create outstanding and impeccably modern cuisine.

Rooms 50 (8 GF) 🐾 **S** £100-£330; **D** £120-£600 (incl. bkfst)* **Facilities** STV WiFi ⓘ🎾 ⚓ 🏊 Gym Saunas Xmas New Year **Conf** Class 40 Board 20 Thtr 60 Del from £250 to £350* **Services** Lift **Parking** 60 **Notes** LB ⊗ Closed 3 Jan-2 Feb Civ Wed 80

L'Horizon Beach Hotel and Spa

★★★★ 86% ◉◉ HOTEL

tel: 01534 743101 **St Brelade's Bay JE3 8EF**
email: lhorizon@handpicked.co.uk **web:** www.handpickedhotels.co.uk/lhorizon
dir: *From airport right at rdbt towards St Brelades & Red Houses. Through Red Houses, hotel 300mtrs on right in centre of bay*

The combination of a truly wonderful setting on the golden sands of St Brelade's Bay, a relaxed atmosphere and excellent facilities prove a winning formula here. Bedrooms are stylish and have a real contemporary feel, all with plasma TVs and a host of extras; many have balconies or terraces and superb sea views. Spacious public areas include a spa and leisure club, a choice of dining options and relaxing lounges.

Rooms 106 (1 fmly) (15 GF) 🐾 **Facilities** Spa STV FTV WiFi ⓘⓘ 🏊 Gym Windsurfing Water skiing Sailing Sauna Steam room ♫ Xmas New Year **Conf** Class 100 Board 50 Thtr 250 **Services** Lift **Parking** 125 **Notes** ⊗ Civ Wed 240

St Brelade's Bay Hotel

★★★★ 81% HOTEL

tel: 01534 746141 **JE3 8EF**
web: www.stbreladesbayhotel.com
dir: *SW corner of island*

The hotel, set in five-acres of gardens, enjoys a fabulous location with unobstructed views overlooking St Brelade's Bay, and a sandy beach right on the doorstep. Bedrooms are beautifully presented and equipped to a very high standard. They include two-bedroom suites, family rooms and superb penthouse suites that have large balconies, and even telescopes. The relaxing public areas include a stylish, comfortable lounge along with a spacious bar. The gardens feature a pool area, terraces for relaxing and eating, and a tennis court. A superb leisure and fitness centre with state-of-the-art equipment is another attraction. Attentive friendly service is guaranteed in the elegant restaurant with its sea views.

Rooms 77 (8 fmly) 🐾 **Facilities** Spa FTV WiFi ⓘ 🎾 🏊 Gym Beauty treatment rooms ♫ Xmas New Year **Conf** Class 30 Board 12 Thtr 60 **Services** Lift **Parking** 90 **Notes** ⊗ Civ Wed 70

Hotel La Place

★★★★ 79% ◉ HOTEL

tel: 01534 744261 **Route du Coin, La Haule JE3 8BT**
email: reservations@hotellaplacejersey.com **web:** www.hotellaplacejersey.com
dir: *Off main St Helier/St Aubin coast road at La Haule Manor B25. Up hill, 2nd left to Red Houses, 1st right. Hotel 100mtrs on right*

Developed around a 17th-century farmhouse, this hotel is well placed for exploration of the island. Attentive, friendly service is very much part of the ethos here. Many bedrooms have benefited from an impressive refurbishment program and offer high levels of quality and comfort; some have private patios and direct access to the pool area. The cocktail bar is popular for pre-dinner drinks, and the stylish lounge is a perfect place to sit back and enjoy the tranquil delights of this peaceful setting. Cuisine is also an important feature here with a menu offering a good range of local, seasonal produce, served in the elegant restaurant.

Rooms 42 (1 fmly) (12 GF) 🐾 **D** £100-£210 (incl. bkfst)* **Facilities** STV WiFi 🎾 Discount at Les Ormes Country Club Xmas New Year **Conf** Class 40 Board 40 Thtr 100 **Parking** 100 **Notes** Civ Wed 100

Beau Rivage Hotel

★★★ 77% HOTEL

tel: 01534 745983 **St Brelade's Bay JE3 8EF**
email: beau@welcome.je **web:** www.jersey.co.uk/hotels/beau
dir: *Sea side of coast road in centre of St Brelade's Bay, 1.5m S of airport*

With direct access to one of Jersey's most popular beaches, residents and non-residents alike are welcome to this hotel's bar and terrace. All of the well-equipped bedrooms are now suites, most have wonderful sea views, and some have the bonus of balconies. Residents have a choice of lounges, plus a sun deck exclusively for their use. A range of dishes, featuring English and Continental cuisine, is available from a selection of menus in either the bar or the main bistro restaurant.

Rooms 12 (12 fmly) (12 smoking) ↟ **D** £60-£280* **Facilities** STV FTV WiFi Games room **Services** Lift **Parking** 16 **Notes** ⊗ RS Nov-Mar Civ Wed 80

Highlands Hotel

★★★ 76% HOTEL

tel: 01534 744288 **Corbiere JE3 8HN**
email: enquiries@highlandshotel.com **web:** www.highlandshotel.com
dir: *3m from Jersey airport. Very close to Corbiere Lighthouse*

This hotel has an enviable location, ideally suited to touring and walking the island, close to the coast and beaches of St Brelades Bay. There are several leisure facilities, including a swimming pool and games room. The restaurant and many of the bedrooms have delightful views. Bedrooms and bathrooms are very pleasantly appointed in a bright and attractive style.

Rooms 49 (5 fmly) ↟ **S** £50-£60; **D** £90-£150 (incl. bkfst)* **Facilities** FTV WiFi ⇘ ⬟ Gym **Services** Lift **Parking** 60 **Notes** Closed Oct-May

■ ST CLEMENT   Map 24

Pontac House Hotel

★★★ 77% HOTEL

tel: 01534 857771 **St Clements Bay JE2 6SE**
email: info@pontachouse.com **web:** www.pontachouse.com
dir: *10 mins from St Helier*

Overlooking the sandy beach of St Clement's Bay, this hotel is located on the south eastern corner of Jersey. Many guests return on a regular basis to experience the friendly, relaxed style of service. The bedrooms, most with splendid views, are comfortable and well equipped. Varied menus, featuring local seafood, are on offer each evening.

Rooms 27 (1 fmly) (5 GF) ↟ **Facilities** FTV WiFi ⬟ **Parking** 35 **Notes** Closed 1 Dec-1 Apr

The Samares Coast Hotel

★★★ 73% HOTEL

tel: 01534 723411 & 873006 **St Clement's Coast Rd JE2 6SB**
email: admin@morvanhotels.com **web:** www.morvanhotels.com
dir: *On main esplanade*

This hotel is situated on the south coast in a prime seafront location with delightful views from the restaurant and many of the bedrooms. All rooms are well appointed and the sea-facing balcony rooms prove especially popular. Facilities include a leisure complex with swimming pool and gym, and there are pleasant gardens. Carefully prepared dishes are offered in the comfortable restaurant.

Rooms 52 (4 annexe) (5 fmly) (14 GF) ↟ **Facilities** STV FTV WiFi ⬟ ⬟ Gym Steam room **Services** Lift **Parking** 35 **Notes** ⊗ Closed Nov-Mar

■ ST HELIER   Map 24

Grand Jersey

★★★★★ 83% ◉◉◉ HOTEL

Hand PICKED
HOTELS
BUILT FOR PLEASURE

tel: 01534 722301 **The Esplanade JE2 3QA**
email: reservations.grandjersey@handpicked.co.uk
web: www.handpickedhotels.co.uk/grandjersey
dir: *Located on St Helier seafront. 10mins from airport*

A local landmark, the Grand Hotel has pleasant views across St Aubin's Bay to the front, and the bustling streets of St Helier to the rear. The hotel is elegant and contemporary in design with a real touch of grandeur throughout. The air-conditioned bedrooms, including six suites, come in a variety of designs, but all have luxurious beds, ottomans and LCD TVs. The spacious public areas, many looking out onto the bay, include the very popular Champagne Lounge, Victoria's brasserie, and the impressive and intimate Tassili fine-dining restaurant. There is a large terrace for alfresco eating in the summer months, and the spa offers an indoor pool, gym and treatment rooms.

Rooms 123 (18 fmly) (6 GF) ↟ **Facilities** Spa STV FTV WiFi ⇘ ⬟ Gym ♫ Xmas New Year **Conf** Class 90 Board 50 Thtr 160 Del from £180 to £230* **Services** Lift Air con **Parking** 27 **Notes** ⊗ Civ Wed 180

■ INSPECTORS' CHOICE

The Club Hotel & Spa

★★★★ ◉◉◉◉ TOWN HOUSE HOTEL

tel: 01534 876500 **Green St JE2 4UH**
email: reservations@theclubjersey.com **web:** www.theclubjersey.com
dir: *5 mins walk from main shopping centre*

This swish, town-house hotel is conveniently located close to the centre of town and features stylish, contemporary decor throughout. All the guest rooms and suites have power showers and state-of-the-art technology including wide-screen LCD TV, DVD and CD systems. The choice of restaurants includes Bohemia, a sophisticated eating option that continues to offer outstanding cuisine. For relaxation there is an elegant spa with a luxurious range of treatments.

Rooms 46 (4 fmly) (4 GF) **S** £99-£445; **D** £99-£445 (incl. bkfst) **Facilities** Spa STV FTV WiFi ⬟ ⬟ Steam room Salt cabin Hydrothermal bench Rasul room New Year **Conf** Class 60 Board 34 Thtr 80 Del from £175 to £245 **Services** Lift Air con **Parking** 32 **Notes** LB ⊗ Closed 24-30 Dec Civ Wed 84

ST HELIER *continued*

HIGHLY RECOMMENDED

The Royal Yacht

★★★★ 84% ❁❁❁ HOTEL

tel: 01534 720511 **The Weighbridge JE2 3NF**
email: reception@theroyalyacht.com web: www.theroyalyacht.com
dir: *In town centre, opposite marina & harbour*

Overlooking the marina and steam clock, the Royal Yacht is thought to be the oldest established hotel on the island. Although it has a long history, it is very much a 21st-century hotel, with state-of-the-art technology in all the bedrooms and the two penthouse suites. There is a range of impressive dining options to suit all tastes, with Sirocco's Restaurant offering high quality local produce. In addition to a choice of bars and conference facilities, guests can enjoy the luxury spa with an indoor pool and gym.

Rooms 110 ⟡ **S** £109-£155; **D** £109-£265 (incl. bkfst)* **Facilities** Spa STV WiFi ⬇ ⊕ Gym ♫ Xmas New Year **Conf** Class 150 Board 40 Thtr 280 **Services** Lift Air con **Notes** LB ⊗ Civ Wed 250

See advert on opposite page

Pomme d'Or Hotel

★★★★ 80% HOTEL

tel: 01534 880110 **Liberation Square JE1 3UF**
email: enquiries@pommedorhotel.com web: www.pommedorhotel.com
dir: *Opposite harbour*

This historic hotel overlooks Liberation Square and the marina, and offers comfortably furnished, well-equipped bedrooms. Popular with the business fraternity, a range of conference facilities and meeting rooms are available. Dining options include The Harbour Room Carvery and the café bar.

Rooms 143 (3 fmly) ⟡ **Facilities** STV FTV WiFi ⬇ Free use of The Aquadome at The Merton Hotel Xmas New Year **Conf** Class 100 Board 50 Thtr 220 **Services** Lift Air con **Notes** ⊗ Civ Wed 100

Radisson Blu Waterfront Hotel, Jersey

★★★★ 80% HOTEL

tel: 01534 671100 & 671173 **The Waterfront, La Rue de L'Etau JE2 3WF**
email: info.jersey@radissonblu.com web: www.radissonblu.com/hotel-jersey
dir: *Follow signs to St Helier. From A2 follow signs to harbour. At rdbt just before harbour take 2nd exit, continue to hotel*

Most of the bedrooms at this purpose-built hotel have fabulous views of the coastline. Facilities include a popular brasserie, cocktail bar, lounges, indoor heated pool, gym, sauna, and steam room. A wide range of meeting rooms provides conference facilities for delegates.

Rooms 195 ⟡ **Facilities** Spa STV FTV WiFi ⬇ HL ⊕ Gym Sauna Steam room Hair salon ♫ Xmas New Year **Conf** Class 184 Board 30 Thtr 400 **Services** Lift Air con **Parking** 80 **Notes** ⊗ Civ Wed 400

Best Western Royal Hotel

★★★ 81% ❁ HOTEL

tel: 01534 726521 & 873006 **David Place JE2 4TD**
email: enquiries@royalhoteljersey.com web: www.royalhoteljersey.com
dir: *From Airport: In St Helier on Victoria Ave, left by Grand Hotel into Peirson Rd. Follow one-way system into Cheapside. Left at filter, follow Ring Rd signs into Rouge Boullion (A14). At rdbt right, stay in right lane, right at lights into Midvale Rd. Through 2 lights, hotel on left*

This long established hotel is located in the centre of town and is within walking distance of the business district and shops. Seasons Restaurant offers a modern approach to dining, and the adjoining bar provides a relaxed venue for residents and locals alike. The bedrooms are individually styled. Extensive conference facilities are available.

Rooms 89 (4 fmly) ⟡ **Facilities** FTV WiFi ⬇ Gym Xmas New Year **Conf** Class 120 Board 80 Thtr 300 **Services** Lift **Parking** 15 **Notes** ⊗ Civ Wed 30

The Norfolk Lodge Hotel

★★★ 77% HOTEL

tel: 01534 722950 & 873006 **Rouge Bouillon JE2 3ZB**
email: admin@morvanhotels.com web: www.morvanhotels.com

Centrally located and just a short walk from the main town, this popular hotel has a large number of regularly returning guests. Bedrooms are well decorated and equipped, and include some on the ground floor. In addition to an indoor swimming pool, the hotel offers regular evening entertainment during the main season. A range of well-prepared dishes is offered at dinner in the spacious restaurant.

Rooms 101 (11 annexe) (8 fmly) (15 GF) ⟡ **Facilities** FTV WiFi ⊕ Children's pool ♫ **Services** Lift **Parking** 40 **Notes** ⊗ Closed Nov-Mar

ST HELIER *continued*

Hampshire Hotel

★★★ 76% ⚜ HOTEL

tel: 01534 724115 **53 Val Plaisant JE2 4TB**
email: info@hampshirehotel.je **web:** www.hampshirehotel.je

Located a short walk from the town centre, this hotel features spacious public areas and comfortable bedrooms. There are premier, standard and family rooms, each with a flat-screen TV. The spacious restaurant features seasonal changing dinner menus of popular dishes; at breakfast a wide choice is offered. The outdoor swimming pool and sun terrace are popular in the summer months.

Rooms 42 (2 fmly) (5 GF) **Facilities** STV WiFi ᐅ ⊼ Xmas New Year **Services** Lift **Parking** 30 **Notes** ⊗

The Monterey Hotel

★★★ 76% HOTEL

tel: 01534 724762 & 873006 **St Saviour's Rd JE2 7LA**
email: monterey@morvanhotels.com **web:** www.morvanhotels.com

Conveniently located for the town, this comfortable hotel has the added benefit of ample parking and a range of leisure facilities including an indoor pool. Bedrooms are well decorated and furnished, and include a number of superior rooms. The relaxing bar area is open all day, and a good range of freshly prepared dishes is offered each evening.

Rooms 73 (6 fmly) (9 GF) **Facilities** FTV WiFi ᐅ ⊛ ⊼ Gym Steam room Xmas New Year **Conf** Class 12 Board 22 Thtr 40 **Services** Lift **Parking** 40 **Notes** ⊗

Fort D'Auvergne Hotel

★★★ 74% HOTEL

tel: 01534 879960 & 731684 **Harve des Pas JE2 4UQ**
email: fort@morvanhotels.com **web:** www.morvanhotels.com

The Fort D'Auvergne Hotel is bordered by the sea and sandy beach on two sides and occupies what is one of the best maritime positions in Jersey's capital. The hotel itself is traditional in style but offers modern amenities including an air-conditioned seafront table d'hôte restaurant and an outstanding luxury indoor pool complex with unrivalled views over the bay. There is only a pedestrian promenade separating the hotel from the sea shore. Dinner is served daily in the restaurant with tables benefiting from uninterrupted sea views.

Rooms 65 (4 fmly) (9 GF) **Facilities** FTV WiFi ⊛ ⊼ Child facilities **Services** Lift **Notes** ⊗ Closed 19 Oct-1 Apr

The Hotel Revere

★★★ 74% HOTEL

tel: 01534 611111 **Kensington Place JE2 3PA**
email: reservations@revere.co.uk **web:** www.revere.co.uk
dir: *From Esplanade left after Grand Hotel*

Situated on the west side of the town and convenient for the centre and harbour side, this hotel dates back to the 17th century and retains many period features. The style here is engagingly different, and bedrooms are individually decorated. There are three dining options and a small sun terrace.

Rooms 56 (2 fmly) (4 GF) **Facilities** FTV WiFi ⊼ ⊼ **Notes** ⊗ Closed Jan Civ Wed 50

Westhill Country Hotel

★★★ 74% COUNTRY HOUSE HOTEL

tel: 01534 723260 **Mont-a-l'abbe JE2 3HB**
email: info@westhillhoteljersey.com **web:** www.westhillhoteljersey.com
dir: *See website for details*

Set in its own beautifully landscaped gardens, this hotel enjoys a prominent position just on the outskirts of St Helier. Service is attentive and guests are guaranteed a warm welcome and genuine hospitality throughout the hotel. The bedrooms are spacious and well equipped; several rooms have commanding views over the gardens to the countryside beyond. Public areas include a stylish lounge bar and popular restaurant. Free WiFi is available in the public areas and the swimming pool proves very popular with guests.

Rooms 90 (20 fmly) (16 GF) **S** £50-£65; **D** £100-£130 (incl. bkfst)* **Facilities** FTV WiFi ⊼ Nature trail Childrens adventure play area ⊼ **Conf** Class 80 Board 40 Thtr 60 **Parking** 75 **Notes** ⊗ Closed early Oct-early Apr Civ Wed 75

Apollo Hotel

★★★ 73% HOTEL

tel: 01534 725441 **St Saviours Rd JE2 4GJ**
email: reservations@huggler.com **web:** www.apollojersey.com
dir: *On St Saviours Rd at junct with La Motte St*

Centrally located, this popular hotel has a relaxed, informal atmosphere. Bedrooms are comfortably furnished and include useful extras. Many guests return regularly to enjoy the variety of leisure facilities, including an outdoor pool with water slide and indoor pool with separate jacuzzi. The cocktail bar is an ideal place for a pre-dinner drink.

Rooms 85 (5 fmly) **Facilities** FTV WiFi ⊛ supervised ⊼ supervised Gym Xmas New Year **Conf** Class 100 Board 80 Thtr 150 **Services** Lift **Parking** 40 **Notes** ⊗

Millbrook House Hotel

★★ 77% HOTEL

tel: 01534 733036 **Rue De Trachy, Millbrook JE2 3JN**
email: millbrook.house@jerseymail.co.uk **web:** www.millbrookhousehotel.com
dir: *1.5m W of town off A1*

Peacefully located in its own grounds, this small, personally-run hotel offers a friendly welcome and relaxing ambience. Bedrooms and bathrooms vary in size; many have pleasant, countryside views. In addition to outdoor seating in the warmer months, guests can relax in the library, maybe with a drink before dinner.

Rooms 24 (2 fmly) (6 GF) **S** £40-£55; **D** £75-£95 (incl. bkfst)* **Facilities** WiFi Putt green **Services** Lift **Parking** 20 **Notes** Closed Oct-16 May

Sarum Hotel

★★ 63% METRO HOTEL

tel: 01534 758163 **19/21 New St Johns Rd JE2 3LD**
email: sarum@welcome.je **web:** www.jersey.co.uk/hotels/sarum
dir: *On NW edge of St Helier, 0.5m from town centre*

This hotel, just 600yds from the beach, offers self-catering bedrooms and a number of suites. The friendly staff provide a warm welcome, and there is a spacious recreational lounge with pool tables, plasma-screen TV and internet access. A garden and outdoor pool are also available. Local restaurants are just a short walk away, and bar snacks are available throughout the day.

Rooms 52 (5 annexe) (6 fmly) (2 GF) (52 smoking) **S** £43-£72; **D** £62-£110* **Facilities** STV FTV WiFi Games room **Services** Lift **Parking** 10 **Notes** LB ⊗

■ ST PETER   Map 24

Greenhills Country Hotel

★★★★ 77% ⊛ COUNTRY HOUSE HOTEL

tel: 01534 481042 **Mont de L'Ecole JE3 7EL**
email: reception@greenhillshotel.com **web:** www.greenhillshotel.com
dir: *Follow signs to St Peter's Village, the A11, turn into Le Mont de l'ecole, Hotel on left*

Located in the rural centre of Jersey, this relaxing country-house hotel, with delightful gardens, has a lovely atmosphere. Bedrooms extend from the main building around the courtyard; all are modern and well equipped with satellite LED TVs, luxurious bathrobes, white duck down duvets and linen. A varied menu, based on fresh local produce, is served in the restaurant, and guests also have use of the Aquadome at the Merton Hotel.

Rooms 31 (2 fmly) (9 GF) **S** £70-£140; **D** £99-£240 (incl. bkfst)* **Facilities** STV FTV WiFi ⤢ Free use of Merton Hotel's Aquadome & Leisure Centre **Conf** Class 12 Board 16 Thtr 20 Del from £100 to £135* **Parking** 40 **Notes** LB ⊗ Closed mid Dec-early Feb Civ Wed 40

■ ST SAVIOUR   Map 24

INSPECTORS' CHOICE

Longueville Manor Hotel

★★★★★ ⊛⊛⊛ ⌘ HOTEL

tel: 01534 725501 **JE2 7WF**
email: info@longuevillemanor.com **web:** www.longuevillemanor.com
dir: *A3 E from St Helier towards Gorey. Hotel 1m on left*

Dating back to the 13th century, there is something very special about Longueville Manor, which is why so many guests return time and again. It is set in 16 acres of grounds including woodland walks, a spectacular rose garden, Victorian kitchen garden and a lake. Bedrooms have great style and individuality boasting fresh flowers, fine embroidered bed linen and a host of extras. The very accomplished cuisine is also a highlight of any stay. In summer the pool and terrace are popular spots, plus there are also croquet and tennis courts. Families are particularly welcome, and there are extra activities arranged for children, including an adventure zone to explore. They also have their own menus and DVD library. The committed team of staff create a welcoming atmosphere and every effort is made to ensure a memorable stay.

Rooms 30 (1 annexe) (7 GF) ⟁ **S** £150-£525; **D** £195-£575 (incl. bkfst)* **Facilities** Spa STV WiFi ⇘ ⤢ ☺ ⚐ Gym Treatment rooms Xmas New Year **Conf** Class 30 Board 30 Thtr 45 **Services** Lift **Parking** 40 **Notes** LB Civ Wed 40

SARK

■ SARK   Map 24

Stocks Hotel

★★★★ 81% ⊛⊛ SMALL HOTEL

tel: 01481 832001 & 832444 **GY10 1SD**
email: reception@stockshotel.com **web:** www.stockshotel.com
dir: *Ferry to Guernsey then to Sark. Tractor bus from harbour to top of island. Chargeable horse & carriage available for transfer to hotel or walk - approx 20 mins*

The island of Sark is a delight. With no cars, transport is provided by horse and cart, tractor or bicycle, making this a very tranquil place. Stocks Hotel has spacious, comfortable rooms, which are attractively appointed. There are several lounges, and a cosy bar, as well as two dining options; the Brasserie is at the poolside and offers al fresco dining, while the main restaurant is more formal. The hotel gardens provide much for the kitchen, and the stables house the hotel's own team of cart pullers.

Rooms 23 (11 annexe) (2 fmly) (3 GF) ⟁ **S** £242.50-£262.50; **D** £260-£280 (incl. bkfst) **Facilities** STV FTV WiFi ⇘ ⤢ Gym Massage treatment room Xmas New Year **Conf** Class 70 Board 12 Thtr 70 Del from £300 to £320 **Notes** LB Closed 3 Jan-1 Mar RS Mar & Nov-Dec

Scotland

ABERDEEN
City of Aberdeen

Map 23 NJ90

See also **Aberdeen Airport**

Mercure Aberdeen Ardoe House Hotel & Spa

★★★★ 81% HOTEL

tel: 01224 860600 **South Deeside Rd, Blairs AB12 5YP**
email: h6626@accor.com **web:** www.mercure.com/AberdeenHotels
dir: *4m W of city off B9077, follow for 3m, hotel on left*

From its elevated position on the banks of the River Dee, this 19th-century baronial-style mansion commands excellent countryside views. Beautifully decorated, thoughtfully equipped bedrooms are located in the main house, and in the more modern extension. Public rooms include a spa and leisure club, a cosy lounge and whisky bar and impressive function facilities.

Rooms 120 (7 fmly) ☎ **S** £90-£240; **D** £100-£250* **Facilities** Spa FTV WiFi ☼ HL ⓢ supervised ☺ Gym Sauna Steam room Dance studio Xmas New Year **Conf** Class 200 Board 150 Thtr 600 **Services** Lift Air con **Parking** 200 **Notes** LB Civ Wed 500

The Chester Hotel

★★★★ 80% ⓢⓢ HOTEL

tel: 01244 327777 **59-63 Queens Rd AB15 4YP**
email: enquiries@chester-hotel.com **web:** www.chester-hotel.com
dir: *From Aberdeen Airport follow signs to Perth A90, at Queens Rd rdbt take first exit left. Hotel is on the right*

The Chester Hotel has recently benefited from a complete refurbishment. Bedrooms are modern and well equipped with lovely beds and quality bedding, along with useful extras for the modern traveller. Robes, slippers and quality branded toiletries are provided as standard. Dining options include relaxed comfort food in the bar area or an award-winning restaurant providing high quality dishes using the best local produce. There is a small boutique spa with a well-equipped gym also available to residents. The Chester is ideally located for the city centre as well as the airport and numerous golf courses.

Rooms 50 (6 annexe) (21 GF) ☎ **S** £99-£330; **D** £119-£350 (incl. bkfst)
Facilities Spa STV FTV WiFi ☼ Gym ♬ Xmas New Year **Conf** Class 80 Board 45 Thtr 220 **Services** Lift **Parking** 46 **Notes** ⊗ Civ Wed 200

Norwood Hall Hotel

★★★★ 79% ⓢⓢ HOTEL

tel: 01224 868951 **Garthdee Rd, Cults AB15 9FX**
email: info@norwood-hall.co.uk **web:** www.norwood-hall.co.uk
dir: *Off A90, at 1st rdbt cross Bridge of Dee, left at rdbt onto Garthdee Rd, B&Q & Sainsburys on left, continue to hotel sign*

This imposing Victorian mansion has retained many of its original features, most notably the fine oak staircase, stained glass and ornately decorated walls and ceilings. Accommodation varies in style from individually designed bedrooms in the main house to the newest contemporary bedrooms. The extensive grounds ensure the hotel is popular as a wedding venue.

Rooms 73 (14 GF) **Facilities** STV FTV WiFi ☼ Xmas New Year **Conf** Class 100 Board 70 Thtr 200 **Services** Lift **Parking** 140 **Notes** ⊗ Civ Wed 150

Malmaison Aberdeen

★★★★ 77% ⓢ HOTEL

tel: 01224 327370 & 0844 693 0649
(Calls cost 5p per minute plus your phone company's access charge) **49-53 Queens Rd AB15 4YP**
email: info.aberdeen@malmaison.com **web:** www.malmaison.com
dir: *A90, 3rd exit into Queens Rd at 3rd rdbt, hotel on right*

Popular with business travellers and as a function venue, this well-established hotel lies east of the city centre. Public areas include an attractive reception lounge and an intimate restaurant featuring a Josper Grill, plus the modern bar which remains a popular choice for many regulars whether it be for a bar meal or bottle of wine from the extensive cellar. There are two styles of accommodation, with the superior rooms being particularly comfortable and well equipped.

Rooms 79 (10 GF) ☎ **Facilities** Spa STV FTV WiFi ☼ Gym Steam room Xmas New Year **Conf** Class 12 Board 25 Thtr 30 **Services** Lift Air con **Parking** 30 **Notes** ⊗

The Aberdeen Altens Hotel

THE
HOTEL
COLLECTION

★★★★ 74% HOTEL

tel: 01224 877000 & 379240 **Souterhead Rd, Altens AB12 3LF**
email: aberdeenaltensreception@thehotelcollection.co.uk
web: www.thehotelcollection.co.uk/hotels/aberdeen-altens-hotel
dir: *Follow A90 & take A956 signed Aberdeen Harbour. 1st exit at rdbt onto Souterhead Rd. Hotel on right*

A great venue for business travellers attending conferences, or those visiting the Granite City on a leisure break, this hotel enjoys a quiet setting and ample parking. An interesting range of dishes are available in the Cairngorm Bar and Restaurant, while guests with time can enjoy the extensive leisure and beauty facilities. Bedrooms have all been recently refurbished and feature a number of thoughtful accessories. A small number of apartments are available for those guests on longer breaks.

Rooms 216 (71 fmly) (48 GF) ☎ **D** £49-£180* **Facilities** FTV WiFi ☼ HL ⓢ Gym Sauna Steam Room Treatment room Xmas New Year **Conf** Class 144 Board 70 Thtr 400 Del from £135 to £170* **Services** Lift **Notes** LB ⊗ Civ Wed

The Craighaar Hotel

★★★★ 73% HOTEL

tel: 01224 712275 **Waterton Rd, Bucksburn AB21 9HS**
email: info@craighaar.co.uk **web:** www.craighaarhotel.com
dir: *From A96 Airport/Inverness onto A947, hotel signed*

Conveniently located for the airport, this welcoming hotel is a popular base for business people and tourists alike. Guests can make use of a range of recently refurbished public areas including the popular brasserie and a welcoming lounge bar with open fire. All bedrooms are well equipped, plus there is a wing of duplex suites that provide additional comfort.

Rooms 53 (6 fmly) (16 GF) ☎ **S** £55-£95; **D** £65-£119 (incl. bkfst)* **Facilities** FTV WiFi ☼ Library **Conf** Class 33 Board 30 Thtr 90 Del £129.50* **Parking** 80 **Notes** LB ⊗ Closed 25-26 Dec RS 24 Dec Civ Wed 40

Maryculter House Hotel

★★★★ 72% HOTEL

tel: 01224 732124 **South Deeside Rd, Maryculter AB12 5GB**
email: info@maryculterhousehotel.com **web:** www.maryculterhousehotel.com
dir: Exit A90 S of Aberdeen onto B9077. Hotel 8m on right, 0.5m beyond Deeside Holiday Park

Set in grounds on the banks of the River Dee, this charming Scottish mansion dates back to medieval times and is now a popular wedding and conference venue. Exposed stonework and open fires feature in the oldest parts of Maryculter House, which also house the recently refurbished Poacher's Pocket lounge and the Priory Restaurant. Bedrooms, many of which overlook the river, are equipped especially with business travellers in mind.

Rooms 40 (1 fmly) (16 GF) S £60-£100; D £80-£120 **Facilities** FTV WiFi Fishing Xmas New Year **Conf** Class 100 Board 50 Thtr 180 Del from £130.50 to £155 **Parking** 65 **Notes** LB Civ Wed 200

Holiday Inn Express Aberdeen

BUDGET HOTEL

tel: 01224 227250
Exhibition & Conference Centre, Parkway East, Bridge of Don AB23 8AJ
email: info@hieaberdeenexhibitioncentre.co.uk **web:** www.hiexpress.co.uk
dir: Follow A90 northbound for Aberdeen Exhibition Conference Centre, located 2m from City Centre

A modern hotel ideal for families and business travellers. Fresh and uncomplicated, the spacious rooms include Sky TV, power shower and tea and coffee-making facilities. Continental buffet breakfast is included in the room rate; other meals may be taken at the nearby family pub or restaurant. See also the Hotel Groups pages.

Rooms 135 (100 fmly) **Conf** Class 16 Board 30 Thtr 48

Premier Inn Aberdeen (Anderson Drive)

BUDGET HOTEL

tel: 0871 527 8006 *(Calls cost 13p per minute plus your phone company's access charge)*
North Anderson Dr AB15 6DW
web: www.premierinn.com
dir: Into Aberdeen from S on A90, follow airport signs. Hotel 1st left after fire station. NB for Sat Nav use AB15 6TP

High quality, budget accommodation ideal for both families and business travellers. Spacious, en suite bedrooms feature tea and coffee making facilities, and Freeview TV in most hotels. Internet access and WiFi are available for a small fee. The adjacent family restaurant features a wide and varied menu. See also the Hotel Groups pages.

Rooms 62

Premier Inn Aberdeen City Centre

BUDGET HOTEL

tel: 0871 527 8008 *(Calls cost 13p per minute plus your phone company's access charge)*
Inverlair House, West North St AB24 5AS
web: www.premierinn.com
dir: A90 onto A9013 into city centre. Take A956 towards King St, 1st left into Meal Market St

Rooms 190

Premier Inn Aberdeen North (Bridge Of Don)

BUDGET HOTEL

tel: 0871 527 8010 *(Calls cost 13p per minute plus your phone company's access charge)*
Ellon Rd, Murcar, Bridge of Don AB23 8BP
web: www.premierinn.com
dir: From city centre take A90 N follow Peterhead signs. At rdbt 2m after Aberdeen Exhibition & Conference Centre, left onto B999. Hotel on right

Rooms 91

Premier Inn Aberdeen South (Portlethen)

BUDGET HOTEL

tel: 0871 527 8012 *(Calls cost 13p per minute plus your phone company's access charge)*
Mains of Balquharn, Portlethen AB12 4QS
web: www.premierinn.com
dir: From A90 follow Portlethen & Badentoy Park signs. Hotel on right

Rooms 92

Premier Inn Aberdeen (Westhill)

BUDGET HOTEL

tel: 0871 527 8004 *(Calls cost 13p per minute plus your phone company's access charge)*
Straik Rd, Westhill AB32 6HF
web: www.premierinn.com
dir: On A944 towards Alford, hotel adjacent to Tesco

Rooms 103

Ibis Aberdeen Centre

AA Advertised

tel: 01224 285820 **15 Shiprow AB11 5BY**
email: H5170@accor.com **web:** www.ibishotel.com

Situated in a convenient location in the heart of Aberdeen, the newly constructed hotel provides a comfortable place to stay in a modern environment. Attractive and spacious bedrooms are equipped with a host of features including flat-screen TVs and WiFi access. Snacks are available 24 hours of the day and breakfast is offered in the stylish restaurant. Parking is available adjacent to the hotel.

Rooms 107 **Facilities** STV FTV WiFi HL **Services** Lift **Notes**

ABERDEEN AIRPORT
City of Aberdeen   Map 23 NJ81

Hallmark Hotel Aberdeen Airport

★★★ 75% HOTEL

tel: 0330 028 3409 **Farburn Ter, Dyce AB21 7DW**
email: aberdeen@hallmarkhotels.co.uk web: www.hallmarkhotels.co.uk
dir: *A96/A947 airport E after 1m turn left at lights. Hotel in 250yds*

This hotel is very convenient for air travellers and for those wishing to explore this lovely Highland area. The spacious, well-equipped bedrooms have all the expected up-to-date amenities. The public areas are welcoming and include a contemporary brasserie. Secure parking and WiFi are also provided.

Rooms 212 (212 annexe) (20 fmly) (107 GF) **Facilities** STV FTV WiFi ⇘ Xmas New Year **Conf** Class 160 Board 120 Thtr 400 **Parking** 150 **Notes** Civ Wed 220

Premier Inn Aberdeen Airport (Dyce)

BUDGET HOTEL

tel: 0871 527 9460 *(Calls cost 13p per minute plus your phone company's access charge)*
Aberdeen Airport Main Terminal, Argyll Way, Dyce AB21 0BN
web: www.premierinn.com
dir: *From N on A96 follow Aberdeen signs. At rdbt 1st exit into Dyce Dr signed Airport. At 2nd lights right into Argyll Rd. Hotel on right. From S on A90 follow Airport & A96 signs. Take A96 (Inverurie road) at 2nd rdbt 3rd exit into Dyce Drive then proceed as above*

High quality, budget accommodation ideal for both families and business travellers. Spacious, en suite bedrooms feature tea and coffee making facilities, and Freeview TV in most hotels. Internet access and WiFi are available for a small fee. The adjacent family restaurant features a wide and varied menu. See also the Hotel Groups pages.

Rooms 100

ABERFOYLE
Stirling   Map 20 NN50

Macdonald Forest Hills Hotel & Resort

★★★★ 79% ⊛ HOTEL

tel: 01877 389500 & 0344 879 9057 **Kinlochard FK8 3TL**
email: general.foresthills@macdonald-hotels.co.uk
web: www.macdonald-hotels.co.uk/foresthills
dir: *A84, A873, A81 to Aberfoyle onto B829*

Situated in the heart of The Trossachs with wonderful views of Loch Ard, this popular hotel forms part of a resort complex offering a range of indoor and outdoor facilities. The main hotel has relaxing lounges and a restaurant that all overlook the landscaped gardens. A separate building houses the leisure centre, lounge bar and bistro.

Rooms 55 (16 fmly) (12 GF) ⋔ **Facilities** Spa STV FTV WiFi ⊗ ⥈ Gym Children's club Snooker Watersports Quad biking Archery Clay pigeon shooting ♫ Xmas New Year **Conf** Class 60 Board 20 Thtr 120 **Services** Lift **Parking** 100 **Notes** Civ Wed 100

ABERLADY
East Lothian   Map 21 NT47

Ducks Inn

⊛⊛ RESTAURANT WITH ROOMS

tel: 01875 870682 **Main St EH32 0RE**
email: kilspindie@ducks.co.uk web: www.ducks.co.uk
dir: *A1 (Bankton junct) take 1st exit to North Berwick. At next rdbt 3rd exit onto A198 signed Longniddry, left towards Aberlady. At T-junct, facing river, right to Aberlady*

The name of this restaurant with rooms is referenced around the building - Ducks Restaurant for award-winning cuisine; Donald's Bistro and the Ducklings informal coffee shop. The warm and welcoming public areas include a great bar offering real ales and various objets d'art. The bedrooms are comfortable and well-appointed with stylish en suites. The team are informal and friendly, taking the time to chat to their guests.

Rooms 23 (1 fmly)

ABINGTON MOTORWAY SERVICE AREA (M74)
South Lanarkshire   Map 21 NS92

Days Inn Abington - M74

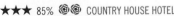

AA Advertised

tel: 01864 502782 **ML12 6RG**
email: abington.hotel@welcomebreak.co.uk web: www.welcomebreak.co.uk
dir: *M74 junct 13, accessible from N'bound and S'bound carriageways*

This modern building offers accommodation in smart, spacious and well-equipped bedrooms, suitable for families and business travellers, and all with en suite bathrooms. Continental breakfast is available and other refreshments may be taken at the nearby family restaurant.

Rooms 54 (50 fmly) (4 smoking) **Facilities** FTV WiFi ⇘ **Conf** Board 10 **Parking** 100

ANSTRUTHER
Fife   Map 21 NO50

The Waterfront

RESTAURANT WITH ROOMS

tel: 01333 312200 **18-20 Shore St KY10 3EA**
email: info@anstruther-waterfront.co.uk web: www.anstruther-waterfront.co.uk
dir: *Off A917 opposite marina*

Situated overlooking the harbour, The Waterfront offers spacious, stylish, contemporary accommodation, with bedrooms located in lovingly restored buildings in a courtyard behind the restaurant. There is a comfortable lounge with a smartly fitted kitchen and dining room, and laundry facilities are available in the granary. Dinner and breakfast are served in the attractive restaurant that offers a comprehensive menu featuring the best of local produce.

Rooms 10 (3 fmly)

ARDUAINE
Argyll & Bute   Map 20 NM71

Loch Melfort Hotel

★★★ 85% ⊛⊛ COUNTRY HOUSE HOTEL

tel: 01852 200233 **PA34 4XG**
email: reception@lochmelfort.co.uk web: www.lochmelfort.co.uk
dir: *On A816, midway between Oban & Lochgilphead*

Enjoying one of the finest locations on the West Coast, this popular, family-run hotel has outstanding views across Asknish Bay towards the Islands of Jura, Scarba and

Shuna. Accommodation is provided in either the balconied rooms of the Cedar wing or the more traditional rooms in the main hotel. Dining options include the main restaurant with stunning views or the more informal bistro.

Rooms 25 (20 annexe) (2 fmly) (10 GF) ↝ S £144-£204; **D** £228-£328 (incl. bkfst & dinner)* **Facilities** WiFi ⇘ 4 moorings Childrens' play park ♫ Xmas New Year **Conf** Class 40 Board 20 Thtr 50 **Parking** 50 **Notes** LB Closed 3 wks beginning Dec & 3 wks mid Jan RS Winter Civ Wed 100

AUCHENCAIRN	Map 21 NX75
Dumfries & Galloway	

HIGHLY RECOMMENDED

Balcary Bay Hotel

★★★ 88% ◉◉ HOTEL

tel: 01556 640217 & 640311 **Shore Rd DG7 1QZ**
email: reservations@balcary-bay-hotel.co.uk **web:** www.balcary-bay-hotel.co.uk
dir: On A711 between Dalbeattie & Kirkcudbright, hotel 2m from Auchencairn

Taking its name from the bay on which it lies, this hotel has lawns running down to the shore. The larger bedrooms enjoy stunning views over the bay, while others overlook the gardens. The comfortable public areas are very relaxing. Imaginative dishes feature at dinner, accompanied by a good wine list.

Rooms 20 (1 fmly) (3 GF) ↝ S £86; **D** £154-£186 (incl. bkfst) **Facilities** FTV WiFi **Parking** 50 **Notes** Closed 1st Sun Dec-1st Fri Feb

AUCHTERARDER	Map 21 NN91
Perth & Kinross	

INSPECTORS' CHOICE

The Gleneagles Hotel

★★★★★ ◉◉◉◉ HOTEL

tel: 01764 662231 & 0800 169 2984 **PH3 1NF**
email: resort.sales@gleneagles.com **web:** www.gleneagles.com
dir: Off A9 at exit for A823 follow signs for Gleneagles Hotel

With its international reputation for high standards, this grand hotel provides something for everyone. A recent change of ownership has resulted in many areas being refurbished. Set in 850 acres of glorious countryside, Gleneagles offers a peaceful retreat, as well as many sporting activities, including the famous championship golf courses. All bedrooms are appointed to a high standard and offer both traditional and contemporary styles. Stylish public areas include various dining options: the Deseo 'Mediterranean Food Market' eaterie; The Strathearn, with two AA Rosettes; as well as inspired cooking at Andrew Fairlie at Gleneagles, a restaurant with four AA Rosettes. There's also the Clubhouse and many bars. The award-winning ESPA spa offers the very latest treatments to restore both body and soul. Service is always professional - the staff are friendly and nothing is too much trouble.

Rooms 232 (115 fmly) (11 GF) **D** fr £255 (incl. bkfst)* **Facilities** Spa STV FTV WiFi ⇘ ⏣ supervised ⚲ supervised ⚲ 54 ⚲ Putt green Fishing ⚲ Gym Falconry Off-road driving Golf Archery Clay shooting Gundog School Horse riding Xmas New Year **Conf** Class 240 Board 60 Thtr 360 **Services** Lift **Parking** 300 **Notes** Civ Wed 360

AVIEMORE	Map 23 NH81
Highland	

Macdonald Aviemore Resort

★★★★ 74% HOTEL   MACDONALD HOTELS & RESORTS

tel: 01479 815100 **PH22 1PN**
email: general@aviemorehighlandresort.com **web:** www.macdonald-hotels.co.uk
dir: From N: Exit A9 to Aviemore (B970). Right at T-junct, through village. Right (2nd exit) at 1st rdbt into Macdonald Aviemore Highland Resort, follow reception signs. From S: Exit A9 to Aviemore, left at T-junct. Immediately after Esso garage, turn left into Resort

The Highlands Hotel is part of the Macdonald Aviemore Resort, which boasts a wide range of activities including a championship golf course. The modern, well-equipped bedrooms suit business, leisure guests and families, and the Scottish Steakhouse offers a fantastic selection of grilled dishes. In addition there is a state-of-the-art gym, spa treatments and a 25 metre pool with a wave machine and flume.

Rooms 151 (10 fmly) (44 GF) **Facilities** Spa STV FTV WiFi ⇘ ⏣ supervised ⚲ 18 Putt green Fishing Gym Steam room Sauna Children's indoor & outdoor playgrounds Xmas New Year **Conf** Class 610 Board 38 Thtr 1000 **Services** Lift **Parking** 500 **Notes** ⊗ Civ Wed 300

AYR	Map 20 NS32
South Ayrshire	

Enterkine Country House

★★★★ 75% ◉◉ COUNTRY HOUSE HOTEL

tel: 01292 520580 **Annbank KA6 5AL**
email: mail@enterkine.com **web:** www.enterkine.com
dir: 5m E of Ayr on B743

This luxurious art deco country mansion dates from the 1930s and retains many original features, notably some splendid bathroom suites. The focus is very much on dining, and in country house tradition there is no bar, drinks being served in the elegant lounge and library. The well-proportioned bedrooms are furnished and equipped to high standards, many with lovely countryside views.

Rooms 14 (8 annexe) (2 fmly) (3 GF) ↝ S £60-£120; **D** £70-£130 (incl. bkfst) **Facilities** FTV WiFi Xmas New Year **Conf** Class 140 Board 140 Thtr 200 Del from £140 to £180 **Parking** 40 **Notes** LB Civ Wed 250

A

AYR *continued*

Fairfield House Hotel

★★★★ 74% HOTEL

tel: 01292 267461 **12 Fairfield Rd KA7 2AS**
email: reservations@fairfieldhotel.co.uk **web:** www.fairfieldhotel.co.uk
dir: *From A77 towards Ayr South (A30). Follow town centre signs, down Miller Rd, left, then right into Fairfield Rd*

Situated in a leafy cul-de-sac close to the esplanade, this hotel enjoys stunning seascapes towards the Isle of Arran. Bedrooms are in either modern or classical styles, the latter featuring impressive bathrooms. Public areas provide stylish, modern rooms in which to relax. Skilfully prepared meals are served in the casual brasserie or elegant restaurant.

Rooms 44 (4 annexe) (3 fmly) (9 GF) **Facilities** FTV WiFi ↳ ⊕ supervised Gym Fitness room Sauna Steam room Xmas New Year **Conf** Class 80 Board 40 Thtr 120 **Services** Lift **Parking** 50 **Notes** ⊗ Civ Wed 150

Mercure Ayr Hotel

★★★ 78% HOTEL

tel: 0844 815 9005 *(Calls cost 5p per minute plus your phone company's access charge)*
Dalblair Rd KA7 1UG
email: info@mercureayr.co.uk **web:** www.mercureayr.co.uk
dir: *M77 towards Prestwick Airport, then A77 Ayr, 1st rdbt 3rd exit, 2nd rdbt straight over, left at lights, then 2nd lights turn left, bottom of road turn right, hotel on left*

This hotel is situated in a central location in Ayr, and many bedrooms benefit from sea views. The property is ideally located for both business and leisure travellers and the area boasts many golf courses within easy reach; indeed the hotel even has its own golf simulator. Bedrooms and bathrooms are presented to a modern standard with a range of extras including free WiFi. A leisure club and Brasserie restaurant are also provided for guests.

Rooms 118 (4 fmly) ↟ **Facilities** FTV WiFi ↳ ⊕ supervised Gym Beauty treatment room **Conf** Class 45 Board 45 Thtr 200 **Services** Lift **Parking** 45 **Notes** ⊗ Civ Wed 75

Premier Inn Ayr A77/Racecourse

BUDGET HOTEL

tel: 0871 527 9416 *(Calls cost 13p per minute plus your phone company's access charge)*
Wheatpark Place KA8 9RT
web: www.premierinn.com
dir: *Phone for directions*

High quality, budget accommodation ideal for both families and business travellers. Spacious, en suite bedrooms feature tea and coffee making facilities, and Freeview TV in most hotels. Internet access and WiFi are available for a small fee. The adjacent family restaurant features a wide and varied menu. See also the Hotel Groups pages.

Rooms 84

Premier Inn Ayr/Prestwick Airport

BUDGET HOTEL

tel: 0871 527 8038 *(Calls cost 13p per minute plus your phone company's access charge)*
Kilmarnock Rd, Monkton KA9 2RJ
web: www.premierinn.com
dir: *At Dutch House Rdbt (at junct of A77 & A78) at Monkton*

Rooms 64

BALLANTRAE	Map 20 NX08
South Ayrshire	

INSPECTORS' CHOICE

Glenapp Castle

★★★★★ ⊛⊛⊛ HOTEL

tel: 01465 831212 **KA26 ONZ**
email: enquiries@glenappcastle.com **web:** www.glenappcastle.com
dir: *S through Ballantrae, cross bridge over River Stinchar, 1st right, hotel gates 1m*

Friendly hospitality and attentive service prevail at this stunning Victorian castle, set in extensive private grounds to the south of the village. Impeccably furnished bedrooms are graced with antiques and period pieces, and include two master rooms and a ground-floor family suite. Breathtaking views of Arran and Ailsa Craig can be enjoyed from the delightful, sumptuous day rooms and from many of the bedrooms. Guests should make a point of walking round the wonderful 36-acre grounds, and take a look at the azalea pond, walled vegetable gardens and restored Victorian greenhouses.

Rooms 24 (2 fmly) (7 GF) ↟ S £275-£485; **D** £450-£670 (incl. bkfst & dinner)*
Facilities FTV WiFi ↳ ⊛ ⊶ Woodland walks Falconry Archery Photography Stargazing New Year **Conf** Class 12 Board 25 Thtr 25 **Services** Lift **Parking** 20 **Notes** LB Civ Wed 40

BALLATER
Aberdeenshire
Map 23 N039

Loch Kinord Hotel
★★★ 79% ⏣ HOTEL

tel: 01339 885229 **Ballater Rd, Dinnet AB34 5JY**
email: stay@lochkinord.com web: www.lochkinord.com
dir: *Between Aboyne & Ballater, on A93, in Dinnet*

Family-run, this roadside hotel is well located for leisure and sporting pursuits. It has lots of character and a friendly atmosphere. There are two bars, one outside and a cosy one inside, plus a dining room with a bold colour scheme. Bedrooms are stylish and have smart bathrooms.

Rooms 20 (3 fmly) (4 GF) ⏣ **Facilities** FTV WiFi ⏃ Xmas **Conf** Class 30 Board 30 Thtr 40 **Parking** 20 **Notes** Civ Wed 50

BALLOCH
West Dunbartonshire
Map 20 NS38

Cameron House on Loch Lomond
★★★★★ 84% ⏣⏣ HOTEL

tel: 01389 755565 **G83 8QZ**
email: reservations@cameronhouse.co.uk web: www.cameronhouse.co.uk
dir: *M8 W junct 30 for Erskine Bridge. A82 for Crainlarich. 14m, at rdbt signed Luss, hotel on right*

Enjoying an idyllic location on the banks of Loch Lomond in over 100 acres of wooded parkland, this stylish hotel offers an excellent range of leisure facilities. These include two golf courses, a world-class spa and a host of indoor and outdoor sporting activities. A choice of restaurants and bars cater for all tastes and include the Scottish-themed Cameron Grill and a fine dining operation, Martin Wishart at Loch Lomond. Bedrooms are stylish, well equipped and many boast wonderful loch views.

Rooms 132 (9 fmly) (18 GF) ⏣ **S** £149-£375; **D** £159-£385 (incl. bkfst)*
Facilities Spa STV WiFi ⏃ HL ⏃ supervised ⏃ 27 ⏃ Fishing ⏃ Gym Squash Motor boat Hairdresser Sea plane Falconry Archery Segways Rib boat Jet Skis Xmas New Year **Conf** Class 180 Board 80 Thtr 300 Del from £195 to £395* **Services** Lift Air con **Parking** 200 **Notes** LB Civ Wed 200

BANCHORY
Aberdeenshire
Map 23 N069

Burnett Arms Hotel
★★★ 74% SMALL HOTEL

tel: 01330 824944 **25 High St AB31 5TD**
email: theburnett@btconnect.com web: www.bw-burnettarms.co.uk
dir: *Town centre on N side of A93*

This popular hotel is located in the heart of the town centre and gives easy access to the many attractions of Royal Deeside. Public areas include a choice of eating and drinking options, with food served in the restaurant, bar and foyer lounge. Bedrooms are thoughtfully equipped and comfortably modern.

Rooms 18 (1 fmly) ⏣ **Facilities** STV FTV WiFi Xmas New Year **Conf** Class 50 Board 50 Thtr 100 **Parking** 22 **Notes** LB

BATHGATE
West Lothian
Map 21 NS96

Premier Inn Livingston (Bathgate)
BUDGET HOTEL

tel: 0871 527 8630 *(Calls cost 13p per minute plus your phone company's access charge)*
Starlaw Rd EH48 1LQ
web: www.premierinn.com
dir: *M8 junct 3A. At 1st rdbt 1st exit (Bathgate). Over bridge, at 2nd rdbt take 1st exit. Hotel 200yds on left*

High quality, budget accommodation ideal for both families and business travellers. Spacious, en suite bedrooms feature tea and coffee making facilities, and Freeview TV in most hotels. Internet access and WiFi are available for a small fee. The adjacent family restaurant features a wide and varied menu. See also the Hotel Groups pages.

Rooms 74

B

BEAULY
Highland **Map 23 NH54**

Priory Hotel
★★★ 75% HOTEL

tel: 01463 782309 & 784920 **The Square IV4 7BX**
email: reservations@priory-hotel.com **web:** www.priory-hotel.com
dir: *Signed from A832, into Beauly, hotel in square on left*

This popular hotel occupies a central location in the town square. Standard and executive rooms are on offer, both providing a good level of comfort and range of facilities. Food is served throughout the day in the modern and comfortable open-plan public areas, with menus offering a first rate choice.

Rooms 38 (3 fmly) (1 GF) ♒ **S** £62.50-£75; **D** £87.50-£115 (incl. bkfst)*
Facilities STV FTV WiFi Xmas New Year **Conf** Class 40 Board 30 Thtr 40 **Services** Lift
Parking 20 **Notes** LB ⊗

BLANTYRE
South Lanarkshire **Map 20 NS65**

Crossbasket Castle
Ⓤ

tel: 01698 829461 **Crossbasket Estate, Stoneymeadow Rd G72 9UE**
email: info@crossbasketcastle.com **web:** www.crossbasketcastle.com
dir: *In High Blantyre close to East Kilbride & the M80/ M74 motorways*

Currently the rating for this establishment is not confirmed. This may be due to a change of ownership or because it has only recently joined the AA rating scheme. For further details please see the AA website: theAA.com

Rooms 9 ♒ **S** £230-£495; **D** £250-£495 (incl. bkfst)* **Facilities** FTV WiFi ⅃ Fishing In room spa treatment ♫ **Conf** Class 150 Board 30 Thtr 350 Del £450* **Services** Lift
Parking 56 **Notes** Civ Wed 300

CALLANDER
Stirling **Map 20 NN60**

Roman Camp Country House Hotel
★★★★ 78% ⊛⊛⊛ COUNTRY HOUSE HOTEL

tel: 01877 330003 **FK17 8BG**
email: mail@romancamphotel.co.uk **web:** www.romancamphotel.co.uk
dir: *N on A84, left at east end of High Street. 300yds to hotel*

Built in the 17th century and originally used as a shooting lodge, this charming country house has a rich history, and has been in the same ownership for over twenty years. Twenty acres of gardens and grounds lead down to the River Teith, and the town centre and its attractions are only a short walk away. Each bedroom is individually and elegantly designed, and offers much pampering comfort. Food is a

highlight of any stay and menus are dominated by high-quality Scottish produce that is sensitively treated by the talented kitchen team. Real fires warm the atmospheric public areas and service is friendly yet professional.

Rooms 15 (4 fmly) (7 GF) ♒ **Facilities** STV FTV WiFi ⅃ Fishing Xmas New Year
Conf Class 60 Board 30 Thtr 120 **Parking** 80 **Notes** LB Civ Wed 150

CLYDEBANK
West Dumbartonshire **Map 20 NS47**

Golden Jubilee Conference Hotel
★★★★ 75% ⊛ HOTEL

tel: 0141 951 6000 **Beardmore St G81 4SA**
email: hotel@goldenjubilee.scot.nhs.uk **web:** www.goldenjubileehotel.com
dir: *M8 junct 19, follow signs for Clydeside Expressway to Glasgow road, then A814 (Dumbarton road), then follow Clydebank Business Park signs. Hotel on left*

Attracting plenty of business and conference custom, this stylish modern hotel lies beside the River Clyde and shares an impressive site with a hospital (although the latter does not intrude). Spacious and imposing public areas include a stylish restaurant that provides innovative contemporary Scottish cooking; the recently added Central Plaza café; and The BBar lounge which offers a more extensive choice of lighter dishes. The leisure facilities include a 15-metre swimming pool, sauna and steam room. All bedrooms come with iMac entertainment systems. The hotel also has a keenly-adhered-to environmental policy.

Rooms 168 **Facilities** STV FTV WiFi ⅃ ⊛ supervised Gym Sauna Steam room Xmas
New Year **Conf** Class 84 Board 27 Thtr 240 **Services** Lift Air con **Parking** 300
Notes ⊗ Civ Wed 170

COMRIE
Perth & Kinross **Map 21 NN72**

Royal Hotel
★★★ 80% ⊛ SMALL HOTEL

tel: 01764 679200 **Melville Square PH6 2DN**
email: reception@royalhotel.co.uk **web:** www.royalhotel.co.uk
dir: *A9 on A822 to Crieff, then B827 to Comrie. Hotel in main square on A85*

The traditional façade gives little indication of the style and elegance to be found inside this long-established hotel located in the village centre. Public areas include a bar and library, a bright modern restaurant and a conservatory-style brasserie. The bedrooms are tastefully appointed and furnished with smart reproduction antiques.

Rooms 13 (2 annexe) **Facilities** STV WiFi Fishing Shooting arranged New Year
Conf Class 10 Board 20 Thtr 20 **Parking** 22 **Notes** Closed 25-26 Dec

CONNEL
Argyll & Bute **Map 20 NM93**

Falls of Lora Hotel
★★★ 73% HOTEL

THE INDEPENDENTS
HOTEL ASSOCIATION

tel: 01631 710483 **Connel Ferry PA37 1PB**
email: enquiries@fallsoflora.com **web:** www.fallsoflora.com

(For full entry see Oban)

COVE
Argyll & Bute
Map 20 NS28

Knockderry House Hotel

★★★★ 76% ◉◉ SMALL HOTEL

---

tel: 01436 842283 **Shore Rd G84 ONX**
email: info@knockderryhouse.co.uk **web:** www.knockderryhouse.co.uk
dir: *A82 to Lochlomondside, left onto A817 signed Garelochhead, through Glen Fruin to A814. Follow Coulport signs. At Coulport left at rdbt, 2m to hotel*

Knockderry House is a stunning example of a mid-19th-century home and features a host of stunning architectural features from famed architect William Leiper. Public areas are warm and welcoming, many featuring original stained-glass windows. Set in expansive grounds with beautiful views of Loch Long, the hotel features modern bedrooms and bathrooms. Hospitality is key to the hotel's success, and friendly staff deliver a high level of personalised service. Scotland's larder is well represented by the output from the kitchen.

Rooms 15 (1 fmly) 🅟 **S** £165-£200; **D** £230-£295ᴬ **Facilities** FTV WiFi New Year **Conf** Class 20 Board 24 Thtr 30 **Parking** 15 **Notes** LB Closed 11-26 Dec Civ Wed 40

CUMBERNAULD
North Lanarkshire
Map 21 NS77

The Westerwood Hotel & Golf Resort

QHOTELS
INSPIRED BY YOU

★★★★ 81% ◉ HOTEL

---

tel: 01236 457171 **1 St Andrews Dr, Westerwood G68 0EW**
email: westerwood@qhotels.co.uk **web:** www.qhotels.co.uk
dir: *M80 junct 6, follow signs for hotel*

This stylish, contemporary hotel enjoys an elevated position within 400 acres at the foot of the Campsie Hills. Accommodation is provided in spacious, bright bedrooms, many with super bathrooms, and day rooms include sumptuous lounges and an airy restaurant; extensive golf, fitness and conference facilities are available.

Rooms 148 (16 fmly) (49 GF) **Facilities** Spa STV WiFi ♦ ⊛ ⅃ 18 ⌗ Putt green Gym Beauty salon Relaxation room Sauna Steam room Xmas New Year **Conf** Class 120 Board 60 Thtr 400 **Services** Lift **Parking** 250 **Notes** Civ Wed 350

Premier Inn Glasgow (Cumbernauld)

BUDGET HOTEL

---

tel: 0871 527 8424 *(Calls cost 13p per minute plus your phone company's access charge)*
4 South Muirhead Rd G67 1AX
web: www.premierinn.com
dir: *From A80, A8011 follow Cumbernauld & town centre signs. Hotel opposite Asda & McDonalds*

High quality, budget accommodation ideal for both families and business travellers. Spacious, en suite bedrooms feature tea and coffee making facilities, and Freeview TV in most hotels. Internet access and WiFi are available for a small fee. The adjacent family restaurant features a wide and varied menu. See also the Hotel Groups pages.

Rooms 37

DALKEITH
Midlothian
Map 21 NT36

Premier Inn Edinburgh A7 (Dalkeith)

BUDGET HOTEL

---

tel: 0871 527 9290 *(Calls cost 13p per minute plus your phone company's access charge)*
Melville Dykes Rd EH18 1AN
web: www.premierinn.com
dir: *Exit A720 at Sheriffhall rdbt onto A7 signed Galashiels/Harwick/Carlisle. At 2nd rdbt take 3rd exit into Melville Dykes Rd (A768). Hotel on left*

High quality, budget accommodation ideal for both families and business travellers. Spacious, en suite bedrooms feature tea and coffee making facilities, and Freeview TV in most hotels. Internet access and WiFi are available for a small fee. The adjacent family restaurant features a wide and varied menu. See also the Hotel Groups pages.

Rooms 40

D

DORNOCH
Highland
Map 23 NH78

Dornoch Castle Hotel

★★★ 78% ◉ HOTEL

---

tel: 01862 810216 **Castle St IV25 3SD**
email: enquiries@dornochcastlehotel.com **web:** www.dornochcastlehotel.com
dir: *2m N of Dornoch Bridge on A9, turn right to Dornoch. Hotel in village centre*

Situated opposite the cathedral, this fully restored ancient castle has become a popular wedding venue. Within the original castle are some splendid themed bedrooms, and elsewhere the more modern bedrooms have all of the expected facilities. There is a character bar and a delightful conservatory restaurant overlooking the garden.

Rooms 23 (3 fmly) (4 GF) 🅟 **S** £65-£75; **D** £129-£185 (incl. bkfst)* **Facilities** FTV WiFi New Year **Conf** Class 40 Board 30 Thtr 60 **Parking** 16 **Notes** ⊗ Closed 24-26 Dec RS early Nov-mid Mar Civ Wed 80

DRYMEN
Stirling
Map 20 NS48

Best Western Buchanan Arms Hotel & Spa

BW Best Western.

★★★ 79% HOTEL

---

tel: 01360 660588 **23 Main St G63 0BQ**
email: info@buchananarms.co.uk **web:** www.buchananarms.co.uk

There has been a lodging on this site since 1760 and although the hotel has significantly changed in this time, it continues to enjoy an excellent location in the heart of the Loch Lomond and Troassachs National Park. Modern bedrooms are complimented by attractive public areas including a spacious conservatory lounge. The Salmon Leap restaurant offers relaxed dining, while the Relax Leisure Club and Haven Spa is the perfect place to kick back and chill out.

Rooms 52 (12 fmly) (4 GF) **Facilities** Spa FTV WiFi ♦ ⊛ Gym Xmas New Year **Conf** Class 80 Board 60 Thtr 200 **Notes** LB ⊗ Civ Wed 180

D

DRYMEN *continued*

Winnock Hotel

★★★ 74% HOTEL

tel: 01360 660245 **The Square G63 OBL**
email: info@winnockhotel.com **web:** www.winnockhotel.com
dir: *From S: M74 onto M8 junct 16b through Glasgow. Follow A809 to Aberfoyle*

Occupying a prominent position overlooking the village green, this popular hotel offers well-equipped bedrooms of various sizes and styles. The public rooms include a bar, a lounge and an attractive formal dining room that serves dishes of good, locally sourced food.

Rooms 73 (18 fmly) (19 GF) 🛏 **S** £39-£89; **D** £128-£178 (incl. bkfst)* **Facilities** FTV WiFi ⛵ Xmas New Year **Conf** Class 60 Board 70 Thtr 140 Del from £69 to £129* **Parking** 60 **Notes** LB ⊗ Civ Wed 150

| DUMBARTON | Map 20 NS37 |
| East Dunbartonshire | |

Premier Inn Dumbarton/Loch Lomond

BUDGET HOTEL

tel: 0871 527 9274 *(Calls cost 13p per minute plus your phone company's access charge)*
Lomondgate Dr G82 2QU
web: www.premierinn.com
dir: *From Glasgow follow A82 towards Crainlarich, right at Lomondgate rdbt onto A813, hotel on right. From N: A82 towards Glasgow, left at Lomondgate rdbt onto A813, hotel on right*

High quality, budget accommodation ideal for both families and business travellers. Spacious, en suite bedrooms feature tea and coffee making facilities, and Freeview TV in most hotels. Internet access and WiFi are available for a small fee. The adjacent family restaurant features a wide and varied menu. See also the Hotel Groups pages.

Rooms 60

| DUMFRIES | Map 21 NX97 |
| Dumfries & Galloway | |

Cairndale Hotel & Leisure Club

★★★ 77% HOTEL

tel: 01387 254111 **English St DG1 2DF**
email: sales@cairndalehotel.co.uk **web:** www.cairndalehotel.co.uk
dir: *From S on M6 take A75 to Dumfries, left at 1st rdbt, cross rail bridge to lights, hotel 1st building on left*

Within walking distance of the town centre, this hotel provides a wide range of amenities, including leisure facilities and an impressive conference and entertainment centre. Bedrooms range from stylish suites to cosy singles. There's a choice of eating options in the evening. The Reivers Restaurant is smartly modern with food to match.

Rooms 91 (22 fmly) (5 GF) 🛏 **S** £69-£129; **D** £89-£169 (incl. bkfst) **Facilities** STV WiFi ⛲ supervised Gym Steam room Sauna Beauty treatment room 🎵 Xmas New Year **Conf** Class 150 Board 50 Thtr 300 **Services** Lift **Parking** 100 **Notes** LB Civ Wed 300

Premier Inn Dumfries

BUDGET HOTEL

tel: 0871 527 8316 *(Calls cost 13p per minute plus your phone company's access charge)*
Annan Rd, Collin DG1 3JX
web: www.premierinn.com
dir: *At rdbt junct of Euroroute bypass (A75) & A780*

High quality, budget accommodation ideal for both families and business travellers. Spacious, en suite bedrooms feature tea and coffee making facilities, and Freeview TV in most hotels. Internet access and WiFi are available for a small fee. The adjacent family restaurant features a wide and varied menu. See also the Hotel Groups pages.

Rooms 82

| DUNBLANE | Map 21 NN70 |
| Stirling | |

AA HOTEL OF THE YEAR
FOR SCOTLAND 2016-2017

Cromlix and Chez Roux

★★★★★ 86% ◉◉◉ ⬤ COUNTRY HOUSE HOTEL

tel: 01786 822125 **Kinbuck FK15 9JT**
email: enquiries@cromlix.com **web:** www.cromlix.com
dir: *M9 towards Stirling/Perth, bypassing Stirling & Dunblane (A9 heading for Perth). Take the turn-off signposted Dunblane/Kinbuck on the B8033. Turn right at the junct for Kinbuck. Follow road through village & continue over the bridge. Entrance gates are 100 yards on left*

Recently purchased by tennis player Andy Murray – who was born in nearby Dunblane – this stunning hotel has been transformed and refurbished to a luxurious standard. Expansive grounds provide seclusion and relaxation and feature a kitchen garden, a loch (stocked with trout; rods available) and tennis court done out in Wimbledon colours. Bedrooms have been lovingly restored and include a number of unique suites. The hotel has its own chapel, a number of welcoming lounges and a billiards room. The modern, light dining space features an open kitchen where guests can observe some masterful cooking being prepared. Service is delivered to an impeccable standard.

Rooms 15 **S** fr £160; **D** fr £180 (incl. bkfst)* **Facilities** FTV WiFi ⛵ ♨ Fishing Archery Falconry display Snooker Outdoor garden games In room spa treatments **Conf** Class 26 Board 26 Thtr 60 Del from £300* **Parking** 51 **Notes** LB ⊗ Civ Wed 50

| DUNDEE | Map 21 NO43 |
| City of Dundee | |

Malmaison Dundee

★★★★ 80% ◉ HOTEL

Malmaison
hotels that dare to be different

tel: 0844 693 0661 *(Calls cost 5p per minute plus your phone company's access charge)*
44 Whitehall Crescent DD1 4AY
web: www.malmaison.com
dir: *A90, right onto riverfront, past airport & adj to train station*

This iconic building has been delightfully restored, and with its gold top, it shines as a beacon of style and quality. Lovingly restored, the public areas are stylish and plush, the staircase is very notable for its ironwork, and the restaurant for its views. Bedrooms are very well appointed and the hotel has a number of meeting rooms available. Cuisine is a feature and a range of menu options are on offer.

Rooms 91 🛏 **Facilities** FTV WiFi Xmas New Year **Conf** Thtr 170 **Services** Lift Air con

Premier Inn Dundee Centre

BUDGET HOTEL

tel: 0871 527 8320 *(Calls cost 13p per minute plus your phone company's access charge)*
Discovery Quay, Riverside Dr DD1 4XA
web: www.premierinn.com
dir: *Follow signs for Discovery Quay, hotel on waterfront*

High quality, budget accommodation ideal for both families and business travellers. Spacious, en suite bedrooms feature tea and coffee making facilities, and Freeview TV in most hotels. Internet access and WiFi are available for a small fee. The adjacent family restaurant features a wide and varied menu. See also the Hotel Groups pages.

Rooms 40

Premier Inn Dundee East

BUDGET HOTEL

tel: 0871 527 8322 *(Calls cost 13p per minute plus your phone company's access charge)*
115-117 Lawers Dr, Panmurefield Village, Broughty Ferry DD5 3UP
web: www.premierinn.com
dir: *From N: A92 (Dundee & Arbroath). Hotel 1.5m after Sainsbury's. From S: A90. At end of dual carriageway follow Dundee to Arbroath signs*

Rooms 59

Premier Inn Dundee (Monifieth)

BUDGET HOTEL

tel: 0871 527 8318 *(Calls cost 13p per minute plus your phone company's access charge)*
Ethiebeaton Park, Arbroath Rd, Monifieth DD5 4HB
web: www.premierinn.com
dir: *From A90 (Kingsway Rd) follow Carnoustie/Arbroath (A92) signs*

Rooms 40

Premier Inn Dundee North

BUDGET HOTEL

tel: 0871 527 8324 *(Calls cost 13p per minute plus your phone company's access charge)*
Camperdown Leisure Park, Dayton Dr, Kingsway DD2 3SQ
web: www.premierinn.com
dir: *2m N of city centre on A90 at junct with A923, adjacent to cinema. At entrance to Camperdown Country Park*

Rooms 78

Premier Inn Dundee West

BUDGET HOTEL

tel: 0871 527 8326 *(Calls cost 13p per minute plus your phone company's access charge)*
Kingsway West DD2 5JU
web: www.premierinn.com
dir: *On A90 towards Aberdeen adjacent to Technology Park rdbt*

Rooms 87

DUNFERMLINE Map 21 NT08
Fife

King Malcolm Hotel

★★★ 74% HOTEL

tel: 01383 722611 **Queensferry Rd KY11 8DS**
email: info@kingmalcolm-hotel-dunfermline.com **web:** www.peelhotels.co.uk
dir: *On A823, S of town*

Located to the south of the city, this purpose-built hotel remains popular with business clientele and is convenient for access to both Edinburgh and Fife. Public rooms include a smart foyer lounge and a conservatory bar, as well as a restaurant. Bedrooms, although not large, are well laid out and well equipped.

Rooms 48 (2 fmly) (24 GF) **Facilities** STV WiFi ♫ Xmas New Year **Conf** Class 60 Board 50 Thtr 150 **Parking** 60 **Notes** Civ Wed 120

Premier Inn Dunfermline

BUDGET HOTEL

tel: 0871 527 8328 *(Calls cost 13p per minute plus your phone company's access charge)*
4-12 Whimbrel Place, Fife Leisure Park KY11 8EX
web: www.premierinn.com
dir: *M90 junct 3 (Forth Road Bridge exit) 1st left at lights signed Duloch Park. 1st left into Fife Leisure Park*

High quality, budget accommodation ideal for both families and business travellers. Spacious, en suite bedrooms feature tea and coffee making facilities, and Freeview TV in most hotels. Internet access and WiFi are available for a small fee. The adjacent family restaurant features a wide and varied menu. See also the Hotel Groups pages.

Rooms 78

DUNOON Map 20 NS17
Argyll & Bute

Selborne Hotel

★★★ 73% HOTEL

tel: 01369 702761 **Clyde St, West Bay PA23 7HU**
email: selborne.dunoon@alfatravel.co.uk **web:** www.leisureplex.co.uk
dir: *From Caledonian MacBrayne pier. Past castle, left into Jane St, right into Clyde St. Ferry crossing to Dunoon via Greenock*

This holiday hotel is situated overlooking the West Bay and provides unrestricted views of the Clyde Estuary towards the Isles of Cumbrae. Tour groups are especially well catered for in this good-value establishment, which offers entertainment most nights. Bedrooms are comfortable and many have sea views.

Rooms 98 (6 fmly) (14 GF) ⚓ **S** £36-£55; **D** £56-£94 (incl. bkfst)* **Facilities** FTV WiFi ⬳ HL Pool table Table tennis ♫ Xmas New Year **Services** Lift **Parking** 30 **Notes** LB ⊗ Closed Dec-Feb (ex Xmas/New Year) RS Nov & Mar

EAST KILBRIDE
South Lanarkshire   Map 20 NS65

Macdonald Crutherland House
★★★★ 74% HOTEL

tel: 01355 577000 & 0344 879 9039 **Strathaven Rd G75 0QZ**
email: crutherland@macdonald-hotels.co.uk
web: www.macdonaldhotels.co.uk/crutherland
dir: Follow A726 signed Strathaven, straight over Torrance rdbt, hotel on left after 250yds

This mansion is set in 37 acres of landscaped grounds two miles from the town centre. Behind its Georgian façade is a very relaxing hotel with elegant public areas plus extensive banqueting and leisure facilities. The bedrooms are spacious and comfortable. Staff provide good levels of attention and enjoyable meals are served in the restaurant.

Rooms 75 (16 fmly) (16 GF) **Facilities** Spa STV WiFi ☉ Gym Sauna Steam room Xmas New Year **Conf** Class 100 Board 50 Thtr 500 **Services** Lift **Parking** 200 **Notes** ⊗ Civ Wed 300

Premier Inn Glasgow East Kilbride Central
BUDGET HOTEL

tel: 0871 527 8450 *(Calls cost 13p per minute plus your phone company's access charge)*
Brunel Way, The Murray G75 0LD
web: www.premierinn.com
dir: M74 junct 5, follow East Kilbride A725 signs, then Paisley A726 signs, left at Murray Rdbt, left into Brunel Way

High quality, budget accommodation ideal for both families and business travellers. Spacious, en suite bedrooms feature tea and coffee making facilities, and Freeview TV in most hotels. Internet access and WiFi are available for a small fee. The adjacent family restaurant features a wide and varied menu. See also the Hotel Groups pages.

Rooms 58

Premier Inn Glasgow East Kilbride (Nerston Toll)
BUDGET HOTEL

tel: 0871 527 8446 *(Calls cost 13p per minute plus your phone company's access charge)*
5 Lee's Burn Court, Nerston G74 3XB
web: www.premierinn.com
dir: M74 junct 5, follow East Kilbride/A725 signs. Into right lane, follow Glasgow/A749 signs. At lights left onto A749 signed East Kilbride Town Centre (A725). Take slip road to Lee's Burn Court

Rooms 44

Premier Inn Glasgow East Kilbride (Peel Park)
BUDGET HOTEL

tel: 0871 527 8448 *(Calls cost 13p per minute plus your phone company's access charge)*
Eaglesham Rd G75 8LW
web: www.premierinn.com
dir: 8m from M74 junct 5 on A726 at rdbt of B764

Rooms 42

EDDLESTON
Scottish Borders   Map 21 NT24

The Horseshoe Restaurant with Rooms
🍽 RESTAURANT WITH ROOMS

tel: 01721 730225 **Edinburgh Rd EH45 8QP**
email: reservations@horseshoeinn.co.uk **web:** www.horseshoeinn.co.uk
dir: A703, 5m N of Peebles

The Horseshoe is five miles north of Peebles and only 18 miles south of Edinburgh. Originally a blacksmith's shop, it has a very good reputation for its delightful atmosphere and excellent cuisine. There are eight luxuriously appointed and individually designed bedrooms. Please note: children are welcome, but dinner is not served to under fives except in the private dining room.

Rooms 8 (1 fmly)

EDINBURGH
City of Edinburgh   Map 21 NT27

INSPECTORS' CHOICE

The Balmoral
★★★★★  HOTEL

ROCCO FORTE
HOTELS
RF

tel: 0131 556 2414 **1 Princes St EH2 2EQ**
email: reservations.balmoral@roccofortehotels.com **web:** www.roccofortehotels.com
dir: Follow city centre signs. Hotel at E end of Princes St, adj to Waverley Station

This elegant hotel enjoys a prestigious address at the top of Princes Street, with fine views over the city and the castle. Bedrooms and suites are stylishly furnished and decorated, all boasting a thoughtful range of extras and impressive marble bathrooms. Hotel amenities include a Roman-style health spa, extensive function facilities, a choice of bars and two very different dining options - Hadrians is a bustling, informal brasserie, while Number One offers excellent Scottish and international fine dining.

Rooms 188 (22 fmly) ☚ **Facilities** Spa STV WiFi ↘ ☉ Gym Xmas New Year **Conf** Class 180 Board 60 Thtr 350 **Services** Lift Air con **Parking** 100 **Notes** ⊗ Civ Wed 120

INSPECTORS' CHOICE

Prestonfield

★★★★★ ◎◎ TOWN HOUSE HOTEL

tel: 0131 225 7800 **Priestfield Rd EH16 5UT**
email: reservations@prestonfield.com **web:** www.prestonfield.com
dir: *A7 towards Cameron Toll. 200mtrs beyond Royal Commonwealth Pool, into Priestfield Rd*

This centuries-old landmark has been lovingly restored and enhanced to provide deeply comfortable and dramatically furnished bedrooms. The building demands to be explored: from the tapestry lounge and the whisky room to the restaurant, where the walls are adorned with pictures of former owners. Facilities and services are up-to-the-minute, and carefully prepared meals are served in the award-winning Rhubarb restaurant.

Rooms 23 (6 GF) ⌁ **Facilities** STV FTV WiFi ⬧ ⬦ 18 Putt green ⬥ Xmas New Year **Conf** Class 500 Board 40 Thtr 700 **Services** Lift **Parking** 250 **Notes** Civ Wed 350

★ **Find out more** about the AA Hotel of the Year for Scotland on page 14

Waldorf Astoria Edinburgh - The Caledonian

★★★★★ 86% ◎◎◎ HOTEL

tel: 0131 222 8888 **Princes St EH1 2AB**
web: www.waldorfastoriaedinburgh.com
dir: *In city centre, on west end of Princes St, adj tp Rutland St & Lothian Rd*

Set in the heart of Scotland's capital city, against the magnificent backdrop of Edinburgh Castle, this former Victorian railway hotel was built in 1903, and hasn't lost any of the charm and character that has made it famous. Spacious bedrooms and en suites offer comfort and luxury, and there is a choice of award-wining restaurants and wonderful public areas. The Guerlain Spa is a popular destination for relaxation and rejuvenation. Many rooms enjoy breath-taking views of the Castle.

Rooms 241 (12 fmly) ⌁ ⬧ **S** £159-£639; **D** £169-£649* **Facilities** Spa STV WiFi ⬧ HI ⬦ Gym Sauna Steam room Xmas New Year **Conf** Class 120 Board 80 Thtr 300 **Del** from £190 to £750* **Services** Lift Air con **Parking** 39 **Notes** LB ⊗ Civ Wed 300

G&V Royal Mile Hotel

★★★★★ 84% ◎ HOTEL

tel: 0131 220 6666 **1 George IV Bridge EH1 1AD**
email: info@gandvhotel.com **web:** www.quorvuscollection.com
dir: *At corner of Royal Mile & George IV Bridge*

Located on the corner of the George IV Bridge and the Royal Mile in the heart of the old town, this hotel's design is strikingly different. Bold use of black and white and vivid colours together with strong patterns creates a stunning impression. Stylish bedrooms, some with great city views, have iPod/AV hook-up, WiFi, coffee machines, and bathrooms with walk-in showers as standard. The buzzing cocktail bar and Cucina Missoni, for modern Italian cuisine, attract locals and residents alike.

Rooms 136 ⌁ **Facilities** Spa STV FTV WiFi ⬧ Gym Xmas New Year **Conf** Class 24 Board 24 Thtr 63 **Services** Lift Air con **Parking** 13

Sheraton Grand Hotel & Spa

★★★★★ 84% ◎ HOTEL

tel: 0131 229 9131 **1 Festival Square EH3 9SR**
email: grandedinburgh@sheraton.com **web:** www.sheraton.com/grandedinburgh
dir: *In city centre. Call for directions/parking*

This modern hotel boasts one of the best spas in Scotland - the external top floor hydro pool is definitely worth a look, while the thermal suite provides a unique venue for serious relaxation. The spacious bedrooms are available in a variety of styles, and the suites prove very popular. There is a wide range of dishes available in the One Square Bar and Restaurant.

Rooms 269 ⌁ **S** £130-£645; **D** £130-£645* **Facilities** Spa STV FTV WiFi ⬧ ⬦ ⬥ Gym Indoor/outdoor hydropool Kinesis studio Thermal suite Fitness studio ⬧ Xmas New Year **Conf** Class 350 Board 120 Thtr 500 **Del** from £240 to £530 **Services** Lift Air con **Parking** 122 **Notes** ⊗ Civ Wed 485

EDINBURGH *continued*

Norton House Hotel & Spa

★★★★ ⊛⊛⊛ ⊜ HOTEL

tel: 0131 333 1275 & 0845 072 7468 *(Calls cost 5p per minute plus your phone company's access charge)* **Ingliston EH28 8LX**
email: nortonhouse@handpicked.co.uk
web: www.handpickedhotels.co.uk/nortonhouse
dir: *Off A8, 5m W of city centre*

This extended Victorian mansion, set in 55 acres of parkland, is peacefully situated just outside the city and is convenient for the airport. The original building dates from 1840, and was bought nearly 40 years later by John Usher of the Scottish brewing family. Today both the contemporary bedrooms and the very spacious, traditional ones have an impressive range of accessories including large flat-screen satellite TVs, DVD/CD players and free high-speed internet access. Executive rooms have more facilities, of course, including MP3 connection and 'television' TVs at the end of the baths. Public areas take in a choice of lounges as well as dining options, with a popular brasserie and the intimate Ushers Restaurant. There is a health club, and a spa which offers a long list of treatments.

Rooms 83 (10 fmly) (20 GF) 🐾 **S** £111-£469; **D** £121-£469 (incl. bkfst)* **Facilities** Spa STV WiFi ↧ HL ⊗ Gym Xmas New Year **Conf** Class 100 Board 60 Thtr 300 Del from £155* **Services** Lift **Parking** 200 **Notes** ⊗ Civ Wed 140

Dalhousie Castle and Aqueous Spa

★★★★ 86% ⊛⊛ HOTEL

tel: 01875 820153 **Bonnyrigg EH19 3JB**
email: info@dalhousiecastle.co.uk web: www.dalhousiecastle.co.uk
dir: *A7 S from Edinburgh through Lasswade/Newtongrange, right at Shell Garage (B704), hotel 0.5m from junct*

A popular wedding venue, this imposing medieval castle sits amid lawns and parkland and even has a falconry. Bedrooms offer a mix of styles and sizes, including richly decorated themed rooms named after various historical figures. The Dungeon restaurant provides an atmospheric setting for dinner, and the less formal Orangery serves food all day. The spa offers many relaxing and therapeutic treatments and hydro facilities.

Rooms 35 (6 annexe) (3 fmly) 🐾 **Facilities** Spa FTV WiFi Fishing Falconry Clay pigeon shooting Archery Xmas New Year **Conf** Class 60 Board 45 Thtr 120 Del from £130 to £200 **Parking** 110 **Notes** Civ Wed 100

Hotel du Vin Edinburgh

★★★★ 81% ⊛ ⊜ TOWN HOUSE HOTEL

tel: 0131 247 4900 **11 Bristo Place EH1 1EZ**
web: www.hotelduvin.com
dir: *M8 junct 1, A720 signed Kilmarnock/W Calder/Edinburgh W. Right at fork, follow A720 signs, merge onto A720. Take exit signed A703. At rdbt take A702/Biggar Rd. 3.5m. Right into Lauriston Pl which becomes Forrest Rd. Right at Bedlam Theatre. Hotel on right*

This hotel offers very stylish and comfortable accommodation; all bedrooms display the Hotel du Vin trademark facilities - air conditioning, free WiFi, plasma TVs, monsoon showers and Egyptian cotton linen to name but a few. Public areas include a whisky snug, and a mezzanine bar that overlooks the brasserie where modern Scottish cuisine is served. For the wine connoisseur there's La Roche tasting room where wines from around the world can be appreciated.

Rooms 47 🐾 **Facilities** STV FTV WiFi ↧ **Conf** Class 10 Board 28 Thtr 30 **Services** Lift Air con **Notes** Civ Wed 28

George Hotel Edinburgh

★★★★ 79% HOTEL

tel: 0131 225 1251 **19-21 George St EH2 2PB**
email: enquiries.thegeorge@principal-hayley.com
web: www.principal-hayley.com
dir: *In city centre*

A long-established hotel, the George enjoys a city centre location. The splendid public areas have many original features such as intricate plasterwork, a marble-floored foyer, and chandeliers. The Tempus Bar offers menus that feature a wide range of dishes to suit most tastes. The elegant, modern bedrooms come in a mix of sizes and styles; the upper ones having fine city views.

Rooms 249 (20 fmly) (4 GF) **Facilities** STV WiFi ↧ HL Xmas New Year **Conf** Class 120 Board 50 Thtr 300 **Services** Lift **Notes** LB ⊗ Civ Wed 300

The Roxburghe Hotel

★★★★ 79% HOTEL

tel: 0131 527 4678 **38 Charlotte Square EH2 4HQ**
email: info@theroxburghe.co.uk web: www.theroxburghe.com
dir: *On corner of Charlotte Sq & George St*

This long-established hotel lies in the heart of the city overlooking Charlotte Square Gardens. Public areas are inviting and include relaxing lounges, a choice of bars (in the evening) and an inner concourse that looks onto a small lawned area. Smart bedrooms come in both classic and contemporary styles. There is a secure underground car park.

Rooms 199 (3 fmly) 🐾 **Facilities** Spa STV FTV WiFi ⊗ Gym Dance studio Sauna Steam room ♫ Xmas New Year **Conf** Class 180 Board 50 Thtr 340 **Services** Lift Air con **Parking** 20 **Notes** ⊗ Civ Wed 280

Malmaison Edinburgh

★★★★ 78% ⊛ HOTEL

tel: 0131 468 5000 & 0844 693 0652
(Calls cost 5p per minute plus your phone company's access charge)
One Tower Place, Leith EH6 7BZ
email: edinburgh@malmaison.com web: www.malmaison.com
dir: *A900 from city centre towards Leith, at end of Leith Walk, through 3 sets of lights, left into Tower St. Hotel on right at end of road*

The trendy Port of Leith is home to this stylish Malmaison. Inside, bold contemporary designs create a striking effect. Bedrooms are comprehensively

E

equipped with CD players, mini-bars and loads of individual touches. Ask for one of the stunning superior rooms for a really memorable stay. The smart brasserie and a café bar are popular with the local clientele.

Rooms 100 (18 fmly) 🐾 **Facilities** STV FTV WiFi ⌖ Gym Xmas New Year **Conf** Class 32 Board 32 Thtr 80 **Services** Lift **Parking** 50 **Notes** Civ Wed 70

Macdonald Holyrood Hotel
★★★★ 77% ◉ HOTEL

tel: 0131 550 4500 & 0370 194 2106 **Holyrood Rd EH8 8AU**
email: general.holyrood@macdonald-hotels.co.uk
web: www.macdonaldhotels.co.uk/holyrood
dir: Parallel to Royal Mile, near Holyrood Palace & Dynamic Earth

Situated just a short walk from Holyrood Palace, this impressive hotel lies next to the Scottish Parliament building. Air-conditioned bedrooms are comfortably furnished, while the Club floor boasts a private lounge. Full business services complement the extensive conference suites.

Rooms 156 (16 fmly) (13 GF) **Facilities** Spa STV FTV WiFi ⌖ ⌖ Gym Sauna Steam room Library Xmas New Year **Conf** Class 100 Board 80 Thtr 200 **Services** Lift Air con **Parking** 38 **Notes** Civ Wed 100

The Bonham Hotel
★★★★ 77% HOTEL

tel: 0131 226 6050 **35 Drumsheugh Gardens EH3 7RN**
email: reserve@thebonham.com **web:** www.thebonham.com
dir: Close to West End & Princes St, 10mins from Haymarket station & 5mins from nearest tramstop

The Bonham Hotel was built in the late 19th century in one of the most sought-after areas of Edinburgh. The three buildings that make up the hotel have been private residences, a medical practice and even a Hall of Residence for Edinburgh University, before becoming a hotel. The property has stylish designs which are sympathetic to the vintage of the buildings. Bedrooms are well appointed, with guest comfort well cared for. The bar and restaurant, like the team here, are warm and welcoming.

Rooms 49 (3 fmly) (6 GF) 🐾 S £89-£499; D £89-£499* **Facilities** FTV WiFi ⌖ HL **Conf** Class 20 Board 26 Thtr 45 Del from £119 to £499* **Services** Lift **Parking** 16 **Notes** LB Civ Wed 70

Novotel Edinburgh Park
★★★★ 77% HOTEL

tel: 0131 446 5600 **15 Lochside Av EH12 9DJ**
email: h6515@accor.com **web:** www.novotel.com
dir: Near Hermiston Gate shopping area

Located just off the city by-pass and within minutes of the airport, this modern hotel offers bedrooms that are spacious and comfortable. The public areas include the open-plan lobby, a bar and a restaurant offering diverse and informal dishes. A swimming pool and small gym are also available to guests.

Rooms 170 (130 fmly) 🐾 **Facilities** WiFi HL ⌖ **Conf** Class 60 Board 40 Thtr 150 **Services** Lift **Parking** 96 **Notes** Civ Wed 90

Novotel Edinburgh Centre
★★★★ 76% HOTEL

tel: 0131 656 3500 **Lauriston Place, Lady Lawson St EH3 9DE**
email: H3271@accor.com **web:** www.novotel.com
dir: From Edinburgh Castle right onto George IV Bridge from Royal Mile. Follow to junct, then right into Lauriston Place. Hotel 700mtrs on right

This modern hotel is located in the centre of the city, close to Edinburgh Castle. Smart and stylish public areas include a cosmopolitan bar, brasserie-style restaurant and indoor leisure facilities. The air-conditioned bedrooms feature a comprehensive range of extras and bathrooms with baths and separate shower cabinets.

Rooms 180 (146 fmly) 🐾 **Facilities** STV WiFi ⌖ HL ⌖ Gym Sauna Steam room Xmas New Year **Conf** Class 50 Board 32 Thtr 80 **Services** Lift Air con **Parking** 15

Ten Hill Place Hotel
★★★★ 74% ◉ HOTEL

tel: 0131 662 2080 **10 Hill Place EH8 9DS**
email: reservations@tenhillplace.com **web:** www.tenhillplace.com
dir: Into Hill Place, opp Festival Theatre. Hotel at end

This centrally located luxury hotel near to the Festival Theatre is owned and operated by the Royal College of Surgeons, with all profits helping to train surgeons around the world. Stylish bedrooms and bathrooms are complimented by a range of welcoming and comfortable public areas including the popular 10 Wine Bar, an interesting wine-themed space, and the award-winning No.10 Restaurant. Limited parking is available on site.

Rooms 77 (4 fmly) (10 GF) 🐾 **Facilities** FTV WiFi ⌖ ⌖ **Services** Lift Air con **Parking** 6

Best Western Kings Manor
★★★ 85% HOTEL

tel: 0131 669 0444 & 468 8003 **100 Milton Road East EH15 2NP**
email: reservations@kingsmanor.com **web:** www.kingsmanor.com
dir: A720 E to Old Craighall junct, left into city, right at A1/A199 junct, hotel 400mtrs on right

Lying on the eastern side of the city and convenient for the by-pass, this hotel is popular with business guests, tour groups and for conferences. It boasts a fine leisure complex and a bright modern bistro, which complements the quality, creative cooking in the main restaurant.

Rooms 94 (8 fmly) (13 GF) 🐾 S £50-£110; D £70-£180 **Facilities** Spa STV FTV WiFi ⌖ ⌖ ⌖ Gym Health & beauty salon Steam room Sauna **Conf** Class 80 Board 60 Thtr 160 Del from £110 to £150 **Services** Lift **Parking** 130 **Notes** Civ Wed 100

Mercure Edinburgh City - Princes Street Hotel
★★★ 77% HOTEL

tel: 0131 226 8400 & 0844 815 9017
(Calls cost 7p per minute plus your phone company's access charge) **Princes St EH2 2DG**
email: info@mercureedinburgh.co.uk **web:** www.mercureedinburgh.co.uk
dir: Opposite Scott Monument & Waverley Station. At east end of Princes St

With an enviable location in the heart of Princes Street, offering excellent views of the castle you really cannot be any more central. The front-facing bedrooms are more spacious; some benefit from a balcony but all are well appointed. The large popular restaurant benefits from the wonderful views.

Rooms 169 (9 fmly) **Facilities** FTV WiFi ⌖ HL New Year **Services** Lift **Notes** ⊗

E

EDINBURGH *continued*

Old Waverley Hotel

★★★ 77% HOTEL

tel: 0131 556 4648 **43 Princes St EH2 2BY**
email: reservations@oldwaverley.co.uk **web:** www.oldwaverley.co.uk
dir: *In city centre, opposite Scott Monument, Waverley Station & Jenners*

Occupying a commanding position opposite Sir Walter Scott's famous monument on Princes Street, this hotel lies right in the heart of the city close to the station. The comfortable public rooms are all on first-floor level and along with front-facing bedrooms enjoy the fine views.

Rooms 86 (5 fmly) **Facilities** WiFi ⇗ Leisure facilities at sister hotel **Services** Lift **Notes** LB ⊗

The Howard

U

tel: 0131 557 3500 **34 Great King St EH3 6QH**
email: reserve@thehoward.com **web:** www.thehoward.com
dir: *E on Queen St, 2nd left, Dundas St. Through 3 lights, right, hotel on left*

Currently the rating for this establishment is not confirmed. This may be due to a change of ownership or because it has only recently joined the AA rating scheme. For further details please see the AA website: theAA.com

Rooms 19 (1 annexe) (3 fmly) (2 GF) ⌂ **S** £89-£260; **D** £99-£380 **Facilities** STV FTV WiFi ⇗ HL Xmas New Year **Conf** Class 28 Board 28 Thtr 28 Del from £160 to £460 **Services** Lift **Parking** 12 **Notes** LB ⊗ Civ Wed 28

Premier Inn Edinburgh A1 (Musselburgh)

BUDGET HOTEL

tel: 0871 527 8358 *(Calls cost 13p per minute plus your phone company's access charge)*
Carberry Rd, Inveresk, Musselburgh EH21 8PT
web: www.premierinn.com
dir: *From A1 follow Dalkeith (A6094) signs. At rdbt turn right, hotel 300yds on right*

High quality, budget accommodation ideal for both families and business travellers. Spacious, en suite bedrooms feature tea and coffee making facilities, and Freeview TV in most hotels. Internet access and WiFi are available for a small fee. The adjacent family restaurant features a wide and varied menu. See also the Hotel Groups pages.

Rooms 60

Premier Inn Edinburgh Airport (Newbridge)

BUDGET HOTEL

tel: 0871 527 9284 *(Calls cost 13p per minute plus your phone company's access charge)*
2A Kirkliston Rd, Newbridge EH28 8SL
web: www.premierinn.com
dir: *M9 junct 1, A89 signed Broxburn. At lights turn right, then 2nd right*

Rooms 119

Premier Inn Edinburgh Central (Lauriston Place)

BUDGET HOTEL

tel: 0871 527 8366 *(Calls cost 13p per minute plus your phone company's access charge)*
82 Lauriston Place, Lady Lawson St EH3 9DG
web: www.premierinn.com
dir: *A8 onto A702 (Lothian Rd). Left into Lauriston Place. Hotel on left*

Rooms 112

Premier Inn Edinburgh City Centre (Haymarket)

BUDGET HOTEL

tel: 0871 527 8368 *(Calls cost 13p per minute plus your phone company's access charge)*
1 Morrison Link EH3 8DN
web: www.premierinn.com
dir: *Adjcent to Edinburgh International Conference Centre*

Rooms 282

Premier Inn Edinburgh City Centre (Princess St)

BUDGET HOTEL

tel: 0871 527 9358 *(Calls cost 13p per minute plus your phone company's access charge)*
122-123 Princes St EH2 4AD
web: www.premierinn.com
dir: *From Edinburgh bypass (A720) onto A702, take A700. NB Princes St is not accessible by car - it is advisable to park in Castle Terrace Car Park EH1 2EW*

Rooms 97

Premier Inn Edinburgh City Centre Royal Mile

BUDGET HOTEL

tel: 0871 527 9644 *(Calls cost 13p per minute plus your phone company's access charge)*
East Market St EH8 8BG
web: www.premierinn.com
dir: *From Waverley train station right into Market St, straight on into East Market St, hotel in 0.4m*

Rooms 127

Premier Inn Edinburgh East

BUDGET HOTEL

tel: 0871 527 8370 *(Calls cost 13p per minute plus your phone company's access charge)*
228 Willowbrae Rd EH8 7NG
web: www.premierinn.com
dir: *M8 junct 1, A720 S for 12m, then A1. At Asda rdbt turn left. In 2m, hotel on left before Esso garage*

Rooms 50

E

Premier Inn Edinburgh Leith Waterfront

BUDGET HOTEL

tel: 0871 527 8360 *(Calls cost 13p per minute plus your phone company's access charge)*
51-53 Newhaven Place, Leith EH6 4TX
web: www.premierinn.com
dir: From A1 follow coast road through Leith. Pass Ocean Terminal, straight ahead at mini-rdbt, 2nd exit signed Harry Ramsden's car park

Rooms 138

Premier Inn Edinburgh Park (The Gyle)

BUDGET HOTEL

tel: 0871 527 9336 *(Calls cost 13p per minute plus your phone company's access charge)*
Edinburgh Park (Airport), 1 Lochside Court EH12 9FX
web: www.premierinn.com
dir: M8 junct 1, A720 (city bypass). At Gogar rdbt 3rd exit follow South Gyle/station signs. Into right lane approaching Gyle rdbt, 3rd exit, follow Edinburgh Park train station signs into Lochside Cres. Straight on at 2 rdbts, 400yds. Hotel on left

Rooms 120

Ibis Budget Edinburgh Park

AA Advertised

tel: 0131 446 5900 **Edinburgh Business Park, 6 Lochside View EH12 9DH**
email: H8710@accor.com **web:** www.ibishotel.com
dir: From W: M8 junct 1. At rdbt take 4th exit, at 2nd rdbt take 3rd exit onto Edinburgh Park. Turn right onto Lochside Ave, then right onto Lochside View, take 1st right to stay on Lochside View. Hotel on left

Modern, budget hotel offering comfortable accommodation in bright and practical bedrooms. Breakfast is self-service and dinner is available in the restaurant.

Rooms 161 (161 fmly) **Facilities** FTV WiFi **Services** Lift

Ibis Edinburgh Centre Royal Mile

AA Advertised

tel: 0131 240 7000 **6 Hunter Square, off The Royal Mile EH1 1QW**
email: H2039@accor.com **web:** www.ibishotel.com
dir: M8/M9/A1 over North Bridge A7 & High St, take 1st right off South Bridge, into Hunter Sq

Modern, budget hotel offering comfortable accommodation in bright and practical bedrooms. Breakfast is self-service and dinner is available in the restaurant.

Rooms 99 (2 GF) **Facilities** STV FTV WiFi **Services** Lift

Ibis Edinburgh Centre South Bridge

AA Advertised

tel: 0131 292 0000 **77 South Bridge EH1 1HN**
email: h8484@accor.com **web:** www.ibishotel.com
dir: From Airport take A8 to City Centre, turn into Queen St, at Picardy Place rdbt take 2nd exit into Leith st, turn right, sharp left onto North Bridge, take 2nd turning on right, Blair St, turn right then 2nd left into Guthrie St, left into Chambers St, left onto South bridge

Modern, budget hotel offering comfortable accommodation in bright and practical bedrooms. Breakfast is self-service and dinner is available in the restaurant.

Rooms 259 (259 fmly) **D** £35-£255* **Facilities** FTV WiFi **Services** Lift Air con

Ibis Styles Edinburgh Centre St Andrew Square

AA Advertised

tel: 0131 292 0200 **19 St Andrew Square EH2 1AU**
email: H9058@accor.com **web:** www.ibishotel.com
dir: Corner of St Andrew Square & Thistle St

Modern, budget hotel offering comfortable accommodation in bright and practical bedrooms. Breakfast is self-service and dinner is available in the restaurant.

Rooms 103 (4 fmly) (5 GF) **Facilities** FTV WiFi HL **Services** Lift Air con

---

INSPECTORS' CHOICE

21212

@@@@ RESTAURANT WITH ROOMS

tel: 0131 523 1030 **3 Royal Ter EH7 5AB**
email: reservations@21212restaurant.co.uk **web:** www.21212restaurant.co.uk
dir: Calton Hill, city centre

A real jewel in Edinburgh's crown, this establishment takes its name from the number of choices at each course on the five-course dinner menu. Located on the prestigious Royal Terrace this is a light and airy, renovated Georgian town house stretching over four floors. The four individually-designed bedrooms epitomise luxury living and the bathrooms certainly have the wow factor. At the heart of this restaurant with rooms is the creative and impressive four AA Rosette award-winning cooking of Paul Kitching. Service throughout is friendly and very attentive.

Rooms 4

INSPECTORS' CHOICE

The Witchery by the Castle

@ RESTAURANT WITH ROOMS

tel: 0131 225 5613 **Castlehill, The Royal Mile EH1 2NF**
email: mail@thewitchery.com **web:** www.thewitchery.com
dir: Top of Royal Mile at gates of Edinburgh Castle

Originally built in 1595, The Witchery by the Castle is situated in a historic building at the gates of Edinburgh Castle. The two luxurious and theatrically decorated suites, known as the Inner Sanctum and the Old Rectory are located above the restaurant and are reached via a winding stone staircase. Filled with antiques, opulently draped beds, large roll-top baths and a plethora of memorabilia, this ancient and exciting establishment is often described as one of the country's most romantic destinations.

Rooms 9 (5 annexe)

E

ELGIN
Moray

Map 23 NJ26

Mansion House Hotel
★★★★ 75% ⊛ HOTEL

tel: 01343 548811 **The Haugh IV30 1AW**
email: reception@mhelgin.co.uk **web:** www.mansionhousehotel.co.uk
dir: Exit A96 into Haugh Rd, then 1st left

Set in grounds by the River Lossie, this baronial mansion is popular with leisure and business guests as well as being a lovely wedding venue. Bedrooms are spacious and many have views of the river. Extensive public areas include a choice of restaurants, with a bistro that contrasts nicely with the classical main restaurant. There is an indoor pool and a beauty and hair salon.

Rooms 23 (6 fmly) (5 GF) ☞ **S** £107-£134; **D** £166.50-£214.50 (incl. bkfst)*
Facilities STV FTV WiFi ⌕ ⌧ supervised Gym Hair studio Beauty treatment room
Conf Class 100 Board 20 Thtr 180 **Parking** 50 **Notes** LB ⊗ Closed 24 Dec-2 Jan
Civ Wed 160

Premier Inn Elgin
BUDGET HOTEL

tel: 0871 527 8372 *(Calls cost 13p per minute plus your phone company's access charge)*
15 Linkwood Way IV30 1HY
web: www.premierinn.com
dir: On A96, 1.5m E of city centre

High quality, budget accommodation ideal for both families and business travellers. Spacious, en suite bedrooms feature tea and coffee making facilities, and Freeview TV in most hotels. Internet access and WiFi are available for a small fee. The adjacent family restaurant features a wide and varied menu. See also the Hotel Groups pages.

Rooms 93

FALKIRK
Falkirk

Map 21 NS88

Premier Inn Falkirk Central
BUDGET HOTEL

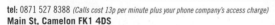

tel: 0871 527 8388 *(Calls cost 13p per minute plus your phone company's access charge)*
Main St, Camelon FK1 4DS
web: www.premierinn.com
dir: From Falkirk A803 signed Glasgow. At mini-rdbt right, continue on A803. At Rosebank rdbt 2nd exit signed Glasgow & Stirling

High quality, budget accommodation ideal for both families and business travellers. Spacious, en suite bedrooms feature tea and coffee making facilities, and Freeview TV in most hotels. Internet access and WiFi are available for a small fee. The adjacent family restaurant features a wide and varied menu. See also the Hotel Groups pages.

Rooms 31

Premier Inn Falkirk (Larbert)
BUDGET HOTEL

tel: 0871 527 8390 *(Calls cost 13p per minute plus your phone company's access charge)*
Glenbervie Business Park, Bellsdyke Rd, Larbert FK5 4EG
web: www.premierinn.com
dir: Just off A88. Approx 1m from M876 junct 2

Rooms 60

FINTRY
Stirling

Map 20 NS68

Culcreuch Castle Hotel & Estate
★★★ 81% ⊛⊛ HOTEL

tel: 01360 860555 **Kippen Rd G63 0LW**
email: info@culcreuch.com **web:** www.culcreuch.com
dir: On B822, 17m W of Stirling

Peacefully located in 1,600 acres of parkland, this ancient castle dates back to 1296. Tastefully restored accommodation is in a mixture of individually themed castle rooms, some with four-poster beds, and more modern courtyard rooms which are suitable for families. Period style public rooms include a bar, serving light meals, an elegant lounge and a wood-panelled dining room.

Rooms 14 (4 annexe) (4 fmly) (4 GF) ☞ **S** £77-£120; **D** £102-£190 (incl. bkfst)*
Facilities STV FTV WiFi ⌕ New Year **Conf** Class 70 Board 30 Thtr 140 Del from £119
to £129* **Parking** 80 **Notes** LB ⊗ Closed 4-18 Jan & 25-26 Dec RS 19 Jan-mid Mar
Civ Wed 110

FORRES
Moray

Map 23 NJ05

Cluny Bank
⊛ RESTAURANT WITH ROOMS

tel: 01309 674304 **69 St Leonards Rd IV36 1DW**
email: info@clunybankhotel.co.uk **web:** www.clunybankhotel.co.uk

Historic, listed Cluny Bank occupies a quiet location within walking distance of the centre of Forres, and is an ideal base for exploring the North East of Scotland. Family-run, the building retains many original architectural features. Public areas include the 'Altyre Bar' with a wide range of whiskies, and 'Franklin's Restaurant' where a real taste of Moray can be experienced. Room service, complimentary WiFi and memorable breakfasts are also provided for guests. AA Friendliest B&B of the Year Award Finalist 2016-2017.

Rooms 7 (1 annexe)

FORT AUGUSTUS
Highland   Map 23 NH30

The Lovat, Loch Ness

★★★★ 80% ●●● HOTEL

tel: 01456 459250 **Loch Ness Side PH32 4DU**
email: info@thelovat.com **web:** www.thelovat.com
dir: *A82 between Fort William & Inverness*

This charming hotel enjoys an elevated position in the pretty town of Fort Augustus with views over Loch Ness. It has impressively styled bedrooms with a host of thoughtful extras. Inviting public areas include a comfortable lounge with a log fire, a stylish brasserie and the contemporary 'Station Road' restaurant where imaginative food is cooked with skill and care. The hotel has an admirable green policy, and the hospitality and commitment to guest care will leave a lasting impression.

Rooms 28 (1 fmly) (7 GF) ✦ **Facilities** FTV WiFi ◊ Beauty treatment room Xmas New Year **Conf** Class 32 Board 24 Thtr 70 **Services** Lift **Parking** 30 **Notes** Closed Jan RS Nov-Mar Civ Wed 150

Inchnacardoch Lodge Hotel

★★★ 72% SMALL HOTEL

tel: 01456 450900 **Inchnacardoch Bay PH32 4BL**
email: happy@inchhotel.com **web:** www.inchhotel.com
dir: *On A82. Turn right before entering Fort Augustus from Inverness*

This 150-year-old former hunting lodge is set on the hillside looking over the south end of Loch Ness, making it a perfect base for exploring the Highlands. Guests can expect the finest hospitality here from staff that are always eager to please. The bedrooms are very individual in style; the Bridal Suite is a very well appointed room with stunning views. The award-winning Yard Restaurant serves dishes based on the plentiful supply of local game and seafood.

Rooms 18 (2 fmly) **S** fr £120 | **D** fr £120 (incl. bkfst)* **Facilities** FTV WiFi Fishing Xmas New Year **Conf** Class 30 Board 26 Thtr 45 Del from £195* **Parking** 30 **Notes** Civ Wed 35

FORTINGALL
Perth & Kinross   Map 20 NN74

Fortingall Hotel

★★★★ 72% ● SMALL HOTEL

tel: 01887 830367 & 829012 **PH15 2NQ**
email: enquiries@fortingall.com **web:** www.fortingallhotel.com
dir: *B846 from Aberfeldy for 6m, left signed Fortingall for 3m. Hotel in village centre*

Appointed to a very high standard, this hotel has plenty of charm. It lies at the foot of wooded hills in the heart of Glen Lyon. All the bedrooms are very well equipped and have an extensive range of thoughtful extras. The comfortable lounge, with its log fire, is ideal for pre-dinner drinks, and the small bar is full of character.

Rooms 10 (1 fmly) **S** £140 | **D** £260-£300 (incl. bkfst & dinner)* **Facilities** STV FTV WiFi ◊ Fishing ⛳ Deer stalking Grouse shoots Munro bagging Clay pigeon Guided walks Cycle hire ♫ Xmas New Year **Conf** Board 20 Thtr 40 Del from £150 to £200* **Parking** 20 **Notes** LB Civ Wed 50

FORT WILLIAM
Highland   Map 22 NN17

Inverlochy Castle Hotel

★★★★★ ●●● COUNTRY HOUSE HOTEL

tel: 01397 702177 **Torlundy PH33 6SN**
email: info@inverlochy.co.uk **web:** www.inverlochycastlehotel.com
dir: *Accessible from either A82 Glasgow-Fort William or A9 Edinburgh-Dalwhinnie. Hotel 3m N of Fort William on A82, in Torlundy*

With Ben Nevis as its backdrop, this imposing and gracious castle sits amidst extensive gardens and grounds overlooking the hotel's own loch. Lavishly appointed in classic country-house style, spacious bedrooms are extremely comfortable and boast flat-screen TVs and laptops with internet access. The sumptuous main hall and lounge provide the perfect setting for afternoon tea or a pre-dinner cocktail, while imaginative modern British cuisine is served in one of three dining rooms. A snooker room and DVD library are also available.

Rooms 17 (6 fmly) ✦ **S** £280-£395 | **D** £335-£465 (incl. bkfst)* **Facilities** STV FTV WiFi ◡ ⛳ Fishing on loch Massage Riding Hunting Stalking Clay pigeon shooting Archery ♫ Xmas New Year **Conf** Class 20 Board 20 Thtr 50 Del from £380* **Parking** 17 **Notes** Civ Wed 80

F

FORT WILLIAM *continued*

Moorings Hotel
★★★★ 76% HOTEL

tel: 01397 772797 **Banavie PH33 7LY**
email: reservations@moorings-fortwilliam.co.uk **web:** www.moorings-fortwilliam.co.uk
dir: *Take A830 N from Fort William, cross Caledonian Canal, 1st right signed Banavie*

Located on the Caledonian Canal next to a series of locks known as Neptune's Staircase and close to Thomas Telford's house, this hotel has a dedicated team offering friendly service. Accommodation comes in three distinct styles; Standard, Superior and the newly-added Executive. These newer rooms with balconies are particularly appealing. Many rooms may offer Canal and/or Ben view. Meals can be taken in the modern new Bistro or alternatively fine dining is offered in the more traditional dining-room.

Rooms 32 (1 fmly) (1 GF) 🐾 **S** £97-£157; **D** £107-£167 (incl. bkfst)* **Facilities** FTV WiFi Gym New Year **Conf** Class 60 Board 40 Thtr 140 Del from £100 to £130* **Parking** 60 **Notes** LB Closed 24-26 Dec Civ Wed 120

Alexandra Hotel
★★★ 74% HOTEL

tel: 01397 702241 **The Parade PH33 6AZ**
email: salesalexandra@strathmorehotels.com **web:** www.strathmorehotels.com
dir: *Off A82. Hotel opposite railway station*

This charming old hotel enjoys a prominent position in the town centre and is just a short walk from all the major attractions. Front-facing bedrooms have views over the town and the spectacular Nevis mountain range. There is a choice of restaurants, including a bistro serving meals until late, along with several stylish and very comfortable lounges.

Rooms 93 (2 fmly) 🐾 **Facilities** WiFi Free use of nearby leisure club 🎵 Xmas New Year **Conf** Class 100 Board 40 Thtr 120 **Services** Lift **Parking** 50

Ben Nevis Hotel & Leisure Club
★★★ 72% HOTEL

tel: 01397 702331 **North Rd PH33 6TG**
email: salesbennevis@strathmorehotels.com **web:** www.strathmorehotels.com
dir: *Off A82*

This popular hotel is ideally situated on the outskirts of Fort William. It provides comfortable, well equipped bedrooms; many with views of the impressive Nevis mountains. The hotel's leisure centre is a firm favourite with guests at the hotel. Recently refurbished public areas include a spacious and welcoming bar with a great selection of whiskies.

Rooms 119 (3 fmly) (30 GF) **Facilities** WiFi ⓢ supervised Gym Beauty salon 🎵 Xmas New Year **Conf** Class 60 Board 40 Thtr 150 **Parking** 100 **Notes** Civ Wed 60

Croit Anna Hotel
★★★ 72% HOTEL

Leisureplex
HOLIDAY HOTELS

tel: 01397 702268 **Achintore Rd, Drimarben PH33 6RR**
email: croitanna@leisureplex.co.uk **web:** www.leisureplex.co.uk
dir: *From Glencoe on A82 into Fort William, hotel 1st on right*

Located on the edge of Loch Linnhe, just two miles out of town, this hotel offers some spacious bedrooms, many with fine views over the loch. There is a choice of two comfortable lounges and a large airy restaurant. The hotel appeals to coach parties and independent travellers alike.

Rooms 90 (5 fmly) (13 GF) **Facilities** FTV WiFi Pool table 🎵 Xmas New Year **Parking** 25 **Notes** ⊗ Closed Dec-Jan (ex Xmas/New Year) RS Nov, Feb & Mar

Premier Inn Fort William
BUDGET HOTEL

tel: 0871 527 8402 *(Calls cost 13p per minute plus your phone company's access charge)*
Loch Iall, An Aird PH33 6AN
web: www.premierinn.com
dir: *N end of Fort William Shopping Centre, just off A82 ring road*

High quality, budget accommodation ideal for both families and business travellers. Spacious, en suite bedrooms feature tea and coffee making facilities, and Freeview TV in most hotels. Internet access and WiFi are available for a small fee. The adjacent family restaurant features a wide and varied menu. See also the Hotel Groups pages.

Rooms 103

F

GALASHIELS
Scottish Borders · Map 21 NT43

Kingsknowes Hotel
★★★ 81% HOTEL

tel: 01896 758375 **Selkirk Rd TD1 3HY**
email: enq@kingsknowes.co.uk **web:** www.kingsknowes.co.uk
dir: *Situated 33m S of Edinburgh on the A7, 2m from Galashiels, 5m from Melrose*

An imposing turreted mansion, this hotel lies in attractive gardens on the outskirts of town close to the River Tweed. It boasts elegant public areas and many spacious bedrooms, some with excellent views. There is a choice of bars, one with a popular menu to supplement the restaurant.

Rooms 12 (2 fmly) ꔹ **S** fr £75; **D** fr £110* **Facilities** FTV WiFi HL **Conf** Class 40 Board 30 Thtr 80 **Parking** 65 **Notes** Civ Wed 75

GATEHOUSE OF FLEET
Dumfries & Galloway · Map 20 NX55

Cally Palace Hotel
★★★★ 75% ⊛ COUNTRY HOUSE HOTEL

tel: 01557 814341 **Cally Dr DG7 2DL**
email: info@callypalace.co.uk **web:** www.callypalace.co.uk
dir: *From M6 & A74, signed A75 Dumfries then Stranraer. At Gatehouse of Fleet right onto B727, left at Cally*

A resort hotel with extensive leisure facilities, this grand 18th-century building is set in 500 acres of forest and parkland that incorporates its own golf course. Bedrooms are spacious and well equipped, while public rooms retain a quiet elegance. The short dinner menu focuses on freshly prepared dishes; a pianist plays most nights and the wearing of jacket and tie is obligatory (for gentlemen).

Rooms 55 (7 fmly) (4 GF) ꔹ **Facilities** STV FTV WiFi ⊗ ⅃ 18 ⅊ Putt green Fishing ꔹ Gym Table tennis Practice fairway Xmas New Year **Conf** Class 40 Board 25 Thtr 40 **Services** Lift **Parking** 100 **Notes** ⊗ Closed Jan-early Feb Civ Wed 130

GLASGOW
City of Glasgow · Map 20 NS56

See also **Clydebank & Uplawmoor**

Blythswood Square
★★★★★ 86% ⊛⊛ HOTEL

PH | principal hayley

tel: 0141 248 8888 **11 Blythswood Square G2 4AD**
email: reserve@blythswoodsquare.com **web:** www.blythswoodsquare.com

Built in 1821, and restored to its former glory, this was the headquarters of the Royal Scottish Automobile Club which was the official start point for the 1955 Monte Carlo Rally. The bedrooms and bathrooms are sumptuous, and include suites and a penthouse. Afternoon tea and cocktails are served in the 35-metre, first-floor Salon Lounge, and the award-winning restaurant occupies the old RSAC's ballroom. The Spa includes a fantastic thermal suite.

Rooms 100 (5 GF) ꔹ **Facilities** Spa STV FTV WiFi ꔹ ⊗ Gym Thermal experience Xmas New Year **Conf** Class 80 Board 80 Thtr 130 Del from £195 to £320 **Services** Lift Air con **Notes** Civ Wed 80

Hotel du Vin at One Devonshire Gardens
★★★★ ⊛⊛⊛ TOWN HOUSE HOTEL

Hotel du Vin & Bistro

tel: 0141 339 2001 & 0844 736 4256
(Calls cost 5p per minute plus your phone company's access charge)
1 Devonshire Gardens G12 0UX
email: info.odg@hotelduvin.com **web:** www.hotelduvin.com
dir: *M8 junct 17, follow signs for A82, in 1.5m left into Hyndland Rd, 1st right, right at mini rdbt, right at end*

Situated in a tree-lined Victorian terrace this luxury 'boutique' hotel has stunning, individually designed bedrooms and suites that have the trademark Egyptian linens and seriously good showers. The oak-panelled Bistro offers a daily-changing menu of both classic and modern dishes with a Scottish influence. Naturally, wine is an important part of the equation here, and knowledgeable staff can guide guests around the impressive wine list.

Rooms 49 (7 GF) ꔹ **Facilities** STV WiFi Gym Beauty treatment room Tennis & Squash facilities at nearby club Xmas New Year **Conf** Class 30 Board 30 Thtr 50 **Notes** LB Civ Wed 70

Malmaison Glasgow
★★★★ 79% ⊛⊛ HOTEL

Malmaison · hotels that dare to be different

tel: 0141 572 1000 & 0844 693 0653
(Calls cost 5p per minute plus your phone company's access charge)
278 West George St G2 4LL
email: reception.glasgow@malmaison.com **web:** www.malmaison.com
dir: *From S & E: M8 junct 18 Charing Cross. From W & N: M8 city centre*

Built around a former church in the historic Charing Cross area, this hotel is a smart, contemporary establishment offering impressive levels of service and hospitality. Bedrooms are spacious and feature a host of modern facilities, such as CD players and mini bars. Dining is a treat here, with French brasserie-style cuisine, backed up by an excellent wine list, served in the original crypt.

Rooms 72 (4 fmly) (19 GF) ꔹ **Facilities** STV WiFi ꔹ New Year **Conf** Class 20 Board 22 Thtr 56 **Services** Lift **Notes** Civ Wed 60

Golden Jubilee Conference Hotel
★★★★ 75% ⊛ HOTEL

tel: 0141 951 6000 **Beardmore St G81 4SA**
email: hotel@goldenjubilee.scot.nhs.uk **web:** www.goldenjubileehotel.com

(For full entry see Clydebank)

GLASGOW *continued*

Grand Central Hotel

★★★★ 75% HOTEL

tel: 0141 240 3700 **99 Gordon St G1 3SF**
email: grandcentralhotel@principal-hayley.com **web:** www.principal-hayley.com
dir: M8 junct 19 towards city centre, turn left at Hope St. Hotel 200mtrs on right

This is the place where John Logie Baird transmitted the world's first long-distance television pictures in 1927, and this 'grand old lady' of the Glasgow hotel scene is appointed to a very good standard. The decor is a blend of contemporary, art deco and original Victorian styles. Bedrooms are well equipped and suit business travellers especially. There is Champagne Central, a glamorous bar, the Tempus Bar and Restaurant, and Deli Central (with direct access to the Central Station) which is an eat-in deli and a take-away. Ample meeting facilities are available, and NCP car parks are nearby.

Rooms 230 (15 fmly) 🐾 **Facilities** FTV WiFi ⬇ New Year **Conf** Class 350 Board 60 Thtr 500 **Services** Lift **Notes** ⊗ Civ Wed 500

Hallmark Hotel Glasgow

★★★★ 74% HOTEL

tel: 0330 028 3407 **27 Washington St G3 8AZ**
email: glasgow@hallmarkhotels.co.uk **web:** www.hallmarkhotels.co.uk
dir: M8 junct 19, follow signs for SECC & Broomielaw. Left at lights

Centrally located, this modern hotel is a short drive from the airport and a short walk from the centre of the city. Bedrooms are generally spacious and boast a range of facilities, including high-speed internet access. Facilities include a brasserie restaurant and an impressive indoor leisure facility.

Rooms 141 (16 fmly) **S** £70-£250; **D** £80-£260* **Facilities** Spa STV FTV WiFi 🕸 supervised Gym **Conf** Class 80 Board 70 Thtr 160 Del from £125 to £165*
Services Lift Air con **Parking** 50 **Notes** LB Civ Wed 150

Holiday Inn Glasgow City Centre - Theatreland

★★★ 82% ⬡ HOTEL

tel: 0141 352 8300 **161 West Nile St G1 2RL**
email: reservations@higlasgow.com **web:** www.holidayinn.co.uk
dir: M8 junct 16, follow signs for Royal Concert Hall, hotel opposite

Built on a corner site close to the Theatre Royal Concert Hall and the main shopping areas, this contemporary hotel features the popular La Bonne Auberge French restaurant, a bar area and conservatory. Recently refurbished bedrooms are well equipped and comfortable; suites are available. Staff are friendly and attentive.

Rooms 113 (20 fmly) (10 smoking) 🐾 **S** £80-£200; **D** £90-£200* **Facilities** STV FTV WiFi **Conf** Class 60 Board 60 Thtr 100 **Services** Lift Air con **Notes** LB ⊗

Novotel Glasgow Centre

★★★ 79% HOTEL

tel: 0141 222 2775 **181 Pitt St G2 4DT**
email: H3136@accor.com **web:** www.novotel.com
dir: M8 junct 18 for Charing Cross. Follow to Sauchiehall St. 3rd right

Enjoying a convenient city centre location and limited parking spaces, this hotel is ideal for both business and leisure travellers. Well-equipped bedrooms are brightly decorated and offer functional design. Modern public areas include a small fitness club and a lively bar serving a range of meals all day. The 'Virtual Concierge' system is available at reception; a great way to learn more about the city.

Rooms 139 (139 fmly) **Facilities** FTV WiFi Gym Sauna Steam room Xmas **Conf** Class 20 Board 20 Thtr 40 **Services** Lift Air con **Parking** 19

Uplawmoor Hotel

★★★ 77% SMALL HOTEL

tel: 01505 850565 **66 Neilston Rd G78 4AF**
email: info@uplawmoor.co.uk **web:** www.uplawmoor.co.uk

(For full entry see Uplawmoor)

Mercure Glasgow City Hotel

★★★ 75% HOTEL

tel: 0844 815 9017 *(Calls cost 5p per minute plus your phone company's access charge)*
201 Ingram St G1 1DQ
email: info@mercureglasgow.co.uk **web:** www.jupiterhotels.co.uk
dir: M8 junct 15, straight through 4 lights, left at 5th into Hanover St, left into George Sq, right into Frederick St. Right at 2nd lights into Ingram St

This hotel enjoys a fantastic location in the heart of Glasgow with great access to shops, bars and restaurants. Bedrooms provide modern accommodation and a host of accessories including flat screen TVs and complimentary WiFi. Extensive conference facilities and the popular Bagio Café Bar mean you may not need to leave the hotel.

Rooms 91 **Facilities** New Year **Conf** Class 40 Board 40 Thtr 80 **Services** Lift **Parking** 30 **Notes** Civ Wed 80

Premier Inn Glasgow (Bearsden)

BUDGET HOTEL

tel: 0871 527 8418 *(Calls cost 13p per minute plus your phone company's access charge)*
279 Milngavie Rd G61 3DQ
web: www.premierinn.com
dir: M8 junct 16, A81. Pass Asda on right. Hotel on left, behind The Burnbrae

High quality, budget accommodation ideal for both families and business travellers. Spacious, en suite bedrooms feature tea and coffee making facilities, and Freeview TV in most hotels. Internet access and WiFi are available for a small fee. The adjacent family restaurant features a wide and varied menu. See also the Hotel Groups pages.

Rooms 61

Premier Inn Glasgow (Bellshill)

BUDGET HOTEL

tel: 0871 527 8421 *(Calls cost 13p per minute plus your phone company's access charge)*
New Edinburgh Rd, Bellshill ML4 3PD
web: www.premierinn.com
dir: M74 junct 5, A725. Follow Bellshill A721 signs, bear left. At rdbt left, follow Tannochside sign. At next rdbt left into Bellziehill Rd. Hotel on right

Rooms 60

Premier Inn Glasgow Buchanan Galleries Hotel

BUDGET HOTEL

tel: 0871 527 9360 *(Calls cost 13p per minute plus your phone company's access charge)*
St Andrew House, 141 West Nile St G1 2RN
web: www.premierinn.com
dir: Phone for detailed directions

Rooms 210

Premier Inn Glasgow (Cambuslang/M74 Jct 2A)

BUDGET HOTEL

tel: 0871 527 8422 *(Calls cost 13p per minute plus your phone company's access charge)*
Cambuslang Investment Park, Off London Rd G32 8YX
web: www.premierinn.com
dir: *At end of M74, turn right at rdbt. At 1st lights turn right, at 2nd lights straight ahead. Hotel on right*

Rooms 76

Premier Inn Glasgow City Centre Argyle St

BUDGET HOTEL

tel: 0141 248 2355 & 0871 527 8436
(Calls cost 13p per minute plus your phone company's access charge) **377 Argyle St G2 8LL**
web: www.premierinn.com
dir: *From S. M8 junct 19, at pedestrian lights left into Argyle St. Hotel 200yds on right*

Rooms 124

Premier Inn Glasgow City Centre (Charing Cross)

BUDGET HOTEL

tel: 0871 527 8438 *(Calls cost 13p per minute plus your phone company's access charge)*
10 Elmbank Gardens G2 4PP
web: www.premierinn.com
dir: *Phone for directions*

Rooms 278

Premier Inn Glasgow City Centre (George Square)

BUDGET HOTEL

tel: 0871 527 8440 *(Calls cost 13p per minute plus your phone company's access charge)*
187 George St G1 1YU
web: www.premierinn.com
dir: *M8 junct 15, into Stirling Rd. Right into Cathedral St. At 1st lights left into Montrose St. Hotel after 1st lights*

Rooms 239

Premier Inn Glasgow City Centre South

BUDGET HOTEL

tel: 0871 527 8442 *(Calls cost 13p per minute plus your phone company's access charge)*
80 Ballater St G5 0TW
web: www.premierinn.com
dir: *M8 junct 21 follow East Kilbride signs, right onto A8 into Kingston St. Right into South Portland St, left into Norfolk St, through Gorbals St into Ballater St*

Rooms 123

Premier Inn Glasgow East

BUDGET HOTEL

tel: 0871 527 8444 *(Calls cost 13p per minute plus your phone company's access charge)*
601 Hamilton Rd, Uddington G71 7SA
web: www.premierinn.com
dir: *At entrance to Glasgow Zoo, adjacent to junct 4 of M73 & M74*

Rooms 68

Premier Inn Glasgow Pacific Quay SECC

BUDGET HOTEL

tel: 0871 527 9340 *(Calls cost 13p per minute plus your phone company's access charge)*
Pacific Quay G51 1DZ
web: www.premierinn.com
dir: *M8 junct 24, left into Helen St, 2nd exit at rdbt, follow Glasgow Science Centre signs. Right into Govan Rd. 1st exit at rdbt into Pacific Dr (pass Science Centre & BBC Scotland). Hotel on left*

Rooms 180

G

citizenM Glasgow

AA Advertised

tel: 020 3519 1111 **60 Renfrew St G2 3BW**
email: supportgla@citizenm.com **web:** www.citizenm.com

Right in the heart of Glasgow, citizenM Glasgow is the height of urban, stylish, business-and-pleasure, boutique accommodation. From the 1 minute check-in promise to the new-media friendly meeting rooms and lobby, this is something different. The bedrooms are stylishly economical, making the most of limited space. They have super-sized beds, blackout blinds, free WiFi, ambient mood lighting, rain shower and a wall-to-wall window above the bed. CanteenM serves breakfast, lunch and dinner, and serves as a 24-hour bar.

Rooms 198 **Facilities** STV FTV WiFi **Notes** ⊗

Ibis Budget Glasgow

AA Advertised

tel: 0141 429 8013 **2a Springfield Quay G5 8NP**
email: H3503@accor.com **web:** www.ibishotel.com
dir: *In central Glasgow, close to Glasgow Central station & SECC*

Modern, budget hotel offering comfortable accommodation in bright and practical bedrooms. Breakfast is self-service and dinner is available in the restaurant.

Rooms 165 ⌕ S £33-£92; D £33-£92* **Facilities** FTV WiFi ⌔ **Services** Lift **Notes** LB

Ibis Glasgow City Centre

AA Advertised

tel: 0141 225 6000 & 619 9000 **220 West Regent St G2 4DQ**
email: H3139@accor.com **web:** www.ibishotel.com

Modern, budget hotel offering comfortable accommodation in bright and practical bedrooms. Breakfast is self-service and meals are also available in the café-bar 24 hours.

Rooms 141 ⌕ **Facilities** FTV WiFi **Services** Lift

GLASGOW *continued*

The Z Hotel Glasgow

AA Advertised

tel: 0141 212 4550 **36 North Frederick St G1 2BS**
email: glasgow@thezhotels.com **web:** www.thezhotels.com
dir: *Located 0.1m from George Sq*

Stay in the heart of Glasgow for an out-of-town price, at Z Glasgow, a converted printworks right next to George Square, with over one hundred bedrooms arranged around a central lightwell over ground and five upper floors. Each room has an en suite wet room, crisp bed linen, 40" TV with Sky, and complimentary WiFi.

Rooms 104 (16 GF) 🐾 **Facilities** STV FTV WiFi ♺ **Services** Lift Air con **Notes** ⊗

G

GLASGOW AIRPORT
Renfrewshire   Map 20 NS46

Premier Inn Glasgow Airport

BUDGET HOTEL

tel: 0871 527 8434 *(Calls cost 13p per minute plus your phone company's access charge)*
Whitecart Rd, Glasgow Airport PA3 2TH
web: www.premierinn.com
dir: *M8 junct 28, follow airport signs for Long Stay & Car Park 3 (Premier Inn signed). At 1st rdbt right into St Andrews Drive. At next rdbt right into Whitecart Rd. Under motorway. Left at garage. Hotel on right*

High quality, budget accommodation ideal for both families and business travellers. Spacious, en suite bedrooms feature tea and coffee making facilities, and Freeview TV in most hotels. Internet access and WiFi are available for a small fee. The adjacent family restaurant features a wide and varied menu. See also the Hotel Groups pages.

Rooms 105

Premier Inn Glasgow (Paisley)

Premier Inn

BUDGET HOTEL

tel: 0871 527 8432 *(Calls cost 13p per minute plus your phone company's access charge)*
Phoenix Retail Park PA1 2BH
web: www.premierinn.com
dir: *M8 junct 28a, A737 signed Irvine, take 1st exit signed Linwood, left at 1st rdbt to Phoenix Park*

Rooms 62

GLENEAGLES

See Auchterarder

GLENFINNAN
Highland   Map 22 NM98

The Prince's House

★★★ 81% ◉◉ SMALL HOTEL

tel: 01397 722246 **PH37 4LT**
email: princeshouse@glenfinnan.co.uk **web:** www.glenfinnan.co.uk
dir: *On A830, 0.5m on right past Glenfinnan Monument. 200mtrs from railway station*

This delightful hotel enjoys a well deserved reputation for fine food and excellent hospitality. The hotel has inspiring views and sits close to where 'Bonnie' Prince Charlie raised the Jacobite standard. Comfortably appointed bedrooms offer pleasing decor. Excellent local game and seafood can be enjoyed in the restaurant and the bar.

Rooms 9 🐾 **S** £75-£90; **D** £125-£195 (incl. bkfst) **Facilities** STV FTV WiFi ♺ New Year **Conf** Class 20 Thtr 40 **Parking** 18 **Notes** LB ⊗ Closed Nov, Xmas, Jan-Feb RS Oct, Dec & Mar

GLENROTHES
Fife   Map 21 NO20

Premier Inn Glenrothes

Premier Inn

BUDGET HOTEL

tel: 0871 527 8454 *(Calls cost 13p per minute plus your phone company's access charge)*
Beaufort Dr, Bankhead Roundabout KY7 4UJ
web: www.premierinn.com
dir: *M90 junct 2a N'bound, A92 to Glenrothes. At 2nd rbt (Bankhead) take 3rd exit. Hotel on left*

High quality, budget accommodation ideal for both families and business travellers. Spacious, en suite bedrooms feature tea and coffee making facilities, and Freeview TV in most hotels. Internet access and WiFi are available for a small fee. The adjacent family restaurant features a wide and varied menu. See also the Hotel Groups pages.

Rooms 65

GRANGEMOUTH
Falkirk   Map 21 NS98

The Grange Manor

★★★★ 76% HOTEL

tel: 01324 474836 **Glensburgh FK3 8XJ**
email: info@grangemanor.co.uk **web:** www.grangemanor.co.uk
dir: *E: M9 junct 6, hotel 200mtrs to right. W: M9 junct 5, A905 for 2m*

Located south of town and close to the M9, this stylish hotel, popular with business and corporate clientele, benefits from hands-on family ownership. It offers spacious, high quality accommodation with superb bathrooms. Public areas include a comfortable foyer area, a lounge bar and a smart restaurant. Cook's bar and restaurant is adjacent to the main house in the converted stables. Staff throughout are very friendly.

Rooms 36 (30 annexe) (6 fmly) (15 GF) **Facilities** FTV WiFi Xmas New Year **Conf** Class 68 Board 40 Thtr 120 **Services** Lift **Parking** 154 **Notes** ⊗ Civ Wed 120

G

GRANTOWN-ON-SPEY
Highland   Map 23 NJ02

Grant Arms Hotel

★★★ 82% HOTEL

tel: 01479 872526 **25-27 The Square PH26 3HF**
email: info@grantarmshotel.com **web:** www.grantarmshotel.com
dir: *Exit A9 N of Aviemore onto A95*

Conveniently located in the centre of the town, this fine hotel is appointed to a high standard yet still retains the building's traditional character. The spacious bedrooms are stylishly presented and very well equipped. The Garden Restaurant is a popular venue for dinner, and lighter snacks can be enjoyed in the comfortable bar. Modern conference facilities are available and the hotel is very popular with birdwatchers and wildlife enthusiasts.

Rooms 50 (7 fmly) ⌁ S £45-£115, **D** £90-£190 (incl. bkfst)* **Facilities** STV FTV WiFi
⤢ Birdwatching & Wildlife Club ♫ Xmas New Year **Conf** Class 30 Board 16 Thtr 70
Del from £105 to £120* **Services** Lift **Notes** LB

GREENOCK
Inverclyde   Map 20 NS27

Premier Inn Greenock

BUDGET HOTEL

tel: 0871 527 8476 *(Calls cost 13p per minute plus your phone company's access charge)*
The Point, 1-3 James Watt Way PA15 2AD
web: www.premierinn.com
dir: A8 to Greenock. At rdbt junct of East Hamilton St & Main St (McDonalds visable on right) take 3rd exit. Hotel on left

High quality, budget accommodation ideal for both families and business travellers. Spacious, en suite bedrooms feature tea and coffee making facilities, and Freeview TV in most hotels. Internet access and WiFi are available for a small fee. The adjacent family restaurant features a wide and varied menu. See also the Hotel Groups pages.

Rooms 62

GRETNA SERVICE AREA (A74(M))
Dumfries & Galloway   Map 21 NY36

Days Inn Gretna Green - M74

WELCOMEBREAK

AA Advertised

tel: 01461 337566 **Welcome Break Service Area DG16 5HQ**
email: gretna.hotel@welcomebreak.co.uk **web:** www.welcomebreak.co.uk
dir: *Between junct 21 & 22 of A74(M) - accessible from both N'bound & S'bound carriageways*

This modern building offers accommodation in smart, spacious and well-equipped bedrooms suitable for families and business travellers, and all with en suite bathrooms. Continental breakfast is available and other refreshments may be taken at the nearby family restaurant.

Rooms 64 (54 fmly) (64 GF) **Facilities** FTV WiFi ⤢ Xmas New Year **Parking** 60

GRETNA (WITH GRETNA GREEN)
Dumfries & Galloway   Map 21 NY36

Smiths at Gretna Green

★★★★ 78% ◉◉ HOTEL   CLASSIC BRITISH HOTELS

tel: 01461 337007 **Gretna Green DG16 5EA**
email: info@smithsgretnagreen.com **web:** www.smithsgretnagreen.com
dir: *From M74 junct 22 follow signs to Old Blacksmith's Shop. Hotel opposite*

Located next to the World Famous Old Blacksmith's Shop Centre just off the motorway linking Scotland and England. The bedrooms offer a spacious environment, complete with flat-screen TVs, DVD players and broadband. Family rooms feature a separate children's area with bunk beds, each with its own TV. Three suites and a penthouse apartment are also available. Open-plan contemporary day rooms lead to the brasserie restaurant; impressive conference and banqueting facilities are provided.

Rooms 56 (6 annexe) (8 fmly) ⌁ **Facilities** STV FTV WiFi ⤢ HL Beauty treatment room
New Year **Conf** Class 100 Board 40 Thtr 250 Del from £115 to £155* **Services** Lift
Air con **Parking** 115 **Notes** Civ Wed 150

The Gables Hotel

★★★ Ⓐ HOTEL

tel: 01461 338300 **1 Annan Rd DG16 5DQ**
email: reservations@gables-hotel-gretna.co.uk **web:** www.gables-hotel-gretna.co.uk
dir: *M74 S or M6/M/4 N follow signs for Gretna. At rdbt at Gretna Gateway take exit onto Annan Rd, hotel 200yds on right*

This Grade II listed hotel is located close to the Gretna Gateway and is ideally located to explore both Galloway and the Border City of Carlisle. Bedrooms offer comfortable and well-appointed accommodation. The main restaurant offers a carte menu with a range of freshly prepared dishes, while Saddlers bar provides light snacks and meals.

Rooms 31 (5 fmly) (10 GF) ⌁ **Facilities** FTV WiFi Xmas New Year **Conf** Class 60
Board 48 Thtr 100 **Parking** 60 **Notes** ⊗ Civ Wed 100

GULLANE
East Lothian   Map 21 NT48

Greywalls and Chez Roux

★★★★★ 86% ◉◉ COUNTRY HOUSE HOTEL

tel: 01620 842144 **Muirfield EH31 2EG**
email: enquiries@greywalls.co.uk **web:** www.greywalls.co.uk
dir: *From Edinburgh follow A1, junct for North Berwick A198 then Gullane. Greywalls is at the end of village on left*

Located in the magnificent East Lothian countryside, Greywalls is just half an hour's drive from Edinburgh, and is located next to the world-famous Muirfield golf course. The hotel offers easy access to some wonderful beaches and there are ten golf courses within five miles. In the grounds are some delightful gardens, and you may be lucky enough to see the beekeeper tending the hives. Inside, public areas are warm and welcoming with an array of seating areas and open fires adding to the charm. Bedrooms are well appointed, in keeping with the style and character of the house. Award-winning food from the Chez Roux team has to be experienced while the hearty breakfast will set you up for the day.

Rooms 23 (6 annexe) (5 GF) ⌁ S £95-£125; **D** £245-£370 (incl. bkfst) **Facilities** FTV
WiFi ⤢ 🏌 Putt green 🏌 Holistic massage Walled gardens Golf retreats ♫ Xmas
New Year **Conf** Class 18 Board 18 Thtr 60 Del from £195 to £295* **Parking** 40
Notes LB Civ Wed 120

INVERARAY
Argyll & Bute
Map 20 NN00

Loch Fyne Hotel & Spa
★★★★ 72% HOTEL

tel: 01499 302980 **Shore St PA32 8XT**
email: lochfyne@crerarhotels.com **web:** www.crerarhotels.com/loch-fyne-hotel-spa
dir: *From A83 Loch Lomond, through town centre on A80 to Lochgilphead. Hotel in 0.5m on the right, overlooking Loch Fyne*

Loch Fyne Hotel & Spa is situated in a stunning location with uninterrupted views across the loch and surrounding landscape, just a short drive from a range of ancient architecture. Public areas include the Clansman restaurant and a large lounge bar with comfy sofas. The bedrooms are modern and well equipped; some rooms have views of the Loch.

Rooms 67 (9 fmly) (15 GF) S £65-£150; D £95-£199 (incl. bkfst)* **Facilities** Spa FTV WiFi Sauna Steam room Xmas New Year **Conf** Class 30 Board 25 Thtr 80 Del from £99 to £199* **Services** Lift **Parking** 60 **Notes** LB Civ Wed 120

INVERGARRY
Highland
Map 22 NH30

Glengarry Castle Hotel
★★★ 82% COUNTRY HOUSE HOTEL

tel: 01809 501254 **PH35 4HW**
email: castle@glengarry.net **web:** www.glengarry.net
dir: *On A82, 0.5m from A82/A87 junct*

This charming country-house hotel is set in 50 acres of grounds on the shores of Loch Oich. The spacious day rooms include comfortable sitting rooms with lots to read and board games to play. The classical dining room boasts an innovative menu that showcases local Scottish produce. The smart bedrooms vary in size and style but all boast magnificent loch or woodland views. The grounds are well worth a look around, with a tennis court and paths along the loch to be found.

Rooms 26 (2 fmly) S £85-£95; D £125-£230 (incl. dinner) **Facilities** FTV WiFi Fishing **Parking** 30 **Notes** Closed mid Nov-mid Mar

INVERGORDON
Highland
Map 23 NH76

Kincraig Castle Hotel
★★★★ 78% COUNTRY HOUSE HOTEL

tel: 01349 852587 **IV18 0LF**
email: info@kincraig-castle-hotel.co.uk **web:** www.kincraig-castle-hotel.co.uk
dir: *Off A9 past Alness towards Tain. Hotel on left 0.25m past Rosskeen Church*

This imposing castle is set in well-tended grounds in an elevated position with views over the Cromarty Firth. It offers smart, individually designed, well-equipped bedrooms with satellite TVs, and inviting public areas that retain the original features. However, it is the friendly service and commitment to guest care that will leave a lasting impression.

Rooms 15 (1 fmly) (1 GF) **Facilities** FTV WiFi 4 Putt green Xmas New Year **Conf** Class 30 Board 24 Thtr 50 **Parking** 30 **Notes** Civ Wed 70

INVERKEILOR
Angus
Map 23 NO64

Gordon's
RESTAURANT WITH ROOMS

tel: 01241 830364 **Main St DD11 5RN**
email: gordonsrest@aol.com **web:** www.gordonsrestaurant.co.uk
dir: *Exit A92 between Arbroath & Montrose into Inverkeilor*

It's worth a detour off the main road to this family-run restaurant with rooms set in the centre of the village. The food in the restaurant has been awarded three AA Rosettes, and the excellent breakfasts are equally memorable. A huge fire dominates the restaurant on cooler evenings. Individually designed rooms all come with contemporary wenge furniture, oversized headboards, chandeliers, high decorative cornice and designer wallpaper. The showcase 'Thistle Suite' is in purple, stone and lavender and has an en suite bathroom with roll-top bath and monsoon shower.

Rooms 5 (1 annexe)

INVERNESS
Highland
Map 23 NH64

Loch Ness Country House Hotel
★★★★ 79% SMALL HOTEL

tel: 01463 230512 **Loch Ness Rd IV3 8JN**
email: info@lochnesscountryhousehotel.co.uk **web:** www.lochnesscountryhousehotel.co.uk
dir: *On A82, 1m from Inverness town boundary*

Built in the Georgian era, this fine house is perfectly situated in its own six acre private Highland estate. The hotel has luxurious bedrooms, four of which are in the garden suite cottages. The stylish restaurant serves the best of local produce and guests have a choice of cosy well-appointed lounges for after dinner drinks. The terrace is ideal for relaxing and has splendid views over the landscaped gardens towards Inverness.

Rooms 13 (2 annexe) (8 fmly) (3 GF) S £90-£215; D £100-£265 (incl. bkfst)* **Facilities** FTV WiFi Xmas New Year **Conf** Class 40 Board 40 Thtr 100 Del from £135 to £295* **Parking** 70 **Notes** LB Civ Wed 150

The New Drumossie Hotel

★★★★ 77% ◉◉ HOTEL

tel: 01463 236451 & 0870 194 2110
(Calls cost 13p per minute plus your phone company's access charge) **Old Perth Rd IV2 5BE**
email: stay@drumossiehotel.co.uk **web:** www.drumossiehotel.co.uk
dir: *From A9 follow signs for Culloden Battlefield, hotel on left after 1m*

Set in nine acres of landscaped hillside grounds south of Inverness, this hotel has fine views of the Moray Firth towards Ben Wyvis. Art deco style decoration together with a country-house atmosphere are found throughout. Service is friendly and attentive, the food imaginative and enjoyable, and the bedrooms spacious and well presented. The main function room is probably the largest in this area.

Rooms 44 (10 fmly) (6 GF) ⋒ **Facilities** STV FTV WiFi HL Fishing New Year **Conf** Class 200 Board 40 Thtr 500 **Services** Lift **Parking** 200 **Notes** Civ Wed 400

Bunchrew House Hotel

★★★★ 75% ◉◉ COUNTRY HOUSE HOTEL

tel: 01463 234917 **Bunchrew IV3 8TA**
email: welcome@bunchrewhousehotel.com **web:** www.bunchrewhousehotel.com
dir: *W on A862. Hotel 2m after canal on right*

Overlooking the Beauly Firth this impressive mansion house dates from the 17th century and retains much original character. Individually styled bedrooms are spacious and tastefully furnished. A wood-panelled restaurant is the setting for artfully constructed cooking and there is a choice of comfortable lounges complete with real fires.

Rooms 16 (4 fmly) (1 GF) ⋒ **Facilities** FTV WiFi Fishing New Year **Conf** Class 30 Board 30 Thtr 80 **Parking** 40 **Notes** Closed 24-27 Dec Civ Wed 92

Glenmoriston Town House Hotel

★★★★ 74% ◉ TOWN HOUSE HOTEL

tel: 01463 223777 **20 Ness Bank IV2 4SF**
email: reception@glenmoristontownhouse.com **web:** www.glenmoristontownhouse.com
dir: *On riverside opposite theatre*

Bold contemporary designs blend seamlessly with the classical architecture of this stylish hotel, situated on the banks of the River Ness. Delightful day rooms include a well-stocked piano bar with a fine selection of malt whiskies and an interesting cocktail menu. Contrast Brasserie features accomplished modern cooking based on the finest Scottish produce. When the weather allows, alfresco eating is possible with views over the River Ness. The sleek, modern, individually designed bedrooms have many facilities including free WiFi, DVD players and flat-screen TVs.

Rooms 30 (15 annexe) (1 fmly) (6 GF) ⋒ **S** £55-£125; **D** £65-£245 (incl. bkfst)*
Facilities STV FTV WiFi ♪ Xmas New Year **Conf** Class 40 Board 60 Thtr 90 **Parking** 40 **Notes** LB ⊗ Civ Wed 70

Mercure Inverness Hotel

★★★ 80% HOTEL

tel: 0844 815 9006 *(Calls cost 7p per minute plus your phone company's access charge)*
Church St IV1 1DX
email: info@mercureinverness.co.uk **web:** www.mercureinverness.co.uk
dir: *From A9 junct A82 Kessock Bridge join A82 Inverness. At rdbt 2nd exit, rdbt straight ahead next rdbt left onto B865. Right at lights continue past church, hotel on left*

The Mercure Inverness Hotel is in an ideal location, with the bustling Inverness city centre to one side, and the attractive River Ness running the length of the other. Spacious public areas, an inviting gym area and comfortable bedrooms can all be found here. The Brasserie serves a wide ranging selection of dishes. On-site parking and complimentary WiFi are added bonuses.

Rooms 118 ⋒ **Facilities** FTV WiFi ⅋ Gym 24 hour gym **Conf** Class 130 Board 90 Thtr 200 **Services** Lift **Parking** 55 **Notes** Civ Wed 200

Best Western Inverness Palace Hotel & Spa   ⓑⓦ Best Western.

★★★ 79% HOTEL

tel: 01463 223243 **8 Ness Walk IV3 5NG**
email: palace@miltonhotels.com **web:** www.invernesspalacehotel.co.uk
dir: *A82 Glenurquhart Rd onto Ness Walk. Hotel 300yds on right opposite Inverness Castle*

Set on the north side of the River Ness close to the Eden Court theatre and a short walk from the town, this hotel has a contemporary look. Recently refurbished bedrooms are comfortable and modern, while public areas feature a Starbucks coffee shop and extensive leisure facilities.

Rooms 89 (48 annexe) (3 fmly) ⋒ **S** £79.90 £179.90, **D** £99.90-£329.90*
Facilities Spa FTV WiFi ⊛ supervised Gym Beautician Sauna Steam room Xmas New Year **Conf** Class 40 Board 30 Thtr 80 Del from £149.90 to £219.90*
Services Lift **Parking** 18 **Notes** Civ Wed 100

Royal Highland Hotel

★★★ 77% HOTEL

tel: 01463 231926 & 251451 **Station Square, Academy St IV1 1LG**
email: info@royalhighlandhotel.co.uk **web:** www.royalhighlandhotel.co.uk
dir: *From A9 into town centre. Hotel next to rail station & Eastgate Retail Centre*

Built in 1858 adjacent to the railway station, the Royal Highland Hotel has a typically grand Victorian foyer with comfortable seating. The contemporary ASH Brasserie and bar is a refreshing venue for both eating and drinking throughout the day. The generally spacious bedrooms are comfortably equipped especially for the business traveller. A recently introduced art gallery showcases an impressive array of artwork.

Rooms 86 (12 fmly) (2 GF) (10 smoking) ⋒ **S** £40-£150; **D** £50-£199 **Facilities** FTV WiFi Xmas New Year **Conf** Class 80 Board 80 Thtr 200 Del from £75 to £175 **Services** Lift **Parking** 8 **Notes** LB Civ Wed 200

Rocpool and Chez Roux

Ⓤ

tel: 01463 240089 **14 Culduthel Rd IV2 4AG**
email: info@rocpool.com **web:** www.rocpool.com
dir: *A9 to Inverness, take exit for Raigmore Hospital then follow signs for city centre. Left at lights onto Southside Rd, right onto Culduthel Rd*

Currently the rating for this establishment is not confirmed. This may be due to a change of ownership or because it has only recently joined the AA rating scheme For further details please see the AA website: theAA.com

Rooms 11 (2 GF) ⋒ **S** £195-£395; **D** £230-£395 (incl. bkfst)* **Facilities** FTV WiFi ⅋ **Conf** Class 16 Board 18 Thtr 20 Del £330* **Services** Air con **Parking** 14 **Notes** LB Civ Wed 20

INVERNESS *continued*

Premier Inn Inverness Centre (Milburn Rd)

BUDGET HOTEL

tel: 0871 527 8544 *(Calls cost 13p per minute plus your phone company's access charge)*
Millburn Rd IV2 3QX
web: www.premierinn.com
dir: *From A9 & A96 junct (Raigmore Interchange, signed Airport/Aberdeen), take B865 towards town centre, hotel 100yds after next rdbt*

High quality, budget accommodation ideal for both families and business travellers. Spacious, en suite bedrooms feature tea and coffee making facilities, and Freeview TV in most hotels. Internet access and WiFi are available for a small fee. The adjacent family restaurant features a wide and varied menu. See also the Hotel Groups pages.

Rooms 55

Premier Inn Inverness Centre (River Ness)

BUDGET HOTEL

tel: 0871 527 9302 *(Calls cost 13p per minute plus your phone company's access charge)*
19-21 Huntly St IV3 5PR
web: www.premierinn.com
dir: *Exit A9 at Longman rdbt, 1st exit into Longman Rd (A82) follow Inverness/Fort William signs. Straight on at 3 rdbts. At Telford St rdbt 1st exit into Wells St. Right into Huntly St. Hotel on right*

Rooms 99

Premier Inn Inverness East

BUDGET HOTEL

tel: 0871 527 8546 *(Calls cost 13p per minute plus your phone company's access charge)*
Beechwood Business Park IV2 3BW
web: www.premierinn.com
dir: *From A9 follow Raigmore Hospital, Police HQ & Inshes Retail Park signs*

Rooms 74

Premier Inn Inverness West

BUDGET HOTEL

tel: 0871 527 9338 *(Calls cost 13p per minute plus your phone company's access charge)*
Glenurquhart Rd IV3 5TD
web: www.premierinn.com
dir: *From A9 exit at Kessock rdbt. At 4th rdbt 2nd exit into Kenneth St. Right at lights into Glenruquhart Rd, pass council offices, 1m, take A82 signed Fort William. Cross Caledonian Canal Bridge. Hotel on right*

Rooms 76

INVERURIE	Map 23 NJ72
Aberdeenshire	

Macdonald Pittodrie House

★★★★ 77% ◉◉ HOTEL

tel: 0121 643 9191 & 0370 194 2111 **Chapel of Garioch, Pitcaple AB51 5HS**
email: gm.pittodrie@macdonald-hotels.co.uk **web:** www.macdonald-hotels.com/pittodrie
dir: *From A96 towards Inverness, pass Inverurie under bridge with lights. Turn left & follow signs*

Set in extensive grounds this house dates from the 15th century and retains many historic features. Public rooms include a gracious drawing room, restaurant, and a cosy bar boasting an impressive selection of whiskies. The well-proportioned bedrooms are found in both the original house and in the extension that was designed to match the existing building.

Rooms 27 (6 fmly) **Facilities** STV FTV WiFi Clay pigeon shooting Quad biking Outdoor activities Xmas New Year **Conf** Class 75 Board 50 Thtr 150 **Parking** 200 **Notes** Civ Wed 120

Thainstone House

★★★★ 77% ◉◉ HOTEL

tel: 01467 621643 **AB51 5NT**
email: thainstone@crerarhotels.com **web:** www.crerarhotels.com/thainstone-house-hotel
dir: *A96 from Aberdeen. Pass by-pass to Kintore. Entrance to hotel at 1st rdbt Thainstone Rdbt. Take 1st left then sharp right to hotel*

Sat in several acres of gardens and meadowlands this former Jacobean house has been developed throughout the centuries. The hotel now provides a choice of bars, lounges and a well equipped games room. Spa facilities include an outdoor hot tub, sauna, pool and gym. Dining is available in the Green Lady restaurant or Stockmans bar.

Rooms 48 (12 GF) 🛏 **S** £89-£169; **D** £99-£169* **Facilities** Spa STV WiFi ⓢ Gym Sauna Steam room Xmas New Year **Conf** Class 100 Board 25 Thtr 200 Del from £150 to £200* **Services** Lift **Parking** 100 **Notes** LB Civ Wed 180

IRVINE	Map 20 NS33
North Ayrshire	

Hallmark Hotel Irvine

★★★★ 70% HOTEL

tel: 0330 028 3415 **46 Annick Rd KA11 4LD**
email: irvine@menzieshotels.co.uk **web:** www.hallmarkhotels.co.uk
dir: *From A78 at Warrix Interchange follow Irvine Central signs. At rdbt 2nd exit (town centre). At next rdbt right onto A71/Kilmarnock. Hotel 100mtrs on left*

Situated on the edge of Irvine with good transportation links (including Prestwick Airport just seven miles away), this is a well-presented hotel that has an extremely friendly team with good customer care awareness. The decor is contemporary throughout, and there is a brasserie-style restaurant, cocktail bar and spacious lounge.

Rooms 128 (14 fmly) (64 GF) **Facilities** STV FTV WiFi ⓣ Fishing Xmas New Year **Conf** Class 140 Board 100 Thtr 280 **Parking** 180 **Notes** LB Civ Wed 200

KELSO	Map 21 NT73
Scottish Borders	

The Roxburghe Hotel, Golf Course and Chez Roux

★★★★ 81% ◉◉ COUNTRY HOUSE HOTEL

tel: 01573 450331 **Heiton TD5 8JZ**
email: hotel@roxburghe.net **web:** www.roxburghe-hotel.com
dir: *From A68 Jedburgh take A698 to Heiton, 3m SW of Kelso*

Outdoor sporting pursuits are popular at this impressive Jacobean mansion owned by the Duke of Roxburghe, and set in 500 acres of woods and parkland bordering the River Teviot. Gracious public areas are the perfect settings for afternoon teas and carefully prepared meals. The elegant bedrooms are individually designed, some by the Duchess herself, and include superior rooms, some with four posters and log fires.

Rooms 22 (6 annexe) (3 fmly) (8 GF) **S** £225-£365; **D** £225-£365 (incl. bkfst)*
Facilities Spa FTV WiFi ⓣ ⌘ 18 Putt green Fishing ⛳ Clay shooting Health & beauty salon Mountain bike hire Falconry Archery Xmas New Year **Conf** Class 20 Board 20 Thtr 50 **Parking** 150 **Notes** Civ Wed 60

KILCHRENAN
Argyll & Bute   Map 20 NN02

The Ardanaiseig Hotel
★★★★ 77% ◎◎ COUNTRY HOUSE HOTEL

tel: 01866 833333 **by Loch Awe PA35 1HE**
email: info@ardanaiseig.com **web:** www.ardanaiseig.com
dir: *A85 at Taynuilt onto B845 to Kilchrenan. Left in front of pub, narrow road signed 'Ardanaiseig Hotel' & 'No Through Road'. Continue for 3m*

Set amid lovely gardens and breathtaking scenery beside the shore of Loch Awe, this peaceful country-house hotel was built in a Scottish baronial style in 1834. Many fine pieces of furniture are evident in the bedrooms and charming day rooms, which include a drawing room, a library bar and an elegant dining room. The bedrooms are individually designed including some with four posters, some with loch views and some with access to the garden; standing on its own by the water is the Boat Shed, a delightful one bedroom suite.

Rooms 18 (4 fmly) (5 GF) ✆ **S** £135-£280; **D** £185-£330* **Facilities** FTV WiFi ⌕ Fishing ⤙ Boating Clay pigeon shooting Bikes for hire In house massage treatments New Year **Parking** 20 **Notes** Civ Wed 50

Taychreggan Hotel
★★★ 83% ◎◎ COUNTRY HOUSE HOTEL

tel: 01866 833211 & 833366 **PA35 1HQ**
email: info@taychregganhotel.co.uk **web:** www.taychregganhotel.co.uk
dir: *W from Crianlarich on A85 to Taynuilt, S for 7m on B845 (single track) to Kilchrenan*

Surrounded by stunning Highland scenery, this stylish and superbly presented hotel, once a drover's cottage, enjoys an idyllic setting in 40 acres of wooded grounds on the shores of Loch Awe. The hotel has a smart bar with adjacent courtyard Orangerie and a choice of quiet lounges with deep, luxurious sofas. A well-earned reputation has been achieved by the kitchen for the skilfully prepared dinners that showcase the local and seasonal Scottish larder. Families, and also dogs and their owners, are welcome.

Rooms 18 (1 fmly) ✆ **S** £136-£324; **D** £136-£324 (incl. bkfst) **Facilities** FTV WiFi Fishing ⤙ Air rifle range Archery Clay pigeon shooting Falconry Mock deer stalk Xmas New Year **Conf** Class 15 Board 20 Del from £180 to £380 **Parking** 40 **Notes** Closed 3 Jan-9 Feb Civ Wed 70

KILLIECRANKIE
Perth & Kinross   Map 23 NN96

INSPECTORS' CHOICE

Killiecrankie Hotel
★★★ ◎◎ SMALL HOTEL

tel: 01796 473220 **PH16 5LG**
email: enquiries@killiecrankiehotel.co.uk **web:** www.killiecrankiehotel.co.uk
dir: *Exit A9 at Killiecrankie onto B8079. Hotel 3m on right*

Originally built in the 1840s, Killiecrankie sits in four acres of wooded grounds with beautifully landscaped gardens; it enjoys a tranquil location by the Pass of Killiecrankie and the River Garry. Public areas include a wood-panelled bar and a cosy sitting room with original artwork, and a blazing fire in colder months. All of the bedrooms are individually decorated, well equipped and have wonderful countryside views.

Rooms 10 (2 GF) ✆ **S** £140-£150; **D** £250-£320 (incl. bkfst & dinner)* **Facilities** FTV WiFi ⌕ ⤙ Xmas New Year **Parking** 20 **Notes** Closed 3 Jan-17 Mar

KILMARNOCK
East Ayrshire   Map 20 NS43

The Fenwick Hotel
★★★ 81% HOTEL

tel: 01560 600478 **Fenwick KA3 6AU**
email: info@thefenwickhotel.co.uk **web:** www.thefenwickhotel.co.uk
dir: *M77 junct 8, B7061 towards Fenwick, follow hotel signs*

The Fenwick Hotel benefits from a great location alongside the M77, with easy links to Ayr, Kilmarnock and Glasgow. The spacious bedrooms are thoughtfully equipped; complimentary WiFi is available throughout the hotel. The bright restaurant offers both formal and informal dining and there is an attractive lounge bar where you can relax and choose from the extensive cocktail list. The hotel also has extensive conference and function facilities.

Rooms 29 (2 fmly) (9 GF) ✆ **Facilities** STV FTV WiFi ⌕ Xmas New Year **Conf** Class 280 Board 150 Thtr 280 **Services** Lift **Parking** 64 **Notes** Civ Wed 110

K

KILMARNOCK *continued*

Premier Inn Kilmarnock

BUDGET HOTEL

tel: 0871 527 8566 *(Calls cost 13p per minute plus your phone company's access charge)*
Moorfield Roundabout, Annadale KA1 2RS
web: www.premierinn.com
dir: *M74 junct 8 signed Kilmarnock (A71). From M77 onto A71 to Irvine. At next rdbt right onto B7064 signed Crosshouse Hospital. Hotel on right*

High quality, budget accommodation ideal for both families and business travellers. Spacious, en suite bedrooms feature tea and coffee making facilities, and Freeview TV in most hotels. Internet access and WiFi are available for a small fee. The adjacent family restaurant features a wide and varied menu. See also the Hotel Groups pages.

Rooms 64

KINCARDINE
Fife   Map 21 NS98

Premier Inn Falkirk North

BUDGET HOTEL

tel: 0871 527 8394 *(Calls cost 13p per minute plus your phone company's access charge)*
Bowtrees Roundabout, Houghs of Airth FK2 8PJ
web: www.premierinn.com
dir: *From N: M9 junct 7 (or from S: M876) towards Kincardine Bridge. On rdbt at end of slip road*

High quality, budget accommodation ideal for both families and business travellers. Spacious, en suite bedrooms feature tea and coffee making facilities, and Freeview TV in most hotels. Internet access and WiFi are available for a small fee. The adjacent family restaurant features a wide and varied menu. See also the Hotel Groups pages.

Rooms 66

KINCLAVEN
Perth & Kinross   Map 21 NO13

Ballathie House Hotel

★★★★ 78% ◎◎ COUNTRY HOUSE HOTEL

tel: 01250 883268 **PH1 4QN**
email: email@ballathiehousehotel.com **web:** www.ballathiehousehotel.com
dir: *From A9, 2m N of Perth, take B9099 through Stanley, follow signs. Or from A93 at Beech Hedge follow signs for hotel, 2.5m*

Set in delightful grounds, this splendid Scottish mansion house combines classical grandeur with modern comfort. Bedrooms range from well-proportioned master rooms to modern standard rooms, and many boast antique furniture and art deco bathrooms. It might be worth requesting one of the Riverside Rooms, a purpose-built development right on the banks of the river, complete with balconies and terraces. The elegant restaurant has views over the River Tay.

Rooms 41 (16 annexe) (2 fmly) (10 GF) ☙ **Facilities** FTV WiFi Fishing ⛳ Xmas New Year **Conf** Class 20 Board 30 Thtr 50 **Services** Lift **Parking** 50 **Notes** Civ Wed 90

KINGUSSIE
Highland   Map 23 NH70

The Cross

◎◎◎ ⬠ RESTAURANT WITH ROOMS

tel: 01540 661166 **Tweed Mill Brae, Ardbroilach Rd PH21 1LB**
email: relax@thecross.co.uk **web:** www.thecross.co.uk
dir: *From lights in Kingussie centre take Ardbroilach Rd, 300yds left into Tweed Mill Brae*

Built as a water-powered tweed mill in the late 19th century, The Cross is situated in the picturesque Cairngorms National Park and surrounded by four acres of riverside grounds that teem with an abundance of wildlife, including red squirrels. Comfortable lounges and a selection of well-appointed bedrooms are offered, and award-winning dinners are served by an open fire in the stone-walled and wood-beamed restaurant.

Rooms 8 (1 fmly)

KIRKCALDY
Fife   Map 21 NT29

Dean Park Hotel

★★★ 77% HOTEL

tel: 01592 261635 **Chapel Level KY2 6QW**
email: reception@deanparkhotel.co.uk **web:** www.deanparkhotel.co.uk
dir: *Signed from A92 Kirkcaldy West junct*

Popular with both business and leisure guests, this hotel has extensive conference and meeting facilities. The bedrooms are spacious, comfortable, well equipped and enjoy modern decor and up-to-date amenities. Public areas include the Dukes Bar & Bistro, and Grill Room which is well-known for its steaks.

Rooms 33 (2 fmly) (5 GF) ☙ **Facilities** STV FTV WiFi Xmas New Year **Conf** Class 125 Board 54 Thtr 250 **Services** Lift **Parking** 250 **Notes** ⊗ Civ Wed 200

LANARK
South Lanarkshire   Map 21 NS84

Best Western Cartland Bridge Hotel

★★★ 73% COUNTRY HOUSE HOTEL

tel: 01555 664426 **Glasgow Rd ML11 9UF**
email: sales@cartlandbridge.co.uk **web:** www.bw-cartlandbridgehotel.co.uk
dir: *A73 through Lanark towards Carluke. Hotel in 1.25m*

Situated in wooded grounds on the edge of the town, this Grade I listed mansion continues to be popular with both business and leisure guests. Public areas feature wood panelling, a gallery staircase and a magnificent dining room. The well-equipped bedrooms vary in size. The hotel has an interesting history and even claims to have a ghost.

Rooms 18 (4 fmly) ☙ **S** £65-£75; **D** £112-£120 (incl. bkfst) **Facilities** FTV WiFi Xmas New Year **Conf** Class 180 Board 50 Thtr 250 Del from £102 to £126 **Parking** 120 **Notes** LB ⊗ Civ Wed 200

LIVINGSTON
West Lothian   Map 21 NT06

Mercure Livingston Hotel
★★★ 76% HOTEL

tel: 0844 815 9102 *(Calls cost 5p per minute plus your phone company's access charge)*
Almondview EH54 6QB
email: info@mercurelivingston.co.uk **web:** www.mercurelivingston.co.uk
dir: *From M8 junct 3 take A899 towards Livingston, exit at Centre Interchange, left at next rdbt, hotel on left*

This large, modern hotel is conveniently located in the town centre with easy access to the M8. Bedrooms offer freedom of space and are comfortably appointed for both business and leisure guests. There is a large open-plan lobby and restaurant area; complementary WiFi is available throughout, and there is also a small but well-appointed leisure club.

Rooms 120 (17 fmly) (55 GF) **Facilities** FTV WiFi ⇗ HL ⊗ Gym Sauna Steam room Xmas New Year **Conf** Class 55 Board 60 Thtr 130 **Parking** 130 **Notes** ⊗ Civ Wed 120

Premier Inn Livingston M8 Jct 3
BUDGET HOTEL

tel: 0871 527 8632 *(Calls cost 13p per minute plus your phone company's access charge)*
Deer Park Av, Deer Park, Knightsbridge EH54 8AD
web: www.premierinn.com
dir. *At M8 junct 3. Hotel opposite rdbt*

High quality, budget accommodation ideal for both families and business travellers. Spacious, en suite bedrooms feature tea and coffee making facilities, and Freeview TV in most hotels. Internet access and WiFi are available for a small fee. The adjacent family restaurant features a wide and varied menu. See also the Hotel Groups pages.

Rooms 107

LOCHGILPHEAD
Argyll & Bute   Map 20 NR88

Cairnbaan Hotel
★★★ 72% HOTEL

tel: 01546 603668 **Crinan Canal, Cairnbaan PA31 8SJ**
email: info@cairnbaan.com **web:** www.cairnbaan.com
dir: *2m N, A816 from Lochgilphead, hotel off B841*

Located on the Crinan Canal, this small hotel offers relaxed hospitality in a delightful setting. Bedrooms are thoughtfully equipped, generally spacious and benefit from stylish decor. Fresh seafood is a real feature in both the formal restaurant and the comfortable bar area. Alfresco dining is popular in the warmer months.

Rooms 12 **Facilities** Xmas **Conf** Class 100 Board 80 Thtr 160 **Parking** 53 **Notes** Civ Wed 120

LOCHINVER
Highland   Map 22 NC02

Inver Lodge and Chez Roux
Ⓤ

tel: 01571 844496 **Iolaire Rd IV27 4LU**
email: stay@inverlodge.com **web:** www.inverlodge.com
dir: *A837 to Lochinver, through village, left after village hall, follow private road for 0.5m*

Currently the rating for this establishment is not confirmed. This may be due to a change of ownership or because it has only recently joined the AA rating scheme. For further details please see the AA website: theAA.com

Rooms 21 (11 GF) ⌁ **S** £160-£195; **D** £250-£530 (incl. bkfst)* **Facilities** FTV WiFi ⇗ Fishing **Parking** 21 **Notes** LB Closed Nov-Mar

LOCKERBIE
Dumfries & Galloway   Map 21 NY18

Kings Arms Hotel
★★ 76% HOTEL

tel: 01576 202410 **High St DG11 2JL**
email: reception@kingsarmshotel.co.uk **web:** www.kingsarmshotel.co.uk
dir: *A74(M), 0.5m into town centre, hotel opposite town hall*

Dating from the 17th century this former inn lies in the town centre. Now a family-run hotel, it provides attractive well-equipped bedrooms with WiFi access. At lunch a menu ranging from snacks to full meals is served in both the cosy bars and the restaurant at dinner.

Rooms 13 (2 fmly) ⌁ **S** £60; **D** £90 (incl. bkfst)* **Facilities** FTV WiFi Xmas New Year **Conf** Class 40 Board 30 Thtr 80 **Parking** 8

Townhead Hotel
★★ 76% SMALL HOTEL

tel. 01576 204627 & 07720 636610 **Townhead St DG11 2AG**
email: thetownhead@gmail.com **web:** www.townheadhotel.co.uk
dir: *Please phone for directions*

This hotel benefits from a great location in the centre of town. Near to the ice rink and train station and easy to find. The intimate lounge bar is popular with locals and residents alike. Bedrooms and bathrooms have been recently refurbished to a good standard and feature widescreen TVs. A wide ranging menu is available in the evenings in the restaurant. Complimentary parking is available.

Rooms 6 (2 fmly) **S** £45-£55; **D** £75-£85 (incl. bkfst)* **Facilities** STV FTV WiFi Xmas New Year **Parking** 20 **Notes** ⊗

L

LOCKERBIE *continued*

Ravenshill House Hotel

★★ 74% HOTEL

tel: 01576 202882 **12 Dumfries Rd DG11 2EF**
email: aaenquiries@ravenshillhotellockerbie.co.uk
web: www.ravenshillhotellockerbie.co.uk
dir: *From A74(M) Lockerbie junct 17 North or 18 South. Follow signs for A709 Dumfries. Hotel 0.5m on right*

Set in spacious gardens on the fringe of the town, this friendly, family-run hotel offers cheerful service and good value, home-cooked meals. Bedrooms are generally spacious and comfortably equipped, including a two-room unit ideal for families.

Rooms 7 (2 fmly) ⌇ **S** £50-£65; **D** £70-£80 (incl. bkfst)* **Facilities** FTV WiFi ⌇
Conf Class 20 Board 12 Thtr 30 **Parking** 35 **Notes** LB Closed 1-7 Jan, 2 wks in Feb & 1 wk in Nov

---

LUSS | Map 20 NS39
Argyll & Bute

The Lodge on Loch Lomond

★★★★ 71% ⊛ HOTEL

tel: 01436 860201 **G83 8PA**
email: res@loch-lomond.co.uk **web:** www.loch-lomond.co.uk
dir: *Off A82, follow sign for hotel*

This hotel is idyllically set on the shores of Loch Lomond. Public areas consist of an open-plan, split-level bar and fine dining restaurant overlooking the loch. The pine-finished bedrooms also enjoy the views and are comfortable, spacious and well equipped; some with saunas, and all with internet access. There is a stunning state-of-the-art leisure suite.

Rooms 47 (17 annexe) (20 fmly) (13 GF) ⌇ **Facilities** STV FTV WiFi ⌇ Fishing Boating Kayaks Canoes Paddleboards Wake boarding Water skies Xmas New Year **Conf** Class 120 Board 80 Thtr 200 **Parking** 120 **Notes** Civ Wed 170

MELROSE | Map 21 NT53
Scottish Borders

HIGHLY RECOMMENDED

Burts Hotel

★★★ 81% ⊛⊛ HOTEL

tel: 01896 822285 **Market Square TD6 9PL**
email: enquiries@burtshotel.co.uk **web:** www.burtshotel.co.uk
dir: *A6091, 2m from A68 3m S of Earlston*

Recognised by its distinctive black-and-white façade and colourful window boxes, in the heart of a small market town, this hotel has been under the same family ownership for almost 40 years. The genuine warmth of hospitality is notable. The smart bedrooms have been individually styled and include WiFi. Food is important at Burts, and the elegant restaurant is well complemented by the range of tasty meals in the bar.

Rooms 20 ⌇ **S** £75; **D** £120-£150 (incl. bkfst)* **Facilities** STV FTV WiFi Salmon fishing Shooting New Year **Conf** Class 20 Board 20 Thtr 38 **Parking** 40 **Notes** Closed 24-26 Dec & 4-11 Jan Civ Wed 30

MILNGAVIE | Map 20 NS57
East Dunbartonshire

Premier Inn Glasgow (Milngavie)

BUDGET HOTEL

tel: 0871 527 8428 *(Calls cost 13p per minute plus your phone company's access charge)* **103 Main St G62 6JQ**
web: www.premierinn.com
dir: *M8 junct 16, follow Milngavie (A879) signs. Approx. 5m. Pass Murray Park Training Ground. Left at lights. Hotel on A81 adjacent to West Highland Gate Beefeater*

High quality, budget accommodation ideal for both families and business travellers. Spacious, en suite bedrooms feature tea and coffee making facilities, and Freeview TV in most hotels. Internet access and WiFi are available for a small fee. The adjacent family restaurant features a wide and varied menu. See also the Hotel Groups pages.

Rooms 61

MONTROSE
Angus

Map 23 NO75

Links Hotel

★★★ 77% HOTEL

tel: 01674 671000 **Mid Links DD10 8RL**
email: reception@linkshotel.com **web:** www.linkshotel.com
dir: *From Montrose High St, turn into John St. After 500mtrs turn right onto Mid Links. Hotel on right*

This Edwardian town house hotel lies in the centre of picturesque Montrose on the Angus coast and is popular with golfers, as it is convenient for many famous courses including the world's fifth oldest; Montrose Links. Hotel facilities include a coffee house, comfortable lounge bar and restaurant. Bedrooms and bathrooms are presented in a traditional style with WiFi and complimentary parking on-site.

Rooms 36 (11 annexe) (4 fmly) (3 GF) ⦿ S £72-£130; D £96-£145 (incl. bkfst)*
Facilities STV FTV WiFi New Year **Conf** Class 60 Board 45 Thtr 120 Del from £145 to £165* **Parking** 38 **Notes** LB Civ Wed 100

MOTHERWELL
North Lanarkshire

Map 21 NS75

Alona Hotel

★★★★ 74% HOTEL

tel: 01698 333888 **Strathclyde Country Park ML1 3RT**
email: gm@alonahotel.co.uk **web:** www.alonahotel.co.uk
dir: *M74 junct 5, hotel approx 250yds on left*

Alona is a Celtic word meaning 'exquisitely beautiful'. This hotel is situated within the idyllic beauty of Strathclyde Country Park, with tranquil views over the picturesque loch and surrounding forests. There is a very contemporary feel, from the open-plan public areas to the spacious and well-appointed bedrooms. WiFi is available throughout. M&D's, Scotland's Family Theme Park, is just next door.

Rooms 51 (24 fmly) (17 GF) ⦿ **Facilities** FTV WiFi ⥮ Xmas New Year **Conf** Class 100 Board 76 Thtr 400 **Services** Lift Air con **Parking** 100 **Notes** ⊗ Civ Wed 250

Premier Inn Glasgow (Motherwell)

BUDGET HOTEL

tel: 0871 527 8430 *(Calls cost 13p per minute plus your phone company's access charge)*
Edinburgh Rd, Newhouse ML1 5SY
web: www.premierinn.com
dir: *From S: M74 junct 5, A725 towards Coatbridge. Take A8 towards Edinburgh, exit at junct 6, follow Lanark signs. Hotel 400yds on right*

High quality, budget accommodation ideal for both families and business travellers. Spacious, en suite bedrooms feature tea and coffee making facilities, and Freeview TV in most hotels. Internet access and WiFi are available for a small fee. The adjacent family restaurant features a wide and varied menu. See also the Hotel Groups pages.

Rooms 60

MUIR OF ORD
Highland

Map 23 NH55

Ord House Hotel

★★ 78% ⊛ SMALL HOTEL

THE CIRCLE

tel: 01463 870492 **Old Dr IV6 7UH**
email: admin@ord-house.co.uk **web:** www.ord-house.co.uk
dir: *Exit A9 at Tore rdbt onto A832. 5m, through Muir of Ord. Left towards Ullapool A832. Hotel 0.5m on left*

Dating back to 1637, this country-house hotel is situated peacefully in wooded grounds and offers brightly furnished and well-proportioned accommodation. Comfortable day rooms reflect the character and charm of the house, with inviting lounges, a cosy snug bar and an elegant dining room where wide-ranging, creative menus are offered.

Rooms 12 (2 fmly) (3 GF) ⦿ S £70-£95; D £105-£155 (incl. bkfst)^ **Facilities** WiFi ⥮ Putt green ⥎ Clay pigeon shooting **Parking** 30 **Notes** LB Closed Nov-Apr

NAIRN
Highland

Map 23 NH85

Golf View Hotel & Spa

★★★★ 75% ⊛ HOTEL

tel: 01667 452301 **Seabank Rd IV12 4HD**
email: golfview@crerarhotels.com **web:** www.crerarhotels.com
dir: *Exit A96 into Seabank Rd, hotel at end on right*

This northern gem has wonderful sea views overlooking the Moray Firth and the Black Isle beyond. The championship golf course at Nairn is adjacent and guests can wander directly onto to the long sandy beach. Guestrooms are of a high standard and the public areas welcoming. As well as all this there are the hotel's own outdoor hot tub, indoor swimming pool, spa bath, gym and Elemis Spa treatments.

Rooms 42 (6 fmly) **Facilities** Spa FTV WiFi ⊛ supervised ⥎ Gym Sauna Steam room Xmas New Year **Conf** Class 40 Board 40 Thtr 100 **Services** Lift **Parking** 40 **Notes** Civ Wed 100

INSPECTORS' CHOICE

Boath House

⊛⊛⊛⊛ RESTAURANT WITH ROOMS

tel: 01667 454896 **Auldearn IV12 5TE**
email: info@boath-house.com **web:** www.boath-house.com
dir: *2m past Nairn on A96, E towards Forres, signed on main road*

Standing in its own 20-acre grounds, this splendid Georgian mansion was built in 1825 for the Dunbar family, but there has been occupation on this site since the 16th century. Guests are welcome to stroll around the gardens which have an ornamental lake, walled garden and secluded seating areas to relax in. The hospitality here is first class; the owners are passionate about what they do, and have an ability to establish a special relationship with their guests that will be particularly remembered. The food is also very memorable; head chef Charlie Lockley is a devotee of slow and organic cooking which also includes using foraged produce. The five-course dinners are a culinary adventure, matched only by the excellence of breakfasts. The house itself is delightful, with inviting lounges and a dining room overlooking a trout loch. The bedrooms, with lake and woodland views, are striking and very comfortable; Orangerie Rooms have their own conservatory.

Rooms 8

NETHY BRIDGE
Highland — Map 23 NJ02

Nethybridge Hotel
★★★ 67% HOTEL

tel: 01479 821203 **PH25 3DP**
email: salesnethybridge@strathmorehotels.com **web:** www.strathmorehotels.com
dir: *A9 onto A95, onto B970 to Nethy Bridge*

This popular tourist and coaching hotel enjoys a central location amidst the majestic Cairngorm Mountains. Bedrooms are stylishly furnished in bold tartans while traditionally styled day rooms include two bars and a popular snooker room. Staff are friendly and keen to please.

Rooms 70 (3 fmly) (7 GF) ⚓ **S** £36.55-£75; **D** £78-£142 (incl. bkfst)* **Facilities** FTV WiFi Putt green Bowling green ♬ Xmas New Year **Conf** Board 50 Thtr 150 Del from £75 to £120* **Services** Lift **Parking** 80 **Notes** LB

NEWTON MEARNS
East Renfrewshire — Map 20 NS55

Premier Inn Glasgow Newton Mearns (M77 Jct 4)

BUDGET HOTEL

tel: 0871 527 9304 *(Calls cost 13p per minute plus your phone company's access charge)*
Greenlaw Crookfur Rd G77 6NP
web: www.premierinn.com
dir: *From N exit M77 junct 4 towards Newton Mearns. At rdbt 1st left. Hotel on left*

High quality, budget accommodation ideal for both families and business travellers. Spacious, en suite bedrooms feature tea and coffee making facilities, and Freeview TV in most hotels. Internet access and WiFi are available for a small fee. The adjacent family restaurant features a wide and varied menu. See also the Hotel Groups pages.

Rooms 60

NEWTON STEWART
Dumfries & Galloway — Map 20 NX46

The Bruce Hotel
★★★ 71% HOTEL

tel: 01671 402294 **88 Queen St DG8 6JL**
email: mail@the-bruce-hotel.com **web:** www.the-bruce-hotel.com
dir: *Exit A75 at Newton Stewart rdbt towards town. Hotel 800mtrs on right*

Named after the Scottish patriot Robert the Bruce, this welcoming hotel is just a short distance from the A75. One of the well-appointed bedrooms features a four-

poster bed, and popular family suites contain separate bedrooms for children. Public areas include a traditional lounge, a formal restaurant and a lounge bar, both offering a good choice of dishes.

Rooms 20 (2 fmly) **S** £50-£80; **D** £60-£90 (incl. bkfst)* **Facilities** FTV WiFi New Year **Conf** Class 50 Board 14 Thtr 100 Del from £70 to £110 **Parking** 14 **Notes** LB

NORTH BERWICK
East Lothian — Map 21 NT58

Macdonald Marine Hotel & Spa
★★★★ 81% ⊛⊛ HOTEL

tel: 01620 897300 & 0344 879 9130 **Cromwell Rd EH39 4LZ**
email: sales.marine@macdonald-hotels.co.uk **web:** www.macdonaldhotels.co.uk/marine
dir: *From A198 turn into Hamilton Rd at lights then 2nd right*

This imposing hotel commands stunning views across the local golf course to the Firth of Forth. Stylish public areas provide a relaxing atmosphere; creative dishes are served in the restaurant and lighter bites in the lounge/bar. Bedrooms come in a variety of sizes and styles, all are well equipped and some are impressively large. The hotel boasts extensive leisure and conference facilities.

Rooms 83 (7 fmly) (9 GF) ⚓ **Facilities** Spa STV FTV WiFi ↳ ⊡ supervised ⇗ supervised Gym Indoor & outdoor hydro pool Thermal areas Xmas New Year **Conf** Class 120 Board 60 Thtr 300 **Services** Lift **Parking** 50 **Notes** Civ Wed 150

OBAN
Argyll & Bute — Map 20 NM82

Manor House Hotel
★★★ 82% ⊛ HOTEL

tel: 01631 562087 **Gallanach Rd PA34 4LS**
email: info@manorhouseoban.com **web:** www.manorhouseoban.com
dir: *Follow MacBrayne Ferries signs, pass ferry entrance for hotel on right*

Handy for the ferry terminal and with views of the bay and harbour, this elegant Georgian residence was built in 1780 as the dower house for the family of the Duke of Argyll. Comfortable and attractive public rooms invite relaxation, while most of the well-equipped bedrooms are furnished with period pieces. Nelson's Bar has stunning views over the bay and fine dining is available in the restaurant. The hotel has its own mooring.

Rooms 11 (1 GF) ⚓ **S** £110-£250; **D** £120-£250 (incl. bkfst)* **Facilities** FTV WiFi New Year **Parking** 20 **Notes** No children 12yrs Closed 25-26 Dec Civ Wed 30

Falls of Lora Hotel

THE INDEPENDENTS
HOTEL ASSOCIATION

★★★ 73% HOTEL

tel: 01631 710483 **Connel Ferry PA37 1PB**
email: enquiries@fallsoflora.com **web:** www.fallsoflora.com
dir: *From Glasgow take A82, A85. Hotel 0.5m past Connel sign 5m before Oban*

Personally run and welcoming, this long-established and thriving holiday hotel enjoys inspiring views over Loch Etive. The spacious ground floor takes in a comfortable, traditional lounge and a cocktail bar with over a hundred whiskies and an open log fire. Guests can eat in the popular, informal bistro, which is open all day. Bedrooms come in a variety of styles, ranging from the cosy standard rooms to high quality luxury rooms.

Rooms 30 (2 fmly) (4 GF) ✎ **S** £47-£66; **D** £77-£174 (incl. bkfst)* **Facilities** FTV WiFi
↳ Child facilities **Conf** Class 20 Board 15 Thtr 45 **Parking** 40 **Notes** LB Closed mid Dec & Jan

Royal Hotel

★★★ 71% HOTEL

tel: 01631 563021 **Argyll Sqaure PA34 4BE**
email: salesroyaloban@strathmorehotels.com **web:** www.strathmorehotels.com
dir: *A82 from Glasgow towards Loch Lomond & Crianlarich then A85, past Loch Awe to Oban*

Well situated in the heart of Oban, just minutes from the ferry terminal and with all the shops on its doorstep, this hotel really is central. The comfortable and well-presented bedrooms differ in size, and all public areas are smart. There is a first-floor restaurant overlooking the town square and a popular lounge bar on the ground floor where food and drink are served all day.

Rooms 91 (3 fmly) ✎ **Facilities** FTV WiFi ♫ Xmas New Year **Conf** Class 60 Board 30 Thtr 140 Del from £69 to £99* **Services** Lift **Parking** 15 **Notes** Civ Wed 100

OLDMELDRUM
Aberdeenshire

Map 23 NJ82

HIGHLY RECOMMENDED

Meldrum House Country Hotel & Golf Course

★★★★ 84% ◉◉ COUNTRY HOUSE HOTEL

tel: 01651 872294 **AB51 0AE**
email: enquiries@meldrumhouse.com **web:** www.meldrumhouse.com
dir: *11m from Aberdeen on A947 - Aberdeen to Banff road*

Set in 350 acres of wooded parkland this imposing baronial country mansion has a golf course as its centrepiece. Tastefully restored to highlight its original character it provides a peaceful retreat. Bedrooms are massive, and like the public rooms, transport guests back to a bygone era, but at the same time provide stylish modern amenities including smart bathrooms.

Rooms 51 (13 annexe) (1 fmly) (6 GF) ✎ **Facilities** FTV WiFi ⅃ 18 Putt green ⛳ Xmas New Year **Conf** Class 200 Board 75 Thtr 200 **Services** Lift **Parking** 70 **Notes** Civ Wed 150

ONICH
Highland

Map 22 NN06

Onich Hotel

★★★ 71% HOTEL

tel: 01855 821214 **PH33 6RY**
email: enquiries@onich-fortwilliam.co.uk **web:** www.onich-fortwilliam.co.uk
dir: *Beside A82, 2m N of Ballachulish Bridge*

Genuine hospitality is part of the appeal of this hotel, which lies right beside Loch Linnhe with gardens extending to its shores. Nicely presented public areas include a choice of inviting lounges and contrasting bars, and views of the loch can be enjoyed from the attractive restaurant. Bedrooms, with pleasing colour schemes, are comfortably modern.

Rooms 26 (6 fmly) ✎ **Facilities** STV FTV WiFi Games room ♫ New Year **Conf** Board 40 Thtr 50 **Parking** 50 **Notes** LB Civ Wed 120

O

PEAT INN
Fife

Map 21 NO40

INSPECTORS' CHOICE

The Peat Inn

RESTAURANT WITH ROOMS

tel: 01334 840206 **KY15 5LH**
email: stay@thepeatinn.co.uk **web:** www.thepeatinn.co.uk
dir: At junct of B940 & B941, 5m SW of St Andrews

This 300-year-old former coaching inn enjoys a rural location, and is close to St Andrews. The Peat Inn is spacious, very well appointed, and offers rooms that all have lounge areas. The inn is steeped in history and for years has proved a real haven for food lovers. The three dining areas create a romantic setting, and chef/owner Geoffrey Smeddle produces excellent, award-winning dishes. Expect welcoming open fires and a relaxed ambiance. An extensive continental breakfast selection is served to guests in their bedrooms each morning.

Rooms 8 (8 annexe) (3 fmly)

PEEBLES
Scottish Borders

Map 21 NT24

Macdonald Cardrona Hotel, Golf & Spa
★★★★ 76% HOTEL

tel: 01896 833600 & 0344 879 9024 **Cardrona EH45 8NE**
email: reception.cardrona@macdonald-hotels.co.uk
web: www.macdonald-hotels.co.uk/cardrona
dir: On A72 between Peebles & Innerleithen, 3m S of Peebles

The rolling hills of the Scottish Borders are a stunning backdrop for this modern, purpose-built hotel. Spacious bedrooms are traditional in style, equipped with a range of extras, and most enjoy fantastic views of countryside. The hotel features some impressive leisure facilities, including an 18-hole golf course, 18-metre indoor pool and state-of-the-art gym.

Rooms 99 (24 fmly) (16 GF) **Facilities** Spa FTV WiFi ♨ HL ☜ ⚓ 18 Putt green Gym Sauna Steam room Xmas New Year **Conf** Class 120 Board 90 Thtr 250 **Services** Lift **Parking** 200 **Notes** Civ Wed 200

PERTH
Perth & Kinross

Map 21 NO12

Murrayshall House Hotel & Golf Course
★★★★ 74% ◉◉ HOTEL

tel: 01738 551171 **New Scone PH2 7PH**
email: info@murrayshall.co.uk **web:** www.murrayshall.co.uk
dir: From Perth take A94 Coupar Angus, 1m from Perth, right to Murrayshall just before New Scone

This imposing country house is set in 350 acres of grounds, including two golf courses, one of which is of championship standard. Bedrooms come in two distinct styles: modern suites in a purpose-built building contrast with more classic rooms in the main building. The Clubhouse bar serves a range of meals all day, while more accomplished cooking can be enjoyed in the Old Masters Restaurant.

Rooms 41 (14 annexe) (17 fmly) (5 GF) ☜ **S** £85; **D** £155* **Facilities** STV FTV WiFi HL ⚓ 36 ⚑ Putt green Driving range New Year **Conf** Class 60 Board 30 Thtr 150 **Parking** 120 **Notes** LB Civ Wed 130

Parklands Hotel
★★★★ 72% ◉◉ SMALL HOTEL

tel: 01738 622451 **2 St Leonards Bank PH2 8EB**
email: info@theparklandshotel.com **web:** www.theparklandshotel.com
dir: M90 junct 10, in 1m left at lights at end of park area, hotel on left

Parklands Hotel is ideally located close to the centre of town, with open views over the South Inch. The enthusiastic proprietors continue to invest heavily in the business and the bedrooms have a smart contemporary feel. Public areas include a choice of restaurants, with a fine dining experience offered in 63@Parklands and more informal dining at the No. 1 The Bank Bistro.

Rooms 15 (3 fmly) (4 GF) ☜ **S** £89.50-£149.50; **D** £99.50-£179.50 (incl. bkfst)* **Facilities** STV WiFi ♨ **Conf** Class 18 Board 20 Thtr 24 Del from £134.50* **Parking** 30 **Notes** LB Closed 26 Dec-6 Jan Civ Wed 40

Best Western Lovat Hotel
★★★ 77% HOTEL

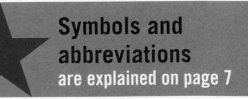

tel: 01738 636555 **90-92 Glasgow Rd PH2 0LT**
email: enquiry@lovat.co.uk **web:** www.lovathotel.co.uk
dir: M90 junct 10, 3rd exit, straight through next 3 rdbts, hotel on right 0.5m after 3rd rdbt

The Lovat Hotel offers a comfortable and relaxing atmosphere just a short walk from the centre of Perth. Accommodation consists of comfortable, modern bedrooms, and guests can enjoy a great dining experience in the 1747 Restaurant and Bar. Residents can also enjoy complimentary access to leisure facilities at the hotel's nearby sister property. Deluxe rooms are available for those looking to splash out on a little extra luxury.

Rooms 30 (1 fmly) (10 GF) ☜ **S** £45-£90; **D** £65-£120 (incl. bkfst)* **Facilities** FTV WiFi ♨ Xmas New Year **Conf** Class 60 Board 30 Thtr 150 Del from £100 to £150* **Parking** 30 **Notes** ⊗ Civ Wed 150

Best Western Queens Hotel
★★★ 73% HOTEL

tel: 01738 442222 **Leonard St PH2 8HB**
email: enquiry@queensperth.co.uk **web:** www.queensperth.co.uk
dir: From M90 follow to 2nd lights, turn left. Hotel on right, opposite railway station

This popular hotel benefits from a central location close to both the bus and rail stations. Bedrooms vary in size and style with top floor rooms offering extra space and excellent views of the town. Public rooms include a smart leisure centre and versatile conference space. A range of meals is served in both the bar and restaurant.

Rooms 50 (4 fmly) **S** £50-£70; **D** £70-£100* **Facilities** FTV WiFi ☜ Gym Steam room Sauna Xmas New Year **Conf** Class 70 Board 50 Thtr 200 Del from £105 to £120* **Services** Lift **Parking** 50 **Notes** LB ⊗ Civ Wed 220

Symbols and abbreviations are explained on page 7

Mercure Perth Hotel

★★★ 73% HOTEL

tel: 0844 815 9105 *(Calls cost 5p per minute plus your phone company's access charge)*
West Mill St PH1 5QP
email: info@mercureperth.co.uk **web:** www.mercureperth.co.uk
dir: *A93/A989 to city centre, left into Caledonian Rd, right at lights onto Old High St, hotel on left*

This former 15th-century watermill has been converted into a modern hotel but still retains the mill stream running through reception under a glass floor. Central to Perth, the hotel is an ideal location for visiting the area or further afield. Contemporary rooms include satellite TV and free WiFi. The hotel has extensive conference facilities, and a popular brasserie where tempting meals are served.

Rooms 76 **Facilities** FTV WiFi ↳ **Conf** Class 50 Board 40 Thtr 120 Del from £99 to £219* **Parking** 55 **Notes** Civ Wed 300

Salutation Hotel

★★★ 73% HOTEL

tel: 01738 630066 **South St PH2 8PH**
email: salessalutation@strathmorehotels.com **web:** www.strathmorehotels.com
dir: *At end of South St on right before River Tay*

Situated at the heart of Perth, the Salutation is reputed to be one of the oldest hotels in Scotland and has been welcoming guests through its doors since 1699. It offers traditional hospitality with all the modern comforts. Bedrooms vary in size and are thoughtfully equipped. An extensive menu is available in the Adam Restaurant, with its impressive barrel-vaulted ceiling and original features.

Rooms 84 (5 fmly) ☏ S £39-£89; D £69-£149 (incl. bkfst) **Facilities** WiFi ↳ HL ♫ Xmas New Year **Conf** Class 180 Board 60 Thtr 300 Del from £99 to £149 **Services** Lift **Notes** LB Civ Wed 150

Premier Inn Perth City Centre

BUDGET HOTEL

tel: 0871 527 9498 *(Calls cost 13p per minute plus your phone company's access charge)*
Mill St PH1 5HZ
web: www.premierinn.com
dir: *M90 junct 10, A912 (City Centre). At mini rdbt into Edinburgh Rd. Through 2 sets of lights. At T-junct left on to Marshall Pl (A989). 1st exit at mini rdbt into Tay St. 2nd left into High St, right into George St. 1st left into Bridge Ln. Continue into Mill St. Hotel on right*

High quality, budget accommodation ideal for both families and business travellers. Spacious, en suite bedrooms feature tea and coffee making facilities, and Freeview TV in most hotels. Internet access and WiFi are available for a small fee. The adjacent family restaurant features a wide and varied menu. See also the Hotel Groups pages.

Rooms 83

PETERHEAD Aberdeenshire Map 23 NK14

Buchan Braes Hotel

★★★★ 76% ⊛ HOTEL

tel: 01779 871471 **Boddam AB42 3AR**
email: info@buchanbraes.co.uk **web:** www.buchanbraes.co.uk
dir: *From Aberdeen take A90, follow Peterhead signs. 1st right in Stirling signed Boddam. 50mtrs, 1st right*

A contemporary hotel located in Boddam that is an excellent base for exploring the attractions of this wonderful part of Scotland. There is an open-plan lounge for drinks and snacks and the Grill Room with an open kitchen that offers a weekly changing, seasonal menu of locally sourced produce. All the bedrooms, including three suites, have 32" flat-screen TVs with satellite channels, king-sized beds and free WiFi.

Rooms 47 (1 fmly) (26 GF) ☏ S £85-£140; D £95-£150 (incl. bkfst)* **Facilities** FTV WiFi ↳ Xmas New Year **Conf** Class 100 Board 130 Thtr 250 **Services** Lift **Parking** 80 **Notes** ⊗ Civ Wed 220

Palace Hotel

★★★ 75% HOTEL

tel: 01779 474821 **Prince St AB42 1PL**
email: info@palacehotel.co.uk **web:** www.palacehotel.co.uk
dir: *A90 from Aberdeen, follow signs to Peterhead, on entering town turn into Prince St, then right into main car park*

This town centre hotel is popular with business travellers and for social events. Bedrooms come in two styles, with the executive rooms being particularly smart and spacious. Public areas include a themed bar, an informal diner reached via a spiral staircase, and a newly refurbished restaurant called The Front Room.

Rooms 64 (1 fmly) (13 GF) ☏ S £65-£80; D £75-£105 (incl. bkfst)* **Facilities** STV FTV WiFi ↳ Snooker & pool table ♫ New Year **Conf** Class 100 Board 60 Thtr 250 **Services** Lift **Parking** 50 **Notes** Civ Wed 250

PITLOCHRY Perth & Kinross Map 23 NN95

Fonab Castle Hotel & Spa

★★★★★ 84% ⊛⊛⊛ HOTEL

tel: 01796 470140 **Foss Rd PH16 5ND**
email: reservations@fonabcastlehotel.com **web:** www.fonabcastlehotel.com
dir: *Pitlochry A9 take Foss Rd junct. Hotel 1st on left*

Nestled on the banks of Loch Faskally with stunning views, this hotel was originally built as a home for the Sandeman family, the sherry and port merchants. Stylish bedrooms are set across the main castle building and more modern annexe. The Brasserie, and lounge both offer panoramic views from the hotel's elevated position, and provide a wide choice of quality produce cooked to the highest standard. Impressive destination spa, pool and gym facilities are available on site.

Rooms 34 (8 annexe) (2 fmly) (10 GF) ☏ S £175-£550; D £175-£550 (incl. bkfst) **Facilities** Spa STV FTV WiFi ↳ ⊛ Thermal & aromatherapy suite Steam room Nail salon Xmas New Year **Conf** Class 100 Board 100 Thtr 150 Del from £250 to £625 **Services** Lift **Parking** 50 **Notes** LB

P

PITLOCHRY *continued*

Knockendarroch

★★★★ 76% ◎◎ SMALL HOTEL

tel: 01796 473473 **Higher Oakfield PH16 5HT**
email: bookings@knockendarroch.co.uk **web:** www.knockendarroch.co.uk
dir: *Central Pitlochry, just off A9*

This secluded hotel has outstanding views over the town and surrounding hills. The individually styled bedrooms are spacious and very well appointed - all have plasma TVs. The traditional, country-style public rooms have large sofas, welcoming open fires and an excellent whisky cabinet. Dinner is served every evening in the award-winning restaurant with only the best of Scottish produce being used. The staff are friendly and attentive.

Rooms 12 (1 GF) ↖ **S** £140-£240; **D** £170-£270 (incl. bkfst & dinner)* **Facilities** FTV WiFi ↻ **Parking** 12 **Notes** LB ⊗ No children 10yrs Closed Dec-Jan

---

POLMONT	Map 21 NS97
Falkirk	

Macdonald Inchyra Hotel and Spa

★★★★ 78% ◎ HOTEL

tel: 01324 711911 **Grange Rd FK2 0YB**
email: inchyra@macdonald-hotels.co.uk **web:** www.macdonaldhotels.co.uk
dir: *2 mins from M9 junct 5*

Ideally placed for the M9 and Grangemouth terminal, this former manor house has been tastefully extended. The hotel provides comprehensive conference facilities and guests will find that The Scottish Steak Club serves the highest quality produce in a contemporary style. The bedrooms are comfortable and most are spacious. A visit to the hotel's luxurious spa and leisure facilities is highly recommended.

Rooms 97 (6 annexe) (35 fmly) (32 GF) **Facilities** Spa FTV WiFi ⏣ ⌣ Gym Steam room Sauna Aromatherapy shower Ice fountain New Year **Conf** Class 300 Board 80 Thtr 750 **Services** Lift **Parking** 500 **Notes** ⊗ Civ Wed 450

Premier Inn Falkirk East

BUDGET HOTEL

tel: 0871 527 8392 *(Calls cost 13p per minute plus your phone company's access charge)*
Beancross Rd FK2 0YS
web: www.premierinn.com
dir: *M9 junct 5, Polmont A9 signs. Hotel on left*

High quality, budget accommodation ideal for both families and business travellers. Spacious, en suite bedrooms feature tea and coffee making facilities, and Freeview TV in most hotels. Internet access and WiFi are available for a small fee. The adjacent family restaurant features a wide and varied menu. See also the Hotel Groups pages.

Rooms 60

PORT APPIN	Map 20 NM94
Argyll & Bute	

Airds Hotel and Restaurant

★★★★ ◎◎◎ ♨ SMALL HOTEL

tel: 01631 730236 **PA38 4DF**
email: airds@airds-hotel.com **web:** www.airds-hotel.com
dir: *From A828 Oban to Fort William rd, turn at Appin signed Port Appin. Hotel 2.5m on left*

Airds shows how appearances can be deceiving, as its modest scale and appearance give little indication of what lies beyond the threshold. Once inside, you are in a luxurious environment where attention to detail and fine food are of paramount importance. The lounges are cosy and inviting, with log fires, welcoming sofas and service that is both top notch and friendly. A stay here is as much about the food as the stunning location, and the kitchen brigade makes full use of the wide range of superb quality produce that is on their doorstep. Both dinner and lunch include options for fish and meat eaters, with the added bonus of superb views across Loch Linnhe. You can also take lunch in the garden or conservatory, while families with young children can take dinner in the conservatory. The well-equipped bedrooms provide style and luxury, while many bathrooms are furnished in marble and have power showers.

Rooms 11 (3 fmly) (2 GF) ↖ **S** fr £245; **D** £305-£510 (incl. bkfst & dinner)* **Facilities** STV FTV WiFi ↻ Putt green ♨ In room massage Xmas New Year **Conf** Class 16 Board 16 Thtr 16 **Parking** 20 **Notes** LB RS Nov-Jan Civ Wed 40

The Pierhouse Hotel

★★★ 80% ◎ SMALL HOTEL

tel: 01631 730302 **PA38 4DE**
email: reservations@pierhousehotel.co.uk **web:** www.pierhousehotel.co.uk
dir: *A828 from Ballachulish to Oban. In Appin right at Port Appin & Lismore ferry sign. After 2.5m left after post office, hotel at end of road*

Nestled on the shores of Loch Linnhe in Port Appin, this hotel offers a warm welcome and relaxing atmosphere with comfortable, contemporary styled bedrooms and wood-burning fires in the Ferry bar and residents' snug lounge. With breathtaking views over the sea loch to the islands of Lismore and Mull, watch the sun set as you dine in the candlelit restaurant which serves freshly prepared, locally sourced seafood and game, simply cooked to perfection.

Rooms 12 (2 fmly) (6 GF) ↖ **Facilities** FTV WiFi ↻ Aromatherapy Massage Sauna Kayaking Walking Cycling New Year **Conf** Class 20 Board 20 Thtr 20 **Parking** 20 **Notes** Closed 25-26 Dec Civ Wed 80

PORTPATRICK
Dumfries & Galloway

Map 20 NW95

Knockinaam Lodge
★★★ ◉◉◉ HOTEL

tel: 01776 810471 **DG9 9AD**
email: reservations@knockinaamlodge.com **web:** www.knockinaamlodge.com
dir: From A77 or A75 follow signs to Portpatrick. Through Lochans. After 2m left at signs for hotel

Any tour of Dumfries and Galloway wouldn't be complete without a stay at this haven of tranquillity and relaxation. Knockinaam Lodge is an extended Victorian house set in an idyllic cove with its own pebble beach (ideal for a private swim in the summer) and sheltered by majestic cliffs and woodlands. Surrounded by 30 acres of delightful grounds, the lodge was the location for a meeting between Churchill and General Eisenhower in World War II. Today, a warm welcome is assured from the proprietors and their committed team, and much emphasis is placed on providing a sophisticated but intimate home-from-home experience. There are just ten suites - each individually designed and all with flat-screen TVs with DVD players, luxury toiletries and complimentary bottled water. The cooking is a real treat and showcases prime Scottish produce on the daily-changing, four-course set menus; guests can always discuss the choices in advance if they wish.

Rooms 10 (1 fmly) ↖ **S** £175-£325; **D** £290-£450 (incl. dinner)* **Facilities** FTV WiFi Fishing 🎣 Shooting Walking Sea fishing Clay pigeon shooting Xmas New Year **Conf** Class 10 Board 16 Thtr 30 **Parking** 20 **Notes** LB Cĩv Wed 40

RENFREW
Hotels are listed under Glasgow Airport

RHU
Argyll & Bute

Map 20 NS28

Rosslea Hall Hotel
★★★ 80% ◉ HOTEL

tel: 01436 439955 **Ferry Rd G84 8NF**
web: www.rossleahallhotel.co.uk
dir: On A814, opposite church

Overlooking the Firth of the Clyde and close to Helensburgh, this imposing mansion is set in its own well tended gardens. Bedrooms and bathrooms are of a good size, are well appointed and cater well for the modern traveller. The eating options include the Conservatory Restaurant which offers dishes cooked with imagination and flair, and overlooks the grounds and the Clyde. The hotel is a popular wedding venue.

Rooms 30 (3 fmly) (2 GF) ↖ **Facilities** STV FTV WiFi Xmas New Year **Conf** Class 60 Board 80 Thtr 150 **Parking** 30 **Notes** LB ⊗ Civ Wed 120

ROY BRIDGE
Highland

Map 22 NN28

The Stronlossit Inn
★★★ 74% SMALL HOTEL

tel: 01397 712253 **PH31 4AG**
email: stay@stronlossit.co.uk **web:** www.stronlossit.co.uk
dir: Exit A82 at Spean Bridge onto A86, signed Roy Bridge. Hotel on left

Appointed to modern standards with the character and hospitality of a traditional hostelry, The Stronlossit Inn is quite a draw for the discerning Highland tourist. The spacious bar is the focal point, with a peat burning fire providing a warm welcome in cooler months; guests can eat in the attractive restaurant. Bedrooms come in a mix of sizes and styles, most being smartly modern and well equipped.

Rooms 10 (5 GF) ↖ **S** £70-£85; **D** £85-£115 (incl. bkfst) **Facilities** WiFi ⋈ **Cont** Class 12 Board 10 Thtr 20 **Del** from £79 to £129 **Parking** 30 **Notes** LB ⊗ No children 17yrs

ST ANDREWS
Fife

Map 21 NO51

Old Course Hotel, Golf Resort & Spa
★★★★★ ◉◉◉ HOTEL

tel: 01334 474371 & 468001 **KY16 9SP**
email: reservations@oldcoursehotel.co.uk **web:** www.oldcoursehotel.co.uk
dir: M90 junct 8, A91 to St Andrews

The five red-star Old Course Hotel, Golf Resort & Spa - a member of The Leading Hotels of the World - borders the world of golf's most famous par four, the 17th 'Road Hole' on the Old Course in St Andrews, the Home of Golf. The hotel has 144 luxurious rooms, including 35 stunning suites, and boasts five dining experiences, overseen by Executive Chef, Martin Hollis: the 3 AA Rosetted Road Hole Restaurant overlooking the Old Course; the AA Rosetted Sands Grill; the world-famous Jigger Inn; the Duke's Clubhouse at their own championship course and the newest addition, Hams Hame Pub & Grill, the closest 19th to the Old Course's 18th green. Whether at the iconic hotel, on the golf course, relaxing in the world-class Kohler Waters Spa or enjoying one of the many food and drink experiences, guests are assured red-star service.

Rooms 144 (5 fmly) (3 GF) ↖ **S** £190-£1380; **D** £240-£1430 (incl. bkfst) **Facilities** Spa STV FTV WiFi ⋈ HL ⌚ ⌘ 18 Putt green Gym Thermal suite ♬ Xmas New Year **Conf** Class 473 Board 259 Thtr 950 **Del** from £249 to £1245 **Services** Lift Air con **Parking** 125 **Notes** ⊗ Civ Wed 180

S

ST ANDREWS *continued*

Fairmont St Andrews, Scotland

★★★★★ 84% HOTEL

tel: 01334 837000 **KY16 8PN**
email: standrews.scotland@fairmont.com **web:** www.fairmont.com/standrews
dir: *Approx 2m from St Andrews on A917 towards Crail*

Sitting just a few miles from St Andrews, overlooking the rugged Fife coastline and the hotel's own championship golf courses, The Fairmont is situated on a 520-acre estate. Bedrooms and bathrooms are spacious and luxuriously appointed. The eating options are The Squire for brasserie-style food, La Cucina for Italian dishes, and The St Andrews Bar and Grill in the clubhouse; for steak and seafood, with The Atrium offering all-day menus. The hotel has an impressive spa and health club. Good standards of service are found throughout.

Rooms 209 (209 fmly) (68 GF) ↖ **D** £177-£550 (incl. bkfst)* **Facilities** Spa STV FTV WiFi ↕ ☜ ⚓ 36 Putt green Gym 106-seat cinema Nail salon Bike hire Dance studio Xmas New Year **Conf** Class 450 Board 168 Thtr 500 Del from £199* **Services** Lift Air con **Parking** 150 **Notes** Civ Wed 550

INSPECTORS' CHOICE

Rufflets Country House

★★★★ COUNTRY HOUSE HOTEL

tel: 01334 472594 **Strathkinness Low Rd KY16 9TX**
email: reservations@rufflets.co.uk **web:** www.rufflets.co.uk
dir: *1.5m W on B939*

Built in 1924 for a Dundee jute baron, this charming property is set in extensive gardens a few minutes' drive from the town centre. The stylish, spacious bedrooms are individually decorated, and include the Gilroy Suite, The Orchard Suite (separate from the main building), and Turret Rooms that have their own seating areas. Public rooms include a well-stocked bar, a choice of inviting lounges and the delightful Terrace Restaurant that serves imaginative, carefully prepared cuisine based on seasonal produce. Impressive conference and banqueting facilities are available in the adjacent Garden Suite. Families are very welcome, and the hotel is a popular wedding venue.

Rooms 24 (5 annexe) (3 fmly) (5 GF) ↖ **S** £100-£200; **D** £150-£350 (incl. bkfst)* **Facilities** STV FTV WiFi ↕ Putt green ⛳ Children's outdoor games New Year **Conf** Class 60 Board 60 Thtr 200 Del from £135 to £215* **Parking** 50 **Notes** Civ Wed 130

Macdonald Rusacks Hotel

★★★★ 79% HOTEL

tel: 01334 474321 & 0344 879 9136 **Pilmour Links KY16 9JQ**
email: general.rusacks@macdonald-hotels.co.uk **web:** www.macdonaldhotels.co.uk
dir: *From A91 W, straight on at rdbt into St Andrews. Hotel 220yds on left*

This long-established hotel enjoys an almost unrivalled location with superb views across the famous golf course. Bedrooms, though varying in size, are comfortably appointed and well equipped. Classically styled public rooms include an elegant reception lounge and a modern restaurant and brasserie bar.

Rooms 70 (1 annexe) (3 fmly) (7 GF) ↖ **Facilities** STV FTV WiFi New Year **Conf** Class 35 Board 20 Thtr 80 **Services** Lift **Parking** 21 **Notes** Civ Wed 60

Hotel du Vin St Andrews

★★★★ 78% TOWN HOUSE HOTEL

tel: 01334 845313 & 472611 **40 The Scores KY16 9AS**
web: www.hotelduvin.com
dir: *M90 junct 3 N over Forth Road Bridge, A92. At rdbt take A914 then A91 signed St Andrews/Cupar*

Hotel du Vin St Andrews is stylish, modern and welcoming. There has been a hotel here for some years but now, having been recently refurbished, the hotel offers guests all the great aspects we have come to know from this very non cookie-cutter hotel brand. Bedrooms are very well equipped; all have free WiFi, Nespresso coffee machines and Egyptian linen. The Bistro offers traditional French dishes while Ma Bells bar offers traditional pub food. Free parking outside the hotel, itself overlooking golden beaches and a mere two minutes' walk from the world-famous Royal and Ancient Golf Club.

Rooms 37 ↖ **S** £109-£285; **D** £109-£285 **Facilities** STV FTV WiFi ↕ HL Xmas New Year **Conf** Class 60 Board 38 Thtr 150 Del from £159 to £250 **Services** Lift **Parking** 7 **Notes** LB Civ Wed 110

Ardgowan Hotel

★★★ 82% ⊚ HOTEL

tel: 01334 472970 **2 Playfair Ter, North St KY16 9HX**
email: info@ardgowanhotel.co.uk **web:** www.ardgowanhotel.co.uk
dir: *A91 onto A917. Hotel 100mtrs from rdbt on left*

The Ardgowan Hotel is ideally located just 200 yards from the Old Course Club House. The university, shops and beach are just a short walk from the hotel as well. This well-presented, family-run hotel was built in 1847 and offers well-appointed bedrooms and en suites. The award-winning restaurant uses the finest quality produce with some great steaks alongside an array of seafood. Playfair's bar is lively, and enjoys good local trade as well as that of the golfers and guests.

Rooms 36 (7 annexe) (4 fmly) (3 GF) ⋒ **Facilities** FTV WiFi ▷ **Notes** Closed 2/3 wks over Xmas

Best Western Scores Hotel

BW Best Western.

★★★ 78% HOTEL

tel: 01334 472451 **76 The Scores KY16 9BB**
email: reception@scoreshotel.co.uk **web:** www.bw-scoreshotel.co.uk
dir: *M90 junct 2a, A92 E. Follow Glenrothes signs then St Andrews signs. Straight on at next 2 rdbts, left into Golf Place, right into The Scores*

Enjoying views over St Andrews Bay, this well-presented hotel is situated only a short pitch from the first tee of the famous Old Course. Bedrooms are impressively furnished and come in various sizes; many are quite spacious. Smart public areas include Champions Grill, offering food all day from breakfast to dinner; Scottish High Teas are served here from 4.30-6.30pm. Alexander's Restaurant opens Thursday, Friday and Saturday evenings.

Rooms 36 (1 fmly) ⋒ **Facilities** FTV WiFi ▷ HL Xmas New Year **Conf** Class 60 Board 40 Thtr 180 **Services** Lift **Parking** 12 **Notes** ⊗ Civ Wed 100

Russell Hotel

★★ 81% ⊚ HOTEL

tel: 01334 473447 **26 The Scores KY16 9AS**
email: enquiries@russellhotelstandrews.co.uk **web:** www.russellhotelstandrews.co.uk
dir: *From A91 left at 2nd rdbt into Golf Place, right in 200yds into The Scores, hotel in 300yds on left*

Lying on the east bay, this friendly, family-run Victorian terrace hotel provides well appointed bedrooms in varying sizes; some enjoy fine sea views. Cosy public areas include a popular bar and an intimate restaurant, both offering a good range of freshly prepared dishes. Situated in St Andrews, said to be 'The Home of Golf', this hotel offers a comprehensive range of golfing breaks, and is convenient for visits to the castle, cathedral and university

Rooms 10 (3 fmly) **Facilities** WiFi ▷ New Year **Notes** ⊗

Premier Inn St Andrews

BUDGET HOTEL

tel: 0871 527 9428 *(Calls cost 13p per minute plus your phone company's access charge)*
Largo Rd KY16 8NH
web: www.premierinn.com
dir: *A91 to St Andrews. Follow signs for Kircaldy (A915). Straight on at 2 rdbts to Largo Rd. Hotel opposite VW car showroom*

High quality, budget accommodation ideal for both families and business travellers. Spacious, en suite bedrooms feature tea and coffee making facilities, and Freeview TV in most hotels. Internet access and WiFi are available for a small fee. The adjacent family restaurant features a wide and varied menu. See also the Hotel Groups pages.

Rooms 65

S

ST FILLANS
Perth & Kinross

Map 20 NN62

The Four Seasons Hotel
★★★ 82% 🏵️🏵️ HOTEL

tel: 01764 685333 **Loch Earn PH6 2NF**
email: info@thefourseasonshotel.co.uk **web:** www.thefourseasonshotel.co.uk
dir: On A85, towards W of village

Set on the edge of Loch Earn, this welcoming hotel and many of its bedrooms benefit from fine views. There is a choice of lounges, including a library, warmed by log fires during winter. Local produce is used to good effect in both the Meall Reamhar restaurant and the more informal Tarken Room.

Rooms 18 (6 annexe) (7 fmly) 🐾 **S** £57-£117; **D** £114-£174 (incl. bkfst)
Facilities FTV WiFi Xmas New Year **Conf** Class 45 Board 38 Thtr 95 Del from £144 to £166* **Parking** 40 **Notes** LB Closed 2 Jan-Feb RS Nov-Dec & Mar Civ Wed 80

SANQUHAR
Dumfries & Galloway

Map 21 NS70

Blackaddie House
🏵️🏵️ RESTAURANT WITH ROOMS

tel: 01659 50270 **Blackaddie Rd DG4 6JJ**
email: ian@blackaddiehotel.co.uk **web:** www.blackaddiehotel.co.uk
dir: 300 yds from A76 on N side of Sanquhar

Overlooking the River Nith, in two acres of secluded gardens, this family-run country house offers friendly and attentive hands-on service. The bedrooms and suites, including family accommodation, are all well-presented and comfortable, with many useful extras provided as standard. The award-winning food, served in the restaurant, with its lovely garden views, is based on prime Scottish ingredients.

Rooms 7 (1 annexe) (1 fmly)

SOUTH QUEENSFERRY
City of Edinburgh

Map 21 NT17

Premier Inn Edinburgh A1 (Newcraighall)
BUDGET HOTEL

tel: 0871 527 8362 (Calls cost 13p per minute plus your phone company's access charge)
91 Newcraighall Rd, Newcraighall EH21 8RX
web: www.premierinn.com
dir: At junct of A1 & A6095 towards Musselburgh

High quality, budget accommodation ideal for both families and business travellers. Spacious, en suite bedrooms feature tea and coffee making facilities, and Freeview TV in most hotels. Internet access and WiFi are available for a small fee. The adjacent family restaurant features a wide and varied menu. See also the Hotel Groups pages.

Rooms 66

Premier Inn Edinburgh (South Queensferry)
BUDGET HOTEL

tel: 0871 527 8364 (Calls cost 13p per minute plus your phone company's access charge)
Builyeon Rd EH30 9YJ
web: www.premierinn.com
dir: M8 junct 2 follow M9 Stirling signs, exit at junct 1a take A8000 towards Forth Road Bridge, at 3rd rdbt 2nd exit into Builyeon Rd. NB do not go onto Forth Road Bridge

Rooms 72

SPEAN BRIDGE
Highland

Map 22 NN28

Smiddy House
🏵️🏵️ 🍽️ RESTAURANT WITH ROOMS

tel: 01397 712335 **Roy Bridge Rd PH34 4EU**
email: enquiry@smiddyhouse.com **web:** www.smiddyhouse.com
dir: In village centre, A82 onto A86

Set in the Great Glen which stretches from Fort William to Inverness, this was once the village smithy, and is now a very friendly restaurant with rooms. The attractive bedrooms, named after places in Scotland, are comfortably furnished and well equipped. A relaxing garden room is available for guest use. Delicious evening meals are served in Russell's restaurant.

Rooms 4 (1 fmly)

SPITTAL OF GLENSHEE
Perth & Kinross

Map 21 NO17

Dalmunzie Castle Hotel
★★★ 81% 🏵️🏵️ COUNTRY HOUSE HOTEL

tel: 01250 885224 **PH10 7QG**
email: reservations@dalmunzie.com **web:** www.dalmunzie.com
dir: On A93 at Spittal of Glenshee, follow signs to hotel

This turreted mansion house sits in a secluded glen in the heart of a glorious 6,500-acre estate, yet is within easy reach of the Glenshee ski slopes. The Edwardian style bedrooms, including spacious tower rooms and impressive four-poster rooms, are furnished with antique pieces. The drawing room enjoys panoramic views over the lawns, and the restaurant serves the finest Scottish produce.

Rooms 17 (1 fmly) **Facilities** STV FTV WiFi ⛳ Fishing 🎵 Xmas **Conf** Class 40 Board 40 Thtr 40 **Services** Lift **Notes** Closed 30 Nov-22 Dec Civ Wed 80

S

STEPPS
North Lanarkshire   Map 20 NS66

Premier Inn Glasgow Stepps (M80 Jct 3)

BUDGET HOTEL

tel: 0871 527 8452 *(Calls cost 13p per minute plus your phone company's access charge)*
Crowwood Roundabout, Cumbernauld Rd G33 6HN
web: www.premierinn.com
dir: *M8 junct 12, A80 (becomes dual carriageway) to Crowwood rdbt, 4th exit back onto A80, hotel 1st left. Or exit M80 at Crowwood rdbt, 3rd exit signed A80 West. Hotel 1st left*

High quality, budget accommodation ideal for both families and business travellers. Spacious, en suite bedrooms feature tea and coffee making facilities, and Freeview TV in most hotels. Internet access and WiFi are available for a small fee. The adjacent family restaurant features a wide and varied menu. See also the Hotel Groups pages.

Rooms 80

STIRLING
Stirling   Map 21 NS79

The Stirling Highland Hotel

THE
HOTEL
COLLECTION

★★★★ 73% ◉ HOTEL

tel: 01786 272727 **Spittal St FK8 1DU**
email: stirling@thehotelcollection.co.uk **web:** www.thehotelcollection.co.uk
dir: *A84 into Stirling. Follow Stirling Castle signs to Albert Hall. Left, left again, follow Castle signs*

Enjoying a location close to the castle and historic town, this atmospheric hotel was previously a high school. Public rooms have been converted from the original classrooms and retain many interesting features. Bedrooms are more modern in style and comfortably equipped. Scholars Restaurant serves traditional and international dishes, and the Headmaster's Study is the ideal venue for enjoying a drink.

Rooms 96 (4 fmly) (28 GF) 🐾 **Facilities** Spa FTV WiFi ❧ HL ⓣ supervised Gym Squash Steam room Dance studio Beauty therapist New Year **Conf** Class 60 Board 40 Thtr 120 Del from £120 to £150* **Services** Lift **Parking** 96 **Notes** Civ Wed 100

Premier Inn Stirling City Centre

BUDGET HOTEL

tel: 0871 527 9472 *(Calls cost 13p per minute plus your phone company's access charge)*
Forthside Way FK8 1QZ
web: www.premierinn.com
dir: *Please see website for detailed directions*

High quality, budget accommodation ideal for both families and business travellers. Spacious, en suite bedrooms feature tea and coffee making facilities, and Freeview TV in most hotels. Internet access and WiFi are available for a small fee. The adjacent family restaurant features a wide and varied menu. See also the Hotel Groups pages.

Rooms 60

Premier Inn Stirling South (M9 Jct 9)

BUDGET HOTEL

tel: 0871 527 9038 *(Calls cost 13p per minute plus your phone company's access charge)*
Glasgow Rd, Whins of Milton FK7 8EX
web: www.premierinn.com
dir: *On A872, 0.25m from M9/M80 junct 9*

Rooms 82

STRANRAER
Dumfries & Galloway   Map 20 NX06

Corsewall Lighthouse Hotel

★★★ 77% ◉ HOTEL

tel: 01776 853220 **Corsewall Point, Kirkcolm DG9 0QG**
email: info@lighthousehotel.co.uk **web:** www.lighthousehotel.co.uk
dir: *A718 from Stranraer to Kirkcolm (approx 8m). Follow hotel signs for 4m*

Looking for something completely different? This is a unique hotel converted from buildings that adjoin a Grade A listed, 19th-century lighthouse set on a rocky coastline. Situated on the headland to the west of Loch Ryan, the lighthouse beam still functions to warn approaching ships. Bedrooms come in a variety of sizes, some reached by a spiral staircase, and like the public areas, are cosy and atmospheric. The cottage suites in the grounds offer greater space. The restaurant menus are based on Scottish produce such as venison and salmon.

Rooms 11 (5 annexe) (4 fmly) (2 GF) (3 smoking) 🐾 **Facilities** FTV WiFi Xmas New Year **Conf** Thtr 20 **Parking** 20 **Notes** ⊗ Civ Wed 28

STRATHAVEN
South Lanarkshire   Map 20 NS74

Rissons at Springvale

◉ RESTAURANT WITH ROOMS

tel: 01357 521131 & 520234 **18 Lethame Rd ML10 6AD**
email: info@rissons.co.uk **web:** www.rissonsrestaurant.co.uk
dir: *A71 into Strathaven, W of town centre off Townhead St*

Guests are assured of a warm welcome at this charming establishment close to the town centre. The bedrooms and bathrooms are stylish and well equipped. The main attraction here is the food - a range of interesting, well-prepared dishes served in Rissons Restaurant.

Rooms 9 (1 fmly)

S

STRATHYRE
Stirling

Map 20 NN51

Creagan House

◉◉ RESTAURANT WITH ROOMS

tel: 01877 384638 **FK18 8ND**
email: eatandstay@creaganhouse.co.uk **web:** www.creaganhouse.co.uk
dir: *0.25m N of Strathyre on A84*

Originally a farmhouse dating from the 17th century, Creagan House has operated as a restaurant with rooms for many years. The baronial-style dining room provides a wonderful setting for the cuisine which is classic French with some Scottish influences. The warm hospitality and attentive service are noteworthy.

Rooms 5 (1 fmly)

STRONTIAN
Highland

Map 22 NM86

Kilcamb Lodge Hotel

★★★★ 76% ◉◉ COUNTRY HOUSE HOTEL

tel: 01967 402257 **PH36 4HY**
email: enquiries@kilcamblodge.co.uk **web:** www.kilcamblodge.co.uk
dir: *Off A861, via Corran Ferry, in the village of Strontian*

This historic house on the shores of Loch Sunart was one of the first stone buildings in the area, and was used as military barracks around the time of the Jacobite uprising. It is situated on the beautiful and peaceful Ardamurchan Peninsula where otters, red squirrels and eagles can be spotted. The suites and bedrooms, with either loch or garden views, are stylishly decorated using designer fabrics and have flat-screen TVs, DVD/CD players, plus bath robes, iced water and even guest umbrellas. Accomplished cooking, utilising much local produce, can be enjoyed in the stylish dining room. Warm hospitality is assured.

Rooms 10 (2 fmly) ☀ **Facilities** FTV WiFi ॐ Fishing Boating Hiking Bird/whale/otter watching Stalking Clay pigeon shooting Xmas New Year **Conf** Class 18 Board 18 Thtr 18 **Parking** 20 **Notes** Closed 2 Jan-1 Feb RS Nov & Feb Civ Wed 120

TAIN
Highland

Map 23 NH78

The Glenmorangie Highland Home at Cadboll

★★★ ◉◉ COUNTRY HOUSE HOTEL

tel: 01862 871671 **Cadboll, Fearn IV20 1XP**
email: relax@glenmorangie.co.uk **web:** www.theglenmorangiehouse.com
dir: *A9 onto B9175 towards Nigg. Follow tourist signs*

This historic Highland Home superbly balances top class service with intimate customer care. Evenings are dominated by the highly successful 'house party' where guests are introduced in the drawing room, sample whiskies, then take dinner (a set six-course meal) together around one long table. Conversation can extend well into the evening. Stylish bedrooms are divided between the traditional main house and some cosy cottages in the grounds. This is an ideal base from which to enjoy the world famous whisky tours.

Rooms 9 (3 annexe) (4 fmly) (3 GF) ☀ **Facilities** FTV WiFi ॐ Archery Beauty treatments Clay pigeon shooting Falconry Xmas New Year **Conf** Board 12 **Parking** 60 **Notes** ⊗ No children 15yrs Civ Wed 60

TARBERT
Argyll & Bute

Map 20 NN30

Stonefield Castle Hotel

Ⓤ

"bespoke"

tel: 01880 820836 & 0843 1787141 **PA29 6YJ**
email: reservations.stonefieldcastle@bespokehotels.com
web: www.bespokehotels.com/stonefieldcastle
dir: *From Glasgow take M8 towards Erskine Bridge onto A82, follow Loch Lomond signs. From Arrochar follow A83 signs through Inveraray & Lochgilphead, hotel on left 2m before Tarbert*

Currently the rating for this establishment is not confirmed. This may be due to a change of ownership or because it has only recently joined the AA rating scheme. For further details please see the AA website: theAA.com

Rooms 36 (20 annexe) (3 fmly) (11 GF) ☀ **S** £140-£220; **D** £145-£225 (incl. bkfst)*
Facilities FTV WiFi ॐ Fishing Xmas New Year **Conf** Class 60 Board 60 Thtr 120
Services Lift **Parking** 70 **Notes** LB Civ Wed 110

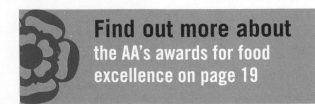

S

THORNHILL
Dumfries & Galloway

Map 21 NX89

The Buccleuch and Queensberry Arms Hotel

★★★ 81% HOTEL

tel: 01848 323101 **112 Drumlanrig St DG3 5LU**
email: info@bqahotel.com **web:** www.bqahotel.com
dir: *On A76 in centre of Thornhill*

This small, family-run hotel is located in the heart of the small town of Thornhill. Inside the hotel has bedrooms that are extremely well appointed and of a high quality. Public areas are warm and welcoming with an open log fire adding to the charm. Food is a strong aspect to the operation with the award-winning chef using local produce where possible.

Rooms 14 (2 annexe) (3 fmly) (2 GF) S £50-£95; **D** £60-£175 (incl. bkfst)
Facilities STV FTV WiFi Xmas New Year **Conf** Class 60 Board 40 Thtr 120 Del from £120 to £175 **Notes** LB

THURSO
Highland

Map 23 ND16

Forss House Hotel

★★★★ 73% SMALL HOTEL

tel: 01847 861201 **Forss KW14 7XY**
email: anne@forsshousehotel.co.uk **web:** www.forsshousehotel.co.uk
dir: *On A836 between Thurso & Reay*

This delightful country house is set in its own 20 acres of woodland and was originally built in 1810. The hotel offers a choice of bedrooms from the traditional styled rooms in the main house to the more contemporary annexe rooms in the grounds. All rooms are very well equipped and well appointed. The beautiful River Forss runs through the grounds and is a firm favourite with fishermen.

Rooms 14 (6 annexe) (1 fmly) (7 GF) S £99-£135; **D** £135-£185 (incl. bkfst)*
Facilities FTV WiFi Fishing **Conf** Class 12 Board 14 Thtr 20 Del from £160 to £195*
Parking 14 **Notes** LB Closed 23 Dec-3 Jan Civ Wed 26

Food Allergies

A recent EU regulation makes it easier for those with food allergies to choose safer foods when eating out. 14 allergens are listed in the regulation, and pubs and restaurants must now list any of these used in the dishes they offer.

TORRIDON
Highland

Map 22 NG95

The Torridon

★★★★ ◉◉◉ COUNTRY HOUSE HOTEL

tel: 01445 791242 **By Achnasheen, Wester Ross IV22 2EY**
email: info@thetorridon.com **web:** www.thetorridon.com
dir: *From A832 at Kinlochewe, A896 towards Torridon 1m, do not turn into village. Hotel on right*

Delightfully set amid inspiring loch and mountain scenery, this elegant Victorian shooting lodge has been beautifully appointed to make the most of its many original features, and the 58 acres of surrounding parkland make it a perfect getaway destination. The attractive bedrooms are individually furnished and most enjoy stunning Highland views; expect to find Egyptian cotton sheets, duck down duvets, flat-screen satellite TVs, iPod docks plus Victorian-style bathrooms; for complete privacy choose The Boathouse on the loch shore. Comfortable day rooms feature fine wood panelling and roaring fires in cooler months. The kitchen team creates award-winning menus based as much as possible on locally sourced ingredients; the hotel has its own herd of cattle. The whisky bar is aptly named, boasting over 300 malts and in-depth tasting notes. Outdoor activities include shooting, cycling and walking.

Rooms 18 (2 GF) **Facilities** STV WiFi Fishing Abseiling Archery Climbing Kayaking Mountain biking Clay pigeon shooting Xmas New Year **Conf** Board 16 Thtr 42 **Services** Lift **Parking** 20 **Notes** Closed 2 Jan-9 Feb RS Nov-Mar Civ Wed 55

T

INSPECTORS' CHOICE

Lochgreen House Hotel

★★★★ ❀❀❀ COUNTRY HOUSE HOTEL

tel: 01292 313343 **Monktonhill Rd, Southwood KA10 7EN**
email: lochgreen@costley-hotels.co.uk web: www.costley-hotels.co.uk
dir: *From A77 follow Prestwick Airport signs. 0.5m before airport take B749 to Troon.
Hotel 1m on left*

Set in immaculately maintained grounds, Lochgreen House is graced by tasteful
extensions which have created stunning public rooms and spacious, comfortable
and elegantly furnished bedrooms. Extra facilities include a coffee shop, gift
shop and beauty treatments in The Retreat. The magnificent Tapestry Restaurant
provides the ideal setting for dinners that are immaculately presented.

Rooms 38 (7 annexe) (17 GF) **Facilities** STV WiFi Beauty treatments Xmas New
Year **Conf** Class 180 Board 50 Thtr 200 **Services** Lift **Parking** 50 **Notes** ⊗
Civ Wed 140

Who are the AA's award-winning hotels? For details see pages 13-15

INSPECTORS' CHOICE

Turnberry Resort, Scotland

★★★★★ ❀❀ HOTEL

tel: 01655 331000 **KA26 9LT**
email: turnberry@luxurycollection.com web: www.turnberryresort.co.uk
dir: *From Glasgow take A77, M77 S towards Stranraer, 2m past Kirkoswald follow
signs for A719 & Turnberry. Hotel 500mtrs on right*

Golf probably springs to mind when this hotel is mentioned, and with good
reason. This famous establishment enjoys magnificent views over to Arran, Ailsa
Craig, and the Mull of Kintyre. Facilities include a world-renowned golf course,
the excellent Colin Montgomerie Golf Academy, a luxurious spa with pool, ESPA
treatments and a techno fitness studio, as well as a host of outdoor pursuits for
both adults and children. Some superbly modern rooms and more traditional,
elegant bedrooms and suites are located in the main hotel, while adjacent
lodges provide more space. The public areas are stunning and include the Grand
Tea Lounge, Ailsa Bar and Lounge, the Duel in the Sun sports bar and 1906
restaurant.

Rooms 157 (40 annexe) (2 fmly) (14 GF) 🐾 **Facilities** Spa STV FTV WiFi ⇗ ⊕
supervised ♨ 45 Putt green Gym Leisure club Turnberry Adventures Turnberry
Performance Academy Xmas New Year Child facilities **Conf** Class 145 Board 80
Thtr 300 **Services** Lift **Parking** 200 **Notes** LB Closed 1 wk Dec & 2 wks Jan
Civ Wed 220

Malin Court

★★★ 80% HOTEL

tel: 01655 331457 **KA26 9PB**
email: info@malincourt.co.uk **web:** www.malincourt.co.uk
dir: On A74 to Ayr then A719 to Turnberry & Maidens

Forming part of the Malin Court Residential and Nursing Home Complex, this friendly and comfortable hotel enjoys delightful views over the Firth of Clyde and Turnberry golf courses. Standard and executive rooms are available; all are well equipped. Public areas are plentiful, with the restaurant serving high teas, dinners and light lunches.

Rooms 18 (9 fmly) **S** £60-£70; **D** £90-£115 (incl. bkfst)* **Facilities** STV WiFi Putt green **Conf** Class 60 Board 30 Thtr 200 Del from £125 to £130* **Services** Lift **Parking** 110 **Notes** ⊗ Closed 1-5 Jan RS Oct-Mar

UPHALL
West Lothian
Map 21 NT07

Macdonald Houstoun House

★★★★ 79% ⑩⑩ HOTEL

MACDONALD
HOTELS & RESORTS

tel: 01506 853831 & 0344 879 9043 **EH52 6JS**
email: houstoun@macdonald-hotels.co.uk **web:** www.macdonaldhotels.co.uk
dir: M8 junct 3 follow Broxburn signs, straight over rdbt, at mini-rdbt turn right towards Uphall, hotel 1m on right

This historic 17th-century tower house lies in beautifully landscaped grounds and gardens, and features a modern leisure club and spa, a choice of dining options, a vaulted cocktail bar and extensive conference and meeting facilities. Stylish bedrooms, some located around a courtyard, are comfortably furnished and well equipped.

Rooms 73 (47 annexe) (12 fmly) (12 GF) 🐾 **S** £75-£245; **D** £75-£245 **Facilities** Spa STV FTV WiFi ▷ ⑤ ♨ Gym Health & beauty salon Xmas New Year **Conf** Class 80 Board 80 Thtr 400 Del from £135 to £300 **Parking** 250 **Notes** LB Civ Wed 200

UPLAWMOOR
East Renfrewshire
Map 20 NS45

Uplawmoor Hotel

★★★ 77% SMALL HOTEL

THE CIRCLE

tel: 01505 850565 **66 Neilston Rd G78 4AF**
email: info@uplawmoor.co.uk **web:** www.uplawmoor.co.uk
dir: M77 junct 2, A736 signed Barrhead & Irvine. Hotel 4m beyond Barrhead

Originally a coaching inn, this friendly hotel is set in a village off the Glasgow to Irvine road. The relaxed restaurant features imaginative dishes, while the popular lounge bar is a great setting for freshly prepared bar meals. The modern bedrooms are both comfortable and well equipped, and Uplawmoor Hotel prides itself on the level of hospitality it provides to guests.

Rooms 14 (1 fmly) 🐾 **S** £65-£75; **D** £89-£99* **Facilities** STV WiFi ▷ **Parking** 40 **Notes** LB ⊗ Closed 26 Dec & 1 Jan

WHITEBRIDGE
Highland
Map 23 NH41

Whitebridge Hotel

★★ 69% HOTEL

tel: 01456 486226 **IV2 6UN**
email: info@whitebridgehotel.co.uk **web:** www.whitebridgehotel.co.uk
dir: A9 onto B851, follow signs to Fort Augustus. Or A82 onto B862 at Fort Augustus

Close to Loch Ness and set amid rugged mountain and moorland scenery, this hotel is popular with tourists, fishermen and deerstalkers. Guests have a choice of more formal dining in the restaurant or lighter meals in the popular cosy bar. Bedrooms are thoughtfully equipped and brightly furnished.

Rooms 12 (3 fmly) **Facilities** WiFi Fishing **Parking** 32 **Notes** Closed 11 Dec-9 Jan

WICK
Highland
Map 23 ND35

Mackay's Hotel

★★★ 81% ⑩ HOTEL

tel: 01955 602323 **Union St KW1 5ED**
email: info@mackayshotel.co.uk **web:** www.mackayshotel.co.uk
dir: Opposite Caithness General Hospital

This well-established hotel is situated just outside the town centre overlooking the River Wick, and enjoys an entrance on to the world's shortest street; Ebenezer Place. MacKay's provides well-equipped, attractive accommodation, suited to both the business and leisure guest. There is a stylish bistro offering food throughout the day and the main bar offers a wide selection of whiskies.

Rooms 30 (2 fmly) 🐾 **S** £79-£92; **D** £89-£165 (incl. bkfst)* **Facilities** FTV WiFi ▷ HL Complimentary use of local gym & pool 🎵 **Conf** Class 100 Board 60 Thtr 200 Del from £130 to £160* **Services** Lift **Notes** LB ⊗ Civ Wed 200

W

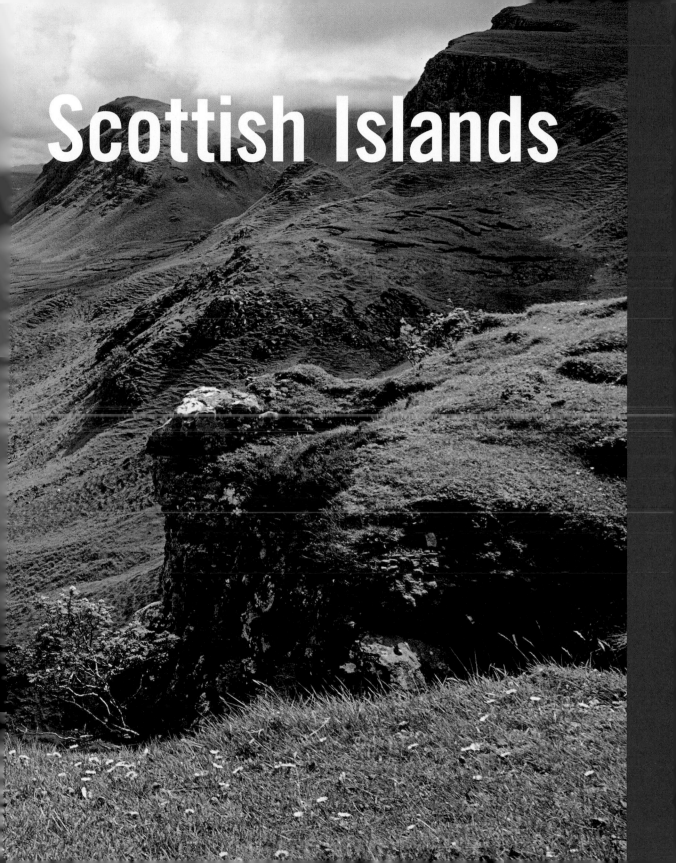

Scottish Islands

ISLE OF HARRIS

TARBERT
Map 22 NB10

Hotel Hebrides
★★★★ 74% @ HOTEL

tel: 01859 502364 **Pier Rd HS3 3DG**
email: stay@hotel-hebrides.com **web:** www.hotel-hebrides.com
dir: *To Tarbert via ferry from Uig (Isle of Skye) or ferry from Ullapool to Stornaway, A859 to Tarbert; or by plane to Stornaway from Glasgow, Edinburgh or Inverness*

Benefiting from an elevated position overlooking the town, this hotel is just a few minutes' walk from the centre. The small, hands-on team extend wonderful hospitality and customer care. The bedrooms are stylishly designed and include WiFi, high speed internet access and flat-screen TVs; the deluxe rooms have iPod docking stations and some rooms have loch and harbour views. Award-winning food is served in the Pierhouse Restaurant. A complimentary bus service is provided to the theatre in the summer months.

Rooms 21 (2 fmly) 🐾 **Facilities** FTV WiFi ↳ 🎵 **Conf** Class 35 Board 35 **Parking** 10 **Notes** ⊗

ISLE OF ISLAY

PORT ASKAIG
Map 20 NR46

Port Askaig Hotel
★★ 64% SMALL HOTEL

tel: 01496 840245 **PA46 7RD**
email: hotel@portaskaig.co.uk **web:** www.portaskaig.co.uk
dir: *At ferry terminal*

The building of this endearing family-run hotel dates back to the 18th-century. The lounge provides fine views over the Sound of Islay to Jura, and there is a choice of bars that are popular with locals - the Snug Bar and the Old Malt Whisky Bar. There is also a beer garden. Traditional dinners and seafood fresh from the harbour are served in the bright 'Starboard' restaurant and a full range of bar snacks and meals is also on offer. The bedrooms are smart and comfortable, and free WiFi is available.

Rooms 13 (2 annexe) (4 fmly) (11 GF) 🐾 **Facilities** WiFi **Parking** 21 **Notes** ⊗

ISLE OF MULL

TOBERMORY
Map 22 NM55

INSPECTORS' CHOICE

Highland Cottage
★★★ @@ SMALL HOTEL

tel: 01688 302030 **24 Breadalbane St PA75 6PD**
email: davidandjo@highlandcottage.co.uk **web:** www.highlandcottage.co.uk
dir: *A848 Craignure/Fishnish ferry terminal, pass Tobermory signs, straight on at mini rdbt across narrow bridge, turn right. Hotel on right opposite fire station*

Providing the highest level of natural and unassuming hospitality, this delightful little gem lies high above the island's capital. Don't be fooled by its side street location, a stunning view over the bay is just a few metres away. 'A country house hotel in town' it is an Aladdin's Cave of collectables and treasures, as well as masses of books and magazines. There are two inviting lounges, one with an honesty bar. The cosy dining room offers memorable dinners and splendid breakfasts. Bedrooms are individual; some have four-posters and all are comprehensively equipped to include TVs and music centres.

Rooms 6 (1 GF) **Facilities** FTV WiFi ↳ **Parking** 6 **Notes** No children 10yrs Closed Nov-Mar

SHETLAND

LERWICK
Map 24 HU44

Shetland Hotel
★★★ 79% HOTEL

tel: 01595 695515 **Holmsgarth Rd ZE1 0PW**
email: reception@shetlandhotel.co.uk **web:** www.shetlandhotels.com
dir: *Opposite ferry terminal, on main road N from town centre*

This purpose-built hotel is centrally opposite the main ferry terminal. Spacious and comfortable bedrooms are situated on three floors, and many look out over the harbour itself. The popular Waterfront Bar & Grill offers diverse, well executed and enjoyable dishes. There is also a Sports Bar on the ground floor.

Rooms 64 (4 fmly) 🐾 **S** £105; **D** £135 (incl. bkfst)* **Facilities** FTV WiFi ↳ **Conf** Class 75 Board 50 Thtr 300 **Services** Lift **Parking** 150 **Notes** ⊗ Closed 25-26 Dec, 1-2 Jan Civ Wed 200

SCALLOWAY
Map 24 HU33

Scalloway Hotel

★★★ 78% ◉◉ SMALL HOTEL

tel: 01595 880444 **Main St ZE1 0TR**
email: info@scallowayhotel.com web: www.scallowayhotel.com
dir: *6m from main port of Lerwick on A970. Situated in Scalloway Main St*

Scalloway is the ancient capital of Shetland; the Scalloway Hotel sits overlooking the waterfront. On offer is warm, friendly service and award-winning food using the best produce that the Shetland Larder can provide.

Rooms 23 🐾 Facilities FTV WiFi ♨ Parking 10 Notes RS 23 Dec-3 Jan

ISLE OF SKYE

ARDVASAR
Map 22 NG60

Ardvasar Hotel

★★★ 74% SMALL HOTEL

tel: 01471 844223 **Sleat IV45 8RS**
email: richard@ardvasar-hotel.demon.co.uk web: www.ardvasarhotel.com
dir: *From ferry, 500mtrs, left signed Ardvasar*

The Isle of Skye is dotted with cosy, welcoming hotels that make touring the island easy and convenient. This hotel ranks highly amongst its peers thanks to great hospitality and a preservation of community spirit. The hotel sits less than five minutes' drive from the Mallaig ferry and provides comfortable bedrooms and a cosy bar lounge for residents. Seafood is prominent on menus, and meals can be enjoyed in either the popular bar or the attractive dining room.

Rooms 10 (4 fmly) Facilities FTV WiFi ♫ Xmas New Year Conf Board 24 Thtr 50
Parking 30

COLBOST
Map 22 NG24

INSPECTORS' CHOICE

The Three Chimneys and House Over-By

◉◉◉ RESTAURANT WITH ROOMS

tel: 01470 511258 **IV55 8ZT**
email: eatandstay@threechimneys.co.uk
web: www.threechimneys.co.uk
dir: *5m W of Dunvegan take B884 signed Glendale. On left beside loch*

Crofters' cottages are as firmly rooted in the terroir as it is possible to be, synonymous with the island and its rugged and wild landscape. Two such crofts form the basis of Eddie and Shirley Spear's restaurant, which over the last 30 years has made its mark, too, on both the local economy and on the island's culinary reputation. This is destination dining. There are also classy bedrooms next door as staying over is a good option given the location. The decor reflects the natural environment, too, being proud of its origins, adding refined touches here and there but guaranteeing a sense of place. That sense of place is enhanced by the stunning views over land and loch. Breakfast is an impressive array of local fish, meats and cheeses, served with fresh home baking and home-made preserves.

The Three Chimneys and House Over-By

Rooms 6 (1 fmly) (6GF)

ISLEORNSAY
Map 22 NG71

Duisdale House Hotel

★★★★ 82% ◉◉ SMALL HOTEL

tel: 01471 833202 **Sleat IV43 8QW**
email: info@duisdale.com web: www.duisdale.com
dir: *7m S of Broadford on A851 towards Armadale. 7m N of Armadale ferry*

This grand Victorian house stands in its own landscaped gardens overlooking the Sound of Sleat. The hotel has a contemporary and chic style which complements the original features of the house. Each bedroom is individually designed and the superior rooms have four-poster beds. The elegant lounge has sumptuous sofas, original artwork and blazing log fires in the colder months.

Rooms 18 (1 fmly) (1 GF) 🐾 S £85-£250; D £85-£395 (incl. bkfst)* Facilities STV
WiFi ♨ Private yacht Outdoor hydropool Xmas New Year Conf Board 28 Thtr 50
Del from £99 to £250* Parking 30 Notes LB ⊗ Civ Wed 58

SCOTTISH ISLANDS

ISLEORNSAY *continued*

INSPECTORS' CHOICE

Kinloch Lodge

★★★ ◉◉◉ COUNTRY HOUSE HOTEL

tel: 01471 833214 & 833333 **Sleat IV43 8QY**
email: reservations@kinloch-lodge.co.uk **web:** www.kinloch-lodge.co.uk
dir: *6m S of Broadford on A851, 10m N of Armadale on A851*

Owned and run in a hands-on fashion by Lord and Lady MacDonald and their family, this hotel enjoys a picture postcard location surrounded by hills and a sea loch. Bedrooms and bathrooms are well appointed and comfortable, and public areas boast numerous open fires and relaxing areas to sit. There is a cookery school run by Claire MacDonald and a shop that sells her famous cookery books and produce.

Rooms 15 (8 annexe) (1 GF) ⌁ **Facilities** STV FTV WiFi Fishing Beauty treatment room Xmas New Year **Conf** Class 20 Board 20 Thtr 20 **Parking** 40

Silver Stars

The AA Silver Star rating denotes a Hotel that we highly recommend. They have a superior level of quality within their star rating, high standards of hospitality, service and cleanliness.

Toravaig House Hotel

★★★ 86% ◉◉ SMALL HOTEL

tel: 01471 820200 & 833231 **Knock Bay, Sleat IV44 8RE**
email: info@toravaig.com **web:** wwwskyehotel.co.uk
dir: *From Skye Bridge, left at Broadford onto A851, hotel 11m on left. Or from ferry at Armadale take A851, hotel 6m on right*

Set in two acres and enjoying panoramic views to the Knoydart Hills, this hotel is a haven of peace, with stylish, well-equipped and beautifully decorated bedrooms. There is an inviting lounge complete with deep sofas and an elegant dining room where delicious meals are the order of the day. The hotel provides a sea-going yacht for guests' exclusive use from April to September.

Rooms 9 ⌁ S £85-£190; **D** £85-£250 (incl. bkfst)* **Facilities** STV WiFi ⌁ Daily excursions (Apr-Sep) on hotel yacht Xmas New Year **Conf** Class 15 Board 15 Thtr 15 Del from £99 to £250* **Parking** 15 **Notes** LB ⊗ No children 5yrs Civ Wed 25

Hotel Eilean Iarmain

★★★ 77% ◉ SMALL HOTEL

THE CIRCLE

tel: 01471 833332 **Sleat IV43 8QR**
email: hotel@eileaniarmain.co.uk **web:** www.eileaniarmain.co.uk
dir: *From Skye Bridge take A87 towards Broadford. Left onto A851 signed Armadale. 8m, left to hotel. Or From Armadale ferry take A851 signed Broadford. 7m to hotel*

A hotel of charm and character, this 19th-century former inn sits by the pier and enjoys fine views across the sea loch. Bedrooms are individual and retain a traditional style, and a stable block has been converted into four delightful suites. Public rooms are cosy and inviting, and the restaurant offers award-winning menus showcasing the island's best produce, especially seafood and game.

Rooms 16 (10 annexe) (4 fmly) (3 GF) ⌁ S £122.50-£197.50; **D** £130-£210 (incl. bkfst)* **Facilities** FTV WiFi Fishing Shooting Art exhibitions Whisky tasting Tweed shop ♫ Xmas New Year **Conf** Class 10 Board 14 Thtr 25 **Parking** 20 **Notes** Civ Wed 30

PORTREE   Map 22 NG44

Cuillin Hills Hotel

★★★★ 76% HOTEL

tel: 01478 612003 **IV51 9QU**
email: info@cuillinhills-hotel-skye.co.uk **web:** www.cuillinhills-hotel-skye.co.uk
dir: *Right 0.25m N of Portree off A855. Follow hotel signs*

This imposing building enjoys a superb location overlooking Portree Bay and the Cuillin Hills. Accommodation is provided in smart, well-equipped rooms that are generally spacious; some rooms are found in an adjacent building. Public areas include comfortable lounges, a Malt Whisky Bar and a newly refurbished restaurant that takes advantage of the views - 'The View'. Service is particularly attentive.

Rooms 29 (7 annexe) (4 fmly) (10 GF) **Facilities** STV FTV WiFi HL Xmas New Year **Parking** 56 **Notes** Civ Wed 45

Bosville Hotel

U

tel: 01478 612846 **9-11 Bosville Ter IV51 9DG**
email: reservations@bosvillehotel.co.uk **web:** www.bosvillehotel.co.uk

This contemporary boutique hotel enjoys a stunning setting overlooking the harbour in Portree from an elevated position; perfectly located for touring the North of Skye and for access to the Outer Hebrides. Recently refurbished throughout, the hotel offers a range of luxurious, comfortable bedrooms, a popular public bar with a great selection of whiskies, and the restaurant - 'Dulse & Brose' - where modern Scottish food is served. You are guaranteed a warm Scottish welcome.

Rooms 20 (1 annexe) (4 fmly) **D** £95-£295 (incl. bkfst)* **Facilities** FTV WiFi **Conf** Class 20 Board 20 Thtr 20 **Parking** 10 **Notes** ⊗

STRUAN   Map 22 NG33

INSPECTORS' CHOICE

Ullinish Country Lodge

 RESTAURANT WITH ROOMS

tel: 01470 572214 **IV56 8FD**
email: ullinish@theisleofskye.co.uk **web:** www.theisleofskye.co.uk
dir: *Take A863 N. Lodge signed on left*

Set in some of Scotland's most dramatic landscape, with views of the Black Cuillin and MacLeod's Tables, this lodge has lochs on three sides. Samuel Johnson and James Boswell stayed here in 1773 and were impressed with the hospitality even then. Hosts Brian and Pam hope to extend the same welcome to their guests today. As you would expect, all bedrooms have amazing views, and come with half-tester beds.

Rooms 6

Wales

A

ABERDARE
Rhondda Cynon Taff

Map 9 SO00

Premier Inn Aberdare

BUDGET HOTEL

tel: 0871 527 8002

(Calls cost 13p per minute plus your phone company's access charge)

Riverside Retail Park, Tirfounders Field CF44 0AH

web: www.premierinn.com

dir: *M4 junct 32, A470 signed Merthyr Tydfil. In approx 10m take A4059 signed Aberdare. Straight on at 1st rdbt, 3rd exit at next rdbt into Fffordd Tirwaun signed Riverside Retail Park, hotel in park*

High quality, budget accommodation ideal for both families and business travellers. Spacious, en suite bedrooms feature tea and coffee making facilities, and Freeview TV in most hotels. Internet access and WiFi are available for a small fee. The adjacent family restaurant features a wide and varied menu. See also the Hotel Groups pages.

Rooms 40

ABERGAVENNY
Monmouthshire

Map 9 SO21

Llansantffraed Court Hotel

★★★★ 81% @@ COUNTRY HOUSE HOTEL

WELSH
RAREBITS
*Hotels of
Distinction*

tel: 01873 840678 **Old Raglan Rd, Llanvihangel Gobion, Clytha NP7 9BA**

email: reception@llch.co.uk **web:** www.llch.co.uk

dir: *At A465 & A40 Abergavenny junct take B4598 signed Usk (do not join A40). Towards Raglan, hotel on left in 4.5m*

In a commanding position and in its own extensive grounds, this very impressive property - a privately owned country-house hotel - has enviable views of the Brecon Beacons. Extensive public areas include a relaxing lounge and a spacious restaurant offering imaginative and enjoyable award-winning dishes. Bedrooms vary in size and reflect the individuality of the building; all are comfortably furnished and provide some thoughtful extras. Extensive parking is available.

Rooms 20 (1 fmly) ✎ **S** £110-£135; **D** £135-£195 (incl. bkfst) **Facilities** STV FTV WiFi ⚐ Putt green Fishing ⚒ Clay pigeon shooting school Xmas New Year Child facilities **Conf** Class 120 Board 100 Thtr 220 Del from £160 to £245 **Services** Lift **Parking** 250 **Notes** LB Civ Wed 200

AA HOTEL OF THE YEAR FOR WALES 2016-2017

Angel Hotel

★★★ 82% @ HOTEL

tel: 01873 857121 **15 Cross St NP7 5EN**

email: mail@angelabergavenny.com **web:** www.angelabergavenny.com

dir: *From A40 & A465 junct follow town centre signs, S of Abergavenny, past rail & bus stations*

Once a coaching inn, this has long been a popular venue for both locals and visitors; the two traditional function rooms and the ballroom are in regular use. In addition there is a comfortable lounge, a relaxed bar and a smart restaurant. In warmer weather there is a central courtyard that is ideal for alfresco eating. The bedrooms include a four-poster room and some that are suitable for families.

Rooms 34 (4 annexe) (2 fmly) ✎ **S** £99-£178; **D** £99-£178 (incl. bkfst)* **Facilities** FTV WiFi ♫ Xmas New Year **Conf** Class 60 Board 60 Thtr 180 Del £150* **Services** Lift **Parking** 30 **Notes** LB Closed 25 Dec Civ Wed 180

ABERGELE
Conwy

Map 14 SH97

The Kinmel

★★★★ 71% @ HOTEL

THE INDEPENDENTS
HOTEL ASSOCIATION

tel: 01745 832014 **St George Rd LL22 9AS**

email: reception@kinmelhotel.co.uk **web:** www.thekinmel.co.uk

dir: *A55 junct 24, hotel entrance on rdbt*

In a rural location at the end of a long drive leading from the A55, parts of this notable, family-run hotel date from the 16th century. However, substantial recent refurbishments have brought into play the stunning new Kinspa and leisure facility along with a range of smart, contemporary bedrooms. The stylish 1786 Brasserie serves modern British cuisine, while a Thai flavoured lighter option is served at Chiang Mai within the spa.

Rooms 42 (8 fmly) (18 GF) ✎ **S** £80-£149; **D** £99-£249 (incl. bkfst) **Facilities** Spa FTV WiFi ⚐ 🏊 Gym Steam room Sauna Hydrotherapy pool Relaxation room Xmas New Year **Conf** Class 100 Board 100 Thtr 250 Del from £129 to £139* **Services** Lift **Parking** 85 **Notes** LB Civ Wed 150

The Kinmel Arms

@@ RESTAURANT WITH ROOMS

tel: 01745 832207 **The Village, St George LL22 9BP**

email: info@thekinmelarms.co.uk **web:** www.thekinmelarms.co.uk

dir: *From A55 junct 24a to St George. E on A55, junct 24. 1st left to Rhuddlan, 1st right into St George. 2nd right*

This converted 17th-century coaching inn stands close to the church in the village of St George. The restaurant specialises in skilfully prepared produce from Wales and north-west England. Friendly, helpful staff will ensure you have a relaxing stay, in one of four attractive suites. All are kitted out with small kitchenettes where continental breakfasts are placed each day to enjoy at your leisure. Each suite is individually designed in a clean, natural style with luxurious bathrooms to match.

Rooms 4

B

ABERSOCH
Gwynedd   Map 14 SH32

Porth Tocyn Hotel

★★★ 81% ◎◎ COUNTRY HOUSE HOTEL

tel: 01758 713303 & 07789 994942 **Bwlch Tocyn LL53 7BU**
email: bookings@porthtocynhotel.co.uk web: www.porthtocynhotel.co.uk
dir: *2.5m S of Abersoch follow Porth Tocyn signs after Sarnbach*

Located above Abersoch with fine views across Cardigan bay, Porth Tocyn is set in its own attractive gardens. Several elegantly furnished sitting rooms are provided with space set aside for families. Bedrooms are comfortably appointed. Award-winning food is served in the restaurant with a formal option and more relaxed menu also available.

Rooms 17 (1 fmly) (3 GF) S £80-£95; D £110-£190 (incl. bkfst)* **Facilities** FTV WiFi ⚓ 🛏 Table tennis **Conf** Class 15 **Parking** 50 **Notes** LB Closed mid Nov-week before Etr RS low season

BANGOR
Gwynedd   Map 14 SH57

Premier Inn Bangor

BUDGET HOTEL

tel: 0871 527 8046 *(Calls cost 13p per minute plus your phone company's access charge)*
Parc Menai, Ffordd Y Parc LL57 4FA
web: www.premierinn.com
dir: *A55 junct 9 (Holyhead, Ysbyty Gwynedd Hospital). Take 3rd exit off rdbt. Hotel next left*

High quality, budget accommodation ideal for both families and business travellers. Spacious, en suite bedrooms feature tea and coffee making facilities, and Freeview TV in most hotels. Internet access and WiFi are available for a small fee. The adjacent family restaurant features a wide and varied menu. See also the Hotel Groups pages.

Rooms 78

BEAUMARIS
Isle of Anglesey   Map 14 SH67

Château Rhianfa

★★★★ 79% ◎ HOTEL

tel: 01248 713656 **Beaumaris LL59 5NS**
email: hello@chateaurhianfa.com web: www.chateaurhianfa.com
dir: *Situated between Menai Bridge & Beaumaris*

Built in the mid-19th century as a dower house in the style of a French chateau, Rhianfa has been carefully restored in recent years to create a luxurious venue.

Mature grounds reach to the shore. Bedrooms are spacious with modern facilities. The bar and lounges are on an upper floor affording spectacular views of Snowdonia and the Menai straits. A choice of Bars is available including the 'Wine Cave' and dinner is a highlight of any stay.

Rooms 19 (3 annexe) (4 GF) **Facilities** FTV WiFi 🛏 🛏 Gym Sauna Xmas New Year **Conf** Class 40 Thtr 50 **Services** Lift **Parking** 40 **Notes** ⊗ Civ Wed 100

The Bulkeley Hotel

★★★ 79% HOTEL

tel: 01248 810415 **Castle St LL58 8AW**
email: reception@bulkeleyhotel.co.uk web: www.bulkeleyhotel.co.uk
dir: *A55 junct 8a to Beaumaris. Hotel in town centre*

A Grade I listed hotel built in 1832, the Bulkeley is just 100 yards from the 13th-century Beaumaris Castle in the centre of town. Friendly staff create a relaxed atmosphere, serving morning til night in a choice of bars, a coffee shop, the fine dining restaurant and bistro. The well-equipped bedrooms and suites, some with four-posters, are generally spacious, and have pretty furnishings. Many of the rooms have fine panoramic views across the Menai Straits to the Snowdonian Mountains.

Rooms 43 (3 fmly) **Facilities** FTV WiFi Xmas New Year **Conf** Class 40 Board 25 Thtr 160 **Services** Lift **Parking** 25 **Notes** Civ Wed 100

HIGHLY RECOMMENDED

Bishopsgate House Hotel

★★ 85% ◎ SMALL HOTEL

tel: 01248 810302 **54 Castle St LL58 8BB**
email: hazel@bishopsgatehotel.co.uk web: www.bishopsgatehotel.co.uk
dir: *From Menai Bridge onto A545 to Beaumaris. Hotel on left in main street*

This immaculately maintained, privately-owned and personally-run small hotel dates back to 1760. It features fine examples of wood panelling and a Chinese Chippendale staircase. Thoughtfully furnished bedrooms are attractively decorated and two have four-poster beds. Quality cooking is served in the elegant restaurant and guests have a comfortable lounge and cosy bar to relax in.

Rooms 9 **Facilities** FTV WiFi 🛏 Xmas New Year **Parking** 8

B

BEDDGELERT
Gwynedd   Map 14 SH54

The Royal Goat Hotel

★★★ 74% HOTEL

THE CIRCLE
Selected by established Hotels

tel: 01766 890224 **LL55 4YE**
email: info@royalgoathotel.co.uk **web:** www.royalgoathotel.co.uk
dir: On A498 at Beddgelert

An impressive building steeped in history, the Royal Goat provides well-equipped accommodation, and carries out an annual programme of refurbishment. Attractively appointed, comfortable public areas include a choice of bars and restaurants, a residents' lounge and function rooms.

Rooms 32 (4 fmly) **Facilities** FTV WiFi Fishing Xmas New Year **Conf** Class 40 Board 30 Thtr 70 **Services** Lift **Parking** 100 **Notes** Closed Jan-14 Feb

BETWS-Y-COED
Conwy   Map 14 SH75

Craig-y-Dderwen Riverside Hotel

★★★★ 78% ⚜ COUNTRY HOUSE HOTEL

tel: 01690 710293 **LL24 0AS**
email: info@snowdoniahotel.com **web:** www.snowdoniahotel.com
dir: A5 to Betws-y-Coed, cross Waterloo Bridge, take 1st left

This Victorian country-house hotel is set in well-maintained grounds alongside the River Conwy, at the end of a tree-lined drive. Views down the river can be enjoyed from the restaurant and deck. Many of the bedrooms have balconies, and the feature rooms include a four-poster bed and a hot tub. There are comfortable lounges and the atmosphere throughout is tranquil and relaxing.

Rooms 18 (2 fmly) (1 GF) (1 smoking) S £105-£145; D £120-£230 (incl. bkfst)* **Facilities** STV FTV WiFi Fishing Badminton Volleyball New Year **Conf** Class 50 Board 50 Thtr 100 **Parking** 50 **Notes** LB Closed 23-26 Dec & 2 Jan-1 Feb Civ Wed 100

Royal Oak Hotel

★★★ 85% ⚜ HOTEL

tel: 01690 710219 **Holyhead Rd LL24 0AY**
email: royaloakmail@btopenworld.com **web:** www.royaloakhotel.net
dir: On A5 in town centre, adjacent to St Mary's Church

Centrally situated in the village, this elegant, privately owned hotel started life as a coaching inn and now provides very comfortable bedrooms with smart, modern en suite bathrooms. The extensive public areas retain much of their original charm

and character. The choice of eating options includes the Grill Bistro, the Stables Bar which is much frequented by locals, and the more formal Llugwy Restaurant.

Royal Oak Hotel

Rooms 27 (1 fmly) S £77.50-£85; D £95-£195 (incl. bkfst)* **Facilities** FTV WiFi New Year **Conf** Class 40 Board 20 Thtr 80 Del from £100 to £195* **Parking** 90 **Notes** LB Closed 25-26 Dec Civ Wed 60

See advert on opposite page

BODELWYDDAN
Denbighshire   Map 14 SJ07

Bodelwyddan Castle Hotel

★★★ 80% HOTEL

WARNER
LEISURE
HOTELS
We've all grown up

tel: 01745 585088 **LL18 5YA**
email: claire.fletcher@bourne-leisure.co.uk **web:** www.warnerleisurehotels.co.uk
dir: Off A55 towards North Wales at junct 25, opposite Marble Church

This Grade II listed Victorian castle is situated on the north Wales coast within easy reach of Snowdonia and Cheshire. The famous Bodelwyddan marble church, set in the valley below, can be seen from the grounds and The National Portrait Gallery is also situated on site. The hotel is entirely adults only and offers a super range of leisure facilities and numerous daily in-house and external activities such as archery, as well as nightly entertainment in the cabaret suite. Packages range from a minimum two-night, half-board stay.

Rooms 233 (123 annexe) (114 GF) **Facilities** Spa FTV WiFi HL Putt green Gym Archery Rifle shooting Football Dancing Xmas New Year **Services** Lift **Parking** 156 **Notes** LB No children 21yrs

BRECON
Powys   Map 9 SO02

Peterstone Court

⚜ RESTAURANT WITH ROOMS

tel: 01874 665387 **Llanhamlach LD3 7YB**
email: info@peterstone-court.com **web:** www.peterstone-court.com
dir: 3m from Brecon on A40 towards Abergavenny

Situated on the edge of the Brecon Beacons, this establishment affords stunning views overlooking the River Usk. The atmosphere is friendly and informal, with no unnecessary fuss. No two bedrooms are alike, but all share comparable levels of comfort, quality and elegance. Public areas reflect similar standards, eclectically styled with a blend of the contemporary and the traditional. Quality produce is cooked with care in a range of enjoyable dishes.

Rooms 12 (4 annexe) (2 fmly)

B

BRIDGEND
Bridgend

Map 9 SS97

Best Western Heronston Hotel & Spa

 Best Western.

★★★ 79% HOTEL

tel: 01656 668811 **Ewenny Rd CF35 5AW**
email: reservations@bestwesternheronstonhotel.co.uk
web: www.bw-heronstonhotel.co.uk
dir: *M4 junct 35, follow signs for Porthcawl, at 5th rdbt left towards Ogmore-by-Sea B4265, hotel 200yds on left*

Situated within easy reach of the town centre and the M4, this large modern hotel offers spacious well-equipped accommodation, including ground-floor rooms. Public areas include an open-plan lounge/bar, attractive restaurant and a smart leisure and fitness club. The hotel also has a choice of function and conference rooms, and ample parking is available.

Rooms 75 (3 fmly) (36 GF) ✆ **S** £70-£120; **D** £80-£130 (incl. bkfst) **Facilities** Spa STV FTV WiFi ⅄ HL ⓢ Gym Steam room Sauna New Year **Conf** Class 80 Board 60 Thtr 250 Del from £105 to £125 **Services** Lift **Parking** 160 **Notes** LB Civ Wed 200

Court Colman Manor

★★★ 66% COUNTRY HOUSE HOTEL

tel: 01656 720212 **Pen-y-Fai CF31 4NG**
email: experience@court-colman-manor.com **web:** www.court-colman-manor.com
dir: *M4 junct 36, A4063 towards Maesteg, after lights 1st exit to Bridgend, under motorway, next right, follow hotel signs*

Dating back to the Tudor times this fine mansion is set in its own peaceful grounds outside Bridgend, and is just a short distance from the M4. The spacious, comfortable bedrooms include ten themed rooms inspired by exotic locations - India, Japan, Morocco etc. The award-winning food served in Bokhara Brasserie is imaginative, and Indian and Mediterranean dishes are included in the choices. Diners can view their meals being prepared in the open-plan kitchen.

Rooms 30 (6 fmly) ✆ **S** £70-£80; **D** £100-£170 (incl. bkfst)* **Facilities** FTV WiFi ⅄ HL Xmas New Year **Conf** Class 60 Thtr 100 **Parking** 180 **Notes** Civ Wed 150

Premier Inn Bridgend Central

BUDGET HOTEL

tel: 0871 527 8146 *(Calls cost 13p per minute plus your phone company's access charge)*
The Derwen CF32 9ST
web: www.premierinn.com
dir: *M4 junct 36, A4061 (signed Bridgend & Pen-y-Bont). Hotel at next rdbt*

High quality, budget accommodation ideal for both families and business travellers. Spacious, en suite bedrooms feature tea and coffee making facilities, and Freeview TV in most hotels. Internet access and WiFi are available for a small fee. The adjacent family restaurant features a wide and varied menu. See also the Hotel Groups pages.

Rooms 69

Premier Inn Bridgend M4 Jct 35

BUDGET HOTEL

tel: 0871 527 8144 *(Calls cost 13p per minute plus your phone company's access charge)*
Pantruthyn Farm, Pencoed CF35 5HY
web: www.premierinn.com
dir: *At M4 junct 35, behind petrol station & McDonalds*

Rooms 60

B

BUILTH WELLS
Powys   Map 9 SO05

Caer Beris Manor Hotel
THE INDEPENDENTS
HOTEL ASSOCIATION

★★★ 79% COUNTRY HOUSE HOTEL

tel: 01982 552601 **LD2 3NP**
email: info@caerberis.com **web:** www.caerberis.com
dir: *From town centre follow A483/Llandovery signs. Hotel on the left. Keep in left hand lane but bear right, straight over mini-rdbt*

Guests can expect a relaxing stay at this friendly and privately-owned boutique, country house hotel that has extensive and attractive landscaped grounds. Bedrooms are individually decorated and furnished to retain the atmosphere of a bygone era. The spacious and comfortable lounge, complete with log fire, and lounge bar continue this theme. Dining is available in the elegant 1896 Restaurant, complete with 16th-century panelling. Those aiming for total relaxation can also indulge in a well-being treatment including massages and facials.

Rooms 23 (2 fmly) (3 GF) ⌁ **S** £80-£90; **D** fr £140 (incl. bkfst)* **Facilities** FTV WiFi ⇘ Fishing ⌁ Clay pigeon shooting Birdwatching Walking holidays Xmas New Year **Conf** Class 75 Board 50 Thtr 100 **Parking** 100 **Notes** LB Civ Wed 200

CAERNARFON
Gwynedd   Map 14 SH46

INSPECTORS' CHOICE

Seiont Manor Hotel
Hand PICKED HOTELS
BUILT FOR PLEASURE

★★★ ◉◉ COUNTRY HOUSE HOTEL

tel: 01286 673366 & 0845 072 7550 *(Calls cost 5p per minute plus your phone company's access charge)* **Llanrug LL55 2AQ**
email: seiontmanor@handpicked.co.uk
web: www.handpickedhotels.co.uk/seiontmanor
dir: *E on A4086, 2.5m from Caernarfon*

A splendid hotel created from authentic farm buildings, set in the tranquil countryside near Snowdonia; the River Seiont flows through the 150-acre grounds. The bedrooms, including junior suites, are individually decorated and have luxurious extra touches; each has either a balcony or patio. The comfortable public rooms are cosy and furnished in country-house style. The kitchen team use the best local produce to provide exciting takes on traditional dishes, and guests can choose to eat in either the award-winning Llwyn y Brain Restaurant or the conservatory brasserie.

Rooms 28 (2 fmly) (14 GF) ⌁ **S** £85-£175; **D** £85-£185 (incl. bkfst)* **Facilities** STV FTV WiFi ⇘ HL ⓢ Fishing Gym Xmas New Year **Conf** Class 40 Board 40 Thtr 100 Del from £135 to £165* **Parking** 60 **Notes** LB ⊗ Civ Wed 100

Premier Inn Caernarfon

BUDGET HOTEL

tel: 0871 527 8180 *(Calls cost 13p per minute plus your phone company's access charge)*
Victioria Dock, Balaclava Rd LL55 1SQ
web: www.premierinn.com
dir: *A55 junct 9, at rdbt 1st exit follow Caernarfon signs. In Caernarfon at rdbt (Morrisons on right) 1st exit, keep in right lane, at next rdbt 4th exit to mini rdbt, hotel opposite*

High quality, budget accommodation ideal for both families and business travellers. Spacious, en suite bedrooms feature tea and coffee making facilities, and Freeview TV in most hotels. Internet access and WiFi are available for a small fee. The adjacent family restaurant features a wide and varied menu. See also the Hotel Groups pages.

Rooms 93

CAERPHILLY
Caerphilly   Map 9 ST18

Premier Inn Caerphilly (Corbetts Lane)

BUDGET HOTEL

tel: 0871 527 8182 *(Calls cost 13p per minute plus your phone company's access charge)*
Corbetts Ln CF83 3HX
web: www.premierinn.com
dir: *M4 junct 32, A470, 2nd left signed Caerphilly. At rdbt 4th exit, at next rdbt 2nd exit. Straight on at next rdbt & at Pwllypant Rdbt, hotel on left*

High quality, budget accommodation ideal for both families and business travellers. Spacious, en suite bedrooms feature tea and coffee making facilities, and Freeview TV in most hotels. Internet access and WiFi are available for a small fee. The adjacent family restaurant features a wide and varied menu. See also the Hotel Groups pages.

Rooms 62

Premier Inn Caerphilly (Crossways)
Premier Inn
BUDGET HOTEL

tel: 0871 527 8184 *(Calls cost 13p per minute plus your phone company's access charge)*
Crossways Business Park, Pontypandy CF83 3NL
web: www.premierinn.com
dir: *M4 junct 32, A470 towards Merthyr Tydfil (junct 4 take A458 towards Caerphilly). At Crossways Business Park (5th rdbt). Hotel on right at McDonald's rdbt*

Rooms 40

CARDIFF
Cardiff   Map 9 ST17

The St David's Hotel & Spa
PH | principal hayley

★★★★★ 82% HOTEL

tel: 029 2045 4045 **Havannah St CF10 5SD**
email: stdavids.reservations@principal-hayley.com **web:** www.principal-hayley.com
dir: *M4 junct 33, A4232 for 9m, follow Cardiff Bay signs, then Techniquest signs, at top exit slip road, 1st left at rdbt, 1st right*

This imposing contemporary building sits in a prime position on Cardiff Bay and has a seven-storey atrium creating a dramatic impression. Leading from the atrium are the practically designed and comfortable bedrooms. Tides Restaurant, adjacent to the stylish cocktail bar, has views across the water to Penarth, and there is a quiet first-floor lounge for guests seeking peace and quiet. A well-equipped spa and extensive business areas complete the package.

C

Rooms 142 🐾 **Facilities** Spa FTV WiFi ♨ HL ⏱ Gym Fitness studio Hydrotherapy pool Aerobics studio ♫ **Conf** Class 110 Board 76 Thtr 270 **Services** Lift Air con **Parking** 60 **Notes** ⊗ Civ Wed 270

Mercure Cardiff Holland House Hotel & Spa
★★★★ 76% HOTEL

tel: 029 2043 5000 **24/26 Newport Rd CF24 0DD**
email: h6622@accor.com **web:** www.mercure.com
dir: M4 junct 33, A4232 to city centre, right at lights facing prison, straight through next lights, hotel car park end of lane facing Magistrates Court

Conveniently located just a few minutes' walk from the city centre, this exciting hotel combines contemporary styling with a genuinely friendly welcome. Bedrooms, including five luxurious suites, are spacious and include many useful extras. A state-of-the-art leisure club and spa is available in addition to a large function room. An eclectic menu provides a varied range of freshly prepared, quality dishes.

Rooms 165 (80 fmly) 🐾 **Facilities** Spa STV WiFi ⏱ Gym **Conf** Class 250 Board 90 Thtr 700 **Services** Lift Air con **Parking** 90 **Notes** Civ Wed 500

Novotel Cardiff Central
★★★★ 76% HOTEL

tel: 029 211 32800 **Schooner Way, Atlantic Wharf CF10 4RT**
email: h5982@accor.com **web:** www.novotel.com
dir: M4 junct 29 onto A48(M), follow signs for city centre

Situated in the heart of the city's development area, this hotel is equally convenient for the centre and Cardiff Bay. Bedrooms vary between standard rooms in the modern extension, and executive rooms in the original wing. There is good seating space in public rooms, and the hotel has a popular leisure club. The Elements Restaurant is an innovative dining concept.

Rooms 138 (100 fmly) 🐾 **S** £95-£595; **D** £105-£605 **Facilities** FTV WiFi ♨ ⏱ Gym Sauna Steam room Xmas New Year **Conf** Class 90 Board 65 Thtr 250 Del from £125 to £195 **Services** Lift Air con **Parking** 120 **Notes** Civ Wed 250

The Angel Hotel
★★★ 79% HOTEL

THE HOTEL COLLECTION

tel: 029 2064 9200 **Castle St CF10 1SZ**
email: angel@thehotelcollection.co.uk **web:** www.thehotelcollection.co.uk
dir: Opposite Cardiff Castle

The Angel is a well-established hotel in the heart of the city, overlooking the famous castle and almost opposite the Millennium Stadium. All bedrooms offer air conditioning and are appointed to a good standard. Public areas include an impressive lobby, a modern restaurant and a selection of conference rooms. There is limited parking at the rear of the hotel.

Rooms 102 (3 fmly) **S** £55-£95; **D** £75-£195* **Facilities** WiFi Xmas New Year **Conf** Class 120 Board 50 Thtr 300 Del from £99 to £139* **Services** Lift Air con **Parking** 60 **Notes** Civ Wed 200

Premier Inn Barry Island (Cardiff Airport)
BUDGET HOTEL

tel: 0871 527 9370 (Calls cost 13p per minute plus your phone company's access charge) **Triangle Site, Fford Y Mileniwm, The Waterfront, Hood Rd CF62 5QN**
web: www.premierinn.com
dir: M4 junct 33 A4232 signed A4050, pass through 8 rdbts, left onto Trinity St, right onto A4055 Broad St. Left after 0.2m.

High quality, budget accommodation ideal for both families and business travellers. Spacious, en suite bedrooms feature tea and coffee making facilities, and Freeview TV in most hotels. Internet access and WiFi are available for a small fee. The adjacent family restaurant features a wide and varied menu. See also the Hotel Groups pages.

Rooms 80

Premier Inn Cardiff City Centre
BUDGET HOTEL

tel: 0871 527 8196 (Calls cost 13p per minute plus your phone company's access charge) **Helmont House, 10 Churchill Way CF10 2HE**
web: www.premierinn.com
dir: M4 junct 29 onto A48(M) towards Cardiff (East & South), 4.5m. Follow Cardiff (East), Docks & A4232 signs. Left at A4161 (Eastern Avenue North). At rdbt 2nd exit onto A4161 (Newport Rd). 2m, left into Station Terrace. Right into Churchill Way

Rooms 200

Premier Inn Cardiff City South
BUDGET HOTEL

tel: 0871 527 8198 (Calls cost 13p per minute plus your phone company's access charge) **Keen Rd CF24 5JT**
web: www.premierinn.com
dir: Follow Cardiff Docks & Bay signs from A48(M), over flyover. At 5th rdbt, 3rd exit. Hotel 1st right, then 1st right again

Rooms 97

CARDIFF *continued*

Premier Inn Cardiff East

BUDGET HOTEL

tel: 0871 527 8200 *(Calls cost 13p per minute plus your phone company's access charge)*
Newport Rd, Castleton CF3 2UQ
web: www.premierinn.com
dir: *M4 junct 28, A48 signed Castleton. 3m, hotel on right*

Rooms 49

Premier Inn Cardiff North

BUDGET HOTEL

tel: 0871 527 8202 *(Calls cost 13p per minute plus your phone company's access charge)*
Pentwyn Rd, Pentwyn CF23 7XH
web: www.premierinn.com
dir: *W'bound: M4 junct 29, A48(M). (E'bound: M4 junct 30, A4232 signs, A48(M) towards Cardiff). Follow Pentwyn signs, 3rd exit at rdbt. Hotel 200yds on right*

Rooms 147

Premier Inn Cardiff (Roath)

BUDGET HOTEL

tel: 0871 527 8194 *(Calls cost 13p per minute plus your phone company's access charge)*
Ipswich Rd, Roath CF23 9AQ
web: www.premierinn.com
dir: *W'bound: M4 junct 29, A48(M). E'bound: M4 junct 30 A48(M). Follow Cardiff (E) Docks & Cardiff Bay signs. Then follow brown signs for David Lloyd Tennis Centre. Into David Lloyd Leisure Club car park, follow hotel signs*

Rooms 75

Premier Inn Cardiff West

BUDGET HOTEL

tel: 0871 527 8204 *(Calls cost 13p per minute plus your phone company's access charge)*
Port Rd, Nantisaf, Wenvoe CF5 6DD
web: www.premierinn.com
dir: *M4 junct 33, S on A4232. Take 2nd exit (signed Airport), 3rd exit at Culverhouse Cross rdbt. Hotel 0.5m on Barry Rd A4050*

Rooms 39

Ibis Budget Cardiff Centre

AA Advertised

tel: 029 2045 8131 **Tyndall St CF10 4BE**
email: H6175@accor.com **web:** www.ibishotel.com
dir: *In central Cardiff, close to city centre & less than 1m from Millennium Stadium*

Modern, budget hotel offering comfortable accommodation in bright and practical bedrooms. Breakfast is self-service and dinner is available in the restaurant.

Rooms 157 (81 fmly) (12 GF) ♠ **Facilities** FTV WiFi HL **Services** Lift **Parking** 45

Ibis Cardiff

AA Advertised

tel: 029 2064 9250 **Churchill Way CF10 2HA**
email: H2936@accor.com **web:** www.ibishotel.com
dir: *M4 junct 29, to junct 29A, A48(M), A48, 2nd exit A4232. Follow signs to City Centre on Newport Rd, left after rail bridge, left after Queen St station*

Modern, budget hotel offering comfortable accommodation in bright and practical bedrooms. Breakfast is self-service and dinner is available in the restaurant.

Rooms 102 (18 GF) ♠ **Facilities** STV FTV WiFi ♨ **Services** Lift

Ibis Cardiff Gate

AA Advertised

tel: 029 2073 3222 **Malthouse Av, Cardiff Gate Business Park, Pontprennau CF23 8RA**
email: H3159@accor.com **web:** www.ibishotel.com
dir: *M4 junct 30, follow Cardiff Service Station signs. Hotel on left*

This modern, budget hotel offers comfortable accommodation in bright and practical bedrooms. Breakfast is self-service and dinner is available in the restaurant.

Rooms 78 (7 fmly) (22 GF) ♠ **D** £38-£250* **Facilities** STV FTV WiFi **Conf** Class 24 Thtr 25 Del £150* **Services** Lift **Parking** 78

CARMARTHEN	Map 8 SN42
Carmarthenshire	

Ivy Bush Royal Hotel

★★★ 77% HOTEL

tel: 01267 235111 **Spilman St SA31 1LG**
email: reception@ivybushroyal.co.uk **web:** www.ivybushroyal.co.uk
dir: *A48 to Carmarthen, over 1st rdbt, at 2nd rdbt right onto A4242. Straight over next 2 rdbts. Left at lights. Hotel on right at top of hill*

This hotel offers spacious, well-equipped bedrooms and bathrooms, a relaxing lounge with outdoor patio seating, and a comfortable restaurant serving a varied selection of carefully prepared meals. Weddings, meetings and conferences are all well catered for at this friendly, family-run establishment.

Rooms 70 (4 fmly) ♠ **S** £65-£80; **D** £80-£100 (incl. bkfst) **Facilities** FTV WiFi ♨ Gym Xmas New Year **Conf** Class 50 Board 40 Thtr 200 Del from £99 to £150 **Services** Lift **Parking** 83 **Notes** LB ⊗ Civ Wed 150

Falcon Hotel

★★★ 75% HOTEL

tel: 01267 234959 & 237152 **Lammas St SA31 3AP**
email: reception@falconcarmarthen.co.uk **web:** www.falconcarmarthen.co.uk
dir: *In town centre pass bus station, left, hotel 200yds on left*

This friendly hotel has been owned and run by the Exton family for over 45 years, and is located in the centre of the town. Bedrooms, some with four-poster beds, are tastefully decorated and have good facilities. There is a comfortable lounge with adjacent bar, and the restaurant offers a varied selection of enjoyable dishes at both lunch and dinner.

Rooms 16 (1 fmly) **Facilities** FTV WiFi ♨ **Conf** Class 50 Board 40 Thtr 80 **Parking** 36 **Notes** LB Closed 26 Dec RS Sun

C

CONWY
Conwy
Map 14 SH77

Castle Hotel Conwy
★★★★ 79% ◉◉ TOWN HOUSE HOTEL

tel: 01492 582800 **High St LL32 8DB**
email: mail@castlewales.co.uk **web:** www.castlewales.co.uk
dir: *A55 junct 18, follow town centre signs, cross estuary (castle on left). Right then left at mini-rdbts onto one-way system. Right at Town Wall Gate, right into Berry St then High St*

This family-run, 16th-century hotel is one of Conwy's most distinguished buildings and offers a relaxed and friendly atmosphere. Bedrooms are appointed to an impressive standard and include a stunning suite and a choice of individually styled rooms. Downstairs, a popular modern bar serving real ales and the award-winning Dawsons restaurant await guests. The new 'Healing Hands' spa-therapy is an added bonus.

Rooms 27 (2 fmly) ☎ **S** £77-£105; **D** £115-£250 **Facilities** FTV WiFi ⋩ Holistic therapy treatment room New Year **Parking** 34 **Notes** LB Closed 25-26 Dec

CRICCIETH
Gwynedd
Map 14 SH43

Bron Eifion Country House Hotel
★★★★ 83% ◉ COUNTRY HOUSE HOTEL

tel: 01766 522385 **LL52 0SA**
email: enquiries@broneifion.co.uk **web:** www.broneifion.co.uk
dir: *A497 between Porthmadog & Pwllheli, 0.5m from Criccieth, on right towards Pwllheli*

This delightful country house, built in 1883, is set in extensive grounds to the west of Criccieth, commanding impressive sea views. Now a privately-owned and personally-run hotel, it provides warm and very friendly hospitality. The interior styling highlights many retained period features. There is a choice of lounges and the very impressive central hall features a minstrels' gallery. The Gin List is not to be missed; 50 varieties served with a selection of accompaniments including pink grapefruit, blueberries and star anise.

Rooms 18 (1 fmly) (1 GF) ☎ **S** £95-£135; **D** £145-£215 (incl. bkfst)*
Facilities FTV WiFi ⋩ Xmas New Year **Conf** Class 150 Board 60 Thtr 150 Del from £125 **Parking** 50 **Notes** ⊗ Civ Wed 150

George IV Hotel
★★★ 72% HOTEL

Leisureplex
HOLIDAY HOTELS

tel: 01766 522168 & 01257 24800 **23-25 High St LL52 0BS**
email: georgeiv.criccieth@alfatravel.co.uk **web:** www.leisureplex.co.uk
dir: *On A497 in town centre*

This hotel stands back from the A497 in the town centre. The bedrooms, which in general are spacious, are attractively furnished and well equipped to meet the needs of both business guests and holidaymakers. George's Brasserie serves a menu based on locally sourced ingredients.

Rooms 80 (5 fmly) ☎ **Facilities** FTV WiFi ♫ Xmas New Year **Services** Lift **Parking** 16 **Notes** ⊗ Closed Jan RS Nov & Feb-Mar

CRICKHOWELL
Powys
Map 9 SO21

Manor Hotel
★★★ 77% ◉ HOTEL

tel: 01873 810212 **Brecon Rd NP8 1SE**
email: info@manorhotel.co.uk **web:** www.manorhotel.co.uk
dir: *On A40, 0.5m from Crickhowell*

This impressive manor house, set in a stunning location, was the birthplace of Sir George Everest, after whom Mount Everest is named. The bedrooms and public areas are elegant, and there are extensive leisure facilities. The restaurant, with panoramic views, is the setting for exciting modern cooking.

Rooms 23 (2 fmly) **D** £85-£120 (incl. bkfst)* **Facilities** STV FTV WiFi ⋩ ⊛ Gym Xmas New Year **Conf** Class 250 Board 150 Thtr 300 Del £145* **Parking** 200 **Notes** LB Civ Wed 150

CWMBRAN
Torfaen
Map 9 ST29

The Parkway Hotel & Spa
★★★★ 78% ◉ HOTEL

tel: 01633 871199 & 486312 **Cwmbran Dr NP44 3UW**
email: enquiries@theparkwayhotel.co.uk **web:** www.parkwayhotelandspa.com
dir: *M4 junct 25a & 26, A4051 follow Cwmbran-Llantarnam Park signs. Right at rdbt, right for hotel*

This purpose-built hotel, in over seven acres of grounds, offers comfortable bedrooms and public areas that will suit a wide range of guests. The coffee shop is an informal eating option throughout the day, and there is fine dining in Ravello's Restaurant. The bedrooms, including suites, interconnecting family rooms and wheelchair access rooms, are stylishly appointed. Additional facilities include a sports centre and conference and meeting facilities.

Rooms 80 (4 fmly) (34 GF) ☎ **S** £65-£195; **D** £75-£250 (incl. bkfst)* **Facilities** Spa FTV WiFi ⋩ ⊛ supervised ⟲ Gym Steam room Sauna Boules Table tennis Chess Badminton Snooker Table ♫ Xmas New Year **Conf** Class 240 Board 100 Thtr 500 Del from £125 to £155* **Services** Lift **Parking** 300 **Notes** LB ⊗ RS Xmas period Civ Wed 500

Premier Inn Cwmbran
BUDGET HOTEL

tel: 0870 111 2851 *(Calls cost 13p per minute plus your phone company's access charge)*
Avondale Rd, Pontrhydyrun NP44 1DE
web: www.premierinn.com
dir: *M4 junct 26, A4501 signed Cwmbran, straight on at next 5 rdbts. At 6th take Pontrhydyrun Rd exit, left into Avondale Rd*

High quality, budget accommodation ideal for both families and business travellers. Spacious, en suite bedrooms feature tea and coffee making facilities, and Freeview TV in most hotels. Internet access and WiFi are available for a small fee. The adjacent family restaurant features a wide and varied menu. See also the Hotel Groups pages.

Rooms 41

D

DEGANWY
Conwy
Map 14 SH77

Quay Hotel & Spa
★★★★ 82% HOTEL

tel: 01492 564100 **Deganwy Quay LL31 9DJ**
email: reservations@quayhotel.co.uk **web:** www.quayhotel.co.uk
dir: *M56, A494, A55 junct 18, straight across 2 rdbts. At lights bear left into The Quay. Hotel on right*

This luxury hotel occupies a stunning position beside the estuary on Deganwy's Quay. What was once an area for railway storage is now a property of modern architectural design. Spacious bedrooms, many with balconies and wonderful views, are decorated individually and boast a host of extras. Four penthouse suites command spectacular views. Extensive spa and leisure facilities and The Grill Room restaurant complete the experience.

Rooms 74 (15 fmly) (30 GF) ⌂ **Facilities** Spa WiFi HL ⌖ supervised Gym Steam & sauna room Hydrotherapy pool ♪ Xmas New Year **Conf** Class 240 Board 90 Thtr 240 **Services** Lift **Parking** 96 **Notes** LB Civ Wed 150

DEVIL'S BRIDGE
Ceredigion
Map 9 SN77

The Hafod Hotel
★★★ 68% HOTEL

tel: 01970 890232 **SY23 3JL**
email: info@thehafodhotel.co.uk **web:** www.thehafodhotel.co.uk
dir: *Exit A44 in Ponterwyd signed Devil's Bridge/Pontarfynach onto A4120, 3m, over bridge. Hotel opposite*

This former hunting lodge dates back to the 17th century and is situated in six acres of grounds. Now a family-owned and run hotel, it provides accommodation suitable for both business and leisure guests. Family rooms and a four-poster room are available. In addition to the dining area and lounge, there are tea rooms.

Rooms 16 (2 fmly) **Facilities** WiFi ⌂ Xmas New Year **Conf** Class 70 Board 40 Thtr 100 **Parking** 200 **Notes** Civ Wed 40

DOLGELLAU
Gwynedd
Map 14 SH71

Penmaenuchaf Hall Hotel
★★★ COUNTRY HOUSE HOTEL

WELSH RAREBITS *Hotels of Distinction*

tel: 01341 422129 **Penmaenpool LL40 1YB**
email: relax@penhall.co.uk **web:** www.penhall.co.uk
dir: *A470 onto A493 to Tywyn. Hotel approx 1m on left*

Built in 1860, this impressive hall stands in 20 acres of formal gardens, grounds and woodland, and enjoys magnificent views across the River Mawddach. Sympathetic restoration has created a comfortable and welcoming hotel with spacious day rooms and thoughtfully furnished bedrooms, some with private balconies. Fresh produce cooked in modern British style is served in an elegant conservatory restaurant, overlooking the countryside.

Rooms 14 (2 fmly) ⌂ **S** £130-£195; **D** £180-£290 (incl. bkfst)* **Facilities** STV FTV WiFi ⌖ Fishing ⌂ Complimentary salmon & trout fishing Coracling In-room massage treatments Xmas New Year **Conf** Class 30 Board 22 Thtr 50 Del from £140 to £210* **Parking** 30 **Notes** LB No children 6yrs Civ Wed 65

EBBW VALE
Blaenau Gwent
Map 9 SO10

Premier Inn Ebbw Vale
BUDGET HOTEL

Premier Inn

tel: 0871 527 8356 *(Calls cost 13p per minute plus your phone company's access charge)*
Victoria Business Park, Waunllwyd NP23 8AN
web: www.premierinn.com
dir: *M4 junct 28, A467 signed Risca, then Brynmawr. At rdbt at Brynithel 1st exit onto A4046, signed Ebbw Vale. At rdbt 3rd exit towards Waunllwyd. At rdbt 1st exit, next left. Hotel adjacent*

High quality, budget accommodation ideal for both families and business travellers. Spacious, en suite bedrooms feature tea and coffee making facilities, and Freeview TV in most hotels. Internet access and WiFi are available for a small fee. The adjacent family restaurant features a wide and varied menu. See also the Hotel Groups pages.

Rooms 44

EGLWYS FACH
Ceredigion Map 14 SN69

Plas Ynyshir Hall Hotel
★★★★ ❀❀❀❀ COUNTRY HOUSE HOTEL

tel: 01654 781209 **SY20 8TA**
email: ynyshir@relaischateaux.com **web:** www.ynyshirhall.co.uk
dir: Fxit A487, 5.5m S of Machynlleth, signed from main road

Set in beautifully landscaped grounds and surrounded by the RSPB Ynys-hir Nature Reserve, Plas Ynyshir Hall is a haven of calm. The house was once owned by Queen Victoria and is surrounded by mountain scenery. Lavishly styled bedrooms, each individually themed around a great painter, provide high standards of luxury and comfort. The lounge and bar, adorned with an abundance of fresh flowers, have different moods. The dining room offers highly accomplished cooking using the best, locally sourced ingredients including herbs, soft fruit and vegetables from the hotel's own kitchen garden, and wild foods gathered nearby. This hotel makes an idyllic location for weddings.

Rooms 10 (3 annexe) (4 GF) ⚲ **S** £250-£1070; **D** £250-£1070 (incl. bkfst)
Facilities FTV WiFi ⚲ ⚲ Treatment rooms Xmas New Year **Conf** Class 20 Board 18 Thtr 25 Del from £395 to £795 **Parking** 20 **Notes** Civ Wed 40

FISHGUARD
Pembrokeshire Map 8 SM93

The Cartref Hotel
★★ 68% HOTEL

tel: 01348 872430 & 0781 330 5235 **15-19 High St SA65 9AW**
email: cartrefhotel@btconnect.com **web:** www.cartrefhotel.co.uk
dir: On A40 in town centre

Personally run by the proprietor, this friendly hotel offers convenient access to the town centre and ferry terminal. Bedrooms are well maintained and include some family rooms. There is also a cosy lounge bar and a welcoming restaurant that looks out onto the high street.

Rooms 10 (2 fmly) ⚲ **S** £50-£60; **D** £75-£85 (incl. bkfst)* **Facilities** FTV WiFi **Parking** 4

HAVERFORDWEST
Pembrokeshire Map 8 SM91

H

Premier Inn Haverfordwest North
BUDGET HOTEL

tel: 0871 527 9546 *(Calls cost 13p per minute plus your phone company's access charge)* **Glanafon Farm House, Fishguard Rd SA62 4BP**
web: www.premierinn.com
dir: From E: A40 to Haverfordwest. At rdbt follow Fishguard (A40) signs. Straight on at next rdbt. At next rdbt (Withybush Rdbt) take 2nd exit to hotel

High quality budget accommodation ideal for both families and business travellers. Spacious, en suite bedrooms feature tea and coffee making facilities, and Freeview TV in most hotels. Internet access and WiFi are available for a small fee. The adjacent family restaurant features a wide and varied menu. See also the Hotel Groups pages.

Rooms 60

HENSOL
Vale of Glamorgan Map 9 ST07

Vale Resort
★★★★ 80% ❀ HOTEL

tel: 01443 667800 **Hensol Park CF72 8JY**
email: reservations@vale-hotel.com **web:** www.vale-hotel.com
dir: M4 junct 34 towards Pendoylan, hotel signed from junct

A wealth of leisure facilities is offered at this large and modern, purpose-built complex, including two golf courses and a driving range plus an extensive health spa with a gym, swimming pool, squash courts, orthopaedic clinic and a range of treatments. Public areas are spacious and attractive, while bedrooms, many with balconies, are well appointed. Meeting and conference facilities are available. Guests can dine in the traditional Vale Grill, a brasserie-style restaurant serving quality fresh ingredients.

Rooms 143 (114 annexe) (15 fmly) (35 GF) ⚲ **Facilities** Spa STV WiFi ⚲ ⚲ ⚲ 36 ⚲ Putt green Fishing Gym Squash Children's club Sat am & school hols Xmas New Year **Conf** Class 280 Board 60 Thtr 700 **Services** Lift Air con **Parking** 450 **Notes** ⊗ Civ Wed 700

KNIGHTON	Map 9 SO27
Powys	

Milebrook House Hotel

★★★ 79% COUNTRY HOUSE HOTEL

tel: 01547 528632 **Milebrook LD7 1LT**
email: hotel@milebrookhouse.co.uk **web:** www.milebrookhouse.co.uk
dir: *2m E of Knighton, on A4113*

Set in three acres of grounds and gardens in the Teme Valley, this charming house dates back to 1760. Over the years since its conversion into a hotel, it has acquired a well-deserved reputation for its warm hospitality, comfortable accommodation and the quality of its cuisine, which uses local produce and home-grown vegetables.

Rooms 10 (2 fmly) (2 GF) **S** £93; **D** £148 (incl. bkfst)* **Facilities** WiFi ⛳ Table tennis Trout fly fishing Xmas New Year **Conf** Class 30 **Parking** 21 **Notes** LB ⊗ No children 8yrs RS Mon lunch

LAMPETER	Map 8 SN54
Ceredigion	

The Falcondale Hotel & Restaurant

★★★★ 78% COUNTRY HOUSE HOTEL

tel: 01570 422910 **Falcondale Dr SA48 7RX**
email: info@thefalcondale.co.uk **web:** www.thefalcondale.co.uk
dir: *800yds W of High St A475 or 1.5m NW of Lampeter - A482*

Built in the Italianate style, this charming Victorian property is set in extensive grounds and beautiful parkland. The individually-styled bedrooms are generally spacious, well equipped and tastefully decorated. Bars and lounges are similarly well appointed with additional facilities including a conservatory and terrace. The award-winning restaurant, with a relaxed and friendly atmosphere, offers menus based on the best seasonal, locally sourced produce.

Rooms 18 (2 fmly) **S** £100-£150; **D** £100-£190 (incl. bkfst)* **Facilities** FTV WiFi ⛳ Xmas New Year **Conf** Class 26 Board 26 Thtr 60 Del £142* **Services** Lift **Parking** 60 **Notes** LB Civ Wed 200

LAUGHARNE	Map 8 SN31
Carmarthenshire	

The Corran Resort & Spa

★★★★ 74% HOTEL

tel: 01994 427417 **East Marsh SA33 4RS**
email: info@thecorran.com **web:** www.thecorran.com
dir: *Take the A40 exit off the M4 towards St Clears, then A4066 towards Pendine & Laugharne. Follow signs to hotel*

Guests will enjoy a unique setting and surroundings at this unusual hotel located in the quiet marshlands of the Carmarthenshire countryside. Bedrooms, mostly located around a courtyard, offer contemporary styling in the interiors while retaining an original 16th-century farmhouse feel to the exterior. A delightful sun terrace is available during warmer months, while the spa with full treatment rooms can be used any time of year. Dinner and breakfast utilise the best quality local produce and are served in the delightful surroundings of the stylish restaurant.

Rooms 21 (16 annexe) (5 fmly) (15 GF) ⛳ **Facilities Spa** STV FTV WiFi ⛳ Gym Xmas New Year **Conf** Class 120 Board 70 Thtr 150 **Parking** 90 **Notes** Civ Wed 150

LLANBEDR	Map 14 SH52
Gwynedd	

Ty Mawr Hotel

★★ 74% HOTEL

tel: 01341 241440 & 07717 080171 **LL45 2NH**
email: info@tymawrhotel.com **web:** www.tymawrhotel.com
dir: *From Barmouth A496 Harlech Rd. In Llanbedr turn right after bridge, hotel 50yds on left, follow brown tourist signs*

Ty Mawr translates as 'Big House' with this particular house located in the picturesque Snowdonia National Park. The attractive grounds, opposite the River Artro, provide a popular beer garden during fine weather. Family-run, with a relaxed, friendly atmosphere, the focus of the hotel is the rustically furnished bar offering a blackboard selection of food and real ales, and the restaurant where a more formal menu is available. Bedrooms are smart and brightly decorated.

Rooms 10 (2 fmly) ⛳ **S** £59; **D** £89 (incl. bkfst)* **Facilities** STV FTV WiFi ⛳ **Parking** 15 **Notes** Closed 24-26 Dec

LLANBERIS	Map 14 SH56
Gwynedd	

The Royal Victoria Hotel Snowdonia

★★★ 73% HOTEL

tel: 01286 870253 **LL55 4TY**
email: enquiries@theroyalvictoria.co.uk **web:** www.theroyalvictoria.co.uk
dir: *On A4086 Caernarfon to Llanberis rd, directly opposite Snowdon Mountain Railway*

This well-established hotel sits near the foot of Snowdon, between the Peris and Padarn lakes. Pretty gardens and grounds make an attractive setting for the many weddings held here. Bedrooms are well equipped. There are spacious lounges and bars, and a large dining room with a conservatory looking out over the lakes.

Rooms 104 (12 annexe) (5 fmly) ⛳ **Facilities** FTV WiFi ♫ Xmas New Year **Conf** Class 60 Board 50 Thtr 100 **Services** Lift **Parking** 70 **Notes** ⊗ Civ Wed 100

LLANDRINDOD WELLS	Map 9 SO06
Powys	

Metropole Hotel & Spa

★★★★ 76% HOTEL

tel: 01597 823700 **Temple St LD1 5DY**
email: info@metropole.co.uk **web:** www.metropole.co.uk
dir: *On A483 in town centre, car park at rear of hotel*

The centre of this famous spa town is dominated by this large Victorian hotel, which has been personally run by the same family for well over 100 years. The lobby leads to Spencers Bar and Brasserie and to the comfortable and elegantly styled lounge. Bedrooms vary in style, but all are spacious and well equipped. Facilities include an extensive range of modern conference and function rooms, as well as the impressive leisure centre. Extensive parking is provided to the rear of the hotel.

Rooms 109 (11 fmly) ⛳ **Facilities Spa** FTV WiFi ⛳ Gym Beauty & holistic treatments Sauna Steam room Xmas New Year **Conf** Class 200 Board 80 Thtr 300 **Services** Lift **Parking** 150 **Notes** Civ Wed 300

LLANDUDNO
Conwy

Map 14 SH78

INSPECTORS' CHOICE

Bodysgallen Hall and Spa
★★★★ COUNTRY HOUSE HOTEL

tel: 01492 584466 **LL30 1RS**
email: info@bodysgallen.com **web:** www.bodysgallen.com
dir: *A55 junct 19, A470 (The Royal Welsh Way) towards Llandudno. Hotel 2m on right*

Situated in the idyllic surroundings of its own parkland and formal gardens, this 17th-century house is in an elevated position, with views towards Snowdonia and across to Conwy Castle. The lounges and dining room have fine antiques and great character. Accommodation is provided in the house, but also in delightfully converted cottages, together with a superb spa. Friendly and attentive service is discreetly offered, while the restaurant features fine local produce prepared with great skill.

Rooms 31 (16 annexe) (4 fmly) (4 GF) 🐾 **S** £160-£385; **D** £180-£435 (incl. bkfst)* **Facilities** Spa STV FTV WiFi 🐾 ⊛ 🏊 Gym Spa treatments Steam room Relaxation room Sauna Xmas New Year **Conf** Class 30 Board 22 Thtr 50 Del from £145* **Parking** 50 **Notes** LB ⊗ No children 6yrs Civ Wed 50

St George's Hotel
★★★★ 81% ⊛ HOTEL

tel: 01492 877544 & 862184 **The Promenade LL30 2LG**
email: sales@stgeorgeswales.co.uk **web:** www.stgeorgeswales.co.uk
dir: *A55, A470, follow to promenade, 0.25m, hotel on corner*

This large and impressive seafront property was the first hotel to be built in the town. Restored to its former glory, the accommodation is of very high quality. The many Victorian features include the splendid, ornate Wedgwood Room restaurant. The terrace restaurant and main lounges overlook the bay; hot and cold snacks are available all day. Many of the thoughtfully equipped bedrooms enjoy sea views.

Rooms 76 (13 fmly) 🐾 **S** £75-£140; **D** £94-£165 (incl. bkfst)* **Facilities** STV FTV WiFi 🐾 In room beauty treatments Xmas New Year **Conf** Class 200 Board 45 Thtr 250 **Services** Lift Air con **Parking** 36 **Notes** LB ⊗ Civ Wed 200

L

LLANDUDNO *continued*

Imperial Hotel

★★★★ 80% HOTEL

tel: 01492 877466 **The Promenade, Vaughan St LL30 1AP**
email: reception@theimperial.co.uk web: www.theimperial.co.uk
dir: *A470 to Llandudno*

The Imperial is a large and impressive hotel, situated on the promenade with lovely views out over the blue flag beaches to the bay, and within easy reach of the town centre and other amenities. Many of the bedrooms have sea views and there are also several suites available. The elegant Chantrey's Restaurant offers a fixed-price, monthly-changing menu that utilises local produce, and The Terrace is the place to relax and enjoy a leisurely lunch or a snack during the day.

Rooms 98 (10 fmly) ↖ Facilities FTV WiFi ⌕ 🕭 Gym Beauty therapist Hairdressing 🎵 Xmas New Year Conf Class 50 Board 50 Thtr 150 Del from £160 to £190*
Services Lift Parking 25 Notes ⊗ Civ Wed 120

Empire Hotel & Spa

★★★★ 78% HOTEL

tel: 01492 860555 **Church Walks LL30 2HE**
email: reservations@empirehotel.co.uk web: www.empirehotel.co.uk
dir: *From Chester, A55 junct 19 for Llandudno. Follow signs to Promenade, turn right at war memorial & left at rdbt. Hotel 100yds on right*

Family run for over 60 years, the Empire offers luxuriously appointed bedrooms with every modern facility. The 'Number 72' rooms in an adjacent house are particularly sumptuous. The indoor pool is overlooked by a lounge and café where snacks are served all day, and in summer an outdoor pool and roof garden are available. The Watkins restaurant offers an interesting fixed-price menu.

Rooms 58 (8 annexe) (1 fmly) (2 GF) ↖ S £70-£125; D £105-£145 (incl. bkfst)*
Facilities Spa STV FTV WiFi ⌕ HL 🕭 🕭 Gym Sauna Steam room Fitness suite New Year Services Lift Air con Parking 57 Notes LB Closed 18-30 Dec

Dunoon Hotel

★★★ 82% HOTEL

tel: 01492 860787 **Gloddaeth St LL30 2DW**
email: reservations@dunoonhotel.co.uk web: www.dunoonhotel.co.uk
dir: *Exit Promenade at war memorial by pier into Gloddaeth St. Hotel 200yds on right*

This impressive, privately-owned hotel is centrally located and offers a variety of well-equipped bedrooms. Elegant public areas include a tastefully appointed restaurant where competently prepared dishes are served together with a good choice of notable, reasonably priced wines. The caring and attentive service is also noteworthy.

Rooms 48 (4 fmly) ↖ S £70-£102; D £120-£144 (incl. bkfst)* Facilities FTV WiFi 🎵 Conf Board 12 Thtr 30 Del from £110 to £130* Services Lift Parking 24 Notes LB Closed mid Dec-early Mar

Cae Mor Hotel

★★★ 75% HOTEL

tel: 01492 878101 **5-6 Penrhyn Crescent LL30 1BA**
email: info@caemorhotel.co.uk web: www.caemorhotel.co.uk
dir: *Exit A55 junct 19, follow A470/Llandudno/Town Centre signs. Straight on at 3 rdbts, right at 4th. Into right lane, right at next rdbt, follow Promenade signs. Straight on at next rdbt, left at next rdbt onto Promenade. Adj to Venue Cymru*

Located in a stunning seafront position adjacent to Venue Cymru, this tastefully renovated Victorian hotel provides a range of thoughtfully furnished bedrooms in minimalist style with smart modern bathrooms. Public areas include a choice of lounges and a stylish restaurant, the setting for imaginative dinners featuring the best of local seasonal produce.

Rooms 23 (2 fmly) (2 GF) ↖ Facilities FTV WiFi Xmas New Year Conf Board 28 Thtr 60 Services Lift Parking 26 Notes LB

Tynedale Hotel

★★★ 73% HOTEL

tel: 01492 877426 **Central Promenade LL30 2XS**
email: enquiries@tynedalehotel.co.uk **web:** www.tynedalehotel.co.uk
dir: *On Promenade opposite bandstand*

Tour groups are well catered for at this privately-owned and personally-run hotel, and regular live entertainment is a feature. Vibrant modern public areas create a unique and comfortable setting, and an attractive seafront patio garden is an additional asset. Bedrooms provide good comfort levels and the staff offer friendly and efficient service.

Rooms 54 (1 fmly) (10 GF) ⌒ **Facilities** FTV WiFi ⌂ ♫ Xmas New Year **Services** Lift **Parking** 15 **Notes** LB ⊗

Hydro Hotel

★★★ 67% HOTEL

tel: 01492 870101 **Neville Crescent LL30 1AT**
email: hydro.llandudno@alfatravel.co.uk **web:** www.leisureplex.co.uk
dir: *Follow signs for theatre to seafront, towards pier*

This large hotel is situated on the promenade overlooking the sea, and offers good, value-for-money, modern accommodation. Public areas are quite extensive and include a choice of lounges, a games/snooker room and a ballroom where entertainment is provided every night. The hotel is a popular venue for coach tour parties.

Rooms 120 (4 fmly) (0 GF) ⌒ **Facilities** WiFi Table tennis Snooker ♫ Xmas New Year **Services** Lift **Parking** 10 **Notes** ⊗ Closed Jan-mid Feb RS Nov-Dec (ex Xmas) & mid Feb-Mar

Premier Inn Llandudno North (Little Orme)

BUDGET HOTEL

tel: 0871 527 8636 *(Calls cost 13p per minute plus your phone company's access charge)*
Colwyn Rd LL30 3AL
web: www.premierinn.com
dir: *A55 junct 20 follow Rhos-on-Sea/Llandrillo-Yn-Rhos/B5115 signs. Onto B5115 (Brompton Ave). Straight on at next 2 rdbts. Hotel on left*

High quality, budget accommodation ideal for both families and business travellers. Spacious, en suite bedrooms feature tea and coffee making facilities, and Freeview TV in most hotels. Internet access and WiFi are available for a small fee. The adjacent family restaurant features a wide and varied menu. See also the Hotel Groups pages.

Rooms 19

The Lilly Restaurant with Rooms

◉ ⌷ RESTAURANT WITH ROOMS

tel: 01492 876513 **West Pde, West Shore LL30 2BD**
email: thelilly@live.co.uk **web:** www.thelilly.co.uk
dir: *Phone for detailed directions*

Located on the seafront on the West Shore with views over the Great Orme, this establishment has bedrooms that offer high standards of comfort, and good facilities. Children are very welcome here, and a relaxed atmosphere is found in Madhatter's Brasserie, which takes its name from Lewis Carroll's *Alice's Adventures in Wonderland*, some of which may have been written while the author was staying on the West Shore. A fine dining restaurant is also available.

Rooms 5

LLANDUDNO JUNCTION
Conwy | Map 14 SH77

Premier Inn Llandudno (Glan-Conwy)

BUDGET HOTEL

tel: 0871 527 8634 *(Calls cost 13p per minute plus your phone company's access charge)*
Afon Conwy LL28 5LB
web: www.premierinn.com
dir: *A55 junct 19. Exit rdbt at A470 (Betws-y-Coed). Hotel immediately on left, opposite petrol station*

High quality, budget accommodation ideal for both families and business travellers. Spacious, en suite bedrooms feature tea and coffee making facilities, and Freeview TV in most hotels. Internet access and WiFi are available for a small fee. The adjacent family restaurant features a wide and varied menu. See also the Hotel Groups pages.

Rooms 69

LLANELLI
Carmarthenshire | Map 8 SN50

Best Western Diplomat Hotel and Spa

Ⓑ Best Western.

★★★ 79% HOTEL

tel: 01554 756156 **Felinfoel SA15 3PJ**
email: reservations@diplomat-hotel-wales.com **web:** www.diplomat-hotel-wales.com
dir: *M4 junct 48, A4138 then B4303, hotel 0.75m on right*

This Victorian mansion, set in mature grounds, has been extended over the years to provide a comfortable and relaxing hotel. The well-appointed bedrooms are located in the main house and there is also a wing of equally comfortable modern rooms. Public areas include Trubshaw's Restaurant, a large function suite and a modern leisure centre.

Rooms 50 (8 annexe) (2 fmly) (4 GF) ⌒ **S** £80-£90; **D** £90-£120 (incl. bkfst)* **Facilities** Spa FTV WiFi ⌂ ⊛ supervised Gym Sauna Steam room ♫ Xmas New Year **Conf** Class 150 Board 100 Thtr 450 Del from £89 to £110 **Services** Lift **Parking** 250 **Notes** LB Civ Wed 300

Ashburnham Hotel

★★★ 70% HOTEL

tel: 01554 834343 & 834455 **Ashburnham Rd, Pembrey SA16 0TH**
email: info@ashburnham-hotel.co.uk **web:** www.ashburnham-hotel.co.uk
dir: *M4 junct 48, A4138 to Llanelli, A484 W to Pembrey. Follow brown information signs*

American aviatrix, Amelia Earhart stayed at this friendly hotel after finishing her historic trans-Atlantic flight in 1928. Public areas include the brasserie restaurant, and the conservatory lounge bar that serves an extensive range of bar meals. Bedrooms, varying from standard to superior, have modern furnishings and facilities. The hotel is licensed for civil ceremonies, and function and conference facilities are also available.

Rooms 13 (2 fmly) **S** £50-£60; **D** £60-£80* **Facilities** STV FTV WiFi ⌂ **Conf** Class 150 Board 80 Thtr 150 **Parking** 100 **Notes** ⊗ RS 24-26 Dec Civ Wed 130

L

LLANELLI continued

Premier Inn Llanelli Central East

BUDGET HOTEL

tel: 0871 527 8638 *(Calls cost 13p per minute plus your phone company's access charge)*
Llandafen Rd SA14 9BD
web: www.premierinn.com
dir: *M4 junct 48, A4138, approx 3m. Hotel on left*

High quality, budget accommodation ideal for both families and business travellers. Spacious, en suite bedrooms feature tea and coffee making facilities, and Freeview TV in most hotels. Internet access and WiFi are available for a small fee. The adjacent family restaurant features a wide and varied menu. See also the Hotel Groups pages.

Rooms 50

Premier Inn Llanelli Central West

BUDGET HOTEL

tel: 0871 527 9342 *(Calls cost 13p per minute plus your phone company's access charge)*
Sandpiper Rd, Sandy Water Park SA15 4SG
web: www.premierinn.com
dir: *M4 junct 48, A4138 towards Llanelli town centre. Then follow Carmarthen signs to Sandy Park rdbt. Hotel on left*

Rooms 28

LLANGAMMARCH WELLS
Powys
Map 9 SN94

The Lake Country House & Spa

★★★★ 75% COUNTRY HOUSE HOTEL

tel: 01591 620202 **LD4 4BS**
email: info@lakecountryhouse.co.uk **web:** www.lakecountryhouse.co.uk
dir: *W from Builth Wells on A483 to Garth (approx 6m). Left for Llangammarch Wells, follow hotel signs*

Expect good old-fashioned values and hospitality at this Victorian country house hotel. In fact, the service is so good that guests may believe they have their own butler. The establishment offers a 9-hole, par 3 golf course, 50 acres of wooded grounds and a spa with a hot tub that overlooks the lake. Bedrooms, some located in an annexe, and some at ground-floor level, are individually styled and have many extra comforts. Traditional afternoon teas are served in the lounge, and award-winning cuisine is provided in the spacious and elegant restaurant.

Rooms 31 (12 annexe) (8 GF) 🐾 **S** £105-£205; **D** £145-£260 (incl. bkfst)
Facilities Spa FTV WiFi ⓣ ♨ 9 ⌣ Putt green Fishing ⚓ Gym Archery Horse riding Mountain biking Quad biking Xmas New Year **Conf** Class 30 Board 25 Thtr 80 Del from £156 to £200 **Parking** 70 **Notes** LB No children 8yrs Civ Wed 100

LLANRWST
Conwy
Map 14 SH86

Maenan Abbey

★★★ 79% COUNTRY HOUSE HOTEL

tel: 01492 660247 **Maenan LL26 0UL**
email: reservations@maenanabbey.co.uk **web:** www.maenanabbey.co.uk
dir: *A55/A470 (junct 19) in direction of Betws y Coed. Hotel 8m on right. From A5 turn onto A470 at Betws y Coed through Llanrwst. Hotel 2m on left*

Maenan Abbey is a small and personally-run country house which is ideally located. Walkers can enjoy the National Park then retire to this quiet, well-equipped hotel. Bedrooms are individually designed with some large family rooms available. Cuisine is a highlight of any stay.

Rooms 14 (3 fmly) (3 smoking) 🐾 **Facilities** FTV WiFi Fishing Guided mountain walks Xmas New Year **Conf** Class 30 Board 30 Thtr 50 **Parking** 60 **Notes** Civ Wed 55

LLANSTEFFAN
Carmarthenshire
Map 8 SN31

Mansion House Llansteffan

 RESTAURANT WITH ROOMS

tel: 01267 241515 & 07768 194539 **Pantyrathro SA33 5AJ**
email: info@mansionhousellansteffan.co.uk
web: www.mansionhousellansteffan.co.uk
dir: *From Carmarthen on B4312 towards Llansteffan, follow brown signs*

Mansion House has been lovingly restored by the current owners, and is set in five acres of grounds with enviable views over the Towy Estuary and Carmarthen Bay. While bedrooms differ in size and style all are well-equipped and complemented by smart bathrooms. With a wealth of quality produce right on the doorstep it's not surprising that the head chef focuses on using seasonal, local, and home-grown produce on the constantly changing, interesting menu. Pre-dinner drinks can be taken in the bar, where there is an excellent range of gins.

Rooms 9 (1 fmly)

LLANTRISANT
Monmouthshire
Map 9 ST39

Premier Inn Llantrisant

BUDGET HOTEL

tel: 0871 527 8640 *(Calls cost 13p per minute plus your phone company's access charge)*
Gwaun Elai, Magden Park CF72 8LL
web: www.premierinn.com
dir: *M4 junct 34, A4119 towards Llantrisant & Rhondda. At 1st rdbt take 2nd exit. At 2nd rdbt take 1st exit*

High quality, budget accommodation ideal for both families and business travellers. Spacious, en suite bedrooms feature tea and coffee making facilities, and Freeview TV in most hotels. Internet access and WiFi are available for a small fee. The adjacent family restaurant features a wide and varied menu. See also the Hotel Groups pages.

Rooms 51

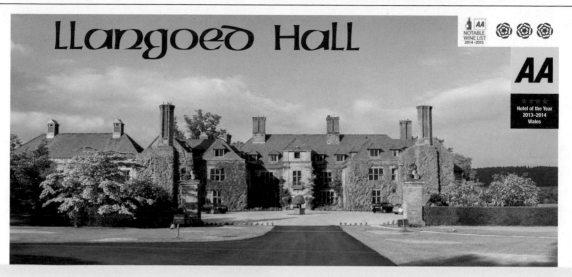

L

L

LLANWDDYN
Powys

Map 15 SJ01

Lake Vyrnwy Hotel & Spa

★★★★ 76% ◉ COUNTRY HOUSE HOTEL

tel: 01691 870692 **Lake Vyrnwy SY10 OLY**
email: info@lakevyrnwyhotel.co.uk **web:** www.lakevyrnwy.com
dir: *On A4393, 200yds past dam turn sharp right into drive*

This elegant Victorian country-house hotel lies in 26,000 acres of woodland above Lake Vyrnwy, and provides a wide range of bedrooms, most with superb views and many with four-poster beds and balconies. Extensive public rooms retain many period features, and informal dining is available in the popular Tower Tavern. Relaxing and rejuvenating treatments are a feature of the stylish health spa.

Rooms 52 (12 fmly) ⤢ **S** £129-£244; **D** £154-£269 (incl. bkfst)* **Facilities** Spa STV FTV WiFi ⬗ ⬲ Fishing Gym Archery Birdwatching Canoeing Kayaking Clay shooting Sailing Fly fishing Cycling Xmas New Year **Conf** Class 80 Board 60 Thtr 200 Del £155* **Services** Lift **Parking** 70 **Notes** Civ Wed 200

LLANWRTYD WELLS
Powys

Map 9 SN84

Lasswade Country House

◉◉ RESTAURANT WITH ROOMS

tel: 01591 610515 **Station Rd LD5 4RW**
email: info@lasswadehotel.co.uk **web:** www.lasswadehotel.co.uk
dir: *Exit A483 into Irfon Terrace, right into Station Rd, 350yds on right*

This friendly establishment on the edge of the town has impressive views over the countryside. Bedrooms are comfortably furnished and well equipped, while the public areas consist of a tastefully decorated lounge, an elegant restaurant with a bar, and an airy conservatory which looks towards the neighbouring hills. The kitchen makes good use of fresh, local produce to provide an enjoyable, award-winning dining experience.

Rooms 8 (1 fmly)

LLYSWEN
Powys

Map 9 SO13

INSPECTORS' CHOICE

Llangoed Hall

★★★★ ◉◉◉ COUNTRY HOUSE HOTEL

tel: 01874 754525 **LD3 0YP**
email: enquiries@llangoedhall.com **web:** www.llangoedhall.com
dir: *On A470 between Brecon & Builth Wells*

Set against the stunning backdrop of the Black Mountains and the Wye Valley, this imposing country house is a haven of peace and quiet. The interior is no less impressive, with a noteworthy art collection complementing the many antiques in day rooms and bedrooms. Comfortable, spacious accommodation is matched by equally inviting lounges.

Rooms 23 ⤢ **S** £145-£350; **D** £195-£600 (incl. bkfst)* **Facilities** FTV WiFi ⬗ HL ⬲ Fishing ⬲ Snooker table Outdoor chess Xmas New Year **Conf** Class 30 Board 30 Thtr 80 **Parking** 50 **Notes** LB ⊗ Civ Wed 80

See advert on page 547

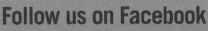

MAESYCWMMER
Caerphilly
Map 9 ST19

Bryn Meadows Golf, Hotel & Spa

★★★★ 76% HOTEL

tel: 01495 225590 **CF82 7SN**
email: reception@brynmeadows.co.uk **web:** www.brynmeadows.wales
dir: M4 junct 28, A467 signed Brynmawr, 10m to Newbridge. Take A472 signed Ystrad Mynach. Hotel off Crown rdbt signed golf course

Surrounded by its own mature parkland and 18-hole golf course, this impressive hotel, golf, leisure and function complex provides a range of high quality, well-equipped bedrooms; several have their own balconies or patio areas. The attractive public areas include a pleasant restaurant which, like many of the bedrooms, enjoys striking views of the golf course and beyond. There are impressive function facilities and the hotel is a popular venue for weddings.

Rooms 42 (4 fmly) (21 GF) ↖ **S** £89-£170; **D** £104-£185* **Facilities** Spa FTV WiFi ⊙ supervised ⅃ 18 Putt green Gym Sauna Steam room Aromatherapy suite Xmas New Year **Conf** Class 70 Board 60 Thtr 120 Del from £95 to £150* **Services** Air con **Parking** 120 **Notes** LB ⊗ Civ Wed 250

MANORBIER
Pembrokeshire
Map 8 SS09

Castlemead

RESTAURANT WITH ROOMS

tel: 01834 871358 **SA70 7TA**
email: castlemeadhotel@aol.com **web:** www.castlemeadhotel.com
dir: A4139 towards Pembroke, B4585 into village, follow signs to beach & castle, establishment on left

Benefiting from a superb location with spectacular views of the bay, the Norman church and Manorbier Castle, this family-run business is friendly and welcoming. Bedrooms, which include some in a converted former coach house at ground floor level, are generally quite spacious and have modern facilities. Public areas include a sea-view residents' lounge and a restaurant accessed by stairs, which is open to non-residents, along with a cosy bar. There are extensive gardens to the rear of the property.

Rooms 8 (3 annexe) (2 fmly)

MERTHYR TYDFIL
Merthyr Tydfil
Map 9 SO00

Premier Inn Merthyr Tydfil

BUDGET HOTEL

tel: 0871 527 8768 *(Calls cost 13p per minute plus your phone company's access charge)*
Pentrebach CF48 4BB
web: www.premierinn.com
dir: M4 junct 32, A470 to Merthyr Tydfil. At rdbt right to Pentrebach (A4060). At next rdbt 3rd exit signed Abergavenny (dual carriageway). Double back at next rdbt by Pentrebach Co-op onto A4060 towards Pentrebach. Left after layby, hotel adjacent to Pentrebach House

High quality, budget accommodation ideal for both families and business travellers. Spacious, en suite bedrooms feature tea and coffee making facilities, and Freeview TV in most hotels. Internet access and WiFi are available for a small fee. The adjacent family restaurant features a wide and varied menu. See also the Hotel Groups pages.

Rooms 62

MISKIN
Rhondda Cynon Taff
Map 9 ST08

Miskin Manor Country Hotel

★★★★ 72% COUNTRY HOUSE HOTEL

tel: 01443 224204 **Pendoylan Rd CF72 8ND**
email: reservations@miskin-manor.co.uk **web:** www.miskin-manor.co.uk
dir: M4 junct 34, A4119, signed Llantrisant, hotel 300yds on left

This historic manor house is peacefully located in 22-acre grounds, yet is only minutes away from the M4. Bedrooms are furnished to a high standard and include some located in converted stables and cottages. Public areas are spacious and comfortable and include a variety of function rooms. The relaxed atmosphere and surroundings ensure this hotel remains popular for wedding functions as well as with business guests. There is a separate modern health and fitness centre which includes a gym, sauna, steam room and swimming pool.

Rooms 43 (9 annexe) (2 fmly) (7 GF) ↖ **Facilities** Spa FTV WiFi ⊙ ⅍ Gym Sauna Steam room Dance studio **Conf** Class 80 Board 65 Thtr 160 Del £155* **Parking** 200 **Notes** Civ Wed 200

MOLD
Flintshire
Map 15 SJ26

Beaufort Park Hotel

★★★ 77% HOTEL

tel: 01352 758646 **Alltami Rd, New Brighton CH7 6RQ**
email: info@beaufortparkhotel.co.uk **web:** www.beaufortparkhotel.co.uk
dir: A55, A494, through Alltami lights, over mini rdbt by petrol station towards Mold, A5119. Hotel 100yds on right

This large, modern hotel is conveniently located a short drive from the North Wales Expressway and offers various styles of spacious accommodation. There are extensive public areas, and several meeting and function rooms are available. There is a wide choice of meals in the formal restaurant and in the popular Arches bar.

Rooms 106 (8 fmly) (32 GF) **Facilities** FTV WiFi Squash ⅃⅃ Xmas New Year **Conf** Class 120 Board 120 Thtr 250 **Parking** 200 **Notes** Civ Wed 220

MONMOUTH
Monmouthshire
Map 10 SO51

#7 Church Street

◉◉ RESTAURANT WITH ROOMS

tel: 01600 712600 **7 Church St NP25 3BX**
email: enquiries@numbersevenchurchstreet.co.uk
dir: Travelling N A40 at lights left turn, T-junct left turn, 2nd right, at rear of car park

Located in the centre of Monmouth #7 Church Street is open for light lunches and dinner and is popular with both guests and locals. Award-winning food is prepared with care and an emphasis on local sourcing and seasonality. Rooms are located above the restaurant and vary in size and shape, a comfortable private guest lounge is also available.

Rooms 8 (2 fmly)

N

NARBERTH
Pembrokeshire

Map 8 SN11

INSPECTORS' CHOICE

Grove
★★★★ ◉◉◉ HOTEL

tel: 01834 860915 **Molleston SA67 8BX**
email: info@thegrove-narberth.co.uk **web:** www.thegrove-narberth.co.uk
dir: A48 to Carmarthen, A40 to Haverfordwest. At A478 rdbt 1st exit to Narberth, through town towards Tenby. At bottom of hill right, 1m, hotel on right

Grove is an elegant 18th-century country house set on a hillside in 24 acres of rolling countryside. The owners have lovingly restored the building with care, combining period features with excellent modern decor. There are bedrooms in the main house, and additional rooms in separate buildings; all are appointed with high levels of quality and comfort. Some bedrooms are on the ground floor, and most have fantastic views out over the Preseli Hills. There are two sumptuous lounge areas, one with an open fire and a small bar, and two separate dining rooms that offer award-winning cuisine. Self-catering cottages are available.

Rooms 20 (3 fmly) (3 GF) **Facilities** FTV WiFi ⬦ In room spa treatments **Parking** 20
Notes Civ Wed

See advert on opposite page

NEATH
Neath Port Talbot

Map 9 SS79

Castle Hotel
★★★ 74% HOTEL

tel: 01639 641119 **The Parade SA11 1RB**
email: info@castlehotelneath.co.uk **web:** www.castlehotelneath.co.uk
dir: M4 junct 43, follow signs for Neath, 500yds past rail station, hotel on right. Car park on left in 50yds

Situated in the town centre, this Georgian property, once a coaching inn, has a wealth of history and plenty of character. Lord Nelson and Lady Hamilton are reputed to have stayed here, although it is a matter of historical fact that the Welsh Rugby Union was founded here in 1881. The hotel provides well-equipped accommodation and pleasant public areas. Bedrooms include family-bedded rooms and one with a four-poster. Green's restaurant provides a good range of dishes at both lunch and dinner. Function and meeting rooms are available.

Rooms 29 (3 fmly) (14 smoking) **Facilities** STV FTV WiFi ⬦ ♫ Xmas New Year
Conf Class 75 Board 50 Thtr 160 **Parking** 26 **Notes** ⊗ Civ Wed 120

NEWCASTLE EMLYN
Carmarthenshire

Map 8 SN34

Gwesty'r Emlyn Hotel
★★★ 81% HOTEL

WELSH
RAREBITS
Hotels of
Distinction

tel: 01239 710317 **Bridge St SA38 9DU**
email: reception@gwestyremlynhotel.co.uk **web:** www.gwestyremlynhotel.co.uk
dir: In town centre

This hotel, in the heart of a busy market town, dates back some 300 years. Appointed to a high standard, the stylish and comfortable bedrooms have luxury bathrooms. The public areas comprise a choice of bars, a cosy seating area and a modern restaurant offering dishes created from good, locally sourced ingredients. There is a gym, a sauna and a spa pool, plus a large function suite for weddings and parties.

Rooms 29 (5 annexe) (5 fmly) (1 GF) ⬦ **S** £49-£70; **D** £70-£120 (incl. bkfst)*
Facilities FTV WiFi ⬦ Gym Sauna Steam room Splash pool Xmas New Year
Conf Class 100 Board 50 Thtr 150 **Parking** 25 **Notes** LB ⊗ Civ Wed 150

GROVE

NARBERTH

Nestling in the heart of the beautiful Pembrokeshire countryside, Grove is one of Wales' finest restaurants and a leading small luxury hotel.

Grove of Narberth is a privately owned luxury country house hotel nestled in the heart of the rolling Pembrokeshire countryside with stunning views of the Preseli Hills. At the Grove you can be assured of a warm Welsh welcome and a truly relaxing stay in real luxury combined with great food and friendly professional service.

Our small luxury hotel really is the perfect setting to unwind in Pembrokeshire, whether it's for a weekend break, an escape from the city or to enjoy a home from home.

Grove is the perfect setting to unwind and enjoy the best of Welsh cuisine, and a truly memorable time in Pembrokeshire.

AA ROSETTE AWARD
FOR CULINARY EXCELLENCE

+44 (0)1834 860915   thegrove-narberth.co.uk   info@thegrove-narberth.co.uk

NEWPORT
Newport

Map 9 ST38

See also **Cwmbran**

The Celtic Manor Resort

★★★★★ 85% ◉◉◉ HOTEL

tel: 01633 413000 & 410262 **Coldra Woods NP18 1HQ**
email: bookings@celtic-manor.com **web:** www.celtic-manor.com
dir: *M4 junct 24, take B4237 towards Newport. Hotel 1st on right*

This hotel is part of the outstanding Celtic Manor Resort. Here there are three challenging golf courses including the Twenty Ten Course specifically designed for the 2010 Ryder Cup; a huge convention centre; superb leisure clubs and two hotels. This hotel has excellent bedrooms, with suites and two Presidential suites, offering good space and comfort. Stylish extensive public areas are set around a spectacular atrium lobby that includes several eating options including The Epicure Experience by Richard Davies. There is a choice of shops and boutiques as well.

Rooms 334 (34 fmly) **Facilities** Spa STV FTV WiFi ↻ ⊕ ⅃ 54 ⚘ Putt green Fishing Gym Golf Academy Clay pigeon shooting Mountain bike trails Games room Archery ♫ Xmas New Year Child facilities **Conf** Class 600 Board 60 Thtr 1500 **Services** Lift Air con **Parking** 1300 **Notes** ⊗ Civ Wed 100

The Manor House

★★★★ 74% HOTEL

tel: 01633 413000 **The Celtic Manor Resort, Coldra Woods NP18 1HQ**
email: bookings@celtic-manor.com **web:** www.celtic-manor.com
dir: *M4 junct 24, B4237 towards Newport. Hotel 1st on right*

Part of the Celtic Manor Resort complex, this 19th-century hotel offers country house charm combined with modern comforts. Sitting in beautiful landscaped gardens, it has traditionally styled bedrooms, three with four-posters. An Asian-inspired restaurant is located in the Hotel with a further number of restaurants located at the main Celtic Manor Resort. Guests have access to all the hotel and leisure facilities at the resort; three challenging golf courses, a superb leisure complex and many other activities suitable for both adults and families.

Rooms 65 (3 fmly) **Facilities** Spa STV FTV WiFi ⊕ supervised ⅃ 18 ⚘ Putt green Fishing Gym Golf academy Adventure golf Archery Clay pigeon shooting ♫ Xmas New Year Child facilities **Conf** Class 80 Board 40 Thtr 200 **Services** Lift Air con **Parking** 1000 **Notes** ⊗ Civ Wed 180

Premier Inn Newport Wales (M4 Jct 24)

BUDGET HOTEL

tel: 0871 527 8814 *(Calls cost 13p per minute plus your phone company's access charge)*
Coldra Junction, Chepstow Rd, Langstone NP18 2NX
web: www.premierinn.com
dir: *M4 junct 24, A48 to Langstone, at next rdbt return towards junct 24. Hotel 50mtrs on left*

High quality, budget accommodation ideal for both families and business travellers. Spacious, en suite bedrooms feature tea and coffee making facilities, and Freeview TV in most hotels. Internet access and WiFi are available for a small fee. The adjacent family restaurant features a wide and varied menu. See also the Hotel Groups pages.

Rooms 81

Ibis Budget Newport

AA Advertised

tel: 01633 859058 **164 Malpas Rd NP20 5PP**
email: H6814@accor.com **web:** www.ibishotel.com
dir: *M4 junct 26, 3rd exit at rdbt onto Malpas Road A4051, turn right, hotel on left*

Modern, budget hotel offering comfortable accommodation in bright and practical bedrooms. Breakfast is self-service and dinner is available in the restaurant.

Rooms 103 **Facilities** FTV WiFi **Services** Lift Air con

NEWPORT
Pembrokeshire

Map 8 SN03

Llys Meddyg

◉◉ RESTAURANT WITH ROOMS

tel: 01239 820008 **East St SA42 0SY**
email: info@llysmeddyg.com **web:** www.llysmeddyg.com
dir: *On A487 in centre of town*

Llys Meddyg is a Georgian town house offering a blend of old and new, with elegant furnishings, deep sofas and a welcoming fire. The owners of the property employed local craftsmen to create a lovely interior that has an eclectic style. The focus of the quality restaurant menu is on fresh, seasonal, locally sourced ingredients. The spacious bedrooms are comfortable and contemporary in design; bathrooms vary in style.

Rooms 8 (3 annexe) (3 fmly)

PEMBROKE
Pembrokeshire

Map 8 SM90

Lamphey Hall Hotel

★★★ 77% HOTEL

tel: 01646 672394 & 07791 896191 **Lamphey SA71 5NR**
email: bookings@lampheyhall.co.uk **web:** www.lampheyhall.co.uk
dir: *From Carmarthen A40 to St Clears. Follow signs for A477, left at Milton*

Set in a delightful village, this very friendly, privately owned and efficiently run hotel offers an ideal base from which to explore the surrounding countryside. Bedrooms are well equipped, comfortably furnished and include family rooms and ground floor rooms. Diners have a choice of three restaurant areas offering an extensive range of dishes. There is also a small lounge, a bar and attractive gardens.

Rooms 10 (1 fmly) (2 GF) **S** £45-£59.50; **D** £65-£89.50 (incl. bkfst)* **Facilities** FTV WiFi **Parking** 32 **Notes** LB

Best Western Lamphey Court Hotel & Spa

 Best Western.

A ★★★★ HOTEL

tel: 01646 672273 **Lamphey SA71 5NT**
email: info@lampheycourt.co.uk **web:** www.lampheycourt.co.uk
dir: M4 then A477 to Pembroke. Left at Milton for Lamphey, hotel on right

This Georgian mansion, on an elevated site, is set in attractive countryside and is perfectly situated for exploring the stunning Pembrokeshire coast, the beaches and the Preseli Hills. Well-appointed bedrooms and family suites are situated in a converted coach house within the grounds. The elegant public areas include both formal and informal dining rooms that feature dishes inspired by local produce. Leisure facilities include a state-of-the-art spa with a swimming pool, gym, sauna, treatment rooms and much more.

Rooms 38 (12 annexe) (7 fmly) (6 GF) **Facilities** Spa FTV WiFi ↘ ⊕ ⊹ Gym Sauna Steam room Beauty & therapy Xmas New Year **Conf** Class 40 Board 30 Thtr 60 **Parking** 50 **Notes** Civ Wed 80

PENARTH Map 9 ST17
Vale of Glamorgan

Holm House Hotel

U

 WELSH RAREBITS Hotels of Distinction

tel: 029 2070 6029 **Marine Pde CF64 3BG**
email: reception@holmhousehotel.co.uk **web:** www.holmhousehotel.com

Currently the rating for this establishment is not confirmed. This may be due to a change of ownership or because it has only recently joined the AA rating scheme. For further details please see the AA website: theAA.com

Rooms 12

Restaurant James Sommerin

◉◉◉ RESTAURANT WITH ROOMS

tel: 029 2070 6559 **The Esplanade CF64 3AU**
email: info@jamessommerinrestaurant.co.uk **web:** www.jamessommerinrestaurant.co.uk

Restaurant James Sommerin stands proudly by the Pier in Penarth with unrivalled views across the Bay, just a short distance from Cardiff centre. Cuisine is accomplished and exciting with three different tasting menus offered in addition to the à la carte, showcasing the passion for food from this innovative chef and his team. The latest addition is the accommodation, which offers comfortable, quality facilities for guests wanting to take full advantage of the interesting and extensive wine list. This is truly a family business; the friendly front of house team are under the watchful eye of Louise Sommerin and often their oldest daughter can be seen assisting in the kitchen.

Rooms 9

PONTYPOOL Map 9 SO20
Torfaen

Premier Inn Pontypool

BUDGET HOTEL

 Premier Inn

tel: 0871 527 8890 *(Calls cost 13p per minute plus your phone company's access charge)*
Tyr'felin, Lower Mill Field NP4 0RH
web: www.premierinn.com
dir: At junct of A4042 & A472

High quality, budget accommodation ideal for both families and business travellers. Spacious, en suite bedrooms feature tea and coffee making facilities, and Freeview TV in most hotels. Internet access and WiFi are available for a small fee. The adjacent family restaurant features a wide and varied menu. See also the Hotel Groups pages.

Rooms 50

PONTYPRIDD Map 9 ST08
Rhondda Cynon Taff

Llechwen Hall Hotel

★★★ 79% ◉ COUNTRY HOUSE HOTEL

tel: 01443 742050 & 743020 **Llanfabon CF37 4HP**
email: enquiries@llechwenhall.co.uk **web:** www.llechwen.co.uk
dir: A470 N towards Merthyr Tydfil. At large rdbt take 3rd exit. At mini rdbt take 3rd exit, hotel signed 0.5m on left

Set on top of a hill with a stunning approach, this country house hotel has served many functions in its 200-year-old history including time as a private school and a magistrates' court. The spacious, individually decorated bedrooms are well equipped; some are situated in the separate coach house nearby. There are ground-floor, twin, double and family bedrooms on offer. The Victorian-style public areas are attractively appointed and the hotel is a popular venue for weddings.

Rooms 20 (8 annexe) (6 fmly) (4 GF) **Facilities** FTV WiFi ↘ Xmas New Year **Conf** Class 80 Board 40 Thtr 200 **Parking** 150 **Notes** Civ Wed 90

PORTHCAWL Map 9 SS87
Bridgend

Seabank Hotel

Leisureplex HOLIDAY HOTELS

★★★ 68% HOTEL

tel: 01656 782261 **Esplanade CF36 3LU**
email: seabank@leisureplex.co.uk **web:** www.leisureplex.co.uk
dir: M4 junct 37, A4229 to Porthcawl seafront

The Seabank Hotel stands in a prime location on the promenade of this seaside town, with panoramic sea views from the majority of bedrooms. Porthcawl has several beaches and coastal walks; the world famous Royal Porthcawl golf course is within easy distance and the cities of Swansea and Cardiff are only a short drive away. The spacious bedrooms are all en suite and there is a lift which serves most bedrooms. There is a spacious restaurant, a lounge bar and a choice of lounges with sea views. The hotel is a popular venue for coach tour parties, as well as weddings and conferences. There is ample parking around the hotel.

Rooms 89 (3 fmly) (5 GF) ⚲ **Facilities** FTV WiFi ♬ Xmas New Year **Services** Lift **Parking** 100 **Notes** ⊗ Closed 2 Jan-10 Feb

P

PORTHMADOG
Gwynedd

Map 14 SH53

Royal Sportsman Hotel
★★★ 82% ◉◉ HOTEL

tel: 01766 512015 **131 High St LL49 9HB**
email: enquiries@royalsportsman.co.uk **web:** www.royalsportsman.co.uk/hotel
dir: Located opposite rdbt where A487 meets A497

This hotel has a very convenient location handy for the coast or for those wishing to visit the National Park or mountain railway. The hotel has a choice of dining options and food is a notable aspect here. Bedrooms are smartly appointed, and there is a spacious lounge. The staff are a friendly team and service is attentive. There is also covered parking available.

Rooms 28 (7 fmly) (9 GF) ⟲ **S** £53-£66; **D** £80-£96 (incl. bkfst) **Facilities** STV FTV WiFi ⮧ Xmas New Year **Conf** Class 30 Board 30 Thtr 50 Del from £110 to £120 **Parking** 17 **Notes** LB Civ Wed 60

PORTMEIRION
Gwynedd

Map 14 SH53

The Hotel Portmeirion
★★★★ 77% ◉◉ HOTEL

WELSH RAREBITS Hotels of Distinction

tel: 01766 770000 & 772440 **Minffordd LL48 6ET**
email: hotel@portmeirion-village.com **web:** www.portmeirion-village.com
dir: 2m W, Portmeirion village is S off A487

Saved from dereliction in the 1920s by Clough Williams-Ellis, the elegant Hotel Portmeirion enjoys one of the finest settings in Wales, located beneath the wooded slopes of the village, overlooking the sandy estuary towards Snowdonia. Many bedrooms have private sitting rooms and balconies with spectacular views. The staff, mostly Welsh-speaking, provide a good mix of warm hospitality and efficient service. Dinner and breakfast include the finest produce.

Rooms 44 (30 annexe) (6 fmly) ⟲ **S** £104-£199; **D** £119-£214 (incl. bkfst)*
Facilities Spa FTV WiFi ⮧ ⚡ ♫ Xmas New Year **Conf** Class 40 Board 30 Thtr 100 **Services** Lift **Parking** 44 **Notes** ⊗ Civ Wed 130

PORT TALBOT
Neath Port Talbot

Map 9 SS78

Premier Inn Port Talbot
BUDGET HOTEL

tel: 0871 527 8896 (Calls cost 13p per minute plus your phone company's access charge)
Baglan Rd, Baglan SA12 8ES
web: www.premierinn.com
dir: M4 junct 41 W'bound. Hotel just off 4th exit at rdbt. M4 junct 42 E'bound, left towards Port Talbot. Take 2nd exit off 2nd rdbt

High quality, budget accommodation ideal for both families and business travellers. Spacious, en suite bedrooms feature tea and coffee making facilities, and Freeview TV in most hotels. Internet access and WiFi are available for a small fee. The adjacent family restaurant features a wide and varied menu. See also the Hotel Groups pages.

Rooms 42

REYNOLDSTON
Swansea

Map 8 SS48

Fairyhill
◉◉ ☺ RESTAURANT WITH ROOMS

tel: 01792 390139 **SA3 1BS**
email: postbox@fairyhill.net **web:** www.fairyhill.net
dir: M4 junct 47, A483, at next rdbt right onto A484. At Gowerton take B4295 for 10m

Peace and tranquillity are never far away at this charming Georgian mansion set in the heart of the beautiful Gower Peninsula. Bedrooms are furnished with care and are filled with many thoughtful extras. There is also a range of comfortable seating areas, with crackling log fires, to choose from. The smart restaurant offers menus based on local produce that are complemented by an excellent wine list.

Rooms 8

RHUDDLAN
Denbighshire

Map 15 SJ07

Premier Inn Rhuddlan
BUDGET HOTEL

tel: 0871 527 8932 (Calls cost 13p per minute plus your phone company's access charge)
Castle View Retail Park, Marsh Rd LL18 5UA
web: www.premierinn.com
dir: A55 junct 27, A525 signed Rhyl. At next rdbt 3rd exit into Station Rd. Next left into Marsh Rd. Hotel on left

High quality, budget accommodation ideal for both families and business travellers. Spacious, en suite bedrooms feature tea and coffee making facilities, and Freeview TV in most hotels. Internet access and WiFi are available for a small fee. The adjacent family restaurant features a wide and varied menu. See also the Hotel Groups pages.

Rooms 44

ROCKFIELD
Monmouthshire

Map 9 SO41

The Stonemill & Steppes Farm Cottages
◉◉ RESTAURANT WITH ROOMS

tel: 01600 775424 **NP25 5SW**
email: bookings@thestonemill.co.uk **web:** www.steppesfarmcottages.co.uk
dir: A48 to Monmouth, take B4233 to Rockfield. 2.6m

Located in a small hamlet just west of Monmouth, close to the Forest of Dean and the Wye Valley, this operation offers accommodation comprising six very well-appointed cottages. The comfortable rooms (available for self-catering or on a B&B basis) have been lovingly restored to retain many original features. In a separate, converted 16th-century barn is Stonemill Restaurant with oak beams, vaulted ceilings and an old cider press. Breakfast is served in the cottages on request. This establishment's location proves handy for golfers, with a choice of many courses in the area.

Rooms 6 (6 fmly)

ROSSETT
Wrexham
Map 15 SJ35

Best Western Hallmark Hotel Chester Llyndir Hall
★★★ 81% HOTEL

tel: 0330 028 3417 **Llyndir Ln LL12 0AY**
email: llyndir@hallmarkhotels.co.uk **web:** www.hallmarkhotels.co.uk
dir: 5m S of Chester on B5445 follow Pulford signs

Located on the English/Welsh border within easy reach of Chester and Wrexham, this elegant manor house lies in several acres of mature grounds. The hotel is popular with both business and leisure guests, and facilities include conference rooms, an impressive leisure centre, a choice of comfortable lounges and a brasserie-style restaurant.

Rooms 48 (3 fmly) (17 GF) ✆ **S** £55-£159; **D** £55-£159* **Facilities** Spa FTV WiFi HL ⌚ supervised Gym Beauty salon Sauna Xmas New Year **Conf** Class 60 Board 40 Thtr 120 Del from £110 to £140* **Parking** 80 **Notes** LB ⊗ Civ Wed 120

RUTHIN
Denbighshire
Map 15 SJ15

Ruthin Castle Hotel
★★★★ 76% ⚜⚜ HOTEL

tel: 01824 702664 **Castle St LL15 2NU**
email: reservations@ruthincastle.co.uk **web:** www.ruthincastle.co.uk
dir: From Manchester M56/A55/A494

This originally medieval building has been many things over the years and now serves as a luxurious hotel. Set in picturesque North Wales, it offers a variety of bedrooms, many of which have been patronised by Royalty. Dinner is in the elegant Berties (another Kingly connection), guests can relax in the octagonal Library bar and there are modern spa and leisure facilities as well as extensive conference rooms also on site.

Rooms 55 (10 fmly) (27 GF) ✆ **Facilities** Spa FTV WiFi ⛲ Gym Thermal Suite Sauna Steam room Xmas New Year **Conf** Class 80 Board 46 Thtr 180 **Services** Lift Air con **Parking** 80 **Notes** LB ⊗ Civ Wed 140

SARN PARK MOTORWAY SERVICE AREA (M4)
Bridgend
Map 9 SS98

Days Inn Bridgend Cardiff - M4

WELCOMEBREAK

AA Advertised

tel: 01656 659218 **Sarn Park Services, M4 Junct 36 CF32 9RW**
email: sarn.hotel@welcomebreak.co.uk **web:** www.welcomebreak.co.uk
dir: M4 junct 36

This modern building offers accommodation in smart, spacious and well-equipped bedrooms, suitable for families and business travellers, and all with en suite bathrooms. Continental breakfast is available and other refreshments may be taken at the nearby family restaurant.

Rooms 40 (15 fmly) (20 GF) (8 smoking) **Facilities** FTV WiFi ⌕ **Parking** 40

SAUNDERSFOOT
Pembrokeshire
Map 8 SN10

HIGHLY RECOMMENDED

St Brides Spa Hotel
★★★★ 84% HOTEL

tel: 01834 812304 **St Brides Hill SA69 9NH**
email: reservations@stbridesspahotel.com **web:** www.stbridesspahotel.com
dir: A478 onto B4310 to Saundersfoot. Hotel above harbour

Set overlooking Carmarthen Bay, this contemporary hotel and spa takes prime position. Many of the stylish, modern bedrooms enjoy sea views and have balconies; there are also luxury apartments in the grounds. The hotel is open-plan and has excellent views of the bay from the split-level lounge areas. Fresh local seafood is a speciality in the modern airy restaurant, which has a terrace for dining alfresco when the weather allows. The destination spa enjoys some of the very best views from the double treatment room and spa pool.

Rooms 46 (12 annexe) (6 fmly) (9 GF) ✆ **Facilities** Spa FTV WiFi ⌕ Gym Thermal suite Hydrotherapy pool Steam & herbal rooms Ice fountain Xmas New Year **Conf** Class 40 Board 34 Thtr 100 **Services** Lift **Parking** 65 **Notes** Civ Wed 90

SOLVA
Pembrokeshire
Map 8 SM82

Crug Glâs Country House
⚜ RESTAURANT WITH ROOMS

tel: 01348 831302 **Abereiddy SA62 6XX**
email: janet@crug-glas.co.uk **web:** www.crug-glas.co.uk
dir: From Solva to St Davids on A487. From St Davids take A487 towards Fishguard. 1st left after Carnhedryn, house signed

This house, on a dairy, beef and cereal farm of approximately 600 acres, is situated about a mile from the coast on the St Davids Peninsula. Comfort, relaxation and flawless attention to detail are provided by the charming host, Janet Evans. Each spacious bedroom has the hallmark of assured design plus a luxury bathroom with both bath and shower; one suite on the top floor has great views. In addition there are two suites in separate buildings.

Rooms 7 (1 fmly)

S

See also **Port Talbot**

Mercure Swansea Hotel

★★★ 79% HOTEL

tel: 0844 815 9081 *(Calls cost 5p per minute plus your phone company's access charge)*
Phoenix Way SA7 9EG
email: sales@mercureswansea.co.uk **web:** www.mercureswansea.co.uk
dir: *M4 junct 44, A48 Llansamlet, left at 3rd lights, right at 1st mini rdbt, left into Phoenix Way at 2nd rdbt. Hotel 800mtrs on right*

Located in the business park area just outside of Swansea, this is a popular hotel with both business and leisure guests. A wide range of dishes are available throughout the day and evening from the relaxing lounge, or the well furnished restaurant. Bedrooms and bathrooms are located over two floors and include standard and executive options. Leisure facilities and a large car park are also provided.

Rooms 119 (24 fmly) (55 GF) **S** £49-£129; **D** £69-£149* **Facilities** FTV WiFi
Gym Sauna Xmas New Year **Conf** Class 80 Board 50 Thtr 180 Del from £95 to £165*
Parking 180 **Notes** Civ Wed 180

Premier Inn Swansea City Centre

BUDGET HOTEL

tel: 0871 527 9060 *(Calls cost 13p per minute plus your phone company's access charge)*
Salubrious Place, Wind St SA1 1EE
web: www.premierinn.com
dir: *M4 junct 42, A483 towards the city centre. Pass Sainsburys on left, right into Salubrious Place, 2nd right, then 3rd exit at mini rdbt*

High quality, budget accommodation ideal for both families and business travellers. Spacious, en suite bedrooms feature tea and coffee making facilities, and Freeview TV in most hotels. Internet access and WiFi are available for a small fee. The adjacent family restaurant features a wide and varied menu. See also the Hotel Groups pages.

Rooms 116

Premier Inn Swansea North

BUDGET HOTEL

tel: 0871 527 9062 *(Calls cost 13p per minute plus your phone company's access charge)*
Upper Forest Way, Morriston SA6 8WB
web: www.premierinn.com
dir: *M4 junct 45, A4067 towards Swansea. In 0.5m at 2nd exit left into Clase Rd. Hotel 400yds on left*

Rooms 63

Premier Inn Swansea Waterfront

BUDGET HOTEL

tel: 0871 577 9212 *(Calls cost 13p per minute plus your phone company's access charge)*
The Waterfront Development, Langdon Rd SA1 8PL
web: www.premierinn.com
dir: *M4 junct 42, A483 towards Swansea/Abertawe (signed Fabian Way). Approx 4.5m. At 2nd lights, left into SA1 Waterfront development. At rdbt take 2nd exit into Langdon Rd. Hotel on left*

Rooms 132

Ibis Swansea

AA Advertised

tel: 01792 638800 **Fabian Way, A483 SA1 8LD**
email: H6653@accor.com **web:** www.ibishotel.com
dir: *M4 junct 42 on to Fabian Way/A483 then west for approx 3.1m. At lights at Swansea dock entrance, turn left, then right at rdbt onto Lagdon Rd. Hotel on right*

Modern, budget hotel offering comfortable accommodation in bright and practical bedrooms. Breakfast is self-service and dinner is available in the restaurant.

Rooms 99 (99 fmly) **Facilities** FTV WiFi ᵇ 18 **Services** Lift **Parking** 100

Bodnant Welsh Food Centre

RESTAURANT WITH ROOMS

tel: 01492 651100 & 651102 **Furnace Farm LL28 5RP**
email: reception@bodnant-welshfood.co.uk **web:** www.bodnant-welshfood.co.uk
dir: *Off A470, 4m from A55 junct 19, follow signs for A470*

Overlooking the River Conwy and neighbouring Bodnant Gardens, this 18th-century farm has been fully restored and is now the home to Bodnant Welsh Food Centre. It is ideally placed to explore the North Wales coastline, Snowdonia, and the nearby surf park. The buildings have been transformed into a tea room, farm shop and wine merchants with a focus on Welsh products. The Hayloft Restaurant serves interesting lunches and dinners, including a 7-course taster menu. A range of room types and sizes can be found in the comfortable accommodation, with a guest lounge and kitchen also available. There is a cookery school on-site, and small conferences and weddings can be accommodated here.

Rooms 6

Atlantic Hotel

★★★ 80% HOTEL

tel: 01834 842881 **The Esplanade SA70 7DU**
email: enquiries@atlantic-hotel.uk.com **web:** www.atlantic-hotel.uk.com
dir: *A478 into Tenby, follow town centre signs (keep town walls on left) right at Esplanade, hotel on right*

This privately-owned and personally-run, friendly hotel has an enviable position looking out over South Beach towards Caldy Island. Bedrooms vary in size and style, but all are well equipped and tastefully appointed. The comfortable public areas include a choice of lounges and in fine weather, guests can also enjoy the cliff-top gardens. Relax in the salt-water swimming pool with jacuzzi, steam room and heated loungers. Dining is offered in Carringtons Restaurant on the lower ground floor.

Rooms 42 (11 fmly) (4 GF) **S** £81-£96; **D** £110-£210 (incl. bkfst) **Facilities** FTV WiFi
Steam room Spa bath **Conf** Board 8 **Services** Lift **Parking** 25 **Notes** LB Closed end Nov-late Jan

Premier Inn Tenby Town Centre

BUDGET HOTEL

tel: 0871 527 9514 *(Calls cost 13p per minute plus your phone company's access charge)*
White Lion St SA70 7ET
web: www.premierinn.com
dir: *A478 into Tenby. Left into Narberth Rd. On bay turn right into White Lion St*

High quality, budget accommodation ideal for both families and business travellers. Spacious, en suite bedrooms feature tea and coffee making facilities, and Freeview TV in most hotels. Internet access and WiFi are available for a small fee. The adjacent family restaurant features a wide and varied menu. See also the Hotel Groups pages.

Rooms 61

TINTERN PARVA
Monmouthshire   Map 4 SO50

Best Western Royal George Hotel

★★★ 79% HOTEL

tel: 01291 689205 **Wye Valley Rd NP16 6SF**
email: royalgeorgetintern@hotmail.com **web:** www.bw-royalgeorgehotel.co.uk
dir: *M48 junct 2, A466, 5m to Tintern, 2nd left*

This privately-owned and personally-run hotel provides comfortable, spacious accommodation, including bedrooms with balconies overlooking the well-tended garden; there are also a number of ground-floor bedrooms. The public areas include a lounge bar and a large function room, and a varied and popular menu is available in either the bar or restaurant. This hotel is an ideal base for exploring the counties of Monmouthshire and Herefordshire.

Rooms 14 (14 annexe) (3 fmly) (10 GF) **S** £65-£105; **D** £80-£120* **Facilities** FTV WiFi ⊠ Xmas New Year **Conf** Class 40 Board 30 Thtr 80 Del from £95 to £140* **Parking** 50 **Notes** LB Civ Wed 70

TREARDDUR BAY
Isle of Anglesey   Map 14 SH27

Trearddur Bay Hotel

★★★ 82% HOTEL

tel: 01407 860301 **LL65 2UN**
email: enquiries@trearddurbayhotel.co.uk **web:** www.trearddurbayhotel.co.uk
dir: *A55 junct 2, left, over 1st rdbt, left at 2nd rdbt, right after approx 2m*

A real seaside theme runs through this bright and welcoming hotel situated only 100 yards from a Blue Flag beach. Bedrooms include a large number of recently refurbished, contemporary rooms; some with balconies and stunning views of the bay. Guests have a choice of dining in the more formal Bay Restaurant, or the Inn at The Bay which has an outdoor area for summer dining. Facilities include function rooms, an indoor swimming pool and children's play area.

Rooms 43 (6 annexe) (6 fmly) (3 GF) **S** £60-£100; **D** £80-£210 (incl. bkfst)* **Facilities** FTV WiFi ⊠ Xmas New Year **Conf** Class 80 Board 60 Thtr 200 Del from £100 to £135* **Parking** 200 **Notes** LB Civ Wed 140

USK
Monmouthshire   Map 9 SO30

The Three Salmons Hotel

★★★ 77% ◉◉ HOTEL

tel: 01291 672133 **Bridge St NP15 1RY**
email: general@threesalmons.co.uk **web:** www.threesalmons.co.uk
dir: *M4 junct 24, A449, 1st exit signed Usk. On entering town, hotel on main road*

The Three Salmons is a 17th-century coaching inn located in the centre of a small market town with friendly, efficient staff that help create a welcoming atmosphere. The food in the contemporary restaurant is very popular. Bedrooms are comfortable and a good range of extras are provided. There is a large function suite ideal for weddings and parties. Parking is secure.

Rooms 24 (14 annexe) (3 fmly) (7 GF) ⚓ **Facilities** FTV WiFi **Conf** Class 80 Board 40 Thtr 110 **Parking** 43 **Notes** Civ Wed 100

Newbridge on Usk

◉ RESTAURANT WITH ROOMS

tel: 01633 451000 & 410262 **Tredunnock NP15 1LY**
email: newbridgeonusk@celtic-manor.com **web:** www.celtic-manor.com
dir: *M4 junct 24, signed Newport, onto B4236. At Ship Inn turn right, over mini rdbt onto Llangybi/Usk road. Turn right opposite Cwrt Bleddyn Hotel, signed Tredunnock, through village & down hill*

This cosy gastropub is tucked away in a beautiful village setting with the River Usk nearby. The well-equipped bedrooms, in a separate building, provide comfort and a good range of extras. Guests can eat at rustic tables around the bar or in the upstairs dining room where award-winning, seasonal food is served; there is also a small private dining room. Breakfast is one of the highlights of a stay with quality local ingredients offered in abundance.

Rooms 6 (2 fmly)

WELSHPOOL
Powys   Map 15 SJ20

The Royal Oak Hotel

★★★ 79% HOTEL

tel: 01938 552217 **The Cross SY21 7DG**
email: royaloak@innmail.co.uk **web:** www.royaloakwelshpool.co.uk
dir: *By lights at junct of A483 & A458*

Standing in the centre of Welshpool, The Royal Oak Hotel was once the Manor House for the Earl of Powys, before being used as a coaching inn for travellers en route to the Welsh Coast. Recently refurbished, a range of bedrooms types offer high levels of comfort and are complimented by very good quality bathrooms. A bustling coffee shop is located on the ground floor, with a number of interconnecting lounges ensuring there is always a quiet corner. The smart dining room offers a range of dishes to suit most tastes both at lunch and dinner. A small secure car park is a welcome additional feature.

Rooms 25 (3 fmly) ⚓ **Facilities** WiFi Xmas New Year **Conf** Class 60 Board 30 Thtr 100 **Parking** 19 **Notes** Civ Wed 100

W

WHITEBROOK	Map 4 SO50
Monmouthshire	

INSPECTORS' CHOICE

The Whitebrook

◉◉◉◉ RESTAURANT WITH ROOMS

tel: 01600 860254 **NP25 4TX**
email: info@thewhitebrook.co.uk **web:** www.thewhitebrook.co.uk
dir: 4m from Monmouth on B4293, left at sign to Whitebrook, 2m on unclassified road, on right

Peacefully located and surrounded by woods and rivers, this delightful restaurant with rooms offers a peaceful escape. All the bedrooms are located above the main restaurant and come in a range of shapes and sizes. All are very comfortably decorated and furnished. The four AA Rosette award-winning food makes great use of the finest local produce and the relaxing surroundings and friendly service provide a memorable dining experience.

Rooms 8

WOLF'S CASTLE	Map 8 SM92
Pembrokeshire	

Wolfscastle Country Hotel

★★★ 79% ◉◉ COUNTRY HOUSE HOTEL

tel: 01437 741225 & 741688 **Wolf's Castle SA62 5LZ**
email: enquiries@wolfscastle.com **web:** www.wolfscastle.com
dir: On A40 in village at top of hill. 6m N of Haverfordwest

This large stone house, a former vicarage, dates back to the mid-19th century and is now a friendly, privately-owned and personally-run hotel. It provides stylish, modern, well-maintained and well-equipped bedrooms. There is a pleasant bar and an attractive restaurant, which has a well deserved reputation for its food.

Rooms 20 (2 fmly) ❧ **S** £75-£105; **D** £110-£145 (incl. bkfst)* **Facilities** STV FTV WiFi New Year **Conf** Class 100 Board 40 Thtr 150 Del £122.50* **Parking** 60 **Notes** Closed 24-26 Dec Civ Wed 100

WREXHAM	Map 15 SJ35
Wrexham	

Premier Inn Wrexham North (A483)

BUDGET HOTEL

tel: 0871 527 9190 (Calls cost 13p per minute plus your phone company's access charge)
Chester Rd, Gresford LL12 8PW
web: www.premierinn.com
dir: On B5445, just off A483 (dual carriageway) near Gresford

High quality, budget accommodation ideal for both families and business travellers. Spacious, en suite bedrooms feature tea and coffee making facilities, and Freeview TV in most hotels. Internet access and WiFi are available for a small fee. The adjacent family restaurant features a wide and varied menu. See also the Hotel Groups pages.

Rooms 60

Premier Inn Wrexham Town Centre

BUDGET HOTEL

tel: 0871 527 9458 (Calls cost 13p per minute plus your phone company's access charge)
Jacques Way LL11 2BY
web: www.premierinn.com
dir: A55 junct 38. At Wrexham Road Interchange, A483. At rdbt 2nd exit signed Wrexham. Exit at junct 5, at next rdbt take A541. Pass football ground, right at lights

Rooms 83

The Lemon Tree

RESTAURANT WITH ROOMS

tel: 01978 261211 **29 Rhosddu Rd LL11 2LP**
email: info@thelemontree.org.uk **web:** www.thelemontree.org.uk
dir: A483 junct 5 follow signs for town centre, pass university & football stadium. Keep left, left at 1st rdbt

A modern and stylish restaurant setting awaits within this unassuming Gothic, Grade II listed building in the heart of Wrexham. The owners have a relaxed approach and offer locally sourced, modern British cuisine in the evenings. Straightforward and good value bedrooms are smartly appointed and comfortable; available in a range of sizes.

Rooms 12

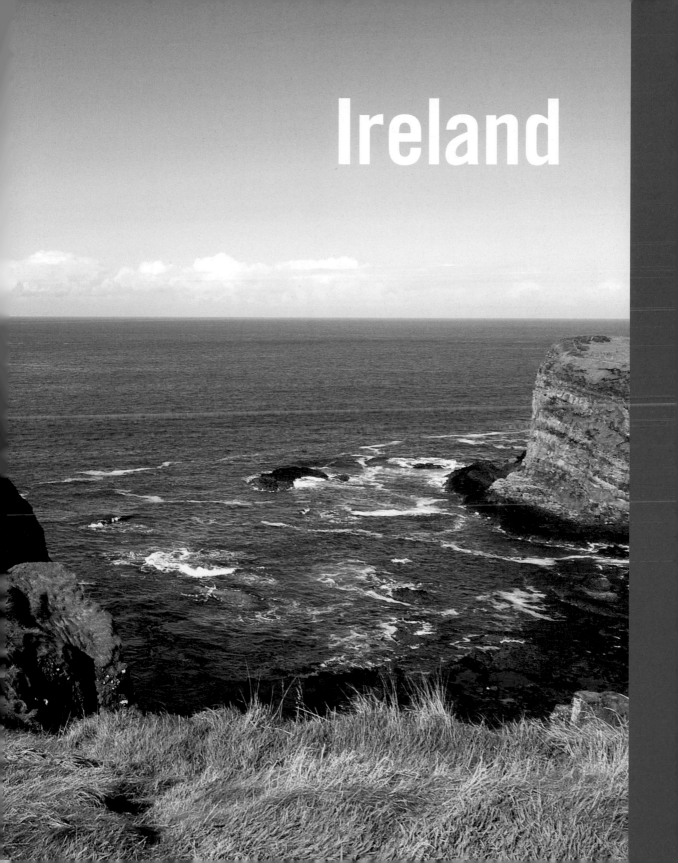

Ireland

Additional Information for Northern Ireland & the Republic of Ireland

Licensing Regulations

Northern Ireland: Public houses open Mon-Sat 11.30-23.00. Sun 12.30-22.00. Hotels can serve residents without restriction. Non-residents can be served 12.30-22.00 on Christmas Day. Children under 18 are not allowed in the bar area and may neither buy nor consume liquor in hotels.

Republic of Ireland: General licensing hours are Mon-Thu 10.30-23.30, Fri & Sat 10.30-00.30. Sun 12.30-23.00 (or 00.30 if the following day is a Bank Holiday). There is no service (except for hotel residents) on Christmas Day or Good Friday.

The Fire Services (NI) Order 2006

This covers establishments accommodating more than six people, which must have a certificate from the Northern Ireland Fire Authority. Places accommodating fewer than six people need adequate exits. AA inspectors check emergency notices, fire fighting equipment and fire exits here.

The Republic of Ireland safety regulations are a matter for local authority regulations. For your own and others' safety, read the emergency notices and be sure you understand them.

Telephone numbers

Area codes for numbers in the Republic of Ireland apply only within the Republic. If dialling from outside check the telephone directory (from the UK the international dialling code is 00 353). Area codes for numbers in Britain and Northern Ireland cannot be used directly from the Republic.

For the latest information on the Republic of Ireland visit the AA Ireland's website: www.TheAA.ie

---

NORTHERN IRELAND

AGHADOWEY
County Londonderry

Map 1 C6

Brown Trout Golf & Country Inn

★★★ 79% HOTEL

IRISH COUNTRY HOTELS

tel: 028 7086 8209 **209 Agivey Rd BT51 4AD**
email: jane@browntroutinn.com **web:** www.browntroutinn.com
dir: *At junct of A54 & B66 junct on road to Coleraine*

Set alongside the Agivey River and featuring its own 9-hole golf course, this welcoming inn offers a choice of spacious accommodation. Comfortably furnished bedrooms are situated around a courtyard area, while the cottage suites also have lounge areas. Home-cooked meals are served in the restaurant and lighter fare is available in the charming lounge bar which has entertainment at weekends.

Rooms 15 (11 fmly) (15 GF) ✿ **Facilities** STV FTV WiFi ▷ ♨ 9 Putt green Gym Game fishing ♫ Xmas New Year **Conf** Class 24 Board 28 Thtr 40 **Parking** 80 **Notes** Civ Wed 80

ANTRIM
County Antrim

Map 1 D5

Holiday Inn Express Antrim

BUDGET HOTEL

tel: 028 9442 5500 **Junction 1 Leisure Park, Ballymena Rd BT41 4LL**
email: reception.antrim@holidayinnexpress.org.uk **web:** www.hiexantrim.co.uk
dir: *At Junction One Shopping Outlet*

Holiday Inn Express Antrim is located at Junction One, Northern Ireland's largest international shopping outlet, and is convenient for Ballymena, Coleraine and Londonderry. Within a short drive are Belfast city centre and the Giant's Causeway. It has 90 stylish bedrooms and 4 modern, purpose-built meeting rooms. A full Irish or Continental breakfast is on offer, while in the evening guests can dine at the Great Room Restaurant, Bar and Lounge. The hotel has a large, secure, car park that is free for all hotel guests. See also the Hotel Groups pages.

Rooms 90 (52 fmly) (10 GF) ✿ **Conf** Class 20 Board 20 Thtr 40

BALLYMENA
County Antrim

Map 1 D5

HIGHLY RECOMMENDED

Galgorm Resort & Spa

★★★★ 88% ❀❀❀ HOTEL

tel: 028 2588 1001 **136 Fenaghy Rd, Galgorm BT42 1EA**
email: reservations@galgorm.com **web:** www.galgorm.com
dir: *1m from Ballymena on A42, between Galgorm & Cullybackey*

Standing in 163 acres of private woodland and sweeping lawns beside the River Maine, this 19th-century mansion offers spacious, comfortable bedrooms. Public areas include a welcoming cocktail bar and elegant restaurant, as well as Gillies, a lively and atmospheric locals' bar. Also on the estate is an equestrian centre and a conference hall.

Rooms 122 (17 fmly) (8 GF) ✿ **Facilities** Spa FTV WiFi ▷ ⓢ supervised ✇ Fishing Gym Clay pigeon shooting Archery Horseriding (all can be arranged off site) ♫ Xmas New Year **Conf** Class 170 Board 30 Thtr 500 **Services** Lift **Parking** 300 **Notes** ⊗ Civ Wed 300

BELFAST
Belfast

Map 1 D5

INSPECTORS' CHOICE

The Merchant Hotel
★★★★★ ◎◎ HOTEL

tel: 028 9023 4888 **16 Skipper St BT1 2DZ**
email: info@themerchanthotel.com **web:** www.themerchanthotel.com
dir: In city centre, 2nd left at Albert Clock into Waring St. Hotel on left

The Merchant Hotel is a magnificent hotel situated in the historic Cathedral Quarter of the city centre. This Grade I listed building has been lovingly and sensitively restored to reveal its original architectural grandeur and interior opulence. All the bedrooms, including five suites, have air-conditioning, high-speed internet access, flat-screen TVs and luxury bathrooms. There are several eating options including the grand and beautifully decorated Great Room Restaurant.

Rooms 62 (17 fmly) ✿ **Facilities** Spa FTV WiFi ♨ Gym Steam room ♫ Xmas New Year **Conf** Class 100 Board 60 Thtr 200 **Services** Lift Air con **Parking** 35 **Notes** ⊗ Civ Wed 130

Malmaison Belfast
★★★★ 79% HOTEL

tel: 0844 693 0650 (Calls cost 5p per minute plus your phone company's access charge)
34-38 Victoria St BT1 3GH
email: belfast@malmaison.com **web:** www.malmaison.com
dir: M1 along Westlink to Grosvenor Rd. Follow city centre signs. Pass City Hall on right, left onto Victoria St. Hotel on right

Situated in a former seed warehouse, this luxurious, contemporary hotel is ideally located for the city centre. Comfortable bedrooms boast a host of modern facilities, while the deeply comfortable, stylish public areas include a popular bar lounge. The 'Home Grown and Local' menu in the brasserie showcases local seasonal ingredients. The warm hospitality is notable.

Rooms 64 (8 fmly) **Facilities** STV WiFi Gym **Conf** Board 22 **Services** Lift **Notes** Civ Wed

Malone Lodge Hotel
★★★★ 78% HOTEL

tel: 028 9038 8000 **60 Eglantine Av BT9 6DY**
email: info@malonelodgehotel.com **web:** www.malonelodgehotelbelfast.com
dir: At hospital rdbt exit towards Boucher Rd, left at 1st rdbt, right at lights at top, then 1st left. Carpark to the rear of hotel

Situated in the leafy suburbs of the university area of south Belfast, this stylish hotel forms the centrepiece of an attractive row of Victorian terraced properties. The hotel has undergone a massive transformation of the exterior, public areas, bar and restaurant, with a rolling bedroom refurbishment also undertaken. The Knife and Fork restaurant offers relaxed and informal dining.

Rooms 54 (7 fmly) **Facilities** FTV WiFi ♫ **Conf** Class 126 Board 48 Thtr 250 **Del** from £124 to £206 **Services** Lift **Parking** 70 **Notes** ⊗ Civ Wed 120

Radisson Blu Hotel Belfast
★★★★ 78% HOTEL

tel: 028 9043 4065 & 9082 0109 **3 Cromac Place BT7 2JB**
email: info.belfast@radissonblu.com **web:** www.radissonblu.co.uk/hotel-belfast
dir: On corner of Ormeau Rd & Cromac St

This modern hotel is in the centre of the regenerated urban area close to the city centre. The bedrooms are stylishly presented, well equipped and all have air conditioning; there is a choice of business suites. Public areas include a spacious lounge bar and the Filini Restaurant, which serves good Italian and Sardinian cuisine. Ample secure parking, and free WiFi (throughout the hotel) are available.

Rooms 120 (11 fmly) **S** £80-£230; **D** £90-£240 (incl. bkfst)* **Facilities** FTV WiFi ♨ Xmas New Year **Conf** Class 70 Board 50 Thtr 150 **Del** from £115 to £265* **Services** Lift Air con **Parking** 120 **Notes** LB ⊗ Civ Wed 90

Premier Inn Belfast City Cathedral Quarter
BUDGET HOTEL

tel: 0871 527 8070 (Calls cost 13p per minute plus your phone company's access charge)
2-6 Waring St BT1 1XY
web: www.premierinn.com
dir: M1 or M2 to Westlink to Grosvenor Rd rdbt, signed city centre. Into Grosvenor Rd. At 2nd lights left, take right lane, right (pass City Hall on right). At end of Chichester St left into Victoria St. Through next 2 lights, left into Waring St. Hotel 300yds on right

High quality, budget accommodation ideal for both families and business travellers. Spacious, en suite bedrooms feature tea and coffee making facilities, and Freeview TV in most hotels. Internet access and WiFi are available for a small fee. The adjacent family restaurant features a wide and varied menu. See also the Hotel Groups pages.

Rooms 171

Premier Inn Belfast City Centre Alfred St
BUDGET HOTEL

tel: 0871 527 8068 (Calls cost 13p per minute plus your phone company's access charge)
Alfred St BT2 8ED
web: www.premierinn.com
dir: M1 or M2 to Westlink. Follow city centre signs. 1st right, 2nd left into Hope St. At 2nd lights left into Bedford St. At next lights right into Ormeau Ave. Left into Alfred St. Underground car park (chargeable) on left

Rooms 148

BELFAST *continued*

Premier Inn Belfast Titanic Quarter

BUDGET HOTEL

tel: 0871 527 9210 *(Calls cost 13p per minute plus your phone company's access charge)*
2A Queens Rd BT3 9FB
web: www.premierinn.com
dir: *From all major routes follow Odyssey Arena signs. From M3 junct 1 exit onto Queens Island, to lights. Hotel on left*

Rooms 122

Etap Belfast

AA Advertised

tel: 028 9032 8126 **35 Dublin Rd BT2 7HE**
email: H7186@accor.com **web:** www.ibishotel.com
dir: *In heart of Belfast city centre, 5mins walk from Belfast Central station*

Modern, budget hotel offering comfortable accommodation in bright and practical bedrooms. Breakfast is self-service and dinner is available in the restaurant.

Rooms 146 🐾 **Facilities** FTV WiFi HL **Services** Lift Air con

BUSHMILLS	Map 1 C6
County Antrim	

HIGHLY RECOMMENDED

Bushmills Inn Hotel

★★★★ 83% @ HOTEL

tel: 028 2073 3000 & 2073 2339 **9 Dunluce Rd BT57 8QG**
email: mail@bushmillsinn.com **web:** www.bushmillsinn.com
dir: *On A2 in village centre*

Enjoying a prominent position in the heart of the village, this hotel offers a range of bedroom styles including spacious, creatively designed rooms that have the latest technology and a small dressing room. The charming public areas feature inglenook turf-burning fires, cosy snugs along with a very popular traditional bar. The restaurant has a well-deserved reputation for its food. The hotel is very popular with golfers; it is close to the Giants Causeway, Bushmills Distillery and the stunning scenery of the Antrim Coast.

Rooms 41 (2 fmly) (20 GF) 🐾 **S** £108–£278; **D** £128–£398* **Facilities** WiFi 🎵 New Year **Conf** Class 30 Board 18 Thtr 40 **Services** Lift **Parking** 70 **Notes** ⊗ Closed 25 Dec

CARRICKFERGUS	Map 1 D5
County Antrim	

Premier Inn Carrickfergus

BUDGET HOTEL

tel: 0871 527 8214 *(Calls cost 13p per minute plus your phone company's access charge)*
The Harbour, Alexandra Pier BT38 8BE
web: www.premierinn.com
dir: *Exit at M2 junct 2, take M5 N onto A2 towards Carrickfergus. Follow Castle/Maritime Area signs. Right at rdbt adjacent to castle. Hotel straight ahead, adjacent to harbour*

High quality, budget accommodation ideal for both families and business travellers. Spacious, en suite bedrooms feature tea and coffee making facilities, and Freeview TV in most hotels. Internet access and WiFi are available for a small fee. The adjacent family restaurant features a wide and varied menu. See also the Hotel Groups pages.

Rooms 49

COLERAINE	Map 1 C6
County Londonderry	

Premier Inn Coleraine

BUDGET HOTEL

tel: 0871 527 8262 *(Calls cost 13p per minute plus your phone company's access charge)*
3 Riverside Park North, Castleroe Rd BT51 3GE
web: www.premierinn.com
dir: *A26 towards Coraine. At rdbt left on A29 (ring road) signed Cookstown/Garragh. At rdbt A54 (Castleroe Rd). Hotel on right*

High quality, budget accommodation ideal for both families and business travellers. Spacious, en suite bedrooms feature tea and coffee making facilities, and Freeview TV in most hotels. Internet access and WiFi are available for a small fee. The adjacent family restaurant features a wide and varied menu. See also the Hotel Groups pages.

Rooms 49

COMBER	Map 1 D5
County Down	

The Old Schoolhouse Inn

@@ RESTAURANT WITH ROOMS

tel: 028 9754 1182 **100 Ballydrain Rd BT23 6EA**
email: info@theoldschoolhouseinn.com **web:** www.theoldschoolhouseinn.com
dir: *A22 to Comber, right at end of road. 0.5m past Castle Espie to property*

Located close to the shore of Strangford Lough, The Old Schoolhouse Inn enjoys a peaceful rural location, and is just a short drive from Comber and 20 minutes from Belfast. This family-run operation is in the capable hands of Will Brown who has learnt his trade in some of London's best kitchens and in establishments closer to home. Bedrooms are spacious and well appointed, while service is warm and genuine. The refurbished restaurant has been awarded two AA Rosettes and serves local produce with flair and imagination.

Rooms 12

CRAWFORDSBURN
County Down

Map 1 D5

HIGHLY RECOMMENDED

The Old Inn

★★★★ 83% @@ HOTEL

tel: 028 9185 3255 **15 Main St BT19 1JH**
email: info@theoldinn.com **web:** www.theoldinn.com
dir: *A2 from Belfast, past Belfast City Airport & Transport Museum. 2m, left at lights onto B20. 1.2m to hotel*

This delightful hotel enjoys a peaceful rural setting just a short drive from Belfast. The property dates from 1614, and many of the day rooms exude charm and character. Individually styled, comfortable bedrooms, some with feature beds, offer modern facilities. The popular bar and intimate restaurant both offer creative menus, and staff throughout are keen to please. Recent extensive investment in The Old Inn's business facilities make this the ideal place for a meeting or conference.

Rooms 31 (1 annexe) (7 fmly) (4 GF) ⚓ **S** £95–£220; **D** £105–£230 (incl. bkfst) **Facilities** STV FTV WiFi ▷ In room spa/massage treatments ♫ Xmas New Year **Conf** Class 120 Board 40 Thtr 150 Del from £135 to £180 **Services** Lift **Parking** 84 **Notes** LB ⊗ RS 25 Dec Civ Wed 100

DUNGANNON
County Tyrone

Map 1 C5

The Cohannon Inn & Auto Lodge

★★ 76% HOTEL

tel: 028 8772 4488 **212 Ballynakilly Rd BT71 6HJ**
email: info@cohannon.com **web:** www.cohannon.com
dir: *400yds from M1 junct 14*

Handy for the M1 and the nearby towns of Dungannon and Portadown, this hotel offers well-maintained bedrooms, located behind the inn complex in a smart purpose-built wing. Public areas are smartly furnished and wide-ranging menus are served throughout the day.

Rooms 42 (20 fmly) (21 GF) (5 smoking) **S** fr £54.95; **D** fr £59.95 **Facilities** FTV WiFi Hair & beauty salon New Year **Conf** Class 100 Board 40 Thtr 160 Del from £75 to £150 **Parking** 160 **Notes** RS 25 Dec

ENNISKILLEN
County Fermanagh

Map 1 C5

Lough Erne Resort

★★★★★ 86% @@@ HOTEL

tel: 028 6632 3230 **Belleek Rd BT93 7ED**
email: info@lougherneresort.com **web:** www.lougherneresort.com
dir: *A46 from Enniskillen towards Donegal, hotel In 3m*

This delightful resort enjoys a peaceful and idyllic setting and boasts championship golf courses, a wonderful Thai spa and a host of outdoor and leisure pursuits. Bedrooms and en suites are spacious, particularly well appointed and include a number of luxury suites. Day rooms are spacious, luxurious and include lounges, bars and restaurants with splendid views. Service is friendly and extremely attentive.

Rooms 120 (61 annexe) **Facilities** Spa STV WiFi ⊙ ♨ 18 Fishing Gym ♫ Xmas New Year **Conf** Class 200 Board 80 Thtr 400 **Services** Lift **Parking** 240 **Notes** ⊗ Civ Wed 300

NORTHERN IRELAND

ENNISKILLEN *continued*

Manor House Country Hotel

★★★★ 83% ◉ COUNTRY HOUSE HOTEL

tel: 028 6862 2200 **Killadeas BT94 1NY**
email: info@manorhousecountryhotel.com **web:** www.manorhousecountryhotel.com
dir: *On B82, 7m N of Enniskillen*

This charming country house hotel enjoys a stunning location on the banks of Lower Lough Erne and is a short drive from the busy town of Enniskillen. Bedrooms are equipped to a very high standard with front-facing rooms having the fabulous lough views. There is a choice of restaurants, and afternoon tea is served in the comfortable lounge with its open fire. The hotel has first-class business, conference and leisure facilities including its own air-conditioned cruiser for tours and corporate events.

Rooms 78 (12 fmly) (12 GF) ↑ **S** £70-£125; **D** £80-£325 (incl. bkfst)*
Facilities FTV WiFi ↕ ⓧ Gym Sauna Steam room ♫ Xmas New Year
Conf Class 120 Board 100 Thtr 400 Del £135* **Services** Lift **Parking** 300 **Notes** ⊗ Civ Wed 300

Killyhevlin Lakeside Hotel

★★★★ 82% HOTEL

IRISH COUNTRY HOTELS

tel: 028 6632 3481 **BT74 6RW**
email: info@killyhevlin.com **web:** www.killyhevlin.com
dir: *2m S of Enniskillen, off A4*

This modern, stylish hotel is situated on the shores of Lough Erne, south of the town. The well-equipped bedrooms are particularly spacious and enjoy fine views of the gardens and lake. The restaurant, informal bar and comfortable lounges all share the views. Staff are friendly and helpful. There are extensive leisure facilities and a spa.

Rooms 71 (42 fmly) (22 GF) ↑ **Facilities** Spa FTV WiFi ↕ ⓧ Fishing Gym Aerobic studio Steam room Sauna Hydrotherapy area Relaxation room ♫ New Year
Conf Class 160 Board 100 Thtr 500 **Services** Lift **Parking** 500 **Notes** ⊗ Closed 25 Dec RS 24 & 26 Dec Civ Wed 250

LIMAVADY	Map 1 C6
County Londonderry	

Roe Park Resort

★★★★ 79% ◉ HOTEL

tel: 028 7772 2222 **BT49 9LB**
email: reservations@roeparkresort.com **web:** www.roeparkresort.com
dir: *On A2 Londonderry-Limavady rd, 1m from Limavady*

This impressive, popular hotel is part of a modern golf resort. The spacious, contemporary bedrooms are well equipped and many have excellent views of the fairways and surrounding estate. The Greens Restaurant provides a refreshing dining experience and the Coach House brasserie offers a lighter menu. The leisure options are extensive.

Rooms 118 (15 fmly) (37 GF) (5 smoking) ↑ **Facilities** Spa FTV WiFi HL ⓧ supervised ↙ 18 Putt green Fishing Gym Driving range Indoor golf academy ♫ Xmas New Year **Conf** Class 190 Board 140 Thtr 450 **Services** Lift **Parking** 350 **Notes** ⊗ Civ Wed 300

LISBURN	Map 1 D5
County Antrim	

Premier Inn Lisburn

BUDGET HOTEL

Premier Inn

tel: 0871 527 8606 *(Calls cost 13p per minute plus your phone company's access charge)*
136-144 Hillsborough Rd BT27 5QY
web: www.premierinn.com
dir: *M1 onto A1 (Sprucefield Rd). Left into Hillsborough Rd. Approx 1.5m, hotel on left*

High quality, budget accommodation ideal for both families and business travellers. Spacious, en suite bedrooms feature tea and coffee making facilities, and Freeview TV in most hotels. Internet access and WiFi are available for a small fee. The adjacent family restaurant features a wide and varied menu. See also the Hotel Groups pages.

Rooms 90

LONDONDERRY
County Londonderry

Map 1 C5

City Hotel

★★★★ 78% HOTEL

tel: 028 7136 5800 **Queens Quay BT48 7AS**
email: reservations@cityhotelderry.com **web:** www.cityhotelderry.com
dir: *Follow city centre signs. Hotel on waterfront*

In a central position overlooking the River Foyle, this stylish, contemporary hotel will appeal to business and leisure guests alike. All bedrooms have excellent facilities including internet access; the executive rooms make particularly good working environments. Meeting and function facilities are extensive and there are good leisure options.

Rooms 158 (16 fmly) **Facilities** FTV WiFi supervised Gym Steam room New Year **Conf** Class 150 Board 80 Thtr 350 **Services** Lift Air con **Parking** 48 **Notes** LB Closed 25 Dec Civ Wed 350

Premier Inn Derry / Londonderry

BUDGET HOTEL

tel: 0871 527 9414 *(Calls cost 13p per minute plus your phone company's access charge)*
Crescent Link BT47 6SA
web: www.premierinn.com
dir: *Phone for detailed directions*

High quality, budget accommodation ideal for both families and business travellers. Spacious, en suite bedrooms feature tea and coffee making facilities, and Freeview TV in most hotels. Internet access and WiFi are available for a small fee. The adjacent family restaurant features a wide and varied menu. See also the Hotel Groups pages.

Rooms 60

MAGHERA
Co Londonderry

Map 1 C5

Ardtara Country House

RESTAURANT WITH ROOMS

tel: 028 7964 4490 **8 Gorteade Rd BT46 5SA**
email: info@ardtara.com **web:** www.ardtara.com

Set in its own extensive gardens Ardtara Country House enjoys a secluded location just a short drive from the beautiful North Antrim Coast and the famous Giant's Causeway. This fine 19th-century house offers guests spacious bedrooms with views over the landscaped gardens. There is a comfortable lounge, a cosy bar and many of the original features have been sympathetically restored. The award-winning restaurant offers the best in fresh seasonal produce and the hearty breakfasts served in the conservatory are not to be missed. The city of Derry is a short drive away as is the challenging Royal Portrush golf course. Ardtara Country House is the AA Guest Accommodation of the Year for Northern Ireland 2016-2017.

Rooms 9

REPUBLIC OF IRELAND

ARDMORE
County Waterford

Map 1 C2

Cliff House Hotel

★★★★ 83% HOTEL

tel: 024 87800 & 87801
email: info@thecliffhousehotel.com **web:** www.thecliffhousehotel.com
dir: *From Dungarvan: N25, signed Cork. Left onto R673. From Youghal: N25 signed Waterford. Right onto R673 signed Ardmore. In Ardmore take Middle Rd to hotel*

This unique property, virtually sculpted into the cliff-face overlooking Ardmore Bay, is just a few minutes' walk from the village. Most of the individually designed bedroom suites and the public rooms enjoy the spectacular sea views, as do the stunning spa and leisure facilities. Rooms are very comfortable and artistically designed, in a palette of colours reflecting the natural setting. Dinner in the award-winning House Restaurant is a particular highlight - the menus feature imaginatively cooked, seasonal and local produce prepared with care and great flair. More casual fare is served in the bar, or on the terrace when weather permits. Some event spaces and valet parking are available.

Rooms 39 (8 fmly) (7 GF) **S** €245-€285; **D** €245-€285 (incl. bkfst)*
Facilities Spa STV FTV WiFi Fishing Gym Sauna Steam room Relaxation room Outdoor pursuits New Year Child facilities **Conf** Class 30 Board 20 Thtr 50 **Services** Lift Air con **Parking** 52 **Notes** LB Closed 24-26 Dec Civ Wed 60

BALLINA
County Mayo

Map 1 B4

Mount Falcon Estate

★★★★ 83% HOTEL

tel: 096 74472
email: info@mountfalcon.com **web:** www.mountfalcon.com
dir: *On N26, 6m from Foxford & 3m from Ballina. Hotel on left*

Dating from 1876, this house has been lovingly restored to its former glory, and has a bedroom extension that is totally in keeping with the original design. Relaxing lounges look out on the 100-acre estate, which has excellent salmon fishing on The Moy plus well-stocked trout lakes. Dinner is served in the original kitchen with choices from a varied and interesting menu; for lunch there is also the Boathole Bar. An air-conditioned gym is available.

Rooms 32 (3 fmly) **Facilities** Spa STV WiFi supervised Fishing Gym Sauna Steam room Driving range New Year **Conf** Class 120 Board 80 Thtr 200 **Services** Lift **Parking** 260 **Notes** Closed 24-27 Dec Civ Wed 200

BALLINA *continued*

Belleek Castle

★★★ 72% ◉◉ HOTEL

tel: 096 22400 **Belleek**
email: info@belleekcastle.com **web:** www.belleekcastle.com
dir: *In Belleek woods, N of Ballina*

This lovely manor house, formerly the ancestral home of the Earl of Arran, is set in wonderful parkland at the head of Belleek Wood on the River Moy estuary. The cosy public lounges are welcoming, and are complemented by a series of banqueting suites that are decorated in a nautical theme. Bedroom accommodation varies in style; all rooms are comfortably appointed. Dinner is the highlight of any visit, offered from a choice of Market or Gourmet set menus. The food is all locally sourced, and the chef has a keen eye for seasonality. The hotel is a popular wedding venue. There is also a museum specialising in armoury and memorabilia from the Spanish Armada.

Rooms 11 (2 fmly) ◈ **S** €80-€100; **D** €160-€220 (incl. bkfst) **Facilities** STV FTV WiFi ◊ Xmas New Year **Conf** Class 60 Board 30 Thtr 100 **Parking** 200 **Notes** LB ⊗ Closed 1 Jan - mid Feb Civ Wed 200

BALLINGEARY	Map 1 B2
County Cork	

Gougane Barra Hotel

★★★ 78% ◉ HOTEL

tel: 026 47069 **Gougane Barra**
email: gouganebarrahotel@eircom.net **web:** www.gouganebarrahotel.com
dir: *On L4643. Exit R584 between N22 at Macroom & N71 at Bantry*

This charming hotel, run by the Lucey family for over five generations, is in an idyllic location on the shores of Gougane Barra Lake, overlooking the tiny Oratory of St. Finbarr, a popular venue for intimate weddings. The bedrooms vary in size, but they are all well decorated, very comfortable and ideal for leisure guests. Chef Katie Lucey prepares menus based on the best local and seasonal ingredients, some from artisan producers. The ground floor includes cosy lounge areas and a traditional bar, with a marquee theatre in the summer months for an innovative experience known as Theatre by the Lake.

Rooms 26 (8 GF) ◈ **S** €69-€78; **D** €109-€129 (incl. bkfst) **Facilities** WiFi Fishing Boating Cycling Hiking **Conf** Class 12 Board 12 Thtr 22 **Parking** 26 **Notes** LB ⊗ Closed 10 Oct-10 Apr Civ Wed 60

BALLYFIN	Map 1 C3
County Laois	

Ballyfin Demesne

★★★★★ ◉◉ HOTEL

tel: 057 8755866 & 8755883
email: info@ballyfin.com **web:** www.ballyfin.com

Nestled in over 600 acres, this lavish Regency mansion has been painstakingly restored, yet all modern conveniences have been incorporated. With only 20 bedrooms, guests at Ballyfin have the feeling of visiting a friend's home; relaxation comes naturally when ensconced in any one of the sumptuously decorated salons, library or the stunning Turner-designed conservatory. Hospitality is key here; a team of butlers are at hand ensuring guests are well cared for at all times. Cuisine is an important element of the Ballyfin experience, with daily created menus on offer, together with suggested wine pairings, many featuring the Bordeaux estates of the Irish 'Wine Geese' who fled following the Battle of Kinsale. Spa treatments are available, as are a number of country pursuits such as falconry, archery, fishing and clay shooting.

Rooms 20 (2 GF) ◈ **Facilities** Spa STV WiFi ◊ ⊛ ♨ Fishing ♣ Gym Clay pigeon Air rifle shooting Archery Falconry Horse riding Xmas New Year **Services** Lift **Notes** ⊗ No children 9yrs Closed Jan Civ Wed 130

BALLYLICKEY	Map 1 B2
County Cork	

Seaview House Hotel

★★★ ◉◉ HOTEL

tel: 027 50073 & 50462
email: info@seaviewhousehotel.com **web:** www.seaviewhousehotel.com
dir: *5km from Bantry, 11km from Glengarriff on N71*

Colourful gardens and glimpses of Bantry Bay through the mature trees frame this delightful country house. Owner Kathleen O'Sullivan's team of staff are exceptionally pleasant, and there is a relaxed atmosphere in the cosy lounges. Guest comfort and good cuisine are top priorities. Bedrooms are spacious and individually styled, and some on the ground floor are appointed to suit less able guests.

Rooms 25 (3 fmly) (5 GF) ⚡ **Facilities** STV FTV WiFi **Conf** Class 30 Board 25 Thtr 25 **Parking** 32 **Notes** LB Closed mid Nov-mid Mar Civ Wed 75

BALLYLIFFIN	Map 1 C6
County Donegal	

Ballyliffin Lodge & Spa

★★★★ 78% ◉ HOTEL

tel: 074 9378200 & 07493 78146 **Shore Rd**
email: info@ballyliffinlodge.com **web:** www.ballyliffinlodge.com
dir: *From Derry take A2 towards Moville, exit for Carndonagh at Quigleys Point. Ballyliffin 10km*

Located in the heart of the village, this property offers a range of very comfortable bedrooms, many of which enjoy panoramic views of Malin Head and the famed Ballyliffin Golf Club. Dinner is served in the open-plan Jacks bar and restaurant, and less formal meals are served in the bar throughout the day. Guests are welcome to use the leisure facilities in the adjoining Crystal Rock Spa, where there is also a hairdressing salon.

Rooms 40 (28 fmly) ⚡ **S** €80-€120; **D** €110-€190 (incl. bkfst)* **Facilities** Spa STV WiFi ⊗ supervised Gym Hair salon Beauty salon Children's play areas ♫ New Year **Conf** Class 250 Board 125 Thtr 400 Del from €89 to €150 **Services** Lift **Parking** 80 **Notes** LB ⊗ Civ Wed 150

BALLYVAUGHAN	Map 1 B3
County Clare	

Gregans Castle

★★★ ◉◉◉ COUNTRY HOUSE HOTEL

tel: 065 7077005
email: stay@gregans.ie **web:** www.gregans.ie
dir: *3.5m S of Ballyvaughan on N67*

This hotel is a hidden gem in The Burren area, and the delightful restaurant and bedrooms enjoy splendid views towards Galway Bay. The Haden family, together with their welcoming staff, offer a high level of personal service. Bedrooms are individually decorated; superior rooms and suites are particularly comfortable; some are on the ground floor and have patio gardens. There are welcoming fires in the comfortable drawing room and the cosy cocktail bar where afternoon tea is served. Dinner is a highlight of any visit; the chef shows a real passion for food which is evident in his cooking of top quality local and organic produce. The area is rich in archaeological, geological and botanical interest, and cycling and walking tours can be organised. There is a beautiful garden to relax in.

Rooms 21 (3 fmly) (7 GF) ⚡ **Facilities** WiFi ↘ ⚓ **Conf** Class 25 Board 14 Thtr 25 **Parking** 25 **Notes** Closed Jan-12 Feb & 30 Nov-Dec Civ Wed 65

BALTIMORE	Map 1 B1
County Cork	

Rolfs Country House

◉ RESTAURANT WITH ROOMS

tel: 028 20289 **Baltimore Hill**
email: info@rolfscountryhouse.com **web:** www.rolfscountryhouse.com
dir: *Before village turn sharp left up hill. House signed*

Situated on a hill above the fishing village of Baltimore, these 400-year-old stone buildings have been successfully converted by the Haffner family. There are ten traditionally furnished en suite bedrooms in an annexe, a cosy bar with an open fire, and a rustic restaurant on two levels. Dinner is served nightly during the high season and at weekends in the winter; the menu features quality meats, artisan cheeses and fish landed at the busy pier. This is a lovely place to stay and the hosts are very friendly.

Rooms 10 (10 annexe)

BARNA (BEARNA)
County Galway

Map 1 B3

The Twelve
★★★★ 80% ◉◉ HOTEL

tel: 091 597000 **Barna Village**
email: enquire@thetwelvehotel.ie **web:** www.thetwelvehotel.ie
dir: Coast road Barna village, 10 mins from Galway

Located just ten minutes west of Galway city, this hotel looks as if it has been on the site for decades. However, once inside the decor is striking and contemporary. The bedrooms come in a number of different sizes, but all are furnished with taste and with guest comfort in mind. The Pins is a vibrant and popular bar and bistro where food is served throughout the day. West Restaurant opens during the evening, and features fine dining from a well-compiled menu of local and seasonal produce. Le Petit Spa offers treatments based on seaweed products.

Rooms 47 (12 fmly) ⚑ **S** €90-€160; **D** €100-€170 (incl. bkfst) **Facilities** STV FTV WiFi ⚑ Beauty treatment room Children's cookery programme Art classes Wine classes ♫ Xmas New Year **Conf** Class 70 Board 60 Thtr 80 Del from €190 to €250 **Services** Lift Air con **Parking** 140 **Notes** LB RS 22-27 Dec Civ Wed 100

BELMULLET
County Mayo

Map 1 A5

The Talbot Hotel
★★★★ 78% ◉◉ HOTEL

tel: 097 20484 **Barrack St**
email: info@thetalbothotel.ie **web:** www.thetalbothotel.ie
dir: On left side as you enter the town

In the heart of Belmullet town, this family-operated boutique property has evolved from its humble beginnings as a grocery store with a bar, to what is now a warm and welcoming hotel. The simple exterior belies the contemporary opulence of the individually designed and decorated bedrooms and suites that make up this comfortable townhouse. It is very much a boutique hotel, with a really welcoming team that have great interest in their guests. The bar is a popular venue with the locals and visitors alike, where quality food is served throughout the day, with seafood a feature. The 1st floor Barony Restaurant opens from Easter to October, and at peak periods, offering an interesting menu of interesting combinations of local and seasonal produce.

Rooms 21 (4 fmly) (8 GF) ⚑ **Facilities** STV FTV WiFi ⚑ ♫ New Year **Conf** Class 100 Board 100 Thtr 180 **Services** Lift Air con **Notes** ⊗ Civ Wed 150

BORRIS
County Carlow

Map 1 C3

Step House Hotel
★★★★ 78% ◉ HOTEL

tel: 059 9773209 **Main St**
email: info@stephousehotel.ie **web:** www.stephousehotel.ie
dir: In Borrisee, please see website for detailed directions

Originating from 1808, The Step House was once part of the Borris House Estate, ancestral home of the High Kings of Leinster. It has been a licensed premises in the Coady family for five generations, and became a hotel in the last decade following a dedicated refurbishment and expansion. Bedrooms are spacious, with many having wonderful views towards Mount Leinster. Dinner in the original kitchen, now the award-winning Cellar Restaurant, is a highlight of a visit, but lighter fare is also served daily in the 1808 bar and the gardens. The hotel has a strong reputation for weddings and family gatherings, and al fresco dining in the well-tended grounds and gardens.

Rooms 20 ⚑ **Facilities** WiFi **Notes** ⊗ Civ Wed 180

CARRICKMACROSS
County Monaghan

Map 1 C4

Shirley Arms Hotel
★★★★ 78% ◉ HOTEL

tel: 042 9673100 **Main St**
email: reception@shirleyarmshotel.ie **web:** www.shirleyarmshotel.ie
dir: N2 to Derry, take Ardee Rd to Carrickmacross

Set at the top of the town, this long established boutique hotel is an imposing 19th-century stone building with a contemporary interior. Bedrooms, in a purpose-built block to the rear, are spacious with clean, minimalist lines; there is also a comfortable suite in the original house overlooking the square. Food is an important element of the business here, with options available throughout the day in The Shirley Bar and award-winning evening dining in Whites Bistro. A night club is available for hire in the basement.

Rooms 25 (2 fmly) ⚑ **S** €85-€125; **D** €130-€230 (incl. bkfst) **Facilities** STV WiFi ⚑ ♫ New Year **Conf** Class 150 Board 200 Thtr 200 **Services** Lift **Parking** 80 **Notes** LB ⊗ Closed 24-26 Dec RS 6 Apr, Good Fri Civ Wed 150

CASHEL
County Galway

Map 1 A4

Cashel House Hotel
★★★ ◉◉ COUNTRY HOUSE HOTEL

tel: 095 31001
email: res@cashel-house-hotel.com **web:** www.cashel-house-hotel.com
dir: S off N59, 1.5km W of Recess, well signed

Cashel House is a mid-19th-century property, standing at the head of Cashel Bay in the heart of Connemara, set amidst secluded, award-winning gardens with woodland walks. Attentive service comes with the perfect balance of friendliness and professionalism from the McEvilly family and their staff. The comfortable lounges have turf fires and antique furnishings. The restaurant offers local produce such as the famous Connemara lamb, and fish from the nearby coast.

Rooms 29 (4 fmly) (6 GF) ⚑ **S** €75-€105; **D** €150-€210 (incl. bkfst)* **Facilities** STV FTV WiFi Garden school Cookery classes Xmas New Year **Parking** 40 **Notes** Closed Jan-10 Feb Civ Wed 120

CAVAN
County Cavan

Map 1 C4

Radisson Blu Farnham Estate Hotel

★★★★ 79% 🏨 HOTEL

tel: 049 4377700 **Farnham Estate**
email: info.farnham@radissonblu.com **web:** www.farnhamestate.com
dir: *From Dublin take N3 to Cavan. From Cavan take Killeshandra road for 3km*

Situated on a 1,300 acre estate, this 16th-century Great House combines old-world grandeur with modern glamour. Interiors are light, airy and contemporary with a relaxing atmosphere. The spacious bedrooms and suites are in the newer building. Interesting dining options are available in the Botanica Restaurant and Wine Goose Cellar Bar. There are extensive banqueting facilities and the health spa offers a range of treatments.

Rooms 158 (50 GF) 🐾 **Facilities** Spa STV WiFi ◊ 🕙 ⤜ 👍 18 Putt green Fishing ⛵ Gym In/Outdoor infinity pool Mint thermal suite Relaxation rooms Walking trails 🎵 Xmas New Year **Conf** Class 150 Board 44 Thtr 380 **Services** Lift **Parking** 600 **Notes** 🐕 Civ Wed 150

Cavan Crystal Hotel

★★★★ 78% 🏨 HOTEL

tel: 049 4360600 **Dublin Rd**
email: info@cavancrystalhotel.com **web:** www.cavancrystalhotel.com
dir: *On outskirts of Cavan town*

Contemporary design using native timber and handcrafted brickwork together with crystal chandeliers make this a particularly distinctive hotel. Expect excellent hospitality from all the highly trained staff. Located on the southern edge of the town, the hotel also features a well-equipped health facility, plus beauty clinic and extensive banquet and conference facilities. Opus One is the award-winning restaurant for dinner, with all-day dining available in The Atrium Bar.

Rooms 85 (2 fmly) (9 GF) **Facilities** WiFi 🕙 supervised Gym Beauty & massage treatments Salon Sauna Steam room **Conf** Class 300 Board 100 Thtr 500 **Services** Lift **Parking** 216 **Notes** Civ Wed

CLAREMORRIS
County Mayo

Map 1 B4

McWilliam Park Hotel

★★★★ 79% HOTEL

tel: 094 9378000
email: info@mcwilliamparkhotel.ie **web:** www.mcwilliampark.ie
dir: *Take Castlebar/Claremorris exit from N17, straight over rdbt. Hotel on right*

McWilliam Park Hotel is situated on the outskirts of Claremorris town just off the N17 between Galway and Sligo. It is approximately 20 minutes from the Knock Marian Shrine and Ireland West Airport Knock. There are comfortable lounges together with extensive conference, banqueting, leisure, and health facilities. The spacious bedrooms are well appointed, with good communication technology. Food is served all day in Kavanagh's bar, and dinner is available each night in J.G's Restaurant which also serves a popular Sunday lunch. Traditional music, social dancing and other entertainment events are held on a regular basis in the McWilliam Suite.

Rooms 103 (19 fmly) (15 GF) 🐾 **S** €95-€125; **D** €150-€190 (incl. bkfst)*
Facilities Spa STV FTV WiFi ◊ 🕙 Gym 🎵 Xmas New Year **Conf** Class 250 Board 80 Thtr 600 **Services** Lift **Parking** 320 **Notes** LB 🐕 Civ Wed 200

CLIFDEN
County Galway

Map 1 A4

Abbeyglen Castle Hotel

★★★★ 80% 🏨 HOTEL

tel: 095 21201 **Sky Rd**
email: info@abbeyglen.ie **web:** www.abbeyglen.ie
dir: *N59 from Galway towards Clifden. Hotel 1km from Clifden on Sky Rd*

The tranquil setting overlooking the town of Clifden, matched with the dedication of the Hughes's father and son team and their dedicated staff, combine to create a magical atmosphere. Now into its fifth decade in hospitality, Abbeyglen Castle has a well-earned reputation, with many guests returning year after year. Well-appointed rooms and very comfortable suites are available, together with a range of relaxing lounge areas. The restaurant features a daily-changing menu of traditional and more modern dishes. Lobster and oysters are a speciality. Many guests enjoy impromptu sessions around the piano in the bar following dinner. Treatment rooms are available.

Rooms 45 (9 GF) 🐾 **S** €125-€150; **D** €198-€250 (incl. bkfst)* **Facilities** STV WiFi 🏊 Putt green Wellness & relaxation centre 🎵 Xmas New Year **Conf** Class 50 Board 40 Thtr 100 Del from €190 to €220* **Services** Lift **Parking** 50 **Notes** LB 🐕 No children 10yrs Closed 8 Jan - 2 Feb

CLONMEL
County Tipperary

Map 1 C2

Hotel Minella

★★★★ 80% 🏨 HOTEL

tel: 052 6122388
email: frontdesk@hotelminella.ie **web:** www.hotelminella.ie
dir: *S of river in town*

This family-run hotel is set in nine acres of well-tended gardens on the banks of the Suir River. The hotel originates from the 1860s, and the public areas include a cocktail bar and a range of lounges; some of the bedrooms are particularly spacious. The leisure centre in the grounds is noteworthy. Two-bedroom holiday homes are also available.

Rooms 90 (8 fmly) (14 GF) (10 smoking) 🐾 **Facilities** FTV WiFi ◊ 🕙 🏊 Fishing ⛵ Gym Beauty treatment room Sauna Steam room **Conf** Class 300 Board 20 Thtr 500 **Services** Lift **Parking** 100 **Notes** 🐕 Closed 24-28 Dec

REPUBLIC OF IRELAND

REPUBLIC OF IRELAND

CONG
County Mayo

Map 1 B4

Ashford Castle

★★★★★ ◎◎ COUNTRY HOUSE HOTEL

THE RED CARNATION HOTEL COLLECTION

tel: 094 9546003
email: ashford@ashfordcastle.com **web:** www.ashfordcastle.com
dir: In Cross, left at church onto R345 signed Cong. Left at hotel sign, through castle gates

Dating from 1228, this magnificent castle is set in over 350 acres of rolling parklands, occupying a stunning position on the edge of Lough Corrib, and has recently completed a multi-million refurbishment. Bedrooms and suites vary in style, but all benefit from a pleasing combination of character, charm and modern comforts. Dinner in the elegant George V Dining Room is a treat, with creative cookery of seasonal ingredients. Less formal dining is available in The Dungeon and other locations on the estate during peak periods. The hotel offers an extensive range of both indoor and outdoor leisure pursuits including falconry, golf, shooting, fishing, an equestrian centre and lake cruising. A spectacular spa and fitness facility has recently been completed in a striking bronze conservatory overlooking the lake.

Rooms 82 (5 fmly) (22 GF) ♠ **Facilities** Spa STV WiFi ⊾ ⊗ ⌘ 9 ≋ Putt green Fishing Gym Archery Clay pigeon Falconry Horse riding Bike hire Lake cruises Water sports ♫ Xmas New Year **Conf** Class 70 Board 32 Thtr 110 **Services** Lift Air con **Parking** 250 **Notes** Civ Wed 160

The Lodge at Ashford Castle

★★★★ 76% ◎ COUNTRY HOUSE HOTEL

THE RED CARNATION HOTEL COLLECTION

tel: 094 9545400 **Ashford Estate**
email: reception@thelodgeac.com **web:** www.thelodgeac.com
dir: From N84 take first turn for Cong, go through Ashford main gates, first left

This charming hotel, as the name suggests, is in the grounds of Ashford Castle; itself a big 5-star sister hotel. The original part of the hotel is Victorian and was the estate manager's house back in the day. The first floor restaurant (there is also a brasserie on the ground floor) offers stunning views over Lough Corrib as do some bedrooms; these are spacious, well equipped and suit leisure travellers. The team are welcoming and friendly.

Rooms 64 (54 annexe) (20 fmly) (20 GF) ♠ **S** €155–€440; **D** €165–€450 (incl. bkfst)* **Facilities** STV FTV WiFi ⊾ ⌘ 9 ≋ Fishing Gym Beauty treatment room Falconry Archery Equestrian Boating Canoeing Kayaking ♫ New Year Child facilities **Conf** Class 80 Board 80 Thtr 200 **Services** Lift **Parking** 80 **Notes** LB Closed Mon-Wed (Nov-Feb) & 24-25 Dec Civ Wed 186

CORK
County Cork

Map 1 B2

Maryborough Hotel & Spa

★★★★ 80% ◎ HOTEL

tel: 021 4365555 **Maryborough Hill, Douglas**
email: info@maryborough.com **web:** www.maryborough.com
dir: From Jack Lynch Tunnel 2nd exit signed Douglas. Right at 1st rdbt, follow Rochestown signs to Fingerpost rdbt. Left, hotel on left in 0.5m

Dating from 1715, this house was renovated and extended to become a fine hotel with beautifully landscaped grounds featuring rare plant species. There are stylish suites in the main house and the bedrooms in the wing are comfortably furnished. The bar and lounge are very popular for the range of food served throughout the day; Zings restaurant offers a mix of classic and contemporary dishes. There are impressive spa, leisure and conference facilities, plus activities for children.

Rooms 93 (6 fmly) ♠ **Facilities** Spa STV WiFi ⊾ ⊗ supervised Gym Sauna Steam room New Year **Conf** Class 250 Board 60 Thtr 500 **Services** Lift **Parking** 300 **Notes** LB ⊗ Closed 24-26 Dec Civ Wed 100

DELGANY
County Wicklow

Map 1 D3

Glenview Hotel

★★★★ 78% ◎◎ HOTEL

tel: 01 2873399 **Glen O' the Downs**
email: sales@glenviewhotel.com **web:** www.glenviewhotel.com
dir: From Dublin city centre follow signs for N11, past Bray on N11 S'bound, exit 9

This hotel is set in lovely terraced gardens overlooking the Glen o' the Downs. The comfortable bedrooms are spacious, and many enjoy the great views over the valley. The impressive public areas include a conservatory bar, lounge and choice of dining options including the first-floor Woodlands Restaurant where dinner is served. The hotel has an excellent range of leisure and conference facilities. A championship golf course and horse riding can be found nearby.

Rooms 70 (11 fmly) (16 GF) ♠ **S** €110–€150; **D** €130–€190* **Facilities** Spa STV WiFi ⊗ ⌘ Gym Aerobics studio Massage Beauty treatment rooms ♫ Xmas New Year **Conf** Class 80 Board 80 Thtr 230 Del €140* **Services** Lift **Parking** 200 **Notes** ⊗ Civ Wed 180

DINGLE (AN DAINGEAN)
County Kerry

Map 1 A2

Dingle Skellig Hotel & Peninsula Spa

★★★★ 80% ◎ HOTEL

tel: 066 9150200
email: reservations@dingleskellig.com **web:** www.dingleskellig.com
dir: N86 to Dingle, hotel on harbour

This modern hotel, close to the town, overlooks Dingle Bay and has spectacular views from many of the comfortably furnished bedrooms and suites. Public areas offer a spacious bar and lounge and a bright, airy restaurant. There are extensive health and leisure facilities, and many family activities are organised in the Fungi Kids Club.

Rooms 113 (10 fmly) (31 GF) ♠ **Facilities** Spa STV FTV WiFi ⊾ ⊗ supervised Gym ♫ New Year Child facilities **Conf** Class 120 Board 100 Thtr 250 **Services** Lift **Parking** 110 **Notes** ⊗ Closed Jan RS Nov-Dec Civ Wed 250

DONEGAL
County Donegal

Map 1 B5

Harvey's Point Hotel

★★★★ 85% ◉◉ HOTEL

tel: 074 9722208 **Lough Eske**
email: stay@harveyspoint.com **web:** www.harveyspoint.com
dir: *N56 from Donegal, then 1st right Loch Eske/Harvey's Point*

Situated by the shores of Lough Eske, a short drive from Donegal Town, this family-run, welcoming hotel is an oasis of relaxation; comfort and attentive guest care are the norm here. A wide range of particularly spacious suites and bedrooms is on offer, together with smaller Garden Suites in the courtyard annexe. The kitchen brigade maintains consistently high standards in The Lakeside Restaurant at dinner, with less formal dining in the atmospheric Harvey's Bar throughout the day. A very popular Sunday buffet lunch is served weekly, with dinner and cabaret entertainment on selected dates during the summer. Breakfast is also a feature of a stay here. Pet friendly accommodation is available.

Rooms 64 (8 annexe) (17 fmly) (28 GF) ♠ **S** €149–€225; **D** €238–€540 (incl. bkfst) **Facilities** STV FTV WiFi ⇗ Beauty treatment rooms Walking tours ♫ Xmas New Year **Conf** Class 200 Board 50 Thtr 200 Del from €179 to €226* **Services** Lift **Parking** 300 **Notes** Closed Mon & Tue Nov–Mar Civ Wed 250

Mill Park Hotel

★★★★ 76% HOTEL

tel: 074 9722880 **The Mullins, Donegal Town**
email: info@millparkhotel.com **web:** www.millparkhotel.com

The Mill Park is located within walking distance of Donegal town. It is a family-owned and operated property, with a friendly and dedicated team that are sure to please with their natural and warm approach. All of the comfortable rooms and suites have been renovated in stylish contemporary decor schemes. All-day dining is available in the Café Bar, a popular destination with the locals, with more formal evening dining in the 1st floor Granary Restaurant that overlooks the main lobby. There is a spacious leisure centre available on a complimentary basis to resident guests, together with treatments and pampering in the Wellness Centre. The hotel has an excellent reputation for its banqueting and conference facilities.

Rooms 115 (10 fmly) (40 GF) ♠ **Facilities** STV FTV WiFi ⇗ ⊛ supervised Gym New Year **Conf** Class 100 Board 40 Thtr 300 **Services** Lift **Parking** 200 **Notes** ⊗ Closed 24–26 Dec Civ Wed 350

The Red Door Country House

◉ RESTAURANT WITH ROOMS

tel: 074 9360289 **Fahan, Inishowen**
email: info@thereddoor.ie **web:** www.thereddoor.ie
dir: *In Fahan village, church on right, The Red Door signed on left*

Nestled among mature trees and landscaped gardens, this warm and welcoming restaurant with rooms stands proudly on the shore of Lough Swilly, in the historic village of Fahan, just south of Buncrana. Dating from 1789, the original features of the house are cleverly combined with contemporary styling. Bedrooms are cosy and comfortable, each individually decorated and all en suite. The house has a fine reputation in the region for the quality of its restaurant for evening dining, and alfresco lunches. Breakfast is also a highlight and is designed to be lingered over.

Rooms 4

DROGHEDA
County Louth

Map 1 D4

Scholars Townhouse Hotel

★★★ 78% ◉◉ HOTEL

tel: 041 983 5410 **King St**
email: info@scholarshotel.com **web:** www.scholarshotel.com
dir: *From West St, continue to St Laurence's Gate. Before the gate, turn left and carry on to the top of the hill. Hotel on the left*

Located less than ten minutes stroll from the centre of Drogheda, this family-owned and operated boutique property was formerly a monastery. Built in the late 19th century, many of the architectural features of the period have been retained in this sympathetic refurbishment. This is also the case with the bedrooms; having previously been monk's cells, space is rather compromised, but they are all en suite, comfortable, with excellent beds and quality fabrics. Food is an important element of the business enjoyed in this warm and welcoming property. All-day dining is available in the Gastrolounge, where craft beers are a feature. Award-winning evening dining is offered in the restaurant. Breakfast is also noteworthy. The hotel is situated on an elevated site amid well-tended grounds and secure car-parking.

Rooms 16 (1 fmly) **S** €75–€95; **D** €89–€140 (incl. bkfst) **Facilities** FTV WiFi ⇗ New Year **Conf** Class 55 Board 18 Thtr 55 **Services** Lift **Parking** 30 **Notes** ⊗ Closed 25–26 Dec Civ Wed 70

DUBLIN
Dublin

Map 1 D4

The Merrion Hotel

★★★★★ ◉◉◉◉ HOTEL

tel: 01 6030600 **21 Upper Merrion St,**
email: info@merrionhotel.com **web:** www.merrionhotel.com
dir: *At top of Upper Merrion St on left, beyond Government buildings on right*

This terrace of gracious Georgian buildings, reputed to have been the birthplace of the Duke of Wellington, embraces the character of many changes of use over 200 years. Bedrooms and suites are spacious, some in the original house; others are in a modern wing overlooking the gardens. They all offer great comfort and a wide range of extra facilities. The lounges retain the charm and opulence of days gone by, while the Cellar bar area is a popular meeting point. Dining options include The Cellar Restaurant specialising in prime local ingredients and, for that very special occasion, the award-winning Restaurant Patrick Guilbaud is Dublin's finest. "Art Tea" is an afternoon tea experience with a difference, where delightful pastries are inspired by works from the hotel's vast art collection.

Rooms 142 (21 GF) (20 smoking) ♠ **Facilities** Spa STV FTV WiFi ⇗ ⊛ Gym Steam room Relaxation area Xmas New Year **Conf** Class 25 Board 25 Thtr 60 **Services** Lift Air con **Parking** 60 **Notes** LB ⊗ Civ Wed 50

DUBLIN *continued*

INSPECTORS' CHOICE

The Shelbourne Dublin, a Renaissance Hotel

★★★★★ ◉◉ HOTEL

tel: 01 6634500 **27 St Stephen's Green,**
email: rhi.dubbr.reservations@renaissancehotels.com **web:** www.theshelbourne.ie
dir: *M1 to city centre, along Parnell St to O'Connell St towards Trinity College, 3rd right into Kildare St, hotel on left*

This Dublin landmark exudes elegance and a real sense of history, having been established in 1824. The public areas are spacious and offer a range of dining and bar options. There is a selection of bedroom styles and suites available, many with commanding views over St. Stephen's Green. No 27 is a popular bar and lounge for casual dining. The Saddle Room is the main restaurant featuring a steak and seafood menu with a contemporary twist, while afternoon tea is served in the elegant Lord Mayor's Lounge. An extensive leisure and fitness facility is also available.

Rooms 265 (7 smoking) ⚲ **S** fr €220; **D** fr €220 **Facilities** Spa STV FTV WiFi ⬡ ⟳ Gym Relaxtion room Thermal facilities Dance studio Hair salon ♫ Xmas **Conf** Class 252 Board 84 Thtr 450 **Services** Lift Air con **Notes** ⊗ Civ Wed 350

The Westbury

★★★★★ 87% ◉◉ HOTEL

tel: 01 6791122 **Grafton St**
email: westbury@doylecollection.com **web:** www.doylecollection.com
dir: *Adjacent to Grafton St, half way between Trinity College & Stephens Green*

Located just off Grafton Street, Dublin's premier shopping district, this is an oasis of calm; guests are well cared for amid smart, contemporary surroundings. Spacious public areas include the relaxing Gallery Lounge where afternoon tea is popular with shoppers taking a break. Decor is smart, featuring many interesting art pieces and sculpture. Balfes is the hotel's buzzing street-level Brasserie bar, while Wilde - The Restaurant is an award-winning elegant grill with an emphasis on seasonal and artisan fare. Bedrooms and suites come in a range of sizes, all are very comfortably appointed with deep large beds, and warm contemporary decor schemes. The Grafton Suite is an event space, augmented by a range of private dining and meeting rooms. Secure underground parking and a fitness suite are available to resident guests.

Rooms 205 (9 fmly) ⚲ **Facilities** STV FTV WiFi ⬡ Gym **Conf** Class 90 Board 46 Thtr 200 **Services** Lift Air con **Parking** 100 **Notes** ⊗ Civ Wed 120

Castleknock Hotel & Country Club

★★★★ 83% ◉ HOTEL

FBD *Hotels & Resorts*

tel: 01 6406300 **Porterstown Rd, Castleknock**
email: info@chcc.ie **web:** www.castleknockhotel.com
dir: *M50 from airport. Exit at junct 6 signed Navan, Cavan & M3, onto N3, becomes M3. Exit at junct 3. At top of slip road 1st left signed Consilla R121. At T-junct left. 1km to hotel*

This modern hotel is set on a golf course only 15 minutes from Dublin. The bedrooms are very comfortable, with all expected modern guest facilities. The spacious public rooms have an airy feel, and some rooms open onto a terrace that overlooks the golf course. The range of food and beverage outlets includes The Park Room, a steak house, a busy all-day brasserie, and The Lime Tree which is open in the evening. Excellent conference and banqueting facilities are available, together with a popular leisure centre.

Rooms 138 (30 fmly) (5 smoking) ⚲ **Facilities** Spa FTV WiFi ⬡ ⟳ supervised ⚴ 18 Gym Sauna Steam room Children's pool ♫ New Year **Conf** Class 140 Board 80 Thtr 400 **Services** Lift **Parking** 200 **Notes** ⊗ Closed 24-26 Dec Civ Wed 200

Radisson Blu St Helens Hotel

★★★★ 82% ◉ HOTEL

Radisson BLU *HOTELS & RESORTS*

tel: 01 2186000 & 2186011 **Stillorgan Rd**
email: info.dublin@radissonblu.com **web:** www.radissonblu.ie/sthelenshotel-dublin
dir: *On N11 Stillorgan dual carriageway*

An early 18th-century period estate houses this hotel, carefully restored with much of the original decor and architectural features still intact. Just 5 km south of the city, close to UCD, there are over a hundred and fifty suites and rooms from which to choose. They are in a modern block to the side and are all very well appointed, many with garden views. The spectacular Orangerie and the Ballroom are popular venues for all day dining, with the AA-Rosetted Italian restaurant, Talavera, located in the original kitchens open each evening. Le Panto is a wonderfully decorated room available for private dining. Fitness suite and beauty facilities are provided, together with extensive meeting and event spaces for up to 300 delegates.

Rooms 151 (22 fmly) (38 GF) ⚲ **Facilities** STV FTV WiFi ⬡ Gym Beauty salon ♫ Xmas New Year **Conf** Class 150 Board 70 Thtr 350 **Services** Lift Air con **Parking** 220 **Notes** ⊗ Civ Wed 240

Clontarf Castle Hotel

★★★★ 81% ◉◉ HOTEL

tel: 01 8332321 & 8534336 **Castle Av, Clontarf**
email: mlong@clontarfcastle.ie **web:** www.clontarfcastle.ie
dir: *M1 towards centre, left at Whitehall Church, left at T-junct, straight on at lights, right at next lights into Castle Ave, hotel on right at rdbt*

Dating back to the 12th century, this castle retains many historic architectural features which have been combined with contemporary styling in the well-equipped bedrooms. Public areas offer relaxing lounges, and modern cuisine is served in Fahrenheit Grill, Indigo Lounge and Knights Bar. The Great Hall is a versatile venue for banqueting and conferences.

Rooms 111 (7 fmly) (11 GF) ⚲ **S** €199-€379; **D** €209-€399 (incl. bkfst)*
Facilities STV WiFi ⬡ Gym Xmas New Year **Conf** Class 250 Board 90 Thtr 600 **Services** Lift Air con **Parking** 134 **Notes** LB ⊗ Civ Wed 400

Crowne Plaza Hotel Dublin - Blanchardstown

★★★★ 79% ⊛ HOTEL

tel: 01 8977777 **The Blanchardstown Centre**
email: info@cpireland.crowneplaza.com **web:** www.cpireland.ie
dir: *M50 junct 6 Blanchardstown*

This landmark building is on the doorstep of a wide range of shops in Blanchardstown. Bedrooms are stylishly decorated with generously sized beds and well appointed en suites. The Sanctuary Bar serves an international range of informal dishes from lunchtime through to the evening, with Italian specialities (pasta dishes and pizzas) served in the evenings in Forchetta Restaurant. Secure underground parking is provided. There is a floor of dedicated boardrooms and meeting facilities, together with banqueting rooms. Secure underground parking is complimentary to resident guests.

Rooms 188 (60 fmly) ⋔ **Facilities** STV FTV WiFi ⇘ HL Gym Sauna ♫ New Year **Conf** Class 300 Board 300 Thtr 500 **Services** Lift Air con **Parking** 250 **Notes** ⊗ Civ Wed 300

Ashling Hotel, Dublin

★★★★ 78% ⊛ HOTEL

tel: 01 6772324 **Parkgate St**
email: info@ashlinghotel.ie **web:** www.ashlinghotel.ie
dir: *Close to River Liffey, opposite Heuston Station*

Situated on the banks of the River Liffey close to the city centre, railway station and law courts, this hotel is on the tram route and just a five-minute walk from Phoenix Park. The property is appointed to a high standard in a contemporary style. The bedrooms are comfortably furnished; the newer ones are more spacious. Food is available in the Iveagh Bar throughout the day and a popular carvery is served at lunchtime; Chesterfield's Brasserie offers a la carte in the evening. Staff are very friendly and service is attentive and professional. Secure multi-storey parking is available.

Rooms 225 (23 fmly) ⋔ **Facilities** STV WiFi **Conf** Class 110 Board 50 Thtr 220 **Services** Lift **Parking** 100 **Notes** ⊗ Closed 24-26 Dec

The Talbot Hotel Stillorgan

★★★★ 78% ⊛ HOTEL

tel: 01 2001800 **Stillorgan Rd, Stillorgan**
email: info@stillorganpark.com **web:** www.stillorganpark.com
dir: *From N11 follow Wexford signs (pass RTE studios on left) through 5 sets of lights. Hotel on left*

The Talbot Hotel Stillorgan is situated on the southern outskirts of the city, close to UCD, the shopping centre and The RTE Studios. Comfortable public areas include a spacious lobby, The Purple Sage Restaurant and a new brasserie/bar serving quality food throughout the day. Bedrooms and suites come in a range of styles and sizes, all well-appointed and comfortable. There are extensive air-conditioned banqueting and conference facilities, a compact gym and a spa with treatment rooms. Generous parking to the rear, makes public transport by bus to the city centre ideal.

Rooms 150 (8 fmly) (4 smoking) ⋔ **Facilities** Spa STV WiFi ⇘ Gym ♫ New Year **Conf** Class 220 Board 130 Thtr 500 **Services** Lift Air con **Parking** 300 **Notes** ⊗ Closed 25 Dec RS 24 Dec Civ Wed 300

Roganstown Hotel and Country Club

★★★★ 77% ⊛ HOTEL

tel: 01 8433118 **Naul Rd, Sword**
web: www.roganstown.com
dir: *Please call or see website for detailed directions*

Developed from the original family home and farm some 10 years ago, Roganstown is now a quality hotel property surrounded by parkland encompassing a golf course and a well equipped leisure centre and spa. Some rooms are in the original farmhouse, with most in a separate modern block around a well landscaped courtyard. The public areas include a cosy bar that doubles as the golf member's area, a busy O'Callaghan's lounge where food is served throughout the day. Finer evening dining takes place in the award-winning McLaughlin's restaurant where the menu features carefully sourced seasonal ingredients cooked with flair. A multi-use conference and events centre is located on the first floor.

Rooms 52 (4 fmly) (20 GF) ⋔ **S** €99-€359; **D** €119-€379* **Facilities** Spa STV WiFi ⇘ ⊛ ♪ 18 Putt green Gym Aerobics studio **Conf** Class 150 Board 128 Thtr 300 Del from €150 to €279* **Services** Lift **Parking** 370 **Notes** LB ⊗ Civ Wed 240

Red Cow Moran Hotel

★★★★ 76% HOTEL

tel: 01 4593650 **Red Cow Complex, Naas Rd**
email: redcowres@moranhotels.com **web:** www.moranhotels.com
dir: *At junct of M50 & N7 on city side of motorway*

Located just off the M50, this hotel is 20 minutes from the airport and close to the city centre via the Luas light rail system. The dedicated team of staff show a genuine willingness to create a memorable stay. Bedrooms are well equipped and comfortable, and the public areas and conference rooms are spacious. Ample free parking is available.

Rooms 123 (21 fmly) (7 smoking) **Facilities** FTV WiFi ⇘ ♫ New Year **Conf** Class 350 Board 150 Thtr 750 **Services** Lift Air con **Parking** 700 **Notes** ⊗ Closed 24-26 Dec Civ Wed 400

Cassidys Hotel

★★★ 78% HOTEL

tel: 01 8780555 **6-8 Cavendish Row, Upper O'Connell St**
email: stay@cassidyshotel.com **web:** www.cassidyshotel.com
dir: *In city centre at N end of O'Connell St*

This long established family-run hotel is located at the northern end of O'Connell Street, in a terrace of red-brick Georgian townhouses, directly opposite the famed Gate Theatre. The warm and welcoming atmosphere created by the hospitable team in Groome's Bar and Bistro adds to the traditional atmosphere. An all-day menu is served, together with a pre-theatre offering. Bedrooms are individually styled and well appointed; many have air conditioning, with executive rooms in a modern block to the side. A residents' gym, conference facilities and limited parking are all available.

Rooms 113 (26 annexe) (3 fmly) (12 GF) (30 smoking) **Facilities** STV WiFi ⇘ Gym **Conf** Class 45 Board 45 Thtr 80 **Services** Lift **Parking** 8 **Notes** ⊗ Closed 24-26 Dec

DUBLIN continued

Maldron Hotel Newlands Cross

★★★ 74% HOTEL

tel: 01 4640140 & 4123301 **Newlands Cross, Naas Rd**
email: newlands@bewleyshotels.com **web:** www.bewleyshotels.com
dir: M50 junct 9, N7 (Naas road). Hotel near junct of N7 & Belgard Rd

This modern hotel is situated on the N7 and close to the M50 and Luas light rail to the city. Bedrooms are spacious and the pricing structure proves popular with families. The Brasserie restaurant is open throughout the day for casual dining and serves a carvery lunch; more formal meals are served in the evening. The hotel also has a comfortable bar where snacks are available, conference rooms, a gym and ample free parking.

Rooms 297 (182 fmly) (62 GF) ⚘ **Facilities** STV WiFi ⤓ Gym ♫ New Year **Conf** Class 18 Board 14 Thtr 50 **Services** Lift **Parking** 200 **Notes** ⊗ Closed 24-26 Dec

The Marker

Ⓤ

tel: 01 6875100 **Grand Canal Square**
email: info@themarker.ie **web:** www.themarkerhoteldublin.com
dir: M50 junct 1, 2nd exit North Wall Quay. Right onto Commons St, right onto Mayor St, right on Guild St, over SB Bridge, left onto Quays. Right onto Forbes St, right onto Hanover Quay

Currently the rating for this establishment is not confirmed. This may be due to a change of ownership or because it has only recently joined the AA rating scheme. For further details please see the AA website: theAA.com

Rooms 187 ⚘ **S** €199-€450; **D** €199-€450* **Facilities** Spa STV FTV WiFi ⤓ ⓢ Gym Sauna Steam room New Year **Conf** Class 180 Board 68 Thtr 250 **Services** Lift Air con **Parking** 13 **Notes** ⊗ Closed 25-26 Dec Civ Wed 250

Dunboyne Castle Hotel & Spa

Hotel description

Minutes from Dublin and easily accessible from Dublin Airport, the award-winning four star Dunboyne Castle Hotel & Spa is one of Ireland's finest hotels, set on 21 acres of picturesque tree-lined grounds. With modern architectural design complementing the beautiful décor of the original Georgian Manor, Dunboyne Castle Hotel and Spa provides a luxurious escape in the tranquil Dunboyne Village, yet close to all the attractions Dublin city offers. Comprising of 145 en suite rooms, 24 hour reception, The Ivy restaurant which holds 2 AA Rosettes, Seoid Spa and a selection of bars. Conference facilities and complimentary WIFI are both available, along with a laundry service and 24 hour room service. Guests arriving by car can avail of ample free car parking.

Room Description

Designed with space and comfort in mind, the over-sized guest rooms have either garden or forest views providing plenty of natural light. The rooms are en suite with bathtub and shower and include bathrobes and a hairdryer. All of the rooms come with an in-room safe, coffee tray, flat-Interactive Smart TV, fridge and ironing set. Further facilities include direct dial telephone, radio, complimentary Wi-Fi access, king-size bed, air conditioning and heating and some with balcony.

Seoid Spa

The hotel grounds include a hot tub, sauna, steam room, solarium, gym and sun terrace, as well as 18 treatment rooms and a hydrotherapy pool. A wide range of spa and massage treatments are available. Guests looking to play a round of golf have the choice of a number of championship courses nearby.

Meals

This hotel offers a large selection of packages including dinner, bed and breakfast.

Location

This country hotel is set in 21 acres of lush landscape in an ideal location, approximately 16 km from Dublin city centre. The centre of Dunboyne is just 100 metres from the hotel's doors and features restaurants, bars and pubs. Shops can be found 5 km away in Blanchardstown Shopping Centre, and Dublin Airport is 21 km from the accommodation.

How To Get There

On leaving Dublin Airport take the M50 heading south. Continue southbound until reaching the Blanchardstown exit (N3). Continue on this road until signs for Clonee and Dunboyne; take this exit. After driving through Clonee village, reach Dunboyne. Drive through the village, and on exiting the village take a left turn, signposted Maynooth. The hotel is on the left-hand side.

Maynooth Road, Dunboyne, Co. Meath • Tel: +353 1 801 3500 • Fax: +353 1 436 6801
Website: www.dunboynecastlehotel.com • Email: sales@dunboynecastlehotel.com

| **DUBLIN AIRPORT** | Map 1 D4 |

Dublin

Crowne Plaza Dublin Northwood

★★★★ 80% ⊛ HOTEL

CROWNE PLAZA
HOTELS & RESORTS

tel: 01 8628888 **Northwood Park, Santry Demesne, Santry**
email: info@crowneplazadublin.ie **web:** www.cpdublin.crowneplaza.com
dir: *M50 junct 4, left into Northwood Park, 1km, hotel on left*

Located within minutes of Dublin Airport, and served by a complimentary shuttle service, this modern hotel is located in Northwood Park, and benefits from an idyllic location overlooking 85 acres of mature woodlands of the former Santry Demesne. Bedrooms come in a variety of styles, and each is comfortable and well appointed. Guests in executive rooms have the use of a lounge facility where a light breakfast is served. The hotel offers a range of dining options, including full room service and a lobby café. There are extensive conference and event rooms at this property, together with a secure multi-storey car park. Guests also have use of a well equipped gymnasium.

Rooms 204 (17 fmly) (5 smoking) ↟ **S** €99-€380; **D** €99-€380* **Facilities** STV FTV WiFi ⋈ HL Gym Xmas New Year **Conf** Class 450 Board 100 Thtr 850 **Services** Lift Air con **Parking** 400 **Notes** ⊗ Civ Wed 300

Clayton Hotel Dublin Airport

★★★★ 78% HOTEL

tel: 01 8711000 & 8711200 **Baskin Ln**
email: info.dublinairport@claytonhotels.com **web:** www.claytonhotels.com
dir: *At end of M50 N'bound, 2nd exit at rdbt (N3C), left at next rdbt*

Conveniently situated for Dublin Airport, this hotel has the added advantage of secure underground long-term parking with a complimentary shuttle bus to the airport. Bedroom accommodation is spacious, and following major refurbishment the rooms and suites are very comfortable and well appointed. The Playwright is a buzzy, atmospheric lobby lounge serving informal meals throughout the day, with more formal dining in The Restaurant each evening, and a popular Carvery operation at lunchtime. There are a number of meeting and boardrooms available, together with a resident's gym.

Rooms 466 (228 fmly) (36 smoking) ↟ **Facilities** FTV WiFi ⋈ Fitness room Xmas **Conf** Class 150 Board 12 Thtr 300 **Services** Lift **Parking** 1150 **Notes** Civ Wed 250

Find out more about the AA's Hotel rating scheme on page 18

| **DUNBOYNE** | Map 1 D4 |

County Meath

Dunboyne Castle Hotel & Spa

★★★★ 79% ⊛⊛ HOTEL

tel: 01 8013500
email: info@dunboynecastlehotel.com **web:** www.dunboynecastlehotel.com
dir: *In Dunboyne take R157 towards Maynooth. Hotel on left*

Located within walking distance of Dunboyne village, this fine property is a successful combination of the traditional and contemporary. Set on over two acres of mature woodland and well-tended grounds, the original house is home to a number of meeting rooms, with the spacious bedrooms in a modern block to the side. All day dining is offered in the Terrace Lounge, with evening meals and breakfast served in the Ivy Restaurant.

Rooms 145 (37 GF) ↟ **S** €81-€350; **D** €99-€450 (incl. bkfst) **Facilities** Spa STV WiFi ⋈ Gym ♫ Xmas New Year **Conf** Class 200 Board 80 Thtr 450 **Services** Lift Air con **Parking** 380 **Notes** LB ⊗ Civ Wed 250

See advert on opposite page

DUNDALK
County Louth

Map 1 D4

Ballymascanlon House Hotel
★★★★ 80% HOTEL

tel: 042 9358200
email: info@ballymascanlon.com **web:** www.ballymascanlon.com
dir: *M1 junct 18 onto N52 signed Dundalk North/R173 at Carlingford. Exit at Faughart rdbt. 1st left at next rdbt. Hotel in approx 1km on left*

This Victorian mansion is set in 130 acres of woodland and landscaped gardens at the foot of the Cooley Mountains. The elegant house and the modern extension make this a very comfortable hotel that has really stylish bedrooms. Public areas include a spacious restaurant, lounge and bar, together with relaxing reading rooms that retain many original architectural features. There is a well-equipped leisure centre, and The Oak Room banqueting facility proves to be very popular for weddings and family occasions.

Rooms 90 (11 fmly) (5 GF) **Facilities** STV FTV WiFi ♨ supervised ⌀ 18 Putt green Gym Steam room Sauna Plunge pool ♫ Xmas New Year **Conf** Class 220 Board 100 Thtr 400 **Services** Lift **Parking** 250 **Notes** ⊗ Civ Wed 300

DUNFANAGHY
County Donegal

Map 1 C6

Arnolds Hotel
★★★ 78% HOTEL

IRISH COUNTRY HOTELS

tel: 074 9136208
email: enquiries@arnoldshotel.com **web:** www.arnoldshotel.com
dir: *N56 from Letterkenny, hotel on left on entering village*

This family-owned and run hotel, situated in a coastal village overlooking sandy beaches and beautiful scenery, is noted for its warm welcome and good food. The public areas and bedrooms are very comfortable; there is a traditional cosy bar with turf fires, a popular bistro that serves food throughout the day, and Seascapes Restaurant where local seafood features on the menu. A recent addition is a popular Café with an interesting menu, open daily with al fresco dining in the garden, weather permitting. There are stables attached to the hotel, with preferential terms for residents. Photographic and painting breaks are available, as is links-based golf. Live music is a regular evening feature in the bar.

Rooms 30 (10 fmly) **S** €59-€95; **D** €118-€150 (incl. bkfst)* **Facilities** FTV WiFi ♨ ♫ New Year **Parking** 60 **Notes** LB ⊗ RS Nov-Apr Civ Wed 90

DURRUS
County Cork

Map 1 B2

INSPECTORS' CHOICE

Blairscove House & Restaurant
RESTAURANT WITH ROOMS

tel: 027 61127
email: mail@blairscove.ie **web:** www.blairscove.ie
dir: *From Durrus on R591 towards Crookhaven, 2.4km, blue gate on right*

Blairscove comprises four elegant suites located in the courtyard of a Georgian country house outside the pretty village of Durrus near Bantry; each room is individually decorated in a contemporary style and has stunning views over Dunmanus Bay and the mountains. The restaurant is renowned for its wide range of hors d'oeuvres and its open wood-fire grill. The piano-playing and candlelight add to a unique dining experience.

Rooms 4 (4 annexe) (1 fmly)

ENNIS
County Clare

Map 1 B3

Temple Gate Hotel
★★★★ 78% HOTEL

tel: 065 6823300 **The Square**
email: info@templegatehotel.com **web:** www.templegatehotel.com
dir: *Exit N18 onto Tulla Rd for 0.25m, hotel on left*

This smart hotel is owned and run by the Madden family and is located in the centre of the town. It incorporates a 19th-century, Gothic-style Great Hall banqueting room. The public areas are well planned and include a comfortable library lounge, popular traditional pub, and Legends Restaurant. Bedrooms are attractive and well equipped with some executive rooms and suites available.

Rooms 70 (3 fmly) (11 GF) (20 smoking) **Facilities** STV FTV WiFi ♨ ♫ New Year **Conf** Class 100 Board 80 Thtr 250 **Services** Lift **Parking** 52 **Notes** ⊗ Closed 25-26 Dec RS 24 Dec Civ Wed 200

ENNISCRONE (INISHCRONE)
County Sligo

Map 1 B5

INSPECTORS' CHOICE

Waterfront House
RESTAURANT WITH ROOMS

tel: 096 37120 **Sea Front, Cliff Rd**
email: relax@waterfronthouse.ie **web:** www.waterfronthouse.ie

Located less than a five minute stroll from the town, Waterfront House has great views of the beach and Killalla Bay. This is a warm and friendly place, with proprietor Martina and her loyal team going to great lengths to ensure guests enjoy their stay. Bedrooms are spacious and very comfortably appointed. The award-winning restaurant has a well-deserved reputation, where the menu features fresh seafood, but there are plenty of other options available. Breakfast is a particular highlight in terms of range and food quality. This is an ideal location for the golf and surfing facilities in the area, or the famed Warm Seaweed Baths!

Rooms 11

ENNISKERRY
County Wicklow

Map 1 D3

Powerscourt Hotel Resort & Spa
★★★★★ 88% HOTEL

tel: 01 2748888 **Powerscourt Estate**
email: info@powerscourthotel.com **web:** www.powerscourthotel.com
dir: *From Dublin take M50, M11, then N11, follow Enniskerry signs. In Enniskerry left up hill, hotel on right*

This very stylish hotel, built in the Palladian style, has a tranquil setting with stunning views over the gardens and woodlands to the Sugar Loaf. The bedrooms and suites are particularly spacious and well appointed with very impressive bathrooms that have TVs, deep tubs and walk-in showers. The luxuriously appointed public areas are airy and spacious with a variety of food options that includes Sika restaurant, Sugar Loaf Lounge and McGills Bar. The hotel also has a stunning spa, two golf courses, and includes fly fishing and equestrian pursuits among its many leisure facilities.

Rooms 200 (39 GF) **Facilities** Spa STV WiFi ♨ ⌀ 36 Putt green Fishing Gym Cycling Mega chess Fitness classes Jogging trails ♫ Xmas New Year **Conf** Class 240 Board 72 Thtr 500 **Services** Lift Air con **Parking** 384 **Notes** ⊗ Civ Wed 400

GALWAY
County Galway

Map 1 B3

The G Hotel

★★★★★ 87% ⓦⓦ HOTEL

tel: 091 865200 **Wellpark, Dublin Rd**
email: info@theg.ie web: www.theghotel.ie
dir: *Phone for detailed directions*

Designed in association with the acclaimed milliner Philip Treacy who hails from the county, this hotel is the epitome of contemporary styling. The public areas include a series of eclectically furnished Signature Lounges, each with its own identity. The cutting-edge design is also apparent in the bedrooms and suites, which are very comfortable and appointed to a high standard. An interesting selection of menus is on offer at dinner each evening in GiGi's, the atmospheric restaurant, and a very popular all-day menu is served in the lounges, including a range of traditional afternoon tea options. The hotel has a number of boardrooms, an events space and an ESPA spa facility. Underground and valet parking is available.

Rooms 101 (2 fmly) ⋔ **Facilities** Spa STV FTV WiFi HL Gym ♬ New Year **Conf** Class 70 Board 70 Thtr 300 **Services** Lift Air con **Parking** 349 **Notes** LB ⊗ Closed 23-26 Dec Civ Wed 90

Glenlo Abbey Hotel

★★★★ 86% ⓦ HOTEL

tel: 091 526666 **Kentfield, Bushypark**
email: info@glenloabbey.ie web: www.glenloabbeyhotel.ie
dir: *2m from Galway City Centre on N59 to Clifden*

The origins of Glenlo Abbey date from 1740 when the original house was built by the Ffrenchs, a wealthy merchant family. It is set on a spacious estate with wonderful views of Lough Corrib, yet only 5km from Galway City on the road to Connemara. Great care has been taken in the refurbishment of the house, with many of the public rooms retaining their proportions and many original features. Most of the accommodation is in a wing to the rear; suites and bedrooms are finished to a very high level, with some featuring lake or garden views. Guests have two restaurants from which to choose, The Pullman Restaurant aboard The Orient Express is a unique dining experience, made up of two carriages from the iconic railway. Golf is available on the estate, which also features stand-alone banqueting facilities.

Rooms 50 (13 fmly) (16 GF) ⋔ **Facilities** WiFi ↳ ⚓ 9 Putt green Fishing ⚓ 21 bay driving range Falconry 134 acre estate for walking/cycling Xmas New Year **Conf** Class 100 Board 50 Thtr 180 **Services** Lift **Notes** ⊗ Civ Wed 100

Ardilaun Hotel & Leisure Club

★★★★ 81% ⓦ HOTEL

tel: 091 521433 **Taylor's Hill**
email: info@theardilaunhotel.ie web: www.theardilaunhotel.ie
dir: *M6 to Galway City West, then follow signs for N59 Clifden, then N6 towards Salthill*

This very smart country-house style hotel, appointed to a high standard, is located on the outskirts of the city near Salthill and has lovely landscaped gardens and ample car parking. The bedrooms have been thoughtfully appointed and the deluxe rooms and suites are particularly spacious. Public areas include a selection of comfortable lounges, the Camilaun Restaurant overlooking the garden and extensive banqueting and leisure facilities. A recent addition is The Ardilaun Bistro, where the menu features artisan seasonal ingredients in a contemporary and inventive style, with much of the produce coming from the walled garden.

Rooms 125 (17 fmly) (8 GF) (16 smoking) ⋔ **Facilities** Spa STV WiFi ⓣ supervised Gym Beauty treatment & analysis rooms Beauty salon ♬ New Year **Conf** Class 280 Board 100 Thtr 650 **Services** Lift **Parking** 380 **Notes** LB Closed 23 Dec pm & 24-26 Dec Civ Wed 650

Park House Hotel & Restaurant

★★★★ 79% ⓦ HOTEL

tel: 091 564924 **Forster St, Eyre Square**
email: reservations@parkhousehotel.ie web: www.parkhousehotel.ie
dir: *In city centre/Eyre Sq*

Situated just off Eyre Square, this well established hotel offers comfortable facilities to suit business or leisure guests. Public areas and bedrooms are well appointed and attractively decorated in traditional schemes. The Park Restaurant has been a popular spot for the people of Galway for many years with less formal yet quality food is served throughout the day in Boss Doyle's bar. Some resident parking is available to the rear.

Rooms 84 ⋔ **Facilities** STV FTV WiFi ↳ ♬ **Services** Lift Air con **Parking** 48 **Notes** ⊗ Closed 24-26 Dec

Radisson Blu Hotel & Spa, Galway

★★★★ 79% HOTEL

Radisson BLU
HOTELS & RESORTS

tel: 091 538300 & 538200 **Lough Atalia Rd**
email: reservations.galway@radissonblu.com
web: www.radissonblu.com/en/hotel-galway
dir: *Overlooking Galway Bay, close to city centre. Call for directions*

This hotel is situated in a prime position on Lough Atalia's waterfront and overlooks Galway Bay. While car parking is available, its location within minutes of both the train and bus stations makes this an ideal place for a car-free break. The striking interior design and levels of comfort are impressive in the bright and airy public areas. Bedrooms are well equipped and there is an executive floor where further privacy and personal service are guaranteed. Dining options include RAW, a rooftop sushi restaurant, or the very popular Marina Grill on the ground floor, offering a varied menu that is sure to please. A range of event spaces are available, capable of accommodating nearly 1000 delegates.

Rooms 261 (5 fmly) S €130-€450; D €140-€450 (incl. bkfst)* **Facilities** Spa STV FTV WiFi ↳ ⓣ supervised Gym Sauna Steam room Salt spa Aerobics studios Xmas New Year **Conf** Class 650 Board 25 Thtr 990 **Services** Lift Air con **Notes** LB ⊗ Civ Wed

The Harbour Hotel

★★★ 74% HOTEL

tel: 091 894800 **New Dock Rd**
email: stay@harbour.ie web: www.harbour.ie
dir: *Phone for directions*

Within a three minute stroll of the bustling and vibrant Quay Street area of Galway, this hotel really is in the centre of things, yet easily accessed without driving through the city. Rooms come in a variety of sizes, all are modern and comfortable. The Harbour Bar is a popular venue for locals and residents alike, where interesting menus are on offer, featuring house-made dishes with seafood being a particular feature. Limited secure parking at a reduced rate and a fitness suite are also available.

Rooms 96 (5 fmly) S €99-€329; D €99-€329 (incl. bkfst) **Facilities** STV FTV WiFi ↳ Fitness room ♬ Xmas New Year **Conf** Class 60 Board 50 Thtr 150 Del from €185 to €399* **Parking** 70 **Notes** LB ⊗ Civ Wed 130

GLASLOUGH	Map 1 C5
County Monaghan	

The Lodge at Castle Leslie Estate

★★★★ 82% ◉◉ HOTEL

tel: 047 88100
email: info@castleleslie.com **web:** www.castleleslie.com
dir: M1 junct 14, N2 to Monaghan, N12 to R185 to Glaslough

Set in 1,000 acres of rolling countryside dotted with mature woodland, The Lodge is the social hub of the Castle Leslie Estate which has been in the Leslie family since the 1660s. The comfortably furnished bedrooms are in the original hunting lodge and the converted stable block. Resident guests have two dining options - Snaffles Restaurant and Conors Bar. There is a spa known as The Victorian Treatment Rooms, a world class equestrian centre, and a private fishing lake. For those who enjoy country pursuits this hotel is ideal for the many walks and interesting flora and fauna that the area has to offer.

Rooms 29 (2 fmly) (10 GF) ☇ **Facilities** Spa STV FTV WiFi ⌇ Fishing Horse riding Kayaking Clay pigeon Falconry Boating Hot air balloon rides **Conf** Class 25 Board 24 Thtr 35 **Services** Lift **Parking** 100 **Notes** ⊗ Closed 24-27 Dec Civ Wed 40

GOREY	Map 1 D3
County Wexford	

Seafield Golf & Spa Hotel

★★★★ 80% ◉◉ HOTEL

tel: 053 942 4000 **Ballymoney**
email: reservations@seafieldhotel.com **web:** www.seafieldhotel.com
dir: M11 exit 22

This ultra-modern hotel is part of a village style resort that includes an 18-hole championship golf course, courtyard family suites and the award-winning Oceo Spa. Set in 225 acres of parkland with mature trees, river-side walks and access onto Ballymoney Beach, the hotel offers contemporary, spacious bedrooms and suites which have views of either the coastline or the golf course. There are two dining options - fine dining in the restaurant, and a more casual option in the bar or on the terrace.

Rooms 101 ☇ **S** €135-€155; **D** €210-€250 (incl. bkfst)* **Facilities** Spa STV WiFi ⌇ ⌖ ⌁ 18 Putt green Gym Playground ♫ New Year **Conf** Class 220 Board 40 Thtr 300 Del from €200 to €250* **Services** Lift **Parking** 200 **Notes** LB ⊗ Civ Wed 280

Amber Springs Hotel

★★★★ 80% ◉ HOTEL

tel: 053 9484000 **Wexford Rd**
email: info@ambersprings.ie **web:** www.ambersspringshotel.ie
dir: 500mtrs from Gorey by-pass at junct 23

This modern hotel, on the Wexford road, is within walking distance of the town. It enjoys a well-earned reputation for families with its dedicated facilities. Bedrooms are spacious and very comfortable, and guests have full use of the leisure facilities. All day dining is offered in Brooks Bar & Grill, with an adult-only space at dinner in the award-winning Farm Steakhouse. Much of the food produce is sourced from the proprietor's farm in the region, specialising in Angus Beef. This is a popular Wedding destination, and has a number of conference spaces. Ample parking is available to the rear.

Rooms 80 (34 fmly) (24 GF) ☇ **Facilities** Spa STV WiFi ⌇ ⌖ supervised Gym Mini golf Petting farm Kids train ♫ New Year **Conf** Class 450 Board 30 Thtr 700 **Services** Lift Air con **Parking** 178 **Notes** ⊗ Closed 25-26 Dec Civ Wed 700

Ashdown Park Hotel

★★★★ 77% ◉ HOTEL

tel: 053 9480500 **The Coach Rd**
email: info@ashdownparkhotel.com **web:** www.ashdownparkhotel.com
dir: N11 junct 22, on approaching Gorey, 1st left (before railway bridge), hotel on left

Situated on an elevated position overlooking the town, this modern hotel has excellent health, leisure and banqueting facilities. There are comfortable lounge areas and two dining options - Ivy, a popular carvery bar, and The Rowan Tree, the first-floor fine dining restaurant open in the evenings. Bedrooms are available in a number of styles; all are spacious and well equipped. Close to a number of golf courses, this property is popular with golfers, and also with families as it is near the beaches.

Rooms 79 (17 fmly) (22 GF) ☇ **Facilities** Spa FTV WiFi ⌇ ⌖ supervised Gym Leisure centre Massage rooms ♫ New Year **Conf** Class 315 Board 100 Thtr 800 **Services** Lift **Parking** 150 **Notes** ⊗ Closed 25 Dec Civ Wed 300

INSPECTORS' CHOICE

Marlfield House Hotel

★★★ ◉◉ COUNTRY HOUSE HOTEL

tel: 053 9421124
email: info@marlfieldhouse.ie **web:** www.marlfieldhouse.com
dir: N11 junct 23, follow signs for Courtown. At Courtown Rd rdbt left for Gorey. Hotel 1m on left

This Regency-style building has been gracefully extended and developed into an excellent hotel. An atmosphere of elegance and luxury permeates every corner of the house, underpinned by truly friendly and professional service led by the Bowe family who are always in evidence. The bedrooms are decorated in keeping with the style of the house, with some really spacious rooms and suites on the ground floor. Dinner in the restaurant is always a highlight of a stay at Marlfield.

Rooms 18 (3 fmly) (6 GF) ☇ **Facilities** STV FTV WiFi ⌇ ⌖ ⌁ Beauty treatment room **Conf** Board 24 Thtr 60 **Parking** 100 **Notes** LB Closed 2 Jan-28 Feb RS Nov-Dec & Mar-Apr Civ Wed 120

KENMARE
County Kerry
Map 1 B2

INSPECTORS' CHOICE

Sheen Falls Lodge

★★★★★ ◉◉ COUNTRY HOUSE HOTEL

tel: 064 6641600
email: info@sheenfallslodge.ie **web:** www.sheenfallslodge.ie
dir: From Kenmare take N71 to Glengarriff over suspension bridge, take 1st left

This former fishing lodge has been developed into a beautiful hotel with a friendly team of professional staff. The cascading Sheen Falls are floodlit at night, forming a romantic backdrop to award-winning cuisine in La Cascade Restaurant. Less formal dining is available in Oscar's Bistro, and the Sun Lounge serves refreshments and light snacks throughout the day. The bedrooms are very comfortably appointed; many of the suites are particularly spacious. The leisure centre and beauty therapy facilities offer a number of exclusive treatments, and outdoor pursuits include walking, fishing, tennis, horse riding and clay pigeon shooting.

Rooms 66 (14 fmly) (14 GF) ✿ **S** €150-€295; **D** €180-€325 (incl. bkfst)⁴
Facilities Spa STV WiFi ☜ ⌣ Fishing ⌣ Gym Table tennis Steam room Clay pigeon shooting Cycling Vintage car rides Library ♫ Xmas New Year Child facilities **Conf** Class 65 Board 50 Thtr 120 **Services** Lift **Parking** 76 **Notes** ⊗ Closed 30 Nov-19 Dec & 2 Jan-1 Feb RS 24-27 Dec Civ Wed 150

Park Hotel Kenmare

★★★★ 86% ◉◉ HOTEL

tel: 064 6641200
email: info@parkkenmare.com **web:** www.parkkenmare.com
dir: On R569 beside golf course at top of town

This hotel is a luxurious house, situated on the famous Ring of Kerry, that has been welcoming guests for over 100 years. Warm hospitality and professional service come naturally to all the team, who endeavour to make guests feel pampered. All the suites and bedrooms are spacious and very well appointed, with either garden or sea views. The elegant restaurant serves very good food, much of it locally sourced, together with fine wines. Samas, a luxury treatment spa is newly opened.

Rooms 46 (3 fmly) ✿ **Facilities** Spa FTV WiFi ☜ ⌣ Putt green ⌣ Gym ♫ Xmas New Year **Conf** Class 40 Board 28 Thtr 60 **Services** Lift **Parking** 60 **Notes** Closed 1-22 Dec & 4 Jan-5 Mar Civ Wed 120

KILKENNY
County Kilkenny
Map 1 C3

Lyrath Estate

★★★★ 86% ◉ HOTEL

tel: 056 7760088 & 77605810 **Old Dublin Rd**
email: reservations@lyrath.com **web:** www.lyrath.com
dir: M9 junct 8 signed Kilkenny. 1st exit at both 1st & 2nd rdbts, hotel 1km

Located a short drive from Kilkenny City, and set in 170 acres of mature parkland and lakeland, this 17th-century house has been carefully restored and greatly expanded to one of the country's largest convention centres, with a myriad of event spaces and public areas. The property is very popular for weddings, held in the public rooms of the main house, some of which retain many of the original architectural features. Bedrooms are predominantly in a separate block, all well-appointed and en suite. Some are available in the original house. There are great dining options to be savoured here, from La Perla the more traditional restaurant, to Yindees a very popular oriental option, and Tuppers bar for all-day dining. Guests have complimentary access to the health club and gym, with spa treatments and a thermal suite available at a supplement

Rooms 139 (24 fmly) (31 GF) ✿ **Facilities** Spa FTV WiFi ☜ ☽ Fishing Gym Private cinema Snooker room Outdoor hydrotherapy pool ♫ New Year **Conf** Class 750 Board 75 Thtr 1500 **Services** Lift Air con **Parking** 420 **Notes** ⊗ Closed 20-27 Dec Civ Wed 100

Langton House Hotel

★★★★ 76% HOTEL

tel: 056 7765133 & 7721728 **69 John St**
email: reservations@langtons.ie **web:** www.langtons.ie
dir: N9 & N10 from Dublin, follow city centre signs on outskirts of Kilkenny, left to Langtons. Hotel 500mtrs on left after lights

This hotel, situated in the heart of the medieval city of Kilkenny, has long had a well-deserved reputation for its genuine hospitality as a vibrant entertainment venue with many strings to its bow. There is a nightclub with free access for guests and up to seven bars to choose from. The most recent addition is the much talked-about Set Theatre, where leading performers take to the stage. There is a range of bedroom options, many in the garden annexe; all are very comfortable and smartly decorated, with the junior suites in the main house being particularly well appointed. Eating options include The Langton, a busy restaurant serving dinner, and the more casual, all-day '67', a lively bar popular with visitors and locals that features live music groups most evenings. The elegant Tea Room is open throughout the day.

Rooms 34 (16 annexe) (4 fmly) (8 GF) (22 smoking) ✿ **Facilities** STV FTV WiFi ♫ New Year **Conf** Class 250 Board 30 Thtr 400 **Services** Air con **Parking** 60 **Notes** ⊗ Closed 25 Dec Civ Wed 252

KILLARNEY
County Kerry — Map 1 B2

The Brehon Killarney
★★★★ 80% @ HOTEL

tel: 0203 5645225 **Muckross Rd**
web: www.thebrehon.com
dir: *1m from Killarney on N71*

This is a spectacular hotel close to Killarney National Park and a 20-minute walk from the town. Public areas are particularly spacious with comfortable mezzanine lounge areas, and a bustling bar where a popular all-day-dining menu is on offer. Danú is the bright and airy award-winning restaurant where breakfast and dinner are served, from an interesting well-compiled menu. The spacious bedrooms and suites are well equipped, many with great views towards the mountains. The hotel offers a specialist Thai spa experience and extensive conference facilities. Other leisure facilities are on offer at their nearby sister hotel.

Rooms 123 (123 fmly) **Facilities** STV FTV WiFi ⏰ **Services** Lift Air con

The Lake Hotel
★★★★ 79% @@ HOTEL

tel: 064 6631035 **Lake Shore, Muckross Rd**
email: info@lakehotel.com **web:** www.lakehotel.com
dir: *N22 to Killarney. Hotel 2km from town on Muckross Rd*

Enjoying a delightful location on the shores of Killarney's lake, this hotel is run by a second generation of the Huggard family together with a dedicated and friendly team. There is a relaxed atmosphere, with log fires and stunning views from the lounges and restaurant. Guests could be lucky enough to see a herd of red deer wander by. The smartly furnished bedrooms have either lake or woodland views; some have balconies and four-poster beds. The spa offers good facilities, and there are cycle paths and lovely walks to enjoy.

Rooms 130 (6 fmly) (23 GF) ⏰ **S** €75-€300; **D** €110-€350 (incl. bkfst)*
Facilities STV FTV WiFi ⏰ ⏰ Fishing ⏰ Gym Beauty treatment room Sauna Steam room ⏰ **Conf** Class 60 Board 40 Thtr 80 Del from €230 to €250* **Services** Lift **Parking** 140 **Notes** LB ⏰ Closed Dec-Jan Civ Wed 60

Castlerosse Hotel & Holiday Homes
★★★ 79% HOTEL

tel: 064 6631144 **Lakes of Killarney**
email: res@castlerosse.ie **web:** www.castlerosse.ie
dir: *From Killarney take R562 signed Killorglin & The Ring of Kerry. Hotel 2.5km from town on left*

This hotel is situated on 6,000 acres overlooking the Lakes of Killarney with the Magillycuddy Mountains as a backdrop. At times guests may be able to spot deer in Killarney National Park. Bedrooms and junior suites are well appointed and comfortable. There is live entertainment most nights in Mulligan's pub. Leisure facilities include a 9-hole parkland golf course, tennis courts, a leisure centre and treatment rooms.

Rooms 120 (27 fmly) (116 GF) ⏰ **S** €75-€95; **D** €100-€180 (incl. bkfst)
Facilities STV FTV WiFi ⏰ ⏰ supervised ⏰ 9 ⏰ Putt green Gym Beauty treatment rooms Cycling Golf & horse riding arranged ⏰ **Conf** Class 100 Board 40 Thtr 200 **Services** Lift **Parking** 100 **Notes** ⏰ Closed Nov-Mar Civ Wed 80

KILLINEY
County Dublin — Map 1 D4

Fitzpatrick Castle Hotel
★★★★ 81% @ HOTEL

tel: 01 2305400 & 2305556
email: reservations@fitzpatricks.com **web:** www.fitzpatrickcastle.com
dir: *From Dun Laoghaire port turn left, on coast road right at lights, left at next lights. Follow to Dalkey, right at Ivory Pub, immediate left, up hill, hotel at top*

This family-owned and operated 18th-century castle is situated in lovely gardens with mature trees and spectacular views over Dublin Bay. The original castle rooms are appointed to a high standard and have four-poster beds, while the rooms in modern wings are spacious, some with balconies. Spacious lounges are comfortably furnished, with extensive leisure and events spaces. The Grill at the Castle is a warm and relaxing evening dining venue, very popular with the local population for early evening dining and family celebrations. The original dungeon makes for an atmospheric pre-dinner location, or perhaps a nightcap. The Lobby lounge serves afternoon tea and informal meals during the day. Spacious car parking, with a coach service direct to the airport is available.

Rooms 113 (36 fmly) ⏰ **S** €99-€269; **D** €109-€309 (incl. bkfst)* **Facilities** STV WiFi ⏰ supervised Gym Beauty/hairdressing salon Sauna Steam room Fitness centre ⏰ Xmas New Year **Conf** Class 250 Board 80 Thtr 500 Del from €170 to €190* **Services** Lift **Parking** 300 **Notes** LB ⏰ RS 25 Dec Civ Wed 400

KILTIMAGH
County Mayo — Map 1 B4

Park Hotel Kiltimagh
★★★ 77% HOTEL

IRISH COUNTRY HOTELS

tel: 094 9374922 **Swinford Rd**
email: info@parkhotelmayo.com **web:** www.parkhotelmayo.com
dir: *N17 onto R322 or R323 (or N60 onto R320) to Kiltimagh*

This smart hotel overlooks the Wetlands Wildlife Park and is within walking distance of Kiltimagh, and just 15 minutes from Ireland West Knock Airport and Knock Marian Shrine. The spacious bedrooms are well appointed. Public areas are attractively decorated and include comfortable lounges, Café Bar, Park Restaurant and banqueting facilities. The Aroma Beauty Spa offers a range of treatments and there is also a fitness centre and steam room. A shuttle coach service operates to the airport, and for guests using the airport, parking can be arranged at the hotel.

Rooms 46 (40 fmly) **Facilities** Spa WiFi ⏰ Gym New Year **Conf** Class 120 Board 60 Thtr 450 **Services** Lift **Parking** 300 **Notes** Civ Wed 350

KINSALE — County Cork — Map 1 B2

The White House

◎ RESTAURANT WITH ROOMS

tel: 021 4772125 **Pearse St, The Glen**
email: info@whitehouse-kinsale.ie **web:** www.whitehouse-kinsale.ie
dir: *In town centre*

Centrally located among the narrow, twisting streets of the charming maritime town of Kinsale, this restaurant with rooms dates from 1850. It is a welcoming hostelry with smart, comfortably appointed contemporary bedrooms. The atmospheric bar and bistro are open for lunch and dinner, with Restaurant d'Antibes also open during the evenings. The varied menu features local fish and beef. The courtyard at the rear makes a perfect setting in summer and there is regular entertainment in the bar.

Rooms 10 (2 fmly)

LEIGHLINBRIDGE — County Carlow — Map 1 C3

Lord Bagenal Inn

★★★★ 76% ◎ HOTEL

tel: 059 9774000 **Main St**
email: info@lordbagenal.com **web:** www.lordbagenal.com
dir: *Just off M9 junct 6 signed Leighlinbridge. On entering N9 about 1km turn left onto R705, hotel 1km on right*

On the banks of the River Barrow in a picturesque village, this attractive inn has its own private marina. Bedrooms are comfortable and well-equipped and the traditional bar is a cluster of cosy rooms with log fires. Fine dining is available in the restaurant. The Lord Bagenal is proud to showcase paintings and sculptures by a wide range of contemporary artists. There is also original porcelain from the Ming and Qing periods on display.

Rooms 39 (3 fmly) (3 GF) ⋒ **S** €70-€100; **D** €95-€140 (incl. bkfst)* **Facilities** STV WiFi ⬎ Guided walks Canoeing Kayaking Cycling ♫ **Conf** Class 80 Board 50 Thtr 450 **Services** Lift **Parking** 120 **Notes** LB ⊗ Closed 25-26 Dec Civ Wed 250

LETTERKENNY — County Donegal — Map 1 C5

Radisson Blu Hotel Letterkenny

★★★★ 79% ◎ HOTEL

tel: 074 9194444 **Paddy Harte Rd**
email: info.letterkenny@radissonblu.com **web:** www.radissonblu.ie/hotel-letterkenny
dir: *N14 into Letterkenny. At Polestar Rdbt take 1st exit, to hotel*

Letterkenny is an ideal base for visiting the many peninsulas of County Donegal. Within walking distance of the town and the retail parks, this hotel offers a range of very comfortable rooms, with all the facilities that today's traveller expects. Guests can dine throughout the day in the popular Port Bar & Grill, or, in the evening, enjoy seafood delights and other good dishes in Brasserie TriBeCa. Well-equipped meeting rooms are available, together with a large conference and banqueting hall. The leisure facilities are complimentary to residents.

Rooms 114 (5 fmly) ⋒ **Facilities** STV WiFi ⬎ ③ Gym Sauna Steam room Sunbed Olympic weights room Xmas New Year **Conf** Class 270 Board 80 Thtr 600 **Services** Lift **Parking** 150 **Notes** ⊗ Civ Wed 200

Downings Bay Hotel

★★★ 75% HOTEL

tel: 074 9155586 & 9155770 **Downings**
email: info@downingsbayhotel.com **web:** www.downingsbayhotel.com
dir: *23m N of Letterkenny on R245. Hotel in village centre*

This friendly family-run hotel is situated on Sheephaven Bay in the picturesque village of Downings. There is a cosy lounge; JC's traditional style bar where an extensive menu is available all day, and The Haven Restaurant which opens for dinner. The bedroom accommodation is spacious and all rooms are comfortable and well appointed. A popular location for families and within easy reach of a number of golf courses, this property hosts occasional musical events, and there is a nightclub open at weekends. Guests have complimentary use of the local leisure centre.

Rooms 40 (8 fmly) (4 smoking) ⋒ **S** €50-€85; **D** €90-€130 (incl. bkfst)* **Facilities** WiFi ⬎ ③ supervised Gym Sauna Steam room Indoor adventure play area ♫ New Year Child facilities **Conf** Class 175 Board 50 Thtr 350 Del from €80 to €125* **Services** Lift Air con **Parking** 40 **Notes** ⊗ Closed 24-26 Dec RS Nov-Mar Civ Wed 80

LIMERICK — County Limerick — Map 1 B3

Limerick Strand Hotel

★★★★ 80% ◎ HOTEL

tel: 061 421800 **Ennis Rd**
email: info@strandlimerick.ie **web:** www.strandlimerick.ie
dir: *From Shannon/Galway follow N18 to Limerick. At Coonagh rdbt follow Ennis Rd into city centre. Hotel on right on banks of river*

This hotel enjoys stunning views over the River Shannon, and all bedrooms are spacious and fitted to a high standard. The public areas make the most of the views, with meeting rooms on the penthouse level. All-day dining is available in the bar, with innovative evening meals served in the River Restaurant. Secure parking is available at a reduced rate for residents.

Rooms 184 (13 fmly) ⋒ **Facilities** Spa STV WiFi ⬎ ③ supervised Gym ♫ Xmas New Year **Conf** Class 400 Board 50 Thtr 600 **Services** Lift Air con **Parking** 203 **Notes** ⊗ Civ Wed 450

Radisson Blu Hotel & Spa Limerick

★★★★ 78% HOTEL

tel: 061 456200 **Ennis Rd**
email: info.limerick@radissonblu.com **web:** www.radissonblu.com/en/hotel-limerick
dir: *On N18 Ennis Rd, close to Limerick city centre*

Situated between Limerick City and Shannon International Airport, this smart hotel is set in 20 acres of parkland and has comfortable lounge areas and a choice of dining options; the contemporary styled Porters Restaurant offers fine dining, while more casual eating can be enjoyed in the Quench Bar. Bedrooms are comfortable, spacious and very well appointed. Guests have complimentary use of the Thermal Suite and outdoor Canadian hot tub in the Rain Spa. There are extensive leisure and corporate facilities, including seven meeting rooms with capacity up to 800 delegates.

Rooms 154 (20 fmly) **Facilities** Spa STV WiFi ③ ⬎ Gym Hair salon Cold fog & tropical rain showers Laconium Steam room Elite training

LISDOONVARNA
County Clare

Map 1 B3

Sheedy's Country House Hotel

★★★ 78% ◉◉ HOTEL

tel: 065 7074026
email: info@sheedys.com **web:** www.sheedys.com
dir: *200mtrs from The Square in town centre*

Dating in part from the 17th century and set in an unrivalled town centre location on the edge of The Burren, this house is full of character and has an intimate atmosphere. Fine cuisine can be enjoyed in the contemporary restaurant, and the bedrooms are spacious and well appointed. Sheedys makes an ideal base for touring as it is close to Doolin, Lahinch Golf Course, and the Cliffs of Moher.

Rooms 11 (1 fmly) (5 GF) ☎ **S** €80-€120; **D** €110-€170 (incl. bkfst)* **Facilities** STV FTV WiFi ☇ **Parking** 20 **Notes** ⊗ Closed mid Oct-Apr

Wild Honey Inn

◉◉ RESTAURANT WITH ROOMS

tel: 065 7074300 **Kincora**
email: info@wildhoneyinn.com **web:** www.wildhoneyinn.com
dir: *N18 from Ennis to Ennistymon. Continue through Ennistymon towards Lisdoonvarna, located on the right at edge of town*

Set in a former hotel dating from the 1860s, when the town prospered as a spa, the Wild Honey Inn has created a solid reputation for its two AA Rosette award-winning cuisine. 'Modern bistro style' is Aidan McGrath's description of the food on offer, served in the comfortable atmospheric bar at both lunch and dinner. Great attention is paid to the provenance of the ingredients, most of which are organic and sourced as close to County Clare as possible. Reservations are not taken. Bedrooms come in a number of styles, and the garden rooms have private patios. Residents have the use of a relaxing lounge, filled with reading material, not surprisingly featuring food and cookery. Breakfast is also a highlight of any visit, with a range of interesting options.

Rooms 14

LUCAN
County Dublin

Map 1 D4

Lucan Spa Hotel

★★★ 70% HOTEL

tel: 01 628 0494 & 630 2300
email: info@lucanspahotel.ie **web:** www.lucanspahotel.ie
dir: *At N4 junct 4a, approx 11km from city centre*

Set in its own grounds and 20 minutes from Dublin Airport, at the start of the M7 the main artery to the West of Ireland, the Lucan Spa is a lovely Georgian house with modern extensions. Originally built to accommodate guests taking the waters at the former Spa, the building retains amny of the architectural features of the period. Bedrooms vary in size but are well equipped. There are two dining options; dinner is served in Honora D Restaurant, and The Ballyneety is for more casual dining. The event space has a good reputation for weddings and conference business.

Rooms 71 (15 fmly) (9 GF) ☎ **S** €55-€109; **D** €69-€198 (incl. bkfst) **Facilities** STV FTV WiFi ☇ Access to Lucan Golf Club opp hotel **Conf** Class 250 Board 80 Thtr 600 Del from €79.50 to €139 **Services** Lift Air con **Parking** 200 **Notes** ⊗ Closed 24-26 Dec Civ Wed 250

MACREDDIN
County Wicklow

Map 1 D3

BrookLodge Hotel & Macreddin Village

★★★★ 82% ◉◉ HOTEL

tel: 0402 36444
email: info@brooklodge.com **web:** www.brooklodge.com
dir: *N11 to Rathnew, R752 to Rathdrum, R753 to Aughrim, follow signs to Macreddin Village*

BrookLodge is a luxurious country-house hotel in a village-style setting which includes an 18-hole golf course, a country pub, a café and food shop. There is a choice of dining options - the award-winning Strawberry Tree Restaurant specialising in organic and wild foods, and the more casual Italian restaurant offering Southern Italian cuisine. Macreddin Village has eighty six bedrooms, many of which feature four-poster or sleigh beds with window seats from which you can admire the stunning views. There are also bedrooms in BrookHall, tailored for guests attending weddings and conferences. The Wells Spa offers extensive treatments and leisure facilities, and there are many outdoor activities including horse riding and mapped walks affording you the opportunity to enjoy the Wicklow countryside.

Rooms 86 (32 annexe) (27 fmly) (4 GF) ☎ **Facilities** Spa STV FTV WiFi ☇ ⊗ ⊰ Putt green Gym Archery Clay pigeon shooting Off road driving Cycling Walking Horse riding New Year **Conf** Class 170 Board 150 Thtr 300 **Services** Lift Air con **Parking** 200 **Notes** Closed 24-25 Dec Civ Wed 200

MALLOW
County Cork   Map 1 B2

Springfort Hall Country House Hotel
★★★ 77% ⊛ HOTEL

tel: 022 21278
email: stay@springfort-hall.com **web:** www.springfort-hall.com
dir: N20 onto R581 at Two Pot House, hotel 500mtrs on right

This 18th-century country manor is tucked away amid tranquil woodlands located just six kilometres from Mallow. There is an attractive oval dining room, a cosy drawing room and lounge bar where bistro-style food is served. The spacious bedrooms are comfortably furnished. There are extensive banqueting and conference facilities, and local amenities include championship golf courses, fishing on the Blackwater and Ballyhass Lakes, and horseracing at Cork.

Rooms 49 (5 fmly) (17 GF) ⟨ **S** €60-€100; **D** €80-€180 (incl. bkfst) **Facilities** STV FTV WiFi ⟨ ♫ **Conf** Class 180 Board 50 Thtr 360 **Parking** 200 **Notes** ⊗ Closed 23-26 Dec Civ Wed 300

MAYNOOTH
County Kildare   Map 1 D4

Carton House Hotel Golf & Spa
★★★★ 79% HOTEL

tel: 01 5052000
email: sales@cartonhouse.com **web:** www.cartonhouse.com
dir: From Dublin Airport follow M50, N4 then M4 towards Sligo. At junct 6 take R449 to Leixlip. Continue to R148. Located 4m outside Maynooth

The Carton House dates from 1739 and many of the features of that period are reflected in the careful renovation of the fine public rooms and event spaces. While some suites of the hotel are also in the original house, most of the bedrooms are in a modern block to the side. They are all spacious and comfortable, fitted out to a high standard. There are a number of dining options on the estate, including The Coach House in the golf club and The Linden Tree. Set in over a thousand acres, there are plenty of walks and cycle paths to be enjoyed. The property has a strong reputation for its many sport training facilities and Spa treatment rooms.

Rooms 165 (12 fmly) (46 GF) ⟨ **Facilities** Spa STV WiFi ⟨ ⊗ ⅃ 36 ⅌ Putt green Fishing Gym Sauna Steam room Xmas New Year **Conf** Class 280 Board 90 Thtr 500 **Services** Lift **Parking** 500 **Notes** ⊗ Civ Wed 200

MOVILLE
County Donegal   Map 1 C6

Redcastle Hotel, Golf & Spa Resort
★★★★ 79% ⊛ HOTEL

tel: 074 9385555 **Inishowen Peninsula**
email: info@redcastlehotel.com **web:** www.redcastlehotel.com
dir: On R238 between Derry & Greencastle

Perched beside the sea in mature parkland just outside Redcastle, this hotel has an enviable position on the Inishowen Peninsula with great views over Lough Foyle. It offers spacious, well-equipped bedrooms; some on the ground floor and some with balconies. The public areas include a range of relaxing lounges with an atmospheric bar where food is served throughout the day, and a large terrace for relaxing when the weather permits. The Edge Restaurant is right on the water's edge, and offers a well thought out menu with interesting options. There is a conference centre and an extensive leisure club offering spa treatments. The hotel has its own private 9-hole golf course, with sea fishing available from the shore.

Rooms 93 (17 fmly) (16 GF) (8 smoking) ⟨ **Facilities** Spa STV FTV WiFi ⟨ ⊗ ⅃ 9 Putt green Fishing ⅃ Gym ♫ New Year **Conf** Class 150 Board 50 Thtr 300 Del from €99 to €169* **Services** Lift **Parking** 200 **Notes** ⊗ Civ Wed 250

MULRANY
County Mayo   Map 1 A4

Mulranny Park Hotel
★★★★ 79% ⊛⊛ HOTEL

tel: 098 36000
email: info@mulrannyparkhotel.ie **web:** www.mulrannyparkhotel.ie
dir: R311 from Castlebar to Newport onto N59. Hotel on right

Set on an elevated site, this property has commanding views over Clew Bay. Originally a railway hotel dating from the late 1800s, it has a range of smart public rooms that retain many of the period features. Bedrooms vary in size but are comfortable and decorated in a contemporary style. Dinner in the Nephin Restaurant is a highlight of any stay, with casual dining available throughout the day in the Waterfront Bar. A programme of activities is offered weekly for resident guests, in addition to a well appointed leisure club.

Rooms 60 (25 fmly) ⟨ **Facilities** WiFi ⟨ ⊗ supervised Gym Steam room Health & beauty Hairdressing Cycling ⅃ New Year **Conf** Class 140 Board 50 Thtr 400 **Services** Lift **Parking** 200 **Notes** ⊗ Closed 4-21 Jan Civ Wed 150

NAVAN
County Meath   Map 1 D4

Bellinter House
★★★★ 74% ⊛⊛ HOTEL

tel: 046 9030900
web: www.bellinterhouse.com
dir: N3 towards Navan, left at Tara Na Ri pub, travel 5 mins, hotel on right

Set in rolling parkland, this Palladian-style Georgian house dates from 1749 and retains much of the scale and architectural features of the period. The decor however is very contemporary in the public areas where comfort and relaxation is key. Bedrooms are mainly set around two courtyards and feature a minimalist approach to decoration, with lots of timber and white surfaces. Dinner in Eden Restaurant in the vaulted basement is a delight, with more casual fare served in the bar throughout the day. Spa treatments are available in The Bathhouse, with weddings and other events in the Refectory.

Rooms 34 (5 fmly) (12 GF) **Facilities** Spa STV FTV WiFi Fishing Steam room Sauna **Conf** Class 30 Board 24 Thtr 50 **Services** Lift **Parking** 80 **Notes** ⊗ Civ Wed 200

Food Allergies

A recent EU regulation makes it easier for those with food allergies to choose safer foods when eating out. 14 allergens are listed in the regulation, and pubs and restaurants must now list any of these used in the dishes they offer.

NEWMARKET-ON-FERGUS
County Clare

Map 1 B3

INSPECTORS' CHOICE

Dromoland Castle Hotel
★★★★★ ◉◉ HOTEL

tel: 061 368144
email: sales@dromoland.ie **web:** www.dromoland.ie
dir: *N18 to Ennis/Galway from Shannon for 8km to 'Dromoland Interchange' signed Quin. Take slip road left, 4th exit at 1st rdbt, 2nd exit at 2nd rdbt. Hotel 500mtrs on left*

Dromoland Castle, dating from the early 18th century, stands on a 375-acre estate and offers extensive indoor leisure activities and outdoor pursuits. The professional team are wholly committed to caring for guests, in a warm and informal manner. The thoughtfully equipped bedrooms and suites vary in style, but they all provide excellent levels of comfort. The magnificent public rooms, warmed by log fires, are no less impressive. The hotel has several dining options; the elegant fine-dining Earl of Thomond Restaurant, where award-winning cuisine is available together with the less formal Fig Tree in the golf clubhouse, and The Gallery, which offers a menu suitable for all day dining.

Rooms 98 (20 fmly) ⚓ **S** €240-€610; **D** €240-€770 (incl. bkfst)* **Facilities Spa** STV WiFi ⓑ ⊙ supervised ⚓ 18 ⚘ Putt green Fishing Gym Archery Clay shooting Mountain bikes Falconry Pony & trap Golf academy ♫ Xmas New Year **Conf** Class 220 Board 80 Thtr 450 Del from €320 to €650* **Services** Lift **Parking** 120 **Notes** LB ⊗ Civ Wed 70

NEWTOWNMOUNTKENNEDY
County Wicklow

Map 1 D3

Druids Glen Resort
★★★★★ 85% ◉◉ HOTEL

tel: 01 2870800
email: reservations@druidsglenresort.com **web:** www.druidsglenresort.com
dir: *N11 S'bound, off at Newtown Mount Kennedy. Follow signs for hotel*

This hotel, situated between the Wicklow Mountains and the coast, has two fabulous golf courses and a range of smart indoor leisure facilities and treatment rooms. Bedrooms have been equipped to the highest standard and service is delivered in a most professional manner, and always with a smile. Guests may choose to dine in Druid's Brasserie or the more formal Flynn's Restaurant.

Rooms 145 (26 fmly) (42 GF) ⚓ **S** €135-€500; **D** €145-€500 (incl. bkfst) **Facilities Spa** STV WiFi ⓑ ⊙ ⚓ 36 Putt green Gym Sauna Steam room Indoor playroom Outdoor playground Giant games ♫ Xmas New Year Child facilities **Conf** Class 180 Board 50 Thtr 400 Del from €235 to €600 **Services** Lift Air con **Parking** 300 **Notes** ⊗ Civ Wed 120

Parkview Hotel
★★★ 70% HOTEL

tel: 01 2015600 **Main St**
email: info@parkviewhotel.ie **web:** www.parkviewhotel.ie

Located in the heart of the Wicklow village of Newtownmountkennedy, 35km south of Dublin City, this modern hotel offers a range of room styles, all of which are very comfortably appointed. The Park Lounge is the hotel main bar, which enjoys a solid reputation for casual dining among the local community. Synnott's Restaurant opens for dinner at peak periods and for private use. The Park Room is a popular wedding venue, catering for events up to 250 guests. Secure car parking available to the rear.

Rooms 60 (4 fmly) **Facilities** STV FTV WiFi Xmas **Conf** Class 250 Thtr 500 **Services** Lift **Parking** 60 **Notes** ⊗ Civ Wed 300

RATHNEW
County Wicklow

Map 1 D3

Tinakilly Country House
★★★★ 78% ◉◉ HOTEL

tel: 0404 69274
email: info@tinakilly.ie **web:** www.tinakilly.ie
dir: *Follow N11/M11 to Rathnew, then R750 towards Wicklow. Entrance to hotel approx 500mtrs from village on left*

An elegant oak-lined avenue leads to Tinakilly House, a Victorian mansion steeped in history. It was built in 1884 for Captain Robert Halpin, Master Mariner and Commander of *SS Great Eastern* who laid the telegraphic cable joining Europe to America. There are lovely garden views from the lounges that have open log fires. Some of the comfortable bedrooms and suites enjoy views over the Irish Sea and bird sanctuary at Broadlough Costal Lagoon. Furnishings throughout reflect the Victorian period yet provide all modern comforts. Fine dining is available in the dining room, and snacks and afternoon tea are served in the drawing room.

Rooms 51 (15 fmly) (14 GF) ⚓ **Facilities** STV WiFi ⓑ ♫ New Year **Conf** Class 70 Board 35 Thtr 90 **Services** Lift **Parking** 60 **Notes** ⊗ Closed 24-26 Dec Civ Wed 100

Hunter's Hotel
★★★ 78% ◉ HOTEL

tel: 0404 40106
email: reception@hunters.ie **web:** www.hunters.ie
dir: *1.5km from village of Rathnew. From Dublin, N11/M11 exit 15, turn left at bridge in Ashford, follow signs to hotel*

One of Ireland's oldest coaching inns, this charming country house was built in 1720 and is full of character and atmosphere. The comfortable bedrooms have wonderful views over prize-winning gardens that border the River Vartry. The restaurant has a good reputation for carefully prepared dishes which make the best use of high quality local produce, including fruit and vegetables from the hotel's own garden.

Rooms 16 (2 fmly) (2 GF) **Facilities** WiFi **Conf** Class 40 Board 16 Thtr 40 **Parking** 50 **Notes** LB ⊗ Closed 24-26 Dec Civ Wed 40

RECESS (SRAITH SALACH)
County Galway   Map 1 A4

INSPECTORS' CHOICE

Lough Inagh Lodge Hotel
★★★ ◎◎ COUNTRY HOUSE HOTEL

tel: 095 34706 & 34694 **Inagh Valley,**
email: inagh@iol.ie **web:** www.loughinaghlodgehotel.ie
dir: From Recess take R344 towards Kylemore

Dating from 1880, this former fishing lodge is akin to a family home, where guests are encouraged to relax and enjoy the peace. Overlooking Lough Inagh, and situated amid the mountains of Connemara, it is in an ideal location for those who enjoy walking and fishing. Bedrooms are individually decorated, some with spacious seating areas, and each is dedicated to an Irish literary figure. There are two cosy lounges where welcoming turf fires are often lit. Informal dining from a bar menu is available during the day. Dinner is a highlight of a visit to the lodge; the menus feature locally sourced produce cooked with care - seafood is a speciality.

Rooms 13 (1 fmly) (4 GF) **Facilities** WiFi Fly fishing Cycling **Conf** Class 20 Board 20 Thtr 20 **Services** Air con **Parking** 16 **Notes** Closed mid Dec-mid Mar Civ Wed 50

ROSCOMMON
County Roscommon   Map 1 B4

Kilronan Castle Estate & Spa
★★★★ 80% ◎◎ HOTEL

tel: 071 9618000 **Ballyfarnon**
email: enquiries@kilronancastle.ie **web:** www.kilronancastle.ie
dir: M4 to N4, exit R299 towards R207 Droim ar Snámh/Drumsna/Droim. Exit R207 for R280, turn left Keadue Rd R284

Located on the shores of Lough Meelagh, this restored Gothic revival castle dates from the early 19th century. It is set in almost 50 acres of rolling park and woodland. Great care has been taken in its restoration, with many of the fine bedrooms and suites in the adjoining, sympathetically-built modern block. The Drawing Room is now a cosy lounge serving food throughout the day. The highlight however is dinner in the Douglas Hyde Restaurant, where the friendly professional team go to great lengths to offer fine food in elegant surroundings. The impressive Spa has a wide range of treatments on offer. There is also a leisure centre together with a wonderful events centre accessed by a tunnel from the main building.

Rooms 84 (9 fmly) ⌂ **S** €149; **D** €189 (incl. bkfst)* **Facilities** Spa FTV WiFi Gym Xmas New Year **Conf** Class 360 Board 60 Thtr 500 **Services** Lift Air con **Parking** 300 **Notes** LB Civ Wed 200

ROSSCARBERY
County Cork   Map 1 B2

Celtic Ross Hotel
★★★ 77% HOTEL

tel: 023 88 48722
email: info@celticross.com **web:** www.celticrosshotel.com
dir: N71 from Cork, through Bandon towards Clonakilty. Follow signs for Skibbereen

This hotel is situated on the edge of Rosscarbery village overlooking Rosscarbery Bay. Public areas are relaxing places, with a variety of lounges, a library, and the Warren Suite which enjoys panoramic views as far as Galley Head. Food is available in the bar throughout the day and evening in the Kingfisher Bar and Bistro. Afternoon tea is a speciality that can be reserved in advance. The spacious bedrooms are comfortable and well-appointed, many with wonderful sea views. There are extensive leisure and banqueting facilities plus music and dancing events on a regular basis. This is a property that enjoys a strong reputation in the region for wedding celebrations and other family occasions.

Rooms 66 (5 fmly) ⌂ **S** €55-€105; **D** €70-€170 (incl. bkfst)* **Facilities** Spa FTV WiFi supervised Gym New Year **Conf** Class 200 Board 60 Thtr 300 Del from €85 to €115* **Services** Lift **Parking** 250 **Notes** LB Closed 24-26 Dec Civ Wed 250

ROSSLARE
County Wexford   Map 1 D2

INSPECTORS' CHOICE

Kelly's Resort Hotel & Spa
★★★★ ◎◎ HOTEL

tel: 053 9132114
email: info@kellys.ie **web:** www.kellys.ie
dir: N25 onto Rosslare/Wexford road, signed Rosslare Strand

The Kelly family have been offering hospitality here since 1895, where together with a dedicated team, they provide very professional and friendly service. The resort overlooks the sandy beach and is within minutes of the ferry port at Rosslare. Bedrooms are thoughtfully equipped and comfortably furnished. The extensive leisure facilities include a smart spa, swimming pools, a crèche, young adults' programme and spacious well-tended gardens. Both the eating options, La Marine Bistro and Beaches restaurant, have been awarded AA Rosettes for the quality of their cuisine.

Rooms 118 (15 fmly) (20 GF) ⌂ **Facilities** Spa STV FTV WiFi supervised Putt green Gym Bowls Badminton Crazy golf Table tennis Snooker Sauna Steam room Child facilities **Conf** Class 30 Board 20 Thtr 30 **Services** Lift **Parking** 150 **Notes** LB Closed early Dec-late Feb

---

SALTHILL

See **Galway**

SKIBBEREEN
County Cork

Map 1 B2

West Cork Hotel

★★★ 77% ⊛ HOTEL

tel: 028 21277 **Ilen St**
email: info@westcorkhotel.com web: www.westcorkhotel.com
dir: *In Skibbereen, N71 into Bridge St, with Baby Hannah's pub on left to right into Ilen St, hotel on right. From Cork Rd, N71 to Schull, left at next rdbt towards town centre, hotel on left*

This charming hotel was built in 1902 and is family owned and run. It is located in the centre of town beside the River Ilen, where guests can enjoy an outdoor drink while sitting on the historic old West Cork railway bridge. There is a cosy lounge with log fire and furnishings and decor successfully mix the best of old and new. Food is available throughout the day in the Railway Bar and in the evening in Kennedy's Restaurant. Bedrooms vary in size and are comfortably furnished, some with riverside views. There are extensive banqueting facilities and ample car parking at the rear of the hotel.

Rooms 34 (4 fmly) ↑ S €55-€90; D €79-€149 (incl. bkfst)* Facilities FTV WiFi Use of facilities at Skibbereen Sports Centre Conf Class 20 Board 24 Thtr 250 Services Lift Parking 100 Notes LB ⊗ Closed 24-28 Dec Civ Wed 300

SLANE
County Meath

Map 1 D4

Conyngham Arms Hotel

★★★ 74% ⊛ HOTEL

tel: 041 984444 **Main St**
email: info@conynghamarms.ie web: www.conynghamarms.ie
dir: *Exit 10 for Navan from M1. Through village, hotel on the left of Main St*

This 17th-century coaching inn has been beautifully refurbished to a high standard of comfort and quality, and is situated in the centre of Slane village, close to Slane Castle and the World Heritage site of Newgrange and many other historical sites. The bedrooms vary in size due to the age of the house and are very smartly appointed with guest comfort in mind. Food is bistro style featuring the best of local produce, and breads and confectionary from their own bakery, served throughout the day in the cosy bar with an open log fire. There is private off-street parking available.

Rooms 15 ↑ S €65-€99; D €89-€139 (incl. bkfst) Facilities FTV WiFi ⓈConf Class 100 Board 50 Thtr 200 Parking 20 Notes LB ⊗ Civ Wed 200

SLIGO
County Sligo

Map 1 B5

Radisson Blu Hotel & Spa Sligo

★★★★ 79% ⊛ HOTEL

tel: 071 9140008 **Rosses Point Rd, Ballincar**
email: info.sligo@radissonblu.com web: www.radissonblu.com/en/hotel-sligo
dir: *From N4 into Sligo to main bridge. Take R291 on left. Hotel 1.5m on right*

Located four kilometres north of the town overlooking Sligo Bay, this contemporary hotel offers standard and business class bedrooms which are all appointed with up-to-date facilities. The Benwiskin bar offers tasty casual dining throughout the day, and for more formal dining in the evening there's Classiebawn Restaurant, featuring local ingredients cooked with international flair. Residents are welcome to use the Healthstyles leisure club during their stay, and relaxing treatment facilities

are also available in the Solas Spa. A range of eleven rooms are provided for meetings and events.

Rooms 132 (13 fmly) (32 GF) ↑ S €150; D €220 (incl. bkfst)* Facilities Spa STV WiFi Ⓢ Gym Steam room Thermal suite Sauna ♫ Xmas New Year Conf Class 420 Board 40 Thtr 750 Del from €130 to €250 Services Lift Air con Parking 320 Notes ⊗ Civ Wed 500

Sligo Park Hotel & Leisure Club

★★★★ 79% ⊛ HOTEL

tel: 071 9190400 **Pearse Rd F91 Y762**
email: sligo@leehotels.com web: www.sligopark.com
dir: *N4 to Sligo take exit S2 Sligo South Carrowroe/R287. Follow signs for Sligo. Hotel 1m on right*

Set in seven acres on the southern side of town, this hotel is well positioned for visiting the many attractions of the north west and Yeats' Country. Bedrooms are spacious and appointed to a high standard. There are two dining options, plus good leisure and banqueting facilities.

Rooms 136 (10 fmly) (52 GF) ↑ S €79-€189; D €89-€199* Facilities WiFi Ⓢ Ⓡ supervised ≋ Gym Holistic treatment suite Plunge pool Steam room ♫ Xmas New Year Conf Class 290 Board 80 Thtr 520 Services Lift Parking 200 Notes LB ⊗ RS 24-26 Dec Civ Wed 520

The Glasshouse

★★★★ 79% HOTEL

tel: 071 9194300 **Swan Point**
email: info@theglasshouse.ie web: www.theglasshouse.ie
dir: *From N4 right at 2nd junct. Left at Post Office into Wine St. Hotel on right*

This landmark building in the centre of town makes a bold statement with its cutting edge design and contemporary decor. Bright cheerful colours are used throughout the hotel; the bedrooms have excellent facilities including LCD TVs, workspace and internet access. There is a buzzing café bar serving food throughout the day, with a board walk for alfresco riverside dining. More formal evening dining takes place in the Kitchen restaurant. Secure underground parking is available together with a fitness suite.

Rooms 116 ↑ S €100-€280; D €120-€300 (incl. bkfst)* Facilities STV FTV WiFi Ⓢ ♫ New Year Conf Class 100 Board 60 Thtr 120 Del from €125 to €150* Services Lift Air con Parking 250 Notes LB ⊗ Closed 24-27 Dec Civ Wed 120

The Riverside Hotel

★★★ 71% HOTEL

tel: 071 9194480 **Riverside**
email: gm@riversidesligo.ie web: www.riversidesligo.ie
dir: *N4, follow city loop as far as Bridge St, turn left at Belfry/Toffs, sign posted Riverside Suites, Hotel 300 mtrs on left hand side*

This recently renovated hotel is perched on the bank of the Garavogue River, less than a 10-minute walk from the centre of the town. A traditional ambience has been created in The Mill Bar, where an all-day dining menu is on offer, with further options available in the bright and airy Riverside Restaurant during the evenings, from an interesting menu. Bedrooms and suites are comfortably appointed with a wide range of TV stations and WiFi available. Other facilities include beauty and hair suites and a gym for the more active. There is an event space suitable for small meetings, and private dining is also available. Free parking is provided in a public area some 300m further down the road.

Rooms 51 ↑ Facilities STV FTV WiFi Ⓢ Gym Hairdresser Natural therapies ♫ New Year Conf Class 80 Board 50 Thtr 130 Services Lift Air con Parking 8 Notes ⊗ Closed 24-26 Dec

STRAFFAN
County Kildare

Map 1 D4

The K Club
★★★★★ ◉◉ COUNTRY HOUSE HOTEL

tel: 01 6017200
email: sales@kclub.ie **web:** www.kclub.ie
dir: From Dublin take N4, exit for R406, hotel on right in Straffan

The K Club is set in 550 acres of rolling woodland. There are two magnificent championship golf courses, and a spa facility that complements the truly luxurious hotel that is the centrepiece of the resort. Public areas, suites and bedrooms are opulently furnished, and many have views of the formal gardens that lead down to the banks of the River Liffey. Additional rooms and family suites are a feature of the recently completed Liffey Wing. Dining options include the elegant River Room, with more informal dining options offered in Legends in the Arnold Palmer Golf Clubhouse, and in The K Thai Restaurant in The Smurfit Clubhouse. The K Club is home of the 2016 Irish Open Golf.

Rooms 134 (30 fmly) (18 GF) ⌕ **S** fr €229, **D** fr €229 (incl. bkfst)* **Facilities** Spa STV FTV WiFi ⓘ supervised ⌕ 36 ⌕ Putt green Fishing ⌕ Gym Beauty salon Fishing tuition Clay pigeon shooting Horse riding Falconry ♫ Xmas New Year Child facilities **Conf** Class 180 Board 160 Thtr 460 **Services** Lift **Parking** 200 **Notes** LB ⊗ Civ Wed 250

Barberstown Castle
★★★★ 78% HOTEL

tel: 01 6288157
email: info@barberstowncastle.ie **web:** www.barberstowncastle.ie
dir: R406, follow signs for Barberstown

With parts dating from the 13th century, this castle hotel provides the very best in standards of comfort. The inviting public areas range from the original keep, which houses one of the restaurant areas, to the warmth of the drawing room and its cocktail bar. Bedrooms, some in a purpose-built wing, are elegantly appointed with relaxing seating areas. The airy Tea Room serves light meals throughout the day. The Castle is a popular venue for weddings and other family occasions.

Rooms 55 (2 fmly) (21 GF) ⌕ **S** €115-€235; **D** €180-€300 (incl. bkfst) **Facilities** STV WiFi ⌕ ♫ New Year **Conf** Class 100 Board 72 Thtr 200 Del from €195 to €245 **Services** Lift **Parking** 200 **Notes** ⊗ Closed 24-26 Dec, Jan-Feb Civ Wed 280

THOMASTOWN
County Kilkenny

Map 1 C3

Mount Juliet Hotel
★★★★ ◉◉◉ COUNTRY HOUSE HOTEL

tel: 056 7773000
email: info@mountjuliet.ie **web:** www. mountjuliet.ie
dir: M7 from Dublin, M9 towards Waterford, exit at junct 9/Stoneyford for hotel

The Mount Juliet Estate is set in 1,500 acres of parkland with a Jack Nicklaus-designed golf course and an equestrian centre. The elegant and spacious public areas of the house retain many of the original architectural features including ornate plasterwork and Adam fireplaces. Bedrooms and suites are elegant and comfortably appointed to a high standard, with more compact rooms available in the Clubhouse annexe, less than a five minute walk away. Award-winning fine dining is on offer in the ornate Lady Helen restaurant overlooking the river; with brasserie style cuisine in Kendal's located in the golf clubhouse. The President's Bar is the location for all-day dining from an interesting menu and an opportunity for al fresco dining when the weather permits. The hotel has an excellent spa and health club, with other country pursuits and activities also available. Some major development is planned for 2016-2017

Rooms 46 (14 annexe) (6 fmly) (7 GF) ⌕ **S** €189-€299; **D** €199-€309 (incl. bkfst) **Facilities** Spa STV WiFi ⓘ supervised ⌕ 18 ⌕ Putt green Fishing ⌕ Gym Archery Cycling Equestrian Estate tours Xmas New Year **Conf** Class 40 Board 20 Thtr 75 **Parking** 200 **Notes** LB ⊗ Civ Wed 100

THURLES
County Tipperary

Map 1 C3

Horse & Jockey Hotel
★★★★ 79% HOTEL

tel: 0504 44192 **Horse & Jockey**
email: info@horseandjockeyhotel.com **web:** www.horseandjockeyhotel.com
dir: 800mtrs from M8 junct 6

Located just off the motorway, this hotel offers smart and well-appointed bedrooms which are very comfortable. Dining options are the Enclosure Bar with a varied menu, and for more formal dining in the evening there is Silks Restaurant. There is also a well-equipped leisure centre with spa treatments and an equestrian themed gift shop. The conference facilities include ten self-contained meeting rooms and a tiered auditorium seating 200 delegates.

Rooms 67 (4 fmly) (15 GF) ⌕ **S** €80-€100; **D** €99-€140 (incl. bkfst)* **Facilities** Spa STV FTV WiFi ⓘ supervised Gym Sauna Steam room Hydrotherapy area ♫ **Conf** Class 24 Board 25 Thtr 200 **Services** Lift **Parking** 450 **Notes** LB ⊗ Closed 25 Dec RS 24 Dec

TRALEE	Map 1 A2
County Kerry	

INSPECTORS' CHOICE

Ballyseede Castle

★★★ ◉◉ HOTEL

tel: 066 7125799
email: info@ballyseedecastle.com **web:** www.ballyseedecastle.com
dir: *On N21 just after junct of N21/N22*

Located within minutes of Tralee town, Ballyseede Castle is steeped in history dating back to 1590 and has been fought over, lived in and lovingly restored to a high standard which still pays homage to its ancient grandeur. The spacious bedrooms are elegantly decorated; some have four-poster beds and antique furnishings. There are gracious reception rooms with original ornamental cornices and marble fireplaces, a carved oak library, a cosy bar and a splendid banqueting hall. The castle stands in its own grounds at the end of a winding drive through formal gardens and natural woodland. All-day dining is available in the atmospheric Pappy's Bar, with more formal evening dining in the award-winning O'Connell Room. The Castle is noted for the quality of its wedding celebrations and other family events.

Rooms 23 (4 fmly) (10 GF) ✿ **Facilities** STV FTV WiFi **Parking** 180 **Notes** ⊗ Closed Jan-3 Mar Civ Wed 130

TULLOW	Map 1 D3
County Carlow	

Mount Wolseley Hotel, Spa & Golf Resort

★★★★ 80% ◉ HOTEL

tel: 059 9180 100
email: info@mountwolseley.ie **web:** www.mountwolseley.ie
dir: *N7 from Dublin. In Naas, take N9 towards Carlow. In Castledermot left for Tullow*

Located on a vast, well landscaped estate long associated with the Wolseley family of motoring fame, this hotel has much to offer. Public areas are very spacious with a large range of suites and bedrooms. Leisure pursuits include a championship golf course together with a popular health centre and Sanctuary Spa facilities. The hotel offers a number of dining options including Aaron's lounge, Fredrick's, and The Wolseley Lounge in the Golf Pavilion.

Rooms 143 (10 fmly) (5 smoking) ✿ **Facilities** Spa STV FTV WiFi ❧ HL ☻ supervised ♨ 18 ⛳ Putt green Gym Childrens play areas Games room ♫ New Year **Conf** Class 288 Board 70 Thtr 750 **Services** Lift Air con **Parking** 160 **Notes** ⊗ Closed 25-26 Dec Civ Wed 450

WATERFORD	Map 1 C2
County Waterford	

Waterford Castle Hotel and Golf Club

★★★★ 80% ◉◉ COUNTRY HOUSE HOTEL

tel: 051 878203 **The Island, Ballinakill**
email: info@waterfordcastleresort.com **web:** www.waterfordcastleresort.com
dir: *From city centre continue onto Dunmore Rd for 2km. At hospital, take exit for Dunmore Rd. Left at 3rd set of lights*

This enchanting and picturesque castle dates back to Norman times and is located on a 320-acre island just a five-minute journey from the mainland by chain-link ferry. Bedrooms vary in style and size, but all are individually decorated and offer high standards of comfort. Dinner is served in the oak-panelled Munster Room, with breakfast taken in the conservatory. The 18-hole golf course is set in beautiful parkland where deer can be seen.

Rooms 19 (3 fmly) (4 GF) **S** €129-€250; **D** €159-€295 (incl. bkfst)* **Facilities** WiFi ❧ ♨ 18 ⛳ Putt green ♣ ♫ **Services** Lift **Parking** 50 **Notes** LB ⊗ Civ Wed 120

Faithlegg House Hotel & Golf Resort

FBD Hotels & Resorts

★★★★ 79% ◉◉ HOTEL

tel: 051 382000 **Faithlegg**
email: reservations@fhh.ie **web:** www.faithlegg.com
dir: *From Waterford follow Dunmore East Rd then Cheekpoint Rd*

This hotel is surrounded by a parkland championship golf course and overlooks the estuary of the River Suir. The house has 14 original bedrooms, and the others in a more contemporary style are in an adjacent modern block. There is a range of comfortable lounges together with comprehensive meeting facilities. The leisure and treatment rooms are the perfect way to work off the food offered in the Roseville Restaurant. Lighter options are served throughout the day in the Piano Bar and in the golf Clubhouse.

Rooms 82 (6 fmly) (30 GF) ✿ **Facilities** Spa FTV WiFi ☻ supervised ♨ 18 ⛳ Putt green Gym Sauna Steam room New Year **Conf** Class 90 Board 44 Thtr 180 **Services** Lift **Parking** 100 **Notes** LB ⊗ Closed 20-27 Dec Civ Wed 220

Granville Hotel

★★★★ 77% ◉ HOTEL

tel: 051 305555 **The Quay**
email: stay@granville-hotel.ie **web:** www.granville-hotel.ie
dir: *N25 to waterfront, hotel opposite clock tower*

Centrally located on the quayside, this long established hotel was originally a coaching house. It is appointed to a very high standard, and retains much of its original character. The bedrooms come in a choice of standard or executive grades; all are well equipped and very comfortable. The Meagher Bar offers food throughout the day, and is a popular lunch venue with shoppers and the business community of Waterford. The Bianconi is an elegant restaurant where evening dinner is served. Friendliness and hospitality are hallmarks of a stay here.

Rooms 100 (5 fmly) (10 smoking) ✿ **S** €90-€150; **D** €120-€240 (incl. bkfst) **Facilities** STV ♫ New Year **Conf** Class 150 Board 30 Thtr 200 **Services** Lift **Parking** 300 **Notes** LB ⊗ Closed 25-26 Dec Civ Wed 200

Tower Hotel

FBD Hotels & Resorts

★★★ 79% HOTEL

tel: 051 862300 **The Mall**
email: info@thw.ie **web:** www.towerhotelwaterford.com
dir: *Opposite Reginald's Tower in town centre. Hotel at end of quay, in the heart of the Viking Triangle*

With a commanding position on The Mall opposite Reginald's Tower, this well established hotel has much to offer. The spacious public areas include conference suites, a choice of dining options and a popular leisure club. Health and beauty treatments are available. A range of bedrooms is on offer; all are comfortably appointed and stylishly decorated. Secure parking is provided to the rear of the building.

Rooms 134 (27 fmly) ⬧ **S** €70-€145; **D** €89-€220* **Facilities** STV FTV WiFi ⬧ supervised Gym Beauty treatment rooms ♫ **Conf** Class 250 Board 80 Thtr 500 **Services** Lift **Parking** 100 **Notes** LB ⊗ Closed 24-28 Dec Civ Wed 400

Dooley's Hotel

★★★ 78% HOTEL

tel: 051 873531 **30 The Quay**
email: hotel@dooleys-hotel.ie **web:** www.dooleys-hotel.ie
dir: *Adjacent to N25, on the Quay on R680*

This hotel has been operating since the 19th century and is approaching its seventh decade in the hospitable hands of the Darrer family and their friendly team. It is situated on the quay overlooking the River Suir at the bus station, within walking distance of the railway station. Dinner is served in the New Ship Restaurant from an interesting menu, and casual dining is available in the Dry Dock Bar. Bedrooms are attractively decorated in keeping with the age of the property and offer a good standard of comfort. There is a convenient public car park opposite the hotel.

Rooms 110 (13 fmly) ⬧ **S** €70-€180; **D** €80-€200 **Facilities** STV WiFi ⬧ ♫ New Year **Conf** Class 150 Board 100 Thtr 240 Del from €175 to €285 **Services** Lift **Notes** LB ⊗ Closed 25-27 Dec RS 24 Dec

WESTPORT
County Mayo

Map 1 B4

Knockranny House Hotel

MANOR HOUSE HOTELS

★★★★ 84% HOTEL

tel: 098 28600
email: info@khh.ie **web:** www.knockrannyhousehotel.ie
dir: *On N5 Westport-Castlebar Rd*

Perched on a height overlooking Westport, with Clew Bay and Croagh Patrick in the distance, this fine family-run property is set in well landscaped grounds. The reception rooms take full advantage of the stunning views, and include The Brehon, a lounge where food is served throughout the day, and La Fougère, the award-winning restaurant that is a real treat to visit. The comfortable furnishings create an inviting and relaxing atmosphere throughout the lounges, bar and restaurant. Bedrooms are very well appointed and come in a number of styles, with the newer ones being particularly spacious. Guests have complimentary use of extensive leisure facilities, with wellbeing treatments on offer in Spa Salveo. There are extensive banqueting and conference facilities.

Rooms 97 (4 fmly) (18 GF) ⬧ **Facilities** Spa STV FTV WiFi ⬧ HL ⬧ Gym ♫ New Year **Conf** Class 350 Board 40 Thtr 600 **Services** Lift **Parking** 150 **Notes** ⊗ Closed 24-26 Dec Civ Wed 250

Hotel Westport Leisure, Spa & Conference

★★★★ 81% HOTEL

tel: 098 25122 **Newport Rd**
email: reservations@hotelwestport.ie **web:** www.hotelwestport.ie
dir: *N5 to Westport. Right at end of Castlebar St, 1st right before bridge, right at lights, left before church. Follow to end of street*

Located in seven acres of woodlands and just a short riverside walk from the town, this hotel offers spacious public areas, including The Islands restaurant and the all-day Maple Bar. Bedrooms come in a range of styles, and are all comfortable and well appointed. Both leisure and business guests are well catered for by the enthusiastic and friendly team who go to great lengths to ensure residents enjoy their stay. This hotel is a popular choice with special interest groups and also families, who enjoy the leisure facilities, and in summer time, the children's club.

Rooms 129 (G7 fmly) (42 GF) (12 smoking) ⬧ **Facilities** Spa STV WiFi ⬧ IIL ⬧ supervised Gym Children's pool Lounger pool Steam room Sauna Fitness suite ♫ Xmas New Year Child facilities **Conf** Class 150 Board 60 Thtr 500 Del from €150 to €250* **Services** Lift **Parking** 220 **Notes** ⊗ Civ Wed 350

Mill Times Hotel Westport

★★★ 73% HOTEL

tel: 098 29200 & 29130 **Mill St**
email: info@milltimeshotel.ie **web:** www.milltimeshotel.ie
dir: *N59 signed town centre, in Bridge St keep in left lane, into Mill St, hotel on left*

This family-run hotel is situated in the centre of Westport, close to the shops and many pubs of this bustling town. It is ideal for visiting north Mayo with its many beaches and golf courses, or as a base for climbing the pilgrimage mountain of Croagh Patrick. Bedrooms are traditional in style and public areas are comfortable. Uncle Sam's café bar is a lively venue with entertainment at weekends. Temptations Restaurant offers good value meals during the evening, and is the venue for a hearty breakfast. Underground parking is provided.

Rooms 34 (6 fmly) **Facilities** WiFi ♫ New Year **Conf** Class 100 Board 60 Thtr 180 **Services** Lift Air con **Parking** 25 **Notes** ⊗ Closed 24-25 Dec Civ Wed 200

WEXFORD
County Wexford

Map 1 D3

Aldridge Lodge Restaurant and Guesthouse

 RESTAURANT WITH ROOMS

tel: 051 389116 **Duncannon**
email: info@aldridgelodge.com **web:** www.aldridgelodge.com

Just a 45-minute drive from the Ferryport at Rosslare, Aldridge Lodge is an ideal first night stop-off following an afternoon sailing from the UK, and it's tempting to return for the final night of a visit to Ireland given the warm welcome. It makes a great base for exploring the many attractions and activities of The Hook Peninsula. Hosts Joanne and Billy, who is also the chef, take a keen interest in their guests - it's no wonder so many of them return, making advance weekend reservations essential. While each of the three guest rooms is warm and cosy, what brings most visitors here is the food. Billy has a strong reputation for his use of local ingredients and seasonality is also very much to the fore. The breakfast experience is also a feature - quality ingredients cooked with skill and care in a relaxed environment.

Rooms 3

Gibraltar

GIBRALTAR

Sunborn Yacht Hotel

★★★★★ 82% ◉ HOTEL

tel: 00 350 200 16100 **Ocean Village GX11 1AA**
email: info@sunborngibraltar.com **web:** www.sunbornhotels.com/gibraltar
dir: *Ocean Village Marina*

This floating hotel is situated in the Ocean Village Marina; the yacht has 189 individually designed bedrooms with up-to-date technology to control the lighting, heating, curtains and televisions; most of the rooms have views over the marina and some rooms have large terraces. The yacht has a range of spacious public areas that include a choice of dining options, lounges, bars, a casino, a spa and leisure facilities.

Rooms 189 (1 fmly) (19 GF) 📞 **S** £130-£259; **D** £135-£285 **Facilities** Spa STV FTV WiFi ⇩ ✻ Gym 🎵 Xmas New Year **Conf** Class 200 Board 80 Thtr 360 **Services** Lift Air con **Parking** 12 **Notes** LB ⊗ Civ Wed 80

Caleta Hotel

★★★★ 81% ◉◉ HOTEL

tel: 00 350 200 76501 **Sir Herbert Miles Rd, PO Box 73 GX11 1AA**
email: reservations@caletahotel.gi **web:** www.caletahotel.com
dir: *Enter Gibraltar via Spanish border & cross runway. At 1st rdbt turn left, hotel in 2km*

For travellers arriving in Gibraltar by plane, the Caleta is an eye-catching coastal landmark that can be spotted from the air if arriving from the east. This imposing and stylish hotel sits on a cliff top and all sea-facing rooms enjoy panoramic views across the straights to Morocco. Bedrooms vary in size and style; some have spacious balconies, flat screen TVs and mini bars. Several dining venues are available, but Nunos provides an award-winning, fine dining Italian experience. The staff are friendly and service is professional.

Rooms 161 (89 annexe) (13 fmly) (80 smoking) **Facilities** Spa STV FTV WiFi ⇩ ✻ supervised Gym Health & beauty club Xmas New Year **Conf** Class 172 Board 85 Thtr 216 **Services** Lift Air con **Parking** 32 **Notes** ⊗ Civ Wed 300

O'Callaghan Eliott Hotel

★★★★ 79% HOTEL

tel: 00 350 200 70500 & 200 75905 **2 Governor's Pde GX11 1AA**
email: eliott@ocallaghanhotels.com **web:** www.ocallaghanhotels.com

Located in the heart of the old town, this hotel provides a convenient central base for exploring the duty-free shopping district and other key attractions on foot. The bedrooms are stylish, spacious and well equipped. The roof-top restaurant provides stunning bay views, while guests can also take a swim in the roof-top pool.

Rooms 123 📞 **Facilities** STV WiFi ✻ Gym 🎵 Xmas New Year **Conf** Class 80 Board 70 Thtr 180 **Services** Lift Air con **Parking** 17 **Notes** ⊗ Civ Wed 120

The Rock Hotel

★★★★ 78% HOTEL

tel: 00 350 200 73000 **Europa Rd GX11 1AA**
email: reservations@rockhotel.gi **web:** www.rockhotelgibraltar.com
dir: *From airport follow tourist board signs. Hotel on left half way up Europa Rd*

Enjoying a prime elevated location directly below the Rock, this long-established art deco styled hotel has been the destination of celebrities and royalty since it was built in 1932. The bedrooms are spacious and well equipped, and many boast stunning coastal views that stretch across the Mediterranean to Morocco. The staff are friendly and service is delivered with flair and enthusiasm. Creative dinners and hearty breakfasts can be enjoyed in the stylish restaurant.

Rooms 104 📞 **Facilities** STV WiFi ✻ supervised Gym Xmas New Year **Conf** Class 120 Board 30 Thtr 150 **Services** Lift Air con **Parking** 10 **Notes** ⊗ RS 5 Oct-1 Apr Civ Wed 200

Acknowledgments

The Automobile Association would like to thank the following photographers, companies and picture libraries for their assistance in the preparation of this book.

Abbreviations for the picture credits are as follows – (t) top; (b) bottom; (c) centre; (l) left; (r) right; (AA) AA World Travel Library

3 Courtesy of the Northcote Hotel, Lancashire; 4 Courtesy of the Grosvenor Pulford Hotel & Spa, Cheshire; 6 Courtesy of The Abode Canterbury, Kent; 7 Courtesy of The Beaumont, London; 9 Courtesy of The Beaumont, London; 10 Courtesy of The Angel Hotel, Abergavenny; 11 AA/Stockbyte; 13l Courtesy of the Northcote Hotel, Lancashire; 13r Courtesy of The Beaumont, London; 13bg AA/C Sawyer; 14l Courtesy of The Cromlix and Chez Roux, Dunblane; 14r Courtesy of The Angel Hotel, Abergavenny; 15 Courtesy of The Manor House Country Hotel, Enniskillen; 14–15bg AA/C Sawyer; 17t Courtesy of Thwaites Hotels; 17b Courtesy of Thwaites Hotels; 18 Courtesy of The Angel Hotel, Abergavenny; 20 Courtesy of The Angel Hotel, Abergavenny; 21 Courtesy of the Northcote Hotel, Lancashire; 22–24 AA; 26 All images courtesy of The Imperial Hotel Blackpool; 27t Courtesy of The Goring, London; 27b Courtesy of The Goring, London; 28–29 AA; 40–41 AA/A Burton; 234–235 AA/J Tims; 252 AA/J Tims; 464 AA/P Trenchard; 476–477 AA/J Henderson; 524–525 AA/AJ Hopkins; 529 AA/S Whitehorne; 530–531 AA/M Sterling; 559 AA/M Bauer; 560–561 AA/C Hill; 592 AA/J Tims.

Every effort has been made to trace the copyright holders, and we apologise in advance for any unintentional omissions or errors. We would be pleased to apply any corrections in a following edition of this publication

GIBRALTAR

COUNTY MAPS

England

1. Bedfordshire
2. Berkshire
3. Bristol
4. Buckinghamshire
5. Cambridgeshire
6. Greater Manchester
7. Herefordshire
8. Hertfordshire
9. Leicestershire
10. Northamptonshire
11. Nottinghamshire
12. Rutland
13. Staffordshire
14. Warwickshire
15. West Midlands
16. Worcestershire

Scotland

17. City of Glasgow
18. Clackmannanshire
19. East Ayrshire
20. East Dunbartonshire
21. East Renfrewshire
22. Perth & Kinross
23. Renfrewshire
24. South Lanarkshire
25. West Dunbartonshire

Wales

26. Blaenau Gwent
27. Bridgend
28. Caerphilly
29. Denbighshire
30. Flintshire
31. Merthyr Tydfil
32. Monmouthshire
33. Neath Port Talbot
34. Newport
35. Rhondda Cynon Taff
36. Torfaen
37. Vale of Glamorgan
38. Wrexham

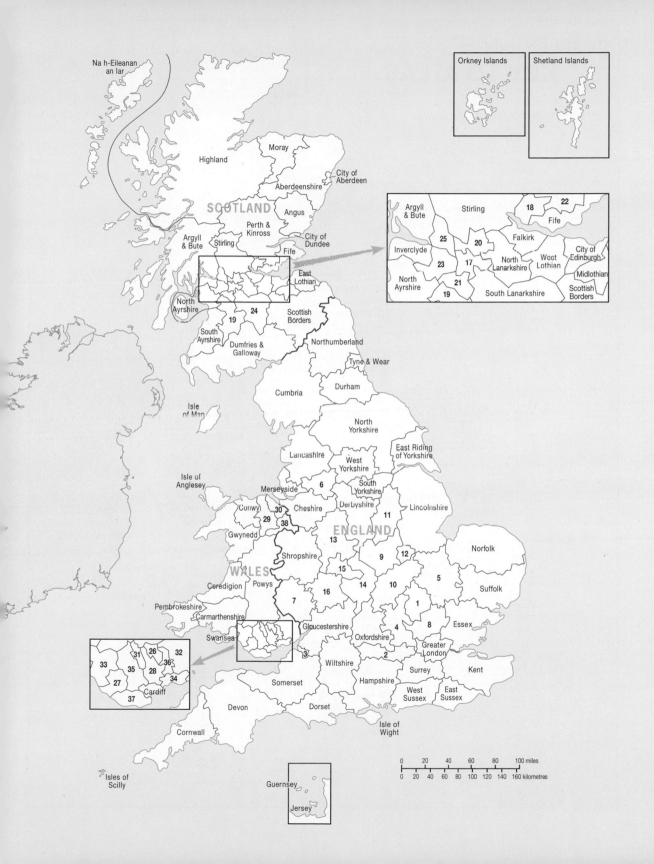

Na h-Eileanan
an Iar

Orkney Islands

Shetland Islands

Highland

Moray

Aberdeenshire

City of
Aberdeen

SCOTLAND

Angus

Perth &
Kinross

City of
Dundee

Argyll
& Bute

Stirling

Fife

East
Lothian

Argyll
& Bute

Stirling

18

22

Fife

Falkirk

Inverclyde

25

20

North
Ayrshire

North
Ayrshire

19

24

23

17

North
Lanarkshire

West
Lothian

City of
Edinburgh

Midlothian

South
Ayrshire

21

South Lanarkshire

Scottish
Borders

Dumfries &
Galloway

Scottish Borders

19

Northumberland

Tyne & Wear

Cumbria

Durham

Isle
of Man

North
Yorkshire

East Riding
of Yorkshire

Lancashire

West
Yorkshire

Isle of
Anglesey

Merseyside

6

South
Yorkshire

Lincolnshire

Conwy

30

Cheshire

Derbyshire

11

29

38

ENGLAND

Gwynedd

13

Norfolk

Shropshire

15

9

12

5

WALES

16

14

10

Suffolk

Ceredigion

Powys

7

1

Pembrokeshire

Carmarthenshire

Swansea

26

32

31

36

Gloucestershire

4

8

Essex

33

35

28

34

3

Oxfordshire

2

Greater
London

27

Cardiff

Wiltshire

Surrey

Kent

37

Somerset

Hampshire

West
Sussex

East
Sussex

Devon

Dorset

Isle of
Wight

Cornwall

Isles of
Scilly

Guernsey

Jersey

| 0 | 20 | 40 | 60 | 80 | 100 miles |

| 0 | 20 | 40 | 60 | 80 | 100 | 120 | 140 | 160 kilometres |

KEY TO ATLAS

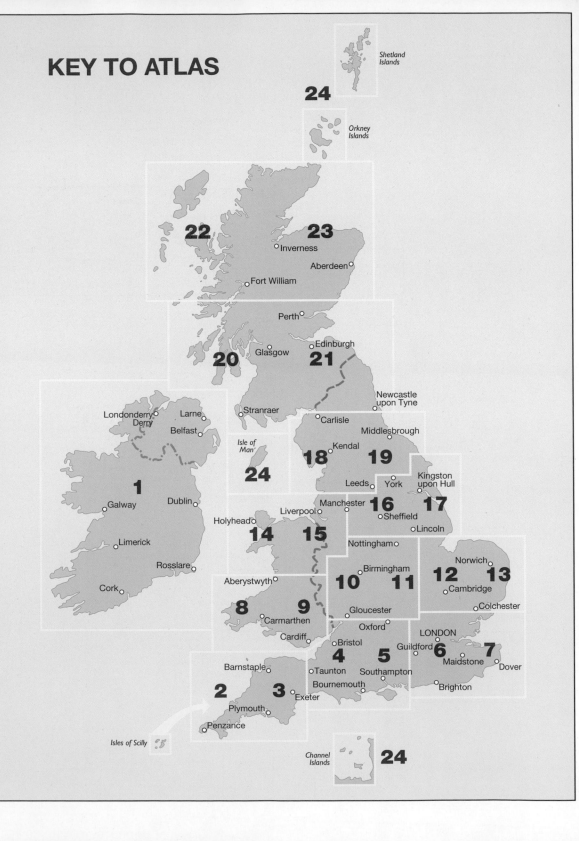

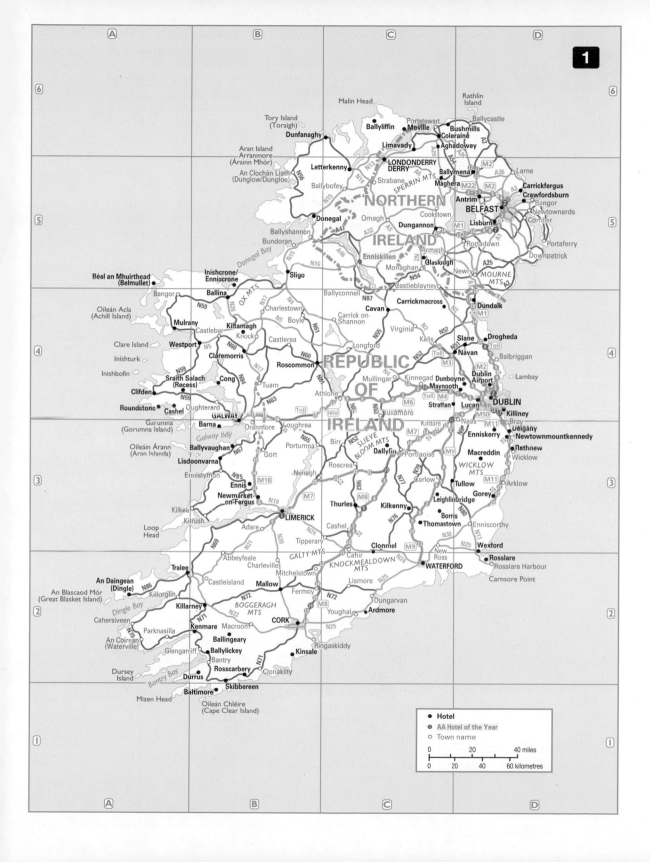

Legend

M6	Motorway/toll motorway	● **Stamford**	Hotel
	Motorway junction full/restricted. Service area	● **Langho**	AA Hotel of the Year
A30	Primary route single/dual carriageway	○ King's Cliffe	Town/Village name
A34	Other A road single/dual carriageway		National boundary
B3400	B road	**ESSEX**	English county name & boundary
	Unclassified road	**CONWY**	Welsh county name & boundary
V	Vehicle ferry	**MORAY**	Scottish county name & boundary
C	Fast vehicle ferry or catamaran		National Park

ISLES OF SCILLY

Bryher
New Grimsby
St Martin's
Higher Town
Tresco
Hugh Town
St Mary's
ISLES OF SCILLY (ST MARY'S)
Old Town
Middle Town
St Agnes

SV

SW

Lundy

Hartland Point
Hartland

Morwenstow

Kilkhampton

Bude
Bude
Bay
Widemouth Bay

Crackington Haven
Week St Mary

Boscastle
Tintagel
A39
A395

Delabole
Camelford

Port Isaac
Penboggett
St Tudy
Bolventor
BODMIN MOOR
Blisland
A30

Polzeath
Rock
A38

Harlyn
Padstow
Wadebridge
A389

Porthcothan
CORNWALL
St Cleer

Mawgan Porth
St Mawgan
Bodmin
A30
A38
Dobwalls
Liske

Newquay
St Columb Major
Lanivet
A389
A38
St Keyne

West Pentire
A392
Roche
Bugle
A391
Lostwithiel
A390

Fraddon
A3058
St Blazey
Golant
V
Pelynt

Perranporth
Summercourt
St Austell
Fowey
Le

St Agnes
A30
Ladock
A3058
St Stephen
A390
Polruan
Polperro

Porthtowan
Marazanvose
Grampound
Pentewan

Portreath
St Day
Carnon Downs
Tregony
Mevagissey

St Ives
St Ives Bay
Gwithian
Truro
Gorran Haven

Zennor
Redruth
A393
A39
Portloe

Lelant
Camborne
A30
St Just-in-Roseland
Veryan

Hayle
Penryn
Portscatho

St Just
A3071
A394
Falmouth
St Mawes

Penzance
Marazion
Constantine

Newlyn
Helston
Mawnan Smith

Land's End
Sennen
St Buryan
Porthleven
Gweek
Manaccan

Land's End
Mousehole
Praa Sands
St Keverne

Porthcurno
Treen
Mount's Bay

Mullion
Coverack

Lizard
Cadgwith
Lizard Point

For continuation pages refer to numbered arrows

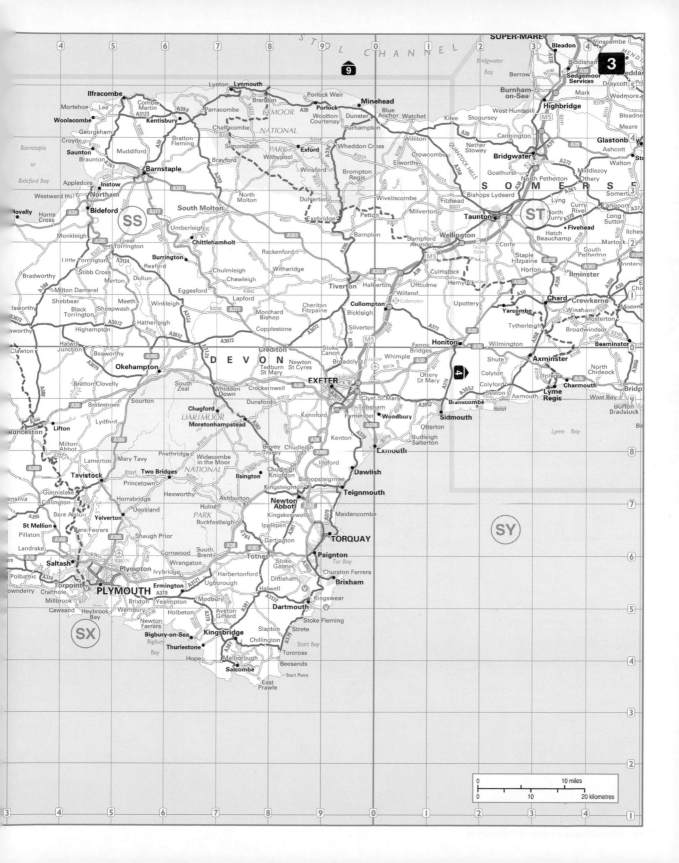

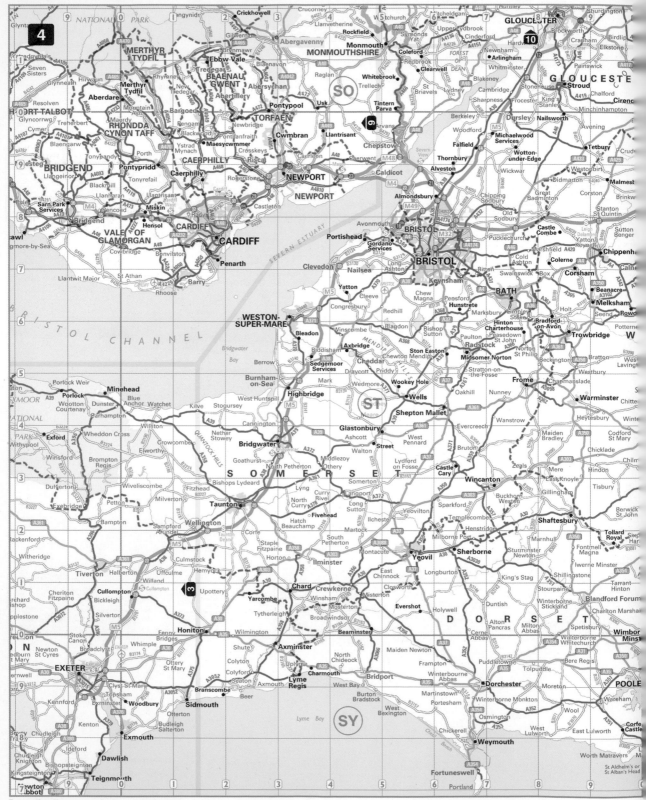

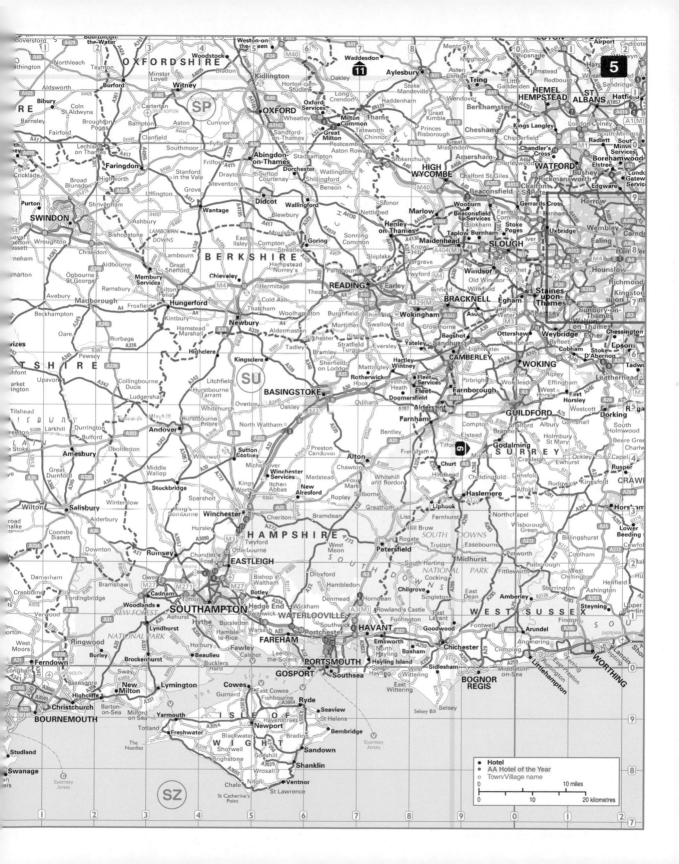

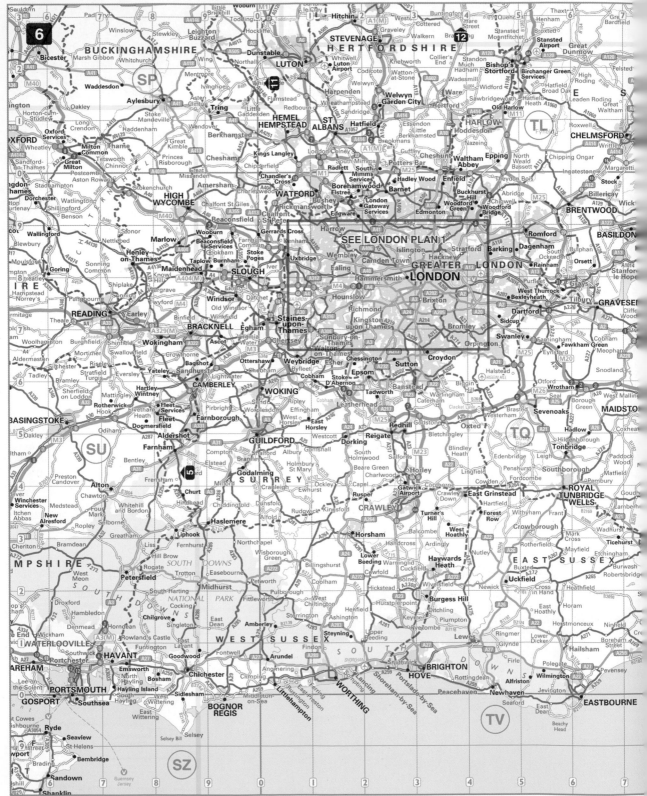

For continuation pages refer to numbered arrows

Hotel
AA Hotel of the Year
Town/Village name

0   10 miles

0   10   20 kilometres

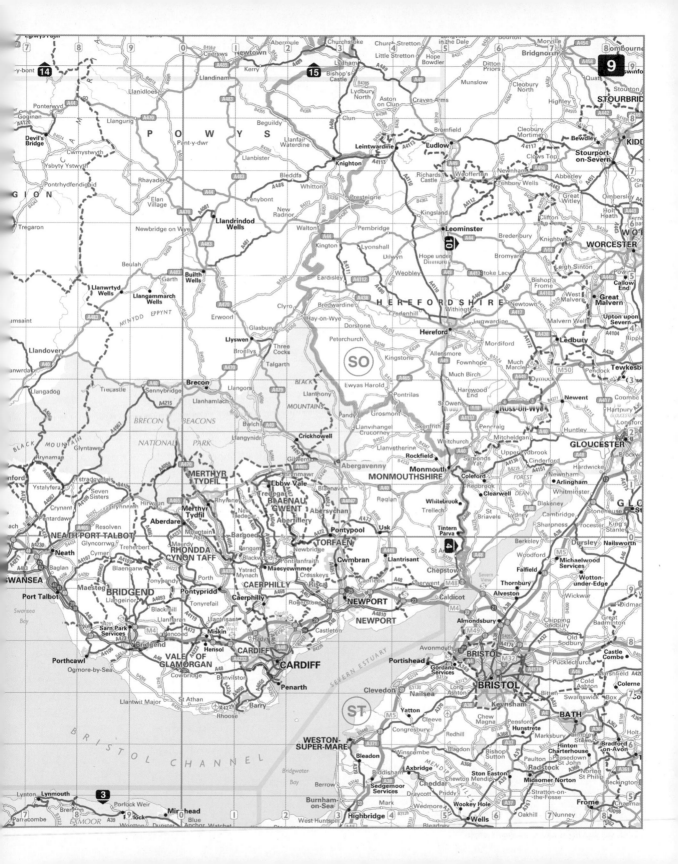

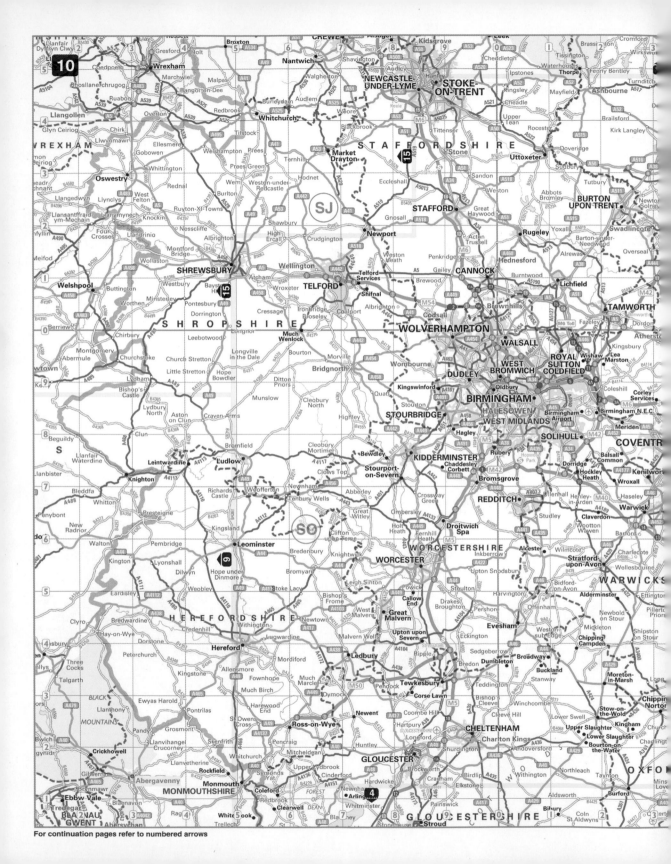

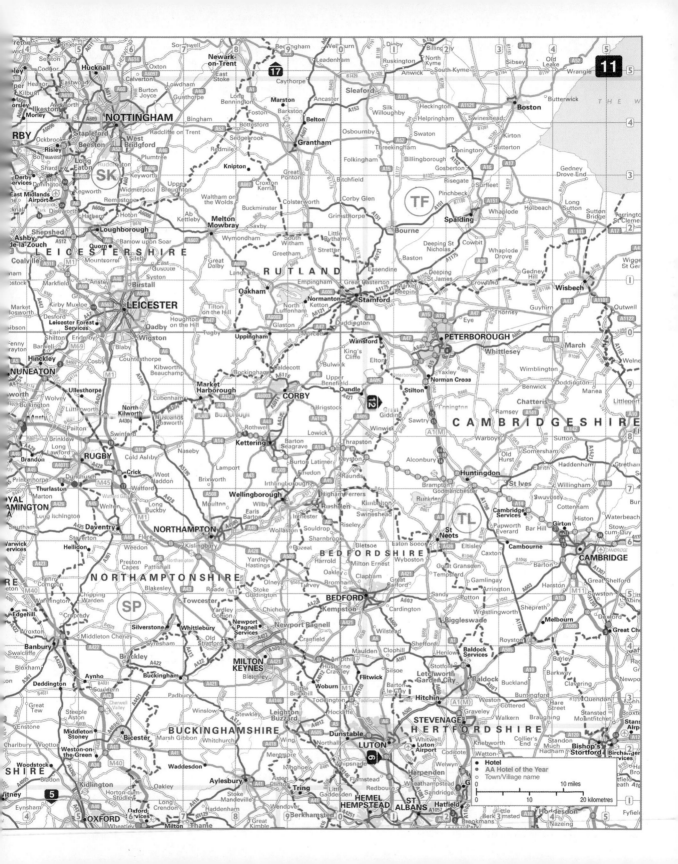

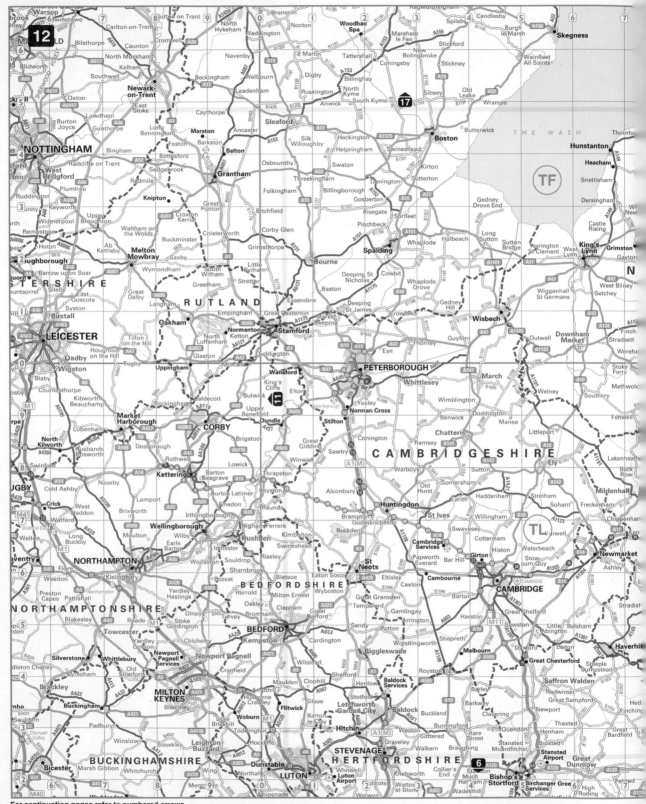

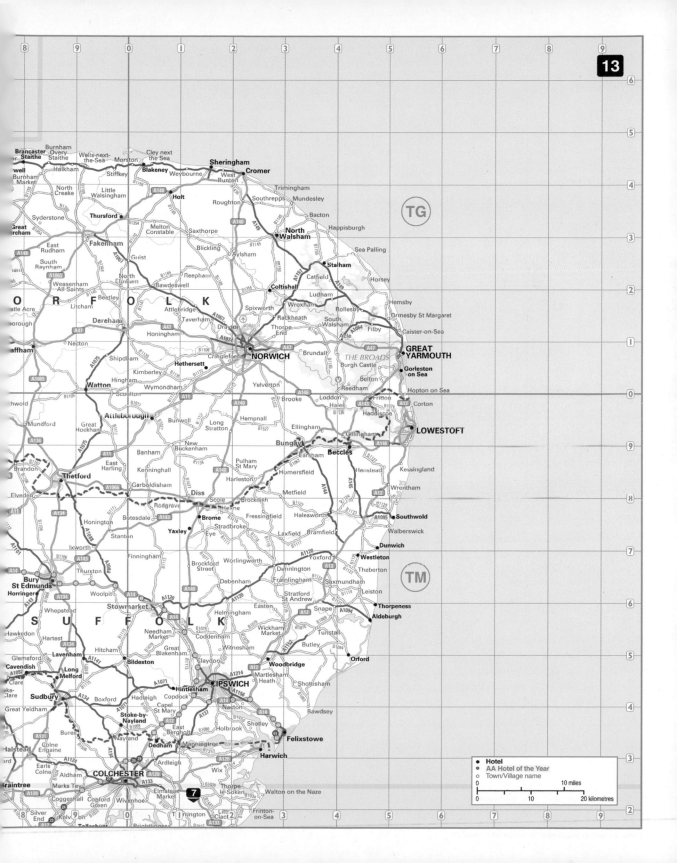

For continuation pages refer to numbered arrows

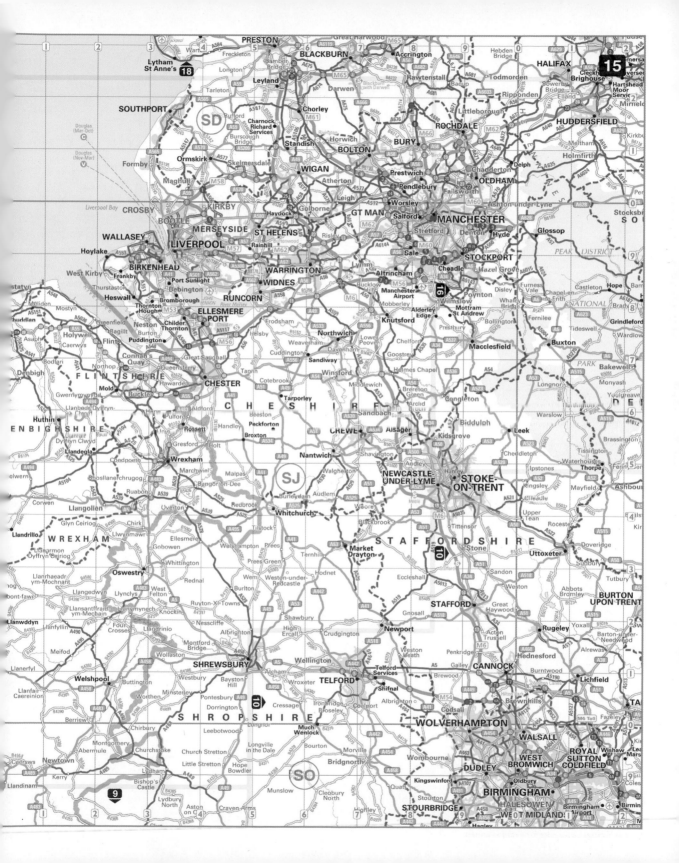

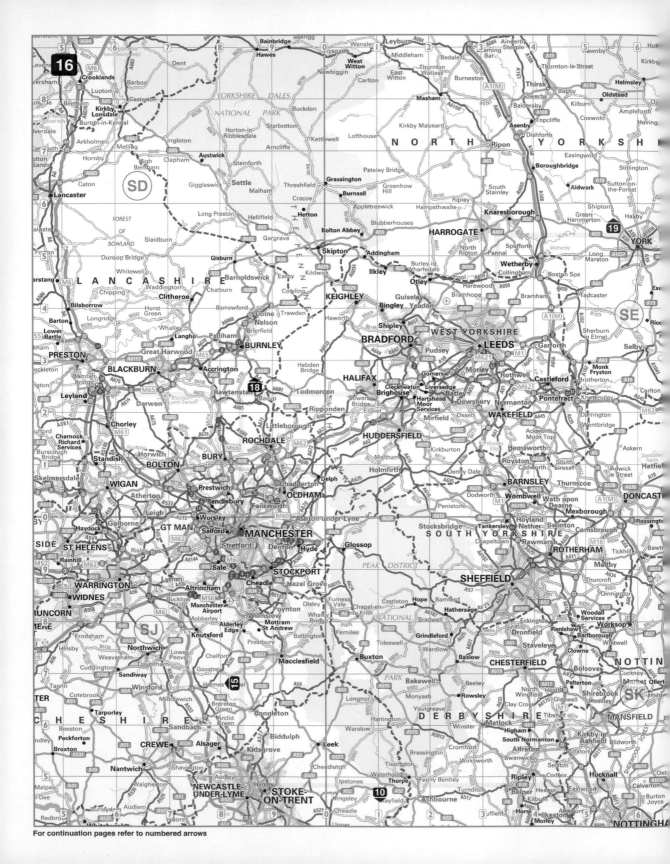

For continuation pages refer to numbered arrows

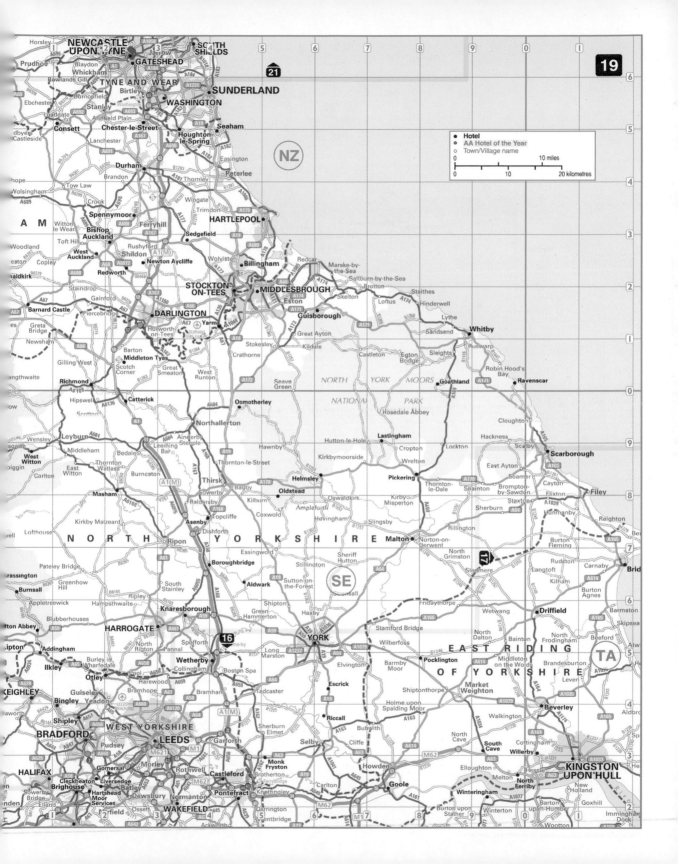

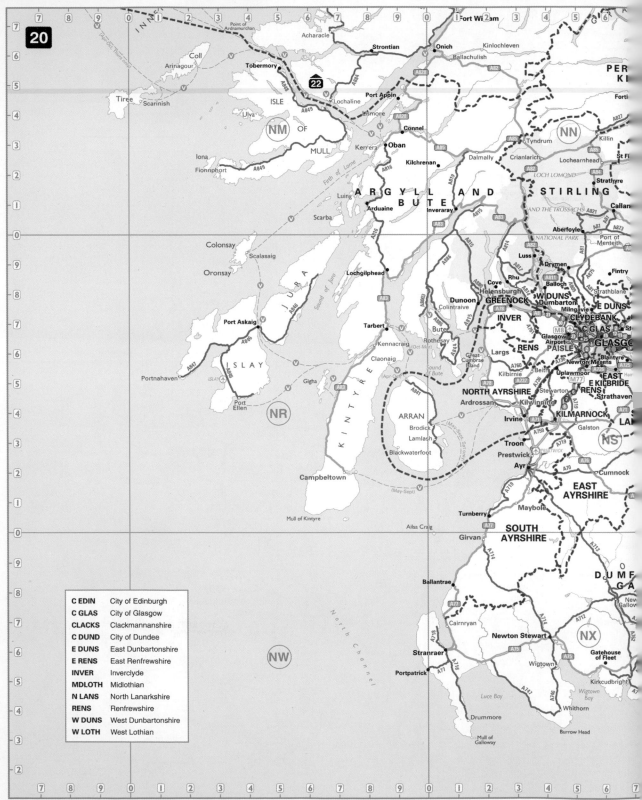

C EDIN	City of Edinburgh
C GLAS	City of Glasgow
CLACKS	Clackmannanshire
C DUND	City of Dundee
E DUNS	East Dunbartonshire
E RENS	East Renfrewshire
INVER	Inverclyde
MDLOTH	Midlothian
N LANS	North Lanarkshire
RENS	Renfrewshire
W DUNS	West Dunbartonshire
W LOTH	West Lothian

For continuation pages refer to numbered arrows

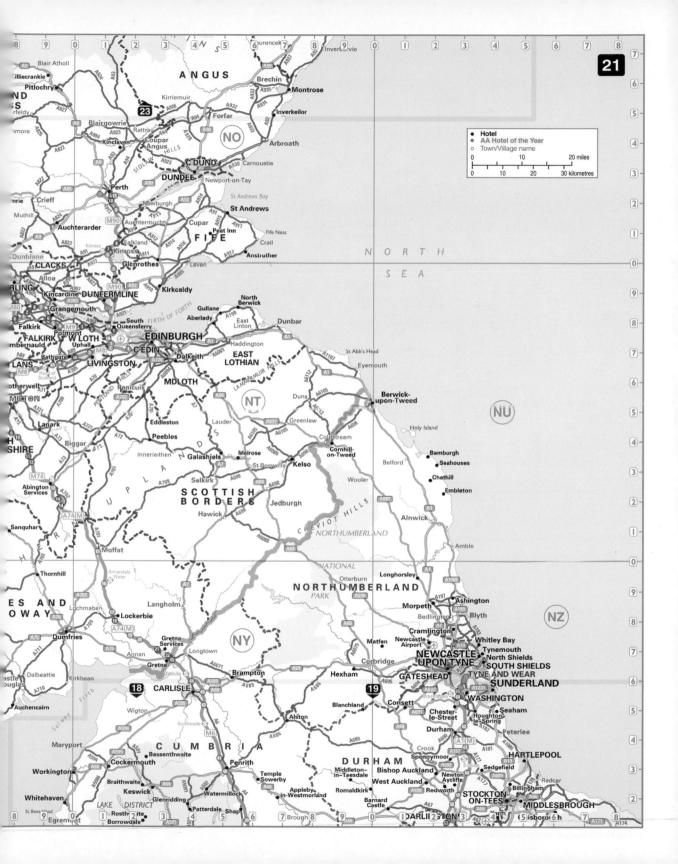

NA

NB

Cape Wrath

Scourie

Inchnada

Lochinver

A894

A837

A835

A835

A832

Ullapool

Gruinard
Bay

Rudha Rhobhanais
(Butt of Lewis)

Port Nis
(Port of Ness)

Cellar
Head

A857

LEWIS

A858

Great
Bernera

Carlabhagh
(Carloway)

OF

Steornabhagh
(Stornoway)

A857

Tiumpan
Head

A866

A858

A859

ISLE

Scarp

NA H–EILEANAN
AN IAR

A859

Taransay

Tairbeart
(Tarbert)

Scalpay

HARRIS

A859

Pabbay

Boreray

Berneray

OUTER HEBRIDES

THE MINCH

THE LITTLE MINCH

Gairloch

A832

A832

Kinlochewe

A832

Achnasheen

Torridon

Shieldaig

A896

NORTH
WEST
HIGHLANDS

NF

A865

NORTH UIST

A867

Loch nam Madadh
(Lochmaddy)

Ronay

A865

Wiay

Uig

A855

A87

ISLE

A850

Colbost

Dunvegan

A863

OF

Struan

Portree

NG

Raasay

Inner Sound

A87

Carinish

A896

A890

SOUTH
UIST

A865

Drynoch

SKYE

Scalpay

Kyle of
Lochalsh

A87

A890

A887

A87

Loch Baghasdail
(Lochboisdale)

Eriskay

Soay

Cuillin Sound

Isleornsay

A851

Ardvasar

Sound of Sleat

Invergarry

BARRA

A888

Bàgh a Chaisteil
(Castlebay)

Sandray

Canna

Rùm

Mallaig

A830

Roy
Bridge

Glenfinnan

A830

Spean Bridge

A82

Mingulay

INNER HEBRIDES

Eigg

Muck

A861

A861

Fort William

NL

(Ar. Oir. Thìre Mòir)

Point of
Ardnamurchan

Acharacle

NM

Strontian

Onich

Kinlochleven

Ballachulish

A82

Coll

Arinagour

Tobermory

A848

A828

Port Appin

Lochaline

Lismore

A828

Tiree

Scarinish

20

ISLE

A849

Ulva

OF

Connel

Kerrera

Oban

A85

Iona

Fionnphort

A849

MULL

A816

Kilchoan

Dalmally

Crianla

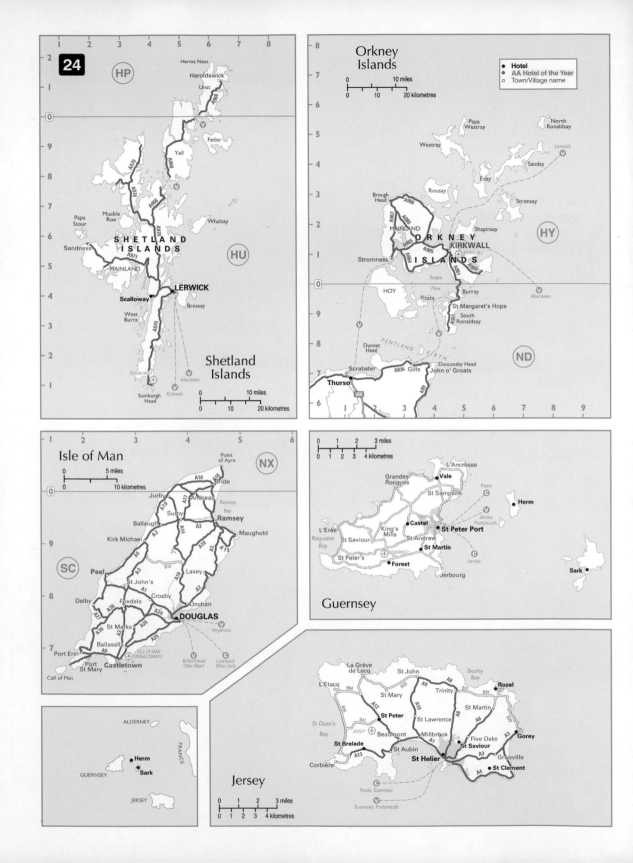

Readers' Report Form

Please send this form to:–
Editor, The Hotel Guide,
Lifestyle Guides,
AA Media,
Fanum House,
Basingstoke RG21 4EA

e-mail: lifestyleguides@theAA.com

Please use this form to recommend any hotel where you have stayed, whether it is included in the guide or not currently listed. You can also help us to improve the guide by completing the short questionnaire on the reverse.

Please note that the AA does not undertake to arbitrate between you and the hotel management, or to obtain compensation or engage in protracted correspondence.

Date

Your name (BLOCK CAPITALS)

Your address (BLOCK CAPITALS)

Post code

E-mail address

Name of hotel

Location

Comments

(please attach a separate sheet if necessary)

Please tick here ☐ if you DO NOT wish to receive details of AA offers or products

PTO

Readers' Report Form *continued*

Have you bought this guide before?   ☐ YES   ☐ NO

Do you regularly use any other, accommodation, restaurant, pub or food guides?   ☐ YES   ☐ NO
If YES, which ones?

Why did you buy this guide? (tick all that apply)

Holiday ☐   Short break ☐   Business travel ☐   Special occasion ☐
Overnight stop ☐   Find a venue for an event e.g. conference ☐
Other (please state)

How often do you stay in hotels? (tick one choice)

More than once a month ☐   Once a month ☐   Once in 2-3 months ☐
Once in six months ☐   Once a year ☐   Less than once a year ☐
Other (please state)

Please answer these questions to help us make improvements to the guide:
Which of these factors are the most important when choosing a hotel? (tick all that apply)

Price ☐   Location ☐   Awards/ratings ☐   Service ☐
Decor/surroundings ☐   Previous experience ☐   Recommendation ☐
Other (please state)

Do you read the editorial features in the guide?   ☐ YES   ☐ NO

Do you use the location atlas?   ☐ YES   ☐ NO

What elements of the guide do you find most useful when choosing somewhere to stay? (tick all that apply)

Description ☐   Photo ☐   Advertisement ☐   Star rating ☐

Is there any other information you would like to see added to this guide?

Readers' Report Form

Please send this form to:–
Editor, The Hotel Guide,
Lifestyle Guides,
AA Media,
Fanum House,
Basingstoke RG21 4EA

e-mail: lifestyleguides@theAA.com

Please use this form to recommend any hotel where you have stayed, whether it is included in the guide or not currently listed. You can also help us to improve the guide by completing the short questionnaire on the reverse.

Please note that the AA does not undertake to arbitrate between you and the hotel management, or to obtain compensation or engage in protracted correspondence.

Date

Your name (BLOCK CAPITALS)

Your address (BLOCK CAPITALS)

Post code

E-mail address

Name of hotel

Location

Comments

(please attach a separate sheet if necessary)

Please tick here ☐ if you DO NOT wish to receive details of AA offers or products

PTO

Readers' Report Form *continued*

Have you bought this guide before? ☐ YES ☐ NO

Do you regularly use any other, accommodation, restaurant, pub or food guides? ☐ YES ☐ NO
If YES, which ones?

Why did you buy this guide? (tick all that apply)

Holiday ☐	Short break ☐	Business travel ☐	Special occasion ☐
Overnight stop ☐	Find a venue for an event e.g. conference ☐		

Other (please state)

How often do you stay in hotels? (tick one choice)

More than once a month ☐	Once a month ☐	Once in 2-3 months ☐
Once in six months ☐ Once a year ☐	Less than once a year ☐	

Other (please state)

Please answer these questions to help us make improvements to the guide:
Which of these factors are the most important when choosing a hotel? (tick all that apply)

Price ☐	Location ☐	Awards/ratings ☐	Service ☐
Decor/surroundings ☐	Previous experience ☐	Recommendation ☐	

Other (please state)

Do you read the editorial features in the guide? ☐ YES ☐ NO

Do you use the location atlas? ☐ YES ☐ NO

What elements of the guide do you find most useful when choosing somewhere to stay? (tick all that apply)

Description ☐	Photo ☐	Advertisement ☐	Star rating ☐

Is there any other information you would like to see added to this guide?